THE CANON & ITS CRITICS

THE CANON & ITS CRITICS
A Multi-Perspective Introduction to Philosophy
Second Edition

Todd M. Furman
McNeese State University

Mitchell Avila
California State University, Fullerton

Boston Burr Ridge, IL Dubuque, IA Madison, WI New York
San Francisco St. Louis Bangkok Bogotá Caracas Kuala Lumpur
Lisbon London Madrid Mexico City Milan Montreal New Delhi
Santiago Seoul Singapore Sydney Taipei Toronto

Higher Education

THE CANON AND ITS CRITICS : A MULTI-PERSPECTIVE
INTRODUCTION TO PHILOSOPHY

This book is printed on acid-free paper.

2 3 4 5 6 7 8 9 0   FGR/FGR   0 9 8 7 6 5

ISBN 0-07-283237-1

Publisher: *Christopher Freitag*
Sponsoring editor: *Jon-David Hague*
Marketing manager: *Lisa Berry*
Senior project manager: *Christina Thornton-Villagomez*
Production Supervisor: *Janean Utley*
Designer: *Cassandra J. Chu*
Cover design: *Glenda King*
Interior design: *John Edeen/Glenda King*
Typeface: *10/12 Minion*
Compositor: *G&S Typesetters, Inc.*
Printer: *Quebecor World/Fairfield*

Library of Congress Cataloging-in-Publication Data

The canon & its critics : a multi-perspective introduction to philosophy /
     [compiled by] Todd M. Furman, Mitchell Avila. — 2nd ed.
        p.   cm.
     Includes bibliographical references.
        ISBN 0-07-283237-1 (pbk. : alk. paper)
        1. Philosophy—Introductions.   I. Title: Canon and its critics.
     II. Furman, Todd M.   III. Avila, Mitchell.
     BD21.C34   2004
     100 — dc21   2003046307

www.mhhe.com

To my mother, Mary L. Furman,
and to my father, Michael G. Furman,
who taught me love and compassion,
self-discipline and perseverance
by example.
— Todd Michael Furman

To Lisa, Grace, and Elliot:
"For now we see as through a glass darkly,
but then we shall see face to face."
—Mitch Avila

CONTENTS

PREFACE

In our experience, philosophical discourse in the past two decades has been marked by unprecedented vibrant energy, vigorous debate, and engaging new developments. Whether the result of ongoing developments within the traditional confines of academic philosophy, or the consequence of critiques and challenges by individuals formerly marginalized from mainstream philosophy, or the fruit of cross-fertilization from interdisciplinary ventures, philosophers have witnessed unparalleled advances resulting in the production of interesting new philosophies. In the past decade, a very different picture of the boundaries and frontiers of philosophy has emerged. A new textbook was necessary in order to respond to these changes. *The Canon and Its Critics* acknowledges these continuing changes while remaining contiguous with the parameters and methodologies of traditional philosophy. Although *The Canon and Its Critics* is a unique text in many ways, we believe it accurately reflects the current practice of philosophy, capturing the exciting changes that are taking place as well as the valued tradition of philosophy.

As the title suggests, one central feature of this text is the juxtaposition of what we call "the canon" with "critics of the canon." By *canon,* we mean both traditional, classic readings in Western philosophy and contemporary approaches by "mainstream" academic philosophers; by *critics,* we mean authors, recent or otherwise, who challenge the classic paradigms, questions, and methods of philosophy, and who, often from a marginal position relative to "mainstream" academic philosophy, argue for reconceptualizing basic philosophical questions, methods, and investigations. The designations *canon* and *critic* are not rigid but flexible. The point of identifying canonical and critical sources is not to pigeonhole certain authors but to identify what we believe is a central, basic dynamic in the practice and methodology of philosophy since Socrates: *the rooting-out and identification of hidden assumptions and invisible presuppositions.*

Some chapters contain all traditional, canonical sources, while other chapters consist solely of critics, and some are a mix of the two. Sometimes the divide between canon and critic falls between authors, and thus they both appear in the *same* chapter; other times the disagreement is over the proper questions or the proper method, so the dialogue between these diverse voices occurs between chapters.

We find we derive a great deal of instructional mileage by including the critics. They stimulate student interest, provoke thoughtful response, illustrate alternative ways of doing philosophy, and even enhance student appreciation of traditional philosophy. Undoubtedly, some of the authors included in this text will be unfamiliar to you, but we encourage you to explore these new voices with your students and judge for yourself if they are making important contributions.

Many instructors share our desire to include traditional classic sources. Because an understanding of the cultural and intellectual history of Western civilization is a necessary component of a liberal arts education, it is a central task of introductory philosophy courses to help students learn who important figures are—such as Plato, Descartes, Locke, Kant, and Sartre—and what traditional positions—idealism, rationalism, and so forth—have been advanced. Put simply, every student who takes an introductory philosophy course should read "The Allegory of the Cave" and Descartes' *Meditations*, among other selections. These readings are time-tested ways of awakening students to the philosophical impulse and discipline, invaluable tools for teaching philosophy.

The critics, as we call them, are also important. There are several reasons to include these voices: (1) They are pedagogically useful. Students find them more interesting, engaging, and relevant than traditional readings alone. We find that we can use these readings to identify clearly the main philosophical issue and to illustrate plainly what sorts of questions philosophers are interested in asking. (2) The selections are interesting in their own right as examples of core philosophical thinking. They are a natural extension of typical ways philosophy has been practiced. (3) These readings and authors allow for a greater representation of cultural, ethnic, and gender diversity than would otherwise be possible—an important and valuable goal. (4) These authors are particularly useful for identifying where the current debate lies, what topics and approaches are 'live' now, and how these current debates are related historically to past discussions.

One important advantage of the canon-and-critic model is that we can include articles and topics that have proven themselves interesting to students. Students are quick to take a reading seriously when they grasp its relevance to their own lives. Additionally, by including readings outside the canon, we are able to add voices that reflect student diversity and the broad range of experiences students bring with them to the classroom. Of course, traditional readings are equally interesting and engaging—precisely the reason they are classics.

One word about what is meant by "multi-perspective." We have been profoundly affected by multicultural approaches to philosophy, and we consider such developments to be among the most important of the last decade. Nonetheless, we do not regard multiculturalism as a central goal in introductory philosophy courses, although it is a legitimate goal in an overall curriculum. Our approach is better characterized as *multi-perspective,* by which we mean that we are intentionally looking for diversity, but a diversity that continues the tradition of dialogue with the canon. We have looked for authors who challenge the tradition but do so from a standpoint that is itself dependent on or an extension of that tradition. Not surprisingly, however, a multi-perspective approach includes a wide array of philosophers representative of diverse philosophical, as well as cultural and ethnic, traditions.

Pedagogical Features

As instructors, we know the value of asking our students to read original, primary sources—an indispensable part of our introductory courses. Students, however, can sometimes find these readings difficult and initially frustrating. *The Canon and Its Critics* was designed to be versatile and adaptable, suitable for a range of students. We began with this typical profile of a student in mind: a first-generation college student, more likely than not to be an ethnic minority, a college freshman or sophomore enrolled in a state college, whose reading skills and minimal background knowledge of Western civilization and world history pose many initial challenges. With the right text and classroom pedagogy, however, such students are ultimately responsive, receptive, and rewarding.

The chief pedagogical features of this text are designed to make it easier for students to read and appreciate primary sources in philosophy. We have found that given an overview of a selection's contents and a road map of signposts to look for, students become increasingly competent and confident readers. We encourage you to make use of the pedagogical features of this text, especially early in the semester, to improve student learning outcomes.

The Canon and Its Critics includes various features designed to make it more accessible to students and more useful to professors.

Flexible Organization   Each of the fourteen chapters is a group of four to seven primary readings organized around a central theme or question. The organizing question for each chapter reflects what we have judged to be a central question philosophers have asked or are currently asking. Each chapter is meant to be self-contained, so that the instructor may move from question to question as he or she chooses, assigning a chapter at a time throughout the semester. Although the chapter unit is the basic organizational structure, each reading selection remains independent within that chapter, making it possible to assign individual reading selections from chapters, rather than entire chapters. Flexibility was a primary issue in the organization of this text, and we encourage you to order the material in whatever manner best suits your particular goals.

Chapter and Selection Introductions   Each chapter begins with a one- to two-page introduction, in which the exact nature of the question itself is clearly laid out. This is especially important for some chapters—personal identity, for example—because without some assistance students often misunderstand the direction and content of the discussion. The chapter introductions also elucidate the practical importance of the topics and explain how various articles within the chapter are related to one another. Again, a minimal investment in stage setting pays off with valuable dividends later in the form of accelerated student learning.

For individual selections, each primary reading begins with a brief introduction that concisely states the thesis of the selection. If the article is more complex, it also provides an overview and analysis of the logical or argumentative structure of the selection. Our aim here is to assist reading comprehension, not to pre-digest the author's work. Finally, short biographies of the authors are included wherever possible.

Reading and Discussion Questions   Each article is preceded by a set of Reading Questions and followed by a set of Discussion Questions. The reading questions are straightforward, easily answered by students as they read the text. *Requiring students to answer the Reading Questions as they read the selections is, in our experience, the best way to improve student comprehension and reading skills.* Students can be expected to turn in these answers as homework or perhaps to write their answers in a journal. (Some instructors may find the Reading Questions useful for in-class quizzes.) The Discussion Questions, on the other hand, are designed to facilitate classroom or small-group discussion but are also useful for journal exercises or as the basis for extended reflective-writing assignments. Whenever appropriate, the Discussion Questions include one or more multicultural questions that ask students to consider the issues raised in the selection from the standpoint of their own cultural heritage or from that of the cultures of other students.

Further Reading Suggestions   After each selection is an annotated list of suggested further readings. We identify the views and general approach of each suggested reading and provide bibliographical information.

Glossary   At the back of the text is a glossary of important terms and phrases from the discipline of philosophy, as well as common foreign phrases. Many of these words, but not all, appear in boldface the first time they occur in a chapter. As a practical matter, at the beginning of the course we encourage students to refer to the glossary and other reference works in the library.

Acknowledgments

Dialogue and discussion are central parts of philosophical method, and we have benefited from helpful and thoughtful conversations not only with each other but also with our colleagues and our students. Thanks especially to James Sennett, David Arthur, Moya Arthur, and Anita Bucklin. The Department of Philosophy at CSU Fullerton provided valuable mailing, copying, and phone assistance. The reference librarians at McNeese State proved to be amazingly resourceful and invaluable. The authors are appreciative of the helpful staff at McGraw-Hill for the invaluable contribution they have made to this second edition, especially Jon-David Hague and Ken King for their continuing support for this project. In addition, we would like to thank the many competent individuals who worked on the production of the book, including Christina Thornton-Villagomez, Sandra Hahn, Cassadra Chu, Glenda King and the staff at G&S Typesetters. Finally, this second edition benefited from the thoughtful reviews of our kind colleagues, including Maria Cimitile, Grand Valley State University; Matthew Lawrence, Long Beach City College; and Barbara Montero, Georgia State University.

Todd Furman

Mitch Avila

INTRODUCTION

What does it mean to be a philosopher? The rich tapestry of ideas called philosophy, now over 2,500 years old, has been woven from the unique contributions of many disparate thinkers. Separated by centuries and by vast distances, philosophers are an unusually diverse group of individuals who have held an astonishing range of views. Among the ranks of philosophers can be found logicians and poets, scientists and artists, theists and atheists, idealists and materialists, infidels and saints, conservatives and radicals, egalitarians and elitists, as well as skeptics and true believers. This is never more true than today; new voices are reshaping philosophy by reinvigorating past debates and opening up new avenues of investigation.

What unites philosophers, however, is more important than what divides them. Philosophers share many things in common. First and foremost, they traditionally share a commitment to careful reasoning and honest reflection. For many philosophers, rationality is a central value, and they place a high premium on reason. Much of the unity of philosophy over the centuries has resulted from each philosopher's principal appeal to reason and argumentation. Philosophers use reason to defend their positions in public forums, continuing an ongoing tradition of engagement, dialogue, and discourse with other philosophers. No matter what views or disagreements arise, all philosophers consider the sincere and uncompromising pursuit of the truth paramount. Sometimes, however, as several authors in this book illustrate, philosophers have challenged the claim that reason is the only reliable guide to forming beliefs. They have argued that the tradition has put too much emphasis on narrowly defined forms of rationality. Nonetheless, even when this claim is made, these critics of rationality make public arguments for other philosophers to consider—arguments that appeal, implicitly at least, to reason. In the spirit of this tradition, you are encouraged to critically examine each philosopher's arguments for yourself, evaluating the reasons for and against his or her particular view.

A second factor uniting philosophers is a common set of questions. Typically philosophers ask questions such as *What is true? What is good? How can I have knowledge? What is ultimately real? What is beautiful?* Although new questions are sometimes added— such as recent inquiries into artificial intelligence and personal identity—the boundaries of philosophy have remained stable over millennia. It would be wrong, however, to suppose that philosophy has a narrow scope; rather, philosophers consider virtually no topic to be outside the scope of philosophical investigation. Philosophers scrutinize science, history, literature, the arts, politics, economics—almost every human intellectual undertaking. It is unlikely that you will take any course in college that has not at one time or another been the object of a philosopher's careful critical examination.

You need not be a professional philosopher to be committed to honest self-reflection. All it takes is a love of the truth, an openness to asking questions, and a willingness to devote time and energy to a reasoned self-analysis. While honest philosophical reflection may challenge and disrupt many of the beliefs you now hold, it will also enhance and enrich the beliefs you continue to hold. Nor is the value of philosophy limited to the investigation of philosophy alone. The methods of philosophy can be applied to almost any discipline and can enhance every human pursuit.

This book will introduce you to philosophy and provide a foundation for your own journey as a philosopher. The readings included here are selected from an intellectual tradition called **Western philosophy.** Rooted in ancient Greek culture, Western philosophy has had an important and far-reaching impact on the thought and culture of Europe and the Americas. There are other philosophical traditions, notably **Eastern philosophy,** which is rooted in the cultures and religious traditions of India and China. Ancient Greek philosophy also influenced **Islamic** (or **Arabic**) **philosophy,** although this world philosophy has diverged historically from the main branch of Western philosophy and now represents a separate and distinct tradition. Although all of these philosophical traditions deserve attention and in-depth study, Western philosophy is the tradition with the greatest importance and significance for students living in the Americas and Europe. Nonetheless, it would be wise to devote part of your college experience to the study of other world philosophies as well.

The readings in this book are organized around two groups of Western philosophy called *the canon* and *the critics.* The labels are imprecise and indefinite, and the distinction between the two groups is somewhat arbitrary. Still, the distinction between the canon and its critics signals an important dynamic at work in philosophy: the continuing dialogue between philosophers and the rigorous challenges philosophers make of each other's work. By *canon* is meant those authors and positions that have withstood the test of time or are now widely represented as mainstream among philosophers. The classics of Western philosophy belong in this category, including the works of seminal figures such as Plato, Descartes, and Hume, as well as the work of many contemporary authors who continue traditional lines of inquiry and accepted methods of analysis. These canonical approaches are increasingly challenged by *critics* who argue against the basic tenets and approaches of this tradition. These critical voices often charge that traditional investigations are hampered by narrow frameworks or distorted by the (supposed) narrow-mindedness of standard philosophy. Although these critical voices object to both the style and content of the philosophy they criticize, they continue the living tradition of philosophy by propagating new and creative arguments that bring the resources of reason and public discourse to centuries-old concerns. Of course, some critics quickly become canonical figures themselves as their arguments prove to be convincing, just as many of philosophy's most canonical authors were once critics of the tradition that preceded them.

Philosophy today is marked by vigorous and vibrant debate. New critiques, from feminists, multi-culturalists, and other groups traditionally outside the ranks of professional philosophers, pose new challenges and updated questions for philosophy. The line between the canon and the critics is even more difficult to distinguish as traditions are challenged and old challenges become new traditions—all while maintaining the timeless commitments to reason, truth, and intellectual honesty. This is an exciting time to be a student of philosophy.

Two philosophers from opposite ends of the history of Western philosophy exemplify the core commitments of this living tradition: the ancient Greek philosopher Socrates and the twentieth-century British philosopher Bertrand Russell. Although each is controversial and their views are not necessarily widely held among contemporary practitioners of philosophy, each is an excellent representation of what it means to be a philosopher and what motivates and drives philosophy. Socrates was willing to die before he would give up practicing philosophy and searching for the truth. Russell, controversial during his life as well, here provides an overview of the basic questions modern philosophy asks.

1 THE APOLOGY AND CRITO
Plato

Although not the first philosopher, Socrates is a pivotal figure in the history of philosophy. He left an important legacy that continues to shape the practice of philosophy. "The unexamined life is not worth living," Socrates said. The self-examination of beliefs and actions as part of an uncompromising and careful pursuit of the truth is a permanent cornerstone of the life lived well. Philosophers today, along with centuries of philosophers who have preceded them, also value critical reflection and careful self-evaluation, even when it leads to skepticism or the rejection of comforting illusions. A life built on the honest and careful pursuit of the truth is more rewarding and intrinsically better than a life shrouded by the clouds of confusion and the darkness of error.

Many powerful groups and individuals, however, have interests that are challenged by the critical examination and questioning of accepted cultural truths. For Socrates, it was the citizens of Athens who were threatened by his questioning and his relentless pursuit of what can be known. The citizens of Athens were willing to tolerate persons who could give persuasive speeches and make great shows of rhetoric, but they had no room for Socrates, whose questioning and investigations threatened to undermine a public culture of conformity to traditional authority. Eventually, the practice of philosophy cost Socrates his life. In 399 B.C.E., Socrates found himself on trial for his life in Athens, on the bogus charge of "corrupting the youth." A great deal was at stake: not just the life of Socrates, but the future direction of philosophy. Would Socrates give in to the pressures of society or continue his pursuit of the truth?

The following two selections—written by Plato, Socrates' most famous student—document Socrates' uncompromising pursuit of the truth and personal integrity. In the first, *The Apology,* Socrates is speaking during his trial, answering his accusers' charges; the second, the *Crito,* takes place in prison, after Socrates' trial, in which he was condemned to die, but before his eventual death a few days later.

As a student, consider who is threatened by your investigation of philosophy. What do others stand to lose if you critically examine your life and your culture's beliefs? What might they gain? What do you stand to gain?

Reading Questions

1. What crimes is Socrates charged with committing?
2. What does the Oracle at Delphi say and how does Socrates respond to it?
3. Does Socrates believe he is wise? Are other persons wise?
4. How does Socrates respond to the charge that his philosophical pursuits have led to his own death?
5. What penalty does Socrates propose instead of death? Why does he believe he deserves this?
6. Why, in the *Crito*, does Socrates refuse to escape from jail and leave Athens?
7. In the *Crito*, what arguments do the 'laws' make against Socrates escaping his punishment?

THE APOLOGY

Socr: I cannot tell you what impression my accusers have made upon you, Athenians: for my own part, I know that they nearly made me forget who I was, so plausible were they; and yet they have scarcely uttered one single word of truth. But of all their many falsehoods, the one which astonished me most, was when they said that I was a clever speaker, and that you must be careful not to let me mislead you. I thought that it was most impudent of them not to be ashamed to talk in that way; for as soon as I open my mouth the lie will be exposed, and I shall prove that I am not a clever speaker in any way at all: unless, indeed, by a clever speaker they mean a man who speaks the truth. If that is their meaning, I agree with them that I am a much greater orator than they. My accusers, then I repeat, have said little or nothing that is true; but from me you shall hear the whole truth. Certainly you will not hear an elaborate speech, Athenians, dressed up, like theirs, with words and phrases. I will say to you what I have to say, without preparation, and in the words which come first, for I believe that my cause is just; so let none of you expect anything else. . . .

. . .

Let us begin again, then, and see what is the charge which has given rise to the prejudice against me, which was what Meletus relied upon when he drew his indictment. What is the calumny which my enemies have been spreading about me? I must assume that they are formally accusing me, and read their indictment. It would run somewhat in this fashion: "Socrates is an evil-doer, who meddles with inquiries into things beneath the earth, and in heaven, and who 'makes the worse appear the better reason,' and who teaches others these same things." That is what they say; and in the Comedy of Aristophanes you yourselves saw a man called Socrates swinging round in a basket, and saying that he walked on the air, and talking a great deal of nonsense about matters of which I understand nothing, either more or less. I do not mean to disparage that kind of knowledge, if there is any man who possesses it. I trust Meletus may never be able to prosecute me for that. But, the truth is, Athenians, I have nothing to do with these matters, and almost all of you are yourselves my witnesses of this. I beg all of you who have ever heard me converse, and they are many, to inform your neighbors and tell them if any of you have ever heard me conversing about such matters, either more or less. That will show you that the other common stories about me are as false as this one.

But, the fact is, that not one of these stories is true; and if you have heard that I undertake to educate men, and exact money from them for so doing, that is not true either. . . .

Perhaps some of you may reply: But, Socrates, what is this pursuit of yours? Whence come these calumnies against you? You must have been engaged in some pursuit out of the common. All these stories and reports of you would have never gone about, if you had not been in some way different from other men. So tell us what your pursuits are, that we may not give our verdict in the dark. I think that that is a fair question, and I will try to explain to you what it is that has raised these calumnies against me, and given me this name. Listen, then: some of you perhaps will think that I am jesting; but I assure you that I will tell you the whole truth. I have gained this name, Athenians, simply by reason of a certain wisdom. But by what kind of wisdom? It is by just that wisdom which is, I believe, possible to men. In that, it may be, I am really wise. But the men of whom I was speaking just now must be wise in a wisdom which is greater than human wisdom, or in some way which I cannot describe, for certainly I know nothing of it myself, and if any man says that I do, he lies and wants to slander me. Do not interrupt me, Athenians, even if you think that I am speaking arrogantly. What I am going to say is not my own: I will tell you who says it, and he is worthy of your credit. I will bring the god of Delphi to be the witness of the fact of my wisdom and of its nature. You remember Chærephon. From youth upwards he was my comrade; and he went into exile with the people, and with the people he returned. And you remember, too, Chærephon's character; how vehement he was in carrying through whatever he took in hand. Once he went to Delphi and ventured to put this question to the oracle,—I entreat you again, my friends, not to cry out,— he asked if there was any man who was wiser than I: and the priestess answered that there was no man. Chærephon himself is dead, but his brother here will confirm what I say.

Now see why I tell you this. I am going to explain to you the origin of my unpopularity. When I heard of the oracle I began to reflect: What can God mean by this dark saying? I know very well that I am not wise, even in the smallest degree. Then what can he mean by saying that I am the wisest of men? It cannot be that he is speaking falsely, for he is a god and cannot lie. And for a long time I was at a loss to understand his meaning: then, very

reluctantly, I turned to seek for it in this manner. I went to a man who was reputed to be wise, thinking that there, if anywhere, I should prove the answer wrong, and meaning to point out to the oracle its mistake, and to say, "You said that I was the wisest of men, but this man is wiser than I am." So I examined the man—I need not tell you his name, he was a politician—but this was the result, Athenians. When I conversed with him I came to see that, though a great many persons, and most of all he himself, thought that he was wise, yet he was not wise. And then I tried to prove to him that he was not wise, though he fancied that he was: and by so doing I made him, and many of the bystanders, my enemies. So when I went away, I thought to myself, "I am wiser than this man: neither of us probably knows anything that is really good, but he thinks that he has knowledge, when he has not, while I, having no knowledge, do not think that I have. I seem, at any rate, to be a little wiser than he is on this point: I do not think that I know what I do not know." Next I went to another man who was reputed to be still wiser than the last, with exactly the same result. And there again I made him, and many other men, my enemies.

Then I went on to one man after another, seeing that I was making enemies every day, which caused me much unhappiness and anxiety: still I thought that I must set God's command above everything. So I had to go to every man who seemed to possess any knowledge, and search for the meaning of the oracle: and, Athenians, I must tell you the truth; verily, by the dog of Egypt, this was the result of the search which I had made at God's bidding. I found that the men, whose reputation for wisdom stood highest, were nearly the most lacking in it; while others, who were looked down on as common people, were much better fitted to learn. . . .

. . .

By reason of this examination, Athenians, I have made many enemies of a very fierce and bitter kind, who have spread abroad a great number of calumnies about me, and people say that I am "a wise man." For the bystanders always think that I am wise myself in any matter wherein I convict another man of ignorance. But, my friends, I believe that only God is really wise: and that by this oracle he meant that men's wisdom is worth little or nothing. I do not think that he meant that Socrates was wise. He only made use of my name, and took me as an example, as though he would say to men, "He among you is the wisest, who, like Socrates, knows that in very truth his wisdom is worth nothing at all." And therefore I shall go about testing and examining every man whom I think wise, whether he be a citizen or a stranger, as God has commanded me; and whenever I find that he is not wise, I point out to him on the part of God that he is not wise. And I am so busy in this pursuit that I have never had leisure to take any part worth mentioning in public matters, or to look after my private affairs. I am in very great poverty by reason of my service to God.

...

(*He is found guilty by 281 votes to 220.*)

I am not vexed at the verdict which you have given, Athenians, for many reasons. I expected that you would find me guilty; and I am not so much surprised at that, as at the numbers of the votes. I, certainly, never thought that the majority against me would have been so narrow. But now it seems that if only thirty votes had changed sides, I should have escaped. . . .

So [Meletus] proposes death as the penalty. Be it so. And what counter-penalty shall I propose to you, Athenians? What I deserve, of course, must I not? What then do I deserve to pay or to suffer for having determined not to spend my life in ease? I neglected the things which most men value, such as wealth, and family interests, and military commands, and popular oratory, and all the political appointments, and clubs, and factions, that there are in Athens; for I thought that I was really too conscientious a man to preserve my life if I engaged in these matters. So I did not go where I should have done no good either to

you or to myself. I went instead to each one of you by himself, to do him, as I say, the greatest of services, and strove to persuade him not to think of his affairs, until he had thought of himself, and tried to make himself as perfect and wise as possible; nor to think of the affairs of Athens, until he had thought of Athens herself; and in all cases to bestow his thoughts on things in the same manner. Then what do I deserve for such a life? Something good, Athenians, if I am really to propose what I deserve; and something good which it would be suitable for me to receive. Then what is a suitable reward to be given to a poor benefactor, who requires leisure to exhort you? There is no reward, Athenians, so suitable for him as a public maintenance in the Prytaneum. It is a much more suitable reward for him than for any of you who has won a victory at the Olympic games with his horse or his chariots. Such a man only makes you seem happy, but I make you really happy: and he is not in want, and I am. So if I am to propose the penalty which I really deserve, I propose this, a public maintenance in the Prytaneum.

...

Perhaps some one will say, "Why cannot you withdraw from Athens, Socrates, and hold your peace?" It is the most difficult thing in the world to make you understand why I cannot do that. If I say that I cannot hold my peace, because that would be to disobey God, you will think that I am not in earnest and will not believe me. And if I tell you that no better thing can happen to a man than to converse every day about virtue and the other matters about which you have heard me conversing and examining myself and others, and that an unexamined life is not worth living, then you will believe me still less. But that is the truth, my friends, though it is not easy to convince you of it. And, what is more, I am not accustomed to think that I deserve any punishment. If I had been rich, I would have proposed as large a fine as I could pay: that would have done me no harm. But I am not rich enough to pay a fine, unless you are willing to fix it at a sum within my means. Perhaps I could pay you a mina: so

I propose that. Plato here, Athenians, and Crito, and Critobulus, and Apollodorus bid me propose thirty minf, and they will be sureties for me. So I propose thirty minf. They will be sufficient sureties to you for the money.

(He is condemned to death.)

CRITO

Crito: But, O my good Socrates, I beseech you for the last time to listen to me and save yourself. For to me your death will be more than a single disaster: not only shall I lose a friend the like of whom I shall never find again, but many persons, who do not know you and me well, will think that I might have saved you if I had been willing to spend money, but that I neglected to do so. And what character could be more disgraceful than the character of caring more for money than for one's friends? The world will never believe that we were anxious to save you, but that you yourself refused to escape.

...

... Take care, Socrates, lest these things be not evil only, but also dishonorable to you and to us. Consider then; or rather the time for consideration is past; we must resolve; and there is only one plan possible. Everything must be done to-night. If we delay any longer, we are lost. O Socrates, I implore you not to refuse to listen to me.

Socr: My dear Crito, if your anxiety to save me be right, it is most valuable: but if it be not right, its greatness makes it all the more dangerous. We must consider then whether we are to do as you say, or not; for I am still what I always have been, a man who will listen to no voice but the voice of the reasoning which on consideration I find to be truest. I cannot cast aside my former arguments because this misfortune has come to me. They seem to me to be as true as ever they were, and I hold exactly the same ones in honor and esteem as I used to: and if we have no better reasoning to substitute for them, I certainly shall not agree to your proposal, not even

though the power of the multitude should scare us with fresh terrors, as children are scared with hobgoblins, and inflict upon us new fines, and imprisonments, and deaths. . . .

...

. . . Now consider whether we still hold to the belief, that we should set the highest value, not on living, but on living well?

Crito: Yes, we do.

Socr: And living well and honorably and rightly mean the same thing: do we hold to that or not?

Crito: We do.

Socr: Then, starting from these premises, we have to consider whether it is right or not right for me to try to escape from prison, without the consent of the Athenians. If we find that it is right, we will try: if not, we will let it alone. I am afraid that considerations of expense, and of reputation, and of bringing up my children, of which you talk, Crito, are only the reflections of our friends, the many, who lightly put men to death, and who would, if they could, as lightly bring them to life again, without a thought. But reason, which is our guide, shows us that we can have nothing to consider but the question which I asked just now: namely, shall we be doing right if we give money and thanks to the men who are to aid me in escaping, and if we ourselves take our respective parts in my escape? Or shall we in truth be doing wrong, if we do all this? And if we find that we should be doing wrong, then we must not take any account either of death, or of any other evil that may be the consequence of remaining quietly here, but only of doing wrong.

...

Ought we never to do wrong intentionally at all; or may we do wrong in some ways, and not in others? Or, as we have often agreed in former times, is it never either good or honorable to do wrong? Have all our former conclusions been forgotten in these few days? Old men as we were, Crito, did we not see, in days gone by, when we were gravely conversing with each other, that we were no better than children? Or is not what we used to say most assuredly the truth, whether the world agrees with us or not? Is not wrong-doing an evil and a shame to the wrong-doer in every case, whether we incur a heavier or a lighter punishment than death as the consequence of doing right? Do we believe that?

Crito: We do.

Socr: Then we ought never to do wrong at all?

Crito: Certainly not.

Socr: Neither, if we ought never do wrong at all, ought we to repay wrong with wrong, as the world thinks we may?

Crito: Clearly not.

Socr: Well then, Crito, ought we to do evil to any one?

Crito: Certainly I think not, Socrates.

Socr: And is it right to repay evil with evil, as the world thinks, or not right?

Crito: Certainly it is not right.

Socr: For there is no difference, is there, between doing evil to a man, and wronging him?

Crito: True.

Socr: Then we ought not to repay wrong with wrong or do harm to any man, no matter what we may have suffered from him. . . .

. . .

Then, my next point, or rather my next question, is this: Ought a man to perform his just agreements, or may he shuffle out of them?

Crito: He ought to perform them.

Socr: Then consider. If I escape without the state's consent, shall I be injuring those whom I ought least to injure, or not? Shall I be abiding by my just agreements or not?

Crito: I cannot answer your question, Socrates. I do not understand it.

Socr: Consider it this way. Suppose the laws and the commonwealth were to come and appear to me as I was preparing to run away (if that is the right phrase to describe my escape) and were to ask, "Tell us, Socrates, what have you in your mind to do? What do you mean by trying to escape, but to destroy us the laws, and the whole city, so far as in you lies? Do you think that a state can exist and not be overthrown, in which the decisions of law are of no force, and are disregarded and set at naught by private individuals?" How shall we

answer questions like that, Crito? Much might be said, especially by an orator, in defense of the law which makes judicial decisions supreme. Shall I reply, "But the state has injured me: it has decided my cause wrongly." Shall we say that?

Crito: Certainly we will, Socrates.

Socr: And suppose the laws were to reply, "Was that our agreement? or was it that you would submit to whatever judgments the state should pronounce?" And if we were to wonder at their words, perhaps they would say, "Socrates, wonder not at our words, but answer us; you yourself are accustomed to ask questions and to answer them. What complaint have you against us and the city, that you are trying to destroy us? Are we not, first, your parents? Through us your father took your mother and begat you. Tell us, have you any fault to find with those of us that are the laws of marriage?" "I have none," I should reply. "Or have you any fault to find with those of us that regulate the nurture and education of the child, which you, like others, received? Did not we do well in bidding your father educate you in music and gymnastic?" "You did," I should say. "Well then, since you were brought into the world and nurtured and educated by us, how, in the first place, can you deny that you are our child and our slave, as your fathers were before you? And if this be so, do you think that your rights are on a level with ours? Do you think that you have a right to retaliate upon us if we should try to do anything to you? You had not the same rights that your father had, or that your master would have had, if you had been a slave. You had no right to retaliate upon them if they ill-treated you, or to answer them if they reviled you, or to strike them back if they struck you, or to repay them evil with evil in any way. And do you think that you may retaliate on your country and its laws? If we try to destroy you, because we think it right, will you in return do all that you can to destroy us, the laws, and your country, and say that in so doing you are doing right, you, the man, who in truth thinks so much of virtue? Or are you too wise to see that your country is worthier, and more august, and more sacred, and holier, and held in higher honor both by the gods and by all men of understanding, than your father and your mother and all your other ancestors; and that it is your bounden duty to reverence it, and to submit to it, and to approach it more humbly than you would approach your father, when it is angry with you; and either to do whatever it bids you to do or to persuade it to excuse you; and to obey in silence if it orders you to endure stripes or imprisonment, or if it send you to battle to be wounded or to die? That is what is your duty. You must not give way, nor retreat, nor desert your post. In war, and in the court of justice, and everywhere, you must do whatever your city and your country bid you to do, or you must convince them that their commands are unjust. But it is against the law of God to use violence to your father or to your mother; and much more so is it against the law of God to use violence to your country." What answer shall we make, Crito? Shall we say that the laws speak truly, or not?

Crito: I think that they do.

Socr: "Then consider, Socrates," perhaps they would say, "if we are right in saying that by attempting to escape you are attempting to injure us. We brought you into the world, we nurtured you, we educated you, we gave you and every other citizen a share of all the good things we could. Yet we proclaim that if any man of the Athenians is dissatisfied with us, he may take his goods and go away whithersoever he pleases: we give that permission to every man who chooses to avail himself of it, so soon as he has reached man's estate, and sees us, the laws, and the administration of our city. No one of us stands in his way or forbids him to take his goods and go wherever he likes, whether it be to an Athenian colony, or to any foreign country, if he is dissatisfied with us and with the city. But we say that every man of you who remains here, seeing how we administer justice, and how we govern the city in other matters, has agreed, by the very fact of remaining here, to do whatso-ever we bid him. And, we say, he who disobeys us, does a threefold wrong: he disobeys us who

are his parents, and he disobeys us who fostered him, and he disobeys us after he has agreed to obey us, without persuading us that we are wrong. Yet we did not bid him sternly to do whatever we told him. We offered him an alternative; we gave him his choice, either to obey us, or to convince us that we were wrong: but he does neither."

…

Then they would say, "Are you not breaking your covenants and agreements with us? And you were not led to make them by force or by fraud: you had not to make up your mind in a hurry. You had seventy years in which you might have gone away, if you had been dis-satisfied with us, or if the agreement had seemed to you unjust. But you preferred neither Lacedfmon nor Crete, though you are fond of saying that they are well governed, nor any other state, either of the Hellenes, or the Barbarians. You went away from Athens less than the lame and the blind and the cripple. Clearly you, far more than other Athenians, were satisfied with the city, and also with us who are its laws: for who would be satisfied with a city which had no laws? And now will you not abide by your agreement? If you take our advice, you will, Socrates: then you will not make yourself ridiculous by going away from Athens."

…

"No, Socrates, be advised by us who have fostered you. Think neither of children, nor of life, nor of any other thing before justice, that when you come to the other world you may be able to make your defense before the rulers who sit in judgment there. It is clear that neither you nor any of your friends will be happier, or juster, or holier in this life, if you do this thing, nor will you be happier after you are dead. Now you will go away wronged, not by us, the laws, but by men. But if you repay evil with evil, and wrong with wrong in this shameful way, and break your agreements and covenants with us, and injure those whom you should least injure, yourself, and your friends, and your country, and us, and so escape, then we shall be angry with you while you live, and when you die our brethren, the laws in Hades, will not receive you kindly; for they know that on earth you did all that you could to destroy us. Listen then to us, and let not Crito persuade you to do as he says."

Know well, my dear friend Crito, that this is what I seem to hear, as the worshippers of Cybele seem, in their frenzy, to hear the music of flutes: and the sound of these words rings loudly in my ears, and drowns all other words. And I feel sure that if you try to change my mind you will speak in vain; nevertheless, if you think that you will succeed, say on.

Crito: I can say no more, Socrates.

Socr: Then let it be, Crito: and let us do as I say, seeing that God so directs us.

Discussion Questions

1. Did Socrates act correctly in the events leading up to his death? Do you believe he had committed a crime against the citizens of Athens? If so, what? Should he have escaped? Why or why not?
2. What, if anything, are you prepared to die for? If you are prepared to die for something, why is it worth your death?
3. Socrates claimed 'the unexamined life is not worth living.' In your view, do most people examine their lives? Why or why not? Should people critically examine their lives? Would this add value to their lives, making them "more worth living"? Or does self-examination only make life more confusing?
4. Who, if anyone, is threatened if you question popularly held beliefs? Are the members of your family or religious group threatened by your asking critical questions that challenge traditions or authority? What other groups might be threatened? What persons or groups might benefit from your questioning?

For Further Reading

Besides *The Apology* and the *Crito*, the final days of Socrates are remembered by Plato in his dialogue *Phaedo*, which contains some of Plato's own philosophy but also recounts Socrates' death and includes a moving discussion of the possibility of immortality for philosophers. A worthwhile study of the method and philosophy of Socrates is found in Gregory Vlastos, *Socrates, Ironist and Moral Philosopher* (1991). An interesting discussion of how the study of philosophy and critical self-examination is perceived as threatening by various interest groups in society can be found in Martha Nussbaum's *Cultivating Humanity* (1997).

2   APPEARANCE AND REALITY
Bertrand Russell

Bertrand Russell (1872–1970) was one of the twentieth century's most prolific philosophers—and one of its most controversial. Russell wrote on numerous topics in contemporary philosophy, mainly in the fields of logic, the philosophical foundations of mathematics, epistemology (the study of knowledge), and metaphysics (the study of ultimate reality). Russell also published on topics relating to morality, religion, and social reform.

Respected by many philosophers, Russell also earned the respect of those outside of philosophy, and in recognition of his contributions to free thought and free speech, he was awarded the Nobel Prize for Literature in 1950. At the same time, Russell's views often ignited controversy. Because of his views on pacifism and nuclear disarmament, he was jailed twice. He was once found unfit to hold an appointment in the Department of Philosophy at the College of the City of New York (now the City University of New York) because inflammatory charges were made against him on the basis of his published writings on marriage and religion. The judge for the case blocked Russell's professorship allegedly to protect the "health, safety, and morals" of society and to prevent the establishment of a "chair of indecency."

This selection is from a short book, *The Problems of Philosophy,* written in 1912 for both philosophers and the general public. The book focuses on two problems that have preoccupied modern philosophy: first, what is the (real) nature of the world and, second, how can we know it? These twin problems are captured in one interesting puzzle: What assurance is there that our sensory appearances are an accurate guide to reality?

Reading Questions

1. What difficulties are posed by attempting to describe completely the color of the table?
2. How are appearances different for painters? How does this complicate the question of what the table really is?
3. What is the 'real' shape of the table? Do we ever know its 'real' shape?
4. Why can't the senses tell us the truth about the object itself? What knowledge, if any, do the senses provide us with?

Is there any knowledge in the world which is so certain that no reasonable man could doubt it? This question, which at first sight might not seem difficult, is really one of the most difficult that can be asked. When we have realized the obstacles in the way of a straightforward and confident answer, we shall be well launched on the study of philosophy—for philosophy is merely the attempt to answer such ultimate questions, not carelessly and dogmatically, as we do in ordinary life and even in the sciences, but critically, after exploring all that makes such questions puzzling, and after realizing all the vagueness and confusion that underlie our ordinary ideas.

In daily life, we assume as certain many things which, on a closer scrutiny, are found to be so full of apparent contradictions that only a great amount of thought enables us to know what it is that we really may believe. In the search for certainty, it is natural to begin with our present experiences, and in some sense, no doubt, knowledge is to be derived from them. But any statement as to what it is that our immediate experiences make us know is likely to be wrong. It seems to me that I am now sitting in a chair, at a table of a certain shape, on which I see sheets of paper with writing or print. By turning my head I see out the window buildings and clouds and the sun. I believe that the sun is about ninety-three million miles from the earth; that it is a hot globe many times bigger than the earth; that, owing to the earth's rotation, it rises every morning, and will continue to do so for an indefinite time in the future. I believe that, if any other normal person comes into my room, he will see the same chairs and tables and books and papers that I see, and that the table which I see is the same as the table which I feel pressing against my arm. All this seems to be so evident as to be hardly worth stating, except in answer to a man who doubts whether I know anything. Yet all this may be reasonably doubted, and all of it requires much careful discussion before we can be sure that we have stated it in a form that is wholly true.

To make our difficulties plain, let us concentrate attention on the table. To the eye it is oblong, brown and shiny, to the touch it is smooth and cool and hard; when I tap on it, it gives out a wooden sound. Any one else who sees and feels and hears the table will agree with this description, so that it might seem as if no difficulty would arise; but as soon as we try to be more precise our troubles begin. Although I believe that the table is 'really' of the same color all over, the parts that reflect light look much brighter than other parts, and some parts look white because of reflected light. I know that, if I move, the parts that reflect the light will be different, so that the apparent distribution of colors on the table will change. It follows that if several people are looking at the table at the same moment, no two of them will see exactly the same distribution of colors, because no two can see it from exactly the same point of view, and any change in the point of view makes some change in the way the light is reflected.

For most practical purposes these differences are unimportant, but to the painter they are all-important: the painter has to unlearn the habit of thinking that things seem to have the color which common sense says they 'really' have, and to learn the habit of seeing things as they appear. Here we have already the beginning of one of the distinctions that cause most trouble in philosophy—the distinction between 'appearance' and 'reality', between what things seem to be and what they are. The painter wants to know what things seem to be, the practical man and the philosopher want to know what they are; but the philosopher's wish to know is stronger than the practical man's, and is more troubled by knowledge as to the difficulties of answering the question.

To return to the table. It is evident from what we have found, that there is no color which preeminently appears to be *the* color of the table, or even of any one particular part of the table—it appears to be of different colors from different points of view, and there is no reason for regarding some of these as more really its color than others. And we know that even from a given point of view the color will seem different by artificial light, or to a color-blind man, or to a man wearing blue spectacles, while in the dark there will be no color at all, though to touch and hearing the table will be unchanged. This color is not something which is inherent in the table, but something depending upon the table and the spectator and the way the light falls on the table. When, in ordinary life, we speak of *the* color of the table, we only mean the sort of color which it will seem to have to a normal spectator from an ordinary point of view under usual conditions of light. But the other colors which appear under other conditions have just as good a right to be considered real; and therefore, to avoid favoritism, we are compelled to deny that, in itself, the table has any one particular color.

The same thing applies to the texture. With the naked eye one can see the grain, but otherwise the table looks smooth and even. If we looked at it through a microscope, we should see roughnesses and hills and valleys, and all sorts of differences that are imperceptible to the naked eye. Which of these is the 'real' table? We are naturally tempted to say that what we see through the microscope is more real, but that in turn would be changed by a still more powerful microscope. If, then, we cannot trust what we see with the naked eye, why should we trust what we see through a microscope? Thus, again, the confidence in our senses with which we began deserts us.

The *shape* of the table is no better. We are all in the habit of judging as to the 'real' shapes of things, and we do this so unreflectingly that we come to think we actually see the real shapes. But, in fact, as we all have to learn if we try to draw, a given thing looks different in shape from every different point of view. If our table is 'really' rectangular, it will look, from almost all points of view, as if it had two acute angles and two obtuse angles. If opposite sides are parallel, they will look as if they converged to a point away from the spectator; if they are of equal length, they will look as if the nearer side were longer. All these things are not commonly noticed in looking at a table, because experience has taught us to construct the 'real' shape from the apparent shape, and the 'real' shape is what interests us as practical men. But the 'real' shape is not what we see; it is something inferred from what we see. And what we see is constantly changing in shape as we move about the room; so that here again the senses seem not to give us the truth about the table itself, but only about the appearance of the table.

Similar difficulties arise when we consider the sense of touch. It is true that the table always gives us a sensation of hardness, and we feel that it resists pressure. But the sensation we obtain depends upon how hard we press the table and also upon what part of the body we press with; thus the various sensations due to various pressures or various parts of the body cannot be supposed to reveal *directly* any definite property of the table, but at most to be *signs* of some property which perhaps *causes* all the sensations, but is not actually apparent in any of them. And the same applies still more obviously to the sounds which can be elicited by rapping the table.

Thus it becomes evident that the real table, if there is one, is not the same as what we immediately experience by sight or touch or hearing. The real table, if there is one, is not *immediately* known to us at all, but must be an inference from what is immediately known. Hence, two very difficult questions at once arise; namely, (1) Is there a real table at all? (2) If so, what sort of object can it be?

Discussion Questions

1. Russell's example of the table is a trivial example. Can you identify some examples where the problem of whether appearance matches reality is not so trivial, examples that affect how we conduct our lives? To what other important human questions—besides the reality of external objects—do appearances fail to provide a careful, complete, and satisfactory answer?
2. Do you think a university is ever justified in rejecting the appointment of a professor because of his or her political and moral beliefs? If not, why not? If yes, under what conditions would it be justifiable to prevent such employment?

For Further Reading

An excellent overview and discussion of Russell's life and philosophy is the entry on Russell in the *Encyclopedia of Philosophy* (published by Macmillan, 1964), a reference work found in most college libraries. In addition, that article includes a useful and thorough bibliography. There are a number of biographical sources for Russell's life, including his own *My Philosophical Development* (1959). For more about how Russell's professorate appointment was blocked, see Paul Edwards' article "How Bertrand Russell Was Prevented from Teaching at the College of the City of New York," published as an appendix to Russell's book *Why I Am Not a Christian* (1927). This book is still widely available and contains some of Russell's controversial writings on religion and morality.

CHAPTER 1

AM I FREE OR DETERMINED?

You may be familiar with the **nature/nurture debate.** On one side of the debate—the nurture side—are those who believe that we act and think the way we do primarily because of our environment—how we are raised, for example. Much can be said in favor of this perspective. For example, most children grow up to hold the same religious views as their parents and many of their parents' values, habits, and preferences as well. Consider how observations concerning domestic violence and child molestation further support the nurture side of the debate: anecdotal and clinical evidence suggests that children who grow up in homes in which they witness spousal abuse or are victims of molestation are more likely to abuse their future children or spouses than children who grow up in nonabusive households, apparently because of environmental influences.

On the other hand, advances in the scientific understanding of human nature, especially genetics, support the *nature* side of the nature/nurture debate. Those on the nature side of the debate contend that our genetic makeup is primarily responsible for how we act and think. For example, some evidence suggests that we can be genetically predisposed to ailments such as alcoholism and mental illness. Perhaps it is not an accident that alcoholism and mental illness tend to run more strongly in genetically related groups (such as families) than in the general population. Some researchers also argue that sexual preference—be it homosexuality or heterosexuality—is due to our genetic makeup.

Which side of the nature/nurture debate is correct is not our primary concern here. Some combination of genetic and environmental factors probably influences our thoughts and behavior. This chapter investigates *the extent* to which our thoughts and actions are shaped, be it by genes or by the environment. Do genetic and environmental factors dictate the course of our lives down to the last detail—whom we will marry, how many children we will have, and what we will name them, for example—or are we free to live our lives according to how we see fit, in whatever manner we choose? This is the question of **free will** and **determinism.**

Some believe that we are not free, that each and every one of our thoughts and actions—from what we choose to eat for breakfast to what our favorite color happens to be—is an inevitable consequence of what has gone before, what philosophers call **antecedent conditions.** Such a view is referred to as determinism, sometimes called **hard determinism.** Determinists are represented in this chapter by Robert Blatchford, an atheist of some import in the early 1900s. The view that at least some human activity is free, known as **libertarianism,** is represented in this chapter by C. A. Campbell.

A third alternative is **soft determinism.** Soft determinists believe that all human activity is the inevitable result of what has gone before—that is, they believe that determinism is true—but insist that humans are free nonetheless. Soft determinists are sometimes called **compatibilists** because they argue that being determined is compatible with being free. In this chapter, A. J. Ayer and Susan Wolf defend various forms of compatibilism. At first glance, soft determinists appear to endorse a contradiction, that humans are simultaneously free and not free. What the soft determinists have in mind, however, is this: in one sense of the word *free,* humans *are not* free, since human activity is the inevitable result of its antecedent conditions. Humans *are* free, however, in other senses of *free.* But in what sense of *free* can we be determined and free at the same time? Surprisingly, compatibilists argue that there are many senses in which we can be free and determined at the same time. For example, we might be determined yet 'free' if what is meant by 'freedom' is "the absence of coercion." In another sense, we might be determined but 'free' if by 'freedom' we mean that we could have acted other than we did (if we had chosen to). The question is, Which sense of freedom is the important one?

For the most part, the determinism debate focuses on a particular sense of 'freedom' called **moral freedom.** A person is considered *morally free* just in case it is fair or appropriate to hold that person morally responsible for his or her actions—that is, when it is appropriate to ascribe *blame* or *praise* to a person's actions. Consider this example. Suppose Tom suffers from Tourette's syndrome, a medical condition that causes involuntary bodily movements, such as tics and jerks, and involuntary vocalizations. Can Tom be held morally responsible for the effects of his Tourette's syndrome? Although Tom is *causally* responsible, clearly Tom is not morally blameworthy or morally responsible for any disturbances caused by his Tourette's syndrome. In other words, it would be unfair to punish Tom because his actions are not morally free; they are not the sort of actions that admit of moral evaluation.

What is it that makes an act *morally free?* This is a source of debate. Soft determinists endorse an analysis of moral freedom that is compatible with human activity being completely determined, while on the other hand, determinists and libertarians believe that it is logically impossible for one to be both determined and morally free. Hence, both determinists and libertarians are categorized as **incompatibilists.**

Suppose for the moment that we are morally free. That is, suppose that we could have acted differently than we did and hence we are morally culpable for our actions. Is that all there is to worry about concerning freedom?

Jean-Paul Sartre and Simone de Beauvoir, two twentieth-century **existentialists,** think otherwise. We might be free to do what we want with respect to any particular option, but if our very options are limited, we are not free in a very important sense of freedom. For example, de Beauvoir believes that society places constraints on women. Women are free to do as they please so long as they stay within certain limits set by a patriarchal society. In this chapter's selection from Sartre, Sartre explores the limits we place on ourselves due to our concern with what others think of us.

3   THE DELUSION OF FREE WILL
Robert Blatchford

Born in Kent, England, Robert Blatchford (1851–1943) evolved from the ranks of a journalist to that of an activist. Early in his career Blatchford championed socialism and publicly rejected Christianity. To these ends,

Blatchford helped found the *Clarion,* a socialist newspaper, and he penned *God and My Neighbor* (1903), a critique of Christianity. Later, however, Blatchford backtracks a bit with respect to his religious convictions. Blatchford becomes a spiritualist when he becomes convinced that his wife's spirit has survived her bodily death. This ultimately results in the publication of *More Things in Heaven and Earth* (1925).

The following selection comes from one of Blatchford's earlier writings, *Not Guilty* (1913). In this selection Blatchford takes up the question of **free will**. Are we free to do as we wish? To this question Blatchford answers yes. Yes, we are free to do as we wish. But Blatchford then asks another important question: *Why do we wish for what we do?*

According to Blatchford, what we wish for, what we desire, is a product of our heredity and environment. And since these factors are not under our control, our choices, based on our desires, are not morally free.

Reading Questions

1. When a man says that his will is free, he means to say what?
2. On what pivotal question does Blatchford believe that the determinism debate hangs?
3. Blatchford believes that the will is ruled by what?
4. How does Blatchford account for a man who hesitates in his choice between two acts?
5. How does Blatchford account for a man doing something he does not want to do?
6. What question does Blatchford ask of the man who believes that he can *do as he likes?*

The free will delusion has been a stumbling block in the way of human thought for thousands of years. Let us try whether common sense and common knowledge cannot remove it.

Free will is a subject of great importance to us in this case; and it is one we must come to with our eyes wide open and our wits wide awake; not because it is very difficult, but because it has been tied and twisted into a tangle of Gordian knots by twenty centuries full of wordy but unsuccessful philosophers.

The free will party claim that man is responsible for his acts, because his will is free to choose between right and wrong.

We reply that the will is not free, and that if it were free man could not know right from wrong until he was taught.

As to the knowledge of good and evil the free will party will claim that conscience is an unerring guide. But I have already proved that conscience does not and cannot tell us what is right and what is wrong: it only reminds us of the lessons we have learnt as to right and wrong.

The "still small voice" is not the voice of God: it is the voice of heredity and environment.

And now to the freedom of the will.

When a man says his will is free, he means that it is free of all control or interference: that it can over-rule heredity and environment.

We reply that the will is ruled by heredity and environment.

The cause of all the confusion on this subject may be shown in a few words.

When the free will party say that man has a free will, they mean that he is free to act as he chooses to act.

There is no need to deny that. *But what causes him to choose?*

That is the pivot upon which the whole discussion turns.

The free will party seem to think of the will as something independent of the man, as something outside him. They seem to think that the will decides without the control of the man's reason.

If that were so, it would not prove the man responsible. "The will" would be responsible, and not the man. It would be as foolish to blame a man for the act of a "free" will, as to blame a horse for the action of its rider.

But I am going to prove to my readers, by appeals to their common sense and common knowledge, that the will is not free; and that it is ruled by heredity and environment.

To begin with, the average man will be against me. He knows that he chooses between two courses every hour, and often every minute, and he thinks his choice is free. But that is a delusion: his choice is not free. He can choose, and does choose. But he can only choose as his heredity and his environment cause him to choose. He never did choose and never will choose except as his heredity and his environment—his temperament and his training—cause him to choose. And his heredity and his environment have fixed his choice before he makes it.

The average man says, "I know that I can act as I wish to act." But what causes him to wish?

The free will party say, "We know that a man can and does choose between two acts." But what settles the choice?

There is a cause for every wish, a cause for every choice; and every cause of every wish and choice arises from heredity, or from environment.

For a man acts always from temperament, which is heredity, or from training, which is environment.

And in cases where a man hesitates in his choice between two acts, the hesitation is due to a conflict between his temperament and his training, or, as some would express it, "between his desire and his conscience."

A man is practicing at a target with a gun, when a rabbit crosses his line of fire. The man has his eye and his sights on the rabbit, and his finger on the trigger. The man's will is free. If he presses the trigger the rabbit will be killed.

Now, how does the man decide whether or not he shall fire? He decides by feeling, and by reason.

He would like to fire, just to make sure that he could hit the mark. He would like to fire, because he would like to have the rabbit for supper. He would like to fire, because there is in him the old, old hunting instinct, to kill.

But the rabbit does not belong to him. He is not sure that he will not get into trouble if he kills it. Perhaps—if he is a very uncommon kind of man—he

feels that it would be cruel and cowardly to shoot a helpless rabbit.

Well. The man's will is free. He can fire if he likes: he can let the rabbit go if he likes. How will he decide? On what does his decision depend?

His decision depends upon the relative strength of his desire to kill the rabbit, and of his scruples about cruelty, and the law.

Not only that, but, if we knew the man fairly well, we could guess how his free will would act before it acted. The average sporting Briton would kill the rabbit. But we know that there are men who would on no account shoot any harmless wild creature.

Broadly put, we may say that the sportsman would will to fire, and that the humanitarian would not will to fire.

Now, as both their wills are free, it must be something outside the wills that makes the difference.

Well. The sportsman will kill, because he is a sportsman: the humanitarian will not kill, because he is a humanitarian.

And what makes one man a sportsman and another a humanitarian? Heredity and environment: temperament and training.

One man is merciful, another cruel, by nature; or one is thoughtful and the other thoughtless, by nature. That is a difference of heredity.

One may have been taught all his life that to kill wild things is "sport"; the other may have been taught that it is inhuman and wrong: that is a difference of environment.

Now, the man by nature cruel or thoughtless, who has been trained to think of killing animals as sport, becomes what we call a sportsman, because heredity and environment have made him a sportsman.

The other man's heredity and environment have made him a humanitarian.

The sportsman kills the rabbit, because he is a sportsman, and he is a sportsman because heredity and environment have made him one.

That is to say the "free will" is really controlled by heredity and environment.

Allow me to give a case in point. A man who had never done any fishing was taken out by a fisherman. He liked the sport, and for some months followed it eagerly. But one day an accident brought home to his mind the cruelty of catching fish with a hook, and he instantly laid down his rod, and never fished again.

Before the change he was always eager to go fishing if invited: after the change he could not be persuaded to touch a line. His will was free all the while. How was it that his will to fish changed to his will not to fish? It was the result of environment. He had learnt that fishing was cruel. The knowledge controlled his will.

But, it may be asked, how do you account for a man doing the thing he does not wish to do?

No man ever did a thing he did not wish to do. When there are two wishes the stronger rules.

Let us suppose a case. A young woman gets two letters by the same post; one is an invitation to go with her lover to a concert, the other is a request that she will visit a sick child in the slums. The girl is very fond of music, and is rather afraid of the slums. She wishes to go to the concert, and to be with her lover; she dreads the foul street and the dirty home, and shrinks from the risk of measles or fever. But she goes to the sick child, and she forgoes the concert. Why?

Because her sense of duty is stronger than her self-love.

Now, her sense of duty is partly due to her nature—that is, to her heredity—but it is chiefly due to environment. Like all of us, this girl was born without any kind of knowledge, and with only the rudiments of a conscience. But she has been well taught, and the teaching is part of her environment.

We may say that the girl is free to act as she chooses, but she *does* act as she has been *taught* that she *ought* to act. This teaching, which is part of her environment, controls her will.

We may say that a man is free to act as he chooses. He is free to act as *he* chooses, but *he* will choose as heredity and environment cause *him* to choose. For heredity and environment have made him that which he is.

A man is said to be free to decide between two courses. But really he is only free to decide in accordance with his temperament and training. . . .

Macbeth was ambitious; but he had a conscience. He wanted Duncan's crown; but he shrank from treason and ingratitude. Ambition pulled him one way, honour pulled him the other way. The opposing forces were so evenly balanced that he seemed unable to decide. Was Macbeth free to choose? To what extent was he free? He was so free that he could arrive at no decision, and it was the influence of his wife that turned the scale to crime.

Was Lady Macbeth free to choose? She did not hesitate. Because her ambition was so much stronger than her conscience that she never was in doubt. She chose as her over-powering ambition compelled her to choose.

And most of us in our decisions resemble either Macbeth or his wife. Either our nature is so much stronger than our training, or our training is so much stronger than our nature, that we decide for good or evil as promptly as a stream decides to run down hill; or our nature and our training are so nearly balanced that we can hardly decide at all.

In Macbeth's case the contest is quite clear and easy to follow. He was ambitious, and his environment had taught him to regard the crown as a glorious and desirable possession. But environment had also taught him that murder, and treason, and ingratitude were wicked and disgraceful.

Had he never been taught these lessons, or had he been taught that gratitude was folly, that honour was weakness, and murder excusable when it led to power, he would not have hesitated at all. It was his environment that hampered his will. . . .

In all cases the action of the will depends upon the relative strength of two or more motives. The stronger motive decides the will; just as the heavier weight decides the balance of a pair of scales. . . .

How, then, can we believe that free will is outside and superior to heredity and environment? . . .

"What! Cannot a man be honest if he choose?" Yes, if he choose. But that is only another way of saying that he can be honest if his nature and his training lead him to choose honesty.

"What! Cannot I please myself whether I drink or refrain from drinking?" Yes. But that is only to say you will not drink because it pleases *you* to be sober. But it pleases another man to drink, because his desire for drink is strong, or because his self-respect is weak.

And you decide as you decide, and he decides as he decides, because you are *you,* and he is *he;* and heredity and environment made you both that which you are.

And the sober man may fall upon evil days, and may lose his self-respect, or find the burden of his trouble greater than he can bear, and may fly to drink for comfort, or oblivion, and may become a drunkard. Has it not been often so?

And the drunkard may, by some shock, or some

disaster, or some passion, or some persuasion, regain his self-respect, and may renounce drink, and lead a sober and useful life. Has it not been often so?

And in both cases the freedom of the will is untouched: it is the change in the environment that lifts the fallen up, and beats the upright down.

We might say that a woman's will is free, and that she could, if she wished, jump off a bridge and drown herself. But she cannot *wish*. She is happy, and loves life, and dreads the cold and crawling river. And yet, by some cruel turn of fortune's wheel, she may become destitute and miserable; so miserable that she hates life and longs for death, and *then* she can jump into the dreadful river and die.

Her will was as free at one time as at another. It is the environment that has wrought the change. Once she could not wish to die: now she cannot wish to live.

The apostles of free will believe that all men's wills are free. But a man can only will that which he is able to will. And one man is able to will. And one man is able to will that which another man is unable to will. To deny this is to deny the commonest and most obvious facts of life. . . .

We all know that we can foretell the action of certain men in certain cases, because we know the men.

We know that under the same conditions Jack Sheppard would steal and Cardinal Manning would not steal. We know that under the same conditions the sailor would flirt with the waitress, and the priest would not; that the drunkard would get drunk, and the abstainer would remain sober. We know that Wellington would refuse a bribe, that Nelson would not run away, that Buonaparte would grasp at power, that Abraham Lincoln would be loyal to his country, that Torquemada would not spare a heretic. Why? If the will is free, how can we be sure, before a test arises, how the will must act?

Simply because we know that heredity and environment have so formed and moulded men and women that under certain circumstances the action of their wills is certain.

Heredity and environment having made a man a thief, he will steal. Heredity and environment having made a man honest, he will not steal.

That is to say, heredity and environment have decided the action of the will, before the time has come for the will to act.

This being so—and we all know that it is so—what becomes of the sovereignty of the will?

Let any man that believes that he can "do as he likes" ask himself *why* he *likes,* and he will see the error of the theory of free will, and will understand why the will is the servant and not the master of the man: for the man is the product of heredity and environment, and these control the will.

As we want to get this subject as clear as we can, let us take one or two familiar examples of the action of the will.

Jones and Robinson meet and have a glass of whisky. Jones asks Robinson to have another. Robinson says, "no thank you, one is enough." Jones says, "all right: have another cigarette." Robinson takes the cigarette. Now, here we have a case where a man refuses a second drink, but takes a second smoke. Is it because he would like another cigarette, but would not like another glass of whisky? No. It is because he knows that it is *safer* not to take another glass of whisky.

How does he know that whisky is dangerous? He has learnt it—from his environment.

"But he *could* have taken another glass if he wished."

But he could not wish to take another, because there was something he wished more strongly—to be safe.

And why did he want to be safe? Because he had learnt—from his environment—that it was unhealthy, unprofitable, and shameful to get drunk. Because he had learnt—from his environment—that it is easier to avoid forming a bad habit than to break a bad habit when formed. Because he valued the good opinion of his neighbours, and also his position and prospects.

These feelings and this knowledge ruled his will, and caused him to refuse the second glass.

But there was no sense of danger, no well-learned lesson of risk to check his will to smoke another cigarette. Heredity and environment did not warn him against that. So, to please his friend, and himself, he accepted.

Now suppose Smith asks Williams to have another glass. Williams takes it, takes several, finally goes home—as he often goes home. Why?

Largely because drinking is a habit with him. And not only does the mind instinctively repeat an action, but, in the case of drink, a physical craving is set up, and the brain is weakened. It is easier to refuse the first glass than the second; easier to refuse the second than the third; and it is very much harder for a man to keep sober who has frequently got drunk.

So, when poor Williams has to make his choice, he has habit against him, he has a physical craving against him, and he has a weakened brain to think with.

"But, Williams could have refused the first glass."

No. Because in his case the desire to drink, or to please a friend, was stronger than his fear of the danger. Or he may not have been so conscious of the danger as Robinson was. He may not have been so well taught, or he may not have been so sensible, or he may not have been so cautious. So that his heredity and environment, his temperament and training, led him to take the drink, as surely as Robinson's heredity and environment led him to refuse it.

And now, it is my turn to ask a question. If the will is "free," if the conscience is a sure guide, how is it that the free will and the conscience of Robinson caused him to keep sober, while the free will and the conscience of Williams caused him to get drunk?

Robinson's will was curbed by certain feelings which failed to curb the will of Williams. Because in the case of Williams the feelings were stronger on the other side.

It was the nature and the training of Robinson which made him refuse the second glass, and it was the nature and the training of Williams which made him drink the second glass.

What had free will to do with it?

We are told that *every* man has a free will, and a conscience.

Now, if Williams had been Robinson, that is to say if his heredity and his environment had been exactly like Robinson's, he would have done exactly as Robinson did.

It was because his heredity and environment were not the same that his act was not the same.

Both men had free wills. What made one do what the other refused to do?

Heredity and environment. To reverse their conduct we should have to reverse their heredity and environment. . . .

Two boys work at a hard and disagreeable trade. One leaves it, finds other work, "gets on," is praised for getting on. The other stays at the trade all his life,

works hard all his life, is poor all his life, and is respected as an honest and humble working man; that is to say, he is regarded by society as Mr. Dorgan was regarded by Mr. Dooely—"he is a fine man, and I despise him."

What causes these two free wills to will so differently? One boy knew more than the other boy. He "knew better." All knowledge is environment. Both boys had free wills. It was in knowledge they differed: environment!

Those who exalt the power of the will, and belittle the power environment, belie their words by their deeds.

For they would not send their children amongst bad companions or allow them to read bad books. They would not say the children have free will and therefore have power to take the good and leave the bad.

They know very well that evil environment has power to pervert the will, and that good environment has power to direct it properly.

They know that children may be made good or bad by good or evil training, and that the will follows the training.

That being so, they must also admit that the children of other people may be good or bad by training.

And if a child gets bad training, how can free will save it? Or how can it be blamed for being bad? It never had a chance to be good. That they know this is proved by their carefulness in providing their own children with better environment.

As I have said before, every church, every school, every moral lesson is a proof that preachers and teachers trust to good environment, and not to free will, to make children good.

In this, as in so many other matters, actions speak louder than words.

That, I hope, disentangles the many knots into which thousands of learned men have tied the simple subject of free will; and disposes of the claim that man is responsible because his will is free. But there is one other cause of error, akin to the subject, on which I should like to say a few words.

We often hear it said that a man is to blame for his conduct because "he knows better."

It is true that men do wrong when they know better. Macbeth "knew better" when he murdered

Duncan. But it is true, also, that we often think a man "knows better," when he does not know better.

For a man cannot be said to know a thing until he believes it. If I am told that the moon is made of green cheese, it cannot be said that I *know* it to be made of green cheese.

Many moralists seem to confuse the words "to know" with the words "to hear."

Jones reads novels and plays opera music on Sunday. The Puritan says Jones "knows better," when he means that Jones has been told that it is wrong to do those things.

But Jones does not know that it is wrong. He has heard someone say that it is wrong, but does not believe it. Therefore it is not correct to say that he knows it.

And, again, as to that matter of belief. Some moralists hold that it is wicked not to believe certain things, and that men who do not believe those things will be punished.

But a man cannot believe a thing he is told to believe: he can only believe a thing which he *can* believe; and he can only believe that which his own reason tells him is true.

It would be no use asking Sir Roger Ball to believe that the earth is flat. He *could not* believe it.

It is no use asking an agnostic to believe the story of Jonah and the whale. He *could not* believe it. He might pretend to believe it. He might try to believe it. But his reason would not allow him to believe it.

Therefore it is a mistake to say that a man "knows better," when the fact is that he has been told "better" and cannot believe what he has been told.

That is a simple matter, and looks quite trivial; but how much ill-will, how much intolerance, how much violence, persecution, and murder have been caused by the strange idea that a man is wicked because *his* reason *cannot* believe that which to another man's reason [is] quite true.

Free will has no power over a man's belief. A man cannot believe by will, but only by conviction. A man cannot be forced to believe. You may threaten him, wound him, beat him, burn him; and he may be frightened, or angered, or pained; but he cannot *believe,* nor can he be made to believe. Until he is convinced.

Now, truism as it may seem, I think it necessary to say here that a man cannot be convinced by abuse, nor by punishment. He can only be convinced by *reason.*

Yes. If we wish a man to believe a thing, we shall find a few words of reason more powerful than a million curses, or a million bayonets. To burn a man alive for failing to believe that the sun goes round the world is not to convince him. The fire is searching, but it does not seem to him to be relevant to the issue. He never doubted that fire would burn; but perchance his dying eyes may see the sun sinking down into the west, as the world rolls on its axis. He dies in his belief. And knows no "better."

Discussion Questions

1. In what way does our picture of the world depend on the background belief that people are *free*? Give some examples of ways in which our actions and beliefs depend on the supposition that people act freely. Then consider ways in which our picture of the world depends on the background belief that people's behavior is *determined*. In general, do we consider people to be free, determined, or some combination of both?

2. Are determinism and your religion compatible? Can both be true? If not, is faith that God exists and that God gave us free will an adequate response to Blatchford's arguments?

3. In what ways do humans express creativity? Is this creativity compatible with determinism? How would Blatchford explain creativity? Do you think that human creativity requires that humans are free? Explain your answer.

4. Do psychological investigations of human behavior presuppose that determinism is true? If not, could psychologists ever hope to explain and predict human behavior? Does

a science of human nature require that humans be conceptualized as part of the natural world, subject to the same natural laws as other objects? Why or why not?

5. Are there any possible circumstances that would satisfy Blatchford that his thesis is false? For example, could scientific experiments disconfirm Blatchford's determinism? Why or why not? What does your answer suggest about the adequacy of Blatchford's thesis?

For Further Reading

This selection comes from *Not Guilty* (1913). To learn more about Blatchford, consult his autobiography, *My Eighty Years* (1931). For an excellent introduction to the problem of free will, see either R. Taylor's *Metaphysics* (1991) or J. Trusted's *Free Will and Responsibility* (1984). For a collection of essays concerning free will and determinism, see *Determinism and Freedom* (1961), edited by Sidney Hook; *Freedom and Determinism* (1966), edited by K. Lehrer; *Essays on Freedom of Action* (1973), edited by T. Honderich; and *Free Will* (1982), edited by G. Watson. For a contemporary defense of determinism, see Honderich's *The Consequences of Determinism* (1988).

4   FREE WILL
Charles Arthur Campbell

C. A. Campbell (1897–1974) spent most of his academic career teaching philosophy at his alma mater, the University of Glasgow. The following selection comes from Campbell's most important work, *On Selfhood and Godhood* (1957), a book comprised of three separate projects. First, Campbell endeavors to make clear the sort of freedom that is (or ought to be) at issue in the free will debate. Second, Campbell attempts to show that humans indeed possess this sort of freedom, and finally, Campbell defends his thesis from possible criticisms.

The relevant sort of freedom in the free will debate is, according to Campbell, 'moral freedom'. What is moral freedom? Campbell writes that "a man can be said to exercise free will in a morally significant sense only insofar as his chosen act is one of which he is the sole cause or author, and only if . . . he 'could have chosen otherwise.'" What evidence does Campbell offer to prove the existence of moral freedom? For Campbell, it is *inner experience* that confirms our moral freedom. Every time we make a *moral effort* to do the right thing, we are directly aware of the fact that we could have done otherwise.

Reading Questions

1. What sort of freedom is at issue in the free will and determinism debate? What is the proper touchstone for determining the sort of freedom at issue?
2. Under what conditions are we the sole author of our actions?

SOURCE: From *On Selfhood and Godhood* by C. A. Campbell. 1957 Allen and Unwin. Reprinted with permission of Routledge, Inc.

3. Why may sole authorship of an act not suffice to make it morally free?
4. Why is a categorical interpretation of "X could have acted otherwise" preferable to a hypothetical interpretation?
5. What 'proof' of moral freedom does Campbell offer?
6. What 'proof' does Campbell offer of the veracity of our "practical" beliefs?
7. How does Campbell attack the 'predictability' argument for determinism?
8. Explain Campbell's response to the claim that free will is unintelligible.

. . .

It is something of a truism that in philosophic enquiry the exact formulation of a problem often takes one a long way on the road to its solution. In the case of the free will problem I think there is a rather special need of careful formulation. For there are many sorts of human freedom; and it can easily happen that one wastes a great deal of labor in proving or disproving a freedom which has almost nothing to do with the freedom which is at issue in the traditional problem of free will. . . .

. . .

Fortunately we can at least make a beginning with a certain amount of confidence. It is not seriously disputable that the kind of freedom in question is the freedom which is commonly recognized to be in some sense a precondition of moral responsibility. . . .

Our first business, then, is to ask, exactly what kind of freedom is it which is required for moral responsibility? And as to method of procedure in this inquiry, there seems to me to be no real choice. I know of only one method that carries with it any hope of success; viz. the critical comparison of those acts for which, on due reflection, we deem it proper to attribute moral praise or blame to the agents, with those acts for which, on due reflection, we deem such judgments to be improper. The ultimate touchstone, as I see it, can only be our moral consciousness as it manifests itself in our more critical and considered moral judgments. . . .

2. The first point to note is that the freedom at issue pertains primarily not to overt acts but to inner acts. . . . We do not consider the acts of a robot to be morally responsible acts; nor do we consider the acts of a man to be so save insofar as they are distinguishable from those of a robot by reflecting an inner life of choice. Similarly, from the other side, if we are satisfied that a person has definitely elected to follow a course which he believes to be wrong, but has been prevented by external

circumstances from translating his inner choice into an overt act, we still regard him as morally blameworthy. Moral freedom, then, pertains to inner acts.

The next point . . . is the simple point that the act must be one of which the person judged can be regarded as the *sole* author. It seems plain enough that if there are any *other* determinants of the act, external to the self, to that extent the act is not an act which the *self* determines, and to that extent not an act for which the self can be held morally responsible. The self is only part-author of the act, and his moral responsibility can logically extend only to those elements within the act of which he is the sole author.

. . .

Thirdly we come to a point over which much recent controversy has raged. We may approach it by raising the following question. Granted an act of which the agent is sole author, does this 'sole authorship' suffice to make the act a morally free act? We may be inclined to think that it does, until we contemplate the possibility that an act of which the agent is sole author might conceivably occur as a necessary expression of the agent's nature; the way in which, e.g., some philosophers have supposed the divine act of creation to occur. This consideration excites a legitimate doubt; for it is far from easy to see how a person can be regarded as a proper subject for moral praise or blame in respect of an act which he *cannot help* performing—even if it be his own 'nature' which necessitates it. Must we not recognize it as a condition of the morally free act that the agent 'could have acted otherwise' than he in fact did? . . .

Now philosophers today are fairly well agreed that it is a postulate of the morally responsible act that the agent 'could have acted otherwise' in *some* sense of that phrase. But sharp differences of opinion have arisen over the way in which the phrase ought to be interpreted. There is a strong disposition to water down its apparent meaning by insisting that it is not (as a postulate of moral responsibility) to be understood as a straightforward categorical proposition, but rather as a disguised hypothetical proposition. All that we really require to be assured of, in order to justify our holding X morally responsible for an act, is, we are told, that X could have acted otherwise *if* he had *chosen* otherwise (Moore, Stevenson); or perhaps that X could have acted otherwise *if* he had had a different character, or *if* he had been placed in different circumstances.

I think it is easy to understand, and even, in a measure, to sympathize with, the motives which induce philosophers to offer these counter-interpretations. It is not just the fact that 'X could have acted otherwise', as a bald categorical statement, is incompatible with the universal sway of causal law—though this is, to some philosophers, a serious stone of stumbling. The more widespread objection is that it at least looks as though it were incompatible with that causal continuity of an agent's character with his conduct which is implied when we believe (surely with justice) that we can often tell the sort of thing a man will do from our knowledge of the sort of man he is.

We shall have to make our accounts with that particular difficulty later. At this stage I wish merely to show that neither of the hypothetical propositions suggested—and I think the same could be shown for any hypothetical alternative—is an acceptable substitute for the categorical proposition 'X could have acted otherwise' as the presupposition of moral responsibility.

Let us look first at the earlier suggestion—'X could have acted otherwise *if* he had chosen otherwise'. Now clearly there are a great many acts with regard to which we are entirely satisfied that the agent is thus situated. We are often perfectly sure that—for this is all it amounts to—if X had chosen otherwise, the circumstances presented no external obstacle to the translation of that choice into action. For example, we often have no doubt at all that X, who in point of fact told a lie, could have told the truth *if* he had so chosen. But does our confidence on this score allay all legitimate doubts about whether X is really blameworthy? Does it entail that X is free in the sense required for moral responsibility? Surely not. The obvious question immediately arises: 'But *could* X have *chosen* otherwise than he did?' It is doubt about

the true answer to *that* question which leads most people to doubt the reality of moral responsibility. Yet on this crucial question the hypothetical proposition which is offered as a sufficient statement of the condition justifying the ascription of moral responsibility gives us no information whatsoever.

Indeed this hypothetical substitute for the categorical 'X could have acted otherwise' seems to me to lack all plausibility unless one contrives to forget why it is, after all, that we ever come to feel fundamental doubts about man's moral responsibility. Such doubts are born, surely, when one becomes aware of certain reputable world-views in religion or philosophy, or of certain reputable scientific beliefs, which in their several ways imply that man's actions are necessitated, and thus could not be otherwise than they in fact are. But clearly a doubt so based is not even touched by the recognition that a man could very often act otherwise *if* he so chose. That proposition is entirely compatible with the necessitarian theories which generate our doubt: indeed it is this very compatibility that has recommended it to some philosophers, who are reluctant to give up either moral responsibility or determinism. The proposition which we *must* be able to affirm if moral praise or blame of X is to be justified is the categorical proposition that X could have acted otherwise because—not if—he could have chosen otherwise; or, since it is essentially the inner side of the act that matters, the proposition simply that X could have chosen otherwise.

...

3. Let me, then, briefly sum up the answer at which we have arrived to our question about the kind of freedom required to justify moral responsibility. It is that a man can be said to exercise free will in a morally significant sense only insofar as his chosen act is one of which he is the sole cause or author, and only if—in the straightforward, categorical sense of the phrase—he 'could have chosen otherwise'.

...

5. That brings me to the second, and more constructive, part of this lecture. From now on I shall be considering whether it is reasonable to believe that man does in fact possess a free will of the kind specified in the first part of the lecture. If so, just how and where within the complex fabric of the volitional

life are we to locate it?—for although free will must presumably belong (if anywhere) to the volitional side of human experience, it is pretty clear from the way in which we have been forced to define it that it does not pertain simply to volition as such; not even to all volitions that are commonly dignified with the name of 'choices'. . . .

...

Suppose one asks the ordinary intelligent citizen *why* he deems it proper to make allowances for X, whose heredity and/or environment are unfortunate. He will tend to reply, I think, in some such terms as these: that X has more and stronger temptations to deviate from what is right than Y or Z, who are normally circumstanced, so that he must put forth a *stronger moral effort* if he is to achieve the same level of external conduct. The intended implication seems to be that X is just as morally praiseworthy as Y or Z *if* he exerts an equivalent moral effort, even though he may not thereby achieve an equal success in conforming his will to the 'concrete' demands of duty. And this implies, again, common sense's belief that *in moral effort* we have something for which a man is responsible *without qualification,* something that is *not* affected by heredity and environment but depends *solely* on the self itself.

Now in my opinion common sense has here, in principle, hit upon the one and only defensible answer. Here, and here alone, so far as I can see, in the act of deciding whether to put forth or withhold the moral effort required to resist temptation and rise to duty, is to be found an act which is free in the sense required for moral responsibility; an act of which the self is sole author, and of which it is true to say that 'it could be' (or, after the event, 'could have been') 'otherwise'. Such is the thesis which we shall now try to establish.

...

. . . [Consider a] situation of moral temptation. 'Is it possible', we must ask, 'for anyone so circumstanced to *dis*believe that he could be deciding otherwise?' The answer is surely not in doubt. When we decide to exert moral effort to resist a temptation, we feel quite certain that we *could* withhold the effort; just as, if we decide to withhold the effort and yield to our desires, we feel quite certain that we *could*

exert it—otherwise we should not blame ourselves afterwards for having succumbed. It may be, indeed, that this conviction is mere self-delusion. But that is not at the moment of our concern. It is enough at present to establish that the act of deciding to exert or to withhold moral effort, as we know it from the inside in actual moral living, belongs to the category of acts which 'could have been otherwise'.

Mutatis mutandis, the same reply is forthcoming if we ask, 'Is it possible for the moral agent in the taking of his decision to disbelieve that he is the *sole* author of that decision?' Clearly he cannot disbelieve that it is *he* who takes the decision. That, however, is not in itself sufficient to enable him, on reflection, to regard himself as *solely* responsible for the act. For his 'character' as so far formed might conceivably be a factor in determining it, and no one can suppose that the constitution of his 'character' is uninfluenced by circumstances of heredity and environment with which *he* has nothing to do. But as we pointed out in the last lecture, the very essence of the moral decision as it is experienced is that it is a decision whether or not to *combat* our strongest desire, and our strongest desire *is* the expression in the situation of our character as so far formed. Now clearly our character cannot be a factor in determining the decision whether or not to *oppose* our character. I think we are entitled to say, therefore, that the act of moral decision is one in which the self is for itself not merely 'author' but 'sole author'.

7. We may pass on, then, to the second phase of our constructive argument; and this will demand more elaborate treatment. Even if a moral agent *qua* making a moral decision in the situation of 'temptation' cannot help believing that he has free will in the sense at issue—a moral freedom between real alternatives, between genuinely open possibilities—are there, nevertheless, objections to a freedom of this kind so cogent that we are bound to distrust the evidence of 'inner experience'?

I begin by drawing attention to a simple point whose significance tends, I think, to be underestimated. If the phenomenological analysis we have offered is substantially correct, no one while functioning as a moral agent can help believing that he enjoys free will. Theoretically he may be completely convinced by determinist arguments, but when actually confronted with a personal situation of conflict between duty and desire he is quite certain that it lies with him here and now whether or not he will rise to duty. It follows that if determinists could produce convincing theoretical arguments against a free will of this kind, the awkward predicament would ensue that man has to deny as a theoretical being what he has to assert as a practical being. Now I think the determinist ought to be a good deal more worried about this than he usually is. He seems to imagine that a strong case on general theoretical grounds is enough to prove that the 'practical' belief in free will, even if inescapable for us as practical beings, is mere illusion. But in fact it proves nothing of the sort. There is no reason whatever why a belief that we find ourselves obliged to hold *qua* practical beings should be required to give way before a belief which we find ourselves obliged to hold *qua* theoretical beings; or, for that matter, vice versa. All that the theoretical arguments of determinism can prove, unless they are reinforced by a refutation of the phenomenological analysis that supports libertarianism, is that there is a radical conflict between the theoretical and the practical sides of man's nature, an antinomy at the very heart of the self. And this is a state of affairs with which no one can easily rest satisfied. I think therefore that the determinist ought to concern himself a great deal more than he does with phenomenological analysis, in order to show, if he can, that the assurance of free will is not really an inexpungable element in man's practical consciousness. There is just as much obligation upon him, convinced though he may be of the soundness of his theoretical arguments, to expose the errors of the libertarian's phenomenological analysis, as there is upon us, convinced though we may be of the soundness of the libertarian's phenomenological analysis, to expose the errors of the determinist's theoretical arguments.

8. However, we must at once begin the discharge of our own obligation. The rest of this lecture will be devoted to trying to show that the arguments which seem to carry most weight with determinists are, to say the least of it, very far from compulsive.

...

These arguments can, I think, be reduced in principle to no more than two: first, the argument from 'predictability'; second, the argument from the alleged meaninglessness of an act supposed to be the self's act and yet not an expression of the self's character. Contemporary criticism of free will seems to me to consist almost exclusively of variations on these two themes. I shall deal with each in turn.

9. . . . Surely it is beyond question (the critic urges) that when we know a person intimately we can foretell with a high degree of accuracy how he will respond to at least a large number of practical situations. One feels safe in predicting that one's dog-loving friend will not use his boot to repel the little mongrel that comes yapping at his heels; or again that one's wife will not pass with incurious eyes (or indeed pass at all) the new hat-shop in the city. So to behave would not be (as we say) 'in character'. But, so the criticism runs, you with your doctrine of 'genuinely open possibilities', of a free will by which the self can diverge from its own character, remove all rational basis from such prediction. You require us to make the absurd supposition that the success of countless predictions of the sort in the past has been mere matter of chance. If you *really* believed in your theory, you would not be surprised if tomorrow your friend with the notorious horror of strong drink should suddenly exhibit a passion for whisky and soda, or if your friend whose taste for reading has hitherto been satisfied with the sporting columns of the newspapers should be discovered on a fine Saturday afternoon poring over the works of Hegel. But of course you *would* be surprised. Social life would be sheer chaos if there were not well-grounded social expectations; and social life is not sheer chaos. Your theory is hopelessly wrecked upon obvious facts.

Now whether or not this criticism holds good against some versions of libertarian theory I need not here discuss. It is sufficient if I can make it clear that against the version advanced in this lecture, according to which free will is localized in a relatively narrow field of operation, the criticism has no relevance whatsoever.

Let us remind ourselves briefly of the setting within which, on our view, free will functions. There is X, the course which we believe we ought to follow, and Y, the course towards which we feel our desire is strongest. The freedom which we ascribe to the agent is the freedom to put forth or refrain from putting forth the moral effort required to resist the pressure of desire and do what he thinks he ought to do.

But then there is surely an immense range of practical situations—covering by far the greater part of life—in which there is no question of a conflict within the self between what he most desires to do and what he thinks he ought to do. Indeed such conflict is a comparatively rare phenomenon for the majority of men. Yet over that whole vast range there is nothing whatever in our version of libertarianism to prevent our agreeing that character determines conduct. In the absence, real or supposed, of any 'moral' issue, what a man chooses will be simply that course which, after such reflection as seems called for, he deems most likely to bring him what he most strongly desires; and that is the same as to say the course to which his present character inclines him.

Over by far the greater area of human choices, then, our theory offers no more barrier to successful prediction on the basis of character than any other theory. For where there is no clash of strongest desire with duty, the free will we are defending has no business. There is just nothing for it to do.

But what about the situations—rare enough though they may be—in which there is this clash and in which free will does therefore operate? Does our theory entail that there at any rate, as the critic seems to suppose, 'anything may happen'?

Not by any manner of means. In the first place, and by the very nature of the case, the range of the agent's possible choices is bounded by what he thinks he ought to do on the one hand, and what he most strongly desires on the other. The freedom claimed for him is a freedom of decision to make or withhold the effort required to do what he thinks he ought to do. There is no question of a freedom to act in some 'wild' fashion, out of all relation to his characteristic beliefs and desires. This so-called 'freedom of caprice', so often charged against the libertarian, is, to put it bluntly, a sheer figment of the critic's imagination, with no habitat in serious libertarian theory. Even in situations where free will does come into play it is perfectly possible, on a view like ours, given the appropriate knowledge of a man's character, to predict within certain limits how he will respond.

But 'probable' prediction in such situations can, I think, go further than this. It is obvious that where desire and duty are at odds, the felt 'gap' (as it were) between the two may vary enormously in breadth in different cases. The moderate drinker and the chronic tippler may each want another glass, and each deem it his duty to abstain, but the felt gap between desire and duty in the case of the former is trivial beside the great gulf which is felt to separate them in the case of the latter. Hence it will take a far harder moral effort for the tippler than for the moderate drinker to achieve the same external result of abstention. So much is matter of common agreement. And we are entitled, I think, to take it into account in prediction, on the simple principle that the harder the moral effort required to resist desire the less likely it is to occur. Thus in the example taken, most people would predict that the tippler will very probably succumb to his desires, whereas there is a reasonable likelihood that the moderate drinker will make the comparatively slight effort needed to resist them. So long as the prediction does not pretend to more than a measure of probability, there is nothing in our theory which would disallow it.

I claim, therefore, that the view of free will I have been putting forward is consistent with predictability of conduct on the basis of character over a very wide field indeed. And I make the further claim that that field will cover all the situations in life concerning which there is any empirical evidence that successful prediction is possible.

10. Let us pass on to consider the second main line of criticism. . . .

'Free will as you describe it is completely unintelligible. On your own showing no *reason* can be given, because there just *is* no reason, why a man decides to exert rather than to withhold moral effort, or vice versa. But such an act—or more properly, such an "occurrence"—it is nonsense to speak of as an act of a *self*. If there is nothing in the self's character to which it is, even in principle, in any way traceable, the self has nothing to do with it. Your so-called "freedom", therefore, so far from supporting the self's moral responsibility, destroys it as surely as the crudest determinism could do.'

If we are to discuss this criticism usefully, it is important, I think, to begin by getting clear about two different senses of the word 'intelligible'.

If, in the first place, we mean by an 'intelligible' act one whose occurrence is in principle capable of being inferred, since it follows necessarily from something (though we may not know in fact from what), then it is certainly true that the libertarian's free will is unintelligible. But that is only saying, is it not, that the libertarian's 'free' act is not an act which follows necessarily from something! This can hardly rank as a *criticism* of libertarianism. It is just a description of it. That there can be nothing unintelligible in *this* sense is precisely what the determinist has got to *prove*.

Yet it is surprising how often the critic of libertarianism involves himself in this circular mode of argument. Repeatedly it is urged against the libertarian, with a great air of triumph, that on his view he can't say *why* I now decide to rise to duty, or now decide to follow my strongest desire in defiance of duty. Of course he can't. If he could he wouldn't be a libertarian. To 'account for' a 'free' act is a contradiction in terms. A free will is *ex hypothesi* the sort of thing of which the request for an *explanation* is absurd. The assumption that an explanation must be in principle possible for the act of moral decision deserves to rank as a classic example of the ancient fallacy of 'begging the question'.

But the critic usually has in mind another sense of the word 'unintelligible'. He is apt to take it for granted that an act which is unintelligible in the above sense (as the morally free act of the libertarian undoubtedly is) is unintelligible in the further sense that we can attach no meaning to it. And this is an altogether more serious matter. If it could really be shown that the libertarian's 'free will' were unintelligible in this sense of being meaningless, that, for myself at any rate, would be the end of the affair. Libertarianism would have been conclusively refuted.

But it seems to me manifest that this can *not* be shown. The critic has allowed himself, I submit, to become the victim of a widely accepted but fundamentally vicious assumption. He has assumed that whatever is meaningful must exhibit its meaningfulness to those who view it from the standpoint of external observation. Now if one chooses thus to limit one's self to the role of external observer, it is, I think, perfectly true that one can attach no meaning to an act which is the act of something we call a 'self'

and yet follows from nothing in that self's character. But then *why should we* so limit ourselves, when what is under consideration is a subjective activity? For the apprehension of subjective acts there is another standpoint available, that of *inner experience*, of the practical consciousness in its actual functioning. If our free will should turn out to be something to which we can attach a meaning from *this* standpoint, no more is required. And no more ought to be expected. For I must repeat that only from the inner standpoint of living experience *could* anything of the nature of 'activity' be directly grasped. Observation from without is in the nature of the case impotent to apprehend the active *qua* active. We can from without observe sequences of states. If into these we read activity (as we sometimes do), this can only be on the basis of what we discern in ourselves from the inner standpoint. It follows that if anyone insists upon taking his criterion of the meaningful simply from the standpoint of external observation, he is really deciding in advance of the evidence that the notion of activity, and *a fortiori* the notion of a free will, is 'meaningless'. He looks for the free act through a medium which is in the nature of the case incapable of revealing it, and then, because inevitably he doesn't find it, he declares that it doesn't exist!

But if, as we surely ought in this context, we adopt the inner standpoint, then (I am suggesting) things appear in a totally different light. From the inner standpoint, it seems to me plain, there is no difficulty whatever in attaching meaning to an act which is the self's act and which nevertheless does not follow from the self's character. So much I claim has been established by the phenomenological analysis, in this and the previous lecture, of the act of moral decision in the face of moral temptation. It is thrown into particularly clear relief where the moral decision is to make the moral effort required to rise to duty. For the very function of moral effort, as it appears to the agent engaged in the act, is to enable the self to act against the line of least resistance, against the line to which his character as so far formed most strongly inclines him. But if the self is thus conscious here of *combating* his formed character, he surely cannot possibly suppose that the act, although his own act, *issues from* his formed character? I submit, therefore, that the self knows very well indeed—from the inner standpoint—what is meant by an act which is the *self's* act and which nevertheless does not follow from the self's *character*.

What this implies—and it seems to me to be an implication of cardinal importance for any theory of the self that aims at being more than superficial—is that the nature of the self is for itself something more than just its character as so far formed. The 'nature' of the self and what we commonly call the 'character' of the self are by no means the same thing, and it is utterly vital that they should not be confused. The 'nature' of the self comprehends, but is not without remainder reducible to, its 'character'; it must, if we are to be true to the testimony of our experience of it, be taken as including also the authentic creative power of fashioning and re-fashioning 'character'.

The misguided, and as a rule quite uncritical, belittlement, of the evidence offered by inner experience has, I am convinced, been responsible for more bad argument by the opponents of free will than has any other single factor. How often, for example, do we find the determinist critic saying, in effect, '*Either* the act follows necessarily upon precedent states, *or* it is a mere matter of chance and accordingly of no moral significance'. The disjunction is invalid, for it does not exhaust the possible alternatives. It seems to the critic to do so only because he *will* limit himself to the standpoint which is proper, and indeed alone possible, in dealing with the physical world, the standpoint of the external observer. If only he would allow himself to assume the standpoint which is not merely proper for, but necessary to, the apprehension of subjective activity, the inner standpoint of the practical consciousness in its actual functioning, he would find himself obliged to recognize the falsity of his disjunction. Reflection upon the act of moral decision as apprehended from the inner standpoint would force him to recognize a *third* possibility, as remote from chance as from necessity, that, namely, of *creative activity*, in which (as I have ventured to express it) nothing determines the act save the agent's doing of it. . . .

Discussion Questions

1. What is 'moral effort'? Can each person exert the same moral effort, or is moral effort itself subject to the effects of heredity and the environment? How do you believe Campbell would answer this question? Do you agree? Why or why not?

2. What is an 'inner experience'? Are inner experiences reliable sources of information? Should we trust our inner experience of freedom? Is it possible to be deceived about our own inner experience of freedom? Could we be determined and yet still feel as if we are free?

3. Suppose inner experiences come into conflict with theoretical or scientific arguments. Should our inner experiences be trusted when they conflict with theoretical and scientific arguments? Why or why not? Are there times when we should trust our inner experiences but other times when we should not? Explain your answer.

For Further Reading

Campbell's major work is his book, *On Selfhood and Godhood* (1957), and many of his essays have been collected in *In Defense of Free Will* (1967). For commentaries on Campbell's work see H. P. Owen's "The Moral and Religious Philosophy of C. A. Campbell," *Religious Studies* 3.

For other defenses of free will see R. Chisholm's "Human Freedom and the Self," in *Free Will* (1982), edited by G. Watson; *Existentialism and Humanism* (1948), by Jean-Paul Sartre; and A. Mele's text *Autonomous Agents* (1995).

5   FREEDOM AND NECESSITY
A. J. Ayer

British philosopher A. J. Ayer (1910–1989) is most famous for his first
book, *Language, Truth, and Logic* (1936), in which he made a strong case
for **logical positivism.** As a logical positivist, Ayer believed that only
certain sorts of sentences could be true and meaningful. These were
sentences that expressed, on the one hand, **logical truths** or **conceptual
truths** or, on the other hand, sentences that were empirically verifiable. As
a positivist, Ayer was skeptical of the truth and meaningfulness of
sentences that expressed moral judgments. How, for example, is one to
empirically verify the claim that a particular act is morally wrong?
Apparently, one cannot. Hence, Ayer believed that such sentences should
be understood as mere expressions of the speaker's preferences—a view
called **emotivism.**

Language, Truth, and Logic was followed by several other important books
including *The Foundations of Empirical Knowledge* (1940), *The Problem of
Knowledge* (1954), and *Probability and Evidence* (1972). In 1973, A. J. Ayer
was knighted for his impressive work as a scholar and a philosopher.

In the following essay, Ayer defends compatibilism, the belief that humans
are determined yet still morally free. Curiously, Ayer begins by noting the
fact that although the evidence in favor of determinism is not conclusive,
problems result for anyone who would deny determinism. For example, if
our actions are not caused, that is, if our actions are merely a matter of
chance, then we would not be responsible for our actions. Given this
unacceptable consequence, Ayer sets out to explain how free will is
compatible with determinism. He begins by noting that moral
responsibility, rather than being at odds with determinism, actually
presupposes determinism. This is true because one is held accountable for
only those sorts of actions that are a result of our character and are,
therefore, predictable. Although they appear contradictory, Ayer contends
that moral freedom and determinism are indeed compatible.

One possible problem with this contention is illustrated by the following
example. The activities of a kleptomaniac (an individual with a neurotic
impulse to steal) are predictable and a function of his or her nature. But
kleptomaniacs are not held morally responsible for their actions. Hence,
Ayer must identify and explain the difference in moral culpability between
an ordinary person who might steal for economic gain and a kleptomaniac,
who steals out of a psychological compulsion. For Ayer, the difference
between the two is this: Because the kleptomaniac is under a compulsion to
steal, he or she is not responsible for stealing. On the other hand, the
ordinary person who steals is (presumably) under no such compulsion and
can therefore be held morally accountable. In other words, the ordinary
person could have done otherwise and is, therefore, responsible for stealing,

Source: From *Philosophical Essays* by A. J. Ayer, 1954. Used by permission of Macmillan Press Ltd.

whereas the kleptomaniac could not have done otherwise and is, therefore, not responsible for stealing. For Ayer, then, moral freedom depends on the extent to which one is or is not compelled to act.

Reading Questions

1. Under what conditions is a person responsible for his or her actions?
2. Is 'feeling as if one has a free will' proof that one has free will?
3. What reasons are there for doubting whether all human actions are subservient to causal laws?
4. How does the determinist account for faulty predictions concerning human behavior?
5. Are persons morally free if it is a matter of chance that they act in one way rather than another?
6. Are we responsible for our own character?
7. Why does moral responsibility presuppose determinism?
8. What is wrong with equating freedom with the 'consciousness of necessity'?
9. With what is freedom properly contrasted?
10. Under what conditions is one constrained?
11. In reference to constraint, explain the difference between a common thief and a diagnosed kleptomaniac.

When I am said to have done something of my own free will it is implied that I could have acted otherwise; and it is only when it is believed that I could have acted otherwise that I am held to be morally responsible for what I have done. For a man is not thought to be morally responsible for an action that it was not in his power to avoid. But if human behavior is entirely governed by causal laws, it is not clear how any action that is done could ever have been avoided. It may be said of the agent that he would have acted otherwise if the causes of his action had been different, but they being what they were, it seems to follow that he was bound to act as he did. Now it is commonly assumed both that men are capable of acting freely, in the sense that is required to make them morally responsible and that human behavior is entirely governed by causal laws: and it is the apparent conflict between these two assumptions that gives rise to the philosophical problem of the freedom of the will.

. . . What is evident, indeed, is that people often believe themselves to be acting freely; and it is to this 'feeling' of freedom that some philosophers appeal when they wish, in the supposed interests of morality, to prove that not all human action is causally determined. But if these philosophers are right in their assumption that a man cannot be acting freely if his action is causally determined, then the fact someone feels free to do, or not to do, a certain action does not prove that he really is so. It may prove that the agent does not himself know what it is that makes him act in one way rather than another: but from the fact that a man is unaware of the causes of his action, it does not follow that no such causes exist.

So much may be allowed to the determinist; but his belief that all human actions are subservient to causal laws still remains to be justified. If, indeed, it is necessary that every event should have a cause, then the rule must apply to human behavior as much as to anything else. But why should it be supposed that every event must have a cause? The contrary is not unthinkable. Nor is the law of universal causation a necessary presupposition of scientific thought. The scientist may try to discover causal laws, and in many cases he succeeds; but sometimes he has to be content with statistical laws, and sometimes he comes upon events which, in the present state of his knowledge, he is not able to subsume under any law at all. In the case of these events he assumes that if he knew more he would be able to discover some law, whether causal or statistical, which would enable him to account for them. And this assumption cannot be disproved. For however far he may have carried his investigation, it is always open to him to carry it further; and it is always conceivable that if he carried it further he would discover the connection which had hitherto escaped him. Nevertheless, it is also conceivable that the events with which he is concerned are not systematically connected with any others: so that the reason why he does not discover the sort of laws that he requires is simply that they do not obtain.

Now in the case of human conduct the search for explanations has not in fact been altogether fruitless. Certain scientific laws have been established; and with the help of these laws we do make a number of successful predictions about the ways in which different people will behave. But these predictions do not always cover every detail. We may be able to predict that in certain circumstances a particular man will be angry, without being able to prescribe the precise form that the expression of his anger will take. We may be reasonably sure that he will shout, but not sure how loud his shout will be, or exactly what words he will use. And it is only a small proportion of human actions that we are able to forecast even so precisely as this. But that, it may be said, is because we have not carried our investigations very far. The science of psychology is still in its infancy and, as it is developed, not only will more human actions be explained, but the explanations will go into greater detail. The ideal of complete explanation may never in fact be attained: but it is theoretically attainable. Well, this may be so: and certainly it is impossible to show *a priori* that it is not so: but equally it cannot be shown that it is. This will not, however, discourage the scientist who, in the field of human behavior, as elsewhere, will continue to formulate theories and test them by the facts. And in this he is justified. For since he has no reason *a priori* to admit that there is a limit to what he can discover, the fact that he also cannot be sure that there is no limit does not make it unreasonable for him to devise theories, nor, having devised them, to try constantly to improve them.

But now suppose it to be claimed that, so far as men's actions are concerned, there is a limit: and that this limit is set by the fact of human freedom. An obvious objection is that in many cases in which a person feels himself to be free to do, or not to do, a certain action, we are even now able to explain, in causal terms, why it is that he acts as he does. But it might be argued

that even if men are sometimes mistaken in believing that they act freely, it does not follow that they are always so mistaken. For it is not always the case that when a man believes that he has acted freely we are in fact able to account for his action in causal terms. A determinist would say that we should be able to account for it if we had more knowledge of the circumstances, and had been able to discover the appropriate natural laws. But until those discoveries have been made, this remains only a pious hope. And may it not be true that, in some cases at least, the reason why we can give no causal explanation is that no causal explanation is available; and that this is because the agent's choice was literally free, as he himself felt it to be?

The answer is that this may indeed be true, inasmuch as it is open to anyone to hold that no explanation is possible until some explanation is actually found. But even so it does not give the moralist what he wants. For he is anxious to show that men are capable of acting freely in order to infer that they can be morally responsible for what they do. But if it is a matter of pure chance that a man should act in one way rather than another, he may be free but he can hardly be responsible. And indeed when a man's actions seem to us quite unpredictable, when, as we say, there is no knowing what he will do, we do not look upon him as a moral agent. We look upon him rather as a lunatic.

To this it may be objected that we are not dealing fairly with the moralist. For when he makes it a condition of my being morally responsible that I should act freely, he does not wish to imply that it is purely a matter of chance that I act as I do. What he wishes to imply is that my actions are the result of my own free choice: and it is because they are the result of my own free choice that I am held to be morally responsible for them.

But now we must ask how it is that I come to make my choice. Either it is an accident that I choose to act as I do or it is not. If it is an accident, then it is merely a matter of chance that I did not choose otherwise; and if it is merely a matter of chance that I did not choose otherwise, it is surely irrational to hold me morally responsible for choosing as I did. But if it is not an accident that I choose to do one thing rather than another, then presumably there is some causal explanation of my choice: and in that case we are led back to determinism.

Again, the objection may be raised that we are not doing justice to the moralist's case. His view is not that it is a matter of chance that I choose to act as I do, but rather that my choice depends upon my character. Nevertheless he holds that I can still be free in the sense that he requires; for it is I who am responsible for my character. But in what way am I responsible for my character? Only, surely, in the sense that there is a causal connection between what I do now and what I have done in the past. It is only this that justifies the statement that I have made myself what I am: and even so this is an over-simplification, since it takes no account of the external influences to which I have been subjected. But, ignoring the external influences, let us assume that it is in fact the case that I have made myself what I am. Then it is still legitimate to ask how it is that I have come to make myself one sort of person rather than another. And if it be answered that it is a matter of my strength of will, we can put the same question in another form by asking how it is that my will has the strength that it has and not some other degree of strength. Once more, either it is an accident or it is not. If it is an accident, then by the same argument as before, I am not morally responsible, and if it is not an accident we are led back to determinism.

Furthermore, to say that my actions proceed from my character or, more colloquially, that I act in character, is to say that my behavior is consistent and to that extent predictable: and since it is, above all, for the actions that I perform in character that I am held to be morally responsible, it looks as if the admission of moral responsibility, so far from being incompatible with determinism, tends rather to presuppose it. But how can this be so if it is a necessary condition of moral responsibility that the person who is held responsible should have acted freely? It seems that if we are to retain this idea of moral responsibility, we must either show that men can be held responsible for actions which they do not freely, or else find some way of reconciling determinism with the freedom of the will.

It is no doubt with the object of effecting this reconciliation that some philosophers have defined freedom as the consciousness of necessity. And by so doing they are able to say not only that a man can be acting freely when his action is causally determined, but even that his action must be causally determined

for it to be possible for him to be acting freely. Nevertheless this definition has the serious disadvantage that it gives to the word 'freedom' a meaning quite different from any that it ordinarily bears. It is indeed obvious that if we are allowed to give the word 'freedom' any meaning that we please, we can find a meaning that will reconcile it with determinism: but this is no more a solution of our present problem than the fact that the word 'horse' could be arbitrarily used to mean what is ordinarily meant by 'sparrow' is a proof that horses have wings. For suppose that I am compelled by another person to do something 'against my will'. In that case, as the word 'freedom' is ordinarily used, I should not be said to be acting freely: and the fact that I am fully aware of the constraint to which I am subjected makes no difference to the matter. I do not become free by becoming conscious that I am not. It may, indeed, be possible to show that my being aware that my action is causally determined is not incompatible with my acting freely: but it by no means follows that it is in this that my freedom consists. Moreover, I suspect that one of the reasons why people are inclined to define freedom as the consciousness of necessity is that they think that if one is conscious of necessity one may somehow be able to master it. But this is a fallacy. It is like someone's saying that he wishes he could see into the future, because if he did he would know what calamities lay in wait for him and so would be able to avoid them. But if he avoids the calamities then they don't lie in the future and it is not true that he foresees them. And similarly if I am able to master necessity, in the sense of escaping the operation of a necessary law, then the law in question is not necessary. And if the law is not necessary, then neither my freedom nor anything else can consist in my knowing that it is.

Let it be granted, then, that when we speak of reconciling freedom with determinism we are using the word 'freedom' in an ordinary sense. It still remains for us to make this usage clear: and perhaps the best way to make it clear is to show what it is that freedom, in this sense, is contrasted with. Now we began with the assumption that freedom is contrasted with causality: so that a man cannot be said to be acting freely if his action is causally determined. But this assumption has led us into difficulties and I now wish to suggest that it is mistaken. For it is not, I think, causality that freedom is to be contrasted with, but constraint. And while it is true that being constrained to do an action entails being caused to do it, I shall try to show that the converse does not hold. I shall try to show that from the fact that my action is causally determined it does not necessarily follow that I am constrained to do it: and this is equivalent to saying that it does not necessarily follow that I am not free.

If I am constrained, I do not act freely. But in what circumstances can I legitimately be said to be constrained? An obvious instance is the case in which I am compelled by another person to do what he wants. In a case of this sort the compulsion need not be such as to deprive one of the power of choice. It is not required that the other person should have hypnotized me, or that he should make it physically impossible for me to go against his will. It is enough that he should induce me to do what he wants by making it clear to me that, if I do not, he will bring about some situation that I regard as even more undesirable than the consequences of the action that he wishes me to do. Thus, if the man points a pistol at my head I may still choose to disobey him: but this does not prevent its being true that if I fall in with his wishes he can legitimately be said to have compelled me. And if the circumstances are such that no reasonable person would be expected to choose the other alternative, then the action that I am made to do is not one for which I am held to be morally responsible.

A similar, but still somewhat different, case is that in which another person has obtained an habitual ascendancy over me. Where this is so, there may be no question of my being induced to act as the other person wishes by being confronted with a still more disagreeable alternative: for if I am sufficiently under his influence this special stimulus will not be necessary. Nevertheless I do not act freely, for the reason that I have been deprived of the power of choice. And this means that I have acquired so strong a habit of obedience that I no longer go through any process of deciding whether or not to do what the other person wants. About other matters I may still deliberate; but as regards the fulfillment of this other person's wishes, my own deliberations have ceased to be a causal factor in my behavior. And it is in this sense that I may be said to be constrained. It is not, however, necessary that such constraint should take the form of subservience to another person. A kleptoma-niac is not a free agent, in respect of his stealing, because he does not go through any process of deciding whether or not to steal. Or rather, if he does go through such a process, it is irrelevant to his behavior. Whatever he resolved to do, he would steal all the same. And it is this that distinguishes him from the ordinary thief.

But now it may be asked whether there is any essential difference between these cases and those in which the agent is commonly thought to be free. No doubt the ordinary thief does go through a process of deciding whether or not to steal, and no doubt it does affect his behavior. If he resolved to refrain from stealing, he could carry his resolution out. But if it be allowed that his making or not making this resolution is causally determined, then how can he be any more free than the kleptomaniac? It may be true that unlike the kleptomaniac he could refrain from stealing if he chose: but if there is a cause, or set of causes, which necessitate his choosing as he does, how can he be said to have the power of choice? Again, it may be true that no one now compels me to get up and walk across the room: but if my doing so can be causally explained in terms of my history or my environment, or whatever it may be, then how am I any more free than if some other person had compelled me? I do not have the feeling of constraint that I have when a pistol is manifestly pointed at my head; but the chains of causation by which I am bound are no less effective for being invisible.

The answer to this is that the cases I have mentioned as examples of constraint do differ from the others: and they differ just in the ways that I have tried to bring out. If I suffered from a compulsion neurosis, so that I got up and walked across the room, whether I wanted to or not, or if I did so because somebody else compelled me, then I should not be acting freely. But if I do it now, I shall be acting freely, just because these conditions do not obtain; and the fact that my action may nevertheless have a cause is, from this point of view, irrelevant. For it is not when my action has any cause at all, but only when it has a special sort of cause, that it is reckoned not to be free.

But here it may be objected that, even if this distinction corresponds to ordinary usage, it is still very irrational. For why should we distinguish, with regard to a person's freedom, between the operations of one sort of cause and those of another? Do not all causes equally necessitate? And is it not therefore arbitrary to say that a person is free when he is necessitated in one fashion but not when he is necessitated in another?

That all causes equally necessitate is indeed a tautology, if the word 'necessitate' is taken merely as equivalent to 'cause': but if, as the objection requires, it is taken as equivalent to 'constrain' or 'compel', then I do not think that this proposition is true. For all that is needed for one event to be the cause of another is that, in the given circumstances, the event which is said to be the effect would not have occurred if it had not been for the occurrence of the event which is said to be the cause, or vice versa, according as causes are interpreted as necessary, or sufficient, conditions: and this fact is usually deducible from some causal law which states that whenever an event of the one kind occurs then, given suitable conditions, an event of the other kind will occur in a certain temporal or spatio-temporal relationship to it. In short, there is an invariable concomitance between the two classes of events; but there is no compulsion, in any but a metaphorical sense. Suppose, for example, that a psycho-analyst is able to account for some aspect of my behavior by referring it to some lesion that I suffered in my childhood. In that case, it may be said that my childhood experience, together with certain other events, necessitates my behaving as I do. But all that this involves is that it is found to be true in general that when people have had certain experiences as children, they subsequently behave in certain specifiable ways; and my case is just another instance of this general law. It is in this way indeed that my behavior is explained. But from the fact that my behavior is capable of being explained, in the sense that it can be subsumed under some natural law, it does not follow that I am acting under constraint.

If this is correct, to say that I could have acted otherwise is to say, first, that I should have acted otherwise if I had so chosen; secondly, that my action was voluntary in the sense in which the actions, say, of the kleptomaniac are not; and thirdly, that nobody compelled me to choose as I did: and these three conditions may very well be fulfilled. When they are fulfilled, I may be said to have acted freely. But this is not to say that it was a matter of chance that I acted as I did, or, in other words, that my action could not be explained. And that my actions should be capable of being explained is all that is required by the postulate of determinism. . . .

Discussion Questions

1. Suppose determinism is true. In this case, would an ordinary thief be any less compelled or constrained than a kleptomaniac? What difference is there between the two? Is there enough difference to say that the thief is 'morally free' whereas the kleptomaniac is not?
2. Suppose an individual were under a compulsion to do good deeds, that is, to help others in time of need and to donate generously to charity. Are this person's actions morally praiseworthy? Are they done freely? Is there any way in which this person could be said to be free, whereas the kleptomaniac cannot?
3. Individuals are held accountable for actions which are considered 'in character'. These actions, however, are also predictable. Does the fact that they are predictable mean that we should not be held accountable for them? Why or why not?
4. Ayer writes, "Either it is an accident that I choose to act as I do or it is not. If it is an accident then it is merely a matter of chance that I did not choose otherwise." Is this an argument in favor of determinism? Why or why not? If determinism is false, does this mean that all our actions are random and therefore not praiseworthy? Explain your answer.

For Further Reading

For works about Ayer see his two autobiographies, *Part of My Life* (1977) and *More of My Life* (1984). For a text about the philosophy of A. J. Ayer see *A. J. Ayer* (1985), by J. Foster. For collections of essays by Ayer see *Philosophical Essays* (1954), *The Concept of a Person and Other Essays* (1963), and *Metaphysics and Common-Sense* (1969). For a collection of essays concerning Ayer's work see *Essays on A. J. Ayer* (1991), by T. Honderich, and *The Philosophy of A. J. Ayer* (1972), edited by L. E. Hahn.

For further defenses of compatibilism see *A System of Logic* (1843), by John Stuart Mill, and *Elbow Room* (1984), by Daniel Dennett. For studies and critiques of compatibilism see *The Metaphysics of Free Will* (1994), by J. M. Fisher; *The Consequences of Determinism* (1988), by T. Honderich; and *An Essay on Free Will* (1983), by Peter Van Inwagen.

6   SANITY AND THE METAPHYSICS OF RESPONSIBILITY
Susan Wolf

In the following selection, Susan Wolf (1952–), a philosopher at Johns Hopkins University, considers a line of argument about the nature of moral freedom, what she calls 'the deep-self view'. According to Wolf, the deep-self view—maintains that "the key to responsibility lies in the fact that responsible agents are those for whom it is not just the case that their actions are within the control of their wills, but also the case that their wills are within the control of their selves in some deeper sense." At first glance such a view is convincing. It explains, for example, why we believe that kleptomaniacs and victims of brainwashing are not responsible for their actions, whereas ordinary persons are.

Wolf, however, believes that the deep-self view needs to be amended. To support her argument Wolf imagines a person born of privilege, JoJo, who is brought up to believe that treating others badly is perfectly acceptable behavior for a ruler like himself. Whenever JoJo has occasion to question his brutal *modus operandi,* he remains satisfied with himself and his behavior. On the deep-self view, JoJo would be responsible for his actions because JoJo could change his ways. There is only one problem: he does not want to.

Is JoJo morally responsible for his actions? Wolf believes he is not because JoJo cannot distinguish what is truly right from wrong in this instance. In essence, according to Wolf, JoJo is not responsible for his actions because he is not *sane.* Hence, Wolf suggests that we add the requirement of sanity to the deep-self view of moral responsibility, what might be called the 'sane deep-self view'.

Reading Questions

1. Explain the difference between 'freedom of action' and 'freedom of the will'.
2. Why are kleptomaniacs not responsible for their actions?
3. Explain the difference between first-order and second-order desires. Also explain—in terms of first- and second-order desires—the conditions under which Frankfurt believes that we are morally free.

SOURCE: "Sanity and the Metaphysics of Responsibility" by Susan Wolf from *Responsibility, Character, and the Emotions,* edited by Ferdinand David Schoeman. Cambridge University Press, 1988. Reprinted with the permission of Cambridge University Press.

4. What, according to Watson, is the difference between a free action and an unfree action?
5. Under what conditions does Taylor believe that we are morally responsible for our actions?
6. Explain the deep-self view.
7. What drawbacks does Wolf attribute to the deep-self view? Why is the deep-self view unconvincing when it is offered as a complete account of the conditions of responsibility?
8. Under what conditions are we deemed sane?
9. Why is the M'Naughten Rule a defective account of sanity?
10. Why is JoJo not responsible for his actions according to the sane deep-self view?
11. Explain the difference between the sane deep-self view and the plain deep-self view.

...

In his seminal article "Freedom of the Will and the Concept of a Person," Harry Frankfurt notes a distinction between freedom of action and freedom of the will. A person has freedom of action, he points out, if she (or he) has the freedom to do whatever she wills to do—the freedom to walk or sit, to vote liberal or conservative, to publish a book or open a store, in accordance with her strongest desires. Even a person who has freedom of action may fail to be responsible for her actions, however, if the wants or desires she has the freedom to convert into action are themselves not subject to her control. Thus, the person who acts under posthypnotic suggestion, the victim of brainwashing, and the kleptomaniac might all possess freedom of action. In the standard contexts in which these examples are raised, it is assumed that none of the individuals is locked up or bound. Rather, these individuals are understood to act on what, at one level at least, must be called *their own desires*. Their exemption from responsibility stems from the fact that their own desires (or at least the ones governing their actions) are not up to them. These cases may be described in Frankfurt's terms as cases of people who possess freedom of action, but who fail to be responsible agents because they lack freedom of the will.

Philosophical problems about the conditions of responsibility naturally focus on an analysis of this latter kind of freedom: What *is* freedom of the will, and under what conditions can we reasonably be thought to possess it? Frankfurt's proposal is to understand freedom of the will by analogy to freedom of action. As freedom of action is the freedom to do whatever one wills to do, freedom of the will is the freedom to will whatever one wants to will. To make this point clearer, Frankfurt introduces a distinction between first-order and second-order desires. first-order desires are desires to do or have various things; second-order desires are desires about what desires to have or what desires to make effective in action. In order for an agent to have both freedom of action and freedom of the will, that agent must be capable of governing his or her actions by first-order desires and capable of governing his or her first-order desires by second-order desires.

Gary Watson's view of free agency—free and responsible agency, that is—is similar to Frankfurt's in holding that an agent is responsible for an action only if the desires expressed by that action are of a particular kind. While Frankfurt identifies the right kind of desires as desires that are supported by second-order desires, however, Watson draws a distinction between "mere" desires, so to speak, and desires that are *values*. According to Watson, the difference between free action and unfree action cannot be analyzed by reference to the logical form of the desires from which these various actions arise, but rather must relate to a difference in the quality of their source. Whereas some of my desires are just appetites or conditioned responses I find myself "stuck with," others are expressions of judgments on my part that the objects I desire are good. Insofar as my actions can be governed by the latter type of desire—governed, that is, by my values or valuational system—they are actions that I perform freely and for which I am responsible.

Frankfurt's and Watson's accounts may be understood as alternate developments of the intuition that in order to be responsible for one's actions, one must be responsible for the self that performs these actions. Charles Taylor, in an article entitled "Responsibility for Self," is concerned with the same intuition. Although Taylor does not describe his view in terms of different levels or types of desire, his view is related, for he claims that our freedom and responsibility depends on our ability to reflect on, criticize, and revise our selves. Like Frankfurt and Watson, Taylor seems to believe that if the characters from which our actions flowed were simply and permanently *given* to us, implanted by heredity, environment, or God, then we would be mere vehicles through which the causal forces of the world traveled, no more responsible than dumb animals or young children or machines. But like the others, he points out that, for most of us, our characters and desires are not so brutely implanted—or, at any rate, if they are, they are subject to revision by our own reflecting, valuing, or second-order desiring selves. We human beings— and as far as we know, only we human beings—have the ability to step back from ourselves and decide whether we are the selves we want to be. Because of this, these philosophers think, we are responsible for our selves and for the actions that we produce.

Although there are subtle and interesting differences among the accounts of Frankfurt, Watson, and Taylor, my concern is with the features of their views that are common to them all. All share the idea that responsible agency involves something more than intentional agency. All agree that if we are responsible agents, it is not just because our actions are within the control of our wills, but because, in addition, our wills are not just psychological states in us, but expressions of characters that come *from* us, or that at any rate are acknowledged and affirmed *by* us. For Frankfurt, this means that our wills must be ruled by our second-order desires; for Watson, that our wills must be governable by our system of values; for Taylor, that our wills must issue from selves that are subject to self-assessment and redefinition in terms of a vocabulary of worth. In one way or another, all these philosophers seem to be saying that the key to responsibility lies in the fact that responsible agents are those for whom it is not just the case that their actions are within the control of their wills, but also the case that their wills are within the control of their *selves* in some deeper sense. Because, at one level, the differences among Frankfurt, Watson, and Taylor may be understood as differences in the analysis or interpretation of what it is for an action to be under the control of this deeper self, we may speak of their separate positions as variations of one basic view about responsibility: the *deep-self view*.

THE DEEP-SELF VIEW

. . .

One virtue [of the deep-self view] is that this view explains a good portion of our pretheoretical intuitions about responsibility. It explains why kleptomaniacs, victims of brainwashing, and people acting under posthypnotic suggestion may not be responsible for their actions, although most of us typically are. In the cases of people in these special categories, the connection between the agents' deep selves and their wills is dramatically severed—their wills are governed not by their deep selves, but by forces external to and independent from them. A different intuition is that we adult human beings can be responsible for our actions in a way that dumb animals, infants, and machines cannot. Here the explanation is not in terms of a split between these beings' deep selves and their wills; rather, the point is that these beings *lack* deep selves altogether. . . .

At a more theoretical level, the deep-self view has another virtue: It responds to at least one way in which the fear of determinism presents itself.

A naive reaction to the idea that everything we do is completely determined by a causal chain that extends backward beyond the times of our births involves thinking that in that case we would have no control over our behavior whatsoever. If everything is determined, it is thought, then what happens happens, whether we want it to or not. A common, and proper, response to this concern points out that determinism does not deny the causal efficacy an agent's desires might have on his or her behavior. On the contrary, determinism in its more plausible forms tends to affirm this connection, merely adding that as one's behavior is determined by one's desires, so one's desires are determined by something else.

Those who were initially worried that determinism implied fatalism, however, are apt to find their fears merely transformed rather than erased. If our desires are governed by something else, they might say, they are not *really* ours after all—or, at any rate, they are ours in only a superficial sense.

The deep-self view offers an answer to this transformed fear of determinism, for it allows us to distinguish cases in which desires are determined by forces foreign to oneself from desires which are determined by one's self—by one's "real," or second-order desiring, or valuing, or deep self, that is. Admittedly, there are cases, like that of the kleptomaniac or the victim of hypnosis, in which the agent acts on desires that "belong to" him or her in only a superficial sense. But the proponent of the deep self view will point out that even if determinism is true, ordinary adult human action can be distinguished from this. Determinism implies that the desires which govern our actions are in turn governed by something else, but that something else will, in the fortunate cases, be our own deeper selves.

This account of responsibility thus offers a response to our fear of determinism; but it is a response with which many will remain unsatisfied. Even if my actions are governed by my desires and my desires are governed by my own deeper self, there remains the question: Who, or what, is responsible for this deeper self? The response above seems only to have pushed the problem further back.

···

...To see why, it will be helpful to consider another example of an agent whose responsibility is in question.

JoJo is the favorite son of Jo the first, an evil and sadistic dictator of a small, undeveloped country. Because of his father's special feelings for the boy, JoJo is given a special education and is allowed to accompany his father and observe his daily routine. In light of this treatment, it is not surprising that little JoJo takes his father as a role model and develops values very much like Dad's. As an adult, he does many of the sorts of things his father did, including sending people to prison or to death or to torture chambers on the basis of whim. He is not *coerced* to do these things, he acts according to his own desires. Moreover, these are desires he wholly *wants* to have. When he steps back and asks, "Do I really want to be this sort of person?" his answer is resoundingly "Yes," for this way of life expresses a crazy sort of power that forms part of his deepest ideal.

In light of JoJo's heritage and upbringing—both of which he was powerless to control—it is dubious at best that he should be regarded as responsible for what he does. It is unclear whether anyone with a childhood such as his could have developed into anything but the twisted and perverse sort of person that he has become. However, note that JoJo is someone whose actions are controlled by his desires and whose desires are the desires he wants to have: That is, his actions are governed by desires that are governed by and expressive of his deepest self.

The Frankfurt–Watson–Taylor strategy that allowed us to differentiate our normal selves from the victims of hypnosis and brainwashing will not allow us to differentiate ourselves from the son of Jo the first. In the case of these earlier victims, we were able to say that although the actions of these individuals were, at one level, in control of the individuals themselves, these individuals themselves, *qua* agents, were not the selves they more deeply wanted to be. In this respect, these people were unlike our happily more integrated selves. However, we cannot say of JoJo that his self, *qua* agent, is not the self he wants it to be. It is the self he wants it to be. From the inside, he feels as integrated, free, and responsible as we do.

Our judgment that JoJo is not a responsible agent is one that we can make only from the outside—from reflecting on the fact, it seems, that his deepest self is not up to him. Looked at from the outside, however, our situation seems no different from his—for in the last analysis, it is not up to any of us to have the deepest selves we do. Once more, the problem seems metaphysical—and not just metaphysical, but insuperable. For, as I mentioned before, the problem is independent of the truth of determinism. Whether we are determined or undetermined, we cannot have created our deepest selves. Literal self-creation is not just empirically, but logically impossible.

If JoJo is not responsible because his deepest self is not up to him, then we are not responsible either. Indeed, in that case responsibility would be impossible for anyone to achieve. But I believe the appearance that literal self-creation is required for freedom and responsibility is itself mistaken.

The deep-self view was right in pointing out that freedom and responsibility require us to have certain distinctive types of control over our behavior and our selves. Specifically, our actions need to be under the control of our selves, and our (superficial) selves need to be under the control of our deep selves. Having seen that these types of control are not enough to guarantee us the status of responsible agents, we are tempted to go on to suppose that we must have yet another kind of control to assure us that even our deepest selves are somehow up to us. But not all the things necessary for freedom and responsibility must be types of power and control. We may need simply to be a certain way, even though it is not within our power to determine whether we are that way or not.

Indeed, it becomes obvious that at least one condition of responsibility is of this form as soon as we remember what, in everyday contexts, we have known all along—namely, that in order to be responsible, an agent must be sane. It is not ordinarily in our power to determine whether we are or are not *sane*. Most of us, it would seem, are lucky, but some of us are not. Moreover, being sane does not necessarily mean that one has any type of power or control an insane person lacks. Some insane people, like JoJo and some political leaders who resemble him, may have complete control of their actions, and even complete control of their acting selves. The desire to be sane is thus not a desire for another form of control; it is rather a desire that one's self be connected to the world in a certain way—we could even say it is a desire that one's self be *controlled by* the world in certain ways and not in others.

This becomes clear if we attend to the criteria for sanity that have historically been dominant in legal questions about responsibility. According to the M'Naughten Rule, a person is sane if (1) he knows what he is doing and (2) he knows that what he is doing is, as the case may be, right or wrong. Insofar as one's desire to be sane involves a desire to know what one is doing—or more generally, a desire to live in the real world—it is a desire to be controlled (to have, in this case, one's *beliefs* controlled) by perceptions and sound reasoning that produce an accurate conception of the world, rather than by blind or distorted forms of response. The same goes for the second constituent of sanity—only, in this case, one's hope is that one's *values* be controlled by processes that afford an accurate conception of the world. . . .

. . .

THE SANE DEEP-SELF VIEW

So far I have argued that the conditions of responsible agency offered by the deep-self view are necessary but not sufficient. Moreover, the gap left open by the deep-self view seems to be one that can be filled only by a metaphysical, and, as it happens, metaphysically impossible addition. I now wish to argue, however, that the condition of sanity, as characterized above, is sufficient to fill the gap. In other words, the deep-self view, supplemented by the condition of sanity, provides a satisfying conception of responsibility. The conception of responsibility I am proposing, then, agrees with the deep-self view in requiring that a responsible agent be able to govern her (or his) actions by her desires and to govern her desires by her deep self. In addition, my conception insists that the agent's deep self be sane, and claims that this is *all* that is needed for responsible agency. By contrast to the plain deep-self view, let us call this new proposal the *sane deep-self view.*

It is worth noting, to begin with, that this new proposal deals with the case of JoJo and related cases of deprived childhood victims in ways that better match our pretheoretical intuitions. Unlike the plain deep-self view, the sane deep-self view offers a way of explaining why JoJo is not responsible for his actions without throwing our own responsibility into doubt. For, although like us, JoJo's actions flow from desires that flow from his deep self, unlike us, JoJo's deep self is itself insane. Sanity, remember, involves the ability to know the difference between right and wrong, and a person who, even on reflection, cannot see that having someone tortured because he failed to salute you is wrong plainly lacks the requisite ability.

. . .

The sane deep-self view thus offers an account of why victims of deprived childhoods as well as victims of misguided societies may not be responsible for their actions, without implying that we are not responsible for ours. The actions of these others are governed by mistaking conceptions of value that the agents in question cannot help but have. Since, as far as we know, our values are not, like theirs, unavoidably mistaken, the fact that these others are not responsible for their actions need not force us to conclude that we are not responsible for ours.

But it may not yet be clear why sanity, in this special sense, should make such a difference—why, in particular, the question of whether someone's values are unavoidably *mistaken* should have any bearing on their status as responsible agents. The fact that the sane deep-self view implies judgments that match our intuitions about the difference in status between characters like JoJo and ourselves provides little support for it if it cannot also defend these intuitions. So we must consider an objection that comes from the point of view we considered earlier which rejects the intuition that a relevant difference can be found.

Earlier, it seemed that the reason JoJo was not responsible for his actions was that although his actions were governed by his deep self, his deep self was not up to him. But this had nothing to do with his deep self's being mistaken or not mistaken, evil or good, insane or sane. If JoJo's values are unavoidably mistaken, our values, even if not mistaken, appear to be just as unavoidable. When it comes to freedom and responsibility, isn't it the unavoidability, rather than the mistakenness, that matters?

Before answering this question, it is useful to point out a way in which it is ambiguous: The concepts of avoidability and mistakenness are not unequivocally distinct. One may, to be sure, construe the notion of avoidability in a purely metaphysical way. Whether an event or state of affairs is unavoidable under this construal depends, as it were, on the tightness of the causal connections that bear on the event's or state of affairs' coming about. In this sense, our deep selves do seem as unavoidable for us as JoJo's and the others' are for them. For presumably we are just as influenced by our parents, our cultures, and our schooling as they are influenced by theirs. In another sense, however, our characters are not similarly unavoidable.

In particular, in the cases of JoJo and the others, there are certain features of their characters that they cannot avoid *even though these features are seriously mistaken, misguided, or bad.* This is so because, in our special sense of the term, these characters are less than fully sane. Since these characters lack the ability to know right from wrong, they are unable to revise their characters on the basis of right and wrong, and so their deep selves lack the resources and the reasons that might have served as a basis for self-correction. Since the deep selves *we* unavoidably have, however, are sane deep selves—deep selves, that is, that unavoidably *contain* the ability to know right from wrong—we unavoidably do have the resources and reasons on which to base self-correction. What this means is that though in one sense we are no more in control of our deepest selves than JoJo et al., it does not follow in our case, as it does in theirs, that we would be the way we are, even if it is a bad or wrong way to be. However, if this does not follow, it seems

to me, our absence of control at the deepest level should not upset us.

Consider what the absence of control at the deepest level amounts to for us: Whereas JoJo is unable to control the fact that, at the deepest level, he is not fully sane, we are not responsible for the fact that, at the deepest level, we are. It is not up to us to have minimally sufficient abilities cognitively and normatively to recognize and appreciate the world for what it is. Also, presumably, it is not up to us to have lots of other properties, at least to begin with—a fondness for purple, perhaps, or an antipathy for beets. As the proponents of the plain deep-self view have been at pains to point out, however, we do, if we are lucky, have the ability to revise our selves in terms of the values that are held by or constitutive of our deep selves. If we are lucky enough both to have this ability and to have our deep selves be sane, it follows that although there is much in our characters that we did not choose to have, there is nothing irrational or objectionable in our characters that we are compelled to keep.

Being sane, we are able to understand and evaluate our characters in a reasonable way, to notice what there is reason to hold on to, what there is reason to eliminate, and what, from a rational and reasonable standpoint, we may retain or get rid of as we please. Being able as well to govern our superficial selves by our deep selves, then, we are able to change the things we find there is reason to change. This being so, it seems that although we may not be *metaphysically* responsible for ourselves—for, after all, we did not create ourselves from nothing—we are *morally* responsible for ourselves, for we are able to understand and appreciate right and wrong, and to change our characters and our actions accordingly.

SELF-CREATION, SELF-REVISION, AND SELF-CORRECTION

At the beginning of this chapter, I claimed that recalling that sanity was a condition of responsibility would dissolve at least some of the appearance that responsibility was metaphysically impossible. To see how this is so, and to get a fuller sense of the sane deep-self view, it may be helpful to put that view into perspective by comparing it to the other views we have discussed along the way.

As Frankfurt, Watson, and Taylor showed us, in order to be free and responsible we need not only to be able to control our actions in accordance with our desires, we need to be able to control our desires in accordance with our deepest selves. We need, in other words, to be able to *revise* ourselves—to get rid of some desires and traits, and perhaps replace them with others on the basis of our deeper desires or values or reflections. However, consideration of the fact that the selves who are doing the revising might themselves be either brute products of external forces or arbitrary outputs of random generation made us wonder whether the capacity for self-revision was enough to assure us of responsibility—and the example of JoJo added force to the suspicion that it was not. Still, if the ability to revise ourselves is not enough, the ability to create ourselves does not seem necessary either. Indeed, when you think of it, it is unclear why anyone should want self-creation. Why should anyone be disappointed at having to accept the idea that one has to get one's start somewhere? It is an idea that most of us have lived with quite contentedly all along. What we do have reason to want, then, is something more than the ability to revise ourselves, but less than the ability to create ourselves. Implicit in the sane deep-self view is the idea that

what is needed is the ability to *correct* (or improve) ourselves.

Recognizing that in order to be responsible for our actions, we have to be responsible for our selves, the sane deep-self view analyzes what is necessary in order to be responsible for our selves as (1) the ability to evaluate ourselves sensibly and accurately, and (2) the ability to transform ourselves insofar as our evaluation tells us to do so. We may understand the exercise of these abilities as a process whereby we *take* responsibility for the selves that we are but did not ultimately create. The condition of sanity is intrinsically connected to the first ability; the condition that we be able to control our superficial selves by our deep selves is intrinsically connected to the second.

The difference between the plain deep-self view and the sane deep-self view, then, is the difference between the requirement of the capacity for self-correction. Anyone with the first capacity can *try* to take responsibility for himself or herself. However, only someone with a sane deep self—a deep self that can see and appreciate the world for what it is—can self-evaluate sensibly and accurately. Therefore, although insane selves can try to take responsibility for themselves, only sane selves will properly be accorded responsibility. . . .

Discussion Questions

1. Does Wolf's position absolve Nazis of their moral responsibility for the Holocaust? Why or why not? What about slave owners? Does Wolf's position imply that these individuals were free? Why or why not? Do you find Wolf's position correct? Explain your answer.
2. Is it possible that sanity is a culturally relative concept? Could the definition of sanity differ from one culture to another, or is sanity a feature of human behavior that transcends cultural boundaries? Does your answer have any implications for Wolf's theory?
3. Consider the case of Jo Jo. Why does Wolf believe that Jo Jo is not responsible for his actions? Do you agree with her judgment? Why or why not?

For Further Reading

For a collection of articles concerning the issue of responsibility and the deep-self position, including Wolf's article "Sanity and the Metaphysics of Responsibility", see *Responsibility, Character, and the Emotions* (1988), edited by D. Schoeman. For other articles by Wolf concerning responsibility see "The Importance of Free Will," *Mind* (90) (1981), 386–403; and "Asymmetrical Freedom," *Journal of Philosophy* (77) (1980), 151–166.

For discussions and criticisms of Wolf's position see "Sanity and Irresponsibility," *Philosophy, Phychiatry, and Psychology* 3 (4) (1996), 293–302, by P. E. Wilson; "Responsibility, Freedom, and Reason," *Ethics* 102 (2) (1992), by J. M. Fisher; and "Understanding and Blaming," *Philosophy and Phenomenological Research* 53 (1) (1993), by L. Vogel.

For further reading on the deep-self view and responsibility not contained in Schoeman, see *The Importance of What We Care About* (1988), a collection of essays by H. Frankfurt, and *Free Will* (1982), edited by G. Wilson

7   NO EXIT
Jean-Paul Sartre

Jean-Paul Sartre (1905–1980) was a leading exponent of the existentialist movement that emanated out of France in the 1930s and 1940s. Sartre's magnum opus of academic philosophy was his lengthy and highly technical *Being and Nothingness* (1957)—first published in French in 1943. But Sartre also brilliantly voiced his philosophical ideas in literature as well: *Nausea* (1938), *The Roads to Freedom* (a trilogy) (1945–1949), *The Flies* (1943), *In Camera* (1944), and *Dirty Hands* (1948). In fact, Sartre was awarded the Nobel Prize for Literature in 1964. Out of principle, however, Sartre refused to accept the award.

Most of Sartre's efforts focused on the issue of human freedom in one way or another. Our selection comes from *In Camera*—which was titled *No Exit* when it was published in English—and is no exception to this rule. As an existentialist Sartre believed that humans are morally free. But Sartre also believed that our options in life are limited by our facticity—the particulars of our situation: our age, sex, height, race, and the like. But within these bounds we are metaphysically and morally free to do as we please. What a shame it would be, then, if we were to unnecessarily limit our freedom any further.

For example, it would be a shame if we were to become overly concerned with what others think of us to the point that we started living the life that we thought they would approve of, instead of the sort of life that we truly desired to live. Or suppose that we fancy ourselves to be this or that—a poet or an athlete, for example. If we deny ourselves opportunities in life because "poets or athletes just do not do those sorts of things," then we are limiting our own freedom to live up to some self-imposed stereotype. To restrict one's choices in order to conform to a role or stereotype is what Sartre would call an act of bad faith. And we should, according to Sartre, definitely avoid acting in bad faith. To act in bad faith is to waste our freedom.

In the following selection, Sartre focuses on the first of these two themes—our concern for the look of the other. It can create a living hell.

SOURCE: From *No Exit* by Jean-Paul Sartre, adapted from the French by Paul Bowles. Copyright ©, 1945, under title HUIS-CLOS, by Librairie Gallimard. Copyright ©, 1945, under title HUIS-CIOS, adapted by Paul Bowles, by Oliver Smith.

Reading Questions

1. What does Inez believe that Cradeau will do to her?
2. What item, and everything that looks remotely like it, has been removed from the room?
3. Why does Cradeau apologize to Inez?
4. Why is Estelle concerned about sitting down on her divan?
5. What can Estelle see? Whom does she see crying?
6. How did Inez, Estelle, and Cradeau die?
7. Where are Inez, Estelle, and Cradeau?
8. Who is the torturer?
9. Estelle does not have a mirror. What must she use for a mirror instead?

Scene: A room. Sparsely furnished. Looks rather like dentist's waiting room. The room is set on a platform that rakes from back down stage. The walls slant outward from back to down stage and the ceiling rakes from middle stage to the back. There is a fireplace and mantel in Right wall; on the mantel are a statue of Cupid and a letter opener. The door is in Center of back wall. There is a window in the Left wall; when the curtains are opened we see that the window has been bricked up. A chandelier hangs Center from ceiling, there being a hole in the ceiling large enough for the chandelier to go through. There is a large ornate gold chair Down Center; a red divan Right and a green divan Left of Center chair.)

(CRADEAU *enters, looks around. Speech nervous, clipped.* BOY *follows.*)

Cradeau: So this is it.

Boy: This is it.

Cradeau: (*Musingly.*) And this is the way it looks.

Boy: This is the way it looks.

Cradeau: I—I suppose in the end you get used to the furnishings.

Boy: That depends. Some people do.

Cradeau: Are all the rooms like this?

Boy: (*Contemptuously.*) No, of course not. We get Chinese, Hindus, blacks, everything. What would they want with stuff like this?

Cradeau: (*Vigorously.*) And what do they think I want with it? God, it's hideous. Oh, well, I was always living with furniture I couldn't stand, anyway. And ideas. And people. I liked it.

Boy: (*Uncomprehending.*) Oh, you won't find it so bad here. You'll see.

Cradeau: (*Mechanically.*) Good. Fine, fine. (*He looks around.*) Just the same, it seems funny to me—you've heard all the stuff they tell back there.

Boy: What about?

Cradeau: Oh—(*Making a vague, wide gesture.*) All this.

Boy: You don't believe all that crap! People who've never been anywhere near here. Because if they had—

Cradeau: Yes!

(*They* BOTH *laugh.*)

(*Becoming suddenly serious again.*) Where are the thumbscrews?

Boy: What?

Cradeau: The thumbscrews, the whips, the racks?

Boy. Are you serious?

Cradeau: (*Looking at him.*) Ah? Oh, good. Yes, I was serious. (*Silence; he walks about. With sudden violence.*) No mirrors, no windows, of course. Nothing breakable. (*With sudden violence.*) And why'd they take away my toothbrush?

Boy: Aha! There's your human dignity coming back!

Cradeau: (*Pounds angrily once on the back of the divan.*) Save your familiarity, my friend. I know where I am and I know why I'm here, but I'll be damned if I'm going to stand for—

Boy: Take it easy. No harm meant. But what do you expect, all the guests ask the same thing. Right away they ask: "Where's the thumbscrews?" And when they say that, I can tell you they're not thinking about that Pepsodent smile of theirs. Then you get 'em calmed down, and about that time they start wanting their toothbrush. Now all I ask is, just stop and think: *why* in hell would you want to brush your teeth here?

Cradeau: (*Quieted.*) Yes, I suppose that's true. Why should I? (*Looks around.*) And why would I want to look in the mirror? As far as the statue goes, fine. There'll probably be plenty of times when I won't be able to look at it enough. (*Working himself up.*) Not enough, see? What the hell, there's nothing to hide. I tell you I'm quite aware of my status here. And why I was sent. Do you want to know what it's like to be here? Is that why you were looking at me like that? All right, I'll tell you. It's like drowning in hot water, with your eyes above the water. (*Whirls about to face mantel.*) And what do you see? A statue of Napoleon! (*Pause.*) What a nightmare! (*Pause.*) That's all right, *you* don't have to say anything. You're probably not allowed to, anyway. I know, I'll shut up. But just don't think it's a shock to me. I knew what was coming. I know the whole score backwards and forwards, behind me and ahead of me. (*He begins walking again. Reflectively.*) So it's no toothbrush. No beds either. You never sleep. Right?

Boy: Right.

Cradeau: I was sure of it! Why *would* you sleep any way? You feel sleepy, it creeps up on you behind the ears first. You feel your eyes shutting, but—sleep? You lie down on the couch, and—fttt! All gone, you're not sleepy any more. You have to rub your eyes, get up and go through the whole thing over again.

Boy: You've got some imagination.

Cradeau: Shut up. I'm not going to make any fuss; I just want to look the whole thing straight in the face. I don't want to give it a chance to knife me from behind where I can't see it. Imagination? Well, then, how's this? You don't get sleepy. Why sleep if you're not sleepy? Correct. Wait a minute, wait a minute! I've got it! Why is it painful to be here? Why would it naturally have to be torture? I've got it! Just because it's life without time off, without a break.

Boy: What d'you mean, break?

Cradeau: What do I mean? (*Suspiciously.*) Look at me. I knew it! That's why you've got that

smug, cocky expression on your face. (*Pause. To himself.*) My God, they're atrophied.

Boy: Just what are you talking about?

Cradeau: Your eyelids. *We* used to close ours. We called it blinking your eyes. A second of darkness, a little black curtain falls and goes back up, and your break is made. It keeps your eyeball moist and blots out the world. Think how restful it would be. A hundred rests in an hour. A hundred little escapes— So? I'm going to live without eyelids? You know it's all the same thing, without eyelids, without sleep. (*Pause.*) No more sleep—But how'm I going to put up with myself? Just try to understand. Try hard. I've got a mean, nasty kind of disposition, you see, and I—I'm sort of used to teasing myself. But I can't—I can't go on doing that all the time. Back there, there were nights. I used to sleep. A wonderful soft sleep, to make up for it. I made myself have simple dreams. There would be a field. A field of grass, that's all. I'd dream I was walking through it. (*Pause.*) Is it daytime?

Boy: Daytime?

Cradeau: Is it light?

Boy: Don't you see the lights are lit?

Cradeau: (*Pause. Then quietly.*) I see. But outside?

Boy: (*Flabbergasted.*) Outside?

Cradeau: Outside! On the other side of the wall?

Boy: There's the hall.

Cradeau: And at the end of the hall?

Boy: More rooms and more halls and stairs.

Cradeau: And then what?

Boy: That's all.

Cradeau: You must have a day off once in a while. Where do you go?

Boy: To see my uncle on the third floor. He's Bell Captain on that floor.

Cradeau: I should have guessed. (*Pause.*) Where's the light-switch here?

Boy: There isn't any.

Cradeau: You mean you can't turn the light off?

Boy: The management can shut off the juice. But I don't remember they ever did it on this floor. We have unlimited service.

Cradeau: All right, so you have to live with your eyes open.

Boy: (*Maliciously, ironically.*) Live?

Cradeau: Let's not split hairs about words. With your eyes open. Forever. Broad daylight in my eyes. And inside my head. (*A wait. Then suddenly.*) And if I were to send that statue through the chandelier, do you think it'd do the trick?

Boy: It's too heavy.

Cradeau: (*Tries to take the statue in his hands.*) You're right. It is too heavy.

(*A silence.*)

Boy: Well, if you won't be needing me any longer, I'll—

Cradeau: (*Jumping.*) You going? (*Pause.*) So long. (*The* Boy *reaches the door.*)

Wait!

(*The* Boy *makes an affirmative gesture.*)

I can ring for you when I want and you have to come?

Boy: Well, yes. But something seems to be wrong with it. Sometimes it works and sometimes it doesn't.

(Cradeau. *goes to the button and presses it.* BELL *rings.*)

Cradeau: It works!

Boy: (*Surprised.*) That's right. So it does! (*He rings.*) But don't get your hopes up; it won't last. Well, excuse me—

Cradeau: (*Makes a movement to detain him.*) I—uh—

Boy: Huh?

Cradeau: No, nothing. (*He goes to the mantel and takes the paper knife.*) What's this?

Boy: Why, a letter-opener.

Cradeau: You have no mail delivery here?

Boy: No.

Cradeau: Then what good is it?

(Boy *shrugs his shoulders.*)

That's all right. You can go.

(Boy *goes out.* Cradeau *is alone. He goes to the statue and pats it with his hand. Sits down. Gets up. Exhibits extreme nervousness as he examines room in detail. At one point walks to window at stage Left, jerks curtains aside, disclosing solid brick wall in place of glass. Goes to the bell and pushes button. Bell does not ring. Tries two or three times. In vain. Then goes to the door and tries to open it. It does not open. He calls, frantically.*)

Boy! Boy!

(*No answer. His fists rain blows on the door, and he continues to call the boy. Then suddenly he becomes calm, goes back and sits down. At this point, the door opens and* Inez *comes in, followed by the* Boy.)

Boy: (*To* Cradeau.) You call?

Cradeau: (Cradeau *is about to reply, but glances at* Inez.) No.

Boy: (*Turning toward* Inez.) Here you are, Madame.

(*Silence from* Inez.)

If you have anything you want to ask—

(*Continued silence.*)

(*Disappointed.*) Usually the guests want a little information—It's all the same to me—Besides, as far as the toothbrush goes, and the statue, and the bell, this gentleman knows all about it and he can answer your questions as well as I can.

(Boy *goes out. Silence.* Cradeau. *does not look at* Inez. *She looks about, then goes brusquely toward* Cradeau.)

Inez: Where is Florence?

(Cradeau. *does not answer.*)

I'm asking you a question. Where is Florence?

Cradeau: I haven't any idea.

Inez: Is that the best you can do? Torture by separation? Well, it's a failure as far as I'm concerned. Florence was a little fool and I don't miss her.

Cradeau: (*Moves to* Inez.) I'm sorry, but—Who are you taking me for?

Inez: You? You're the torturer, I suppose.

Cradeau: (*Jumps, then begins to laugh. Moves down.*) That's very funny! You came in, you took one look at me, and you thought: "That's the man who's going to torture me." What a mistake! That stupid bellboy should have introduced us. Torturer! Let me do the honors. Vincent Cradeau, journalist and writer. Since we seem to be sharing the same quarters, Madame—? (*Moves to sit Center.*)

Inez: (*Drily.*) Inez Serrano—Mademoiselle.

Cradeau: Good. fine! Well, the ice is broken. Now do you find I have the face of a torturer? (*Pause.*) And would you kindly tell me just how you can recognize one?

Inez: They look as if they were afraid.

Cradeau: Afraid. That's crazy. And of whom? Of their victims?

Inez: (*Stubbornly, looking away. Crosses above divan Right.*) I know what I'm talking about. I've seen my own face in the mirror.

Cradeau: In the mirror? (*Looks around.*) This place is impossible. They've taken everything that looks remotely like a mirror out of here. (*A pause.*) Well, anyway, I can assure you *I'm* not afraid. I don't take the situation lightly, and I'm fully aware of its seriousness, but I'm not afraid.

Inez: (*Shrugging her shoulders.*) That's your business. (*A pause. Insolently.*) Do you ever, by any chance, go out for a stroll?

Cradeau: The door's bolted.

Inez: (*Sits divan Right.*) Well, so much the worse.

Cradeau: I can understand that you're not exactly happy to find me in here with you. And as a matter of fact I'd rather be alone myself. I'd like the chance to get a few things straight in my mind. Put my life in order, as it were. But I'm sure we can get used to each other. I don't talk, I don't even move around much, and I make very little noise. The only thing is, if you don't mind my suggesting it, we should keep up the greatest politeness toward each other. It will be our best defense.

Inez: (*In a dead voice.*) I'm not a polite person.

Cradeau: I'll be polite for both of us.

(*A silence.* CRADEAU *is seated. His mouth twitches.* INEZ *walks back and forth in the room.*)

Inez: (*Stopping to look at him, with intense distaste.*) Your mouth.

Cradeau: (*Coming out of a dream.*) I beg your pardon?

Inez: Do you think it would be possible to stop twitching your mouth? It's going around like a top there, under your nose.

Cradeau: I'm extremely sorry. I didn't realize.

Inez: That's just the trouble.

(CRADEAU *resumes his tic automatically.*)

There! You make a point of being polite, but you leave your face out in the open. You're not alone, and you have no right to inflict the sight of your fear on me.

Cradeau: (CRADEAU *rises and walks toward her.*) You're not afraid?

Inez: What good would it do? Fear was for *before,* while we still had hope.

Cradeau: (*Gently.*) There's no more hope, that I know, but we're still *before.* Whatever it's to be, it hasn't begun yet, you know, Mlle. Serrano.

Inez: I know. (*A wait.*) And so? What's going to happen?

Cradeau: I don't know. I'm just waiting.

(*A silence.* CRADEAU *goes back and sits down.* INEZ *resumes her striding about.* CRADEAU's *mouth still twitches, then, after a glance at* INEZ, *he buries his face in his hands. The door opens and* ESTELLE *and the* BOY *enter.* ESTELLE *looks at* CRADEAU, *with his face still in his hands.*)

Estelle: (*Hysterically to* CRADEAU.) No! No, no! Don't take your hands away! I know what's behind! You have no face!

(CRADEAU *takes his hands away.*)

Oh! (*A pause. With surprise.*) I don't know you.

Cradeau: I'm not the torturer, Madame.

Estelle: I didn't think that's who you were. I—I thought someone was trying to play a joke on me. (*To the* BOY, *anxiously.*) Are you still expecting someone else?

Boy: No one else is coming.

Estelle: (*Calmed.*) Oh! Then we're going to be all alone, just the three of us? Oh! (*She begins to laugh.*)

Cradeau: (*Dryly.*) It's not a laughing matter.

Estelle: (*Continuing her laughter. Moves back of divan Left.*) Oh, I know, but these divans are so hideous. And look how they've set them out in a row. I feel as if it were New Year's and I were visiting my Aunt Marie. Each one has his own divan, I suppose. This one's mine? (*To the* BOY.) But I shall *never* be able to sit down on it! It's frightful! I'm in turquoise and it's upholstered in spinach *green.*

Inez: Would you like mine?

Estelle: (*Going to Right of divan.*) That burgundy one? It's awfully nice of you, but I'm afraid it wouldn't be much better. Oh, well, what can one expect? Each one gets his little prize. Mine's the green one. I'll keep it. (*Pause. Reflectively.*) Actually the only one that could possibly match at *all* is the one this gentleman's sitting on.

(*Silence.*)

Inez: (*Snaps.*) Did you hear, Cradeau?

Cradeau: (*Jumping.*) The divan. Oh, excuse me! (*He gets up.*) It's yours, Madame. (*Crosses down to divan Left.*)

Estelle: Thank you. (*Moves up of chair Center. She takes off her coat and throws it on the chair. A wait.*) Since we're all going to live together, I think we should make each other's acquaintance. I am Estelle Delaunay.

(CRADEAU *bows and is about to introduce himself, but* INEZ *steps stolidly in front of him.*)

Inez: (*To* ESTELLE.) Inez Serrano. I'm delighted!

Cradeau: (*Bows again.*) Vincent Cradeau. (*Sits Left.*)

Boy: Do you need me for anything?

Estelle: No, that's all. I'll ring for you.

(BOY *bows and goes out.*)

Inez: (*In the tone one uses to soothe a child who has fallen down.*) You're very lovely to look at, and I'm very happy. I wish I had some flowers to make you feel more at home.

Estelle: Flowers? Oh, yes. I always loved flowers. But they'd wither here, it's so hot. Oh dear! The important thing, I suppose, is to keep in a good humor. You, ah—

Inez: Yes, last week, and you?

Estelle: I? Yesterday. The funeral isn't over yet. (*She speaks perfectly naturally, looking out over audience's heads as if she were seeing the things she describes.*) The wind is blowing my sister's veil around. She's doing *all* she can to cry. Oh, come, try a little harder than that! There! *Two* tears, two tiny little tears shining under the crepe. Gabrielle is terribly ugly this morning. She's holding onto her sister's arm. She doesn't dare cry because it would make her mascara run. I must say that in her place, I'd—Well, after all, she *was* my best friend.

Inez: (*Fascinated.*) Did you suffer very much?

Estelle: No. I was barely conscious.

Inez: What did you—

Estelle: Pneumonia. (*Continuing the same business as before.*) Well, it's over. They're leaving. Good morning! Good morning! Such a lot of handshaking! My husband is abso-

lutely ill, he's so unhappy. He stayed at home. (*To* INEZ.) And you?

Inez: Gas.

Estelle: (*To* CRADEAU.) And you?

Cradeau: Twelve bullets in my carcass.

(ESTELLE *makes a gesture, shocked.*)

I'm sorry. (*Rises—moves up Left.*) I'm afraid I'm not a very high-class corpse.

Estelle: Oh, no, but I mean, if you only wouldn't use such crude words. It's—it's a little *disgusting!* And after all, what does it mean? You know, it may very well be that we've all never been so much alive as we are right now. If we must absolutely give a name to this— state of affairs, I suggest we call it absence. It *sounds* so much nicer. Have you been absent long?

Cradeau: About a month.

Estelle: Where are you from?

Cradeau: (*Crosses to Right Center.*) Paris.

Estelle: Have you anyone left back there?

Cradeau: My wife. (*Looking out over audience.*) She came to the jail every other day. They wouldn't let her in. She's looking in through the bars, now. Doesn't know yet that I'm absent, but she suspects. Now she's leaving. She's all in black. So much the better, she won't have to change. The sun is nice and bright and she's in black, there in the empty streets, with those big eyes, like a victim's— Agh! She gets on my nerves!

(*A silence.* CRADEAU *goes and sits down in the Right divan and buries his face in his hands.*)

Inez: Estelle!

Estelle: (*Rises, crosses Left of* CRADEAU.) Excuse me, Monsieur Cradeau!

Cradeau: I beg your pardon?

Estelle: You're sitting on my divan.

Cradeau: I'm sorry. (*He gets up; crosses to divan Left.*)

Estelle: You look so wrapped up.

Cradeau: (*Sits Left.*) I'm putting my life in order.

(INEZ *bursts out laughing.*)

(*With vexation.*) It might be better for some people if they did the same thing.

Inez: My life is all in order. Completely in order. It did it all by itself back there, and I don't need to bother about it here. (*Sits Right.*)

Cradeau: Really? You think it's that simple? (*He wipes his forehead with his hand; rises.*) What heat! May I? (*He starts to take off his jacket.*)

Estelle: Oh, don't! (*More gently.*) No, please. I can't *stand* men in their shirtsleeves.

Cradeau: (CRADEAU *puts it back on.*) That's all right. (*A pause.*) I used to spend all night in the copy room. It was always hot as a jungle in there. (*Pause. Same business as before.*) It *is* hot as the jungle in there right now. It's night out.

Estelle: So it is. Already night. Millicent is getting undressed, getting ready for bed. How fast time flies, there.

Inez: It's night. They've closed up my room and sealed the door. And the room is empty and dark.

Cradeau: They've put their coats on the backs of the chairs and rolled their shirtsleeves up above their elbows. It smells of men and cigar smoke. (*Silence.*) I used to like to live that way, with men around in their shirtsleeves. (*Sits Left.*)

Estelle: (*Dryly.*) Well, we don't happen to have the same tastes. That's all *that* proves. (*To* INEZ.) And you, did *you* like men in shirtsleeves?

Inez: (*flatly, looking at her nails.*) Shirts or no shirts, I'm not very fond of men anyway.

Estelle: (ESTELLE *looks at them both with stupefaction.*) But *why, why* have they put us together?

Inez: (*Suppressing a laugh.*) What's that?

Estelle: I look at you both and I think of how we're going to live together—I somehow expected to find friends, relatives.

Inez: A lovely friend with a hole in the middle of his face!

Estelle: Yes, that one, too. He used to do a rhumba like an absolute professional—But why have they put us, *us,* together?

Cradeau: Well, it's just chance. They put the people in wherever they can, in the order of their arrival. (*To* INEZ.) What are you laughing at?

Inez: At you and your chance. Do you need to be reassured that badly? They leave nothing to chance

Estelle: (*Timidly.*) Perhaps we've met somewhere before?

Inez: Never, I'd never have forgotten you.

Estelle: Or maybe we had friends in common. Don't you know the Dubois-Seymours?

Inez: I doubt it very much.

Estelle: They're always entertaining. Everyone goes.

Inez: What do they do?

Estelle: (*Surprised.*) Do? Why nothing. They have that big place at Cannes and—

Inez: I was a secretary.

Estelle: (*With a little step backward.*) Oh, really? Well, then, of course!—(*A wait.*) And you, Mr. Cradeau?

Cradeau: I never left Paris. I found trouble enough right there.

Estelle: In that case you must be right. It's pure chance that brought us together.

Inez: Chance! Thou this furniture is here by chance. It's just an accident that the divan on the right is dark green and the one on the left is red. An accident? Well, then try changing them around and let me know how it comes out? And the statue, is that there by chance, too? And this heat, this heat? (*Pause.*) I tell you, everything has been planned. Down to the last detail and with the greatest of care. This room was *made* for us. It was waiting for us.

Estelle: But why should it be? Everything about it is so ugly, so hard and angular. I always hated angles.

Inez: D'you think *I* lived in a room like this? (*A pause.*)

Estelle: Then you think everything has been arranged?

Inez: Everything. And we're well matched, too.

Estelle: And it's not by chance that *you* happen to be sitting opposite *me*? (*A pause. Musingly.*) What are they waiting for?

Inez: I don't know, but they're waiting, don't worry.

Estelle: I can't stand it when I think someone expects me to do something. Right away I have the most *awful* urge to do just the contrary.

Inez: Well, go ahead! Do it! You don't even know what it is they want you to do.

Estelle: (*Tapping her foot.*) It's unbearable. And something's supposed to happen to me because of you two? (*She looks at them.*)

Because of you two! I've seen faces that meant something to me right off. And yours say nothing at all.

Cradeau: (*Who has been pondering, rises, crosses up of* INEZ. *Brusquely, to* INEZ.) Come, now, why are we together? You've already said too much. Go on to the end.

Inez: (*A little astonished.*) I don't know anything about it.

Cradeau: We've *got* to know. (*He reflects a moment.*)

Inez: If only each one of us had the courage to tell—

Cradeau: What?

(*Pause.*)

Inez: Estelle?

Estelle: Yes?

Inez: What did you do? Why have you been sent here?

Estelle: (*With animation.*) But I don't *know!* I haven't the vaguest *idea!* I even have a feeling it must be a mistake! (*To* INEZ.) Don't smile. Think of all the people who—who become absent every day. They come here by the thousands and are taken care of by mere underlings, uneducated employees. How could there help being an error now and then? Don't laugh at the idea. It's perfectly reasonable. (*To* CRADEAU.) And you, why don't you say something? Perhaps they didn't make a mistake in my case, but perhaps they did in yours. (*To* INEZ.) And yours, too, maybe. Don't you think it's *better* to think we're here by mistake?

Inez: Is that all you have to tell us?

Estelle: What more do you want to know? I have nothing to hide. I was an orphan, had no money, and I was trying to bring up my younger brother. There was an old friend of my father's who wanted to marry me, and he had a good deal of money and was rather nice, so I accepted. What would you have done in my place? My brother's health was terribly delicate and it was frightfully difficult to give him the kind of care he needed. I lived six years with my husband without even a shadow of trouble or unhappiness. Then two years ago I met the man I was really meant for. We both knew it the minute we saw each other, and he wanted me to run off with him but naturally I wouldn't. After that I had my pneumonia. That's all. Of course I suppose I *could* be blamed in a way, for having sacrificed my youth to an old man. (*To* CRADEAU.) Do you think that's wrong?

Cradeau: Certainly not. (*Pause.*) Do *you* think it's wrong to live according to your principles?—

Estelle: I don't see how anyone could be blamed for it.

Cradeau: I edited a newspaper that had a reputation for telling the truth. I had a bold policy. The truth, whether they liked it or not, and the hell with consequences. That was my motto. They called me a fearless journalist. I always came out against war. Pacifist, not the milksop kind, but militantly against all war, any war. After Danzig I went right ahead preaching the gospel of peace. France fell. Was I supposed to change all my principles because they happened to find favor with the Germans? My enemies denounced me as a traitor. They said I had sold out. Fools! I was for the brotherhood of man. But mine was a lost cause. And the fools had their way in the end. They shot me. I folded my arms and they shot me. Where's the blame there? What did I do wrong?

Estelle: (*Puts her hand on his arm.*) You did nothing wrong. You're—

Inez: (*Rises, finishes in a tone of sarcasm.*) A hero. (*Pause.*) And so it was simple as that!

Cradeau: Well, almost. Perhaps not quite. (*Moves to Left, sits.*)

Inez: It was lucky you had no responsibilities toward anyone. You weren't married, I take it.

Cradeau: (*Guiltily.*) Well, yes, I had a wife. (*Defiantly.*) What about her? I took her out of the gutter to marry her.

Estelle: (*Triumphantly, to* INEZ.) You see! You see!

Inez: (*Moves up of divan Right. Grimly.*) I see, (*A pause.*) Who are you putting this act on for anyway? We're all in this together.

Estelle: (*Insolently.*) Together?

Inez: (*With brutality.*) Criminals together. We're in hell, my little friend, and there's never any mistake there. People are not damned for nothing.

Estelle: Stop it!

Inez: (*Raising her voice.*) In hell! Damned! Damned!

Estelle: Stop! Will you stop? I forbid you to use coarse words like that.

Inez: (*Quietly. Moving up of* ESTELLE *to Left Center.*) I said damned. Did you hear that, Salvation Nell? And you, too, you great big clean-cut hero, (*Persuasively*) We had our day, didn't we? People suffered, they were through agonies because of us and we thought it was pretty amusing. It's got to be paid for now.

Cradeau: (*Rises, moving Left. Raising his hand menacingly.*) Will you shut up?

Inez: (*Looks at him without fear, but with great surprise.*) Ah! (*Pause.*) Wait! Now I understand! I see why they've put us together.

Cradeau: (*Nervously, up of divan Left.*) Be careful what you say. We don't want to hear it, anyway. We know we're here. Isn't that enough for you?

Inez: Oh, no! You've got to hear this! This is too good to keep secret. (*Pause.*) It's pretty clever! Very clever! There's no physical torture, right? No nail-pulling and roasting over the flames. And yet we're in hell. And nobody else is coming. No one. We're together, just the three of us, from now on.

Cradeau: (*In a low voice.*) I know it.

Inez: Well, this is the point: they've made a saving in their hired help. That's all. The customers serve themselves. It's like a cafeteria.

Estelle: What do you mean?

Inez: Each one of us is the torturer for the other two.

(*A pause as they take this in. Finally.*)

Cradeau: (*Crosses to Left of* INEZ.) I won't provide your tortures for you. I have nothing against you and I don't want anything to do with you. Nothing. It's perfectly simple. So there you are. Each one into his little corner. It's a game. You here, you here, and I'll be here. And silence. Not a word. (INEZ *sits divan Right.*) It's not so hard, is it? Each one of us has enough to do thinking about himself. I could stay ten thousand years without speaking.

Estelle: (*ingenuously.*) I have to be quiet?

Cradeau: Yes. And we'll be—we'll be saved. Just be quiet. Look inside yourself, never lift your head once. Agreed?

Inez: Agreed.

Estelle: (*Wistfully, after a moment's hesitation.*) I agree.

Cradeau: Well, goodbye. (*He goes to his divan and sits with his head in his hands. Silence.*)

(INEZ *begins to sing to herself.* ESTELLE *busies herself with her make-up. She puts on powder and looks about for a mirror anxiously. Searches in her handbag. Finally turns to* CRADEAU.)

Estelle: I'm sorry, you wouldn't have a mirror—? (CRADEAU *does not answer.*)

A mirror, (*Rises, moves to* CRADEAU.) a little hand-mirror, you know, anything.

(CRADEAU *still does not answer.* ESTELLE *pouts a little, moves to Center.*)

If you're going to leave me all alone, at least you might get me a looking glass.

(CRADEAU *remains without looking up, head in hands.*)

Inez: (*Eager to please.*) I have one in my bag! (*She digs in her handbag. With vexation.*) It's gone! They must have taken it when I came in here.

Estelle: (*Weakly.*) What a bore! (*Sits Center.*)

(*Pause. She shuts her eyes and seems to be about to faint.* INEZ *rushes forward and holds her up.*)

Inez: What's the matter?

Estelle: (ESTELLE *opens her eyes and smiles.*) I feel so strange. (*She runs her hand feebly over her body.*) Don't you ever feel that way? When I can't see myself in the mirror, I can't even feel myself, and I begin to wonder if I really exist at all.

Inez: (*Looking fixedly at her.*) You're very lucky. I always feel myself inside. (*Sits.*)

Estelle: Oh, yes, inside—Everything that goes on in one's head is so vague it puts me to sleep. (*A pause.*)

There are six huge mirrors in my bedroom. I can always see them but they can't see me. They reflect the couch, the rug, the window. How empty it is, a mirror, if I can't see myself in it! Whenever I had to talk to anyone, I always arranged it so that I *could* see myself in one. I talked and I could *see* myself talking. I could see how I *looked* to other people and that sort of kept me awake. (*Desperately.*) My make-up! I'm sure I've put it on all wrong—I simply can't go on through all eternity without a mirror!

Inez: (*All this as if to a child again.*) Wouldn't you like me to be your mirror? Come, I invite you over to my house. (*Indicating place on divan Right.*) Sit down on my divan.

Estelle: (*Pointing to* Cradeau.) But—

Inez: We won't pay any attention to him.

Estelle: (*Rising; fearfully.*) We're going to hurt each other. You said so yourself.

Inez: Do I look as if I wanted to hurt you?

Estelle: (*Hesitantly.*) You never know. (*Crosses to sit Right of* Inez.)

Inez: It's *you* who'll hurt *me.* But what does it matter? If I've got to suffer, it might as well be because of you. Sit down. Closer. Come over here closer to me. Look into my eyes. What do you see?

Estelle: I see myself very tiny. I can hardly see myself.

Inez: I see you. All of you. Ask me questions. You'll see no mirror could be so faithful.

Estelle: (Estelle, *embarrassed, turns toward* Cradeau, *as if to ask his help.*) Monsieur Cradeau! I'm sure we're annoying you with our silly chatter!

(Cradeau *does not answer.*)

Inez: Let him be. He doesn't count any more. We're all alone. Go on, ask me questions.

Estelle: Is my lipstick on straight?

Inez: Come here. Let's see. Not very. (*Leaning back to look.*)

Estelle: Oh, I knew it! Fortunately, (*She looks toward* Cradeau *out of the corner of her eye.*) nobody saw me. I'll start over again.

Inez: That's better. No, no! Follow the line of the lips. I'll guide your hand. (*She does so.*) There—there—that's it!

Estelle: Is it as good as it was a little while ago, when I came in?

Inez: (*With satisfaction.*) Better. Heavier. More cruel. Just the right make-up for Hell.

Estelle: (*Not seeming to notice.*) Hm! And it's all right? (*Petulantly.*) Oh, it's such a nuisance, I can't judge for myself! You *swear* it's all right?

Inez: (*As if asking an opinion.*) Do you think I'd lie to you, my sweet?

Estelle: *Swear* it looks all right.

Inez: You're beautiful.

Estelle: (*Runs it all together.*) But have you any taste? I mean, do you have *my* taste? Oh, it's *so* awfull It's so nerve-racking!

Inez: I have the same taste as you, because I like you. Look at me, straight *at* me. Smile at me. I'm not ugly either. Don't you think I'm better than a mirror?

Estelle: (*Distraught.*) I don't know. You're a little terrifying. My reflection in the mirror was *caught* there, you know, and I could do what I wanted with it. I knew it so well—I'm going to smile. It'll go all the way into your eyes and Heaven only knows what'll happen to it there.

Inez: And who's stopping you from catching *me?* (*They look at each other.* Estelle *smiles, a little fascinated.*)

Won't you call me "Inez"?

Estelle: (*Squirms slightly.*) It's awfully hard for me to call women by their first names.

Inez: (*Matter-of-factly.*) Especially secretaries, I suppose. (*As if startled.*) What's that you've got there on your cheek? It looks like a pimple.

Estelle: (*Jumping.*) On my cheek? How frightful! Where?

Inez: (*Laughs.*) You see? I'm a mirror to catch little mice in, and you're my little mouse. I've got you. (*Exaggeratedly reassuring.*) It's all right. There's nothing, nothing at all. You see? Suppose the mirror should begin to lie? Or if I should shut my eyes and wouldn't look at you, then what would you do with all that beauty? But don't worry, my eyes will stay wide open. I *have* to look at you. And I'll be nice, ve-ry nice. But you'll call me Inez.

(*Pause.*)

Estelle: You like me, Inez?

Inez: Very much.

(*A pause.*)

Estelle: (*Poutingly, indicating* Cradeau *with a nod of her head.*) I wish he'd look at me, too. . . .

Discussion Questions

1. To what extent is your freedom limited by your concern for what others think of you?
2. To what extent is your freedom limited by the expectations your family has for you?
3. To what extent is your freedom limited by the expectations you have for yourself?
4. To what extent do you think that others limit their freedom out of a concern for what you think of them?
5. To what extent is it possible to live without being concerned about how others view you? Would it be a good or bad thing for society if we did not care about what others thought of us?

For Further Reading

Sartre's major philosophical effort is *Being and Nothingness* (1957). Some of his best literary efforts include *Nausea* (1938), *The Flies* (1943), and *Dirty Hands* (1948). For works on Sartre see *Sartre* (1975) by A. C. Danto and *The Cambridge Companion to Sartre* (1992) edited by Christina Howells. For an excellent introduction to existentialism see *Existentialism from Dostoevsky to Sartre* (1956) by Walter Kaufmann.

8 THE SECOND SEX
Simone de Beauvoir

Simone de Beauvoir (1908–1986), like Sartre, was an influential exponent of the existential movement that emanated out of France in the 1930s and 1940s. In fact, Beauvoir and Sartre collaborated to found an avant-garde journal, *Les Temps Modernes* in 1945. Besides being collaborators, Sartre and Beauvoir shared intimate relations over the course of their lives. However, their relationship always remained *open* and they never married.

Beauvoir's most famous philosophical works are *The Ethics of Ambiguity* (1947) and *The Second Sex* (1949). Our selection comes from *The Second Sex*, considered a landmark in the evolution of feminist thought. According to Beauvoir, women are morally free in theory, but they exist as *other*, a subordinate role, in our patriarchal society. And as such, women are not as free as they ought to be.

Reading Questions

1. Why is asking the question *What is a woman?* significant?
2. Are the terms *masculine* and *feminine* symmetrical?
3. What did Aristotle say about women?
4. Why is it that women have gained only what men have been willing to grant?
5. What is the basic trait of women?

Source: From *The Second Sex* by Simone de Beauvoir, translated by H. M. Parshley, copyright 1952 and renewed 1980 by Alfred A. Knopf, a division of Random House, Inc. Used by permission of Alfred A. Knopf, a division of Random House, Inc.

6. Why has the liberation of the working class been slow?
7. Why may woman fail to lay claim to the status of subject?
8. What philosopher first took up the cause of women?
9. How do poor Southern whites and mediocre men console themselves?
10. What conception of happiness does Beauvoir reject?
11. What peculiarity signalizes the situation of women?

. . . What is a woman?

To state the question is, to me, to suggest, at once, a preliminary answer. The fact that I ask it is in itself significant. A man would never get the notion of writing a book on the peculiar situation of the human male. But if I wish to define myself, I must first of all say: "I am a woman"; on this truth must be based all further discussion. A man never begins by presenting himself as an individual of a certain sex; it goes without saying that he is a man. The terms *masculine* and *feminine* are used symmetrically only as a matter of form, as on legal papers. In actuality the relation of the two sexes is not quite like that of two electrical poles, for man represents both the positive and the neutral, as is indicated by the common use of *man* to designate human beings in general; whereas woman represents only the negative, defined by limiting criteria, without reciprocity. In the midst of an abstract discussion it is vexing to hear a man say: "You think thus and so because you are a woman"; but I know that my only defense is to reply: "I think thus and so because it is true," thereby removing my subjective self from the argument. It would be out of the question to reply: "And you think the contrary because you are a man," for it is understood that the fact of being a man is no peculiarity. A man is in the right in being a man; it is the woman who is in the wrong. It amounts to this: just as for the ancients there was an absolute vertical with reference to which the oblique was defined, so there is an absolute human type, the masculine. Woman has ovaries, a uterus; these peculiarities imprison her in her subjectivity, circumscribe her within the limits of her own nature. It is often said that she thinks with her glands. Man superbly ignores the fact that his anatomy also includes glands, such as the testicles, and that they secrete hormones. He thinks of his body as a direct and normal connection with the world, which he believes he apprehends objectively, whereas he regards the body of

woman as a hindrance, a prison, weighed down by everything peculiar to it. "The female is a female by virtue of a certain *lack* of qualities," said Aristotle; "we should regard the female nature as afflicted with a natural defectiveness." And St. Thomas for his part pronounced woman to be an "imperfect man," an "incidental" being. This is symbolized in Genesis where Eve is depicted as made from what Bossuet called "a supernumerary bone" of Adam.

Thus humanity is male and man defines woman not in herself but as relative to him; she is not regarded as an autonomous being. Michelet writes: "Woman, the relative being. . . ." And Benda is most positive in his *Rapport d'Uriel:* "The body of man makes sense in itself quite apart from that of woman, whereas the latter seems wanting in significance by itself. . . . Man can think of himself without woman. She cannot think of herself without man." And she is simply what man decrees; thus she is called "the sex," by which is meant that she appears essentially to the male as a sexual being. For him she is sex—absolute sex, no less. She is defined and differentiated with reference to man and not he with reference to her; she is the incidental, the inessential as opposed to the essential. He is the Subject, he is the Absolute—she is the Other.

The category of the *Other* is as primordial as consciousness itself. In the most primitive societies, in the most ancient mythologies, one finds the expression of a duality—that of the Self and the Other. This duality was not originally attached to the division of the sexes; it was not dependent upon any empirical facts. It is revealed in such works as that of Granet on Chinese thought and those of Dumézil on the East Indies and Rome. The feminine element was at first no more involved in such pairs as Varuna-Mitra, Uranus-Zeus, Sun-Moon, and Day-Night than it was in the contrasts between Good and Evil, lucky and unlucky auspices, right and left, God and Lucifer.

Otherness is a fundamental category of human thought.

Thus it is that no group ever sets itself up as the One without at once setting up the Other over against itself. If three travelers chance to occupy the same compartment, that is enough to make vaguely hostile "others" out of all the rest of the passengers on the train. In small-town eyes all persons not belonging to the village are "strangers" and suspect; to the native of a country all who inhabit other countries are "foreigners"; Jews are "different" for the anti-Semite, Negroes are "inferior" for American racists, aborigines are "natives" for colonists, proletarians are the "lower class" for the privileged.

Lévi-Strauss, at the end of a profound work on the various forms of primitive societies, reaches the following conclusion: "Passage from the state of Nature to the state of Culture is marked by man's ability to view biological relations as a series of contrasts; duality, alternation, opposition, and symmetry, whether under definite or vague forms, constitute not so much phenomena to be explained as fundamental and immediately given data of social reality." These phenomena would be incomprehensible if in fact human society were simply a *Mitsein* or fellowship based on solidarity and friendliness. Things become clear, on the contrary, if, following Hegel, we find in consciousness itself a fundamental hostility toward every other consciousness; the subject can be posed only in being opposed—he sets himself up as the essential, as opposed to the other, the inessential, the object.

But the other consciousness, the other ego, sets up a reciprocal claim. The native traveling abroad is shocked to find himself in turn regarded as a "stranger" by the natives of neighboring countries. As a matter of fact, wars, festivals, trading, treaties, and contests among tribes, nations, and classes tend to deprive the concept *Other* of its absolute sense and to make manifest its relativity; willy-nilly, individuals and groups are forced to realize the reciprocity of their relations. How is it, then, that this reciprocity has not been recognized between the sexes, that one of the contrasting terms is set up as the sole essential, denying any relativity in regard to its correlative and defining the latter as pure otherness? Why is it that women do not dispute male sovereignty? No subject will readily volunteer to become the object, the

inessential; it is not the Other who, in defining himself as the Other, establishes the One. The Other is posed as such by the One in defining himself as the One. But if the Other is not to regain the status of being the One, he must be submissive enough to accept this alien point of view. Whence comes this submission in the case of woman?

There are, to be sure, other cases in which a certain category has been able to dominate another completely for a time. Very often this privilege depends upon inequality of numbers—the majority imposes its rule upon the minority or persecutes it. But women are not a minority, like the American Negroes or the Jews; there are as many women as men on earth. Again, the two groups concerned have often been originally independent; they may have been formerly unaware of each other's existence, or perhaps they recognized each other's autonomy. But a historical event has resulted in the subjugation of the weaker by the stronger. The scattering of the Jews, the introduction of slavery into America, the conquests of imperialism are examples in point. In these cases the oppressed retained at least the memory of former days; they possessed in common a past, a tradition, sometimes a religion or a culture.

The parallel drawn by Bebel between women and the proletariat is valid in that neither ever formed a minority or a separate collective unit of mankind. And instead of a single historical event it is in both cases a historical development that explains their status as a class and accounts for the membership of *particular individuals* in that class. But proletarians have not always existed, whereas there have always been women. They are women in virtue of their anatomy and physiology. Throughout history they have always been subordinated to men and hence their dependency is not the result of a historical event or a social change—it was not something that *occurred*. The reason why otherness in this case seems to be an absolute is in part that it lacks the contingent or incidental nature of historical facts. A condition brought about at a certain time can be abolished at some other time, as the Negroes of Haiti and others have proved; but it might seem that a natural condition is beyond the possibility of change. In truth, however, the nature of things is no more immutably given, once for all, than is historical reality. If woman seems to be the inessential which never becomes the essential, it is because she herself fails to bring about this change. Proletarians say "We"; Negroes also. Regarding themselves as subjects, they transform the bourgeois, the whites, into "others." But women do not say "We," except at some congress of feminists or similar formal demonstration; men say "women," and women use the same word in referring to themselves. They do not authentically assume a subjective attitude. The proletarians have accomplished the revolution in Russia, the Negroes in Haiti, the Indo–Chinese are battling for it in Indo–China; but the women's effort has never been anything more than a symbolic agitation. They have gained only what men have been willing to grant; they have taken nothing, they have only received.

The reason for this is that women lack concrete means for organizing themselves into a unit which can stand face to face with the correlative unit. They have no past, no history, no religion of their own; and they have no such solidarity of work and interest as that of the proletariat. They are not even promiscuously herded together in the way that creates community feeling among the American Negroes, the ghetto Jews, the workers of Saint-Denis, or the factory hands of Renault. They live dispersed among the males, attached through residence, housework, economic condition, and social standing to certain men—fathers or husbands—more firmly than they are to other women. If they belong to the bourgeoisie, they feel solidarity with men of that class, not with proletarian women; if they are white, their allegiance is to white men, not to Negro women. The proletariat can propose to massacre the ruling class, and a sufficiently fanatical Jew or Negro might dream of getting sole possession of the atomic bomb and making humanity wholly Jewish or black; but woman cannot even dream of exterminating the males. The bond that unites her to her oppressors is not comparable to any other. The division of the sexes is a biological fact, not an event in human history. Male and female stand opposed within a primordial *Mitsein*, and woman has not broken it. The couple is a fundamental unity with its two halves riveted together, and the cleavage of society along the line of sex is impossible. Here is to be found the basic trait of woman: she is the Other in a totality of which the two components are necessary to one another.

One could suppose that this reciprocity might have facilitated the liberation of woman. When Hercules sat at the feet of Omphale and helped with her spinning, his desire for her held him captive; but why did she fail to gain a lasting power? To revenge herself on Jason, Medea killed their children; and this grim legend would seem to suggest that she might have obtained a formidable influence over him through his love for his offspring. In *Lysistrata* Aristophanes gaily depicts a band of women who joined forces to gain social ends through the sexual needs of their men; but this is only a play. In the legend of the Sabine women, the latter soon abandoned their plan of remaining sterile to punish their ravishers. In truth woman has not been socially emancipated through man's need—sexual desire and the desire for offspring—which makes the male dependent for satisfaction upon the female.

Master and slave, also, are united by a reciprocal need, in this case economic, which does not liberate the slave. In the relation of master to slave the master does not make a point of the need that he has for the other; he has in his grasp the power of satisfying this need through his own action; whereas the slave, in his dependent condition, his hope and fear, is quite conscious of the need he has for his master. Even if the need is at bottom equally urgent for both, it always works in favor of the oppressor and against the oppressed. That is why the liberation of the working class, for example, has been slow.

Now, woman has always been man's dependent, if not his slave; the two sexes have never shared the world in equality. And even today woman is heavily handicapped, though her situation is beginning to change. Almost nowhere is her legal status the same as man's, and frequently it is much to her disadvantage. Even when her rights are legally recognized in the abstract, long-standing custom prevents their full expression in the mores. In the economic sphere men and women can almost be said to make up two castes; other things being equal, the former hold the better jobs, get higher wages, and have more opportunity for success than their new competitors. In industry and politics men have a great many more positions and they monopolize the most important posts. In addition to all this, they enjoy a traditional prestige that the education of children tends in every way to support, for the present enshrines the past—and in the past all history has been made by men. At the present time, when women are beginning to take part in the affairs of the world, it is still a world that belongs to men—they have no doubt of it at all and women have scarcely any. To decline to be the Other, to refuse to be a party to the deal—this would be for women to renounce all the advantages conferred upon them by their alliance with the superior caste. Man-the-sovereign will provide woman-the-liege with material protection and will undertake the moral justification of her existence; thus she can evade at once both economic risk and the metaphysical risk of a liberty in which ends and aims must be contrived without assistance. Indeed, along with the ethical urge of each individual to affirm his subjective existence, there is also the temptation to forgo liberty and become a thing. This is an inauspicious road, for he who takes it—passive, lost, ruined—becomes henceforth the creature of another's will, frustrated in his transcendence and deprived of every value. But it is an easy road; on it one avoids the strain involved in undertaking an authentic existence. When man makes of woman the *Other*, he may, then, expect her to manifest deep-seated tendencies toward complicity. Thus, woman may fail to lay claim to the status of subject because she lacks definite resources, because she feels the necessary bond that ties her to man regardless of reciprocity, and because she is often very well pleased with her role as the *Other*.

But it will be asked at once: how did all this begin? It is easy to see that the duality of the sexes, like any duality, gives rise to conflict. And doubtless the winner will assume the status of absolute. But why should man have won from the start? It seems possible that women could have won the victory; or that the outcome of the conflict might never have been decided. How is it that this world has always belonged to the men and that things have begun to change only recently? Is this change a good thing? Will it bring about an equal sharing of the world between men and women?

These questions are not new, and they have often been answered. But the very fact that woman *is the Other* tends to cast suspicion upon all the justifications that men have ever been able to provide for it. These have all too evidently been dictated by men's interest. A little-known feminist of the seventeenth century, Poulain de la Barre, put it this way: "All that has been written about women by men should be suspect, for the men are at once judge and party to the lawsuit." Everywhere, at all times, the males have displayed their satisfaction in feeling that they are the lords of creation. "Blessed be God . . . that He did not make me a woman," say the Jews in their morning prayers, while their wives pray on a note of resignation: "Blessed be the Lord, who created me according to His will." The first among the blessings for which Plato thanked the gods was that he had been created free, not enslaved; the second, a man, not a woman. But the males could not enjoy this privilege fully unless they believed it to be founded on the absolute and the eternal; they sought to make the fact of their supremacy into a right. "Being men, those who have made and compiled the laws have favored their own sex, and jurists have elevated these laws into principles," to quote Poulain de la Barre once more.

Legislators, priests, philosophers, writers, and scientists have striven to show that the subordinate position of woman is willed in heaven and advantageous on earth. The religions invented by men reflect this wish for domination. In the legends of Eve and Pandora men have taken up arms against women. They have made use of philosophy and theology, as the quotations from Aristotle and St. Thomas have shown. Since ancient times satirists and moralists have delighted in showing up the weaknesses of women. We are familiar with the savage indictments hurled against women throughout French literature. Montherlant, for example, follows the tradition of Jean de Meung, though with less gusto. This hostility may at times be well founded, often it is gratuitous; but in truth it more or less successfully conceals a desire for self-justification. As Montaigne says, "It is easier to accuse one sex than to excuse the other." Sometimes what is going on is clear enough. For instance, the Roman law limiting the rights of woman cited "the imbecility, the instability of the sex" just when the weakening of family ties seemed to threaten the interests of male heirs. And in the effort to keep the married woman under guardianship, appeal was made in the sixteenth century to the authority of St. Augustine, who declared that "woman is a creature neither decisive nor constant," at a time when the single woman was thought capable of managing her property. Montaigne understood clearly how arbitrary and unjust was woman's appointed lot: "Women are not in the wrong when they decline to accept the rules laid down for them, since the men make these rules without consulting them. No wonder intrigue and strife abound." But he did not go so far as to champion their cause.

It was only later, in the eighteenth century, that genuinely democratic men began to view the matter objectively. Diderot, among others, strove to show that woman is, like man, a human being. Later John Stuart Mill came fervently to her defense. But these philosophers displayed unusual impartiality. In the nineteenth century the feminist quarrel became again a quarrel of partisans. One of the consequences of the industrial revolution was the entrance of women into productive labor, and it was just here that the claims of the feminists emerged from the realm of theory and acquired an economic basis, while their opponents became the more aggressive. Although landed property lost power to some extent, the bourgeoisie clung to the old morality that found the guarantee of private property in the solidity of the family. Woman was ordered back into the home the more harshly as her emancipation became a real menace. Even within the working class the men endeavored to restrain woman's liberation, because they began to see the women as dangerous competitors—the more so because they were accustomed to work for lower wages.

In proving woman's inferiority, the antifeminists then began to draw not only upon religion, philosophy, and theology, as before, but also upon science—biology, experimental psychology, etc. At most they were willing to grant "equality in difference" to the *other sex*. That profitable formula is most significant; it is precisely like the "equal but separate" formula of the Jim Crow laws aimed at the North American Negroes. As is well known, this so-called equalitarian segregation has resulted only in the most extreme discrimination. The similarity just noted is in no way due to chance, for whether it is a race, a caste, a class, or a sex that is reduced to a position of inferiority, the methods of justification are the same. "The eternal feminine" corresponds to "the black soul" and to "the Jewish character." True, the Jewish problem is on the whole very different from the other two—to the anti-Semite the Jew is not so much an inferior as he is an enemy for whom there is to be granted no place on earth, for whom annihilation is the fate desired. But there are deep similarities between the situation of woman and that of the Negro. Both are being emancipated today from a like paternalism, and the former master class wishes to "keep them in their place"—that is, the place chosen for them. In both cases the former masters lavish more or less sincere eulogies, either on the virtues of "the good Negro" with his dormant, childish, merry soul—the submissive Negro—or on the merits of the woman who is "truly feminine"—that is, frivolous, infantile, irresponsible—the submissive woman. In both cases the dominant class bases its argument on a state of affairs that it has itself created. As George Bernard Shaw puts it, in substance, "The American white relegates the black to the rank of shoeshine boy; and he concludes from this that the black is good for nothing but shining shoes." This vicious circle is met with in all analogous circumstances; when an individual (or a group of individuals) is kept in a situation of inferiority, the fact is that he *is* inferior. But the significance of the verb *to be* must be rightly understood here; it is in bad faith to give it a static value when it really has the dynamic Hegelian sense of "to have become." Yes, women on the whole *are* today inferior to men; that is, their situation affords them fewer possibilities. The question is: should that state of affairs continue?

Many men hope that it will continue; not all have given up the battle. The conservative bourgeoisie still see in the emancipation of women a menace to their morality and their interests. Some men dread feminine competition. Recently a male student wrote in the *Hebdo-Latin*: "Every woman student who goes into medicine or law robs us of a job." He never questioned his rights in this world. And economic interests are not the only ones concerned. One of the benefits that oppression confers upon the oppressors is that the most humble among them is made to *feel* superior; thus, a "poor white" in the South can console himself with the thought that he is not a "dirty nigger"—and the more prosperous whites cleverly exploit this pride.

Similarly, the most mediocre of males feels himself a demigod as compared with women. It was much easier for M. de Montherlant to think himself a hero when he faced women (and women chosen for his purpose) than when he was obliged to act the man among men—something many women have done better than he, for that matter. And in September 1948, in one of his articles in the *Figaro littéraire*, Claude Mauriac—whose great originality is admired by all—could write regarding woman: "*We* listen on a tone [*sic!*] of polite indifference . . . to the most brilliant among them, well knowing that her wit reflects more or less luminously ideas that come from *us*."

Evidently the speaker referred to is not reflecting the ideas of Mauriac himself, for no one knows of his having any. It may be that she reflects ideas originating with men, but then, even among men there are those who have been known to appropriate ideas not their own; and one can well ask whether Claude Mauriac might not find more interesting a conversation reflecting Descartes, Marx, or Gide rather than himself. What is really remarkable is that by using the questionable *we* he identifies himself with St. Paul, Hegel, Lenin, and Nietzsche, and from the lofty eminence of their grandeur looks down disdainfully upon the bevy of women who make bold to converse with him on a footing of equality. In truth, I know of more than one woman who would refuse to suffer with patience Mauriac's "tone of polite indifference."

I have lingered on this example because the masculine attitude is here displayed with disarming ingenuousness. But men profit in many more subtle ways from the otherness, the alterity of woman. Here is miraculous balm for those afflicted with an inferiority complex, and indeed no one is more arrogant toward women, more aggressive or scornful, than the man who is anxious about his virility. Those who are not fear-ridden in the presence of their fellow men are much more disposed to recognize a fellow creature in woman; but even to these the myth of woman, the Other, is precious for many reasons. They cannot be blamed for not cheerfully relinquishing all the benefits they derive from the myth, for they realize what they would lose in relinquishing woman as they fancy her to be, while they fail to realize what they have to gain from the woman of tomorrow. Refusal to pose oneself as the Subject, unique and absolute, requires great self-denial. Furthermore, the vast majority of men make no such claim explicitly. They do not *postulate* woman as inferior, for today they are too thoroughly imbued with the ideal of democracy not to recognize all human beings as equals.

In the bosom of the family, woman seems in the eyes of childhood and youth to be clothed in the same social dignity as the adult males. Later on, the young man, desiring and loving, experiences the resistance, the independence of the woman desired and loved; in marriage, he respects woman as wife and mother, and in the concrete events of conjugal life she stands there before him as a free being. He can therefore feel that social subordination as

between the sexes no longer exists and that on the whole, in spite of differences, woman is an equal. As, however, he observes some points of inferiority—the most important being unfitness for the professions—he attributes these to natural causes. When he is in a co-operative and benevolent relation with woman, his theme is the principle of abstract equality, and he does not base his attitude upon such inequality as may exist. But when he is in conflict with her, the situation is reversed: his theme will be the existing inequality, and he will even take it as justification for denying abstract equality.

So it is that many men will affirm as if in good faith that women *are* the equals of man and that they have nothing to clamor for, while *at the same time* they will say that women can never be the equals of man and that their demands are in vain. It is, in point of fact, a difficult matter for man to realize the extreme importance of social discriminations which seem outwardly insignificant but which produce in woman moral and intellectual effects so profound that they appear to spring from her original nature. The most sympathetic of men never fully comprehend woman's concrete situation. And there is no reason to put much trust in the men when they rush to the defense of privileges whose full extent they can hardly measure. We shall not, then, permit ourselves to be intimidated by the number and violence of the attacks launched against women, nor to be entrapped by the self-seeking eulogies bestowed on the "true woman," nor to profit by the enthusiasm for woman's destiny manifested by men who would not for the world have any part of it.

We should consider the arguments of the feminists with no less suspicion, however, for very often their controversial aim deprives them of all real value. If the "woman question" seems trivial, it is because masculine arrogance has made of it a "quarrel"; and when quarreling, one no longer reasons well. People have tirelessly sought to prove that woman is superior, inferior, or equal to man. Some say that, having been created after Adam, she is evidently a secondary being; others say on the contrary that Adam was only a rough draft and that God succeeded in producing the human being in perfection when He created Eve. Woman's brain is smaller; yes, but it is relatively larger. Christ was made a man; yes, but perhaps for his greater humility. Each argument at once suggests its opposite, and both are often fallacious. If we are to gain understanding, we must get out of these ruts; we must discard the vague notions of superiority, inferiority, equality which have hitherto corrupted every discussion of the subject and start afresh.

Very well, but just how shall we pose the question? And, to begin with, who are we to propound it at all? Man is at once judge and party to the case; but so is woman. What we need is an angel—neither man nor woman—but where shall we find one? Still, the angel would be poorly qualified to speak, for an angel is ignorant of all the basic facts involved in the problem. With a hermaphrodite we should be no better off, for here the situation is most peculiar; the hermaphrodite is not really the combination of a whole man and a whole woman, but consists of parts of each and thus is neither. It looks to me as if there are, after all, certain women who are best qualified to elucidate the situation of woman. Let us not be misled by the sophism that because Epimenides was a Cretan he was necessarily a liar; it is not a mysterious essence that compels men and women to act in good or in bad faith, it is their situation that inclines them more or less toward the search for truth. Many of today's women, fortunate in the restoration of all the privileges pertaining to the estate of the human being, can afford the luxury of impartiality—we even recognize its necessity. We are no longer like our partisan elders; by and large we have won the game. In recent debates on the status of women the United Nations has persistently maintained that the equality of the sexes is now becoming a reality, and already some of us have never had to sense in our femininity an inconvenience or an obstacle. Many problems appear to us to be more pressing than those which concern us in particular, and this detachment even allows us to hope that our attitude will be objective. Still, we know the feminine world more intimately than do the men because we have our roots in it, we grasp more immediately than do men what it means to a human being to be feminine; and we are more concerned with such knowledge. I have said that there are more pressing problems, but this does not prevent us from seeing some importance in asking how the fact of being women will affect our lives. What opportunitites precisely have been given us and what withheld? What fate awaits our younger sisters, and what directions should they take? It is significant that books by women on women are in general animated in our day less by a wish to demand our rights than by an effort toward clarity and understanding. As we emerge from an era of excessive controversy, this book is offered as one attempt among others to confirm that statement.

But it is doubtless impossible to approach any human problem with a mind free from bias. The way in which questions are put, the points of view assumed, presuppose a relativity of interest; all characteristics imply values, and every objective description, so called, implies an ethical background. Rather than attempt to conceal principles more or less definitely implied, it is better to state them openly at the beginning. This will make it unnecessary to specify on every page in just what sense one uses such words as *superior, inferior, better, worse, progress, reaction,* and the like. If we survey some of the works on woman, we note that one of the points of view most frequently adopted is that of the public good, the general interest; and one always means by this the benefit of society as one wishes it to be maintained or established. For our part, we hold that the only public good is that which assures the private good of the citizens; we shall pass judgment on institutions according to their effectiveness in giving concrete opportunities to individuals. But we do not confuse the idea of private interest with that of happiness, although that is another common point of view. Are not women of the harem more happy than women voters? Is not the housekeeper happier than the workingwoman? It is not too clear just what the word *happy* really means and still less what true values it may mask. There is no possibility of measuring the happiness of others, and it is always easy to describe as happy the situation in which one wishes to place them.

In particular those who are condemned to stagnation are often pronounced happy on the pretext that happiness consists in being at rest. This notion we reject, for our perspective is that of existentialist ethics. Every subject plays his part as such specifically through exploits or projects that serve as a mode of transcendence; he achieves liberty only through a continual reaching out toward other liberties. There is no justification for present existence other than its expansion into an indefinitely open future. Every time transcendence falls back into immanence, stagnation, there is a degradation of existence into the "*en-soi*"— the brutish life of subjection to given conditions— and of liberty into constraint and contingence. This downfall represents a moral fault if the subject consents to it; if it is inflicted upon him, it spells frustration and oppression. In both cases it is an absolute evil. Every individual concerned to justify his existence feels that his existence involves an undefined need to transcend himself, to engage in freely chosen projects.

Now, what peculiarly signalizes the situation of woman is that she—a free and autonomous being like all human creatures—nevertheless finds herself living in a world where men compel her to assume the status of the Other. They propose to sta-

bilize her as object and to doom her to immanence since her transcendence is to be overshadowed and forever transcended by another ego (*conscience*) which is essential and sovereign. The drama of woman lies in this conflict between the fundamental aspirations of every subject (ego)—who always regards the self as the essential—and the compulsions of a situation in which she is the inessential. How can a human being in woman's situation attain fulfillment? What roads are open to her? Which are blocked? How can independence be recovered in a state of dependency? What circumstances limit woman's liberty and how can they be overcome? These are the fundamental questions on which I would fain throw some light. This means that I am interested in the fortunes of the individual as defined not in terms of happiness but in terms of liberty. . . .

Discussion Questions

1. Are men and women equal?
2. Are men and women treated as equals in our society?
3. If women are not treated as equals in our society, why do they accept this situation?
4. What sort of changes would need to be made before we could say that our society treated men and women equally? Should we make these changes?
5. Do we raise boys in the same way that we raise girls? If not, why not?

For Further Reading

Simone de Beauvoir's major philosophical efforts are *The Ethics of Ambiguity* (1948) and *The Second Sex* (1953). For examples of her literary work see *She Came to Stay* (1943) and *All Men Are Mortal* (1946).

   For studies of Beauvoir's life and philosophy see *Simone de Beauvoir, The Making of an Intellectual Woman* (1994) by T. Moi and *Philosophy as Passion: The Thinking of Simone de Beauvoir* (1996) by K. Vintges. For a study of the relationships between the philosophies of Beauvoir, Sartre, and Merleau-Ponty see *Situation and Human Existence: Freedom, Subjectivity and Society* (1990) by S. Kruks.

CHAPTER 2

IS ARTIFICIAL INTELLIGENCE POSSIBLE?

Consider the following session between therapist and patient:

Patient: Men are all alike.
Therapist: In what way?
Patient: They're always bugging us about something or other.
Therapist: Can you think of a specific example?
Patient: Well, my boyfriend made me come here.
Therapist: Your boyfriend made you come here.
Patient: He says I'm depressed much of the time.
Therapist: I am sorry to hear that you are depressed.
Patient: It's true. I am unhappy.
Therapist: Do you think coming here will help you not to be unhappy?
Patient: I need some help, that much seems certain.
Therapist: What would it mean to you if you got some help?
Patient: Perhaps I could learn to get along with my mother.
Therapist: Tell me more about your family.
Patient: My mother takes care of me.
Therapist: Who else in your family takes care of you?
Patient: My father.
Therapist: Your father.
Patient: You are like my father in some ways.
Therapist: What resemblance do you see?
Patient: You are not very aggressive but I think you don't want me to notice that.
Therapist: What makes you think that I am not very aggressive?
Patient: You don't argue with me.
Therapist: Why do you think that I don't argue with you?
Patient: You are afraid of me.
Therapist: Does it please you to believe that I am afraid of you?
Patient: My father is afraid of everybody.
Therapist: What else comes to mind when you think of your father?

Patient: Bullies.

Therapist: Does that have anything to do with the fact that your boyfriend made you come here?*

The amazing fact about this session is that the therapist is not human. Instead, the therapist is ELIZA, a computer program written in 1966 by Massachusetts Institute of Technology (M.I.T.) professor Joseph Weizenbaum. Following a simple set of instructions, ELIZA constructs *intelligent* responses to patient input to mimic the role of a Rogerian psychotherapist. Although initially impressive, further interaction between ELIZA and the patient would eventually reveal that the therapist is a fraud.

Programs such as ELIZA marked the humble beginnings of research into **artificial intelligence** (AI), the attempt to make computer systems capable of solving problems that normally require human intelligence to solve. Other examples include GTP, a program designed in the late 1950s to work geometry problems, and DENDRAL, designed to calculate the molecular structure of chemicals.

Many researchers, however, view AI as more than an attempt to create intelligent computers; it can also be used to explore the very nature of the human mind. If intelligent machines perform the same functions as human minds, they reason, then the intelligent machine is an excellent model for understanding the human mind. Of course, this hope assumes that computer brains and human brains operate in the same way, a tenuous assumption because human brains and (most) computers possess dissimilar architectures. The neurons of the brain are interconnected or 'netted' together in a way quite unlike the serial structure of the computer's circuitry. Today, however, AI researchers are beginning to design and work with computer architectures that attempt to mirror the architecture of the human brain. Such an approach to creating an artificial brain or cognitive system is referred to as a **connectionist** approach or a **neural network** approach.

Replicating the physical structure of the brain may not, however, be necessary to achieve dramatic results. In May 1997, Grand Master Garry Kasparov, the best (human) chess player the world has ever known, sat down to play a six-game match with Deep Blue, a chess program running on an IBM supercomputer capable of massive **parallel-processing**—dividing up a larger problem into smaller problems and working on a number of the smaller problems simultaneously. Deep Blue won the match with two wins, one loss, and three draws. For the first time ever, a computer could be said to be the best chess player in the world. Other computers, also capable of parallel-processing, have shown signs of being able to learn, that is, to alter and augment their programming based on *experience,* instead of simply relying on the 'knowledge' contained in their initial programs. The robot COG developed at the M.I.T. Artificial Intelligence Laboratory is a leading example.

This chapter focuses on three interrelated questions about the nature of intelligence, the possibility of artificial machine intelligence, and the possibility of machine consciousness. These questions raise further questions. For example, consider a computer/android such as Lt. Commander Data from the television series *Star Trek: The Next Generation.* Is Data conscious? If so, is he a person, entitled to rights like other persons? And if physical machines can be conscious, is there any remaining reason to claim that the human mind and brain are not one and the same thing? Moreover, if the mind and brain are one and the same, does this mean that we cease to exist when our brains stop functioning? Is there no afterlife?

---

* Dorothy Hunshaw Patent, *The Quest for Artificial Intelligence* (1986), pp. 26–27.

9 COMPUTING MACHINERY AND INTELLIGENCE
Alan Mathison Turing

Born in London, A. M. Turing (1912–1952)—part mathematician, part logician, and part pioneering computer scientist—built computers as early as the 1940s, when they were still constructed using vacuum tubes. Machines of that era were unreliable, generated copious amounts of heat, and had very little computing power despite their huge size. For example, ENIAC, the first electronic computer ever built, weighed over 30 tons and was larger than a house. ENIAC also required its own air-conditioning system to prevent overheating. Nonetheless, Turing grasped the theoretical potential of computers and predicted that they would eventually become extremely powerful and would someday complete a variety of complex intellectual assignments more accurately and faster than humans.

Suppose computers have or will have this capacity, that is, that they can complete a variety of intellectual tasks as well as or better than humans. Would it be fair to say that these machines think and are intelligent? In the following article, Turing proposes a test—the **Turing Test,** as it has come to be known—for determining whether a particular machine is intelligent. Turing also defends the claim that machines will, someday, be able to pass the Turing Test—quite a boast when one remembers that this article was written in 1950.

Reading Questions

1. Describe the imitation game. How is it related to the original question of whether a machine can think?
2. Does Turing believe that machines will be able to succeed at playing the imitation game? Why?
3. Explain the theological objection. How does Turing respond?
4. What is the mathematical objection? What response does Turing offer to this objection?
5. Explain the argument from consciousness and Turing's response.
6. What is Lady Lovelace's objection? What is Turing's response?
7. What is the argument from informality of behavior? How does Turing respond?

1. THE IMITATION GAME

I propose to consider the question, 'Can machines think?' This should begin with definitions of the meaning of the terms 'machine' and 'think'. The definitions might be framed so as to reflect so far as possible the normal use of the words, but this attitude is dangerous. If the meaning of the words 'machine' and 'think' are to be found by examining how they are commonly used it is difficult to escape the conclusion that the meaning and the answer to the question, 'Can machines think?' is to be sought in a statistical survey such as a Gallup poll. But this is absurd. Instead of attempting such a definition I shall replace the question by another, which is

---

SOURCE: "Computing Machinery and Intelligence" by A. M. Turing, from *Mind* 59, no. 236, pp. 4–30. 1950 by Oxford University Press. Reprinted with permission of Oxford University Press.

closely related to it and is expressed in relatively unambiguous words.

The new form of the problem can be described in terms of a game which we call the 'imitation game'. It is played with three people, a man (A), a woman (B), and an interrogator (C) who may be of either sex. The interrogator stays in a room apart from the other two. The object of the game for the interrogator is to determine which of the other two is the man and which is the woman. He knows them by labels X and Y, and at the end of the game he says either 'X is A and Y is B' or 'X is B and Y is A'. The interrogator is allowed to put questions to A and B thus:

C: Will X please tell me the length of his or her hair?

Now suppose X is actually A, then A must answer. It is A's object in the game to try and cause C to make the wrong identification. His answer might therefore be 'My hair is shingled, and the longest strands are about nine inches long.'

In order that tones of voice may not help the interrogator the answers should be written, or better still, typewritten. The ideal arrangement is to have a teleprinter communicating between the two rooms. Alternatively the question and answers can be repeated by an intermediary. The object of the game for the third player (B) is to help the interrogator. The best strategy for her is probably to give truthful answers. She can add such things as 'I am the woman, don't listen to him!' to her answers, but it will avail nothing as the man can make similar remarks.

We now ask the question, 'What will happen when a machine takes the part of A in this game?' Will the interrogator decide wrongly as often when the game is played like this as he does when the game is played between a man and a woman? These questions replace our original, 'Can machines think?'

2. CRITIQUE OF THE NEW PROBLEM

As well as asking, 'What is the answer to this new form of the question', one may ask, 'Is this new question a worthy one to investigate?' This latter question we investigate without further ado, thereby cutting short an infinite regress.

The new problem has the advantage of drawing a fairly sharp line between the physical and the intellectual capacities of a man. No engineer or chemist claims to be able to produce a material which is indistinguishable from the human skin. It is possible that at some time this might be done, but even supposing this invention available we should feel there was little point in trying to make a 'thinking machine' more human by dressing it up in such artificial flesh. The form in which we have set the problem reflects this fact in the condition which prevents the interrogator from seeing or touching the other competitors, or hearing their voices. Some other advantages of the proposed criterion may be shown up by specimen questions and answers. Thus:

Q: Please write me a sonnet on the subject of the Forth Bridge.
A: Count me out on this one. I never could write poetry.
Q: Add 34957 to 70764
A: (Pause about 30 seconds and then give as answer) 105621.
Q: Do you play chess?
A: Yes.
Q: I have K at my K1, and no other pieces. You have only K at K6 and R at R1. It is your move. What do you play?
A: (After a pause of 15 seconds) R-R8 mate.

The question and answer method seems to be suitable for introducing almost any one of the fields of human endeavor that we wish to include. We do not wish to penalize the machine for its inability to shine in beauty competitions, nor to penalize a man for losing in a race against an airplane. The conditions of our game make these disabilities irrelevant. The 'witnesses' can brag, if they consider it advisable, as much as they please about their charms, strength or heroism, but the interrogator cannot demand practical demonstrations.

...

6. CONTRARY VIEWS ON THE MAIN QUESTION

We may now consider the ground to have been cleared and we are ready to proceed to the debate on our question, 'Can machines think?' and the variant of it quoted at the end of the last section. We cannot altogether abandon the original form of the problem, for opinions will differ as to the appropriateness of the substitution and we must at least listen to what has to be said in this connection.

It will simplify matters for the reader if I explain first my own beliefs in the matter. Consider first the more accurate form of the question. I believe that in about fifty years' time it will be possible to program computers, with a storage capacity of about 10^9, to make them play the imitation game so well that an average interrogator will not have more than 70 percent chance of making the right identification after five minutes of questioning. The original question, 'Can machines think?' I believe to be too meaningless to deserve discussion. Nevertheless I believe that at the end of the century the use of words and general educated opinion will have altered so much that one will be able to speak of machines thinking without expecting to be contradicted. I believe further that no useful purpose is served by concealing these beliefs. The popular view that scientists proceed inexorably from well-established fact to well-established fact, never being influenced by any unproved conjecture, is quite mistaken. Provided it is made clear which are proved facts and which are conjectures, no harm can result. Conjectures are of great importance since they suggest useful lines of research.

I now proceed to consider opinions opposed to my own.

(1) The Theological Objection

Thinking is a function of man's immortal soul. God has given an immortal soul to every man and woman, but not to any other animal or to machines. Hence no animal or machine can think.

I am unable to accept any part of this, but will attempt to reply in theological terms. I should find the argument more convincing if animals were classed with men, for there is a greater difference, to my mind, between the typical animate and the inanimate than there is between man and the other animals. The arbitrary character of the orthodox view becomes clearer if we consider how it might appear to a member of some other religious community. How do Christians regard the Moslem view that women have no souls? But let us leave this point aside and return to the main argument. It appears to me that the argument quoted above implies a serious restriction of the omnipotence of the Almighty. It is admitted that there are certain things that He cannot do such as

making one equal to two, but should we not believe that He has freedom to confer a soul on an elephant if He sees fit? We might expect that He would only exercise this power in conjunction with a mutation which provided the elephant with an appropriately improved brain to minister to the needs of this soul. An argument of exactly similar form may be made for the case of machines. It may seem different because it is more difficult to 'swallow'. But this really only means that we think it would be less likely that He would consider the circumstances suitable for conferring a soul. The circumstances in question are discussed in the rest of this paper. In attempting to construct such machines we should not be irreverently usurping His power of creating souls, any more than we are in the procreation of children: rather we are, in either case, instruments of His will providing mansions for the souls that He creates.

However, this is mere speculation. I am not very impressed with theological arguments whatever they may be used to support. Such arguments have often been found unsatisfactory in the past. In the time of Galileo it was argued that the texts, "And the sun stood still ... and hasted not to go down about a whole day" (Joshua x. 13) and "He laid the foundations of the earth, that it should not move at any time" (Psalm cv. 5) were an adequate refutation of the Copernican theory. With our present knowledge such an argument appears futile. When that knowledge was not available it made a quite different impression.

(2) The 'Heads in the Sand' Objection

"The consequences of machines thinking would be too dreadful. Let us hope and believe that they cannot do so."

This argument is seldom expressed quite so openly as in the form above. But it affects most of us who think about it at all. We like to believe that Man is in some subtle way superior to the rest of creation. It is best if he can be shown to be *necessarily* superior, for then there is no danger of him losing his commanding position. The popularity of the theological argument is clearly connected with this feeling. It is likely to be quite strong in intellectual people, since they value the power of thinking more highly than others, and are more inclined to base their belief in the superiority of Man on this power.

I do not think that this argument is sufficiently substantial to require refutation. Consolation would be more appropriate: perhaps this should be sought in the transmigration of souls.

(3) The Mathematical Objection

There are a number of results of mathematical logic which can be used to show that there are limitations to the powers of discrete-state machines. The best known of these results is known as Gödel's theorem, and shows that in any sufficiently powerful logical system statements can be formulated which can neither be proved nor disproved within the system, unless possibly the system itself is inconsistent. There are other, in some respects similar, results due to Church, Kleene, Rosser, and Turing. The latter result is the most convenient to consider, since it refers directly to machines, whereas the others can only be used in a comparatively indirect argument: for instance if Gödel's theorem is to be used we need in addition to have some means of describing logical systems in terms of machines, and machines in terms of logical systems. The result in question refers to a type of machine which is essentially a digital computer with an infinite capacity. It states that there are certain things that such a machine cannot do. If it is rigged up to give answers to questions as in the imitation game, there will be some questions to which it will either give a wrong answer, or fail to give an answer at all however much time is allowed for a reply. There may, of course, be many such questions, and questions which cannot be answered by one machine may be satisfactorily answered by another. We are of course supposing for the present that the questions are of the kind to which an answer 'Yes' or 'No' is appropriate, rather than questions such as 'What do you think of Picasso?' The questions that we know the machines must fail on are of this type, "Consider the machine specified as follows. . . . Will this machine ever answer 'Yes' to any question?" The dots are to be replaced by a description of some machine in a standard form. . . . When the machine described bears a certain comparatively simple relation to the machine which is under interrogation, it can be shown that the answer is either wrong or not forthcoming. This is the mathematical result: it is argued that it proves a disability of machines to which the human intellect is not subject.

The short answer to this argument is that although it is established that there are limitations to the powers of any particular machine, it has only been stated, without any sort of proof, that no such limitations apply to the human intellect. But I do not think this view can be dismissed quite so lightly. Whenever one of these machines is asked the appropriate critical question, and gives a definite answer, we know that this answer must be wrong, and this gives us a certain feeling of superiority. Is this feeling illusory? It is no doubt quite genuine, but I do not think too much importance should be attached to it. We too often give wrong answers to questions ourselves to be justified in being very pleased at such evidence of fallibility on the part of the machines. Further, our superiority can only be felt on such an occasion in relation to the one machine over which we have scored our petty triumph. There would be no question of triumphing simultaneously over *all* machines. In short, then, there might be men cleverer than any given machine, but then again there might be other machines cleverer again, and so on.

Those who hold to the mathematical argument would, I think, mostly be willing to accept the imitation game as a basis for discussion. Those who believe in the two previous objections would probably not be interested in any criteria.

(4) The Argument from Consciousness

This argument is very well expressed in Professor Jefferson's Lister Oration for 1949, from which I quote. "Not until a machine can write a sonnet or compose a concerto because of thoughts and emotions felt, and not by the chance fall of symbols, could we agree that machine equals brain—that is, not only write it but know that it had written it. No mechanism could feel (and not merely artificially signal, an easy contrivance) pleasure at its successes, grief when its valves fuse, be warmed by flattery, be made miserable by its mistakes, be charmed by sex, be angry or depressed when it cannot get what it wants."

This argument appears to be a denial of the validity of our test. According to the most extreme form of this view the only way by which one could be sure that a machine thinks is to *be* the machine and to feel oneself thinking. One could then describe these feelings to the world, but of course no one would be justified in taking any notice. Likewise according to this view the only way to know that a *man* thinks is to be that particular man. It is in fact the solipsist point of view. It may be the most logical view to hold but it makes communication of ideas difficult. A is liable to believe 'A thinks but B does not' while B believes 'B thinks but A does not'. Instead of arguing continually over this point it is usual to have the polite convention that everyone thinks.

I am sure that Professor Jefferson does not wish to adopt the extreme and solipsist point of view. Probably he would be quite willing to accept the imitation game as a test. The game (with the player B omitted) is frequently used in practice under the name of *viva voce* to discover whether some one really understands something or has 'learnt it parrot fashion'. Let us listen in to a part of such a *viva voce*:

Interrogator: In the first line of your sonnet which reads 'Shall I compare thee to a summer's day', would not 'a spring day' do as well or better?

Witness: It wouldn't scan.

Interrogator: How about 'a winter's day'? That would scan all right.

Witness: Yes, but nobody wants to be compared to a winter's day.

Interrogator: Would you say Mr. Pickwick reminded you of Christmas?

Witness: In a way.

Interrogator: Yet Christmas is a winter's day, and I do not think Mr. Pickwick would mind the comparison.

Witness: I don't think you're serious. By a winter's day one means a typical winter's day, rather than a special one like Christmas.

And so on. What would Professor Jefferson say if the sonnet-writing machine was able to answer like this in the *viva voce*? I do not know whether he would regard the machine as 'merely artificially signaling' these answers, but if the answers were as satisfactory and sustained as in the above passage I do not think he would describe it as 'an easy contrivance'. This phrase is, I think, intended to cover such devices as the inclusion in the machine of a record of someone reading a sonnet, with appropriate switching to turn it on from time to time.

In short then, I think that most of those who support the argument from consciousness could be persuaded to abandon it rather than be forced into the solipsist position. They will then probably be willing to accept our test.

I do not wish to give the impression that I think there is no mystery about consciousness. There is, for instance, something of a paradox connected with any attempt to localize it. But I do not think these mysteries necessarily need to be solved before we can answer the question with which we are concerned in this paper.

(5) Arguments from Various Disabilities

These arguments take the form, "I grant you that you can make machines do all the things you have mentioned but you will never be able to make one to do X." Numerous features X are suggested in this connection. I offer a selection:

> Be kind, resourceful, beautiful, friendly, have initiative, have a sense of humor, tell right from wrong, make mistakes, fall in love, enjoy strawberries and cream, make someone fall in love with it, learn from experience, use words properly, be the subject of its own thought, have as much diversity of behavior as a man, do something really new.

No support is usually offered for these statements. I believe they are mostly founded on the principle of scientific induction. A man has seen thousands of machines in his lifetime. From what he sees of them he draws a number of general conclusions. They are ugly, each is designed for a very limited purpose, when required for a minutely different purpose they are useless, the variety of behavior of any one of them is very small, etc., etc. Naturally he concludes that these are necessary properties of machines in general. Many of these limitations are associated with the very small storage capacity of most machines. (I am assuming that the idea of storage capacity is extended in some way to cover machines other than discrete-state machines. The exact definition does not matter as no mathematical accuracy is claimed in the present discussion.) A few years ago, when very little had been heard of digital computers, it was possible to elicit much incredulity concerning them, if one mentioned their properties without describing their construction. That was presumably due to a similar application of the principle of scientific induction. These applications of the principle are of course largely unconscious. When a burnt child fears the fire and shows that he fears it by avoiding it, I should say that he was applying scientific induction. (I could of course also describe his behavior in many other ways.) The works and customs of mankind do not seem to be very suitable material to which to apply scientific induction. A very large part of space-time must be investigated, if reliable results are to be obtained. Otherwise we may (as most English children do) decide that everybody speaks English, and that it is silly to learn French.

There are, however, special remarks to be made about many of the disabilities that have been mentioned. The inability to enjoy strawberries and cream may have struck the reader as frivolous. Possibly a machine might be made to enjoy this delicious dish, but any attempt to make one do so would be idiotic. What is important about this disability is that it contributes to some of the other disabilities, e.g., to the difficulty of the same kind of friendliness occurring between man and machine as between white man and white man, or between black man and black man.

The claim that "machines cannot make mistakes" seems a curious one. One is tempted to retort, "Are they any the worse for that?" But let us adopt a more sympathetic attitude, and try to see what is really meant. I think this criticism can be explained in terms of the imitation game. It is claimed that the interrogator could distinguish the machine from the man simply by setting them a number of problems in arithmetic. The machine would be unmasked because of its deadly accuracy. The reply to this is simple. The machine (programmed for playing the game) would not attempt to give the *right* answers to the arithmetic problems. It would deliberately introduce mistakes in a manner calculated to confuse the interrogator. A mechanical fault would probably show itself through an unsuitable decision as to what sort of a mistake to make in the arithmetic. Even this interpretation of the criticism is not sufficiently sympathetic. But we cannot afford the space to go into it much further. It seems to me that this criticism depends on a confusion between two kinds of mistake. We may call them 'errors of functioning' and 'errors of conclusion'. Errors of functioning are due to some mechanical or electrical fault which causes the machine to behave otherwise than it was designed to do. In philosophical discussions one likes to ignore the possibility of such errors; one is therefore discussing 'abstract machines'.

These abstract machines are mathematical fictions rather than physical objects. By definition they are incapable of errors of functioning. In this sense we can truly say that 'machines can never make mistakes'. Errors of conclusion can only arise when some meaning is attached to the output signals from the machine. The machine might, for instance, type out mathematical equations, or sentences in English. When a false proposition is typed we say that the machine has committed an error of conclusion. There is clearly no reason at all for saying that a machine cannot make this kind of mistake. It might do nothing but type out repeatedly '0 = 1'. To take a less perverse example, it might have some method for drawing conclusions by scientific induction. We must expect such a method to lead occasionally to erroneous results.

The claim that a machine cannot be the subject of its own thought can of course only be answered if it can be shown that the machine has *some* thought with *some* subject matter. Nevertheless, 'the subject matter of a machine's operations' does seem to mean something, at least to the people who deal with it. If, for instance, the machine was trying to find a solution of the equation $x^2 - 40x - 11 = 0$ one would be tempted to describe this equation as part of the machine's subject matter at that moment. In this sort of sense a machine undoubtedly can be its own subject matter. It may be used to help in making up its own programs, or to predict the effect of alterations in its own structure. By observing the results of its own behavior it can modify its own programs so as to achieve some purpose more effectively. These are possibilities of the near future, rather than Utopian dreams.

The criticism that a machine cannot have much diversity of behavior is just a way of saying that it cannot have much storage capacity. Until fairly recently a storage capacity of even a thousand digits was very rare.

The criticisms that we are considering here are often disguised forms of the argument from consciousness. Usually if one maintains that a machine *can* do one of these things, and describes the kind of method that the machine could use, one will not make much of an impression. It is thought that the method (whatever it may be, for it must be mechanical) is really rather base. Compare the parenthesis in Jefferson's statement quoted [above].

(6) Lady Lovelace's Objection

Our most detailed information of Babbage's Analytical Engine comes from a memoir by Lady Lovelace. In it she states, "The Analytical Engine has no pretensions to *originate* anything. It can do *whatever we know how to order it* to perform" (her italics). This statement is quoted by Hartree who adds: "This does not imply that it may not be possible to construct electronic equipment which will 'think for itself', or in which, in biological terms, one could set up a conditioned reflex, which would serve as a basis for 'learning'. Whether this is possible in principle or not is a stimulating and exciting question, suggested by some of these recent developments. But it did not seem that the machines constructed or projected at the time had this property."

I am in thorough agreement with Hartree over this. It will be noticed that he does not assert that the machines in question had not got the property, but rather that the evidence available to Lady Lovelace did not encourage her to believe that they had it. It is quite possible that the machines in question had in a sense got this property. For suppose that some discrete-state machine has the property. The Analytical Engine was a universal digital computer, so that, if its storage capacity and speed were adequate, it could by suitable programming be made to mimic the machine in question. Probably this argument did not occur to the Countess or to Babbage. In any case there was no obligation on them to claim all that could be claimed.

This whole question will be considered again under the heading of learning machines.

A variant of Lady Lovelace's objection states that a machine can 'never do anything really new'. This may be parried for a moment with the saw, 'There is nothing new under the sun'. Who can be certain that 'original work' that he has done was not simply the growth of the seed planted in him by teaching, or the effect of following well-known general principles. A better variant of the objection says that a machine can never 'take us by surprise'. This statement is a more direct challenge and can be met directly. Machines take me by surprise with great frequency. This is largely because I do not do sufficient calculation to decide what to expect them to do, or rather because, although I do a calculation, I do it in a hurried, slipshod fashion, taking risks. Perhaps I say to myself, 'I suppose the voltage here ought to be the same as there: anyway let's assume it is'. Naturally I am often wrong, and the result is a surprise

for me for by the time the experiment is done these assumptions have been forgotten. These admissions lay me open to lectures on the subject of my vicious ways, but do not throw any doubt on my credibility when I testify to the surprises I experience.

I do not expect this reply to silence my critic. He will probably say that such surprises are due to some creative mental act on my part, and reflect no credit on the machine. This leads us back to the argument from consciousness, and far from the idea of surprise. It is a line of argument we must consider closed, but it is perhaps worth remarking that the appreciation of something as surprising requires as much of a 'creative mental act' whether the surprising event originates from a man, a book, a machine or anything else.

The view that machines cannot give rise to surprises is due, I believe, to a fallacy to which philosophers and mathematicians are particularly subject. This is the assumption that as soon as a fact is presented to a mind all consequences of that fact spring into the mind simultaneously with it. It is a very useful assumption under many circumstances, but one too easily forgets that it is false. A natural consequence of doing so is that one then assumes that there is no virtue in the mere working out of consequences from data and general principles.

(7) Argument from Continuity in the Nervous System

The nervous system is certainly not a discrete-state machine. A small error in the information about the size of a nervous impulse impinging on a neuron, may make a large difference to the size of the outgoing impulse. It may be argued that, this being so, one cannot expect to be able to mimic the behavior of the nervous system with a discrete-state system.

It is true that a discrete-state machine must be different from a continuous machine. But if we adhere to the conditions of the imitation game, the interrogator will not be able to take any advantage of this difference. The situation can be made clearer if we consider some other simpler continuous machine. A differential analyzer will do very well. (A differential analyzer is a certain kind of machine not of the discrete-state type used for some kinds of calculation.) Some of these provide their answers in a typed form, and so are suitable for taking part in the game. It would not be possible for a digital computer to predict exactly what answers the differential analyzer would give to a problem, but it would be quite capable of giving the right sort of answer. For instance, if asked to give the value of π (actually about 3.1416) it would be reasonable to choose at random between the values 3.12, 3.13, 3.14, 3.15, 3.16 with the probabilities of 0.05, 0.15, 0.55, 0.19, 0.06 (say). Under these circumstances it would be very difficult for the interrogator to distinguish the differential analyzer from the digital computer.

(8) The Argument from Informality of Behavior

It is not possible to produce a set of rules purporting to describe what a man should do in every conceivable set of circumstances. One might for instance have a rule that one is to stop when one sees a red traffic light, and to go if one sees a green one, but what if by some fault both appear together? One may perhaps decide that it is safest to stop. But some further difficulty may well arise from this decision later. To attempt to provide rules of conduct to cover every eventuality, even those arising from traffic lights, appears to be impossible. With all this I agree.

From this it is argued that we cannot be machines. I shall try to reproduce the argument, but I fear I shall hardly do it justice. It seems to run something like this. 'If each man had a definite set of rules of conduct by which he regulated his life he would be not better than a machine. But there are no such rules, so men cannot be machines.' The undistributed middle is glaring. I do not think the argument is ever put quite like this, but I believe this is the argument used nevertheless. There may however be a certain confusion between 'rules of

conduct' and 'laws of behavior' to cloud the issue. By 'rules of conduct' I mean precepts such as 'Stop if you see red lights', on which one can act, and of which one can be conscious. By 'laws of behavior' I mean laws of nature as applied to a man's body such as 'if you pinch him he will squeak'. If we substitute 'laws of behavior which regulate his life' for 'laws of conduct by which he regulates his life' in the argument quoted the undistributed middle is no longer insuperable. For we believe that it is not only true that being regulated by laws of behavior implies being some sort of machine (though not necessarily a discrete-state machine), but that conversely being such a machine implies being regulated by such laws. However, we cannot so easily convince ourselves of the absence of complete laws of behavior as of complete rules of conduct. The only way we know of for finding such laws is scientific observation, and we certainly know of no circumstances under which we could say, 'We have searched enough. There are no such laws.'

We can demonstrate more forcibly that any such statement would be unjustified. For suppose we could be sure of finding such laws if they existed. Then given a discrete-state machine it should certainly be possible to discover by observation sufficient about it to predict its future behavior, and this within a reasonable time, say a thousand years. But this does not seem to be the case. I have set up on the Manchester computer a small program using only 1000 units of storage, whereby the machine supplied with one sixteen figure number replies with another within two seconds. I would defy anyone to learn from these replies sufficient about the program to be able to predict any replies to untried values.

Discussion Questions

1. Suppose there are a finite number of moves in a game of chess. If you discovered that the chess program that just beat you simply had a massive list containing the correct move for every possible position, would the machine/program be intelligent? What do you believe Turing would say about this machine's 'intelligence'?

2. If a computer/android such as Lt. Commander Data of the television series *Star Trek: The Next Generation* could be constructed, would it be intelligent? Would it be conscious? What differences are there between Data and humans? Do these differences mean that Data is not a person? Would it be immoral to kill Data?

3. Suppose that machines with artificial intelligence and consciousness were created by human beings. Would this have any effect on our beliefs about the existence (or nonexistence) of souls? Explain your response.

4. Currently it seems as if computers can only *think* about what they have been programmed to think about. Do you believe that machines will ever be capable of creativity? Is creativity something that can be programmed into a machine? What does your answer say about human creativity?

For Further Reading

For biographical information about Turing see *Alan Turing: The Enigma* (1983), by A. Hodges. For Turing's collected works see *Collected Works of A. M. Turing* (1992), edited by D. C. Ince. For selections concerning Turing's test see *The Philosophy of Artificial Intelligence* (1990), edited by M. Boden, and *Readings in Philosophy of Psychology* (1980), vol. 1, edited by N. Block. See John Searle, *Minds, Brains, and Programs* (1980), for a view sharply critical of Turing's approach to measuring machine intelligence.

10   MACHINE CONSCIOUSNESS
William G. Lycan

William G. Lycan (1945–) teaches philosophy at the University of North Carolina at Chapel Hill, where he devotes his philosophical research to the nature of mind, knowledge, and language.

Lycan is a proponent of **functionalism.** Functionalism is a theory of mind that equates S being in mental state X to S's having particular sorts of reactions to particular sorts of inputs. For example, some person S is in the mental state called 'being in pain' if S reacts to pain inputs (cuts and bruises) with the appropriate pain reaction (moving away from their causes, crying out, and so forth). After all, no one actually observes the conscious mental state of another person, but only infers a person's conscious state from his or her behavior.

Functionalism raises interesting questions for AI researchers. If a computer/android responded to injury in the appropriate way, would the android have the mental state 'being in pain'? If so, would the android be conscious? Lycan explores this question in the following selection. His answer is "yes, it would be conscious": all of the reasons one has for believing that other people are conscious turn out to be reasons that one could have for believing that a machine is conscious.

Reading Questions

1. How does Lycan define intelligence? Are computers capable of intelligence based on this definition?
2. What objections are raised against the claim that Harry has a mental life? How does the example of Henrietta answer these objections?

SOURCE: From *Consciousness* by William G. Lycan. © 1978 by The MIT Press. Used by permission of The MIT Press.

3. What moral conundrum does the possibility of machine consciousness raise? How is this problem related to the issue of animal rights?

4. What does it mean to be free according to Lycan? Are machines capable of free choice?

Artificial Intelligence is, very crudely, the science of getting machines to perform jobs that normally require intelligence and judgment. Researchers at any number of AI labs have designed machines that prove mathematical theorems, play chess, sort mail, guide missiles, assemble auto engines, diagnose illnesses, read stories and other written texts, and converse with people in a rudimentary way. This is, we might say, intelligent behavior.

But what is this 'intelligence'? As a first pass, I suggest that intelligence of the sort I am talking about is a kind of flexibility, a responsiveness to contingencies. A dull or stupid machine must have just the right kind of raw materials presented to it in just the right way, or it is useless: the electric can opener must have an appropriately sized can fixed under its drive wheel *just so,* in order to operate at all. Humans (most of us, anyway) are not like that. We deal with the unforeseen. We take what comes and make the best of it, even though we may have had no idea what it would be. We play the ball from whatever lie we are given, and at whatever angle to the green; we read and understand texts we have never seen before; we find our way back to Chapel Hill after getting totally lost in downtown Durham (or downtown Washington, D.C., or downtown Lima, Peru).

Our pursuit of our goals is guided while in progress by our ongoing perception and handling of interim developments. Moreover, we can pursue any number of different goals at the same time, and balance them against each other. We are sensitive to contingencies, both external and internal, that have a very complex and unsystematic structure.

It is almost irresistible to speak of *information* here, even if the term were not as trendy as it is. An intelligent creature, I want to say, is an *information-sensitive* creature, one that not only *registers* information through receptors such as sense-organs but somehow stores and manages and finally uses that information. Higher animals are intelligent beings in this sense, and so are we, even though virtually nothing is known about how we organize or manage the vast, seething profusion of information that comes our way. And there is one sort of machine that is information-sensitive also: the digital computer. A computer *is* a machine specifically designed to be fed complexes of information, to store them, manage them, and produce appropriate theoretical or practical conclusions on demand. Thus, if artificial intelligence is what one is looking for, it is no accident that one looks to the computer.

Yet a computer has two limitations in common with machines of less elite and grandiose sorts, both of them already signaled in the characterization I have just given. First, a (present-day) computer must be *fed* information, and the choice of what information to feed and in what form is up to a human programmer or operator. (For that matter, a present-day computer must be plugged into an electrical outlet and have its switch turned to ON, but this is a very minor contingency given the availability of nuclear power packs.) Second, the *appropriateness* and effectiveness of a computer's output depends entirely on what the programmer or operator had in mind and goes on to make of it. A computer has intelligence in the sense I have defined, but has no judgment, since it has no goals and purposes of its own and no internal sense of appropriateness, relevance, or proportion.

For essentially these reasons—that computers are intelligent in my minimal sense, and that they are nevertheless limited in the two ways I have mentioned—AI theorists, philosophers, and intelligent laymen have inevitably compared computers to human minds, but at the same time debated both technical and philosophical questions raised by this comparison. The questions break down into three main groups or types: (A) Questions of the form "Will a computer ever be able to do X?" where X is something that intelligent humans can do. (B) Questions of the form "Given that a computer can or could do X, have we any reason to think that it does X in the same way that humans do X?" (C) Questions of the form "Given that some futuristic supercomputer were able to do X, Y, Z, . . ., for some arbitrarily large range and variety of human activities, would that show that the computer had property P?" where P is some feature held to be centrally, vitally characteristic of human minds, such as thought, consciousness, feeling, sensation, emotion, creativity, or freedom of the will.

Questions of type A are empirical questions and cannot be settled without decades, perhaps centuries, of further research—compare ancient and medieval speculations on the question of whether a machine could ever fly. Questions of type B are brutely empirical too, and their answers are unavailable to AI researchers *per se*, lying squarely in the domain of cognitive psychology, a science or alleged science barely into its infancy. Questions of type C are philosophical and conceptual, and so I shall essay to answer them all at one stroke.

Let us begin by supposing that all questions of types A and B have been settled affirmatively—that one day we might be confronted by a much-improved version of Hal, the soft-spoken computer in Kubrick's *2001* (younger readers may substitute *Star Wars'* C3PO or whatever subsequent cinematic robot is the most lovable). Let us call this more versatile machine "Harry." Harry (let us say) is humanoid in form—he is a miracle of miniaturization and has lifelike plastic skin—and he can converse intelligently on all sorts of subjects, play golf *and* the viola, write passable poetry, control his occasional nervousness pretty well, make love, prove mathematical theorems (of course), show envy when outdone, throw gin bottles at annoying children, etc., etc. We may suppose he fools people into thinking he is human. Now the question is, is Harry really a *person*? Does he have thoughts, feelings, and so on? Is he actually conscious, or is he just a mindless walking hardware store whose movements are astoundingly *like* those of a person?

Plainly his acquaintances would tend from the first to see him as a person, even if they were aware of his dubious antecedents. I think it is a plain psychological fact, if nothing more, that we could not help treating him as a person, unless we resolutely made up our minds, on principle, not to give him the time of day. But how could we really tell that he is conscious?

Well, how do we really tell that any humanoid creature is conscious? How do you tell that I am conscious, and how do I tell that you are? Surely we tell, and decisively, on the basis of our standard behavioral tests for mental states . . . : We know that a human being has such-and-such mental states when it behaves, to speak very generally, in the ways we take to be appropriate to organisms that are in those states. (The point is of course an epistemological one only, no metaphysical implications intended or tolerated.) We know for practical purposes that a creature has a mind when it fulfills all the right criteria. And by hypothesis, Harry fulfills all our behavioral criteria with a vengeance; moreover, he does so *in the right way* (cf. questions of type B): the processing that stands causally behind his behavior is just like ours. It follows that we are at least *prima facie* justified in believing him to be conscious.

We have not *proved* that he is conscious, of course—any more than you have proved that I am conscious. An organism's merely behaving in a certain way is no logical guarantee of sentience; from my point of view it is at least imaginable, a bare logical possibility, that my wife, my daughter, and my chairman are not conscious, even though I have excellent, overwhelming behavioral reason to think that they are. But for that matter, our "standard behavioral tests" for mental states yield practical or moral certainty only so long as the situation is not palpably extraordinary or bizarre. A human chauvinist—in this case, someone who denies that Harry has thoughts and feelings, joys and sorrows—thinks precisely that Harry is as bizarre as they come. But *what is bizarre about him?* There are quite a few chauvinist answers to this, but what they boil down to, and given our hypothesized facts all they could boil down to, are two differences between Harry and ourselves: his *origin* (a laboratory is not a proper mother), and the *chemical composition of his anatomy,* if his creator has used silicon instead of carbon, for example. To exclude him from our community for either or both of *those* reasons seems to me to be a clear case of racial or ethnic prejudice (literally) and nothing more. I see no obvious way in which either a creature's origin or its subneuroanatomical chemical composition should matter to its psychological processes or any respect of its mentality.

My argument can be reinforced by a thought-experiment . . . : Imagine that we take a normal human being, Henrietta, and begin gradually replacing parts of her with synthetic materials—first a few prosthetic limbs, then a few synthetic arteries, then some neural fibers, and so forth. Suppose that the surgeons who perform the successive operations (particularly the neurosurgeons) are so clever and skillful that Henrietta survives in fine style: her intelligence, personality, perceptual acuity, poetic abilities, etc., remain just as they were before. But after the replacement process has eventually gone on to completion, Henrietta will have become an artifact—at least, her body will then be nothing but a collection of artifacts. Did she lose consciousness at some point during the sequence of operations, despite her continuing to behave and respond normally? When? It is hard to imagine that there is some privileged portion of the human nervous system that is for some reason indispensable, even though kidneys, lungs, heart, and any given bit of brain could in principle be replaced by a prosthesis (for *what* reason?); and it is also hard to imagine that there is some *proportion* of the nervous system such that removal of more than that proportion causes loss of consciousness or sentience despite perfect maintenance of all intelligent capacities.

If this quick but totally compelling defense of Harry and Henrietta's personhood is correct, then the two, and their ilk, will have not only mental lives like ours, but *moral* lives like ours, and moral rights and privileges accordingly. Just as origin and physical constitution fail to affect psychological personhood, if a creature's internal organization is sufficiently like ours, so do they fail to affect moral personhood. We do not discriminate against a person who has a wooden leg, or a mechanical kidney, or a nuclear heart regulator; no more should we deny any human or civil right to Harry or Henrietta on grounds of their origin or physical makeup, which they cannot help.

But this happy egalitarianism raises a more immediate question: *In real life,* we shall soon be faced with medium-grade machines, which have some intelligence and are not "mere" machines like refrigerators or typewriters but which fall far short of flawless human simulators like Harry. For AI researchers may well build machines that will appear to have some familiar mental capacities but not others. The most obvious example is that of a sensor or perceptron, which picks up information from its immediate environment, records it, and stores it in memory for future printout. (We already have at least crude machines of this kind. When they become versatile and sophisticated enough, it will be quite natural to say that they see or hear and that they remember.) But the possibility of "specialist" machines of this kind raises an unforeseen contin-

gency: There is an enormous and many-dimensional range of possible beings in between our current "mere" machines and our fully developed, flawless human simulators; we have not even begun to think of all the infinitely possible variations on this theme. And once we do begin to think of these hard cases, we will be at a loss as to where to draw the 'personhood' line between them. How complex, eclectic, and impressive must a machine be, and in what respects, before we award it the accolade of personhood and/or of consciousness? There is, to say the least, no clear answer to be had *a priori,* Descartes' notorious view of animals to the contrary notwithstanding.

This typical philosophical question would be no more than an amusing bonbon, were it not for the attending moral conundrum: What moral rights would an intermediate or marginally intelligent machine have? Adolescent machines of this sort will confront us much sooner than will any good human simulators, for they are easier to design and construct; more to the moral point, they will be designed mainly as *labor-saving devices,* as servants who will work for free, and servants of this kind are (literally) made to be exploited. If they are intelligent to any degree, we should have qualms in proportion.

I suggest that this moral problem, which may become a real and pressing one, is parallel to the current debate over animal rights. Luckily I have never wanted to cook and eat my Compaq Portable.

Suppose I am right about the irrelevance of biochemical constitution to psychology; and suppose I was also right about the coalescing of the notions *computation, information, intelligence.* Then our mentalized theory of computation suggests in turn a computational theory of mentality, and a computational picture of the place of human beings in the world. In fact, philosophy aside, that picture has already begun to get a grip on people's thinking—as witness the filtering down of computer jargon into contemporary casual speech—and that grip is not going to loosen. Computer science is the defining technology of our time, and in this sense the computer is the natural cultural successor to the steam engine, the clock, the spindle, and the potter's wheel. Predictably, an articulate computational theory of the mind has also gained credence among professional psychologists and philosophers. I have been trying to support it here and elsewhere; I shall say no more about it for now, save to note again its near-indispensability in accounting for intentionality (noted), and to address the ubiquitous question of computer creativity and freedom.

Soft-determinism or libertarianism may be true of humans. But many people have far more rigidly deterministic intuitions about computers. Computers, after all, (let us all say it together:) "only do what they are told/programmed to do"; they have no spontaneity and no freedom of choice. But human beings choose all the time, and the ensuing states of the world often depend entirely on these choices. Thus the "computer analogy" supposedly fails.

The alleged failure of course depends on what we think freedom really is. As a soft-determinist, I think that to have freedom of choice in acting is (roughly) for one's action to proceed out of one's own desires, deliberation, will, and intention, rather than being compelled or coerced by external forces regardless of my desires or will. As before, free actions are not *uncaused* actions. My free actions are those that *I* cause, i.e., that are caused by my own mental processes rather than by something pressing on me from the outside. I have argued . . . that I am free in that my beliefs, desires, deliberations, and intentions are all functional or computational states and processes within me that do interact in characteristic ways to produce my behavior. Note now that the same response vindicates our skilled human-simulating machines from the charge of puppethood. The word "robot" is often used as a veritable synonym for "puppet," so it may seem that Harry and Henrietta are paradigm cases of *un*free mechanisms that "only do what they are programmed to do." This is a slander—for two reasons:

First, even an ordinary computer, let alone a fabulously sophisticated machine like Harry, is in a way unpredictable. You are at its mercy. You *think* you know what it is going to do; you know what it should do, what it is supposed to do, but there is no guarantee—and it may do something *awful* or at any rate something that you could not have predicted and could not figure out if you tried with both hands. This practical sort of unpredictability would be multiplied a thousandfold in the case of a machine

as complex as the human brain, and it is notably characteristic of *people*.

The unpredictability has several sources. (i) Plain old physical defects, as when Harry's circuits have been damaged by trauma, stress, heat, or the like. (ii) Bugs in one or more of his programs. (I have heard that once upon a time, somewhere, a program was written that had not a single bug in it, but this is probably an urban folk tale.) (iii) Randomizers, quantum-driven or otherwise; elements of Harry's behavior may be *genuinely*, physically random. (iv) Learning and analogy mechanisms; if Harry is equipped with these, as he inevitably would be, then his behavior-patterns will be modified in response to his experimental input from the world, which would be neither controlled nor even observed by us. *We don't know where he's been.* (v) The relativity of reliability to goal-description. This last needs a bit of explanation.

People often say things like, "A computer just crunches binary numbers; provided it isn't broken, it just chugs on mindlessly through whatever flipflop settings are predetermined by its electronic makeup." But such remarks ignore the multileveled character of real computer programming. At any given time, . . . a computer is running *each of any number of* programs, depending on how it is described and on the level of functional organization that interests us. True, it is always crunching binary numbers, but in crunching them it is also doing any number of more esoteric things. And (more to the point) what counts as a mindless, algorithmic procedure at a very low level of organization may constitute, at a higher level, a hazardous do-or-die heuristic that might either succeed brilliantly or (more likely) fail and leave its objective unfulfilled.

As a second defense, remember that Harry too has beliefs, desires, and intentions (provided my original argument is sound). If this is so, then his behavior normally proceeds out of his own mental processes rather than being externally compelled; and so he satisfies the definition of freedom-of-action formulated above. In most cases it will be appropriate to say that Harry could have done other than what he did do (but in fact chose after some ratiocination to do what he did, instead). Harry acts in the same sense as that in which we act, though one might continue to quarrel over what sense that is.

Probably the most popular remaining reason for doubt about machine consciousness has to do with the raw qualitative character of experience. Could a mere bloodless runner-of-programs have states that *feel to it* in any of the various dramatic ways in which our mental states feel to us?

The latter question is usually asked rhetorically, expecting a resounding answer "NO!!" But I do not hear it rhetorically, for I do not see why the negative answer is supposed to be at all obvious, even for machines as opposed to biologic humans. Of course there is an incongruity *from our human point of view* between human feeling and printed circuitry or silicon pathways; that is to be expected, since we are considering those high-tech items from an external, third-person perspective and at the same time comparing them to our own first-person feels. But argumentatively, that *Gestalt* phenomenon counts for no more in the present case than it did in that of human consciousness, viz., for nothing, especially if my original argument about Harry was successful in showing that biochemical constitution is irrelevant to psychology. What matters to mentality is not the stuff of which one is made, but the complex way in which that stuff is organized. If after years of close friendship we were to open Harry up and find that he is stuffed with microelectronic gadgets instead of protoplasm, we would be taken aback—no question. But our *Gestalt* clash on the occasion would do nothing *at all* to show that Harry does not have his own right inner qualitative life. If an objector wants to insist that computation alone cannot provide consciousness with its qualitative character, the objector will have to take the initiative and come up with a further, substantive argument to show why not. We have already seen that such arguments have failed wretchedly for the case of humans; I see no reason to suspect that they would work any better for the case of robots. We must await further developments. But at the present stage of inquiry I see no compelling feel-based objection to the hypothesis of machine consciousness.

Discussion Questions

1. Suppose that an android outwardly responds to injuries in a manner consistent with being in pain. Is it reasonable to believe that the android *feels* the (physical) pain of its injuries? Can a machine ever *feel* the (mental) pain of losing a loved one? For that matter, could a machine ever *feel* love for another being? How would a functionalist like Lycan respond?

2. Lycan suggests that intelligent machines might possess rights. Can you imagine treating a machine as if it were a moral agent? Would the rights of a machine ever outweigh the rights of humans? Explain your answers. Does it matter that these machines were built by us, that we are their "creators"?

3. Lycan suggests that it is possible for the actions of intelligent machines to be free. Suppose that an intelligent machine is acting on "its" desires. Does this mean the machine can be held (morally) accountable for its actions? Did the machine have any choice concerning its programmed desires? Are machines any different from humans in this way?

For Further Reading

Lycan's major work in philosophy of mind is *Consciousness* (1987). The following anthologies have articles that concern functionalism and philosophy of mind: *Readings in the Philosophy of Psychology*, vol. 1, edited by N. Block; *The Nature of Mind* (1991), edited by D. M. Rosenthal; and *Mind and Cognition: A Reader* (1989), edited by Lycan.

For a collection of papers concerned with various objections to functionalism see *Identity, Cause and Mind* (1984) by S. Shoemaker. Also see *Philosophical Perspectives 4: Action Theory and Philosophy of Mind* (1990), edited by James Tomberlin.

11   WHAT THE HUMAN MIND CAN DO THAT THE COMPUTER CAN'T
Morton M. Hunt

With dozens of books and hundreds of articles to his credit, Morton M. Hunt (1920 –) is a prolific author who writes with clarity about psychology and science in popular magazines such as *Harper's, The New Yorker,* and *The Saturday Evening Post.*

In the following article Hunt raises major theoretical objections for AI researchers who hope to duplicate the feats of the human mind. Viewed from the outside (as Turing and Lycan suggest), a sophisticated android appears conscious of its surroundings. But is it? Is it conscious in the same way that you and I are? Hunt argues that one key difference between human and machine consciousness is that humans are *conscious of being conscious.* Humans not only experience the world around them but are aware of—they *experience*—the fact that they experience the world. In other words, humans are self-conscious beings.

Are machines self-conscious? As of yet, the answer seems to be no, and one wonders whether such machines could ever be developed. But suppose that an android were developed that appeared to be self-conscious. Hunt doubts whether such machines could ever learn things from scratch as children do; moreover, human thought is fluid, flowing from one interest to the next. Computers, by contrast, focus only on whatever they have been expressly programmed to focus on and are incapable of taking an interest in what they are doing. Could a machine ever have a passion for reading the works of Jane Austen or *The Bhagavad-Gita?* Not according to Hunt.

Reading Questions

1. Why does Hunt claim that a computer can never be conscious? What part of the human mental life cannot be replicated in computers?
2. Explain why Hunt believes that HACKER, a program that examines and modifies its own problem-solving strategies, is not conscious.
3. Why does Hunt believe that self-awareness is so important? What role does it play for us?
4. Is a machine capable of having a desire? Can a machine be motivated?
5. Even though the program POLITICS can simulate human reasoning to some extent, what deficiencies does Hunt attribute to POLITICS?

Like creative acts, there are a number of important mental phenomena that have not yet been simulated by any computer program and, many cognitive scientists believe, probably never will be. Surprisingly, most of these are everyday aspects of our mental lives that we take for granted and that seem as natural and uncomplicated to us as eating and sleeping.

The first is that obvious, seemingly simple, but largely ineluctable phenomenon, consciousness. To philosophers through the centuries, and to psychologists of recent decades, this concept has proven as elusive as a drop of mercury under one's finger, but the only question we need ask ourselves here is: Can a machine be conscious? Let's say the current is on, the machine has a program stored in it, you address it from a terminal and, in response, it goes through various steps of solving a problem in very much the way a human being would. Now ask yourself: Was it conscious of its cognitive processes as you were of yours? The question answers itself: There is no reason to suppose so. Nothing built into any existing program that I have heard of is meant to, or does, as far as one can tell, yield a state corresponding to consciousness.

Much of our own thinking, to be sure, takes place outside of consciousness, but the results of these processes become conscious, and each of us *experiences* those conscious thoughts: we know them to be taking place in our own minds. We not only think, but perceive ourselves thinking. Artificial intelligence has no analog to this. As Donald Norman put it—and he was only one of many cognitive scientists who made similar remarks to me—"We don't have any programs today that are self-aware or that even begin to approach consciousness such as human beings have. I see this as a critical difference between human intelligence and artificial intelligence. The human mind is aware of itself as an identity, it can introspect, it can examine its own ideas and react to them—not just with thoughts about them but with emotions. We can't begin to simulate consciousness on a computer, and perhaps never will."

Not everyone would agree that consciousness may forever remain impossible to simulate, but what is clear is that it cannot be simulated at present—and for one very good reason: it remains the least understood and most puzzling of psychological phenomena. I am aware of my own thoughts, to be sure, but what is this 'I'? How do I distinguish the 'I' from the identity of other people or the rest of the world? Surely it is not a matter of the borders of my physical being, for in the dark, or blindfolded and bound, or even cut off by spinal anesthesia from all feeling, I would know myself: the borders are those of thought, not body. Actually, the question "What is this 'I'?" rarely concerns us, for we experience our own identity as a self-evident reality. But that ineluctable sense of I-ness does not exist in any computer; there is no evidence that any computer program has ever realized that it is itself, running in a particular machine, and not a similar program, running on another machine somewhere else.

Cognitive science does offer at least a rudimentary explanation of consciousness: it is thought to be the product of our internalizing the real world in our minds in symbolic form. We perceive not only the real world but also our own mental representation of it; the experience of the difference between the two results in self-awareness. We recognize that there is not only a real world but a simulacrum of it within us; therefore there must be an *us: cogito ergo sum,* yet again. The thought that we have thoughts is the crucial one that becomes consciousness; it is what Douglas Hofstadter, in *Gödel, Escher, Bach,* calls a "strange loop" of the mind, an interaction between different levels, a self-reinforcing resonance. "The self," he says, "comes into being at the moment it has the power to reflect itself." We contemplate our thoughts, but the awareness of doing so is itself a thought, and the foundation of consciousness.

Perhaps the key factor is that consciousness develops in us as a result of our cognitive history. . . . [T]he infant gradually becomes capable of thinking about external objects by means of mental images and symbols stored in memory. The newborn does not seem to be aware of the boundaries between itself and the rest of the world, but it perceives them more and more distinctly as its internal image of the world builds up. Consciousness emerges as a product of the child's mental development. The computer, in contrast, though it may acquire an ever-larger store of information, has no such sense or experience of its own history. Nor does it recognize that what is in its memory is a representation of something outside. To the computer, what is in its system is what *is;* it does not contemplate its thoughts as thoughts, but as the only reality. How could it, then, be aware of itself as an individual?

Some AI enthusiasts do, however, argue that if a program examines its own problem-solving behavior and modifies it to improve it, as HACKER does, this is the equivalent of consciousness; so says Pamela McCorduck in *Machines Who Think*. John McCarthy of Stanford University, one of America's leading computer scientists, goes even further: he says it is possible to ascribe beliefs, free will, consciousness, and wants to a machine. In his view, even as simple a machine as a thermostat can be said to have beliefs (presumably the thermostat "believes" that the optimum temperature is the one it is set for). But such talk is either metaphorical or, more likely, anthropomorphic; it reads into the machine what the human observer feels, much as primitive people attribute rage to the volcano and prudence to the ant. There is no reason to suppose HACKER or a thermostat experience anything like awareness of the self; they merely respond to certain incoming stimuli with mechanical reactions. HACKER, to be sure, does register corrections in its program for future use, but so does a vine, growing around an obstruction. It seems most unlikely that anywhere within HACKER some small voice says, "I made an error, but I'm correcting it and I'll do better next time."

What difference does it make? If a machine can respond to its own errors and correct them, what does it matter that it isn't aware of doing so?

It matters a lot. Awareness of self is the essence of what being alive means to us. If, through some accident, you remained able to talk and reason but could not realize that you were doing so, would you not be as dead, from your own viewpoint, as if your brain had been destroyed?

More than that, with awareness of self we become conscious of the alternatives in our thoughts; we become conscious of our choices, and of our ability to will the things we choose to do. Choice and will are difficult to account for within a scientific psychology, since it views existence as a continuum in which no phenomenon occurs uncaused. If no event is, itself, a first cause, but is the product of antecedent forces, then the experience of choice and of will must be illusory; the acts of choosing and of willing, though they seem to be within our power, must be products of all that has happened to us in the past and is happening at the moment.

And yet when we are conscious of our alternatives, that self-awareness is another level of causality—a set of influences in addition to those of the past and present. We are not automata, weighing all the pros and cons of any matter and inevitably acting in accord with our calculations. In mathematical decision theory, the totally rational human being does just that and always selects the most advantageous option; so does a well-designed computer program. But in reality we are aware of our own decision making, and that awareness in itself brings other forces to bear upon the decision—emotional responses to the situation, loyalties, moral values, a sense of our own identity—and these resonances, these loops of thought, affect the outcome.

A simple example: you are annoyed by something a friend has said or done, you fume about it, you imagine a conversation in which the two of you argue about it, you prepare your crushing remarks—and suddenly perceive all this as from a distance; in perspective, you see yourself as an outsider might see you, question your own thoughts and feeling, alter them, and, as a result, accept the friend's behavior and dismiss your anger, or, perhaps, call the friend and talk the matter over amicably.

Another example: like every writer I know, when I am writing a first draft I rattle away at the typewriter, setting down words; but once I see them I think, That isn't quite right—that's not only exactly what I mean, and tinker and revise and rewrite until the words are right. But it wasn't that the first words didn't say what I meant; rather, in seeing my thoughts, I had thoughts about them; the strange loop yielded something like freedom—the freedom to make a different choice among my thoughts. If the experiences of choice and will are not what they seem to be, they nonetheless reflect real processes that produce results different from those that would come about without them.

In any case, there is no doubt that we do not experience our thought processes as automatic but as within our control. . . .

But what does "want" mean? Can a machine want? In a sense; if its program calls for it to assign different weights to various subgoals and goals it will proceed to choose that option which its program reckons to have the greatest numerical value. All very neat and simple. Human beings are far less neat and far more complicated. We often desire things but lack the motivation to pursue them; conversely, we are sometimes so strongly motivated by beliefs, values, and emotions that we pursue a particular goal with a devotion far beyond what any realistic evaluation would warrant.

Of all the components in human motivation, the one least likely ever to be simulated by a computer is our capacity to find things interesting. It is a mystifying phenomenon. Why do we find any matter interesting? What makes us want to know about, or understand, something—especially something that has no practical value for us, such as the age of the universe or when human beings first appeared on earth? Why do we want to know if there is life elsewhere in the cosmos, if its replies to our messages could not arrive back here for centuries? Why did Pythagoras feel so powerfully impelled to prove his celebrated theorem?

This tendency in us, some cognitive scientists believe, is an intrinsic characteristic of our nervous system. We are driven to think certain thoughts, and to pursue certain goals, by an inherent neurological restlessness, a need to do something with the thoughts in our minds and with the world they represent. The computer, in contrast, is a passive system: its goals and the strength of its drive to reach them are those given it by its designer. Left to itself, it will sit inert, awaiting further orders. We will not; we look for new goals, and, to reach them, are forced to solve problems we did not have before; we do not let well enough alone.

Why don't we? Call it restlessness, call it curiosity, or perhaps, like the historian Huizinga, call it playfulness. Other animals play, but with us playfulness becomes cognitive: we play with our ideas, and afterward with the real-world counterparts of those ideas. How would you simulate that on a machine? Allen Newell and a few other AI researchers say there is no reason why a program could not be designed to be curious and to create new goals for itself, but they are a small minority; most cognitive scientists think otherwise. Yet even if a machine could be programmed to cast about in some way for new goals and new problems, it would do so because it had been programmed to; it wouldn't do so because it wanted to. It wouldn't give a damn.

And that would be bound to affect the kinds of new problems it chose to tackle and the strength of its

motivation to solve them. Maybe the biggest difference between artificial and human intelligence is just that simple: we care about the things we choose to do. Solving a new problem, discovering some new fact, visiting a new place, reading a new book, all make us feel good; that's why we do them. But how would one make a computer feel good? Some AI people have built rewards into their programs: if the machine makes right decisions, its program is automatically altered to strengthen that kind of response, and so it learns. Theoretically, a program could be rewarded if it did something new and different, so that its tendency would be not to maintain itself, unchanged, but to keep changing. But would it *want* to do so or *like* doing so? And lacking that, would there be any meaning to its changes? Perhaps computer-written music and poetry have been unimpressive because the computer itself was neither pleased nor displeased by its own product, as every creative artist is. Without that test, it wasn't able to tell whether it had created a work of genius or a piece of trash. And it didn't care.

We, on the other hand, care—and care most of all about those thoughts which express moral values. Each of us is not just an information processor but the product of a particular culture and its belief system. We perceive the world through the special focus of the values we have learned from parents, schools, books, and peers. Those values become a part of our decision-making processes; in making many of our choices, we weight the alternatives in accordance with our moral, religious, and political beliefs.

This aspect of human thinking can be, and has been, simulated on the machine, . . . in the form of the simulations of political decision making created by Jaime Carbonell and his colleagues. . . . POLITICS has simulated the reasoning of either a conservative or a liberal considering what the United States should do if, for instance, Russia were to build nuclear submarines. Both as conservative and as liberal, POLITICS flawlessly came to conclusions consonant with the assumptions it was programmed to draw upon. Carbonell's purpose was to test his theoretical model of the way in which ideology affects the decision-making process; he did not suggest that POLITICS could be developed into a machine that could do our political thinking for us. But his work does have two important implications for this discussion of what the human mind can do that the computer can't do.

First, even though POLITICS can simulate archetypal conservative or liberal political reasoning, it does so in a wholly predictable way; it produces decisions Carbonell could foresee because they are based entirely on the terms and conditions he had put into it. But that is not the way human beings think. Within any party or ideological group, there is a wide range of variations in how individuals interpret the tenets of that ideology. There are always mavericks, dissenters, and innovators, without whom every party, every church, and every culture would atrophy and die.

Second, within any given ideological group, some people have the emotional maturity, the richness of human experience, and the soundness of judgment to use its tenets wisely; others do not, and use them foolishly. This is not to say that wise persons will reach the same conclusions everywhere; I would not want the wisest judge in Russia, India, or Iran to hear a civil liberties case in which I was accused of slandering the state. But if it is true that within any culture, its ethical system has internal validity, some of its people will interpret those beliefs wisely, others foolishly, and the majority somewhere in between. Moral wisdom is not so much the product of a special method of reasoning as of an ability to harmonize moral beliefs with fundamental individual and societal needs. I do not see how artificial intelligence can simulate that.

Will artificial intelligence, then, ever outstrip human intelligence? Yes, astronomically—in certain ways; and clearly it is already doing so. But in other ways it does not now match our powers, much less exceed them, and seems unlikely to do so soon. And in still other ways it seems incapable of simulating human intellectual functioning at all.

For until it acquires perceptual systems as sophisticated as our own, it will not be able to learn directly from the environment. But the development of such systems is bound to prove more difficult, by many orders of magnitude, than the creation of a living cell—a feat not now imaginable—and lacking such perceptual systems, the machine will remain dependent on the human being for its information.

But that is the least of it. Until artificial intelligence can duplicate human mental development from birth onward; until it can absorb the intricacies and subtleties of cultural values; until it can acquire consciousness of self; until it becomes capable of playfulness and curiosity; until it can create new goals for itself, unplanned and uninstigated by any human programmer; until it is motivated not by goals alone but by some restless compulsion to be doing and exploring; until it can care about, and be pleased or annoyed by, its own thoughts; until it can make wise moral judgments—until all these conditions exist, the computer, it seems to me, will not match or even palely imitate the most valuable aspects of human thinking.

There is no doubt that the computer has already transformed our lives, and will continue to do so. But its chief influence will continue to be its utility as a tool. Supercalculators have radically changed, and will continue to change, all human institutions that require reckoning. Artificial intelligence will reconstruct many areas of problem solving—everything from the practice of medicine to literary and historical research and the investigation of the cosmos—and in so doing will change our ways of thinking as profoundly as did the invention of writing. Tools have powerful effects on the thinking of those who use them (the plow radically altered humankind's view of itself and of the world around it), but tools of the mind have the most powerful effects of all. Still, they are our tools, we their users.

But is it not possible that the computer will take over, outthink us, make our decisions for us, become our ruler? Not unless we assign it the power to make our decisions. Joseph Weizenbaum, in *Computer Power and Human Reason,* passionately argues that the computer represents a major danger to humanity not because it can forcibly take over but because we are heedlessly allowing it to make decisions for us in areas where we alone ought to make them. He sees the problem as a moral one rather than a struggle between human and machine: we ought not let the computer function as a psychotherapist, ought not rely on it to tell us whether to bomb civilian enemy targets or only military ones, ought not have it function as a judge in court.

Of course we ought not, but is there any real danger that we will? I hope not; I think not. The computer does not set its own goals: we do, and we human beings are jealous of our own powers. We have often delegated them to some leader—a human being, like ourselves, but one we took to be a greater person than we. Or we have asked some god (who often looks like us, enlarged) to make our decisions for us. But would we ever delegate our intellectual responsibilities to a machine that we ourselves created? I doubt it. Though human beings have often enough been fools, I find it hard to believe that we would ever be foolish enough to think our machines wiser than we; at least, not as long as we are aware of, and proud of, the human difference.

Discussion Questions

1. Hunt believes that programs are not self-conscious, even if they monitor and adjust themselves. Is he right? Would it be possible to program self-consciousness into a computer?
2. According to Hunt, humans are not automata, mechanically calculating our next move. For example, emotions, loyalties, and moral values affect our decisions. But given the emotions, loyalties, and moral values an individual has at any given time, is that person's next move not inevitable? If not, why not? If so, then how can an individual be said to control his or her actions?
3. Part of the claim that machines are not self-conscious appears to depend on the fact that we fully understand how computers work. Suppose we fully understood the human mind. Would this make a difference in how we experienced our own consciousness?
4. If, from the outside and for all intents and purposes, it appeared as if a machine were self-conscious, would it matter that it might not be conscious in the same way that humans are? Should the machine be treated as if it were conscious? What would Hunt say?

For Further Reading

For introductions to artificial intelligence, see M. A. Boden, *Artificial Intelligence and Natural Man* (1987) and *The Philosophy of Artificial Life* (1996), and A. J. Clark, *Microcognition: Philosophy, Cognitive Science, and Parallel Distributed Processing* (1989).

For texts discussing the limits of artificial intelligence, see *What Computers "Still" Can't Do: A Critique of Artificial Intelligence* (1992) by H. L. Dreyfus, and *The Emperor's New Mind* (1989) by Roger Penrose. See also *How to Build a Person: A Prolegomenon* (1989) by J. L. Pollock for a defense of functionalism and the possibility of artificial persons. For possible future trends in artificial intelligence, see *Future Directions in Artificial Intelligence* (1991), edited by Flach and Meersman.

12 MINDS, BRAINS, AND PROGRAMS
John Searle

In the following essay John Searle (1932–) adopts a view similar to Morton Hunt's: There are some things that computer brains cannot do that human brains can. While Turing and Lycan have suggested that machines are (theoretically) capable of being intelligent—and perhaps even having

Source: "Minds, Brains, and Programs" by John Searle, from *The Behavioral and Brain Sciences,* vol. 3, pp. 417–24. Cambridge: Cambridge University Press. Cambridge University Press, 1980. Reprinted with the permission of Cambridge University Press.

feelings and mental states—questions remain. Does intelligence imply consciousness and comprehension? Searle believes that it does and constructs a thought experiment that shows that machines are incapable of consciousness or comprehension. From this thought experiment, he concludes that machines cannot be intelligent despite what Turing claims. This famous thought experiment is known as "the Chinese room."

How does the Chinese room work? Consider this similar example: Suppose that a monkey was trained to bubble in scantron sheets according to a particular pattern. And suppose that this pattern matched the answer key to Dr. Smith's next physics test. If the monkey were allowed to take Dr. Smith's test, should Dr. Smith believe that she had a promising young primate on her hands? Probably not, even if the monkey outscored the rest of the class.

John Searle teaches philosophy at the University of California, Berkeley, and is widely regarded for his research in the philosophy of language and, more recently, in the philosophy of mind.

Reading Questions

1. What is the difference between strong and weak AI? What claims do the strong AI proponents make about what their programs, such as Schank's, are capable of doing?
2. Describe the Chinese room experiment. What is it supposed to prove?
3. What is the systems reply to the Chinese room example? How does Searle respond to the systems reply?
4. What consequence results from speaking of 'subsystems' to shore up the system's reply?
5. What is the robot reply to the Chinese room example? How does Searle respond to the robot reply?

What psychological and philosophical significance should we attach to recent efforts at computer simulations of human cognitive capacities? In answering this question, I find it useful to distinguish what I will call "strong" AI from "weak" or "cautious" AI (Artificial Intelligence). According to weak AI, the principal value of the computer in the study of the mind is that it gives us a very powerful tool. For example, it enables us to formulate and test hypotheses in a more rigorous and precise fashion. But according to strong AI, the computer is not merely a tool in the study of the mind; rather, the appropriately programmed computer really *is* a mind, in the sense that computers given the right programs can be literally said to *understand* and have other cognitive states. In strong AI, because the programmed computer has cognitive states, the programs are not mere tools that enable

us to test psychological explanations; rather, the programs are themselves the explanations.

I have no objection to the claims of weak AI, at least as far as this article is concerned. My discussion here will be directed at the claims I have defined as those of strong AI, specifically the claim that the appropriately programmed computer literally has cognitive states and that the programs thereby explain human cognition. When I hereafter refer to AI, I have in mind the strong version, as expressed by these two claims.

I will consider the work of Roger Schank and his colleagues at Yale (Schank & Abelson 1977), because I am more familiar with it than I am with any other similar claims, and because it provides a very clear example of the sort of work I wish to examine. But nothing that follows depends upon the details of Schank's programs. The same arguments would apply to Winograd's SHRDLU (Winograd 1973), Weizenbaum's ELIZA (Weizenbaum 1965), and indeed any Turing machine simulation of human mental phenomena.

Very briefly, and leaving out the various details, one can describe Schank's program as follows: the aim of the program is to simulate the human ability to understand stories. It is characteristic of human beings' story-understanding capacity that they can answer questions about the story even though the information that they give was never explicitly stated in the story. Thus, for example, suppose you are given the following story: "A man went into a restaurant and ordered a hamburger. When the hamburger arrived it was burned to a crisp, and the man stormed out of the restaurant angrily, without paying for the hamburger or leaving a tip." Now, if you are asked "Did the man eat the hamburger?" you will presumably answer, "No, he did not." Similarly, if you are given the following story: "A man went into a restaurant and ordered a hamburger; when the hamburger came he was very pleased with it; and as he left the restaurant he gave the waitress a large tip before paying his bill," and you are asked the question "Did the man eat the hamburger?" you will presumably answer, "Yes, he ate the hamburger." Now Schank's machines can similarly answer questions about restaurants in this fashion. To do this, they have a "representation" of the sort of information that human beings have about restaurants, which enables them to answer such questions as those above, given these sorts of stories. When the machine is given the story and then asked the question, the machine will print out answers of the sort that we would expect human beings to give if told similar stories. Partisans of strong AI claim that in this question and answer sequence the machine is not only simulating a human ability but also

1. that the machine can literally be said to *understand* the story and provide the answers to questions, and
2. that what the machine and its program do *explains* the human ability to understand the story and answer questions about it.

Both claims seem to me to be totally unsupported by Schank's work, as I will attempt to show in what follows.

One way to test any theory of the mind is to ask oneself what it would be like if my mind actually worked on the principles that the theory says all minds work on. Let us apply this test to the Schank program with the following *Gedankenexperiment*. Suppose that I'm locked in a room and given a large batch of Chinese writing. Suppose furthermore (as is indeed the case) that I know no Chinese, either written or spoken, and that I'm not even confident that I could recognize Chinese writing as Chinese writing distinct from, say, Japanese writing or meaningless squiggles. To me, Chinese writing is just so many meaningless squiggles. Now suppose further that after this first batch of Chinese writing I am given a second batch of Chinese script together with a set of rules for correlating the second batch with the first batch. The rules are in English, and I understand these rules as well as any other native speaker of English. They enable me to correlate one set of formal symbols with another set of formal symbols, and all that "formal" means here is that I can identify the symbols entirely by their shapes. Now suppose also that I am given a third batch of Chinese symbols together with some instructions, again in English, that enable me to correlate elements of this third batch with the first two batches, and these rules instruct me how to give back certain Chinese symbols with certain sorts of shapes in response to certain sorts of shapes given me in the third batch. Unknown to me, the people who are giving me all of these symbols call the first batch "a script," they call the second batch a "story," and they call the third batch "questions." Furthermore, they call the symbols I give them back in response to the third batch "answers to the questions," and the set of rules in English that they gave me, they call "the program." Now just to complicate the story a little, imagine that these people also give me stories in English, which I understand, and they then ask me questions in English about these stories, and I give them back answers in English. Suppose also that after a while I get so good at following the instructions for manipulating the Chinese symbols and the programmers get so good at writing the programs that from the external point of view—that is, from the point of view of somebody outside the room in which I am locked—my answers to the questions are absolutely indistinguishable from those of native Chinese speakers. Nobody just looking at my answers can tell that I don't speak a word of Chinese. Let us also suppose that my answers to the English questions are, as they no doubt would be, indistinguishable from those of other native English speakers, for the simple reason that I am a native English speaker. From the external point of view—from the point of view of someone reading my "answers"—the answers to the Chinese questions and the English questions are equally good. But in the Chinese case, unlike the English case, I produce the answers by manipulating uninterpreted formal symbols. As far as the Chinese is concerned, I simply behave like a computer; I perform computational operations on formally specified elements. For the purposes of the Chinese, I am simply an instantiation of the computer program.

Now the claims made by strong AI are that the programmed computer understands the stories and that the program in some sense explains human understanding. But we are now in a position to examine these claims in light of our thought experiment.

1. As regards the first claim, it seems to me quite obvious in the example that I do not understand a word of the Chinese stories. I have inputs and outputs that are indistinguishable from those of the native Chinese speaker, and I can have any formal program you like, but I still understand nothing. For the same reasons, Schank's computer understands nothing of any stories, whether in Chinese, English, or whatever, since in the Chinese case the computer is me, and in cases where the computer is not me, the computer has nothing more than I have in the case where I understand nothing.

2. As regards the second claim, that the program explains human understanding, we can see that the computer and its program do not provide sufficient conditions of understanding since the computer and the program are functioning, and there is no understanding. But does it even provide a necessary condition or a significant contribution to understanding? One of the claims made by the supporters of strong AI is that when I understand a story in English, what I am doing is exactly the same—or perhaps more of the same—as what I was doing in manipulating the Chinese symbols. It is simply more formal symbol manipulation that distinguishes the case in English, where I do understand, from the case in Chinese, where I don't. I have not demonstrated that this claim is false, but it would certainly appear an incredible claim in the example. Such plausibility as the claim has derives from the supposition that we can construct a program that will have the same inputs and outputs as native speakers, and in addition we assume that speakers have some level of description where they are also instantiations of a program. On the basis of these two assumptions we assume that even if Schank's program isn't the whole story about understanding, it may be part of the story. Well, I suppose that is an empirical possibility, but not the slightest reason has so far been given to believe that it is true, since what is suggested—though certainly not demonstrated—by the example is that the computer program is simply irrelevant to my understanding of the story. In the Chinese case I have everything that artificial intelligence can put into me by way of a program, and I understand nothing; in the English case I understand everything, and there is so far no reason at all to suppose that my understanding has anything to do with computer programs, that is, with computational operations on purely formally specified elements. As long as the program is defined in terms of computational operations on purely formally defined elements, what the example suggests is that these by themselves have no interesting connection with understanding. They are certainly not sufficient conditions, and not the slightest reason has been given to suppose that they are necessary conditions or even that they make a significant contribution to understanding. Notice that the force of the argument is not simply that different machines can have the same input and output while operating on different formal principles—that is not the point at all. Rather, whatever purely formal principles you put into the computer, they will not be sufficient for understanding, since a human will be able to follow the formal principles without understanding anything. No reason whatever has been offered to suppose that such principles are necessary or even contributory, since no reason has been given to suppose that when I understand English I am operating with any formal program at all.

. . .

I have had the occasions to present this example to several workers in artificial intelligence, and, interestingly, they do not seem to agree on what the proper reply to it is. I get a surprising variety of replies, and in what follows I will consider the most common of these (specified along with their geographic origins).

...

I. THE SYSTEMS REPLY (BERKELEY)

"While it is true that the individual person who is locked in the room does not understand the story, the fact is that he is merely part of a whole system, and the system does understand the story. The person has a large ledger in front of him in which are written the rules, he has a lot of scratch paper and pencils for doing calculations, he has 'data banks' of sets of Chinese symbols. Now, understanding is not being ascribed to the mere individual; rather it is being ascribed to this whole system of which he is a part."

My response to the systems theory is quite simple: let the individual internalize all of these elements of the system. He memorizes the rules in the ledger and the data banks of Chinese symbols, and he does all the calculations in his head. The individual then incorporates the entire system. There isn't anything at all to the system that he does not encompass. We can even get rid of the room and suppose he works outdoors. All the same, he understands nothing of the Chinese, and *a fortiori* neither does the system, because there isn't anything in the system that isn't in him. If he doesn't understand, then there is no way the system could understand because the system is just a part of him.

Actually I feel somewhat embarrassed to give even this answer to the systems theory because the theory seems to me so unplausible to start with. The idea is that while a person doesn't understand Chinese, somehow the *conjunction* of that person and bits of paper might understand Chinese. It is not easy for me to imagine how someone who was not in the grip of an ideology would find the idea at all plausible. Still, I think many people who are committed to the ideology of strong AI will in the end be inclined to say something very much like this; so let us pursue it a bit further. According to one version of this view, while the man in the internalized systems example doesn't understand Chinese in the sense that a native Chinese speaker does (because, for example, he doesn't know

that the story refers to restaurants and hamburgers, etc.), still "the man as a formal symbol manipulation system" *really does understand Chinese.* The subsystem of the man that is the formal symbol manipulation system for Chinese should not be confused with the subsystem for English.

So there are really two subsystems in the man; one understands English, the other Chinese, and "it's just that the two systems have little to do with each other." But, I want to reply, not only do they have little to do with each other, they are not even remotely alike. The subsystem that understands English (assuming we allow ourselves to talk in this jargon of "subsystems" for a moment) knows that the stories are about restaurants and eating hamburgers, he knows that he is being asked questions about restaurants and that he is answering questions as best he can by making various inferences from the content of the story, and so on. But the Chinese system knows none of this. Whereas the English subsystem knows that "hamburgers" refer to hamburgers, the Chinese subsystem knows only that "squiggle squiggle" is followed by "squoggle squoggle." All he knows is that various formal symbols are being introduced at one end and manipulated according to rules written in English, and other symbols are going out at the other end. The whole point of the original example was to argue that such symbol manipulation by itself couldn't be sufficient for understanding Chinese in any literal sense because the man could write "squoggle squoggle" after "squiggle squiggle" without understanding anything in Chinese. And it doesn't meet that argument to postulate subsystems within the man, because the subsystems are no better off than the man was in the first place; they still don't have anything even remotely like what the English-speaking man (or subsystem) has. Indeed, in the case as described, the Chinese subsystem is simply a part of the English subsystem, a part that engages in meaningless symbol manipulation according to rules in English.

Let us ask ourselves what is supposed to motivate the systems reply in the first place; that is, what *independent* grounds are there supposed to be for saying that the agent must have a subsystem within him that literally understands stories in Chinese? As far as I can tell the only grounds are that in the example I have the same input and output as native Chinese speakers and a program that goes from one to the other. But the whole point of the examples has been to try to show that that couldn't be sufficient for understanding, in the sense in which I understand stories in English, because a person, and hence the set of systems that go to make up a person, could have the right combination of input, output, and program and still not understand anything in the relevant literal sense in which I understand English. The only motivation for saying there *must* be a subsystem in me that understands Chinese is that I have a program and I can pass the Turing test; I can fool native Chinese speakers. But precisely one of the points at issue is the adequacy of the Turing test. The example shows that there could be two "systems," both of which pass the Turing test, but only one of which understands; and it is no argument against this point to say that since they both pass the Turing test they must both understand, since this claim fails to meet the argument that the system in me that understands English has a great deal more than the system that merely processes Chinese. In short, the systems reply simply begs the question by insisting without argument that the system must understand Chinese.

Furthermore, the systems reply would appear to lead to consequences that are independently absurd. If we are to conclude that there must be cognition in me on the grounds that I have a certain sort of input and output and a program in between, then it looks like all sorts of noncognitive subsystems are going to turn out to be cognitive. For example, there is a level of description at which my stomach does information processing, and it instantiates any number of computer programs, but I take it we do not want to say that it has any understanding. But if we accept the systems reply, then it is hard to see how we avoid saying that stomach, heart, liver, and so on, are all understanding subsystems, since there is no principled way to distinguish the motivation for saying the Chinese subsystem understands from saying that the stomach understands. It is, by the way, not an answer to this point to say that the Chinese system has information as input and output and the stomach has food and food products as input and output, since from the point of view of the agent, from my point of view, there is no information in either the food or the Chinese—the Chinese is just so many meaningless squiggles. The information in the Chinese case is solely in the eyes of the programmers and the interpreters, and there is nothing to prevent them from treating the input and output of my digestive organs as information if they so desire.

This last point bears on some independent problems in strong AI, and it is worth digressing for a moment to explain it. If strong AI is to be a branch of psychology, then it must be able to distinguish those systems that are genuinely mental from those that are not. It must be able to distinguish the principles on which the mind works from those on which nonmental systems work; otherwise it will offer us no explanations of what is specifically mental about the mental. And the mental-nonmental distinction cannot be just in the eye of the beholder but it must be intrinsic to the systems; otherwise it would be up to any beholder to treat people as nonmental and, for example, hurricanes as mental if he likes. But quite often in the AI literature the distinction is blurred in ways that would in the long run prove disastrous to the claim that AI is a cognitive inquiry. McCarthy, for example writes, "Machines as simple as thermostats can be said to have beliefs, and having beliefs seems to be a characteristic of most machines capable of problem solving performance" (McCarthy, 1979). Anyone who thinks strong AI has a chance as a theory of the mind ought to ponder the implications of that remark. We are asked to accept it as a discovery of strong AI that the hunk of metal on the wall that we use to regulate the temperature has beliefs in exactly the same sense that we, our spouses, and our children have beliefs, and furthermore that "most" of the other machines in the room—telephone, tape recorder, adding machine, electric light switch—also have beliefs in this literal sense. It is not the aim of this article to argue against McCarthy's point, so I will simply assert the following without argument. The study of the mind starts with such facts as that humans have beliefs, while thermostats, telephones, and adding machines don't. If you get a theory that denies this point you have produced a counterexample to the theory and the theory is false. One gets the impression that people in AI who write this sort of thing think they can get away with it because they don't really take it seriously, and they don't think anyone else will either. I propose for a moment at least, to take it seriously. Think hard for one minute about what would be necessary to establish that that hunk of metal on the wall over there had real beliefs, beliefs with direction of fit, propositional content, and conditions of satisfaction; beliefs that had the possibility of being strong beliefs or weak beliefs; nervous, anxious, or secure beliefs; dogmatic, rational, or superstitious beliefs: blind faiths or hesitant cogitations: any kind of beliefs. The thermostat is not a candidate. Neither is stomach, liver, adding machine, or telephone. However, since we are taking the idea seriously, notice that its truth would be fatal to strong AI's claim to be a science of the mind. For the now the mind is the mind from thermostats and livers. And if McCarthy were right, strong AI wouldn't have a hope of telling us that.

II. THE ROBOT REPLY (YALE)

"Suppose we wrote a different kind of program from Schank's program. Suppose we put a computer inside a robot, and this computer would not just take in formal symbols as input and give out formal symbols as output, but rather would actually operate the robot in such a way that the robot does something very much like perceiving, walking, moving about, hammering nails, eating, drinking—anything you like. The robot would, for example, have a television camera attached to it that enabled it to 'see', it would have arms and legs that enabled it to 'act', and all of this would be controlled by its computer 'brain'. Such a robot would, unlike Schank's computer, have genuine understanding and other mental states."

The first thing to notice about the robot reply is that it tacitly concedes that cognition is not solely a matter of formal symbol manipulation, since this reply adds a set of causal relation with the outside world. But the answer to the robot reply is that the addition of such "perceptual" and "motor" capacities adds nothing by way of understanding, in particular, or intentionality, in general, to Schank's original program. To see this, notice that the same thought experiment applies to the robot case. Suppose that instead of the computer inside the robot, you put me inside the room and, as in the original Chinese case, you give me more Chinese symbols with more instructions in English for matching Chinese symbols to Chinese symbols and feeding back Chinese symbols to the outside. Suppose, unknown to me, some of the Chinese symbols that come to me come from a television camera attached to the robot and other Chinese symbols that I am giving out serve to make the motors inside the robot move the robot's legs or arms. It is important to emphasize that all I am doing is manipulating formal symbols: I know none of these other facts. I am receiving "information" from the robot's "perceptual" apparatus, and I am giving out "instructions" to its motor apparatus without knowing either of these facts. I am the robot's homunculus, but unlike the traditional homunculus, I don't know what's going on. I don't understand anything except the rules for symbol manipulation. Now in this case I want to say that the robot has no intentional states at all; it is simply moving about as a result of its electrical wiring and its program. And furthermore, by instantiating the program I have no intentional states of the relevant type. All I do is follow formal instructions about manipulating formal symbols.

Discussion Questions

1. If Searle is right—if computers are categorically incapable of understanding—does this give us reason to believe that something immaterial (that is, mind or soul) is involved in consciousness and understanding? What feature of computers makes them incapable of understanding? Is it their material nature? If not, then what?

2. What evidence do we have for believing that other people are conscious or that they understand? Do we have any more reason to believe that other people are conscious than we have for believing that someone in the Chinese room understands Chinese?

3. What reason do you have for believing that you understand English? Could these reasons also imply that a computer understands English? Why or why not?

For Further Reading

For Searle's work related to artificial intelligence and the philosophy of mind, see *Minds, Brains, and Programs* (1980); *Intentionality* (1983); *Minds, Brains and Science* (1984); and *The Rediscovery of the Mind* (1992). For a text on Searle's philosophy, see *John Searle and His Critics* (1991), edited by Lepore and van Gulick. The Chinese room argument is discussed in *The Mind's I* (1981), edited by Dennett and Hofstadter. For additional reading concerning the prospects for artificial intelligence, see *Android Epistemology* (1995), edited by Ford, Glymour, and Hayes; and *Artificial Intelligence: The Case Against* (1987), edited by R. Born.

CHAPTER 3

AM I A MIND,
A BODY, OR BOTH?

As seen in Chapter 2, the prospect of **artificial intelligence** (AI) raises some interesting questions: Can intelligent machines be constructed? How about conscious machines? Or can AI simply hope for machines that—from the outside—*appear* to be intelligent and conscious but lack understanding and mental states, including the ability to feel pain and sorrow? The ability to create a conscious machine may depend on whether the mind is material or not. If the mind is an immaterial substance—for example, a soul—then the quest for artificial intelligence might be doomed to failure, since minds apparently cannot be made out of circuits, wires, and transistors.

Are human minds immaterial? Or are they nothing more than brain matter? Or are human minds some combination of the physical and the immaterial? In Western culture, many talk as if mind and matter are two distinct entities, but they also assume that mind and matter do in fact interact. On the one hand, the body affects the mind. For example, an injury to the brain often corresponds to a diminished mental life, while the foods and medications we consume affect our feelings and experiences. On the other hand, our minds appear to affect our bodies: As I mentally will that my hands type out these words, my physical body follows my intentions. But there are important and troubling issues here. If human minds and bodies are composed of two entirely distinct substances, how is it possible for the physical and the immaterial to interact? Additionally, what is the relationship between mind and matter? Does the physical control the mental, or vice versa; or is the relationship one of give and take?

Questions of this sort fall into an area of philosophy known as **metaphysics,** which is the study of the nature of reality (what is ultimately real?). Our current topic, the mind-body problem, is only one area of metaphysics; other areas include the nature of the universe and the existence of God, topics covered in later chapters.

Notice that the answer we give to the question "What is ultimately real?" impacts our understanding of the relationship between mind and matter. **Idealism** is one answer. It maintains that there are only immaterial substances—minds and their contents—so there is no interaction between mind and matter, since everything is immaterial. **Materialism,** on the other hand, maintains that everything that exists is physical. Mental events, on this view, are just physical events—the mind is nothing more than the brain—so, again, there is no interaction between (immaterial) mind and matter.

However, both materialists and idealists have the same problem: to explain how one substance can have such widely variant qualities. Idealists, such as George Berkeley, must explain how supposedly physical objects, such as chairs and desks, are actually only mental substances, whereas materialists must explain how the mind is merely a property of physical processes within the brain. An alternative to both views is **dualism.** Dualists, such as René Descartes, believe there are two sorts of substances: mind and matter. But this view has its own difficulties. If we claim that the mind is mental substance and the brain is physical, how do these fundamentally different substances interact with each other?

Dualists can be divided according to their account of the nature of the supposed "interaction" between mind and body. Cartesian dualism, named after its proponent Descartes, holds that the mind can affect the body and vice versa. For example, Cartesian dualists believe both that one can *will* one's arm to rise (a mental event), thereby *causing* one's arm to rise (a physical event) and that when one's arm is burned (a physical event), this results in feeling pain (a mental event). Cartesian dualism is perhaps the most popular form of dualism, partly because it accords with a standard Judeo-Christian worldview.

In contrast to Cartesian dualism, **epiphenomenalism** holds that a one-sided interaction occurs between the mind and body: bodily events have an effect on the mental, but mental events have no causal effect on the body. The mind passively observes the life of the body.

There are two other (rather strange) forms of dualism to mention. Both forms hold that humans are composed of two substances, mind and body, but that these two substances have no causal influence on each other. **Occasionalists,** such as French philosopher Nicholas Malebranche (1638–1715), believe that what happens in the mind is accurately reflected in the actions of the body, and vice versa, because God wills it to be the case. If one wills one's arm to rise (a mental event), God causes the relevant physical event (the arm raising) to happen. Or, in the case that one's arm is burned (a physical event), God causes the appropriate pain (a mental event) to occur in one's mind. **Parallelism,** advocated by the German philosopher Leibniz (1646–1716), is similar to occasionalism in that it maintains that mental events accurately reflect and parallel what happens to the body, and vice versa, but for parallelism the harmony between mind and body is not the result of God's active and continued intervention. Rather, mind and body run according to a harmony preestablished by God. The mind and body are like two separate clocks: God winds up the clocks, sets them to the same time, and then lets them run. The mind and body thus keep in step but without the continued intervention of God.

Perhaps, though, the mind-body dilemma rests on a mistake: the attempt to treat with scientific accuracy and precision concepts that are not empirical. By avoiding language about nonobservable entities such as thoughts and intentions, **behaviorism,** advocated by B. F. Skinner, attempts to investigate human behavior without becoming embroiled in the mind-body problem. This strategy, however, creates problems of its own.

The stakes in the mind-body debate are high. If, for example, the materialists hold the winning hand, then our hopes to survive our bodily death (and perhaps our belief in God) might be overly optimistic. But then again, if materialism is true, one has the complication of trying to explain how humans possess free will—the ability to choose what they will do without that choice being the inevitable result of what has gone before.

In the following selections, dualism is represented by J. P. Moreland and critiqued by both Gilbert Ryle and the behaviorist B. F. Skinner, while J. J. C. Smart defends materialism. Although a selection from Descartes does not appear in this chapter, a selection containing his argument for dualism appears in Chapter 6, Reading 28; you may wish to read it as a supplement. In brief, Descartes attempts to establish dualism in the following manner: If something is true of X but not Y, then X and Y are not the same thing. The existence of the body is dubitable, since one might falsely believe that one has a body when one does not, but the existence of the mind is indubitable, since we are directly aware of our thoughts. Therefore, mind and body are not the same thing.

13 DUALISM DEFENDED
J. P. Moreland

J. P. Moreland (1948–) holds a master's degree in theology and a Ph.D. in philosophy, and currently teaches at the Talbot School of Theology at Biola University. As his academic credentials suggest, Moreland's interests include the philosophy of religion, but also ethics and applied ethics, especially euthanasia.

Moreland is a proponent of Cartesian dualism, which he calls 'substance dualism,' the claim that humans are composed of both an immaterial substance (mind or soul) and a physical substance (body). He begins his defense of dualism by attempting to make belief in immaterial souls more palatable to nonbelievers, while simultaneously attempting to discredit materialism. Moreland points out that persons actually (and routinely) believe in the existence of numerous sorts of immaterial entities. For instance, the existence of numbers, goodness, theories, universals, and the laws of logic are unproblematic even though all of these things are immaterial. Physicalism (or materialism), on the other hand, is problematic since it cannot explain the existence of numbers, theories, and so forth. Additionally, whereas physicalism maintains that the mind and the brain are one and the same thing, Moreland counters that there are distinct differences between minds (or mental states) and brains (or brain states). For instance, individuals have first-person access to their own mental states, but no one has first-person access to his or her brain states. Therefore, minds and brains are not one and the same thing.

Moreland concludes by defending dualism against another competitor, the emergent property view (EPV), a form of **epiphenomenalism.** Among other things, Moreland faults EPV for suggesting that the mental component of persons is a silent partner in the mind-body relationship: the body affects the mind, but the mind has no influence on the body. If this were true, reasons Moreland, then there would be no rational agent directing your actions—a view that runs counter to ordinary experience.

Reading Questions

1. Briefly explain physicalism in the context of the mind-body debate.
2. Explain the difference between property dualism and substance dualism.
3. Why does Moreland believe that physicalism is inadequate as a worldview?

SOURCE: From *Scaling the Secular City* by J. P. Moreland. Baker Books, 1987. Used by permission of Baker Book House Company.

4. Other than numbers, what entities are considered nonphysical?
5. Why does the falsity of physicalism not refute mind-body physicalism? Explain your answer.
6. Under what conditions can X and Y be considered identical?
7. What reasons are there for denying that thoughts are identical to physical events in the brain?
8. Does the subjectivity of experience count against physicalism?
9. What problem arises for the physicalist concerning personal identity?
10. What problems does Moreland identify with epiphenomenalism?

Dualism Defined

The mind/body problem focuses on two main issues. First, is a human being composed of just one ultimate component or two? Second, if the answer is two, how do these two relate to one another? Physicalism is one solution to the problem. As a general worldview, physicalism holds that the only thing which exists is matter (where matter is defined by an ideal, completed form of physics). Applied to the mind/body problem, physicalism asserts that a human being is just a physical system. There is no mind or soul, just a brain and central nervous system. Dualism is the opponent of physicalism and it asserts that in addition to the body, a human being also has a nonphysical component called a soul, mind, or self (words which will be used interchangeably for our purposes).

There are two main varieties of dualism—property dualism and substance dualism. . . .

. . .

Property dualists hold that the mind is a property of the body. As Richard Taylor puts it, "A person is a living physical body having mind, the mind consisting, however, of nothing but a more or less continuous series of conscious or unconscious states and events . . . which are the effects but never the causes of bodily activity." This view is call *epiphenomenalism*. The mind is to the body as smoke is to fire. Smoke is different from fire, but smoke does not cause anything. Smoke is a byproduct of fire. Similarly, mind is a byproduct of the body which does not cause anything. It just "rides" on top of the events in the body. Body events cause mind as a byproduct. The mind is a property of the body which ceases to exist when the body ceases to function.

Though some theists have denied it recently, the historic Christian view has been substance dualism. The mind, distinct from the body, is a real substance which can cause things to happen by acting and which can exist when the body ceases to function.

Dualism Defended

Problems with Physicalism as a General Worldview

Physicalism as a worldview holds that everything that exists is nothing but a single spatio-temporal system which can be completely described in terms of some ideal form of physics. Matter/energy is all that exists. God, souls, and nonphysical abstract entities do not exist. If physicalism is true at the worldview level, then obviously, mind/body physicalism would follow. But is physicalism adequate as a worldview? Several factors indicate that it is not.

First, if theism is true, then physicalism as a worldview is false. God is not a physical being. Second, a number of people have argued that numbers exist and that they are abstract, nonphysical entities (e.g., sets, substances, or properties). Several arguments can be offered for the existence of numbers, but two appear frequently. For one thing, mathematics claims to give us knowledge. But if this is so, there must be something that mathematics is about. Just as the biologist *discovers* biological truths about biological objects (organisms), so the mathematician often *discovers* mathematical truths (he does not invent them all the time) and these truths are about mathematical objects. If one denies the existence of numbers, then it is hard to rescue mathematics as a field which conveys knowledge about something. Without numbers, mathematics becomes merely an internally consistent game which is invented.

. . .

Some have argued that values, in addition to God and numbers, exist and are not physical. Certain objects (persons, animals) and certain events (helping a stranger, for example) have a nonphysical property of worth or goodness. Furthermore, moral laws are often held to be absolute, objective realities (e.g., one should not torture babies). But if certain objects possess goodness, and if certain moral laws are objective realities, then physicalism must be false, because the property of goodness and the nature of moral laws are not physical. For example, it makes no sense to ask how much goodness weighs, or to ask where a moral law exists. Such realities are not physical.

[Additionally], if physicalism is true, it is hard to see what one should make of the existence and nature of theories, meanings, concepts, propositions, the laws of logic, and truth itself. . . .

. . .

The entities listed have caused a lot of difficulty for physicalists. They have spent a good deal of time trying to do away with numbers, values, propositions, laws of logic, and universals by reducing them to notions compatible with physicalism. But these reductionist attempts have failed and physicalism as a worldview cannot adequately handle the existence of these entities. Theism can embrace them, however, by holding that God created these nonphysical entities and sustains them in existence. The falsity of physicalism as a worldview does not refute mind/body physicalism. One could hold to the existence of numbers and values but deny the existence of the soul. But much of the motivation for mind/body physicalism has been the desire to argue for physicalism at the worldview level. If physicalism at that level is false, then part of the reason for holding to mind/body physicalism is removed. For example, just because one cannot see the soul, weigh it, or say where it is, it does not follow that the soul does not exist. One cannot see, weigh, or locate numbers or values, but they still exist.

Problems with Mind/Body Physicalism

In order to facilitate an understanding of some of the arguments against mind/body physicalism, we must first examine the nature of identity. Suppose you know that someone named J. P. Moreland exists and that the author of this book exists. Assume further that you do not know that J. P. Moreland wrote this book. If someone asked you whether J. P. Moreland is identical to the author of this book, how would you decide? How would you determine that the "two" individuals are identical instead of being two different people? If you could find something true of

J. P. Moreland which is not true of the author of this book or vice versa, then they would be different people. They could not be identical. For example, if J. P. Moreland is married to Hope Moreland but the author of this book is not, they would be different people. On the other hand, if everything true of one is true of the other, "they" would be one person.

In general, if "two" things are identical, then whatever is true of the one is true of the other, since in reality only one thing is being discussed. However, if something is true of the one which is not true of the other, then they are two things and not one. This is sometimes called the indiscernibility of identicals and is expressed as follows:

$$(x)\,(y)\,[(x = y){\rightarrow}(P)\,(Px \leftrightarrow Py)]$$

For any entities x and y, if x and y are really the same thing, then for any property P, P is true of x if and only if P is true of y. If x is the mind and y is a part or state of the body (e.g., the brain), then if physicalism is true, x must be identical to y. On the other hand, if something is true of the mind which is not true of some part or state of the body, then the mind is not identical to the body and physicalism is false. This would be true even if the mind and body are inseparable. . . .

Every time something happens in the mind (someone has a thought of an ice cream cone), some event may be going on in the brain which could be described by a neurophysiologist. In general, brain events may always have mental events that correlate with them and vice versa. They may be inseparable in that one does not occur without the other in an embodied person. But this does not mean that the mental thought is identical to the brain event. The redness and roundness of an apple, though inseparable, are not identical. The property of having three sides (trilaterality) and the property of having three angles (triangularity) always go together. They are inseparable. But they are not identical. Physicalists must not only show that mental and brain phenomena are inseparable to make their case. They must also show that they are identical. With this in mind let us turn to some arguments for dualism.

The Distinctiveness of Mental and Physical Properties Mental events include thoughts, feelings of pain, the experience of being a person, or a sense image or picture of a ball in my mind. Physical events are events in the brain or central nervous system which can be described exhaustively using terms of chemistry, physics, and (for now) biology. The difficulty for physicalism is that mental events do not seem to have properties that hold for physical events. My thought of Kansas City is not ten centimeters long, it does not weigh anything, it is not located anywhere (it is not two inches from my left ear). Nor is it identical to any behavior or tendency to behave in a certain way (shouting "Kansas City" when I hear the name *George Brett*). But the brain event associated with this thought may be located inside my head, it may have a certain chemical composition and electrical current, and so forth. My afterimage of a ball (the impression of the ball present to my consciousness when I close my eyes after seeing the ball) may be pink, but nothing in my brain is pink. Mental events and properties have different attributes and therefore they are not identical.

…

The Experience of First-Person Subjectivity   The subjective character of experience is hard to capture in physicalist terms. The simple fact of consciousness is a serious difficulty for physicalism. To see this consider the following. Suppose a deaf scientist became the world's leading expert on the neurology of hearing. It would be possible for him to know and describe everything there is to the physical processes involved in hearing. However, something would still be left out of such a description—the experience of what it is like to be a human who hears. As Howard Robinson puts it:

> The notion of *having something as an object of experience* is not, *prima facie*, a physical notion; it does not figure in any physical science. *Having something as an object of experience* is the same as the subjective feel or the *what it is like* of experience.

Subjective states of experience exist. My experience of what it is like to be me, to hear a bird or see a tree, exists, and I have a first-person subjectivity to it. Such first-person experiences of my own self or "I" which has experiences cannot be reduced to a third-person "he" or "it," because the latter do not describe the experience itself or its first-person standpoint. A physicalist, scientific description of the world leaves out this character of subjective awareness. Such a description characterizes the world in impersonal, third-person terms (e.g., "there exists an object with such and such properties and states") and leaves

out the first-person, subjective experience itself (e.g., "I feel sad and food tastes sour to me").

…

Personal Identity   Imagine a wooden table which had all its parts removed one by one and replaced with metal parts. When the top and all the legs were replaced would it still be the same table? The answer would seem to be no. In fact, it would be possible to take all the original wooden parts and rearrange them into the original table. Even when the table had just one leg replaced, it would not literally be the same table. It would be a table similar to the original.

Losing old parts and gaining new ones changes the identity of the object in question. But now a question arises regarding persons. Am I literally the same self that I was a moment ago? Are my baby pictures really pictures of *me* or are they pictures of an ancestor of me who resembles me? I am constantly losing physical parts. I lose hair and fingernails; atoms are constantly being replaced, and every seven years my cells are almost entirely replaced. Do I maintain literal, absolute identity through change or not?

Substance dualists argue that persons do maintain absolute identity through change, because they have, in addition to their bodies, a soul that remains constant through change, and personal identity is constituted by sameness of soul, not sameness of body.

Physicalists have no alternative but to hold that personal identity is not absolute. Usually they argue that persons are really ancestral chains of successive "selves" which are connected with one another in some way. At each moment a new self exists (since the self or physical organism is constantly in flux, losing and gaining parts) and this self resembles the self prior to and after it. The relation of resemblance between selves plus the fact that later selves have the same memories as earlier selves and the body of each self traces a continuous path through space when the whole chain of selves is put together, constitute a relative sense of personal identity.

So substance dualists hold to a literal, absolute sense of personal identity and physicalists hold to a loose, relative sense of personal identity which amounts to a stream of successive selves held together into "one" person by resemblance between each self (also called a person stage), similarity of memory, and spatial continuity. For the physicalist, a person becomes a spacetime worm (i.e., a path traced through space and time).

The person is the entire path marked off at the time and place of his birth and death. At any given moment and location where "I" happen to be, "I" am not a person, just a person stage. The person is the whole path. So there is no literal sameness through change.

But now certain problems arise from physicalism. First, why should "I" ever fear the future? When it gets here, "I" will not be present; rather, another self who looks like me will be there but "I" will have ceased to exist. Second, why should anyone be punished? The self who did the crime in the past is not literally the same self who is present at the time of punishment. Physicalism seems to require a radical readjustment of our common-sense notions of future expectations and past actions because both presuppose a literal identity of the same self present in past, present, and future.

Third, physicalists not only have difficulty handling the unity of the self through time, but also cannot explain the unity of the self at a given time. As Harvard philosopher W. V. O. Quine puts it, according to physicalism the self becomes a sum or heap of scattered physical parts. The unity of the self is like the unity of an assembly of building blocks. If I have a pain in my foot while I am thinking about baseball, each is a distinct experience involving different physical parts. There is no self which *has* each experience. The self is merely a bundle or heap of parts and experiences. It has no real unity. The dualist says that the soul is diffused throughout the body and it is present before each experience. The soul has each experience. The unity of the consciousness is due to the fact that the same soul is the possessor of each and every experience of the consciousness. But the physicalist must say that each experience is possessed by different parts of the body and there is no real unity. However, my own experience of the unity of my consciousness shows this unity to be genuine and not arbitrary. *I* have my experiences. They are all *mine*. Physicalism does not adequately explain this fact.

...

THE ORIGIN OF MIND

We have seen that there are good reasons for holding that strict physicalism is false. But most physicalists are recalcitrant. If they embrace dualism at all, they embrace epiphenomenalism. ...

...

[But] there are ... serious difficulties with epiphenomenalism. To see these we must first clarify what epiphenomenalism involves. The view is also called holism, and when mind is seen to emerge through the coming together of the matter in a certain way (for instance, through the evolution of the central nervous system and brain) the position is called the emergent property view (EPV). Here are four main features of the EPV.

The Emergent Property View

Wholes and Parts   In nature, wholes are often greater than the sum of their parts. Nature exhibits a hierarchy of systems—subatomic particles, atoms, molecules, cells, organs, whole organisms. Each level has properties of the wholes at that level which are not properties of their constituent parts. For example, water has the property of being wet, but this property is not true of either hydrogen or oxygen. Similarly, the mind is a property of the brain.

Levels of Explanation and Complementarity   Each level in the hierarchy can be explained by using concepts appropriate at that level. Further, all the levels are complementary. For example, an explanation of a person's behavior could be given at a psychological level which used the concepts *beliefs, desires,* or *fears.* The same behavior could be given an explanation at the neurophysiological level using the concepts *neurons, synapses,* and so forth. These two levels of explanation are not in competition; they complement one another by offering descriptions of the same behavior at different levels.

Causation between Levels   Lower levels in the hierarchy cause things to happen at higher levels but not vice versa. When it comes to persons, events at the physical level can be characterized in terms of physical laws which make no reference to the causal efficaciousness of future events (e.g., the purposes of the agent) or higher levels of organization. The events at the physical level obey deterministic physical laws and mental events are mere by-products.

Resultant View of the Self   The self is not some mental substance added to the brain from the "outside" when the brain reaches a certain level of complexity. It is an emergent property which supervenes upon the brain. The self becomes a discontinuous series of mental events when mental properties are instanced in different brain events. The self is a series of events which "ride" on top of the brain. Consider the following diagram:

$$M_1 \quad M_2 \quad M_3 \quad M_4$$
$$\uparrow \quad \uparrow \quad \uparrow \quad \uparrow$$
$$B_1 \rightarrow B_2 \rightarrow B_3 \rightarrow B_4$$

Suppose M_1 is the mental state of seeing an apple from a distance of five feet. It is a *mental* state since it involves the conscious awareness of seeing the apple, and conscious awareness is something true of minds and not matter. Now suppose M_2 is the mental state of seeing the apple from one foot, M_3 the state of feeling a pain on the toe, and M_4 the state of hearing a plane fly overhead. B_1 through B_4 are brain states which are associated with each mental state.

Three things stand out immediately. First, B_1 through B_4 stand in rigid physical, causal relations with one another. B_1 causes B_2 and so on. There is no room for a rational agent to intervene in this causal sequence. Mental agents do not act here. The physical level determines all the action. Mental states are mere byproducts of their physical states as smoke is a byproduct of fire.

Second, there is no unified, enduring self at the mental level. According to substance dualism, the self is not identical to its states; it *has* its states. The mind *has* its thoughts and experiences and the same mind can have two experiences at the same time (hearing a plane and seeing an apple) or it can have one experience followed by another. The *self* is present at both experiences and underlies the change of experiences.

When a leaf goes from green to red, green does not become red. Rather, green leaves and is replaced by red *in* the leaf. The leaf is the same substance present at both ends of the process. When a substance gains or loses properties, *it* remains the same while properties come and go. They are replaced. Red replaces green. The EPV says that M_1 through M_4 are properties of the body. There is no enduring mental substance which has them. There is just one mental property at one time which leaves and is replaced by another mental property at another time. The "self" is a series of mental events where mental properties are had by physical states.

Third, it is hard to see what sense can be given to intentionality. How is it that M_1 is of or about an apple? M_1 is just a dummy, a free rider on B_1. At best, B_1 would just be a state caused by light waves from the apple but it is hard to see how this would cause M_1 to be really a state *about* that apple. Even if it were, what difference would it make? Any further body states (the act of touching the apple or eating it) would be caused totally by brain states and make no reference to mental states at all.

It should now be clear why epiphenomenalism was ruled out as an inadequate account of the necessary features of rationality. It cannot account for the existence of intentionality, it leaves no room for genuine rational agency to freely choose mental beliefs, and there is no enduring "I" to be present through the process of thought. . . .

Discussion Questions

1. Is it possible that God is a physical being? In other words, are theism and physicalism compatible? If physicalism is true, must God necessarily not exist? Why or why not?
2. Do numbers exist? If so, in what sense? Is the question of whether or not numbers exist relevant to the mind-body problem? Explain your answer.
3. Suppose that destroying a particular piece of your brain meant that you would forever lose a particular memory. Is this relevant to the mind-body problem? How would it affect your views?
4. Do you believe in near-death experiences? What about out-of-body experiences? Why or why not? If these experiences are real, do they support dualism? Could there be some physical explanation for these experiences besides substance dualism?

For Further Reading

For an introduction to the mind-body problem, see *Metaphysics* (1991), by R. Taylor; *The Mind-Body Problem: A Guide to the Current Debate* (1994), edited by R. Warner; and *Mind and Brain: A Dialogue on the Mind-Body Problem* (1996), by R. J. Gennaro.

The classic defense of dualism is Descartes' *Meditations on First Philosophy* (1641). For other defenses of dualism, see *The Case for Dualism* (1989), edited by J. R. Smythies; *The Self and Its Brain: An Argument for Interactionism* (1983), edited by Popper and Eccles; and *Objections to Physicalism* (1993), edited by H. Robinson. For two critiques of dualism, see *A Materialist Theory of Mind* (1993), by D. M. Armstrong, and *Body and Mind* (1970), by K. Campbell.

14 THE DOGMA OF THE GHOST IN THE MACHINE
Gilbert Ryle

Gilbert Ryle (1900–1976) of Oxford University concerned himself with the standard questions of philosophy, but also turned philosophy back onto itself and pursued meta-philosophical questions—questions about the nature of philosophy itself: What makes a question philosophical? How does one solve a philosophical problem? What counts as a satisfactory solution to a philosophical problem?

Under the heading of proper philosophical solutions, Ryle believed that he had identified a common sort of mistake made by philosophers, what he called 'category-mistakes'. A category-mistake occurs when one speaks of one sort of thing as if it were another sort of thing. If you talk about apples as if they were political parties, you make a category mistake (that is, it's nonsense to speak of *conservative* or *liberal* apples). Ryle believed that a colossal category-mistake was responsible for belief in the existence of immaterial entities such as souls. In short, Ryle believed that Cartesian dualism—the *official doctrine,* as Ryle called it—rested on a basic mistake.

Consider the following example. Suppose a fan wanted to meet the 1998 Chicago Bulls and was introduced to Jordan, Rodman, Pippen, and the rest. Suppose the fan then asked when he would be able to meet not just the players but the Chicago Bulls proper. What would we think? We would think that the fan was a bit confused. His mistake is to treat 'the Chicago Bulls' as if the team itself were a player, someone to meet and converse with—a category-mistake of treating 'the Chicago Bulls' as if it belonged to the category 'player' rather than 'team'. Notice that talk about the tenacity, athleticism, or artistry of 'the Chicago Bulls' perpetuates and compounds this mistake, and at a certain point it lulls us into falsely thinking of 'the Chicago Bulls' as a real and existent thing, despite the fact that it cannot be seen, touched, or heard.

SOURCE: From *The Concept of Mind* by Gilbert Ryle. London: Hutchinson & Co., 1949. Used by permission of Routledge Ltd.

According to Ryle, the mistaken belief in the existence of immaterial minds has a similar genesis. Ultimately, the belief in the existence of immaterial minds (souls) is the result of making a category-mistake concerning mental events. Ryle explains exactly how this happens.

Reading Questions

1. What is the "official doctrine"?
2. Explain the supposed differences between mind and matter.
3. Why can adherents of the official doctrine not know for certain that other people have minds of their own? Explain your answer.
4. Explain one of Ryle's examples of a category-mistake.
5. What is the origin of the Cartesian category-mistake?
6. What is the major theoretical obstacle to dualism according to Ryle? Why is this such a difficult problem?

(I) THE OFFICIAL DOCTRINE

There is a doctrine about the nature and place of minds which is so prevalent among theorists and even among laymen that it deserves to be described as the official theory. Most philosophers, psychologists, and religious teachers subscribe, with minor reservations, to its main articles and, although they admit certain theoretical difficulties in it, they tend to assume that these can be overcome without serious modifications being made to the architecture of the theory. It will be argued here that the central principles of the doctrine are unsound and conflict with the whole body of what we know about minds when we are not speculating about them.

The official doctrine, which hails chiefly from Descartes, is something like this. With the doubtful exceptions of idiots and infants in arms every human being has both a body and a mind. Some would prefer to say that every human being is both a body and a mind. His body and his mind are ordinarily harnessed together, but after the death of the body his mind may continue to exist and function.

Human bodies are in space and are subject to the mechanical laws which govern all other bodies in space. Bodily processes and states can be inspected by external observers. So a man's bodily life is as much a public affair as are the lives of animals and reptiles and even as the careers of trees, crystals and planets.

But minds are not in space, nor are their operations subject to mechanical laws. The workings of one mind are not witnessable by other observers; its career is private. Only I can take direct cognizance of the states and processes of my own mind. A person therefore lives through two collateral histories, one consisting of what happens in and to his body, the other consisting of what happens in and to his mind. The first is public, the second private. The events in the first history are events in the physical world, those in the second are events in the mental world.

It has been disputed whether a person does or can directly monitor all or only some of the episodes of his own private history; but, according to the official doctrine, of at least some of these episodes he has direct and unchallengeable cognizance. In consciousness, self-consciousness, and introspection he is directly and authentically apprised of the present states and operations of his mind. He may have great or small uncertainties about concurrent and adjacent episodes in the physical world, but he can have none about at least part of what is momentarily occupying his mind.

It is customary to express this bifurcation of his two lives and of his two worlds by saying that the things and events which belong to the physical world, including his own body, are external, while the workings of his own mind are internal. This antithesis of outer and inner is of course meant to be construed as a metaphor, since minds, not being in space, could not be described as being spatially inside anything else, or as having things going on spatially inside themselves. But relapses from this good intention are common and theorists are found speculating how stimuli, the physical sources of which are yards or miles outside a person's skin, can generate mental responses inside his skull, or how decisions framed inside his cranium can set going movements of his extremities.

Even when 'inner' and 'outer' are construed as metaphors, the problem of how a person's mind and body influence one another is notoriously charged with theoretical difficulties. What the mind wills, the legs, arms and the tongue execute; what affects the ear and the eye has something to do with what the mind perceives; grimaces and smiles betray the mind's moods and bodily castigations lead, it is hoped, to moral improvement. But the actual transactions between the episodes of the private history and those of the public history remain mysterious, since by definition they can belong to neither series. They could not be reported among the happenings described in a person's autobiography of his inner life, but nor could they be reported among those described in someone else's biography of that person's overt career. They can be inspected neither by introspection nor by laboratory experiment. They are theoretical shuttlecocks which are forever being bandied from the physiologist back to the psychologist and from the psychologist back to the physiologist.

Underlying this partly metaphorical representation of the bifurcation of a person's two lives there is a seemingly more profound and philosophical assumption. It is assumed that there are two different kinds of existence or status. What exists or happens may have the status of physical existence, or it may have the status of mental existence. Somewhat as the faces of coins are either heads or tails, or somewhat as living creatures are either male or female, so, it is supposed, some existing is physical existing, other existing is mental existing. It is a necessary feature of what has physical existence that it is in space and time; it is a necessary feature of what has mental existence that it is in time but not in space. What has physical existence is composed of matter, or else is a function of matter; what has mental existence consists of consciousness, or else is a function of consciousness.

There is thus a polar opposition between mind and matter, an opposition which is often brought out as follows. Material objects are situated in a common field, known as 'space', and what happens to one body in one part of space is mechanically connected with what happens to other bodies in other parts of space. But mental happenings occur in insulated fields, known as 'minds', and there is, apart maybe

from telepathy, no direct causal connection between what happens in one mind and what happens in another. Only through the medium of the public physical world can the mind of one person make a difference to the mind of another. The mind is its own place and in his inner life each of us lives the life of a ghostly Robinson Crusoe. People can see, hear and jolt one another's bodies, but they are irremediably blind and deaf to the workings of one another's minds and inoperative upon them.

What sort of knowledge can be secured of the workings of a mind? On the one side, according to the official theory, a person has direct knowledge of the best imaginable kind of the workings of his own mind. Mental states and processes are (or are normally) conscious states and processes, and the consciousness which irradiates them can engender no illusions and leaves the door open for no doubts. A person's present thinkings, feelings and willings, his perceivings, rememberings and imaginings are intrinsically 'phosphorescent'; their existence and their nature are inevitably betrayed to their owner. The inner life is a stream of consciousness of such a sort that it would be absurd to suggest that the mind whose life is that stream might be unaware of what is passing down it.

True, the evidence adduced recently by Freud seems to show that there exist channels tributary to this stream, which run hidden from their owner. People are actuated by impulses the existence of which they vigorously disavow; some of their thoughts differ from the thoughts which they acknowledge; and some of the actions which they think they will to perform they do not really will. They are thoroughly gulled by some of their own hypocrisies and they successfully ignore facts about their mental lives which on the official theory ought to be patent to them. Holders of the official theory tend, however, to maintain that anyhow in normal circumstances a person must be directly and authentically seized of the present state and workings of his own mind.

Besides being currently supplied with these alleged immediate data of consciousness, a person is also generally supposed to be able to exercise from time to time a special kind of perception, namely inner perception, or introspection. He can take a (non-optical) 'look' at what is passing in his mind. Not only can he view and scrutinize a flower through his sense of sight and listen to and discriminate the notes of a bell through his sense of hearing; he can also reflectively or introspectively watch, without any bodily organ of sense, the current episodes of his inner life. This self-observation is also commonly supposed to be immune from illusion, confusion or doubt. A mind's report of its own affairs have a certainty superior to the best that is possessed by its reports of matters in the physical world. Sense-perceptions can, but consciousness and introspection cannot, be mistaken or confused.

On the other side, one person has no direct access of any sort to the events of the inner life of another. He cannot do better than make problematic inferences from the observed behavior of the other person's body to the states of mind which, by analogy from his own conduct, he supposes to be signalized by that behavior. Direct access to the workings of a mind is the privilege of that mind itself; in default of such privileged access, the workings of one mind are inevitably occult to everyone else. For the supposed arguments from bodily movements similar to their own to mental workings similar to their own would lack any possibility of observational corroboration. Not unnaturally, therefore, an adherent of the official theory finds it difficult to resist this consequence of his premises, that he has no good reason to believe that there do exist minds other than his own. Even if he prefers to believe that to other human bodies there are harnessed minds not unlike his own, he cannot claim to be able to discover their individual characteristics, or the particular things that they undergo and do. Absolute solitude is on this showing the ineluctable destiny of the soul. Only our bodies can meet.

As a necessary corollary of this general scheme there is implicitly prescribed a special way of construing our ordinary concepts of mental powers and operations. The verbs, nouns and adjectives, with which in ordinary life we describe the wits, characters and higher-grade performances of the people with whom we have do, are required to be construed as signifying special episodes in their secret histories, or else as signifying tendencies for such episodes to occur. When someone is described as knowing, believing or guessing something, as hoping, dreading, intending or shirking something, as designing this or being amused at that, these verbs are supposed to denote the occurrence of specific modifications in

his (to us) occult stream of consciousness. Only his own privileged access to this stream in direct awareness and introspection could provide authentic testimony that these mental-conduct verbs were correctly or incorrectly applied. The onlooker, be he teacher, critic, biographer or friend, can never assure himself that his comments have any vestige of truth. Yet it was just because we do in fact all know how to make such comments, make them with general correctness and correct them when they turn out to be confused or mistaken, that philosophers found it necessary to construct their theories of the nature and place of minds. Finding mental-conduct concepts being regularly and effectively used, they properly sought to fix their logical geography. But the logical geography officially recommended would entail that there could be no regular or effective use of these mental-conduct concepts in our descriptions of, and prescriptions for, other people's minds.

(2) THE ABSURDITY OF THE OFFICIAL DOCTRINE

Such in outline is the official theory. I shall often speak of it, with deliberate abusiveness, as 'the dogma of the Ghost in the Machine'. I hope to prove that it is entirely false, and false not in detail but in principle. It is not merely an assemblage of particular mistakes. It is one big mistake and a mistake of a special kind. It is, namely, a category-mistake. It represents the facts of mental life as if they belonged to one logical type or category (or range of types or categories), when they actually belong to another. The dogma is therefore a philosopher's myth. In attempting to explode the myth I shall probably be taken to be denying well-known facts about the mental life of human beings, and my plea that I aim at doing nothing more than rectify the logic of mental-conduct concepts will probably be disavowed as mere subterfuge.

I must first indicate what is meant by the phrase 'category-mistake'. This I do in a series of illustrations.

A foreigner visiting Oxford or Cambridge for the first time is shown a number of colleges, libraries, playing fields, museums, scientific departments and administrative offices. He then asks 'But where is the University? I have seen where the members of the Colleges live, where the Registrar works, where the scientists experiment and the rest. But I have not yet seen the University in which reside and work the members of your University.' It has then to be explained to him that the University is not another collateral institution, some ulterior counterpart to the colleges, laboratories and offices which he has seen. The University is just the way in which all that he has already seen is organized. When they are seen and when their coordination is understood, the University has been seen. His mistake lay in his innocent assumption that it was correct to speak of Christ Church, the Bodleian Library, the Ashmolean Museum *and* the University, to speak, that is, as if 'the University' stood for an extra member of the class of which these other units are members. He was mistakenly allocating the University to the same category as that to which the other institutions belong.

The same mistake would be made by a child witnessing the march-past of a division, who, having had pointed out to him such and such battalions, batteries, squadrons, etc., asked when the division was going to appear. He would be supposing that a division was a counterpart to the units already seen, partly similar to them and partly unlike them. He would be shown his mistake by being told that in watching the battalions, batteries and squadrons marching past he had been watching the division marching past. The march-past was not a parade of battalions, batteries, squadrons *and* a division; it was a parade of the battalions, batteries and squadrons *of* a division.

One more illustration. A foreigner watching his first game of cricket learns what are the functions of the bowlers, the batsmen, the fielders, the umpires, and the scorers. He then says 'But there is no one left on the field to contribute the famous element of team-spirit. I see who does the bowling, the batting, and the wicket-keeping; but I do not see whose role it is to exercise *esprit de corps.*' Once more, it would have to be explained that he was looking for the wrong type of thing. Team-spirit is not another cricketing-operation supplementary to all of the other special tasks. It is, roughly, the keenness with which each of the special tasks is performed, and performing a task keenly is not performing two tasks. Certainly exhibiting team-spirit is not the same thing as bowling or catching, but nor is it a third thing such that we can say that the bowler first bowls *and* then exhibits team-spirit or that a fielder is at a given moment *either* catching *or* displaying *esprit de corps.*

These illustrations of category-mistakes have a common feature which must be noticed. The mistakes were made by people who did not know how to wield the concepts *University, division* and *team-spirit.* Their puzzles arose from inability to use certain items in the English vocabulary.

The theoretically interesting category-mistakes are those made by people who are perfectly competent to apply concepts, at least in the situations with which they are familiar, but are still liable in their abstract thinking to allocate those concepts to logical types to which they do not belong. An instance of a mistake of this sort would be the following story. A student of politics has learned the main differences between the British, the French, and the American Constitutions, and has learned also the differences and connections between the Cabinet, Parliament, the various Ministries, the Judicature and the Church of England. But he still becomes embarrassed when asked questions about the connections between the Church of England, the Home Office and the British Constitution. For while the Church and the Home Office are institutions, the British Constitution is not another institution in the same sense of that noun. So interinstitutional relations which can be asserted or denied to hold between the Church and the Home Office cannot be asserted or denied to hold between either of them and the British Constitution. 'The British Constitution' is not a term of the same logical type as 'the Home Office' and 'the Church of England'. In a partially similar way, John Doe may be a relative, a friend, an enemy or a stranger to Richard Roe; but he cannot be any of these things to the Average Taxpayer. He knows how to talk sense in certain sorts of discussions about the Average Taxpayer, but he is baffled to say why he could not come across him in the street as he can come across Richard Roe.

It is pertinent to our main subject to notice that, so long as the student of politics continues to think of the British Constitution as a counterpart to the other institutions, he will tend to describe it as a mysteriously occult institution; and so long as John Doe continues to think of the Average Taxpayer as a fellow-citizen, he will tend to think of him as an elusive insubstantial man, a ghost who is everywhere yet nowhere.

My destructive purpose is to show that a family of radical category-mistakes is the source of the double-life theory. The representation of a person as a ghost mysteriously ensconced in a machine derives from this argument. Because, as is true, a person's thinking, feeling and purposive doing cannot be described solely in the idioms of physics, chemistry, and physiology, therefore they must be described in counterpart idioms. As the human body is a complex organized unit, so the human mind must be another complex organized unit, though one made of a different sort of stuff and with a different sort of structure. Or, again, as the human body, like any other parcel of matter, is a field of causes and effects, so the mind must be another field of causes and effects, though not (Heaven be praised) mechanical causes and effects.

(3) THE ORIGIN OF THE CATEGORY-MISTAKE

One of the chief intellectual origins of what I have yet to prove to be the Cartesian category-mistake seems to be this. When Galileo showed that his methods of scientific discovery were competent to provide a mechanical theory which should cover every occupant of space, Descartes found in himself two conflicting motives. As a man of scientific genius he could not but endorse the claims of mechanics, yet as a religious and moral man he could not accept, as Hobbes accepted, the discouraging rider to those claims, namely that human nature differs only in degree of complexity from clockwork. The mental could not be just a variety of the mechanical.

He and subsequent philosophers naturally but erroneously availed themselves of the following escape- route. Since mental-conduct words are not to be construed as signifying the occurrence of mechanical processes, they must be construed as signifying the occurrence of non-mechanical processes; since mechanical laws explain movements in space as the effects of other movements in space, other laws must explain some of the non-spatial workings of minds as the effects of other non-spatial workings of minds. The difference between the human behaviors which we describe as intelligent and those which we describe as unintelligent must be a difference in their causation; so, while some movements of human tongues and limbs are the effects of mechanical causes, others must be the effects of non-mechanical causes, i.e., some issue from movements of particles of matter, others from workings of the mind.

The differences between the physical and the mental were thus represented as differences inside the common framework of the categories of 'thing', 'stuff', 'attribute', 'state', 'process', 'change', 'cause' and 'effect'. Minds are things, but different sorts of things from bodies; mental processes are causes and effects, but different sorts of causes and effects from bodily movements. And so on. Somewhat as the foreigner expected the University to be an extra edifice, rather like a college but also considerably different, so the repudiators of mechanism represented minds as extra centers of causal processes, rather like machines but also considerably different from them. Their theory was a para-mechanical hypothesis.

That this assumption was at the heart of the doctrine is shown by the fact that there was from the beginning felt to be a major theoretical difficulty in explaining how minds can influence and be influenced by bodies. How can a mental process, such as willing, cause spatial movements like the movements of the tongue? How can a physical change in the optic nerve have among its effects a mind's perception of a flash of light? This notorious crux by itself shows the logical mold into which Descartes pressed his theory of the mind. It was the self-same mold into which he and Galileo set their mechanics. Still unwittingly adhering to the grammar of mechanics, he tried to avert disaster by describing minds in what was merely an obverse vocabulary. The workings of minds had to be described by the mere negatives of the specific descriptions given to bodies; they are not in space, they are not motions, they are not modifications of matter, they are not accessible to public observation. Minds are not bits of clockwork, they are just bits of not-clockwork.

As thus represented, minds are not merely ghosts harnessed to machines, they are themselves just spectral machines. Though the human body is an engine, it is not quite an ordinary engine, since some of its workings are governed by another engine inside it— this interior governor-engine being one of a very special sort. It is invisible, inaudible and it has no size or weight. It cannot be taken to bits and the laws it obeys are not those known to ordinary engineers. Nothing is known of how it governs the bodily engine.

A second major crux points the same moral. Since, according to the doctrine, minds belong to the same category as bodies and since bodies are rigidly governed by mechanical laws, it seemed to many theorists to follow that minds must be similarly governed by rigid non-mechanical laws. The physical world is a deterministic system, so the mental world must be a deterministic system. Bodies cannot help the modifications that they undergo, so minds cannot help pursuing the careers fixed for them. *Responsibility, choice, merit* and *demerit* are therefore inapplicable concepts—unless the compromise solution is adopted of saying that the laws governing mental processes, unlike those governing physical processes, have the congenital attribute of being only rather rigid. The problem of the freedom of the will was the problem how to reconcile the hypothesis that minds are to be described in terms drawn from the categories of mechanics with the knowledge that higher-grade human conduct is not of a piece with the behavior of machines.

...

If my argument is successful, there will follow some interesting consequences. First, the hallowed contrast between Mind and Matter will be dissipated, but dissipated not by either of the equally hallowed absorptions of Mind by Matter or of Matter by Mind, but in quite a different way. For the seeming contrast of the two will be shown to be as illegitimate as would be the contrast of 'she came home in a flood of tears' and 'she came home in a sedan-chair'. The belief that there is a polar opposition between Mind and Matter is the belief that they are terms of the same logical type.

It will also follow that both idealism and materialism are answers to an improper question. The 'reduction' of the material world to mental states and processes, as well as the 'reduction' of mental states and processes to physical states and processes, presuppose the legitimacy of the disjunction 'Either there exist minds or there exist bodies (but not both)'. It would be like saying, 'Either she bought a left-hand and a right-hand glove or she bought a pair of gloves (but not both)'.

It is perfectly proper to say, in one logical tone of voice, that there exist minds and to say, in another logical tone of voice, that there exist bodies. But these expressions do not indicate two different species of existence, for 'existence' is not a generic word like 'colored' or 'sexed'. They indicate two different senses of 'exist', somewhat as 'rising' has different senses in 'the tide is rising', 'hopes are rising', and 'the average age of death is rising'. A man would be thought to be making a poor joke who said that three things are now rising, namely the tide, hopes and the average age of death. It would be just as good or bad a joke to say that there exist prime numbers and Wednesdays and public opinions and navies; or that there exist both minds and bodies. . . .

Discussion Questions

1. Does Ryle establish the nonexistence of immaterial minds, or does he merely describe how the belief arose? Is his explanation of the mistake enough to convince you that in fact it is a mistake? Why or why not?
2. Identify any other category-mistakes that you can think of. Does anything important depend on these mistakes?

For Further Reading

For Ryle's major work concerning the philosophy of mind and attack on dualism, see *The Concept of Mind* (1949). For collections of Ryle's work, see *Collected Papers* (1971); *On Thinking* (1979), edited by K. Kolenda; and *Aspects of Mind* (1993), edited by R. Meyer. Biographical information about Ryle can be found in *Gilbert Ryle: An Introduction to His Philosophy* (1980), by W. Lyons, and *Ryle: A Collection of Critical Essays* (1960), edited by Wood and Pitcher.

15 BEHAVIORISM
B. F. Skinner

Continuing a line of thought initiated by John B. Watson (1878–1958), American psychologist B. F. Skinner (1904–1990) sought to make psychology and the study of human behavior a true science. Among other things, this meant that psychology must explain human behavior in terms of visible, observable phenomena instead of appealing to nonobservable, invisible, postulated entities, such as the mind and the will, or Freudian inventions such as the id, ego, and superego.

But Skinner did not explain human behavior using the language of the (mechanistic) functioning of a material brain and central nervous system either. For Skinner, these sorts of explanations also lacked true explanatory power. Skinner's goal was to dispense with all talk of inner states (mental, physical, or otherwise) in order to develop a precise and scientific understanding of human behavior. The difficulty with referring to inner states is that they cannot be measured precisely and thus cannot be accurately replicated in laboratory experiments. As long as the science of human behavior employs spurious 'magical' explanations that are not grounded in repeatable, empirically verifiable observations, it will always be a deficient science, according to Skinner.

Skinner conceptualized humans as creatures that respond to and are conditioned by—in uniform, predictable ways—external stimuli in their environment. Known as **behaviorism,** Skinner's position is accepted as commonsensical by many today: A child will act in a particular way when the desired behavior is rewarded and deviant behavior punished; an adult's fear of dogs is not irrational when that individual had been attacked by a dog as a child. Consistently applied, however, behaviorism may lead to some seemingly difficult conclusions. Not only does it dismiss all talk of minds, but it leaves little or no room for freedom and choice: Our actions are always and only the function of environmental conditioning.

Reading Questions

1. What liability does Skinner associate with looking for the causes of actions inside things?
2. Why is the study of the nervous system not useful in the prediction and control of human behavior?
3. Why are psychic inner causes considered by Skinner to be fictional?
4. What sorts of variables are immediately available for analysis when we analyze human behavior?
5. Why does Skinner contend that you can make a horse drink if you lead it to water?
6. Does Skinner deny the existence of inner states? Of what use are they?
7. Why does Skinner reject social forces as important to understanding human behavior?

SOURCE: *Science and Human Behavior* by B. F. Skinner, Copyright © 1953 by Prentice-Hall, Inc. Reprinted by permission of Prentice-Hall, Inc., Upper Saddle River, NJ.

INNER "CAUSES"

Every science has at some time or other looked for causes of action inside the things it has studied. Sometimes the practice has proved useful, sometimes it has not. There is nothing wrong with an inner explanation as such, but events which are located inside a system are likely to be difficult to observe. For this reason we are encouraged to assign properties to them without justification. Worse still, we can invent causes of this sort without fear of contradiction. The motion of a rolling stone was once attributed to its *vis viva*. The chemical properties of bodies were thought to be derived from the *principles* or *essences* of which they were composed. Combustion was explained by the *phlogiston* inside the combustible object. Wounds healed and bodies grew well because of a *vis medicatrix*. It has been especially tempting to attribute the behavior of a living organism to the behavior of an inner agent, as the following examples may suggest.

Neural Causes

The layman uses the nervous system as a ready explanation of behavior. The English language contains hundreds of expressions which imply such a causal relationship. At the end of a long trial we read that the jury shows signs of *brain fag*, that the *nerves* of the accused are *on edge*, that the wife of the accused is on the verge of a *nervous breakdown*, and that his lawyer is generally thought to have lacked the *brains* needed to stand up to the prosecution. Obviously, no direct observations have been made of the nervous systems of any of these people. Their "brains" and "nerves" have been invented on the spur of the moment to lend substance to what might otherwise seem a superficial account of their behavior.

The sciences of neurology and physiology have not divested themselves entirely of a similar practice. Since techniques for observing the electrical and chemical processes in nervous tissue had not yet been developed, early information about the nervous system was limited to its gross anatomy. Neural processes could only be inferred from the behavior which was said to result from them. Such inferences were legitimate enough as scientific theories, but they could not justifiably be used to explain the very behavior upon which they were based. The hypotheses of the early physiologist may have been sounder than those of the layman, but until independent evidence could be obtained, they were no more satisfactory as explanations of behavior. Direct information about many of the chemical and electrical processes in the nervous system is now available. Statements about the nervous system are no longer necessarily inferential or fictional. But there is still a measure of circularity in much physiological explanation, even in the writings of specialists. In World War I a familiar disorder was called "shell shock." Disturbances in behavior were explained by arguing that violent explosions had damaged the structure of the nervous system, though no direct evidence of such damage was available. In World War II the same disorder was classified as "neuropsychiatric." The prefix seems to show a continuing unwillingness to abandon explanations in terms of hypothetical neural damage.

Eventually a science of the nervous system based upon direct observation rather than inference will describe the neural states and events which immediately precede instances of behavior. We shall know the precise neurological conditions which immediately precede, say, the response, "No, thank you." These events in turn will be found to be preceded by other neurological events, and these in turn by others. This series will lead us back to events outside the nervous system and, eventually, outside the organism. [Later] we shall consider external events of this sort in some detail. We shall then be better able to evaluate the place of neurological explanations of behavior. However, we may note here that we do not have and may never have this sort of neurological information at the moment it is needed in order to predict a specific instance of behavior. It is even more unlikely that we shall be able to alter the nervous system directly in order to set up the antecedent conditions of a particular instance. The causes to be sought in the nervous system are, therefore, of limited usefulness in the prediction and control of specific behavior.

Psychic Inner Causes

An even more common practice is to explain behavior in terms of an inner agent which lacks physical dimensions and is called "mental" or "psychic." The purest form of the psychic explanation is seen in the animism of primitive peoples. From the immobility of the body after death it is inferred that a spirit responsible for movement has departed. The *enthusiastic* person is, as the etymology of the word implies, energized by a "god within." It is only a modest refinement to attribute every feature of the behavior of the physical organism to a corresponding feature of the "mind" or of some inner "personality." The inner man is regarded as driving the body very much as the man at the steering wheel drives a car. The inner man wills an action, the outer executes it. The inner loses his appetite, the outer stops eating. The inner man wants and the outer man gets. The inner has the impulse which the outer obeys.

It is not the layman alone who resorts to these practices, for many reputable psychologists use a similar dualistic system of explanation. The inner man is sometimes personified clearly, as when delinquent behavior is attributed to a "disordered personality," or he may be dealt with in fragments, as when behavior is attributed to mental processes, faculties, and traits. Since the inner man does not occupy space, he may be multiplied at will. It has been argued that a single physical organism is controlled by several psychic agents and that its behavior is the resultant of their several wills. The Freudian concepts of the ego, superego, and id are often used in this way. They are frequently regarded as nonsubstantial creatures, often in violent conflict, whose defeats or victories lead to the adjusted or maladjusted behavior of the physical organism in which they reside.

Direct observation of the mind comparable with the observation of the nervous system has not proved feasible. It is true that many people believe that they observe their "mental states" just as the physiologist observes neural events, but another interpretation of what they observe is possible, as we shall see [later]. Introspective psychology no longer pretends to supply direct information about events which are the causal antecedents, rather than the mere accompaniments, of behavior. It defines its "subjective" events in ways which strip them of any usefulness in a causal analysis. The events appealed to in early mentalistic explanations of behavior have remained beyond the reach of observation. Freud insisted upon this by emphasizing the role of the unconscious—a frank recognition that important mental processes are not directly observable. The Freudian literature supplies many examples of behavior from which unconscious wishes, impulses,

instincts, and emotions are inferred. Unconscious thought-processes have also been used to explain intellectual achievements. Though the mathematician may feel that he knows "how he thinks," he is often unable to give a coherent account of the mental processes leading to the solution of a specific problem. But any mental event which is unconscious is necessarily inferential, and the explanation is therefore not based upon independent observations of a valid cause.

The fictional nature of this form of inner cause is shown by the ease with which the mental process is discovered to have just the properties needed to account for the behavior. When a professor turns up in the wrong classroom or gives the wrong lecture, it is because his *mind* is, at least for the moment, *absent*. If he forgets to give a reading assignment, it is because it has slipped his *mind* (a hint from the class may re*mind* him of it). He begins to tell an old joke but pauses for a moment, and it is evident to everyone that he is trying to make up his *mind* whether or not he has already used the joke that term. His lectures grow more tedious with the years, and questions from the class confuse him more and more, because his *mind* is failing. What he says is often disorganized because his *ideas* are confused. He is occasionally unnecessarily emphatic because of the force of his *ideas*. When he repeats himself, it is because he has an *idée fixe*; and when he repeats what others have said, it is because he borrows his *ideas*. Upon occasion there is nothing in what he says because he lacks *ideas*. In all this it is obvious that the mind and the ideas, together with their special characteristics, are being invented on the spot to provide spurious explanations. A science of behavior can hope to gain very little from so cavalier a practice. Since mental or psychic events are asserted to lack the dimensions of physical science, we have an additional reason for rejecting them.

Conceptual Inner Causes

The commonest inner causes have no specific dimensions at all, either neurological or psychic. When we say that a man eats *because* he is hungry, smokes a great deal *because* he has the tobacco habit, fights *because* of the instinct of pugnacity, behaves brilliantly *because* of his intelligence, or plays the piano well *because* of his musical ability, we seem to be referring to causes. But on analysis these phrases prove to be merely redundant descriptions. A single set of facts is described by the two statements: "He eats" and "He is hungry." A single set of facts is described by the two statements: "He smokes a great deal" and "He has the smoking habit." A single set of facts is described by the two statements: "He plays well" and "He has musical ability." The practice of explaining one statement in terms of the other is dangerous because it suggests that we have found the cause and therefore need search no further. Moreover, such terms as "hunger," "habit," and "intelligence" convert what are essentially the properties of a process or relation into what appear to be things. Thus we are unprepared for the properties eventually to be discovered in the behavior itself and continue to look for something which may not exist.

THE VARIABLES OF WHICH BEHAVIOR IS A FUNCTION

The practice of looking inside the organism for an explanation of behavior has tended to obscure the variables which are immediately available for a scientific analysis. These variables lie outside the organism, in its immediate environment and in its environmental history. They have a physical status to which the usual techniques of science are adapted, and they make it possible to explain behavior as other subjects are explained in science. These independent variables are of many sorts and their relations to behavior are often subtle and complex, but we cannot hope to give an adequate account of behavior without analyzing them.

Consider the act of drinking a glass of water. This is not likely to be an important bit of behavior in anyone's life, but it supplies a convenient example. We may describe the topography of the behavior in such a way that a given instance may be identified quite accurately by any qualified observer. Suppose now we bring someone into a room and place a glass of water before him. Will he drink? There appear to be only two possibilities: either he will or he will not. But we speak of the *chances* that he will drink, and this notion may be refined for scientific use. What we want to evaluate is the *probability* that he will drink. This may range from virtual certainty that drinking will occur to virtual certainty that it will not. The very considerable problem of how to measure such a

probability will be discussed later. For the moment, we are interested in how the probability may be increased or decreased.

Everyday experience suggests several possibilities, and laboratory and clinical observations have added others. It is decidedly not true that a horse may be led to water but cannot be made to drink. By arranging a history of severe deprivation we could be "absolutely sure" that drinking would occur. In the same way we may be sure that the glass of water in our experiment will be drunk. Although we are not likely to arrange them experimentally, deprivations of the necessary magnitude sometimes occur outside the laboratory. We may obtain an effect similar to that of deprivation by speeding up the excretion of water. For example, we may induce sweating by raising the temperature of the room or by forcing heavy exercise, or we may increase the excretion of urine by mixing salt or urea in food taken prior to the experiment. It is also well known that loss of blood, as on a battlefield, sharply increases the probability of drinking. On the other hand, we may set the probability at virtually zero by inducing or forcing our subject to drink a large quantity of water before the experiment.

If we are to predict whether or not our subject will drink, we must know as much as possible about these variables. If we are to induce him to drink, we must be able to manipulate them. In both cases, moreover, either for accurate prediction or control, we must investigate the effect of each variable quantitatively with the methods and techniques of a laboratory science.

Other variables may, of course, affect the result. Our subject may be "afraid" that something has been added to the water as a practical joke or for experimental purposes. He may even "suspect" that the water has been poisoned. He may have grown up in a culture in which water is drunk only when no one is watching. He may refuse to drink simply to prove that we cannot predict or control his behavior. These possibilities do not disprove the relations between drinking and the variables listed in the preceding paragraphs; they simply remind us that other variables may have to be taken into account. We must know the history of our subject with respect to the behavior of drinking water, and if we cannot eliminate social factors from the situation, then we must know the history of his personal relations to people resembling the experimenter. Adequate prediction in any science requires information about all relevant variables, and the control of a subject matter for practical purposes makes the same demands.

Other types of "explanation" do not permit us to dispense with these requirements or to fulfill them in any easier way. It is of no help to be told that our subject will drink provided he was born under a particular sign of the zodiac which shows a preoccupation with water or provided he is the lean and thirsty type or was, in short, "born thirsty." Explanations in terms of inner states or agents, however, may require some further comment. To what extent is it helpful to be told, "He drinks because he is thirsty"? If to be thirsty means nothing more than to have a tendency to drink, this is mere redundancy. If it means that he drinks because of a state of thirst, an inner causal event is invoked. If this state is purely inferential—if no dimensions are assigned to it which would make direct observation possible—it cannot serve as an explanation. But if it has physiological or psychic properties, what role can it play in a science of behavior?

The physiologist may point out that several ways of raising the probability of drinking have a common effect: they increase the concentration of solutions in the body. Through some mechanism not yet well understood, this may bring about a corresponding change in the nervous system which in turn makes drinking more probable. In the same way, it may be argued that all these operations make the organism "feel thirsty" or "want a drink" and that such a psychic state also acts upon the nervous system in some unexplained way to induce drinking. In each case we have a causal chain consisting of three links: (1) an operation performed upon the organism from without—for example, water deprivation; (2) an inner condition—for example, physiological or psychic thirst; and (3) a kind of behavior—for example, drinking. Independent information about the second link would obviously permit us to predict the third without recourse to the first. It would be a preferred type of variable because it would be nonhistoric; the first link may lie in the past history of the organism, but the second is a current condition. Direct information about the second link is, however, seldom, if ever, available. Sometimes we infer the second link from the third: an animal is judged to be thirsty if it

drinks. In that case, the explanation is spurious. Sometimes we infer the second link from the first: an animal is said to be thirsty if it has not drunk for a long time. In that case, we obviously cannot dispense with the prior history.

The second link is useless in the *control* of behavior unless we can manipulate it. At the moment, we have no way of directly altering neural processes at appropriate moments in the life of a behaving organism, nor has any way been discovered to alter a psychic process. We usually set up the second link through the first: we make an animal thirsty, in either the physiological or the psychic sense, by depriving it of water, feeding it salt, and so on. In that case, the second link obviously does not permit us to dispense with the first. Even if some new technical discovery were to enable us to set up or change the second link directly, we should still have to deal with those enormous areas in which human behavior is controlled through manipulation of the first link. A technique of operating upon the second link would increase our control of behavior, but the techniques which have already been developed would still remain to be analyzed.

The most objectionable practice is to follow the causal sequence back only as far as a hypothetical second link. This is a serious handicap both in a theoretical sense and in the practical control of behavior. It is no help to be told that to get an organism to drink we are simply to "make it thirsty" unless we are also told how this is to be done. When we have obtained the necessary prescription for thirst, the whole proposal is more complex than it need be. Similarly, when an example of maladjusted behavior is explained by saying that the individual is "suffering from anxiety," we have still to be told the cause of the anxiety. But the external conditions which are then invoked could have been directly related to the maladjusted behavior. Again, when we are told that a man stole a loaf of bread because "he was hungry," we have still to learn of the external conditions responsible for the "hunger." These conditions would have sufficed to explain the theft.

The objection to inner states is not that they do not exist, but that they are not relevant in a functional analysis. We cannot account for the behavior of any system while staying wholly inside it; eventually we must turn to forces operating upon the organism from without. Unless there is a weak spot in our causal chain so that the second link is not lawfully determined by the first, or the third by the second, then the first and third links must be lawfully related. If we must always go back beyond the second link for prediction and control, we may avoid many tiresome and exhausting digressions by examining the third link as a function of the first. Valid information about the second link may throw light upon this relationship but can in no way alter it.

A FUNCTIONAL ANALYSIS

The external variables of which behavior is a function provide for what may be called a causal or functional analysis. We undertake to predict and control the behavior of the individual organism. This is our "dependent variable"—the effect for which we are to find the cause. Our "independent variables"—the causes of behavior—are the external conditions of which behavior is a function. Relations between the two—the "cause-and-effect relationships" in behavior—are the laws of a science. A synthesis of these laws expressed in quantitative terms yields a comprehensive picture of the organism as a behaving system.

This must be done within the bounds of a natural science. We cannot assume that behavior has any peculiar properties which require unique methods or special kinds of knowledge. It is often argued that an act is not so important as the "intent" which lies behind it, or that it can be described only in terms of what it "means" to the behaving individual or to others whom it may affect. If statements of this sort are useful for scientific purposes, they must be based upon observable events, and we may confine ourselves to such events exclusively in a functional analysis. We shall see later that although such terms as "meaning" and "intent" appear to refer to properties of behavior, they usually conceal references to independent variables. This is also true of "aggressive," "friendly," "disorganized," "intelligent," and other terms which appear to describe properties of behavior but in reality refer to its controlling relations.

The independent variables must also be described in physical terms. An effort is often made to avoid the labor of analyzing a physical situation by guessing what it "means" to an organism or by distinguishing between the physical world and a psychological world of "experience." This practice also reflects a confusion between dependent and independent variables. The events affecting an organism must be capable of description in the language of physical science. It is sometimes argued that certain "social forces" or the "influences" of culture or tradition are exceptions. But we cannot appeal to entities of this sort without explaining how they can affect both the scientist and the individual under observation. The physical events which must then be appealed to in such an explanation will supply us with alternative material suitable for a physical analysis.

By confining ourselves to these observable events, we gain a considerable advantage, not only in theory, but in practice. A "social force" is no more useful in manipulating behavior than an inner state of hunger, anxiety, or skepticism. Just as we must trace these inner events to the manipulable variables of which they are said to be functions before we may put them to practical use, so we must identify the physical events through which a "social force" is said to affect the organism before we can manipulate it for purposes of control. In dealing with the directly observable data we need not refer to either the inner state or the outer force.

Discussion Questions

1. How much of human behavior can Skinner account for? Can he account for all that we do and experience? Or are some areas left out? For instance, what about inner thoughts that we keep to ourselves, thoughts that do not necessarily lead to any particular action?

2. Skinner believed that studying the nervous system was of little help in understanding human behavior. But Skinner wrote this in 1953, and the science of neurology has made

great advances since that time. Given these advances in the scientific study of the brain, do you think Skinner would continue to hold this position? Why or why not?

3. Consider 'falling in love'. Can the experience of falling in love be completely and thoroughly described using only observable descriptions of external behavior? If we had an exhaustive list of all the behaviors a person who had fallen in love performed, would we know all there is to know about being in love?

For Further Reading

Skinner's defense of behaviorism can be found in numerous works, including *The Behavior of Organisms* (1938), *Science and Human Behavior* (1953), *Beyond Freedom and Dignity* (1971), and *About Behaviorism* (1974). For biographical information see Skinner's autobiographies: *Particulars of My Life* (1976), *The Shaping of a Behaviorist* (1979), and *A Matter of Consequences* (1983).

For other introductions to behaviorism see *Philosophy of Psychology* (1974), edited by S. C. Brown; *Matter and Consciousness* (1984), by Patricia M. Churchland; and *Scientific Psychology, Principles and Approaches* (1965), edited by Wolman and Nagel. For critiques of behaviorism see *Brainstorms* (1978), by Daniel Dennett; *The Science of Mind* (1991), by Owen Flanagan; and *Psychological Explanation* (1968), by J. Fodor.

16   SENSATIONS AND BRAIN PROCESSES
J. J. C. Smart

J. J. C. Smart (1920 –) was born and educated in England but moved to Australia in 1950 to take the Chair of Philosophy at Adelaide University. Smart eventually found his way to the Institute of Advanced Studies at the Australian National University in 1976 and became an Emeritus Professor in 1985.

As a philosopher Smart is best known for his defense of **act utilitarianism** and **materialism.** His major publications in these areas are *An Outline of a System of Utilitarian Ethics* (1961) and *Philosophy and Scientific Realism* (1963).

It is Smart's materialism that interests us here. As a materialist, Smart believes that nothing exists in the world except for those entities that physicists work with: physical entities such as atoms and molecules, and the things of which they are made. As such, Smart flatly rejects the dualist's picture of the universe—immaterial minds interacting with our physical brains. Physical brain states/brain processes such as being in pain do not causally lead to, or correlate with, a separate immaterial state of consciousness of being in pain because there are nothing but physical entities. Conscious states such as being in pain are nothing other than— that is, are identical to—particular physical brain states. But if this is true, Smart has a lot of explaining to do because we seem to talk about brain states and mental states as if they are very different things. In the following article Smart attempts to refute various objections to his mind-brain identity theory.

Reading Questions

1. What is the one thing that seems to be left outside of the physico-chemical picture of the world?
2. Does Smart believe that there are philosophical arguments that compel us to be dualists?
3. Exactly what does the thesis "sensations are brain processes" claim?
4. What sense of identity does the brain-process doctrine assert?
5. What are the objections to the view that the processes reported in sensation statements are in fact processes in the brain? Hint: There are seven different objections.
6. Does Smart believe that the materialist can rule out epiphenomenalism? If not, why not?
7. What principle favors the brain-process theory over epiphenomenalism?

. . . It seems to me that science is increasingly giving us a viewpoint whereby organisms are able to be seen as physico-chemical mechanisms: it seems that even the behavior of man himself will one day be explicable in mechanistic terms. There does seem to be, so far as science is concerned, nothing in the world but increasingly complex arrangements of physical constituents. All except for one place: in consciousness. That is, for a full description of what is going on in a man you would have to mention not only the physical processes in his tissue, glands, nervous system, and so forth, but also his states of consciousness: his visual, auditory, and tactual sensations, his aches and pains. That these should be *correlated* with brain processes does not help, for to say that they are *correlated* is to say that they are something "over and above." You cannot correlate something with itself. You correlate footprints with burglars, but not Bill Sikes the burglar with Bill Sikes the burglar. So sensations, states of consciousness, do seem to be the one sort of thing left outside the physicalist picture, and for various reasons I just cannot believe that this can be so. That everything should be explicable in terms of physics (together of course with descriptions of the ways in which the parts are put together—roughly, biology is to physics as radio-engineering is to electro-magnetism) except the occurrence of sensations seems to me to be frankly unbelievable. Such sensations would be "nomological danglers," to use Feigl's expression. It is not often realized how odd would be the laws whereby these nomological danglers would dangle. It is sometimes asked, "Why can't there be psycho-physical laws which are of a novel sort, just as the laws of electricity and magnetism were novelties from the standpoint of

Newtonian mechanics?" Certainly we are pretty sure in the future to come across new ultimate laws of a novel type, but I expect them to relate simple constituents: for example, whatever ultimate particles are then in vogue. I cannot believe that ultimate laws of nature could relate simple constituents to configurations consisting of perhaps billions of neurons (and goodness knows how many billion billions of ultimate particles) all put together for all the world as though their main purpose in life was to be a negative feedback mechanism of a complicated sort. Such ultimate laws would be like nothing so far known in science. They have a queer "smell" to them. I am just unable to believe in the nomological danglers themselves, or in the laws whereby they would dangle. If any philosophical arguments seemed to compel us to believe in such things, I would suspect a catch in the argument. In any case it is the object of this paper to show that there are no philosophical arguments which compel us to be dualists. . . .

. . . Why should not sensations just be brain processes of a certain sort? There are, of course, well-known (as well as lesser-known) philosophical objections to the view that reports of sensations are reports of brain-processes, but I shall try to argue that these arguments are by no means as cogent as is commonly thought to be the case.

Let me first try to state more accurately the thesis that sensations are brain processes. It is not the thesis that, for example, "after-image" or "ache" means the same as "brain process of sort *X*" (where "*X*" is replaced by a description of a certain sort of brain process). It is that, in so far as "after-image" or "ache" is a report of a process, it is a report of a process that *happens to be* a brain process. It follows that the thesis does not claim that sensation statements can be *translated* into statements about brain processes. Nor does it claim that the logic of a sensation statement is the same as that of a brain-process statement. All it claims is that in so far as a sensation statement is a report of something, that something is in fact a brain process. Sensations are nothing over and above brain processes. Nations are nothing "over and above" citizens, but this does not prevent the logic of nation statements being very different from the logic of citizen statements, nor does it insure the translatability of nation statements into citizen statements. (I do not, however, wish to assert that the relation of sensation statements to brain-process statements is very like that of nation statements to citizen statements. Nations do not just *happen to be* nothing over and above citizens, for example. I bring in the "nations" example merely to make a negative point: that the fact that the logic of A-statements is different from that of B-statements does not insure that A's are anything over and above B's.)

Remarks on identity: When I say that a sensation is a brain process or that lightning is an electric discharge, I am using "is" in the sense of strict identity. (Just as in the—in this case necessary—proposition "7 is identical with the smallest prime number greater than 5.") When I say that a sensation is a brain process or that lightning is an electric discharge I do not mean just that the sensation is somehow spatially or temporally continuous with the brain process or that the lightning is just spatially or temporally continuous with the discharge. When on the other hand I say that the successful general is the same person as the small boy who stole the apples I mean only that the successful general I see before me is a time slice of the same four-dimensional object of which the small boy stealing apples is an earlier time slice. However, the four-dimensional object which has the general-I-see-before-me for its late time slice is identical in the strict sense with the four-dimensional object which has the small-boy-stealing-apples for an early time slice. I distinguish these two senses of "is identical with" because I wish to make it clear that the brain-process doctrine asserts identity in the *strict* sense.

I shall now discuss various possible objections to the view that the processes reported in sensation statements are in fact processes in the brain. Most of us have met some of these objections in our first year as philosophy students. All the more reason to take a good look at them. Others of the objections will be more recondite and subtle.

Objection 1: Any illiterate peasant can talk perfectly well about his after-images, or how things look or feel to him, or about his aches and pains, and yet he may know nothing whatever about neurophysiology. A man may, like Aristotle, believe that the brain is an organ for cooling the body without any impairment of his ability to make true statements about his sensations. Hence the things we are talking about when we describe our sensations cannot be processes in the brain.

Reply: You might as well say that a nation of slug-abeds, who never saw the morning star or knew of its existence, or who had never thought of the expression "the Morning Star," but who used the expression "the Evening Star" perfectly well, could not use this expression to refer to the same entity as we refer to (and describe as) "the Morning Star."

You may object that the Morning Star is in a sense not the very same thing as the Evening Star, but only something spatio-temporally continuous with it. That is, you may say that the Morning Star is not the Evening Star in the strict sense of "identity" that I distinguished earlier. I can perhaps forestall this objection by considering the slug-abeds to be New Zealanders and the early risers to be Englishmen. Then the thing the New Zealanders describe as "the Morning Star" could be the very same thing (in the strict sense) as the Englishmen describe as "the Evening Star." And yet they could be ignorant of this fact.

There is, however, a more plausible example. Consider lightning. Modern physical science tells us that lightning is a certain kind of electrical discharge due to ionization of clouds of water-vapor in the atmosphere. This, it is now believed, is what the true nature of lightning is. Note that there are not two things: a flash of lightning and an electrical discharge. There is one thing, a flash of lightning, which is described scientifically as an electrical discharge to the earth from a cloud of ionized water-molecules. The case is not at all like that of explaining a footprint by reference to a burglar. We say that what lightning really is, what its true nature as revealed by science is, is an electric discharge. (It is not the true nature of a footprint to be a burglar.)

To forestall irrelevant objections, I should like to make it clear that by "lightning" I mean the publicly observable physical object, lightning, not a visual sense-datum of lightning. I say that the publicly observable physical object lightning is in fact the electric discharge, not just a correlate of it. The sense-datum, or at least the having of the sense-datum, the "look" of lightning, may well in my view be a correlate of the electric discharge. For in my view it is a brain state *caused* by the lightning. But we should no more confuse sensations of lightning with lightning than we confuse sensations of a table with the table.

In short, the reply to Objection 1 is that there can be contingent statements of the form "A is identical with B," and a person may well know that something is an A without knowing that it is a B. An illiterate peasant might well be able to talk about his sensations without knowing about his brain processes, just as he can talk about lightning though he knows nothing of electricity.

Objection 2: It is only a contingent fact (if it is a fact) that when we have a certain kind of sensation there is a certain kind of process in our brain. Indeed it is possible, though perhaps in the highest degree unlikely, that our present physiological theories will be as out of date as the ancient theory connecting mental processes with goings on in the heart. It follows that when we report a sensation we are not reporting a brain-process.

Reply: The objection certainly proves that when we say "I have an after-image" we cannot *mean* something of the form "I have such and

such a brain-process." But this does not show that what we report (having an after-image) is not *in fact* a brain process. "I see lightning" does not *mean* "I see an electric discharge." Indeed, it is logically possible (though highly unlikely) that the electrical discharge account of lightning might one day be given up. Again, "I see the Evening Star" does not *mean* the same as "I see the Morning Star," and yet "the Evening Star and the Morning Star are one and the same thing" is a contingent proposition. Possibly Objection 2 derives some of its apparent strength from a "Fido"–Fido theory of meaning. If the meaning of an expression were what the expression named, then of course it *would* follow from the fact that "sensation" and "brain-process" have different meanings that they cannot name one and the same thing.

Objection 3: Even if Objections 1 and 2 do not prove that sensations are something over and above brain-processes, they do prove that the qualities of sensations are something over and above the qualities of brain-processes. That is, it may be possible to get out of asserting the existence of irreducibly psychic processes, but not out of asserting the existence of irreducibly psychic *properties.* For suppose we identify the Morning Star with the Evening Star. Then there must be some properties which logically imply that of being the Morning Star, and quite distinct properties which entail that of being the Evening Star. Again, there must be some properties (for example, that of being a yellow flash) which are logically distinct from those in the physicalist story. . . .

Now how do I get over the objection that a sensation can be identified with a brain process only if it has some phenomenal property, not possessed by brain processes, whereby one-half of the identification may be, so to speak, pinned down?

My suggestion is as follows. When a person says, "I see a yellowish-orange after-image," he is saying something like this: "*There is something going on which is like what is going on when* I have my eyes open, am awake, and there is an orange illuminated in good light in front of me, that is, when I really see an orange." (And there is no reason why a person should not say the same thing when he is having a veridical sense-datum, so long as we construe "like" in the last sentence in such a sense that something can be like itself.) Notice that the italicized words, namely "there is something going on which is like what is going on when," are all quasi-logical or topic-neutral words. This explains why the ancient Greek peasant's reports about his sensations can be neutral between dualistic metaphysics or my materialistic metaphysics. It explains how sensations can be brain-processes and yet how those who report them need know nothing about brain-processes. For he reports them only very abstractly as "something going on which is like what is going on when . . ." Similarly, a person may say "someone is in the room," thus reporting truly that the doctor is in the room, even though he has never heard of doctors. (There are not two people in the room: "someone" *and* the doctor.) This account of sensation statements also explains the singular elusiveness of "raw feels"—why no one seems to be able to pin any properties on them. Raw feels, in my view, are colorless for the very same reason that *something* is colorless. This does not mean that sensations do not have properties, for if they are brain-processes they certainly have properties. It only means that in speaking of them as being like or unlike one another we need not know or mention these properties.

This, then, is how I would reply to Objection 3. The strength of my reply depends on the possibility of our being able to report that one thing is like another without being able to state the respect in which it is like. I am not sure whether this is so or not, and that is why I regard Objection 3 as the strongest with which I have to deal.

Objection 4: The after-image is not in physical space. The brain-process is. So the after-image is not a brain-process.

Reply: This is an *ignoratio elenchi.* I am not arguing that the after-image is a brain-process,

but that the experience of having an after-image is a brain-process. It is the *experience* which is reported in the introspective report. Similarly, if it is objected that the after-image is yellowy-orange but that a surgeon looking into your brain would see nothing yellowy-orange, my reply is that it is the experience of seeing yellowy-orange that is being described, and this experience is not a yellowy-orange something. So to say that a brain-process cannot be yellowy-orange is not to say that a brain-process cannot in fact be the experience of having a yellowy-orange after-image. There is, in a sense, no such thing as an after-image or a sense-datum, though there is such a thing as the experience of having an image, and this experience is described indirectly in material object language, not in phenomenal language, for there is no such thing. We describe the experience by saying, in effect, that it is like the experience we have when, for example, we really see a yellowy-orange patch on the wall. Trees and wallpaper can be green, but not the experience of seeing or imagining a tree or wallpaper. (Or if they are described as green or yellow this can only be in a derived sense.)

Objection 5: It would make sense to say of a molecular movement in the brain that it is swift or slow, straight or circular, but it makes no sense to say this of the experience of seeing something yellow.

Reply: So far we have not given sense to talk of experiences as swift or slow, straight or circular. But I am not claiming that "experience" and "brain-process" mean the same or even that they have the same logic. "Somebody" and "the doctor" do not have the same logic, but this does not lead us to suppose that talking about somebody telephoning is talking about someone over and above, say, the doctor. The ordinary man when he reports an experience is reporting that something is going on, but he leaves it open as to what sort of thing is going on, whether in a material solid medium, or perhaps in some sort of gaseous medium, or even perhaps in some sort of nonspatial medium (if this makes sense). All that I am saying is that "experience" and "brain-process" may in fact refer to the same thing, and if so we may easily adopt a convention (which is not a change in our present rules for the use of experience words but an addition to them) whereby it would make sense to talk of an experience in terms appropriate to physical processes.

Objection 6: Sensations are private, brain processes are *public.* If I sincerely say, "I see a yellowish-orange after-image" and I am not making a verbal mistake, then I cannot be wrong. But I can be wrong about a brain-process. The scientist looking into my brain might be having an illusion. Moreover, it makes sense to say that two or more people are observing the same brain-process but not that two or more people are reporting the same inner experience.

Reply: This shows that the language of introspective reports has a different logic from the language of material processes. It is obvious that until the brain-process theory is much improved and widely accepted there will be no *criteria* for saying "Smith has an experience of such-and-such a sort" *except* Smith's introspective reports. So we have adopted a rule of language that (normally) what Smith says goes.

Objection 7: I can imagine myself turned to stone and yet having images, aches, pains, and so on.

Reply: I can imagine that the electrical theory of lightning is false, that lightning is some sort of purely optical phenomenon. I can imagine that lightning is not an electrical discharge. I can imagine that the Evening Star is not the Morning Star. But it is. All the objection shows is that "experience" and "brain-process" do not have the same meaning. It does not show that an experience is not in fact a brain process. . . .

I have now considered a number of objections to the brain-process thesis. I wish now to conclude by some remarks on the logical status of the thesis itself. U. T. Place seems to hold that it is a straight-out scientific hypothesis. If so, he is partly right and partly wrong. If the issue is between (say) a brain-process thesis and a heart thesis, or a liver thesis, or a kidney thesis, then the issue is a purely empirical one, and the verdict is overwhelmingly in favor of the brain. The right sorts of things don't go on in the heart, liver, or kidney, nor do these organs possess the right sort of complexity of structure. On the other hand, if the issue is between a brain-or-heart-or-liver-or-kidney thesis (that is, some form of materialism) on the one hand and epiphenomenalism on the other hand, then the issue is not an empirical one. For there is no conceivable experiment which could decide between materialism and epiphenomenalism. This latter issue is not like the average straight-out empirical issue in science, but like the issue between the nineteenth-century English naturalist Philip Gosse and the orthodox geologists and paleontologists of his day. According to Gosse, the earth was created about 4000 B.C. exactly as described in *Genesis,* with twisted rock strata, "evidence" of erosion, and so forth, and all sorts of fossils, all in their appropriate strata, just as if the usual evolutionist story had been true. Clearly this theory is in a sense irrefutable: no evidence can possibly tell against it. Let us ignore the theological setting in which Philip Gosse's hypothesis had been placed, thus ruling out objections of a theological kind, such as "what a queer God who would go to such elaborate lengths to deceive us." Let us suppose that it is held that the universe just *began* in 4004 B.C. with the initial conditions just everywhere as they were in 4004 B.C., and in particular that our own planet began with sediment in the rivers, eroded cliffs, fossils in the rocks, and so on. No scientist would ever entertain this as a serious hypothesis, consistent though it is with all possible evidence. The hypothesis offends against the principles of parsimony and simplicity. There would be far too many brute and inexplicable facts. Why are pterodactyl bones just as they are? No explanation in terms of the evolution of pterodactyls from earlier forms of life would any longer be possible. We would have millions of facts about the world as it was in 4004 B.C. that just have to be *accepted.*

The issue between the brain-process theory and epiphenomenalism seems to be of the above sort. (Assuming that a behavioristic reduction of introspective reports is not possible.) If it be agreed that there are no cogent philosophical arguments which force us into accepting dualism, and if the brain process theory and dualism are equally consistent with the facts, then the principles of parsimony and simplicity seem to me to decide overwhelmingly in favor of the brain-process theory. As I pointed out earlier, dualism involves a large number of irreducible psychophysical laws (whereby the "nomological danglers" dangle) of a queer sort, that just have to be taken on trust, and are just as difficult to swallow as the irreducible facts about the paleontology of the earth with which we are faced on Philip Gosse's theory.

Discussion Questions

1. Would Skinner find Smart's explanation of consciousness satisfactory? Why or why not? What are the differences between their accounts? Are these differences significant? Which view do you find to be stronger?

2. Suppose Smart's physico-chemical explanation is correct. Does this affect religious explanations of human life? If so, in what ways? Is life after death possible based on this explanation? What about free will? Why or why not?

3. Suppose the materialist explanation of consciousness is true. What explanation would materialists give for basic human experiences such as being happy, being sad, having a purpose in life, falling in love, being afraid, and so forth? Would all of these experiences be reduced to mere states of the brain? Why or why not? Does materialism offer an adequate explanation of these experiences?

For Further Reading

Smart's major work on materialism is *Philosophy and Scientific Realism* (1963). For a collection of essays on Smart's views, see *Metaphysics and Morality* (1987), edited by P. Pettit. Materialism is also defended in *A Neurocomputational Perspective* (1989), by Patricia M. Churchland, and *Materialism: An Affirmative History and Definition* (1995), by R. C. Vitzthum.

For critiques of materialism see *The Immaterial Self* (1991), by J. Foster; *Perception, Mind and Personal Identity* (1994), by D. H. Lund; and *Matter and Sense* (1982), by H. Robinson. See also *Objections to Physicalism* (1996), edited by H. Robinson, and *Materialism and the Mind-Body Problem* (1971), edited by D. M. Rosenthal.

CHAPTER 4

HOW DOES SOCIETY SHAPE MY IDENTITY?

Each of us has an identity, a unique set of personal traits that define us as individuals. This includes our tastes and preferences, our choices and desires, as well as our self-understanding of who we are and our place in the world. Where does that identity come from? Is it something we are each individually responsible for? Or is our identity a result of social forces, largely outside of our control? This is a crucial question, for if our identity impacts our life prospects, how individuals acquire their 'sense-of-themselves' is a vital concern. This chapter explores that question by examining the ways in which some philosophers have argued that society shapes who we are. Instead of discussions on these issues in general terms, the following selections focus on two areas of particular relevance for today's troubled society: gender identity and racial identity. Where do our beliefs about gender come from? How exactly do these roles affect our beliefs and our future? Do members of racial minorities see the world in a different light than do the members of the racial majority? Does the racial majority view and treat members of the minority any differently than its own members? If so, what impact does all of this have on society? How can things be improved?

In the first selection, "Gender Personality and the Reproduction of Mothering," Nancy Chodorow examines some of the processes affecting gender identity and how these processes limit the possibilities open to women—processes that are, unfortunately, self-perpetuating. If Chodorow is right, then whether society is truly just with respect to its treatment of women is an open question. Are women truly free to be who they want to be in our culture, or does society choose their roles for them? Do women actually prefer to be mothers, teachers, and nurses, or is this just what is expected of them?

Susan Bordo also investigates various social forces that affect women. In her article, "Anorexia Nervosa: Psychopathology as the Crystallization of Culture," Bordo links these forces to the negative, and often destructive, perception many women have of their bodies. Is the increasing prevalence of anorexia nervosa a manifestation of social stereotypes gone horribly wrong? Would anorexia nervosa be less prevalent if less emphasis were placed on physical beauty or if ideals of feminine beauty were more realistic and healthy?

In the next two selections, Frantz Fanon and Clyde Warrior provide a firsthand glimpse of the experience of racial minority, the experience of being black and Native American, respectively. Interestingly, both Fanon and Warrior suggest that the morale of minorities can be improved through cultural education, that is, by learning about their rich cultural heritage. Clyde Warrior also emphasizes the need for autonomy, the freedom for a people to govern their own fate. He writes, "For the sake of our psychic stability as well as our physical well-being we must be free men and exercise free choices. We must make decisions about our own destinies. We must be able to learn and profit by our own mistakes. Only then can we become competent and prosperous communities." The accounts of Fanon and Warrior raise troubling questions about how minority identity is shaped and whether the social construction of identity restricts the freedom and self-definition of racial minorities.

The final selection looks at both gender and racial identity, focusing on the role language plays in creating our social identities and self-conception. Why consider the role language plays? One reason is that language may not merely be a neutral representation of the world—instead, language itself may fundamentally distort our understanding of the world, perhaps in harmful and injurious ways. Robert Baker, in the last reading of this chapter, argues that the grammatical structure of metaphors used to describe race, sexual intercourse, and gender is part of a pattern of prejudice and oppression—social realities made real and reinforced through language. The harmful effects of racial and sexual language, including the way it shapes the identity of each of us, remain invisible until uncovered and exposed. Perhaps then new ways of speaking about race and gender can help to shape our identities in directions that liberate humans from past patterns of discrimination and injustice.

17 GENDER PERSONALITY AND THE REPRODUCTION OF MOTHERING
Nancy Chodorow

Gender is a complex phenomenon, and there is no single way in which we experience either maleness or femaleness. Nonetheless, when viewed from a sociological standpoint, certain behavior patterns and institutions emerge. Chief among these are the gendered roles of child care and parenting: Women have been and continue to be the primary caretakers of children. What explanations can be offered for this?

Nancy Chodorow (1944–), a sociologist at the University of California, Berkeley, has written an influential account of the gendered pattern of mothering. In *The Reproduction of Mothering,* a groundbreaking text in feminist psychoanalysis, Chodorow considers why, given all of the changes that have occurred throughout history, women continue to be assigned primary responsibility for raising children. Rejecting the claim that women are naturally more suited for mothering, Chodorow offers a psychoanalytic account of the formation of gender identity. Suitability for mothering is not the simple adoption of a cultural gender role, but a formative, psychological event that constructs the self-identity of girls in such a way that they are more suited to the task of mothering. According to this theory, because primary caretakers are women ('mothers'), girls can identify continuously with their

SOURCE: *The Reproduction of Mothering: Psychoanalysis and the Sociology of Gender* by Nancy Chodorow. Berkeley, CA: University of California Press. Copyright © 1978 by The Regents of the University of California. Used with permission from The University of California Press.

mothers, whereas boys must break with that early childhood identity, a break experienced as an oedipal crisis. Girls, as a result, define themselves in terms of their social and personal relationships (for example, 'the sister-of- . . .' or 'the daughter-of- . . .'), more readily adopting the gendered role of mothering. Boys, on the other hand, define themselves as solitary individuals, alone and separate, and thus they move more readily outside the confines of the family. Furthermore, this complex psychoanalytic process is maintained through social and economic institutions. Appropriating Marxist theory, Chodorow postulates a reciprocal relationship between capitalism and the family that ensures that girls continue to become mothers.

Reading Questions

1. Why does the fact that women mother require an explanation in terms of social structure?
2. What does psychoanalytic theory contribute to the project of explaining the social origins of mothering? According to psychoanalysts what is the origin of personality?
3. What results from the fact that women have been primarily parented by a woman?
4. How are relationships and the need to participate in relationships shaped differently for women than they are for men?
5. How does men's lack of emotional availability contribute to women adopting the role of mother?
6. How does the 'reproduction of mothering' in women result in women being primarily located and placed in the domestic sphere?
7. What does it mean that social reproduction is asymmetrical?

In spite of the apparently close tie between women's capacities for childbearing and lactation on the one hand and their responsibilities for child care on the other, and in spite of the probable prehistoric convenience (and perhaps survival necessity) of a sexual division of labor in which women mothered, biology and instinct do not provide adequate explanations for how women come to mother. Women's mothering as a feature of social structure requires an explanation in terms of social structure. Conventional feminist and social psychological explanations for the genesis of gender roles—girls and boys are "taught" appropriate behaviors and "learn" appropriate feelings—are insufficient both empirically and methodologically to account for how women become mothers.

Methodologically, socialization theories rely inappropriately on individual intention. Ongoing social structures include the means for their own reproduction—in the regularized repetition of social processes, in the perpetuation of conditions which require members' participation, in the genesis of legitimizing ideologies and institutions, and in the psychological as well as physical reproduction of people to perform necessary roles. Accounts of socialization help to explain the perpetuation of ideologies about gender roles. However, notions of appropriate behavior, like coercion, cannot in themselves produce parenting. Psychological capacities and a particular object-relational stance are central and definitional to parenting in a way that they are not to many other roles and activities.

Women's mothering includes the capacities for its own reproduction. This reproduction consists in the production of women with, and men without, the particular psychological capacities and stance which go into primary parenting. Psychoanalytic theory provides us with a theory of social reproduction that explains major features of personality development and the development of psychic structure, and the differential development of gender personality in particular. Psychoanalysts argue that personality both results from and consists in the ways a child appropriates, internalizes, and organizes early experiences in their family—from the fantasies they have, the defenses they use, the ways they channel and redirect drives in this object-relational context. A person subsequently imposes this intrapsychic structure, and the fantasies, defenses, and relational modes and preoccupations which go with it, onto external social situations. This reexternalization (or mutual reexternalization) is a major constituting feature of social and interpersonal situations themselves.

Psychoanalysis, however, has not had an adequate theory of the reproduction of mothering. Because of the teleological assumption that anatomy is destiny, and that women's destiny includes primary parenting, the ontogenesis of women's mothering has been largely ignored, even while the genesis of a wide variety of related disturbances and problems has been accorded widespread clinical attention. Most psychoanalysts agree that the basis for parenting is laid for both genders in the early relationship to a primary caretaker. Beyond that, in order to explain why *women* mother, they tend to rely on vague notions of a girl's subsequent identification with her mother, which makes her and not her brother a primary parent, or on an unspecified and uninvestigated innate femaleness in girls, or on logical leaps from lactation or early vaginal sensations to caretaking abilities and commitments.

The psychoanalytic account of male and female development, when reinterpreted, gives us a developmental theory of the reproduction of women's mothering. Women's mothering reproduces itself through differing object-relational experiences and differing psychic outcomes in women and men. As a result of having been parented by a woman, women are more likely than men to seek to be mothers, that is, to relocate themselves in a primary mother-child relationship, to get gratification from the mothering relationship, and to have psychological and relational capacities for mothering.

The early relation to a primary caretaker provides in children of both genders both the basic capacity to participate in a relationship with the features of the early parent-child one, and the desire to create this intimacy. However, because women mother, the early experience and preoedipal relationship differ for boys and girls. Girls retain more concern with early childhood issues in relation to their mother, and a sense of self involved with these issues. Their attachments therefore retain more preoedipal aspects. The greater length and different nature of their preoedipal experience, and their continuing preoccupation with the issues of this period, mean that women's sense of self is continuous with others and that they retain capacities for primary identification, both of which enable them to experience the empathy and lack of reality sense needed by a cared-for infant. In men, these qualities have been curtailed, both because they are early treated as an opposite by their mother and because their later attachment to her must be repressed. The relational basis for mothering is thus extended in women, and inhibited in men, who experience themselves as more separate and distinct from others.

The different structure of the feminine and masculine oedipal triangle and process of oedipal experience that results from women's mothering contributes further to gender personality differentiation and the reproduction of women's mothering. As a result of this experience, women's inner object world, and the affects and issues associated with it, are more actively sustained and more complex than men's. This means that women define and experience themselves relationally. Their heterosexual orientation is always in internal dialogue with both oedipal and preoedipal mother-child relational issues. Thus, women's heterosexuality is triangular and requires a third person—a child—for its structural and emotional completion. For men, by contrast, the heterosexual relationship alone recreates the early bond to their mother; a child interrupts it. Men, moreover, do not define themselves in relationship and have come to suppress relational capacities and repress relational needs. This prepares them to participate in the affect-denying world of alienated work, but not to fulfill women's needs for intimacy and primary relationships.

The oedipus complex, as it emerges from the asymmetrical organization of parenting, secures a psychological taboo on parent-child incest and pushes boys and girls in the direction of extrafamilial heterosexual relationships. This is one step toward the reproduction of parenting. The creation and maintenance of the incest taboo and of heterosexuality in girls and boys are different, however. For boys, superego formation and identification with their father, rewarded by the superiority of masculinity, maintain the taboo on incest with their mother, while heterosexual orientation continues from their earliest love relation with her. For girls, creating them as heterosexual in the first place maintains the taboo. However, women's heterosexuality is not so exclusive as men's. This makes it easier for them to accept or seek a male substitute for their fathers. At the same time, in a male-dominant society, women's exclusive emotional heterosexuality is not so necessary, nor is her repression of love for her father. Men are more likely to initiate relationships, and women's economic dependence on men pushes them anyway into heterosexual marriage.

Male dominance in heterosexual couples and marriage solves the problem of women's lack of heterosexual commitment and lack of satisfaction by making women more reactive in the sexual bonding process. At the same time, contradictions in heterosexuality help to perpetuate families and parenting by ensuring that women will seek relations to children and will not find heterosexual relationships alone satisfactory. Thus, men's lack of emotional availability and women's less exclusive heterosexual commitment help ensure women's mothering.

Women's mothering, then, produces psychological self-definition and capacities appropriate to mothering in women, and curtails and inhibits these capacities and this self-definition in men. The early experience of being cared for by a woman produces a fundamental structure of expectations in women and men concerning mothers' lack of separate interests from their infants and total concern for their infants' welfare. Daughters grow up identifying with these mothers, about whom they have such expectations. This set of expectations is generalized to the assumption that women naturally take care of children of all ages and the belief that women's "maternal" qualities can and should be extended to the nonmothering work that they do. All these results of women's mothering have ensured that women will mother infants and will take continuing responsibility for children.

The reproduction of women's mothering is the basis for the reproduction of women's location and responsibilities in the domestic sphere. This mothering, and its generalization to women's structural location in the domestic sphere, links the contemporary social organization of gender and social organization of production and contributes to the reproduction of each. That women mother is a fundamental organizational feature of the sex-gender system: It is basic to the sexual division of labor and generates a psychology and ideology of male dominance as well as an ideology about women's capacities and nature. Women, as wives and mothers, contribute as well to the daily and generational reproduction, both physical and psychological, of male workers and thus to the reproduction of capitalist production.

Women's mothering also reproduces the family as it is constituted in male-dominant society. The sexual and familial division of labor in which women mother creates a sexual division of psychic organization and orientation. It produces socially gendered women and men who enter into asymmetrical heterosexual relationships; it produces men who react to, fear, and act superior to women, and who put most of their energies into the nonfamilial work world and do not parent. Finally, it produces women who turn their energies toward nurturing and caring for children—in turn reproducing the sexual and familial division of labor in which women mother.

Social reproduction is thus asymmetrical. Women in their domestic role reproduce men and children physically, psychologically, and emotionally. Women in their domestic role as houseworkers reconstitute themselves physically on a daily basis and reproduce themselves as mothers, emotionally and psychologically, in the next generation. They thus contribute to the perpetuation of their own social roles and position in the hierarchy of gender.

Institutionalized features of family structure and the social relations of reproduction reproduce themselves. A psychoanalytic investigation shows that women's mothering capacities and commitments, and the general psychological capacities and wants which are the basis of women's emotion work, are built developmentally into feminine personality. Because women are themselves mothered by women, they grow up with the relational capacities and needs, and psychological definition of self-in-relationship, which commits them to mothering. Men, because they are mothered by women, do not. Women mother daughters, who, when they become women, mother.

Discussion Questions

1. Who raised you during your infancy and as a young child? Did your father or other male figure care for you during this time? How would Chodorow say those early experiences shaped your gender identity today? Does your experience confirm her thesis? Why or why not?

2. How have gender roles changed in the past 10 years? List some specific differences in expected behavior from men and women in your cultural group. How have these changed from earlier gender roles? Are these changes good or bad? Are the changes (if any) better or worse for individuals?

3. Is it possible for males and females to equitably share child-rearing duties? What economic changes would have to occur in order for men and women to share equally in raising children? To what extent do current economic factors influence the organizational structure of today's families? Explain your answer.

4. Would most men feel comfortable marrying a woman who held a much better job than they did? Would most men give up their careers to stay home and rear the children so that their wives could continue their careers? Would most men feel satisfied playing such a role? Would Chodorow's theory explain your answer? If so, how? If not, why not?

For Further Reading

For recent work by Chodorow in feminist psychoanalysis see *Feminism and Psychoanalytic Theory* (1989), and *Femininities, Masculinities, Sexualities: Freud and Beyond* (1994).

For a general introduction to feminist psychoanalysis see *Psychoanalysis and Gender: An Introductory Reader* (1996), edited by R. Minsky. For other important work in this area see J. Mitchell, *Psychoanalysis and Feminism* (1974), and Carol Gilligan, *In a Different Voice: Psychological Theories and Women's Development* (1982). A critique of feminist psychoanalysis can be found in *Gender Trouble: Feminism and the Subversion of Identity* (1990), by Judith Butler.

18   ANOREXIA NERVOSA: PSYCHOPATHOLOGY AS THE CRYSTALLIZATION OF CULTURE
Susan Bordo

Perhaps you know someone with an eating disorder or you yourself have had an eating disorder. Eating disorders such as anorexia nervosa and bulimia are increasingly common psychological disorders. You might think that philosophy has no bearing on medical or psychological disorders such as these, but according to Susan Bordo (1947–), a philosopher at the University of Kentucky, these pathologies are the 'crystallization' of underlying cultural disorders, created in part by distorting philosophical doctrines.

Bordo has earned a reputation both as a feminist philosopher and for her work on Descartes. These two strands of research come together in the following selection. Bordo analyzes various factors contributing to the

Source: "Anorexia Nervosa: Psychopathology as the Crystallization of Culture" by Susan Bordo, from *Philosophical Forum* (17), pp. 73–104. Used with permission from Blackwell Publishers.

increase of anorexia nervosa and bulimia in Western societies. The first contributing factor is philosophical. **Western philosophy**—as influenced by Descartes—has essentially divided human existence into two substances, material body and spiritual mind. Unfortunately, the material, the body, is conceptualized as alien and corrupting, a rogue force that the spiritual side must control. Second, the feeling of control one experiences through conquering hunger and weight becomes intoxicating—especially in a world as topsy-turvy as our own, where our fate often seems outside our control. Disciplining the body provides women with a satisfying feeling of self-control. Finally, Bordo argues that the self-starvation that characterizes anorexia is a means by which women, at some deep level of consciousness, reject or minimize those bodily characteristics that identify them as female, a devalued status in contemporary culture.

What does this account contribute to an understanding of social identity? Bordo's analysis suggests that the struggle over identity occurs not just at a psychological level (as Chodorow demonstrates) but at the level of the body itself: the site of the struggle over gender identity is the body.

Reading Questions

1. Is the incidence of eating disorders increasing or decreasing?
2. Who is most likely to suffer from an eating disorder?
3. Are images of beauty fixed over time?
4. Explain the dualist axis. How does it contribute to the existence of eating disorders?
5. Explain the control axis. How does it contribute to the existence of eating disorders?
6. Explain the gender/power axis. How does it contribute to the existence of eating disorders?

PREFATORY NOTE

In 1983, preparing to teach an interdisciplinary course in "Gender, Culture, and Experience," I felt the need for a topic that would enable me to bring feminist theory alive for a generation of students that seemed increasingly suspicious of feminism. My sister, Binnie Klein, who is a therapist, suggested that I have my class read Kim Chernin's *The Obsession: Reflection on the Tyranny of Slenderness*. I did, and I found my Reagan-era students suddenly sounding like the women in the consciousness raising sessions that had first made me aware of the fact that my problems as a woman were not mine alone. While delighted to have happened on a topic that was intensely meaningful to them, I was also disturbed by what I was reading in their journals and hearing in the privacy of my office. I had identified deeply with the general themes of Chernin's book. But my own disordered relations with food had never reached the point of anorexia or bulimia, and I was not prepared for the discovery that large numbers of my students were starving, binging, purging, and filled with self-hatred and desperation. I began to read everything I could find on eating disorders. I found that while the words and diaries of patients were enormously illuminating, most of the clinical theory was not very helpful. The absence of cultural perspective—particularly relating to the situation of women—was striking.

As a philosopher, I was also intrigued by the classically dualistic language my students often used to describe their feelings, and I decided to incorporate a section on contemporary attitudes toward the body in my metaphysics course. There, I discovered that although it was predominantly my female students who experienced their lives as a perpetual battle with their bodies, quite a few of my male students expressed similar ideas when writing about running. I found myself fascinated by what seemed to me to be the cultural emergence of a set of attitudes about the body which, while not new *as ideas,* were finding a special kind of embodiment in contemporary culture, and I began to see all sorts of evidence for this cultural hypothesis. "Anorexia Nervosa: Psychopathology as the Crystallization of Culture," first published in 1985, was the result of my initial exploration of the various cultural axes to which my students' experiences guided me in my "Gender, Culture, and Experience" and metaphysics courses. Other essays followed, and ultimately a book, *Unbearable Weight: Feminism, Western Culture, and the Body,* further exploring eating disorders through other cultural interconnections and intersections: the historically female disorders, changes in historical attitudes toward what constitutes "fat" and "thin," the structural tensions of consumer society, the postmodern fascination with re-making the self.

Since I began this work in 1983, my then-tentative intuitions have progressively been validated, as I have watched body practices and attitudes that were a mere ripple on the cultural scene assume a central place in the construction of contemporary subjectivity. In 1995, old clinical generalizations positing a distinctive class, race, family and "personality" profile of the woman most likely to develop an eating disorder no longer hold, as images of the slender, tight body become ever-more widely deployed, asserting their homogenizing power over other cultural ideals of beauty, other cultural attitudes toward female appetite and desire. The more generalized obsession with control of the body which I first began to notice in the early eighties now supports burgeoning industries in exercise equipment, diet products and programs, and cosmetic surgery—practices which are engaged in by greater numbers and more diverse groups of people all the time. On television, "infomercials" hawking stomach-flatteners, miracle diet plans, and wrinkle-dissolving cosmetics have become as commonplace as aspirin ads. As the appearance of our bodies has become more and more important to personal and professional success, the incidence of eating disorders has risen, too, among men. All of this has led to an explosion of written material, media attention and clinical study, much of it strongly bearing out my observations and interpretations. I have not,

however, incorporated any new studies or statistics into the piece reprinted here. With the exception of a few endnotes, it appears substantially as it did in its original version.

I. STATEMENT OF PROBLEM AND THEORETICAL FRAMEWORK

Psychopathology, as Jules Henry has said, "is the final outcome of all that is wrong with a culture." In no case is this more strikingly true than in the case of anorexia nervosa and bulimia, barely known a century ago, yet reaching epidemic proportions today. Far from being the result of a superficial fashion phenomenon, these disorders, I will argue, reflect and call our attention to some of the central ills of our culture—from our historical heritage of disdain for the body, to our modern fear of loss of control over our futures, to the disquieting meaning of contemporary beauty ideals in an era of greater female presence and power than ever before.

Changes in the incidence of anorexia have been dramatic: In 1945, when Ludwig Binswanger chronicled the now famous case of Ellen West, he was able to say that "from a psychiatric point of view we are dealing here with something new, with a new symptom." In 1973, Hilde Bruch, one of the pioneers in understanding and treating eating disorders, could still say that anorexia was "rare indeed." Today, in 1984, it is estimated that as many as one in every 200–250 women between the ages of 13 and 22 suffer from anorexia, and that anywhere from 12 to 33% of college women control their weight through vomiting, diuretics, and laxatives. The New York Center for the Study of Anorexia and Bulimia reports that in the first five months of 1984, it received 252 requests for treatment, as compared to the 30 requests received in all of 1980. Even discounting for increased social awareness of eating disorders, and a greater willingness of sufferers to report their illness, these statistics are startling and provocative. So, too, is the fact that 90% of all anorexics are women, and that of the 5,000 people each year who have their intestines removed to lose weight 80% are women.

Anorexia nervosa is clearly, as Paul Garfinkel and David Garner call it, a "multidetermined disorder," with familial, perceptual, cognitive and possibly biological factors interacting in varying combinations in different individuals to produce a "final common pathway." Over the last several years, with growing evidence, not only of an overall increase in frequency of the disease, but of its higher incidence in certain populations, attention has begun to turn, too, to cultural factors as significant in the pathogenesis of eating disorders. Until very recently, however, the most that one could expect in the way of cultural or social analysis, with very few exceptions, was the (unavoidable) recognition that anorexia is related to the increasing emphasis that fashion has placed on slenderness over the last 15 years. This, unfortunately, is only to replace one mystery with another, more profound mystery than the first.

What we need to ask is *why* our culture is so obsessed with keeping our bodies slim, tight, and young that when 500 people were asked, in a recent poll, what they feared most in the world, 190 replied "getting fat." In an age when our children regularly have nightmares of nuclear holocaust, that as adults we should give *this* answer—that we most fear "getting fat"—is far more bizarre than the anorexic's misperceptions of her body image, or the bulimic's compulsive vomiting. The nightmares of nuclear holocaust and our desperate fixation on our bodies as arenas of control—perhaps one of the few available arenas of control we have left in the twentieth-century—are not unconnected, of course. The connection, if explored, could be significant, de-mystifying, instructive.

So, too, do we need to explore the fact that it is women who are most oppressed by what Kim Chernin calls "the tyranny of slenderness," and that this particular oppression is a post-nineteen-sixties, post-feminist phenomenon. In the fifties, by contrast, with women once again out of the factories and safely immured in the home, the dominant ideal of female beauty was exemplified by Marilyn Monroe—hardly your androgynous, athletic, adolescent body type. At the peak of her popularity, Monroe was often described as "femininity incarnate," "femaleness embodied"; last term, a student of mine described her as "a cow." Is this merely a change in what size hips, breasts, and waist are considered attractive, or has the very idea of incarnate femaleness come to have a different meaning, different associations, the capacity to stir up different fantasies and images, for the culture of the eighties? These are the sorts of questions that need to be addressed if we are

to achieve a deep understanding of the current epidemic of eating disorders.

The central point of intellectual orientation for this paper is expressed in its subtitle. I take the psychopathologies that develop within a culture, far from being anomalies or aberrations, as characteristic expressions of that culture, as the crystallization, indeed, of much that is wrong with it. For that reason they are important to examine, as keys to cultural self-diagnosis and self-scrutiny. "Every age," says Christopher Lasch, "develops its own peculiar forms of pathology, which express in exaggerated form its underlying character structure." The only thing with which I would disagree in this formulation, with respect to anorexia, is the idea of the expression of an underlying, unitary cultural character structure. Anorexia appears less as the extreme expression of a character structure than as a remarkably over-determined *symptom* of some of the multi-faceted and heterogeneous distresses of our age. Just as it functions in a variety of ways in the psychic economy of the anorexic individual, so a variety of cultural currents or streams converge in anorexia, find their perfect, precise expression in it.

I will call those streams or currents "axes of continuity": *axes* because they meet or converge in the anorexic syndrome; *continuity* refers to the fact that when we place or locate anorexia on these axes, its family resemblances and connections with other phenomena emerge.... The three axes that I will discuss in this paper (although they by no means exhaust the possibilities for cultural understanding of anorexia) are *the dualist axis, the control axis, and the gender/power axis.*

...

II. THE DUALIST AXIS

I will begin with the most general and attenuated axis of continuity—the one that begins with Plato, winds its way to its most lurid expression in Augustine, and finally becomes metaphysically solidified and "scientized" by Descartes. I am referring, of course, to our dualistic heritage: the view that human existence is bifurcated into two realms or substances—the bodily or material, on the one hand, and the mental or spiritual, on the other.... Let me briefly describe its central features: ...

First, the body is experienced as alien, as the not-self, the not-me. *It* is "fastened and glued" to me, "nailed" and "riveted" to me, as Plato describes it in the *Phaedo.* For Descartes, it is the brute material envelope for the inner and essential self, the thinking thing—ontologically distinct from it, as mechanical in its operations as a machine, comparable to animal existence. *Second,* the body is experienced as *confinement* and *limitation:* a "prison," a "swamp," a "cage," a "fog"—all images which occur in Plato, Descartes, and Augustine—from which the soul, will, or mind struggle to escape. "The enemy ['the madness of lust'] held my will in his power and from it he made a chain and shackled me," says Augustine. In all three, images of the soul being "dragged" by the body are prominent. The body is "heavy, ponderous," as Plato describes it; it exerts a downward pull. *Third,* the body is the *enemy,* as Augustine explicitly describes it time and again, and as Plato and Descartes strongly suggest in their diatribes against the body as the source of obscurity and confusion in our thinking. "A source of countless distractions by reason of the mere requirement of food," says Plato, "liable also to diseases which overtake and impede us in the pursuit of truth. . . ."

Finally, whether as an impediment to reason, or as the home of the "slimy desires of the flesh" (as Augustine calls them), the body is the locus of all that which threatens our attempts at *control.* It overtakes, it overwhelms, it erupts and disrupts. This situation, for the dualist, becomes an incitement to battle the unruly forces of the body, to show it who is boss. For, as Plato says, "Nature orders the soul to rule and govern and the body to obey and serve." All three, Plato, Augustine, and, most explicitly, Descartes provide instructions, rules or models of how to gain control over the body, with the ultimate aim—for this is what it finally boils down to—of learning to live without it. That is: to achieve intellectual independence from the lure of its illusions, to become impervious to its distractions, and most importantly, to kill off its desires and hungers. . . .

. . .

This is what many anorexics describe as their ultimate goal. "[I want] to reach the point," as one put it, "when I don't need to eat at all." Kim Chernin recalls her surprise when after fasting, her hunger returned: "I realized [then] that my secret goal in dieting must have been the intention to kill off my appetite completely."

. . .

For these women, hunger is experienced as an alien invader, marching to the tune of its own seemingly arbitrary whims, disconnected from any normal self-regulating mechanisms. How could it be so connected? For, it is experienced as coming from an area *outside* the self. One patient of Bruch's says she ate breakfast because "my stomach wanted it," expressing here the same sense of alienation from her hungers (and her physical self) that Augustine expresses when he speaks of his "captor," "the law of sin that was in my member." . . .

While the body is experienced as alien and outside, the soul or will is described as being trapped or confined in this alien "jail," as one woman describes it. "I feel caught in my body," "I'm a prisoner in my body" is the theme that is repeated again and again. A typical fantasy, as it is for Plato, is of total liberation from the bodily prison: "I wish I could get out of my body entirely and fly!" "Please dear God, help me. . . . I want to get out of my body, I want to get out!" . . .

Anorexia is not a philosophical attitude; it is a debilitating affliction. Yet quite often a highly conscious and articulate scheme of images and associations—one could go as far as to call it a metaphysics—is presented by these women. The scheme is strikingly Augustinian, with evocations of Plato. This is not to say, of course, that anorexics are followers of Plato or Augustine, but that in the anorexic's "metaphysics" elements are made explicit, historically grounded in Plato and Augustine, that run deep in our culture. As Augustine often speaks of the "two wills" within him, "one the servant of the flesh, the other of the spirit," who "between them tore my soul apart," so the anorexic describes a "spiritual struggle," a "contest between good and evil," often conceived explicitly as a battle between mind or will and appetite or body. . . .

In this battle, thinness represents a triumph of the will over body, and the thin body (i.e., the non-body) is associated with "absolute purity, hyperintellectuality and transcendence of the flesh. My soul seemed to grow as my body waned; I felt like one of those early Christian saints who starved themselves in the desert sun. I felt invulnerable, clean and hard as the bones etched into my silhouette." Fat (i.e., becoming *all* body) is associated with the "taint" of matter and flesh, "wantonness," mental stupor and mental decay....

III. THE CONTROL AXIS

...

. . . Looking now at contemporary American life, a second axis of continuity emerges on which to locate anorexia. I will call it the *control axis.*

The anorexic, typically, experiences her life as well as her hungers as being out of control. She is a perfectionist, and can never fulfill the tasks she sets to her own rigorous standards. She is torn by conflicting and contradictory expectations and demands, wanting to shine in all areas of student life, confused about where to place most of her energies, what to focus on, as she develops into an adult. Characteristically, her parents expect a great deal of her in the way of individual achievement (as well as physical appearance, particularly her father), yet have made most important decisions for her. Usually, the anorexic syndrome emerges, *not* as a conscious decision to get as thin as possible, but as the result of her having begun a diet fairly casually, often at the suggestions of a parent, having succeeded splendidly in taking off five or ten pounds, and then gotten *hooked* on the intoxicating feeling of accomplishment and control.

Recalling her anorexic days, Aimée Liu recreates her feelings:

> The sense of accomplishment exhilarates me, spurs me to continue on and on. It provides a sense of purpose and shapes my life with distractions from insecurity .... I shall become an expert [at losing weight]....
> The constant downward trend [of the scale] somehow comforts me, gives me visible proof that I can exert control.

The diet, she realizes "is the one sector of my life over which I and I alone wield total control."

The frustrations of starvation, the rigors of the constant exercise and physical activity in which anorexics engage, the pain of the numerous physical complications of anorexia do not trouble the anorexic; indeed, her ability to ignore them is further proof to her of her mastery of her body. "This was something I could control," says one of Bruch's

patients, "I still don't know what I look like or what size I am, but I know my body can take anything." . . .

Surely we must recognize in this last honest and explicit statement a central *modus operandi* for the control of contemporary bourgeois anxiety. Consider: compulsive jogging and marathon-running, often despite shin-splints and other painful injuries, with intense agitation over missed days, or not meeting goals for particular runs. Consider the increasing popularity of triathlon events like the "Iron Man," which appear to have no other purpose than to allow people to find out how far they can push their bodies before collapsing. . . .

None of this is to dispute that the contemporary concern with fitness has non-pathological, non-dualist dimensions as well. Particularly for women, who have historically suffered from the ubiquity of rape and abuse, from the culturally instilled conviction of our own helplessness, and from lack of access to facilities and programs for rigorous physical training, the cultivation of strength, agility, and confidence has a clearly positive dimension. Nor are the objective benefits of daily exercise and concern for nutrition in question here. My focus, rather, is on a subjective stance, increasingly more prominent over the last five years, which, although preoccupied with the body and deriving narcissistic enjoyment from its appearance, takes little pleasure in the *experience* of embodiment. Rather, the fundamental identification is with mind (or will), ideals of spiritual perfection, fantasies of absolute control.

Not everyone, of course, for whom physical training is a part of daily routine exhibits such a stance. Here, an examination of the language of female body-builders is illustrative. Body-building is particularly interesting because on the surface it appears to have the very opposite structure from anorexia: The body-builder is, after all, building the body *up*, not whittling it down. Body-building develops strength. We imagine the body-builder as someone who is proud, confident, and, perhaps most of all, conscious of and accepting of her physicality. This is, indeed, how some female body-builders experience themselves:

> I feel . . . tranquil and stronger [says Lydia Cheng]. Working out creates a high everywhere in my body. I feel the heat. I feel the muscles rise, I see them blow out, flushed with lots of blood. . . . My whole body is

sweating, and there's few things I love more than working up a good sweat. That's when I really feel like a woman.

Yet a sense of joy in the body as active and alive is *not* the most prominent theme among the women interviewed by Trix Rosen in *Strong and Sexy*. Many of them, rather, talk about their bodies in ways that are disquietingly resonant with typical anorexic themes.

There is the same emphasis on will, purity, and perfection: "I've learned to be a stronger person with a more powerful will . . . pure concentration, energy and spirit." "I want to be as physically perfect as possible." "Body-building suits the perfectionist in me." "My goal is to have muscular perfection." Compulsive exercisers—who Dinitia Smith, in an article for *New York* magazine, calls "The New Puritans"—speak in similar terms: Kathy Krauch, a New York art director who bikes twelve miles a day and swims two-and-a-half, says she is engaged in "a quest for perfection." Mike Frankfurt, in describing his motivation for marathon running, speaks of "the purity about it." These people, Smith emphasizes, care little about their health: "They pursue self-denials as an end in itself, out of an almost mystical belief in the purity it confers."

Among body-builders, as for anorexics, there are the same unnerving conceptualizations of the body as alien, the not-self:

> I'm constantly amazed by my muscles. The first thing I do when I wake up in the morning is look down at my "abs" and flex my legs to see if the "cuts" are there. . . . My legs have always been my most stubborn part, and I want them to develop so badly. Every day I can see things happening to them. . . . I don't flaunt my muscles as much as I thought I would. I feel differently about them; they are my product and I protect them by wearing sweaters to keep them warm.

Most strikingly, there is the same emphasis on *control,* on feeling one's life to be fundamentally out of control, and on the feeling of accomplishment derived from total mastery of the body. That sense of mastery, like the anorexic's, appears derived from two sources. First, there is the reassurance that one can overcome all physical obstacles, push oneself to any extremes in pursuit of one's goals (which, as we have seen, is a characteristic motivation of compulsive runners, as well). Second, and most dramatic (it is spoken of time and

again by female body-builders), is the thrill of being in total charge of the shape of one's body. . . .

The sense of security derived from the attainment of this goal appears, first of all, as the pleasure of control and independence. "Nowadays," says Michael Sacks, associate professor of psychiatry at Cornell Medical College, "people no longer feel they can control events outside themselves—how well they do in their jobs or in their personal relationships, for example—but they can control the food they eat and how far they can run. Abstinence, tests of endurance, are ways of proving their self-sufficiency." . . .

. . .

IV. THE GENDER /POWER AXIS

Ninety percent of all anorexics are women. We do not need, of course, to know that particular statistic to realize that the contemporary "tyranny of slenderness" is far from gender neutral. Women are more obsessed with their bodies than men, less satisfied with them, and permitted less latitude with them by themselves, by men, and by the culture. In a recent *Glamour* magazine poll of 33,000 women, 75% said that they thought they were "too fat." Yet by Metropolitan Life Insurance Tables—although they are themselves notoriously affected by cultural standards—only 25% of these women were heavier than the specified standards, and a full 30% were *below.* The anorexic's distorted image of her body—her inability to see it as anything but "too fat," while more extreme, is not radically discontinuous, then, from fairly common female misperceptions.

Consider, too, actors like Nick Nolte and William Hurt, who are permitted a certain amount of softening, of thickening about the waist, while still retaining romantic lead status. Individual style, wit, the projection of intelligence, experience, and effectiveness still go a long way for men, even in our fitness-obsessed culture. But no female can achieve the status of romantic or sexual ideal without the appropriate *body.* That body, if we use television commercials as a gauge, has gotten steadily leaner over the past ten years. What used to be acknowledged as extremes required of high fashion models only is now the dominant image that beckons to high school and college women. Over and over, extremely slender women students complain of hating their thighs, or their stomachs (the anorexic's most dreaded danger spot); often, they express concern and anger over frequent teasing by their boyfriends: Janey, a former student, is 5'10" and weighs 132 pounds. Yet her boyfriend calls her "Fatso" and "Big Butt" and insists she should be 110 pounds because "that's what Brooke Shields weighs." He calls this "constructive criticism," and seems to experience extreme anxiety over the possibility of her gaining any weight: "I can tell it bothers her yet I still continue to badger her about it. I guess that I think that if I continue to remind her things will change faster. . . ." This sort of relationship—within which the woman's weight has become a focal issue—is not at all atypical, as I've discovered from student journals and papers.

· · ·

What is the meaning of these gender associations in the anorexic? I propose that there are two levels of meaning. One has to do with fear and disdain for traditional female *roles* and social limitations. The other has to do, more profoundly, with a deep fear of "The Female," with all its more nightmarish archetypal associations: voracious hungers and sexual insatiability. Let us examine each of these levels in turn.

Adolescent anorexics express characteristic fears about growing up to be mature, sexually developed, and potentially reproductive women. "I have a deep fear," says one, "of having a womanly body, round and fully developed. I want to be tight and muscular and thin." Cherry Boone O'Neill speaks explicitly of her "fear of womanhood." If only she could stay thin, says yet another, "I would never have to deal with having a woman's body; like Peter Pan I could stay a child forever." The choice of Peter Pan is telling here—what she means is, stay a *boy* forever. . . .

· · ·

Some authors interpret these symptoms as a species of unconscious feminist protest, involving anger at the limitations of the traditional female role, rejection of values associated with it, and fierce rebellion against allowing their futures to develop in the same direction as their mothers' lives. In her portrait of the typical anorexic family configuration, Bruch describes nearly all of the mothers as submissive to their husbands, while very controlling of their children. Practically all had had promising careers which they gave up to care for their husbands and families full-time, a task they take very seriously, although often expressing frustration and dissatisfaction.

Certainly, many anorexics appear to experience anxiety over falling into the lifestyle they associate with their mothers. It is a prominent theme in Aimée Liu's *Solitaire*. Another woman describes her feeling that she is "full of my mother . . . she is in me even if she isn't there" in nearly the same breath as she complains of her continuous fear of being "not human . . . of ceasing to exist." And Ellen West, nearly a century earlier, had quite explicitly equated becoming fat with the inevitable (for a woman of her time) confinements of domestic life and the domestic stupor she associates with it:

> Dread is driving me mad . . . the consciousness that ultimately I will lose everything; all courage, all rebelliousness, all drive for doing; that it—my little world—will make me flabby, flabby and fainthearted and beggarly. . . .

Several of my students with eating disorders reported that their anorexia had developed after their families had dissuaded or forbidden them from embarking on a traditionally male career.

· · ·

It is important to recognize, too, that the anorexic is terrified and repelled, not only by the traditional female domestic role—which she associates with mental lassitude and weakness—but by a certain archetypal image of the female: as hungering, voracious, all-needing, and all-wanting. It is this image that shapes and permeates her experience of her own hunger for food as insatiable and out-of-control, which makes her feel that if she takes just one bite, she won't be able to stop.

Let's explore this image. Let's break the tie with food and look at the metaphor: Hungering. Voracious. Extravagantly and excessively needful. Without restraint. Always wanting. Always wanting too much affection, reassurance, emotional and sexual contact and attention. This is how many women frequently experience themselves, and, indeed, how many men experience women. "Please, please God, keep me from telephoning him," prays the heroine in Dorothy Parker's classic "The Telephone Call," experiencing her need for reassurance and contact as being as out-of-control and degrading as the anorexic experiences her desire for food. The male counterpart to this is found in someone like Paul Morel in Lawrence's *Sons and Lovers*: "Can you never like things without clutching them as if you wanted to pull the heart out of them?" he accuses Miriam as she fondles a flower, "Why don't you have a bit more restraint, or reserve, or something. . . . You're always begging things to love you, as if you were a beggar for love. Even the flowers, you have to fawn on them." How much psychic authenticity do these images carry in 1980s America? One woman in my class provided a stunning insight into the connection between her perception of herself and the anxiety of the compulsive dieter: "You know," she said, "the anorexic is always convinced she is taking up too much space, eating too much, wanting food too much. I've never felt that way, but I've often felt that I was *too much*—too much emotion, too much need, too loud and demanding, too much *there*, if you know what I mean."

The most extreme cultural expressions of the fear of woman-as-too-much—which almost always revolve around her sexuality—are strikingly full of eating and hungering metaphors. "Of woman's unnatural, *insatiable* lust, what country, what village doth not complain?" queries Burton in *The Anatomy of Melancholy*. "You are the true hiennas," says Walter Charleton, "that allure us with the fairness of your skins, and when folly hath brought us within your reach, you leap upon us and *devour* us."

The mythology/ideology of the devouring, insatiable female (which, as we have seen, is the internalized image the anorexic has of her female self) tends historically to wax and wane. But not without rhyme or reason. In periods of gross environmental and social crisis, such as characterized the period of the witch-hunts in the fifteenth and sixteenth centuries, it appears to flourish. "All witchcraft comes from carnal lust, which is in women *insatiable*," say Kramer and Sprenger, authors of the official witch-hunters handbook, *Malleus Malificarum*. For the sake of fulfilling the "*mouth* of the womb . . . [women] consort even with the devil."

Anxiety over women's uncontrollable hungers appears to peak, as well, during periods when women are becoming independent, and asserting themselves politically and socially. The second half of the nineteenth century, concurrent with the first feminist wave discussed earlier, saw a virtual "flood" (as Peter Gay calls it) of artistic and literary images of the dark, dangerous, and evil female: "sharp-teethed, devouring" Sphinxes, Salomés and Delilahs, "biting, tearing,

murderous women." "No century," claims Gay, "depicted woman as vampire, as castrator, as killer, so consistently, so programmatically, and so nakedly as the nineteenth." . . .

. . .

On the gender/power axis the female body appears, then, as the unknowing medium of the historical ebbs and flows of the fear of woman-as-too-much. That, as we have seen, is how the anorexic experiences her female, bodily self: as voracious, wanton, needful of forceful control by her male will. Living in the tide of cultural backlash against the second major feminist wave, she is not alone in these images. Christopher Lasch, in *The Culture of Narcissism*, speaks of what he describes as "the apparently aggressive overtures of sexually liberated women" which "convey to many males the same message—that women are *voracious, insatiable*," and call up "early fantasies of a possessive, suffocating, *devouring* and castrating mother." (emphasis added)

Our contemporary beauty ideals, on the other hand, seemed purged, as Kim Chernin puts it, "of the power to conjure up memories of the past, of all that could remind us of a woman's mysterious power." The ideal, rather, is an "image of a woman in which she is not yet a woman": Darryl Hannah as the lanky, new-born mermaid in *Splash;* Lori Singer (appearing virtually anorexic) as the reckless, hyper-kinetic heroine of *Footloose;* The Charlie Girl; "Cheryl Tiegs in shorts, Margaux Hemingway with her hair wet, Brooke Shields naked on an island. . . ." The dozens of teen-age women who appear in coke commercials, in jeans commercials, in chewing gum commercials.

The images suggest amused detachment, casual playfulness, flirtatiousness without demand, and lightness of touch. A refusal to take sex, death, or politics too deadly seriously. A delightfully unconscious relationship to her body. The twentieth century has seen this sort of feminine ideal before, of course: When, in the 1920s, young women began to flatten their breasts, suck in their stomachs, bob their hair, and show off long colt-like legs, they believed they were pursuing a new freedom and daring that demanded a carefree, boyish style. If the traditional female hour glass suggested anything, it was confinement and immobility. Yet the flapper's freedom, as Mary McCarthy's and Dorothy Parker's short stories brilliantly reveal, was largely an illusion—as any obsessively cultivated sexual style must inevitably be. Although today's images may suggest androgynous independence, we need only consider who is on the receiving end of the imagery in order to confront the pitiful paradox involved.

Watching the commercials are thousands of anxiety-ridden women and adolescents (some of whom are likely the very ones appearing in the commercials) with anything *but* an unconscious relation to their bodies. They are involved in an absolutely contradictory state of affairs, a totally no-win game: caring desperately, passionately, obsessively about attaining an ideal of coolness, effortless confidence, and casual freedom. Watching the commercials is a little girl, perhaps ten years old, who I saw in Central Park, gazing raptly at her father, bursting with pride: "Daddy, guess what? I lost two pounds!" And watching the commercials is the anorexic, who associates her relentless pursuit of thinness with power and control, but who in fact destroys her health and imprisons her imagination. She is surely the most startling and stark illustration of how cavalier power relations are with respect to the motivations and goals of individuals, yet how deeply they are etched on our bodies, and how well our bodies serve them.

Discussion Questions

1. Do you know someone with an eating disorder? What do you believe to be the cause of the disorder? Are social factors involved? Could anything have been done to prevent the disorder?

2. Why is the incidence of eating disorders higher among women than among men? How would Bordo explain this phenomenon? Do you agree? Is her view convincing? Why or why not?

3. Gather some women's magazines and the Sunday edition of a major newspaper. How are women's bodies represented in ads and pictures? What ideal picture of a woman's body do these media sources suggest? Are these images harmful? Why or why not?

4. Women now play more sports than they did several generations ago. Has this had any effect on women's self-image and conception of their bodies? What change do you think Bordo's analysis of eating disorders might predict for women who play sports? Are those changes occurring? Why or why not?

5. Consider your own cultural or ethnic group. Is the body experienced as something "alien" that must be controlled? List some ways that confirm and deny the thesis that bodies are experienced as an alien force in your culture. Do you experience your body as "alien," something you must fight to control?

6. Are the standards for "beauty" as rigorous for men as they are for women? Why or why not? What is the best explanation of this? If there is no difference, are they still a problem? Why or why not?

For Further Reading

For further work by Bordo concerning the body see "Eating Disorders: The Feminist Challenge to the Concept of Pathology" in *The Body in Medical Thought and Practice* (1992), edited by D. Leder; and "Docile Bodies, Rebellious Bodies" in *Writing the Politics of Difference* (1991), edited by H. Silverman. See especially Bordo's *Unbearable Weight: Feminism, Western Culture and the Body* (1993). See also *Gender/Body/Knowledge: Feminist Reconstructions of Being and Knowing* (1989), edited by Alison Jaggar and Susan Bordo.

For Bordo's work concerning objectivity see "Feminist Skepticism and the 'Maleness' of Philosophy," *Journal of Philosophy* 85 (1988), 619–629; and *The Fight to Objectivity: Essays on Cartesianism and Culture* (1987). Bordo's article "Feminist Skepticism and the

'Maleness' of Philosophy" has generated several responses, which can be found in volume 7 (Summer 1992) of the journal *Hypatia*.

19 THE FACT OF BLACKNESS
Frantz Fanon

Frantz Fanon (1925–1961) was an important black voice against colonialism. Tragically, Fanon died of leukemia before he had completed his work on the debilitating (psychological) effects of living under colonialism. In the following selection, from *Black Skin, White Masks,* Fanon draws on both psychology and philosophy to paint a vivid picture of the struggle over self-identity that characterizes the lives of black men and women who lived under colonial rule.

In a Eurocentric world full of racism, self-loathing is not uncommon; but how does this self-destructive identity form? This selection from Fanon describes the processes through which he and others who lived under colonial rule came to understand their own identity. Fanon is relying on a philosophical model of self-identity first proposed by Hegel, an important and influential nineteenth-century philosopher. According to Hegel's account, individuals do not define themselves; that is, no one creates his or her own identity. Instead, identity and self-conception come through being recognized by the 'other', that is, by being acknowledged by other persons. Personal identity, then, is necessarily a social process of mutual recognition. In this selection, Fanon uses the metaphor of being seen to dissect the processes that create the social identity of blacks who struggle under colonialism. As Fanon traces the development of his own identity, he discovers a prison created by how he is perceived by white society: "Look, a Negro!"

(*Note:* Fanon's discussion includes the use of racial terms now considered offensive.)

Reading Questions

1. How does a black man come to experience his own being through others?
2. Why does Fanon conclude that a black man must be black in relation to a white man, but that the converse is not true?
3. How does Fanon's response to being perceived as a Negro change?
4. What processes lead up to Fanon seeing himself as an object? What does this mean, to see yourself as an object?
5. What changes occur to Fanon's self-identity when he gives an angry response to the comment "Look how handsome . . ."?
6. Why is Fanon locked into an 'infernal circle'?

SOURCE: From *Black Skin, White Masks* by Frantz Fanon, translated by Charles Lam Markmann. Copyright © 1967 Grove Press, Inc. Used by permission of Grove/Atlantic, Inc.

"Dirty nigger!" Or simply, "Look, a Negro!"

I came into the world imbued with the will to find a meaning in things, my spirit filled with the desire to attain to the source of the world, and then I found that I was an object in the midst of other objects.

Sealed into that crushing objecthood, I turned beseechingly to others. Their attention was a liberation, running over my body suddenly abraded into non-being, endowing me once more with an agility that I had thought lost, and by taking me out of the world, restoring me to it. But just as I reached the other side, I stumbled, and the movements, the attitudes, the glances of the other fixed me there, in the sense in which a chemical solution is fixed by a dye. I was indignant; I demanded an explanation. Nothing happened. I burst apart. Now the fragments have been put together again by another self.

As long as the black man is among his own, he will have no occasion, except in minor internal conflicts, to experience his being through others. There is of course the moment of "being for others," of which Hegel speaks, but every ontology is made unattainable in a colonized and civilized society. It would seem that this fact has not been given sufficient attention by those who have discussed the question. In the *Weltanschauung* of a colonized people there is an impurity, a flaw that outlaws any ontological explanation. Someone may object that this is the case with every individual, but such an objection merely conceals a basic problem. Ontology—once it is finally admitted as leaving existence by the wayside—does not permit us to understand the being of the black man. For not only must the black man be black; he must be black in relation to the white man. Some critics will take it on themselves to remind us that this proposition has a converse. I say that this is false. The black man has no ontological resistance in the eyes of the white man. Overnight the Negro has been given two frames of reference within which he has had to place himself. His metaphysics, or, less pretentiously, his customs and the sources on which they were based, were wiped out because they were in conflict with a civilization that he did not know and that imposed itself on him.

The black man among his own in the twentieth century does not know at what moment his inferiority comes into being through the other. Of course I have talked about the black problem with friends, or, more rarely, with American Negroes. Together we protested, we asserted the equality of all men in the world. In the Antilles there was also that little gulf that exists among the almost-white, the mulatto, and the nigger. But I was satisfied with an intellectual understanding of these differences. It was not really dramatic. And then. . . .

And then the occasion arose when I had to meet the white man's eyes. An unfamiliar weight burdened me. The real world challenged my claims. In the white world the man of color encounters difficulties in the development of his bodily schema. Consciousness of the body is solely a negating activity. It is a third-person consciousness. The body is surrounded by an atmosphere of certain uncertainty. I know that if I want to smoke, I shall have to reach out my right arm and take the pack of cigarettes lying at the other end of the table. The matches, however, are in the drawer on the left, and I shall have to lean back slightly. And all these movements are made not out of habit but out of implicit knowledge. A slow composition of my *self* as a body in the middle of a spatial and temporal world—such seems to be the schema. It does not impose itself on me; it is, rather, a definitive structuring of the self and of the world—definitive because it creates a real dialectic between my body and the world.

For several years certain laboratories have been trying to produce a serum for "denegrification"; with all the earnestness in the world, laboratories have sterilized their test tubes, checked their scales, and embarked on researches that might make it possible for the miserable Negro to whiten himself and thus to throw off the burden of that corporeal malediction. Below the corporeal schema I had sketched a historico-racial schema. The elements that I used had been provided for me not by "residual sensations and perceptions primarily of a tactile, vestibular, kinesthetic, and visual character," but by the other, the white man, who had woven me out of a thousand details, anecdotes, stories. I thought that what I had in hand was to construct a physiological self, to balance space, to localize sensations, and here I was called on for more.

"Look, a Negro!" It was an external stimulus that flicked over me as I passed by. I made a tight smile.

"Look, a Negro!" It was true. It amused me.

"Look, a Negro!" The circle was drawing a bit tighter. I made no secret of my amusement.

"Mama, see the Negro! I'm frightened!" Frightened! Frightened! Now they were beginning to be afraid of me. I made up my mind to laugh myself to tears, but laughter had become impossible.

I could no longer laugh, because I already knew that there were legends, stories, history, and above all *historicity,* which I had learned about from Jaspers. Then, assailed at various points, the corporeal schema crumbled, its place taken by a racial epidermal schema. In the train it was no longer a question of being aware of my body in the third person but in a triple person. In the train I was given not one but two, three places. I had already stopped being amused. It was not that I was finding febrile coordinates in the world. I existed triply: I occupied space. I moved toward the other . . . and the evanescent other, hostile but not opaque, transparent, not there, disappeared. Nausea . . .

I was responsible at the same time for my body, for my race, for my ancestors. I subjected myself to an objective examination, I discovered my blackness, my ethnic characteristics; and I was battered down by tom-toms, cannibalism, intellectual deficiency, fetishism, racial defects, slave-ships, and above all else, above all: "Sho' good eatin'."

On that day, completely dislocated, unable to be abroad with the other, the white man, who unmercifully imprisoned me, I took myself far off from my own presence, far indeed, and made myself an object. What else could it be for me but an amputation, an excision, a hemorrhage that spattered my whole body with black blood? But I did not want this revision, this thematization. All I wanted was to be a man among other men. I wanted to come lithe and young into a world that was ours and to help to build it together.

But I rejected all immunization of the emotions. I wanted to be a man, nothing but a man. Some identified me with ancestors of mine who had been enslaved or lynched: I decided to accept this. It was on the universal level of the intellect that I understood this inner kinship—I was the grandson of slaves in exactly the same way in which President Lebrun was the grandson of tax-paying, hardworking peasants. In the main, the panic soon vanished.

In America, Negroes are segregated. In South America, Negroes are whipped in the streets, and Negro strikers are cut down by machine-guns. In West Africa, the Negro is an animal. And there beside me, my neighbor in the university, who was born in Algeria, told me: "As long as the Arab is treated like a man, no solution is possible."

"Understand, my dear boy, color prejudice is something I find utterly foreign. . . . But of course, come in, sir, there is no color prejudice among us. . . . Quite, the Negro is a man like ourselves. . . . It is not because he is black that he is less intelligent than we are. . . . I had a Senegalese buddy in the army who was really clever. . . ."

Where am I to be classified? Or, if you prefer, tucked away?

"A Martinican, a native of 'our' old colonies."

Where shall I hide?

"Look at the nigger! . . . Mama, a Negro! . . . Hell, he's getting mad. . . . Take no notice, sir, he does not know that you are as civilized as we. . . ."

My body was given back to me sprawled out, distorted, recolored, clad in mourning in that white winter day. The Negro is an animal, the Negro is bad, the Negro is mean, the Negro is ugly; look, a nigger, it's cold, the nigger is shivering, the nigger is shivering because he is cold, the little boy is trembling because he is afraid of the nigger, the nigger is shivering with cold, that cold that goes through your bones, the handsome little boy is trembling because he thinks that the nigger is quivering with rage, the little white boy throws himself into his mother's arms: Mama, the nigger's going to eat me up.

All round me the white man, above the sky tears at its navel, the earth rasps under my feet, and there is a white song, a white song. All this whiteness that burns me. . . .

I sit down at the fire and I become aware of my uniform. I had not seen it. It is indeed ugly. I stop there, for who can tell me what beauty is?

Where shall I find shelter from now on? I felt an easily identifiable flood mounting out of the countless facets of my being. I was about to be angry. The fire was long since out, and once more the nigger was trembling.

"Look how handsome that Negro is! . . ."

"Kiss the handsome Negro's ass, madame!"

Shame flooded her face. At last I was set free from my rumination. At the same time I accomplished two things: I identified my enemies and I made a scene. A grand slam. Now one would be able to laugh.

The field of battle having been marked out, I entered the lists.

What? While I was forgetting, forgiving, and wanting only to love, my message was flung back in my face like a slap. The white world, the only honorable one, barred me from all participation. A man was expected to behave like a man. I was expected to behave like a black man—or at least like a nigger. I shouted a greeting to the world and the world slashed away my joy. I was told to stay within bounds, to go back where I belonged.

They would see, then! I had warned them, anyway. Slavery? It was no longer even mentioned, that unpleasant memory. My supposed inferiority? A hoax that it was better to laugh at. I forgot it all, but only on condition that the world not protect itself against me any longer. I had incisors to test. I was sure they were strong. And besides. . . .

What! When it was I who had every reason to hate, to despise, I was rejected? When I should have been begged, implored, I was denied the slightest recognition? I resolved, since it was impossible for me to get away from an *inborn complex,* to assert myself as a BLACK MAN. Since the other hesitated to recognize me, there remained only one solution: to make myself known.

I move slowly in the world, accustomed now to seek no longer for upheaval. I progress by crawling. And already I am being dissected under white eyes, the only real eyes. I am *fixed.* Having adjusted their microtomes, they objectively cut away slices of my reality. I am laid bare. I feel, I see in those white faces that it is not a new man who has come in, but a new kind of man, a new genus. Why, it's a Negro!

I slip into corners, and my long antennae pick up the catch-phrases strewn over the surface of things—nigger underwear smells of nigger—nigger teeth are white—nigger feet are big—the nigger's barrel chest—I slip into corners, I remain silent, I strive for anonymity, for invisibility. Look, I will accept the lot, as long as no one notices me!

"Oh, I want you to meet my black friend. . . . Aimé Césaire, a black man and a university gradu-

ate. . . . Marian Anderson, the finest of Negro singers. . . . Dr. Cobb, who invented white blood, is a Negro. . . . Here, say hello to my friend from Martinique (be careful, he's extremely sensitive). . . ."

Shame. Shame and self-contempt. Nausea. When people like me, they tell me it is in spite of my color. When they dislike me, they point out that it is not because of my color. Either way, I am locked into the infernal circle.

I turn away from these inspectors of the Ark before the Flood and I attach myself to my brothers, Negroes like myself. To my horror, they too reject me. They are almost white. And besides they are about to marry white women. They will have children faintly tinged with brown. Who knows, perhaps little by little. . . .

I had been dreaming.

"I want you to understand, sir, I am one of the best friends the Negro has in Lyon."

The evidence was there, unalterable. My blackness was there, dark and unarguable. And it tormented me, pursued me, disturbed me, angered me.

Negroes are savages, brutes, illiterates. But in my own case I knew that these statements were false. There was a myth of the Negro that had to be destroyed at all costs. The time had long since passed when a Negro priest was an occasion for wonder. We had physicians, professors, statesmen. Yes, but something out of the ordinary still clung to such cases. "We have a Senegalese history teacher. He is quite bright. . . . Our doctor is colored. He is very gentle."

It was always the Negro teacher, the Negro doctor; brittle as I was becoming, I shivered at the slightest pretext. I knew, for instance, that if the physician made a mistake it would be the end of him and of all those who came after him. What could one expect, after all, from a Negro physician? As long as everything went well, he was praised to the skies, but look out, no nonsense, under any conditions! The black physician can never be sure how close he is to disgrace. I tell you, I was walled in: No exception was made for my refined manners, or my knowledge of literature, or my understanding of the quantum theory.

Discussion Questions

1. Detail the stages of Fanon's evolving self-identity. What changes occur and why? Have other ethnic groups experienced the same changes? Does the self-identity of women follow a similar path? How about the identity of gays and lesbians?

2. Is it important to know about your own cultural heritage? Why or why not? What do you know about your own ethnic cultural background? How does this shape your own identity?

3. Is Fanon correct that whites can define themselves without reference to blacks, but that blacks must define themselves necessarily in reference to whites? Why or why not?

4. Do you have different expectations for whites and blacks? In what ways? How were these different expectations formed? Are they problematic? If a person holds different expectations for different races, does this make him or her a racist? Why or why not?

For Further Reading

Besides *Black Skin, White Masks* (1952), Fanon's other major work is *The Wretched of the Earth* (1961). Essays by Fanon are collected in *A Dying Colonialism* (1965), and *Toward the African Revolution* (1964).

For works on Fanon and Fanon's thought see *Fanon* (1970), by D. Caute; *Black Soul, White Artifact* (1983), by O. Mannoni; and *Frantz Fanon: Social and Political Thought* (1977), by E. Hansen. For a collection of essays devoted to "black-existentialism" see *Existence in Black: An Anthology of Black Existential Philosophy* (1997), edited by L. R. Gordon. There is an interesting article relating this selection by Fanon to the Rodney King riots in Los Angeles; see "'Look, a Negro!'," by Robert Gooding-Williams, in *Reading Rodney King/Reading Urban Uprising* (1993), edited by Robert Gooding-Williams.

---

20   WE ARE NOT FREE
Clyde Warrior

A Ponca Indian, Clyde Warrior (1939–1968), was a renowned Indian dancer and singer, as well as a founding member of the National Indian Youth Council (NIYC). Warrior and others—Shirley Hill Witt, Joan Noble, Mel Thom, and Herbert Blatchford—founded the NIYC in 1961 out of dissatisfaction with the National Congress of American Indians (NCAI)—at that time the *de facto* mouthpiece for voicing Indian concerns to the U.S. government.

As Warrior saw it, the NCAI was too accommodating to the federal government and the concerns of whites. Warrior's alternative was a proactive organization that would seek autonomy for Indians, reclaiming their pride as a people—"Red Power." With the help of notables such as Marlon Brando and Jane Fonda, Warrior advanced the efforts of the NIYC, focusing attention on the plight of American Indians. One way he did this

SOURCE: Reprinted from *RedPower: The American Indians Fight for Freedom* by Alvin M. Josephy, Jr., by permission of the University of Nebraska Press. Copyright © 1971 by Alvin M. Josephy, Jr. Copyright © 1999 by The University of Nebraska.

was by organizing "fish-ins." In defiance of (Washington) state authority, Indians gathered to assert their right to fish in their traditional fishing grounds by doing just that. Ultimately, what Warrior and the NIYC set in motion resulted in Indians legally reclaiming their rights to fish in specified waters and, more importantly, a renewed Indian activism.

The following selection comes from a 1967 speech Warrior made before the National Commission on Rural Poverty. Rejecting handouts and government interference, he demands self-rule and Indian self-autonomy. This was the path to reclaiming dignity and self-definition.

Reading Questions

1. Explain the difference between being materially rich and spiritually rich.
2. How does Warrior define freedom?
3. What does Warrior dislike about Indian children growing up in the American school system?
4. Would economic prosperity solve all of the problems facing Indians today?
5. What would help today's Indians?
6. Why should America be concerned about the welfare of Indians today?
7. Explain Warrior's thoughts concerning Indians assimilating into American culture.

Most members of the National Indian Youth Council can remember when we were children and spent many hours at the feet of our grandfathers listening to stories of the time when the Indians were a great people, when we were free, when we were rich, when we lived the good life. At the same time we heard stories of droughts, famines and pestilence. It was only recently that we realized that there was surely great material deprivation in those days, but that our old people felt rich because they were free. They were rich in things of the spirit, but if there is one thing that characterizes Indian life today it is poverty of the spirit. We still have human passions and depth of feeling (which may be something rare in these days), but we are poor in spirit because we are not free—free in the most basic sense of the word. We are not allowed to make those basic human choices and decisions about our personal life and about the destiny of our communities which is the mark of free mature people. We sit on our front porches or in our yards, and the world and our lives in it pass us by without our desires or aspirations having any effect.

We are not free. We do not make choices. Our choices are made for us; we are the poor. For those of us who live on reservations these choices and decisions are made by federal administrators, bureaucrats, and their "yes men," euphemistically called tribal governments. Those of us who live in non-reservation areas have our lives controlled by local white power elites. We have many rulers. They are called social workers, "cops," school teachers, churches, etc., and now OEO employees. They call us into meetings to tell us what is good for us and how they've programmed us, or they come into our homes to instruct us and their manners are not always what one would call polite by Indian standards or perhaps by any standards. We are rarely accorded respect as fellow human beings. Our children come home from school to us with shame in their hearts and a sneer on their lips for their home and parents. We are the "poverty problem" and that is true; and perhaps it is also true that our lack of reasonable choices, our lack of freedoms, our poverty of spirit is not unconnected with our material poverty.

The National Indian Youth Council realizes there is a great struggle going on in America now between those who want more "local" control of programs and those who would keep the power and the purse strings in the hands of the federal government. We are unconcerned with that struggle, because we know that no one is arguing that the dispossessed, the poor, be given any control over their own destiny. The local white power elites who protest the loudest against federal control are the very ones who would keep us poor in spirit and worldly goods in order to enhance their own personal and economic station in the world.

Nor have those of us on reservations fared any better under the paternalistic control of federal administrations. In fact, we shudder at the specter of what seems to be the forming alliances in Indian areas between federal administrators and local elites. Some of us fear that this is the shape of things to come in the War on Poverty effort. Certainly, it is in those areas where such an alliance is taking place that the poverty program seems to be "working well." That is to say, it is in those areas of the country where the federal government is getting the least "static" and where federal money is being used to bolster the local power structure and local institutions. By "everybody being satisfied," I mean the people who count and the Indian or poor does not count.

Let us take the Head Start Program as an instance. We are told in the not-so-subtle racist vocabulary of the modern middle class that our children are "deprived." Exactly what they are deprived of seems to be unstated. We give our children love, warmth and respect in our homes and the qualities necessary to be a warm human being. Perhaps many of them get into trouble in their teens because we have given them too much warmth, love, passion, and respect. Perhaps they have a hard time reconciling themselves to being a number on an IBM card. Nevertheless, many educators and politicians seem to assume that we, the poor, the Indians, are not capable of handling our own affairs and even raising our own children and that state institutions must do that job for us and take them away from us as soon as they can. My grandmother said last week, "Train your child well now for soon she will belong to her teacher and the schools." Many of our fears about the Head Start Program which we had from listening to the vocabulary of educators and their intentions were not justified, however. In our rural areas the program seems to have turned out to be just a federally subsidized kindergarten which no one seems to take too seriously. It has not turned

out to be, as we feared, an attempt to "re-thread" the "twisted head" of the child from a poor home. Head Start, as a program, may not have fulfilled the expectations of elitist educators in our educational colleges, and the poor may not be ecstatic over the results, but local powers are overjoyed. This is the one program which has not upset any one's apple cart and which has strengthened local institutions in an acceptable manner, acceptable at least to our local "patrons."

Fifty years ago the federal government came into our communities and by force carried most of our children away to distant boarding schools. My father and many of my generation lived their childhoods in an almost prison-like atmosphere. Many returned unable even to speak their own language. Some returned to become drunks. Most of them had become white haters or that most pathetic of all modern Indians—Indian haters. Very few ever became more than very confused, ambivalent and immobilized individuals—never able to reconcile the tensions and contradictions built inside themselves by outside institutions. As you can imagine, we have little faith in such kinds of federal programs devised for our betterment nor do we see education as a panacea for all ills. In recent days, however, some of us have been thinking that perhaps the damage done to our communities by forced assimilation and directed acculturative programs was minor compared to the situation in which our children now find themselves. There is a whole generation of Indian children who are growing up in the American school system. They still look to their relatives, my generation, and my father's to see if they are worthy people. But their judgment and definition of what is worthy is now the judgment most Americans make. They judge worthiness as competence and competence as worthiness. And I am afraid me and my fathers do not fare well in the light of this situation and judgment. Our children are learning that their people are not worthy and thus that they individually are not worthy. Even if by some stroke of good fortune, prosperity was handed to us "on a platter" that still would not soften the negative judgment our youngsters have of their people and themselves. As you know, people who feel themselves to be unworthy and feel they cannot escape this unworthiness turn to drink and crime and self-destructive acts. Unless there is some way that we as Indian individuals and communities can prove ourselves competent and worthy in the eyes of our youngsters there will be a generation of Indians grow to adulthood whose reaction to their situation will make previous social ills seem like a Sunday School picnic.

For the sake of our children, for the sake of the spiritual and material well-being of our total community we must be able to demonstrate competence to ourselves. For the sake of our psychic stability as well as our physical well-being we must be free men and exercise free choices. We must make decisions about our own destinies. We must be able to learn and profit by our own mistakes. Only then can we become competent and prosperous communities. We must be free in the most literal sense of the word—not sold or coerced into accepting programs for our own good, not of our own making or choice. Too much of what passes for "grass-roots democracy" on the American scene is really a slick job of salesmanship. It is not hard for sophisticated administrators to sell tinsel and glitter programs to simple people—programs which are not theirs, which they do not understand and which cannot but ultimately fail and contribute to already strong feelings of inadequacy. Community development must be just what the word implies, Community Development. It cannot be packaged programs wheeled into Indian communities by outsiders which Indians can "buy" or once again brand themselves as unprogressive if they do not "cooperate." Even the best of outside programs suffer from one very large defect—if the program falters helpful outsiders too often step in to smooth over the rough spots. At that point any program ceases to belong to the people involved and ceases to be a learning experience for them. Programs must be Indian creations, Indian choices, Indian experiences. Even the failures must be Indian experiences because only then will Indians understand why a program failed and not blame themselves for some personal inadequacy. A better program built upon the failure of an old program is the path of progress. But to achieve this experience, competence, worthiness, sense of achievement and the resultant material prosperity Indians must have the responsibility in the ultimate sense of the word.

Indians must be free in the sense that other more prosperous Americans are free. Freedom and prosperity are different sides of the same coin and there can be no freedom without complete responsibility. And I do not mean the fictional responsibility and democracy of passive consumers of programs; programs which emanate from and whose responsibility for success rests in the hands of outsiders—be they federal administrators or local white elitist groups.

Many of our young people are captivated by the lure of the American city with its excitement and promise of unlimited opportunity. But even if educated they come from powerless and inexperienced communities and many times carry with them a strong sense of unworthiness. For many of them the promise of opportunity ends in the gutter on the skid rows of Los Angeles and Chicago. They should and must be given a better chance to take advantage of the opportunities they have. They must grow up in a decent community with a strong sense of personal adequacy and competence.

America cannot afford to have whole areas and communities of people in such dire social and economic circumstances. Not only for her economic well-being but for her moral well being as well. America has given a great social and moral message to the world and demonstrated (perhaps not forcefully enough) that freedom and responsibility as an ethic is inseparable from and, in fact, the "cause" of the fabulous American standard of living. America has not however been diligent enough in promulgating this philosophy within her own borders. American Indians need to be given this freedom and responsibility which most Americans assume as their birth right. Only then will poverty and powerlessness cease to hang like the sword of Damocles over our heads stifling us. Only then can we enjoy the fruits of the American system and become participating citizens—Indian Americans rather than American Indians.

Perhaps, the National Indian Youth Council's real criticism is against a structure created by bureaucratic administrators who are caught in this American myth that all people assimilate into American society, that economics dictates assimilation and integration. From the experience of the National Indian Youth Council, and in reality, we cannot emphasize and recommend strongly enough the fact that no one integrates and disappears into American society. What ethnic groups do is not integrate into American society and economy individually, but enter into the mainstream of American society as a people, and in particular as communities of people. The solution to Indian poverty is not "government programs" but in the competence of the person and his people. The real solution to poverty is encouraging the competence of the community as a whole.

[The] National Indian Youth Council recommends for "openers" that to really give these people "the poor, the dispossessed, the Indians," complete freedom and responsibility is to let it become a reality not a much-heard-about dream and let the poor decide for once, what is best for themselves. . . .

Discussion Questions

1. How were Native Americans portrayed in your history books in elementary school? Were Indians portrayed as civilized or savages, simpletons or intelligent persons? How have they been portrayed in the media, for example, in the movies? What effects might these portrayals have on Native American children?
2. How much autonomy and independence should Native American tribes have? Should they be allowed to govern their own affairs apart from the oversight of a federal government? Explain your answer. Would you agree that other ethnic groups should have the same level of local autonomy? Why or why not?
3. Identify some specific ways in which Native Americans have been denied autonomy. How has this denial of self-governance prevented these tribes from flourishing? Has your ethnic or cultural group been prevented from flourishing by similar denials of group autonomy? Why or why not?
4. Many would argue that America is guilty of attempted genocide against American Indians. Consider the implications of that claim. If true, are American Indians owed reparations? If true, would it be an act of self-hatred for Native Americans to assimilate into a culture that nearly annihilated them?
5. What is the difference between the terms "American Indian" and "Native American"? What connotations are associated with each? Is there some reason to prefer one term over the other?

For Further Reading

For biographical information on Clyde Warrior see *Like a Hurricane* (1996), by P. C. Smith and R. A. Warrior. The idea of Red Power is discussed in *Custer Died for Your Sins* (1969), by V. Deloria, Jr.; *The New Indians* (1968), by S. Steiner; and *Red Power: The American Indians' Fight for Freedom* (1971), edited by A. M. Josephy, Jr. For a history of Native Americans sensitive to the Native American perspective, see *The American Indian: Prehistory to the Present* (1980), by A. M. Gibson. *Native America in the Twentieth Century: An Encyclopedia* (1996), edited by M. B. Davis, is a good source for information about twentieth-century Native Americans.

To learn more about the NIYC see "'Rise Up, Make Haste. Our People Need Us!' The National Indian Youth Council and the Origins of the Red Power Movement" and "Activities of the National Indian Youth Council," both available through the NIYC (318 Elm St. S.E., Albuquerque, NM).

21 "PRICKS" AND "CHICKS": A PLEA FOR "PERSONS"
Robert Baker

Robert Baker's article, reprinted next, has been anthologized many times and has been the occasion for much reflection and discussion. Baker's focus is language and the way language shapes culture, in turn shaping our personal identity. Key to his argument is the claim that how we *identify* a thing reflects our *conception* of that thing. By looking at the words we use to identify the race and gender of a person, we uncover how race and gender are conceived. The words we use don't merely refer to things, pointing them out for others to see, but instead both reflect and shape our conception of that thing. Throughout this article, Baker will be addressing some particularly offensive uses of language: crude and troubling language about race, sex, and gender. The purpose of this analysis, however, is not to focus on their crudeness or vulgarity, but rather to explore the 'grammar' of these metaphors and what that grammar reveals about gender and racial prejudice. This strategy has a practical advantage: it lets the reader evaluate the proposition that language does not just reflect a conception of the world, but in addition helps to shape and mold that world.

There are a number of questions to ask as you read this passage. Do these metaphorical terms actually *reflect* cultural attitudes or are they in some way misrepresentative? Does this language merely *reflect* cultural attitudes, or does it also *shape* and *construct* them? Would a change in language result in a corresponding change in our conceptions about race and sexuality? And finally, what accounts for the permanence of these offensive terms?

(The reader is cautioned that the following selection contains a frank analysis of vulgar and offensive words.)

Reading Questions

1. What, according to Baker, is the relationship between the metaphorical use of terms—such as "boy" for an African American—and cultural conceptual structures?
2. What changes occurred in the language used to refer to African Americans? What significance does Baker attach to these linguistic changes?
3. What do the pronouns of English identify as the most important characteristic of humans? How does the example of "over" and "under" illustrate this?
4. Why does Baker believe that animal and plaything terms for women are offensive and denigrating?
5. What does the comparison between a tennis partner and a sex partner show about what it means to be a male's sexual partner? How is this related to cultural paradigms for sexual intercourse?
6. Explain why Baker does not believe that anatomical differences between men and women adequately explain the asymmetry of metaphorical language for sexual intercourse.

I. IDENTIFICATION AND CONCEPTION

Until the 1960s, Afro-Americans were identified by such terms as "Negro" and "colored" (the respectable terms) and by the more disreputable "nigger," "spook," "kink," and so on. Recently there has been an unsuccessful attempt to replace the respectable identifications with such terms as "African," and "Afro-American," and a more successful attempt to replace them with "black." The most outspoken champions of this linguistic reform were those who argued that nonviolence must be abandoned for Black Power (Stokely Carmichael, H. Rap Brown), that integration must be abandoned in favor of separation (the Black Muslims: Malcolm X, Muhammad Ali), and that Afro-Americans were an internal colony in the alien world of Babylon who must arm themselves against the possibility of extermination (the Black Panthers: Eldridge Cleaver, Huey Newton). All of these movements and their partisans wished to stress that Afro-Americans were different from other Americans and could not be merged with them because the difference between the two was as great as that between black and white. Linguistically, of course, "black" and "white" are antonyms; and it is precisely this sense of oppositeness that those who see the Afro-American as alienated, separated, and nonintegratable wish to capture with the term "black." Moreover, as any good dictionary makes clear, in some contexts "black" is synonymous with "deadly," "sinister," "wicked," "evil," and so forth. The new militants were trying to create just this picture of the black man—civil rights and Uncle Tomism are dead, the ghost of Nat Turner is to be resurrected, freedom now or pay the price, the ballot or the bullet, violence is as American as cherry pie.—The new strategy was that the white man would either give the black man his due or pay the price in violence. Since conceptually a "black man" was an object to be feared ("black" can be synonymous with "deadly," and so on), while a "colored man" or a "Negro" was not, the new strategy required that the "Negro" be supplanted by the "black man." White America resisted the proposed linguistic reform quite vehemently, until hundreds of riots forced the admission that the Afro-American was indeed black.

II. WAYS OF IDENTIFYING WOMEN

It may at first seem trivial to note that women (and men) are identified sexually; but conceptually this is extremely significant. To appreciate the significance of this fact it is helpful to imagine a language in which proper names and personal pronouns do not reflect the sex of the person designated by them (as they do in our language). I have been told that in some oriental languages pronouns and proper names reflect social status rather than sex, but whether or not there actually exists such a language is irrelevant, for it is easy enough to imagine what one would be like. Let us then imagine a language where the proper names are sexually neutral (for example, "Xanthe"), so that one cannot tell from hearing a name whether the person so named is male or female, and where the personal pronouns in the language are "under" and "over." "Under" is the personal pronoun appropriate for all those who are younger than thirty, while "over" is appropriate to persons older than thirty. In such a language, instead of saying such things as "Where do you think *he* is living now?" one would say such things as "Where do you think *under* is living now?"

What would one say about a cultural community that employed such a language? Clearly, one would say that they thought that for purposes of intelligible communication it was more important to know a person's age grouping than the person's height, sex, race, hair color, or parentage. (There are many actual cultures, of course, in which people are identified by names that reflect their parentage; for example, Abu ben Adam means Abu son of Adam.) I think that one would also claim that this people would not have reflected these differences in the pronominal structure of their language if they did not believe that the differences between unders and overs was such that a statement would frequently have one meaning if it were about an under and a different meaning if it were about an over. For example, in feudal times if a serf said, "My lord said to do this," that assertion was radically different from "Freeman John said to do this," since (presumably) the former had the status of a command while the latter did not. Hence the conventions of Middle English required that one refer to people in such a way as to indicate their social status. Analogously, one would not distinguish between pronominal references according to the age differences in the persons referred to were there no shift in meaning involved.

If we apply the lesson illustrated by this imaginary language to our own, I think that it should be clear that since in our language proper nouns and pronouns reflect sex rather than age, race, parentage, social status, or religion, we believe one of the most important things one can know about a person is that person's sex. (And, indeed, this is the first thing one seeks to determine about a newborn babe—our first question is almost invariably "Is it a boy or a girl?") Moreover, we would not reflect this important difference pronominally did we not also believe that statements frequently mean one thing when applied to males and something else when applied to females. Perhaps the most striking aspect of the conceptual discrimination reflected in our language is that man is, as it were, essentially human, while woman is only accidentally so.

This charge may seem rather extreme, but consider the following synonyms (which are readily confirmed by any dictionary). "Humanity" is synonymous with "mankind" but not with "womankind." "Man" can be substituted for "humanity" or "mankind" in any sentence in which the terms "mankind" or "humanity" occur without changing the meaning of the sentence, but significantly, "woman" cannot. Thus, the following expressions are all synonymous with each other: "humanity's great achievements," "mankind's great achievements," and "man's great achievements." "Woman's great achievements" is not synonymous with any of these. To highlight the degree to which women are excluded from humanity, let me point out that it is something of a truism to say that "man is a rational animal," while "woman is a rational animal" is quite debatable. Clearly, if "man" in the first assertion embraced both men and women, the second assertion would be just as much a truism as the first. Humanity, it would seem, is a male prerogative. (And hence, one of the goals of woman's liberation is to alter our conceptual structure so that someday "mankind" will be regarded as an improper and vestigial ellipsis for "humankind," and "man" will have no special privileges in relation to "human being" that "woman" does not have.)

The major question before us is, "How are women conceived of in our culture?" I have been trying to answer this question by talking about how they are identified. I first considered pronominal identification; now I wish to turn to identification through other types of noun phrases. Methods of non-pronominal identification can be discovered by determining which terms can be substituted for "woman" in such sentences as "Who is that woman over there?" without changing the meaning of the sentence. Virtually no term is interchangeable with "woman" in that sentence for all speakers on all occasions. Even "lady," which most speakers would accept as synonymous with "woman" in that sentence, will not do for a speaker who applies the term "lady" only to those women who display manners, poise, and sensitivity. In most contexts, a large number of students in one or more of my classes will accept the following types of terms as more or less interchangeable with "woman." (An asterisk indicates interchanges acceptable to both males and females; a plus sign indicates terms restricted to black students only. Terms with neither an asterisk nor a plus sign are acceptable by all males but are not normally used by females.)

A. NEUTRAL TERMS: *lady, *gal, *girl (especially with regard to a co-worker in an office or factory), *+sister, *broad (originally in the animal category, but most people do not think of the term as now meaning pregnant cow)

B. ANIMAL: *chick, bird, fox, vixen, filly, bitch (Many do not know the literal meaning of the term. Some men and most women construe this use as pejorative; they think of "bitch" in the context of "bitchy," that is, snappy, nasty, and so forth. But a large group of men claim that it is a standard nonpejorative term of identification—which may perhaps indicate that women have come to be thought of as shrews by a large subclass of men.)

C. PLAYTHING: babe, doll, cuddly

D. GENDER (association with articles of clothing typically worn by those in the female gender role): skirt, hem

E. SEXUAL: snatch, cunt, ass, twat, piece (of ass, and so forth), lay, pussy (could be put in the animal category, but most users associated it with slang expression indicating the female pubic region), +hammer (related to anatomical analogy between a hammer and breasts). There are many other usages, for example, "bunny," "sweat hog," but these were not recognized as standard by as many as ten percent of any given class.

The students in my classes reported that the most frequently used terms of identification are in the neutral and animal classifications (although men in their forties claim to use the gender classifications quite a bit) and that the least frequently used terms of identification are sexual. Fortunately, however, I am not interested in the frequency of usage but only in whether the use is standard enough to be recognized as an identification among some group or other. (Recall that "brown" was not a standardized term of identification and hence we could not make sense out of "Who was the brown who planned Washington, D.C.?" Similarly, one has trouble with "Who was the breasts who planned Washington, D.C.?" but not with "Who was the babe (doll, chick, skirt, and so forth) who planned Washington, D.C.?")

Except for two of the animal terms, "chick" and "broad"—but note that "broad" is probably neutral today—women do not typically identify themselves in sexual terms, in gender terms, as playthings, or as animals; *only males use nonneutral terms to identify women.* Hence, it would seem that there is a male conception of women and a female conception. Only males identify women as "foxes," "babes," "skirts," or "cunts" (and since all the other nonneutral identifications are male, it is reasonable to assume that the identification of a woman as a "chick" is primarily a male conception that some women have adopted).

What kind of conception do men have of women? Clearly they think that women share certain properties with certain types of animals, toys, and playthings; they conceive of them in terms of the clothes associated with the female gender role; and, last (and, if my classes are any indication, least frequently), they conceive of women in terms of those parts of their anatomy associated with sexual intercourse, that is, as the identification "lay" indicates quite clearly, as sexual partners.

The first two nonneutral male classifications, animal and plaything, are *prima facie* denigrating (and I mean this in the literal sense of making one like a "nigger"). Consider the animal classification. . . .

With one exception all of the animal terms reflect a male conception of women either as domesticated servants or as pets, or as both. Indeed, some of the terms reflect a conception of women first as pets and then as servants. Thus, when a pretty, cuddly little chick grows older, she becomes a very useful servant—the egg-laying hen.

...

In considering plaything identifications, only one sentence is necessary. *All the plaything identifications are clearly denigrating since they assimilate women to the status of mindless or dependent objects.* "Doll" is to male paternalism what "boy" is to white paternalism.

Up to this point in our survey of male conceptions of women, every male identification, without exception, has been clearly antithetical to the conception of women as human beings (recall that "man" was synonymous with "human," while "woman" was not). Since the way we talk of things, and especially the way we identify them, is the way in which we conceive of them, any movement dedicated to breaking the bonds of female servitude must destroy these ways of identifying and hence of conceiving of women. Only when both sexes find the terms "babe," "doll," "chick," "broad," and so forth, as objectionable as "boy" and "nigger" will women come to be conceived of as independent *human beings.*

The two remaining unexamined male identifications are gender and sex. There seems to be nothing objectionable about gender identifications per se. That is, women are metaphorically identified as skirts because in this culture, skirts, like women, are peculiarly female. Indeed, if one accepts the view that the slogan "female and proud" should play the same role for the women's liberation movement that the slogan "Black is beautiful" plays for the black-liberation movement, then female clothes should be worn with the same pride as Afro clothes. (Of course, one can argue that the skirt, like the cropped-down Afro, is a sign of bondage, and hence both the item of clothing and the identification with it are to be rejected—that is, cropped-down Afros are to Uncle Tom what skirts are to Uncle Mom.)

...

What is objectionable in the animal and plaything identifications is not the fact that some of these identifications reflect a sexual context but rather that—regardless of the context—these identifications reflect a conception of women as mindless servants (whether animate or inanimate is irrelevant). The point is not that men ought not to think of women in sexual terms but that they ought to think of them as human beings; and the slogan *men should not think of women as sex objects* is only appropriate when a man thinking of a woman as a sexual partner automatically conceives of her as something less than human. The point about *sex objects* is not merely that it is inappropriate for a man, when, for example, listening to a woman deliver a serious academic paper, to imagine having sexual intercourse with the woman; it is inappropriate, of course, but much in the same way that it is inappropriate to imagine playing tennis with the speaker. The difference between a tennis partner and a sex partner is that whereas there is nothing degrading about a woman's being thought of as a tennis partner, there seems to be something *degrading* about her being thought of as a man's sex partner in our society—at least outside of the circumscribed context of a love relationship. (Note that it would be inappropriate, but not necessarily degrading to the woman, for a man in the audience to imagine courting the woman, having an affair with the woman, or marrying the woman; it does degrade the woman for the man to mentally undress the woman, or imagine an act of sexual intercourse between them.) The reason why unadorned sexual partnership is degrading to the female is that in this relationship the female is conceptualized, and treated not merely as a mindless thing productive of male pleasure, but as an *object* in the Kantian sense of the term—as a person whose autonomy has been violated. Or, to put the point differently, the reason why it is degrading for a woman to be conceptualized as a sexual partner is because *rape* is our paradigm of unadorned sexual intercourse.

IV. OUR CONCEPTION OF SEXUAL INTERCOURSE

Consider the terms we use to identify coitus, or more technically, the terms that function synonymously with "had sexual intercourse with" in a sentence of the form "A had sexual intercourse with B." The following is a list of some commonly used synonyms (numerous others that are not as widely used have been omitted, for example, "diddled," "laid pipe with"):

screwed
laid
fucked
had

did it with (to)
banged
balled
humped
slept with
made love to

Now, for a select group of these verbs, names for males are the subjects of sentences with active constructions (that is, where the subjects are said to be doing the activity); and names for females require passive constructions (that is, they are the recipients of the activity—whatever is done is done to them). Thus, we would not say "Jane did it to Dick," although we would say "Dick did it to Jane." Again, Dick bangs Jane, Jane does not bang Dick; Dick humps Jane, Jane does not hump Dick. In contrast, verbs like "did it with" do not require an active role for the male; thus, "Dick did it with Jane and Jane with Dick." Again, Jane may make love to Dick, just as Dick makes love to Jane; and Jane sleeps with Dick as easily as Dick sleeps with Jane. (My students were undecided about "laid." Most thought that it would be unusual indeed for Jane to lay Dick, unless she played the masculine role of seducer-agressor.)

The sentences thus form the following pairs. (Those nonconjoined singular noun phrases where a female subject requires a passive construction are marked with a cross. An asterisk indicates that the sentence in question is not a sentence of English if it is taken as synonymous with the italicized sentence heading the column.)

Dick had sexual intercourse with Jane
Dick screwed Jane+
Dick laid Jane+
Dick fucked Jane+
Dick had Jane+
Dick did it to Jane+
Dick banged Jane+
Dick humped Jane+
Dick balled Jane (?)
Dick did it with Jane
Dick slept with Jane
Dick made love to Jane
Jane had sexual intercourse with Dick
Jane was banged by Dick
Jane was humped by Dick
* Jane was done by Dick

Jane was screwed by Dick
Jane was laid by Dick
Jane was fucked by Dick
Jane was had by Dick
Jane balled Dick (?)
Jane did it with Dick
Jane slept with Dick
Jane made love to Dick
*Jane screwed Dick
*Jane laid Dick
*Jane fucked Dick
*Jane had Dick
*Jane did it to Dick
*Jane banged Dick
*Jane humped Dick

These lists make clear that within the standard view of sexual intercourse, males, or at least names for males, seem to play a different role than females, since male subjects play an active role in the language of screwing, fucking, having, doing it, and perhaps, laying, while female subjects play a passive role.

The asymmetrical nature of the relationship indicated by the sentences marked with a cross is confirmed by the fact that the form "_ed with each other" is acceptable for the sentences not marked with a cross, but not for those that require a male subject. Thus:

Dick and Jane had sexual intercourse with each other
Dick and Jane made love to each other
Dick and Jane slept with each other
Dick and Jane did it with each other
Dick and Jane balled with each other (*?)
*Dick and Jane banged with each other
*Dick and Jane did it to each other
*Dick and Jane had each other
*Dick and Jane fucked each other
*Dick and Jane humped each other
*(?)Dick and Jane laid each other
*Dick and Jane screwed each other

It should be clear, therefore, that our language reflects a difference between the male and female sexual roles, and hence that we conceive of the male and female roles in different ways. The question that now arises is, "What difference in our conception of the male and female sexual roles requires active constructions for males and passive for females?"

One explanation for the use of the active construction for males and the passive construction for females is that this grammatical asymmetry merely reflects the natural physiological asymmetry between men and women: the asymmetry of "to screw" and "to be screwed," "to insert into" and "to be inserted into." That is, it might be argued that the difference between masculine and feminine grammatical roles merely reflects a difference naturally required by the anatomy of males and females. This explanation is inadequate. Anatomical differences do not determine how we are to conceptualize the relation between penis and vagina during intercourse. Thus one can easily imagine a society in which the female normally played the active role during intercourse, where female subjects required active constructions with verbs indicating copulation, and where the standard metaphors were terms like "engulfing"—that is, instead of saying "he screwed her," one would say "she engulfed him." It follows that the use of passive constructions for female subjects of verbs indicating copulation does not reflect differences determined by human anatomy but rather reflects those generated by human customs.

What I am going to argue next is that the passive construction of verbs indicating coitus (that is, indicating the female position) can *also* be used to indicate that a person is being harmed. I am then going to argue that the metaphor involved would only make sense if we conceive of the female role in intercourse as that of a person being harmed (or being taken advantage of).

Passive constructions of "fucked," "screwed," and "had" indicate the female role. They also can be used to indicate being harmed. Thus, in all of the following sentences, Marion plays the female role: "Bobbie fucked Marion"; "Bobbie screwed Marion"; "Bobbie had Marion"; "Marion was fucked"; "Marion was screwed"; and "Marion was had." All of the statements are equivocal. They might literally mean that someone had sexual intercourse with Marion (who played the female role); or they might mean, metaphorically, that Marion was deceived, hurt, or taken advantage of. Thus, we say things as "I've been screwed" ("fucked," "had," "taken," and so on) when we have been treated unfairly, been sold shoddy merchandise, or conned out of valuables. Throughout this essay I have been arguing that metaphors are applied to things only if what the term *actually* applies to shares one or more properties with what the term *metaphorically* applies to. Thus, the female sexual role must have something in common with being conned or being sold shoddy merchandise. The only common property is that of being harmed, deceived, or taken advantage of. *Hence we conceive of a person who plays the female sexual role as someone who is being harmed* (that is, "screwed," "fucked," and so on).

It might be objected that this is clearly wrong, since the unsignated terms do not indicate someone's being harmed, and hence we do not conceive of having intercourse as being harmed. The point about the unsignated terms, however, is that they can take both females and males as subjects (in active constructions) and thus *do not pick out the female role*. This demonstrates that we conceive of sexual roles in such a way that only females are thought to be taken advantage of in intercourse.

The best part of solving a puzzle is when all the pieces fall into place. If the subjects of the passive construction are being harmed, presumably the subjects of the active constructions are doing harm, and, indeed, we do conceive of these subjects in precisely this way. Suppose one is angry at someone and wishes to express malevolence as forcefully as possible without actually committing an act of physical violence. If one is inclined to be vulgar one can make the sign of the erect male cock by clenching one's fist while raising one's middle finger, or by clenching one's fist and raising one's arm and shouting such things as "screw you," "up yours," or "fuck you." In other words, one of the strongest possible ways of telling someone that you wish to harm him is to tell him to assume the female sexual role relative to you. Again, to say to someone "go fuck yourself" is to order him to harm himself, while to call someone a "mother fucker" is not so much a play on his Oedipal fears as to accuse him of being so low that he would inflict the greatest imaginable harm (fucking) upon that person who is most dear to him (his mother). . . .

Discussion Questions

1. It has been over 25 years since Baker first wrote this article. Do we still use the same metaphorical terms to describe sexual intercourse and women? What new terms are now commonly used? Are they still as problematic as previous language? Do the new metaphors still retain the same gender asymmetry?

2. Do metaphorical terms used for sexual intercourse reflect our beliefs about sexual intercourse, or do they shape and construct those beliefs? Or perhaps these metaphorical terms do neither or both. Explain your view.

3. Silently consider the following example. Write down your answer and then discuss it with your group or class. Does this riddle support Baker's argument? Why or why not?

   A child is brought into a hospital emergency room in need of surgery. The surgeon examines the boy and states, "I cannot operate on the child; he is my son." The surgeon is not the boy's father. What is the relationship between the child and the surgeon?

4. What words are now used to refer to North Americans who descended from Africa? What changes have happened over the past 40 years? Do these changes correspond to new cultural attitudes toward this racial group? Does the new language reflect changing conceptions or was it part of causing these new perceptions? Would cultural conceptions have changed without these new words?

5. What words are commonly used to describe your cultural or ethnic group in this culture? What is the history of these words? How did they originate? Does the use of these words pose any problems or difficulties for members of your cultural or ethnic group? Why or why not?

For Further Reading

There are several useful sources for continuing the dialogue Baker has begun. See especially *Sexist Language,* edited by Mary Vetterling-Braggin (1981), which contains this article as well as several responses and a helpful bibliography. This book also includes Stephanie Ross's article "How Words Hurt," in which Ross analyzes how metaphors function to create oppressive language. For an interesting and contrasting analysis of visual images, see Terry Winant's "How Ordinary (Sexist) Discourse Resists Radical (Feminist) Critique," reprinted in *Hypatia Reborn,* edited by Azizah Y. al-Hibri and Margaret A. Simons (1990).

CHAPTER 5

WHAT IS THE NATURE OF THE UNIVERSE?

W hat is the nature of the universe? This question can be asked and answered on many different levels. For example, it is a question about the *origins* of the universe: Where did the universe come from? It is also a question about the *contents* or *substance* of the universe: What is the universe made of? And it is a question about how the universe *works:* How do the contents of the universe relate to each other? These questions constitute a field of philosophy called **metaphysics.**

Historically, philosophy has focused on the second question. Philosophers sought to understand the universe by investigating—or, more precisely, speculating about—the basic substance of the universe, what it was made of. It was hoped that discovering what 'stuff' the universe was made of would lead to an understanding of how the universe worked. And then, perhaps, one could control nature, instead of being at its mercy.

This inquiry into the nature of substance has very deep roots, predating even Plato (427–347 B.C.E.) and Aristotle (384–322 B.C.E). As far as can be determined, the Ionians— Thales (c. 624–545 B.C.E.), Anaximander (c. 610–545 B.C.E.), and Anaximenes (c. 580–500 B.C.E.)—were the first Western philosophers to consider the question. Today, the investigations of the Ionians look very amateurish. Anaximenes, for example, believed that everything was made out of air, either a condensed form of air or a rarefied form of air. However mistaken, the efforts of the Ionians nonetheless represented a profound change. Instead of appealing to the gods as an explanation of how and why the universe worked and operated as it did, the Ionians sought an understanding based on an investigation of the universe itself—the first small steps toward a true science.

This chapter picks up the debate over the substance of the universe in the seventeenth century with René Descartes (1596–1650), and then John Locke (1632–1704), and George Berkeley (1685–1753). Interestingly, the positions these three took about the nature of substance are primarily influenced by their divergent views about **epistemology** (the investigation of how knowledge is acquired and what can be known). The selections by Descartes, Locke, and Berkeley are not, then, only a record of their views on the nature of substance, but also an insight into their beliefs about the limits of human understanding.

One of the most important challenges to metaphysics has come from David Hume (1711–1776). Hume asks whether or not metaphysics is possible: Are rational speculations into the nature of the universe ever justified? Or are these conjectures idle fancy? In the selection included in this chapter, Hume attacks a basic principle of metaphysics, the principle of cause and effect. By making some simple distinctions, Hume shows that there is no warrant for our belief in cause and effect. And since this principle underlies most of our beliefs about the world, these beliefs are without foundation as well.

The final selection comes from A. J. Ayer (1910–1989), a representative of **logical positivism** or positivism. Positivists endorse a particular theory about the meaningfulness of sentences, what is called the **verifiability criterion** of meaning. Roughly, the theory claims that a sentence is meaningful only if it can be verified. For example, the sentence "The dog has fleas" is meaningful only if the conditions under which the sentence would be true (or false) can be stated (in terms that can be empirically verified). Since those conditions are perfectly clear in this particular case, the sentence has meaning. If, however, such conditions cannot be stated for a sentence, then the sentence in question is utterly without meaning. And this is exactly what Ayer believes is true about metaphysics. The 'truth-conditions' for most metaphysical sentences cannot be stated. Hence, those sentences are meaningless. Logical positivism 'solves' metaphysical problems by eliminating the questions. For example, the problem of free will and determinism disappears if the empirical conditions that verify claims such as "I have free will" cannot be stated.

22 SUBSTANCE
René Descartes

Born in La Haye, France, René Descartes (1596–1650) left an indelible mark on philosophy, mathematics, and the sciences. Descartes began his education at La Flèche but eventually transferred to Poitiers, where he completed his formal education. By and large, Descartes was unhappy with the scholastic education—a blend of the philosophy of Aristotle and Roman Catholicism—he received. Being a theist, Descartes focused his complaints on that part of his education concerned with the works of Aristotle, specifically Aristotle's science.

For Descartes, Aristotle's science merely described the *what*—the events that took place in the world—rather than the *how* or the *why*. Explaining the phenomenon of falling bodies by referring to their heaviness, as did Aristotle, did not satisfy Descartes. Hence, Descartes set out to create a new science (or scientific method) to replace Aristotle's. This project resulted in several important works by Descartes, including *Rules for the Direction of the Mind* (1620), *The World* (1630), *Discourse on the Method for Properly Conducting Reason and Searching for Truth in the Sciences* (1637), *Meditations on First Philosophy* (1641), and *Principles of Philosophy* (1644).

The following selection comes from the *Principles of Philosophy* and concerns the nature of **substance.** For Descartes, the primary and sole characteristic of substance, matter, or body is that it is extended in space; that is, it has three dimensions. But why should this be all that substance

SOURCE: From *The Philosophical Works of Descartes*, Vols. 1–2, by Elizabeth S. Haldane and G. R. T. Ross (eds./trans.). © 1931 by Cambridge University Press. Used by permission of Cambridge University Press.

amounts to? Do various substances not have particular densities or textures? Descartes answers that "the nature of matter or of body in its universal aspect, does not consist in its being hard, or heavy, or colored, or one that affects our senses in some other way, but solely in the fact that it is a substance extended in length, breadth and depth. . . . [Since] reason shows us that weight, color, and all the other qualities of the kind that is perceived in corporeal matter, may be taken from it, it remaining meanwhile entire: it thus follows that the nature of body depends on none of these."

Reading Questions

1. What are the two ultimate classes of real things? What classes pertain to extended substance?
2. What is Descartes' understanding of substance? What is the one and only true substance?
3. How can one be sure that substance (other than God) exists?
4. What is the principal property of corporeal substance?
5. What are the reasons for our having a certain knowledge of material things?
6. Why is it that the nature of body consists not in weight, nor in hardness, nor color, and so on, but in extension alone?
7. In what sense is space no different from corporeal substance?
8. Why does Descartes believe that vacuums cannot exist?
9. Why does Descartes believe that matter is infinitely divisible?
10. How much substance is there in the universe?
11. What explains the variations in matter?
12. What is motion?

PRINCIPLE XLVIII

That all the objects of our perceptions are to be considered either as things or the affections of things, or else as eternal truths; and the enumeration of things.

I distinguish all the objects of our knowledge either into things or the affections of things, or as eternal truths having no existence outside our thought. Of the things we consider as real, the most general are *substance, duration, order, number,* and possibly such other similar matters as range through all the classes of real things. I do not however observe more than two ultimate classes of real things—the one is intellectual things, or those of the intelligence, that is, pertaining to the mind or to thinking substance, the other is material things, or that pertaining to extended substance, i.e., to body. Perception, volition, and every mode of knowing and willing, pertain to thinking substance; while to extended substance pertain magnitude or extension in length, breadth and depth, figure, movement, situation, divisibility into parts themselves

divisible, and such like. Besides these, there are, however, certain things which we experience in ourselves and which should be attributed neither to mind nor body alone, but to the close and intimate union that exists between the body and mind as I shall later on explain in the proper place. Such are the appetites of hunger, thirst, etc., and also the emotions or passions of the mind which do not subsist in mind or thought alone, as the emotions of anger, joy, sadness, love, etc.; and, finally all the sensations such as pain, pleasure, light and color, sounds, odors, tastes, heat, hardness, and all other tactile qualities.

. . .

PRINCIPLE LI

What substance is, and that it is a name which we cannot attribute in the same sense to God and to His creatures.

As regards these matters which we consider as being things or modes of things, it is necessary that we should examine them here one by one. By substance, we can understand nothing else than a thing which so exists that it needs no other thing in order to exist. And in fact only one single substance can be understood which clearly needs nothing else, namely, God. We perceive that all other things can exist only by the help of the concourse of God. That is why the word substance does not pertain *univoce* to God and to other things, as they say in the schools, that is, no common signification for this appellation which will apply equally to God and to them can be distinctly understood.

PRINCIPLE LII

That it may be attributed univocally to the soul and to body, and how we know substance.

Created substances, however, whether corporeal or thinking, may be conceived under this common concept; for they are things which need only the concurrence of God in order to exist. But yet substance cannot be first discovered merely from the fact that it is a thing that exists, for that fact alone is not observed by us. We may, however, easily discover it by means of any one of its attributes because it is a common notion that nothing is possessed of no attributes, properties, or qualities. For this reason, when we perceive any attribute, we therefore conclude that some existing thing or substance to which it may be attributed, is necessarily present.

PRINCIPLE LIII

That each substance has a principal attribute, and that the attribute of the mind is thought, while that of body is extension.

But although any one attribute is sufficient to give us a knowledge of substance, there is always one principal property of substance which constitutes its nature and essence, and on which all the others depend. Thus extension in length, breadth and depth, constitutes the nature of corporeal substance; and thought constitutes the nature of thinking substance. For all else that may be attributed to body presupposes extension, and is but a mode of this extended thing; as everything that we find in mind is but so many diverse forms of thinking. Thus, for example, we cannot conceive figure but as an extended thing, nor

movement but as in an extended space; so imagination, feeling, and will, only exist in a thinking thing. But, on the other hand, we can conceive extension without figure or action, and thinking without imagination or sensation, and so on with the rest; as is quite clear to anyone who attends to the matter.

...

PRINCIPLE LXIII

How we may have distinct conceptions of thought and extension, inasmuch as the one constitutes the nature of mind, and the other that of body.

We may likewise consider thought and extension as constituting the natures of intelligence and corporeal substance; and then they must not be considered otherwise than as the very substances that think and are extended, i.e., as mind and body; for we know them in this way very clearly and distinctly. It is moreover more easy to know a substance that thinks, or an extended substance, than substance alone, without regarding whether it thinks or is extended. For we experience some difficulty in abstracting the notions that we have of substance from those of thought or extension, for they in truth do not differ but in thought, and our conception is not more distinct because it comprehends fewer properties, but because we distinguish accurately that which it does comprehend from all other notions.

...

PRINCIPLE I

What are the reasons for our having a certain knowledge of material things?

Although we are all persuaded that material things exist, yet because we have doubted this before and have placed it in the rank of the prejudices of our childhood, it is now requisite that we should inquire into the reasons through which we may accept this truth with certainty. To begin with we feel that without doubt all our perceptions proceed from some thing which is different from our mind. For it is not in our power to have one perception rather than another, since each one is clearly dependent on the object which affects our senses. It is true that we may inquire whether that object is God, or some other different from God. But inasmuch as we perceive, or rather are stimulated by sense to apprehend clearly and distinctly a matter which is extended in length, breadth, and depth, the various parts of which have various figures and motions, and give rise to the sensations we have of colors, smells, pains, etc., if God immediately and of Himself presented to our mind the idea of this extended matter, or merely permitted it to be caused in us by some other object which possessed no extension, figure, or motion, there would be nothing to prevent Him from being regarded as a deceiver. For we clearly apprehend this matter as different from God, or ourselves, or our mind, and appear to discern very plainly that the idea of it is due to objects outside of ourselves to which it is absolutely similar. But God cannot deceive us, because deception is repugnant to His nature, as has been explained. And hence we must conclude that there is an object extended in length, breadth, and depth, and possessing all those properties which we clearly perceive to pertain to extended objects. And this extended object is called by us either body or matter.

...

PRINCIPLE III

That the perceptions of the senses do not teach us what is really in things, but merely that whereby they are useful or hurtful to man's composite nature.

It will be sufficient for us to observe that the perceptions of the sense are related simply to the intimate union which exists between body and mind, and that while by their means we are made aware of what in external bodies can profit or hurt this union, they do not present them to us as they are in themselves unless occasionally and accidentally. For [after this observation] we shall without difficulty set aside all the prejudices of the senses and in this regard rely upon our understanding alone, by reflecting carefully on the ideas implanted therein by nature.

PRINCIPLE IV

That the nature of body consists not in weight, nor in hardness, nor color and so on, but in extension alone.

In this way we shall ascertain that the nature of matter or of body in its universal aspect, does not

consist in its being hard, or heavy, or colored, or one that affects our senses in some other way, but solely in the fact that it is a substance extended in length, breadth and depth. For as regards hardness we do not know anything of it by sense, excepting that the portions of the hard bodies resist the motion of our hands when they come in contact with them; but if, whenever we moved our hands in some direction, all the bodies in that part retreated with the same velocity as our hands approached them, we should never feel hardness; and yet we have no reason to believe that the bodies which recede in this way would on this account lose what makes them bodies. It follows from this that the nature of body does not consist in hardness. The same reason shows us that weight, color, and all the other qualities of the kind that is perceived in corporeal matter, may be taken from it, it remaining meanwhile entire: it thus follows that the nature of body depends on none of these.

...

PRINCIPLE XI

In what sense it may be said that space is not different from corporeal substance.

And it will be easy for us to recognize that the same extension which constitutes the nature of body likewise constitutes the nature of space, nor do the two mutually differ, excepting as the nature of the genus or species differs from the nature of the individual, provided that, in order to discern the idea that we have of any body, such as stone, we reject from it all that is not essential to the nature of body. In the first place, then, we may reject hardness, because if the stone were liquefied or reduced to powder, it would no longer possess hardness, and yet would not cease to be a body; let us in the next place reject color, because we have often seen stones so transparent that they had no color; again we reject weight, because we see that fire although very light is yet body; and finally we may reject cold, heat, and all the other qualities of the kind either because they are not considered as in the stone, or else because with the change of their qualities the stone is not for that reason considered to have lost its nature as body. After examination we shall find that there is nothing remaining in the idea of body excepting that it is extended in length, breadth, and depth; and this is comprised in our idea of space, not only of that which is full of body, but also of that which is called a vacuum.

...

PRINCIPLE XVI

That it is contrary to reason to say that there is a vacuum or space in which there is absolutely nothing.

As regards a vacuum in the philosophic sense of the word, i.e., a space in which there is no substance, it is evident that such cannot exist, because the extension of space or internal place, is not different from that of body. For, from the mere fact that a body is extended in length, breadth, or depth, we have reason to conclude that it is a substance, because it is absolutely inconceivable that nothing should possess extension, we ought to conclude also that the same is true of the space which is supposed to be void, i.e., that since there is in it extension, there is necessarily also substance.

...

PRINCIPLE XVIII

How the prejudice concerning the absolute vacuum is to be corrected.

We have almost all lapsed into this error from the beginning of our lives, for, seeing that there is no necessary connection between the vessel and the body it contains, we thought that God at least could remove all the body contained in the vessel without its being necessary that any other body should take its place. But in order that we may be able to correct this error, it is necessary to remark that while there is no connection between the vessel and that particular body which it contains, there is an absolutely necessary one between the concave figure of the vessel and the extension considered generally which must be comprised in this cavity; so that there is not more contradiction in conceiving a mountain without a valley, than such a cavity without the extension which it contains, or this extension without the substance which is extended, because nothing, as has already been frequently remarked, cannot have extension. And therefore, if it is asked what would happen if

God removed all the body contained in a vessel without permitting its place being occupied by another body, we shall answer that the sides of the vessel will thereby come into immediate contiguity with one another. For two bodies must touch when there is nothing between them, because it is manifestly contradictory for these two bodies to be apart from one another, or that there should be a distance between them, and yet that this distance should be nothing; for distance is a mode of extension, and without extended substance it cannot therefore exist.

...

PRINCIPLE XX

That from this may be demonstrated the non-existence of atoms.

We also know that there cannot be any atoms or parts of matter which are indivisible of their own nature [as certain philosophers have imagined]. For however small the parts are supposed to be, yet because they are necessarily extended we are always able in thought to divide any one of them into two or more parts; and thus we know that they are divisible. For there is nothing which we can divide in thought, which we do not thereby recognize to be divisible; and therefore if we judged it to be indivisible, our judgment would be contrary to the knowledge we have of the matter. And even should we suppose that God had reduced some portion of matter to a smallness so extreme that it could not be divided into smaller, it would not for all that be properly termed indivisible. For though God had rendered the particle so small that it was beyond the power of any creature to divide it, He could not deprive Himself of His power of division, because it is absolutely impossible that He should lessen His own omnipotence as was said before. And therefore, absolutely speaking, its divisibility remains [to the smallest extended particle] because from its nature it is such.

PRINCIPLE XXI

That extension of the world is likewise indefinite.

We likewise recognize that this world, or the totality of corporeal substance, is extended without limit, because wherever we imagine a limit we are not only still able to imagine beyond that limit spaces indefinitely extended, but we perceive these to be in reality such as we imagine them, that is to say that they contain in them corporeal substance indefinitely extended. For, as has been already shown very fully, the idea of extension that we perceive in any space whatever is quite evidently the same as the idea of corporeal substance.

PRINCIPLE XXII

Thus the matter of the heavens and of the earth is one and the same, and there cannot be a plurality of worlds.

It is thus not difficult to infer from all this, that the earth and heavens are formed of the same matter, and that even were there an infinitude of worlds, they would all be formed of this matter; from which it follows that there cannot be a plurality of worlds, because we clearly perceive that the matter whose nature consists in its being an extended substance only, now occupies all the imaginable spaces where these other worlds could alone be, and we cannot find in ourselves the idea of any other matter.

PRINCIPLE XXIII

That all the variety in matter, or all the diversity of its forms, depends on motion.

There is therefore but one matter in the whole universe, and we know this by the simple fact of its being extended. All the properties which we clearly perceive in it may be reduced to the one, viz. that it can be divided, or moved according to its parts, and consequently is capable of all these affections which we perceive can arise from the motion of its parts. For its partition by thought alone makes no difference to it; but all the variation in matter, or diversity in its forms, depends on motion. This the philosophers have doubtless observed, inasmuch as they have said that nature was the principle of motion and rest, and by nature they understood that by which all corporeal things become such as they are experienced to be.

PRINCIPLE XXIV

What motion is in common parlance.

But motion (i.e., local motion, for I can conceive no other kind, and do not consider that we ought to conceive any other in nature), in the vulgar sense, is nothing more than the *action by which any body passes from one place to another*. And just as we have remarked above that the same thing may be said to change and not to change its place at the same time, we can say that it moves and does not move at the same time. For he who is seated in a ship setting sail, thinks he is moving when he looks at the shore he has left, and considers it as fixed, but not if he regards the vessel he is on, because he does not change his position in reference to its parts. Likewise, because we are accustomed to think that there is no motion without action and that in rest there is cessation of action, the person thus seated may more properly be said to be in repose than in motion, since he is not conscious of any action in himself.

PRINCIPLE XXV

What movement properly speaking is.

But if, looking not to popular usage, but to the truth of the matter, let us consider what ought to be understood by motion according to the truth of the thing; we may say, in order to attribute a determinate nature to it, that it is the *transference of one part of matter or one body from the vicinity of those bodies that are in immediate contact with it, and which we regard as in repose, into the vicinity of others*. By *one body* or by a *part of matter* I understand all that which is transported together, although it may be composed of many parts which in themselves have other motions. And I say that it is the *transportation* and not either the force or the action which transports, in order to show that the motion is always in the mobile thing, not in that which moves; for these two do not seem to me to be accurately enough distinguished. Further, I understand that it is a mode of the mobile thing and not a substance, just as figure is a mode of the figured thing, and repose of that which is at rest. . . .

Discussion Questions

1. Does modern science still hold to Descartes' model of substance? What does modern science tell us is the basic stuff of the universe? How is this similar to or different from Descartes' view? Does the existence of vacuums undermine Descartes' understanding of substance? Why or why not?
2. To what extent does the fact that an atom of, say, gold cannot be split into two smaller pieces of gold undermine Descartes' understanding of substance?
3. Does it make sense to speak of 'real' nonextended things such as souls or God? Are these things just as 'real' as material substance?

For Further Reading

Two excellent collections of Descartes' work are *The Philosophical Works of Descartes* (1911), translated by Haldane and Ross, and *The Philosophical Writings of Descartes* (1984), translated by Cottingham, Stoothoff, Murdoch, and Kenny. Cottingham and Kenny also have excellent introductory texts to the philosophy of Descartes; see *Descartes* (1986) and *Descartes* (1968), respectively.

For texts featuring extended discussion of the nature of substance—including Descartes' views—see *Substance: Its Nature and Existence* (1997), by J. Hoffman and G. Rosenkrantz; *Descartes, Spinoza, Leibniz: The Concept of Substance in Seventeenth-Century Metaphysics* (1993), by Roger Woolhouse; and *The Rationalists* (1988), by J. Cottingham.

For a timeless introduction to the origins of metaphysics, beginning with the Ionians, see *The Idea of Nature* (1945), by R. G. Collingwood.

23   OF OUR COMPLEX IDEAS OF SUBSTANCES
John Locke

Englishman John Locke (1632–1704) is considered by many to be the founder of British empiricism. Essentially, adherents of **empiricism** believe that all knowledge is acquired through, or dependent on, experience. Locke was especially critical of the notion of innate ideas as an explanation of how knowledge is acquired. If humans are to have an idea, such as the idea of substance, that idea must come through experience—no one is born with an intuitive understanding of substance. What, then, does experience reveal about the nature of substance?

To answer this question, Locke makes a number of distinctions. First, he distinguishes simple ideas from complex ideas. By simple ideas Locke has in mind an idea that cannot be broken down into further, smaller and simpler, components. For example, a color, a sound, a texture, a taste, and an odor are all simple ideas; they cannot be reduced to a simpler idea. The idea of a chair, on the other hand, is a complex idea because it is comprised of multiple simple ideas in conjunction with one another: the color is red or blue, the fabric is smooth or rough, the back is straight or curved, and so forth.

Second, Locke makes a distinction between **primary qualities** and **secondary qualities.** An object's primary qualities are those qualities that are inseparable from it: its solidity and extension, for example. And an object's secondary qualities are its powers to act on human senses to produce certain ideas in the mind. For example, a gold coin has a particular size and solidity; these are its primary qualities. But the coin also produces a golden color in the mind when perceived; its color is one of the coin's secondary qualities. If the coin had a particular texture, say smooth, when it was touched, this would be another of the coin's secondary qualities.

Now let us relate Locke's two distinctions to the notion of substance. Locke tells us that the belief that a particular object, say a particular gold coin, exists is due to various simple ideas constantly conjoined together in a particular way, forming the complex idea of a coin. And humans naturally believe that there is something behind the simple ideas that produce them. But as for this underlying stuff, the simple idea's substratum, although it is surely there, Locke has no evidence as to its nature.

Reading Questions

1. Is belief in substance well founded? How does one come to have an idea of particular sorts of substances? Does one have a clear idea of substance proper?
2. How rational is it to believe in the substance of spirit as compared to believing in corporeal substance?
3. What is substance? What sorts of simple ideas make up one's complex idea of corporeal substance?
4. If one's senses were different, say sharper, would one's view of the world be the same? For example, would gold look the same if one had microscopic vision?

---

1. The Mind being, as I have declared, furnished with a great number of the simple Ideas, conveyed in by the Senses, as they are found in exterior things, or by Reflection on its own Operations, takes notice also, that a certain number of these simple Ideas go constantly together; which being presumed to belong to one thing, and Words being suited to common apprehensions, and made use of for quick dispatch, are called so united in one subject, by one name; which by inadvertency we are apt afterward to talk of and consider as one simple Idea, which indeed is a complication of many Ideas together; because, as I have said, not imagining how these simple Ideas can subsist by themselves, we accustom our selves, to suppose some Substratum, wherein they do subsist, and from which they do result, which therefore we call Substance.

2. So that if any one will examine himself concerning his *Notion of pure Substance in general,* he will find he has no other Idea of it at all, but only a Supposition of he knows not what support of such Qualities, which are capable of producing simple Ideas in us; which Qualities are commonly called Accidents. If any one should be asked, what is the subject wherein color or weight inheres, he would have nothing to say, but the solid extended parts: And if he were demanded, what is it, that that Solidity and Extension inhere in, he would not be in a much better case, than the Indian . . ., who, saying that the World was supported by a great elephant, was asked, what the elephant rested on; to which his answer was, a great tortoise: But being again pressed to know what gave support to the broad-backed tortoise, replied, something, he knew not what. And thus here, as in all other cases, where we use Words without having clear and distinct Ideas, we talk like children; who, being questioned, what such a thing is, which they know not, readily give this satisfactory answer, that it is

something; which in truth signifies no more, when so used, either by children or men, but that they know not what; and that the thing they pretend to know, and talk of, is what they have no distinct Idea of at all, and so are perfectly ignorant of it, and in the dark. The Idea then we have, to which we give the general name Substance, being nothing, but the supposed, but unknown support of those Qualities, we find existing, which we imagine cannot subsist, *sine re substante,* without something to support them, we call that Support Substantia; which, according to the true import of the word, is in plain English, *standing under,* or *upholding.*

3. An obscure and relative Idea of Substance in general being thus made, we come to have the *Ideas of particular sorts of Substances,* by collecting such combinations of simple Ideas, as are by Experience and Observation of Men's Senses taken notice of to exist together, and are therefore supposed to flow from the particular internal Constitution, or unknown Essence of that Substance. Thus we come to have the Ideas of a man, horse, gold, water, etc. of which Substances, whether any one has any other clear Idea, farther than of certain simple Ideas coexisting together, I appeal to every one's own Experience. 'Tis the ordinary Qualities, observable in iron, or a diamond, put together, that make the true complex Idea of those Substances, which a smith, or a jeweller, commonly knows better than a philosopher; who, whatever substantial forms he may talk of, has no other Idea of those Substances, than what is framed by a collection of those simple Ideas which are to be found in them; only we must take notice, that our complex Ideas of Substances, besides all these simple Ideas they are made up of, have always the confused Idea of *something* to which they belong, and in which they subsist: and therefore when we speak of any sort of Substance, we say it is a *thing* having such or such Qualities, as Body is a *thing* that is extended, figured, and capable of motion; a Spirit a *thing* capable of thinking; and so hardness, friability, and power to draw iron, we say, are Qualities to be found in a Loadstone. These, and the like fashions of speaking intimate, that the Substance is supposed always *something* besides the Extension, Figure, Solidity, Motion, Thinking, or other observable Ideas, though we know not what it is.

4. Hence when we talk or think of any particular sort of corporeal Substances, as *horse, stone,* etc. though the Idea, we have of either of them, be but the Complication, or Collection of those several simple Ideas of sensible Qualities, which we use to find united in the thing called *horse* or *stone,* yet because we cannot conceive, how they should subsist alone, nor one in another, we suppose them existing in, and supported by some common subject; which Support we denote by the name Substance, though it be certain, we have no clear, or distinct Idea of that *thing* we suppose a Support.

5. The same happens concerning the Operations of the Mind, viz. Thinking, Reasoning, Fearing, etc. which we concluding not to subsist of themselves, nor apprehending how they can belong to Body, or be produced by it, we are apt to think these the Actions of some other Substance, which we call Spirit; whereby yet it is evident, that having no other Idea or Notion, of Matter, but *something* wherein those many sensible Qualities, which affect our Senses, do subsist; by supposing a Substance, wherein Thinking, Knowing, Doubting, and a power of Moving, etc. do subsist, *We have as clear a Notion of the Substance of Spirit, as we have of Body;* the one being supposed to be (without knowing what it is) the Substratum to those simple Ideas we have from without; and the other supposed (with a like ignorance of what it is) to be the Substratum to those Operations, which we experiment in our selves within. 'Tis plain then, that the Idea of corporeal Substance in Matter is as remote from our Conceptions, and Apprehensions, as that of Spiritual Substance, or Spirit; and therefore from our not having any notion of the Substance of Spirit, we can no more conclude its non-Existence, than we can, for the same reason, deny the Existence of Body: It being as rational to affirm, there is no Body, because we have no clear and distinct Idea of the Substance of Matter; as to say, there is no Spirit, because we have no clear and distinct Idea of the Substance of a Spirit.

6. Whatever therefore be the secret and abstract Nature of Substance in general, all the Ideas we have of particular distinct sorts of Substances, are nothing but several Combinations of simple Ideas, coexisting in such, though unknown, Cause of their Union, as makes the whole subsist of itself. 'Tis by

such Combinations of simple Ideas and nothing else, that we represent particular sorts of Substances to our selves; such are the Ideas we have of their several species in our Minds; and such only do we, by their specific Names, signify to others, v.g., *man, horse, sun, water, iron,* upon hearing which Words, every one who understands the Language, frames in his Mind a Combination of those several simple Ideas, which he has usually observed, or fancied to exist together under that denomination; all which he supposes to rest in, and be, as it were, adherent to that unknown common Subject, which inheres not in any thing else. Though in the mean time it be manifest, and every one upon Enquiry into his own thoughts, will find that he has no other Idea of any Substance, v.g., let it be *gold, horse, iron, man, vitriol, bread,* but what he has barely of those sensible Qualities, which he supposes to inhere, with a supposition of such a Substratum, as gives as it were a support to those Qualities, or simple Ideas, which he has observed to exist united together. Thus the Idea of the *sun,* what is it, but an aggregate of those several simple Ideas, bright, hot, roundish, having a constant regular motion, at a certain distance from us, and, perhaps, some other: as he who thinks and discourses of the Sun, has been more or less accurate, in observing those sensible Qualities, Ideas, or Properties, which are in that thing, which he calls the Sun.

...

9. The Ideas that make our complex ones of corporeal Substances, are of these three sorts. *First,* the Ideas of the primary Qualities of things, which are discovered by our Senses, and are in them even when we perceive them not, such are the bulk, figure, number, situation, and motion of the parts of Bodies, which are really in them, whether we take notice of them or no. *Secondly,* The sensible secondary Qualities, which depending on these, are nothing but the Powers, those Substances have to produce several Ideas in us by our Senses; which Ideas are not in the things themselves, otherwise than as any thing is in its Cause. *Thirdly,* The aptness we consider in any Substance, to give or receive such alterations of primary Qualities, as that the Substance so altered, should produce in us different Ideas from what it did before, these are

called active and passive Powers: All which Powers, as far as we have any Notice or Notion of them, terminate only in sensible simple Ideas. For whatever alteration a Loadstone has the Power to make in the minute particles of iron, we should have no Notion of any Power it had at all to operate on iron, did not its sensible Motion discover it; and I doubt not, but there are a thousand Changes, that Bodies we daily handle, have a Power to cause in one another, which we never suspect, because they never appear in sensible effects.

10. Powers therefore, justly make a great part of our complex Ideas of Substances. He, that will examine his complex Idea of Gold, will find several of its Ideas, that make it up, to be only Powers, as the Power of being melted, but of not spending itself in the Fire; of being dissolved in *Aqua Regia,* are Ideas, as necessary to make up our complex Idea of Gold, as its color and weight: which if duly considered, are also nothing but different Powers. For to speak truly, yellowness is not actually in Gold; but is a Power in Gold, to produce that Idea in us by our Eyes, when placed in a due light: and the heat, which we cannot leave out of our Idea of the Sun, is no more really in the Sun, than the white color it introduces into wax. These are both equally Powers in the Sun, operating, by the Motion and Figure of its insensible Parts, so on a Man, as to make him have the Idea of Heat; and so on Wax, as to make it capable to produce in a Man the Idea of White.

11. Had we Senses acute enough to discern the minute particles of Bodies, and the real Constitution on which their sensible Qualities depend, I doubt not but they would produce quite different Ideas in us; and that which is now the yellow color of Gold, would then disappear, and instead of it we should see an admirable texture of parts of a certain size and figure. This Microscopes plainly discover to us: for what to our naked Eyes produces a certain color, is by thus augmenting the acuteness of our Senses, discovered to be quite a different thing; and thus altering, as it were, the proportion of the Bulk of the minute parts of a colored Object to our usual Sight, produces different Ideas, from what it did before. Thus Sand, or pounded Glass, which is

opaque, and white to the naked Eye, is pellucid in a Microscope; and a Hair seen this way, loses its former color, and is in a great measure pellucid, with a mixture of some bright sparkling colors, such as appear from the refraction of diamonds, and other pellucid Bodies. Blood to the naked Eye appears all red; but by a good Microscope, wherein its lesser parts appear, shows only some few Globules of Red, swimming in a pellucid Liquor; and how these red Globules would appear, if Glasses could be found, that yet could magnify them 1000, or 10000 times more, is uncertain.

…

14. But to return to the Matter in hand, the Ideas we have of Substances, and the ways we come by them; I say our specific Ideas of Substances are nothing else but a Collection of a certain number of simple Ideas, considered as united in one thing. These Ideas of Substances, though they are commonly called simple Apprehensions, and the Names of them simple Terms; yet in effect, are complex and compounded. Thus the Idea which an English-man signifies by the Name Swan is white color, long neck, red beak, black legs, and whole feet, and all these of a certain size, with a power of swimming in the water, and making a certain kind of noise, and, perhaps, to a Man, who has long observed those kind of Birds, some other Properties, which all terminate in sensible simple Ideas, all united in one common subject.

…

29. To conclude, Sensation convinces us, that there are solid extended Substances; and Reflection, that there are thinking ones: Experience assures us of the Existence of such Beings; and that the one hath a power to move Body by impulse, the other by thought; this we cannot doubt of. Experience, I say, every moment furnishes us with the clear Ideas, both of the one, and the other. But beyond these Ideas, as received from their proper Sources, our Faculties will not reach. If we would enquire farther into their Nature, Causes, and Manner, we perceive not the Nature of Extension, clearer than we do of Thinking. If we would explain them any farther, one is as easy as the other; and there is no more difficulty, to conceive how a Substance we know not, should by thought set Body into motion, than how a Substance we know not, should by impulse set Body into motion. So that we are no more able to discover, wherein the Ideas belonging to Body consist, than those belonging to Spirit. From whence it seems probable to me, that the simple Ideas we receive from Sensation and Reflection, are the Boundaries of our Thoughts; beyond which, the Mind, whatever efforts it would make, is not able to advance one jot; nor can it make any discoveries, when it would prie into the Nature and hidden Causes of those Ideas.

Discussion Questions

1. Is there any reason to believe that there is something behind the simple ideas that form the idea of an object? Why should there be a substance at all?
2. Suppose humans had different sensory capacities and our perception of the world changed. For example, you might be able to see in infrared or hear ultrasonic sound. Given that your perception of the world would change if your senses were differently composed, is there any reason to suppose that you now know what the world really looks like? How would Locke answer this question? Is he correct?
3. Many persons do in fact differ in sensory capacities—lacking sight or hearing, for example. How is their knowledge of the world altered? How would Locke explain these different conceptions of the world?
4. A swan, for example, is a complex idea formed by a conjunction of simple ideas. Does this imply that the world is constructed by you? Do you see the world as it is or as you construct it? Are there really swans or does the mind simply refer to a common collection of simple ideas as a swan?

For Further Reading

For a collection of Locke's work see *The Clarendon Edition of the Works of Locke* (1975), edited by P. H. Nidditch. For biographical information concerning Locke, see *The Cambridge Companion to Locke* (1994), edited by V. Chappell. A general introduction to the philosophy of John Locke can be found in *Locke* (1983) and *The Empiricists* (1988), both by R. Woolhouse. J. L. Mackie's text, *Problems from Locke* (1976), is also helpful.

24 OF THE PRINCIPLES OF HUMAN KNOWLEDGE
George Berkeley

The metaphysics of Irishman Bishop George Berkeley (1685–1753) stand in stark contrast to those of Descartes and Locke. Whereas both Descartes and Locke believed in the existence of corporeal bodies (material substances), Berkeley did not. Berkeley believed that materialism— as a belief in the existence of material bodies—leads to skepticism, and eventually, to atheism.

But why should Berkeley believe this? Assume that Locke is right in believing that our notion of a particular substance is a complex idea composed of a collection of simple ideas. And assume that those simple ideas are not the object itself. In this case, we can never know the object itself, since all that we have to work with are our (simple) ideas of it. That is, we could never be sure that our (complex) ideas accurately represented their objects. In fact, we could never be sure that there are real existent things behind, and responsible for, our complex ideas of existent things. Hence, materialism ends in skepticism.

Rather than embrace skepticism, Berkeley found a clever way around it. If things *are* nothing more than our perceptions of them, then we could not be mistaken about their nature, nor could we be wrong about their existence, since there they are, right in front of our mind's eye. But this view leaves Berkeley with some explaining to do. First, from where do our ideas of particular things originate if not from their corresponding corporeal bodies? And second, what happens to an object when it is not being perceived? It would seem that Berkeley would have to say that it did not exist, because to be is to be perceived.

The existence of God provides the answer on both counts. First, God produces our perceptions of particular bodies. And second, God perceives everything all of the time; hence, objects continue to exist when not perceived by us because God perceives them.

The following selection contains Berkeley's thoughts concerning *substance* and comes from his *Treatise Concerning the Principles of Human Knowledge.*

Reading Questions

1. Do thoughts, passions, or ideas formed by the imagination exist independently of the mind?
2. What does it mean to say that something exists?
3. What is the one and only true substance? Why is it impossible for there to be an unthinking substance?
4. How does Berkeley critique the notion that matter is an inert, senseless substance, in which extension, figure, and motion subsist?
5. On what does the tenet of extended movable substances existing without mind depend?
6. Is the supposition of the existence of external bodies necessary to explain the ideas that we have of extended bodies?
7. What is the ultimate cause of ideas?
8. Does one have control over what one perceives? What does this demonstrate?
9. What is the difference between real things and ideas or images of things?

It is evident to anyone who takes a survey of the *objects* of human knowledge that they are either ideas actually imprinted on the senses, or else such as are perceived by attending to the passions and operations of the mind, or lastly, ideas formed by help of memory and imagination—either compounding, dividing, or barely representing those originally perceived in the aforesaid ways. By sight I have the ideas of light and colors, with their several degrees and variations. By touch I perceive, for example, hard and soft, heat and cold, motion and resistance, and of all these more and less either as to quantity or degree. Smelling furnishes me with odors, the palate with tastes, and hearing conveys sounds to the mind in all their variety of tone and composition. And as several of these are observed to accompany each other, they come to be marked by one name, and so to be reputed as one thing. Thus, for example, a certain color, taste, smell, figure, and consistence having been observed to go together, are accounted one distinct thing signified by the name "apple"; other collections of ideas constitute a stone, a tree, a book, and the like sensible things—which as they are pleasing or disagreeable excite the passions of love, hatred, joy, grief, and so forth.

2. But, besides all that endless variety of ideas or objects of knowledge, there is likewise something which knows or perceives them and exercises divers operations, as willing, imagining, remembering, about them. This perceiving, active being is what I call "mind," "spirit," "soul," or "myself." By which words I do not denote any one of my ideas, but a thing entirely distinct from them, wherein they exist or, which is the same thing, whereby they are perceived—for the existence of an idea consists in being perceived.

3. That neither our thoughts, nor passions, nor ideas formed by the imagination exist without the mind is what everybody will allow. And it seems no less evident that the various sensations or ideas imprinted on the sense, however blended or combined together (that is, whatever objects they compose), cannot exist otherwise than in a mind perceiving them.—I think an intuitive knowledge may be obtained of this by anyone that shall attend to what is meant by the term "exist" when applied to sensible things. The table I write on I say exists, that is, I see and feel it; and if I were out of my study I should say it existed—meaning thereby that if I was in my study I might perceive it, or that some other spirit actually does perceive it. There was an odor, that is, it was smelled, there was a sound, that is to say, it was heard; a color or figure, and it was perceived by sight or touch. This is all that I can understand by these and the like expressions. For as to what is said of the absolute existence of unthinking things without any relation to their being perceived, that seems perfectly unintelligible. Their *esse* is *percipi*, nor is it possible they should have any existence out of the minds or thinking things which perceive them.

4. It is indeed an opinion strangely prevailing amongst men that houses, mountains, rivers, and, in a word, all sensible objects have an existence, natural or real, distinct from their being perceived by the understanding. But with how great an assurance and acquiescence soever this principle may be entertained in the world, yet whoever shall find in his heart to call it in question may, if I mistake not, perceive it to involve a manifest contradiction. For what are the forementioned objects but the things we perceive by sense? And what do we perceive besides our own ideas or sensations? And is it not plainly repugnant that any one of these, or any combination of them, should exist unperceived?

5. If we thoroughly examine this tenet it will, perhaps, be found at bottom to depend on the doctrine of *abstract ideas*. For can there be a nicer strain of abstraction than to distinguish the existence of sensible objects from their being perceived, so as to conceive them existing unperceived? Light and colors, heat and cold, extension and figures—in a word, the things we see and feel—what are they but so many sensations, notions, ideas, or impressions on the sense? And is it possible to separate, even in thought, any of these from perception? For my part, I might as easily divide a thing from itself. I may, indeed, divide in my thoughts, or conceive apart from each other, those things which, perhaps, I never perceived by sense so divided. Thus I imagine the trunk of a human body without the limbs, or conceive the smell of a rose without thinking on the rose itself. So far, I will not deny, I can abstract—if that may properly be called "abstraction" which extends only to the conceiving separately such objects as it is possible may really exist or be actually perceived asunder. But my conceiving or imagining power does not extend beyond the possibility of real existence or perception. Hence, as it is impossible for me to see or feel anything without an actual sensation of that thing, so it is impossible for me to conceive in my thoughts any sensible thing or object distinct from the sensation or perception of it.

6. Some truths there are so near and obvious to the mind that a man need only open his eyes to see them. Such I take this important one to be, to wit, that all the choir of heaven and furniture of the earth, in a word, all those bodies which compose the mighty frame of the world, have not any subsistence without a mind—that their *being* is to be perceived or known, that, consequently, so long as they are not actually perceived by me or do not exist in my mind or that of any other created spirit, they must either have no existence at all or else subsist in the mind of some eternal spirit—it being perfectly unintelligible, and involving all the absurdity of abstraction, to attribute to any single part of them an existence independent of a spirit. To be convinced of which, the reader need only reflect, and try to separate in his own thoughts, the *being* of a sensible thing from its *being perceived*.

7. From what has been said it follows there is not any other substance than *spirit*, or that which perceives. But, for the fuller proof of this point, let it be considered the sensible qualities are color, figure, motion, smell, taste, and such like—that is, the ideas perceived by sense. Now, for an idea to exist in an unperceiving thing is a manifest contradiction, for to have an idea is all one as to perceive; that, therefore, wherein color, figure, and the like qualities exist must perceive them; hence it is clear there can be no unthinking substance or *substratum* of those ideas.

8. But, say you, though the ideas themselves do not exist without the mind, yet there may be things like them, whereof they are copies or resemblances, which things exist without the mind in an unthinking substance. I answer, an idea can be like nothing but an idea; a color or figure can be like nothing but another color or figure. If we look but ever so little into our thoughts, we shall find it impossible for us to conceive a likeness except only between our ideas. Again, I ask whether those supposed originals or external things, of which our ideas are the pictures or representations, be themselves perceivable or no? If they are, then they are ideas and we have gained our point; but if you say they are not, I appeal to anyone whether it be sense to assert a color is like something which is invisible; hard or soft, like something which is intangible; and so of the rest.

9. Some there are who make a distinction betwixt *primary* and *secondary* qualities. By the former they mean extension, figure, motion, rest, solidity or impenetrability, and number; by the latter they denote all other sensible qualities, as colors, sounds, tastes, and so forth. The ideas we have of these they

acknowledge not to be the resemblances of anything existing without the mind, or unperceived, but they will have our ideas of the primary qualities to be patterns or images of things which exist without the mind, in an unthinking substance which they call "matter." By "matter," therefore, we are to understand an inert, senseless substance, in which extension, figure, and motion do actually subsist. But it is evident from what we have already shown that extension, figure, and motion are only ideas existing in the mind, and that an idea can be like nothing but another idea, and that consequently neither they nor their archetypes can exist in an unperceiving substance. Hence it is plain that the very notion of what is called "matter" or "corporeal substance" involves a contradiction in it.

10. They who assert that figure, motion, and the rest of the primary or original qualities do exist without the mind in unthinking substances do at the same time acknowledge that colors, sounds, heat, cold, and suchlike secondary qualities do not—which they tell us are sensations existing in the mind alone, that depend on and are occasioned by the different size, texture, and motion of the minute particles of matter. This they take for an undoubted truth which they can demonstrate beyond all exception. Now, if it be certain that those original qualities are inseparably united with the other sensible qualities, and not, even in thought, capable of being abstracted from them, it plainly follows that they exist only in the mind. But I desire anyone to reflect and try whether he can, by any abstraction of thought, conceive the extension and motion of a body without all other sensible qualities. For my own part, I see evidently that it is not in my power to frame an idea of a body extended and moved, but I must withal give it some color or other sensible quality which is acknowledged to exist only in the mind. In short, extension, figure, and motion, abstracted from all other qualities, are inconceivable. Where therefore the other sensible qualities are, there must these be also, to wit, in the mind and nowhere else.

11. Again, *great* and *small, swift* and *slow* are allowed to exist nowhere without the mind, being entirely relative, and changing as the frame or position of the organs of sense varies. The extension, therefore, which exists without the mind is neither great nor small, the motion neither swift nor slow; that is, they are nothing at all. But, say you, they are extension in general, and motion in general: thus we see how much the tenet of extended movable substances existing without the mind depends on that strange doctrine of *abstract ideas.* And here I cannot but remark how nearly the vague and indeterminate description of matter or corporeal substance, which the modern philosophers are run into by their own principles, resembles that antiquated and so much ridiculed notion of *materia prima,* to be met with in Aristotle and his followers. Without extension, solidity cannot be conceived; since, therefore, it has been shown that extension exists not in an unthinking substance, the same must also be true of solidity.

12. That number is entirely the creature of the mind, even though the other qualities be allowed to exist without, will be evident to whoever considers that the same thing bears a different denomination of number as the mind views it with different respects. Thus the same extension is one, or three, or thirty-six, according as the mind considers it with reference to a yard, a foot, or an inch. Number is so visibly relative and dependent on men's understanding that it is strange to think how anyone should give it an absolute existence without the mind. We say one book, one page, one line; all these are equally units, though some contain several of the others. And in each instance it is plain the unit relates to some particular combination of ideas arbitrarily put together by the mind.

13. Unity I know some will have to be a simple or uncompounded idea accompanying all other ideas into the mind. That I have any such idea answering the word "unity" I do not find; and if I had, methinks I could not miss finding it; on the contrary, it should be the most familiar to my understanding, since it is said to accompany all other ideas and to be perceived by all the ways of sensation and reflection. To say no more, it is an *abstract idea.*

14. I shall further add that, after the same manner as modern philosophers prove certain sensible qualities to have no existence in matter, or without the mind, the same thing may be likewise proved of all other sensible qualities whatsoever. Thus, for instance, it is said that heat and cold are affections only of the mind, and not at all patterns of real

beings existing in the corporeal substances which excite them, for that the same body which appears cold to one hand seems warm to another. Now, why may we not as well argue that figure and extension are not patterns or resemblances of qualities existing in matter, because to the same eye at different stations, or eyes of a different texture at the same station, they appear various and cannot, therefore, be the images of anything settled and determinate without the mind? Again, it is proved that sweetness is not really in the sapid thing, because, the thing remaining unaltered, the sweetness is changed into bitter, as in case of a fever or otherwise vitiated palate. Is it not as reasonable to say that motion is not without the mind, since if the succession of ideas in the mind become swifter, the motion, it is acknowledged, shall appear slower without any alteration in any external object?

15. In short, let anyone consider those arguments which are thought manifestly to prove that colors and tastes exist only in the mind, and he shall find they may with equal force be brought to prove the same thing of extension, figure, and motion. Though it must be confessed this method of arguing does not so much prove that there is no extension or color in an outward object as that we do not know by sense which is the true extension or color of the object. But the arguments foregoing plainly show it to be impossible that any color or extension at all, or other sensible quality whatsoever, should exist in an unthinking subject without the mind, or, in truth, that there should be any such thing as an outward object.

16. But let us examine a little the received opinion.—It is said extension is a mode or accident of matter, and that matter is the *substratum* that supports it. Now I desire that you would explain what is meant by matter's "supporting" extension. Say you, I have no idea of matter and, therefore, cannot explain it. I answer, though you have no positive, yet, if you have any meaning at all, you must at least have a relative idea of matter; though you know not what it is, yet you must be supposed to know what relation it bears to accidents, and what is meant by its supporting them. It is evident "support" cannot here be taken in its usual or literal sense—as when we say that pillars support a building; in what sense therefore must it be taken?

17. If we inquire into what the most accurate philosophers declare themselves to mean by "material substance," we shall find them acknowledge they have no other meaning annexed to those sounds but the idea of being in general together with the relative notion of its supporting accidents. The general idea of being appears to me the most abstract and incomprehensible of all other; and as for its supporting accidents, this, as we have just now observed, cannot be understood in the common sense of those words; it must, therefore, be taken in some other sense, but what that is they do not explain. So that when I consider the two parts or branches which make the signification of the words "material substance," I am convinced there is no distinct meaning annexed to them. But why should we trouble ourselves any further in discussing this material *substratum* or support of figure and motion and other sensible qualities? Does it not suppose they have an existence without the mind? And is not this a direct repugnancy and altogether inconceivable?

18. But, though it were possible that solid, figured, movable substances may exist without the mind, corresponding to the ideas we have of bodies, yet how is it possible for us to know this? Either we must know it by sense or by reason. As for our senses, by them we have the knowledge only of our sensations, ideas, or those things that are immediately perceived by sense, call them what you will; but they do not inform us that things exist without the mind, or unperceived, like to those which are perceived. This the materialists themselves acknowledge. It remains therefore that if we have any knowledge at all of external things, it must be by reason, inferring their existence from what is immediately perceived by sense. But what reason can induce us to believe the existence of bodies without the mind, from what we perceive, since the very patrons of matter themselves do not pretend there is any necessary connection betwixt them and our ideas? I say it is granted on all hands (and what happens in dreams, frenzies, and the like, puts it beyond dispute) that it is possible we might be affected with all the ideas we have now, though no bodies existed without resembling them. Hence it is evident the supposition of external bodies is not necessary for the producing our ideas; since it is granted they are produced sometimes, and might possibly be produced always in the

same order we see them in at present, without their concurrence.

...

24. It is very obvious, upon the least inquiry into our own thoughts, to know whether it be possible for us to understand what is meant by "the absolute existence of sensible objects in themselves, or without the mind." To me it is evident those words mark out either a direct contradiction or else nothing at all. And to convince others of this, I know no readier or fairer way than to entreat they would calmly attend to their own thoughts; and if by this attention the emptiness or repugnancy of those expressions does appear, surely nothing more is requisite for their conviction. It is on this, therefore, that I insist, to wit, that "the absolute existence of unthinking things" are words without a meaning, or which include a contradiction. This is what I repeat and inculcate, and earnestly recommend to the attentive thoughts of the reader.

25. All our ideas, sensations, or the things which we perceive, by whatsoever names they may be distinguished, are visibly inactive—there is nothing of power or agency included in them. So that one idea or object of thought cannot produce or make any alteration in another. To be satisfied of the truth of this, there is nothing else requisite but a bare observation of our ideas. For since they and every part of them exist only in the mind, it follows that there is nothing in them but what is perceived; but whoever shall attend to his ideas, whether of sense or reflection, will not perceive in them any power or activity; there is, therefore, no such thing contained in them. A little attention will discover to us that the very being of an idea implies passiveness and inertness in it, insomuch that it is impossible for an idea to do anything or, strictly speaking, to be the cause of anything; neither can it be the resemblance or pattern of any active being, as is evident from sec. 8. Whence it plainly follows that extension, figure, and motion cannot be the cause of our sensations. To say, therefore, that these are the effects of powers resulting from the configuration, number, motion, and size of corpuscles must certainly be false.

26. We perceive a continual succession of ideas, some are anew excited, others are changed or totally disappear. There is, therefore, some cause of these ideas, whereon they depend and which produces and changes them. That this cause cannot be any quality or idea or combination of ideas is clear from the preceding section. It must therefore be a substance; but it has been shown that there is no corporeal or material substance: it remains, therefore, that the cause of ideas is an incorporeal, active substance or spirit.

27. A spirit is one simple, undivided, active being—as it perceives ideas it is called "the understanding," and as it produces or otherwise operates about them it is called "the will." Hence there can be no *idea* formed of a soul or spirit; for all ideas whatever, being passive and inert (*vide* sec. 25), they cannot represent unto us, by the way of image or likeness, that which acts. A little attention will make it plain to anyone that to have an idea which shall be like that active principle of motion and change of ideas is absolutely impossible. Such is the nature of *spirit*, or that which acts, that it cannot be of itself perceived, but only by the effects which it produces. If any man shall doubt of the truth of what is here delivered, let him but reflect and try if he can frame the idea of any power or active being, and whether he has ideas of two principal powers marked by the names "will" and "understanding," distinct from each other as well as from a third idea of substance or being in general, with a relative notion of its supporting or being the subject of the aforesaid powers—which is signified by the name "soul" or "spirit." This is what some hold; but, so far as I can see, the words "will," "soul," "spirit" do not stand for different ideas or, in truth, for any idea at all, but for something which is very different from ideas, and which, being an agent, cannot be like unto, or represented by, any idea whatsoever. [Though it must be owned at the same time that we have some notion of soul, spirit, and the operations of the mind, such as willing, loving, hating—inasmuch as we know or understand the meaning of those words.]

28. I find I can excite ideas in my mind at pleasure, and vary and shift the scene as oft as I think fit. It is no more than willing, and straightway this or that idea arises in my fancy; and by the same power it is obliterated and makes way for another. This making and unmaking of ideas does very properly denominate the mind active. Thus much is certain

and grounded on experience; but when we talk of unthinking agents or of exciting ideas exclusive of volition, we only amuse ourselves with words.

29. But, whatever power I may have over my own thoughts, I find the ideas actually perceived by sense have not a like dependence on my will. When in broad daylight I open my eyes, it is not in my power to choose whether I shall see or no, or to determine what particular objects shall present themselves to my view; and so likewise as to the hearing and other senses; the ideas imprinted on them are not creatures of my will. There is therefore some *other* will or spirit that produces them.

30. The ideas of sense are more strong, lively, and distinct than those of the imagination; they have likewise a steadiness, order, and coherence, and are not excited at random, as those which are the effects of human wills often are, but in a regular train or series, the admirable connection whereof sufficiently testifies the wisdom and benevolence of its Author. Now the set rules or established methods wherein the mind we depend on excites in us the ideas of sense are called "the laws of nature"; and these we learn by experience, which teaches us that such and such ideas are attended with such and such other ideas in the ordinary course of things.

31. This gives us a sort of foresight which enables us to regulate our actions for the benefit of life. And without this we should be eternally at a loss; we could not know how to act anything that might procure us the least pleasure or remove the least pain of sense. That food nourishes, sleep refreshes, and fire warms us; that to sow in the seedtime is the way to reap in the harvest; and in general that to obtain such or such ends, such or such means are conducive—all this we know, not by discovering any necessary connection between our ideas, but only by the observation of the settled laws of nature, without which we should be all in uncertainty and confusion, and a grown man no more know how to manage himself in the affairs of life than an infant just born.

32. And yet this consistent, uniform working which so evidently displays the goodness and wisdom of that Governing Spirit whose Will constitutes the laws of nature, is so far from leading our thoughts to Him that it rather sends them awandering after second causes. For when we perceive certain ideas of sense constantly followed by other ideas, and we know this is not of our own doing, we forthwith attribute power and agency to the ideas themselves and make one the cause of another, than which nothing can be more absurd and unintelligible. Thus, for example, having observed that when we perceive by sight a certain round, luminous figure, we at the same time perceive by touch the idea or sensation called "heat," we do from thence conclude the sun to be the cause of heat. And in like manner perceiving the motion and collision of bodies to be attended with sound, we are inclined to think the latter an effect of the former.

33. The ideas imprinted on the senses by the Author of Nature are called "real things"; and those excited in the imagination, being less regular, vivid, and constant, are more properly termed "ideas" or "images of things" which they copy and represent. But then our sensations, be they never so vivid and distinct, are nevertheless ideas, that is, they exist in the mind, or are perceived by it, as truly as the ideas of its own framing. The ideas of sense are allowed to have more reality in them, that is, to be more strong, orderly, and coherent than the creatures of the mind; but this is no argument that they exist without the mind. They are also less dependent on the spirit, or thinking substance which perceives them, in that they are excited by the will of another and more powerful spirit; yet still they are *ideas;* and certainly no idea, whether faint or strong, can exist otherwise than in a mind perceiving it. . . .

. . .

Discussion Questions

1. Berkeley suggests that something does not exist if it is not perceived. Can you imagine that this is in fact true? For example, does a sunset not exist if it is not perceived?
2. Can you know with certainty that there are any other thinking beings? Furthermore, how can you be sure that anything other than the portion of the universe that you are currently perceiving exists?

3. Berkeley infers from the fact that you cannot control your perceptions that some other spirit must be ultimately responsible for the content of your perceptions. Is this a reasonable inference? Can you give another explanation that would account for this?

For Further Reading

Berkeley's works are collected in *The Works of George Berkeley* (1948), edited by A. Luce and T. Jessop. For biographical information concerning Berkeley see A. Luce, *The Life of George Berkeley, Bishop of Cloyne* (1949). For a general introduction to the philosophy of Berkeley see *The Empiricists* (1988), by Roger Woolhouse, and *Locke, Berkeley, Hume: Central Themes* (1971), by Jonathan Bennett. For a work focusing on Berkeley's immaterialism see *Berkeley's Immaterialism* (1945), by A. Luce, and *Berkeley: The Philosophy of Immaterialism* (1974), by I. Tipton.

25 SKEPTICAL DOUBTS CONCERNING THE OPERATIONS OF THE UNDERSTANDING
David Hume

Born in Edinburgh, Scotland, David Hume (1711–1776) is regarded as a leading spokesperson for empiricism. Central to his empiricism is a distinction between **conceptual truths** known through reason and **matters of fact** known through experience.

Consider these examples. The sentence "All bachelors are unmarried men" is true and furthermore is known to be true by simply reflecting on the concepts contained in the sentence. Sentences such as this express a *conceptual truth*, what Hume calls a 'relation of ideas'. On the other hand, sentences such as "Frank is a bachelor" express what Hume calls *matters of fact*. The truth of these propositions depends on whether they accurately represent the world. Matters of fact require an empirical investigation to be known for certain. In other words, "Frank is a bachelor" is true only if Frank is, in fact, not married—a truth that can be verified only by examining the world, that is, through experience.

This distinction between conceptual truths and matters of fact is sometimes called Hume's fork. It can be applied to any truth claim, including the claims of metaphysics. Consider the notion of cause and effect. Is our idea of cause and effect a conceptual truth or a matter of fact? It does not appear to be the case that the principle of cause and effect is a conceptual truth, known the same way that "all bachelors are unmarried" is known. So it must be known through experience. Is there, however, any experiential evidence for the notion of cause and effect? Surprisingly, Hume says no. When one billiard ball hits another, does it cause it to move? Hume points out that we don't actually see one billiard ball 'cause' the other one to move. Instead, what we have—what we experience strictly speaking—is the mere conjunction of three events: one ball moving toward the other, both in contact, and then both balls moving away from each other. Where is the cause and effect? Watch the balls closely: Can you see the cause and effect? All that can be observed, insists Hume, is mere correlation, not causation. Beliefs in cause-and-effect relationships are thus unwarranted. As a result, very little is known about the world, since most of our claims are based on 'cause-and-effect' reasoning.

Reading Questions

1. Explain the distinction between *relations of ideas* and *matters of fact*.
2. Can the truth of a *matter of fact* be demonstrated?
3. On what relation are all *matters of fact* founded?
4. Is belief in cause and effect *a priori* or is it based on experience?
5. What is the foundation of all conclusions from experience?
6. Why is it impossible to establish that "the future will be conformable to the past" by any argument from experience?

20. All the objects of human reason or enquiry may naturally be divided into two kinds, to wit, relations of ideas, and matters of fact. Of the first kind are the sciences of geometry, algebra, and arithmetic; and in short, every affirmation which is either intuitively or demonstratively certain. That the square of the hypotenuse is equal to the square of the two sides, is a proposition which expresses a relation between these figures. That three times five is equal to the half of thirty, expresses a relation between these numbers. Propositions of this kind are discoverable by the mere operation of thought, without dependence on what is anywhere existent in the universe. Though there never were a circle or triangle in nature, the truths demonstrated by Euclid would forever retain their certainty and evidence.

21. Matters of fact, which are the second objects of human reason, are not ascertained in the same manner; nor is our evidence of their truth, however great, of a like nature with the foregoing. The contrary of every matter of fact is still possible; because it can never imply a contradiction, and is conceived by the mind with the facility and distinctness, as if ever so conformable to reality. *That the sun will not rise tomorrow* is no less intelligible a proposition, and implies no more contradiction than the affirmation, *that it will rise*. We should in vain, therefore, attempt to demonstrate its falsehood. Were it demonstratively false, it would imply a contra-

diction, and could never be distinctly conceived by the mind.

It may, therefore, be a subject worthy of curiosity, to enquire what is the nature of that evidence which assures us of any real existence and matter of fact, beyond the present testimony of our senses, or the records of our memory. This part of philosophy, it is observable, has been little cultivated, either by the ancients or moderns; and therefore our doubts and errors, in the prosecution of so important an enquiry, may be the more excusable; while we march through such difficult paths without any guide or direction. They may even prove useful, by exciting curiosity, and destroying that implicit faith and security, which is the bane of all reasoning and free enquiry. The discovery of defects in the common philosophy, if any such there be, will not, I presume, be a discouragement, but rather an incitement, as is usual, to attempt something more full and satisfactory than has yet been proposed to the public.

22. All reasonings concerning matter of fact seem to be founded on the relation of *cause and effect*. By means of that relation alone we can go beyond the evidence of our memory and senses. If you were to ask a man, why he believes any matter of fact, which is absent; for instance, that his friend is in the

country, or in France; he would give you a reason; and this reason would be some other fact; as a letter received from him, or the knowledge of his former resolutions and promises. A man finding a watch or any other machine in a desert island, would conclude that there had once been men in that island. All our reasonings concerning fact are of the same nature. And here it is constantly supposed that there is a connection between the present and that which is inferred from it. Were there nothing to bind them together, the inference would be entirely precarious. The hearing of an articulate voice and rational discourse in the dark assures us of the presence of some person: Why? because these are the effects of the human make and fabric, and closely connected with it. If we anatomize all the other reasonings of this nature, we shall find that they are founded on the relation of cause and effect, and that this relation is either near or remote, direct or collateral. Heat and light are collateral effects of fire, and the one effect may justly be inferred from the other.

23. If we would satisfy ourselves, therefore, concerning the nature of that evidence, which assures us of matters of fact, we must enquire how we arrive at the knowledge of cause and affect.

I shall venture to affirm, as a general proposition, which admits of no exception, that the knowledge of this relation is not, in any instance, attained by reasonings *a priori;* but arises entirely from experience, when we find that any particular objects are constantly conjoined with each other. Let an object be presented to a man of ever so strong natural reason and abilities; if that object be entirely new to him, he will not be able, by the most accurate examination of its sensible qualities, to discover any of its causes or effects. Adam, though his rational faculties be supposed, at the very first, entirely perfect, could not have inferred from the fluidity and transparency of water that it would suffocate him, or from the light and warmth of fire that it would consume him. No object ever discovers, by the qualities which appear to the senses, either the causes which produced it, or the effects which will arise from it; nor can our reason, unassisted by experience, ever draw any inference concerning real existence and matter of fact.

24. This proposition, *that causes and effects are discoverable, not by reason but by experience,* will readily be admitted with regard to such objects, as we remember to have once been altogether unknown to us; since we must be conscious of the utter inability, which we then lay under, of foretelling what would arise from them. Present two smooth pieces of marble to a man who has no tincture of natural philosophy; he will never discover that they adhere together in such a manner as to require great force to separate them in a direct line, while they make so small a resistance to a lateral pressure. Such events, as bear little analogy to the common course of nature, are also readily confessed to be known only by experience; nor does any man imagine that the explosion of gunpowder, or the attraction of a lodestone, could ever be discovered by arguments *a priori.* In like manner, when an effect is supposed to depend upon an intricate machinery or secret structure of parts, we make no difficulty in attributing all our knowledge of it to experience. Who will assert that he can give the ultimate reason, why milk or bread is proper nourishment for a man, not for a lion or a tiger?

But the same truth may not appear at first sight, to have the same evidence with regard to events, which have become familiar to us from our first appearance in the world, which bear close analogy to the whole course of nature, and which are supposed to depend on the simple qualities of objects, without any secret structure of parts. We are apt to imagine that we could discover these effects by the mere operation of our reason, without experience. We fancy, that were we brought on a sudden into this world, we could at first have inferred that one billiard-ball would communicate motion to another upon impulse; and that we needed not to have waited for the event, in order to pronounce with certainty concerning it. Such is the influence of custom, that, where it is strongest, it not only covers our natural ignorance, but even conceals itself, and seems not to take place, merely because it is found in the highest degree.

25. But to convince us that all the laws of nature, and all the operations of bodies without exception, are known only by experience, the following reflections may, perhaps, suffice. Were any object presented to us, and were we required to pronounce

concerning the effect, which will result from it, without consulting past observation; after what manner, I beseech you, must the mind proceed in this operation? It must invent or imagine some event which it ascribes to the object as its effect; and it is plain that this invention must be entirely arbitrary. The mind can never possibly find the effect in the supposed cause, by the most accurate scrutiny and examination. For the effect is totally different from the cause, and consequently can never be discovered in it. Motion in the second billiard-ball is a quite distinct event from motion in the first; nor is there anything in the one to suggest the smallest hint of the other. A stone or piece of metal raised into the air, and left without any support, immediately falls: but to consider the matter *a priori,* is there anything we discover in this situation which can beget the idea of a downward, rather than an upward, or any other motion, in the stone or metal?

And as the first imagination or invention of a particular effect, in all natural operations, is arbitrary, where we consult not experience; so must we also esteem the supposed tie or connection between the cause and effect, which binds them together, and renders it impossible that any other effect could result from the operation of that cause. When I see, for instance, a billiard-ball moving in a straight line towards another; even suppose motion in the second ball should by accident be suggested to me, as the result of their contact or impulse; may I not conceive, that a hundred different events might as well follow from the cause? May not both these balls remain at absolute rest? May not the first ball return in a straight line, or leap off from the second in any line or direction? All these suppositions are consistent and conceivable. Why then should we give the preference to one, which is no more consistent or conceivable than the rest? All our reasonings *a priori* will never be able to show us any foundation for this preference.

In a word, then, every effect is a distinct event from its cause. It could not, therefore, be discovered in the cause, and the first invention or conception of it, *a priori,* must be entirely arbitrary. And even after it is suggested, the conjunction of it with the cause must appear equally arbitrary; since there are always many other effects, which, to reason, must seem fully as consistent and natural. In vain, therefore, should

we pretend to determine any single event, or infer any cause or effect, without the assistance of observation and experience.

26. Hence we may discover the reason why no philosopher, who is rational and modest, has ever pretended to assign the ultimate cause of any natural operation, or to show distinctly the action of that power, which produces any single effect in the universe. It is confessed, that the utmost effort of human reason is to reduce the principles, productive of natural phenomena, to a greater simplicity, and to resolve the many particular effects into a few general causes, by means of reasonings from analogy, experience, and observation. But as to the causes of these general causes, we should in vain attempt their discovery; nor shall we ever be able to satisfy ourselves, by any particular explication of them. These ultimate springs and principles are totally shut up from human curiosity and enquiry. Elasticity, gravity, cohesion of parts, communication of motion by impulse; these are probably the ultimate causes and principles which we shall ever discover in nature; and we may esteem ourselves sufficiently happy; if, by accurate enquiry and reasoning, we can trace up the particular phenomena to, or near to, these general principles. The most perfect philosophy of the natural kind only staves off our ignorance a little longer: as perhaps the most perfect philosophy of the moral or metaphysical kind serves only to discover larger portions of it. Thus the observation of human blindness and weakness is the result of all philosophy, and meets us at every turn, in spite of our endeavors to elude or avoid it.

27. Nor is geometry, when taken into the assistance of natural philosophy, ever able to remedy this defect, or lead us into the knowledge of ultimate causes, by all that accuracy of reasoning of which it is so justly celebrated. Every part of mixed mathematics proceeds upon the supposition that certain laws are established by nature in her operations; and abstract reasonings are employed, either to assist experience in the discovery of these laws, or to determine their influence in particular instances, where it depends upon any precise degree of distance and quantity. Thus, it is a law of motion, discovered by experience, that the moment or force of any body in motion is in

the compound ratio or proportion of its solid contents and its velocity; and consequently, that a small force may remove the greatest obstacle or raise the greatest weight, if, by any contrivance or machinery, we can increase the velocity of that force, so as to make it an overmatch for its antagonist. Geometry assists us in the application of this law, by giving us the just dimensions of all the parts and figures which can enter into any species of machine; but still the discovery of the law itself is owing merely to experience, and all the abstract reasonings in the world could never lead us one step towards the knowledge of it. When we reason *a priori*, and consider merely any object or cause, as it appears to the mind, independent of all observation, it never could suggest to us the notion of any distinct object, such as its effect; much less, show us the inseparable and inviolable connection between them. A man must be very sagacious who could discover by reasoning that crystal is the effect of heat, and ice and cold, without being previously acquainted with the operation of these qualities.

PART II

28. But we have not yet attained any tolerable satisfaction with regard to the question first proposed. Each solution still gives rise to a new question as difficult as the foregoing, and leads us on to farther enquiries. When it is asked, *What is the nature of all our reasonings concerning matter of fact?* the proper answer seems to be, that they are founded on the relation of cause and effect. When again it is asked, *What is the foundation of all our reasonings and conclusions concerning that relation?* it may be replied in one word, Experience. But if we still carry on our sifting humor, and ask, *What is the foundation of all conclusions from experience?* this implies a new question, which may be of more difficult solution and explication. Philosophers, that give themselves airs of superior wisdom and sufficiency, have a hard task when they encounter persons of inquisitive dispositions, who push them from every corner to which they retreat, and who are sure at last to bring them to some dangerous dilemma. The best expedient to prevent this confusion, is to be modest in our pretensions; and even to discover the difficulty ourselves before it is objected to us. By this means, we may make a kind of merit of our very ignorance.

I shall content myself, in this section, with an easy task, and shall pretend only to give a negative answer to the question here proposed. I say then, that, even after we have experience of the operations of cause and effect, our conclusions from that experience are *not* founded on reason or any process of the understanding. This answer we must endeavor both to explain and to defend.

29. It must certainly be allowed, that nature has kept us at a great distance from all her secrets, and has afforded us only the knowledge of a few superficial qualities of objects; while she conceals from us those powers and principles on which the influence of those objects entirely depends. Our senses inform us of the color, weight, and consistence of bread; but neither sense nor reason can ever inform us of those qualities which fit it for the nourishment and support of the human body. Sight or feeling conveys an idea of the actual motion of bodies; but as to that wonderful force or power, which would carry on a moving body for ever in a continued change of place, and which bodies never lose but by communicating it to others; of this we cannot form the most distant conception. But notwithstanding this ignorance of natural powers and principles, we always presume, when we see like sensible qualities, that they have like secret powers, and expect that effects, similar to those which we have experienced, will follow from them. If a body of like color and consistence with that bread, which we have formerly eat, be presented to us, we make no scruple of repeating the experiment and foresee, with certainty, like nourishment and support. Now this is a process of the mind or thought, of which I would willingly know the foundation. It is allowed on all hands that there is no known connection between the sensible qualities and the secret powers; and consequently, that the mind is not led to form such a conclusion concerning their constant and regular conjunction, by anything which it knows of their nature. As to past *experience*, it can be allowed to give *direct* and *certain* information of those precise objects only, and that precise period of time, which fell under its cognizance: but why this experience should be extended to future times, and to other objects, which for aught we know, may be only in appearance similar; this is the main question on which I would insist.

The bread, which I formerly eat, nourished me; that is, a body of such sensible qualities was, at that time, endued with such secret powers: but does it follow, that other bread must also nourish me at another time, and that like sensible qualities must always be attended with like secret powers? The consequence seems nowise necessary. At least, it must be acknowledged that there is here a consequence drawn by the mind; that there is a certain step taken; a process of thought, and an inference, which wants to be explained. These two propositions are far from being the same, *I have found that such an object has always been attended with such effect,* and *I foresee, that other objects, which are, in appearance, similar, will be attended with similar effects.* I shall allow, if you please, that one proposition may justly be inferred from the other: I know, in fact, that it always is inferred. But if you insist that the inference is made by a chain of reasoning, I desire you to produce that reasoning. The connection between these propositions is not intuitive. There is required a medium, which may enable the mind to draw such an inference, if indeed it be drawn by reasoning and argument. What that medium is, I must confess, passes my comprehension; and it is incumbent on those to produce it, who assert that it really exists, and is the origin of all our conclusions concerning matter of fact.

30. This negative argument must certainly, in process of time, become altogether convincing, if many penetrating and able philosophers shall turn their enquiries this way and no one be ever able to discover any connecting proposition of intermediate step, which supports the understanding in this conclusion. But as the question is yet new, every reader may not trust so far to his own penetration, as to conclude, because an argument escapes his enquiry, that therefore it does not really exist. For this reason it may be requisite to venture upon a more difficult task; and enumerating all the branches of human knowledge, endeavor to show that none of them can afford such an argument.

All reasonings may be divided into two kinds, namely, demonstrative reasoning, or that concerning relations of ideas, and moral reasoning, or that concerning matter of fact and existence. That there are no demonstrative arguments in the case seems evident; since it implies no contradiction that the course of nature may change, and that an object, seemingly like those which we have experienced, may be attended with different or contrary effects. May I not clearly and distinctly conceive that a body, falling from the clouds, and which, in all other respects, resembles snow, has yet the taste of salt or feeling of fire? Is there any more intelligible proposition than to affirm, that all the trees will flourish in December and January, and decay in May and June? Now whatever is intelligible, and can be distinctly conceived, implies no contradiction, and can never be proved false by any demonstrative argument or abstract reasoning *a priori.*

If we be, therefore, engaged by arguments to put trust in past experience, and make it the standard of our future judgement, these arguments must be probable only, or such as regard matter of fact and real existence, according to the division above mentioned. But that there is no argument of this kind, must appear, if our explication of that species of reasoning be admitted as solid and satisfactory. We have said that all arguments concerning existence are founded on the relation of cause and effect; that our knowledge of that relation is derived entirely from experience; and that all our experimental conclusions proceed upon the supposition that the future will be conformable to the past. To endeavor, therefore, the proof of this last supposition by probable arguments, or arguments regarding existence, must be evidently going in a circle, and taking that for granted, which is the very point in question.

31. In reality, all arguments from experience are founded on the similarity which we discover among natural objects, and by which we are induced to expect effects similar to those which we have found to follow from such objects. And though none but a fool or madman will ever pretend to dispute the authority of experience, or to reject that great guide of human life, it may surely be allowed a philosopher to have so much curiosity at least as to examine the principle of human nature, which gives this mighty authority to experience, and makes us draw advantage from that similarity which nature has placed among different objects. From causes which appear *similar* we expect similar effects. This is the sum of all

our experimental conclusions. Now it seems evident that, if this conclusion were formed by reason, it would be as perfect at first, and upon one instance, as after ever so long a course of experience. But the case is far otherwise. Nothing so like as eggs; yet no one, on account of this appearing similarity, expects the same taste and relish in all of them. It is only after a long course of uniform experiments in any kind, that we attain a firm reliance and security with regard to a particular event. Now where is that process of reasoning which, from one instance, draws a conclusion, so different from that which it infers from a hundred instances that are nowise different from that single one? This question I propose as much for the sake of information, as with an intention of raising difficulties. I cannot find, I cannot imagine any such reasoning. But I keep my mind still open to instruction, if any one will vouchsafe to bestow it on me.

32. Should it be said that, from a number of uniform experiments, we *infer* a connection between the sensible qualities and the secret powers; this, I must confess, seems the same difficulty, couched in different terms. The question still recurs, on what process of argument this *inference* is founded? Where is the medium, the interposing ideas, which join propositions so very wide of each other? It is confessed that the color, consistence, and other sensible qualities of bread appear not, of themselves, to have any connection with the secret powers of nourishment and support. For otherwise we could infer these secret powers from the first appearance of these sensible qualities, without the aid of experience; contrary to the sentiment of all philosophers, and contrary to plain matter of fact. Here, then, is our natural state of ignorance with regard to the powers and influence of all objects. How is this remedied by experience? It only shows us a number of uniform effects, resulting from certain objects, and teaches us that those particular objects, at that particular time, were endowed with such powers and forces. When a new object, endowed with similar sensible qualities, is produced, we expect similar powers and forces, and look for a like effect. From a body of like color and consistence with bread we expect like nourishment and support. But this surely is a step or progress of the mind, which wants to be explained. When a man says, *I have found, in all past instances, such sensible qualities conjoined with such secret powers:* And when he says, *Similar sensible qualities will always be conjoined with similar secret powers,* he is not guilty of a tautology, nor are these propositions in any respect the same. You say that the one proposition is an inference from the other. But you must confess that the inference is not intuitive; neither is it demonstrative: Of what nature is it, then? To say it is experimental, is begging the question. For all inferences from experience suppose, as their foundation, that the future will resemble the past, and that similar powers will be conjoined with similar sensible qualities. If there be any suspicion that the course of nature may change, and that the past may be no rule for the future, all experience becomes useless, and can give rise to no inference or conclusion. It is impossible, therefore, that any arguments from experience can prove this resemblance of the past to the future; since all these arguments are founded on the supposition of that resemblance. Let the course of things be allowed hitherto ever so regular; that alone, without some new argument or inference, proves not that, for the future, it will continue so. In vain do you pretend to have learned the nature of bodies from your past experience. Their secret nature, and consequently all their effects and influence, may change, without any change in their sensible qualities. This happens sometimes, and with regard to some objects: Why may not it happen always, and with regard to all objects? What logic, what process of argument secures you against this supposition? My practice, you say, refutes my doubts. But you mistake the purport of my question. As an agent, I am quite satisfied in the point; but as a philosopher, who has some share of curiosity, I will not say skepticism, I want to learn the foundation of this inference. No reading, no enquiry has yet been able to remove my difficulty, or give me satisfaction in a matter of such importance. Can I do better than to propose the difficulty to the public, even though, perhaps, I have small hopes of obtaining a solution? We shall at least, by this means, be sensible of our ignorance, if we do not augment our knowledge.

33. I must confess that a man is guilty of unpardonable arrogance who concludes, because an argument has escaped his own investigation, that

therefore it does not really exist. I must also confess that, though all the learned, for several ages, should have employed themselves in fruitless search upon any subject, it may still, perhaps, be rash to conclude positively that the subject must, therefore, pass all human comprehension. Even though we examine all the sources of our knowledge, and conclude them unfit for such a subject, there may still remain a suspicion, that the enumeration is not complete, or the examination not accurate. But with regard to the present subject, there are some considerations which seem to remove all this accusation of arrogance or suspicion of mistake.

It is certain that the most ignorant and stupid peasants—nay infants, nay even brute beasts—improve by experience, and learn the qualities of natural objects, by observing the effects which result from them. When a child has felt the sensation of pain from touching the flame of a candle, he will be careful not to put his hand near any candle; but will expect a similar effect from a cause which is similar in its sensible qualities and appearance. If you assert, therefore, that the understanding of the child is led into this conclusion by any process of argument or ratiocination, I may justly require you to produce that argument; nor have you any pretense to refuse so - equitable a demand. You cannot say that the argument is abstruse, and may possibly escape your enquiry; since you confess that it is obvious to the capacity of a mere infant. If you hesitate, therefore, a moment, or if, after reflection, you produce any intricate or profound argument, you, in a manner, give up the question, and confess that it is not reasoning which engages us to suppose the past resembling the future, and to expect similar effects from causes which are, to appearance, similar. This is the proposition which I intended to enforce in the present section. If I be right, I pretend not to have made any mighty discovery. And if I be wrong, I must acknowledge myself to be indeed a very backward scholar; since I cannot now discover an argument which, it seems, was perfectly familiar to me long before I was out of my cradle.

Discussion Questions

1. Undoubtedly you know something about how bread nourishes the body. Does the fact that you now *know* how bread nourishes refute or blunt Hume's skeptical arguments? Does nutritional science refute Hume? Why or why not?
2. Some scientific truths have been independently verified time and time again—the ideal gas law, for example. Is this a refutation of Hume's skeptical arguments?
3. Hume admits that only a madman would truly doubt the authority of experience. Why, then, should you be bothered by his skeptical arguments? Do his arguments serve a purpose that justifies struggling with them? If so, what?
4. Hume writes "Philosophers, that give themselves airs of superior wisdom and sufficiency, have a hard task when they encounter persons of inquisitive dispositions, who push them from every corner to which they retreat, and who are sure at last to bring them to some dangerous dilemma. The best expedient to prevent this confusion, is to be modest in our pretensions; and even to discover the difficulty ourselves before it is objected to us. By this means, we may make a kind of merit of our very ignorance." What does Hume mean by this? Do you agree?

For Further Reading

For a collection of Hume's work see *The Philosophical Works of David Hume* (1875), edited by Green and Grose. For biographical information see *The Life of David Hume* (1954), by E. C. Mossner. For an introduction to the philosophy of Hume see *Hume* (1975), by T. Penelhum; *The Philosophy of David Hume* (1941), by Norman Kemp Smith; *Hume's Philosophy of Human Nature* (1932), by J. Laird; and *Hume* (1977), by Barry Stroud.

For discussions of Hume's views concerning causation see *The Secret Connexion* (1989), by G. Strawson; *Hume and the Problem of Causation* (1981), by T. Beauchamp and A. Rosenberg; and *The Nature of Causation* (1976), edited by M. Brand. Hume's skepticism is treated in *Hume's Skepticism in the Treatise of Human Nature* (1985), by R. J. Fogelin.

26   THE ELIMINATION OF METAPHYSICS
A. J. Ayer

British philosopher A. J. Ayer (1910–1989) was a leading proponent of logical positivism. As a logical positivist Ayer believed that only certain sorts of sentences can be true and meaningful. These sentences either express logical (conceptual) truths or are empirically verifiable (testable). The verifiability criteria is similar to Hume's fork, except that it is about meaning, not truth *per se*. Ayer claims that since most metaphysical statements are neither logical truths nor empirically verifiable, they are utterly meaningless—pure nonsense. It is no wonder, then, that philosophers have had such a hard time making advances in the field of metaphysics: It is hard to reach a consensus when arguing over nothing.

Needless to say, logical positivism was not well received by many philosophers—no one appreciates being told that their life's work is pointless. Nevertheless, logical positivism was quite fashionable for a time, from the mid-1920s through the 1950s. Today, however, logical positivists are a threatened species. The decline can be traced to some difficulties facing the positivist. For example, how does the positivist handle universal claims such as "All men are mortal"? Certainly, this statement is meaningful even though it is difficult—if not impossible—to explain how such a statement could be verified. More important, what happens when positivism is turned upon itself? Is the principle of verification itself verifiable? Probably not.

Reading Questions

1. Explain Ayer's first strategy for attacking metaphysicians who claim knowledge of a reality that transcends the phenomenal world.
2. What is required to overthrow a system of transcendent metaphysics?
3. How does Ayer's attack on metaphysics differ from Kant's?
4. Explain the criterion of verifiability.
5. Explain the difference between verifiability and verifiability in principle.
6. Explain the difference between the strong and weak sense of the term *verifiability*.
7. Explain how the criterion of verifiability handles the debate between the monist and the pluralist.
8. How does Ayer define a metaphysical sentence?
9. How is the metaphysician misled into believing in substance?
10. Where does the postulation of real nonexistent entities come from?

The traditional disputes of philosophers are, for the most part, as unwarranted as they are unfruitful. The surest way to end them is to establish beyond question what should be the purpose and method of a philosophical enquiry. And this is by no means so difficult a task as the history of philosophy would lead one to suppose. For if there are any questions which science leaves it to philosophy to answer, a straightforward process of elimination must lead to their discovery.

We may begin by criticizing the metaphysical thesis that philosophy affords us knowledge of a reality transcending the world of science and common sense. Later on, when we come to define metaphysics and account for its existence, we shall find that it is possible to be a metaphysician without believing in a transcendent reality; for we shall see that many metaphysical utterances are due to the commission of logical errors, rather than to a conscious desire on the part of their authors to go beyond the limits of experience. But it is convenient for us to take the case of those who believe that it is possible to have knowledge of a transcendent reality as a starting-point for our discussion. The arguments which we use to refute them will subsequently be found to apply to the whole of metaphysics.

One way of attacking a metaphysician who claimed to have knowledge of a reality which transcended the phenomenal world would be to enquire from what premises his propositions were deduced. Must he not begin, as other men do, with the evidence of his senses? And if so, what valid process of reasoning can possibly lead him to the conception of a transcendent reality? Surely from empirical premises nothing whatsoever concerning the properties, or even the existence, of anything super-empirical can legitimately be inferred. But this objection would be met by a denial on the part of the metaphysician that his assertions were ultimately based on the evidence of his senses. He would say that he was endowed with a faculty of intellectual intuition which enabled him to know facts that could not be known through sense-experience. And even if it could be shown that he was relying on empirical premises, and that his venture into a non-empirical world was therefore logically unjustified, it would not follow that the assertions which he made concerning this nonempirical world could not be true. For the fact

that a conclusion does not follow from its putative premise is not sufficient to show that it is false. Consequently one cannot overthrow a system of transcendent metaphysics merely by criticizing the way in which it comes into being. What is required is rather a criticism of the nature of the actual statements which comprise it. And this is the line of argument which we shall, in fact, pursue. For we shall maintain that no statement which refers to a "reality" transcending the limits of all possible sense-experience can possibly have any literal significance; from which it must follow that the labors of those who have striven to describe such a reality have all been devoted to the production of nonsense.

It may be suggested that this is a proposition which has already been proved by Kant. But although Kant also condemned transcendent metaphysic, he did so on different grounds. For he said that the human understanding was so constituted that it lost itself in contradictions when it ventured out beyond the limits of possible experience and attempted to deal with things in themselves. And thus he made the impossibility of a transcendent metaphysics, not, as we do, a matter of logic, but a matter of fact. He asserted, not that our minds could not conceivably have had the power of penetrating beyond the phenomenal world, but merely that they were in fact devoid of it. And this leads the critic to ask how, if it is possible to know only what lies within the bounds of sense-experience, the author can be justified in asserting that real things do exist beyond, and how he can tell what are the boundaries beyond which the human understanding may not venture, unless he succeeds in passing them himself. As Wittgenstein says, "in order to draw a limit to thinking, we should have to think both sides of this limit," a truth to which Bradley gives a special twist in maintaining that the man who is ready to prove that metaphysics is impossible is a brother metaphysician with a rival theory of his own.

Whatever force these objections may have against the Kantian doctrine, they have none whatsoever against the thesis that I am about to set forth. It cannot here be said that the author is himself overstepping the barrier he maintains to be impassable. For the fruitlessness of attempting to transcend the limits of possible sense-experience will be deduced, not from a psychological hypothesis concerning the actual constitution of the human mind, but from the rule which determines the literal significance of language. Our charge against the metaphysician is not that he attempts to employ the understanding in a field where it cannot profitably venture, but that he produces sentences which fail to conform to the conditions under which alone a sentence can be literally significant. Nor are we ourselves obliged to talk nonsense in order to show that all sentences of a certain type are necessarily devoid of literal significance. We need only formulate the criterion which enables us to test whether a sentence expresses a genuine proposition about a matter of fact, and then point out that sentences under consideration fail to satisfy it. And this we shall now proceed to do. We shall first of all formulate the criterion in somewhat vague terms, and then give the explanations which are necessary to render it precise.

The criterion which we use to test the genuineness of apparent statements of fact is the criterion of verifiability. We say that a sentence is factually significant to any given person, if, and only if, he knows how to verify the proposition which it purports to express—that is, if he knows what observations would lead him, under certain conditions, to accept the proposition as being true, or reject it as being false. If, on the other hand, the putative proposition is of such a character that the assumption of its truth, or falsehood, is consistent with any assumption whatsoever concerning the nature of his future experience, then, as far as he is concerned, it is, if not a tautology, a mere pseudo-proposition. The sentence expressing it may be emotionally significant to him; but it is not literally significant. And with regard to questions the procedure is the same. We enquire in every case what observations would lead us to answer the question, one way or the other; and, if none can be discovered, we must conclude that the sentence under consideration does not, as far as we are concerned, express a genuine question, however strongly its grammatical appearance may suggest that it does.

As the adoption of this procedure is an essential factor in the argument of this book, it needs to be examined in detail.

In the first place, it is necessary to draw a distinction between practical verifiability, and verifiability in principle. Plainly we all understand, in many cases believe, propositions which we have not in fact taken steps to verify. Many of these are propositions which we could verify if we took enough trouble. But there remain a number of significant propositions, concerning matters of fact, which we could not verify even if we chose; simply because we lack the practical means of placing ourselves in the situation where the relevant observations could be made. A simple and familiar example of such a proposition is the proposition that there are mountains on the farther side of the moon. No rocket has yet been invented which would enable me to go and look at the farther side of the moon, so that I am unable to decide the matter by actual observation. But I do know what observations would decide it for me, if, as is theoretically conceivable, I were once in a position to make them. And therefore I say that the proposition is verifiable in principle, if not in practice, and is accordingly significant. On the other hand, such a metaphysical pseudo-proposition as "the Absolute enters into, but is itself incapable of, evolution and progress," is not even in principle verifiable. For one cannot conceive of an observation which would enable one to determine whether the Absolute did, or did not, enter into evolution and progress. Of course it is possible that the author of such a remark is using English words in a way in which they are not commonly used by English-speaking people, and that he does, in fact, intend to assert something which could be empirically verified. But until he makes us understand how the proposition that he wishes to express would be verified, he fails to communicate anything to us. And if he admits, as I think the author of the remark in question would have admitted, that his words were not intended to express either a tautology or a proposition which was capable, at least in principle, of being verified, then it follows that he has made an utterance which has no literal significance even for himself.

A further distinction which we must make is the distinction between the "strong" and "weak" sense of the term "verifiable." A proposition is said to be verifiable, in the strong sense of the term, if, and only if, its truth could be conclusively established in experience. But it is verifiable, in the weak sense, if it is possible for experience to render it probable. In which sense are we using the term when we say that a putative proposition is genuine only if it is verifiable?

It seems to me that if we adopt conclusive verifiability as our criterion of significance, as some positivists have proposed, our argument will prove too much. Consider, for example, the case of general propositions of law—such propositions, namely, as "arsenic is poisonous"; "all men are mortal"; "a body tends to expand when it is heated." It is of the very nature of these propositions that their truth cannot be established with certainty by any finite series of observations. But if it is recognized that such general propositions of law are designed to cover an infinite number of cases, then it must be admitted that they cannot, even in principle, be verified conclusively. And then, if we adopt conclusive verifiability as our criterion of significance, we are logically obliged to treat these general propositions of law in the same fashion as we treat the statements of the metaphysician.

In face of this difficulty, some positivists have adopted the heroic course of saying that these general propositions are indeed pieces of nonsense, albeit an essentially important type of nonsense. But here the introduction of the term "important" is simply an attempt to hedge. It serves only to mark the authors' recognition that their view is somewhat too paradoxical, without in any way removing the paradox. Besides, the difficulty is not confined to the case of general propositions of law, though it is there revealed most plainly. It is hardly less obvious in the case of propositions about the remote past. For it must surely be admitted that, however strong the evidence in favor of historical statements may be, their truth can never become more than highly probable. And to maintain that they also constituted an important, or unimportant, type of nonsense would be unplausible, to say the very least. Indeed, it will be our contention that no proposition, other than a tautology, can possibly be anything more than a probable hypothesis. And if this is correct, the principle that a sentence can be factually significant only if it expresses what is conclusively verifiable is self-stultifying as a criterion of significance. For it leads to the conclusion that it is impossible to make a significant statement of fact at all.

Nor can we accept the suggestion that a sentence should be allowed to be factually significant if, and only if, it expresses something which is definitely confutable by experience. Those who adopt this course assume that, although no finite series of observations is ever sufficient to establish the truth of a hypothesis beyond all possibility of doubt, there are crucial cases in which a single observation, or series of observations, can definitely confute it. But, as we shall show later on, this assumption is false. A hypothesis cannot be conclusively confuted any more than it can be conclusively verified. For when we take the occurrence of certain observations as proof that a given hypothesis is false, we presuppose the existence of certain conditions. And though, in any given case, it may be extremely improbable that this assumption is false, it is not logically impossible. We shall see that there need be no self-contradiction in holding that some of the relevant circumstances are other than we have taken them to be, and consequently that the hypothesis has not really broken down. And if it is not the case that any hypothesis can be definitely confuted, we cannot hold that the genuineness of a proposition depends on the possibility of its definite confutation.

Accordingly, we fall back on the weaker sense of verification. We say that the question that must be asked about any putative statement of fact is not, Would any observations make its truth or falsehood logically certain? but simply, Would any observations be relevant to the determination of its truth or falsehood? And it is only if a negative answer is given to this second question that we conclude that the statement under consideration is nonsensical.

To make our position clearer, we may formulate it in another way. Let us call a proposition which records an actual or possible observation an experiential proposition. Then we may say that it is the mark of a genuine factual proposition, not that it should be equivalent to an experiential proposition, or any finite number of experiential propositions, but simply that some experiential propositions can be deduced from it in conjunction with certain other premises without being deducible from those other premises alone.

This criterion seems liberal enough. In contrast to the principle of conclusive verifiability, it clearly does not deny significance to general propositions or to propositions about the past. Let us see what kinds of assertion it rules out.

A good example of the kind of utterance that is condemned by our criterion as being not even false but nonsensical would be the assertion that the world of sense-experience was altogether unreal. It must, of course, be admitted that our senses do sometimes deceive us. We may, as the result of having sensations, expect certain other sensations to be obtainable which are, in fact, not obtainable. But, in all such cases, it is further sense-experience that informs us of the mistakes that arise out of sense-experience. We say that the senses sometimes deceive us, just because the expectations to which our sense-experiences give rise do not always accord with what we subsequently experience. That is, we rely on our senses to substantiate or confute the judgements which are based on our sensations. And therefore the fact that our perceptual judgements are sometimes found to be erroneous has not the slightest tendency to show that the world of sense-experience is unreal. And, indeed, it is plain that no conceivable observation, or series of observations could have any tendency to show that the world revealed to us by sense-experience was unreal. Consequently, anyone who condemns the sensible world as a world of mere appearance, as opposed to reality, is saying something which, according to our criterion of significance, is literally nonsensical.

An example of a controversy which the application of our criterion obliges us to condemn as fictitious is provided by those who dispute concerning the number of substances that there are in the world. For it is admitted both by monists, who maintain that reality is one substance, and by pluralists, who maintain that reality is many, that it is impossible to imagine any empirical situation which would be relevant to the solution of their dispute. But if we are told that no possible observation could give any probability either to the assertion that reality was one substance or to the assertion that it was many, then we must conclude that neither assertion is significant. We shall see later on that there are genuine logical and empirical questions involved in the dispute between monists and pluralists. But the metaphysical question concerning "substance" is ruled out by our criterion as spurious.

A similar treatment must be accorded to the controversy between realists and idealists, in its metaphysical aspect. A simple illustration, which I have made use of in a similar argument elsewhere, will help to demonstrate this. Let us suppose that a picture is discovered and the suggestion made that it was painted by Goya. There is a definite procedure for dealing with such a question. The experts examine the picture to see in what way it resembles the accredited works of Goya, and to see if it bears any marks which

are characteristic of a forgery; they look up contemporary records for evidence of the existence of such a picture, and so on. In the end, they may still disagree, but each one knows what empirical evidence would go to confirm or discredit his opinion. Suppose, now, that these men have studied philosophy, and some of them proceed to maintain that this picture is a set of ideas in the perceiver's mind, or in God's mind, others that it is objectively real. What possible experience could any of them have which would be relevant to the solution of this dispute one way or the other? In the ordinary sense of the term "real," in which it is opposed to "illusory," the reality of the picture is not in doubt. The disputants have satisfied themselves that the picture is real, in this sense, by obtaining a correlated series of sensations of sight and sensations of touch. Is there any similar process by which they could discover whether the picture was real, in the sense in which the term "real" is opposed to "ideal"? Clearly there is none. But, if that is so, the problem is fictitious according to our criterion. This does not mean that the realist-idealist controversy may be dismissed without further ado. For it can legitimately be regarded as a dispute concerning the analysis of existential propositions, and so as involving a logical problem which, as we shall see, can be definitively solved. What we have just shown is that the question at issue between idealists and realists becomes fictitious when, as is often the case, it is given a metaphysical interpretation.

There is no need for us to give further examples of the operation of our criterion of significance. For our object is merely to show that philosophy, as a genuine branch of knowledge, must be distinguished from metaphysics. We are not now concerned with the historical question how much of what has traditionally passed for philosophy is actually metaphysical. We shall, however, point out later on that the majority of the "great philosophers" of the past were not essentially metaphysicians, and thus reassure those who would otherwise be prevented from adopting our criterion by considerations of piety.

As to the validity of the verification principle, in the form in which we have stated it, a demonstration will be given in the course of this book. For it will be shown that all propositions which have factual content are empirical hypotheses; and that the function of an empirical hypothesis is to provide a rule for the anticipation of experience. And this means that every empirical hypothesis must be relevant to some actual, or possible, experience, so that a statement which is not relevant to any experience is not an empirical hypothesis, and accordingly has no factual content. But this is precisely what the principle of verifiability asserts.

It should be mentioned here that the fact that the utterances of the metaphysician are nonsensical does not follow simply from the fact that they are devoid of factual content. It follows from that fact, together with the fact that they are not *a priori* propositions. And in assuming that they are not *a priori* propositions, we are once again anticipating the conclusions of a later chapter in this book. For it will be shown there that *a priori* propositions, which have always been attractive to philosophers on account of their certainty, owe this certainty to the fact that they are tautologies. We may accordingly define a metaphysical sentence as a sentence which purports to express a genuine proposition, but does, in fact, express neither a tautology nor an empirical hypothesis. And as tautologies and empirical hypotheses form the entire class of significant propositions, we are justified in concluding that all metaphysical assertions are nonsensical. Our next task is to show how they come to be made.

The use of the term "substance," to which we have already referred, provides us with a good example of the way in which metaphysics mostly comes to be written. It happens to be the case that we cannot, in our language, refer to the sensible properties of a thing without introducing a word or phrase which appears to stand for the thing itself as opposed to anything which may be said about it. And, as a result of this, those who are infected by the primitive superstition that to every name a single real entity must correspond assume that it is necessary to distinguish logically between the thing itself and any, or all, of its sensible properties. And so they employ the term "substance" to refer to the thing itself. But from the fact that we happen to employ a single word to refer to a thing, and make that word the grammatical subject of the sentences in which we refer to the sensible appearances of the thing, it does not by any means follow that the thing itself is a "simple entity," or that it cannot be defined in terms of the totality of its appearances. It is true that in talking of "its" appearances we appear to distinguish the thing from the appearances, but that is simply an accident of linguistic usage. Logical analysis

shows that what makes these "appearances" the "appearances of" the same thing is not their relationship to an entity other than themselves, but their relationship to one another. The metaphysician fails to see this because he is misled by a superficial grammatical feature of his language.

A simpler and clearer instance of the way in which a consideration of grammar leads to metaphysics is the case of the metaphysical concept of Being. The origin of our temptation to raise questions about Being, which no conceivable experience would enable us to answer, lies in the fact that, in our language, sentences which express existential propositions and sentences which express attributive propositions may be of the same grammatical form. For instance, the sentences "Martyrs exist" and "Martyrs suffer" both consist of a noun followed by an intransitive verb, and the fact that they have grammatically the same appearance leads one to assume that they are of the same logical type. It is seen that in the proposition "Martyrs suffer," the members of a certain species are credited with a certain attribute, and it is sometimes assumed that the same thing is true of such a proposition as "Martyrs exist." If this were actually the case, it would, indeed, be as legitimate to speculate about the Being of martyrs as it is to speculate about their suffering. But, as Kant pointed out, existence is not an attribute. For, when we ascribe an attribute to a thing, we covertly assert that it exists: so that if existence were itself an attribute, it would follow that all positive existential propositions were tautologies, and all negative existential propositions self-contradictory; and this is not the case. So that those who raise questions about Being which are based on the assumption that existence is an attribute are guilty of following grammar beyond the boundaries of sense.

A similar mistake has been made in connection with such propositions as "Unicorns are fictitious." Here again the fact that there is a superficial grammatical resemblance between the English sentences "Dogs are faithful" and "Unicorns are fictitious," and between the corresponding sentences in other languages, creates the assumption that they are of the same logical type. Dogs must exist in order to have the property of being faithful, and so it is held that unless unicorns in some way existed they could not have the property of being fictitious. But, as it is plainly self-contradictory to say that fictitious objects exist, the device is adopted of saying that they are real in some non-empirical sense— that they have a mode of real being which is different from the mode of being of existent things. But since there is no way of testing whether an object is real in this sense, as there is for testing whether it is real in the ordinary sense, the assertion that fictitious objects have a special non-empirical mode of real being is devoid of all literal significance. It comes to be made as a result of the assumption that being fictitious is an attribute. And this is a fallacy of the same order as the fallacy of supposing that existence is an attribute, and it can be exposed in the same way.

In general, the postulation of real non-existent entities results from the superstition, just now referred to, that, to every word or phrase that can be the grammatical subject of a sentence, there must somewhere be a real entity corresponding. For as there is no place in the empirical world for many of these "entities," a special non-empirical world is invoked to house them. To this error must be attributed, not only the utterances of a Heidegger, who bases his metaphysics on the assumption that "Nothing" is a name which is used to denote something peculiarly mysterious, but also the prevalence of such problems as those concerning the reality of propositions and universals whose senselessness, though less obvious, is no less complete.

These few examples afford a sufficient indication of the way in which most metaphysical assertions come to be formulated. They show how easy it is to write sentences which are literally nonsensical without seeing that they are nonsensical. And thus we see that the view that a number of the traditional "problems of philosophy" are metaphysical, and consequently fictitious, does not involve any incredible assumptions about the psychology of philosophers.

Among those who recognize that if philosophy is to be accounted a genuine branch of knowledge it must be defined in such a way as to distinguish it from metaphysics, it is fashionable to speak of the metaphysician as a kind of misplaced poet. As his statements have no literal meaning, they are not subject to any criteria of truth or falsehood: but they may still serve to express, or arouse, emotion, and thus be subject to ethical or aesthetic standards. And it is suggested that they may have considerable value, as means of moral inspiration, or even as works of art. In this way, an attempt is made to compensate the metaphysician for his extrusion from philosophy.

I am afraid that this compensation is hardly in accordance with his deserts. The view that the metaphysician is to be reckoned among the poets appears to rest on the assumption that both talk nonsense. But this assumption is false. In the vast majority of cases the sentences which are produced by poets do have literal meaning. The difference between the man who uses language scientifically and the man who uses it emotively is not that the one produces sentences which are incapable of arousing emotion, and the other sentences which have no sense, but that the one is primarily concerned with the expression of true propositions, the other with the creation of a work of art. Thus, if a work of science contains true and important propositions, its value as a work of science will hardly be diminished by the fact that they are inelegantly expressed. And similarly, a work of art is not necessarily the worse for the fact that all the propositions comprising it are literally false. But to say that many literary works are largely composed of falsehoods, is not to say that they are composed of pseudo-propositions. It is, in fact, very rare for a literary artist to produce sentences which have no literal meaning. And where this does occur, the sentences are carefully chosen for their rhythm and balance. If the author writes nonsense, it is because he considers it most suitable for bringing about the effects for which his writing is designed.

The metaphysician, on the other hand, does not intend to write nonsense. He lapses into it through being deceived by grammar, or through committing errors of reasoning, such as that which leads to the view that the sensible world is unreal. But it is not the mark of a poet simply to make mistakes of this sort. There are some, indeed, who would see in the fact that the metaphysician's utterances are senseless a reason against the view that they have aesthetic value. And, without going so far as this, we may safely say that it does not constitute a reason for it.

It is true, however, that although the greater part of metaphysics is merely the embodiment of humdrum errors, there remain a number of metaphysical passages which are the work of genuine mystical feeling; and they may more plausibly be held to have moral or aesthetic value. But, as far as we are concerned, the distinction between the kind of metaphysics that is produced by a philosopher who has been duped by grammar, and the kind that is produced by a mystic who is trying to express the inexpressible, is of no great importance: what is important to us is to realize that even the utterances of the metaphysician who is attempting to expound a vision are literally senseless; so that henceforth we may pursue our philosophical researches with as little regard for them as for the more inglorious kind of metaphysics which comes from a failure to understand the workings of our language.

Discussion Questions

1. Consider the criterion of verifiability. Is it plausible? Can you give an alternative criterion that would be better? Should the criterion of verifiability itself be verifiable? What problems would this pose? Then consider this question: Why is a criterion of meaningfulness needed at all?

2. Consider the following sentences. "All men are mortal"; "Abortion is morally wrong"; "God exists"; and "The painting is beautiful." Would a positivist consider any of these sentences to be meaningful? If so, which ones? If not, why not? Do you agree? Why or why not?

For Further Reading

For works about Ayer see his two autobiographies, *Part of My Life* (1977) and *More of My Life* (1984). For analyses of Ayer's philosophy see *A. J. Ayer* (1985), by J. Foster; *Essays on A. J. Ayer* (1991), edited by T. Honderich; and *The Philosophy of A. J. Ayer* (1972), edited by L. E. Hahn. For collections of essays by Ayer see *Philosophical Essays* (1954), *The Concept of a Person and Other Essays* (1963), and *Metaphysics and Common-Sense* (1969). Logical positivism is discussed in a number of places, including *Logical Positivism in Perspective* (1987), edited by B. Gower; *Essential Readings in Logical Positivism* (1981), edited by O. Hanfling; *Logical Positivism* (1981), by O. Hanfling; and *Classics of Analytic Philosophy* (1990), edited by R. Ammerman.

CHAPTER 6

HOW CAN I HAVE KNOWLEDGE?

What is knowledge? How much knowledge is possible? Both of these questions fall into an area of philosophy known as **epistemology.** Roughly, epistemologists seek to understand both the nature of knowledge and the extent to which humans possess it. As could be expected, there are a number of different and competing views within epistemology. For example, some skeptical philosophers believe that humans are capable of little or no knowledge. Other philosophers, sometimes called **cognitivists,** agree that knowledge is possible, but they disagree about how much we can know or the means by which we come to know things. For example, some cognitivists believe that humans are born with a certain amount of innate knowledge, while others claim that the human mind is essentially empty at birth and that knowledge derives from sensory experience or the use of reason.

The first selection is taken from one of Plato's most famous dialogues, *The Republic.* For Plato, ultimate reality can be known, but this reality cannot be seen with one's eyes. The real world is known through reason; our senses, according to Plato, only give us impressions of a shadowy world of appearances. For Plato, a particular thing, say a beautiful vase, is neither real nor knowable; rather, what is real and knowable is "beauty itself" and the "idea of a vase." For example, consider the case of triangles. Do we know what triangles are? Of course, but have we ever seen one *really?* No, says Plato, since all physical "triangles" around us are merely approximations of the true idea of a triangle. Nonetheless, it does make sense to talk about triangles, and Plato believed that things such as the idea of a triangle actually exist as immaterial entities called *Forms.* True knowledge, argues Plato, is knowledge of the Form of a thing, not its physical instantiation.

The next two selections come from René Descartes and David Hume. They represent two opposing sides in a perennial debate between epistemologists, the debate between **rationalism** and **empiricism.** Rationalists and empiricists disagree over how basic knowledge about the world is acquired. Rationalists, such as Descartes, believe that the mind, on its own power, can come to a (nearly) complete and accurate understanding of the world, independently of sense experience. In contrast, empiricists, such as Hume, maintain that "there is nothing in the mind that was not first in the senses." This means that any knowledge we possess is gained solely through sensory experience.

Kant, the author of the chapter's fourth reading, attempts to synthesize rationalism and empiricism. On the one hand, Kant sides with empiricists and argues that "all our knowledge begins with experience." But Kant holds that the fact that knowledge begins with experience does not mean that knowledge comes exclusively from experience, as the empiricists claim. Kant writes "though all our knowledge begins with experience, it by no means follows that all arises out of experience. For, on the contrary, it is quite possible that our empirical knowledge is a compound of that which we receive through impressions, and that which the faculty of cognition supplies from itself." Hence, Kant also sides with the rationalists inasmuch as "[a priori] principles are the indispensable basis of the possibility of experience itself." Granted this nexus, Kant traces out the possibilities of human knowledge.

William James, in the fifth reading, advocates a view called **pragmatism.** As the name suggests, pragmatism holds that a belief is true if believing it to be true is more useful than believing it to be false. For example, if the sciences are able to offer a better explanation of how and why light behaves as it does by describing light as a particle, then it is true that light is a particle. If for some reason it becomes more useful to describe and think of light in different terms—as a wave, for example—then this new way of thinking about light becomes the truth. And if for some reason it becomes more useful to describe light as both a particle and a wave, then the truth is that light is both a particle and a wave. Roughly put, the truth is whatever works best.

The views of Paul Feyerabend, selection six of this chapter, are similar to those of William James. Typically we think of science as a discipline that methodically employing the scientific method marches forward, increasing our knowledge of the world. But, Feyerabend claims, science does not progress methodically forward, step by step. Not only do scientists have a false picture of how science actually works, but if they would only admit that there are other means for acquiring knowledge of the world, our understanding of the world would increase even more quickly.

The final article presents a very different picture of how we come to know what is true. Responding to recent criticisms that traditional epistemology has depended on an oversimplified conception of knowledge, John Greco argues that knowledge is achieved by virtuous persons. Virtue epistemology, as it is called, is in many ways like virtue ethics (see Chapter 8, Reading 45). Both trace their roots back to Aristotle and claim that human knowledge—of the world and morality, respectively—is best understood as the result of 'good' or 'virtuous' persons exercising their judgment in a balanced and reasoned manner.

27 THE ALLEGORY OF THE CAVE
Plato

The written record of **Western philosophy** traces its roots to Plato (c. 428–348 B.C.E), but Plato is famous not only because he is the first major figure in Western philosophy. His importance also derives from the fact that his philosophy shaped almost every philosophical investigation that followed him. In fact, Alfred North Whitehead has said that the rest of philosophy is little more than a footnote to Plato.

Born in Athens to an aristocratic family of both political power and financial means, Plato had political aspirations for a time. But when democracy began to emerge in ancient Greece, Plato's family lost much of its political leverage. Instead of politics, then, Plato became a student of Socrates and took up the study of philosophy. After Socrates' death in 399 B.C.E., Plato left Athens and traveled for a time. After visiting Italy, Sicily, and perhaps even Egypt, Plato eventually returned to Athens and founded the *Academy* in 385 B.C.E.—the first university of the Western world. The *Academy* remained open, in one form or another, until 529 C.E. and included Aristotle among its famous students.

The following selection comes from Books V and VII of *The Republic*. In it, Plato makes several different points. First, material objects, the physical things that make up the world around us, are not what is ultimately real. That is, particular things we see, such as beautiful vases, particular triangles, or particular acts of justice, are not ultimate reality. What is ultimately real, permanent, and immutable are Ideas— for example, the idea of beauty itself, of triangularity itself, and of justice itself. Moreover, Plato believes that these Ideas—what he calls the Forms—have an (immaterial, but real) existence independent of the human mind.

Second, since authentic knowledge can only be knowledge of what is truly real, knowledge consists of recognizing and contemplating the Forms. So, strictly speaking, we cannot *know* that a (material) vase is beautiful. But we can possess knowledge of the Idea of beauty itself, the Idea of a vase itself, and so on. Of course, Plato recognizes that most people consider the material world to be the real world. As a result, most people base their lives on imperfect renderings of ultimate reality. They may think they have knowledge, but they actually have only a shadowy glimpse of what is truly real. Ironically, when these persons are told of their error and are shown the true nature of knowledge and reality, they often find these truths preposterous, blinding, or disorienting.

Reading Questions

1. According to Plato, what is a philosopher?
2. What is the difference between knowledge and opinion?
3. How does Socrates answer those who do not believe in the existence of an absolute and unchanging Idea of Beauty or Justice?
4. To what extent do beautiful things exist?
5. What is one's initial reaction when one is liberated and compelled to gaze on the real truth (the light)?
6. How do those who have not ventured outside of "the cave of ignorance and illusion" respond to the teachings of those who have?
7. How do those who have seen the truth respond to the evil state of man?

. . . [H]e who dislikes learning, especially in youth, when he has no power of judging what is good and what is not, such a one we maintain not to be a philosopher or a lover of knowledge, just as he who refuses his food is not hungry, and may be said to have a bad appetite and not a good one?

Very true, he said.

Whereas he who has a taste for every sort of knowledge and who is curious to learn and is never satisfied, may be justly termed a philosopher? Am I not right?

Glaucon said: If curiosity makes a philosopher, you will find many a strange being will have a title to the name. All the lovers of sights have a delight in learning, and must therefore be included. Musical amateurs, too, are a folk strangely out of place among philosophers, for they are the last persons in the world who would come to anything like a philosophical discussion if they could help; while they run about at the Dionysiac festivals as if they had let out their ears for the season to hear every chorus, and miss no performance either in town or country. Now are we to maintain that all these and any who have similar tastes, as well as the professors of quite minor arts, are philosophers?

Certainly not, I replied; they are only an imitation.

He said: Who then are the true philosophers?

Those, I said, who are lovers of the vision of truth.

That is also good, he said; but I should like to know what you mean?

To another, I replied, I might have a difficulty in explaining; but I am sure that you will admit a proposition which I am about to make.

What is the proposition?

That since beauty is the opposite of ugliness, they are two?

Certainly.

And inasmuch as they are two, each of them is one?

True again.

And of just and unjust, good and evil, and of every other form, the same remark holds: taken singly, each of them is one; but from the various combinations of them with actions and bodies and with one another, they are seen in all sorts of lights and appear many?

Very true.

And this is the distinction which I draw between the sight-loving, art-loving, practical class which you have mentioned, and those of whom I am speaking, and who are alone worthy of the name of philosophers.

How do you distinguish them? he said.

The lovers of sounds and sights, I replied, are, as I conceive, fond of fine tones and colors and forms and all the artificial products that are made out of them, but their mind is incapable of seeing or loving absolute beauty.

The fact is plain, he replied.

Few are they who are able to attain to this ideal beauty and contemplate it.

Very true.

And he who, having a sense of beautiful things, has no sense of absolute beauty, or who, if another lead him to a knowledge of that beauty, is unable to follow—of such a one I ask, Is he awake or in a dream only? Reflect: is not the dreamer, sleeping or waking, one who likens dissimilar things, who puts the copy in the place of the real object?

I should certainly say that such a one was dreaming.

But he who, on the contrary, recognizes the existence of absolute beauty and is able to contemplate both the Idea and the objects which participate in it, neither putting the objects in the place of the Idea nor the Idea in the place of the objects—is he a dreamer, or is he awake?

He is wide awake.

And since he knows, it would be right to describe his state of mind as knowledge, and the state of mind of the other, who opines only, as opinion?

Certainly.

. . .

This being premised, I would ask the gentleman who is of opinion that there is no absolute or unchangeable Idea of beauty, but only a number of beautiful things—he, I say, your lover of beautiful sights, who cannot bear to be told that the beautiful is one, and the just is one, or that anything is one—to him I would appeal, saying, Will you be so very kind, sir, as to tell us whether, of all these beautiful things, there is one which will not be found ugly; or of the just, which will not be found unjust; or of the holy, which will not also seem unholy?

No, he replied; these things must, from different points of view, be found both beautiful and ugly; and the same is true of the rest.

And do not the many which are doubles appear no less plainly to be halves?

Quite true.

And things great and small, heavy and light, will not be denoted by the names which we happen to use first any more than by the opposite names?

True; both names will always attach to all of them.

If so, can any one of those many things be said to be, rather than not to be, that which we happen to have termed it?

He replied: They are like the punning riddles which are asked at feasts or the children's puzzle about the eunuch aiming at the bat, with what he hit him, as they say in the puzzle, and upon what the bat was sitting. The individual objects of which I am speaking are also a riddle, and have a double sense: nor can you fix them in your mind, either as being or not-being, or both, or neither.

Then what will you do with them? I said. Can they have a better place than between being and not-being? For they are clearly not in greater darkness or negation than not-being, or more full of light and existence than being.

That is quite true, he said.

Thus then we seem to have discovered that the many notions which the multitude entertain about the beautiful and about all other things are tossing about in some region which is half-way between pure being and pure not-being?

We have.

...

And now, I said, let me show in a figure how far our nature is enlightened or unenlightened:—Behold! human beings housed in an underground cave, which has a long entrance open towards the light and as wide as the interior of the cave; here they have been from their childhood, and have their legs and necks chained, so that they cannot move and can only see before them, being prevented by the chains from turning round their heads. Above and behind them a fire is blazing at a distance, and between the fire and the prisoners there is a raised way; and you will see, if you look, a low wall built along the way, like the screen which marionette players have in front of them, over which they show the puppets.

I see.

And do you see, I said, men passing along the wall carrying all sorts of vessels, and statues and figures of animals made of wood and stone and various materials, which appear over the wall? While carrying their burdens, some of them, as you would expect, are talking, others silent.

You have shown me a strange image, and they are strange prisoners.

Like ourselves, I replied; for in the first place do you think they have seen anything of themselves, and of one another, except the shadows which the fire throws on the opposite wall of the cave?

How could they do so, he asked, if throughout their lives they were never allowed to move their heads?

And of the objects which are being carried in like manner they would only see the shadows?

Yes, he said.

And if they were able to converse with one another, would they not suppose that the things they saw were the real things?

Very true.

And suppose further that the prison had an echo which came from the other side, would they not be sure to fancy when one of the passers-by spoke that the voice which they heard came from the passing shadow?

No question, he replied.

To them, I said, the truth would be literally nothing but the shadows of the images.

That is certain.

And now look again, and see in what manner they would be released from their bonds, and cured of their error, whether the process would naturally be as follows. At first, when any of them is liberated and compelled suddenly to stand up and turn his neck round and walk and look towards the light, he will suffer sharp pains; the glare will distress him, and he will be unable to see the realities of which in his former state he had seen the shadows; and then conceive someone saying to him that what he saw before was an illusion, but that now, when he is approaching nearer to being and his eye is turned towards more real existence, he has a clearer vision,—what will be his reply? And you may further imagine that his instructor is pointing to the objects as they pass and requiring him to name them,—will he not be perplexed? Will he not fancy that the shadows which he formerly saw are truer than the objects which are now shown to him?

Far truer.

And if he is compelled to look straight at the light, will he not have a pain in his eyes which will make him turn away to take refuge in the objects of vision which he can see, and which he will conceive to be in reality clearer than the things which are now being shown to him?

True, he said.

And suppose once more, that he is reluctantly dragged up that steep and rugged ascent, and held fast until he is forced into the presence of the sun himself, is he not likely to be pained and irritated? When he approaches the light his eyes will be dazzled, and he will not be able to see anything at all of what are now called realities.

Not all in a moment, he said.

He will require to grow accustomed to the sight of the upper world. And first he will see the shadows best, next the reflections of men and other objects in the water, and then the objects themselves; and, when he turned to the heavenly bodies and the heaven itself, he would find it easier to gaze upon the light of the moon and the stars at night than to see the sun or the light of the sun by day?

Certainly.

Last of all he will be able to see the sun, not turning aside to the illusory reflections of him in the water, but gazing directly at him in his own proper place, and contemplating him as he is.

Certainly.

He will then proceed to argue that this is he who gives the seasons and the years, and is the guardian of all that is in the visible world, and in a certain way the cause of all things which he and his fellows have been accustomed to behold?

Clearly, he said, he would arrive at this conclusion after what he had seen.

And when he remembered his old habitation, and the wisdom of the cave and his fellow-prisoners, do you not suppose that he would felicitate himself on the change, and pity them?

Certainly, he would.

And if they were in the habit of conferring honors among themselves on those who were quickest to observe the passing shadows and to remark which of them went before and which followed after and which were together, and who were best able from these observations to divine the future, do you think that he would be eager for such honors and glories, or envy those who attained honor and sovereignty among those men? Would he not say with Homer,

'Better to be a serf, laboring for a landless master',

and to endure anything, rather than think as they do and live after their manner?

Yes, he said, I think that he would consent to suffer anything rather than live in this miserable manner.

Imagine once more, I said, such a one coming down suddenly out of the sunlight, and being replaced in his old seat; would he not be certain to have his eyes full of darkness?

To be sure, he said.

And if there were a contest, and he had to compete in measuring the shadows with the prisoners who had never moved out of the cave, while his sight was still weak, and before his eyes had become steady (and the time which would be needed to acquire this new habit of sight might be very considerable), would he not make himself ridiculous? Men would say of him that he had returned from the place above with his eyes ruined; and that it was better not even to think of ascending; and if anyone tried to loose another and lead him up to the light, let them only catch the offender, and they would put him to death.

No question, he said.

This entire allegory, I said, you may now append, dear Glaucon, to the previous argument; the prison-house is the world of sight, the light of the fire is the power of the sun, and you will not misapprehend me if you interpret the journey upwards to be the ascent of the soul into the intellectual world according to my surmise, which, at your desire, I have expressed—whether rightly or wrongly God knows. But, whether true or false, my opinion is that in the world of knowledge the Idea of good appears last of all, and is seen only with an effort; although, when seen, it is inferred to be the universal author of all things beautiful and right, parent of light and of the lord of light in the visible world, and the immediate and supreme source of reason and truth in the intellectual; and that this is the power upon which he who would act rationally either in public or private life must have his eye fixed.

I agree, he said, as far as I am able to understand you.

Moreover, I said, you must agree once more, and not wonder that those who attain to this vision are unwilling to take any part in human affairs; for their souls are ever hastening into the upper world where they desire to dwell; which desire of theirs is very natural, if our allegory may be trusted.

Yes, very natural.

And is there anything surprising in one who passes from divine contemplations to the evil state of man, appearing grotesque and ridiculous; if, while his eyes are blinking and before he has become accustomed to the surrounding darkness, he is compelled to fight in courts of law, or in other places, about the images or the shadows of images of justice, and must strive against some rival about opinions of these things which are entertained by men who have never yet seen the true justice?

Anything but surprising, he replied.

Anyone who has common sense will remember that the bewilderments of the eyes are of two kinds and arise from two causes, either from coming out of the light or from going into the light, and, judging that the soul may be affected in the same way, will not give way to foolish laughter when he sees anyone whose vision is perplexed and weak; he will first ask whether that soul of man has come out of the brighter life and is unable to see because unaccustomed to the dark, or having turned from darkness to the day is dazzled by excess of light. And he will count the one happy in his condition and state of being, and he will pity the other; or, if he have a mind to laugh at the soul which comes from below into the light, this laughter will not be quite so laughable as that which greets the soul which returns from above out of the light into the cave.

That, he said, is a very just distinction.

But then, if I am right, certain professors of education must be wrong when they say that they can put a knowledge into the soul which was not there before, like sight into blind eyes.

They undoubtedly say this, he replied.

Whereas our argument shows that the power and capacity of learning exists in the soul already; and that just as if it were not possible to turn the eye from darkness to light without the whole body, so too the instrument of knowledge can only by the movement of the whole soul be turned from the world of becoming to that of being, and learn by degrees to endure the sight of being, and of the brightest and best of being, or in other words, of the good.

Very true. . . .

Discussion Questions

1. What liberates a person from "the cave of ignorance and illusion" according to Plato? How can you be sure that you know what is truly real on Plato's theory? Is this a defensible view? Why or why not?
2. A triangle is defined as "three lines that intersect in a plane." Have you ever actually seen a "real" triangle? How would Plato answer this question? Are there such things as actual triangles? Why or why not?
3. Is Plato a rationalist; that is, does he think that knowledge comes from reason? What role does reason play in his theory? What role does sensory experience play in his theory?
4. Are there other world philosophies or world religions that are like Plato insofar as they regard this world as a shadowy imperfect world and regard ultimate reality to be far different from the world around us? If so, which ones are they? Why do you think such philosophical or religious views would be attractive to persons?

For Further Reading

For a collection of Plato's dialogues see *The Collected Dialogues of Plato* (1961), edited by E. Hamilton and H. Cairns. Several of Plato's dialogues are relevant to his epistemology, including *Meno, Phaedo, Republic, Theaetetus, Timaeus,* and *Laws.* For an excellent account of Plato's epistemology see *Plato's Theory of Knowledge* (1960), by F. M. Cornford. For introductions to Plato's thought in general see *Plato's Thought* (1980), by G. Grube, and *Plato's Theory of Ideas* (1951), by W. D. Ross.

28 MEDITATIONS ON FIRST PHILOSOPHY
René Descartes

René Descartes (1596–1650) was born in a town now named in his honor, Descartes, France. Although Descartes made crucial contributions to the fields of optics, geometry, mathematics, and science, arguably his most important contributions were to philosophy, for which he is often described as the Father of Modern Philosophy. Unfortunately for Descartes, his intellectual genius eventually caught the attention of Queen Christina of Sweden, who invited him to serve as her philosophy instructor. After Descartes ran out of excuses, he reluctantly agreed to her request and moved to Sweden, whereupon Descartes was compelled by the Queen to instruct her in philosophy shortly after daybreak. This proved to be a grueling trial for Descartes, a frail man and a notorious late-riser. In the end, Descartes died of pneumonia—after less than one year in Queen Christina's service.

Descartes was a rationalist and believed that the mind, guided by reason alone, is capable of discovering the more important truths about the world. In fact, the following reading, taken from Descartes' *Meditations on First Philosophy* (1641), is Descartes' famous "argument" for this view. Descartes begins his *Meditations* by employing "methodological skepticism". That is, Descartes inspects the entire stock of his beliefs and dismisses as false any belief that can be doubted in the least. The surviving beliefs—and whatever can be logically inferred from them—are those things that we can know with certainty and are the basis for all of our knowledge about the world.

So what can we know with certainty? At first, it looks as if very little can be known with certainty. For example, Descartes discovers that he is forced to dismiss all of his beliefs that depend on sensory experience, since the senses deceive us on occasion. As a result, Descartes is even forced to doubt that he has a body, since his *knowledge* of his body is based on data from his senses. Eventually, however, Descartes does discover something that he cannot doubt: that he is a "thinking thing" and therefore exists. This is the origin of Descartes' often quoted sentence, **cogito ergo sum:** "I think, therefore I am." Although this sentence does not appear in the *Meditations*, the basic concept does. Descartes can doubt everything except for one crucial fact—that he is a thing that is doubting. Therefore, he exists.

While discovering that he exists, Descartes simultaneously discovers a most useful rule: Whatever he very clearly and distinctly perceives is true. And using this very simple rule, Descartes sets out to reclaim the knowledge he lost to methodological skepticism. The first step in this process is to establish the existence of God. If God's existence can be established, Descartes believes that he can (more or less) trust his senses again, since God—being no deceiver—would not have given us a strong desire to trust our senses if in fact these senses were unworthy of such trust. And since Descartes believes that he can prove the existence of God, the world that was once in doubt is known with certainty again.

Reading Questions

1. Which sort of opinions does Descartes reject as false? Which sort does he accept as true?
2. Does Descartes believe that our senses are to be trusted?
3. Can Descartes be sure that he is not dreaming?
4. Can Descartes be sure that he is not deceived by an evil genius?
5. What is the first truth of which Descartes is certain?
6. What is a thinking thing?
7. To what extent does one's knowledge of an external body—a piece of wax, for example—depend on one's senses?
8. What is Descartes' general rule for identifying the truth?
9. Is Descartes sure that his ideas of external things emanate from external things? Is Descartes sure that his ideas of external things accurately resemble their objects?
10. Can something come from nothing? Can something come from something less perfect than itself? Could Descartes have invented the idea of God on his own?
11. What role does God play in validating the accuracy of one's senses?

MEDITATION I
OF THE THINGS OF
WHICH WE MAY DOUBT

1. Several years have now elapsed since I first became aware that I had accepted, even from my youth, many false opinions for true, and that consequently what I afterward based on such principles was highly doubtful; and from that time I was convinced of the necessity of undertaking once in my life to rid myself of all the opinions I had adopted, and of commencing anew the work of building from the foundation, if I desired to establish a firm and abiding superstructure in the sciences. But as this enterprise appeared to me to be one of great magnitude, I waited until I had attained an age so mature as to leave me no hope that at any stage of life more advanced I should be better able to execute my design. On this account, I have delayed so long that I should henceforth consider I was doing wrong were I still to consume in deliberation any of the time that now remains for action. Today, then, since I have opportunely freed my mind from all cares and am happily disturbed by no passions, and since I am in the secure possession of leisure in a peaceable retirement, I will at length apply myself earnestly and freely to the general overthrow of all my former opinions.

2. But, to this end, it will not be necessary for me to show that the whole of these are false—a point, perhaps, which I shall never reach; but as even now my reason convinces me that I ought not the less carefully to withhold belief from what is not entirely certain and indubitable, than from what is manifestly false, it will be sufficient to justify the rejection of the whole if I shall find in each some ground for doubt. Nor for this purpose will it be necessary even to deal with each belief individually, which would be truly an endless labor; but, as the removal from below of the foundation necessarily involves the downfall of the whole edifice, I will at once approach the criticism of the principles on which all my former beliefs rested.

3. All that I have, up to this moment, accepted as possessed of the highest truth and certainty, I received either from or through the senses. I observed, however, that these sometimes misled us; and it is the part of prudence not to place absolute confidence in that by which we have even once been deceived.

4. But it may be said, perhaps, that, although the senses occasionally mislead us respecting minute objects, and such as are so far removed from us as to be beyond the reach of close observation, there are yet many other of their ... [reports], of the truth of which it is manifestly impossible to doubt; as for example, that I am in this place, seated by the fire, clothed in a winter dressing gown, that I hold in my hands this piece of paper, with other intimations of the same nature. But how could I deny that I possess these hands and this body, and withal escape being classed with persons in a state of insanity, whose

brains are so disordered and clouded by dark bilious vapors as to cause them pertinaciously to assert that they are monarchs when they are in the greatest poverty; or clothed in gold and purple when destitute of any covering; or that their head is made of clay, their body of glass, or that they are gourds? I should certainly be not less insane than they, were I to regulate my procedure according to examples so extravagant.

5. Though this be true, I must nevertheless here consider that I am a man, and that, consequently, I am in the habit of sleeping, and representing to myself in dreams those same things, or even sometimes others less probable, which the insane think are presented to them in their waking moments. How often have I dreamt that I was in these familiar circumstances, that I was dressed, and occupied this place by the fire, when I was lying undressed in bed? At the present moment, however, I certainly look upon this paper with eyes wide awake; the head which I now move is not asleep; I extend this hand consciously and with express purpose, and I perceive it; the occurrences in sleep are not so distinct as all this. But I cannot forget that, at other times I have been deceived in sleep by similar illusions; and, attentively considering those cases, I perceive so clearly that there exist no certain marks by which the state of waking can ever be distinguished from sleep, that I feel greatly astonished; and in amazement I almost persuade myself that I am now dreaming.

6. Let us suppose, then, that we are dreaming, and that all these particulars—namely, the opening of the eyes, the motion of the head, the forth-putting of the hands—are merely illusions; and even that we really possess neither an entire body nor hands such as we see. Nevertheless it must be admitted at least that the objects which appear to us in sleep are, as it were, painted representations which could not have been formed unless in the likeness of realities; and, therefore, that those general objects, at all events, namely, eyes, a head, hands, and an entire body, are not simply imaginary, but really existent. For, in truth, painters themselves, even when they study to represent sirens and satyrs by forms the most fantastic and extraordinary, cannot bestow upon them natures absolutely new, but can only make a certain medley of the members of different animals; or if they chance to imagine something so novel that

nothing at all similar has ever been seen before, and such as is, therefore, purely fictitious and absolutely false, it is at least certain that the colors of which this is composed are real. And on the same principle, although these general objects, viz. a body, eyes, a head, hands, and the like, be imaginary, we are nevertheless absolutely necessitated to admit the reality at least of some other objects still more simple and universal than these, of which, just as of certain real colors, all those images of things, whether true and real, or false and fantastic, that are found in our consciousness, are formed.

7. To this class of objects seem to belong corporeal nature in general and its extension; the figure of extended things, their quantity or magnitude, and their number, as also the place in, and the time during, which they exist, and other things of the same sort.

8. We will not, therefore, perhaps reason illegitimately if we conclude from this that Physics, Astronomy, Medicine, and all the other sciences that have for their end the consideration of composite objects, are indeed of a doubtful character; but that Arithmetic, Geometry, and the other sciences of the same class, which regard merely the simplest and most general objects, and scarcely inquire whether or not these are really existent, contain somewhat that is certain and indubitable: for whether I am awake or dreaming, it remains true that two and three make five, and that a square has but four sides; nor does it seem possible that truths so apparent can ever fall under a suspicion of falsity or incertitude.

9. Nevertheless, the belief that there is a God who is all powerful, and who created me, such as I am, has, for a long time, obtained steady possession of my mind. How, then, do I know that he has not arranged that there should be neither earth, nor sky, nor any extended thing, nor figure, nor magnitude, nor place, providing at the same time, however, for the rise in me of the perceptions of all these objects, and the persuasion that these do not exist otherwise than as I perceive them? And further, as I sometimes think that others are in error respecting matters of which they believe themselves to possess a perfect knowledge, how do I know that I am not also deceived each time I add together two and three, or number the

sides of a square, or form some judgment still more simple, if more simple indeed can be imagined? But perhaps Deity has not been willing that I should be thus deceived, for he is said to be supremely good. If, however, it were repugnant to the goodness of Deity to have created me subject to constant deception, it would seem likewise to be contrary to his goodness to allow me to be occasionally deceived; and yet it is clear that this is permitted.

10. Some, indeed, might perhaps be found who would be disposed rather to deny the existence of a Being so powerful than to believe that there is nothing certain. But let us for the present refrain from opposing this opinion, and grant that all which is here said of a Deity is fabulous: nevertheless, in whatever way it be supposed that I reach the state in which I exist, whether by fate, or chance, or by an endless series of antecedents and consequents, or by any other means, it is clear (since to be deceived and to err is a certain defect) that the probability of my being so imperfect as to be the constant victim of deception, will be increased exactly in proportion as the power possessed by the cause, to which they assign my origin, is lessened. To these reasonings I have assuredly nothing to reply, but am constrained at last to avow that there is nothing of all that I formerly believed to be true of which it is impossible to doubt, and that not through thoughtlessness or levity, but from cogent and maturely considered reasons; so that henceforward, if I desire to discover anything certain, I ought not the less carefully to refrain from assenting to those same opinions than to what might be shown to be manifestly false.

11. But it is not sufficient to have made these observations; care must be taken likewise to keep them in remembrance. For those old and customary opinions perpetually recur—long and familiar usage giving them the right of occupying my mind, even almost against my will, and subduing my belief; nor will I lose the habit of deferring to them and confiding in them so long as I shall consider them to be what in truth they are, viz, opinions to some extent doubtful, as I have already shown, but still highly probable, and such as it is much more reasonable to believe than deny. It is for this reason I am persuaded that I shall not be doing wrong, if, taking an opposite judgment of deliberate design, I become my own deceiver, by supposing, for a time, that all those opinions are entirely false and imaginary, until at length, having thus balanced my old by my new prejudices, my judgment shall no longer be turned aside by perverted usage from the path that may conduct to the perception of truth. For I am assured that, meanwhile, there will arise neither peril nor error from this course, and that I cannot for the present yield too much to distrust, since the end I now seek is not action but knowledge.

12. I will suppose, then, not that Deity, who is . . . [supremely] good and the fountain of truth, but that some malignant demon, who is at once exceedingly potent and deceitful, has employed all his artifice to deceive me; I will suppose that the sky, the air, the earth, colors, figures, sounds, and all external things, are nothing better than the illusions of dreams, by means of which this being has laid snares for my credulity; I will consider myself as without hands, eyes, flesh, blood, or any of the senses, and as falsely believing that I am possessed of these; I will continue resolutely fixed in this belief, and if indeed by this means it be not in my power to arrive at the knowledge of truth, I shall at least do what is in my power, viz, suspend my judgment, and guard with settled purpose against giving my assent to what is false, and being imposed upon by this deceiver, whatever be his power and artifice. But this undertaking is arduous, and a certain indolence insensibly leads me back to my ordinary course of life; and just as the captive, who, perchance, was enjoying in his dreams an imaginary liberty, when he begins to suspect that it is but a vision, dreads awakening, and conspires with the agreeable illusions that the deception may be prolonged; so I, of my own accord, fall back into the train of my former beliefs, and fear to arouse myself from my slumber, lest the time of laborious wakefulness that would succeed this quiet rest, in place of bringing any light of day, should prove inadequate to dispel the darkness that will arise from the difficulties that have now been raised.

MEDITATION II
OF THE NATURE OF THE HUMAN MIND; AND THAT IT IS MORE EASILY KNOWN THAN THE BODY

1. The Meditation of yesterday has filled my mind with so many doubts, that it is no longer in my power to forget them. Nor do I see, meanwhile, any principle

on which they can be resolved; and, just as if I had fallen all of a sudden into very deep water, I am so greatly disconcerted as to be unable either to plant my feet firmly on the bottom or sustain myself by swimming on the surface. I will, nevertheless, make an effort, and try anew the same path on which I had entered yesterday, that is, proceed by casting aside all that admits of the slightest doubt, not less than if I had discovered it to be absolutely false; and I will continue always in this track until I shall find something that is certain, or at least, if I can do nothing more, until I shall know with certainty that there is nothing certain. Archimedes, that he might transport the entire globe from the place it occupied to another, demanded only a point that was firm and immovable; so, also, I shall be entitled to entertain the highest expectations, if I am fortunate enough to discover only one thing that is certain and indubitable.

2. I suppose, accordingly, that all the things which I see are false (fictitious); I believe that none of those objects which my fallacious memory represents ever existed; I suppose that I possess no senses; I believe that body, figure, extension, motion, and place are merely fictions of my mind. What is there, then, that can be esteemed true? Perhaps this only, that there is absolutely nothing certain.

3. But how do I know that there is not something different altogether from the objects I have now enumerated, of which it is impossible to entertain the slightest doubt? Is there not a God, or some being, by whatever name I may designate him, who causes these thoughts to arise in my mind? But why suppose such a being, for it may be I myself am capable of producing them? Am I, then, at least not something? But I before denied that I possessed senses or a body; I hesitate, however, for what follows from that? Am I so dependent on the body and the senses that without these I cannot exist? But I had the persuasion that there was absolutely nothing in the world, that there was no sky and no earth, neither minds nor bodies; was I not, therefore, at the same time, persuaded that I did not exist? Far from it; I assuredly existed, since I was persuaded. But there is I know not what being, who is possessed at once of the highest power and the deepest cunning, who is constantly employing all his ingenuity in deceiving

me. Doubtless, then, I exist, since I am deceived; and, let him deceive me as he may, he can never bring it about that I am nothing, so long as I shall be conscious that I am something. So that it must, in fine, be maintained, all things being maturely and carefully considered, that this proposition . . . I am, I exist, is necessarily true each time it is expressed by me, or conceived in my mind.

. . .

6. But as to myself, what can I now say that I am, since I suppose there exists an extremely powerful, and, if I may so speak, malignant being, whose whole endeavors are directed toward deceiving me? Can I affirm that I possess any one of all those attributes of which I have lately spoken as belonging to the nature of body? After attentively considering them in my own mind, I find none of them that can properly be said to belong to myself. To recount them were idle and tedious. Let us pass, then, to the attributes of the soul. The first mentioned were the powers of nutrition and walking; but, if it be true that I have no body, it is true likewise that I am capable neither of walking nor of being nourished. Perception is another attribute of the soul; but perception too is impossible without the body; besides, I have frequently, during sleep, believed that I perceived objects which I afterward observed I did not in reality perceive. Thinking is another attribute of the soul; and here I discover what properly belongs to myself. This alone is inseparable from me. I am—I exist: this is certain; but how often? As often as I think; for perhaps it would even happen, if I should wholly cease to think, that I should at the same time altogether cease to be. I now admit nothing that is not necessarily true. I am therefore, precisely speaking, only a thinking thing, that is, a mind, understanding, or reason, terms whose signification was before unknown to me. I am, however, a real thing, and really existent; but what thing? The answer was, a thinking thing.

. . .

8. But what, then, am I? A thinking thing, it has been said. But what is a thinking thing? It is a thing that doubts, understands, conceives, affirms, denies, wills, refuses; that imagines also, and perceives.

. . .

10. From this I begin to know what I am with somewhat greater clearness and distinctness than heretofore. But, nevertheless, it still seems to me, and I cannot help believing, that corporeal things, whose images are formed by thought which fall under the senses, and are examined by the same, are known with much greater distinctness than that I know not what part of myself which is not imaginable; although, in truth, it may seem strange to say that I know and comprehend with greater distinctness things whose existence appears to me doubtful, that are unknown, and do not belong to me, than others of whose reality I am persuaded, that are known to me, and appertain to my proper nature; in a word, than myself. But I see clearly what is the state of the case. My mind is apt to wander, and will not yet submit to be restrained within the limits of truth. Let us therefore leave the mind to itself once more, and, according to it every kind of liberty permit it to consider the objects that appear to it from without, in order that, having afterward withdrawn it from these gently and opportunely and fixed it on the consideration of its being and the properties it finds in itself, it may then be the more easily controlled.

11. Let us now accordingly consider the objects that are commonly thought to be the most easily, and likewise the most distinctly known, viz, the bodies we touch and see; not, indeed, bodies in general, for these general notions are usually somewhat more confused, but one body in particular. Take, for example, this piece of wax; it is quite fresh, having been but recently taken from the beehive; it has not yet lost the sweetness of the honey it contained; it still retains somewhat of the odor of the flowers from which it was gathered; its color, figure, size, are apparent (to the sight); it is hard, cold, easily handled; and sounds when struck upon with the finger. In fine, all that contributes to make a body as distinctly known as possible, is found in the one before us. But, while I am speaking, let it be placed near the fire—what remained of the taste exhales, the smell evaporates, the color changes, its figure is destroyed, its size increases, it becomes liquid, it grows hot, it can hardly be handled, and, although struck upon, it emits no sound. Does the same wax still remain after this change? It must be admitted that it does remain; no one doubts it, or judges

otherwise. What, then, was it I knew with so much distinctness in the piece of wax? Assuredly, it could be nothing of all that I observed by means of the senses, since all the things that fell under taste, smell, sight, touch, and hearing are changed, and yet the same wax remains.

12. It was perhaps what I now think, viz, that this wax was neither the sweetness of honey, the pleasant odor of flowers, the whiteness, the figure, nor the sound, but only a body that a little before appeared to me conspicuous under these forms, and which is now perceived under others. But, to speak precisely, what is it that I imagine when I think of it in this way? Let it be attentively considered, and, retrenching all that does not belong to the wax, let us see what remains. There certainly remains nothing, except something extended, flexible, and movable. But what is meant by flexible and movable? Is it not that I imagine that the piece of wax, being round, is capable of becoming square, or of passing from a square into a triangular figure? Assuredly such is not the case, because I conceive that it admits of an infinity of similar changes; and I am, moreover, unable to compass this infinity by imagination, and consequently this conception which I have of the wax is not the product of the faculty of imagination. But what now is this extension? Is it not also unknown? for it becomes greater when the wax is melted, greater when it is boiled, and greater still when the heat increases; and I should not conceive clearly and according to truth, the wax as it is, if I did not suppose that the piece we are considering admitted even of a wider variety of extension than I ever imagined, I must, therefore, admit that I cannot even comprehend by imagination what the piece of wax is, and that it is the mind alone which perceives it. I speak of one piece in particular; for as to wax in general, this is still more evident. But what is the piece of wax that can be perceived only by the understanding or mind? It is certainly the same which I see, touch, imagine; and, in fine, it is the same which, from the beginning, I believed it to be. But (and this it is of moment to observe) the perception of it is neither an act of sight, of touch, nor of imagination, and never was either of these, though it might formerly seem so, but is simply an intuition of the mind, which may be imperfect and confused, as it formerly was, or very clear and distinct, as it is at

present, according as the attention is more or less directed to the elements which it contains, and of which it is composed.

13. But, meanwhile, I feel greatly astonished when I observe the weakness of my mind, and its proneness to error. For although, without at all giving expression to what I think, I consider all this in my own mind, words yet occasionally impede my progress, and I am almost led into error by the terms of ordinary language. We say, for example, that we see the same wax when it is before us, and not that we judge it to be the same from its retaining the same color and figure: whence I should forthwith be disposed to conclude that the wax is known by the act of sight, and not by the intuition of the mind alone, were it not for the analogous instance of human beings passing on in the street below, as observed from a window. In this case I do not fail to say that I see the men themselves, just as I say that I see the wax; and yet what do I see from the window beyond hats and cloaks that might cover artificial machines, whose motions might be determined by springs? But I judge that there are human beings from these appearances, and thus I comprehend, by the faculty of judgment alone which is in the mind, what I believed I saw with my eyes.

...

MEDITATION III
OF GOD: THAT HE EXISTS

1. I will now close my eyes, I will stop my ears, I will turn away my senses from their objects, I will even efface from my consciousness all the images of corporeal things; or at least, because this can hardly be accomplished, I will consider them as empty and false; and thus, holding converse only with myself, and closely examining my nature, I will endeavor to obtain by degrees a more intimate and familiar knowledge of myself. I am a thinking (conscious) thing, that is, a being who doubts, affirms, denies, knows a few objects, and is ignorant of many,—who loves, hates, wills, refuses, who imagines likewise, and perceives; for, as I before remarked, although the things which I perceive or imagine are perhaps

nothing at all apart from me and in themselves, I am nevertheless assured that those modes of consciousness which I call perceptions and imaginations, in as far only as they are modes of consciousness, exist in me.

2. And in the little I have said I think I have summed up all that I really know, or at least all that up to this time I was aware I knew. Now, as I am endeavoring to extend my knowledge more widely, I will use circumspection, and consider with care whether I can still discover in myself anything further which I have not yet hitherto observed. I am certain that I am a thinking thing; but do I not therefore likewise know what is required to render me certain of a truth? In this first knowledge, doubtless, there is nothing that gives me assurance of its truth except the clear and distinct perception of what I affirm, which would not indeed be sufficient to give me the assurance that what I say is true, if it could ever happen that anything I thus clearly and distinctly perceived should prove false; and accordingly it seems to me that I may now take as a general rule, that all that is very clearly and distinctly apprehended (conceived) is true.

...

[I]t is necessary at this stage to divide all my thoughts into certain classes, and to consider in which of these classes truth and error are, strictly speaking, to be found.

...

7. But among these ideas, some appear to me to be innate, others adventitious, and others to be made by myself (factitious); for, as I have the power of conceiving what is called a thing, or a truth, or a thought, it seems to me that I hold this power from no other source than my own nature; but if I now hear a noise, if I see the sun, or if I feel heat, I have all along judged that these sensations proceeded from certain objects existing out of myself; and, in fine, it appears to me that sirens, hippogryphs, and the like, are inventions of my own mind. But I may even perhaps come to be of opinion that all my ideas are of the class which I call adventitious, or that they are all innate, or that they are all factitious; for I have not yet clearly discovered their true origin.

8. What I have here principally to do is to consider, with reference to those that appear to

come from certain objects without me, what grounds there are for thinking them like these objects. The first of these grounds is that it seems to me I am so taught by nature; and the second that I am conscious that those ideas are not dependent on my will, and therefore not on myself, for they are frequently presented to me against my will, as at present, whether I will or not, I feel heat; and I am thus persuaded that this sensation or idea of heat is produced in me by something different from myself, viz., by the heat of the fire by which I sit. And it is very reasonable to suppose that this object impresses me with its own likeness rather than any other thing.

9. But I must consider whether these reasons are sufficiently strong and convincing. When I speak of being taught by nature in this matter, I understand by the word nature only a certain spontaneous impetus that impels me to believe in a resemblance between ideas and their objects, and not a natural light that affords a knowledge of its truth. But these two things are widely different; for what the natural light shows to be true can be in no degree doubtful, as, for example, that I am because I doubt, and other truths of the like kind; inasmuch as I possess no other faculty whereby to distinguish truth from error, which can teach me the falsity of what the natural light declares to be true, and which is equally trustworthy; but with respect to seemingly natural impulses, I have observed, when the question related to the choice of right or wrong in action, that they frequently led me to take the worse part; nor do I see that I have any better ground for following them in what relates to truth and error.

10. Then, with respect to the other reason, which is that because these ideas do not depend on my will, they must arise from objects existing without me, I do not find it more convincing than the former, for just as those natural impulses, of which I have lately spoken, are found in me, notwithstanding that they are not always in harmony with my will, so likewise it may be that I possess some power not sufficiently known to myself capable of producing ideas without the aid of external objects, and, indeed, it has always hitherto appeared to me that they are formed during sleep, by some power of this nature, without the aid of aught external.

11. And, in fine, although I should grant that they proceeded from those objects, it is not a necessary consequence that they must be like them. On the contrary, I have observed, in a number of instances, that there was a great difference between the object and its idea. Thus, for example, I find in my mind two wholly diverse ideas of the sun; the one, by which it appears to me extremely small draws its origin from the senses, and should be placed in the class of adventitious ideas; the other, by which it seems to be many times larger than the whole earth, is taken up on astronomical grounds, that is, elicited from certain notions born with me, or is framed by myself in some other manner. These two ideas cannot certainly both resemble the same sun; and reason teaches me that the one which seems to have immediately emanated from it is the most unlike.

12. And these things sufficiently prove that hitherto it has not been from a certain and deliberate judgment, but only from a sort of blind impulse, that I believed existence of certain things different from myself, which, by the organs of sense, or by whatever other means it might be, conveyed their ideas or images into my mind and impressed it with their likenesses.

…

[W]ithout doubt, those [ideas] that represent substances are something more, and contain in themselves, so to speak, more objective reality that is, participate by representation in higher degrees of being or perfection, than those that represent only modes or accidents. . . .

…

14. Now, it is [also] manifest by the natural light that there must at least be as much reality in the efficient and total cause as in its effect; for whence can the effect draw its reality if not from its cause? And how could the cause communicate to it this reality unless it possessed it in itself? And hence it follows, not only that what is cannot be produced by what is not, but likewise that the more perfect, in other words, that which contains in itself more reality, cannot be the effect of the less perfect; and this is not only evidently true of those effects, whose reality is actual or formal, but likewise of ideas, whose reality is only considered as objective.

…

17. But, among these my ideas, besides that which represents myself, respecting which there can be here no difficulty, there is one that represents a God; others that represent corporeal and inanimate things; others angels; others animals; and, finally, there are some that represent men like myself.

18. But with respect to the ideas that represent other men, or animals, or angels, I can easily suppose that they were formed by the mingling and composition of the other ideas which I have of myself, of corporeal things, and of God, although they were, apart from myself, neither men, animals, nor angels.

19. And with regard to the ideas of corporeal objects, I never discovered in them anything so great or excellent which I myself did not appear capable of originating. . . .

. . .

22. There only remains, therefore, the idea of God, in which I must consider whether there is anything that cannot be supposed to originate with myself. By the name God, I understand a substance infinite, eternal, immutable, independent, all-knowing, all-powerful, and by which I myself, and every other thing that exists, if any such there be, were created. But these properties are so great and

excellent, that the more attentively I consider them the less I feel persuaded that the idea I have of them owes its origin to myself alone. And thus it is absolutely necessary to conclude, from all that I have before said, that God exists.

. . .

MEDITATION VI
OF THE EXISTENCE OF MATERIAL THINGS, AND OF THE REAL DISTINCTION BETWEEN THE MIND AND BODY OF MAN

1. There now only remains the inquiry as to whether material things exist.

. . . [A]s God is no deceiver, it is manifest that he does not of himself and immediately communicate those ideas [of corporeal things] to me, nor even by the intervention of any creature in which their objective reality is not formally, but only eminently, contained. For as he has given me no faculty whereby I can discover this to be the case, but, on the contrary, a very strong inclination to believe that those ideas arise from corporeal objects, I do not see how he could be vindicated from the charge of deceit, if in truth they proceeded from any other source, or were produced by other causes than corporeal things: and accordingly it must be concluded, that corporeal objects exist. . . .

Discussion Questions

1. Can you be certain that you are not dreaming right now? Is it possible that you are dreaming at this time? Why or why not?
2. Can you be sure that you are not being deceived by an evil genius right now? Or, for example, that all of your experiences are the result of some mad scientific experiment? Why or why not? If you are not absolutely positive, why in fact do you not believe these things to be true?
3. Explain carefully how Descartes believes he knows that God exists. Can Descartes be certain of his proof of God's existence before he has disproved the possibility of an evil genius bent on deceiving him? Or does Descartes have to disprove the possibility of an evil genius before he can prove that God exists? Explain your answer.
4. Supposing that God's existence cannot be proved, could Descartes still be certain about anything? If God existed, would this be a reason to be sure, for example, that chairs and tables exist? Why or why not?
5. Suppose Descartes can prove the existence of God. Can Descartes also prove that this God is not a deceiver, that is, that God is not a trickster bent on deceiving him? Explain your answer. How would Descartes answer this question? Is his answer defensible?

For Further Reading

Two excellent collections of Descartes' work are *The Philosophical Works of Descartes* (1911), translated by Haldane and Ross, and *The Philosophical Writings of Descartes* (1984), translated by Cottingham, Stoothoff, Murdoch, and Kenny. Cottingham and Kenny also have excellent introductory texts to the philosophy of Descartes, *Descartes* (1986) and *Descartes* (1968), respectively. For an introduction to rationalism see *The Rationalists* (1988), by J. Cottingham. For discussions of skepticism, including Cartesian skepticism, see *Knowledge of the External World* (1991), by B. Aune; *Scepticism* (1990), by C. Hookway; and *The Skeptical Tradition* (1983), edited by M. Burnyeat.

29   OF THE ORIGIN OF IDEAS
David Hume

The empiricism of Scottish philosopher David Hume (1711–1776) is an important historical contrast to Descartes' rationalism. Consider the statement "All bachelors are unmarried men." According to Hume, this statement is true and can be known as true simply by reflecting on the concepts involved in the sentence. A statement such as "All bachelors are unmarried men" expresses a conceptual truth, what Hume calls a *relation of ideas*. So far, Hume and Descartes would agree, except that then Hume adds an important caveat: **Conceptual truths** or relations of ideas provide us with no important information whatsoever about the world around us. Conceptual truths are merely truths about language, not about the world.

On the other hand, statements such as "Frank is a bachelor" report something concrete about the world: there is a bachelor and his name is Frank. Hume calls sentences of this sort **matters of fact.** For Hume, matters of fact can only be verified by an appeal to sensory experience, and hence, concludes Hume, all meaningful knowledge about the world comes *exclusively through our senses.*

This simple distinction between *matters of fact* and *conceptual truths* has far-reaching implications. If Hume's distinction is legitimate, then all knowledge about the world must be dependent solely on sense perception; otherwise one is, at best, only guessing. Moreover, if a truth claim cannot be defended by an appeal to actual or possible sensory perception, then this claim is unintelligible.

Reading Questions

1. What is the difference between the perception (or sensation) of X and the memory of X?
2. What is the difference between thoughts (or ideas) and impressions?
3. What are the limits of our powers to imagine new things?

4. What is the relationship between ideas and impressions? Which come first? What evidence does Hume offer as proof?
5. What is one to make of a philosophical term which cannot be traced back to some particular impression?

OF THE ORIGIN OF IDEAS

11. Every one will readily allow, that there is a considerable difference between the perceptions of the mind, when a man feels the pain of excessive heat, or the pleasure of moderate warmth, and when he afterwards recalls to his memory this sensation, or anticipates it by his imagination. These faculties may mimic or copy the perceptions of the senses; but they never can entirely reach the force and vivacity of the original sentiment. The utmost we say of them, even when they operate with greatest vigor, is, that they represent their object in so lively a manner, that we could *almost* say we feel or see it: But, except the mind be disordered by disease or madness, they never can arrive at such a pitch of vivacity, as to render these perceptions altogether undistinguishable. All the colors of poetry, however splendid, can never paint natural objects in such a manner as to make the description be taken for a real landskip. The most lively thought is still inferior to the dullest sensation.

We may observe a like distinction to run through all the other perceptions of the mind. A man in a fit of anger, is actuated in a very different manner from one who only thinks of that emotion. If you tell me, that any person is in love, I easily understand your meaning, and form a just conception of his situation; but never can mistake that conception for the real disorders and agitations of the passion. When we reflect on our past sentiments and affections, our thought is a faithful mirror, and copies its objects truly; but the colors which it employs are faint and dull, in comparison of those in which our original perceptions were clothed. It requires no nice discernment or metaphysical head to mark the distinction between them.

12. Here therefore we may divide all the perceptions of the mind into two classes or species, which are distinguished by their different degrees of force and vivacity. The less forcible and lively are commonly denominated *Thoughts* or *Ideas.* The other species want a name in our language, and in most others; I suppose, because it was not requisite for any, but philosophical purposes, to rank them under a general term or appellation. Let us, therefore, use a little freedom, and call them *Impressions;* employing that word in a sense somewhat different from the usual. By the term *impression,* then, I mean all our more lively perceptions, when we hear, or see, or feel, or love, or hate, or desire, or will. And impressions are distinguished from ideas, which are the less lively perceptions, of which we are conscious, when we reflect on any of those sensations or movements above mentioned.

13. Nothing, at first view, may seem more unbounded than the thought of man, which not only escapes all human power and authority, but is not even restrained within the limits of nature and reality. To form monsters, and join incongruous shapes and appearances, costs the imagination no more trouble than to conceive the most natural and familiar objects. And while the body is confined to one planet, along which it creeps with pain and difficulty; the thought can in an instant transport us into the most distant regions of the universe; or even beyond the universe, into the unbounded chaos, where nature is supposed to lie in total confusion. What never was seen, or heard of, may yet be conceived; nor is any thing beyond the power of thought, except what implies an absolute contradiction.

But though our thought seems to possess this unbounded liberty, we shall find, upon a nearer examination, that it is really confined within very narrow limits, and that all this creative power of the mind amounts to no more than the faculty of compounding, transposing, augmenting, or diminishing the materials afforded us by the senses and experience. When we think of a golden mountain, we only join two consistent ideas, *gold,* and *mountain,* with which we were formerly acquainted. A virtuous horse we can conceive; because, from our own feeling, we can conceive virtue; and this we may unite to the figure and shape of a horse, which is an animal familiar to us. In short, all the materials of thinking are derived either from our outward or inward sentiment: the mixture and composition of these belongs alone to the mind and will. Or, to express myself in philosophical language, all our ideas or more feeble perceptions are copies of our impressions or more lively ones.

14. To prove this, the two following arguments will, I hope, be sufficient. First, when we analyze our thoughts or ideas, however compounded or sublime, we always find that they resolve themselves into such simple ideas as were copied from a precedent feeling or sentiment. Even those ideas, which, at first view, seem the most wide of this origin, are found, upon a nearer scrutiny, to be derived from it. The idea of God, as meaning an infinitely intelligent, wise, and good Being, arises from reflecting on the operations of our own mind, and augmenting, without limit, those qualities of goodness and wisdom. We may prosecute this enquiry to what length we please; where we shall always find, that every idea which we examine is copied from a similar impression. Those who would assert that this position is not universally true nor without exception, have only one, and that an easy method of refuting it; by producing that idea, which, in their opinion, is not derived from this source. It will then be incumbent on us, if we would maintain our doctrine, to produce the impression, or lively perception, which corresponds to it.

15. Secondly. If it happen, from a defect of the organ, that a man is not susceptible of any species of sensation, we always find that he is as little susceptible of the correspondent ideas. A blind man can form no notion of colors; a deaf man of sounds. Restore either of them that sense in which he is deficient; by opening this new inlet for his sensations, you also open an inlet for the ideas; and he finds no difficulty in conceiving these objects. The case is the same, if the object, proper for exciting any sensation, has never been applied to the organ. A Laplander or Negro has no notion of the relish of wine. And though there are few or no instances of a like deficiency in the mind, where a person has never felt or is wholly incapable of a sentiment or passion that belongs to his species; yet we find the same observation to take place in a less degree. A man of mild manners can form no idea of inveterate revenge or cruelty; nor can a selfish heart easily conceive the heights of friendship and generosity. It is readily allowed, that other beings may possess many senses of which we can have no conception; because the ideas of them have never been introduced to us in the only manner by which an idea can have access to the mind, to wit, by the actual feeling and sensation.

16. There is, however, one contradictory phenomenon, which may prove that it is not absolutely impossible for ideas to arise, independent of their correspondent impressions. I believe it will readily be allowed, that the several distinct ideas of color, which enter by the eye, or those of sound, which are conveyed by the ear, are really different from each other; though, at the same time, resembling. Now if this be true of different colors, it must be no less so of the different shades of the same color; and each shade produces a distinct idea, independent of the rest. For if this should be denied, it is possible, by the continual gradation of shades, to run a color insensibly into what is most remote from it; and if you will not allow any of the means to be different, you cannot, without absurdity, deny the extremes to be the same. Suppose, therefore, a person to have enjoyed his sight for thirty years, and to have become perfectly acquainted with colors of all kinds except one particular shade of blue, for instance, which it never has been his fortune to meet with. Let all the different shades of that color, except that single one, be placed before him, descending gradually from the deepest to the lightest; it is plain that he will perceive a blank, where that shade is wanting, and will be sensible that there is a greater distance in that place between the contiguous colors than in any other. Now I ask, whether it be possible for him, from his own imagination, to supply this deficiency, and raise up to himself the idea of that particular shade, though it had never been conveyed to him by his senses? I believe there are few but will be of opinion that he can: and this may serve as a proof that the simple ideas are not always, in every instance, derived from the correspondent impressions; though this instance is so singular, that it is scarcely worth our observing, and does not merit that for it alone we should alter our general maxim.

17. Here, therefore, is a proposition, which not only seems, in itself, simple and intelligible; but, if a proper use were made of it, might render every dispute equally intelligible, and banish all that jargon, which has so long taken possession of metaphysical reasonings, and drawn disgrace upon them. All ideas, especially abstract ones, are naturally faint and obscure: the mind has but a slender hold of them: they are apt to be confounded with other resembling ideas; and when we have often employed any term, though without a distinct meaning, we are apt to imagine it has a determinate idea annexed to it. On the contrary, all impressions, that is, all sensations, either outward or inward, are strong and vivid: the limits between them are more exactly determined: nor is it easy to fall into any error or mistake with regard to them. When we entertain, therefore, any suspicion that a philosophical term is employed without any meaning or idea (as is but too frequent), we need but enquire, *from what impression is that supposed idea derived?* And if it be impossible to assign any, this will serve to confirm our suspicion. By bringing ideas into so clear a light we may reasonably hope to remove all dispute, which may arise, concerning their nature and reality.

Discussion Questions

1. Is Hume right when he claims that the impression of X always precedes the idea of X? Can you have an idea of a thing without having an impression of it? Could you have an idea of a thing without having impressions of the constituent parts that make up this thing?
2. Can someone blind from birth have a concept (or idea) of color? Why or why not?
3. Suppose Hume is right. What are the implications of Hume's theory for the pursuit of scientific knowledge? Are there claims that science makes now that it could not make if Hume was correct? Why or why not? Does the success of science prove that Hume is wrong? Explain your answer.

For Further Reading

For a collection of Hume's work see *The Philosophical Works of David Hume* (1875), edited by Green and Grose. For biographical information on Hume see *The Life of David Hume* (1954), by E. C. Mossner. For an introduction to Hume's philosophy see *Hume* (1975), by T. Penelhum; *The Philosophy of David Hume* (1941), by Norman Kemp Smith; *Hume's Philosophy of Human Nature* (1932), by J. Laird; and *Hume* (1977), by Barry Stroud. For a discussion of skepticism, including Hume's skepticism, see *Knowledge of the External World* (1991), by B. Aune; *Scepticism* (1990), by C. Hookway; *The Skeptical Tradition* (1983), edited by M. Burnyeat; and *Hume's Skepticism in the Treatise of Human Nature* (1985), by R. J. Fogelin.

30   THE CRITIQUE OF PURE REASON
Immanuel Kant

Immanuel Kant (1724–1804), born in Königsberg, East Prussia (in what is now Germany), is said to never have traveled more than a few miles from his hometown during his entire life. Be that as it may, Kant's philosophical thought has had an effect felt around the world. Today Kant's philosophy, from his ethics to his metaphysics, is required study for any serious student of philosophy.

Kant had been a relatively average philosopher, until, as Kant tells it, he was "awoken from his dogmatic slumber" by the philosophy of David Hume. In Hume's *Treatise of Human Nature* (1739) and *Enquiry Concerning Human Understanding* (1748), Kant discovered some rather startling and skeptical conclusions regarding the powers of human reason. If Hume was right, then metaphysical knowledge, knowledge about the ultimate nature of the world, was well beyond the scope of human reason—a conclusion Kant set out to refute. In response, Kant wrote *The Critique of Pure Reason* in 1781 and then revised it and published it again in 1787. This book, from which this reading is drawn, became one of the most important philosophical works ever written, and, although very difficult, a careful study of this book can be very rewarding.

Kant begins by making several distinctions. One is the distinction between **analytic judgments** and **synthetic judgments,** which is roughly akin to Hume's distinction between *relations of idea* and *matters of fact.* According to Kant, an analytic judgment is one where the predicate of the sentence is 'contained' within the subject of the sentence. For example, consider the sentence "All bodies are extended." The subject of the sentence is "bodies" and the predicate is "extension." Says Kant, when one thinks of a body, one *necessarily* thinks of it as a thing that is extended. Hence, the predicate "extension" is contained within the concept of the subject, "body." Such sentences are called analytic. The important thing about analytic sentences is that they can be known **a priori,** that is, before or 'prior' to experience.

Now consider the sentence "Frank is a bachelor." The subject of the sentence is "Frank" and the predicate is "bachelor." When one thinks of Frank, one need not necessarily conceive of Frank being unmarried— that is, the predicate is *not* contained within the subject. These kinds of judgments, for Kant, are called synthetic judgments, that is, their truth depends on putting together or 'synthesizing' two separate concepts. Such knowledge depends on experience and is known **a posteriori,** that is, after experience.

So, in general, analytic statements are *a priori* and synthetic statements are *a posteriori.* Is a synthetic a priori judgment possible? Kant claims it is. For example, consider the rather simple mathematical judgment "7 + 5 = 12." At first, one might think that this sentence, and all mathematical sentences, are analytic. That is, one might think that the predicate "12" is contained in the subject "7 + 5" because one immediately recognizes the fact that 7 + 5 equals 12. But, in fact, the predicate is not contained in the subject of a mathematical statement. This becomes clear when we consider a more complicated statement such as "74 × 18 = 1332." In this situation, one's mind certainly does not leap from the subject, "74 × 18," straight to the predicate, "1332," which it should, if the predicate is contained within the subject. Hence, Kant concludes that mathematical statements are synthetic and not analytic as Hume supposed.

More important, however, the truth of "74 × 18 = 1332" can be known *a priori,* without experience. If Kant is correct about this, he has demonstrated the possibility of synthetic *a priori* judgments—and the existence of synthetic *a priori* judgments makes it possible (in theory) to refute Hume's skeptical pronouncements.

Reading Questions

1. Does knowledge begin and end with experience?
2. What does Kant mean by the term "knowledge *a priori*"? What does Kant mean by the term "knowledge *a posteriori*"?
3. Explain the difference between pure and impure knowledge *a priori*.
4. What is a judgment *a priori*? What is a judgment absolutely *a priori*?
5. Are empirical judgments capable of being absolutely certain?
6. How can one distinguish between pure knowledge and empirical knowledge?
7. Why does Kant believe that the very possibility of experience rests on *a priori* principles?
8. What is the difference between analytic and synthetic judgments? Why are analytic judgments called explicative? Why are synthetic judgments called augmentative?
9. Are mathematical judgments synthetic or analytic?
10. What is the (proper) problem of pure reason? What are the consequences for metaphysics if synthetic knowledge *a priori* is impossible?

I. OF THE DIFFERENCE BETWEEN PURE AND EMPIRICAL KNOWLEDGE

That all our knowledge begins with experience there can be no doubt. For how is it possible that the faculty of cognition should be awakened into exercise otherwise than by means of objects which affect our senses, and partly of themselves produce representations, partly rouse our powers of understanding into activity, to compare, to connect, or to separate these, and so to convert the raw material of our sensuous impressions into a knowledge of objects, which is called experience? In respect of time, therefore, no knowledge of ours is antecedent to experience, but begins with it.

But, though all our knowledge begins with experience, it by no means follows that all arises out of experience. For, on the contrary, it is quite possible that our empirical knowledge is a compound of that which we receive through impressions, and that which the faculty of cognition supplies from itself (sensuous impressions giving merely the *occasion*), an addition which we cannot distinguish from the original element given by sense, till long practice has made us attentive to, and skillful in separat-

ing it. It is, therefore, a question which requires close investigation, and not to be answered at first sight, whether there exists a knowledge altogether independent of experience, and even of all sensuous impressions? Knowledge of this kind is called *a priori*, in contradistinction to empirical knowledge, which has its sources *a posteriori*, that is, in experience.

But the expression, "*a priori*," is not as yet definite enough adequately to indicate the whole meaning of the question above started. For, in speaking of knowledge which has its sources in experience, we are wont to say, that this or that may be known *a priori*, because we do not derive this knowledge immediately from experience, but from a general rule, which, however, we have itself borrowed from experience. Thus, if a man undermined his house, we say, "he might know *a priori* that it would have fallen;" that is, he needed not to have waited for the experience that it did actually fall. But still, *a priori*, he could not know even this much. For, that bodies are heavy, and, consequently, that they fall when their supports are taken away, must have been known to him previously, by means of experience.

By the term "knowledge *a priori*," therefore, we shall in the sequel understand, not such as is independent of this or that kind of experience, but such as is absolutely so of *all* experience. Opposed to this is empirical knowledge, or that which is possible only *a posteriori*, that is, through experience. Knowledge *a priori* is either pure or impure. Pure knowledge *a priori* is that with which no empirical element is mixed up. For example, the proposition, "Every change has a cause," is a proposition *a priori*, but impure, because change is a conception which can only be derived from experience.

II. THE HUMAN INTELLECT, EVEN IN AN UNPHILOSOPHICAL STATE, IS IN POSSESSION OF CERTAIN COGNITIONS "*A PRIORI*"

The question now is as to a *criterion*, by which we may securely distinguish a pure from an empirical cognition. Experience no doubt teaches us that this or that object is constituted in such and such a manner, but not that it could not possibly exist otherwise. Now, in the first place, if we have a proposition which contains the idea of necessity in its very conception, it is a judgement *a priori*; if, moreover, it is not derived from any other proposition, unless from one equally involving the idea of necessity, it is absolutely *a priori*. Secondly, an empirical judgement never exhibits strict and absolute, but only assumed and comparative universality (by induction); therefore, the most we can say is—so far as we have hitherto observed, there is no exception to this or that rule. If, on the other hand, a judgement carries with it strict and absolute universality, that is, admits of no possible exception, it is not derived from experience, but is valid absolutely *a priori*.

Empirical universality is, therefore, only an arbitrary extension of validity, from that which may be predicated of a proposition valid in most cases, to that which is asserted of a proposition which holds good in all; as, for example, in the affirmation, "All bodies are heavy." When, on the contrary, strict universality characterizes a judgement, it necessarily indicates another peculiar source of knowledge, namely, a faculty of cognition *a priori*. Necessity and strict universality, therefore, are infallible tests for distinguishing pure from empirical knowledge, and are inseparably connected with each other. But as in the use of these criteria the empirical limitation is sometimes more easily detected than the contingency of the judgement, or the unlimited universality which we attach to a judgement is often a more convincing proof than its necessity, it may be advisable to use the criteria separately, each being by itself infallible.

Now, that in the sphere of human cognition we have judgements which are necessary, and in the strictest sense universal, consequently pure *a priori*, it will be an easy matter to show. If we desire an example from the sciences, we need only take any proposition in mathematics. If we cast our eyes upon the commonest operations of the understanding, the proposition, "Every change must have a cause," will amply serve our purpose. In the latter case, indeed, the conception of a cause so plainly involves the conception of a necessity of connection with an effect, and of a strict universality of the law, that the very notion of a cause would entirely disappear, were we to derive it, like Hume, from a frequent association of what happens with that which precedes, and the habit thence originating of connecting representations—the necessity inherent in the judgement being therefore merely subjective. Besides, without seeking for such examples of principles existing *a priori* in cognition, we might easily show that such principles are the indispensable basis of the possibility of experience itself, and consequently prove their existence *a priori*. For whence could our experience itself acquire certainty, if all the rules on which it depends were themselves empirical, and consequently fortuitous? No one, therefore, can admit the validity of the use of such rules as first principles. But, for the present, we may content ourselves with having established the fact, that we do possess and exercise a faculty of pure *a priori* cognition; and, secondly, with having pointed out the proper tests of such cognition, namely, universality and necessity.

Not only in judgements, however, but even in conceptions, is an *a priori* origin manifest. For example, if we take away by degrees from our conceptions of a body all that can be referred to mere sensuous experience—color, hardness or softness, weight, even impenetrability—the body will then vanish; but the space which it occupied still remains, and this it is utterly impossible to annihilate in thought. Again, if we take away, in like manner, from our empirical conception of any object, corporeal or incorporeal, all properties which mere experience has taught us to connect with it, still we cannot think away those through which we cogitate it as substance, or adhering to substance, although our conception of substance is more determined than that of an object. Compelled, therefore, by that necessity with which the conception of substance forces itself upon us, we must confess that it has its seat in our faculty of cognition *a priori*.

…

IV. OF THE DIFFERENCE BETWEEN ANALYTICAL AND SYNTHETICAL JUDGEMENTS

In all judgements wherein the relation of a subject to the predicate is cogitated (I mention affirmative judgements only here; the application to negative will be very easy), this relation is possible in two different ways. Either the predicate B belongs to the subject A, as somewhat which is contained (though covertly) in the conception A; or the predicate B lies completely out of the conception A, although it stands in connection with it. In the first instance, I term the judgement *analytical*, in the second, *synthetical*. Analytical judgements (affirmative) are therefore those in which the connection of the predicate with the subject is cogitated through identity; those in which this connection is cogitated without identity, are called synthetical judgements. The former may be called *explicative*, the latter *augmentative* judgements; because the former add in the predicate nothing to the conception of the subject, but only analyze it into its constituent conceptions, which were thought already in the subject, although in a confused manner; the latter add to our conceptions of the subject a predicate which was not contained in it, and which no analysis could ever have discovered therein. For example, when I say, "All bodies are extended," this is an analytical judgement. For I need not go beyond the conception of *body* in order to find extension connected with it, but merely analyze the conception, that is, become conscious of the manifold properties which I think in that conception, in order to discover this

predicate in it: it is therefore an analytical judgement. On the other hand, when I say, "All bodies are heavy," the predicate is something totally different from that which I think in the mere conception of a body. By the addition of such a predicate, therefore, it becomes a synthetical judgement.

Judgements of experience, as such, are always synthetical. For it would be absurd to think of grounding an analytical judgement on experience, because in forming such a judgement I need not go out of the sphere of my conceptions, and therefore recourse to the testimony of experience is quite unnecessary. That "bodies are extended" is not an empirical judgement, but a proposition which stands firm *a priori*. For before addressing myself to experience, I already have in my conception all the requisite conditions for the judgement, and I have only to extract the predicate from the conception, according to the principle of contradiction, and thereby at the same time become conscious of the necessity of the judgement, a necessity which I could never learn from experience. On the other hand, though at first I do not at all include the predicate of weight in my conception of body in general, that conception still indicates an object of experience, a part of the totality of experience, to which I can still add other parts; and this I do when I recognize by observation that bodies are heavy. I can cognize beforehand by analysis the conception of body through the characteristics of extension, impenetrability, shape, etc., all which are cogitated in this conception. But now I extend my knowledge, and looking back on experience from which I had derived this conception of body, I find weight at all times connected with the above characteristics, and therefore I synthetically add to my conceptions this as a predicate, and say, "All bodies are heavy." Thus it is experience upon which rests the possibility of the synthesis of the predicate of weight with the conception of body, because both conceptions, although the one is not contained in the other, still belong to one another (only contingently, however), as parts of a whole, namely, of experience, which is itself a synthesis of intuitions.

But to synthetical judgements *a priori*, such aid is entirely wanting. If I go out of and beyond the conception A, in order to recognize another B as connected with it, what foundation have I to rest on, whereby to render the synthesis possible? I have here no longer the advantage of looking out in the sphere of experience for what I want. Let us take, for example, the proposition, "Everything that happens has a cause." In the conception of "*something that happens*," I indeed think an existence which a certain time antecedes, and from this I can derive analytical judgements. But the conception of a cause lies quite out of the above conception, and indicates something entirely different from "that which happens," and is consequently not contained in that conception. How then am I able to assert concerning the general conception—"that which happens"—something entirely different from that conception, and to recognize the conception of cause although not contained in it, yet as belonging to it, and even necessarily? what is here the unknown = X, upon which the understanding rests when it believes it has found, out of the conception A a foreign predicate B, which it nevertheless considers to be connected with it? It cannot be experience, because the principle adduced annexes the two representations, cause and effect, to the representation existence, not only with universality, which experience cannot give, but also with the expression of necessity, therefore completely *a priori* and from pure conceptions. Upon such synthetical, that is augmentative propositions, depends the whole aim of our speculative knowledge *a priori*; for although analytical judgements are indeed highly important and necessary, they are so, only to arrive at that clearness of conceptions which is requisite for a sure and extended synthesis, and this alone is a real acquisition.

V. IN ALL THEORETICAL SCIENCES OF REASON, SYNTHETICAL JUDGEMENTS "*A PRIORI*" ARE CONTAINED AS PRINCIPLES

1. Mathematical judgements are always synthetical. Hitherto this fact, though incontestably true and very important in its consequences, seems to have escaped the analysts of the human mind, nay, to be in complete opposition to all their conjectures. For as it was found that mathematical conclusions all proceed according to the principle of contradiction (which the nature of every apodeictic certainty requires), people became persuaded that the fundamental principles of the science also were recognized and admitted in the same way. But the notion is fallacious; for although a synthetical proposition can certainly be discerned by means of the principle of contradiction, this is possible only when another synthetical proposition precedes, from which the latter is deduced, but never of itself.

Before all, be it observed, that proper mathematical propositions are always judgements *a priori*, and not empirical, because they carry along with them the conception of necessity, which cannot be given by experience. If this be demurred to, it matters not; I will then limit my assertion to *pure* mathematics, the very conception of which implies that it consists of knowledge altogether non-empirical and *a priori*.

We might, indeed, at first suppose that the proposition $7 + 5 = 12$ is a merely analytical proposition, following (according to the principle of contradiction) from the conception of a sum of seven and five. But if we regard it more narrowly, we find that our conception of the sum of seven and five contains nothing more than the uniting of both sums into one, whereby it cannot at all be cogitated what this single number is which embraces both. The conception of twelve is by no means obtained by merely cogitating the union of seven and five; and we may analyze our conception of such a possible sum as long as we will, still we shall never discover in it the notion of twelve. We must go beyond these conceptions, and have recourse to an intuition which corresponds to one of the two—our five fingers, for example, or like Segner in his *Arithmetic* five points, and so by degrees, add the units contained in the five given in the intuition, to the conception of seven. For I first take the number 7, and, for the conception of 5 calling in the aid of the fingers of my hand as objects of intuition, I add the units, which I before took together to make up the number 5, gradually now by means of the material image my hand, to the number 7, and by this process, I at length see the number 12 arise. That 7 should be added to 5, I have certainly cogitated in my conception of a sum $= 7 + 5$, but not that this sum was equal to 12. Arithmetical propositions are therefore always synthetical, of which we may become more clearly convinced by trying large numbers. For it will thus become quite evident that, turn and twist our conceptions as we may, it is impossible, without having recourse to intuition, to arrive at the sum total or product by means of the mere analysis of our conceptions. Just as little is any principle of pure geometry analytical. "A straight line between two points is the shortest," is a synthetical proposition. For my conception of *straight* contains no notion of *quantity*, but is merely *qualitative*. The conception of the *shortest* is therefore wholly an addition, and by no analysis can it be extracted from our conception of a straight line. Intuition must therefore here lend its aid, by means of which, and thus only, our synthesis is possible.

Some few principles preposited by geometricians are, indeed, really analytical, and depend on the principle of contradiction. They serve, however, like identical propositions, as links in the chain of method, not as principles—for example $a = a$, the whole is equal to itself, or $(a + b) > a$, the whole is greater than its part. And yet even these principles themselves, though they derive their validity from pure conceptions, are only admitted in mathematics because they can be presented in intuition. What causes us here commonly to believe that the predicate of such apodeictic judgements is already contained in our conception, and that the judgement is therefore analytical, is merely the equivocal nature of the expression. We must join in thought a certain predicate to a given conception, and this necessity cleaves already to the conception. But the question is, not what we must join in thought to the given conception, but what we really think therein, though only obscurely, and then it becomes manifest that the predicate pertains to these conceptions, necessarily indeed, yet not as thought in the conception itself, but by virtue of an intuition, which must be added to the conception.

2. The science of *natural philosophy* (physics) contains in itself synthetical judgements *a priori,* as principles. I shall adduce two propositions. For instance, the proposition, "In all changes of the material world, the quantity of matter remains unchanged"; or, that, "In all communication of motion, action and reaction must always be equal." In both of these, not only is the necessity, and therefore their origin *a priori* clear, but also that they are synthetical propositions. For in the conception of matter, I do not cogitate its permanency, but merely its presence in space, which it fills. I therefore really go out of and beyond the conception of matter, in order to think on to it something *a priori,* which I did not think in it.

The proposition is therefore not analytical, but synthetical, and nevertheless conceived *a priori;* and so it is with regard to the other propositions of the pure part of natural philosophy.

3. As to *metaphysics,* even if we look upon it merely as an attempted science, yet, from the nature of human reason, an indispensable one, we find that it must contain synthetical propositions *a priori*. It is not merely the duty of metaphysics to dissect, and thereby analytically to illustrate the conceptions which we form *a priori* of things; but we seek to widen the range of our *a priori* knowledge. For this purpose, we must avail ourselves of such principles as add something to the original conception—something not identical with, nor contained in it, and by means of synthetical judgements *a priori,* leave far behind us the limits of experience; for example, in the proposition, "the world must have a beginning," and such like. Thus metaphysics, according to the proper aim of the science, consists merely of synthetical propositions *a priori*.

VI. THE UNIVERSAL PROBLEM OF PURE REASON

It is extremely advantageous to be able to bring a number of investigations under the formula of a single problem. For in this manner, we not only facilitate our own labor, inasmuch as we define it clearly to ourselves, but also render it more easy for others to decide whether we have done justice to our undertaking. The proper problem of pure reason, then, is contained in the question: "How are synthetical judgements *a priori* possible?"

That metaphysical science has hitherto remained in so vacillating a state of uncertainty and contradiction, is only to be attributed to the fact that this great problem, and perhaps even the difference between analytical and synthetical judgements, did not sooner suggest itself to philosophers. Upon the solution of this problem, or upon sufficient proof of the impossibility of synthetical knowledge *a priori,* depends the existence or downfall of the science of metaphysics. Among philosophers, David Hume came the nearest of all to this problem; yet it never acquired in his mind sufficient precision, nor did he regard the question in its universality. On the contrary, he stopped short at the synthetical proposition of the connection of an effect with its cause (*principium causalitatis*), insisting that such proposition *a priori* was impossible. According to his conclusions, then, all that we term metaphysical science is a mere delusion, arising from the fancied insight of reason into that which is in truth borrowed from experience, and to which habit has given the appearance of necessity. Against this assertion, destructive to all pure philosophy, he would have been guarded, had he had our problem before his eyes in its universality. For he would then have perceived that, according to his own argument, there likewise could not be any pure mathematical science, which assuredly cannot exist without synthetical propositions *a priori*—an absurdity from which his good understanding must have saved him.

In the solution of the above problem is at the same time comprehended the possibility of the use of pure reason in the foundation and construction of all sciences which contain theoretical knowledge *a priori* of objects, that is to say, the answer to the following questions:

How is pure mathematical science possible?
How is pure natural science possible?

Respecting these sciences, as they do certainly exist, it may with propriety be asked, *how* they are possible?—for that they must be possible is shown by the fact of their really existing. But as to metaphysics, the miserable progress it has hitherto made, and the fact that of no one system yet brought forward, as far as regards its true aim, can it be said that this science really exists, leaves any one at liberty to doubt with reason the very possibility of its existence.

Yet, in a certain sense, this kind of knowledge must unquestionably be looked upon as *given*; in other words, metaphysics must be considered as really existing, if not as a science, nevertheless as a natural disposition of the human mind (*metaphysica naturalis*). For human reason, without any instigations imputable to the mere vanity of great knowledge, unceasingly progresses, urged on by its own feeling of need, towards such questions as cannot be answered by any empirical application of reason, or principles derived therefrom; and so there has ever really existed in every man some system of metaphysics. It will always exist, so soon as reason awakes to the exercise of its power of speculation. And now the

question arises: "How is metaphysics, as a natural disposition, possible?" In other words, how, from the nature of universal human reason, do those questions arise which pure reason proposes to itself, and which it is impelled by its own feeling of need to answer as well as it can?

But as in all the attempts hitherto made to answer the questions which reason is prompted by its very nature to propose to itself, for example, whether the world had a beginning, or has existed from eternity, it has always met with unavoidable contradictions, we must not rest satisfied with the mere natural disposition of the mind to metaphysics, that is, with the existence of the faculty of pure reason, whence, indeed, some sort of metaphysical system always arises; but it must be possible to arrive at certainty in regard to the question whether we know or do not know the things of which metaphysics treats. We must be able to arrive at a decision on the subjects of its questions, or on the ability or inability of reason to form any judgement respecting them; and therefore either to extend with confidence the bounds of our pure reason, or to set strictly defined and safe limits to its action. This last question, which arises out of the above universal problem, would properly run thus: "How is metaphysics possible as a science?"

Thus, the critique of reason leads at last, naturally and necessarily, to science; and, on the other hand, the dogmatical use of reason without criticism leads to groundless assertions, against which others equally specious can always be set, thus ending unavoidably in skepticism.

Besides, this science cannot be of great and formidable prolixity, because it has not to do with objects of reason, the variety of which is inexhaustible, but merely with Reason herself and her problems; problems which arise out of her own bosom, and are not proposed to her by the nature of outward things, but by her own nature. And when once Reason has previously become able completely to understand her own power in regard to objects which she meets with in experience, it will be easy to determine securely the extent and limits of her attempted application to objects beyond the confines of experience.

We may and must, therefore, regard the attempts hitherto made to establish metaphysical science dogmatically as non-existent. For what of analysis, that is, mere dissection of conceptions, is contained in one or other, is not the aim of, but only a preparation for metaphysics proper, which has for its object the extension, by means of synthesis, of our *a priori* knowledge. And for this purpose, mere analysis is of course useless, because it only shows what is contained in these conceptions, but not how we arrive, *a priori,* at them; and this it is her duty to show, in order to be able afterwards to determine their valid use in regard to all objects of experience, to all knowledge in general. But little self-denial, indeed, is needed to give up these pretensions, seeing the undeniable, and in the dogmatic mode of procedure, inevitable contradictions of Reason with herself, have long since ruined the reputation of every system of metaphysics that has appeared up to this time. It will require more firmness to remain undeterred by difficulty from within, and opposition from without, from endeavoring, by a method quite opposed to all those hitherto followed, to further the growth and fruitfulness of a science indispensable to human reason—a science from which every branch it has borne may be cut away, but whose roots remain indestructible. . . .

Discussion Questions

1. What is an analytic judgment? Give some examples. Is Kant right when he claims that mathematics is not analytic? How about the theorems of geometry?
2. How might Hume evaluate Kant's proposals? With which ideas would Hume agree? With which would he disagree?

For Further Reading

For an introduction to the philosophy of Kant see *The Cambridge Companion to Kant* (1992), edited by Paul Guyer. For commentaries on Kant's *Critique of Pure Reason* see *Kant and the Claims of Knowledge* (1987), by Paul Guyer; *A Commentary to Kant's Critique of Pure Reason* (1923), by Norman Kemp Smith; and *Kant's "Critique of Pure Reason": An Introductory Text* (1983), by H. Palmer. For additional biographical information concerning Kant see *The Life of Immanuel Kant* (1986), by J. H. W. Stuckenberg.

31   WHAT PRAGMATISM MEANS
William James

William James (1842–1910) was an American-born psychologist and philosopher with an M. D. from Harvard. James first achieved fame in the field of psychology with his *Principles of Psychology* (1890), a massive description of the various schools of thought then present within the field of psychology. But James' interest in psychology was always a thinly veiled interest in larger, philosophical questions. Eventually his natural inclinations got the better of him and he gave himself over to the study of philosophy. James was primarily interested in epistemology, as well as the rationality of religious belief. In both areas he followed the lead of **pragmatism,** a philosophy first developed by American philosopher C. S. Peirce (1839–1914).

As a theory of truth (or knowledge), James' pragmatism—which Peirce believed to be different from his own—represents a radical departure from the classic epistemologies of Plato, Descartes, Hume, and Kant. Whether one believed that humans could know the truth or not, truth had been construed as something objective, fixed, and unchanging—something to be either discovered or not discovered. But pragmatists reject this analysis of truth. Truth, instead, is whatever works, whatever has the most 'cash value'. The following selection comes from *Pragmatism* (1907), James' major defense and explication of pragmatism.

Reading Questions

1. How does the pragmatic method propose to handle metaphysical disputes?
2. What is truth according to James?
3. How do the rationalist and pragmatist differ with respect to their treatment of the truth?
4. Does pragmatism exclude theological ideas or beliefs?

Some years ago, being with a camping party in the mountains, I returned from a solitary ramble to find every one engaged in a ferocious metaphysical dispute. The *corpus* of the dispute was a squirrel—a live squirrel supposed to be clinging to one side of a tree trunk; while over against the tree's opposite side a human being was imagined to stand. This human witness tries to get sight of the squirrel by moving rapidly round the tree, but no matter how fast he goes, the squirrel moves as fast in the opposite direction, and always keeps the tree between himself and the man, so that never a glimpse of him is caught. The resultant metaphysical problem now is this: *Does the man go round the squirrel or not?* He goes round the tree, sure enough, and the squirrel is on the tree; but does he go round the squirrel? In the unlimited leisure of the wilderness, discussion had been worn threadbare. Every one had taken sides, and was obstinate; and the numbers on both sides were even. Each side, when I appeared therefore appealed to me to make it a majority. Mindful of the scholastic adage that whenever you meet a contradiction you must make a distinction, I immediately sought and found one, as follows: "Which party is right," I said, "depends on what you *practically mean* by 'going round' the squirrel. If you mean passing from the north of him to the east, then to the south, then to the west, and then to the north of him again, obviously the man does go round him, for he occupies these successive positions. But if on the contrary you mean being first in front of him, then on

the right of him, then behind him, then on his left, and finally in front again, it is quite as obvious that the man fails to go round him, for by the compensating movements the squirrel makes, he keeps his belly turned towards the man all the time, and his back turned away. Make the distinction, and there is no occasion for any farther dispute. You are both right and both wrong according as you conceive the verb 'to go round' in one practical fashion or the other."

Although one or two of the hotter disputants called my speech a shuffling evasion, saying they wanted no quibbling or scholastic hairsplitting, but meant just plain honest English "round," the majority seemed to think that the distinction had assuaged the dispute.

I tell this trivial anecdote because it is a peculiarly simple example of what I wish now to speak of as *the pragmatic method*. The pragmatic method is primarily a method of settling metaphysical disputes that otherwise might be interminable. Is the world one or many?—fated or free?—material or spiritual?—here are notions either of which may or may not hold good of the world; and disputes over such notions are unending. The pragmatic method in such cases is to try to interpret each notion by tracing its respective practical consequences. What difference would it practically make to any one if this notion rather than that notion were true? If no practical difference whatever can be traced, then the alternatives mean practically the same thing, and all dispute is idle. Whenever a dispute is serious, we ought to be able to show some practical difference that must follow from one side or the other's being right.

A glance at the history of the idea will show you still better what pragmatism means. The term is derived from the same Greek word πραγμα [*pragma*], meaning action, from which our words "practice" and "practical" come. It was first introduced into philosophy by Mr. Charles Peirce in 1878. In an article entitled "How to Make Our Ideas Clear," in the *Popular Science Monthly* for January of that year Mr. Peirce, after pointing out that our beliefs are really rules for action, said that, to develop a thought's meaning, we need only determine what conduct it is fitted to produce: that conduct is for us its sole significance. And the tangible fact at the root of all our thought distinctions, however subtle, is that there is no one of them so fine as to consist in anything but a possible difference of practice. To attain perfect clearness in our thoughts of an object, then, we need only consider what conceivable effects of a practical kind the object may involve—what sensations we are to expect from it, and what reactions we must prepare. Our conception of these effects, whether immediate or remote, is then for us the whole of our conception of the object, so far as that conception has positive significance at all.

This is the principle of Peirce, the principle of pragmatism. It lay entirely unnoticed by anyone for twenty years, until I, in an address before Professor Howison's philosophical union at the University of California, brought it forward again and made a special application of it to religion. By that date (1898) the times seemed ripe for its reception. The word "pragmatism" spread, and at present it fairly spots the pages of the philosophic journals. On all hands we find the "pragmatic movement" spoken of, sometimes with respect, sometimes with contumely, seldom with clear understanding. It is evident that the term applies itself conveniently to a number of tendencies that hitherto have lacked a collective name, and that it has "come to stay."

To take in the importance of Peirce's principle, one must get accustomed to applying it to concrete cases. I found a few years ago that Ostwald, the illustrious Leipzig chemist, had been making perfectly distinct use of the principle of pragmatism in his lectures on the philosophy of science, though he had not called it by that name.

"All realities influence our practice," he wrote me, "and that influence is their meaning for us. I am accustomed to put questions to my classes in this way: In what respects would the world be different if this alternative or that were true? If I can find nothing that would become different, then the alternative has no sense."

That is, the rival views mean practically the same thing, and meaning, other than practical, there is for us none. Ostwald in a published lecture gives this example of what he means. Chemists have long wrangled over the inner constitution of certain bodies called "tautomerous." Their properties seemed equally consistent with the notion that an instable hydrogen atom oscillates inside of them, or that they are instable mixtures of two bodies. Controversy raged, but never was decided. "It would never have begun," says Ostwald, "if the combatants had asked themselves what particular experimental fact could have been made different by one or the other view being correct. For it would then have appeared that no difference of fact could possibly ensue; and the quarrel was as unreal as if, theorizing in primitive times about the raising of dough by yeast, one party should have invoked a 'brownie,' while another insisted on an 'elf' as the true cause of the phenomenon."

It is astonishing to see how many philosophical disputes collapse into insignificance the moment you subject them to this simple test of tracing a concrete consequence. There can *be* no difference anywhere that doesn't *make* a difference elsewhere—no difference in abstract truth that doesn't express itself in a difference in concrete fact and in conduct consequent upon that fact, imposed on somebody, somehow, somewhere, and somewhen. The whole function of philosophy ought to be to find out what definite difference it will make to you and me, at definite instants of our life, if this world formula or that world formula be the true one.

There is absolutely nothing new in the pragmatic method. Socrates was an adept at it. Aristotle used it methodically. Locke, Berkeley, and Hume made momentous contributions to truth by its means. Shadworth Hodgson keeps insisting that realities are only what they are "known as." But these forerunners of pragmatism used it in fragments: they were preluders only. Not until in our time has it generalized itself, become conscious of a universal mission, pretended to a conquering destiny. I believe in that destiny, and I hope I may end by inspiring you with my belief.

...

So much for the pragmatic method! You may say that I have been praising it rather than explaining it to you, but I shall presently explain it abundantly enough by showing how it works on some familiar problems. Meanwhile the word pragmatism has come to be used in a still wider sense, as meaning also a certain *theory of truth*. I mean to give a whole lecture to the statement of that theory, after first paving the way, so I can be very brief now. But brevity is hard to follow, so I ask for your redoubled attention for a quarter of an hour. If much remains obscure, I hope to make it clearer in the later lectures.

...

... [T]eachers [of pragmatism] say, "truth" in our ideas and beliefs means the same thing that it means in science. It means, they say, nothing but this, *that ideas (which themselves are but parts of our experience) become true just insofar as they help us to get into satisfactory relation with other parts of our experience*, to summarize them and get about among them by conceptual shortcuts instead of following the interminable succession of particular phenomena. Any idea upon which we can ride, so to speak; any idea that will carry us prosperously from any one part of our experience to any other part, linking things satisfactorily, working securely, simplifying, saving labor; is true for just so much, true in so far forth, true *instrumentally*. This is the "instrumental" view of truth taught so successfully at Chicago, the view that truth in our ideas means their power to "work," promulgated so brilliantly at Oxford.

...

You will probably be surprised to learn ... that Messrs. Schiller's and Dewey's theories have suffered a hailstorm of contempt and ridicule. All rationalism has risen against them. In influential quarters Mr. Schiller, in particular, has been treated like an impudent schoolboy who deserves a spanking. I should not mention this, but for the fact that it throws so much sidelight upon that rationalistic temper to which I have opposed the temper of pragmatism. Pragmatism is uncomfortable away from facts. Rationalism is comfortable only in the presence of abstractions. This pragmatist talk about truths in the plural, about their utility and satisfactoriness,

about the success with which they "work," etc., suggests to the typical intellectualist mind a sort of coarse lame second-rate makeshift article of truth. Such truths are not real truth. Such tests are merely subjective. As against this, objective truth must be something nonutilitarian, haughty, refined, remote, august, exalted. It must be an absolute correspondence of our thoughts with an equally absolute reality. It must be what we *ought* to think unconditionally. The conditioned ways in which we *do* think are so much irrelevance and matter for psychology. Down with psychology, up with logic, in all this question!

See the exquisite contrast of the types of mind! The pragmatist clings to facts and concreteness, observes truth at its work in particular cases, and generalizes. Truth, for him, becomes a class name for all sorts of definite working values in experience. For the rationalist it remains a pure abstraction, to the bare name of which we must defer. When the pragmatist undertakes to show in detail just *why* we must defer, the rationalist is unable to recognize the concretes from which his own abstraction is taken. He accuses us of *denying* truth; whereas we have only sought to trace exactly why people follow it and always ought to follow it. Your typical ultra-abstractionist fairly shudders at concreteness: other things equal, he positively prefers the pale and spectral. If the two universes were offered, he would always choose the skinny outline rather than the rich thicket of reality. It is so much purer, clearer, nobler.

...

Now pragmatism, devoted though she be to facts, has no ... materialistic bias as ordinary empiricism labors under. Moreover, she has no objection whatever to the realizing of abstractions, so long as you get about among particulars with their aid and they actually carry you somewhere. Interested in no conclusions but those which our minds and our experiences work out together, she has no *a priori* prejudices against theology. *If theological ideas prove to have a value for concrete life, they will be true, for pragmatism, in the sense of being good for so much. For how much more they are true, will depend entirely on their relations to the other truths that also have to be acknowledged. ...*

Discussion Questions

1. Does pragmatism allow for more than one truth? Why or why not? If so, does this make sense? Does it make sense that something can go from being true, to being false, to being true again?
2. Can the pragmatist explain how we have moral knowledge? What would the pragmatist have to say about moral standards? Are there absolute moral truths according to pragmatism? Explain your answer.
3. Suppose humans have free will. Would the world look any different if humans lacked free will; that is, would it appear any different to humans if there were no free will? Why is this question important to the pragmatist? How does the answer affect the free will and determinism debate? Is there any practical difference between believing in free will and not believing in free will?

For Further Reading

James' works are collected in *The Works of William James* (1975), edited by Burkhardt, Bowers, and Skrupselis. James' main publications are *The Principles of Psychology* (1890), *The Will to Believe and Other Essays* (1897), *The Varieties of Religious Experience* (1903), *Pragmatism* (1907), and *The Meaning of Truth* (1909). For biographical information and an introduction to James' pragmatism, see *William James* (1987), by G. E. Meyers; *The Thought and Character of William James* (1935), by R. B. Perry; and *The Cambridge Companion to William James* (1997), edited by R. A. Putnam. For information concerning pragmatism in general see *The Origins of Pragmatism* (1968), by A. J. Ayer; *Four Pragmatists* (1974), by I. Scheffler; and *Meaning and Action* (1968), by H. S. Thayer.

32   AGAINST METHOD
Paul Feyerabend

Scientific method is an important part of the practice of science and, as such, instruction in the procedures of proper scientific method is an important part of the education of college undergraduates and future scientists. Proper scientific method emphasizes carefully designed procedures, such as statistical analysis, that aim to ensure that the results of scientific inquiry remain free of any bias caused by the investigator's distortions. Scientific method, in short, guarantees objectivity. To be a successful researcher in a scientific field, you must demonstrate an ability to create carefully designed studies that implement procedures that ensure objectivity, since, according to science's own interpretation of its success, past progress made by science was primarily the result of a standard, uniform method of investigation.

But does science actually progress this way? Is there in fact only one method—the scientific method—that helps us to discover the truth? What if, alternatively, there are many methods? Would the insistence of

SOURCE: From *Against Method* by Paul Feyerabend (Verso Books, 1993). Copyright © 1975, 1988, 1993 by Paul Feyerabend. Used by permission of Verso Books.

science upon a single method actually impede human knowledge instead of promoting it? According to Paul Feyerabend (1924–1996), a former professor at the University of California, Berkeley, the answer is yes.

According to Feyerabend's reading of the history of science, scientists themselves have in fact used multiple methods of inquiry—in contradiction to the 'official' picture science has of itself. Science, according to Feyerabend, is too often a mere **ideology,** that is, the partisan convictions of zealots blinded to points of view outside their own. On Feyerabend's account, science actually shares a number of features with mythological thinking. This, however, isn't necessarily bad. The problem with science is not that it has mythological elements in it, but that it refuses to openly admit to them and stubbornly insists on enforcing upon society a narrow and limited method of pursuing truth. But democratic, pluralistic societies need not accept the attempt at dominance by science; that is, society should reject science's effort to prescribe its method as the only proper way of discovering the truth or of justifying claims to knowledge. Rather, all methods of pursuing truth should be considered legitimate. The ideology of science should be treated like any other ideology, such as religious and political ideologies—taught only in private, parochial institutions to persons wishing to be indoctrinated into the superiority of the scientific method.

Reading Questions

1. Why is science both pernicious and unrealistic according to Feyerabend?
2. How are science and myth alike according to Feyerabend's summary of Horton's research?
3. How do most scientists respond to the basic ideas and beliefs of their discipline? How is this similar to mythological thinking?
4. Why does Feyerabend believe that science "reigns supreme"? Why does he conclude that there must be a separation between state and science?
5. What is the "fairy-tale" explanation of the success of science?
6. What reasons are there for rejecting the "fairy-tale" picture of science?
7. What assumptions are necessary to support the widely held view of how science works? What reasons does Feyerabend give to reject these assumptions?
8. In order to understand nature, what must we do, according to Feyerabend?
9. How does Feyerabend believe that science, which he regards as an ideology, should be taught in a pluralistic society such as ours?

Thus science is much closer to myth than a scientific philosophy is prepared to admit. It is one of the many forms of thought that have been developed by man, and not necessarily the best. It is conspicuous, noisy, and impudent, but it is inherently superior only for those who have already decided in favor of a certain ideology, or who have accepted it without ever having examined its advantages and its limits. And as the accepting and rejecting of ideologies should be left to the individual it follows that the separation of state and church must be complemented by the separation of state and science,

that most recent, most aggressive, and most dogmatic religious institution. Such a separation may be our only chance to achieve a humanity we are capable of, but have never fully realized.

The idea that science can, and should, be run according to fixed and universal rules, is both unrealistic and pernicious. It is *unrealistic,* for it takes too simple a view of the talents of man and of the circumstances which encourage, or cause, their development. And it is *pernicious,* for the attempt to enforce the rules is bound to increase our professional qualifications at the expense of our humanity. In addition, the idea is *detrimental to science,* for it neglects the complex physical and historical conditions which influence scientific change. It makes our science less adaptable and more dogmatic: every methodological rule is associated with cosmological assumptions, so that using the rule we take it for granted that the assumptions are correct. Naive falsificationism takes it for granted that the laws of nature are manifest and not hidden beneath disturbances of considerable magnitude. Empiricism takes it for granted that sense experience is a better mirror of the world than pure thought. Praise of argument takes it for granted that the artifices of Reason give better results than the unchecked play of our emotions. Such assumptions may be perfectly plausible *and even true.* Still, one should occasionally put them to a test. Putting them to a test means that we stop using the methodology associated with them, start doing science in a different way and see what happens. Case studies such as those reported in the preceding chapters show that such tests occur all the time, and that they speak *against* the universal validity of any rule. All methodologies have their limitations and the only 'rule' that survives is 'anything goes'.

The change of perspective brought about by these discoveries leads once more to the long-forgotten problem of the excellence of science. It leads to it for the first time in *modern* history, for modern science *overpowered* its opponents, it did not *convince* them. Science took over by *force,* not by argument (this is especially true of the former colonies where science and the religion of brotherly love were introduced as a matter of course, and without consulting, or arguing with, the inhabitants). Today we realize that rationalism, being bound to science, cannot give us any assistance in the issue between science and myth and we also know, from inquiries of an entirely different kind, that myths are vastly better than rationalists have dared to admit. Thus we are now *forced* to raise the question of the excellence of science. An examination then reveals that science and myth overlap in many ways, that the differences we think we perceive are often *local* phenomena which may turn into similarities elsewhere and that fundamental discrepancies are results of different *aims* rather than of different methods trying to reach one and the same

'rational' end (such as, for example, 'progress', or increase of content, or 'growth').

To show the surprising similarities of myth and science, I shall briefly discuss an interesting paper by Robin Horton, entitled 'African Traditional Thought and Western Science'.[1] Horton examines African mythology and discovers the following features: the quest for theory is a quest for unity underlying apparent complexity. The theory places things in a causal context that is wider than the causal context provided by common sense: both science and myth cap common sense with a theoretical superstructure. There are theories of different degrees of abstraction and they are used in accordance with the different requirements of explanation that arise. Theory construction consists in breaking up objects of common sense and in reuniting the elements in a different way. Theoretical models start from analogy but they gradually move away from the pattern on which the analogy was based. And so on.

These features, which emerge from case studies no less careful and detailed than those of Lakatos, refute the assumption that science and myth obey different principles of formation (Cassirer), that myth proceeds without reflection (Dardel), or speculation (Frankfurt, occasionally). Nor can we accept the idea . . . that myth has an essentially pragmatic function or is based on ritual. Myth is much closer to science than one would expect from a philosophical discussion. It is closer to science than even Horton himself is prepared to admit.

To see this, consider some of the *differences* Horton emphasizes. According to Horton, the central ideas of a myth are regarded as sacred. There is anxiety about threats to them. One 'almost never finds a confession of ignorance' and events 'which seriously defy the established lines of classification in the culture where they occur' evoke a 'taboo reaction'. Basic beliefs are protected by this reaction as well as by the device of 'secondary elaborations' which, in our terms, are series of *ad hoc* hypotheses. Science, on the other hand, is characterized by an 'essential

---

1. Originally published in *Africa,* Vol. 7, 1967, pp. 87–155. I am quoting from the abbreviated reprint in Max Marwick (ed.), *Witchcraft and Sorcery,* Penguin Books, 1970, pp. 342ff.

skepticism'; 'when failures start to come thick and fast, defense of the theory switches inexorably to attack on it'. This is possible because of the 'openness' of the scientific enterprise, because of the pluralism of ideas it contains and also because 'whatever defies or fails to fit into the established category system is not something horrifying, to be isolated or expelled. On the contrary, it is an intriguing 'phenomenon'—a starting-point and a challenge for the invention of new classifications and new theories. . . . A field study of science itself shows a very different picture.

Such a study reveals that, while some scientists may proceed as described, the great majority follow a different path. Skepticism is at a minimum; it is directed against the view of the opposition and against minor ramifications of one's own basic ideas, never against the basic ideas themselves. Attacking the basic ideas evokes taboo reactions which are no weaker than are the taboo reactions in so-called primitive societies. Basic beliefs are protected by this reaction as well as by secondary elaborations, as we have seen, and whatever fails to fit into the established category system or is said to be incompatible with this system is either viewed as something quite horrifying or, more frequently, *it is simply declared to be non-existent*. Nor is science prepared to make a theoretical pluralism the foundation of research. Newton reigned for more than 150 years, Einstein briefly introduced a more liberal point of view only to be succeeded by the Copenhagen Interpretation. The similarities between science and myth are indeed astonishing.

But the fields are even more closely related. The massive dogmatism I have described is not just a *fact,* it has also a most important *function. Science would be impossible without it*. 'Primitive' thinkers showed greater insight into the nature of knowledge than their 'enlightened' philosophical rivals. It is, therefore, necessary to re-examine our attitude towards myth, religion, magic, witchcraft and towards all those ideas which rationalists would like to see forever removed from the surface of the earth (without having so much as looked at them—a typical taboo reaction).

There is another reason why such a re-examination is urgently required. The rise of modern science coincides with the suppression of non-Western tribes by Western invaders. The tribes are not only physically suppressed, they also lose their intellectual independ-ence and are forced to adopt the bloodthirsty religion of brotherly love—Christianity. The most intelligent members get an extra bonus: they are introduced into the mysteries of Western Rationalism and its peak—Western Science. Occasionally this leads to an almost unbearable tension with tradition (Haiti). In most cases the tradition disappears without the trace of an argument, one simply becomes a slave both in body and in mind. Today this development is gradu-ally reversed—with great reluctance, to be sure, but it is reversed. Freedom is regained, old traditions are rediscovered, both among the minorities in Western countries and among large populations in non-Western continents. *But science still reigns supreme*. It reigns supreme because its practitioners are *unable to understand*, and *unwilling to condone*, different ide-ologies, because they have the *power* to enforce their wishes, and because they *use* this power just as their ancestors used *their* power to force Christianity on the peoples they encountered during their conquests. Thus, while an American can now choose the religion he likes, he is still not permitted to demand that his children learn magic rather than science at school. There is a separation between state and church, there is no separation between state and science.

And yet science has no greater authority than any other form of life. Its aims are certainly not more important than are the aims that guide the lives in a religious community or in a tribe that is united by a myth. At any rate, they have no business restricting the lives, the thoughts, the education of the members of a free society where everyone should have a chance to make up his own mind and to live in accordance with the social beliefs he finds most acceptable. The separation between state and church must therefore be complemented by the separation between state and science.

We need not fear that such a separation will lead to a breakdown of technology. There will always be people who prefer being scientists to being the mas-ters of their fate and who gladly submit to the mean-est kind of (intellectual and institutional) slavery provided they are paid well and provided also there are some people around who examine their work and sing their praise. Greece developed and progressed because it could rely on the services of unwilling slaves. We shall develop and progress with the help of the numerous *willing* slaves in universities and laboratories who provide us with pills, gas, electricity, atom bombs, frozen dinners and, occasionally, with a few interesting fairy-tales. We shall treat these slaves well, we shall even listen to them, for they have occasionally some interesting stories to tell, but we shall *not* permit them to impose their ideology on our children in the guise of 'progressive' theories of education. We shall not permit them to teach the fancies of science as if they were the only factual statements in existence. This separation of science and state may be our only chance to overcome the hectic barbarism of our scientific-technical age and to achieve a humanity we are capable of, but have never fully realized. Let us, therefore, in conclusion review the arguments that can be adduced for such a procedure.

The image of 20th-century science in the minds of scientists and laymen is determined by technological miracles such as color television, the moon shots, the infra-red oven, as well as by a somewhat vague but still quite influential rumor, or fairy-tale, concerning the manner in which these miracles are produced.

According to the fairy-tale the success of science is the result of a subtle, but carefully balanced combination of inventiveness and control. Scientists have *ideas*. And they have special *methods* for improving ideas. The theories of science have passed the test of method. They give a better account of the world than ideas which have not passed the test.

The fairy-tale explains why modern society treats science in a special way and why it grants it privileges not enjoyed by other institutions.

Ideally, the modern state is ideologically neutral. Religion, myth, prejudices *do* have an influence, but only in a roundabout way, through the medium of politically influential *parties*. Ideological principles *may* enter the governmental structure, but only via a majority vote, and after a lengthy discussion of possible consequences. In our schools the main religions are taught as *historical phenomena*. They are taught as parts of the truth only if the parents insist on a more direct mode of instruction. It is up to them to decide about the religious education of their children. The financial support of ideologies does not exceed the financial support granted to parties and to private groups. State and ideology, state and church, state and myth, are carefully separated.

State and science, however, work closely together. Immense sums are spent on the improvement of scientific ideas. Bastard subjects such as the philosophy of science which have not a single discovery to their credit profit from the boom of the sciences. Even human relations are dealt with in a scientific manner, as is shown by education programs, proposals for prison reform, army training, and so on. Almost all scientific subjects are compulsory subjects in our schools. While the parents of a six-year-old child can decide to have him instructed in the rudiments of Protestantism, or in the rudiments of the Jewish faith, or to omit religious instruction altogether, they do not have a similar freedom in the case of the sciences. Physics, astronomy, history *must* be learned. They cannot be replaced by magic, astrology, or by a study of legends.

Nor is one content with a merely *historical* presentation of physical (astronomical, historical, etc.) facts and principles. One does not say: *some people believe* that the earth moves round the sun while others regard the earth as a hollow sphere that contains the sun, the planets, the fixed stars. One says: the earth *moves* round the sun—everything else is sheer idiocy.

Finally, the manner in which we accept or reject scientific ideas is radically different from democratic decision procedures. We accept scientific laws and scientific facts, we teach them in our schools, we make them the basis of important political decisions, but without ever having subjected them to a vote. *Scientists* do not subject them to a vote—or at least this is what they say—and *laymen* certainly do not subject them to a vote. Concrete proposals are occasionally discussed, and a vote is suggested. But the procedure is not extended to general theories and scientific facts. Modern society is 'Copernican' not because Copernicanism has been put on a ballot, subjected to a democratic debate and then voted in with a simple majority; it is 'Copernican' because the *scientists* are Copernicans and because one accepts their cosmology as uncritically as one once accepted the cosmology of bishops and cardinals.

···

The reason for this special treatment of science is, of course, our little fairy-tale: if science has found a method that turns ideologically contaminated ideas into true and useful theories, then it is indeed not mere ideology, but an objective measure of all ideologies. It is then not subjected to the demand for a separation between state and ideology.

But the fairy-tale is false, as we have seen. There is no special method that guarantees success or makes it probable. Scientists do not solve problems because they possess a magic wand—methodology, or a theory of rationality—but because they have studied a problem for a long time, because they know the situation fairly well, because they are not too dumb (though that is rather doubtful nowadays when almost anyone can become a scientist), and because the excesses of one scientific school are almost always balanced by the excesses of some other school. (Besides, scientists only rarely solve their problems, they make lots of mistakes, and many of their solutions are quite useless.) Basically there is hardly any difference between the process that leads to the announcement of a new scientific law and the process preceding passage of a new law in society: one informs either all citizens or those immediately concerned, one collects 'facts' and prejudices, one discusses the matter, and one finally votes. But while a democracy makes some effort to *explain* the process so that everyone can understand it, scientists either *conceal* it, or *bend* it, to make it fit their sectarian interests.

No scientist will admit that voting plays a role in his subject. Facts, logic, and methodology alone decide—this is what the fairy-tale tells us. But how do facts decide? What is their function in the advancement of knowledge? We cannot *derive* our theories from them. We cannot give a *negative* criterion by saying, for example, that good theories are theories which can be refuted, but which are not yet contradicted by any fact. A principle of falsification that removes theories because they do not fit the facts would have to remove the whole science (or it would have to admit that large parts of science are irrefutable). The hint that a good theory *explains more* than its rivals is not very realistic either. True: new theories often predict new things—but almost always at the expense of things already known. Turning to logic we realize that even the simplest demands *are not* satisfied in scientific practice, and *could not be* satisfied, because of the complexity of the material. The ideas which scientists use to present the known and to advance into the unknown are only rarely in agreement with the strict injunctions of logic or pure mathematics and the attempt to make them conform would rob science of the elas-

ticity without which progress cannot be achieved. We see: facts alone are not strong enough for making us accept, or reject, scientific theories, the range they leave to thought is *too wide;* logic and methodology eliminate too much, they are *too narrow*. In between these two extremes lies the ever-changing domain of human ideas and wishes. And a more detailed analysis of successful moves in the game of science ('successful' from the point of view of the scientists themselves) shows indeed that there is a wide range of freedom that *demands* a multiplicity of ideas and *permits* the application of democratic procedures (ballot-discussion-vote) but that is actually closed by power politics and propaganda. *This is where the fairy-tale of a special method assumes its decisive function.* It conceals the freedom of decision which creative scientists and the general public have even inside the most rigid and the most advanced parts of science by a recitation of 'objective' criteria and it thus protects the big-shots (Nobel Prize winners; heads of laboratories, of organizations such as the AMA, of special schools; 'educators'; etc.) from the masses (laymen; experts in non-scientific fields; experts in other fields of science): only those citizens count who were subjected to the pressures of scientific institutions (they have undergone a long process of education), who succumbed to these pressures (they have passed their examinations), and who are now firmly convinced of the truth of the fairy-tale. This is how scientists have deceived themselves and everyone else about their business, but without any real disadvantage: they have more money, more authority, more sex appeal than they deserve, and the most stupid procedures and the most laughable results in their domain are surrounded with an aura of excellence. It is time to cut them down in size, and to give them a more modest position in society.

This advice, which only few of our well-conditioned contemporaries are prepared to accept, seems to clash with certain simple and widely-known facts.

Is it not a fact that a learned physician is better equipped to diagnose and to cure an illness than a layman or the medicine-man of a primitive society? Is it not a fact that epidemics and dangerous individual diseases have disappeared only with the beginning of modern medicine? Must we not admit that technology has made tremendous advances since the rise of modern science? And are not the moon-shots a most impressive and undeniable proof of its excellence? These are some of the questions which are thrown at the impudent wretch who dares to criticize the special position of the sciences.

The questions reach their polemical aim only if one assumes that the results of science *which no one will deny* have arisen without any help from non-scientific elements, and that they cannot be improved by an admixture of such elements either. 'Unscientific' procedures such as the herbal lore of witches and cunning men, the astronomy of mystics, the treatment of the ill in primitive societies are totally without merit. *Science alone* gives us a useful astronomy, an effective medicine, a trustworthy technology. One must also assume that science owes its success to the correct method and not merely to a lucky accident. It was not a fortunate cosmological guess that led to progress, but the correct *and cosmologically neutral* handling of data. These are the assumptions we must make to give the questions the polemical force they are supposed to have. Not a single one of them stands up to closer examination.

Modern astronomy started with the attempt of Copernicus to adapt the old ideas of Philolaos to the needs of astronomical predictions. Philolaos was not a precise scientist, he was a muddleheaded Pythagorean, as we have seen, and the consequences of his doctrine were called 'incredibly ridiculous' by a professional astronomer such as Ptolemy. Even Galileo, who had the much improved Copernican version of Philolaos before him, says: 'There is no limit to my astonishment when I reflect that Aristrarchus and Copernicus were able to make reason to conquer sense that, in defiance of the latter, the former became mistress of their belief'. 'Sense' here refers to the experiences which Aristotle and others had used to show that the earth must be at rest. The 'reason' which Copernicus opposes to their arguments is the very mystical reason of Philolaos combined with an equally mystical faith ('mystical' from the point of view of today's rationalists) in the fundamental character of circular motion. I have shown that modern astronomy and modern dynamics could not have advanced without this unscientific use of antediluvian ideas.

While astronomy profited from Pythagoreanism and from the Platonic love for circles, medicine profited from herbalism, from the psychology, the metaphysics, the physiology of witches, midwives, cunning men, wandering druggists. It is well known that 16th- and 17th-century medicine while theoretically hypertrophic was quite helpless in the face of disease (and stayed that way for a long time after the 'scientific revolution'). Innovators such as Paracelsus fell back on the earlier ideas and improved medicine. Everywhere science is enriched by unscientific methods and unscientific results, while procedures which have often been regarded as essential parts of science are quietly suspended or circumvented.

The process is not restricted to the early history of modern science. It is not merely a consequence of the primitive state of the sciences of the 16th and 17th centuries. Even today science can and does profit from an admixture of unscientific ingredients. An example . . . is the revival of traditional medicine in Communist China. When the Communists in the fifties forced hospitals and medical schools to teach the ideas and the methods contained in the *Yellow Emperor's Textbook of Internal Medicine* and to use them in the treatment of patients, many Western experts were aghast and predicted the downfall of Chinese medicine. What happened was the exact opposite. Acupuncture, moxibustion, pulse diagnosis have led to new insights, new methods of treatment, new problems both for the Western and for the Chinese physician. And those who did not like to see the state meddling in scientific matters should remember the sizeable chauvinism of science: for most scientists the slogan 'freedom for science' means the freedom to indoctrinate not only those who have joined them, but the rest of society as well. . . .

Combining this observation with the insight that science has no special method, we arrive at the result that the separation of science and non-science is not only artificial but also detrimental to the advancement of knowledge. If we want to understand nature, if we want to master our physical surroundings, then we must use *all* ideas, *all* methods, and not just a small selection of them. The assertion, however, that there is no knowledge outside science—*extra scientiam nulla salus*—is nothing but another and most convenient fairy-tale. Primitive tribes have more detailed classifications of animals and plants than contemporary scientific zoology and botany, they know remedies whose effectiveness astounds physicians (while the pharmaceutical industry already smells here a new source of income), they have means of influencing their fellow men which science for a long time regarded as non-existent (Voodoo), they solve difficult problems in ways which are still not quite understood (building of the pyramids; Polynesian travels), there existed a highly developed and internationally known astronomy in the old Stone Age, this astronomy was factually adequate *as well as* emotionally satisfying, *it solved both physical and social problems* (one cannot say the same about modern astronomy) and it was tested in very simple and ingenious ways (stone observatories in England and in the South Pacific; astronomical schools in Polynesia . . .). There was the domestication of animals, the invention of rotating agriculture, new types of plants were bred and kept pure by careful avoidance of cross fertilization, we have chemical inventions, we have a most amazing art that can compare with the best achievements of the present. True, there were no collective excursions to the moon, but single individuals, disregarding great dangers to their soul and their sanity, rose from sphere to sphere until they finally faced God himself in all His splendor while others changed into animals and back into humans again. At all times man approached his surroundings with wide open senses and a fertile intelligence, at all times he made incredible discoveries, at all times we can learn from his ideas.

Modern science, on the other hand, is not at all as difficult and as perfect as scientific propaganda wants us to believe. A subject such as medicine, or physics, or biology appears difficult only because it is taught badly, because the standard instructions are full of redundant material, and because they start too late in life. During the war, when the American Army needed physicians within a very short time, it was suddenly possible to reduce medical instruction to half a year (the corresponding instruction manuals have disappeared long ago, however. Sci-

ence may be simplified during the war. In peacetime the prestige of science demands greater complication.) And how often does it not happen that the proud and conceited judgment of an expert is put in its proper place by a layman! Numerous inventors built 'impossible' machines. Lawyers show again and again that an expert does not know what he is talking about. Scientists, especially physicians, frequently come to different results so that it is up to the relatives of the sick person (or the inhabitants of a certain area) to decide *by vote* about the procedure to be adopted. How often is science improved, and turned into new directions by non-scientific influences! It is up to us, it is up to the citizens of a free society to either accept the chauvinism of science without contradiction or to overcome it by the counterforce of public action. Public action was used against science by the Communists in China in the fifties, and it was again used, under very different circumstances, by some opponents of evolution in California in the seventies. Let us follow their example and let us free society from the strangling hold of an ideologically petrified science just as our ancestors freed *us* from the strangling hold of the One True Religion!

The way towards this aim is clear. A science that insists on possessing the only correct method and the only acceptable results is ideology and must be separated from the state, and especially from the process of education. One may teach it, but only to those who have decided to make this particular superstition their own. On the other hand, a science that dropped such totalitarian pretensions is no longer independent and self-contained, and it can be taught in many different combinations (myth and modern cosmology might be one such combination). Of course, every business has the right to demand that its practitioners be prepared in a special way, and it may even demand acceptance of a certain ideology (I for one am against the thinning out of subjects so that they become more and more similar to each other; whoever does not like present-day Catholicism should leave it and become a Protestant, or an Atheist, instead of ruining it by such inane changes as mass in the vernacular). That is true of physics, just as it is true of religion, or of prostitution. But such special ideologies, such special skills have no room in the process of *general education* that prepares a citizen for his role in society. A mature citizen is not a man who has been *instructed* in a special ideology, such as Puritanism, or critical rationalism, and who now carries this ideology with him like a mental tumor, a mature citizen is a person who has learned how to make up his mind and who has then *decided* in favor of what he thinks suits him best. He is a person who has a certain mental toughness (he does not fall for the first ideological street singer he happens to meet) and who is therefore able *consciously to choose* the business that seems to be most attractive to him rather than being swallowed by it. To prepare himself for his choice he will study the major ideologies as *historical phenomena,* he will study science as a historical phenomenon and not as the one and only sensible way of approaching a problem. He will study it together with other fairytales such as the myths of 'primitive' societies so that he has the information needed for arriving at a free decision. An essential part of a general education of this kind is acquaintance with the most outstanding propagandists in all fields, so that the pupil can build up his resistance against all pro-

paganda, including the propaganda called 'argument'. It is only *after* such a hardening procedure that he will be called upon to make up his mind on the issue rationalism–irrationalism, science–myth, science–religion, and so on. His decision in favor of science—assuming he chooses science—will then be much more 'rational' than any decision in favor of science is today. At any rate—science and the schools will be just as carefully separated as religion and the schools are separated today. Scientists will of course participate in governmental decisions, for everyone participates in such decisions. But they will not be given overriding authority. It is the *vote* of *everyone concerned* that decides fundamental issues such as the teaching methods used, or the truth of basic beliefs such as the theory of evolution, or the quantum theory, and not the authority of big-shots hiding behind a nonexisting methodology. There is no need to fear that such a way of arranging society will lead to undesirable results. Science itself uses the method of ballot, discussion, vote, though without a clear grasp of its mechanism, and in a heavily biased way. But the rationality of our beliefs will certainly be considerably increased.

Discussion Questions

1. In what ways is science like a religion? What similarities and differences are there between the two? Given your answer, do you agree with Feyerabend that democratic society ought to treat science as it treats religious faith? Why or why not?

2. What is Feyerabend's vision of an ideal society? Can you construct his picture of an ideal society from his essay? Would such a society be desirable to you? Would you wish to live in it? Why or why not?

3. How do the media portray scientists and the scientific method? For example, how is science portrayed on public television programs (such as *Nova*), shows funded principally by the National Science Foundation and federal grants? How is it portrayed on weekly and nightly network news programs? How is it portrayed on cable channels such as the Discovery Channel and TLC? Would Feyerabend say these are accurate pictures of science? Why or why not? Do you believe, after having read Feyerabend, that these portrayals are distorted?

4. Are there any areas of our lives where science exercises too much authority and control? How about, for example, in areas related to health? How about raising and disciplining children? Should we trust the conclusions of science in every area of our lives? Why or why not?

For Additional Reading

This selection is from Feyerabend's *Against Method* (1975), perhaps the book that he is most famous for. Other recommended books by Feyerabend include *Farewell to Reason* (1987) and *Science in a Free Society* (1978). Feyerabend's autobiography is also worthwhile; see *Killing Time: The Autobiography of Paul Feyerabend* (1995). See also John Preston, *Feyerabend: Philosophy, Science, and Society* (1997) and *Beyond Reason: Essays on the Philosophy of Paul Feyerabend*, edited by Gonzalo Muneavar (1991). Feyerabend's position has been strongly influenced by Thomas S. Kuhn's *The Structure of Scientific Revolutions* (1962).

33   VIRTUES IN EPISTEMOLOGY
John Greco

John Greco (1961–) received his Ph.D. in philosophy in 1989 from Brown University and currently teaches at Fordham University in New York. Greco's research has always been tightly focused on issues in epistemology, and he is the author of *Putting Skeptics in Their Place* (2000) and several journal articles focused on skepticism and virtue epistemology.

When does someone, *S,* know that some fact, *p,* is the case? One school of thought, the Reliabilists, claims that *S* knows that *p is S*'s (true) belief that *p* is the outcome of a reliable cognitive process. But Greco demonstrates that this account of knowledge is lacking—not all reliably formed beliefs should count as knowledge. For example, *"suppose that S suffers from a rare sort of brain lesion, one effect of which is to cause the victim to believe that he has a brain lesion. However, S has no evidence that he has such a condition, and even has evidence against it. . . . It seems clear that S's belief that he has a brain lesion is unjustified, although (by hypothesis) it has been caused by a highly reliable cognitive process."*

If, however, *S* believed that he had a brain lesion as the result of some (reliable) epistemic virtue—as opposed to a quirky consequence of his brain lesion—*S* would know that he had a brain lesion. Hence, Greco offers the following account of knowledge. *"S has knowledge regarding p if and only if S believes that truth regarding p because S believes p out of intellectual virtue."*

Reading Questions

1. What is the structure of knowledge according to foundationalism?
2. What is the structure of knowledge according to coherentism?
3. What is epistemic justification?
4. What is the well-known objection to coherentism?
5. What is Sosa's general account of epistemic justification?

SOURCE: From *Handbook of Epistemology,* edited by Paul Moser, copyright by Oxford University Press. Used by permission of Oxford University Press, Inc.

6. What is animal knowledge?
7. What is reflective knowledge?
8. What is generic reliabilism?
9. Why does reliability seem insufficient for epistemic justification?
10. How does Montmarquet's account of intellectual virtue differ from Sosa's?
11. How does Zagzebski define intellectual virtue?
12. What is the main difference between Sosa's account of intellectual virtue and Zagzebski's?
13. Why is Zagzebski's account of knowledge too strong?
14. How does Greco define subjective justification?
15. Explain Hume's skeptical argument about *unobserved* matters of fact.
16. Explain Hume's skeptical argument about matters of fact.
17. What mistake does agent reliabilism expose in Hume's first skeptical argument?
18. What mistake does agent reliabilism expose in Hume's second skeptical argument?
19. What did Gettier's paper purport to show?
20. Why is it appropriate to credit S with true belief in cases of knowledge but not in the two Gettier cases?

What is a virtue in epistemology? In the broadest sense, a virtue is an excellence of some kind. In epistemology, the relevant kind of excellence will be "intellectual." But then what is an intellectual virtue? Some philosophers have understood intellectual virtues to be broad cognitive abilities or powers. On this view, intellectual virtues are innate faculties or acquired habits that enable a person to arrive at truth and avoid error in some relevant field. For example, Aristotle defined "intuitive reason" as the ability to grasp first principles, and he defined "science" as the ability to demonstrate further truths from these first principles. Some contemporary authors add accurate perception, reliable memory, and various kinds of good reasoning to the list of intellectual virtues. These authors follow Aristotle in the notion that intellectual virtues are cognitive abilities or powers, but they loosen the requirements for what count as such.

Other authors have understood the intellectual virtues quite differently, however. On their view intellectual virtues are more like personality traits than cognitive abilities or powers. For example, intellectual courage is a trait of mind that allows one to persevere in one's ideas. Intellectual open-mindedness is a trait of mind that allows one to be receptive to the ideas of others. Among these authors, however, there is disagreement about why such personality traits count as virtues. Some think it is because they are truth-conducive, increasing one's chances of arriving at true beliefs while avoiding false beliefs. Others think that such traits are virtues independently of their connection to truth—they would be virtues even if they were not truth-conducive at all.

Who is right about the nature of the intellectual virtues? One might think that this is a matter of semantics—that different authors have simply decided to use the term "intellectual virtue" in different ways. In the essay that follows I will argue that there is some truth to this analysis. However, it is not the whole truth. This is because epistemologists invoke the notion of an intellectual virtue for specific reasons, in the context of addressing specific problems in epistemology. In effect, they make claims that understanding the intellectual virtues in a certain way allows us to solve those problems. And of course claims like that are substantive, not merely terminological. In Part One of this essay I will review some recent history of epistemology, focussing on ways in which the intellectual virtues have been invoked to solve specific epistemological problems. The purpose of this part is to give a sense of the contemporary landscape that has emerged, and to clarify some of the disagreements among those who invoke the virtues in epistemology. In Part Two I will explore some epistemological problems in greater detail. The purpose of this part is to defend a particular approach in virtue epistemology by displaying its power in addressing these problems.

PART ONE. HISTORY AND LANDSCAPE

1. Sosa's Virtue Perspectivism

The intellectual virtues made their contemporary debut in a series of papers by Ernest Sosa. In those papers Sosa is primarily concerned with two problems in the theory of knowledge. The first is the debate between foundationalism and coherentism. The second is a series of objections that have been raised against reliabilism.

a. Foundationalism and Coherentism Foundationalism and coherentism are positions regarding the structure of knowledge. According to foundationalism, knowledge is like a pyramid: A solid foundation of knowledge grounds the entire structure, providing the support required by knowledge at the higher levels. According to coherentism, knowledge is like a raft: Different parts of the structure are tied together via relations of mutual support, with no part of the whole playing a more fundamental role than do others. Let us use the term "epistemic justification" to name whatever property it is that turns mere true belief into knowledge. We may then define "pure coherentism" as holding that only coherence contributes to epistemic justification, and we may define "pure foundationalism" as holding that coherence does not contribute to epistemic justification at all. In the papers that introduce the notion of an intellectual virtue, Sosa argues that neither pure coherentism nor pure foundationalism can be right.

Against pure coherentism is the well-known objection that there can be highly coherent belief-systems that are nevertheless largely divorced from reality. But then coherence cannot be the only thing that matters for epistemic justification. Sosa presses this basic point in various ways. For one, consider the victim of Descartes' evil demon. By hypothesis, the victim's beliefs are as coherent as our own. That is, they are members of a coherent system of beliefs, tied together by a great number and variety of logical and quasi-logical relations. Suppose that by chance some few of those beliefs are also true. Surely they do not amount to knowledge, although both true and coherent.

Another way that Sosa argues the point is to highlight the importance of experience for epistemic justification. Consider that any human being will have perceptual beliefs with few connections to other beliefs in her total belief system. For example, my perceptual belief that there is a bird outside my window has few logical relations to other beliefs that I have. But then one can generate counterexamples to pure coherentism by means of the following recipe. First, replace my belief that there is a bird outside my window with the belief that there is squirrel outside my window. Second, make whatever few other changes are necessary to preserve coherence. For example, replace my belief that I seem to see a bird with the belief that I seem to see a squirrel. Clearly, the overall coherence of the new belief system will be about the same as that of the first. This is because coherence is entirely a function of relations among beliefs, and those relations are about the same in the two systems. But it seems wrong that the new belief about the squirrel is as well justified as the old belief about the bird, for my sensory experience is still such that I seem to see a bird, and do not seem to see a squirrel. Again, coherence cannot be the only thing that contributes to epistemic justification.

However, there is an equally daunting problem for pure foundationalism, although the way to see it is less direct. Consider how foundationalism might account for my knowledge that there is a bird outside the window. Since the knowledge in question is perceptual, it is plausible to say that it is grounded in sensory experience. Specifically, it is plausible to say that my belief that there is a bird outside the window is epistemically justified because it is grounded in a visual experience of a particular phenomenal quality. What is more, this explains the difference in epistemic status between my belief about the bird and the belief about the squirrel above. In the latter case, there is no grounding in sensory experience of a relevant sort. But here a problem lurks. Consider the foundationalist epistemic principle invoked above, that is, that a particular sort of sensory experience, with a particular phenomenal quality, justifies the belief that there is a bird outside the window. Is this to be understood as a fundamental principle about epistemic justification, or is it to be understood as an instance of some more general principle? If we say the former, then there would seem to be an infinite number of such principles, with no hope for unity among them. In effect, we would be committed to saying that such principles, in all their number and variety, merely state brute facts about epistemic justification. This is hardly a satisfying position. The more attractive view is that such principles are derived. But then there is more work to be done. Something more fundamental about epistemic justification remains to be explained.

This is where the notion of an intellectual virtue is useful, Sosa argues. Virtues in general are excellences of some kind; more specifically, they are innate or acquired dispositions to achieve some end. Intellectual virtues, Sosa argues, will be dispositions to achieve the intellectual ends of grasping truths and avoiding falsehoods. This notion of an intellectual virtue can be used to give a general account of epistemic justification as follows:

> A belief $B(p)$ is epistemically justified for a person S (that is, justified in the sense required for knowledge) if and only if $B(p)$ is produced by one or more intellectual virtues of S.

This account of justification, Sosa argues, allows us to explain the unifying ground of the foundationalist's epistemic principles regarding perceptual beliefs. Specifically, such principles describe various intellectually virtuous dispositions. Thus human beings are gifted with perceptual powers or abilities; that is, dispositions to reliably form beliefs about the environment on the basis of sensory inputs of various modalities. Such abilities are relative to circumstances and environment, but they are abilities nonetheless. The foundationalist's epistemic principles relating perceptual beliefs to their experiential grounds can now be understood as describing or explicating these various abilities.

And the payoff does not end there. For it is possible to give similar accounts of other sources of justification traditionally recognized by foundationalism. Because they are reliable, such faculties as memory, introspection and logical intuition count as intellectual virtues, and therefore give rise to epistemic justification for their respective products. In a similar fashion, various kinds of deductive and inductive reasoning reliably take one from true belief to further true belief, and hence count as virtues in their own right. By defining epistemic justification in terms of intellectual virtue, Sosa argues, we get a unified account of all the sources of justification traditionally recognized by foundationalism.

Once the foundationalist makes this move, however, pure foundationalism becomes untenable. We said that perception, memory and the like are sources

of epistemic justification because they are intellectual virtues. But now coherence has an equal claim to be an intellectual virtue, and hence an equal claim to be a source of epistemic justification. The intellectual virtues were characterized as cognitive abilities or powers; as dispositions that reliably give rise to true belief under relevant circumstances and in a relevant environment. We may now think of coherence—or more exactly, coherence-seeking reason—as just such a power. In our world, in normal circumstances, coherence-seeking reason is also a reliable source of true belief and hence a source of epistemic justification.

Finally, Sosa argues, we are now in a position to recognize two kinds of knowledge. First, there is "animal knowledge," enjoyed by any being whose true beliefs are the products of intellectual virtue. But second, there is "reflective knowledge," which further requires a coherent perspective on one's beliefs and their source in intellectual virtue. We may also label the latter kind of knowledge "human knowledge," recognizing that the relevant sort of reflective coherence is a distinctively human virtue. More exactly,

S has animal knowledge regarding p only if
1. p is true, and
2. S's belief $B(p)$ is produced by one or more intellectual virtues of S.

S has reflective knowledge regarding p only if

1. p is true,
2. S's belief $B(p)$ is produced by one or more intellectual virtues of S, and
3. S has a true perspective on $B(p)$ as being produced by one or more intellectual virtues, where such perspective is itself produced by an intellectual virtue of S.

b. Reliabilism
Let us define generic reliabilism as follows.

> A belief $B(p)$ is epistemically justified for S if and only if $B(p)$ is the outcome of a sufficiently reliable cognitive process, that is, a process that is sufficiently truth-conducive.

Generic reliabilism is a powerful view. For one, it accounts for a wide range of our pre-theoretical intuitions regarding which beliefs have epistemic justification. Thus reliabilism explains why beliefs caused by perception, memory, introspection, logical intuition, and sound reasoning are epistemically justified, and it explains why beliefs caused by hallucination, wishful thinking, hasty generalization, and other unreliable processes are not. The view also provides a powerful resource against well-known skeptical arguments. For example, a variety of skeptical arguments trade on the assumption that our cognitive faculties must be vindicated as reliable in order to count as sources of epistemic justification. Because it seems impossible to provide such vindication in a noncircular way, a broad skeptical conclusion threatens. Generic reliabilism cuts off this kind of skeptical reasoning at its roots, with the idea that epistemic justification requires *de facto* reliability rather than vindicated reliability: The difference between knowledge and mere opinion is that the former is grounded in cognitive processes that are in fact reliable in this world.

The view is powerful, but subject to a variety of problems. One of these is that reliability seems insufficient for epistemic justification. To see why, consider the following case. Suppose that *S* suffers from a rare sort of brain lesion, one effect of which is to cause the victim to believe that he has a brain lesion. However, *S* has no evidence that he has such a condition, and even has evidence against it. We can imagine, for example, that he has just been given a clean bill of health by competent neurologists. It seems clear that *S*'s belief that he has a brain lesion is unjustified, although (by hypothesis) it has been caused by a highly reliable cognitive process.

The foregoing case seems to show that reliability is not sufficient for epistemic justification. A second case seems to show that reliability is not necessary for epistemic justification. Consider again Descartes' victim of an evil demon. We said that, by hypothesis, the victim's belief system is as coherent as our own. We may now add that the victim bases her beliefs on her experience as we do, and reasons to new beliefs as we do. Clearly, the victim's beliefs cannot amount to knowledge, because she is the victim of massive deception. But still, it seems wrong to say that her beliefs are not justified at all. Let us follow Sosa and call this "the new evil demon problem" for reliabilism. According to simple reliabilism, epistemic justification is entirely a matter of reliability. But the demon victim's beliefs are not reliably formed. The problem for reliabilism is to explain why the victim's beliefs are nevertheless justified.

Sosa argues that both of the above problems can be solved by invoking the notion of an intellectual virtue. Consider the case of the epistemically serendipitous brain lesion. What the case shows is that not all reliable cognitive processes give rise to epistemic justification. On the contrary, the reliabilist must place some kind of restriction on the kind of processes that do so. Sosa's suggestion is that the relevant processes are those which are grounded in the knower's intellectual virtues; that is, her cognitive abilities or powers. Because the belief about the brain lesion does not arise in this way, making this move allows the reliabilist to deny that the belief is epistemically justified.

Now consider the new evil demon problem. Clearly the beliefs of the demon victim are not reliably formed, and therefore lack something important for knowledge. But notice that there are two ways that a belief can fail by way of reliability. One way is that something goes wrong "from the skin inward." For example, the subject might fail to respond appropriately to her sensory experience, or might fail to reason appropriately from her beliefs. Another way to go wrong, however, is "from the skin outward." Perhaps there is no flaw to be found downstream from experience and belief, but one's cognitive faculties are simply not fitted for one's environment. It is this second way that the demon victim fails. Internally speaking, she is in as good working order as we are. Externally speaking, however, her epistemic condition is a disaster. But then there is a straightforward sense in which even the victim's beliefs are internally justified, Sosa argues. Namely, they are beliefs that result from intellectual virtues.

We saw earlier that Sosa endorses the following account of epistemic justification.

> A belief *B(p)* is epistemically justified for a person *S* if and only if *B(p)* is produced by one or more intellectual virtues of *S*.

According to Sosa, we need only add that whether a cognitive faculty counts as a virtue is relative to an environment. The victim's perception and reasoning powers are not reliable in her demon environment, and hence are not virtues relative to her world. But those same faculties are reliable, and therefore do count as virtues, relative to the actual world. Accordingly, we have a sense in which the demon victim's beliefs are internally justified although not reliably formed. In fact, Sosa argues, they are internally justified in every respect relevant for animal knowledge.

Finally, it is possible to define a further kind of internal justification associated with reflective knowledge. Remember that reflective knowledge requires a perspective on one's beliefs and their sources in intellectual virtue. The victim of a deceiving demon might also enjoy such a perspective, together with the broad coherence that this entails. This perspective and coherence provides the basis for a further kind of internal justification, Sosa argues.

2. Moral Models of Intellectual Virtue

According to Sosa, an intellectual virtue is a reliable cognitive ability or power. Coherence-seeking reason is thus an intellectual virtue if reliable, but so are perception, memory, and introspection. Other philosophers have argued against this characterization of the intellectual virtues, however. For example, James Montmarquet's account differs from Sosa's in at least three major respects.

First, cognitive powers such as perception and reason do not count as intellectual virtues at all according to Montmarquet. Rather, on his view the virtues are conceived as personality traits, or qualities of character, such as intellectual courage and intellectual carefulness. In this way the intellectual virtues are analogous to the moral virtues, such as moral temperance and moral courage.

Second, Montmarquet argues that it is a mistake to characterize the intellectual virtues as reliable, or truth-conducive. This is because we can conceive of possible worlds, such as Descartes' demon world, where the beliefs of intellectually virtuous persons are almost entirely false. But traits such as intellectual courage and intellectual carefulness would remain virtues even in such a world, Montmarquet argues. Likewise, we can conceive of worlds where intellectual laziness and carelessness reliably produce true beliefs. But again, traits like laziness and carelessness would remain vices even in such worlds. Therefore, Montmarquet concludes, the intellectual virtues cannot be defined in terms of their reliability. Montmar-

quet's alternative is to define the virtues in terms of a desire for truth. According to this model, the intellectual virtues are those personality traits that a person who desires the truth would want to have.

Finally, on Montmarquet's view the exercise and nonexercise of the intellectual virtues are under our control, and are therefore appropriate objects of praise and blame. When one faces a truck approaching at high speed, one cannot help but perceive accordingly. However, one can control whether one takes a new idea seriously, or considers a line of argument carefully. Hence we have a third way in which Montmarquet's account of the intellectual virtues departs from Sosa's.

It is clear that Montmarquet's account of the intellectual virtues has affinities with Aristotle's account of the moral virtues. Hence Montmarquet thinks of the intellectual virtues as personality traits or qualities; he emphasizes the importance of proper motivation, and he holds that the exercise of the virtues is under our control. A philosopher who follows Aristotle's model of the moral virtues even more closely is Linda Zagzebski. In fact, Zagzebski criticizes Aristotle for maintaining a strong distinction between the intellectual and moral virtues, arguing that the former are best understood as a subset of the latter.

According to Zagzebski, all virtues are acquired traits of character that involve both a motivational component and a reliable success component. Hence, all moral virtues involve a general motivation to achieve the good, and are reliably successful in doing so. All intellectual virtues involve a general motivation to achieve true belief, and are reliably successful in doing so. But since the true is a component of the good, Zagzebski argues, intellectual virtues can be understood as a subset of the moral virtues. In addition to their general motivation and reliability, each virtue can be defined in terms of its specific or characteristic motivational structure. For example, moral courage is the virtue according to which a person is motivated to risk danger when something of value is at stake, and is reliably successful at doing so. Benevolence is the virtue according to which a person is motivated to bring about the well-being of others, and is reliably successful at doing so. Likewise, intellectual courage is the virtue according to which a person is motivated to be persevering in her own ideas, and is reliably successful at doing so.

One advantage of understanding the intellectual virtues this way, Zagzebski argues, is that it allows the following account of knowledge. First, Zagzebski defines an "act of intellectual virtue."

> An act of intellectual virtue A is an act that arises from the motivational component of A, is something a person with virtue A would (probably) do in the circumstances, is successful in achieving the end of the A motivation, and is such that the agent acquires a true belief through these features of the act.

We may then define knowledge as follows:

   S has knowledge regarding p if and only if

1. p is true, and
2. S's true belief $B(p)$ arises out of acts of intellectual virtue.

Since the truth condition is redundant in the above definition, we may say alternatively:

> S has knowledge regarding p if and only if S's believing p arises out of acts of intellectual virtue.

Even more so than Montmarquet, Zagzebski adopts Aristotle's account of the moral virtues as her model for understanding the intellectual virtues. Thus on her account (a) the intellectual virtues are understood as acquired traits of character, (b) their acquisition is partly under our control, (c) both their possession and exercise are appropriate objects of moral praise, and (d) both their lack and nonexercise can be appropriate objects of moral blame. It is noteworthy that Zagzebski's account departs from Sosa's on all of these points. Thus for Sosa the intellectual virtues are cognitive abilities rather than character traits; they need not be acquired, and their acquisition and use need not be under one's control. On Sosa's account, the possession and exercise of the intellectual virtues are grounds for praise, but this need not be praise of a moral sort. Hence we praise people for their keen perception and sound reasoning, but this is more like praise for an athlete's prowess than like praise for a hero's courage.

On the face of things, therefore, there would seem to be a significant disagreement over the nature of the intellectual virtues. But at this point it might be suggested that the issue is merely terminological. What Zagzebski means by a virtue is something close to what Aristotle means by a moral vir-

tue, and therefore natural cognitive powers such as perception and memory do not count as virtues on her meaning of the term. Sosa has adopted a different sense of the term, however, according to which anything that has a function has virtues. In this sense, a virtue is a characteristic excellence of some sort, and reliable perception and reliable memory qualify as intellectual excellences. But to see this as a terminological dispute obscures a substantive one. This comes out if we recall that both Sosa and Zagzebski offer accounts of knowledge in terms of their respective notions of intellectual virtue. The substantive question is now this: Which account of the intellectual virtues better serves this purpose? Sosa also invokes the intellectual virtues to address the dispute between foundationalism and coherentism over the structure of knowledge. Here we may ask again: Which notion of the intellectual virtues is best suited for this purpose?

Once the question regarding the nature of the intellectual virtues is framed this way, however, it seems clear that Zagzebski's account is too strong. Consider first the idea that knowledge arises out of acts of intellectual virtue. On Zagzebski's account, this means that knowledge must manifest dispositions that both (a) involve a certain motivational structure and (b) involve relevant kinds of voluntary control. But neither of these requirements seems necessary for knowledge.

Consider a case of simple perceptual knowledge: You are crossing the street in good light, you look to your left, and you see that a large truck is moving quickly toward you. It would seem that you know that there is a truck moving toward you independently of any control, either over the ability to perceive such things in general, or over this particular exercise of that ability. Neither is it required that one have a motivation to be open-minded, careful, or the like. On the contrary, it would seem that you know that there is a truck coming toward you even if you are motivated *not* to be open-minded, careful, or the like. . . .

It seems clear that an account of the intellectual virtues modeled on Aristotle's account of the moral virtues is apt for addressing a variety of epistemological concerns. It is a mistake, however, to generalize from such concerns to an account of knowledge per se. As we have seen, the moral model is ill suited for that purpose, since it will result in an account of knowledge that is too strong.

3. Wisdom and Understanding

Perhaps one place where the moral model is useful is in accounts of "higher grade" epistemic achievements such as wisdom and understanding. According to Zagzebski, wisdom has clear moral dimensions. Thus wisdom unifies the knowledge of the wise person, but also her desires and values. This is why it is impossible for wisdom to be misused, she argues, and why it is incoherent to talk of a person that is wise but immoral. Also, wisdom is achieved only through extensive life experience, and hence takes time to acquire. Therefore, Zagzebski argues, wisdom is best understood on a moral model of the intellectual virtues, either because it is such a virtue itself, or because it is the product of such virtues. This seems plausible, especially if we mean wisdom to include practical wisdom, or wisdom regarding how one ought to live. But again, it would be a mistake to generalize from an account of wisdom to an account of knowledge per se. I suggest that Zagzebski's account of wisdom is plausible precisely because we think that wisdom is harder to achieve than knowledge. The stronger conditions implied by Zagzebski's account therefore seem more appropriate here than in a general account of knowledge.

I have argued that Zagzebski's position benefits from a distinction between knowledge and wisdom. By maintaining this distinction, it is possible to resist putting conditions on knowledge per se that are appropriate only for knowledge of a higher grade. In a similar fashion, Sosa's position benefits from a distinction between knowledge and understanding. To see how this is so, it is useful to notice a tension in Sosa's thinking.

Recall that Sosa makes a distinction between animal knowledge and reflective knowledge. One has animal knowledge as long as one's true belief has its source in a reliable cognitive faculty. One has reflective knowledge only if one's first-order belief also fits into a coherent perspective, which perspective must include a belief that one's first-order belief has its reliable source. Sometimes Sosa writes as if animal knowledge is real knowledge, while reflective knowledge amounts to a higher achievement still. In other

places Sosa's evaluation of animal knowledge is less enthusiastic. Hence he calls it "servomechanic" and "mere animal" knowledge, and in one place suggests that the label is "metaphorical." Either way, however, it is clear that Sosa thinks animal knowledge is of a lesser kind than reflective knowledge.

The tension is now this: As we saw above, Sosa holds that the virtue of coherence is its reliability. Like perception, memory and introspection, reason-seeking coherence makes its contribution to epistemic justification and knowledge because it is reliable. But then why should reflective knowledge be of a higher kind than animal knowledge? If the difference between animal and reflective knowledge is a coherent perspective, and if the value of coherence is its reliability, it would seem that the distinction between animal knowledge and reflective knowledge is at most a difference in degree rather than in kind. Moreover, we have no good reason to think that a person with reflective knowledge will always be more reliable than a person with only animal knowledge; that is, it seems clearly possible that the cognitive virtues of a person without an epistemic perspective could be more reliable than the cognitive virtues of a person with it. But then reflective knowledge is not necessarily higher than animal knowledge, even in degree.

Here is a different problem for Sosa's view. Suppose we take what seems to be Sosa's considered position, which is that human knowledge is reflective knowledge. On this view a broad skepticism threatens, because it seems clear that in a typical case most people lack the required epistemic perspective; that is, in the typical case most people lack beliefs about the source of their first-order belief, and whether that source is reliable. For example, in most cases where I have a belief that there is a bird outside my window, I do not have further beliefs about the source of that belief, or about the reliability of that source. Sosa's response to this kind of objection is to stress that the required epistemic perspective need only be implicit. Thus he writes,

> [A person judging shapes on a screen] is justified well enough in taking it that, in his circumstances, what looks to have a certain shape does have that shape. He implicitly trusts that connection, as is revealed by his inferential 'habit' of moving from experiencing the look to believing the seen object to have the

corresponding shape. So the 'belief' involved is a highly implicit belief, manifested chiefly in such a 'habit'. . . .

But it is important to maintain a distinction between (a) implicit beliefs and (b) habits or dispositions for forming beliefs. One reason we need the distinction is because often there are such dispositions where there are no such beliefs. For example, simple pattern recognition in perception involves dispositions of amazing subtlety and complexity—that is, dispositions to go from perceptual cues to beliefs about external stimuli. But it is highly implausible to attribute *beliefs* about such perceptual cues, and about their connections to external stimuli, to perceivers. It is implausible to attribute such beliefs to adult perceivers, not to mention small children and animals. But all perceivers, small children and animals included, have the relevant dispositions to form perceptual beliefs.

Moreover, there is a second reason for Sosa to insist on the distinction between implicit beliefs and dispositions for forming beliefs. For without it, his distinction between animal knowledge and reflective knowledge collapses. Recall that even animal knowledge requires a source in reliable cognitive abilities or powers; that is, it requires a source in intellectual virtues. But the virtues required for animal knowledge just are dispositions for forming beliefs. If we identify such dispositions with a perspective on one's beliefs, then there will be no difference between animal and reflective knowledge. Therefore, Sosa's position seems to result in skepticism regarding reflective knowledge. In order to maintain a distinction between animal and reflective knowledge at all, we must understand one's epistemic perspective to involve beliefs about one's first-order beliefs and their sources, and not just dispositions for forming first-order beliefs. But then it is implausible that human beings typically have an epistemic perspective, and therefore implausible that human beings typically have reflective knowledge.

In the preceding paragraphs we have identified two problems for Sosa's position. First, Sosa's distinction between animal and reflective knowledge seems unmotivated, given his claim that the virtue of coherence is its reliability. If that claim is correct, then there is no good reason for thinking that reflective knowledge is of a higher kind than animal knowledge, or that the two belong to significantly different kinds at all. Second, if we do maintain the distinction, then the result seems to be a broad skepticism with respect to reflective (or human) knowledge. This is because most human beings fail to have the required epistemic perspective. Both these problems can be solved, however, if we recognize two plausible claims: (a) that there is a distinction in kind between knowledge and understanding and (b) that coherence has a distinctive value through its contribution to understanding. The first problem is solved because this allows us to make a principled distinction between nonreflective knowledge and reflective knowledge: In virtue of its greater coherence through an epistemic perspective, reflective knowledge involves a kind of understanding that nonreflective knowledge lacks. The second problem is solved because this allows us to drop the requirement of an epistemic perspective for human knowledge: Nonreflective knowledge is real knowledge, and even real human knowledge. Reflective knowledge is of a higher grade and of a rarer sort, involving a special kind of understanding. On this view we still get a skeptical conclusion regarding reflective knowledge, because it will still be the case that few human beings have the kind of perspective that reflective knowledge requires. But the sting is taken out of this conclusion if we recognize that it is a special kind of understanding, rather than knowledge per se, that people so often lack. We never thought that such understanding was wide-spread in the first place, and so a skeptical conclusion in this regard is just what we would expect.

In effect, I am making the same diagnosis of Sosa's account of knowledge as I did of Zagzebski's, and I am suggesting the same solution. In both cases I have argued that the requirements they put on knowledge are too strong, and that therefore their accounts have unattractive skeptical results. And in both cases the solution is to distinguish between knowledge per se and some epistemic value of a higher grade. This allows us to weaken the requirements on knowledge so as to make it generally attainable, and at the same time recognize the intellectual virtues that Zagzebski and Sosa want to emphasize.

However, one question remains: Why should the special kind of understanding involved in an epistemic perspective constitute a distinctive epistemic value? Granting that understanding is a distinctive epistemic value over and above knowledge per se, and granting that coherence contributes to that distinctive value, why should the particular sort of understanding involved in an epistemic perspective constitute a distinctive epistemic value all of its own? Consider that understanding has traditionally been understood in terms of knowledge of causes. Thus understanding involves knowledge of why things exist, how they work, and how they are related. This is why it is plausible that coherence contributes to understanding: coherence in general, and especially explanatory coherence, contributes to a grasp of exactly these matters. But then why should reflective knowledge, or understanding regarding the sources of one's first-order beliefs, be considered a distinctive kind of understanding, with its own distinctive epistemic value? Why should it be different from understanding about how humans came to exist, or what causes plants to grow, or how the mind is related to the body? Obviously, reflective knowledge is distinctive by virtue of its subject matter—it concerns one's first-order beliefs and their source in reliable cognitive faculties. But the relevant question concerns why reflective knowledge is distinctive *epistemically:* Why should reflective knowledge be of a different *epistemic* kind than coherent understanding regarding other things?

It seems to me that there is no good answer to this question. On the contrary, the above considerations show that reflective knowledge is not a distinctive epistemic kind at all. The important distinction is not between animal knowledge and reflective knowledge, but between knowledge per se and understanding per se.

PART TWO. A VIRTUE ACCOUNT OF KNOWLEDGE

In Part One, we saw that different virtue theorists defend different, seemingly incompatible accounts of the intellectual virtues. In this context I argued for an irenic conclusion: that different kinds of intellectual virtue or excellence are best suited to address different issues in epistemology. In particular, I argued (1) that a minimalist notion of the intellectual virtues, in which the virtues are conceived as reliable cognitive abilities or powers, is best suited for an account of knowledge;

and (2) that stronger notions of the intellectual virtues are best suited to address a range of other issues.

In Part Two, I will pursue the idea that a minimalist, reliabilist notion of the intellectual virtues is useful for constructing an account of knowledge. I will do so by addressing three important issues for a theory of knowledge: the challenge of skepticism, Gettier problems, and the problem of explaining why knowledge is more valuable than mere true belief. By defining knowledge in terms of the intellectual virtues so conceived, it is possible to adequately address all three of these issues. But first it will be helpful to make some general comments about virtue, epistemic justification, and knowledge.

1. Agent Reliabilism

Recall generic reliabilism and the conditions it lays down for epistemic justification:

> A belief $B(p)$ is epistemically justified if and only if $B(p)$ is the outcome of a sufficiently reliable cognitive process.

We saw that these conditions are too weak, as is demonstrated by the case of the epistemically serendipitous brain lesion. The lesson to be learned from that case is that not all reliable cognitive processes give rise to epistemic justification and knowledge. Such considerations gave rise to an account in terms of intellectual virtue.

> A belief $B(p)$ is epistemically justified for a person S if and only if $B(p)$ is produced by one or more intellectual virtues of S; that is, by one or more of S's cognitive abilities or powers.

Here the key is to make the cognitive agent the seat of reliability, thereby moving from generic reliabilism to agent reliabilism. By restricting the relevant processes to those grounded in the knower's abilities or powers, we effectively disallow strange and fleeting processes, including brain lesions and the like, from giving rise to epistemic justification.

Recall also that this way of thinking allows an account of internal justification, or the kind of justification enjoyed even by the victim of Descartes' evil demon. Thus Sosa suggested:

> A belief $B(p)$ is epistemically justified for S relative to environment E if and only if $B(p)$ is produced by one

or more cognitive dispositions that are intellectual virtues in E.

Notice that on this account the beliefs of the demon's victim are as justified as ours, so long as we relativize to the same environment. This kind of justification is "internal" because it is entirely a function of factors "from the skin inward," or better, "from the mind inward." This is insured by relativizing justification to external environments.

Finally, it is possible to define a sense of subjective justification, or a sense in which a belief is justified from the knower's own point of view. We have already seen that knowledge must be reliably formed. Many have had the intuition that, in addition to this, a knower must be aware that her belief is reliably formed. One way to cash out such awareness is to require an epistemic perspective on the relevant belief, but I have argued that an account in these terms is too strong for a requirement on knowledge. Nevertheless, a kind of awareness of reliability is manifested in the very dispositions that constitute one's cognitive abilities: The fact that a person interprets experience one way rather than another, or draws one inference rather than another, manifests an awareness of sorts that some relevant evidence is a reliable indication of some relevant truth. Or at least this is so if the person is trying to form her beliefs accurately in the first place—if the person is in the normal mode of trying to believe what is true, as opposed to what is convenient, or comforting, or politically correct. We may use these considerations to define a sense of subjective justification that is not too strong to be a requirement on knowledge.

A belief $B(p)$ is subjectively justified for S if and only if $B(p)$ is produced by cognitive dispositions that S manifests when S is motivated to believe what is true.

In cases of knowledge such dispositions will also be virtues, since they will be objectively reliable in addition to being well motivated. But even in cases where S is not reliable, she may nevertheless have justified beliefs in this sense, since her believing may nevertheless manifest well-motivated dispositions.

Because the notion of intellectual virtue employed in the above definitions is relatively weak, the account of epistemic justification and knowledge that results is relatively weak as well: there is no strong motivation condition, no control condition, and

no condition requiring an epistemic perspective. In the sections that follow, I will argue that this minimalist approach is just what is needed in a theory of knowledge.

2. Skepticism

A number of skeptical arguments have been prominent in the theory of knowledge. These arguments constitute philosophical problems in the following sense: They begin from premises that seem eminently plausible, and proceed by seemingly valid reasoning to conclusions that are outrageously implausible. On this view, skeptical arguments present a theoretical problem rather than a practical problem. The task for a theory of knowledge is to identify some mistake in the skeptical argument and to replace it with something more adequate. Two of the most difficult of these problems come from Hume. The first concerns our knowledge of unobserved matters of fact. The second concerns our knowledge of empirical facts in general.

a. Skepticism about Unobserved Matters of Fact

According to Hume's first argument, we can know nothing about the world that we do not currently observe. For example, I can't know that my next sip of coffee will taste like coffee, or even that my cat will not sprout wings and fly away.

Here is how Hume's reasoning goes. First, he points out that everything we believe about unobserved matters of fact depends on previous observations. Thus I believe that coffee tastes a certain way because I have tasted coffee before, and I believe that cats do not have wings or fly because I have had previous dealings with cats. But such beliefs depend on an additional assumption as well, Hume argues. For my observations about coffee and cats are relevant only if I assume that things such as coffee and cats act in regular ways. In other words, I must assume that my previous observations of things give some indication of their future behavior. But how is that assumption to be justified? Hume argues that it cannot be, and that therefore all our beliefs about unobserved matters of fact are themselves unjustified.

Well, why can't the assumption be justified? Hume's answer is straightforward: The assumption is itself a belief about unobserved matters of fact, and so any attempt to justify it must fall into circular reasoning. Consider that I can justify my assumption that things act in regular ways only by relying on previous observations—I have observed that they do. But these observations of past regular behavior are relevant for establishing additional regular behavior only if I assume the very thing I am trying to establish— that things behave in regular ways!

Hume's argument can be put more formally as follows.

1. All our beliefs about unobserved matters of fact depend for their evidence on (a) previous observations and (b) the assumption (Al) that observed cases are a reliable indication of unobserved cases; that things behave (and will continue to behave) in regular ways.
2. But (Al) is itself a belief about an unobserved matter of fact.
3. Therefore, assumption (Al) depends for its evidence on (Al).(1,2)
4. Circular reasoning does not give rise to justification.
5. Therefore, (Al) is unjustified. (3,4)
6. Therefore, all our beliefs about unobserved matters of fact depend for their evidence on an unjustified assumption. (1,5)
7. Beliefs that depend for their evidence on an unjustified assumption are themselves unjustified
8. Therefore, none of our beliefs about unobserved matters of fact are justified.(6,7)

b. Skepticism about the World

Here is another argument from Hume—this one concerning all our knowledge of matters of fact about the world, whether observed or unobserved. The argument belongs to a family of skeptical arguments, all of which claim (a) that our knowledge of the world depends on how things appear through the senses and (b) that there is no good inference from the way things appear to the way things actually are. Here is the argument put formally

1. All of our beliefs about the world depend, at least in part, on the way things appear to us via the senses.
2. The nature of this dependency is broadly evidential—the fact that things in the world

appear a certain way is often our reason for thinking that they are that way.
3. Therefore, if I am to know how things in the world actually are, it must be via some good inference from how things appear to me.(1,2)
4. But there is no good inference from the way things appear to the way things are.
5. Therefore, I cannot know how things in the world actually are.(3,4)

This argument is a powerful one. Premises (1) and (2) say only that our beliefs about the world depend for their evidence on the way things appear to us. That seems undeniable. Premise (4) is the only remaining independent premise, and there are excellent reasons for accepting it. One reason mirrors the first argument from Hume above. Specifically, our beliefs about the world depend for their evidence on (a) sensory appearances but also (b) an assumption (A2) that the way things appear is a reliable indication of the way things are. But assumption (A2) is itself a belief about the world, and so any attempt to justify it would depend on that very assumption. Hence there can be no noncircular inference from sensory appearances to reality.

Here is a second reason in favor of premise (4). Even if a noncircular inference from appearances to reality were possible in principle, no such inference would be psychologically plausible. In other words, it would not be plausible that such an inference is actually used when we form beliefs about objects on the basis of sensory appearances. This is because an inference takes us from belief to belief, but we do not typically have beliefs about appearances. In the typical case, we form our beliefs about objects in the world without forming beliefs about appearances at all, much less inferring beliefs about the world from beliefs about appearances.

c. Where the Skeptical Arguments Go Wrong

Notice that the two skeptical arguments from Hume cannot be dismissed on the usual grounds. For example, neither argument demands certainty for knowledge, nor does either depend on a controversial metaphysics. On the contrary, the various premises of Hume's arguments are consistent with innocent assumptions about the standards for knowledge, the ontology of appearances, the relationship between mind and world, and the like. The real problem is that circular reasoning cannot give rise to knowledge, and our reasoning about things in the world, whether observed or unobserved, seems to be circular. Once again, the task for a theory of knowledge is to identify the mistake in the arguments. *Something* in the arguments is not innocent, and an adequate theory of knowledge should explain what that it is.

Agent reliabilism provides such explanations. Consider first Hume's argument concerning our beliefs about unobserved matters of fact. That argument begins with the claim that all such beliefs depend on an assumption: that observed cases are a reliable indication of unobserved cases. Another way to put Hume's claim is as follows: that our evidence for unobserved matters of fact must always contain some such assumption among its premises. But why does Hume think that? I suggest that Hume's claim is based on a widespread but mistaken assumption about knowledge and evidence. Namely, that there must be a necessary relation between an item of knowledge and the evidence that grounds it. In cases of deductive knowledge the relation will be logical. But even inductive knowledge, Hume thinks, must involve some quasi-logical relation. That is why our evidence for beliefs about unobserved matters of fact needs a premise about observed cases being a reliable indication of unobserved cases: It is only through some such premise that a quasi-logical relation, this time a probability relation, is established.

Agent reliabilism allows a straightforward diagnosis of this line of reasoning: It is a mistake to think that there must be a necessary relation between evidence and knowledge. On the contrary, knowledge requires evidence that is *in fact* reliable, as opposed to evidence that is necessarily reliable. More exactly, knowledge requires that the knower be in fact reliable in the way that she forms her beliefs on the basis of her evidence. But if that is right, then Hume is wrong to think that our beliefs about unobserved matters of fact depend on assumption (A1) for their evidence.

Agent reliabilism also explains where Hume's second skeptical argument goes wrong. That argument begins with the claim that beliefs about the world depend on the way things appear for their evidence, and concludes from this that knowledge of the world requires a good inference from appearances to reality.

But this line of reasoning depends on an implicit assumption: that sensory appearances ground beliefs about the world by means of an *inference*. This assumption is mistaken, however, and agent reliabilism explains why.

Let us define an inference as a movement from premise-beliefs to a conclusion-belief on the basis of their contents and according to a general rule. According to agent reliabilism, this is one way that a belief can be evidentially grounded, since using a good inference-rule is one way that a belief can be reliably formed. But that is not the only way that an evidential relation can be manifested—not every movement in thought constitutes an inference from premise-beliefs to a conclusion-belief according to a general rule. For example, the movement from sensory appearances to belief does not. When one forms a perceptual belief about the world, it is not the case that one first forms a belief about how things appear, and then infers that the way things appear is probably the way things are. Rather, the process is more direct than that. In a typical case of perception, one reliably moves from appearances to reality without so much as a thought about the appearances themselves, and without doing anything like following a rule of inference. Put simply, our perceptual powers are not reasoning powers.

It might be objected that the present point is merely a verbal one—I have rejected the assumption that the evidence of sensory appearances is inferential, but only by employing a restricted sense of "inference." But this objection misses a more substantive point. Namely, that not all movements in thought can be evaluated by the criteria governing inferences in the narrower sense defined above. In particular, to ask whether there is a good inference from sensory appearances to reality misunderstands the way that sensory appearances function as evidence for our beliefs about the world. This is the mistake that Hume's second argument makes, and agent reliabilism explains why it is a mistake.

4. Gettier Problems

According to agent reliabilism, knowledge is true belief produced by the intellectual virtues of the believer, where intellectual virtues are understood to be reliable cognitive abilities or powers. This account of knowledge explains a wide range of our pre-theoretical intuitions regarding which cases do and do not count as knowledge. For example, the account continues to have the advantages of reliabilism: It explains why beliefs resulting from perception, memory, introspection, logical intuition, and sound reasoning typically count as knowledge, and it explains why beliefs resulting from hallucination, wishful thinking, and other unreliable processes do not. Moreover, the account handles cases that have been deemed problematic for generic reliabilism, such as the case of the serendipitous brain lesion, and the case described in the new evil demon problem. Nevertheless, more needs to be said in light of certain other cases. Specifically, in this section I will argue that agent reliabilism has the resources to address a wide range of "Gettier problems."

In 1963, Edmund Gettier wrote a short paper purporting to show that knowledge is not true justified belief. His argument proceeded by way of two counterexamples, each of which seemed to show that a belief could be both true and justified and yet not amount to knowledge. Here are two examples that are in the spirit of Gettier's originals.

Case 1.   On the basis of excellent reasons, *S* believes that her co-worker, Mr. Nogot, owns a Ford: Nogot testifies that he owns a Ford, and this is confirmed by *S*'s own relevant observations. From this *S* infers that someone in her office owns a Ford. As it turns out, *S*'s evidence is misleading and Nogot does not in fact own a Ford. However, another person in *S*'s office, Mr. Havit, does own a Ford, although *S* has no reason for believing this.

Case 2.   Walking down the road, *S* seems to see a sheep in the field and on this basis believes that there is a sheep in the field. However, due to an unusual trick of light, *S* has mistaken a dog for a sheep, and so what she sees is not a sheep at all. Nevertheless, unsuspected by *S*, there is a sheep in another part of the field.

In both of these cases the relevant belief seems justified, at least in senses of justification that empha-

size the internal or the subjective, and in both cases the relevant belief is true. Yet in neither case would we be inclined to judge that the person in question has knowledge.

These examples show that internal and/or subjective justification is not sufficient for knowledge. Put another way, they show that knowledge requires some stronger relation between belief and truth. From the perspective of a virtue theory, there is a natural way to think of this stronger relation, for it is natural to distinguish between (a) achieving some end by luck or accident and (b) achieving the end through the exercise of one's abilities (or virtues). This suggests the following difference between Gettier cases and cases of knowledge. In Gettier cases, *S* believes the truth, but it is only by accident that she does so. In cases of knowledge, however, it is no accident that *S* believes the truth. Rather, in cases of knowledge *S* believes the truth as the result of her own cognitive abilities—her believing the truth can be credited to her, as opposed to dumb luck or blind chance.

This suggestion is on the right track, but more needs to be said. Here is why. I said that the difference between Gettier cases and cases of knowledge is that in the latter, but not the former, it is to *S*'s credit that she believes the truth. Put another way, in cases of knowledge *S* is responsible for believing the truth, because she believes it as the result of her own cognitive abilities. But in the Gettier cases above, *S* does exercise her cognitive abilities, and this is partly why she believes the truth. Hence it is not clear that Gettier cases and cases of knowledge can be distinguished as I have suggested—it is not clear why it is appropriate to credit *S* with true belief in cases of knowledge, and appropriate to deny credit in Gettier cases. Again, more needs to be said.

The first thing to note is that attributions of credit imply attributions of causal responsibility. As I suggested above, to give *S* credit for her true belief is to say that she "is responsible" for her believing the truth—that her believing the truth "is the result" of her own abilities or virtues. This is in fact a general phenomenon. According to Aristotle, actions deserving moral credit "proceed from a firm and unchangeable character." When we give credit for an athletic feat, we imply that it is the result of athletic ability, as opposed to good luck, or cheating, or a hapless opponent. In all such cases, an attribution of credit implies an attribution of causal responsibility for the action in question—it implies that the cause of the action is relevant abilities (or virtues) in the actor.

The second thing to note is that attributions of causal responsibility display an interesting pragmatics. Specifically, when we say that Y occurs because X occurs, or that Y's occurring is due to X's occurring, we mark out X's occurring as a particularly important or salient part of the causal story behind Y's occurring. For example, to say that the fire occurred because of the explosion is not to say that the explosion caused the fire all by itself. Rather, it is to say that the explosion is a particularly important part, perhaps the most important part, of the whole story. Or to change the example: To say that the fire occurred because of S's negligence is not to say that S's negligence caused the fire all by itself. Rather, it is to say that S's negligence is a particularly salient part, perhaps the most salient part, of the set of relevant factors that caused the fire.

What determines salience? Any number of things might, but two kinds of consideration are particularly important for present purposes. First, salience is often determined by what is *abnormal* in the case. For example, we will say that sparks caused the fire if the presence of sparks in the area is not normal. That explanation misfires, however, if we are trying to explain the cause of a fire in a welding shop, where sparks are flying all the time. Second, salience is often determined by our *interests and purposes*. If the thing to be explained is smoke coming from the engine, for example, we will look for the part that needs to be replaced. Here it is perfectly appropriate to say that the cause of the smoke is the malfunctioning carburetor, although clearly a faulty carburetor cannot cause smoke all by itself.

And now the important point is this: Since attributions of credit imply attributions of causal responsibility, the former inherit the pragmatics of the latter. Specifically, to say that S's believing the truth is to her credit is to say that S's cognitive abilities, her intellectual virtues, are an important part of the causal story regarding how S came to believe the truth. It is to say that S's cognitive abilities are a particularly salient part, perhaps the most salient part, of the total set of relevant causal factors.

We may now return to the diagnosis of Gettier problems that was suggested earlier. There I said that in Gettier cases S believes the truth, but it is only by accident that she does so. This was opposed to cases of knowledge, where it is to S's credit that she believes the truth, because she does so as the result of her own cognitive abilities. However, this diagnosis led to the following question: Why is it appropriate to credit S with true belief in cases of knowledge, but not in the two Gettier cases above, given that in all these cases S's abilities are part of the causal story regarding how S came to have a true belief? We now have an answer to that question: In cases of knowledge, but not in Gettier cases, S's abilities are a *salient* part of the causal story regarding how S came to have a true belief. It is plausible, in fact, that our cognitive abilities have a kind of "default" salience, owing to our interests and purposes as information-sharing beings. In Gettier cases, however, this default salience is trumped by something abnormal in the case. For example, someone in the office owns a Ford, but it is not the person S thinks it is. There is a sheep in the field, but it is not in the place that S is looking. In these cases it is only good luck that S ends up with a true belief, which is to say that S's believing the truth cannot be put down to her abilities.

These considerations suggest the following account of knowledge.

S has knowledge regarding p if and only if

1. S's belief $B(p)$ is *subjectively* justified in the following sense: $B(p)$ is produced by cognitive dispositions that S manifests when S is motivated to believe what is true,
2. S's belief $B(p)$ is *objectively* justified in the following sense: $B(p)$ is produced by one or more intellectual virtues of S; that is, by one or more of S's cognitive abilities or powers, and

3. *S* believes the truth regarding *p* *because S* believes *p* out of intellectual virtue. Alternatively: The intellectual virtues that result in *S*'s believing the truth regarding *p* are an important necessary part of the total set of causal factors that give rise to *S*'s believing the truth regarding *p*.

If we stipulate that intellectual virtues involve a motivation to believe the truth, we may collapse the above account as follows.

> *S* has knowledge regarding *p* if and only if *S* believes the truth regarding *p* because *S* believes *p* out of intellectual virtue.

5. The Value Problem

In recent work Linda Zagzebski has called attention to the value problem for knowledge. An adequate account of knowledge, she points out, ought to explain why knowledge is more valuable than mere true belief. The account of knowledge presented above readily suggests an answer to that problem.

Recall Aristotle's distinction between (a) achieving some end by luck or accident and (b) achieving the end through the exercise of one's abilities (or virtues). It is only the latter kind of action, Aristotle argues, that is both intrinsically valuable and constitutive of human flourishing. "Human good," he writes, "turns out to be activity of soul exhibiting excellence." In this discussion Aristotle is clearly concerned with intellectual virtue as well as moral virtue: His position is that the successful exercise of one's intellectual virtues is both intrinsically good and constitutive of human flourishing.

If this is correct then there is a clear difference in value between knowledge and mere true belief. In cases of knowledge, we achieve the truth through the exercise of our own cognitive abilities or powers, which are a kind of intellectual virtue. Moreover, we can extend the point to include other kinds of intellectual virtue as well. It is plausible, for example, that the successful exercise of intellectual courage is also intrinsically good, and also constitutive of the best intellectual life. And of course there is a long tradition that says the same about wisdom and the same about understanding. On the view I am suggesting, there are a plurality of intellectual virtues, and their successful exercise gives rise to a plurality of epistemic goods. The best intellectual life—intellectual flourishing, so to speak—is rich with all of these.

Discussion Questions

1. Greco believes that his analysis of knowledge helps us identify the mistakes in Hume's skeptical arguments concerning our knowledge of matters of fact. How might Greco respond to the following argument? In order to know that *p* one must be able to rule out the possibility that one is deceived by an evil genius. But no one is able to rule out the possibility that one is deceived by an evil genius. Therefore, one is unable to know that *p*.

2. Do you believe that one must be able to rule out the possibility that one is deceived by an evil genius in order to know that *p*?

3. Greco believes that *S* has knowledge regarding *p* if *S* believes the truth regarding *p* because *S* believes *p* out of intellectual virtue. But suppose that *S* would drop his belief that *p* if he was fed a piece of false information regarding the truth-value of *p*. Does *S* really know that *p* before he is led astray? What do you believe Greco would say about this case?

4. Greco believes that knowledge is more valuable than mere true belief. Do you agree? If knowledge (justified true belief) is more valuable than mere true belief, what are the implications regarding our religious beliefs?

For Further Reading

For a general introduction to epistemology see *The Blackwell Guide to Epistemology* (1999) coedited by Greco and Ernest Sosa. For Greco's views concerning skepticism see *Putting Skeptics in Their Place* (2000) by John Greco. For a collection of essays concerning virtue epistemology see *Virtue Epistemology* (2001) edited by Fairweather and Zagzebski. For an excellent survey of the Gettier problem see *Analysis of Knowledge, a Decade of Research* (1983) by Robert K. Shope.

CHAPTER 7

IS OBJECTIVITY POSSIBLE
OR DESIRABLE?

Except perhaps for **pragmatists,** most Western philosophers have assumed that truth and knowledge are **objective** and that claims about the world—that the earth is round, for example—are not, and cannot be, true for me but false for you.

These assumptions have shaped epistemology in two ways. First, if knowledge is objective, it follows that there is a single truth for any particular question about the world. Hence, given a particular question about the world, all investigations and investigators should reach the same result. That is, **Western philosophy** assumes that the subjectivity of an investigator does not influence his or her investigations into the truth—or, more precisely, his or her subjectivity *should* not influence the investigation. Is this possible? Is it possible for our personal beliefs and opinions not to influence our investigations into the truth? Those that defend the possibility of 'objective' knowledge say that it is, so long as investigators partition off their passions and emotions.

This leads to the second way the objectivity assumption has influenced epistemology: the contrast between reason and emotion. Reason is often characterized as the polar opposite of emotion such that while reason leads to knowledge, emotion leads the investigator astray or confuses him or her about what is real and true. In this contrast between reason and emotion, there has been an implicit, and sometimes explicit, assumption in Western philosophy that men are better at discovering truth and knowledge than women, because men are capable of controlling their emotions whereas women supposedly have an almost insurmountable natural disposition to be emotional, and thereby irrational.

Some feminists, of course, have countered that such characterizations of women are inaccurate. More important, feminist philosophers have also critiqued the notion that only purely objective investigations can yield knowledge. In the first reading of this chapter, Alison Jaggar argues that emotion and knowledge are inextricably linked to one another. In the second reading, Lorraine Code continues this critique by challenging the myth that subjectivity plays no role in acquiring knowledge. Among other factors, race, class, and gender have a profound impact on the production of knowledge, according to Code. In fact, the so-called truth invariably serves the narrow interests of society's dominant group.

Catharine MacKinnon also believes that reliance on objectivity alone is a deeply flawed epistemological method. Moreover, this method ultimately works against the interests of women in particular. Thus, she rejects objectivity as an adequate method, but nonetheless believes that women can and have come to know their own true interests. They can do so, argues MacKinnon, through participation in consciousness-raising groups—a method unique to feminism.

Richard Rorty, the author of the chapter's fourth selection, offers a neo-pragmatist perspective on objectivity. Truth, Rorty contends, is not correspondence with the way the world actually is, but is instead 'what is good for us to believe'. Rorty argues that a claim is not true because it properly mirrors the world; rather, a claim is true if believing it works to our favor. He argues that the tradition of objectivity has in fact not produced the results hoped for. Thus, continued allegiance to that tradition would be wishful thinking at best and denial at worst.

The next two selections extend our exploration of objectivity in a new direction by considering the idea of a *standpoint*. Initially, objectivity might be defined as a perspective free from the bias of any observer or a perspective free from any particular person's standpoint, what is sometimes called a 'view from nowhere'. A 'view from nowhere' is defined as the view of *no one* in particular and comes from the title of a book by Thomas Nagel. However, even Nagel believes that a completely objective standpoint, a view from nowhere, would be inadequate.

Is there a standpoint—a view from somewhere—that we ought to occupy when investigating the world and our place in it? Sandra Harding and bell hooks advocate occupying a 'marginal standpoint', that is, a standpoint from the position of persons on the periphery or margins of society. According to Sandra Harding such a standpoint will help reveal hidden cultural assumptions that otherwise would distort our beliefs about the world. Bell hooks writes about her own effort to discover the true meaning of solidarity and resistance with those in the margins.

The chapter's final selection comes from Friedrich Nietzsche, who might be considered the intellectual grandfather of all the chapter's preceding authors. In Western culture it was Nietzsche who first questioned not just the possibility of objectivity but the value thereof. In the chapter's selection by Nietzsche, Nietzsche focuses on the former and illustrates how the attempts of philosophers to be objective are not as objective as they think they are.

34   LOVE AND EMOTION IN FEMINIST EPISTEMOLOGY
Alison Jaggar

Born in Sheffield, England, Alison Jaggar (1942–) has been at the forefront of feminist philosophy and women's studies for the past 20 years. Among her important works and collaborations are *Feminist Frameworks (1978)*, with Paula Rothenberg; *Feminist Politics and Human Nature* (1983); *Gender/Body/Knowledge* (1989), with Susan Bordo; *Living with Contradictions* (1993); and *A Companion to Feminist Philosophy* (1998). Today, Jaggar serves as the director of women's studies at the

SOURCE: Reprinted from "Love and Emotion in Feminist Epistemology" by Alison M. Jaggar, *Inquiry*, 1989, by permission of Scandinavian University Press, Oslo, Norway.

University of Colorado, Boulder, where she teaches courses in both philosophy and women's studies.

The following selection comes from one of Jaggar's best-known articles, *"Love and Emotion in Feminist Epistemology."* In it Jaggar attacks the claim that "trustworthy knowledge" is possible only through "methods that neutralized the values and emotions" of the investigators. Jaggar contends that such an arrangement is incoherent, or naive at best, since emotions, values, and knowledge are intimately interconnected. She argues that emotional reactions to various experiences help shape what we consider valuable, and our values in turn shape our understanding and knowledge of the world. But then again, our current understanding of the world impacts how we view the world and our emotional responses to it. Thus, Jaggar concludes there is no such thing as an objective observer, that is, an observer completely unaffected by emotion. To suppose that knowledge can be achieved only by distancing the investigator from his or her emotions is a mistake since knowledge is, at least in part, a function of our emotions.

Moreover, Jaggar also observes that "the norms and values that predominate tend to serve the interest of the dominant group" and thus in "a capitalist, white supremacist, and male-dominant society, the predominate values will tend to be those that serve the interest of rich white men." This happens both by distancing our emotions from ourselves and by allowing only certain emotions to be felt. Jaggar believes, however, that some individuals are capable of breaking the stranglehold of the dominant ideology and of having emotional responses that do not correspond to the values of society's dominant group—what she calls "outlaw" emotions. These "outlaw" emotions include a woman's response to being called "baby" or "honey" by her *well-intentioned* male boss and the reaction of an adult African American male to being called "boy" by a *well-intentioned* white man. For Jaggar, these outlaw emotions are signposts that may identify injustices in contemporary society; if so, the only question left is whether we will heed them.

Reading Questions

1. What role do the emotions play in the positivist's epistemology?
2. Explain how it is that emotions are socially constructed. What do the emotions that we experience reflect?
3. To what extent is science "value free"?
4. In what way is emotion a necessary component of knowledge?
5. What is problematic about referring to "people"?
6. Why is the cultural stereotype of women as emotional on shaky ground?
7. Why do stereotypes persist?
8. What are "outlaw emotions"? What sort of people are more likely to feel "outlaw emotions"?
9. In what way are "outlaw" emotions helpful?
10. Under what conditions are emotions appropriate?

...

. . . British empiricism, succeeded in the nineteenth century by positivism, took its epistemological task to be the formulation of rules of inference that would guarantee the derivation of certain knowledge from the "raw data" supposedly given directly to the senses. Empirical testability became accepted as the hallmark of natural science; this, in turn, was viewed as the paradigm of genuine knowledge. Epistemology often was equated with the philosophy of science, and the dominant methodology of positivism prescribed that truly scientific knowledge must be capable of intersubjective verification. Because values and emotions had been defined as variable and idiosyncratic, positivism stipulated that trustworthy knowledge could be established only by methods that neutralized the values and emotions of individual scientists.

Recent approaches to epistemology have challenged some fundamental assumptions of the positivist epistemological model. Contemporary theorists of knowledge have undermined once-rigid distinctions between analytic and synthetic statements, between theories and observations and even between facts and values. Thus far, however, few challenged the purported gap between emotion and knowledge. In this paper, I wish to begin bridging this gap through the suggestion that emotions may be helpful and even necessary rather than inimical to the construction of knowledge. My account is exploratory in nature and leaves many questions unanswered. It is not supported by irrefutable arguments or conclusive proofs; instead, it should be viewed as a preliminary sketch for an epistemological model that will require much further development before its workability can be established.

...

Emotions as Social Constructs

We tend to experience our emotions as involuntary individual responses to situations, responses that are often (though, significantly, not always) private in the sense that they are not perceived as directly and immediately by other people as they are by the subject of the experience. The apparently individual and involuntary character of our emotional experience often is taken as evidence that emotions are presocial, instinctive responses, determined by our biological constitution. This inference, however, is quite mistaken. Although it is probably true that the physiological disturbances characterizing emotions (facial grimaces, changes in the metabolic rate, sweating, trembling, tears and so on) are continuous with the instinctive responses of our prehuman ancestors, and also that the ontogeny of emotions to some extent recapitulates their phylogeny, mature human emotions are neither instinctive nor biologically determined. Instead, they are socially constructed on several levels.

The most obvious way in which emotions are socially constructed is that children are taught deliberately what their culture defines as appropriate responses to certain situations: to fear strangers, to enjoy spicy food, or to like swimming in cold water. On a less conscious level, children also learn what their culture defines as the appropriate ways to express the emotions that it recognizes. Although there may be cross-cultural similarities in the expression of some apparently universal emotions, there are also wide divergences in what are recognized as expressions of grief, respect, contempt, or anger. On an even deeper level, cultures construct divergent understandings of what emotions are. For instance, English metaphors and metonymies are said to reveal a "folk" theory of anger as a hot fluid contained in a private space within an individual and liable to dangerous public explosion. By contrast, the Ilongot, a people of the Philippines, apparently do not understand the self in terms of a public/private distinction and consequently do not experience anger as an explosive internal force: for them, rather, it is an interpersonal phenomenon for which an individual may, for instance, be paid.

Further aspects of the social construction of emotion are revealed through reflection on emotion's intentional structure. If emotions necessarily involve judgments, then obviously they require concepts, which may be seen as socially constructed ways of organizing and making sense of the world. For this reason, emotions simultaneously are made possible and limited by the conceptual and linguistic resources of a society. This philosophical claim is borne out by empirical observation of the cultural variability of emotion. Although there is considerable overlap in the emotions identified by many cultures, at least some emotions are historically or culturally specific, including perhaps *ennui, angst,* the Japanese *amai* (in which one clings to another, affiliative love) and the response of "being a wild pig," which occurs among the Gururumba, a horticultural people living in the New Guinea Highlands. Even apparently universal emotions, such as anger or love, may vary crossculturally. We have just seen that the Ilongot experience of anger apparently is quite different from the contemporary western experience. Romantic love was invented in the Middle Ages in Europe and since that time has been modified considerably; for instance, it is no longer confined to the nobility, and it no longer needs to be extramarital or unconsummated. In some cultures, romantic love does not exist at all.

Thus there are complex linguistic and other social preconditions for the experience, that is, for the existence of human emotions. The emotions that we experience reflect prevailing forms of social life. For instance, one could not feel or even be betrayed in the absence of social norms about fidelity: it is inconceivable that betrayal or indeed any distinctively human emotion could be experienced by a solitary individual in some hypothetical presocial state of nature. There is a sense in which any individual's guilt or anger, joy or triumph, presupposes the existence of a social group capable of feeling guilt, anger, joy, or triumph. This is not to say that group emotions historically precede or are logically prior to the emotions of individuals; it is to say that individual experience is simultaneously social experience. In later sections, I shall explore the epistemological and political implications of this social rather than individual understanding of emotion.

Emotions as Active Engagements

We often interpret our emotions as experiences that overwhelm us rather than as responses we consciously choose: that emotions are to some extent involuntary is part of the ordinary meaning of the term "emotion." Even in daily life, however, we recognize that emotions are not entirely involuntary and we try to gain control over them in various ways, ranging from mechanistic behavior modification techniques designed to sensitize or desensitize our feeling responses to various situations to cognitive techniques designed to help us think differently

about situations. For instance, we might try to change our response to an upsetting situation by thinking about it in a way that will either divert our attention from its more painful aspects or present it as necessary for some larger good.

Some psychological theories interpret emotions as chosen on an even deeper level, interpreting them as actions for which the agent disclaims responsibility. For instance, the psychologist Averell likens the experience of emotion to playing a culturally recognized role: we ordinarily perform so smoothly and automatically that we do not realize we are giving a performance. He provides many examples demonstrating that even extreme and apparently totally involving displays of emotion in fact are functional for the individual and/or the society. For example, when students were asked to record their experiences of anger or annoyance over a two-week period, they came to realize that their anger was not as uncontrollable and irrational as they had assumed previously, and they noted the usefulness and effectiveness of anger in achieving various social goods. Averell notes, however, that emotions often are useful in attaining their goals only if they are interpreted as passions rather than as actions. He cites the case of one subject led to reflect on her anger, who later wrote that it was less useful as a defense mechanism when she became conscious of its function.

The action/passion dichotomy is too simple for understanding emotion, as it is for other aspects of our lives. Perhaps it is more helpful to think of emotions as habitual responses that we may have more or less difficulty in breaking. We claim or disclaim responsibility for these responses depending on our purposes in a particular context. We could never experience our emotions entirely as deliberate actions, for then they would appear nongenuine and inauthentic, but neither should emotions be seen as nonintentional, primal, or physical forces with which our rational selves are forever at war. As they have been socially constructed, so may they be reconstructed, although describing how this might happen would require a long and complicated story.

Emotions, then, are wrongly seen as necessarily passive or involuntary responses to the world. Rather, they are ways in which we engage actively and even construct the world. They have both "mental" and "physical" aspects, each of which conditions the other; in some respects, they are chosen, but in others they are involuntary; they presuppose language and a social order. Thus, *they* can be attributed only to what are sometimes called "whole persons," engaged in the ongoing activity of social life.

EMOTION, EVALUATION, AND OBSERVATION

Emotions and values are closely related. The relation is so close, indeed, that some philosophical accounts [i.e., emotivist accounts] of what it is to hold or express certain values reduce these phenomena to nothing more than holding or expressing certain emotional attitudes. [But] simple emotivism [is] certainly too crude an account of what it is to hold a value; on this account, the intentionality of value judgments vanishes and value judgments become nothing more than sophisticated grunts and groans. Nevertheless, the grain of important truth in emotivism is its recognition that values presuppose emotions to the extent that emotions provide the experiential basis for values. If we had no emotional responses to the world, it is inconceivable that we should ever come to value one state of affairs more highly than another.

Just as values presuppose emotions, so emotions presuppose values. The object of an emotion—that is, the object of fear, grief, pride, and so on—is a complex state of affairs that is appraised or evaluated by the individual. For instance, my pride in a friend's achievement necessarily incorporates the value judgment that my friend has done something worthy of admiration.

Emotions and evaluations, then, are logically or conceptually connected. Indeed, many evaluative terms derive directly from words for emotions: "desirable," "admirable," "contemptible," "despicable," "respectable," and so on. Certainly it is true (pace J. S. Mill) that the evaluation of a situation as desirable or dangerous does not entail it is universally desired or feared but it does entail that desire (or fear) is viewed generally as an appropriate response to the situation. If someone is unafraid in a situation generally perceived as dangerous, her lack of fear requires further explanation; conversely, if someone is afraid without evident danger, then her fear is denounced as irrational or pathological. Thus, every emotion presupposes an evaluation of some aspect of the environment while, conversely, every evaluation or appraisal of the situation implies that those who share that evaluation will share, *ceteris paribus,* a predictable emotional response to the situation.

The rejection of [simple emotivism] and the recognition of intentional elements in emotion already incorporate a realization that observation influences and indeed partially constitutes emotion. We have seen already that distinctively human emotions are not simple instinctive responses to situations or events; instead, they depend essentially on the ways that we perceive those situations and events, as well on the ways that we have learned or decided to respond to them. Without characteristically human perceptions of and engagements in the world, there would be no characteristically human emotions.

Just as observation directs, shapes, and partially defines emotion, so too emotion directs, shapes, and even partially defines observation. Observation is not simply a passive process of absorbing impressions or recording stimuli; instead, it is an activity of selection and interpretation. What is selected and how it is interpreted are influenced by emotional attitudes. On the level of individual observation, this influence always has been apparent to common sense, which notes that we remark very different features of the world when we are happy, depressed, fearful, or confident. Social scientists are now exploring this influence of emotion on perception. One example is the so-called Honi phenomenon, named after the subject Honi who, under identical experimental conditions, perceived strangers' heads as changing in size but saw her husband's head as remaining the same.

The most obvious significance of this sort of example is to illustrate how the individual experience of emotion focuses our attention selectively, directing, shaping and even partially defining our observations, just as our observations direct, shape and partially define our emotions. In addition, the example argues for the social construction of what are taken in any situation to be undisputed facts. It shows how these facts rest on intersubjective agreements that consist partly in shared assumptions about "normal" or appropriate emotional responses to situations. Thus these examples suggest that certain emotional attitudes are involved on a deep level in all observation, in the intersubjectively verified and so supposedly dispassionate observations of science as well as in the common perceptions of daily life. In the next section, I shall elaborate this claim.

EPISTEMOLOGY

The Myth of Dispassionate Investigation

As we have seen already, western epistemology has tended to view emotion with suspicion and even hostility. This derogatory western attitude towards emotion, like the earlier western contempt for sensory observation, fails to recognize that emotion, like sensory perception, is necessary to human survival. Emotions prompt us to act appropriately, to approach some people and situations and to avoid others, to caress or cuddle, fight or flee. Without emotion, human life would be unthinkable. Moreover, emotions have an intrinsic as well as an instrumental value. Although not all emotions are enjoyable or even justifiable, as we shall see, life without any emotion would be life without any meaning.

Within the context of western culture, however, people often have been encouraged to control or even suppress their emotions. Consequently, it is not unusual for people to be unaware of their emotional state or to deny it to themselves and others. This lack of awareness, especially combined with a neopositivist understanding of emotion [i.e., the emotivist understanding] that construes it just as a feeling of which one is aware, lends plausibility to the myth of dispassionate investigation. But lack of awareness of emotions certainly does not mean that emotions are not present subconsciously or unconsciously, or that subterranean emotions do not exert a continuing influence on people's articulated values and observations, thoughts and actions.

Within the positivist tradition, the influence of emotion usually is seen only as distorting or impeding observation or knowledge. Certainly it is true that contempt, disgust, shame, revulsion, or fear may inhibit investigation of certain situations or phenomena. Furiously angry or extremely sad people often seem quite unaware of their surroundings or even their own conditions; they may fail to hear or may systematically misinterpret what other people say. People in love are notoriously oblivious to many aspects of the situation around them.

In spite of these examples, however, positivist epistemology recognizes that the role of emotion in the construction of knowledge is not invariably deleterious and that emotions may make a valuable contribution to knowledge. But the positivist tradition will allow emotion to play only the role of suggesting hypotheses for emotion. Emotions are allowed this because the so-called logic of discovery sets no limits on the idiosyncratic methods that investigators may use for generating hypotheses.

When hypotheses are to be tested, however, positivist epistemology imposes the much stricter logic of justification. The core of this logic is replicability, a criterion believed capable of eliminating or cancelling out what are conceptualized as emotional as well as evaluative biases on the part of individual investigators. The conclusions of western science thus are presumed "objective," precisely in the sense that they are uncontaminated by the supposedly "subjective" values and emotions that might bias individual investigators.

But if, as has been argued, the positivist distinction between discovery and justification is not viable, then such a distinction is incapable of filtering out values in science. For example, although such a split, when built into the western scientific method, generally is successful in neutralizing the idiosyncratic or unconventional values of individual investigators, it has been argued that it does not, indeed cannot, eliminate generally accepted social values. These values are implicit in the identification of the problems that are considered worthy of investigation, in the selection of the hypotheses that are considered worthy of testing, and in the solutions to the problems that are considered worthy of acceptance. The science of past centuries provides ample evidence of the influence of prevailing social values, whether seventeenth century atomistic physics or nineteenth century competitive interpretations of natural selection.

Of course, only hindsight allows us to identify clearly the values that shaped the science of the past and thus to reveal the formative influence on science of pervasive emotional attitudes, attitudes that typically went unremarked at the time because they were shared so generally. For instance, it is now glaringly evident that contempt for (and perhaps fear of) people of color is implicit in nineteenth century anthropology's interpretations and even constructions of anthropological facts. Because we are closer to them, however, it is harder for us to see how certain emotions, such as sexual possessiveness or the need to dominate others, currently are accepted as guiding principles in twentieth century sociobiology or even defined as part of reason within political theory and economics.

Values and emotions enter into the science of the past and the present not only on the level of scientific practice but also on the metascientific level, as answers to various questions: What is science? How should it be practiced? And what is the status of scientific investigation versus nonscientific modes of enquiry? For instance, it is claimed with increasing frequency that the modern western conception of science, which identifies knowledge with power and views it as a weapon for dominating nature, reflects the imperialism, racism and misogyny of the societies that created it. Several feminist theorists have argued that modern epistemology itself may be viewed as an expression of certain emotions alleged to be especially characteristic of males in certain periods, such as separation anxiety and paranoia or an obsession with control and fear of contamination.

Positivism views values and emotions as alien invaders that must be repelled by a stricter application of the scientific method. If the foregoing claims are correct, however, the scientific method and even its positivist construals themselves incorporate values and emotions. Moreover, such an incorporation seems a necessary feature of all knowledge and conception of knowledge. Therefore, rather than repressing emotion in epistemology it is necessary to rethink the relation between knowledge and emotion and construct a conceptual model that demonstrates the mutually constitutive rather than oppositional relation between reason and emotion. Far from precluding the possibility of reliable knowledge, emotion as well as value must be shown as necessary to such knowledge. Despite its classical antecedents and like the ideal of disinterested enquiry, the ideal of dispassionate enquiry is an impossible dream, but a dream nonetheless, or perhaps a myth that has exerted enormous influence on western epistemology. Like all myths, it is a form of ideology that fulfills certain social and political functions.

The Ideological Function of the Myth

So far, I have spoken very generally of people and their emotions, as though everyone experienced similar emotions and dealt with them in similar ways. It is an axiom of feminist theory, however, that all generalizations about "people" are suspect. The divisions in our society are so deep, particularly the divisions of race, class, and gender, that many feminist theorists would claim that talk about people in general is ideologically dangerous because such talk obscures the fact that no one is simply a person but instead is constituted fundamentally by race, class, and gender. Race, class, and gender shape every aspect of our lives, and our emotional constitution is not excluded. Recognizing this helps us to see more clearly the political functions of the myth of the dispassionate investigator.

Feminist theorists have pointed out that the western tradition has not seen everyone as equally emotional. Instead, reason has been associated with members of dominant political, social, and cultural groups and emotion with members of subordinate groups. Prominent among those subordinate groups in our society are people of color, except for supposedly "inscrutable orientals," and women.

Although the emotionality of women is a familiar cultural stereotype, its grounding is quite shaky. Women appear to be more emotional than men because they, along with some groups of people of color, are permitted and even required to express emotion more openly. In contemporary western culture, emotionally inexpressive women are suspect as not being real women, whereas men who express their emotions freely are suspected of being homosexual or in some other way deviant from the masculine ideal. Modern western men, in contrast with Shakespeare's heroes, for instance, are required to present a facade of coolness, lack of excitement, even boredom, to express emotion only rarely and then for relatively trivial events, such as sporting occasions, where the emotions expressed are acknowledged to be dramatized and so are not taken entirely seriously. Thus, women in our society form the main-group allowed or even expected to feel emotion. A woman may cry in the face of disaster, and a man of color may gesticulate, but a white man merely sets his jaw.

White men's control of their emotional expression may go to the extremes of repressing their emotions, failing to develop emotionally, or even losing the capacity to experience many emotions. Not uncommonly, these men are unable to identify what they are feeling, and even they may be surprised, on occasion, by their own apparent lack of emotional response to a situation, such as a death, where emotional reaction is perceived appropriate. In some married couples, the wife implicitly is assigned the job of feeling emotion for both of them. White, college-educated men increasingly enter therapy in order to learn how to "get in touch with" their emotions, a project other men may ridicule as weakness. In therapeutic situations, men may learn that they are just as emotional as women but less adept at identifying their own or others' emotions. In consequence, their emotional development may be relatively rudimentary; this may lead to moral rigidity or insensitivity. Paradoxically, men's lacking awareness of their own emotional responses frequently results in their being more influenced by emotion rather than less.

Although there is no reason to suppose that the thoughts and actions of women are any more influenced by emotion than the thoughts and actions of men, the stereotypes of cool men and emotional women continue to flourish because they are confirmed by an uncritical daily experience. In these circumstances, where there is a differential assignment of reason and emotion, it is easy to see the ideological function of the myth of the dispassionate investigator. It functions, obviously, to bolster the epistemic authority of the currently dominant groups, composed largely of white men, and to discredit the observations and claims of the currently subordinate groups including, of course, the observations and claims of many people of color and women. The more forcefully and vehemently the latter groups express their observations and claims, the more emotional they appear and so the more easily they are discredited. The alleged epistemic authority of the dominant groups then justifies their political authority.

The previous section of this paper argued that dispassionate inquiry was a myth. This section has shown that the myth promotes a conception of epistemological justification vindicating the silencing of those, especially women, who are defined culturally as the bearers of emotion and so are perceived as more "subjective," biased, and irrational. In our present social context, therefore, the ideal of the dispassionate investigator is a classist, racist, and especially masculinist myth.

Emotional Hegemony and Emotional Subversion

As we have seen already, mature human emotions are neither instinctive nor biologically determined, although they may have developed out of presocial, instinctive responses. Like everything else that is human, emotions in part are socially constructed; like all social constructs, they are historical products, bearing the marks of the society that constructed them. Within the very language of emotion, in our basic definitions and explanations of what it is to feel pride or embarrassment, resentment or contempt, cultural norms and expectations are embedded. Simply describing ourselves as angry, for instance, presupposes that we view ourselves as having been wronged, victimized by the violation of some social norm. Thus, we absorb the standards and values of our society in the very process of learning the language of emotion, and those standards and values are built into the foundation of our emotional constitution.

Within a hierarchical society, the norms and values that predominate tend to serve the interest of the dominant groups. Within a capitalist, white supremacist, and male-dominant society, the predominate values will tend to be those that serve the interests of rich white men. Consequently, we are all likely to develop an emotional constitution that is quite inappropriate for feminism. Whatever our color, we are likely to feel what Irving Thalberg has called "visceral racism"; whatever our sexual orientation, we are likely to be homophobic; whatever our class, we are likely to be at least somewhat ambitious and competitive; whatever our sex, we are likely to feel contempt for women. The emotional responses may be rooted in us so deeply that they are relatively impervious to intellectual argument and may recur even when we pay lip service to changed intellectual convictions.

By forming our emotional constitution in particular ways, our society helps to ensure its own perpetuation. The dominant values are implicit in responses taken to be precultural or acultural, our so-called gut responses. Not only do these conservative responses hamper and disrupt our attempts to live in or prefigure alternative social forms but also, and insofar as we take them to be natural responses, they limit our vision theoretically. For instance, they limit our capacity for outrage; they either prevent us from despising or encourage us to despise; they lend plausibility to the belief that greed and domination are inevitable human motivations; in sum, they blind us to the possibility of alternative ways of living.

This picture may seem at first to support the positivist claim that the intrusion of emotion only disrupts the process of seeking knowledge and distorts the results of that process. The picture, however, is not complete; it ignores the fact that people do not always experience the conventionally acceptable emotions. They may feel satisfaction rather than embarrassment when their leaders make fools of themselves. They may feel resentment rather than gratitude for welfare payments and hand-me-downs. They may be attracted to forbidden modes of sexual expression. They may feel revulsion for socially sanctioned ways of treating children or animals. In other words, the hegemony that our society exercises over people's emotional constitution is not total.

People who experience conventionally unacceptable, or what I call "outlaw," emotions often are subordinated individuals who pay a disproportionately high price for maintaining the status quo. The social situation of such people makes them unable to experience the conventionally prescribed emotions: for instance, people of color are more likely to experience anger than amusement when a racist joke is recounted, and women subjected to male sexual banter are less likely to be flattered than uncomfortable or even afraid.

When unconventional emotional responses are experienced by isolated individuals, those concerned may be confused, unable to name their experience; they may even doubt their own sanity. Women may come to believe that they are "emotionally disturbed" and that the embarrassment or fear aroused in them by male sexual innuendo is prudery or paranoia. When certain emotions are shared or validated by others, however, the basis exists for forming a subculture defined by perceptions, norms, and values that systematically oppose the prevailing perceptions, norms, and values. By constituting the basis for such a subculture, outlaw emotions may be politically (because epistemologically) subversive.

Outlaw emotions are distinguished by their incompatibility with the dominant perceptions and values, and some, though certainly not all, of these outlaw emotions are potentially or actually feminist emotions. Emotions become feminist when they incorporate feminist perceptions and values, just as emotions are sexist or racist when they incorporate sexist or racist perceptions and values. For example, anger becomes feminist anger when it involves the perception that the persistent importuning endured by one woman is a single instance of a widespread pattern of sexual harassment, and pride becomes feminist pride when it is evoked by realizing that a certain person's achievement was possible only because that individual overcame specifically gendered obstacles to success.

Outlaw emotions stand in a dialectical relation to critical social theory: at least some are necessary to developing a critical perspective on the world, but they also presuppose at least the beginnings of such a perspective. Feminists need to be aware of how we can draw on some of our outlaw emotions in constructing feminist theory and also of how the increasing sophistication of feminist theory can contribute to the reeducation, refinement, and eventual reconstruction of our emotional constitution.

Outlaw Emotions and Feminist Theory

The most obvious way in which feminist and other outlaw emotions can help in developing alternatives to prevailing conceptions of reality is by motivating new investigations. This is possible because, as we saw earlier, emotions may be long-term as well as momentary; it makes sense to say that someone continues to be shocked or saddened by a situation, even if she is at the moment laughing heartily. As we have seen already, theoretical investigation is always purposeful, and observation is always selective. Feminist emotions provide a political motivation for investigation and so help to determine the selection of problems as well as the method by which they are investigated. Susan Griffin makes the same point when she characterizes feminist theory as following "a direction determined by pain, and trauma, and compassion and outrage."

As well as motivating critical research, outlaw emotions may also enable us to perceive the world differently than we would from its portrayal in conventional descriptions. They may provide the first indications that something is wrong with the way alleged facts have been constructed, with accepted understandings of how things are. Conventionally unexpected or inappropriate emotions may precede our conscious recognition that accepted descriptions and justifications often conceal as much as reveal the prevailing state of affairs. Only when we reflect on our initially puzzling irritability, revulsion, anger, or fear, may we bring to consciousness our "gut-level" awareness that we are in a situation of coercion, cruelty, injustice, or danger. Thus, conventionally inexplicable emotions, particularly, though not exclusively, those experienced by women, may lead us to make subversive observations that challenge dominant conceptions of the status quo. They may help us to realize that what are taken generally to be facts have been constructed in a way that obscures the reality of subordinated people, especially women's reality.

But why should we trust the emotional responses of women and other subordinated groups? . . .

I suggest that emotions are appropriate if they are characteristic of a society in which all humans (and perhaps some nonhuman life too) thrive, or if they are conducive to establishing such a society. For instance, it is appropriate to feel joy when we are developing or exercising our creative powers, and it is appropriate to feel anger and perhaps disgust in those situations where humans are denied their full creativity or freedom. Similarly, it is appropriate to feel fear if those capacities are threatened in us.

This suggestion obviously is extremely vague and may even verge on the tautological. How can we apply it in situations where there is disagreement over what is or is not disgusting or exhilarating or unjust? Here I appeal to a claim for which I have argued elsewhere: the perspective on reality that is available from the standpoint of the oppressed, which in part at least is the standpoint of women, is a perspective that offers a less partial and distorted and therefore more reliable view. Oppressed people have a kind of epistemological privilege insofar as they have easier access to this standpoint and therefore a better chance of ascertaining the possible beginnings of a society in which all could thrive. For this reason, I would claim that the emotional responses of oppressed people in general, and often of women in particular, are more likely to be appropriate than the emotional responses of the dominant class. That is, they are more likely to incorporate reliable appraisals of situations.

. . .

Some Implications of Recognizing the Epistemic Potential of Emotion

Accepting that appropriate emotions are indispensable to reliable knowledge does not mean, of course, that uncritical feeling may be substituted for supposedly dispassionate investigation. Nor does it mean that the emotional responses of women and other members of the underclass are to be trusted without question. Although our emotions are epistemologically indispensable, they are not epistemologically indisputable. Like all our faculties, they may be misleading, and their data, like all data, are always subject to reinterpretation and revision. Because emotions are not presocial, physiological responses to unequivocal situations, they are open to challenge on various grounds. They may be dishonest or self-deceptive, they may incorporate inaccurate or partial perceptions, or they may be constituted by oppressive values. Accepting the indispensability of appropriate emotions to knowledge means no more (and no less) than that discordant emotions should be attended to seriously and respectfully rather than condemned, ignored, discounted, or suppressed.

Just as appropriate emotions may contribute to the development of knowledge so the growth of knowledge may contribute to the development of appropriate emotions. For instance, the powerful insights of feminist theory often stimulate new emotional responses to past and present situations. Inevitably, our emotions are affected by the knowledge that the women on our faculty are paid systematically less than the men, that one girl in four is subjected to sexual abuse from heterosexual men in her own family, and that few women reach orgasm in heterosexual intercourse. We are likely to feel different emotions towards older women or people of color as we reevaluate our standards of sexual attractiveness or acknowledge that Black is beautiful. The new emotions evoked by feminist insights are likely in turn to stimulate further feminist observations and insights, and these may generate new directions in both theory and political practice. There is a continuous feedback loop between our emotional constitution and our theorizing such that each continually modifies the other and is in principle inseparable from it.

The ease and speed with which we can reeducate our emotions unfortunately is not great. Emotions are only partially within our control as individuals. Although affected by new information, they are habitual responses not quickly unlearned. Even when we come to believe consciously that our fear or shame or revulsion is unwarranted, we may still continue to experience emotions inconsistent with our conscious politics. We may still continue to be anxious for male approval, competitive with our comrades and sisters and possessive with our lovers. These unwelcome, because apparently inappropriate, emotions should not be suppressed or denied; instead, they should be acknowledged and subjected to critical scrutiny. The persistence of such recalcitrant emotions probably demonstrates how fundamentally we have been constituted by the dominant world view, but it may also indicate superficiality or other inadequacy in our emerging theory and politics. We can only start from where we are—beings who have been created in a cruelly racist, capitalist, and male-dominated society that has shaped our bodies and our minds, our perceptions, our values and our emotions, our language and our systems of knowledge.

The alternative epistemological model that I suggest displays the continuous interaction between how we understand the world and who we are as people. It shows how our emotional responses to the world change as we conceptualize it differently and how our changing emotional responses then stimulate us to new insights. The model demonstrates the need for theory to be self-reflexive, to focus not only on the outer world but also on ourselves and our relation to that world, to examine critically our social location, our actions, our values, our perceptions and our emotions. The model also shows how feminist and other critical social theories are indispensable psychotherapeutic tools because they provide some insights necessary to a full understanding of our emotional constitution. Thus, the model explains how the reconstruction of knowledge is inseparable from the reconstruction of ourselves.

. . .

CONCLUSION

The claim that emotion is vital to systematic knowledge is only the most obvious contrast between the conception of theoretical investigation that I have sketched here and the conception provided by positivism. For instance, the alternative approach emphasizes that what we identify as emotion is a conceptual abstraction from a complex process of human activity that also involves acting, sensing, and evaluating. This proposed account of theoretical construction demonstrates the simultaneous necessity for and interdependence of faculties that our culture has abstracted and separated from each other: emotion and reason, evaluation and perception, observation and action. The model of knowing suggested here is nonhierarchical and antifoundationalist; instead, it is appropriately symbolized by the radical feminist metaphor of the upward spiral. Emotions are neither more basic than observation, reason, or action in building theory, nor secondary to them. Each of these human faculties reflects an aspect of human knowing inseparable from the other aspects. Thus, to borrow a famous phrase from a Marxian context, the development of each of these faculties is a necessary condition for the development of all. . . .

Discussion Questions

1. Jaggar claims that it is inconceivable that we should ever come to value one state of affairs more highly than another if we had no emotional responses to the world. How does she defend this claim? Do you agree or disagree? Are there other ways of judging states of affairs besides emotional responses? Why or why not?

2. To what extent do one's class, race, gender, and sexual preference influence the way one perceives the world? Why do you believe that in general whites and African Americans reacted so differently to the O. J. Simpson verdict? Was this due to a difference in *perception,* that is, in actually seeing things differently? Why or why not?

3. Describe carefully the role emotions play in Jaggar's thesis. Why have traditional episte-mologies rejected this role for emotions? Do you think there are good reasons for exclud-ing emotions from our search for truth? Why or why not?

4. Can emotions play an important role in generating scientific knowledge? Why or why not? How would Jaggar answer this question? Do you agree with her view? Explain your answer.

For Further Reading

Jaggar's major publications and collaborations include *Feminist Frameworks: Alternative Theoretical Accounts of the Relationships between Women and Men* (1978), *Feminist Politics and Human Nature* (1983), *Gender/Body/Knowledge* (1989), *Living with Contradictions: Ethical Controversies in Contemporary Feminism* (1993), and *A Companion to Feminist Philosophy* (1998). The last book is a recommended introduction to feminist philosophy. There are several excellent books and anthologies exploring the notion of objectivity and feminist epistemology in general: *Feminist Epistemologies* (1993), edited by Alcoff and Potter; *A Mind of One's Own* (1993), edited by Antony and Witt; *Toward a Feminist Epistemology* (1991), by Jane Duran; *Whose Science? Whose Knowledge?* (1991), by Sandra Harding; and *Science as Social Knowledge* (1990), by Helen Longino.

35   TAKING SUBJECTIVITY INTO ACCOUNT
Lorraine Code

Lorraine Code (1937–) has been a perennial critic of traditional epistemologies, what she calls *"S-knows-that-p"* epistemologies. *S-knows-that-p* epistemologies assume that a person, *S,* knows some proposition, *p,* just in case *S* satisfies a certain set of conditions. These conditions may include, for example, "*p* is true," "*S* believes that *p,*" "*S* is justified in believing that *p,*" "*S*'s belief that *p* does not rest on a false belief," and so forth. Notice that *S-knows-that-p* epistemologies assume that it does not matter who *S* is; that is, *S*'s subjectivity makes no difference in the assessment of *S*'s claims to knowledge. And thus knowledge claims, especially scientific claims, are assumed to be objective and unbiased.

According to Code, however, this is a mistake. In this reading, Code illustrates this thesis by examining psychologist Philippe Rushton and his claim that "Orientals as a group are more intelligent, more family-oriented, more law-abiding and less sexually promiscuous than whites, and that whites are superior to blacks in all the same respects." Code finds Rushton's research suspect for all sorts of reasons—reasons, however, that would be ignored and overlooked by traditional *S-knows-that-p* epistemologies. Thus we require a more inclusive epistemological method, which Code outlines at the end of her essay.

Lorraine Code is a professor of philosophy and director of graduate studies in philosophy at York University in Toronto. Code teaches philosophy, women's studies, and political theory. Her major publications include *Epistemic Responsibility* (1987), *What Can She Know?* (1991), and *Rhetorical Spaces (1995).*

Reading Questions

1. How does Code characterize traditional epistemology?
2. In what way does Code's proposed epistemology differ from traditional epistemology? What (new) category plays a prominent role in her epistemology? Why does she include this new category?
3. How does Code demonstrate that it is dangerous to ignore questions about subjectivity in the name of objectivity and value-neutrality?
4. Why does Code find it hard to believe that Rushton's research is objective?
5. How should epistemological investigation be expanded to handle troubling knowledge claims such as Rushton's?
6. How might Rushton's research be seen as symptomatic of the moral health of our society?
7. With what conception of knowledge does Code wish to replace *S-knows-that-p* epistemologies?

. . .

[T]he dominant epistemologies of modernity, with their Enlightenment legacy and later infusion with positivist-empiricist principles, have defined themselves around ideals of pure objectivity and value-neutrality. These ideals are best suited to govern evaluations of the knowledge of knowers who can be considered capable of achieving a "view from nowhere" that allows them, through the autonomous exercise of their reason, to transcend particularity and contingency. The ideals presuppose a universal, homogeneous, and essential human nature that allows knowers to be substitutable for one another. Indeed, for "*S-knows-that-p*" epistemologies, knowers worthy of that title can act as "surrogate knowers" who are able to put themselves in anyone else's place and know her or his circumstances and interests in just the same way as she or he would know them. Hence those circumstances and interests are deemed epistemologically irrelevant. Moreover, by virtue of their professed disinterestedness, these ideals erase the possibility of analyzing the interplay between emotion and reason, and obscure connections between knowledge and power. Hence they lend support to the conviction that cognitive products are as

neutral—as politically innocent—as the processes that allegedly produce them. Such epistemologies implicitly assert that if one cannot see "from nowhere" (or equivalently, from an ideal observation position that could be anywhere and everywhere)— if one cannot take up an epistemological position that mirrors the "original position" of "the moral point of view"—then one cannot *know* anything at all. If one cannot transcend subjectivity and the particularities of its "locations," then there is no knowledge worth analyzing.

. . .

The project of remapping the epistemic terrain that I envisage is subversive, even anarchistic, in challenging and seeking to displace some of the most sacred principles of standard Anglo-American epistemologies. It abandons the search for—denies the possibility of—the disinterested and dislocated view from nowhere. More subversively, it asserts the political investedness of most knowledge-producing activity, and insists upon the accountability—the epistemic responsibilities—of knowing subjects to the community, not just to the evidence.

Because my engagement in the project is prompted, specifically, by a conviction that *gender* must be put in place as a primary analytic category, I start by assuming that it is impossible to sustain the presumption of gender-neutrality that is central to standard epistemologies: the presumption that gender has nothing to do with knowledge, that the mind has no sex, that reason is alike in all men, and "man" embraces "woman?" But gender is not an enclosed category, for it is interwoven, always, with such other sociopolitical-historical locations as class, race, and ethnicity, to mention only a few. It is experienced differently, and plays differently into structures of power and dominance, at its diverse intersections with other specificities. From these multiply describable locations the world looks quite different from the way it might look "from nowhere." Homogenizing those differences under a range of standard or "typical" instances always invites the question "standard or typical for whom?" Answers to that question must, necessarily, take subjectivity into account.

My thesis, then, is that a "variable construction" hypothesis requires epistemologists to pay as much attention to the nature and situation—the location—of S as they commonly pay to the content of p; that a constructivist reorientation requires epistemologists to take subjective factors—factors that pertain to the circumstances of the subject, S, centrally into account in evaluative and justificatory procedures. Yet the socially located, critically dialogical nature of this reoriented epistemological project preserves a realist commitment which ensures that it will not slide into subjectivism. This caveat is vitally important. Although I shall conclude this essay with a plea for a hybrid breed of relativism, my contention will be that realism and relativism are by no means incompatible. Hence although I argue the need to excise the positivist side of the positivist-empiricist couple, I retain a modified commitment to the empiricist side, for several reasons.

...

I want to suggest that . . . it is deceptive and dangerous to ignore questions about subjectivity in the name of objectivity and value-neutrality. To do so, I turn to an example that is now notorious, at least in Canada.

Psychologist Philippe Rushton claims to have demonstrated that "Orientals as a group are more intelligent, more family-oriented, more law-abiding and less sexually promiscuous than whites, and that whites are superior to Blacks in all the same respects." Presented as "facts" that "science [i.e., an allegedly scientific psychology] has proved . . ." using an objective, statistical methodology, Rushton's findings carry a presumption in favor of their reliability *because* they are products of objective research. The "Science has proved . . ." rhetoric creates a public presumption in favor of taking them at face value, believing them true until they are proven false. It erects a screen, a blind, behind which the researcher, like any other occupant of the S place, can abdicate accountability to anything but "the facts"; can present himself as a neutral, infinitely replicable vehicle through which data pass *en route* to becoming knowledge. He can claim to have fulfilled his epistemic obligations if, "withdraw[ing] to . . . [his] professional self"; he can argue that he has been "objective"; detached, disinterested in his research. The rhetoric of objectivity and value-neutrality places the burden of proof on the challenger rather than the fact-finder, and judges her guilty of intolerance, dogmatism, or ideological excess if she cannot make her challenge good. That same rhetoric generates a conception of knowledge for its own sake that at once effaces accountability requirements and threatens the dissolution of viable intellectual and moral community.

I have noted that the "Science has proved . . ." rhetoric derives from the sociopolitical influence of the philosophies of science that incorporate and are underwritten by "S-knows-that-p" epistemologies. Presented as the findings of a purely neutral observer who "discovered" facts about racial inferiority and superiority in controlled observation conditions, so that he could not, rationally, withhold assent, Rushton's results ask the community to be equally objective and neutral in assessing them. These requirements are at once reasonable and troubling. They are reasonable because the empiricist-realist component that, I have urged, is vital to any emancipatory epistemology makes it a mark of competent, responsible inquiry to approach even the most unsavory truth claims seriously, albeit critically. But the requirements are troubling in their implicit appeal to a doxastic involuntarism that becomes an escape hatch from the demands of subjective accountability. The implicit claim is that empirical inquiry is not only a neutral and impersonal process, but also an inexorable one: it is compelling, even coercive, in what it turns up, to the extent that an inquirer *cannot,* rationally, withhold assent. He has no choice but to believe that *p,* however unpalatable it may be. The individualism and presumed disinterestedness of the paradigm reinforces this claim.

It is difficult, however, to believe in the *coincidence* of Rushton's discoveries; and they could only be compelling in that strong sense if they could be shown to be purely coincidental—brute fact— something he came upon as he might bump into a wall. Talk about his impartial reading of the data assumes such hard facticity: the facticity of a blizzard, or a hot sunny day. "Data" is the problematic term here, suggesting that facts presented themselves neutrally to Rushton' s observing eye, as though they were literally given, not sought or made. Yet it is not easy, with Rushton, to conceive of his "data" in perfect independence from ongoing debates about race, sex, and class.

These difficulties are compounded when Rushton's research is juxtaposed against analogous projects in other places and times. In her book, *Sexual Science,* Cynthia Russett documents the intellectual climate of the nineteenth century, when claims for racial and sexual equality were threatening upheavals in the social order. She notes that, just at that time, there was a concerted effort among scientists to produce studies that would demonstrate the "natural" sources of racial and sexual inequality. Given its aptness to the climate of the times, it is hard to believe that this research was "dislocated," prompted by a disinterested spirit of objective, neutral factfinding. It is equally implausible, at a time when racial and sexual unrest is again threatening the complacency of the liberal dream—and meeting with strong conservative efforts to contain it—that it could be purely by coincidence that Rushton reaches the conclusions he does. Consider Rushton's contention that, evolutionarily, as the brain increases in size, the genitals shrink; Blacks have larger genitals, ergo. . . . Leaving elementary logical fallacies aside, it is impossible not to hear echoes of nineteenth-century medical science's "proofs" that, for women, excessive mental activity interferes with the proper functioning of the uterus; hence, permitting women to engage in higher intellectual activity impedes performance of their proper reproductive roles.

The connections Rushton draws between genital and brain size, and conformity to idealized patterns of good, liberal, democratic citizenship, trade upon analogous normative assumptions. The rhetoric of stable, conformist family structure as the site of controlled, utilitarian sexual expression is commonly enlisted to sort the "normal" from the "deviant" and to promote conservative conceptions of the selfimage a society should have of itself. The idea that the dissolution of "the family" (= the nuclear, twoparent, patriarchal family) threatens the destruction of civilized society has been deployed to perpetuate white male privilege and compulsory heterosexuality, especially for women. It has been invoked to preserve homogeneous WASP values from disruption by "unruly"(= not law-abiding; sexually promiscuous) elements. Rushton's contention that "naturally occurring" correlations can explain the demographic distribution of tendencies to unruliness leaves scant room for doubt about the appropriate route for a society concerned about its self-image to take: suppress unruliness. As Julian Henriques puts a similar point, by a neat reversal, the "black person becomes the cause of racism whereas the white person's prejudice is seen as a natural effect of the information-processing mechanisms." The "facts" that Rushton produces are simply presented to the scholarly and lay communities so that they allegedly "speak for themselves" on two levels: both roughly, as data, and in more formal garb, as research findings. What urgently demands analysis is the process by which these "facts" are inserted into a public arena that is prepared to receive them, with the result that inquiry stops right where it should begin.

My point is that it is not enough just to be more rigorously empirical in adjudicating such controversial knowledge claims with the expectation that biases that may have infected the "context of discovery" will be eradicated in the purifying processes of justification. Rather, the scope of epistemological investigation has to expand to merge with moral-political inquiry, acknowledging that "facts" are always infused with values, and that both facts and values are open to ongoing critical debate. It would be necessary to demonstrate the innocence of descriptions (their derivation from pure data) and to show the perfect congruence of descriptions with "the described" in order to argue that descriptive theories have no normative force. Their assumed innocence licenses an evasion of the accountability that socially concerned communities have to demand of their producers of knowledge. Only the most starkly positivistic epistemology merged with the instrumental rationality it presupposes could presume that inquirers are accountable only to the evidence. Evidence is *selected*, not found, and selection procedures are open to scrutiny. Nor can critical analysis stop there, for the funding and institutions that enable inquirers to pursue certain projects and not others explicitly legitimize the work. So the lines of accountability are long and interwoven; only a genealogy of their multiple strands can begin to unravel the issues.

What, then, should occur within epistemic communities to ensure that scientists and other knowers cannot conceal bias and prejudice, cannot claim *a right not to know* about their background assumptions, and the significance of their locations?

The crux of my argument is that the phenomenon of the disinterested inquirer is the exception rather than the rule; that there are no dislocated truths, and that some facts about the locations and interests at the source of inquiry are always pertinent to questions about freedom and accountability. Hence I am arguing, in agreement with Naomi Scheman, that:

> Feminist epistemologists and philosophers of science *along with others who have been the objects of knowledge-as-control* [have to] understand and . . . pose alternatives to the epistemology of modernity. As it has been central to this epistemology to guard its products from contamination by connection to the particularities of its producers, it must be central to the work of its critics and to those who would create genuine alternatives to remember those connections. . . .

There can be no doubt that research is—often imperceptibly—shaped by presuppositions and interests external to the inquiry itself, which cannot be filtered out by standard, objective, disinterested epistemological techniques.

In seeking to explain what makes Rushton possible, the point cannot be to exonerate him as a mere product of his circumstances and times. Rushton accepts grants and academic honors in his own name, speaks "for himself" in interviews with the press, and claims credit where credit is to be had. He upholds the validity of his findings. Moreover, he participates fully in the rhetoric of the autonomous, objective inquirer. Yet although Rushton is plainly accountable for the sources and motivations of his projects, he is not singly responsible. Such research is legitimated by the community and speaks in a discursive space that is made available, prepared for it. So scrutinizing Rushton's "scientific" knowledge claims demands an examination of the moral and intellectual health of a community that is infected by racial and sexual injustices at every level. Rushton may have had reasons to believe that his results would be welcome.

. . .

Knowing other people in relationships requires constant learning: how to be with them, respond to them, act toward them. In this respect it contrasts markedly with the immediacy of common, sense-perceptual paradigms. In fact, if exemplary "bits" of knowledge were drawn from situations where people have to *learn* to know, rather than from taken-for-granted adult expectations, the complexity of knowing even the simplest things would not so readily be masked, and the fact that knowledge is *qualitatively* variable would be more readily apparent. Consider the strangeness of traveling in a country and culture where one has to suspend judgment about how to identify and deal with things from simple artifacts, to flora and fauna, to customs and cultural phenomena. These experiences remind epistemologists of how tentative a process making everyday observations and judgments really is.

Knowledge of other people develops, operates, and is open to interpretation at various levels; it admits of degree in ways that knowing that "the book is red" does not. Such knowledge is not primarily propositional: I can know that Alice is clever, and not *know* her very well at all in a "thicker" sense. Knowing "facts" (= the standard "S-knows-that-p" substitutions) is part of such knowing, but the knowledge involved is more than, and different from, its propositional parts. Nor is this knowledge reducible to the simple, observational knowledge of the traditional paradigms. The fact that it is acquired differently, interactively, relationally, differentiates it both as process and as product from standard propositional knowledge. Yet its status as knowledge disturbs the smooth surface of the paradigm structure. The contrast between its multidimensional, multiperspectival character and the stark simplicity of standard paradigms requires philosophers to reexamine the practice of granting exemplary status to those paradigms. "Knowing how" and "knowing that" are implicated, but they do not begin to tell the whole story.

...

Problems about determining criteria for justifying claims to know another person—the utter unavailability of necessary and sufficient conditions, the complete inadequacy of "*S*-knows-that-*p*" paradigms—must account for philosophical reluctance to count this as knowledge that bears epistemological investigation. Yet my suggestion that such knowledge is a model for a wide range of knowledge, and is not merely inchoate and unmanageable, recommends itself the more strongly in view of the extent to which cognitive practice is grounded upon such knowledge. I am thinking not just of everyday interactions with other people, but of the specialized knowledge—such as Rushton's—that claims institutional authority. Educational theory and practice, psychology, sociology, anthropology, law, some aspects of medicine and philosophy, politics, history and economics, all depend for their credibility upon knowing people. Hence it is all the more curious that observation-based knowledge of material objects, and the methodology of the physical sciences, hold such relatively unchallenged sway as the paradigm—and paragon—of intellectual achievement. The results of according observational paradigms continued veneration are evident in the reductive approaches of behaviorist psychology. They are apparent in parochial impositions of meaning upon the practices of other cultures still characteristic of some areas of anthropology; and in the simple translation of present-day descriptions into past cultural contexts that characterizes some historical and archeological practice. But feminist, hermeneutic, and postmodern critiques are slowly succeeding in requiring objectivist social scientists to reexamine their presuppositions and practices. In fact, it is methodological disputes within the social sciences—and the consequent unsettling of positivistic hegemony—that, according to Susan Hekman, have set the stage for the development of a productive, postmodern approach to epistemology for contemporary feminists.

I am not proposing that knowing other people become *the* new epistemological paradigm, but rather that it has a strong claim to exemplary status in the epistemologies that feminist and other case-by-case analyses will produce. I am proposing further that, if epistemologists require a model drawn from "scientific" inquiry, then a reconstructed, interpretive social science, liberated from positivistic constraints, will be a better resource than natural science—or physics—for knowledge as such.

...

5. RELATIVISM AFTER ALL?

The project I am proposing, then, requires a new *geography* of the epistemic terrain: one that is no longer primarily a physical geography, but a population geography that develops qualitative analyses of subjective positions and identities and of the social-political structures that produce them. Because differing social positions generate variable constructions of reality, and afford different perspectives on the world, the revisionary stages of this project will consist in case-by-case analyses of the knowledge produced in specific social positions. These analyses derive from a recognition that knowers are always *somewhere*—and at once limited and enabled by the specificities of their locations. It is an interpretive project, alert to the possibility of finding generalities, commonalities within particulars—hence of the explanatory potential that opens up when such commonalities can be delineated. But it is wary of the reductivism that results when commonalities are presupposed or forced. It has no ultimate foundation, but neither does it float free, for it is grounded in experiences and practices, in the efficacy of dialogic negotiation and of action.

36 CONSCIOUSNESS RAISING
Catharine A. MacKinnon

Catharine MacKinnon (1946–), professor of law at the University of Michigan Law School, has written extensively on issues in the law relating to gender equality, particularly sexual harassment and pornography. Notably, in a number of contexts MacKinnon has offered critiques of objectivity, claiming that objectivity is essentially a flawed method of gaining knowledge. As such, women, in particular, should not adopt objectivity as their sole standard method for acquiring knowledge.

But how can we acquire knowledge, then, if not simply through objectivity? In her book *A Feminist Theory of the State,* MacKinnon answers that question. She develops a hybrid Marxist-feminist social / political theory. One perennial issue that arises for both Marxism and feminism is the problem of *false consciousness.* False consciousness is the problem that people who live under oppressive social conditions often do not know their own best interests because they adopt the worldview of the ruling social group and become unwitting coconspirators with those who constrain and enslave them. Some have argued that women's consciousness is false consciousness when women view the world using the categories and thought forms that serve the interests of others, that is, when they view it using the standards of objectivity. This poses a thorny question: If women find themselves under false consciousness, not knowing their own true interests, how can they come to discover their actual true interests?

MacKinnon looks to the history of feminism for an answer. How did women come to a higher level of consciousness about their own status as women in the first place? Through consciousness-raising groups, that is, through sharing, speaking, listening, and examining their own lives in a group situation. Through this process, women in consciousness-raising groups came to a group awareness of their own status in society *as women.*

Reading Questions

1. What sorts of things occurred in consciousness-raising groups? How were these groups alike or different?
2. What does MacKinnon mean by saying that the "fact of consciousness-raising groups . . . presupposes the discovery . . . [women] were there to make"?
3. Why was it necessary that men not be present in these groups?
4. What concrete, specific issues were raised and examined in consciousness-raising groups?
5. Summarize MacKinnon's description of the standard (nonfeminist) view of epistemology and its purpose.

Source: Reprinted by permission of the author from *Toward a Feminist Theory of the State,* by Catharine A. MacKinnon, Cambridge, Mass.: Harvard University Press, Copyright © 1989 Catharine A. MacKinnon.

6. What is the relationship between the mind of the researcher and social reality according to social science? Why must the limits of the mind be overcome?
7. Describe the relationship between women as knowers and social reality according to the feminist method of consciousness raising.

...

Consciousness raising is the process through which the contemporary radical feminist analysis of the situation of women has been shaped and shared. As feminist method and practice, consciousness raising is not confined to groups explicitly organized or named for that purpose. In fact, consciousness raising as discussed here was often not practiced in consciousness-raising groups. Such groups were, however, one medium and forum central to its development as a method of analysis, mode of organizing, form of practice, and technique of political intervention. The characteristic structure, ethic, process, and approach to social change which mark such groups as a development in political theory and practice are integral to many of the substantive contributions of feminist theory. The key to feminist theory consists in its way of knowing. Consciousness raising is that way. "[An] oppressed group must at once shatter the self-reflecting world which encircles it and, at the same time, project its own image onto history. In order to discover its own identity as distinct from that of the oppressor, it has to become visible to itself. All revolutionary movements create their own way of seeing." One way to analyze feminism as a theory is to describe the process of consciousness raising as it occurred in consciousness-raising groups.

As constituted in the 1960s and 1970s, consciousness-raising groups were many women's first explicit contact with acknowledged feminism. Springing up spontaneously in the context of friendship networks, colleges and universities, women's centers, neighborhoods, churches, and shared work or workplaces, they were truly grassroots. Many aimed for diversity in age, marital status, occupation, education, physical ability, sexuality, race and ethnicity, class, or political views. Others chose uniformity on the same bases. Some groups proceeded biographically, each woman presenting her life as she wished to tell it. Some moved topically, using subject focuses such as virginity crises, relations among women, mothers, body image, and early sexual experiences to orient discussion. Some read books and shared literature. Some addressed current urgencies as they arose, supporting women through difficult passages or encouraging them to confront situations they had avoided. Many developed a flexible combination of formats. Few could or wanted to stick to a topic if a member was falling apart, yet crises were seldom so clarifying or continuous as entirely to obviate the need for other focus.

Participants typically agreed on an ethic of openness, honesty, and self-awareness. If a member felt she could not discuss an intimate problem or felt coerced to do so, this was typically taken as a group failure. Other usual norms included a commitment to attend meetings and to keep information confidential. Although leadership patterns often emerged, and verbal and emotional skills recognizably varied, equality within the group was a goal that reflected a value of nonhierarchical organization and a commitment to confronting sources of inequality on the basis of which members felt subordinated or excluded.

What brought women to these groups is difficult to distinguish from what happened once they were there. As with any complex social interaction, from laboratory experiment to revolution, it is often difficult to separate the assumptions from the discoveries, the ripeness of conditions from the precipitating spark. Where does consciousness come from? The effectiveness of consciousness raising is difficult to apportion between the process itself and the women who choose to engage in it. The initial recruiting impulse seems to be a response to an unspecific, often unattached, but just barely submerged discontent that in some inchoate way women relate to being female. It has not escaped most women's attention that their femaleness defines much of who they can be. Restrictions, conflicting demands, intolerable but necessarily tolerated work, the accumulation of constant small irritations and indignities of everyday existence have often been justified on the basis of sex. Consciousness raising coheres and claims these impressions.

Feminists tend to believe that most if not all women resent women's status on some level of their being; even women's defense of their status can be a response to that status. Why some women take the step of identifying their situation with their status as women, transforming their discontents into grievances, is a crucial unanswered question of feminism (or, for that matter, of Marxism). What brings people to be conscious of their oppression as common rather than remaining on the level of bad feelings, to see their group identity as a systematic necessity that benefits another group, is the first question of organizing. The fact that consciousness-raising groups were there presupposes the discovery that they were there to make. But what may have begun as a working assumption becomes a working discovery: women are a group, in the sense that a shared reality of treatment exists sufficient to provide a basis for identification—at least enough to begin talking about it in a group of women. This often pre-articulate consensus shapes a procedure, the purpose of which becomes to unpack the concrete moment-to-moment meaning of being a woman in a society that men dominate, by looking at how women see their everyday experience in it. Women's lives are discussed in all their momentous triviality, that is, as they are lived through. The technique explores the social world each woman inhabits through her speaking of it, through comparison with other women's experiences, and through women's experiences of each other in the group itself. Metaphors of hearing and speaking commonly evoke the transformation women experience from silence to voice. As Toni McNaron put it, "within every story I have ever heard from a woman, I have found some voice of me. The details are of course unique to the speaker—they are our differences. But the meaning which they make is common to us all. I will not understand what is common without hearing the details which reveal it to me." The particularities become facets of the collective understanding within which differences constitute rather than undermine collectivity.

The fact that men were not physically present was usually considered necessary to the process. Although the ways of seeing that women have learned in relation to men were very much present or there would be little to discuss, men's temporary concrete absence helped women feel more free of the immediate imperative to compete for male attention and approval, to be passive or get intimidated, or to support men's version of reality. It made speech possible. With these constraints at some remove, women often found that the group confirmed awarenesses they had hidden, including from themselves. Subjects like sexuality, family, body, money, and power could be discussed more openly. The pain of women's roles and women's stake in them could be confronted critically, without the need every minute to reassure men that these changes were not threatening to them or to defend women's breaking of roles as desirable. The all-woman context valued women to each other as sources of insight, advice, information, stimulation, and problems. By providing room for women to be close, these groups demonstrated how far women were separated and how that separation deprived women of access to the way their treatment is systematized. "People who are without names, who do not know themselves, who have no culture, experience a kind of paralysis of consciousness. The first step is to connect and learn to trust one another." This context for serious confrontation also revealed how women had been trivialized to each other. Pamela Allen called these groups "free space." She meant a respectful context for interchange within which women could articulate the inarticulate, admit the inadmissible. The point of the process was not so much that hitherto-undisclosed facts were unearthed or that denied perceptions were corroborated or even that reality was tested, although all these happened. It was not only that silence was broken and that speech occurred. The point was, and is, that this process moved the reference point for truth and thereby the definition of reality as such. Consciousness raising alters the terms of validation by creating community through a process that redefines what counts as verification. This process gives both content and form to women's point of view.

Concretely, consciousness-raising groups often focused on specific incidents and internal dialogue: what happened today, how did it make you feel, why did you feel that way, how do you feel now? Extensive attention was paid to small situations and denigrated pursuits that made up the common life of women in terms of energy, time, intensity, and definition—prominently, housework and sexuality. Women said things like this:

I am nothing when I am by myself. In myself, I am nothing. I only know I exist because I am needed by someone who is real, my husband, and by my children. My husband goes out into the real world. Other people recognize him as real, and take him into account. He affects other people and events. He does things and changes things and they are different afterwards. I stay in my imaginary world in this house, doing jobs that I largely invent, and that no-one cares about but myself. I do not change things. The work I do changes nothing; what I cook disappears, what I clean one day must be cleaned again the next. I seem to be involved in some sort of mysterious process.

Intercourse was interrogated: how and by whom it is initiated, its timing, woman's feelings during and after, its place in relationships, its meaning, its place in being a woman. Other subjects included interactions in routine situations like walking down the street, talking with bus drivers, interacting with cocktail waitresses. Women's stories—work and how they came to do it; children; sexual history, including history of sexual abuse—were explored. Adrienne Rich reflects the process many women experienced and the conclusion to which many women came:

I was looking desperately for clues, because if there were no clues then I thought I might be insane. I wrote in a notebook about this time: "Paralyzed by the sense that there exists a mesh of relationships—e.g., between my anger at the children, my sensual life, pacifism, sex (I mean sex in its broadest significance, not merely sexual desire)—an interconnectedness which, if I could see it, make it valid, would give me back myself, make it possible to function lucidly and passionately. Yet I grope in and out among these dark webs." I think I began at this point to feel that politics was not something "out there" but something "in here" and of the essence of my condition.

Woman's self-concept emerged: who she thinks she is, how she was treated in her family, who they told her she was (the pretty one, the smart one), how she resisted, how that was responded to, her feelings now about her life and herself, her account of how she came to feel that way, whether other group members experience her the way she experiences herself, how she carries her body and delivers her mannerisms, the way she presents herself and interacts in the group. Contradictions between messages tacitly conveyed and messages explicitly expressed inspired insightful and shattering criticism, as with women who behave seductively while complaining that men accost them. Complicity in oppression acquires concrete meaning as women emerge as shapers of reality as well as shaped by it. A carefully detailed and critically reconstructed composite image is built of women's experienced meaning of "being a woman." From women's collective perspective, a woman embodies and expresses a moment-to-moment concept of herself in the way she walks down the street, structures a household, pursues her work and friendships, shares her sexuality—a certain concept of how she has survived and who she survives as. A minute-by-minute moving picture is created of women becoming, refusing, sustaining their condition.

Interactions usually overlooked as insignificant if vaguely upsetting proved good subjects for detailed scrutiny. A woman mentions the way a man on the subway looked at her. How did this make her feel? Why does she feel so degraded? so depressed? Why can the man make her hate her body? How much of this feeling comes from her learned distrust of how men use her sexually? Does this show up in other areas of her life? Do other women feel this way? What form of power does this give the man? Do all men have, or exercise, such power? Could she have done anything at the time? Can the group do anything now? Women learn that the entire structure of sexual domination, the tacit relations of deference and command, can be present in a passing glance.

Realities hidden under layers of valued myth were unmasked simply by talking about what happens every day, such as the hard physical labor performed by the average wife and mother, the few women who feel strictly vaginal orgasms and the many who pretend they do. Women confronted collectively the range of overt violence represented in the life experience of their group of women, women who might previously have appeared "protected." They found fathers who raped them; boyfriends who shot at them; doctors who aborted them when they weren't pregnant or sterilized them "accidentally"; psychoanalysts who so-called seduced them, committing them to mental hospitals when they exposed them; mothers who committed suicide or lived to loathe themselves more when they failed; employers who fired them for withholding sexual favors or unemployment offices that refused benefits when they quit, finding their reason personal and uncompelling. Women learned that men see and treat women from their angle of vision, and they learned the content of that vision.

These details together revealed and documented the kind of world women inhabit socially and some of what it feels like for them to inhabit it, how women are systematically deprived of a self and how that process of deprivation constitutes socialization to femininity. In consciousness raising, women become aware of this reality as at once very specific— a woman's social condition and self-concept as it is lived through by her—and as a social reality in which all women more or less participate, however diversely, and in which all women can be identified. Put another way, although a woman's specific race or class or physiology may define her among women, simply being a woman has a meaning that decisively defines all women socially, from their most intimate moments to their most anonymous relations. This social meaning, which is unattached to any actual anatomical differences between the sexes, or to any realities of women's response to it, pervades everyday routine to the point that it becomes a reflex, a habit. Sexism is seen to be all of a piece and so much a part of the omnipresent background of life that a massive effort of collective concentration is required even to discern that it has edges. Consciousness raising is such an effort. Taken in this way, consciousness means a good deal more than a set of ideas. It constitutes a lived knowing of the social reality of being female.

What women become conscious of—the substance of radical feminist analysis—is integral to this process. Perhaps most obviously, it becomes difficult to take seriously accounts of women's roles or personal qualities based on nature or biology, except as authoritative appeals that have shaped women according to them. Combing through women's lives event by event, detail by detail, it is no mystery that women are who they are, given the way they have been treated. Patterns of treatment that would create feelings of incapacity in anybody are seen to connect seamlessly with acts of overt discrimination to deprive women of tools and skills, creating by force the status they are supposed to be destined for by anatomy. Heterosexuality, supposed natural, is found

to be forced on women moment to moment. Qualities pointed to as naturally and eternally feminine— nurturance, intuition, frailty, quickness with their fingers, orientation to children—or characteristics of a particular subgroup of women—such as married women's supposed talent for exacting, repetitive, simple tasks, or Black women's supposed interest in sex—look simply like descriptions of the desired and required characteristics of particular occupants of women's roles. Meredith Tax summarized this insight: "We didn't get this way by heredity or by accident. We have been molded into these deformed postures, pushed into these service jobs, made to apologize for existing, taught to be unable to do anything requiring any strength at all, like opening doors or bottles. We have been told to be stupid, to be silly."

...

Theories of right knowing are epistemologies. An epistemology is a story of a relation between knower and known. In the history of thought, this relation has been variously cast as a relation between subject and object, value and fact, phenomena and noumena, mind and matter, world and representation, text or evidence and interpretation, and other polarities and antinomies. The point of such distinctions is to establish an account of how knowing connects with what one purports to know. One purpose of this has been to establish an authoritative account of the real in order to expose errors and delusions conclusively in an agreed-upon way. The point is to establish world in mind. Science, for example, seeks empirical certainty over opinion or fiction or delusion or faith. All approaches to knowledge set up modes by which to tell whether what one thinks is real, is real. This connection embodies what is called methodology; adherence to it defines what is called rationality. Method thus puts into operation a way of acquiring that knowledge that a particular epistemological stance approves as real.

Scientific epistemology defines itself in the stance of "objectivity," whose polar opposite is subjectivity. Socially, men are considered objective, women subjective. Objectivity as a stance toward the world erects two tests to which its method must conform: distance and aperspectivity. To perceive reality accurately, one must be distant from what one is looking at and view it from no place and at no time in particular, hence from all places and times at once. This stance defines the relevant world as that which can be objectively known, as that which can be known in this way. An epistemology decisively controls not only the form of knowing but also its content by defining how to proceed, the process of knowing, and by confining what is worth knowing to that which can be known in this way.

The posture scientific epistemology takes toward its world defines the basic epistemic question as a problem of the relation between knowledge—where knowledge is defined as a replication or reflection or copy of reality—and objective reality, defined as that world which exists independent of any knower or vantage point, independent of knowledge or the process of coming to know, and, in principle, knowable in full. For science, the tests of reality are replicability and measurability, the test of true meaning is intersubjective communicability, the test of rationality is formal (axiomatic) logical consistency, and the test of usefulness, as in technology, is whether it can be done.

Social science attempts to view the social world objectively, as physical science has viewed the physical world. One effect has been to uncover many roots of what has previously been taken as the simply given. That which previously was used as explanation becomes that which is to be explained. The scientifically real is found to embody many determinants that science sees as getting in the way of knowing social reality, to the extent they can be accounted for by that reality. In this perspective, for example, psychology traditionally constructs problems of personality, development, and psychosis as intervening within the knower between knowledge and reality, producing distortions from some combination of the person's "nature" and "nurture." Thus Piaget's stages of cognitive development can be viewed as progressive stages of epistemological growth, cognitively grasping the world at a given developmental stage. There is seldom any questioning of the objective "out there" reality of the world the child is attempting to come to know, the possibly distinct and changing object world the child inhabits.

Consistent with this approach, social science attacks the problem of its own knowing largely in terms of the limitations on the "in here" of the knower, with concern for how these limits can be overcome, exorcised, or contained. Its model of knowledge posits a mind needing to overstep its determinants in order to get outside itself in order to get at the facts. Otherwise, it is thought, the mind will only propagate and project its delusions, its determinants, the limitations of its experiences, onto social reality, remaining forever trapped within itself. The movement to uncover the sources of social experience has thus also been a movement that has devalued these sources by regarding them as barriers or distortions between the knower and the known. If social knowledge can be interpreted in terms of the social determinants of the knower, it is caused. Therefore, its truth value, in this definition of tests for truth, is undercut. If it has a time or place—or gender—it becomes doubtful because situated.

Feminist method as practiced in consciousness raising, taken as a theory of knowing about social being, pursues another epistemology. Women are presumed able to have access to society and its structure because they live in it and have been formed by it, not in spite of those facts. Women can know society because consciousness is part of it, not because of any capacity to stand outside it or oneself. This stance locates the position of consciousness, from which one knows, in the standpoint and time frame of that attempting to be known. The question is not whether objective reality exists but whether that concept accesses the is-ness of the world. Feminist epistemology asserts that the social process of being a woman is on some level the same process as that by which woman's consciousness becomes aware of itself as such and of its world. Mind and world, as a matter of social reality, are taken as interpenetrated. Knowledge is neither a copy nor a miscopy of reality, neither representative nor misrepresentative as the scientific model would have it, but a response to living in it. Truth is in a sense a collective experience of truth, in which "knowledge" is assimilated to consciousness, a consciousness that exists as a reality in the world, not merely in the head. This epistemology does not at all deny that a relation exists between thought and some reality other than thought, or between human activity (mental or otherwise) and the products of that activity. Rather, it redefines the epistemological issue from being the scientific one, the relation between knowledge and objective reality, to a problem of the relation of consciousness to social being. This move contextualizes verification, rendering epistemology, in the words of Jane Flax, "the study of the life situation of consciousness, an inquiry which is ultimately political and historical."

An epistemology preempts the definition of reality when its criteria for conclusiveness become taken for granted, as constituting "reality itself," as rules or standards in terms of which other forms of knowing are tested. For science, these criteria are distance and aperspectivity. Though apparently general, and asserted by science as not constructs of reality but ways of getting at it, they have specific social roots and implications. These include devaluing as biased and unreliable the view from the inside and within the moment, and the perspective from the bottom of the social order. For science not only etches itself on the world through its technology, making the world a scientific place in which to live, but also propagates itself through its picture of social reality. This picture exists complete with those categories that a scientific epistemology can perceive as real. Social science provides no account of this prior picture of social reality upon which its "empirically derived" explanations are then superimposed, which its data then "confirm." Because social science is crippled by its mythos as distanced and aperspectival, it cannot give an account of the social reality it approaches because it cannot give an account of its approach.

The social power of science creates a reality that conforms to its image. Conflicting views of reality, although they retain a subcultural or subconscious life and power, are authoritatively defined as unreal or irrational. Sanctions behind the ruling reality construction range from whatever happens inside people who never seem to have conscious thoughts of different ways of being, to bad grades in school, jailing, and mental hospitalization for those who do. The choice of an epistemology is, in Kuhn's words, "like the choice between competing political institutions" because it *is* a choice of political institution—one that women never chose.

Consciousness raising discovered that one form of the social existence of male power is inside women. In this form, male power becomes self-enforcing. Women become "thingified in the head." Once incarnated, male superiority tends to be reaffirmed and reinforced in what can be seen as well as in what can be

done. So male power both is and is not illusory. As it justifies itself, namely as natural, universal, unchangeable, given, and morally correct, it is illusory; but the fact that it is powerful is no illusion. Power is a social relation. Given the imperatives of women's lives, the necessity to avoid punishment—from self-rejection to involuntary incarceration to suicide—it is not irrational for women to see themselves in a way that makes their necessary compliance tolerable, even satisfying. Living each day reconvinces everyone, women and men alike, of male hegemony, which is hardly a myth, and of women's innate inferiority and men's innate superiority, a myth that each day's reliving makes difficult to distinguish meaningfully from reality.

The deepest paradox of consciousness raising and its most potent contribution is that it affirms that there both is and can be another reality for women by doing nothing but examining the current society's deadest ends. Effectively, the process redefines women's feelings of discontent as indigenous to their situation rather than to themselves as crazy, maladjusted, hormonally imbalanced, bitchy, or ungrateful. It is validating to comprehend oneself as devalidated rather than as invalid. Women's feelings are interpreted as appropriate responses to their conditions. This analysis need not posit that feelings are asocial or universally correct as a representation of experience. Nor does it mean that women who feel what they are supposed to feel validate the society that forces them to feel that way. The distinction between "in here" and "out there" made in society through scientific objectivity is, however, seen to operate as a legitimating ideology that supports men's views of what women should think and be by powerfully stigmatizing as irrational and unreal women's feelings of rage and rebellion, by individualizing them, and by keeping the "privacy" (that is isolation) of home and sexual life from being comprehended as gender's collective realities.

...

Discussion Questions

1. Why does MacKinnon not accept 'scientifically objective' studies of women's lives as adequate? What is wrong with an 'objective' analysis of gender, for example? Explain MacKinnon's position and why she regards consciousness-raising groups as a superior method. Do you agree with her? Why or why not?

2. Have you ever been a member of a group that has explored personal issues in ways similar to consciousness-raising groups? If so, what was your experience like? If not, why not? Is it because these groups are not valuable or for some other reason? Why do you think more people do not participate in such groups? How would MacKinnon answer this question? Do you agree with her view? Why or why not?
3. Consider this critique of consciousness-raising groups: Instead of helping women to see the truth about their lives, these groups actually indoctrinated women into believing they were oppressed in ways they were not. Do you believe this ever happens in consciousness-raising groups? If so, why? Do you have any evidence for your position? How would MacKinnon respond to this criticism?

For Further Reading

This selection is from MacKinnon's book *A Feminist Theory of the State* (1989). MacKinnon has been influential in shaping sexual harassment laws; see her *Sexual Harassment of Working Women* (1970). MacKinnon is also widely known for her views on pornography, especially as developed in *Only Words* (1993). For material on consciousness-raising see Mary C. Lynn, ed., *Women's Liberation in the Twentieth Century* (1975); Liz Stanley and Sue Wise, *Breaking Out Again: Feminist Ontology and Epistemology* (1993); Sheila Rowbotham, *Women's Consciousness, Man's World* (1973); Pamela Allen, *Free Space: A Perspective on the Small Group in Women's Liberation* (1970); and Toni McNaron, *The Power of Person: Women Coming into Their Own* (1982).

   For more on MacKinnon's critique of objectivity see Sally Haslanger, "Objective Reality, Male Reality, and Social Construction," in *Women, Knowledge, and Reality*, edited by Ann Garry and Marilyn Pearsall (1996). For alternative readings on feminism and objectivity see the suggested readings after Reading 38 in Chapter 7.

37   SOLIDARITY OR OBJECTIVITY?
Richard Rorty

American philosophy has made a unique contribution to the problem of how beliefs should be justified, that is, defended as true. American **pragmatism,** advanced by such notable philosophers as Charles Peirce, William James, and John Dewey, holds that persons possess knowledge insofar as their ideas 'work' or make a difference in the way persons act. For example, a scientist's knowledge of a particular chemical compound might be justified insofar as that knowledge can be used to make actual predictions and to create new technologies.

In the following essay, American philosopher Richard Rorty (1931–), now at Stanford University, reinterprets pragmatism as 'what it is good for *us* to believe'. Rorty's pragmatism defends particular standards of justification by explaining how, in fact, certain cultures have actually gone about separating

Source: From *Objectivity, Relativism, and Truth: Philosophical Papers,* Vol. 1, by Richard Rorty. Copyright © 1991 Cambridge University Press. Reprinted with the permission of Cambridge University Press.

mere opinion from true belief. Standards of justification, on Rorty's view, are internal to cultures, and thus there is no way to avoid being culturally biased—ethnocentric—in debating standards of truth. Whatever standards of justification we use to assess truth claims, they are always going to be our standards, that is, the standards of our culture. There is no sense in attempting to deny this unavoidable cultural component to our philosophical projects. There are no transcultural standards by which to judge truth claims. Even if there were, there are still no transcultural ways of justifying these standards over others.

None of this means that truth can't be separated from error, or justified belief distinguished from mere opinion, but it does mean that the view that our beliefs are true insofar as they correspond to the way the world actually is should be abandoned. Tomorrow may produce better beliefs, that is, ones that work better and are more pragmatically valuable for *us*.

Reading Questions

1. What are solidarity and objectivity and how are these two ways humans try to give sense to their lives?
2. How has the search for truth been characterized in Western culture? How have Plato and the Enlightenment represented this approach to truth?
3. Who are the 'realists'? What do they believe about how truth is justified?
4. Who are the 'pragmatists'? What do they believe about justification and truth?
5. What three views have been characterized as relativism? Which view does the pragmatist hold?
6. Why does Rorty believe that pragmatism should not be termed relativism?
7. According to Rorty, why does contemporary culture want to avoid relativism?
8. What dilemma does pragmatism pose for realists? Which horn of the dilemma does Rorty believe pragmatists should grasp? Why?
9. What is Nietzsche's picture of truth and how humans should pursue it? In what ways does this conception of truth match Rorty's own view?

There are two principal ways in which reflective human beings try, by placing their lives in a larger context, to give sense to those lives. The first is by telling the story of their contribution to a community. This community may be the actual historical one in which they live, or another actual one, distant in time or place, or a quite imaginary one, consisting perhaps of a dozen heroes and heroines selected from history or fiction or both. The second way is to describe themselves as standing in immediate relation to a nonhuman reality. This relation is immediate in the sense that it does not derive from a relation between such a reality and their tribe, or their nation, or their imagined band of comrades. I shall say that stories of the former kind exemplify the desire for solidarity, and that stories of the latter kind exemplify the desire for objectivity. Insofar as a person is seeking solidarity, she does not ask about the relation between the practices of the chosen community and something outside that community. Insofar as she seeks objectivity, she distances herself from the actual persons around her not by thinking of herself as a member of some other real, or imaginary group, but rather by attaching herself to something which can be described without reference to any particular human beings.

The tradition in Western culture which centers around the notion of the search for Truth, a tradition which runs from the Greek philosophers through the Enlightenment, is the clearest example of the attempt to find a sense in one's existence by turning away from solidarity to objectivity. The idea of Truth as something to be pursued for its own sake, not because it will be good for oneself, or for one's real or imaginary community, is the central theme of this tradition. It was perhaps the growing awareness by the Greeks of the sheer diversity of human communities which stimulated the emergence of this ideal. A fear of parochialism, of being confined within the horizons of the group into which one happens to be born, a need to see it with the eyes of a stranger, helps produce the skeptical and ironic tone characteristic of Euripides and Socrates. Herodotus' willingness to take the barbarians seriously enough to describe their customs in detail may have been a necessary prelude to Plato's claim that the way to transcend skepticism is to envisage a common goal of humanity—a goal set by human nature rather than by Greek culture. The combination of Socratic alienation and Platonic hope gives rise to the idea of the intellectual as someone who is in touch with the nature of things, not by way of the opinions of his community, but in a more immediate way.

Plato developed the idea of such an intellectual by means of distinctions between knowledge and opinion, and between appearance and reality. Such distinctions conspire to produce the idea that rational inquiry should make visible a realm to which nonintellectuals have little access, and of whose very existence they may be doubtful. In the Enlightenment, this notion became concrete in the adoption of the Newtonian physical scientist as a model of the intellectual. To most thinkers of the eighteenth century, it seemed clear that the access to Nature which physical science had provided should now be followed by the establishment of social, political, and economic institutions which were in accordance with Nature. Ever since, liberal social thought has centered around social reform as made possible by objective knowledge of what human beings are like—not knowledge of what Greeks or Frenchmen or Chinese are like, but of humanity as such. We are the heirs of this objectivist tradition, which centers around the assumption that we must step outside our community long enough to examine it in the light of something which transcends it, namely, that which it has in common with every other actual and possible human community. This tradition dreams of an ultimate community which will have transcended the distinction between the natural and the social, which will exhibit a solidarity which is not parochial because it is the expression of an ahistorical human nature. Much of the rhetoric of contemporary intellectual life takes for granted that the goal of scientific inquiry into man is to understand "underlying structures," or "culturally invariant factors," or "biologically determined patterns."

Those who wish to ground solidarity in objectivity—call them "realists"—have to construe truth as correspondence to reality. So they must construct a metaphysics which has room for a special relation between beliefs and objects which will differentiate true from false beliefs. They also must argue that there are procedures of justification of belief which are natural and not merely local. So they must construct an epistemology which has room for a kind of justification which is not merely social but natural, springing from human nature itself, and made possible by a link between that part of nature and the rest of nature. On their view, the various procedures which are thought of as providing rational justification by one or another culture may or may not really *be* rational. For to be truly rational, procedures of justification *must* lead to the truth, to correspondence to reality, to the intrinsic nature of things.

By contrast, those who wish to reduce objectivity to solidarity—call them "pragmatists"—do not require either a metaphysics or an epistemology. They view truth as, in William James' phrase, what is good for *us* to believe. So they do not need an account of a relation between beliefs and objects called 'correspondence', nor an account of human cognitive abilities which ensures that our species is capable of entering into that relation. They see the gap between truth and justification not as something to be bridged by isolating a natural and transcultural sort of rationality which can be used to criticize certain cultures and praise others, but simply as the gap between the actual good and the possible better. From a pragmatist point of view, to say that what is rational for us now to believe may not be *true*, is simply to say that somebody may come up with a better idea. it is to say that there is always room for improved belief, since new evidence, or new hypotheses, or a whole new vocabulary, may come along. For pragmatists, the desire for objectivity is not the desire to escape the limitations of one's community, but simply the desire for as much intersubjective agreement as possible, the desire to extend the reference of "us" as far as we can. Insofar as pragmatists make a distinction between knowledge and opinion, it is simply the distinction between topics on which such agreement is relatively easy to get and topics on which agreement is relatively hard to get.

"Relativism" is the traditional epithet applied to pragmatism by realists. Three different views are commonly referred to by this name. The first is the view that every belief is as good as every other. The second is the view that "true" is an equivocal term, having as many meanings as there are procedures of justification. The third is the view that there is nothing to be said about either truth or rationality apart from descriptions of the familiar procedures of justification which a given society—*ours*—uses in one or another area of inquiry. The pragmatist holds the ethnocentric third view. But he does not hold the self-refuting first view, nor the eccentric second view. He thinks that his views are better than the realists', but he does not think that his views correspond to the nature of things. He thinks that the very flexibility of the word "true"—the fact that it is merely an expression of commendation—insures its univocity. The term "true," on his account, means the same in all cultures, just as equally flexible terms like "here," "there," "good," "bad," "you," and "me" mean the same in all cultures. But the identity of meaning is, of course, compatible with diversity of reference, and with diversity of procedures for assigning the terms. So he feels free to use the term "true" as a general term of commendation in the same way as his realist opponent does—and in particular to use it to commend his own view.

However, it is not clear why "relativist" should be thought an appropriate term for the ethnocentric third view, the one which the pragmatist *does* hold. For the pragmatist is not holding a positive theory which says that something is relative to something else. He is, instead, making the purely *negative* point that we should drop the traditional distinction between knowledge and opinion, construed as the distinction between truth as correspondence to reality and truth as a commendatory term for well-justified beliefs. The reason that the realist calls this

negative claim "relativistic" is that he cannot believe that anybody would seriously deny that truth has an intrinsic nature. So when the pragmatist says that there is nothing to be said about truth save that each of us will commend as true those beliefs which he or she finds good to believe, the realist is inclined to interpret this as one more positive theory about the nature of truth: a theory according to which truth is simply the contemporary opinion of a chosen individual or group. Such a theory would, of course, be self-refuting. But the pragmatist does not have a theory of truth, much less a relativistic one. As a partisan of solidarity, his account of the value of cooperative human inquiry has only an ethical base, not an epistemological or metaphysical one. Not having *any* epistemology, *a fortiori* he does not have a relativistic one.

The question of whether truth or rationality has an intrinsic nature, of whether we ought to have a positive theory about either topic, is just the question of whether our self-description ought to be constructed around a relation to human nature or around a relation to a particular collection of human beings, whether we should desire objectivity or solidarity. It is hard to see how one could choose between these alternatives by looking more deeply into the nature of knowledge, or of man, or of nature. Indeed, the proposal that this issue might be so settled begs the question in favor of the realist, for it presupposes that knowledge, man, and nature *have* real essences which are relevant to the problem at hand. For the pragmatist, by contrast, "knowledge" is, like "truth," simply a compliment paid to the beliefs which we think so well justified that, for the moment, further justification is not needed. An inquiry into the nature of knowledge can, on his view, only be a sociohistorical account of how various people have tried to reach agreement on what to believe.

. . .

I think that putting the issue in such moral and political terms, rather than in epistemological or metaphilosophical terms, makes clearer what is at stake. For now the question is not about how to define words like "truth" or "rationality" or "knowledge" or "philosophy," but about what self-image our society should have of itself. The ritual invocation of the "need to avoid relativism" is most comprehensible as an expression of the need to preserve certain habits of contemporary European life. These are the habits nurtured by the Enlightenment, and justified by it in terms of an appeal of Reason, conceived as a transcultural human ability to correspond to reality, a faculty whose possession and use is demonstrated by obedience to explicit criteria. So the real question about relativism is whether these same habits of intellectual, social, and political life can be justified by a conception of rationality as criterionless muddling through, and by a pragmatist conception of truth.

I think that the answer to this question is that the pragmatist cannot justify these habits without circularity, but then neither can the realist. The pragmatists' justification of toleration, free inquiry, and the quest for undistorted communication can only take the form of a comparison between societies which exemplify these habits and those which do not, leading up to the suggestion that nobody who has experienced both would prefer the latter. It is exemplified by Winston Churchill's defense of democracy as the worst form of government imaginable, except for all the others which have been tried so far. Such justification is not by reference to a criterion, but by reference to various detailed practical advantages. It is circular only in that the terms of praise used to describe liberal societies will be drawn from the vocabulary of liberal societies themselves. Such praise has to be in *some* vocabulary, after all, and the terms of praise current in primitive or theocratic or totalitarian societies will not produce the desired result. So the pragmatist admits that he has no ahistorical standpoint from which to endorse the habits of modern democracies he wishes to praise. These consequences are just what partisans of solidarity expect. But among partisans of objectivity they give rise, once again, to fears of the dilemma formed by ethnocentrism on the one hand and relativism on the other. Either we attach a special privilege to our own community, or we pretend an impossible tolerance for every other group.

I have been arguing that we pragmatists should grasp the ethnocentric horn of this dilemma. We should say that we must, in practice, privilege our own group, even though there can be no noncircular justification for doing so. We must insist that the fact that nothing is immune from criticism does not mean that we have a duty to justify everything.

We Western liberal intellectuals should accept the fact that we have to start from where we are, and that this means that there are lots of views which we simply cannot take seriously. To use Neurath's familiar analogy, we can *understand* the revolutionary's suggestion that a sailable boat can't be made out of the planks which make up ours, and that we must simply abandon ship. But we cannot take his suggestion seriously. We cannot take it as a rule for action, so it is not a live option. For some people, to be sure, the option *is* live. These are the people who have always hoped to become a New Being, who have hoped to be converted rather than persuaded. But we—the liberal Rawlsian searchers for consensus, the heirs of Socrates, the people who wish to link their days dialectically each to each—cannot do so. Our community—the community of the liberal intellectuals of the secular modern West—wants to be able to give a *post factum* account of any change of view. We want to be able, so to speak, to justify ourselves to our earlier selves. This preference is not built into us by human nature. It is just the way *we* live now.

...

My suggestion that the desire for objectivity is in part a disguised form of the fear of the death of our community echoes Nietzsche's charge that the philosophical tradition which stems from Plato is an attempt to avoid facing up to contingency, to escape from time and chance. Nietzsche thought that realism was to be condemned not only by arguments from its theoretical incoherence, the sort of argument we find in Putnam and Davidson, but also on practical, pragmatic, grounds. Nietzsche thought that the test of human character was the ability to live with the thought that there was no convergence. He wanted us to be able to think of truth as:

> a mobile army of metaphors, metonyms, and anthromorphisms—in short a sum of human relations, which have been enhanced, transposed, and embellished poetically and rhetorically and which after long use seem firm, canonical, and obligatory to a people.

Nietzsche hoped that eventually there might be human beings who could and did think of truth in this way, but who still liked themselves, who saw themselves as *good* people for whom solidarity was *enough*.

I think that pragmatism's attack on the various structure-content distinctions which buttress the realist's notion of objectivity can best be seen as an attempt to let us think of truth in this Nietzschean way, as entirely a matter of solidarity. That is why I think we need to say, despite Putnam, that "there is only the dialogue," only *us*, and to throw out the last residues of the notion of "transcultural rationality." But this should not lead us to repudiate, as Nietzsche sometimes did, the elements in our movable host which embody the ideas of Socratic conversation, Christian fellowship, and Enlightenment science. Nietzsche ran together his diagnosis of philosophical realism as an expression of fear and resentment with his own resentful idiosyncratic idealizations of silence, solitude, and violence. Post-Nietzschean thinkers like Adorno and Heidegger and Foucault have run together Nietzsche's criticisms of the metaphysical tradition on the one hand with his criticisms of bourgeois civility, of Christian love, and of the nineteenth century's hope that science would make the world a better place to live, on the other. I do not think that there is any interesting connection between these two sets of criticisms. Pragmatism seems to me, as I have said, a philosophy of solidarity rather than of despair. From this point of view, Socrates' turn away from the gods, Christianity's turn from an Omnipotent Creator to the man who suffered on the Cross, and the Baconian turn from science as contemplation of eternal truth to science as instrument of social progress, can be seen as so many preparations for the act of social faith which is suggested by a Nietzschean view of truth.

The best argument we partisans of solidarity have against the realistic partisans of objectivity is Nietzsche's argument that the traditional Western metaphysico-epistemological way of firming up our habits simply isn't working anymore. It isn't doing its job. It has become as transparent a device as the postulation of deities who turn out, by a happy coincidence, to have chosen *us* as their people. So the pragmatist suggestion that we substitute a "merely" ethical foundation for our sense of community—or, better, that we think of our sense of community as having no foundation except shared hope and the trust created by such sharing—is put

forward on practical grounds. It is *not* put forward as a corollary of a metaphysical claim that the objects in the world contain no intrinsically action-guiding properties, nor of an epistemological claim that we lack a faculty of moral sense, nor of a semantical claim that truth is reducible to justification. It is a suggestion about how we might think of ourselves in order to avoid the kind of resentful belatedness—characteristic of the bad side of Nietzsche—which now characterizes much of high culture. This resentment arises from the realization, which I referred to at the beginning of this chapter, that the Enlightenment's search for objectivity has often gone sour.

The rhetoric of scientific objectivity, pressed too hard and taken too seriously, has led us to people like B. F. Skinner on the one hand and people like Althusser on the other—two equally pointless fantasies, both produced by the attempt to be "scientific" about our moral and political lives. Reaction against scientism led to attacks on natural science as a sort of false god. But there is nothing wrong with science, there is only something wrong with the attempt to divinize it, the attempt characteristic of realistic philosophy. This reaction has also led to attacks on liberal social thought of the type common to Mill and Dewey and Rawls as a mere ideological superstructure, one which obscures the realities of our situation and represses attempts to change that situation. But there is nothing wrong with liberal democracy, nor with the philosophers who have tried to enlarge its scope. There is only something wrong with the attempt to see their efforts as failures to achieve something which they were not trying to achieve—a demonstration of the "objective" superiority of our way of life over all other alternatives. There is, in short, nothing wrong with the hopes of the Enlightenment, the hopes which created the Western democracies. The value of the ideals of the Enlightenment is, for us pragmatists, just the value of some of the institutions and practices which they have created. In this essay I have sought to distinguish these institutions and practices from the philosophical justifications for them provided by partisans of objectivity, and to suggest an alternative justification.

Discussion Questions

1. Could any group appeal to solidarity to justify their beliefs? For example, could a religious sect defend their beliefs on the basis that they were good for them to believe? Or, for example, could creationists defend their rejection of evolution on the basis that it was good for them to believe in creation? Why or why not? How would Rorty answer these questions? Does he have an adequate response in your view?

2. Do we have "solidarity" in this culture, that is, enough to reach a consensus on standards to justify truth claims? Or is our culture so fragmented that there is never enough "solidarity" to reach a consensus? In what areas is consensus possible? In what areas is it not? Is this a problem for Rorty's account? Why or why not?

3. Can you think of some beliefs that were once pragmatically justified (because they worked or were good for the group to believe) and that we now reject? Why do we reject them now? Were they always wrong? Why or why not?

4. Does Rorty have the conceptual resources to explain why racism is wrong? Could racism ever be "good for us to believe"? Explain your view. How would Rorty likely respond here? Is his view adequate? Why or why not?

For Further Reading

This essay has been widely anthologized. One source is Rorty's *Philosophical Papers,* volumes 1–3 (1991). Another source is *Post-Analytic Philosophy,* edited by John Rajchmann and Cornel West (1985). The latter book is helpful because it places Rorty in context with a number of other contemporary philosophers who are struggling with similar issues; it also has a helpful essay by Rajchmann at the beginning. Another source with a similar perspective is *After Philosophy,* edited by Kenneth Baynes, James Bohman, and Thomas McCarthy (1987); this anthology contains other writings by authors whose perspectives complement Rorty's and a helpful bibliography.

   For discussions of Rorty's appropriation of pragmatism see Gary S. Brodsky, "Rorty's Interpretation of Pragmatism" *18,* pp. 311–337, and Abraham Edel, "A Missing Dimension in Rorty's Use of Pragmatism" *21,* pp. 21–38, both in the journal *Transactions of the Charles S. Peirce Society.* See also *Richard Rorty: Prophet and Poet of the New Pragmatism* (1994), by David Hall. For a more critical analysis of Rorty's postmodernism see *After the Demise of the Tradition: Rorty, Critical Theory, and the Fate of Philosophy,* by Kai Nielsen. Rorty is most widely known for his book *Philosophy and the Mirror of Nature* (1979), which is highly recommended.

38 "STRONG OBJECTIVITY": A RESPONSE TO THE NEW OBJECTIVITY QUESTION
Sandra Harding

Objectivity might be defined as neutrality or observer-independence. This definition suggests that a truth claim should be free from observer bias and not depend on the fact that a particular person is conducting the

SOURCE: From *Synthese,* vol. 104, 1995, pp. 331–349, "'Strong Objectivity': A Response to the New Objectivity Question," by Sandra Harding. Copyright © Kluwer Academic Publishing, 1995. With permission from the publisher.

investigation. Yet every person, including scientists, does look at the world from a particular perspective, one shaped by personal and cultural facts. While objectivity as neutrality may represent an ideal, it might also be inherently impossible since there are no investigations conducted *without* observers who inhabit particular circumstances. Hence, critics of objectivity argue that hidden cultural assumptions invariably distort any investigation of the truth. Moreover, it is practically impossible to discover all of the hidden assumptions that distort scientific inquiry.

On the other hand, there might be a method that would help reveal and make apparent these hidden cultural assumptions. Standpoint theorists argue that the hidden cultural assumptions that distort the conclusions of science can be made visible by beginning one's investigation from marginal perspectives. Instead of attempting to occupy a 'view from nowhere'— which is not only impossible but dangerous if it misleads us into believing that we have a neutral, transcultural point of view—standpoint theorists suggest that we first recognize that all thought unavoidably begins from *somewhere.* Once that is understood, the task becomes not how to avoid looking at the world from somewhere, but rather how to decide from *which* 'somewhere' we are going to examine the world. Which standpoint should we occupy, given that we will necessarily occupy some standpoint? If the goal is to maximize objectivity by revealing hidden cultural bias, then the standpoint should reveal hidden cultural bias. According to standpoint theorists, this is the standpoint from the margins, that is, a standpoint from the perspective of persons who have been marginalized from mainstream social groups. Because these groups occupy the periphery of society, their point of view is more likely to reveal the hidden assumptions that perpetuate injurious falsehoods and insidious distortions. (Of course, merely being 'marginalized' would not make their standpoint less likely to contain its own biases: their standpoint may reveal some bias while hiding others.)

This essay is from Sandra Harding (1935–), a philosopher with joint appointments at the University of Delaware and the University of California, Los Angeles. Harding has written extensively on feminism and the philosophy of science. Here she argues that taking a 'view from somewhere,' in particular, from a marginal standpoint, does not make social science less objective; instead, it maximizes objectivity.

Reading Questions

1. How is inequality built in to standpoint theories?
2. Why must research projects start from marginal lives?
3. Why does Harding contend that standpoint theory is not only about marginal lives?
4. How does the dominant ideology affect what is seen about such topics as rape, women's work, and sexual harassment? How do standpoint theories attempt to overcome this limitation?
5. Why does Harding reject the view that there are essential features to women's lives?
6. Why is it wrong to categorize standpoint theory as, for example, merely an epistemology or merely a philosophy of science?

7. Why can we never claim to know the truth? What does it mean to say a theory is "less false"?
8. Why does Harding propose that objectivity is the "indigenous resource" of Northern forms of democracy? How will we respond to objectivity if it is characterized this way?

...

Standpoint theories argue that what we do in our social relations both enables and limits (it does not determine) what we can know. Standpoint theories, in contrast to empiricist epistemologies, begin from the recognition of social inequality; their models of society are conflict models, in contrast to the consensus model of liberal political philosophy assumed by empiricists. All human thought necessarily can be only partial; it is always limited by the fact of having only a particular historical location—of not being able to be everywhere and see everything, and of being "contained" by cultural assumptions that become visible only from outside that culture (hence: "medieval thought", Renaissance thought, etc.). However, standpoint theories are concerned with a distinctive dimension of social location that is more pernicious than these kinds of "positionality," and that is difficult to grasp from within the empiricist assumptions of modern scientific rationality. In hierarchically organized societies, the daily activities of people in the ruling groups tend to set distinctive limits on their thought, limits that are not created by the activities of the subjugated groups. Administrative-managerial activities, including the work of the natural and social sciences, is the form of "ruling" in our contemporary modern societies, and the conceptual frameworks of our disciplines are shaped by administrative-managerial priorities, just as pre-scientific observations of nature are shaped by other cultural priorities. Such priorities do enable gaining the kinds of information administrators need to function effectively, but they also distort and limit our understanding of just what brings about daily social relations and interactions with nature, and they make it difficult to think possible any different kind of interactions. In order to gain a causal critical view of the interests and values that constitute the dominant conceptual projects, one must start one's thought, one's research project, from outside those conceptual schemes and the activities that generate them; one must start from the lives excluded as origins of their design—from "marginal lives."

The fundamental features of the standpoint proposal can be grasped most quickly by looking at *what it is not*. Those constrained by the old objectivity question will tend to distort standpoint theory by perceiving it only through the conceptual choices offered by "Objectivity or relativism: which side are you on?" They often construct it as just a variant of empiricism or, alternatively, as a kind of gynocentrism, special pleading, or unreasonably claimed privileged positionality. On such a reading, empiricism is politics-free, and standpoint theory is asserting epistemological/scientific privilege for one group at the expense of the equally valuable/distorted perceptions of other groups. Or, it is simply substituting one politics for another, and all political positions—the master's and the slave's, that of the rich and of the poor, the colonizer's and the colonized's, the rapist's and his victim's—all are equally valuable and/or distorted. This interpretation of difference as merely diversity is a serious misunderstanding of social realities, as well as of standpoint claims. Standpoint theory leads us to turn such a way of posing the alternatives into a topic for historical analysis: "What forms of social relations make *this* conceptual framework—the 'view from nowhere' versus 'special pleading'—so useful, and for what purposes?"

Not about Only Marginal Lives

First, standpoint theory is not only about how to get a less limited understanding of marginal lives—women's lives, for example. Instead, research is to *start off* from such locations (not to take as truth what people in those locations think or say) in order to explain not only those lives but also the rest of the micro and macro social order, including human interactions with nature and the philosophies that have been developed to explain sciences. The standpoint of women, as Dorothy Smith puts the point, enables us to understand women's lives, men's lives, and the relations between the two through concepts and hypotheses arising from women's lives rather than only ones arising from the lives of those assigned administrative/managerial work, a group that includes sociologists (and philosophers). The point is to produce systematic causal accounts of how the natural and social orders are organized such that the everyday lives of women and men, our activities and beliefs, end up in the forms that they do.

Grounded, but Not in the Conventional Way, in Women's Experiences

The phrase 'women's experiences' can be read in an empiricist way such that these experiences are assumed to be constituted prior to the social. Standpoint theory challenges this kind of reading. For a researcher to start from women's lives is not necessarily to take one's research problems in the terms in which women perceive or articulate their problems—and this is as true for women as it is for men thinkers. The dominant ideology restricts what everyone is permitted to see and shapes everyone's consciousness. Women, like men, have had to learn to think of sexual harassment not as a matter of "boys will be boys," but as a violation of women's civil rights. Marital rape was a legal and, for most people, conceptual impossibility until collective political struggle and theorizing resulted in its articulation in the law. European American feminists, like the rest of European Americans, are only beginning to learn how to conceptualize many of our issues in anti-Eurocentric terms. Women, too, have held distorted beliefs about our bodies, our minds, nature and society, and numerous men have made important contributions to feminist analyses—John Stuart Mill, Marx, Engels, and many contemporary scholars in history, sociology, economics, philosophy, literary and art criticism, etc. Moreover, it is obvious that "women's experience" does not automatically generate feminist analyses, since the former always exists but only occasionally does the latter emerge. Standpoint theorists are not making the absurd claim that feminist work simply flows from women's experiences.

Feminist knowledge is not a "neutral" elaboration of women's experiences, or what women say about their lives, but a collective political and theoretical achievement. Women's experiences and what women say are important guides to the new questions we can ask about nature, sciences, and social relations. However, the *answers* to such questions must be sought elsewhere than in women's experiences, since the latter are shaped by national and international policies and practices that are formulated and enacted far away from our daily lives—by Supreme Court decisions, international trade agreements, military policies on the other side of the world, etc. Standpoint theory is not calling for phenomenologies of women's world, or for ethnocentric (gynocentric) accounts. Nor is it arguing that only women can generate feminist knowledge; it is not an "identity politics" project. Men, too, can learn to start their thought from women's lives, as many have done. These misunderstandings come about because objectivism insists that the only alternatives to its view from nowhere are special interest claims and ethno-knowledges that can be understood only within a relativist epistemology. However, institutionalized power imbalances give starting off from the lives of those who least benefit from such imbalances a critical edge for generating theoretically and empirically more accurate and comprehensive accounts. Feminist accounts of marital rape, sexual harassment, women's double-day of work or women's different and valuable forms of moral reason are capable of conceptualizing phenomena that were heretofore invisible because they start off from outside the dominant paradigms and conceptual schemes.

No Essential Woman's Life

Next, standpoint theory is not arguing that there is some kind of essential, universal woman's life from which feminists (male and female) should start their thought. In any particular research situation, one is to start off research from the lives of those who have been disadvantaged by, excluded from the benefits of, the dominant conceptual frameworks. What can we learn about that framework by starting from their lives? For example, what can we learn about biological models of the human body, or of human evolution, psychological and philosophical models of moral reasoning, historical models of social change and of progress, philosophical models of rationality, etc., by starting off thought about them from the lives of women of different races, ethnicities, classes and sexualities whose natures and activities each of these models defines as inferior in partially different ways?

The point here is that these kinds of models have also been used to define other groups—racial, ethnic, economic, etc.—as inferior. We can learn some similar and some new things about the conceptual frameworks of the disciplines by starting off thought about the latter from, for example, the lives of slaves, or "orientals," workers, etc. Moreover, "woman" and the homogeneity of "women" is an elitist fiction. These categories in everyday life are multiple and contradictory, and the theorization of this fact by women of color and others who *started off their thought from women of color's lives* is one of the great strengths of contemporary feminist thought. This "matrix theory" developed by women of color enables us to think how each of us has a determinate social location in the matrix of social relations that is constituted by gender, class, race, sexuality and whatever other macro forces shape our particular part of the social order. Women are located at many positions in this matrix, and starting thought from each such group of lives can be useful for understanding social phenomena (including our relations with nature) that have effects on those lives.

Consciousness Not Determined by Social Location

For standpoint theorists, we each have a determinate location in such a social matrix, but that location does not *determine* one's consciousness. The availability of competing discourses enables men, for example, to think and act in feminist ways. They are still obviously men, who are thereby in determinate relations to women and men in every class and race; such relations cannot be changed simply by willing them. They can work to eliminate male supremacy, but no matter what they do, they will still be treated with the privilege (or suspicion!) accorded to men by students, sales people, other intellectuals, etc. A parallel account can be given about women, of course.

An Epistemology, a Philosophy of Science, a Sociology of Knowledge, and a Method for Doing Research

Several disciplines have competed to disown standpoint theory. Some philosophers claim it is only a sociology; some sociologists reject it as only an epistemology. Some scientists and philosophers have insisted that it could not have any implications for the natural sciences since it is concerned with intentionality, and physical nature is not intentional.

It is more useful to see it as all of these projects: a philosophy of knowledge, a philosophy of science, a sociology of knowledge, and a proposed research method. Each such project must always make assumptions about the others; for example, every philosophy of science must make epistemological assumptions about the nature and conditions for knowledge in general, historical ones about which procedures for producing knowledge have been most successful in the past, and sociological ones about how communities that have produced the best knowledge claims in the past have been organized. In periods of what we could refer to as "normal philosophy," these background assumptions can safely be left unexamined; but when skepticism arises about the adequacy of fundamental assumptions in any one of these areas, the others all present themselves as candidates for reexamination. Our beliefs face the tribunal of experience as a network, as Quine points out, and none are immune from possible revision when a misfit between belief and observation arises. Feminist challenges to conventional bodies of knowledge have forced reexamination of empiricist assumptions about the organization of scientific communities, ideals of the knower, the known, and how knowledge should be produced, rational reconstructions of the growth of scientific knowledge, and scientific method in the sense of "how to do good research." Standpoint theory's claims must find support and have effects in all of these fields.

Asymmetrical Falsity and Truth in Scientific Practice

Standpoint theory claims that starting from women's lives is a way of gaining less false and distorted results of research. However, one gratuitously asks for trouble if one equates such claims with ones to truth or truth-likeness. This is a general point about scientific claims, not one peculiar to standpoint theories or to feminist philosophies of science. The claim that a result of research is "less false" is sufficient to capture what we can establish about the processes producing such a research result, and attributions of truth or truth-likeness are too strong for scientific claims. We do not have to be claiming to approximate the one true story about nature or social relations in order for it to make sense to argue that our account is less false than some specified set of competitors to it. For one thing, all that scientific processes could in principle produce are claims less false than competing ones as a hypothesis is tested against some chosen set of rivals—the dominant hypothesis, or another new one. Moreover, as a matter of principle one is never to assume that such processes generate what one can know to be true, since empirical claims have to be held open to future revision on the basis of empirical evidence and conceptual shifts. To put the point a familiar way, our best theories are always underdetermined by the evidence. As a glance at the history of science shows, nature says "yea" to many competing and, from our perspective, quite fantastic accounts of its regularities and their underlying causal tendencies; our best theories are only consistent with nature, not uniquely coherent with natural laws that are "out there" for our detection.

Standpoint approaches were developed both to explain the surprising results of feminist research and to guide future research. They show us how to detect values and interests that constitute scientific projects, ones that do not vary between legitimated observers, and the difference between those values and interests that enlarge and those that limit our descriptions, explanations and understandings of nature and social relations. Standpoint approaches provide a map, a method, for maximizing a strong objectivity that can function more effectively for knowledge projects faced with the problem of sciences that have been constituted by the values and interests of the most powerful social groups.

Standpoint theory has become a site for some of the most pressing contemporary discussions about post-foundationalism, realism versus constructivism, identity politics and epistemologies, the role of experience in producing knowledge, alternatives to both the "view from nowhere" and relativism, and other issues controversial in the philosophy and social studies of science more generally. Although it rejects and tries to move beyond many of the distorting features of modernity's conceptual framework, it also retains central commitments of that tradition. One is to the importance of the notion of objectivity.

OBJECTIVITY: AN INDIGENOUS RESOURCE OF THE MODERN NORTH?

Objectivity is an important value for cultures that value sciences, and its value spreads to other cultures as they import Northern forms of democracy, their epistemologies and sciences. This is not to say that Northerners are particularly good at democracy or maximizing objectivity, or have any corner on the ideals. And, of course, Northern forms of these ideals are widely criticized by many Third World intellectuals, as they are by feminists, as ideologies that have justified excluding and exploiting the already less powerful. Nevertheless, 'objective' defines for many people today how they think of themselves: we are fair; we make decisions by principle, not by whim or fiat; we are against "might makes right"; we are rational; we can find ways to live together that value our cultural diversity . . . and so forth. I am not saying that everyone who claims objectivity in fact maximizes it, but that such an ideal is deeply embedded in the ethic and rhetoric of democracy at personal, communal, and institutional levels. The notion is centered in natural and many social science discourses, in jurisprudence, in public policy, in many areas where decisions about how to organize social relations are made. Thus, while the diverse arguments for abandoning the notion are illuminating and important to keep in mind, to do so is to adopt a "bohemian" strategy; it is to do "something else" besides try to struggle on the terrain where philosophies, science projects and social policies are negotiated. Why not, instead, think of objectivity as an "indigenous resource" of the modern North? It needs updating, rehabilitation, so that it is capable of functioning effectively in the science-based society that the North has generated and that many now say is its major cultural export.

What of the epistemological status of this strong objectivity program itself? What limitations arise from the particular historical projects from which it started off? No doubt there are many such limitations, but four easily come to mind. First, the strong objectivity program is, indeed, a science project. It relegitimates scientific rationality (and a modern European form of it) in a world where many think the power of this rationality should be limited. Now the "context of discovery" and the values and interests shared within a research community are to be added to the phenomena to be analyzed with scientific rationality.

Second, this strong objectivity program and the standpoint theory that supports it originate in the North, and draw upon the historical and cultural legacies of those cultures—for example, European Marxian and feminist legacies. Thinkers in other cultures may well prefer to draw on the riches of their own legacies in order to develop resources for blocking "might makes right" in the realm of knowledge production. Third, one can wonder if the delinking of objectivity from the neutrality ideal can succeed eventually in bypassing the gender-coding of objectivity as inherently masculine (and European, bourgeois, etc.)? Or does the logic of discovery become feminized (no neutrality) leaving the logic of justification masculinized as usual (here seeking neutrality can be useful)?

Finally, it is hard to imagine this strong objectivity program effectively enacted right away within the present day culture and practices of sciences, which are largely resistant to the interpretive and critical skills and resources necessary to detect values and interests in the conceptual frameworks of scientific projects. Natural scientists are not trained to do this work, and they often are hostile to sharing authority about nature, let alone about how science should be done, with any individuals or groups that they conceptualize as "outside science." And yet, we should not be too pessimistic since mainstream concerns to bring science under more democratic control, the global and local social changes to which such terms as "diversity" and "multiculturalism" point, and the ever increasing adoption of feminist projects into mainstream cultures and practices (albeit without the label "feminist") offer hope that the borders of scientific culture and practice, too, can become more permeable to these tendencies.

To conclude, the strong objectivity program is one response to the new objectivity question. It is not perfect, but it does have considerable advantages over the alternatives so far in sight.

Discussion Questions

1. Is it possible to take a standpoint not one's own? Can we look at the world from the point of view of other persons? What methods could be used to enhance our ability to do so? How about film, novels, and so forth? Explain your answer.

2. The arts, including painting, film, literature, and music, are often considered capable of helping us to become aware of standpoints other than our own. Does your own experience confirm this? Give some specific examples that support your answer. Would creating art be an important method of communicating your own personal standpoint and the standpoint of your community for the benefit of others who do not share your standpoint? Explain your answer.

3. Suppose you were studying the problem of poverty, with the goal of understanding it in order to respond properly to it. What standpoint would Harding say you should occupy in order to advance your investigation? Why? How would this standpoint differ from the standpoint of an economist, for example? What other standpoints might you occupy? Which of these would be the most beneficial to your project, according to Harding? Why? Do you agree with Harding's recommendation or not?

4. Is it possible for a single person to occupy multiple standpoints, for example, as a young person, as a midwesterner, as an athlete, and as a female? If not, why not? If so, do these standpoints differ according to how they see particular issues and concerns, or do these multiple standpoints combine to form one unified perspective? Explain your answer.

For Further Reading

Harding has written extensively on feminist philosophy of science. See especially *The Science Question in Feminism* (1986); *Whose Science? Whose Knowledge? Thinking from Women's Lives* (1991); and, more recently, *Is Science Multicultural? Postcolonialism, Feminisms, and Epistemologies* (1998). In each of these books and other articles, she progressively develops her concept of "strong objectivity." See also "Rethinking Standpoint Epistemology: What Is Strong Objectivity?" in *Feminist Epistemologies,* edited by Linda Alcoff and Elizabeth Potter (1993).

A classic essay on the feminist standpoint is Nancy Hartsock's "The Feminist Standpoint: Developing the Ground for a Specifically Feminist Historical Materialism," in *Discovering Reality,* edited by Sandra Harding and Merrill B. Hintikka (1983). For two different perspectives on objectivity, one critical and one positive, see Susan Bordo, *The Flight to Objectivity* (1987), and Nicholas Rescher, *Objectivity: The Obligations of Impersonal Reason* (1997). For an overview of feminist approaches to science see *Feminism and Science,* edited by Evelyn Fox Keller and Helen E. Longino (1996).

39   CHOOSING THE MARGIN AS A SPACE OF RADICAL OPENNESS
bell hooks

In some ways it is too easy to write and talk about the 'other' or the 'voice from the margin'—to appropriate rhetoric about 'embracing the other'. After all, many colleges and universities are places of relative privilege and prestige; speech about embracing the other and standing in the margins sounds a bit hollow when it bounces off the walls of a university lecture hall. For example, what does it really mean to 'stand in solidarity' with those who have felt the effects of poverty? Is thinking about poverty from the standpoint of the poor as simple as a thought experiment in a sociology course or watching a video in an ethics course?

bell hooks (1952–) has struggled with these problems. What does it actually mean to stand in the margins, to be in solidarity with those on the edges of society? For hooks, a standpoint from the margins is a place of radical possibility, a place of promise and hope that comes from the critical perspective marginal spaces create. It also comes at a great price.

Reading Questions

1. What choice does moving "out of one's place" pose?
2. In what different ways is language a place of struggle?
3. What is the importance of remembering for hooks?
4. How is the margin not merely a site of deprivation? What possibilities does it create?

SOURCE: From *Yearning: Race, Gender, and Cultural Politics,* by bell hooks, 1990. Used by permission of the Institute for Social and Cultural Change.

5. What did hooks' experience teach her about the problems posed by academic discourse about the "other"?
6. What is the difference between the margin as a place of resistance and the margin as a place of deprivation? From which place does hooks believe well-meaning academics want her to speak? Why does she resist this?

As a radical standpoint, perspective, position, "the politics of location" necessarily calls those of us who would participate in the formation of counter-hegemonic cultural practice to identify the spaces where we begin the process of re-vision. When asked, "What does it mean to enjoy reading *Beloved*, admire *Schooldaze*, and have a theoretical interest in post-structural theory?" (one of the "wild" questions posed by the Third World Cinema Focus Forum), I located my answer concretely in the realm of oppositional political struggle. Such diverse pleasures can be experienced, enjoyed even, because one transgresses, moves "out of one's place." For many of us, that movement requires pushing against oppressive boundaries set by race, sex, and class domination. Initially, then, it is a defiant political gesture. Moving, we confront the realities of choice and location. Within complex and ever shifting realms of power relations, do we position ourselves on the side of colonizing mentality? Or do we continue to stand in political resistance with the oppressed, ready to offer our ways of seeing and theorizing, of making culture, towards that revolutionary effort which seeks to create space where there is unlimited access to the pleasure and power of knowing, where transformation is possible? This choice is crucial. It shapes and determines our response to existing cultural practice and our capacity to envision new, alternative, oppositional aesthetic acts. It informs the way we speak about these issues, the language we choose. Language is also a place of struggle.

To me, the effort to speak about issues of "space and location" evoked pain. The questions raised compelled difficult explorations of "silences"—unaddressed places within my personal and artistic evolution. Before I could consider answers, I had to face ways these issues were intimately connected to intense personal emotional upheaval regarding place, identity, desire. In an intense all-night-long conversation with Eddie George (member of Black Audio Film Collective) talking about the struggle of oppressed people to come to voice, he made the very "down" comment that "ours is a broken voice." My response was simply that when you hear the broken voice you also hear the pain contained within that brokenness—a speech of suffering; often it's that sound nobody wants to hear. Stuart Hall talks about the need for a "politics of articulation." He and Eddie have engaged in dialogue with me in a deeply soulful way, hearing my struggle for words. It is this dialogue between comrades that is a gesture of love; I am grateful.

I have been working to change the way I speak and write, to incorporate in the manner of telling a sense of place, of not just who I am in the present but where I am coming from, the multiple voices within me. I have confronted silence, inarticulateness. When I say, then, that these words emerge from suffering, I refer to that personal struggle to name that location from which I come to voice—that space of my theorizing.

Often when the radical voice speaks about domination we are speaking to those who dominate. Their presence changes the nature and direction of our words. Language is also a place of struggle. I was just a girl coming slowly into womanhood when I read Adrienne Rich's words, "That is the oppressor's language, yet I need it to talk to you." This language that enabled me to attend graduate school, to write a dissertation, to speak at job interviews, carries the scent of oppression. Language is also a place of struggle. The Australian aborigines say "that smell of the white man is killing us." I remember the smells of my childhood, hot water corn bread, turnip greens, fried pies. I remember the way we talked to one another, our words thickly accented Black Southern speech. Language is also a place of struggle. We are wedded in language, have our being in words. Language is also a place of struggle. Dare I speak to oppressed and oppressor in the same voice? Dare I speak to you in a language that will move beyond the boundaries of domination—a language that will not bind you, fence you in, or hold you? Language is also a place of struggle. The oppressed struggle in language to recover ourselves, to reconcile, to re-unite, to renew. Our words are not without meaning, they are an action, a resistance. Language is also a place of struggle.

It is no easy task to find ways to include our multiple voices within the various texts we create—in film, poetry, feminist theory. Those are sounds and images that mainstream consumers find difficult to understand. Sounds and scenes which cannot be appropriated are often that sign everyone questions, wants to erase, to "wipe out." I feel it even now, writing this piece when I gave it talking and reading, talking spontaneously, using familiar academic speech now and then, "talking the talk"—using Black vernacular speech, the intimate sounds and gestures I normally save for family and loved ones. Private speech in public discourse, intimate intervention, making another text, a space that enables me to recover all that I am in language, I find so many gaps, absences in this written text. To cite them at least is to let the reader know something has been missed, or remains there hinted at by words—there in the deep structure.

Throughout *Freedom Charter,* a work which traces aspects of the movement against racial apartheid in South Africa, this statement is constantly repeated: *our struggle is also a struggle of memory against forgetting.* In much new, exciting cultural practice, cultural texts—in film, Black literature, critical theory—there is an effort to remember that is expressive of the need to create spaces where one is able to redeem and reclaim the past, legacies of pain, suffering, and triumph in ways that transform present reality. Fragments of memory are not simply represented as flat documentary but constructed to give a "new take" on the old, constructed to move us into a different mode of articulation. We see this in films like *Dreaming Rivers* and *Illusions,* and in books like *Mama Day* by Gloria Naylor. Thinking again about space and location, I heard the statement "our struggle is also a struggle of memory against forgetting"; a politicization of memory that distinguishes nostalgia, that longing for something to be as once it was, a kind of useless act, from that remembering that serves to illuminate and transform the present.

I have needed to remember, as part of a self-critical process where one pauses to reconsider choices and location, tracing my journey from small town Southern Black life, from folk traditions, and church experience to cities, to the university, to neighborhoods that are not racially segregated, to places where I see for the first time independent cinema, where I read critical theory, where I write theory. Along that trajectory, I vividly recall efforts to silence my coming to voice. In my public presentation I was able to tell stories, to share memories. Here again I only hint at them. The opening essay in my book, *Talking Back,* describes my effort to emerge as critical thinker, artist, and writer in a context of repression. I talk about punishment, about mama and daddy aggressively silencing me, about the censorship of Black communities. I had no choice. I had to struggle and resist to emerge from that context and then from other locations with mind intact, with an open heart. I had to leave that space I called home to move beyond boundaries, yet I needed also to return there. We sing a song in the Black church tradition that says, "I'm going up the rough side of the mountain on my way home." Indeed the very meaning of "home" changes with experience of decolonization, of radicalization. At times, home is nowhere. At times, one knows only extreme estrangement and alienation. Then home is no longer just one place. It is locations. Home is that place which enables and promotes varied and everchanging perspectives, a place where one discovers new ways of seeing reality, frontiers of difference. One confronts and accepts dispersal and fragmentation as part of the construction of a new world order that reveals more fully where we are, who we can become, an order that does not demand forgetting. "Our struggle is also a struggle of memory against forgetting."

This experience of space and location is not the same for Black folks who have always been privileged, or for Black folks who desire only to move from underclass status to points of privilege; not the same for those of us from poor backgrounds who have had to continually engage in actual political struggle both within and outside Black communities to assert an aesthetic and critical presence. Black folks coming from poor, underclass communities, who enter universities or privileged cultural settings unwilling to surrender every vestige of who we were before we were there, all "sign" of our class and cultural "difference," who are unwilling to play the role of "exotic Other," must create spaces within that culture of domination if we are to survive whole, our souls intact. Our very presence is a disruption. We are often as much an "Other," a threat to Black people from privileged class backgrounds who do not understand or share our perspectives, as we are to uninformed white folks. Everywhere we go there is pressure to silence our voices, to co-opt and undermine them. Mostly, of course, we are not there. We never "arrive" or "can't stay." Back in those spaces where we come from, we kill ourselves in despair, drowning in nihilism, caught in poverty, in addiction, in every postmodern mode of dying that can be named. Yet when we few remain in that "other" space, we are often too isolated, too alone. We die there, too. Those of us who live, who "make it," passionately holding on to aspects of that "downhome" life we do not intend to lose while simultaneously seeking new knowledge and experience, invent spaces of radical openness. Without such spaces we would not survive. Our living depends on our ability to conceptualize alternatives, often improvised. Theorizing about this experience aesthetically, critically is an agenda for radical cultural practice.

For me this space of radical openness is a margin—a profound edge. Locating oneself there is difficult yet necessary. It is not a "safe" place. One is always at risk. One needs a community of resistance.

In the preface to *Feminist Theory: From Margin to Center,* I expressed these thoughts on marginality:

> To be in the margin is to be part of the whole but outside the main body. As black Americans living in a small Kentucky town, the railroad tracks were a daily reminder of our marginality. Across those tracks were paved streets, stores we could not enter, restaurants we could not eat in, and people we could not look directly in the face. Across those tracks was a world we could work in as maids, as janitors, as prostitutes, as long as it was in a service capacity. We could enter that world but we could not live there. We had always to return to the margin, to cross the tracks to shacks and abandoned houses on the edge of town.
>
> There were laws to ensure our return. Not to return was to risk being punished. Living as we did—on the edge—we developed a particular way of seeing reality. We looked both from the outside in and from the inside out. We focused our attention on the center as well as on the margin. We understood both. This mode of seeing reminded us of the existence of a whole universe, a main body made up of both margin and

center. Our survival depended on an ongoing public awareness of the separation between margin and center and an ongoing private acknowledgement that we were a necessary, vital part of that whole.

> This sense of wholeness, impressed upon our consciousness by the structure of our daily lives, provided us with an oppositional world-view—a mode of seeing unknown to most of our oppressors, that sustained us, aided us in our struggle to transcend poverty and despair, strengthened our sense of self and our solidarity.

Though incomplete, these statements identify marginality as much more than a site of deprivation; in fact I was saying just the opposite, that it is also the site of radical possibility, a space of resistance. It was this marginality that I was naming as a central location for the production of a counterhegemonic discourse that is not just found in words but in habits of being and the way one lives. As such, I was not speaking of a marginality one wishes to lose—to give up or surrender as part of moving into the center—but rather of a site one stays in, clings to even, because it nourishes one's capacity to resist. It offers to one the possibility of radical perspective from which to see and create, to imagine alternatives, new worlds.

This is not a mythic notion of marginality. It comes from lived experience. Yet I want to talk about what it means to struggle to maintain that marginality even as one works, produces, lives, if you will, at the center. I no longer live in that segregated world across the tracks. Central to life in that world was the ongoing awareness of the necessity of opposition. When Bob Marley sings, "We refuse to be what you want us to be, we are what we are, and that's the way it's going to be," that space of refusal, where one can say no to the colonizer, no to the downpressor, is located in the margins. And one can only say no, speak the voice of resistance, because there exists a counterlanguage. While it may resemble the colonizer's tongue, it has undergone a transformation, it has been irrevocably changed. When I left that concrete space in the margins, I kept alive in my heart ways of knowing reality which affirm continually not only the primacy of resistance but the necessity of a resistance that is sustained by remembrance of the past, which includes recollections of broken tongues giving us ways to speak that decolonize our minds, our very beings. Once mama said to me as I was about to go again to the predominantly white university, "You can take what the white people have to offer, but you do not have to love them." Now understanding her cultural codes, I know that she was not saying to me not to love people of other races. She was speaking about colonization and the reality of what it means to be taught in a culture of domination by those who dominate. She was insisting on my power to be able to separate useful knowledge that I might get from the dominating group from participation in ways of knowing that would lead to estrangement, alienation, and worse—assimilation and co-optation. She was saying that it is not necessary to give yourself over to them to learn. Not having been in those institutions, she knew that I might be faced again and again with situations where I would be "tried," made to feel as though a central requirement of my being accepted would mean participation in this system of exchange to ensure my success, my "making it." She was reminding me of the necessity of opposition and simultaneously encouraging me not to lose that radical perspective shaped and formed by marginality.

Understanding marginality as position and place of resistance is crucial for oppressed, exploited, colonized people. If we only view the margin as a sign marking the despair, a deep nihilism penetrates in a destructive way the very ground of our being. It is there in that space of collective despair that one's creativity, one's imagination is at risk, there that one's mind is fully colonized, there that the freedom one longs for is lost. Truly the mind that resists colonization struggles for freedom of expression. The struggle may not even begin with the colonizer; it may begin within one's segregated, colonized community and family. So I want to note that I am not trying to romantically re-inscribe the notion of that space of marginality where the oppressed live apart from their oppressors as "pure." I want to say that these margins have been both sites of repression and sites of resistance. And since we are well able to name the nature of that repression we know better the margin as site of deprivation. We are more silent when it comes to speaking of the margin as site of resistance. We are more often silenced when it comes to speaking of the margin as site of resistance.

Silenced. During my graduate years I heard myself speaking often in the voice of resistance. I cannot say

that my speech was welcomed. I cannot say that my speech was heard in such a way that it altered relations between colonizer and colonized. Yet what I have noticed is that those scholars, most especially those who name themselves radical critical thinkers, feminist thinkers, now fully participate in the construction of a discourse about the "Other." I was made "Other" there in that space with them. In that space in the margins, that lived-in segregated world of my past and present. They did not meet me there in that space. They met me at the center. They greeted me as colonizers. I am waiting to learn from them the path of their resistance, of how it came to be that they were able to surrender the power to act as colonizers. I am waiting for them to bear witness, to give testimony. They say that the discourse on marginality, on difference has moved beyond a discussion of "us and them." They do not speak of how this movement has taken place. This is a response from the radical space of my marginality. It is a space of resistance. It is a space I choose.

I am waiting for them to stop talking about the "Other," to stop even describing how important it is to be able to speak about difference. It is not just important what we speak about, but how and why we speak. Often this speech about the "Other" is also a mask, an oppressive talk hiding gaps, absences, that space where our words would be if we were speaking, if there were silence, if we were there. This "we" is that "us" in the margins, that "we" who inhabit marginal space that is not a site of domination but a place of resistance. Enter that space. Often this speech about the "Other" annihilates, erases: "No need to hear your voice when I can talk about you better than you can speak about yourself. No need to hear your voice. Only tell me about your pain. I want to know your story. And then I will tell it back to you in a new way. Tell it back to you in such a way that it has become mine, my own. Re-writing you, I write myself anew. I am still author, authority. I am still the colonizer, the speaking subject, and you are now at the center of my talk." Stop. We greet you as liberators. This "we" is that "us" in the margins, that "we" who inhabit marginal space that is not a site of domination but a place of resistance. Enter that space. This is an intervention. I am writing to you. I am speaking from a place in the margins where I am different, where I see things differently. I am talking about what I see.

Speaking from margins. Speaking in resistance. I open a book. There are words on the back cover, *Never in the Shadows Again*. A book which suggests the possibility of speaking as liberators. Only who is speaking and who is silent? Only who stands in the shadows—the shadow in a doorway, the space where images of Black women are represented voiceless, the space where our words are invoked to serve and support, the space of our absence. Only small echoes of protest. We are re-written. We are "Other." We are the margin. Who is speaking and to whom? Where do we locate ourselves and comrades?

Silenced. We fear those who speak about us, who do not speak to us and with us. We know what it is like to be silenced. We know that the forces that silence us, because they never want us to speak, differ from the forces that say speak, tell me your story. Only do not speak in a voice of resistance. Only speak from that space in the margin that is a sign of deprivation, a wound, an unfulfilled longing. Only speak your pain.

This is an intervention. A message from that space in the margin that is a site of creativity and power, that inclusive space where we recover ourselves, where we move in solidarity to erase the category colonized/colonizer. Marginality as site of resistance. Enter that space. Let us meet there. Enter that space. We greet you as liberators.

Spaces can be real and imagined. Spaces can tell stories and unfold histories. Spaces can be interrupted, appropriated, and transformed through artistic and literary practice.

As Pratibha Parma notes, "The appropriation and use of space are political acts."

To speak about that location from which work emerges, I choose familiar politicized language, old codes, words like "struggle, marginality, resistance." I choose these words knowing that they are no longer popular or "cool"—hold onto them and the political legacies they evoke and affirm, even as I work to change what they say, to give them renewed and different meaning.

I am located in the margin. I make a definite distinction between that marginality which is imposed by oppressive structures and that marginality one chooses as site of resistance—as location of radical openness and possibility. This site of resistance is continually formed in that segregated culture of opposition that is our critical response to domination. We come to this space through suffering and pain, through struggle. We know struggle to be that which pleasures, delights, and fulfills desire. We are transformed, individually, collectively, as we make radical creative space which affirms and sustains our subjectivity, which gives us a new location from which to articulate our sense of the world.

Discussion Questions

1. Consider your own social status: your job, the school you attend, your economics class, and so forth. Do you occupy a privileged position or a position on the periphery? How difficult would it be for you to hypothetically occupy a marginal standpoint? If you already occupy a marginal standpoint, how difficult would it be to occupy a privileged position? What changes would you have to make in order to be in solidarity with those on the margins? Would such a standpoint be possible for you?

2. To what degree are persons who have suffered prejudice and injustice responsible for provoking change and creating resistance? To what degree are others who have not suffered these injustices also responsible? How do you believe hooks would answer this question? Do you agree with her view or not?

3. bell hooks as a black woman chooses to stand in the margins with other women and with other black Americans. Could she also do this effectively with other oppressed groups? For example, would hooks be effective taking up the cause of exploited farm laborers in the western United States? Does she have an obligation to do so? Why or why not?

For Further Reading

bell hooks has written numerous books on feminism and race and also a number of critical studies on the visual arts. Among the recommended books by hooks are *Ain't I a Woman: Black Women and Feminism* (1982), *Feminist Theory from Margin to Center* (1984), *Outlaw Culture: Resisting Representation* (1994), and *Art on My Mind: Visual Politics* (1995).

40 BEYOND GOOD AND EVIL
Friedrich Nietzsche

Born in Prussia in 1844, Friedrich Nietzsche was one of Germany's most original and influential philosophers. Interpreting his philosophy is difficult, partly because of the style in which much of it is written, but also because of the subtlety of his ideas and his use of irony and humor. As a result, Nietzsche's philosophy is prone to many distortions and partisan uses. The biographical details of his life only exacerbate this tendency to distort Nietzsche's philosophy. The child of a Lutheran minister, his father went insane during the last years of his life, a few years after Nietzsche was born. Not only did Nietzsche sternly reject the God of Lutheranism and his father, but tragically, in 1989, Nietzsche himself also went insane, spending the last years of his life in an asylum until his death in 1900.

Western philosophy loves to think of itself as objectively searching for the truth. In the following selection, however, Nietzsche points out the various ways in which metaphysicians, logicians, and ethicists fail to achieve objectivity on a host of issues. And this is no surprise to Nietzsche since he argues that philosophers believe what they believe and develop arguments after the fact to support their prejudices.

But Nietzsche does not simply criticize philosophers for their failure to achieve objectivity in their quest for the truth. Nietzsche questions the very value of their quest for the objective truth. Truthfulness of an opinion is not what matters. The question is how far an opinion is life-furthering, life-preserving, species-preserving, and perhaps species-rearing.

Reading Questions

1. Supposing that truth is a woman, what then?
2. What dogmatic philosophies have been caricatures?
3. What was Plato's dogmatic error?
4. What question have we finally risked asking?
5. What is the fundamental belief of metaphysicians?
6. In spite of the value of truth, what values for life might be higher and more fundamental?
7. By what is the conscious thinking of a philosopher secretly influenced?
8. Does the falseness of an opinion matter?
9. What causes philosophers to be regarded half-distrustfully and half-mockingly?
10. To understand the metaphysics of a philosopher, what question should one ask?

11. What happens when a philosophy begins to believe itself?
12. What is the Kantian question? With what question does Nietzsche replace it?
13. If philosophy is not a world explanation, what is it?
14. What does Schopenhauer believe is absolutely and completely known to us?
15. Why does Nietzsche believe that there is a family resemblance of all Indian, Greek, and German philosophizing?
16. How should one use the terms *cause* and *effect*?

Supposing that Truth is a woman—what then? Is there not ground for suspecting that all philosophers, in so far as they have been dogmatists, have failed to understand women—that the terrible seriousness and clumsy importunity with which they have usually paid their addresses to Truth, have been unskilled and unseemly methods for winning a woman? Certainly she has never allowed herself to be won; and at present every kind of dogma stands with sad and discouraged mien—*if*, indeed, it stands at all! For there are scoffers who maintain that it has fallen, that all dogma lies on the ground—nay more, that it is at its last gasp. But to speak seriously, there are good grounds for hoping that all dogmatising in philosophy, whatever solemn, whatever conclusive and decided airs it has assumed, may have been only a noble puerilism and tyronism; and probably the time is at hand when it will be once and again understood *what* has actually sufficed for the basis of such imposing and absolute philosophical edifices as the dogmatists have hitherto reared: perhaps some popular superstition of immemorial time (such as the soul-superstition, which, in the form of subject- and ego-superstition, has not yet ceased doing mischief): perhaps some play upon words, a deception on the part of grammar, or an audacious generalisation of very restricted, very personal, very human—all-too-human facts. The philosophy of the dogmatists, it is to be hoped, was only a promise for thousands of years afterwards, as was astrology in still earlier times, in the service of which probably more labour, gold, acuteness, and patience have been spent than on any actual science hitherto: we owe to it, and to its "super-terrestrial" pretensions in Asia and Egypt, the grand style of architecture. It seems that in order to inscribe themselves upon the heart of humanity with everlasting claims, all great things have first to wander about the earth as enormous and awe-inspiring caricatures: dogmatic philosophy has been a caricature of

this kind—for instance, the Vedanta doctrine in Asia, and Platonism in Europe. Let us not be ungrateful to it, although it must certainly be confessed that the worst, the most tiresome, and the most dangerous of errors hitherto has been a dogmatist error—namely, Plato's invention of Pure Spirit and the Good in Itself. But now when it has been surmounted, when Europe, rid of this nightmare, can again draw breath freely and at least enjoy a healthier—sleep, we, *whose duty is wakefulness itself*, are the heirs of all the strength which the struggle against this error has fostered. It amounted to the very inversion of truth, and the denial of the *perspective*—the fundamental condition—of life, to speak of Spirit and the Good as Plato spoke of them; indeed one might ask, as a physician: "How did such a malady attack that finest product of antiquity, Plato? Had the wicked Socrates really corrupted him? Was Socrates after all a corrupter of youths, and deserved his hemlock?" But the struggle against Plato, or—to speak plainer, and for the "people"—the struggle against the ecclesiastical oppression of millenniums of Christianity (for Christianity is Platonism for the "people"), produced in Europe a magnificent tension of soul, such as had not existed anywhere previously; with such a tensely-strained bow one can now aim at the furthest goals. As a matter of fact, the European feels this tension as a state of distress, and twice attempts have been made in grand style to unbend the bow: once by means of Jesuitism, and the second time by means of democratic enlightenment—which, with the aid of liberty of the press and newspaper-reading, might, in fact, bring it about that the spirit would not so easily find itself in "distress"! (The Germans invented gunpowder—all credit to them! but they again made things square—they invented printing.) But we, who are neither Jesuits, nor democrats, nor even sufficiently Germans, we *good Europeans*, and free, *very* free spirits—we have it still, all the distress of spirit and all the tension of its bow! And perhaps also the arrow, the duty, and, who knows? *the goal to aim at.* . . .

PREJUDICES OF PHILOSOPHERS

The Will to Truth, which is to tempt us to many a hazardous enterprise, the famous Truthfulness of which all philosophers have hitherto spoken with respect, what questions has this Will to Truth not laid before us! What strange, perplexing, questionable questions! It is already a long story; yet it seems as if it were hardly commenced. Is it any wonder if we at last grow distrustful, lose patience, and turn impatiently away? That this Sphinx teaches us at last to ask questions ourselves? *Who* is it really that puts questions to us here? *What* really is this "Will to Truth" in us? In fact we made a long halt at the question as to the origin of this Will—until at last we came to an absolute standstill before a yet more fundamental question. We inquired about the *value* of this Will. Granted that we want the truth: *why not rather* untruth? And uncertainty? Even ignorance? The problem of the value of truth presented itself before us—or was it we who presented ourselves before the problem? Which of us is the Œdipus here? Which the Sphinx? It would seem to be a rendezvous of questions and notes of interrogation. And could it be believed that it at last seems to us as if the problem had never been propounded before, as if we were the first to discern it, get a sight of it, and *risk raising* it. For there is risk in raising it, perhaps there is no greater risk.

2

"*How could* anything originate out of its opposite? For example, truth out of error? or the Will to Truth out of the will to deception? or the generous deed out of selfishness? or the pure sun-bright vision of the wise man out of covetousness? Such genesis is impossible; whoever dreams of it is a fool, nay, worse than a fool; things of the highest value must have a different origin, an origin of *their own*—in this transitory, seductive, illusory, paltry world, in this turmoil of delusion and cupidity, they cannot have their source. But rather in the lap of Being, in the intransitory, in the concealed God, in the 'Thing-in-itself'—*there* must be their source, and nowhere else!"—This

mode of reasoning discloses the typical prejudice by which meta-physicians of all times can be recognised, this mode of valuation is at the back of all their logical procedure; through this "belief" of theirs, they exert themselves for their "knowledge," for something that is in the end solemnly christened "the Truth." The fundamental belief of metaphysicians is *the belief in antitheses of values.* It never occurred even to the wariest of them to doubt here on the very threshold (where doubt, however, was most necessary); though they had made a solemn vow, "*de omnibus dubitandum.*" For it may be doubted, firstly, whether antitheses exist at all; and secondly, whether the popular valuations and antitheses of value upon which metaphysicians have set their seal, are not perhaps merely superficial estimates, merely provisional perspectives, besides being probably made from some corner, perhaps from below—"frog perspectives," as it were, to borrow an expression current among painters. In spite of all the value which may belong to the true, the positive, and the unselfish, it might be possible that a higher and more fundamental value for life generally should be assigned to pretence, to the will to delusion, to selfishness, and cupidity. It might even be possible that *what* constitutes the value of those good and respected things, consists precisely in their being insidiously related, knotted, and crocheted to these evil and apparently opposed things—perhaps even in being essentially identical with them. Perhaps! But who wishes to concern himself with such dangerous "Perhapses"! For that investigation one must await the advent of a new order of philosophers, such as will have other tastes and inclinations, the reverse of those hitherto prevalent—philosophers of the dangerous "Perhaps" in every sense of the term. And to speak in all seriousness, I see such new philosophers beginning to appear.

3

Having kept a sharp eye on philosophers, and having read between their lines long enough, I now say to myself that the greater part of conscious thinking must be counted amongst the instinctive functions, and it is so even in the case of philosophical thinking; one has here to learn anew, as one learned anew about heredity and "innateness." As little as the act of birth comes into consideration in the whole process and procedure of heredity, just as little is "being-conscious" *opposed* to the instinctive in any decisive sense; the greater part of the conscious thinking of a philosopher is secretly influenced by his instincts, and forced into definite channels. And behind all logic and its seeming sovereignty of movement, there are valuations, or to speak more plainly, physiological demands, for the maintenance of a definite mode of life. For example, that the certain is worth more than the uncertain, that illusion is less valuable than "truth": such valuations, in spite of their regulative importance for *us*, might notwithstanding be only superficial valuations, special kinds of *niaiserie*, such as may be necessary for the maintenance of beings such as ourselves. Supposing, in effect, that man is not just the "measure of things." . . .

4

The falseness of an opinion is not for us any objection to it: it is here, perhaps, that our new language sounds most strangely. The question is, how far an opinion is life-furthering, life-preserving, species-preserving, perhaps species-rearing; and we are fundamentally inclined to maintain that the falsest opinions (to which the synthetic judgments *a priori* belong), are the most indispensable to us; that without a recognition of logical fictions, without a comparison of reality with the purely *imagined* world of the absolute and immutable, without a constant counterfeiting of the world by means of numbers, man could not live—that the renunciation of false opinions would be a renunciation of life, a negation of life. *To recognise untruth as a condition of life*: that is certainly to impugn the traditional ideas of value in a dangerous manner, and a philosophy which ventures to do so, has thereby alone placed itself beyond good and evil.

5

That which causes philosophers to be regarded half-distrustfully and half-mockingly, is not the oft-repeated discovery how innocent they are—how often and easily they make mistakes and lose their way, in short, how childish and childlike they are,—but that there is not enough honest dealing with them, whereas they all raise a loud and virtuous outcry when the problem of truthfulness is even hinted at in the remotest manner. They all pose as though their real opinions had been discovered and attained through the self-evolving of a cold, pure, divinely indifferent dialectic (in contrast to all sorts of mystics, who, fairer and foolisher, talk of "inspiration"); whereas, in fact, a prejudiced proposition, idea, or "suggestion," which is generally their heart's desire abstracted and refined, is defended by them with arguments sought out after the event. They are all advocates who do not wish to be regarded as such, generally astute defenders, also, of their prejudices, which they dub "truths,"—and *very* far from having the conscience which bravely admits this to itself; very far from having the good taste of the courage which goes so far as to let this be understood, perhaps to warn friend or foe, or in cheerful confidence and self-ridicule. The spectacle of the Tartuffery of old Kant, equally stiff and decent, with which he entices us into the dialectic by-ways that lead (more correctly mislead) to his "categorical imperative"—makes us fastidious ones smile, we who find no small amusement in spying out the subtle tricks of old moralists and ethical preachers. Or, still more so, the hocus-pocus in mathematical form, by means of which Spinoza has, as it were, clad his philosophy in mail and mask—in fact, the "love of *his* wisdom," to translate the term fairly and squarely—in order thereby to strike terror at once into the heart of the assailant who should dare to cast a glance on that invincible maiden, that Pallas Athene:—how much of personal timidity and vulnerability does this masquerade of a sickly recluse betray!

6

It has gradually become clear to me what every great philosophy up till now has consisted of—namely, the confession of its originator, and a species of involuntary and unconscious auto-biography; and moreover that the moral (or immoral) purpose in every philosophy has constituted the true vital germ out of which the entire plant has always grown. Indeed, to understand how the abstrusest metaphysical assertions of a philosopher have been arrived at, it is always well (and wise) to first ask oneself: "What morality do they (or does he) aim at?" Accordingly, I do not believe that an "impulse to knowledge" is the father of philosophy; but that another impulse, here as elsewhere, has only made use of knowledge (and mistaken knowledge!) as an instrument. But whoever considers the fundamental impulses of man with a view to determining how far they may have here acted as *inspiring* genii (or as demons and cobolds), will find that they have all practised philosophy at one time or another, and that each one of them would have been only too glad to look upon itself as the ultimate end of existence and the legitimate *lord* over all the other impulses. For every impulse is imperious, and as *such*, attempts to philosophise. To be sure, in the case of scholars, in the case of really scientific men, it may be otherwise—"better," if you will; there may really be such a thing as an "impulse to knowledge," some kind of small, independent clock-work, which, when well wound up, works away industriously to that end, *without* the rest of the scholarly impulses taking any material part therein. The actual "interests" of the scholar, therefore, are generally in quite another direction—in the family, perhaps, or in money-making, or in politics; it is, in fact, almost indifferent at what point of research his little machine is placed, and whether the hopeful young worker becomes a good philologist, a mushroom specialist, or a chemist; he is not *characterised* by becoming this or that. In the philosopher, on the contrary, there is absolutely nothing impersonal; and above all, his morality furnishes a decided and decisive testimony as to *who he is,*—that is to say, in what order the deepest impulses of his nature stand to each other.

...

8

There is a point in every philosophy at which the "conviction" of the philosopher appears on the scene; or, to put it in the words of an ancient mystery:

> *Adventavit asinus,*
> *Pulcher et fortissimus.*

9

You desire to *live* "according to Nature"? Oh, you noble Stoics, what fraud of words! Imagine to yourselves a being like Nature, boundlessly extravagant, boundlessly indifferent, without purpose or consideration, without pity or justice, at once fruitful and barren and uncertain: imagine to yourselves *indifference* as a power—how *could* you live in accordance with such indifference? To live—is not that just endeavouring to be otherwise than this Nature? Is not living valuing, preferring, being unjust, being limited, endeavouring to be different? And granted that your imperative, "living according to Nature," means actually the same as "living according to life"—how could you do *differently?* Why should you make a principle out of what you yourselves are, and must be? In reality, however, it is quite otherwise with you: while you pretend to read with rapture the canon of your law in Nature, you want something quite the contrary, you extraordinary stage-players and self-deluders! In your pride you wish to dictate your morals and ideals to Nature, to Nature herself, and to incorporate them therein; you insist that it shall be Nature "according to the Stoa," and would like everything to be made after your own image, as a vast, eternal glorification and generalism of Stoicism! With all your love for truth, you have forced yourselves so long, so persistently, and with such hypnotic rigidity to see Nature *falsely,* that is to say, Stoically, that you are no longer able to see it otherwise—and to crown all, some unfathomable superciliousness gives you the Bedlamite hope that *because* you are able to tyrannise over yourselves—Stoicism is self-tyranny—Nature will also allow herself to be tyrannised over: is not the Stoic a *part* of Nature? ... But this is an old and everlasting story: what happened in old times with the Stoics still happens today, as soon as ever a philosophy begins to believe in itself. It always creates the world in its own image; it cannot do otherwise; philosophy is this tyrannical impulse itself, the most spiritual Will to Power, the will to "creation of the world," the will to the *causa prima.*

...

11

It seems to me that there is everywhere an attempt at present to divert attention from the actual influence which Kant exercised on German philosophy, and especially to ignore prudently the value which he set upon himself. Kant was first and foremost proud of his Table of Categories; with it in his hand he said: "This is the most difficult thing that could ever be undertaken on behalf of metaphysics." Let us only understand this "could be"! He was proud of having *discovered* a new faculty in man, the faculty of synthetic judgment *a priori*. Granting that he deceived himself in this matter; the development and rapid flourishing of German philosophy depended nevertheless on his pride, and on the eager rivalry of the younger generation to discover if possible something—at all events "new faculties"—of which to be still prouder!—But let us reflect for a moment—it is high time to do so. "How are synthetic judgments *a priori* possible?" Kant asks himself—and what is really his answer? "*By means of a means* (faculty)"—but unfortunately not in five words, but so circumstantially, imposingly, and with such display of German profundity and verbal flourishes, that one altogether loses sight of the comical *niaiserie allemande* involved in such an answer. People were beside themselves with delight over this new faculty, and the jubilation reached its climax when Kant further discovered a moral faculty in man—for at that time Germans were still moral, not yet dabbling in the "Politics of hard fact." Then came the honeymoon of German philosophy. All the young theologians of the Tübingen institution went immediately into the groves—all seeking for "faculties." And what did they not find—in that innocent, rich, and still youthful period of the German spirit, to which Romanticism, the malicious fairy, piped and sang, when one could not yet distinguish between "finding" and "inventing"! Above all a faculty for the "transcendental"; Schelling christened it, intellectual intuition, and thereby gratified the most earnest longings of the naturally pious-inclined Germans. One can do no greater wrong to the whole of this exuberant and eccentric movement (which was really youthfulness, notwithstanding that it disguised itself so boldly in hoary and senile conceptions), than to take it seriously, or even treat it with moral indignation. Enough, however—the world grew older, and the dream vanished. A time came when people rubbed their foreheads, and they still rub them today. People had been dreaming, and first and foremost—old Kant. "By means of a means (faculty)"—he had said, or at least meant to say. But, is that—an answer? An explanation? Or is it not rather merely a repetition of the question? How does opium induce sleep? "By means of a means (fac-

ulty)," namely the *virtus dormitiva*, replies the doctor in Moliere,

> *Quia est in eo virtus dormitiva,*
> *Cujus est natura sensus assoupire.*

But such replies belong to the realm of comedy, and it is high time to replace the Kantian question, "How are synthetic judgments *a priori* possible?" by another question, "Why is belief in such judgments *necessary?*"—in effect, it is high time that we should understand that such judgments must be *believed* to be true, for the sake of the preservation of creatures like ourselves; though they still might naturally be *false* judgments! Or, more plainly spoken, and roughly and readily—synthetic judgments *a priori* should not "be possible" at all; we have no right to them; in our mouths they are nothing but false judgments. Only, of course, the belief in their truth is necessary, as plausible belief and ocular evidence belonging to the perspective view of life. And finally, to call to mind the enormous influence which "German philosophy"—I hope you understand its right to inverted commas (goose)?—has exercised throughout the whole of Europe, there is no doubt that a certain *virtus dormitiva* had a share in it; thanks to German philosophy, it was a delight to the noble idlers, the virtuous, the mystics, the artists, the three-fourths Christians, and the political obscurantists of all nations, to find an antidote to the still overwhelming sensualism which overflowed from the last century into this, in short—"*sensus assoupire.*" . . .

12

As regards materialistic atomism, it is one of the best refuted theories that have been advanced, and in Europe there is now perhaps no one in the learned world so unscholarly as to attach serious signification to it, except for convenient everyday use (as an abbreviation of the means of expression)—thanks chiefly to the Pole Boscovich: he and the Pole Copernicus have hitherto been the greatest and most successful opponents of ocular evidence. For whilst Copernicus has persuaded us to believe, contrary to all the senses, that the earth does *not* stand fast, Boscovich has taught us to abjure the belief in the last thing that "stood fast" of the earth—the belief in "substance," in "matter," in the earth-residuum, and particle-atom: it is the greatest triumph over the senses that has hitherto been gained on earth. One must, however, go still further, and also declare war, relentless war to the knife, against the "atomistic requirements" which still lead a dangerous after-life in places where no one suspects them, like the more celebrated "metaphysical requirements": one must also above all give the finishing stroke to that other and more portentous atomism which Christianity has taught best and longest, the *soul-atomism*. Let it be permitted to designate by this expression the belief which regards the soul as something indestructible, eternal, indivisible, as a monad, as an *atomon: this* belief ought to be expelled from science! Between ourselves, it is not at all necessary to get rid of "the soul" thereby, and thus renounce one of the oldest and most venerated hypotheses—as happens frequently to the clumsiness of naturalists, who can hardly touch on the soul without immediately losing it. But the way is open for new acceptations and refinements of the soul-hypothesis; and such conceptions as "mortal soul," and "soul of subjective multiplicity," and "soul as social structure of the instincts and passions," want henceforth to have legitimate rights in science. In that the *new* psychologist is about to put an end to the superstitions which have hitherto flourished with almost tropical luxuriance around the idea of the soul, he is really, as it were, thrusting himself into a new desert and a new distrust—it is possible that the older psychologists had a merrier and more comfortable time of it; eventually, however, he finds that precisely thereby he is also condemned to *invent*—and, who knows? perhaps to *discover* the new.

13

Psychologists should bethink themselves before putting down the instinct of self-preservation as the cardinal instinct of an organic being. A living thing seeks above all to *discharge* its strength—life itself is *Will to Power;* self-preservation is only one of the indirect and most frequent *results* thereof. In short, here, as everywhere else, let us beware of *superfluous* teleological principles!—one of which is the instinct of self-preservation (we owe it to Spinoza's inconsistency). It is thus, in effect, that method ordains, which must be essentially economy of principles.

14

It is perhaps just dawning on five or six minds that natural philosophy is only a world-exposition and world-arrangement (according to us, if I may say so!) and *not* a world-explanation; but in so far as it is based on belief in the senses, it is regarded as more, and for a long time to come must be regarded as more—namely, as an explanation. It has eyes and fingers of its own, it has ocular evidence and palpableness of its own: this operates fascinatingly, persuasively, and *convincingly* upon an age with fundamentally plebeian tastes—in fact, it follows instinctively the canon of truth of eternal popular sensualism. What is clear, what is "explained"? Only that which can be seen and felt—one must pursue every problem thus far. Obversely, however, the charm of the Platonic mode of thought, which was an *aristocratic* mode, consisted precisely in *resistance to* obvious sense-evidence—perhaps among men who enjoyed even stronger and more fastidious senses than our contemporaries, but who knew how to find a higher triumph in remaining masters of them: and this by means of pale, cold, grey conceptional networks which they threw over the motley whirl of the senses—the mob of the senses, as Plato said. In this overcoming of the world, and interpreting of the world in the manner of Plato, there was an *enjoyment* different from that which the physicists of to-day offer us—and likewise the Darwinists and antiteleologists among the physiological workers, with their principle of the "smallest possible effort," and the greatest possible blunder. "Where there is nothing more to see or to grasp, there is also nothing more for men to do"—that is certainly an imperative different from the Platonic one, but it may notwithstanding be the right imperative for a hardy, labourious race of machinists and bridge-builders of the future, who have nothing but *rough* work to perform.

15

To study physiology with a clear conscience, one must insist on the fact that the sense-organs are *not* phenomena in the sense of the idealistic philosophy; as such they certainly could not be causes! Sensualism, therefore, at least as regulative hypothesis, if not as heuristic principle. What? And others say even that the external world is the work of our organs? But then our body, as a part of this external world, would be the work of our organs! But then our organs themselves would be the work of our organs! It seems to me that this is a complete *reductio ad absurdum*, if the conception *causa sui* is something fundamentally absurd. Consequently, the external world is *not* the work of our organs—?

16

There are still harmless self-observers who believe that there are "immediate certainties"; for instance, "I think," or as the superstition of Schopenhauer puts it, "I will"; as though cognition here got hold of its object purely and simply as "the thing in itself," without any falsification taking place either on the part of the subject or the object. I would repeat it, however, a hundred times, that "immediate certainty," as well as "absolute knowledge" and the "thing in itself," involve a *contradictio in adjecto*; we really ought to free ourselves from the misleading significance of words! The people on their part may think that cognition is knowing all about things, but the philosopher must say to himself: "When I analyse the process that is expressed in the sentence, 'I think,' I find a whole series of daring assertions, the argumentative proof of which would be difficult, perhaps impossible: for instance, that it is *I* who think, that there must necessarily be something that thinks, that thinking is an activity and operation on the part of a being who is thought of as a cause, that there is an 'ego,' and finally, that it is already determined what is to be designated by thinking—that I *know* what thinking is. For if I had not already decided within myself what it is, by what standard could I determine whether that which is just happening is not perhaps 'willing' or 'feeling'? In short, the assertion 'I think,' assumes that I *compare* my state at the present moment with other states of myself which I know, in order to determine what it is; on account of this retrospective connection with further 'knowledge,' it has, at any rate, no immediate certainty for me."—In place of the "immediate certainty" in which the people may believe in the special case, the philosopher thus finds a series of metaphysical questions presented to him, veritable conscience questions of the intellect, to wit: "From whence did I get the notion of 'thinking'? Why do I believe in cause and effect? What gives me the right to speak of an 'ego,' and even of an 'ego' as cause, and finally of an 'ego' as cause of thought?" He who ventures to answer these metaphysical questions at once by an appeal to a sort of *intuitive* perception, like the person who says, "I think, and know that this, at least, is true, actual, and certain"—will encounter a smile and two notes of interrogation in a philosopher nowadays. "Sir," the philosopher will perhaps give him to understand, "it is improbable that you are not mistaken, but why should it be the truth?"

17

With regard to the superstitions of logicians, I shall never tire of emphasising a small, terse fact, which is unwillingly recognised by these credulous minds—namely, that a thought comes when "it" wishes, and not when "I" wish; so that it is a *perversion* of the facts of the case to say that the subject "I" is the condition of the predicate "think." *One* thinks; but that this "one" is precisely the famous old "ego," is, to put it mildly, only a supposition, an assertion, and assuredly not an "immediate certainty." After all, one has even gone too far with this "one thinks"—even the "one" contains an *interpretation* of the process, and does not belong to the process itself. One infers here according to the usual grammatical formula—"To think is an activity; every activity requires an agency that is active; consequently" . . . It was pretty much on the same lines that the older atomism sought, besides the operating "power," the material particle wherein it resides and out of which it operates—the atom. More rigorous minds, however, learnt at last to get along without this "earth-residuum," and perhaps some day we shall accustom ourselves, even from the logician's point of view, to get along without the little "one" (to which the worthy old "ego" has refined itself).

18

It is certainly not the least charm of a theory that it is refutable; it is precisely thereby that it attracts the more subtle minds. It seems that the hundred-times-refuted theory of the "free will" owes its persistence to this charm alone; some one is always appearing who feels himself strong enough to refute it.

19

Philosophers are accustomed to speak of the will as though it were the best-known thing in the world; indeed, Schopenhauer has given us to understand that the will alone is really known to us, absolutely and completely known, without deduction or addition. But it again and again seems to me that in this case Schopenhauer also only did what philosophers are in the habit of doing—he seems to have adopted a *popular prejudice* and exaggerated it. Willing—seems to me to be above all something *complicated*, something that is a unity only in name—and it is precisely in a name that popular prejudice lurks, which has got the mastery over the inadequate precautions of philosophers in all ages. So let us for once be more cautious, let us be "unphilosophical": let us say that in all willing there is firstly a plurality of sensations, namely, the sensation of the condition *"away from which* we go," the sensation of the condition *"towards which* we go," the sensation of this *"from"* and *"towards"* itself, and then besides, an accompanying muscular sensation, which, even without our putting in motion "arms and legs," commences its action by force of habit, directly we "will" anything. Therefore, just as sensations (and indeed many kinds of sensations) are to be recognised as ingredients of the will, so, in the second place, thinking is also to be recognised; in every act of the will there is a ruling thought;—and let us not imagine it possible to sever this thought from the "willing," as if the will would then remain over! In the third place, the will is not only a complex of sensation and thinking, but it is above all an *emotion,* and in fact the emotion of the command. That which is termed "freedom of the will" is essentially the emotion of supremacy in respect to him who must obey: "I am free, 'he' must obey"—this consciousness is inherent in every will; and equally so the straining of the attention, the straight look which fixes itself exclusively on one thing, the unconditional judgment that "this and nothing else is necessary now," the inward certainty that obedience will be rendered—and whatever else pertains to the position of the commander. A man who *wills* commands something within himself which renders obedience, or which he believes renders obedience. But now let us notice what is the strangest thing about the will,—this affair so extremely complex, for which the people have only one name. Inasmuch as in the given circumstances we are at the same time the commanding *and* the obeying parties, and as the obeying party we know the sensations of constraint, impulsion, pressure, resistance, and motion, which usually commence immediately after the act of will; inasmuch as, on the other hand, we are accustomed to disregard this duality, and to deceive ourselves about it by means of the synthetic term "I": a whole series of erroneous conclusions, and consequently of false judgments about the will itself, has become attached to the act of willing—to such a degree that he who wills believes firmly that willing *suffices* for action. Since in the majority of cases there has only been exercise of will when the effect of the command—consequently obedience, and therefore action—was to be *expected,* the *appearance* has translated itself into the sentiment, as if there were a *necessity of effect;* in a word, he who wills believes with a fair amount of certainty that will and action are somehow one; he ascribes the success, the carrying out of the willing, to the will itself, and thereby enjoys an increase of the sensation of power which accompanies all success. "Freedom of Will"—that is the expression for the complex state of delight of the person exercising volition, who commands and at the same time identifies himself with the executor of the order—who, as such, enjoys also the triumph over obstacles, but thinks within himself that it was really his own will that overcame them. In this way the person exercising volition adds the feelings of delight of his successful executive instruments, the useful "underwills" or under-souls—indeed, our body is but a social structure composed of many souls—to his feelings of delight as commander. *L'effet c'est moi:* what happens here is what happens in every well-constructed and happy commonwealth, namely, that the governing class identifies itself with the successes of the commonwealth. In all willing it is absolutely a question of commanding and obeying, on the basis, as already said, of a social structure composed of many "souls"; on which account a philosopher should claim the right to include willing-as-such within the sphere of morals—regarded as the doctrine of the relations of supremacy under which the phenomenon of "life" manifests itself.

20

That the separate philosophical ideas are not anything optional or autonomously evolving, but grow up in connection and relationship with each other; that, however suddenly and arbitrarily they seem to appear in the history of thought, they nevertheless belong just as much to a system as the collective members of the fauna of a Continent—is betrayed in the end by the circumstance: how unfailingly the most diverse philosophers always fill in again a definite fundamental scheme of *possible* philosophies. Under an invisible spell, they always revolve once more in the same orbit; however independent of each other they may feel themselves with their critical or systematic wills, something within them leads them, something impels them in definite order the one after the other—to wit, the innate methodology and relationship of their ideas. Their thinking is, in fact, far less a discovery than a re-recognising, a remembering, a return and a home-coming to a far-off, ancient common-household of the soul, out of which those ideas formerly grew: philosophising is so far a kind of atavism of the highest order. The wonderful family resemblance of all Indian, Greek, and German philosophising is easily enough explained. In fact, where there is affinity of language, owing to the common philosophy of grammar—I mean owing to the unconscious domination and guidance of similar grammatical functions—it cannot but be that everything is prepared at the outset for a similar development and succession of philosophical systems; just as the way seems barred against certain other possibilities of world-interpretation. It is highly probable that philosophers within the domain of the Ural-Altaic languages (where the conception of the subject is least developed) look otherwise "into the world," and will be found on paths of thought different from those of the Indo Germans and Mussulmans, the spell of certain grammatical functions is ultimately also the spell of *physiological* valuations and racial conditions.—So much by way of rejecting Locke's superficiality with regard to the origin of ideas.

21

The *causa sui* is the best self-contradiction that has yet been conceived, it is a sort of logical violation and unnaturalness; but the extravagant pride of man has managed to entangle itself profoundly and frightfully with this very folly. The desire for "freedom of will" in the superlative, metaphysical sense, such as still holds sway, unfortunately, in the minds of the half-educated, the desire to bear the entire and ultimate responsibility for one's actions oneself, and to absolve God, the world, ancestors, chance, and society therefrom, involves nothing less than to be precisely this *causa sui*, and, with more than Munchausen daring, to pull oneself up into existence by the hair, out of the slough of nothingness. If any one should find out in this manner the crass stupidity of the celebrated conception of "free will" and put it out of his head altogether, I beg of him to carry his "enlightenment" a step further, and also put out of his head the contrary of this monstrous conception of "free will": I mean "non-free will," which is tantamount to a misuse of cause and effect. One should not wrongly *materialise* "cause" and "effect," as the natural philosophers do (and whoever like them naturalise in thinking at present), according to the prevailing mechanical doltishness which makes the cause press and push until it "effects" its end; one should use "cause" and "effect" only as pure *conceptions,* that is to say, as conventional fictions for the purpose of designation and mutual understanding,—*not* for explanation. In "being-in-itself" there is nothing of "casual-connection," of "necessity," or of "psychological non-freedom; there the effect does *not* follow the cause, there "law" does not obtain. It is *we* alone who have devised cause, sequence, reciprocity, relativity, constraint, number, law, freedom, motive, and purpose; and when we interpret and intermix this symbol-world, as "being in itself," with things, we act once more as we have always acted—*mythologically.* The "non-free will" is mythology; in real life it is only a question of *strong* and *weak* wills.—It is almost always a symptom of what is lacking in himself, when a thinker, in every "casual-connection" and "psychological necessity," manifests something of compulsion, indigence, obsequiousness, oppression, and non-freedom; it is suspicious to have such feelings—the person betrays himself. And in general, if I have observed correctly, the "non-freedom of the will" is regarded as a problem from two entirely opposite standpoints, but always in a profoundly *personal* manner: some will not give up their "responsibility," their belief in *themselves,* the personal right to *their* merits, at any price (the vain races belong to this class); others on the contrary, do not wish to be answerable for anything, or blamed for anything, and owing to an inward self-contempt, seek *to get out of the business,* no matter how. The latter, when they write books, are in the habit at present of taking the side of criminals; a sort of socialistic sympathy is their favourite disguise. And as a matter of fact, the fatalism of the weak-willed embellishes itself surprisingly when it can pose as "*la religion de la souffrance humaine*"; that is *its* "good taste."

22

Let me be pardoned, as an old philologist who cannot desist from the mischief of putting his finger on bad modes of interpretation, but "Nature's conformity to law," of which you physicists talk so proudly, as though—why, it exists only owing to your interpretation and bad "philology." It is no matter of fact, no "text," but rather just a naïvely humanitarian adjustment and perversion of meaning, with which you make abundant concessions to the democratic instincts of the modern soul! "Everywhere equality before the law—Nature is not different in that respect, nor better than we": a fine instance of secret motive, in which the vulgar antagonism to everything privileged and autocratic—likewise a second and more refined atheism—is once more disguised. "*Ni dieu, ni maître*"—that, also, is what you want; and therefore "Cheers for natural law!"—is it not so? But, as has been said, that is interpretation, not text; and somebody might come along, who, with opposite intentions and modes of interpretation, could read out of the same "Nature," and with regard to the same phenomena, just the tyrannically inconsiderate and relentless enforcement of the claims of power—an interpreter who should so place the unexceptionalness and unconditionalness of all "Will to Power" before your eyes, that almost every word, and the word "tyranny" itself, would eventually seem unsuitable, or like a weakening and softening metaphor—as being too human; and who should, nevertheless, end by asserting the same about this world as you do, namely, that it has a "necessary" and "calculable" course, *not,* however, because laws obtain in it, but because they are absolutely *lacking,* and every power

effects its ultimate consequences every moment. Granted that this also is only interpretation—and you will be eager enough to make this objection?—well, so much the better.

23

All psychology hitherto has run aground on moral prejudices and timidities, it has not dared to launch out into the depths. In so far as it is allowable to recognise in that which has hitherto been written, evidence of that which has hitherto been kept silent, it seems as if nobody had yet harboured the notion of psychology as the Morphology and *Development-doctrine of the Will to Power,* as I conceive of it. The power of moral prejudices has penetrated deeply into the most intellectual world, the world apparently most indifferent and unprejudiced, and has obviously operated in an injurious, obstructive, blinding, and distorting manner. A proper physio-psychology has to contend with unconscious antagonism in the heart of the investigator, it has "the heart" against it: even a doctrine of the reciprocal conditionalness of the "good" and the "bad" impulses, causes (as refined immorality) distress and aversion in a still strong and manly conscience—still more so, a doctrine of the derivation of all good impulses from bad ones. If, however, a person should regard even the emotions of hatred, envy, covetousness, and imperiousness as life-conditioning emotions, as factors which must be present, fundamentally and essentially, in the general economy of life (which must, therefore, be further developed if life is to be further developed), he will suffer from such a view of things as from sea-sickness. And yet this hypothesis is far from being the strangest and most painful in this immense and almost new domain of dangerous knowledge; and there are in fact a hundred good reasons why every one should keep away from it who *can* do so! On the other hand, if one has once drifted hither with one's bark, well! very good! now let us set our teeth firmly! let us open our eyes and keep our hand fast on the helm! We sail away right *over* morality, we crush out, we destroy perhaps the remains of our own morality by daring to make our voyage thither—but what do *we* matter! Never yet did a *profounder* world of insight reveal itself to daring travellers and adventurers, and the psychologist who thus "makes a sacrifice"—it is *not* the *sacrifizio dell' intelletto*, on the contrary!—will at least be entitled to demand in return that psychology shall once more be recognised as the queen of the sciences, for whose service and equipment the other sciences exist. For psychology is once more the path to the fundamental problems.

Discussion Questions

1. What is the difference between objectivity and subjectivity? Which do we value more and why? Do we value objectivity and subjectivity differently depending on the circumstance?

2. What would you think of a person who places no value on being objective? Would you respect that person? What would their life be like? Would this be an honorable or dishonorable life? Would you like this person as your friend or neighbor? How about as your political leader or college professor? What does your answer tell us about the importance we place on objectivity?

3. Nietzsche was very critical of Christianity. From the previous reading, why do you think this was? What critique do you think he made or would make of Christianity and other forms of theism? Do you agree with this criticism? Why or why not?

For Further Reading

The literature on Nietzsche is immense. For a good introduction to Nietzsche's philosophy see *The Portable Nietzsche* (1954) or *Nietzsche, Philosopher, Psychologist, Antichrist* (1950) both by Walter Kaufman. One problem with much of the literature on Nietzsche is that it tends to be partisan and controversial. The essays in the following books tend to avoid the pitfalls or partisan interpretations: Robert Solomon, editor, *Nietzsche: A Collection of Critical Essays* (1973); Robert Solomon and Kathleen M. Higgins, editors, *Reading Nietzsche* (1988); Peter R. Sedgwick, editor, *Nietzsche: A Critical Reader* (1995); and Harold Bloom, editor, *Friedrich Nietzsche* (1987). For a philosophical and biographical overview, see Frederick Copleston, *Friedrich Nietzsche: Philosopher of Culture* (1975).

CHAPTER 8

WHAT AM I OBLIGATED TO DO?

At some point in your life you have undoubtedly struggled with a difficult decision. Perhaps you made a promise that was later difficult to keep, or perhaps you struggled with the decision of whether or not to tell the truth to a friend, a parent, or an employer. Maybe you have struggled with more weighty problems, such as whether or not to have an abortion or to fight in a war. These problems pose difficult ethical dilemmas. How can we decide what to do? How can we become moral persons?

Ethics is that part of philosophy that examines and attempts to understand the nature of morality. Unlike metaphysics and epistemology, which ask what *is* the case and how can it be *known*, **normative moral theories** attempt to discover what *ought* to be the case. This is the difference between, on the one hand, discovering the world as it actually exists and, on the other hand, determining how it should exist. In order to determine what ought to be the case, ethicists investigate and analyze the meaning of such ideas as 'good', 'bad', 'right', 'wrong', and so forth.

One initial question is, what sort of things are properly described by the adjectives 'good', 'right', 'bad', and 'wrong'? Typically, these descriptive adjectives are applied to either the *outcome* of an action, the *action* itself, or the *person* performing the action. Ethical theories vary according to which feature of a moral situation the theory considers most significant. Accordingly, ethical theories generally fall into one of three groups: **deontological theories** analyze the *actions*; **consequentialism** focuses on the *results* or *outcomes* of actions, what philosophers call 'states of affairs'; and **virtue theory** examines our character, what it means to be a good *person*.

The first of these theories, deontological ethics, focuses on actions themselves. Many forms of deontological ethics are rule- or principle-based theories; Immanuel Kant, in Reading 44, argues for this kind of deontological theory. For deontologists like Kant, an action is correct inasmuch as it follows a true *moral law* or *principle*: Good actions are principled actions and moral agents have an obligation to follow moral laws. What about the effects caused by a person's actions? Should it matter if the outcome of an action is good or bad? While deontologists believe that, as a matter of fact, good consequences often do result from following moral laws, this in and of itself is not what makes an action good. What makes a particular action the *right* action—what *ought* to be done—is not whether the action produces good consequences, but whether or not it conforms to a moral principle.

For example, you ought to keep your promises, not because good things happen when you do—sometimes bad consequences result from keeping promises—but because your actions should conform to the moral principle of keeping the promises you make. But which moral principles are true? Most deontologists are **rationalists** and assert that some truths, including moral principles, can be known through reason. Reason, then, determines which moral principles are true and thus which actions are morally obligatory.

Consequentialists disagree. Most consequentialists are **empiricists** who believe that knowledge, including moral knowledge, comes from experience. John Stuart Mill, in the third selection of this chapter, is a good example of an empiricist and a consequentialist. A key question for Mill is whether or not moral agents can make good moral judgments based on experience. Mill answers yes, because experience teaches us which actions will produce the best state of affairs, that is, the best consequences. Past experience provides evidence about which actions produce the most happiness, just as it also shows us which actions generally produce suffering and unhappiness. When making decisions, consequentialists rely on our collective experience to decide which action is most likely to produce the best consequences. Note, however, that the best consequence is not one that merely benefits you, regardless of how it affects those around you. The right course of action is the one that produces the greatest happiness *for everyone,* even if it causes you some personal unhappiness. Consider the example of telling the truth. Sometimes telling the truth will result in *personal* unhappiness, such as embarrassment, but overall, experience shows that telling the truth most often creates the greatest amount of happiness *for everyone.* Although consequentialists agree that sometimes (very rarely) telling the truth is not the best action to perform, the testimony of experience is clear: Telling the truth produces better consequences than lying.

Virtue theorists, such as Aristotle in the fifth reading of this chapter, have a distinct theoretical focus on morality. Rather than focusing on actions or on the results of actions, virtue theory examines the moral character of persons, what is called **virtue.** It is *good people* that are the source of good actions and the cause of good outcomes. Good persons have virtues by which they determine the right way to conduct their lives. Virtuous persons also use the valuable resources of reason and experience—just like deontologists and consequentialists—but for most virtue theorists, the central issue ethicists ought to be exploring is the nature of virtue and how it can be created in everyone.

Some persons, however, doubt that any type of ethical investigation makes sense at all. They argue that since morality evidently varies from culture to culture, even from person to person, moral beliefs are inherently subjective, always personal, and therefore never objectively true. Because there are no moral truths, they assert, each of us should respect the moral codes of other persons. This is the challenge of **cultural relativism,** a challenge James Rachels considers in the second reading of this chapter. Although deontologists, consequentialists, and virtue theorists disagree about many things, they all agree that unless cultural relativism is false, there is little reason to argue about the differences between competing moral theories.

First, though, we begin by looking at the relationship between religion and ethics. Some persons believe that philosophy, with its tools of reason and analysis, has nothing important to tell us about ethics because it is God that determines what is right and wrong. On this view, an action is required because God has commanded it and is prohibited because God has forbidden it. If so, then there is little reason to explore such theories as deontology and consequentialism. But as Yeager Hudson argues in the first selection of this chapter, even God has good reasons for commanding us—reasons it turns out that are the same for God as for us. If there is a God, then, God is just as interested in the outcome of the debate between deontologist and consequentialists as we are.

41 THE INDEPENDENCE OF ETHICS FROM RELIGION
Yeager Hudson

Many people believe that moral rules are obligatory because God commands them. This is called **divine command theory,** and according to this view, what makes something right or wrong depends on whether or not it violates a command God has given. For example, if divine command theory is true, then murder is wrong just because God commanded that murder is impermissible. On the other hand, if God had not commanded that murder is wrong or if God commanded us to commit murder, then it would be the morally correct thing to do.

Could this theory be correct? While some philosophers defend divine command theory, almost all recognize that there are some problems. One problem is that if an action is correct because God commanded it, then couldn't God command us to do things that we intuitively regard as inherently immoral? Consider the story of God commanding Abraham to sacrifice his son. (In Jewish and Christian traditions, this son is Isaac; in Muslim traditions, the son is identified as Ishmael.) Did Abraham do the right thing by obeying—or attempting to obey—God's command to sacrifice his son? We certainly wouldn't allow anyone to do the same today, no matter how earnestly they claimed to be following the will of God! If so, then should we regard Abraham as a violent and murderous patriarch, and not as a hero of religious faith?

In this selection, Yeager Hudson (1931–), a philosopher at Colby College, argues against the divine command theory of ethics. Moral duties, Hudson contends, are known by reason and are part of a universal law, called natural law, that is true in all cultures and in all times. As a result, if God commanded us to torture innocent persons, God would be wrong. Just as God can't make $3 + 3 = 7$, God can't make torturing innocent people good. Of course, as Hudson notes, if God is omniscient (all-knowing), God would never command such a thing in the first place.

Reading Questions

1. For the Romans, how were the principles of morality related to God and to human reason? How can they be known?
2. For Thomas Aquinas, what is the distinction between the first and second premises we use when legislating laws? How does this help explain why we have different rules in different cultures?
3. Why does Hudson conclude that Descartes is wrong to believe that God could make $2 + 2 = 7$? Must God conform to the principles of logic and mathematics?
4. According to Hudson, what did anthropologists discover about moral differences as their science matured?

Source: From 'The Independence Of Ethics From Religion' by Yeager Hudson from *The Philosophy of Religion*, pp. 237–247. Copyright © 1991 by Mayfield Publishing company. Reprinted by permission of The McGraw-Hill Companies.

5. How does the example of the controversy about abortion show that persons who hold different moral beliefs do not hold differences about the underlying principles themselves?
6. What does Hudson say we should do with any teaching that contradicts the requirements of rational morality? What examples does he give?
7. What does Hudson think that persons who are religious are likely to believe about the world of science? How is this similar to how religion may interpret the moral requirements of reason?

MORALITY AND NATURAL LAW

It comes as a great surprise to some to learn that during much of the history of the West, even in the Christian tradition, the divine command theory has not been the standard or accepted position. Among the ancient Greeks . . . morality was believed to be grounded in human rationality and had nothing to do with religion or the gods. The Romans developed a concept of law that recognized the objectivity of the principles of government as well as those of the detailed legislative regulations enacted and enforced by governments. The Romans also seem to be the originators of the concept of natural law, not only as a term to describe the regularities in the operation of the material world but also to name the principles recognized by human reason as valid for the regulation of human moral and political life. These principles have nothing to do with the gods or religion, but are written, as it were, into the very structure of reality itself and are discoverable by any humans who take the trouble to reason carefully. This, according to the Romans, is the reason that fundamental moral and social values are so similar from one culture to another despite their great differences in details.

This concept of natural law as the source both of political and moral law came to be incorporated into the thinking of the West and eventually found its way into Christian theology, where it was called the law of God. This view was refined and elaborated in detail by the great Catholic theologian of the Middle Ages, Thomas Aquinas (1224–1274). And though Thomas taught that Christian revelation is a source of knowledge about what God commands, he explicitly rejected the divine command theory of morality, teaching instead that an eternal law provides the foundation both of God's commandments and of the insights about morality that come from human reason.

According to Thomas, natural law is universal, the same for all time and place. Local variations in human law and in moral prescriptions (apart from inattention to, or misunderstanding of, what natural law requires) arise from the differences of circumstances to which natural law comes to be applied. Civil law is thus the result of applying natural law to the specific circumstances of a society. Lawmaking in human parliaments is not actually a process of *making* laws; rather, it is a process of *discovering* what natural law, applied to these local conditions, requires. Thomas says that legislating is like the use of a syllogism, whose first premise is natural law (and thus identical for all times and places), whose second premise is a description of the conditions to which the law is to apply, and whose conclusion is the piece of civil legislation. An example may serve to make his point clearer: When we legislate such matters as speed limits, the stable, unchanging natural law (the first premise) is a dictate about concern for the safety of all persons, but the specific application of that concern differs because the hazards vary from place to place. If we legislate for a congested area or an area near a school (second premise), then the conclusion (civil law) is a slow speed limit. But if we legislate for open countryside, where persons are not likely to be walking in the road, this different second premise, along with the same first premise of natural law, permits a faster speed. In every case, however, what makes the specific law right (assuming that it is properly made) is its foundation in natural law.

Now natural law as a source for civil legislation and for moral rules is valid for all societies alike and is accessible to all rational persons in whatever time or place; it is not connected with any one religion. This means that morality is founded on principles independent of religion and of God. Its laws are rather like the laws of logic and mathematics, which are similarly universal and binding on all rational beings, human and divine. . . .

Some philosophers, such as Descartes, insisted that the omnipotence of God requires what we might call a divine command theory of logic and mathematics—that is, they claimed that the principles of reasoning are created by God and derive their truth from the fact that God prescribes them. This amounts to saying that $2 + 2 = 4$ is true because God says it is, not that God says it is because it is true. It also implies that if God had said that $2 + 2 = 7$, this would have been true instead. But we argued that such a situation clearly renders all meaning and understanding impossible. Not even God himself could actually *think* such things, for they are simply impossible—they destroy the conditions under which thinking can occur or claims can have meaning. There seem to be overwhelming reasons to believe that even an omnipotent deity must conform to the principles of logic and mathematics if such a deity wishes to think or to create a world. What we have playfully called a divine command theory of logic and mathematics is, in the final reckoning, unintelligible and must be rejected. Logic and mathematics are in a sense antecedent to the will of God and govern that will so that even God cannot violate these principles.

The argument is much the same for the principles of morality. It amounts to saying that God forbids inflicting gratuitous suffering on the innocent because to do so is wrong, and not that it is wrong because God forbids it. This means that moral right and wrong are independent of God's will. Like the principles of mathematics, those of morality are objective, binding even on God, and thus not changeable by divine decree. If God declared that $3 + 3 = 7$, God would be wrong; if God declared that torturing the innocent is a moral duty, God would also be wrong. Of course, if God is omniscient in any proper sense of the word, he would never assert such a mathematical claim; similarly, if God is morally good, he would never make any such moral claim. There is an objective natural law from which morality can be inferred by any rational person, whether as religious believer or not. At least in principle, everyone who reasons carefully enough and succeeds in transcending the biases of his or her culture should arrive at the same set of fundamental moral principles binding for all.

INDEPENDENCE OF ETHICS FROM RELIGION

If there is indeed a natural law, valid for all time, written so to speak into the structure of reality and detectable by any carefully thinking rational being, why is it that moral beliefs seem to differ so drastically from one generation to another and from one culture to another? Should we not expect that reasonable persons would come to the same conclusions about what morality requires?

The belief that moral principles differ greatly from culture to culture and from age to age has been widespread, especially in the twentieth century, and has been buttressed by the campaign of anthropology against intolerant ethnocentrism. The efforts of anthropologists to engender a spirit of tolerance toward the beliefs and practices of other cultures was certainly justified by Westerners' arrogant, unthinking assumption of superiority and their attempts to impose their own beliefs and practices on the rest of the world. The result of these anthropologists' efforts was the spread of the concept of cultural relativism during the early years of this century. As anthropology matured, however, and as studies of non-Western cultures became more careful and detailed, the moral differences that had seemed so drastic at first came to be seen as differences in details; underlying moral principles were, in fact, remarkably similar across cultures.

A celebrated instance, often cited in anthropological literature on the controversy over relativism, is the custom among certain Eskimo groups of leaving the elderly to die once they become frail and unable to keep up with the migrations of the group. This practice was initially thought to imply a disrespect, even a moral disregard, for the elderly and was cited as a radical contrast to the veneration of the elderly in certain Asian societies and the respectful care for the aged in Western culture. Closer study revealed that the practice was grounded not in different beliefs about what is morally right, but in different beliefs about human afterlife. The Eskimos regard respect and care for the elderly to be an important moral value just as Asians and Westerners do. Leaving the aged to die is in fact an expression of their esteem because they believe that life in the next world begins at precisely the level of physical strength and health the individual possesses at the time of death. From this point of view, to keep old persons alive until they are bedridden and helpless would condemn them to an eternity of weakness and wretchedness.

Dramatic surface differences in moral beliefs, then, often prove to reflect differences in beliefs about situations to which moral principles are applied, not differences about the principles themselves. Another example closer to home may further serve to illustrate the point. In contemporary Western societies, there is a heated controversy about abortion. One group maintains that abortion is morally unacceptable because it is an abominable act of murder; another holds that during the early weeks of pregnancy abortion is morally permissible under certain circumstances. There might seem to be sharp disagreement here about fundamental principles of morality, with one group holding human life to be sacrosanct and the other (as it is sometimes accused) disregarding this sanctity. The difference, however, has nothing to do with basic moral principles; both groups regard human life as sacred and murder as wrong. They differ only on the issue of whether or not the fertilized ovum is a human being during the early stages of its development. If it is, then to kill it (without strong justification, such as saving the mother's life) is clearly morally wrong. If it is not yet a human being, however, then removing it is not murder and is sometimes morally justifiable.

Many moral disputes seem to be of this sort. What appears to be a radical disagreement about a moral principle is actually a disagreement about the facts to which the principle is being applied. Rational, conscientious people seem nearly always to agree about the basic principles of morality: that murder, lying, stealing, cheating, torture and such things are wrong. Most disagreement seems to involve the definition of these moral terms and whether a particular instance is or is not a case of murder, lying, and so on. Other differences relate to cases where the demands of morality conflict—a murder can be prevented only by lying; the killing of a large number of persons can be prevented only by killing a crazed fanatic, and so on—and value judgments have to be made about which principle is the more pressing. Differences of this sort, however, are also to be decided by the exercise of human reason, and although there will often

be room for conscientious, rational disagreement, careful and open-minded reasoning should lead at least to mutual understanding and, in principle, to a narrowing of differences. . . .

What we have discovered about the relationship of human rationality to moral understanding implies that ultimately there is no place for conflict about the basic requirements of morality. When differences appear, they must be understood as arising from different perspectives on the situations to which the principles apply (assuming that preconceived positions have been set aside and open rational discussion is joined). Morality is a matter of rational inquiry. It involves the exercise of a faculty—reason—that is the same in all normal human persons without regard to culture, religion, or time in history. Like the laws of logic and mathematics, the principles of morality bind every rational being, human and divine; they are not the product of divine command. This fact implies that religious believers do not have greater access to morality than anyone else and that religious leaders are in no better position to make pronouncements about morality than any other rational persons—just as they are in no better position to know what logic or mathematics implies or what scientific truth involves. . . .

Thus the notion that morality would collapse if belief in God or practice of religion disappeared is totally misguided. The statements by Nietzsche and Dostoevsky that the death of God means that all things are permitted reflect a childish understanding of morality. Such a notion resembles the idea that the only reason why the child should keep out of the cookie jar is that his mother will slap his hand if she catches him; when Mother is not looking, everything is permitted. But there is a reason for what morality requires and forbids, and that reason remains valid and binding on rational persons whether Mother is watching or not, and whether there is a God to enforce it or not. We should stay out of the cookie jar because eating too many sweets is harmful to our health; we should refrain from lying because lying undermines the social intercourse on which a good life is dependent. In other words, we should refrain from what morality forbids because such things really are wrong and their being wrong has nothing to do with whether or not they are commanded by God.

THE RELATIONSHIP OF
RATIONAL TO RELIGIOUS ETHICS

...

These insights imply that any teaching that contradicts the properly reasoned-out requirements of rational morality must be rejected. The person who claims the right to kill because he believes the voice of spirits told him to is not thereby justified. The person who claims the right to lie and cheat because she believes her government told her to is not thereby justified. The person who claims the right to kidnap or torture because he believes his religion tells him to is not thereby justified. The only thing that can justify acting contrary to a rational moral injunction is a rational argument showing that some other course of action takes moral precedence in the particular case. For example, the only justification I have for killing another human being is the clear realization that I have no other way to stop that person from killing others. Nothing takes precedence over rational moral commandments except other rational moral commandments supported by even stronger moral arguments, or arguments showing that the alternative course of action is even more urgent morally. In many cases, of course, what is required is difficult to ascertain. Sometimes there will be very good moral reasons supporting more than one incompatible course of action and no definitive way of deciding among these courses. These are the kinds of practical difficulties that accompany any kind of moral judgment, and in dealing with them one must proceed with considerable humility, recognizing one's fallibility and acting on one's most conscientious best judgment.

The principle, however, remains clear. When the requirement of rational morality can be ascertained, nothing else (except a more pressing moral requirement) can overrule it. This means that if a religion or a religious leader commands what rational morality forbids or forbids what rational morality commands, the requirement of rational morality must prevail. We have seen already that this should never happen provided those who speak on behalf of religion make open-minded and conscientious use of their reasoning faculty. But we know that sometimes the teachings of an earlier era, based on an underdeveloped science or an incomplete understanding of the world, become enshrined even when the advancement of

human knowledge has shown them to be inadequate. When pronouncements from religious authorities clash with the discoveries of science, a conflict may ensue. This was the case with the church's condemnation of Galileo's scientific findings (a matter of some embarrassment to the Church today) and continues today in some sects' positions concerning evolution.

This may sound like an attempt to drive religion out of the moral arena altogether. Actually, it is nothing of the sort—any more than the recognition of the independence of science from religion in an attempt to enjoin religions from having anything to say about the findings of science or the world to which those findings pertain. Science offers descriptions and explanations of how phenomena occur in the material world. These descriptions and explanations make no reference to gods and no pronouncements about the significance of the findings for the human spirit. But persons who believe in God are likely to believe that the world that science describes is a realm of divine creation and that the order scientists discover in the world is the result of God's orderly plan. Religious persons may also interpret the facts that science discovers as evidence of God's love and care for his human creatures and may find in them great significance for the worth of human existence. They may also sense the appropriateness of our taking an attitude of reverence for the world because they regard it as God's creation. None of these factors clashed with science nor suggests any area of conflict between the legitimate work of science and that of religion.

In a similar way, religion may interpret the requirements of rationality as commanded and supported by God. We have seen that the validity of these requirements does not derive from God's command, but it is entirely likely that a wise and loving God would command that we behave in accordance with the rules of morality. Religion can offer incentives for living moral lives that may supplement for believers the incentive that reasonable persons already recognize in the nature of moral situations.

Furthermore, religions can place additional obligations on believers beyond those required by secular morality, provided they do not contradict anything required by universal human morality. Morality forbids gratuitous cruelty and requires truth telling of all persons; these injunctions may very well be a part of religious morality as well. But Christianity may also require believers to attend mass or to say certain prayers. Rational morality does not require such things, but neither does it forbid them, so there is no inconsistency between the two moral codes. If a religious group, however, forbids the use of blood transfusions to save the life of a child, there may be situations where this conflicts with rational morality, which requires taking appropriate measures to save the life, in which case the religious injunction must yield.

We conclude, then, that religion and ethics are separate realms independent of each other. Morality is not derived from the teachings of religion nor from the will of God. Rather, it is discovered, like the laws of logic and mathematics, by the proper use of human reason. It applies to all human beings alike, whether they are devotees of one religion or another, or of none. Because religion in the past has often been active in teaching morality and promoting moral behavior, however, we hope and expect that it will continue to do so in the future. . . .

Discussion Questions

1. Should theistic religions such as Judaism, Christianity, and Islam regard Abraham as an important founding figure if he was willing to sacrifice his son? Was Abraham correct to attempt to do this? What does the story of Abraham imply about religion and morality? Does it show that something is correct if God commands it? Or, perhaps, does it show that religions are not in fact deeply committed to being moral at all? Should Abraham be highly regarded as a founding hero of religious faith or dismissed as a man with murderous intent?

2. According to Hudson, both sides of the abortion debate share a common moral principle, that it is wrong to commit murder. Do you agree that both sides share the same moral principle? Do defenders of abortion hold moral principles that their opponents do not? Similarly, do those who oppose abortion hold different moral principles than those who support it? In your view, is the abortion controversy about moral principles or is it about something else, such as whether or not killing the fetus is the same thing as murder?

3. Suppose a religious person told you that God had commanded him or her to commit violence against persons who did not share his or her religious faith. What would you say to this person? Would you try to convince them they were wrong? If so, how would you do that? Could you convince them they were wrong without also appealing to religion?

4. What kinds of moral disagreements are there in contemporary culture between persons who are not religious and those who are? What is the basis for these moral controversies? Does everyone, both those who are religious and those who are not, share the same moral principles? Why or why not? Does your answer support Hudson's claim that there is a rationally defensible moral order true for all persons?

For Further Reading

In recent years, there has been a revival of interest in divine command theories of moral obligation. Articles on this topic are regularly published in *Faith and Philosophy: A Journal of the Society of Christian Philosophers*, such as "The Virtue of Obedience," by Philip Quinn (vol. 15, pp. 445–461), and "Divine Command, Divine Will, and Moral Obligation," by Mark Murphy (vol. 15, pp. 3–27). See also several articles in *Christian Theism and the Problems of Philosophy*, edited by Michael Beaty (1990), including "An Argument for Divine Command Ethics," by Philip Quinn, and "Some Suggestions for Divine Command Theorists," by William Alston. For books on this topic, see Philip Quinn, *Divine Commands and Moral Requirements* (1978), and Richard Mouw, *The God Who Commands* (1990).

42 THE CHALLENGE OF CULTURAL RELATIVISM
James Rachels

In this selection, James Rachels begins with the observation that "different cultures have different moral codes." What conclusions can be drawn from this fact? Many persons draw the conclusion that this observation implies that there can be no universal or cross-cultural moral standards, and thus, there is no point in claiming that one view is correct or incorrect. Consequently there is no reason to believe that there is any 'objective truth' in morality. Although this conclusion is popular, Rachels argues that it is mistaken. Not only is the argument for this conclusion not logically valid, but moreover, there are positive reasons for rejecting it. For example, Rachels argues that if there is no objective moral truth, the idea of social reform would not make sense. Moreover, even cultural standards themselves could not be used to decide what course of action we ought to take. Additionally, Rachels asserts that there might not be as many differences in cultural values as is sometimes thought—and that some rules, necessary conditions for societies to exist, are universally true.

This is not to claim that there is nothing to learn from the cultural relativist's argument. According to Rachels, there are two important lessons implied by the argument's premise that different cultures have different moral standards: first, that many so-called moral judgments may only be mere cultural products; and second, as a result, that an open mind is necessary to pursue moral truth.

Reading Questions

1. What is 'cultural relativism'? What reasons have been offered in support of it?
2. What is the 'cultural differences argument'? Why does Rachels believe that it is not valid, that is, that the conclusion does not follow from the premise?
3. If we accepted cultural relativism, why would we be unable to criticize our own cultural moral code?
4. Why would we probably have to give up on the idea of social reform if we accepted cultural relativism, according to Rachels?
5. Why does Rachels believe there might be less disagreement between cultures than there seems to be?
6. How does Rachels argue that all societies will have at least some moral rules in common? What sort of rules would these be?
7. What two lessons does Rachels believe we ought to draw from the insight that different cultures have different moral codes?

Darius, a king of ancient Persia, was intrigued by the variety of cultures he encountered in his travels. He had found, for example, that the Callatians (a tribe of Indians) customarily ate the bodies of their dead fathers. The Greeks, of course, did not do that— the Greeks practiced cremation and regarded the funeral pyre as the natural and fitting way to dispose of the dead. Darius thought that a sophisticated

Source: From *The Elements of Moral Philosophy*, 2nd ed., by James Rachels. Copyright © 1993, The McGraw-Hill Companies. Reprinted by permission of The McGraw-Hill Companies.

understanding of the world must include an appreciation of such differences between cultures. One day, to teach this lesson, he summoned some Greeks who happened to be present at his court and asked them what they would take to eat the bodies of their dead fathers. They were shocked, as Darius knew they would be, and replied that no amount of money could persuade them to do such a thing. Then Darius called in some Callatians, and while the Greeks listened asked them what they would take to burn their dead fathers' bodies. The Callatians were horrified and told Darius not even to mention such a dreadful thing.

This story, recounted by Herodotus in his *History,* illustrates a recurring theme in the literature of social science: different cultures have different moral codes. What is thought right within one group may be utterly abhorrent to the members of another group, and vice versa. Should we eat the bodies of the dead or burn them? If you were a Greek, one answer would seem obviously correct; but if you were a Callatian, the opposite would seem equally certain.

It is easy to give additional examples of the same kind. Consider the Eskimos. They are a remote and inaccessible people. Numbering only about 25,000, they live in small, isolated settlements scattered mostly along the northern fringes of North America and Greenland. Until the beginning of this century, the outside world knew little about them. Then explorers began to bring back strange tales.

Eskimo customs turned out to be very different from our own. The men often had more than one wife, and they would share their wives with guests, lending them for the night as a sign of hospitality. Moreover, within a community, a dominant male might demand—and get—regular sexual access to other men's wives. The women, however, were free to break these arrangements simply by leaving their husbands and taking up with new partners—free, that is, so long as their former husbands chose not to make trouble. All in all, the Eskimo practice was a volatile scheme that bore little resemblance to what we call marriage.

But it was not only their marriage and sexual practices that were different. The Eskimos also seemed to have less regard for human life. Infanticide, for example, was common. Knud Rasmussen, one of the most famous early explorers, reported that he met one woman who had borne twenty children but had killed ten of them at birth. Female babies, he found,

were especially liable to be destroyed, and this was permitted simply at the parents' discretion, with no social stigma attached to it. Old people also, when they became too feeble to contribute to the family, were left out in the snow to die. So there seemed to be, in this society, remarkably little respect for life.

To the general public, these were disturbing revelations. Our own way of living seems so natural and right that for many of us it is hard to conceive of others living so differently. And when we do hear of such things, we tend immediately to categorize those other peoples as "backward" or "primitive." But to anthropologists and sociologists, there was nothing particularly surprising about the Eskimos. Since the time of Herodotus, enlightened observers have been accustomed to the idea that conceptions of right and wrong differ from culture to culture. If we assume that *our* ideas of right and wrong will be shared by all peoples at all times, we are merely naive.

CULTURAL RELATIVISM

To many thinkers, this observation—"Different cultures have different moral codes"—has seemed to be the key to understanding morality. The idea of universal truth in ethics, they say, is a myth. The customs of different societies are all that exist. These customs cannot be said to be "correct" or "incorrect," for that implies we have an independent standard of right and wrong by which they may be judged. But there is no such independent standard; every standard is culture-bound. The great pioneering sociologist William Graham Sumner, writing in 1906, put the point like this:

> The "right" way is the way which the ancestors used and which has been handed down. The tradition is its own warrant. It is not held subject to verification by experience. The notion of right is in the folkways. It is not outside of them, of independent origin, and brought to test them. In the folkways, whatever is, is right. This is because they are traditional, and therefore contain in themselves the authority of the ancestral ghosts. When we come to the folkways we are at the end of our analysis.

This line of thought has probably persuaded more people to be skeptical about ethics than any other single thing. *Cultural Relativism,* as it has been called, challenges our ordinary belief in the objectivity and universality of moral truth. It says, in effect, that there is no such thing as universal truth in ethics; there are only the various cultural codes, and nothing more. Moreover, our own code has no special status; it is merely one among many.

As we shall see, this basic idea is really a compound of several different thoughts. It is important to separate the various elements of the theory because, on analysis, some parts of the theory turn out to be correct, whereas others seem to be mistaken. As a beginning, we may distinguish the following claims, all of which have been made by cultural relativists:

1. Different societies have different moral codes.
2. There is no objective standard that can be used to judge one societal code better than another.
3. The moral code of our own society has no special status; it is merely one among many.
4. There is no "universal truth" in ethics—that is, there are no moral truths that hold for all peoples at all times.
5. The moral code of a society determines what is right within that society; that is, if the moral code of a society says that a certain action is right, then that action *is* right, at least within that society.
6. It is mere arrogance for us to try to judge the conduct of other peoples. We should adopt an attitude of tolerance toward the practices of other cultures.

Although it may seem that these six propositions go naturally together, they are independent of one another, in the sense that some of them might be true even if others are false. In what follows, we will try to identify what is correct in Cultural Relativism, but we will also be concerned to expose what is mistaken about it.

THE CULTURAL DIFFERENCES ARGUMENT

Cultural Relativism is a theory about the nature of morality. At first blush it seems quite plausible. However, like all such theories, it may be evaluated by subjecting it to rational analysis; and when we analyze Cultural Relativism we find that it is not so plausible as it first appears to be.

The first thing we need to notice is that at the heart of Cultural Relativism there is a certain *form of argument*. The strategy used by cultural relativists is to argue from facts about the differences between cultural outlooks to a conclusion about the status of morality. Thus we are invited to accept this reasoning:

(1) The Greeks believed it was wrong to eat the dead, whereas the Callatians believed it was right to eat the dead.
(2) Therefore, eating the dead is neither objectively right nor objectively wrong. It is merely a matter of opinion, which varies from culture to culture.

Or, alternatively:

(1) The Eskimos see nothing wrong with infanticide, whereas Americans believe infanticide is immoral.
(2) Therefore, infanticide is neither objectively right nor objectively wrong. It is merely a matter of opinion, which varies from culture to culture.

Clearly, these arguments are variations of one fundamental idea. They are both special cases of a more general argument, which says:

(1) Different cultures have different moral codes.
(2) Therefore, there is no objective "truth" in morality. Right and wrong are only matters of opinion, and opinions vary from culture to culture.

We may call this the *Cultural Differences Argument*. To many people, it is very persuasive. But from a logical point of view, is it a *sound* argument?

It is not sound. The trouble is that the conclusion does not really follow from the premise—that is, even if the premise is true, the conclusion still might be false. The premise concerns what people *believe:* in some societies, people believe one thing; in other societies, people believe differently. The conclusion, however, concerns *what really is the case.* The trouble is that this sort of conclusion does not follow logically from this sort of premise.

Consider again the example of the Greeks and Callatians. The Greeks believed it was wrong to eat the dead; the Callatians believed it was right. Does it follow, *from the mere fact that they disagreed,* that there is no objective truth in the matter? No, it does not follow; for it *could* be that the practice was objectively right (or wrong) and that one or the other of them was simply mistaken.

To make the point clearer, consider a very different matter. In some societies, people believe the earth is flat. In other societies, such as our own, people believe the earth is (roughly) spherical. Does it follow, *from the mere fact that they disagree,* that there is no "objective truth" in geography? Of course not; we would never draw such a conclusion because we realize that, in their beliefs about the world, the members of some societies might simply be wrong. There is no reason to think that if the world is round everyone must know it. Similarly, there is no reason to think that if there is moral truth everyone must know it. The fundamental mistake in the Cultural Differences Argument is that it attempts to derive a substantive conclusion about a subject (morality) from the mere fact that people disagree about it.

It is important to understand the nature of the point that is being made here. We are *not* saying (not yet, anyway) that the conclusion of the argument is false. Insofar as anything being said here is concerned, it is still an open question whether the conclusion is true. We *are* making a purely logical point and saying that the conclusion does not *follow from* the premise. This is important, because in order to determine whether the conclusion is true, we need arguments in its support. Cultural Relativism proposes this argument, but unfortunately the argument turns out to be fallacious. So it proves nothing.

THE CONSEQUENCES OF TAKING CULTURAL RELATIVISM SERIOUSLY

Even if the Cultural Differences Argument is invalid, Cultural Relativism might still be true. What would it be like if it were true?

In the passage quoted above, William Graham Sumner summarizes the essence of Cultural Relativism. He says that there is no measure of right and wrong other than the standards of one's society: "The notion of right is in the folkways. It is not outside of them, of independent origin, and brought to test them. In the folkways, whatever is, is right."

Suppose we took this seriously. What would be some of the consequences?

1. *We could no longer say that the customs of other societies are morally inferior to our own.* This, of course, is one of the main points stressed by Cultural Relativism. We would have to stop condemning other societies merely because they are "different." So long as we concentrate on certain examples, such as the funerary practices of the Greeks and Callatians, this may seem to be a sophisticated, enlightened attitude.

   However, we would also be stopped from criticizing other, less benign practices. Suppose a society waged war on its neighbors for the purpose of taking slaves. Or suppose a society was violently anti-Semitic and its leaders set out to destroy the Jews. Cultural Relativism would preclude us from saying that either of these practices was wrong. We would not even be able to say that a society tolerant of Jews is *better* than the anti-Semitic society, for that would imply some sort of transcultural standard of comparison. The failure to condemn *these* practices does not seem "enlightened"; on the contrary, slavery and anti-Semitism seem wrong *wherever* they occur. Nevertheless, if we took Cultural Relativism seriously, we would have to admit that these social practices also are immune from criticism.

2. *We could decide whether actions are right or wrong just by consulting the standards of our society.* Cultural Relativism suggests a simple test for determining what is right and what is wrong: all one has to do is ask whether the action is in accordance with the code of one's society. Suppose a resident of South Africa is wondering whether his country's policy of *apartheid*—rigid racial segregation—is morally correct. All he has to do is ask whether this policy conforms to his society's moral code. If it does, there is nothing to worry about, at least from a moral point of view.

   This implication of Cultural Relativism is disturbing because few of us think that our society's code is perfect—we can think of ways it might be improved. Yet Cultural Relativism would not only forbid us from criticizing the codes of *other* societies; it would stop us from criticizing our *own.* After all, if right and wrong are relative to culture, this must be true for our own culture just as much as for others.

3. *The idea of moral progress is called into doubt.* Usually, we think that at least some changes in our society have been for the better. (Some, of course, may have been changes for the worse.)

Consider this example: Throughout most of Western history the place of women in society was very narrowly circumscribed. They could not own property; they could not vote or hold political office; with a few exceptions, they were not permitted to have paying jobs; and generally they were under the almost absolute control of their husbands. Recently much of this has changed, and most people think of it as progress.

If Cultural Relativism is correct, can we legitimately think of this as progress? Progress means replacing a way of doing things with a *better* way. But by what standard do we judge the new ways as better? If the old ways were in accordance with the social standards of their time, then Cultural Relativism would say it is a mistake to judge them by the standards of a different time. Eighteenth-century society was, in effect, a different society from the one we have now. To say that we have made progress implies a judgment that present-day society is better, and that is just the sort of transcultural judgment that, according to Cultural Relativism, is impermissible.

Our idea of social *reform* will also have to be reconsidered. A reformer such as Martin Luther King, Jr., seeks to change his society for the better. Within the constraints imposed by Cultural Relativism, there is one way this might be done. If a society is not living up to its own ideals, the reformer may be regarded as acting for the best: the ideals of the society are the standard by which we judge his or her proposals as worthwhile. But the "reformer" may not challenge the ideals themselves, for those ideals are by definition correct. According to Cultural Relativism, then, the idea of social reform makes sense only in this very limited way.

These three consequences of Cultural Relativism have led many thinkers to reject it as implausible on its face. It does make sense, they say, to condemn some practices, such as slavery and anti-Semitism, wherever they occur. It makes sense to think that our own society has made some moral progress, while admitting that it is still imperfect and in need of reform. Because Cultural Relativism says that these judgments make no sense, the argument goes, it cannot be right.

WHY THERE IS LESS DISAGREEMENT THAN IT SEEMS

The original impetus for Cultural Relativism comes from the observation that cultures differ dramatically in their views of right and wrong. But just how much do they differ? It is true that there are differences. However, it is easy to overestimate the extent of those differences. Often, when we examine what *seems* to be a dramatic difference, we find that the cultures do not differ nearly as much as it appears.

Consider a culture in which people believe it is wrong to eat cows. This may even be a poor culture, in which there is not enough food; still, the cows are not to be touched. Such a society would *appear* to have values very different from our own. But does it? We have not yet asked why these people will not eat cows. Suppose it is because they believe that after death the souls of humans inhabit the bodies of animals, especially cows, so that a cow may be someone's grandmother. Now do we want to say that their values are different from ours? No; the difference lies elsewhere. The difference is in our belief systems, not in our values. We agree that we shouldn't eat Grandma; we simply disagree about whether the cow *is* (or could be) Grandma.

The general point is this. Many factors work together to produce the customs of a society. The society's values are only one of them. Other matters, such as the religious and factual beliefs held by its members and the physical circumstances in which they must live, are also important. We cannot conclude, then, merely because customs differ, that there is a disagreement about *values.* The difference in customs may be attributable to some other aspect of social life. Thus there may be less disagreement about values than there appears to be.

Consider the Eskimos again. They often kill perfectly normal infants, especially girls. We do not approve of this at all; a parent who did this in our society would be locked up. Thus there appears to be a great difference in the values of our two cultures. But suppose we ask *why* the Eskimos do this. The explanation is not that they have less affection for their children or less respect for human life. An Eskimo family will always protect its babies if conditions permit. But they live in a harsh environment, where food is often in short supply. A fundamental postulate of Eskimo thought is: "Life is hard, and the margin of safety small." A family may want to nourish its babies but be unable to do so.

As in many "primitive" societies, Eskimo mothers will nurse their infants over a much longer period of time than mothers in our culture. The child will take nourishment from its mother's breast for four years, perhaps even longer. So even in the best of times there are limits to the number of infants that one mother can sustain. Moreover, the Eskimos are a nomadic people—unable to farm, they must move about in search of food. Infants must be carried, and a mother can carry only one baby in her parka as she travels and goes about her outdoor work. Other family members can help, but this is not always possible.

Infant girls are more readily disposed of because, first, in this society the males are the primary food providers—they are the hunters, according to the traditional division of labor—and it is obviously important to maintain a sufficient number of food gatherers. But there is an important second reason as well. Because the hunters suffer a high casualty rate, the adult men who die prematurely far outnumber the women who die early. Thus if male and female infants survived in equal numbers, the female adult population would greatly outnumber the male adult population. Examining the available statistics, one writer concluded that "were it not for female infanticide . . . there would be approximately one-and-a-half times as many females in the average Eskimo local group as there are food-producing males."

So among the Eskimos, infanticide does not signal a fundamentally different attitude toward children. Instead, it is a recognition that drastic measures are sometimes needed to ensure the family's survival. Even then, however, killing the baby is not the first option considered. Adoption is common; childless couples are especially happy to take a more fertile couple's "surplus." Killing is only the last resort. I emphasize this in order to show that the raw data of the anthropologists can be misleading; it can make the differences in values between cultures appear greater than they are. The Eskimos' values are not all that different from our values. It is only that life forces upon them choices that we do not have to make.

HOW ALL CULTURES HAVE SOME VALUES IN COMMON

It should not be surprising that, despite appearance, the Eskimos are protective of their children. How could it be otherwise? How could a group survive that did *not* value its young? This suggests a certain argument, one which shows that all cultural groups must be protective of their infants:

(1) Human infants are helpless and cannot survive if they are not given extensive care for a period of years.
(2) Therefore, if a group did not care for its young, the young would not survive, and the older members of the group would not be replaced. After a while the group would die out.
(3) Therefore, any cultural group that continues to exist must care for its young. Infants that are *not* cared for must be the exception rather than the rule.

Similar reasoning shows that other values must be more or less universal. Imagine what it would be like for a society to place no value at all on truth telling. When one person spoke to another, there would be no presumption at all that he was telling the truth—for he could just as easily be speaking falsely. Within that society, there would be no reason to pay attention to what anyone says. (I ask you what time it is, and you say "Four o'clock." But there is no presumption that you are speaking truly; you could just as easily have said the first thing that came into your head. So I have no reason to pay attention to your answer—in fact, there was no point in my asking you in the first place!) Communication would then be extremely difficult, if not impossible. And because complex societies cannot exist without regular communication among their members, society would become impossible. It follows that in any complex society there *must* be a presumption in favor of truthfulness. There may of course be exceptions to this rule: there may be situations in which it is thought to be permissible to lie. Nevertheless, these will be exceptions to a rule that *is* in force in the society.

Let me give one further example of the same type. Could a society exist in which there was no prohibition on murder? What would this be like? Suppose people were free to kill other people at will, and no one thought there was anything wrong with it. In such a "society," no one could feel secure. Everyone would have to be constantly on guard. People who wanted to survive would have to avoid other people as much as possible. This would inevitably result in individuals trying to become as self-sufficient as possible—after all, associating with others would be dangerous. Society on any large scale would collapse. Of course, people might band together in smaller groups with others that they *could* trust not to harm them. But notice what this means: they would be forming smaller societies that *did* acknowledge a rule against murder. The prohibition of murder, then, is a necessary feature of all societies.

There is a general theoretical point here, namely, that *there are some moral rules that all societies will have in common, because those rules are necessary for society to exist.* The rules against lying and murder are two examples. And in fact, we do find these rules in force in all viable cultures. Cultures may differ in what they regard as legitimate exceptions to the rules, but this disagreement exists against a background of agreement on the larger issues. Therefore, it is a mistake to overestimate the amount of difference between cultures. Not *every* moral rule can vary from society to society.

WHAT CAN BE LEARNED FROM CULTURAL RELATIVISM

At the outset, I said that we were going to identify both what is right and what is wrong in Cultural Relativism. Thus far I have mentioned only its mistakes: I have said that it rests on an invalid argument, that it has consequences that make it implausible on its face, and that the extent of cultural disagreement is far less than it implies. This all adds up to a pretty thorough repudiation of the theory. Nevertheless, it is still a very appealing idea, and the reader may have the feeling that all this is a little unfair. The theory *must* have something going for it, or else why has it been so influential? In fact, I think there *is* something right about Cultural Relativism, and now I want to say what that is. There are two lessons we should learn from the theory, even if we ultimately reject it.

1. Cultural Relativism warns us, quite rightly, about the danger of assuming that all our preferences are based on some absolute rational standard. They are not. Many (but not all) of our practices are merely peculiar to our society, and it is easy to lose sight of that fact. In reminding us of it, the theory does a service.

Funerary practices are one example. The Callatians, according to Herodotus, were "men who eat their fathers"—a shocking idea, to us at least. But eating the flesh of the dead could be understood as a sign of respect. It could be taken as a symbolic act that says: We wish this person's spirit to dwell within us. Perhaps this was the understanding of the Callatians. On such a way of thinking, burying the dead could be seen as an act of rejection, and burning the corpse as positively scornful. If this is hard to imagine, then we may need to have our imaginations stretched. Of course we may feel a visceral repugnance at the idea of eating human flesh in any circumstances. But what of it? This repugnance may be, as the relativists say, only a matter of what is customary in our particular society.

There are many other matters that we tend to think of in terms of objective right and wrong, but that are really nothing more than social conventions. Should women cover their breasts? A publicly exposed breast is scandalous in our society, whereas in other cultures it is unremarkable. Objectively speaking, it is neither right nor wrong—there is no objective reason why either custom is better. Cultural Relativism begins with the valuable insight that many of our practices are like this—they are only cultural products. Then it goes wrong by concluding that, because *some* practices are like this, *all* must be.

2. The second lesson has to do with keeping an open mind. In the course of growing up, each of us has acquired some strong feelings: we have learned to think of some types of conduct as acceptable, and others we have learned to regard as simply unacceptable. Occasionally, we may find those feelings challenged. We may encounter someone who claims that our feelings are mistaken. For example, we may have been taught that homosexuality is immoral, and we may feel quite uncomfortable around gay people and see them as alien and "different." Now someone suggests that this may be a mere prejudice; that there is nothing evil about homosexuality; that gay people

are just people, like anyone else, who happen, through no choice of their own, to be attracted to others of the same sex. But because we feel so strongly about the matter, we may find it hard to take this seriously. Even after we listen to the arguments, we may still have the unshakable feeling that homosexuals *must*, somehow, be an unsavory lot.

Cultural Relativism, by stressing that our moral views can reflect the prejudices of our society, provides an antidote for this kind of dogmatism. When he tells the story of the Greeks and Callatians, Herodotus adds:

> For if anyone, no matter who, were given the opportunity of choosing from amongst all the nations of the world the set of beliefs which he thought best, he would inevitably, after careful consideration of their relative merits, choose that of his own country. Everyone without exception believes his own native customs, and the religion he was brought up in, to be the best.

Realizing this can result in our having more open minds. We can come to understand that our feelings are not necessarily perceptions of the truth—they may be nothing more than the result of cultural conditioning. Thus when we hear it suggested that some element of our social code is *not* really the best and we find ourselves instinctively resisting the suggestion, we might stop and remember this. Then we may be more open to discovering the truth, whatever that might be.

We can understand the appeal of Cultural Relativism, then, even though the theory has serious shortcomings. It is an attractive theory because it is based on a genuine insight—that many of the practices and attitudes we think so natural are really only cultural products. Moreover, keeping this insight firmly in view is important if we want to avoid arrogance and have open minds. These are important points, not to be taken lightly. But we can accept these points without going on to accept the whole theory.

Discussion Questions

1. Rachels argues that if you accepted cultural relativism, then you wouldn't be able to make sense of moral reform or progress, including, for example, the work of Martin Luther King, Jr., or Cesar Chavez. What is Rachels' argument? Do you agree that we have made moral progress in the area of civil rights? If so, how do you know that we have made *moral* progress? Does this imply that there is a cross-cultural moral standard against which progress is measured?

2. Are there some moral beliefs that you once held that you no longer believe are true? Why did you change your mind? What would Rachels say this implies about morality?

3. Is one culture or society ever justified in interfering in the affairs of another culture? If so, give some examples (actual or hypothetical) of when such interference is justified. What makes it morally justifiable? Then, give some examples of when interfering with another culture has not been justifiable. What made these interferences unjustifiable?

4. Can advocates of cultural relativism provide a convincing account of moral progress, that is, of the progress that has been made in such areas as slavery, apartheid, child labor, and female genital mutilation? Why or why not? If so, how would the cultural relativist explain the apparent phenomena of moral progress? If not, does this count as a definitive reason against cultural relativism?

For Further Reading

This selection is from Rachels' book *Elements of Moral Philosophy* (1978), a good introduction to ethical theory, including a useful and helpful discussion of virtue ethics. Rachels' most widely discussed article is "Active and Passive Euthanasia," *New England Journal of Medicine*, vol. 292 (pp. 78–80); this article has been widely anthologized in applied ethics texts.

The case for moral relativism was best made by the sociologists William Graham Sumner in his 1907 book *Folkways* and Ruth Benedict in her 1946 book *Patterns of Culture.* For an additional critique of ethical relativism see *Morality: An Introduction to Ethics* (1972), by Bernard Williams. Additional philosophical investigations of relativism have been made by David Wong in *Moral Relativity* (1984).

43   WHAT UTILITARIANISM IS
John Stuart Mill

Consequentialist theories hold that an action is correct insofar as it promotes good consequences. This view seems intuitively correct: How could it not be right to promote good consequences? Certainly, it makes sense to claim that the best thing to do is promote good consequences. But there is a special problem here for consequentialists: What do the words 'best' and 'good' refer to? It does not appear that some thing or event is the 'best' or is 'good' in the same way it is 'red' or 'tall' or 'fast'. After all, it can be observed that a ball is red, a building is tall, and a train is fast—but can the 'goodness' of an action be observed?

As it turns out, most consequentialists are also empiricists. Empiricism is the epistemological theory that holds that knowledge comes only through experience. The question arises, then, that if knowledge comes only through experience, then is there sensory capacity that can be used to experience 'goodness' and 'badness'? Can 'goodness' be seen or felt? Obviously, not in the same way that other qualities of things can be known. One difficulty for consequentialists, then, is not whether or not it is correct to promote the best consequences, but rather how it is possible to know what the best consequences are. Is there some way to know what is 'best' or 'good' through experience?

Yes, says John Stuart Mill. Mill is a **utilitarian.** Utilitarians are consequentialists who believe that actions are right inasmuch as they promote happiness (sometimes referred to as 'utility'). The right course of action is the one that creates the greatest amount of happiness. But a new question arises: What is happiness? Mill's answer is that happiness is pleasure and the absence of pain. For this reason, Mill's theory is regarded as a hedonic form of consequentialism. **Hedonism** is the view that pleasure is a good that ought to be promoted. Mill's utilitarianism is a form of hedonism because, according to Mill, happiness should be understood in hedonistic terms, that is, as pleasure and the absence of pain. Thus, the best actions are the ones that promote the greatest balance of pleasure over pain. Notice this important feature of Mill's account: Pleasure and pain can be experienced. We can know therefore, from past experience, which actions predictably promote pleasure, and therefore happiness, and which actions promote pain, and therefore unhappiness. Notice as well that Mill argues that when determining the right thing to do, all of the pleasure and pain produced must be taken into account. Mill rejects **egoism,** the view that each person should promote only his or her own happiness. Rather, Mill's utilitarianism holds that the correct action to perform is the one that promotes the best consequences for all, that is, the action that produces the greatest amount of happiness for everyone.

John Stuart Mill (1806–1873) was an important nineteenth-century English philosopher who is generally regarded as one of the most important defenders of personal liberty. This selection is from chapter 2 of Mill's *Utilitarianism,* considered along with *On Liberty* and *The Subjection of Women* to be one of his three most important works. Most of Mill's attention in this piece is focused on refuting objections to the doctrine of utilitarianism, but just as often "the best offense is a good defense," Mill's refutation is also a powerful argument for promoting the greatest happiness.

Reading Questions

1. How does Mill respond to the objection that the sources of pleasure for humans and for swine are the same?
2. What is the difference between the quality of pleasure and the quantity of pleasure? Why does Mill introduce this distinction?
3. What is Mill's explanation for why people sometimes choose the lower pleasure to the higher pleasure?
4. What is the objection that happiness is unattainable? What is Mill's response?
5. According to Mill, what would the average person require in order to live an enviable life? What stands in the way of the happiness of ordinary people?
6. Does Mill believe that in order to promote the greatest happiness persons should always advance the general interests of society? Why or why not?
7. How does Mill respond to the objection that there is not enough time to calculate the effects of one's actions before one acts?

. . .

The creed which accepts, as the foundation of morals, Utility, or the Greatest-happiness Principle, holds that actions are right in proportion as they tend to promote happiness, wrong as they tend to produce the reverse of happiness. By happiness is intended pleasure and the absence of pain; by unhappiness, pain and the privation of pleasure. To give a clear view of the moral standard set up by the theory, much more requires to be said; in particular, what things it includes in the ideas of pain and pleasure, and to what extent this is left an open question. But these supplementary explanations do not affect the theory of life on which this theory of morality is grounded,—namely, that pleasure, and freedom from pain, are the only things desirable as ends; and that all desirable things (which are as numerous in the utilitarian as in any other scheme) are desirable either for the pleasure inherent in themselves, or as means to the promotion of pleasure and the prevention of pain.

Now, such a theory of life excites in many minds, and among them in some of the most estimable in feeling and purpose, inveterate dislike. To suppose that life has (as they express it) no higher end than pleasure,—no better and nobler object of desire and pursuit,—they designate as utterly mean and groveling; as a doctrine worthy only of swine, to whom the followers of Epicurus were, at a very early period, contemptuously likened: and modern holders of the doctrine are occasionally made the subject of equally polite comparisons by its German, French, and English assailants.

When thus attacked, the Epicureans have always answered, that it is not they, but their accusers, who represent human nature in a degrading light, since the accusation supposes human beings to be capable of no pleasures except those of which swine are capable. If this supposition were true, the charge could not be gainsaid, but would then be no longer an imputation; for, if the sources of pleasure were precisely the same to human beings and to swine, the rule of life which is good enough for the one would be good enough for the other. The comparison of the Epicurean life to that of beasts is felt as degrading, precisely because a beast's pleasures do not satisfy a human being's conceptions of happiness. Human beings have faculties more elevated than the animal appetites; and, when once made conscious of them, do not regard any thing as happiness which does not include their gratification. I do not, indeed, consider the Epicureans to have been by any means faultless in drawing out their scheme of consequences from the utilitarian principle. To do this in any sufficient manner, many Stoic as well as Christian elements require to be included. But there is no known Epicurean theory of life which does not assign to the pleasures of the intellect, of the feelings and imagination, and of the moral sentiments, a much higher value as pleasures than to those of mere sensation. It must be admitted, however, that utilitarian writers in general have placed the superiority of mental over bodily pleasures chiefly in the greater permanency, safety, uncostliness, etc., of the former,—that is, in their circumstantial advantages rather than in their intrinsic nature. And, on all these points, utilitarians have fully proved their case; but they might have taken the other, and, as it may be called, higher ground, with entire consistency. It is quite compatible with the principle of utility to recognize the fact, that some *kinds* of pleasure are more desirable and more valuable than others. It would be absurd, that while, in estimating all other things, quality is considered as well as quantity, the estimation of pleasures should be supposed to depend on quantity alone.

If I am asked what I mean by difference of quality in pleasures, or what makes one pleasure more valuable than another, merely as a pleasure, except its being greater in amount, there is but one possible answer. Of two pleasures, if there be one to which all or almost all who have experience of both give a decided preference, irrespective of any feeling of moral obligation to prefer it, that is the more desirable pleasure. If one of the two is, by those who are competently acquainted with both, placed so far above the other that they prefer it, even though

knowing it to be attended with a greater amount of discontent, and would not resign it for any quantity of the other pleasure which their nature is capable of, we are justified in ascribing to the preferred enjoyment a superiority in quality, so far outweighing quantity, as to render it, in comparison, of small account.

Now, it is an unquestionable fact, that those who are equally acquainted with and equally capable of appreciating and enjoying both do give a most marked preference to the manner of existence which employs their higher faculties. Few human creatures would consent to be changed into any of the lower animals, for a promise of the fullest allowance of a beast's pleasures: no intelligent human being would consent to be a fool, no instructed person would be an ignoramus, no person of feeling and conscience would be selfish and base, even though they should be persuaded that the fool, the dunce, or the rascal is better satisfied with his lot than they are with theirs. They would not resign what they possess more than he for the most complete satisfaction of all the desires which they have in common with him. If they ever fancy they would, it is only in cases of unhappiness so extreme, that, to escape from it, they would exchange their lot for almost any other, however undesirable in their own eyes. A being of higher faculties requires more to make him happy, is capable probably of more acute suffering, and certainly accessible to it at more points, than one of an inferior type; but, in spite of these liabilities, he can never really wish to sink into what he feels to be a lower grade of existence. We may give what explanation we please of this unwillingness; we may attribute it to pride, a name which is given indiscriminately to some of the most and to some of the least estimable feelings of which mankind are capable; we may refer it to the love of liberty and personal independence,—an appeal to which was with the Stoics one of the most effective means for the inculcation of it; to the love of power, or to the love of excitement, both of which do really enter into and contribute to it: but its most appropriate appellation is a sense of dignity, which all human beings possess in one form or other, and in some, though by no means in exact, proportion to their higher faculties, and which is so essential a part of the happiness of those in whom it is strong, that nothing which conflicts with it could be, otherwise than momentarily, an object of desire to them. Whoever supposes that this preference takes place at a sacrifice of happiness; that the superior being, in any thing like equal circumstances, is not happier than the inferior,— confounds the two very different ideas of happiness and content. It is indisputable, that the being whose capacities of enjoyment are low has the greatest chance of having them fully satisfied; and a highly endowed being will always feel that any happiness which he can look for, as the world is constituted, is imperfect. But he can learn to bear its imperfections, if they are at all bearable; and they will not make him envy the being who is indeed unconscious of the imperfections, but only because he feels not at all the good which those imperfections qualify. It is better to be a human being dissatisfied, than a pig satisfied; better to be Socrates dissatisfied, than a fool satisfied. And if the fool or the pig are of a different opinion, it is because they only know their own side of the question. The other party to the comparison knows both sides.

It may be objected, that many who are capable of the higher pleasures, occasionally, under the influence of temptation, postpone them to the lower. But this is quite compatible with a full appreciation of the intrinsic superiority of the higher. Men often, from infirmity of character, make their election for the nearer good, though they know it to be the less valuable, and this no less when the choice is between two bodily pleasures than when it is between bodily and mental. They pursue sensual indulgences to the injury of health, though perfectly aware that health is the greater good. It may be further objected, that many who begin with youthful enthusiasm for every thing noble, as they advance in years sink into indolence and selfishness. But I do not believe that those who undergo this very common change voluntarily choose the lower description of pleasures in preference to the higher. I believe, that, before they devote themselves exclusively to the one, they have already become incapable of the other. Capacity for the nobler feelings is in most natures a very tender plant, easily killed, not only by hostile influences, but by mere want of sustenance; and, in the majority of young persons, it speedily dies away if the occupations to which their position in life has devoted them, and the society into which it has thrown them, are not favorable to keeping that higher capacity in

exercise. Men lose their high aspirations as they lose their intellectual tastes, because they have not time or opportunity for indulging them; and they addict themselves to inferior pleasures, not because they deliberately prefer them, but because they are either the only ones to which they have access, or the only ones which they are any longer capable of enjoying. It may be questioned, whether any one, who has remained equally susceptible to both classes of pleasures, ever knowingly and calmly preferred the lower; though many in all ages have broken down in an ineffectual attempt to combine both.

From this verdict of the only competent judges, I apprehend there can be no appeal. On a question, which is the best worth having of two pleasures, or which of two modes of existence is the most grateful to the feelings, apart from its moral attributes and from its consequences, the judgment of those who are qualified by knowledge of both, or, if they differ, that of the majority among them, must be admitted as final. And there needs be the less hesitation to accept this judgment respecting the quality of pleasures, since there is no other tribunal to be referred to even on the question of quantity. What means are there of determining which is the acutest of two pains, or the intensest of two pleasurable sensations, except the general suffrage of those who are familiar with both? Neither pains nor pleasures are homogeneous, and pain is always heterogeneous with pleasure. What is there to decide whether a particular pleasure is worth purchasing at the cost of a particular pain, except the feelings and judgment of the experienced? When, therefore, those feelings and judgment declare the pleasures derived from the higher faculties to be preferable *in kind,* apart from the question of intensity, to those of which the animal nature, disjoined from the higher faculties, is susceptible, they are entitled on this subject to the same regard.

According to the Greatest-happiness Principle, as above explained, the ultimate end, with reference to and for the sake of which all other things are desirable (whether we are considering our own good or that of other people), is an existence exempt as far as possible from pain, and as rich as possible in enjoyments, both in point of quantity and quality; the test of quality, and the rule for measuring it against quantity, being the preference felt by those, who in their opportunities of experience, to which must be added their habits of self-consciousness and self-observation, are best furnished with the means of comparison. This, being, according to the utilitarian opinion, the end of human action, is necessarily also the standard of morality: which may accordingly be defined, the rules and precepts for human conduct, by the observance of which an existence such as has been described might be, to the greatest extent possible, secured to all mankind; and not to them only, but, so far as the nature of things admits, to the whole sentient creation.

Against this doctrine, however, arises another class of objectors, who say that happiness, in any form, cannot be the rational purpose of human life and action; because, in the first place, it is unattainable: and they contemptuously ask, What right hast thou to be happy? a question which Mr. Carlyle clinches by the addition, What right, a short time ago, hadst thou even *to be?* Next, they say that men can do *without* happiness; that all noble human beings have felt this, and could not have become noble but by learning the lesson of Entsagen, or renunciation; which lesson, thoroughly learnt and submitted to, they affirm to be the beginning and necessary condition of all virtue.

The first of these objections would go to the root of the matter, were it well founded; for, if no happiness is to be had at all by human beings, the attainment of it cannot be the end of morality, or of any rational conduct. Though, even in that case, something might still be said for the utilitarian theory; since utility includes not solely the pursuit of happiness, but the prevention or mitigation of unhappiness: and, if the former aim be chimerical, there will be all the greater scope and more imperative need for the latter, so long at least as mankind think fit to live, and do not take refuge in the simultaneous act of suicide recommended under certain conditions by Novalis. When, however, it is thus positively asserted to be impossible that human life should be happy, the assertion, if not something like a verbal quibble, is at least an exaggeration. If by happiness be meant a continuity of highly pleasurable excitement, it is evident enough that this is impossible. A state of exalted pleasure lasts only moments, or in some cases, and with some intermissions, hours or days; and is the occasional brilliant flash of enjoyment, not its permanent and steady flame. Of this the philosophers who have taught that happiness is the end of life were as fully aware as those who taunt them. The happiness which they meant was not a life of rapture, but moments of such, in an existence made up of few and transitory pains, many and various pleasures, with a decided predominance of the active over the passive, and having, as the foundation of the whole, not to expect more from life than it is capable of bestowing. A life thus composed, to those who have been fortunate enough to obtain it, has always appeared worthy of the name of "happiness." And such an existence is even now the lot of many, during some considerable portion of their lives. The present wretched education and wretched social arrangements are the only real hindrance to its being attainable by almost all.

Now, there is absolutely no reason in the nature of things why an amount of mental culture sufficient to give an intelligent interest in these objects of contemplation should not be the inheritance of every one born in a civilized country. As little is there an inherent necessity that any human being should be a selfish egotist, devoid of every feeling or care but those which center in his own miserable individuality. Something far superior to this is sufficiently common even now to give ample earnest of what the human species may be made. Genuine private affections, and a sincere interest in the public good, are possible, though in unequal degrees, to every rightly brought up human being. In a world in which there is so much to interest, so much to enjoy, and so much also to correct and improve, every one who has this moderate amount of moral and intellectual requisites is capable of an existence which may be called enviable; and unless such a person, through bad laws, or subjection to the will of others, is denied the liberty to use the sources of happiness within his reach, he will not fail to find this enviable existence, if he escape the positive evils of life, the great sources of physical and mental suffering,—such as indigence, disease, and the unkindness, worthlessness, or premature loss, of objects of affection. The main stress of the problem lies, therefore, in the contest with these calamities, from which it is a rare good fortune entirely to escape; which, as things now are, cannot be obviated, and often cannot be, in any material degree, mitigated. Yet no one, whose opinion deserves a moment's consideration, can doubt that most of the great positive evils of the world are in themselves removable, and will, if human affairs continue to improve, be in the end reduced within narrow limits. Poverty, in any sense implying suffering, may be completely extinguished by the wisdom of society, combined with the good sense and providence of individuals. . . .

I must again repeat, what the assailants of utilitarianism seldom have the justice to acknowledge, that the happiness which forms the utilitarian standard of what is right in conduct is not the agent's own happiness, but that of all concerned; as, between his own happiness and that of others, utilitarianism requires him to be as strictly impartial as a disinterested and benevolent spectator. In the golden rule of Jesus of Nazareth, we read the complete spirit of the ethics of utility. To do as you would be done by, and to love your neighbor as yourself, constitute the ideal perfection of utilitarian morality. As the means of making the nearest approach to this ideal, utility would enjoin, first, that laws and social arrangements should place the happiness or (as, speaking practically, it may be called) the interest of every individual as nearly as possible in harmony with the interest of the whole; and, secondly, that education and opinion, which have so vast a power over human character, should so use that power as to establish in the mind of every individual an indissoluble association between his own happiness and the good of the whole,—especially between his own happiness, and the practice of such modes of conduct, negative and positive, as regard for the universal happiness prescribes,—so that not only he may be unable to conceive the possibility of happiness to himself, consistently with conduct opposed to the general good, but also that a direct impulse to promote the general good may be in every individual one of the habitual motives of action, and the sentiments connected therewith may fill a large and prominent place in every human being's sentient existence. If the impugners of the utilitarian morality represented it to their own minds in this its true character, I know not what recommendation possessed by any other morality they could possibly affirm to be wanting to it; what more beautiful or more exalted developments of human nature any other ethical system can be supposed to foster; or what springs of action, not accessible to the utilitarian, such systems rely on for giving effect to their mandates.

The objectors to utilitarianism cannot always be charged with representing it in a discreditable light. On the contrary, those among them who entertain any thing like a just idea of its disinterested character sometimes find fault with its standard as being too high for humanity. They say it is exacting too much to require that people shall always act from the inducement of promoting the general interests of society. But this is to mistake the very meaning of a standard of morals, and confound the rule of action with the motive of it. It is the business of ethics to tell us what are our duties, or by what test we may know them; but no system of ethics requires that the sole motive of all we do shall be a feeling of duty: on the contrary, ninety-nine hundredths of all our actions are done from other motives, and rightly so done, if the rule of duty does not condemn them. It is the more unjust to utilitarianism that this particular misapprehension should be made a ground of objection to it, inasmuch as utilitarian moralists have gone beyond almost all others in affirming that the motive has nothing to do with the morality of the action, though much with the worth of the agent. He who saves a fellow-creature from drowning does what is morally right, whether his motive be duty, or the hope of being paid for his trouble: he who betrays the friend that trusts him is guilty of a crime, even if his object be to serve another friend to whom he is under greater obligations. But to speak only of actions done from the motive of duty, and in direct obedience to principle: it is a misapprehension of the utilitarian mode of thought to conceive it as implying that people should fix their minds upon so wide a generality as the world or society at large. The great majority of good actions are intended, not for the benefit of the world, but for that of individuals, of which the good of the world is made up; and the thoughts of the most virtuous man need not on these occasions travel beyond the particular persons concerned, except so far as is necessary to assure himself, that, in benefiting them, he is not violating the rights—that is, the legitimate and authorized expectations—of any one else. The multiplication of happiness is, according to the utilitarian ethics, the object of virtue: the occasions on which any person (except one in a thousand) has it in his power to do this on an extended scale—in other words, to be a public benefactor—are but exceptional; and on these occasions alone is he called on to consider public utility: in every other case, private utility, the interest or happiness of some few persons, is all he has to attend to. Those alone, the influence of whose actions extends to society in general, need concern themselves habitually about so large an object. In the case of abstinences indeed,— of things which people forbear to do from moral considerations, though the consequences in the particular case might be beneficial,—it would be unworthy of an intelligent agent not to be consciously aware that the action is of a class, which, if practiced generally, would be generally injurious, and that this is the ground of the obligation to abstain from it. The amount of regard for the public interest implied in this recognition is no greater than is demanded by every system of morals; for they all enjoin to abstain from whatever is manifestly pernicious to society.

The same considerations dispose of another reproach against the doctrine of utility, founded on a still grosser misconception of the purpose of a standard of morality, and of the very meaning of the words "right" and "wrong." It is often affirmed, that utilitarianism renders men cold and unsympathizing; that it chills their moral feelings towards individuals; that it makes them regard only the dry and hard consideration of the consequences of actions, not taking into their moral estimate the qualities from which those actions emanate. If the assertion means that they do not allow their judgment respecting the rightness or wrongness of an action to be influenced by their opinion of the qualities of the person who does it, this is a complaint, not against utilitarianism, but against having any standard of morality at all: for certainly no known ethical standard decides an action to be good or bad because it is done by a good or a bad man; still less because done by an amiable, a brave, or a benevolent man, or the contrary. These considerations are relevant, not to the estimation of actions, but of persons; and there is nothing in the utilitarian theory inconsistent with the fact, that there are other things which interest us in persons besides the rightness and wrongness of their actions. The Stoics indeed, with the paradoxical misuse of language which was part of their system, and by which they strove to raise themselves above all concern about any thing but virtue, were fond of saying, that he who has that, has every thing; that he, and only he, is rich, is beautiful, is a king. But no claim of this description is made for the virtuous man by the utilitarian doctrine. Utilitarians are quite aware that there are other desirable possessions and qualities besides virtue, and are perfectly willing to allow to all of them their full worth. They are also aware that a right action does not necessarily indicate a virtuous character; and that actions which are blamable often proceed from qualities entitled to praise. When this is apparent in any particular case, it modifies their estimation, not certainly of the act, but of the agent. I grant that they are, notwithstanding, of opinion, that, in the long-run, the best proof of a good character is good actions; and resolutely refuse to consider any mental disposition as good, of which the predominant tendency is to produce bad conduct. This makes them unpopular with many people: but it is an unpopularity which they must share with every one who regards the distinction between right and wrong in a serious light; and the reproach is not one which a conscientious utilitarian need be anxious to repel.

If no more be meant by the objection than that many utilitarians look on the morality of actions, as measured by the utilitarian standard, with too exclusive a regard, and do not lay sufficient stress upon the other beauties of character which go towards making a human being lovable or admirable, this may be admitted. Utilitarians who have cultivated their moral feelings, but not their sympathies nor their artistic perceptions, do fall into this mistake; and so do all other moralists under the same conditions. What can be said in excuse for other moralists is equally available for them; namely, that, if there is to be any error, it is better that it should be on that side. As a matter of fact, we may affirm that among utilitarians, as among adherents of other systems, there is every imaginable degree of rigidity and of laxity in the application of their standard: some are even puritanically rigorous, while others are as indulgent as can possibly be desired by sinner or by sentimentalist. But, on the whole, a doctrine which brings prominently forward the interest that mankind have in the repression and prevention of conduct which violates the moral law, is likely to be inferior to no other in turning the sanctions of opinion against such violations. It is true, the question, What does violate the moral law? is one on which those who recognize different standards of morality are likely now and then to differ. But difference of opinion on moral questions was not first introduced into the world by utilitarianism; while that doctrine does supply, if not always an easy, at all events a tangible and intelligible, mode of deciding such differences.

Again: defenders of utility often find themselves called upon to reply to such objections as this,—that there is not time, previous to action, for calculating and weighing the effects of any line of conduct on the general happiness. This is exactly as if any one were to say that it is impossible to guide our conduct by Christianity, because there is not time, on every occasion on which any thing has to be done, to read through the Old and New Testaments. The answer to the objection is, that there has been ample time; namely, the whole past duration of the human species. During all that time, mankind have been learning by experience the tendencies of actions, on which experience all the prudence as well as all the morality of life are dependent. People talk as if the commencement of this course of experience had hitherto been put off, and as if, at the moment when some man feels tempted to meddle with the property or life of another, he had to begin considering for the first time whether murder and theft are injurious to human happiness. Even then, I do not think that he would find the question very puzzling; but, at all events, the matter is now done to his hand. It is truly a whimsical supposition, that, if mankind were agreed in considering utility to be the test of morality, they would remain without any agreement as to what *is* useful, and would take no measures for having their notions on the subject taught to the young, and enforced by law and opinion. There is no difficulty in proving any ethical standard whatever to work ill, if we suppose universal idiocy to be conjoined with it: but, on any hypothesis short of that, mankind must by this time have acquired positive beliefs as to the effects of some actions on their happiness; and the beliefs which have thus come down are the rules of morality for the multitude, and for the philosopher, until he has succeeded in finding better. That philosophers might easily do this, even now, on many subjects; that the received code of ethics is by no means of divine right; and that mankind have still much to learn as to the effects of actions on the general happiness,—I admit, or, rather, earnestly maintain. The corollaries from the principle of utility, like the precepts of every practical art, admit of indefinite improvement; and, in a progressive state of the human mind, their improvement is perpetually going on. But to consider the rules of morality as improv-

able is one thing; to pass over the intermediate generalizations entirely, and endeavor to test each individual action directly by the first principle, is another. It is a strange notion, that the acknowledgment of a first principle is inconsistent with the admission of secondary ones. To inform a traveller respecting the place of his ultimate destination is not to forbid the use of landmarks and direction-posts on the way. The proposition that happiness is the end and aim of morality does not mean that no road ought to be laid down to the goal, or that persons going thither should not be advised to take one direction rather than another. Men really ought to leave off talking a kind of nonsense on this subject which they would neither talk nor listen to on other matters of practical concernment. Nobody argues that the art of navigation is not founded on astronomy, because sailors cannot wait to calculate the "Nautical Almanac." Being rational creatures, they go to sea with it ready calculated; and all rational creatures go out upon the sea of life with their minds made up on the common questions of right and wrong, as well as on many of the far more difficult questions of wise and foolish. And this, as long as foresight is a human quality, it is to be presumed they will continue to do. Whatever we adopt as the fundamental principle of morality, we require subordinate principles to apply it by: the impossibility of doing without them, being common to all systems, can afford no argument against any one in particular; but gravely to argue as if no such secondary principles could be had, and as if mankind had remained till now, and always must remain, without drawing any general conclusions from the experience of human life, is as high a pitch, I think, as absurdity has ever reached in philosophical controversy.

The remainder of the stock arguments against utilitarianism mostly consist in laying to its charge the common infirmities of human nature, and the general difficulties which embarrass conscientious persons in shaping their course through life. We are told that an utilitarian will be apt to make his own particular case an exception to moral rules; and, when under temptation, will see an utility in the breach of a rule greater than he will see in its observance. But is utility the only creed which is able to furnish us with excuses for evil-doing, and means of cheating our own conscience? They are afforded in abundance by all doctrines which recognize as a fact in morals the existence of conflicting considerations; which all doctrines do that have been believed by sane persons. It is not the fault of any creed, but of the complicated nature of human affairs, that rules of conduct cannot be so framed as to require no exceptions, and that hardly any kind of action can safely be laid down as either always obligatory or always condemnable. There is no ethical creed which does not temper the rigidity of its laws by giving a certain latitude, under the moral responsibility of the agent, for accommodation to peculiarities of circumstances; and under every creed, at the opening thus made, self-deception and dishonest casuistry get in. There exists no moral system under which there do not arise unequivocal cases of conflicting obligation. These are the real difficulties; the knotty points both in the theory of ethics, and in the conscientious guidance of personal conduct. They are overcome practically with greater or with less success according to the intellect and virtue of the individual; but it can hardly be pretended that any one will be the less qualified for dealing with them, from possessing an ultimate standard to which conflicting rights and duties can be referred. If utility is the ultimate source of moral obligations, utility may be invoked to decide between them when their demands are incompatible. Though the application of the standard may be difficult, it is better than none at all . . .

Discussion Questions

1. What is the distinction between higher and lower pleasures? Give some examples of each. Do you agree that there are pleasures of different *qualities?* Why or why not?
2. Would it ever promote the greatest happiness to violate the rights of individuals? Why or why not? Do rights, such as the rights to life, property, and privacy, promote the greatest happiness of all? Why or why not?
3. Is the greatest happiness promoted when each person looks after his or her own happiness? Or is the greatest happiness promoted when everyone advances the happiness of all?
4. What makes people happy? What does the collective experience of your cultural group, religion, or community group teach about what makes persons happy? Is being happy the same thing as being moral? Why or why not?

For Further Reading

It is interesting to compare Mill's utilitarianism with his classic defense of liberties in *On Liberty* (1859). An important early advocate for utilitarianism (and, at one time, Mill's tutor) was Jeremy Bentham; see especially his *An Introduction to the Principles of Morals and Legislation* (1789). Perhaps the most important modern utilitarian is Derek Parfit, whose 1986 book, *Reasons and Persons,* is especially noteworthy.

There are numerous anthologies of scholarly articles on utilitarianism. Among the best are Amartya Sen and Bernard Williams, eds., *Utilitarianism and Beyond,* (1982); J. J. C. Smart and B. Williams, eds., *Utilitarianism For and Against* (1973); and Samuel Scheffler, ed., *Consequentialism and Its Critics* (1988).

44   THE CATEGORICAL IMPERATIVE
Immanuel Kant

Immanuel Kant (1724–1804) had a wide impact on the shape and history of philosophy after him, particularly in the areas of metaphysics and epistemology. But Kant also made significant contributions to ethics, particularly through a relatively short book entitled *Foundations of the*

Metaphysics of Morals. Few books in the history of philosophy have been as widely read or as important and significant as this small book. Although a challenging article, you'll find the time spent with this selection a worthwhile and rewarding investment.

Kant is a chief proponent of deontological ethics. The word 'deontology' means the study of duty but is used to describe moral theories that regard actions—not the consequences of actions—as morally significant. Deontological moral theories hold that actions are moral insofar as they conform to moral rules or principles. Kant rejects the view that actions are right insofar as they produce good consequences or result in greater happiness. Rather, actions have worth only insofar as they are performed according to the demands of duty expressed through moral laws. Kant had grown up in a pietist Lutheran home in which morality was conceived of as obedience to universally valid principles that admitted of no exceptions. Lutheranism held that these moral laws had their source in the will of God—literally the commandments of God—but as a mature philosopher Kant sought a more careful and sophisticated explanation of these moral laws.

If morality is conformity to timeless, universal laws, then where do these laws come from and how can we know them? Kant rejects the view that laws come from empirical sources, such as, for example, the study of human nature. Even if the study of human nature yielded interesting results, it still would give us insight only about humanity, but Kant's moral laws are universal and hold for all moral agents, including, if they exist, God, angels, spirits, and even extraterrestrials (Kant imagines the inhabitants of Mercury and Saturn). The source, then, for these laws must be something in common among all moral agents, something in the very nature of the possibility of taking moral action. For Kant this source is the *rational will.*

Expanding on the concept of a rational will, Kant argues that "reason is practical," by which he means that reason alone is enough to motivate the will—a view denied by Hume. The will, Kant maintains, is capable of being moved by the *conception* or *idea* of law. The laws or principles that are capable of moving the will are determined by reason and have a special name: *imperatives.* Some imperatives are hypothetical imperatives and have the form of a hypothetical, an 'If . . . then . . .' statement. For example, the principle "If you wish to do well in school, then attend class regularly" is a hypothetical imperative. It states that if you have a particular end or goal (a telos), then you ought to do such and such. But Kant was primarily interested in *categorical imperatives.* A categorical imperative has no 'if-clause' and instructs moral agents categorically (without exception) to "do such and such" or "don't do such and such." Consider this additional example: "If you want to be considered trustworthy by your acquaintances, keep your promises." This looks like a moral statement, but it is not, because it is a hypothetical imperative—you may or may not want to be considered trust-worthy by your friends. For Kant, moral principles must have a categorical form, in this case, "Keep your promises"—period, regardless of whether or not you want other people to consider you a trustworthy person.

For Kant, there is one categorical imperative, and in this selection we see two versions of it, called the First and Second Versions of the Categorical Imperative. The first version is "Act as though the maxim of your action were by your will to become a universal law of nature." The second version is "Act so that you treat humanity, whether in your own person or in that of another, always as an end and never as a means only."

Reading Questions

1. What conclusion does Kant draw from the fact that it is impossible to discern by experience whether an action was the result of moral duty?
2. Why does Kant argue that we can't derive our conception of morality from examples, such as the examples of Christ (the Holy One)?
3. What reasons does Kant give for concluding that we must derive moral laws from the general concept of rational being?
4. What is the difference between the practical good and the 'pleasant'? How is this difference related to the difference between what is objective and what is subjective?
5. What is the difference between a hypothetical and categorical imperative?
6. Kant argues that if one conceives of a categorical imperative, the content is known at once. Explain his argument and how he concludes that the maxim that determines our actions must conform to a universal law.
7. Explain how the categorical imperative shows that it is wrong to borrow money by making a false promise.
8. How does Kant explain the times when we violate (transgress) our moral duties?
9. What is the difference between an end and a means? How is this distinction connected to the difference between objective and subjective grounds for action?
10. What imperative does Kant conclude from the observation that "rational nature exists as an end in itself"?
11. How does Kant explain why it is wrong to borrow money by lying using the practical imperative (the second version of the categorical imperative)?
12. Why did all previous attempts at discovering principles of morality fail according to Kant?

If we have up until now drawn our notion of duty from the common uses of our practical reason, it is not the case that we have treated it as an empirical notion. On the contrary, when we attend to the experience of men's conduct, we meet frequent and, as we sometimes agree, just complaints that one cannot find a single certain example of the disposition to act from pure duty. Although many things are done in conformity *with duty*, it is nevertheless always doubtful whether they are done strictly *from duty* such that they have a moral worth. Hence there have always been philosophers who have completely denied that the disposition to act from pure duty actually exists in humans, and have thus ascribed everything to a more or less refined self-love. . . .

In fact, it is absolutely impossible to discern by experience with complete certainty a single case in which the maxim of an action, however right in itself, rested simply on moral grounds and on the conception of duty. Sometimes it happens that with the sharpest self-examination we can find nothing beside the moral principle of duty which could have been powerful enough to move us to this or that action and to so great a sacrifice. But we cannot from this infer with certainty that it was not really some secret impulse of self-love, under the false appearance of duty, that was the actual determining cause of the will. We like to flatter ourselves by falsely taking credit for a more noble motive; whereas in fact we can never, even by the strictest examination, get completely behind the secret springs of action. Thus, when the question is one of moral worth, it is not with the actions which we see that concern us, but rather the inward principles which we do not see.

Moreover, we cannot better serve the wishes of those who ridicule all morality as a mere chimera of human imagination, vainly over stepping its bounds, than by conceding to them that notions of duty must be drawn only from experience. . . . I am willing to admit out of love of humanity that even most of our actions are correct, but if we look closer at them we everywhere come upon the dear self which is always prominent, and it is this (the self) that the actions have in view—not the strict command of duty which often requires self-denial. Without being an enemy of virtue, the cool observer—who does not mistake the desire for the good, however impressive, for the reality of achieving it—may sometimes doubt whether true virtue is actually found anywhere in the world. . . .

When we add further that, unless we deny that the notion of morality has any truth or reference to any possible object, we must admit that its law must be valid, not merely for men, but for all rational creatures generally—and not merely under certain contingent conditions or with exceptions, but with absolute necessity, then it is clear that no experience could enable us to infer even the possibility of absolutely certain and universal laws. . . .

Nor could anything be more fatal to morality than that we should wish to derive it from examples. For every supposed example that is set before me must first itself be tested by principles of morality, to determine whether it is worthy to serve as an original example, that is, as a pattern for other actions. But by itself, it cannot authoritatively furnish the conception of morality. Even the Holy One of the Gospels must first be compared with our ideal of moral perfection before we can recognize Him as Holy; and so He says of Himself, "Why call Me (whom you see) good; none is good (the model of good) but God only (whom you do not see)?" But from where did we derive the conception of God as the supreme good? Simply from the idea of moral perfection, which reason frames a priori and connects inseparably with the notion of a free will. Thus we see that imitation finds no place at all in morality, and examples serve only for encouragement. So examples demonstrate

that what the law commands is feasible and make visible and specific what the practical rule expresses only generally. . . .

From what has been said, it is clear that (1) all moral concepts have their origin completely a priori in the reason, whether it be common ordinary reason or speculative reason; that (2) they cannot be obtained by abstraction from any empirical, and therefore merely contingent, knowledge; that (3) it is just this purity of their origin that makes them worthy to serve as our supreme practical principle, and that in proportion to the degree that we add anything empirical to them, we detract from their genuine influence and from the absolute value of actions; and that (4) it is not only of the greatest necessity, in a purely speculative point of view, but is also of the greatest practical importance, to derive these notions and laws from pure reason in order to present them pure and unmixed, and thus to determine the compass of this practical or pure rational knowledge. . . . In so doing, we must not make moral principles dependent on the particular nature of human reason . . . but since moral laws ought to hold good for every rational creature, we must derive them from the general concept of a rational being. . . .

Everything in nature works according to laws. Rational beings alone have the faculty of acting according to the conception of laws, that is according to principles: only rational beings have a will. Since the deduction of actions from principles requires reason, the will is nothing but practical reason. If reason infallibly determines the will, then if the actions of such a being are recognized as *objectively* necessary, then they are *subjectively* necessary also. As such, the will is a faculty whose sole purpose is to choose what reason independent of inclination recognizes as practically necessary, that is, as good. But if reason itself does not sufficiently determine the will, such that the will is subject also to subjective conditions (particular impulses and motives) which do not always coincide with the objective conditions—in a word, if the will does not itself completely accord with reason (which is actually the case with men)—then the actions objectively recognized as necessary are now subjectively contingent. The determination of such a will according to objective laws is called obligation, that is to say, the relation of the objective laws to a will that is not thoroughly good is conceived as the obligatory determination of the will of a rational being by principles of reason—which the will does not naturally or necessarily follow.

This conception of an objective principle, in so far as it is obligatory for a will, is called a *command* (of reason), and the formula of this command is called an *imperative.*

All imperatives are expressed by the word "ought," and thereby indicate the relation of an objective law of reason to a will (which is not subjectively constituted to be necessarily obligated or constrained by it). An imperative says that something would be good to do or to forbear, but says it to a will which does not always do a thing just because it is conceived to be good to do. The *practical good,* however, determines the will by means of the concepts of reason, and consequently not from subjective causes, but *objectively,* that is on principles which are valid for every rational being as such. It is distinguished from the *pleasant,* as that which influences the will only by means of sensation from merely *subjective* causes, valid only for the sense of this or that one, and not as a principle of reason, which holds for every one. . . .

Now all imperatives command either *hypothetically* or *categorically.* The former represent the practical necessity of a possible action as means to another end that is willed (or at least which one might possibly will). The categorical imperative would be that which represented an action as objectively necessary in itself without reference to another end.

. . . If now the action is good only as a means to something else, then the imperative is hypothetical; if it is conceived as good in itself and consequently as being necessarily the principle of a will which of itself conforms to reason, then it is categorical. . . .

Accordingly the hypothetical imperative only says that the action is good for some purpose, possible or actual. . . . The categorical imperative which declares an action to be objectively necessary in itself without reference to any purpose, i.e., without any other end, is valid as a logically certain (practical) principle. . . .

. . . The question of how the imperative of morality is possible, is undoubtedly one, the only one, demanding a solution, as this is not at all hypothetical, and the objective necessity which it presents cannot rest on any hypothesis, as is the case with hypothetical imperatives. We must never forget that we cannot proceed by using examples, in other words

empirically, to demonstrate whether there is such an imperative (of morality) at all, or if, as is feared by some, all those which seem to be categorical may yet be at bottom hypothetical. For example, consider the precept "Thou shalt not promise deceitfully." It is assumed that the necessity of this is not a mere counsel to avoid some other evil and thus does not mean something like "Thou shalt not make a lying promise, lest if it become known thou shouldst destroy thy credit"—because an action of this kind must be regarded as evil in itself and so the imperative of the prohibition must be categorical. Thus we cannot show with certainty in any example that the will was determined merely by the law, without any other spring of action, although it may appear to be so. For it is always possible that fear of disgrace, perhaps also obscure dread of other dangers, may have a secret influence on the will. . . .

We shall therefore have to investigate *a priori* the possibility of a categorical imperative, as we have not in this case the advantage of its reality being given in experience, so that elucidating its possibility should only be required for its explanation, not for its establishment. In the meantime it may be discerned beforehand that the categorical imperative alone has the purport of a practical law; all the rest may indeed be called principles of the will but not laws, since whatever is only necessary for the attainment of some arbitrary purpose may be considered as in itself contingent. In this case, we can at any time be free from the precept if we give up the purpose. But the unconditional command, on the contrary, leaves the will no liberty to choose the opposite and consequently it alone carries with it that necessity which we require in a law. . . .

In this problem we will first inquire whether the mere conception of a categorical imperative may not perhaps supply us also with the formula of it, containing the proposition which alone can be a categorical imperative. . . .

When I conceive of a hypothetical imperative, in general I do not know beforehand what it will contain until I am given the condition. But when I conceive a categorical imperative, I know at once what it contains. For as the imperative contains besides the law only the necessity that the maxims shall conform to this law, while the law contains no conditions restricting it, there remains nothing but the general statement that the maxim of the action should conform to a universal law. It is this conformity alone that the imperative properly represents as necessary. [Note: A maxim is a subjective principle of action, and must be distinguished from the objective principle, namely, practical law. The former, the maxim, contains the practical rule set by reason according to the conditions of the subject (often its ignorance or its inclinations). It is the principle on which the subject acts. The law is the objective principle valid for every rational being. . . .]

There is therefore but one categorical imperative, namely, this: *Act only on that maxim whereby you can at the same time will that it should become a universal law.*

Now if all imperatives of duty can be deduced from this one imperative as from their principle, then . . . we shall be able to show what we understand by it and what this notion means.

Since the universality of the law constitutes what is properly called nature in the most general sense (as to form), that is, the existence of things so far as they are determined by general laws, the imperative of duty may be expressed thus: *Act as if the maxim of your action were to become by your will a universal law of nature.*

We will now enumerate a few duties, adopting the usual division of them into duties to ourselves and to others, and into perfect and imperfect duties.

1. A man reduced to despair by a series of misfortunes feels wearied of life, but is still so far in possession of his reason that he can ask himself whether it would not be contrary to his duty to himself to take his own life. Now he asks whether the maxim of his action could become a universal law of nature. His maxim is: "From self-love I adopt it as a principle to shorten my life when its longer duration is likely to bring more evil than satisfaction." It is then simply asked whether this principle founded on self-love can become a universal law of nature. Now we see at once a contradiction: a system of nature in which it should be a law to destroy life by means of the very feeling whose special nature it is to impel to the improvement of life would contradict itself. Therefore it could not exist as a system of nature and hence that maxim cannot possibly exist as a universal law of nature. Consequently, it is wholly inconsistent with the supreme principle of all duty.

2. Another finds himself forced by necessity to borrow money. He knows that he will not be able to repay it, but sees also that nothing will be lent to him unless he firmly promises to repay it in a definite time. He desires to make this promise, but he still has sufficient conscience to ask himself: "Is it not unlawful and inconsistent with duty to get out of a difficulty in this way?" Suppose however that he resolves to do so. If so, then the maxim of his action would be expressed thus: "Whenever I find myself in want of money, I will borrow money and promise to repay it, although I know that I never can do so." Now this principle of self-love (or of one's own advantage) may perhaps be consistent with my whole future welfare— but the question before us is this: "Is it right?" If I change the hint of self-love into universal law, and restate the question thus: "How would it be if my maxim were a universal law?" then I see at once that it could never hold as a universal law of nature, but would necessarily contradict itself. For suppose it were a universal law that everyone when he finds himself in a difficulty should be able to promise whatever he pleases, with the purpose of not keeping his promise. Then the promise itself would become impossible, as well as the end that one might have in mind for it, since no one would believe anything was promised to him and would ridicule all such statements as vain pretense.

3. A third finds in himself a talent which, with the help of some cultivation, might make him a useful man in many respects. But he finds himself in comfortable circumstances and prefers to indulge in pleasure rather than to take pains in enlarging and improving his happy natural capacities. He asks, however, whether, besides agreeing with his inclination to indulgence, his maxim of neglecting his natural gifts also agrees with duty. He sees at once that a system of nature could indeed subsist with such a universal law, even though men (like the South Sea islanders) should let their talents rest and resolve to devote their lives merely to idleness, amusement, and propagation of their species—in a word, to pleasure. But he cannot possibly will that this should ever become a universal law of nature or that it be implanted in us as such by a natural instinct, for, as a rational being, he necessarily wills that his faculties be developed, since they serve him and have been given to him for all sorts of possible purposes.

4. A fourth, who lives in prosperity, while he sees that other persons must contend with great wretchedness and that he could help them, thinks to himself: "What concern is it of mine? Let everyone be as happy as Heaven pleases, or as he can make himself; I will take nothing from him nor even envy him. I wish only to not contribute anything to his welfare or to his assistance in distress!" Now no doubt if such a mode of thinking were a universal law, the human race might very well subsist (and without a doubt, better than in that state in which everyone talks of sympathy and good-will but does nothing). . . . But although it is possible that a universal law of nature might exist in accordance with his maxim, it is impossible to will that such a principle should have the validity of a universal law of nature. For a will which resolved this would contradict itself, inasmuch as many cases might occur in which one would need the love and sympathy of others, but during which times, by the law of nature which he himself willed, he would have deprived himself of all hope of the aid he so desires.

These are a few of the many actual duties, or at least what we regard as such, which derive from the one principle we laid down. We must be able to will that a maxim of our action should be a universal law. This is the canon of the moral evaluation of action generally. Some actions are of such a character that their maxim cannot without contradiction be even thought of as a universal law of nature, far from it being possible that we could actually will that it should be so. For other actions, this intrinsic impossibility is not found, but it is still impossible to will that their maxim should be a universal law of nature, since such a will would contradict itself. . . . Thus it has been demonstrated that all duties depend, in terms of the nature of obligation (and not the object of the action), on one principle.

If now we reflect on occasions when we transgress duty, we shall find that we in fact do not will that our maxim should be a universal law, for that is impossible for us. Rather, we will that the opposite should remain a universal law and, because of an inclination we possess, desire the freedom to make an exception in our own favor for just this once only. Consequently if we considered such cases from one and the same point of view, namely, that of reason, we should find

a contradiction in our own will: that a certain principle should be *objectively* necessary as a universal law, and yet *subjectively* should not be universal, but admit of exceptions. . . . This proves that we really do recognize the validity of the categorical imperative and (with all respect for it) allow ourselves only a few exceptions, which we think unimportant and forced upon us. . . .

The question before us now is this: "Is it a necessary law for all rational beings that they should always judge their actions according to maxims which they can themselves will should serve as universal laws?" If it is so, then it must be connected (altogether *a priori*) with the very conception of the will of a rational being generally. . . .

The will is conceived as the faculty of committing oneself to action in accordance with the conception of certain laws. Such a faculty can be found only in rational beings. Now that which serves the will as the objective ground of its self-determination is the *end*, and, if this is assigned by reason alone, is an end for all rational beings. On the other hand, that which merely contains the ground of possibility of the action, whose result is an end, this is called the *means*. The subjective ground of the desire is the incentive, the objective ground of the volition is the motive. This leads to the distinction between subjective ends, which rest on springs, and objective ends, which depend on motives valid for every rational being. . . . The ends that a rational being proposes to himself arbitrarily as the goal of his actions are always relative, i.e., subject ends, since it is only their relation to the particular desires of the subject that gives them their worth. Therefore, they cannot furnish universal principles necessary for all rational beings, that is to say, they are not practical laws. Hence relative (subjective) ends only give rise to hypothetical imperatives.

Supposing, however, that there were something whose existence possesses in itself an absolute worth, something which, being an end in itself, could be a source of definite laws. If so, then this thing alone would be the source of a possible categorical imperative, i.e., a practical law.

Now, I say, man—and more generally any rational being—exists as an end in himself, not merely as a means to be arbitrarily used by this or that will. In all his actions, whether they concern himself or other rational beings, he must be always regarded at the same time as an end. All objects of our personal inclinations have only a conditional worth, for if the inclinations and the desires founded on them did not exist, then their object (their end) would be without value. But these inclinations, themselves being sources of want, are so far from having an absolute worth, that on the other hand, it must be the universal wish of every rational being to be wholly free from them. . . . Beings whose existence depends not on our will but on nature's, if they are not rational beings, have only a relative value as means, and are therefore called "things." Rational beings, on the contrary, are called "persons," because their very nature identifies them as ends in themselves, that is as something which must not be used merely as means, and thus, as objects of respect, restricting arbitrary action against them. Such beings, therefore, are not merely subjective ends whose existence has a worth for us as the result of our action, but are rather objective ends whose existence is as an end in itself. . . .

If then there is a supreme practical principle or, in respect of the human will, a categorical imperative, it must be one which, because it is an end in itself, depends on the conception of what is necessarily an end for everyone and which constitutes an objective principle of will. Thus it serves as a universal practical law. The foundation of this principle is this: rational nature exists as an end in itself. Man necessarily conceives his own existence as being so; insofar as is true, this is merely a subjective principle of human actions. But because every other rational being regards its existence similarly, and does so on the basis of the same rational principle that holds for me, it follows that this principle is at the same time an objective principle, from which, as a supreme practical law, all laws of the will must be capable of being deduced. Therefore the practical imperative is this: *Act so as to treat humanity, whether in your own person or in that of any other, always as an end and never as means only.* We will now inquire whether this can be carried out in practice.

To use the previous examples:

First, under the head of necessary duty to oneself, he who contemplates suicide should ask himself whether his action can be consistent with the idea of humanity as an end in itself. If he destroys himself in order to escape from painful circumstances, he uses a person (himself) merely as a mean to maintain a tolerable condition up to the end of life. But a man is not a thing, that is to say, something which can be used merely as means. A man must, in all his actions, always consider himself as an end. I cannot, therefore, dispose in any way of a man, including my own person, so as to mutilate him, damage, or kill him. . . .

Second, as regards necessary duties and strict obligation towards others: He who is thinking of making a lying promise to others will see at once that he would be using another man merely as a means and that this person would not at the same time will the same end for himself. For the person whom I use for my own purposes by such a promise cannot possibly assent to my actions toward him and, therefore, cannot himself contain the end of this action. This violation of the principle of humanity in other men is more obvious if we take in examples of attacks on the freedom and property of others. In these cases it is clear that those who transgress the rights of men intend to use the person of others merely as a means, without considering that as rational beings they ought always to be regarded also as ends, capable of containing in themselves the end of the very same action.

Third, as regards contingent (meritorious) duties to oneself, it is not enough to say that the action does not violate our human dignity as ends in ourselves: the action must also harmonize with it. Now humans are capable of greater perfection. To neglect this possibility might perhaps be consistent with the maintenance of humanity as an end in itself, but not with the advancement of this end.

Fourth, as regards meritorious duties towards others, the natural end which all men have is their own happiness. Now humanity might indeed exist even if no one contributed anything to the happiness of others (provided no one did not intentionally withdraw anything from another), but in the end, if everyone does not aim to advance the ends of others, then this would only harmonize negatively—not positively—with humanity as an end in itself. For the ends of any subject who is an end in himself ought, as far as possible, to be my ends as well. . . .

On this principle, all maxims are rejected which are inconsistent with the will itself being a universal legislator. Thus the will is not simply subject to the law per se, but subject in such a manner that it regards itself as legislating the law itself and is, on this ground only, subject to the law which it considers itself to be the author. . . .

Thus the principle according to which every human will wills that all its maxims constitute universal laws would be the categorical imperative. Because the idea of universal legislation is not based on interest, it alone among all possible imperatives can be unconditional. Or better still, converting the proposition, if there is a categorical imperative (i.e., a law by the will of every rational being), it can only command that everything be done from maxims willed by a will that simultaneously wills that it itself (as a will) should give universal laws. Only in that case are the practical principle and the imperative unconditional, since they cannot be based on any interest.

Looking back now on all previous attempts to discover the principle of morality, it is no wonder why they all failed. It was seen that man was bound to laws by duty, but it was not seen that the laws to which he is subject are those which he gives himself, even though they are at the same time universal. Nor was it seen that he is only bound to act in conformity with his own will, a will which by its nature, however, must give universal laws. When man was conceived only as subject to a law (no matter what), then this law required some need or compulsion, through either desire or repulsion, to determine its content. Because the law did not originate from his own will, this will was obliged to act in a certain manner according to something else other than law itself. As a result, all the effort spent in finding a supreme principle of duty was irrevocably wasted. One never arrived at duty, but only at the necessity of acting from a certain interest. Whether this interest was private or public, the imperative that resulted was always conditional and thus incapable of being a moral command. The supreme practical principle I will, therefore, call the principle of *autonomy* of the will, as opposed to every other, which I accordingly consider as *heteronomy*.

Discussion Questions

1. Review the difference between actions being done from duty and according to duty. Do you agree with Kant that only actions done from duty have moral worth?

2. Kant believed that the categorical imperative implied that it is always wrong to tell a lie, without exception. Explain how the categorical imperative entails that always telling a lie is wrong. Do you agree that one always has a duty to tell the truth? Why or why not?

3. Kant argues that we are bound by laws that we ourselves create. Some persons believe that this means therefore that the laws or principles we legislate are relative to us. Kant thought, however, that these rules or principles are universal, applicable to all moral agents. Explain how Kant can hold that moral laws are nothing other than the laws that we create and nonetheless are universally binding on all persons.

4. Compare Kant to Mill in Reading 43 of this chapter. Kant illustrates the Categorical Imperative with the examples of (a) the person contemplating suicide, (b) promise keeping, (c) cultivating one's talents, and (d) being a Good Samaritan. What conclusion would a utilitarian reach in each example? Is it the same conclusion? If different, how is it different? Which theory do you think is better, Kant's or Mill's?

For Further Reading

For detailed discussions of Kant's ethical theory see *Dignity and Practical Reason in Kant's Moral Theory* (1992), by Thomas E. Hill; *The Autonomy of Reason: A Commentary on Kant's "Groundwork of the Metaphysics of Morals"* (1973), by Robert Paul Wolff; and *Constructions of Reason: Explorations of Kant's Practical Philosophy,* by Onora O'Neill.

Other ethicists who develop deontological moral theories include David Gauthier, *Morals by Agreement* (1986); Alan Gewirth, *Reason and Morality* (1978); and Alan Donagan, *The Theory of Morality* (1977). The most influential recent explication of Kant's ideas has been in the work of John Rawls. A difficult, but important, account is found in Rawls' "Kantian Constructivism in Moral Theory: The Dewey Lectures," *Journal of Philosophy*, 77 (1980), 515–572. Another neo-Kantian account is George Lucas' essay "Moral Order and the Constraints of Agency," anthologized in *New Essays in Metaphysics* (1987), edited by Robert Neville.

45 NICOMACHEAN ETHICS
Aristotle

Born in Greece in 384 B.C.E., Aristotle joined Plato's Academy when he was 17 years old and spent the next 20 years there until the death of Plato. Later, Aristotle would found his own school, the Lyceum, in Athens and would spend three years as the tutor of the son of the King of Macedon, Alexander the Great.

Although a student of Plato, Aristotle developed his own ideas in new and different directions—and indeed became one of Plato's harshest critics. While Plato's metaphysics focused on unchanging, transcendent, universal forms, Aristotle turned his attention to the investigation of concrete actual instances. As a result, Aristotle made important contributions not only to philosophy, but also to science. Among his numerous writings are works on logic, physics, and natural history (studies of animals and plants), as well as philosophy. These writings would later have an important impact on the development of both Islamic philosophy and the philosophy of Thomas Aquinas.

In this selection, Aristotle develops an account of morality, called **virtue ethics.** Virtue ethics is a character-based ethic which holds that moral actions are right and good insofar as they flow from virtuous characters; bad or wrong actions are the results of vices or vicious characters. For Aristotle, a virtue is a mean or balance between two vices. For example, the virtue of generosity lies between the extremes of miserliness, on the one hand, and lavish wastefulness, on the other hand: A generous person neither squanders money by giving away too much on lavish frivolities nor greedily keeps money like the hoarding miser. Bravery is another example of a virtue. This virtue lies between the extremes of cowardice and rashness: The brave person is neither a coward nor a rash and impulsive person. But a virtue is more than just a mean between two vices—it is also an excellence. What does this mean? Aristotle considered rationality to be the unique characteristic of humans. An excellent human, he argued, was one that excelled at being human, that is, at doing what humans do best— living a life according to the dictates of reason. The virtues, then, are excellencies exhibited by the rational human.

This selection is from Books I and II of Aristotle's *Nicomachean Ethics,* which is 10 books long. Aristotle begins by exploring what it means to say that happiness (*eudaimonia* in Greek) is the good for humanity. It is a classic statement and representation of ancient Greek moral thought and ideals.

1. What makes an end the chief good? Why should we try to determine what that good is?
2. How does Aristotle define happiness? How is it related to other choices we make?
3. How is the function of a thing related to the good for that thing? What does Aristotle say is the unique function of humanity?
4. Why are the virtues not passions?
5. Why are the virtues not faculties?
6. What is the 'intermediate'? How does it help define the specific nature of virtue?
7. How does Aristotle define virtue in terms of the mean, the rational, and the man of practical wisdom?
8. Between what two extremes (vices) is courage a mean? Between what two extremes is temperance a mean?
9. Why, according to Aristotle, is it not an easy task to be good?

All human activities aim at some good: some goods subordinate to others

1. EVERY art and every inquiry, and similarly every action and pursuit, is thought to aim at some good; and for this reason the good has rightly been declared to be that at which all things aim. But a certain difference is found among ends; some are activities, others are products apart from the activities that produce them. Where there are ends apart from the actions, it is the nature of the products to be better than the activities.

Now, as there are many actions, arts, and sciences, their ends also are many; the end of the medical art is health, that of shipbuilding a vessel, that of strategy victory, that of economics wealth. But where such arts fall under a single capacity—as bridle-making and the other arts concerned with the equipment of horses fall under the art of riding, and this and every military action under strategy, in the same way other arts fall under yet others—in all of these the ends of the master arts are to be preferred to all the subordinate ends; for it is for the sake of the former that the latter are pursued. It makes no difference whether the activities themselves are the ends of the actions, or something else apart from the activities, as in the case of the sciences just mentioned.

The science of the good for man is politics

2. Suppose, then, there is some end of the things we do, which we desire for its own sake (everything else being desired for the sake of this), and if we do not choose everything for the sake of something else (since the process would go on to infinity, so that our

desire would be empty and vain), clearly this must be the good and the chief good.

Will not the knowledge of it, then, have a great influence on life? Shall we not, like archers who have a mark to aim at, be more likely to hit upon what is right? If so, we must try, in outline at least, to determine what it is, and of which of the sciences or capacities it is the object. It would seem to belong to the most authoritative art and that which is most truly the master art. And politics appears to be of this nature; for it is this that ordains which of the sciences should be studied in a state, and which each class of citizens should learn and up to what point they should learn them; and we see even the most highly esteemed of capacities to fall under this, e.g., strategy, economics, rhetoric. Now, since politics uses the rest of the sciences, and since, again, it legislates as to what we are to do and what we are to abstain from, the end of this science must include those of the others, so that this end must be the good for man. . . .

WHAT IS THE GOOD FOR MAN?

It is generally agreed to be happiness, but there are various views as to what happiness is. What is required at the start is an unreasoned conviction about the facts, such as is produced by a good upbringing

4. Let us resume our inquiry and state, in view of the fact that all knowledge and every pursuit aims at some good, what it is that we say political science aims at and what is the highest of all goods achievable by action.

As far as what to call it, there is much agreement. Both average persons and superior persons say that it is happiness, and identify living well and doing well with being happy; but with regard to what happiness is they differ, and the many do not give the same account as the wise. For the former think it is some plain and obvious thing, like pleasure, wealth, or honour; they differ, however, from one another—and often even the same man identifies it with different things, with health when he is ill, with wealth when he is poor; but, conscious of their ignorance, they admire those who proclaim some great ideal that is above their comprehension. . . .

7. Let us again return to the good we are seeking, and ask what it can be. It seems different in different actions and arts; it is different in medicine, in strategy, and in the other arts likewise.

What then is the good of each? Surely that for whose sake everything else is done. In medicine this is health, in strategy victory, in architecture a house, in any other sphere something else, and in every action and pursuit the end; for it is for the sake of this that all men do whatever else they do. Therefore, if there is an end for all that we do, this will be the good achievable by action, and if there are more than one, these will be the goods achievable by action.

So the argument has by a different course reached the same point; but we must try to state this even more clearly. Since there are evidently more than one end, and we choose some of these (e.g., wealth, flutes, and in general instruments) for the sake of something else, clearly not all ends are final ends; but the chief good is evidently something final. Therefore, if there is only one final end, this will be what we are seeking, and if there are more than one, the most final of these will be what we are seeking.

Now we call that which is in itself worthy of pursuit more final than that which is worthy of pursuit for the sake of something else, and that which is never desirable for the sake of something else more final than the things that are desirable both in themselves and for the sake of that other thing, and therefore we call final without qualification that which is always desirable in itself and never for the sake of something else.

Now such a thing happiness, above all else, is held to be; for this we choose always for itself and never for the sake of something else, but honour, pleasure, reason, and every virtue we choose indeed for themselves (for if nothing resulted from them we should still choose each of them), but we choose them also for the sake of happiness, judging that by means of them we shall be happy. Happiness, on the other hand, no one chooses for the sake of these, nor, in general, for anything other than itself. . . .

Presumably, however, to say that happiness is the chief good seems a platitude, and a clearer account of what it is is still desired. This might perhaps be given, if we could first ascertain the function of man. For just as for a flute-player, a sculptor, or any artist—and in fact for all things that have a function—the good and the 'well' is thought to reside in the function, so would it seem to be for man, if he has a function. Have the carpenter, then, and the tanner certain functions or activities, and has man none? Is he born without a function? Or as eye, hand, foot, and in general each of the parts evidently has a function, may one lay it down that man similarly has a function apart from all these?

What then can this be? Life seems to belong even to plants, but we are seeking what is peculiar to man. Let us exclude, therefore, the life of nutrition and growth. Next there would be a life of perception, but *it* also seems to be shared even by the horse, the ox, and every animal.

There remains, then, an active life of the element that has a rational principle; of this, one part has such a principle in the sense of being obedient to one, the other in the sense of possessing one and exercising thought. And, as 'life of the rational element' also has two meanings, we must state that life in the sense of activity is what we mean; for this seems to be the more proper sense of the term. Now if the function of man is an activity of soul which follows or implies a rational principle, . . . human good turns out to be activity of soul in accordance with virtue, and if there are more than one virtue, in accordance with the best and most complete.

But we must add 'in a complete life'. For one swallow does not make a summer, nor does one day; and so too one day, or a short time, does not make a man blessed and happy. . . .

DEFINITION OF MORAL VIRTUE

The genus of moral virtue: it is a state of character, not a passion, nor a faculty

5. Next we must consider what virtue is. Since things that are found in the soul are of three kinds—passions, faculties, states of character—virtue must be one of these.

By passions I mean appetite, anger, fear, confidence, envy, joy, friendly feeling, hatred, longing, emulation, pity, and in general the feelings that are accompanied by pleasure or pain.

By faculties the things in virtue of which we are said to be capable of feeling these, e.g., of becoming angry or being pained or feeling pity.

By states of character the things in virtue of which we stand well or badly with reference to the passions, e.g., with reference to anger we stand badly if we feel it violently or too weakly, and well if we feel it moderately; and similarly with reference to the other passions.

Now neither the virtues nor the vices are *passions*, because we are not called good or bad on the ground of our passions, but are so called on the ground of our virtues and our vices, and because we are neither praised nor blamed for our passions (for the man who feels fear or anger is not praised, nor is the man who simply feels anger blamed, but the man who feels it in a certain way), but for our virtues and our vices we *are* praised or blamed.

Again, we feel anger and fear without choice, but the virtues are modes of choice or involve choice. Further, in respect of the passions we are said to be moved, but in respect of the virtues and the vices we are said not to be moved but to be disposed in a particular way.

For these reasons also they are not *faculties*; for we are neither called good or bad, nor praised or blamed, for the simple capacity of feeling the passions; again, we have the faculties by nature, but we are not made good or bad by nature; we have spoken of this before.

If, then, the virtues are neither passions nor faculties, all that remains is that they should be *states of character*. Thus we have stated what virtue is in respect of its genus.

The differentia of moral virtue: it is a disposition to choose the mean

6. We must, however, not only describe virtue as a state of character, but also say what sort of state it is.

We may remark, then, that every virtue or excellence both brings into good condition the thing of which it is the excellence and makes the work of that thing be done well; e.g., the excellence of the eye makes both the eye and its work good; for it is by the excellence of the eye that we see well. Similarly the excellence of the horse makes a horse both good in itself and good at running and at carrying its rider and at awaiting the attack of the enemy. Therefore, if this is true in every case, the virtue of man also will be the state of character which makes a man good and which makes him do his own work well.

How this is to happen we have stated already, but it will be made plain also by the following consideration of the specific nature of virtue. In everything that is continuous and divisible it is possible to take more, less, or an equal amount, and that either in terms of the thing itself or relatively to us; and the equal is an intermediate between excess and defect. By the intermediate in the object I mean that which is equidistant from each of the extremes, which is one and the same for all men; by the intermediate relatively to us that which is neither too much nor too little—and this is not one, nor the same for all.

For instance, if ten is many and two is few, six is the intermediate, taken in terms of the object; for it exceeds and is exceeded by an equal amount; this is intermediate according to arithmetical proportion. But the intermediate relatively to us is not to be taken so; if ten pounds are too much for a particular person to eat and two too little, it does not follow that the trainer will order six pounds; for this also is perhaps too much for the person who is to take it, or too little—too little for Milo, too much for the beginner in athletic exercises. The same is true of running and wrestling. Thus a master of any art avoids excess and defect, but seeks the intermediate and chooses this—the intermediate not in the object but relatively to us.

If it is thus, then, that every art does its work well—by looking to the intermediate and judging its works by this standard (so that we often say of good works of art that it is not possible either to take away or to add anything, implying that excess and defect destroy the goodness of works of art, while the mean preserves it; and good artists, as we say, look to this in their work), and if, further, virtue is more exact and better than any art, as nature also is, then virtue must have the quality of aiming at the intermediate. I mean moral virtue; for it is this that is concerned with passions and actions, and in these there is excess, defect, and the intermediate. For instance, both fear and confidence and appetite and anger and pity and in general pleasure and pain may be felt both too much and too little, and in both cases not well; but to feel them at the right times, with reference to the right objects, towards the right people, with the right motive, and in the right way, is what is both intermediate and best, and this is characteristic of virtue. Similarly with regard to actions also there is excess, defect, and the intermediate. Now virtue is concerned with passions and actions, in which excess is a form of failure, and so is defect, while the intermediate is praised and is a form of success; and being praised and being successful are both characteristics of virtue. Therefore virtue is a kind of mean, since, as we have seen, it aims at what is intermediate. . . .

For men are good in but one way, but bad in many.

Virtue, then, is a state of character concerned with choice, lying in a mean, i.e., the mean relative to us, this being determined by a rational principle, and by that principle by which the man of practical wisdom would determine it. Now it is a mean between two vices, that which depends on excess and that which depends on defect; and again it is a mean because the vices respectively fall short of or exceed what is right in both passions and actions, while virtue both finds and chooses that which is intermediate. Hence in respect of its substance and the definition which states its essence virtue is a mean, with regard to what is best and right an extreme.

But not every action nor every passion admits of a mean; for some have names that already imply badness, e.g., spite, shamelessness, envy, and in the case of actions adultery, theft, murder; for all of these and suchlike things imply by their names that they are themselves bad, and not the excesses or deficiencies of them. It is not possible, then, ever to

be right with regard to them; one must always be wrong. Nor does goodness or badness with regard to such things depend on committing adultery with the right woman, at the right time, and in the right way, but simply to do any of them is to go wrong.

It would be equally absurd, then, to expect that in unjust, cowardly, and voluptuous action there should be a mean, an excess, and a deficiency; for at that rate there would be a mean of excess and of deficiency, an excess of excess, and a deficiency of deficiency. But as there is no excess and deficiency of temperance and courage because what is intermediate is in a sense an extreme, so too of the actions we have mentioned there is no mean nor any excess and deficiency, but however they are done they are wrong; for in general there is neither a mean of excess and deficiency, nor excess and deficiency of a mean.

The above proposition illustrated by reference to particular virtues

7. We must, however, not only make this general statement, but also apply it to the individual facts. For among statements about conduct those which are general apply more widely, but those which are particular are more genuine, since conduct has to do with individual cases, and our statements must harmonize with the facts in these cases. We may take these cases from our table.

With regard to feelings of fear and confidence courage is the mean; of the people who exceed, he who exceeds in fearlessness has no name (many of the states have no name), while the man who exceeds in confidence is rash, and he who exceeds in fear and falls short in confidence is a coward.

With regard to pleasures and pains—not all of them, and not so much with regard to the pains—the mean is temperance, the excess self-indulgence. Persons deficient with regard to the pleasures are not often found; hence such persons also have received no name. But let us call them 'insensible'.

With regard to giving and taking of money the mean is liberality, the excess and the defect prodigality and meanness. In these actions people exceed and fall short in contrary ways; the prodigal exceeds in spending and falls short in taking, while the mean man exceeds in taking and falls short in spending. (At present we are giving a mere outline or summary, and are satisfied with this; later these states will be more exactly determined.) With regard to money there are also other dispositions—a mean, magnificence, an excess, tastelessness and vulgarity, and a deficiency, niggardliness; these differ from the states opposed to liberality, and the mode of their difference will be stated later.

With regard to honour and dishonour the mean is proper pride, the excess is known as a sort of 'empty vanity', and the deficiency is undue humility . . . .

With regard to anger also there is an excess, a deficiency, and a mean. Although they can scarcely be said to have names, yet since we call the intermediate person good-tempered let us call the mean good temper; of the persons at the extremes let the one who exceeds be called irascible, and his vice irascibility, and the man who falls short an unirascible sort of person, and the deficiency unirascibility.

There are also three other means, which have a certain likeness to one another, but differ from one another: for they are all concerned with intercourse in words and actions, but differ in that one is concerned with truth in this sphere, the other two with pleasantness; and of this one kind is exhibited in giving amusement, the other in all the circumstances of life. We must therefore speak of these too, that we may the better see that in all things the mean is praiseworthy and the extremes neither praiseworthy nor right, but worthy of blame. Now most of these states also have no names, but we must try, as in the other cases, to invent names ourselves so that we may be clear and easy to follow.

With regard to truth, then, the intermediate is a truthful sort of person and the mean may be called truthfulness, while the pretence which exaggerates is boastfulness and the person characterized by it a boaster, and that which understates is mock modesty and the person characterized by it mock-modest.

With regard to pleasantness in the giving of amusement the intermediate person is ready-witted and the disposition ready-wit, the excess is buffoonery and the person characterized by it a buffoon, while the man who falls short is a sort of boor and his state is boorishness.

With regard to the remaining kind of pleasantness, that which is exhibited in life in general, the man who is pleasant in the right way is friendly and the mean is friendliness, while the man who exceeds is an obsequious person if he has no end in view, a flatterer if he is aiming at his own advantage, and the man who falls short and is unpleasant in all circumstances is a quarrel-some and surly sort of person.

There are also means in the passions and concerned with the passions, since shame is not a virtue and yet praise is extended to the modest man. Even in these matters, one man is said to be intermediate and another exceed, as for instance the bashful man who is ashamed of everything; while he who falls short or is not ashamed of anything at all is shameless, and the intermediate person is modest.

Righteous indignation is a mean between envy and spite, and these states are concerned with the pain and pleasure that are felt at the fortunes of our neighbours; the man who is characterized by righteous indignation is pained at undeserved good fortune, the envious man, going beyond him, is pained at all good fortune, and the spiteful man falls so far short of being pained that he even rejoices. . . .

The mean is hard to attain, and is grasped by perception, not by reasoning

9. That moral virtue is a mean, then, and in what sense it is so, and that it is a mean between two vices, the one involving excess, the other deficiency, and that it is such because its character is to aim at what is intermediate in passions and in actions, has been sufficiently stated.

Hence also it is no easy task to be good. For in everything it is no easy task to find the middle, e.g., to find the middle of a circle is not for everyone but for him who knows; so, too, anyone can get angry—that is easy—or give or spend money; but to do this to the right person, to the right extent, at the right time, with the right motive, and in the right way, *that* is not for everyone, nor is it easy; wherefore goodness is both rare and laudable and noble.

Discussion Questions

1. Would a virtuous person ever tell a lie? Why or why not? How is Aristotle's answer to this question like or unlike the answers given by Mill and Kant earlier in this chapter?
2. Would a person who simply avoided harming other persons or interfering in the affairs of other persons be virtuous on Aristotle's account? Is it enough to say someone is a 'good' person if all he or she does is refrain from hurting or harming other persons? Do you agree or disagree with Aristotle's position?
3. List some virtues (or character traits) that are valued in your cultural or ethnic group. What vices are associated with each virtue? Are there two vices associated with each virtue? Which virtues are the most important in your culture?
4. Which is the best way to ensure that persons predictably do what is morally required: (a) by being virtuous persons with good characters formed by habit, (b) by following rules, or (c) by making the right decision in individual circumstances? Explain your answer.
5. Are the virtues the same in every culture? If so, why? If they differ from culture to culture, does this count against Aristotle's theory? Is Aristotle's account of virtue a theory that could apply to every culture? Why or why not?

For Further Reading

Many parts of the *Nicomachean Ethics* warrant further investigation, especially Aristotle's discussion of friendship (Book Eight) and justice (Book Five). For a collection of excellent essays on Aristotle's ethics, see Amélie Oksenberg Rorty, ed., *Essays on Aristotle's Ethics* (1980). That collection contains a number of essays on the concept of *eudaimonia,* on virtue as a mean, and on the good for persons.

Additional work has been done on virtue ethics in this century. Alasdair MacIntyre's book *After Virtue* (1981) has been very influential. Besides the work of MacIntyre, see also Philippa Foot, *Virtues and Vices and Other Essays in Moral Philosophy* (1979). For a different development of a virtue theory that emphasizes how agents 'see' the correct thing to do, see John McDowell, "Virtue and Reason," *The Monist* 62 (1979), 331–350. This article is reprinted in Stanley G. Clarke and Evan Simpson, eds., *Anti-Theory in Ethics and Moral Conservatism* (1989), which contains a number of essays sympathetic to virtue theory, as well as a helpful bibliography.

CHAPTER 9

WHAT DOES IT MEAN TO BE MORAL?

The classic moral theories of the Western philosophical tradition discussed in the previous chapter—**consequentialism, deontological theory,** and **virtue theory**—each claim to offer universal, transcultural models of determining right and wrong behavior. This is especially true of the theories of Mill and Kant and is implicit in the article by Rachels that cultural relativism is conceptually confused. Such claims, however, often offend contemporary sensibilities. Is it really the case that moral theorists have described ethical standards that are transcultural and universal? Or have they merely adopted conveniently held local truths and treated them as if they were something more?

In one way or another, each author in this chapter considers traditional Western moral theory to be inadequate. Two of the articles in this chapter are by the controversial ethicist Peter Singer, who is represented here by an article on famine relief and animal rights. Singer does not deny the value of moral theory—his concern is that we haven't taken it seriously enough. In both articles, he relies on moral theory to arrive at conclusions that strike many persons as counterintuitive, but Singer insists that as rational human beings, we soberly consider what our own moral principles demand of us and live accordingly.

Other authors take issue with the parochial nature of traditional moral philosophy, charging it with either a cultural bias or a male bias. Herbert Fingarette, in the second selection, challenges us to expand our cultural and moral horizons. He examines the **Confucian** tradition and compares it to Western conceptions of morality that depend upon widely held assumptions about the centrality of choice and responsibility. We need not go outside our own cultural boundaries, however, in order to challenge traditional moral theory, as the two other authors in this chapter make clear.

In the third selection, Carol Gilligan identifies a way in which gender has distorted traditional moral theory. Gilligan proposes that there are two 'voices' used to analyze moral problems and make moral decisions. The 'justice' voice has been predominantly used by men and represents the type of moral reasoning that is overrepresented in traditional moral theory. Women, on the other hand, often use a 'care' voice, but this valid approach to moral reasoning has not made much impact on philosophical ethics, since women have only recently begun to make contributions as philosophers. In the last article, Brian Luke uses the 'care' voice that Gilligan identifies to enlarge the circle of our moral reasoning in a new direction—to include nonhuman species. Our empathetic identification with animals, according to Luke, not only is a valid moral response—something never imagined by traditional moral theories—but also obligates us to work for animal liberation.

46   FAMINE, AFFLUENCE, AND MORALITY
Peter Singer

Many consequentialist theories, including utilitarianism, are quite simple. They generally have two central requirements: first to promote good consequences and second to promote good consequences for everyone, regardless of any connection or relationship to these persons. This last requirement means that geographical distance between persons should not matter when calculating which course of action will produce the best consequences.

Although simple in form, consequentialist theories can have radical implications. In this selection, Peter Singer (1946–), an ethicist at Princeton University, proposes a very simple form of consequentialism that nonetheless, if adopted, would call for fundamental social change. Unlike Mill, Singer doesn't attempt to define the meaning of the predicates 'good' and 'best'. He assumes that, for the purposes of his argument, there is an adequate, shared conception of what is good and bad. Overall, Singer aims to construct an argument from premises that are uncontroversial and not contentious. For example, rather than claiming that individuals must promote good consequences, Singer considers the weaker claim, that you only need "prevent something bad from happening" when it is in your power to do so. Even this weak claim, however, when combined with the claim that distance between persons should not enter into our moral calculations, has far-reaching implications.

Reading Questions

1. What does Singer assume is bad? Do most people agree with this view?
2. Why does Singer argue that proximity and distance shouldn't be taken into account?
3. According to Singer, what is wrong with the argument that each person only has an obligation to give £5 (about $8) to famine relief?
4. What is wrong with our current concept of charity?
5. According to Singer, are philosophers in a position to make judgments about major public policy issues? Do philosophers know enough that they ought to take action now?

SOURCE: From Singer, Peter; "Famine, Affluence and Morality," *Philosophy and Public Affairs,* vol. 1. Copyright © 1972 by Princeton University Press. Reprinted by permission of Princeton University Press.

As I write this, in November 1971, people are dying in East Bengal from lack of food, shelter, and medical care. The suffering and death that are occurring there now are not inevitable, not unavoidable in any fatalistic sense of the term. Constant poverty, a cyclone, and a civil war have turned at least nine million people into destitute refugees; nevertheless, it is not beyond the capacity of the richer nations to give enough assistance to reduce any further suffering to very small proportions. The decisions and actions of human beings can prevent this kind of suffering. Unfortunately, human beings have not made the necessary decisions. At the individual level, people have, with very few exceptions, not responded to the situation in any significant way. Generally speaking, people have not given large sums to relief funds; they have not written to their parliamentary representatives demanding increased government assistance; they have not demonstrated in the streets, held symbolic fasts, or done anything else directed toward providing the refugees with the means to satisfy their essential needs. At the governmental level, no government has given the sort of massive aid that would enable the refugees to survive for more than a few days. Britain, for instance, has given rather more than most countries. It has, to date, given £14,750,000. For comparative purposes, Britain's share of the non-recoverable development costs of the Anglo-French Concorde project is already in excess of £275,000,000, and on present estimates will reach £440,000,000. The implication is that the British government values a supersonic transport more than thirty times as highly as it values the lives of the nine million refugees. Australia is another country which, on a per capita basis, is well up in the "aid to Bengal" table. Australia's aid, however, amounts to less than one-twelfth of the cost of Sydney's new opera house. The total amount given, from all sources, now stands at about £65,000,000. The estimated cost of keeping the refugees alive for one year is £464,000,000. Most of the refugees have now been in the camps for more than six months. The World Bank has said that India needs a minimum of £300,000,000 in assistance from other countries before the end of the year. It seems obvious that assistance on this scale will not be forthcoming. India will be forced to choose between letting the refugees starve or diverting funds from her own development program, which will mean that more of her own people will starve in the future.

These are the essential facts about the present situation in Bengal. So far as it concerns us here, there is nothing unique about this situation except its magnitude. The Bengal emergency is just the latest and most acute of a series of major emergencies in various parts of the world, arising both from natural and from man-made causes. There are also many parts of the world in which people die from malnutrition and lack of food independent of any special emergency. I take Bengal as my example only because it is the present concern, and because the size of the problem has ensured that it has been given adequate publicity. Neither individuals nor governments can claim to be unaware of what is happening there.

What are the moral implications of a situation like this? In what follows, I shall argue that the way people in relatively affluent countries react to a situation like that in Bengal cannot be justified; indeed, the whole way we look at moral issues—our moral conceptual scheme—needs to be altered, and with it, the way of life that has come to be taken for granted in our society.

In arguing for this conclusion I will not, of course, claim to be morally neutral. I shall, however, try to argue for the moral position that I take, so that anyone who accepts certain assumptions, to be made explicit, will, I hope, accept my conclusion.

I begin with the assumption that suffering and death from lack of food, shelter, and medical care are bad. I think most people will agree about this, although one may reach the same view by different routes. I shall not argue for this view. People can hold all sorts of eccentric positions, and perhaps from some of them it would not follow that death by starvation is in itself bad. It is difficult, perhaps impossible, to refute such positions, and so for brevity I will henceforth take this assumption as accepted. Those who disagree need read no further.

My next point is this: if it is in our power to prevent something bad from happening, without thereby sacrificing anything of comparable moral importance, we ought, morally, to do it. By "without sacrificing anything of comparable moral importance" I mean without causing anything else comparably bad to happen, or doing something that is wrong in itself, or failing to promote some moral good, comparable in significance to the bad thing that we can prevent. This principle seems almost as uncontroversial as the last one. It requires us only to prevent what is bad, and not to promote what is good, and it requires this of us only when we can do it without sacrificing anything that is, from the moral point of view, comparably important. I could even, as far as the application of my argument to the Bengal emergency is concerned, qualify the point so as to make it: if it is in our power to prevent something very bad from happening, without thereby sacrificing anything morally significant, we ought, morally, to do it. An application of this principle would be as follows: if I am walking past a shallow pond and see a child drowning in it, I ought to wade in and pull the child out. This will mean getting my clothes muddy, but this is insignificant, while the death of the child would presumably be a very bad thing.

The uncontroversial appearance of the principle just stated is deceptive. If it were acted upon, even in its qualified form, our lives, our society, and our world would be fundamentally changed. For the principle takes, firstly, no account of proximity or distance. It makes no moral difference whether the person I can help is a neighbor's child ten yards from me or a Bengali whose name I shall never know, ten thousand miles away. Secondly, the principle makes no distinction between cases in which I am the only person who could possibly do anything and cases in which I am just one among millions in the same position.

I do not think I need to say much in defense of the refusal to take proximity and distance into account. The fact that a person is physically near to us, so that we have personal contact with him, may make it more likely that we *shall* assist him, but this does not show that we *ought* to help him rather than another who happens to be further away. If we accept any principle of impartiality, universalizability, equality, or whatever, we cannot discriminate against someone merely because he is far away from us (or we are far away from him). Admittedly, it is possible that we are in a better position to judge what needs to be done to help a person near to us than one far away, and perhaps also to provide the assistance we judge to be necessary. If this were the case, it would be a reason for helping those near to us first. This may once have been a justification for being more concerned with the poor in one's own town than with famine victims in India. Unfortunately for those who like to keep their moral responsibilities limited, instant communication and swift transportation have changed the situation. From the moral point of view, the development of the world into a "global village" has made an important, though still unrecognized, difference to our moral situation. Expert observers and supervisors, sent out by famine relief organizations or permanently stationed in famine-prone areas, can direct our aid to a refugee in Bengal almost as effectively as we could get it to someone on our own block. There would seem, therefore, to be no possible justification for discriminating on geographical grounds.

There may be a greater need to defend the second implication of my principle—that the fact that there are millions of other people in the same position, in respect to the Bengali refugees, as I am, does not make the situation significantly different from a situation in which I am the only person who can prevent something very bad from occurring. Again, of course, I admit that there is a psychological difference between the cases; one feels less guilty about doing nothing if one can point to others, similarly placed, who have also done nothing. Yet this can make no real difference to our moral obligations. Should I consider that I am less obliged to pull the drowning child out of the pond if on looking around I see other people, no further away than I am, who have also noticed the child but are doing nothing? One has only to ask this question to see the absurdity of the view that numbers lessen obligation. It is a view that is an ideal excuse for inactivity; unfortunately most of the major evils—poverty, overpopulation, pollution—are problems in which everyone is almost equally involved.

The view that numbers do make a difference can be made plausible if stated in this way: if everyone in circumstances like mine gave £5 to the Bengal Relief Fund, there would be enough to provide food, shelter, and medical care for the refugees; there is no reason why I should give more than anyone else in the same circumstances as I am; therefore I have no obligation to give more than £5. Each premise in this argument is true, and the argument looks sound. It may convince us, unless we notice that it is based on a hypothetical premise, although the conclusion is not stated hypothetically. The argument would be sound if the conclusion were: if everyone in circumstances like mine were to give £5, I would have no obligation to give more than £5. If the conclusion were so stated, however, it would be obvious that the argument has no bearing on a situation in which it is not the case that everyone else gives £5. This, of course, is the actual situation. It is more or less certain that not everyone in circumstances like mine will give £5. So there will not be enough to provide the needed food, shelter, and medical care. Therefore by giving more than £5 I will prevent more suffering than I would if I gave just £5.

It might be thought that this argument has an absurd consequence. Since the situation appears to be that very few people are likely to give substantial amounts, it follows that I and everyone else in similar circumstances ought to give as much as possible, that is, at least up to the point at which by giving more one would begin to cause serious suffering for oneself and one's dependents—perhaps even beyond this point to the point of marginal utility, at which by giving more one would cause oneself and one's dependents as much suffering as one would prevent in Bengal. If everyone does this, however, there will be more than can be used for the benefit of the refugees, and some of the sacrifice will have been unnecessary. Thus, if everyone does what he ought to do, the result will not be as good as it would be if everyone did a little less than he ought to do, or if only some do all that they ought to do.

The paradox here arises only if we assume that the actions in question—sending money to the relief funds—are performed more or less simultaneously, and are also unexpected. For if it is to be expected that everyone is going to contribute something, then clearly each is not obliged to give as much as he would have been obliged to had others not been giving too. And if everyone is not acting more or less simultaneously, then those giving later will know how much more is needed, and will have no obligation to give more than is necessary to reach this amount. To say this is not to deny the principle that people in the same circumstances have the same obligations, but to point out that the fact that others have given, or may be expected to give, is a relevant circumstance: those giving after it has become known that many others are giving and those giving before are not in the same circumstances. So the seemingly absurd consequence of the principle I have put forward can occur only if people are in error about the actual circumstances—that is, if they think they are giving when others are not, but in fact they are giving when others are. The result of everyone doing what he really ought to do cannot be worse than the result of everyone doing less than he ought to do, although the result of everyone doing what he reasonably believes he ought to do could be.

If my argument so far has been sound, neither our distance from a preventable evil nor the number of other people who, in respect to that evil, are in the same situation as we are, lessens our obligation to mitigate or prevent that evil. I shall therefore take as established the principle I asserted earlier. As I have already said, I need to assert it only in its qualified form: if it is in our power to prevent something very bad from happening, without thereby sacrificing anything else morally significant, we ought, morally, to do it.

The outcome of this argument is that our traditional moral categories are upset. The traditional distinction between duty and charity cannot be drawn, or at least, not in the place we normally draw it. Giving money to the Bengal Relief Fund is regarded as an act of charity in our society. The bodies which collect money are known as "charities." These organizations see themselves in this way—if you send them a check, you will be thanked for your "generosity." Because giving money is regarded as an act of charity, it is not thought that there is anything wrong with not giving. The charitable man may be praised, but the man who is not charitable is not condemned. People do not feel in any way ashamed or guilty about spending money on new clothes or a new car instead of giving it to famine relief. (Indeed, the alternative does not occur to them.) This way of looking at the matter cannot be justified. When we buy new clothes not to keep ourselves warm but to look "well-dressed" we are not providing for any important need. We would not be sacrificing anything significant if we were to continue to wear our old clothes, and give the money to famine relief. By doing so, we would be preventing another person from starving. It follows from what I have said earlier that we ought to give money away, rather than spend it on clothes which we do not need to keep us warm. To do so is not charitable, or generous. Nor is it the kind of act which philosophers and theologians have called "supererogatory"—an act which it would be good to do, but not wrong not to do. On the contrary, we ought to give the money away, and it is wrong not to do so.

I am not maintaining that there are no acts which are charitable, or that there are no acts which it would be good to do but not wrong not to do. It may be possible to redraw the distinction between duty and charity in some other place. All I am arguing here is that the present way of drawing the distinction, which makes it an act of charity for a man living at the level of affluence which most people in the "developed nations" enjoy to give money to save someone else from starvation, cannot be supported. It is beyond the scope of my argument to consider whether the distinction should be redrawn or abolished altogether. There would be many other possible ways of drawing the distinction—for instance, one might decide that it is good to make other people as happy as possible, but not wrong not to do so.

Despite the limited nature of the revision in our moral conceptual scheme which I am proposing, the revision would, given the extent of both affluence and famine in the world today, have radical implications. These implications may lead to further objections, distinct from those I have already considered. I shall discuss two of these.

One objection to the position I have taken might be simply that it is too drastic a revision of our moral scheme. People do not ordinarily judge in the way I have suggested they should. Most people reserve their moral condemnation for those who violate some moral norm, such as the norm against taking another person's property. They do not condemn those who indulge in luxury instead of giving to famine relief. But given that I did not set out to present a morally neutral description of the way people make moral judgments, the way people do in fact judge has nothing to do with the validity of my conclusion. My conclusion follows from the principle which I advanced earlier, and unless that principle is rejected, or the arguments shown to be unsound, I think the conclusion must stand, however strange it appears.

It might, nevertheless, be interesting to consider why our society, and most other societies, do judge differently from the way I have suggested they should. In a well-known article, J. O. Urmson suggests that the imperatives of duty, which tell us what we must do, as distinct from what it would be good to do but not wrong not to do, function so as to prohibit behavior that is intolerable if men are to live together in society. This may explain the origin and continued existence of the present division between acts of duty and acts of charity. Moral attitudes are shaped by the needs of society, and no doubt society needs people who will observe the rules that make social existence tolerable. From the point of view of a particular society, it is essential to prevent violations of norms against killing, stealing, and so on. It is quite inessential, however, to help people outside one's own society.

If this is an explanation of our common distinction between duty and supererogation, however, it is not a justification of it. The moral point of view requires us to look beyond the interests of our own society. Previously, as I have already mentioned, this may hardly have been feasible, but it is quite feasible now. From the moral point of view, the prevention of the starvation of millions of people outside our society must be considered at least as pressing as the upholding of property norms within our society.

It has been argued by some writers, among them Sidgwick and Urmson, that we need to have a basic moral code which is not too far beyond the capacities of the ordinary man, for otherwise there will be a general breakdown of compliance with the moral code. Crudely stated, this argument suggests that if we tell people that they ought to refrain from murder and give everything they do not really need to famine relief, they will do neither, whereas if we tell them that they ought to refrain from murder and that it is good to give to famine relief but not wrong not to do so, they will at least refrain from murder. The issue here is: Where should we draw the line between conduct that is required and conduct that is good although not required, so as to get the best possible result? This would seem to be an empirical question, although a very difficult one. One objection to the Sidgwick-Urmson line of argument is that it takes insufficient account of the effect that moral standards can have on the decisions we make. Given a society in which a wealthy man who gives five percent of his income to famine relief is regarded as most generous, it is not surprising that a proposal that we all ought to give away half our incomes will be thought to be absurdly unrealistic. In a society which held that no man should have more than enough while others have less than they need, such a proposal might seem narrow-minded. What it is possible for a man to do and what he is likely to do are both, I think, very greatly influenced by what people around him are doing and expecting him to do. In any case, the possibility that by spreading the idea that we ought to be doing very much more than we are to relieve famine we shall bring about a general breakdown of moral behavior seems remote. If the stakes are an end to widespread starvation, it is worth the risk. Finally, it should be emphasized that these considerations are relevant only to the issue of what we should require from others, and not to what we ourselves ought to do.

The second objection to my attack on the present distinction between duty and charity is one which has from time to time been made against utilitarianism. It follows from some forms of utilitarian theory that we all ought, morally, to be working full time to increase the balance of happiness over misery. The position I have taken here would not lead to this conclusion in all circumstances, for if there were no bad occurrences that we could prevent without sacrificing something of comparable moral importance, my argument would have no application. Given the present conditions in many parts of the world, however, it does follow from my argument that we ought, morally, to be working full time to relieve great suffering of the sort that occurs as a result of famine or other disasters. Of course, mitigating circumstances can be adduced—for instance, that if we wear ourselves out through overwork, we shall be less effective than we would otherwise have been. Nevertheless, when all considerations of this sort have been taken into account, the conclusion remains: we ought to be preventing as much suffering as we can without sacrificing something else of comparable moral importance. This conclusion is one which we may be reluctant to face. I cannot see, though, why it should be regarded as a criticism of the position for which I have argued, rather than a criticism of our ordinary standards of behavior. Since most people are self-interested to some degree, very few of us are likely to do everything that we ought to do. It would, however, hardly be honest to take this as evidence that it is not the case that we ought to do it.

It may still be thought that my conclusions are so wildly out of line with what everyone else thinks and has always thought that there must be something wrong with the argument somewhere. In order to show that my conclusions, while certainly contrary to

contemporary Western moral standards, would not have seemed so extraordinary at other times and in other places, I would like to quote a passage from a writer not normally thought of as a way-out radical, Thomas Aquinas. Now, according to the natural order instituted by divine providence, material goods are provided for the satisfaction of human needs. Therefore the division and appropriation of property, which proceeds from human law, must not hinder the satisfaction of man's necessity from such goods. Equally, whatever a man has in superabundance is owed, of natural right, to the poor for their sustenance. So Ambrosius says, and it is also to be found in the *Decretum Gratiani:* "The bread which you withhold belongs to the hungry; the clothing you shut away, to the naked; and the money you bury in the earth is the redemption and freedom of the penniless."

It is sometimes said, though less often now than it used to be, that philosophers have no special role to play in public affairs, since most public issues depend primarily on an assessment of facts. On questions of fact, it is said, philosophers as such have no special expertise, and so it has been possible to engage in philosophy without committing oneself to any position on major public issues. No doubt there are some issues of social policy and foreign policy about which it can truly be said that a really expert assessment of the facts is required before taking sides or acting, but the issue of famine is surely not one of these. The facts about the existence of suffering are beyond dispute. Nor, I think, is it disputed that we can do something about it, either through orthodox methods of famine relief or through population control or both. This is therefore an issue on which philosophers are competent to take a position. The issue is one which faces everyone who has more money than he needs to support himself and his dependents, or who is in a position to take some sort of political action. These categories must include practically every teacher and student of philosophy in the universities of the Western world. If philosophy is to deal with matters that are relevant to both teachers and students, this is an issue that philosophers should discuss.

Discussion, though, is not enough. What is the point of relating philosophy to public (and personal) affairs if we do not take our conclusions seriously? In this instance, taking our conclusion seriously means acting upon it. The philosopher will not find it any easier than anyone else to alter his attitudes and way of life to the extent that, if I am right, is involved in doing everything that we ought to be doing. At the very least, though, one can make a start. The philosopher who does so will have to sacrifice some of the benefits of the consumer society, but he can find compensation in the satisfaction of a way of life in which theory and practice, if not yet in harmony, are at least coming together.

Discussion Questions

1. What reasons do persons give for not supporting famine relief? How would Singer respond to these objections? Which view do you believe is true and why?

2. Mill argued that the greatest happiness was promoted when persons took care of themselves and those immediately around them. Singer argues that we should ignore the distance between persons and should not necessarily prefer ourselves or our immediate families to other persons, no matter how distant those persons. What reasons are there in support of both Mill's and Singer's positions? Are their views compatible? If so, how can they be joined into a single account? If not, which view is best?

3. Singer noted that Aquinas, a representative of the Catholic tradition, would be supportive of his views. Do other world religions also support Singer's argument that we ought to support famine relief? What about other ethnic and cultural traditions? Do they also support a position similar to Singer's? What do your answers imply about the adequacy of Singer's argument?

For Further Reading

Besides this article, Singer is most widely known for his work on animal welfare; see *Animal Liberation* (1975).

The classic argument against famine relief is by Garrett Hardin in *The Limits of Altruism* (1977). For a discussion of the issues Hardin raises see George R. Lucas and Thomas Ogletree, eds., *Lifeboat Ethics* (1976). For views of other philosophers on practical questions of famine relief and hunger, see Onora O'Neill, *Faces of Hunger: An Essay on Poverty, Justice, and Development* (1985); Jean Drèhze and Amartya Sen, eds., *The Political Economy of Hunger* (1990); and Drèhze and Sen, *Hunger and Political Action* (1989).

47   A WAY WITHOUT A CROSSROADS
Herbert Fingarette

A number of authors in this text argue that unless we occupy standpoints outside of our own cultural traditions, we will never be able to identify the hidden assumptions that underlie our conceptual schemes. In this selection, Herbert Fingarette considers the Confucian moral tradition, reflecting on it not only because of the inherent value of that tradition, but also for what it helps to reveal about our own conception of morality.

Source: Pp. 18–22, 24–27, 34–36 from *Confucius: The Secular as Sacred* by Herbert Fingarette. Copyright © 1972 by Herbert Fingarette. Reprinted by permission of HarperCollins Publishers, Inc.

Study of the Confucian tradition makes apparent some otherwise invisible deeply rooted assumptions in the Judeo-Christian foundations of Western morality: the way in which notions of choice and responsibility are assumed and taken for granted. Left unchallenged, it appears as if there are no alternative ways to conceptualize morality without incorporating notions of choice and responsibility. But as the Confucian tradition makes apparent, these common notions are by no means necessary for a rich moral tradition.

Herbert Fingarette (1921–) is Professor Emeritus of Philosophy at the University of California, Santa Barbara. He has made extensive and innovative contributions to the philosophical study of Eastern philosophical traditions, as well as to law, criminal insanity, and, more recently, to the critical appraisal of the disease model of alcoholism.

Reading Questions

1. What typical Western notions are absent from the Confucian understanding of humanity?
2. What is the *Tao?* What is *li?* How are these two Confucian ideas related?
3. What does it mean that the spiritually noble person arrives at a condition, as opposed to a place?
4. Why does Fingarette conclude that the Confucian ideal of following the Way does not allow for choice?
5. What is the Confucian definition of responsibility? How is the Confucian notion of responsibility future oriented, as opposed to the Western conception of responsibility being oriented toward the past?
6. Describe the Confucian ideal of moral education. How does this differ from Western conceptions of moral education?
7. How should a person respond who fails to conform to the moral order?

Confucius in his teachings in the *Analects* does not elaborate on the language of choice or responsibility. He occasionally uses terms roughly akin to these. But they are not developed or elaborated in the ways so characteristic of their central import in Western philosophical and religious understanding of man. To be specific, Confucius does not elaborate the language of choice and responsibility as these are intimately intertwined with the idea of the ontologically ultimate power of the individual to select from genuine alternatives to create his own spiritual destiny, and with the related ideas of spiritual guilt, and repentance or retribution for such guilt.

Precisely because we of the West are so deeply immersed in a world conceived in just such terms, it is profitable for us to see the world in quite another way, in Confucius' way. He was, after all, profoundly concerned to understand man and man's place in society.

He was dedicated to defining and illuminating what we would call moral issues. He was a great and an original teacher. How, then, could Confucius omit this whole complex of notions centering around "choice" and "responsibility"?

We must recognize at once that the absence of a developed language of choice and responsibility does not imply a failure to choose or to be responsible. Some men were more responsible than others in Confucius' day as in ours. It is also obvious that men made choices in ancient China. I am not so sure we can speak as confidently about guilt, repentance or retributive punishment in the sense we use these words, but also the realities which we use these words to designate did not exist. The notion of punishment, which did exist in ancient China, was that of deterrent punishment—not due retribution to cleanse guilt, but a stern "lesson" or literal crippling which would deter future malfeasance.

However, without arguing this latter point here, we can allow that in the case of "choice" and "responsibility," the realities they designate did indeed exist. Yet, although we in the West have an elaborated language in which to express these realities and to trace out their inner shape and dynamics in detail, Confucius (and his contemporaries) did not possess such a language. And they had no significant concern with these moral realities so central to their contemporaries, the peoples of Greece and the Near East.

Perhaps the most revealing way to begin to bring out this "omission" is to consider the primary imagery in the *Analects*. It centers around the "*Tao.*" *Tao* is a Way, a path, a road, and by common metaphorical extensions it becomes in ancient China the right Way of life, the Way of governing, the ideal Way of human existence, the Way of the Cosmos, the generative-normative Way (Pattern, path, course) of existence as such. (In the *Analects*, "*Tao*" never takes its rare but possible alternative sense as "word" or "speak.")

The imagery in the *Analects* is dominated by the metaphor of traveling the road. Written characters that occur typically and frequently in the text are those meaning path, way, walk, tracks, follow, go through, from, to, enter, leave, arrive, advance, upright, crooked, level, smooth, stop, position.

The notion of a Way is, not surprisingly, congenial to the central Confucian notion of *li*, rite or ceremony. *Li*, for Confucius, is the explicit and detailed pattern of that great ceremony which is social intercourse, the humane life. The transition from the image of walking the true Path uprightly to carrying out a ceremony properly is an easy and congenial one. We may even think of *li* as the map or the specific road-system which is *Tao*.

It is easy, if one is so inclined, to develop this path-imagery to bring in the notions of choice, decision, responsibility. We should need only to introduce the derivative image of the crossroads, an obvious elaboration of *Tao* imagery to us. Yet this image, so perfectly suited, so plainly available for use as a metaphor for choice, is *never* used in the *Analects*.

Indeed the image of the crossroads is so natural and even insistently available as an element of any richly elaborated path-imagery that only the most profound commitment to the idea of the cosmos as basically unambiguous, as a single, definite order, could make it possible to ignore in the metaphor the image of the crossroads as a challenge to the traveler on the Way. This Confucian commitment to a single, definite order is also evident when we note what Confucius sees as the alternative to rightly treading the true Path: it is to walk crookedly, to get lost or to abandon the Path. That is, the only "alternative" to the one Order is disorder, chaos.

Where does one finally arrive if one follows the Way? Is there a goal that puts an end to the travel? The imagery of Confucius does not lead us to dwell upon the person arriving at a destined or ideal place, whether it be depicted as harbor, home or golden city. Instead, the spiritually noble man arrives at a condition rather than a place, the condition of following the Way without effort and properly. He arrives at that tranquil state that comes from appreciating that it is the following of the Way itself that is of ultimate and absolute value. Thus in this respect it does not take time to "reach" the goal since one does not have to arrive at any particular point on the map: to reach the goal is simply to set oneself to treading the Path now—properly, with correct appreciation of its intrinsic and ultimate significance.

One can be truly following the Way at whatever the level of one's personal development and skill in the Way, whatever the level of one's learning—for a wholehearted commitment to learning the Way is itself the Way for those who are not yet perfected in the Way. However, although the learner may be following the Way for the learner, he cannot rest; his burden is heavy for he is the apprentice, not yet the Master, the *jen* man, the man perfected in *li*, the truly noble man.

The basic conception of man in the *Analects* is that he is a being born into the world—more especially into society—with the potentiality to be shaped into a truly human form. There is, to begin with, the raw stuff, the raw material. This must be elaborated by learning and culture, shaped and controlled by *li*. Either this "cutting, filing, chiseling and polishing" is done well or poorly. If it is well done, through painstaking and properly directed effort by the person and good training by his teachers, then to that extent he will walk straight upon the Way. If there is a failure to shape according to the ideal, then by virtue of this defect he will deviate from the Way.

Thus there is no *genuine* option: either one follows the Way or one fails. To take any other "route" than the Way is not a genuine road but a failure through weakness to follow *the* route. Neither the doctrine nor the imagery allows for choice, if we mean by choice a selection, by virtue of the agent's powers, of one out of several equally real options. Instead it puts the task in terms of either using one's powers to walk the Way or being too weak, *without* power, and of going crookedly nowhere, falling or weaving about pointlessly in quest of the mirages of profit, advantage and personal comfort.

It is true that the Master said: "If a man doesn't constantly ask himself, 'What about this, what about this?' I can do nothing about him." Our own tendency, reading this isolated remark, may be to read this as a concern with choice. But it need not be so at all. It need not be read as "What about this—which of the alternatives, to do it or not to do it, shall I choose?" Instead, one may suppose that the notion of equally valid alternatives is not implied, that there is presumed to be only one right thing to do and that the question then means in effect, "What about this, *is* it right; is it the Way?" Put in more general terms, the task is not conceived as a choice but as the attempt to characterize some object or action as objectively right or not. The moral task is to make a proper classification, to locate an act within the scheme of *li*.

...

The notion of choice as a central feature of man's existence is only one element in a closely related complex of notions, and the absence of such a concept of choice reflects the absence of the rest of this complex. Among the chief notions closely linked to choice are moral responsibility, guilt, deserved (retributive) punishment and repentance.

Sometimes when we speak of a person as responsible for something, we refer merely to his role as a critical causal factor in bringing it about. The problem of meaning here is complex, but the general drift in this usage is to treat responsibility as a matter of production or causality rather than moral obligation.

This causal notion of responsibility is quite familiar to the ancient Chinese. There is no lack of explicit discussion of the question who or what brought about a certain state of affairs. But of course it is not discussed under a heading translatable as "responsibility." For the root sense of the latter term is the moral one, and its use with respect to mere causality is a de-moralized derivative use. The root of "responsible" is of course

not "cause" or "produce" but "respond"; the root question is: Who must respond for the way things go? One who is obligated to respond for the way things go will have some actual or potential causal connection with the way things go, but not everyone who has a causal connection with the way things go is obligated to respond for how they do.

The intense concern of Confucius that a person should carry out his duties and act according to what is right reflects one aspect of our notion of responsibility. But if this were all that was characteristic of our notion of responsibility, it would be redundancy— another way of saying that one should carry out one's duties and act rightly. What gives distinct content to the idea of responsibility is derived from the root "response." Herein lies the peculiarly personal commitment—*I* answer for this deed; it is mine—and this in turn links the notion of (moral) responsibility to those of guilt, deserved punishment and repentance. It is the one who must respond whose response may involve guilt, acceptance of punishment, repentance, restitution or merit, pride, reward.

The issues in the West can become confused because of a certain sort of utilitarian view to the effect that responsibility is ultimately a purely causal notion. On this view, "responsibility" ought to be considered merely as a matter of diagnosing past causes in order to influence future events; sanctions and reward are assignable anywhere in the human causal chain that promises future prevention. If present sanctions will deter future malfeasance, then they are justified; if sanctions will not deter, or if in a particular case they would increase tendencies to malfeasance, then countersanctions are indicated. The ground for and value of repentance lie entirely in the future deterrent consequences of repentance, not in any relation to the moral aspect of the past deed. Such value as guilt-feelings have must on this view be justified by an analogous rationale. Subtler and more complex forms of utilitarian views have been emphasized in recent philosophical discussion, but these do not eliminate the possibility of the type of confusion so evidently generated by the simpler view. The fact that Confucius uses language that pertains to sanctions for law-breaking has led translators to render this as "punishment" and naturally misleads the unalerted reader to suppose that Confucius understood and used our concept of punishment (with its root implication of moral guilt).

The view that never appears in Confucius, the view that is peculiar to the Graeco-Hebraic-Christian tradition and for the most part profoundly contrasting with utilitarianism, is that punishment is justified not simply by its consequences but because it is *deserved* by virtue of what went before. Punishment is an appropriate moral response to prior guilty wrongdoing by a morally responsible agent. Repentance, in turn, is not simply a device which is appropriate or not depending on *its* psychological consequences; it is repentance *for* the past deed. Repentance is a moral response to a past wrongdoing for which one is morally responsible. Guilt is a moral (or spiritual) property accruing by virtue of accomplished wrong.

If punishment is given and received as a genuine moral experience, it is a kind of payment of a moral debt—a clearing of the slate. Of course a person may as a consequence also be inclined to be more averse to similar future wrongdoing, to the guilt-feeling it involves as well as to the quite nonmoral discomfort and pain of the punishment. And if repentance is genuine, it constitutes an expression of repugnance with oneself for one's former course of conduct, an acknowledgment of moral guilt, and therefore it is expressed in a recommitment to a different course in the future. Thus normally the *consequences* of guilt, punishment and repentance upon moral character and upon morality-related behavior are likely to be salutary. There is a utilitarian value here. But the moral *ground* for each, that which gives it its moral status, is the past wrongdoing for which one was (morally) responsible. Were "punishment," "guilt" and "repentance" to be unrelated to prior moral wrong for which the person was responsible, we would have social engineering rather than morality—and this was precisely why Confucius took the use of "punishments" as a main target and saw his own positive teaching as in direct contrast.

For Confucius moral education consists in learning the codes of *li*, in studying literature, music and the civilizing arts in general. One's own effort provides the "push," but it is the intrinsic nobility of the goal that provides the "pull." It is by *being* a spiritually noble man that the teacher—or Prince—draws others into the direction of the Way. It is the Way that has power, and this power is effortless, invisible, magical. It is characteristic of the *Analects* that

in every case, except for one clearly late "Legalist" insertion, the use of sanctions and punishment is explicitly contrasted as the undesirable alternative to the use of virtue *(te)*, of humaneness *(jen)*, of ceremonial propriety *(li)* and of such related strategies as "yielding" *(jang)*. The *Analects* present the issue flatly: either one can govern by *li* and "yielding" or one can't; if one can't, then there is no use deceiving ourselves, and we might as well turn to "punishment," to sanctions and rewards. For these can influence people in a coercive way or by payment; but they are not truly human (i.e., moral) ways, nor do they establish a truly human life. Lacking any concept of moral guilt, or of moral responsibility as the ground for guilt and hence punishment as *moral* retribution, Confucius could see no humane potentiality in the use of sanctions.

In the preceding . . . , I have considered the possibility that Confucius does concern himself in substance with choice, responsibility, punishment as moral desert, guilt and repentance. The conclusions reached may be summarized as follows. Although the opportunity for explicitly and richly elaborating the notion of choice is latent in the central imagery of the Path, that opportunity is with remarkable thoroughness ignored. And, although there are isolated references to a moral illness, self-accusations, and inner examination—each potentially so fertile and apt for use by one concerned with responsibility, guilt and repentance—none of these is developed or in any way further remarked upon by Confucius. They remain isolated, *ad hoc* metaphors, very possibly with an ironic or topical meaning in their original context, a meaning now lost in the cryptic saying handed down to us. Finally, although there is more frequent and systematic reference to shame, this is associated with specific external possessions, conduct or status; it is a moral sentiment focused upon one's status and conduct in relation to the world rather than an inward charge against one's stained, corrupt self. The absence of the choice-responsibility-guilt complex of concepts, taken in the textual context, warrants the inference in connection with such an insightful philosopher of human nature and morality, that the concepts in question and their related imagery, were not rejected by Confucius but rather were simply not present in his thinking at all.

The language and imagery that *is* elaborated and that forms the main frame of Confucius' thought presents a different but intelligible and harmonious picture to us. Man is not an ultimately autonomous being who has an inner and decisive power, intrinsic to him, a power to select among real alternatives and thereby to shape a life for himself. Instead he is born as "raw material" who must be civilized by education and thus become a truly human man. To do this he must aim at the Way, and the Way must—through its nobility and the nobility of those who pursue it—attract him. This outcome is not conceived as one that enhances a personal power as over against society or the physical environment, but rather as one that sharpens and steadies a person's "aim" or orientation to the point where he can undeviatingly walk the one true Way: he is a civilized human being. Walking the Way incarnates in him the vast spiritual dignity and power that reside in the Way. One who walks the Way rather than going astray, who does so "naturally," "yielding" rather than forcing, such a man lives a life of personal dignity and fulfillment, of social harmony with others based on mutual respect allowing to each just such a life.

Therefore the central moral issue for Confucius is not the responsibility of a man for deeds he has by his own free will chosen to perform, but the factual questions of whether a man is properly taught the Way and whether he has the desire to learn diligently. The proper response to a failure to conform to the moral order *(li)* is not self-condemnation for a free and responsible, though evil, choice, but self-reeducation to overcome a mere defect, a lack of power, in short a lack in one's "formation." The Westerner's inclination to press at this point the issue of personal responsibility for lack of diligence is precisely the sort of issue that is never even raised in the *Analects*.

To summarize finally in a schematic way, moral problems resolve into one of four forms for Confucius: (1) the wrongdoer is not well enough educated to be able to recognize and properly classify what is according to the Way and what is not; (2) the wrongdoer has not yet learned the requisite skills to follow the Way in some respect; (3) the wrongdoer has not *persisted* in the required effort (this is conceived as a matter of strength, not choice); (4) the wrongdoer knows enough to go through some of the motions, but he is not totally committed to the Way, and he is then either erratic or he systematically perverts the outer forms of *li* to serve personal profit.

Confucius' vision provides no basis for seeing man as a being of tragedy, of inner crisis and guilt; but it does provide a socially oriented, action-oriented view which provides for personal dignity. Moreover, when we place the comments made here in the larger context of Confucius' view of man, a context further discussed in the other essays in this book, we see then that the images of the inner man and of his inner conflict are not essential to a concept of man as a being whose dignity is the consummation of a life of subtlety and sophistication, a life in which human conduct can be intelligible in natural terms and yet be attuned to the sacred, a life in which the practical, the intellectual and the spiritual are equally revered and are harmonized in the one act—the act of *li*.

Discussion Questions

1. Is Fingarette's account compatible with Aristotle's virtue account? Why or why not? How about with Mill and with Kant? Why or why not?

2. How would punishment in Western society be different if we followed the model Fingarette proposes here? How might prisons, courts, punishments, and trials be different? Would these changes be good? Why or why not?

3. Does Fingarette's discussion of Taoist approaches to morality show that moral behavior is relative to cultures? Or does it show that our own moral standards are limited and narrow? What reasons would there be to change our own conception of morality to match a Taoist model?

For Further Reading

This selection is from *Confucius—The Secular as Sacred* (1969). Other books of particular interest by Fingarette include *The Self in Transformation* (1963), *Heavy Drinking: The Myth of Alcoholism as a Disease* (1988), and *Death: Philosophical Soundings* (1996). For a discussion of Fingarette's philosophy and a complete bibliography of his books and articles see *Rules, Rituals, and Responsibility,* edited by Mary I. Bockover (1991).

A helpful introduction to Confucianism can be found in David E. Cooper's *World Philosophies* (1996). For discussions of Confucianism and ethics see Tu Wei-Ming, *Way, Learning, and Politics* (1993); Wm. Theodore de Bary and Tu Weiming, eds., *Confucianism and Human Rights* (1998); Heiner Roetz, *Confucian Ethics of the Axial Age* (1993); and A. S. Cua, *Ethical Argumentation* (1985). Confucian ethics also play a role in the moral philosophy of Robert C. Neville, who often combines it with aspects of Christian ethics and theology; see especially his *The Puritan Smile* (1987) and *Behind the Masks of God* (1991).

48   IMAGES OF RELATIONSHIP
Carol Gilligan

Examining Western moral traditions from a standpoint outside of these traditions may reveal various ways in which these traditions unknowingly incorporate hidden and narrow biases, that is, the way in which undefended and unanalyzed hidden assumptions unwarrantedly determine a particular picture of moral behavior. But such distortions are not evident only from a cross-cultural perspective. Inasmuch as most philosophical ethicists have been males, it would not be surprising if this fact has shaped and contributed to their moral reflection. Even if they had the best of intentions, the social differences between men and women suggest that standard moral theories ought to be critically examined for evidence of a male bias.

Carol Gilligan (1936–), a moral psychologist at New York University, in the process of studying adolescent moral development, developed a detailed and far-reaching analysis of standard moral theories. Her book *In a Different Voice,* published in 1984, had an immediate impact on both the field of moral development and philosophical moral theory. In that book, she proposed that men and women tend to conceptualize moral problems differently: Men tend to use a 'justice' voice while women tend to use a 'care' voice. Each voice differs partly due to a different conception of the self. These differences are rooted in distinct patterns of psychological development. (Gilligan's view is similar to that of Nancy Chodorow in Chapter 4, Reading 17 of this book.) Insofar as males, due to the processes that determine their psychological development, consider themselves as separate atomistic individuals, they tend to characterize morality in terms of roles and responsibilities. Consider this analogy. If persons were like automobiles—that is, if persons were essentially separate, self-directed,

SOURCE: Reprinted by permission of the publisher from *In a Different Voice: Psychological Theory and Women's Development* by Carol Gilligan, pp. 24–32, 51–55, 57–59, 62, 63, Cambridge, Mass.: Harvard University Press, Copyright © 1982, 1983 by Carol Gilligan.

and independently directed in the same way that cars are—what system of morality would best suit them? One that prevents them from running into each other, that is, a system of laws, rules, and rights. But females, Gilligan discovers, typically have a different conception of the self, viewing themselves as part of a web of connections. In this case, morality takes the form of preserving relationships and of responding responsibly to the needs of others—that is, caring for others.

In this selection, Gilligan describes how boys and girls have different responses to distinct moral dilemmas. She uses a standard investigative technique developed by Piagetian moral psychologist Lawrence Kohlberg to evaluate a child's or adult's level of moral development. Subjects are asked to respond to a hypothetical dilemma, called the Heinz dilemma. Based on their answers, they are scored on a scale from zero to six. Gilligan's research led her to believe that not only do women have basically different responses to this dilemma than men, but, more important, the scale used to evaluate moral development was itself conceptually biased, constructed upon a deeply male conception of morality and self-identity. While Gilligan's critique is primarily and initially aimed at Kohlberg's theory, philosophers were quick to realize that her critique could be extended to most Western moral theories, especially those theories that assumed a narrowly defined conception of the self—a conception that generalized only from the collective experience of males.

Reading Questions

1. How does Freud respond to the difficulties of fitting women's experience into his theory? Why does this difficulty arise?
2. How does Jake respond to the Heinz dilemma?
3. How is Jake's response scored on Kohlberg's scale? What type of moral thinking does Jake exhibit?
4. How does Amy respond to the Heinz dilemma?
5. How is Amy's response scored on Kohlberg's scale? Does this fit her own impression of herself?
6. How does Amy's response challenge the way Kohlberg's interviews are conducted?
7. Characterize the differences between Amy's and Jake's separate approaches to conflict and choice.
8. How does Claire's response to the Heinz dilemma change over time? Does this correspond to changes in her moral life?
9. Describe Claire's "guiding principle of connection."
10. How is abortion a problem of relationships for Claire?

In 1914, with his essay "On Narcissism," Freud swallows his distaste at the thought of "abandoning observation for barren theoretical controversy" and extends his map of the psychological domain. Tracing the development of the capacity to love, which he equates with maturity and psychic health, he locates its origins in the contrast between love for the mother and love for the self. But in thus dividing the world of love into narcissism and "object" relationships, he finds that while men's development becomes clearer, women's becomes increasingly opaque. The problem arises because the contrast between mother and self yields two different images of relationships. Relying on the imagery of men's lives in charting the course of human growth, Freud is unable to trace in women the development of relationships, morality, or a clear sense of self. This difficulty in fitting the logic of his theory to women's experience leads him in the end to set women apart, marking their relationships, like their sexual life, as "a 'dark continent' for psychology."

Thus the problem of interpretation that shadows the understanding of women's development arises from the differences observed in their experience of relationships. To Freud, though living surrounded by women and otherwise seeing so much and so well, women's relationships seemed increasingly mysterious, difficult to discern, and hard to describe. While this mystery indicates how theory can blind observation, it also suggests that development in women is masked by a particular conception of human relationships. Since the imagery of relationships shapes the narrative of human development, the inclusion of women, by changing that imagery, implies a change in the entire account.

The shift in imagery that creates the problem in interpreting women's development is elucidated by the moral judgments of two eleven-year-old children, a boy and a girl, who see, in the same dilemma, two very different moral problems. While current theory brightly illuminates the line and logic of the boy's thought, it casts scant light on that of the girl. The choice of a girl whose moral judgments elude existing categories of developmental assessment is meant to highlight the issue of interpretation rather than to exemplify sex differences per se. Adding a new line of interpretation, based on the imagery of the girl's thought, makes it possible not only to see development where previously development was not discerned but also to consider differences in the understanding of relationships without scaling these differences from better to worse.

The two children were in the same sixth-grade class at school and were participants in the rights and responsibilities study, designed to explore different conceptions of morality and self. The sample selected for this study was chosen to focus the variables of gender and age while maximizing developmental potential by holding constant, at a high level, the factors of intelligence, education, and social class that have been associated with moral development, at least as measured by existing scales. The two children in question, Amy and Jake, were both bright and artic-

ulate and, at least in their eleven-year-old aspirations, resisted easy categories of sex-role stereotyping, since Amy aspired to become a scientist while Jake preferred English to math. Yet their moral judgments seem initially to confirm familiar notions about differences between the sexes, suggesting that the edge girls have on moral development during the early school years gives way at puberty with the ascendance of formal logical thought in boys.

The dilemma that these eleven-year-olds were asked to resolve was one in the series devised by Kohlberg to measure moral development in adolescence by presenting a conflict between moral norms and exploring the logic of its resolution. In this particular dilemma, a man named Heinz considers whether or not to steal a drug which he cannot afford to buy in order to save the life of his wife. In the standard format of Kohlberg's interviewing procedure, the description of the dilemma itself—Heinz's predicament, the wife's disease, the druggist's refusal to lower his price—is followed by the question, "Should Heinz steal the drug?" The reasons for and against stealing are then explored through a series of questions that vary and extend the parameters of the dilemma in a way designed to reveal the underlying structure of moral thought.

Jake, at eleven, is clear from the outset that Heinz should steal the drug. Constructing the dilemma, as Kohlberg did, as a conflict between the values of property and life, he discerns the logical priority of life and uses that logic to justify his choice:

> For one thing, a human life is worth more than money, and if the druggist only makes $1,000, he is still going to live, but if Heinz doesn't steal the drug, his wife is going to die. (*Why is life worth more than money?*) Because the druggist can get a thousand dollars later from rich people with cancer, but Heinz can't get his wife again. (*Why not?*) Because people are all different and so you couldn't get Heinz's wife again.

Asked whether Heinz should steal the drug if he does not love his wife, Jake replies that he should, saying not only is there "a difference between hating and killing" but also, if Heinz were caught, "the judge would probably think it was the right thing to do." Asked about the fact that, in stealing, Heinz would be breaking the law, he says that "the laws have mistakes, and you can't go writing up a law for everything that you can imagine."

Thus, while taking law into account and recognizing his function in maintaining social order (the judge, Jake says, "should give Heinz the lightest possible sentence"), he also sees the law as man-made and therefore subject to error and change. Yet his judgment that Heinz should steal the drug, like his view of the law as having mistakes, rests on the assumption of agreement, a societal consensus around moral values that allows one to know and expect others to recognize what is "the right thing to do."

Fascinated by the power of logic, this eleven-year-old boy locates truth in math, which, he says, is "the only thing that is totally logical." Considering the moral dilemma to be "sort of like a math problem with humans," he sets it up as an equation and proceeds to work out the solution. Since his solution is rationally derived, he assumes that anyone following reason would arrive at the same conclusion and thus that a judge would also consider stealing to be the right thing for Heinz to do. Yet he is also aware of the limits of logic. Asked whether there is a right answer to moral problems, Jake replies that "there can only be right and wrong in judgment," since the parameters of action are variable and complex. Illustrating how actions undertaken with the best of intentions can eventuate in the most disastrous of consequences, he says, "like if you give an old lady your seat on the trolley, if you are in a trolley crash and the seat goes through the window, it might be that reason that the old lady dies."

Theories of developmental psychology illuminate well the position of this child, standing at the juncture of childhood and adolescence, at what Piaget describes as the pinnacle of childhood intelligence, and beginning through thought to discover a wider universe of possibility. The moment of preadolescence is caught by the conjunction of formal operational thought with a description of self still anchored in the factual parameters of his childhood world—his age, his town, his father's occupation, the substance of his likes, dislikes, and beliefs. Yet as his self-description radiates the self-confidence of a child who has arrived, in Erickson's terms, at a favorable balance of industry over inferiority—competent, sure of himself, and knowing full well the rules of the game—so his emergent capacity for formal thought, his ability to think about thinking and to reason things out in a logical way, frees him from dependence on authority and allows him to find solutions to problems by himself.

This emergent autonomy follows the trajectory that Kohlberg's six stages of moral development trace, a three-level progression from an egocentric understanding of fairness based on individual need (stages one and two), to a conception of fairness anchored in the shared conventions of societal agreement (stages three and four), and finally to a principled understanding of fairness that rests on the free-standing logic of equality and reciprocity (stages five and six). While this boy's judgments at eleven are scored as conventional on Kohlberg's scale, a mixture of stages three and four, his ability to bring deductive logic to bear on the solution of moral dilemmas, to differentiate morality from law, and to see how laws can be considered to have mistakes points toward the principled conception of justice that Kohlberg equates with moral maturity.

In contrast, Amy's response to the dilemma conveys a very different impression, an image of development stunted by a failure in logic, an inability to think for herself. Asked if Heinz should steal the drug, she replies in a way that seems evasive and unsure:

Well, I don't think so. I think there might be other ways besides stealing it, like if he could borrow the money or make a loan or something, but he really shouldn't steal the drug—but his wife shouldn't die either.

Asked why he should not steal the drug, she considers neither property nor law but rather the effect that theft could have on the relationship between Heinz and his wife:

If he stole the drug, he might save his wife then, but if he did, he might have to go to jail, and then his wife might get sicker again, and he couldn't get more of the drug, and it might not be good. So, they should really just talk it out and find some other way to make the money.

Seeing in the dilemma not a math problem with humans but a narrative of relationships that extend over time, Amy envisions the wife's continuing need for her husband and the husband's continuing concern for his wife and seeks to respond to the druggist's need in a way that would sustain rather than sever connection. Just as she ties the wife's survival to the preservation of relationships, so she considers the value of the wife's life in a context of relationships, saying that it would be wrong to let her die because, "if she died, it hurts a lot of people and it hurts her." Since Amy's moral judgment is grounded in the belief that, "if somebody has something that would keep somebody alive, then it's not right not to give it to them," she considers the problem in the dilemma to arise not from the druggist's assertion of rights but from his failure of response.

As the interviewer proceeds with the series of questions that follow from Kohlberg's construction of the dilemma, Amy's answers remain essentially unchanged, the various probes serving neither to elucidate nor to modify her original response. Whether or not Heinz loves his wife, he still shouldn't steal or let her die; if it were a stranger dying instead, Amy says that "if the stranger didn't have anybody near or anyone she knew," then Heinz should try to save her life, but he should not steal the drug. But as the interviewer conveys through the repetition of questions that the answers she gave were not heard or not right, Amy's confidence begins to diminish, and her replies became more constrained and unsure. Asked again why Heinz should not steal the drug, she simply repeats, "Because it's not right." Asked again to explain why, she states again that theft would not be a good solution, adding lamely, "if he took it, he might not know how to give it to his wife, and so his wife still might die." Failing to see the dilemma as a self-contained problem in moral logic, she does not discern the internal structure of its resolution; as she constructs the problem differently herself, Kohlberg's conception completely evades her.

Instead, seeing a world comprised of relationships rather than of people standing alone, a world that coheres through human connection rather than through systems of rules, she finds the puzzle in the dilemma to lie in the failure of the druggist to respond to the wife. Saying that "it is not right for someone to die when their life could be saved," she assumes that if the druggist were to see the consequences of his refusal to lower his price, he would realize that "he should just give it to the wife and then have the husband pay back the money later." Thus she considers the solution to the dilemma to lie in making the wife's condition more salient to the drug-gist or, that failing, in appealing to others who are in a position to help.

Just as Jake is confident the judge would agree that stealing is the right thing for Heinz to do, so Amy is confident that, "if Heinz and the druggist had talked it out long enough, they could reach something besides stealing." As he considers the law to have "mistakes," so she sees this drama as a mistake, believing that "the world should just share things more and then people wouldn't have to steal." Both children thus recognize the need for agreement but see it as mediated in different ways—he impersonally through systems of logic and law, she personally through communication in relationship. Just as he relies on the conventions of logic to deduce the solution to this dilemma, assuming these conventions to be shared, so she relies on a process of communication, assuming connection and believing that her voice will be heard. Yet while his assumptions about agreement are confirmed by the convergence in logic between his answers and the questions posed, her assumptions are belied by the failure of communication, the interviewer's inability to understand her response.

Although the frustration of the interview with Amy is apparent in the repetition of questions and its ultimate circularity, the problem of interpretation is focused by the assessment of her response. When considered in the light of Kohlberg's definition of the stages and sequence of moral development, her moral judgments appear to be a full stage lower in maturity than those of the boy. Scored as a mixture of stages two and three, her responses seem to reveal a feeling of powerlessness in the world, an inability to think systematically about the concepts of morality or law, a reluctance to challenge authority or to examine the logic of received moral truths, a failure even to conceive of acting directly to save a life or consider that such action, if taken, could possibly have an effect. As her reliance on relationships seems to reveal a continuing dependence and vulnerability, so her belief in communication as the mode through which to resolve moral dilemmas appears naive and cognitively immature.

Yet Amy's description of herself conveys a markedly different impression. Once again, the hallmarks of the preadolescent child depict a child secure in her sense of herself, confident in the substance of her beliefs, and sure of her ability to do something of value in the world. Describing herself at eleven as "growing and changing," she says that she "sees some things differently now, just because I know myself really well now, and I know a lot more about the world." Yet the world she knows is a different world from that refracted by Kohlberg's construction of Heinz's dilemma. Her world is a world of relationships and psychological truths where an awareness of the connection between people gives rise to a recognition of responsibility for one another, a perception of the need for response. Seen in this light, her understanding of morality as arising from the recognition of relationship, her belief in communication as the mode of conflict resolution, and her conviction that the solution to the dilemma will follow from its compelling representation seem far from naive or cognitively immature. Instead, Amy's judgments contain the insights central to an ethic of care, just as Jake's judgments reflect the logic of the justice approach. Her incipient awareness of the "method of truth," the central tenet of nonviolent conflict resolution, and her belief in the restorative activity of care, lead her to see the actors in the dilemma arrayed not as opponents in a contest of rights but as members of a network of relationships on whose continuation they all depend. Consequently her solution to the dilemma lies in activating the network by communication, securing the inclusion of the wife by strengthening rather than severing connections.

But the different logic of Amy's response calls attention to the interpretation of the interview itself. Conceived as an interrogation, it appears instead as a dialogue, which takes on moral dimensions of its own, pertaining to the interviewer's uses of power and to the manifestations of respect. With this shift in the conception of the interview, it immediately becomes clear that the interviewer's problem in understanding Amy's response stems from the fact that Amy is answering a different question from the one the interviewer thought had been posed. Amy is considering not *whether* Heinz should act in this situation ("*should* Heinz steal the drug?") but rather *how* Heinz should act in response to his awareness of his wife's need ("Should Heinz *steal* the drug?"). The interviewer takes the mode of action for granted, presuming it to be a matter of fact; Amy assumes the necessity for action and considers what form it

should take. In the interviewer's failure to imagine a response not dreamt of in Kohlberg's moral philosophy lies the failure to hear Amy's question and to see the logic in her response, to discern that what appears, from one perspective, to be an evasion of the dilemma signifies in other terms a recognition of the problem and a search for a more adequate solution.

Thus in Heinz's dilemma these two children see two very different moral problems—Jake a conflict between life and property that can be resolved by logical deduction, Amy a fracture of human relationship that must be mended with its own thread. Asking different questions that arise from different conceptions of the moral domain, the children arrive at answers that fundamentally diverge, and the arrangement of these answers as successive stages on a scale of increasing moral maturity calibrated by the logic of the boy's response misses the different truth revealed in the judgment of the girl. To the question, "What does he see that she does not?" Kohlberg's theory provides a ready response, manifest in the scoring of Jake's judgements a full stage higher than Amy's in moral maturity; to the question, "What does she see that he does not?" Kohlberg's theory has nothing to say. Since most of her responses fall through the sieve of Kohlberg's scoring system, her responses appear from his perspective to lie outside the moral domain.

Yet just as Jake reveals a sophisticated understanding of the logic of justification, so Amy is equally sophisticated in her understanding of the nature of choice. Recognizing that "if both the roads went in totally separate ways, if you pick one, you'll never know what would happen if you went the other way," she explains that "that's the chance you have to take, and like I said, it's just really a guess." To illustrate her point "in a simple way," she describes her choice to spend the summer at camp:

> I will never know what would have happened if I had stayed here, and if something goes wrong at camp, I'll never know if I stayed here if it would have been better. There's really no way around it because there's no way you can do both at once, so you've got to decide, but you'll never know.

In this way, these two eleven-year-old children, both highly intelligent and perceptive about life, though in different ways, display different modes of moral understanding, different ways of thinking about conflict and choice. In resolving Heinz's dilemma, Jake relies on theft to avoid confrontation and turns to the law to mediate the dispute. Transposing a hierarchy of power into a hierarchy of values, he defuses a potentially explosive conflict between people by casting it as an impersonal conflict of claims. In this way, he abstracts the moral problem from the impersonal situation, finding in the logic of fairness an objective way to decide who will win the dispute. But this hierarchical ordering, with its imagery of winning and losing and the potential for violence which it contains, gives way in Amy's construction of the dilemma to a network of connection, a web of relationships that is sustained by a process of communication. With this shift, the moral problem changes from one of unfair domination, the imposition of property over life, to one of unnecessary exclusion, the failure of the druggist to respond to the wife.

...

Claire, a participant in the college student study, was interviewed first as a senior in college and then again at the age of twenty-seven. When asked, as a senior, how she would describe herself to herself, she answers "confused," saying that she "should be able to say, 'Well, I'm such and such,'" but instead she finds herself "more unsure now than I think I have ever been." Aware that "people see me in a certain way," she has come to find these images contradictory and constraining, "kind of found myself being pushed, being caught in the middle: I should be a good mother and daughter; I should be, as a college woman, aggressive and high-powered and career-oriented." Yet as the feeling of being caught in the middle has turned, in her senior year, into a sense of being constrained to act, of "being pushed to start making decisions for myself," she has "come to realize that all these various roles just aren't exactly right." ...

...

Caught by the interviewer's request for self-description at a time when she is resisting "categorizing or classifying myself," she finds it "hard to start defining what I'm in the process of undefining," the self that, in the past, would "try to push my feelings under the rug" so as not to create any "repercussions." Describing herself as "loving," she is caught

between the two contexts in which that term now applies: an underground world that sets her "apart from others, apart from their definitions of me," and a world of connections that sets her apart from herself. In trying to explain her sense of herself as at once separate and connected, she encounters a problem with "terminology" when trying to convey a new understanding of both self and relationship:

> I'm trying to tell you two things. I'm trying to be myself alone, apart from others, apart from their definitions of me, and yet at the same time I'm doing just the opposite, trying to be with or relate to— whatever the terminology is—I don't think they are mutually exclusive.

In this way she ties a new sense of separation to a new experience of connection, a way of being with others that allows her also to be with herself.

...

Again Claire is caught, but in a different way, not between the contradictory expectations of others but between a responsiveness to others and to herself. Sensing that these modes of response "aren't mutually exclusive," she examines the moral judgment that in the past kept them apart. Formerly, she considered "a moral way of looking" to be one that focused on "responsibility to others"; now she has come to question what seemed in the past a self-evident truth, that "in doing what's right for others, you're doing what's right for yourself." She has, she says, "reached the point where I don't think I can be any good to anyone unless I know who I am."

In the process of seeking to "discover what's me," she has begun to "get rid of all these labels and things I just don't see on my own," to separate her perceptions from her former mode of interpretation and to look more directly at others as well as herself. Thus, she has come to observe "faults" in her mother, whom she perceives as endlessly giving, "because she doesn't care if she hurts herself doing it. She doesn't realize—well, she does realize, that in hurting herself, she hurts people very close to her." Measured against a standard of care, Claire's ideal of self-sacrifice gives way to a vision of "a family where everyone is encouraged to become an individual and at the same time everybody helps others and receives help from them."

Bringing this perspective to Heinz's dilemma, Claire identifies the same moral problem as the eleven-year-old Amy, focusing not on the conflict of rights, but on the failure of response. Claire believes that Heinz should steal the drug ("His wife's life was much more important than anything. He should have done anything to save her life"), but she counters the rights construction with her own interpretation. Although the druggist "had a right, I mean he had a legal right, I also think he had the moral obligation to show compassion in this case. I don't think he had the right to refuse." In tying the necessity for Heinz's action to the fact that "the wife needed him at this point to do it; she couldn't have done it, and it's up to him to do for her what she needs," Claire elaborates the same concept of responsibility that was articulated by Amy. They both equate responsibility with the need for response that arises from the recognition that others are counting on you and that you are in a position to help.

Whether Heinz loves his wife or not is irrelevant to Claire's decision, not because life has priority over affection, but because his wife "is another human being who needs help." Thus the moral injunction to act stems not from Heinz's feelings about his wife but from his awareness of her need, an awareness mediated not by identification but by a process of communication. Just as Claire considers the druggist morally responsible for his refusal, so she ties morality to the awareness of connection, defining the moral person as one who, in acting, "seriously considers the consequences to everybody involved." Therefore, she criticizes her mother for "neglecting her responsibility to herself" at the same time that she criticizes herself for neglecting her responsibility to others.

Although Claire's judgments of Heinz's dilemma for the most part do not fit the categories of Kohlberg's scale, her understanding of the law and her ability to articulate its function in a systematic way earn her a moral maturity score of stage four. Five years later, when she is interviewed at the age of twenty-seven, this score is called into question because she subsumes the law to the considerations of responsibility that informed her thinking about the druggist, Heinz, and his wife. Judging the law now in terms of whom it protects, she extends her ethic of responsibility to a broader vision of societal connection. But the disparity between this vision and the justice conception causes her score on Kohlberg's scale to regress.

During the time when Claire's moral judgments appeared to regress, her moral crisis was resolved. Having taken Kohlberg's course, she suspected that what she had experienced as growth was not progress in his terms. Thus, when she received the letter asking if she would be willing to be interviewed again, she thought:

> My God, what if I have regressed. It seems to me that at one stage of my life, I would have been able to answer these dilemmas with a lot more surety and said, "Yes, this is absolutely right and this is absolutely wrong." And I am just sinking deeper and deeper into the mire of uncertainty. I am not sure if that is good or bad at this point, but I think there has been, in that sense, a direction.

Contrasting an absolute standard of judgment with her own experience of the complexity of moral choice, she introduces the question of direction, the interpretation of her own development.

The question of interpretation recurs throughout the text of her interview at age twenty-seven when, married and about to start medical school, she reflects on her experience of crisis and describes the changes in her life and thought. Speaking of the present, she says that "things have fallen into place," but immediately corrects her phrasing since "that sounds like somebody else put them together, and that's not what happened." The problem of interpretation, however, centers on describing the mode of connection. The connection itself is apparent in Claire's description of herself which she says, "sounds sort of strange," as she characterizes herself as "maternal, with all its connotations." Envisioning herself "as a physician, as a mother," she says that "it's hard for me to think about myself without thinking about other people around me that I am giving to." Like Amy, Claire ties her experience of self to activities of care and connection. Joining the image of her mother with that of herself, she sees herself as a maternal physician, as preparing, like Amy, to become a scientist who takes care of the world.

...

Impatient now with Heinz's dilemma, she structures it starkly as a contrast between the wife's life and the druggist's greed, seeing in the druggist's preoccupation with profit a failure of understanding as well of response. Life is worth more than money because "everybody has the right to live." But then she shifts her perspective, saying, "I'm not sure I want to phrase it that way." In her rephrasing, she replaces the hierarchy of rights with a web of relationships. Through this replacement, she challenges the premise of separation underlying the notion of rights and articulates a "guiding principle of connection." Perceiving relationships as primary rather than as derived from separation, considering the interdependence of people's lives, she envisions "the way things are" and "the way things should be" as a web of interconnection where "everybody belongs to it and you all come from it." Against this conception of social reality, the druggist's claim stands in fundamental contradiction. Seeing life as dependent on connection, as sustained by activities of care, as based on a bond of attachment rather than a contract of agreement, she believes that Heinz should steal the drug, whether or not he loves his wife, "by virtue of the fact that they are both there." Although a person may not like someone else, "you have to love someone else, because you are inseparable from them. In a way it's like loving your right hand; it is part of you. That other person is part of that giant collection of everybody." Thus she articulates an ethic of responsibility that stems from an awareness of interconnection: "The stranger is still another person belonging to that group, people you are connected to by virtue of being another person."

Claire describes morality as "the constant tension between being part of something larger and a sort of self-contained entity," and she sees the ability to live with that tension as the source of moral character and strength. This tension is at the center of the moral dilemmas she has faced which were conflicts of responsibility that pertained to an issue of truth and turned on the recognition of relationship. The problem of truth became apparent to her when, after college, she worked as a counselor in an abortion clinic and was told that, if a woman wanted to see what was evacuated from her uterus she should be told "You can't see anything now. It just looks like jelly at this point." Since this description clashed with the moral turmoil Claire felt while working at the clinic, she decided that she "had to face up to what was going on." Thus she decided to look at a fetus evacuated in a late abortion, and in doing so, she came to the realization that:

> I just couldn't kid myself anymore and say there was nothing in the uterus, just a tiny speck. This is not true, and I knew it wasn't true, but I sort of had to see it. And yet at the same time I knew that's what was going on. I also believed that it was right; it should have happened. But I couldn't say, "well this is right and this is wrong." I was just constantly torn.

When she measured the world by eye and relied on her perceptions in defining what was happening and what was true, the absolutes of moral judgment dissolved. As a result, she was "constantly torn" and mired in uncertainty with respect to the issue of abortion, but she was also able to act in a more responsible way:

> I struggled with it a whole lot. Finally, I just had to reconcile myself—I really do believe this, but it is not an easy thing that you can say without emotions and maybe regret—that, yes, life is sacred, but the quality of life is also important, and it has to be the determining thing in this particular case. The quality of that mother's life, the quality of an unborn child's life— I have seen too many pictures of babies in trash cans and that sort of thing, and it is so easy to say, "Well, either/or," and it just isn't like that. And I had to be able to say, "Yes this is killing, there is no way around it, but I am willing to accept that, but I am willing to go ahead with it, and it's hard." I don't think I can explain it. I don't think I can really verbalize the justification.

Claire's inability to articulate her moral position stems in part from the fact that hers is a contextual judgment, bound to the particulars of time and place, contingent always on "that mother" and that "unborn child" and thus resisting a categorical formulation. To her, the possibilities of imagination outstrip the capacity of generalization. But this sense of being unable to verbalize or explain the rationale for her participation in abortion counseling, an inability that could reflect the inadequacy of her moral thought, could also reflect the fact that she finds in the world no validation of the position she is trying to convey, a position that is neither pro-life nor pro-choice but based on a recognition of the continuing connection between the life of the mother and the life of the child.

Thus Claire casts the dilemma not as a contest of rights but as a problem of relationships, centering on a question of responsibility which in the end must be faced. If attachment cannot be sustained, abortion may be the better solution, but in either case morality lies in recognizing connection, taking responsibility for the care of the child. Although there are times when "killing like that is necessary, it shouldn't become too easy," as it does "if it is removed from you. If the fetus is just jelly, that is removed from you. Southeast Asia is further removed from you." Thus morality and the preservation of life are contingent on sustaining connection, seeing the consequences of action by keeping the web of relationships intact, "not allowing somebody else to do the killing for you without taking the responsibility." Again an absolute judgment yields to the complexity of relationships. The fact that life is sustained by connection leads her to affirm the "sacred tie" of life rather than "the sacredness of life at all costs," and to articulate an ethic of responsibility while remaining cognizant of the issue of rights. . . .

Discussion Questions

1. Identify a moral dilemma you experienced recently. How could this dilemma be described from a justice perspective, that is, in terms of rights and roles? How could this dilemma be described from a care perspective, that is, in terms of responsibility and relationship?

2. How is abortion generally conceptualized in the media, in terms of rights or in terms of relationship? How does Gilligan think women actually approach abortion decisions, from a care perspective or a justice perspective? When women make choices for or against abortion, do they generally consider the rights of the unborn fetus? Or do they base their decisions typically on various responsibilities to themselves, to their unborn fetuses, and to others around them? What do your answers imply about the adequacy of Gilligan's theory?

3. Care tends to be exercised in private, domestic settings. Could care ever be a widely held public moral value? In what ways is care public now? In what ways is it not? Would it be desirable to make care a public norm? Why or why not?

4. Do Gilligan's findings support the claim that morality is relative? Is the right thing to do relative to one's gender, different for males and females? Or is Gilligan's distinction between justice and care still compatible with a single moral standard for everyone?

For Further Reading

Gilligan's book *In a Different Voice* (1983) created an enormous response and a great deal of secondary literature. One of the best sources for early responses to Gilligan is *Women and Moral Theory*, edited by Eva Feder Kittay and Diana T. Meyers (1987). In hindsight, *Women and Moral Theory* is somewhat dated, an early struggle between Gilligan's new paradigm and old standard paradigms of moral philosophy. Gilligan's later work has taken her early thesis in new and more important directions. See especially *Between Voice and Silence,* by Gilligan, Jill Taylor, and Amy Sullivan (1995), and *Meeting at the Crossroads,* by Gilligan and Lyn Mikel Brown (1992). Several recent works by philosophers who have seriously considered care and relationship include J. Kellenberger, *Relationship Morality* (1995); Diana Tietjens Meyers, *Subjection and Subjectivity* (1994); Morwenna Griffiths, *Feminisms and the Self: The Web of Identity* (1995); and Susan J. Hekman, *Moral Voices, Moral Selves: Carol Gilligan and Feminist Moral Theory* (1995).

Much feminist ethics is not centered around an ethic of care. For a sample of the variety of feminist approaches to ethics see *Living with Contradictions: Controversies in Feminist Social Ethics,* edited by Alison M. Jaggar (1994), which focuses primarily on controversies in applied ethics. For a more theoretical approach see Claudia Card, editor, *Feminist Ethics* (1991). Two other feminist authors who have written influential books on feminist approaches to ethics include Nel Noddings, *Caring: A Feminine Approach to Ethics and Moral Education* (1986), and Sara Ruddick, *Maternal Thinking* (1990).

49   ALL ANIMALS ARE EQUAL
Peter Singer

In recent decades, we have learned that systematic unequal treatment of persons due to their race or gender is immoral and that the racial and sexual oppression that results must end. Part of this process has been to recognize the ways in which we have inconsistently and arbitrarily applied our moral principles. What possible reasons can there be to treat racial minorities and women as inferior persons? There are none.

But why stop with racial and sexual discrimination? Why not more consistently apply our moral principles beyond just the human race? In this selection, Peter Singer (1946–) argues that we ought to extend our moral principles to cover animals, as well as humans. Just as racism and sexism are wrong, so is *speciesism*; and just as our moral principles demand racial and sexual liberation, so too they demand *animal liberation*. Singer relies on a consequentialist moral theory to argue that because suffering is bad, and because animals suffer, then it is wrong to make animals suffer. This is a relatively simple and straightforward claim, but would, like his argument for famine relief earlier in this chapter (Reading 46), require fundamental social change.

Reading Questions

1. According to Singer, are there important differences between humans and other animals? What does this mean for differences in rights for humans and animals?
2. What is the difference between equal consideration and equal treatment? What does the basic principle of equality require?
3. How does Singer think we should respond to scientific studies that show differences between the races and sexes? What does this imply about the principle of equality?
4. What is speciesism? Why must we condemn it?
5. Why is suffering important for Bentham? Why is it not like other characteristics such as the ability to do math?
6. According to Singer, how do we know that animals feel pain?
7. What differences between humans and animals to prefer animals to humans for experimentation purposes? What does this argument imply for using human infants or retarded persons for experimental purposes?
8. What is wrong with the 'sanctity of human life' view? How does the example of a brain damaged infant support Singer's argument?
9. What middle position does Singer think we need between the lives of the retarded and the lives of pigs and dogs in order to avoid speciesism?

SOURCE: Reprinted by permission of the author from Peter Singer, *Animal Liberation*, revised edition, Ecco, New York, 2002. © Peter Singer 1975, 1990, 2002.

"Animal Liberation" may sound more like a parody of other liberation movements than a serious objective. The idea of "The Rights of Animals" actually was once used to parody the case for women's rights. When Mary Wollstonecraft, a forerunner of today's feminists, published her *Vindication of the Rights of Women* in 1792, her views were widely regarded as absurd, and before long an anonymous publication appeared entitled *A Vindication of the Rights of Brutes*. The author of this satirical work (now known to have been Thomas Taylor, a distinguished Cambridge philosopher) tried to refute Mary Wollstonecraft's arguments by showing that they could be carried one stage further. If the argument for equality was sound when applied to women, why should it not be applied to dogs, cats, and horses? The reasoning seemed to hold for these "brutes" too; yet to hold that brutes had rights was manifestly absurd; therefore the reasoning by which this conclusion had been reached must be unsound, and if unsound when applied to brutes, it must also be unsound when applied to women, since the very same arguments had been used in each case.

In order to explain the basis of the case for the equality of animals, it will be helpful to start with an examination of the case for the equality of women. Let us assume that we wish to defend the case for women's rights against the attack by Thomas Taylor. How should we reply?

One way in which we might reply is by saying that the case for equality between men and women cannot validly be extended to nonhuman animals. Women have a right to vote, for instance, because they are just as capable of making rational decisions about the future as men are; dogs, on the other hand, are incapable of understanding the significance of voting, so they cannot have the right to vote. There are many other obvious ways in which men and women resemble each other closely, while humans and animals differ greatly. So, it might be said, men and women are similar beings and should have similar rights, while humans and nonhumans are different and should not have equal rights.

The reasoning behind this reply to Taylor's analogy is correct up to a point, but it does not go far enough. There *are* important differences between humans and other animals, and these differences must give rise to *some* differences in the rights that each have. Recognizing this obvious fact, however, is no barrier to the case for extending the basic principle of equality to nonhuman animals. The differences that exist between men and women are equally undeniable, and the supporters of Women's Liberation are aware that these differences may give rise to different rights. Many feminists hold that women have the right to an abortion on request. It does not follow that since these same feminists are campaigning for equality between men and women they must support the right of men to have abortions too. Since a man cannot have an abortion, it is meaningless to talk of his right to have one. Since a dog can't vote, it is meaningless to talk of its right to vote. There is no reason why either Women's Liberation or Animal Liberation should get involved in such nonsense. The extension of the basic principle of equality from one group to another does not imply that we must treat both groups in exactly the same way, or grant exactly the same rights to both groups. Whether we should do so will depend on the nature of the members of the two groups. The basic principle of equality does not require equal or identical *treatment*; it requires equal *consideration*. Equal consideration for different beings may lead to different treatment and different rights.

So there is a different way of replying to Taylor's attempt to parody the case for women's rights, a way that does not deny the obvious differences between humans and nonhumans but goes more deeply into the question of equality and concludes by finding nothing absurd in the idea that the basic principle of equality applies to so-called "brutes." At this point such a conclusion may appear odd; but if we examine more deeply the basis on which our opposition to discrimination on grounds of race or sex ultimately rests, we will see that we would be on shaky ground if we were to demand equality for blacks, women, and other groups of oppressed humans while denying equal consideration to nonhumans. To make this clear we need to see, first, exactly why racism and sexism are wrong.

When we say that all human beings, whatever their race, creed, or sex, are equal, what is it that we are asserting? Those who wish to defend hierarchical, inegalitarian societies have often pointed out that by whatever test we choose it simply is not true that all humans are equal. Like it or not we must face the fact that humans come in different shapes and sizes; they come with different moral capacities, different intellectual abilities, different amounts of benevolent feeling and sensitivity to the needs of others, different abilities to communicate effectively, and different capacities to experience pleasure and pain. In short, if the demand for equality were based on the actual equality of all human beings, we would have to stop demanding equality.

Still, one might cling to the view that the demand for equality among human beings is based on the actual equality of the different races and sexes. Although, it may be said, humans differ as individuals there are no differences between the races and sexes *as such*. From the mere fact that a person is black or a woman we cannot infer anything about that person's intellectual or moral capacities. This, it may be said, is why racism and sexism are wrong. The white racist claims that whites are superior to blacks, but this is false—although there are differences among individuals, some blacks are superior to some whites in all of the capacities and abilities that could conceivably be relevant. The opponent of sexism would say the same: a person's sex is no guide to his or her abilities, and this is why it is unjustifiable to discriminate on the basis of sex.

The existence of individual variations that cut across the lines of race or sex, however, provides us with no defense at all against a more sophisticated opponent of equality, one who proposes that, say, the interests of all those with IQ scores below 100 be given less consideration than the interests of those with ratings over 100. Perhaps those scoring below the mark would, in this society, be made the slaves of those scoring higher. Would a hierarchical society of this sort really be so much better than one based on race or sex? I think not. But if we tie the moral principle of equality to the factual equality of the different races or sexes, taken as a whole, our opposition to racism and sexism does not provide us with any basis for objecting to this kind of inegalitarianism.

There is a second important reason why we ought not to base our opposition to racism and sexism on any kind of actual equality, even the limited kind that asserts that variations in capacities and abilities are spread evenly between the different races and sexes: we can have no absolute guarantee that these capacities and abilities really are distributed evenly, without

regard to race or sex, among human beings. So far as actual abilities are concerned there do seem to be certain measurable differences between both races and sexes. These differences do not, of course, appear in each case, but only when averages are taken. More important still, we do not yet know how much of these differences is really due to the different genetic endowments of the different races and sexes, and how much is due to poor schools, poor housing, and other factors that are the result of past and continuing discrimination. Perhaps all of the important differences will eventually prove to be environmental rather than genetic. Anyone opposed to racism and sexism will certainly hope that this will be so, for it will make the task of ending discrimination a lot easier; nevertheless it would be dangerous to rest the case against racism and sexism on the belief that all significant differences are environmental in origin. The opponent of, say, racism who takes this line will be unable to avoid conceding that *if* differences in ability do after all prove to have some genetic connection with race, racism would in some way be defensible.

Fortunately there is no need to pin the case for equality to one particular outcome of a scientific investigation. The appropriate response to those who claim to have found evidence of genetically based differences in ability between the races or sexes is not to stick to the belief that the genetic explanation must be wrong, whatever evidence to the contrary may turn up: instead we should make it quite clear that the claim to equality does not depend on intelligence, moral capacity, physical strength, or similar matters of fact. Equality is a moral idea, not an assertion of fact. There is no logically compelling reason for assuming that a factual difference in ability between two people justifies any difference in the amount of consideration we give to their needs and interests. *The principle of the equality of human beings is not a description of an alleged actual equality among humans: it is a prescription of how we should treat humans.*

Jeremy Bentham, the founder of the reforming utilitarian school of moral philosophy, incorporated the essential basis of moral equality into his system of ethics by means of the formula: "Each to count for one and none for more than one." In other words, the interests of every being affected by an action are to be taken into account and given the same weight as the like interests of any other being. A later utilitarian, Henry Sidgwick, put the point in this way: "The good of any one individual is of no more importance, from the point of view (if I may say so) of the Universe, than the good of any other." More recently the leading figures in contemporary moral philosophy have shown a great deal of agreement in specifying as a fundamental presupposition of their moral theories some similar requirement which operates so as to give everyone's interests equal consideration—although these writers generally cannot agree on how this requirement is best formulated.

It is an implication of this principle of equality that our concern for others and our readiness to consider their interests ought not to depend on what they are like or on what abilities they may possess. Precisely what this concern or consideration requires us to do may vary according to the characteristics of those affected by what we do: concern for the well-being of a child growing up in America would require that we teach him to read; concern for the well-being of a pig may require no more than that we leave him alone with other pigs in a place where there is adequate food and room to run freely. But the basic element— the taking into account of the interests of the being, whatever those interests may be—must, according to the principle of equality, be extended to all beings, black or white, masculine or feminine, human or nonhuman.

Thomas Jefferson, who was responsible for writing the principle of the equality of men into the American Declaration of Independence, saw this point. It led him to oppose slavery even though he was unable to free himself fully from his slaveholding background. He wrote in a letter to the author of a book that emphasized the notable intellectual achievements of Negroes in order to refute the then common view that they had limited intellectual capacities:

> Be assured that no person living wishes more sincerely than I do, to see a complete refutation of the doubts I have myself entertained and expressed on the grade of understanding allotted to them by nature, and to find that they are on a par with ourselves . . . but whatever be their degree of talent it is no measure of their rights. Because Sir Isaac Newton was superior to others in understanding, he was not therefore lord of the property or person of others.

Similarly when in the 1850s the call for women's rights was raised in the United States a remarkable black feminist named Sojourner Truth made the same point in more robust terms at a feminist convention:

> . . . they talk about this thing in the head; what do they call it? ["Intellect," whispered someone near by:] That's it. What's that got to do with women's rights or Negroes' rights? If my cup won't hold but a pint and yours holds a quart, wouldn't you be mean not to let me have my little half-measure full?

It is on this basis that the case against racism and the case against sexism must both ultimately rest; and it is in accordance with this principle that the attitude that we may call "speciesism," by analogy with racism, must also be condemned. Speciesism—the word is not an attractive one, but I can think of no better term—is a prejudice or attitude of bias toward the interests of members of one's own species and against those of members of other species. It should be obvious that the fundamental objections to racism and sexism made by Thomas Jefferson and Sojourner Truth apply equally to speciesism. If possessing a higher degree of intelligence does not entitle one human to use another for his own ends, how can it entitle humans to exploit nonhumans for the same purpose?

Many philosophers and other writers have proposed the principle of equal consideration of interests, in some form or other, as a basic moral principle; but not many of them have recognized that this principle applies to members of other species as well as to our own. Jeremy Bentham was one of the few who did realize this. In a forward-looking passage written at a time when black slaves had been freed by the French but in the British dominions were still being treated in the way we now treat animals, Bentham wrote:

> The day *may* come when the rest of the animal creation may acquire those rights which never could have been withholden from them but by the hand of tyranny. The French have already discovered that the blackness of the skin is no reason why a human being should be abandoned without redress to the caprice of a tormentor. It may one day come to be recognized that the number of the legs, the villosity of the skin, or the termination of the *os sacrum* are reasons equally insufficient for abandoning a sensitive being to the same fate. What else is it that should trace the insuperable line? Is it the faculty of reason, or

perhaps the faculty of discourse? But a full-grown horse or dog is beyond comparison a more rational, as well as a more conversable animal, than an infant of a day or a week or even a month, old. But suppose they were otherwise, what would it avail? The question is not, Can they *reason*? nor Can they *talk*? but, *Can they suffer?*

In this passage Bentham points to the capacity for suffering as the vital characteristic that gives a being the right to equal consideration. The capacity for suffering—or more strictly, for suffering and/or enjoyment or happiness—is not just another characteristic like the capacity for language or higher mathematics. Bentham is not saying that those who try to mark "the insuperable line" that determines whether the interests of a being should be considered happen to have chosen the wrong characteristic. By saying that we must consider the interests of all beings with the capacity for suffering or enjoyment Bentham does not arbitrarily exclude from consideration any interests at all—as those who draw the line with reference to the possession of reason or language do. The capacity for suffering and enjoyment is *a prerequisite for having interests at all*, a condition that must be satisfied before we can speak of interests in a meaningful way. It would be nonsense to say that it was not in the interests of a stone to be kicked along the road by a schoolboy. A stone does not have interests because it cannot suffer. Nothing that we can do to it could possibly make any difference to its welfare. A mouse, on the other hand, does have an interest in not being kicked along the road, because it will suffer if it is.

If a being suffers there can be no moral justification for refusing to take that suffering into consideration. No matter what the nature of the being, the principle of equality requires that its suffering be counted equally with the like suffering—in so far as rough comparisons can be made—of any other being. If a being is not capable of suffering, or of experiencing enjoyment or happiness, there is nothing to be taken into account. So the limit of sentience (using the term as a convenient if not strictly accurate shorthand for the capacity to suffer and/or experience enjoyment) is the only defensible boundary of concern for the interests of others. To mark this boundary by some other characteristic like intelligence or rationality would be to mark it in an arbitrary manner. Why not choose some other characteristic, like skin color?

The racist violates the principle of equality by giving greater weight to the interests of members of his own race when there is a clash between their interests and the interests of those of another race. The sexist violates the principle of equality by favoring the interests of his own sex. Similarly the speciesist allows the interests of his own species to override the greater interests of members of other species. The pattern is identical in each case. . . .

Do animals other than humans feel pain? How do we know? Well, how do we know if anyone, human or nonhuman, feels pain? We know that we ourselves can feel pain. We know this from the direct experiences of pain that we have when, for instance, somebody presses a lighted cigarette against the back of our hand. But how do we know that anyone else feels pain? We cannot directly experience anyone else's pain, whether that "anyone" is our best friend or a stray dog. Pain is a state of consciousness, a "mental event," and as such it can never be observed. Behavior like writhing, screaming, or drawing one's hand away from the lighted cigarette is not pain itself; nor are the recordings a neurologist might make of activity within the brain observations of pain itself. Pain is something that we feel, and we can only infer that others are feeling it from various external indications.

In theory, we *could* always be mistaken when we assume that other human beings feel pain. It is conceivable that our best friend is really a very cleverly constructed robot, controlled by a brilliant scientist so as to give all the signs of feeling pain, but really no more sensitive than any other machine. We can never know, with absolute certainty, that this is not the case. But while this might present a puzzle for philosophers, none of us has the slightest real doubt that our best friends feel pain just as we do. This is an inference, but a perfectly reasonable one, based on observations, of their behavior in situations in which we would feel pain, and on the fact that we have every reason to assume that our friends are beings like us, with nervous systems like ours that can be assumed to function as ours do, and to produce similar feelings in similar circumstances.

If it is justifiable to assume that other humans feel pain as we do, is there any reason why a similar inference should be unjustifiable in the case of other animals?

Nearly all the external signs which lead us to infer pain in other humans can be seen in other species, especially the species most closely related to us—other species of mammals, and birds. Behavioral signs—writhing, facial contortions, moaning, yelping or other forms of calling, attempts to avoid the source of pain, appearance of fear at the prospect of its repetition, and so on—are present. In addition, we know that these animals have nervous systems very like ours, which respond physiologically as ours do when the animal is in circumstances in which we would feel pain: an initial rise of blood pressure, dilated pupils, perspiration, an increased pulse rate, and, if the stimulus continues, a fall in blood pressure. Although humans have a more developed cerebral cortex than other animals, this part of the brain is concerned with thinking functions rather than with basic impulses, emotions, and feelings. These impulses, emotions, and feelings are located in the diencephalon, which is well developed in many other species of animals, especially mammals and birds.

We also know that the nervous systems of other animals were not artificially constructed to mimic the pain behavior of humans, as a robot might be artificially constructed. The nervous systems of animals evolved as our own did, and in fact the evolutionary history of humans and other animals, especially mammals, did not diverge until the central features of our nervous systems were already in existence. A capacity to feel pain obviously enhances a species' prospects of survival, since it causes members of the species to avoid sources of injury. It is surely unreasonable to suppose that nervous systems which are virtually identical physiologically, have a common origin and a common evolutionary function, and result in similar forms of behavior in similar circumstances should actually operate in an entirely different manner on the level of subjective feelings. . . .

Animals can feel pain. As we saw earlier, there can be no moral justification for regarding the pain (or pleasure) that animals feel as less important than the same amount of pain (or pleasure) felt by humans. But what exactly does this mean, in practical terms? To prevent misunderstanding I shall spell out what I mean a little more fully.

If I give a horse a hard slap across its rump with my open hand, the horse may start, but it presumably feels little pain. Its skin is thick enough to protect it against a mere slap. If I slap a baby in the same way, however, the baby will cry and presumably does feel pain, for its skin is more sensitive. So it is worse to slap a baby than a horse, if both slaps are administered with equal force. But there must be some kind of blow—I don't know exactly what it would be, but perhaps a blow with a heavy stick—that would cause the horse as much pain as we cause a baby by slapping it with our hand. That is what I mean by "the same amount of pain" and if we consider it wrong to inflict that much pain on a baby for no good reason then we must, unless we are speciesists, consider it equally wrong to inflict the same amount of pain on a horse for no good reason.

There are other differences between humans and animals that cause other complications. Normal adult human beings have mental capacities which will, in certain circumstances, lead them to suffer more than animals would in the same circumstances. If, for instance, we decided to perform extremely painful or lethal scientific experiments on normal adult humans, kidnaped at random from public parks for this purpose, every adult who entered a park would become fearful that he would be kidnaped. The resultant terror would be a form of suffering additional to the pain of the experiment. The same experiments performed on nonhuman animals would cause less suffering since the animals would not have the anticipatory dread of being kidnapped and experimented upon. This does not mean, of course, that it would be right to perform the experiment on animals, but only that there is a reason, which is *not* speciesist, for preferring to use animals rather than normal adult humans, if the experiment is to be done at all. It should be noted, however, that this same argument gives us a reason for preferring to use human infants—orphans perhaps—or retarded humans for experiments, rather than adults, since infants and retarded humans would also have no idea of what was going to happen to them. So far as this argument is concerned non-human animals and infants and retarded humans are in the same category; and if we use this argument to justify experiments on nonhuman animals we have to ask ourselves whether we are also prepared to allow experiments on human infants and retarded adults; and if we make a distinction between animals and these humans, on what basis can we do it, other than a barefaced—and morally indefensible—preference for members of our own species? . . .

So far I have said a lot about the infliction of suffering on animals, but nothing about killing them. This omission has been deliberate. The application of the principle of equality to the infliction of suffering is, in theory at least, fairly straightforward. Pain and suffering are bad and should be prevented or minimized, irrespective of the race, sex, or species of the being that suffers. How bad a pain is depends on how intense it is and how long it lasts, but pains of the same intensity and duration are equally bad, whether felt by humans or animals.

The wrongness of killing a being is more complicated. I have kept, and shall continue to keep, the question of killing in the background because in the present state of human tyranny over other species the more simple, straightforward principle of equal consideration of pain or pleasure is a sufficient basis for identifying and protesting against all the major abuses of animals that humans practice. Nevertheless, it is necessary to say something about killing.

Just as most humans are speciesists in their readiness to cause pain to animals when they would not cause a similar pain to humans for the same reason, so most humans are speciesists in their readiness to kill other animals when they would not kill humans. We need to proceed more cautiously here, however, because people hold widely differing views about when it is legitimate to kill humans, as the continuing debates over abortion and euthanasia attest. Nor have moral philosophers been able to agree on exactly what it is that makes it wrong to kill humans, and under what circumstances killing a human being may be justifiable.

Let us consider first the view that it is always wrong to take an innocent human life. We may call this the "sanctity of life" view. People who take this view oppose abortion and euthanasia. They do not usually, however, oppose the killing of nonhumans—so perhaps it would be more accurate to describe this view as the "sanctity of *human* life" view.

The belief that human life, and only human life, is sacrosanct is a form of speciesism. To see this, consider the following example.

Assume that, as sometimes happens, an infant has been born with massive and irreparable brain damage. The damage is so severe that the infant can never be any more than a "human vegetable," unable to talk, recognize other people, act independently of others, or develop a sense of self-awareness. The parents of the infant, realizing that they cannot hope for any improvement in their child's condition and being in any case unwilling to spend, or ask the state to spend, the thousands of dollars that would be needed annually for proper care of the infant, ask the doctor to kill the infant painlessly.

Should the doctor do what the parents ask? Legally, he should not, and in this respect the law reflects the sanctity of life view. The life of every human being is sacred. Yet people who would say this about the infant do not object to the killing of nonhuman animals. How can they justify their different judgments? Adult chimpanzees, dogs, pigs, and many other species far surpass the brain-damaged infant in their ability to relate to others, act independently, be self-aware, and any other capacity that could reasonably be said to give value to life. With the most intensive care possible, there are retarded infants who can never achieve the intelligence level of a dog. Nor can we appeal to the concern of the infant's parents, since they themselves, in this imaginary example (and in some actual cases), do not want the infant kept alive.

The only thing that distinguishes the infant from the animal, in the eyes of those who claim it has a "right to life," is that it is, biologically, a member of the species Homo sapiens, whereas chimpanzees, dogs, and pigs are not. But to use *this* difference as the basis for granting a right to life to the infant and not to the other animals is, of course, pure speciesism. It is exactly the kind of arbitrary difference that the most crude and overt kind of racist uses in attempting to justify racial discrimination.

This does not mean that to avoid speciesism we must hold that it is as wrong to kill a dog as it is to kill a normal human being. The only position that is irredeemably speciesist is the one that tries to make the boundary of the right to life run exactly parallel to the boundary of our own species. Those who hold the sanctity of life view do this because while distinguishing sharply between humans and other animals they allow no distinctions to be made within our own species, objecting to the killing of the severely retarded and the hopelessly senile as strongly as they object to the killing of normal adults.

To avoid speciesism we must allow that beings which are similar in all relevant respects have a similar right to life—and mere membership in our own biological species cannot be a morally relevant criterion for this right. Within these limits we could still hold that, for instance, it is worse to kill a normal adult human, with a capacity for self-awareness, and the ability to plan for the future and have meaningful relations with others, than it is to kill a mouse, which presumably does not share all of these characteristics; or we might appeal to the close family and other personal ties which humans have but mice do not have to the same degree; or we might think that it is the consequences for other humans, who will be put in fear of their own lives, that makes the crucial difference; or we might think it is some combination of these factors, or other factors altogether.

Whatever criteria we choose, however, we will have to admit that they do not follow precisely the boundary of our own species. We may legitimately hold that there are some features of certain beings which make their lives more valuable than those of other beings; but there will surely be some nonhuman animals whose lives, by any standards, are more valuable than the lives of some humans. A chimpanzee, dog, or pig, for instance, will have a higher degree of self-awareness and a greater capacity for meaningful relations with others than a severely retarded infant or someone in a state of advanced senility. So if we base the right to life on these characteristics we must grant these animals a right to life as good as, or better than, such retarded or senile humans.

Now this argument cuts both ways. It could be taken as showing that chimpanzees, dogs, and pigs, along with some other species, have a right to life and we commit a grave moral offense whenever we kill them, even when they are old and suffering and our intention is to put them out of their misery. Alternatively one could take the argument as showing that the severely retarded and hopelessly senile have no right to life and may be killed for quite trivial reasons, as we now kill animals.

Since the focus of this book is on ethical questions concerning animals and not on the morality of euthanasia I shall not attempt to settle this issue finally. I think it is reasonably clear, though, that while both of the positions just described avoid speciesism, neither is entirely satisfactory. What we need is some middle position which would avoid speciesism but would not make the lives of the retarded and senile as cheap as the lives of pigs and dogs now are, nor make the lives of pigs and dogs so sacrosanct that we think it wrong to put them out of hopeless misery. What we must do is bring nonhuman animals within our sphere of moral concern and cease to treat their lives as expendable for whatever trivial purposes we may have. At the same time, once we realize that the fact that a being is a member of our own species is not in itself enough to make it always wrong to kill that being, we may come to reconsider our policy of preserving human lives at all costs, even when there is no prospect of a meaningful life or of existence without terrible pain. . . .

Discussion Questions

1. In what ways are animals made to suffer in contemporary society? For what purposes do we cause animals to suffer or to die? Are most persons aware of the level of animal suffering or not? If they were, would it make a difference in what they choose to eat or what they choose to purchase? For example, if you knew that an animal suffered to make a pair of leather shoes, would you purchase those shoes?

2. Is there a relevant difference between eating animals that were raised in deplorable conditions (such as on a so-called factory farm) and eating animals that lived in natural conditions? For example, is it worse to eat beef from cows that suffered while in overcrowded feed lots than to eat venison from deer we hunt and kill? How about the difference between 'caged' chickens and 'free-range' chickens? Finally, does suffering matter when we consume animal products, such as milk, cheese, and eggs? If given a choice

between eggs from chickens that didn't suffer and those that did, would it be morally wrong to purchase eggs from animals that were made to suffer?

3. Some ranchers and farmers argue that the animals they raise for human consumption would not ever have come into existence if it were not for the purpose of providing food for humans. So, for example, most cattle would not exist were it not for the beef industry; this is also true for poultry and pigs. Does this make a difference in whether or not it is permissible to kill and eat these animals? Is it less wrong to kill an animal that would not exist if it was not eventually going to be killed and eaten? Does it matter if the animal suffers while it is alive?

4. Suppose we knew that we could vastly improve the lives of all future generations of humans through experimenting on several hundred human infants a year for a decade or so. Suppose further that this experimentation caused the infants to suffer intense pain for significant periods of time. Would it be permissible to do so? Why or why not? What do you think Singer would say about this? What does this imply about the suitability of his position?

For Further Reading

This selection was taken from *Animal Liberation* (1975), which is widely available. Singer has written a number of other books, including *One World: The Ethics of Globalization* (2002), *Practical Ethics* (1993), and *Writings on an Ethical Life* (2001). Additional reading sources on animal welfare can be found at the end of the article by Brian Luke (Reading 50 of this chapter).

50   JUSTICE, CARING, AND ANIMAL LIBERATION
Brian Luke

Opponents of our culture's current treatment of animals argue that certain practices, such as vivisection, hunting, and factory farming, are immoral and therefore ought to cease. Typically these arguments proceed by extending rights to animals (essentially a **deontological** strategy) or by objecting to animal suffering (essentially a **consequentialist** or **utilitarian** strategy). But in this selection, Brian Luke, a philosopher at the University of Dayton, argues that these types of defenses of animal welfare not only are inadequate, but fail to capture the actual objections persons have to animal abuse. The problem, Luke suggests, is that defenders of animal liberation such as Peter Singer are making arguments in a 'justice' framework, while in practice, advocates of animal liberation are operating on a 'care' model.

Gilligan's care ethic emphasized empathetic response to persons in need and the importance of making contextualized judgments instead of relying upon rules. Similarly, Luke contends that an empathetic response to animal suffering is both the reason why we respond to animal suffering in the first place and a morally adequate foundation for animal liberation.

Reading Questions

1. What is Regan's argument for animal liberation? What does Luke believe is wrong with it?
2. What is Singer's argument for animal liberation? Why does Luke believe it is flawed?
3. Explain the basis of Luke's opposition to animal abuse. Why does he believe that this is a 'care' response?
4. What four examples does Luke give to illustrate that care for animals is the normal state of humans? Explain how these examples support his thesis.
5. What is the chief mechanism for forestalling sympathetic responses to animals? Explain how it functions.
6. How do cover stories, denials of harm, denials of animal subjectivity, and derogation of sympathies for animals protect industries that abuse animals? How do these mechanisms block caring responses?

Carol Gilligan has described justice and caring as two distinct moral frameworks or orientations to ethical concerns. The *justice* framework is characterized by abstraction, the application of general rules of conduct, an emphasis on restraining aggression, and a concern for consistency and the fair resolution of conflicting claims and interests. The *caring* framework, on the other hand, is characterized by its focus on the concrete and particular, its emphasis on the maintenance and extension of connection, and by its concern for responsiveness and the satisfaction of needs. Animal liberation is often framed as a justice issue, though, I will suggest, it may more appropriately be understood in terms of caring.

By *animal liberation* I mean opposition to institutions of animal exploitation such as vivisection, hunting, and animal farming. Two prominent philosophical defenders of animal liberation are Tom Regan and Peter Singer. Both work exclusively within the justice framework, presenting animal liberation as a matter of consistency and fair treatment, rather than in terms of responsiveness and the satisfaction of needs. We can start to see how the justice approach is ill-suited for animal liberation by considering the arguments of Regan and Singer.

Regan attempts to move the reader from a commitment to the respectful treatment of humans to a like commitment to the respectful treatment of normal adult mammals. Regan points out that we do not in general think it is justifiable to harm one human to benefit others—we would object, for example, to killing a healthy man against his will in order to use his organs to save three sick persons. We do, however,

think it appropriate to harm one animal to benefit other animals, human or otherwise; at least this is the way that vivisection, hunting, and animal farming are usually justified.

Regan argues that we are being inconsistent in treating humans and other mammals differently in this respect. The notion of inconsistency here is not self-contradiction but contradiction with the formal principles of justice, according to which like individuals should be treated alike. Now we protect humans against being vivisected, farmed, or hunted, presumably because such treatment would harm them through the infliction of pain and death. But Regan has shown in the first three chapters of his book that pain and death are also harms to normal adult mammals. So these animals are just as deserving of protection from vivisection, farming, and hunting as are humans. Because both humans and other mammals are harmed by pain and death, the two groups are relevantly similar, and we are inconsistent to treat them so differently.

The flaw in this argument I wish to emphasize is the move from the same kinds of harms to relevant similarity. Most of us would admit that pain and death are harms for both humans and other animals. But this by itself does not show that humans and other animals are relevantly similar with respect to assessing the moral status of these common harms. Regan allows that certain capacities may be unique to humans, and it is conceivable that the presence of uniquely human capacities in an individual is relevant to the justifiability of harming that individual, even when the type of harm in question is one that can be imposed on nonhumans. In fact, according to Kantian theories, only rational individuals can be directly wronged. A Kantian could hold that killing is a harm both to humans and other animals, but that the wrongness of the harm arises only from its impingement upon the victim's rationality. Thus, killing a rational human would require special justification not needed for killing a nonrational animal, even though both are harmed by being killed.

I am not saying that I agree with Kantianism or with the idea that there are uniquely human capacities. I am only saying that as long as Regan's readers are willing to embrace these theories, they can without inconsistency reject Regan's move from "death and pain are harms for both humans and other animals" to "killing and inflicting pain require the same justification for both humans and other animals." Since this move is crucial to his argument as a whole, they can consistently reject Regan's case for animals' rights.

Essentially the same type of maneuver allows rejection of Singer's argument for animal liberation. Like Regan, Singer attempts to move the reader, through considerations of consistency, from commitments concerning the appropriate treatment of humans to similar commitments concerning the appropriate treatment of animals. Singer starts not with respect for humans but with opposition to racism and sexism. Singer argues that anyone who opposes racism and sexism does so on the basis of a principle of equal consideration, according to which we must give equal consideration to the interests of all people, regardless of their race or sex. But animals, at least all those capable of feeling pleasure or pain, have interests, so there is no reason, according to Singer, why they should be excluded from the scope of this principle of equal consideration. But animal farming and vivisection, Singer maintains, are considered acceptable practices only because we tend to give the interests of nonhumans much less consideration than the similar interests of humans. This devaluation of interests solely on the basis of species Singer calls *speciesism,* and he thinks his argument shows that we are inconsistent to oppose sexism and racism but not speciesism.

As with Regan, however, anyone willing to accept a Kantian view can reject Singer's entire argument without inconsistency. Singer presumes that opposition

to sexism and racism must be based on the principle of equal consideration of interests. One could maintain, however, that sexism and racism are objectionable because they are disrespectful of the rationality of members of the oppressed races and sex. One could then consistently exclude nonhumans from moral consideration by holding that they lack the rational capacities of humans.

Again I emphasize that I am not endorsing Kantianism here. I am just showing that Regan's and Singer's arguments fail on their own terms. Both writers insist that they are relying on reason alone, and not emotion, to establish their animal liberationist conclusions. But the crucial step in their arguments, that humans and other animals are relevantly similar, cannot be established by reason alone.

…

As arguments, justice-based approaches to animal liberation fail. The justice orientation also fails to capture the moral outlooks of many in the animal liberation movement. Justice-oriented writers cast the issue as, fundamentally, a comparison between the treatment of humans and the treatment of other animals. According to Regan, we harm animals to benefit others, we do not do this to humans (generally speaking), but there is no relevant difference between humans and animals to justify the dissimilar treatment. Thus animals are treated unfairly by comparison to the treatment of humans. For Singer, the comparative unfairness is in opposing sexism and racism but not opposing speciesism, when again there is no relevant difference between humans and other animals to support the distinction. For both Regan and Singer, and other writers within the justice framework, the basic moral judgment concerns the discrepancy between the treatment of humans and the treatment of other similar animals. What is called into question is the fairness, or what they more often refer to as the consistency, of a society that treats two relevantly similar groups of individuals in such totally different ways.

The emphasis on the consistency of the agent and the focus on comparing the treatment of humans and the treatment of other animals are quite distant from my motivations and those of others in the animal liberation movement. My opposition to the institutionalized exploitation of animals is not based on a *comparison* between human and animal treatment, but on a consideration of the abuse of the animals *in and of itself.* I respond directly to the needs and the plight of the animals used in hunting, farming, and vivisection. In objecting to these practices I am not comparing the treatment of humans and animals, and thinking "this is unfair because humans are protected from such usage." I am appalled by the abuses themselves—shooting, trapping, and poisoning; branding, castrating, forcibly impregnating, separating mother and young, tail docking, debeaking, confining, transporting in cattle cars, and slaughtering; burning, cutting, gassing, starving, asphyxiating, decapitating, decompressing, irradiating, electrocuting, freezing, crushing, paralyzing, amputating, excising organs, removing parts of the brain, socially isolating, inducing addiction, and imposing disease—these acts are repellent because of what they do to the animals. My moral condemnation of the acts arises directly from my sympathy for the animals, and is independent of the question of whether humans are protected from such abuse. To the extent that humans are also treated in these ways I object to that, too, but again, out of sympathy, and not considerations of fairness.

Let me give some examples of discourse that clearly show the sort of direct responsiveness I am talking about. A 1983 study on the psychology of slaughter contains quotes from college students who worked on a farm as part of their curriculum. One 19-year-old woman wrote:

> The first time I went into the slaughter room I had just haltered and pulled a steer into the waiting line. I could tell that the steer sensed what was going to happen to him. He was doing anything to get away. Then when I walked into the slaughter room I was amazed at the amount of blood. It was an awful feeling to look at that steer with its eyes open and his feet pointing up, so I had to look at the ceiling. Mr.——told me to cut off the head with a saw. I couldn't do it so I left. I guess slaughtering affects me more than the usual person because I raised calves for 4-H at home and became quite attached to them—but I *don't* butcher them.

A 19-year-old man wrote:

> It's pretty gross. I don't like having the dry heaves all day. Plus, I feel really bad for the cow. It's bad seeing a big animal turned into hamburger.

...

The reactions described here are not comparative judgments of justice, such as "cutting off this steer's head is wrong because we don't do that to humans," but rather revulsion at bloodshed, pity for an animal struggling for his life, memories of animal friends, a sense of the loss and the waste of "a big animal turned into hamburger"—all elements of caring.

...

In response to the criticism that their justice approach misses the fundamental importance of direct sympathetic responsiveness in the actual motivations of activists, Regan and Singer could point out that their work is not descriptive but normative—that is, that they are not trying to describe animal rights activists and their psyches but, rather, to set out the best reasons we have for accepting the animal rights position. Such a response would be inadequate in two ways. First, it is doubtful that justice-based arguments do present the best reasons for animal liberation, given that those arguments are unsound, as I have shown above. More importantly, this response would incompletely characterize the projects Singer and Regan take for themselves, since, besides attempting to construct sound arguments, both writers explicitly indicate that they also want to further the animal liberation movement. This second part of their project, I would suggest, makes it incumbent upon them to attend to the actual motivations of activists. Arguments with little relation to the ethics of those who already affirm animal liberation are unlikely to bring new members into the movement or to help present activists maintain their commitment. Those of us who write or speak to move others should make presentations consonant with the real processes by which individuals come to reject animal farming, vivisection, and hunting.

...

The disposition to care for animals is not the unreliable quirk of a few, but is rather the normal state of humans generally. As Andrée Collard puts it: "Our common bond with animals is *natural* (of nature), *normal* (of the norm), and healthy *(wholesome)*." If we shift our attention away from animal exploitation to other cultural phenomena, we can see the strength and depth of the human-animal bond. I will mention just four examples:

(1) Animal companions. The practice of befriending animals, in its cross-cultural prevalence and its frequently avid pursuit, demonstrates the strength and depth of human interest in and affection for non-human animals. Approximately half of all contemporary Americans and Europeans live with nonhuman animals, or "pets," at any given time. Many Westerners do keep animals merely as status symbols, objects of domination, emblems of masculinity, or even as pieces of furniture. More commonly, however, the animals we live with are seen as companions and family members. In one survey, for example, companionship, love and affection, and pleasure, ranked respectively as the top three self-reported "advantages of owning a pet." Indigenous people also commonly befriend non-human animals. And as in the industrialized West, when they do so their animal companions receive great attention and affection, and are viewed as family and community members.

(2) Therapy. Many people either socially withdrawn or in depressed states have been helped through the companionship of animals. These people were unable to interact positively with other humans, but could establish a connection with a friendly animal, often a dog or a cat. This reinforces what most of us already recognize, that bonds with animals are sometimes *easier* to establish and maintain than bonds with humans.

(3) Rescue. You may recall from 1988 the plight of three California gray whales off the coast of Point Barrow, Alaska. The iceholes through which the whales were surfacing to breathe were in the process of freezing over, which would result in the whales drowning. A rescue attempt was mounted, which ultimately cost $5.8 million and directly involved local subsistence whalers, professional biologists, environmental activists, 150 journalists, the oil industry, U.S. National Guard, and the U.S. and Soviet federal governments. If we ask why the rescue was pursued at such great lengths, a cynical answer in terms of the self-interest of the participants would be to some extent correct. But to leave it at that would give a very superficial and distorted understanding of the final cause of the rescue. The participation of these groups in the whales' rescue served their interests only by virtue of a deep and widespread concern for the whales' well-being among people generally. The media, for example, cannot play to emotions people do not have: whale rescues boost ratings because people care about whales, especially whales who have become individualized through their special circumstances.

(4) Expiation. James Serpell describes the almost universal presence, in cultures that hunt or slaughter animals, of mechanisms for mediating the guilt that such exploitation engenders. Mechanisms that soothe the consciences of those who harm animals take many forms. Consider the following: many African tribes perform elaborate cleansing and purification ceremonies after killing an animal, others apologize to the slain. Ancient Babylonian priests, as part of the rite of animal sacrifice, would whisper in the slaughtered victim's ear: "This deed was done by all the gods; I did not do it." The Nuer people of the Sudan justify their consumption of cattle blood by claiming that periodic bleeding is beneficial to the animals' health. The Ainu of Japan also claim to benefit the bears they eat by maintaining that bears want to return to the spirit realm from which they came. Western civilization has its own expiatory myths, most outstandingly the biblical fable of divinely granted dominion over animals, and the scientific denial of animal subjectivity (originally expressed as *Cartesian animal automatism,* now more circumspectly maintained as *operational behaviorism*).

All these rituals and myths serve in some way to reduce the guilt feelings of those who harm animals. The general occurrence of guilt-mediating mechanisms around systems of animal exploitation contradicts the notion that humans are naturally indifferent toward animal welfare. People are generally inclined *against* harming animals: otherwise, there would be no need for social mechanisms that make killing somewhat more bearable—the exploitation of animals would be as straightforward as, say, drinking water or breathing air.

Attention to social phenomena such as befriending animals, therapeutic human-animal relationships, animal rescues and the ubiquity of expiatory mechanisms around animal exploitation brings a realization of the depth of the human-animal connection. This realization shifts the question, from Regan's and Singer's "How can we get people to oppose animal exploitation, given that they don't care?" to "How does animal exploitation continue, given that people do care?" The answer I would give to the latter question is that animal exploitation continues with great difficulty. Enormous amounts of social energy are expended to forestall, undermine, and override our sympathies for animals, so that vivisection, animal farming, and hunting can continue.

It is worth examining the mechanisms developed for subverting opposition to animal exploitation — the vast scope of these mechanisms underscores the continual threat human sympathies pose to the animal exploitation industries. Moreover, knowledge of the strategies used to block sympathetic opposition to animal exploitation focuses activism. Rather than constructing justice-based arguments with a view toward charging animal exploiters with inconsistency, we might better resist those corporate and personal manipulations deployed to forestall the expression of our sympathies for animals in animal liberationist politics.

Perhaps the most significant mechanism for forestalling opposition to animal exploitation in our society is reference to supposed divine permission. The idea of a biblical mandate to dominate animals can be applied in defense of any of the animal exploitation industries. Of course, this attempt to pass responsibility to God begs the question of our responsibility for choosing to affirm a nominally anthropocentric religion rather than an explicitly vegetarian religion such as Jainism. Also, Christians or Jews who might attempt to defer responsibility for animal exploitation to God are acting in bad faith, insofar as they are denying their responsibility for choosing to emphasize one biblical passage over another — for instance, Genesis 2:4–25 (in which animals are created after man, to be his helpers) rather than Genesis 1:1–2:3 (in which animals are created before humans, and are recognized as good independently of their relations with humans).

The deferral of responsibility for human exploitation of animals to God is naggingly incomplete without some suggestion as to why God would give "dominion" to humans. Men in the West have filled in this lacuna through the meticulous elaboration of a theory of nonhuman inferiority based on their supposedly deficient rationality. I argued above that if people are determined to maintain a notion of non-

human inferiority, we cannot prove them to be inconsistent. In that sense we cannot prove that humans and other animals are moral equals. It is crucial to recognize the converse, however — namely, that neither can human superiority be objectively proven. Even if one could show that normal adult humans are more rational than nonhuman animals, there is still the insuperable problem of proving that beings of greater rationality have a right to exploit beings of lesser rationality. The doctrine of human supremacy may be consistent, but so is its denial — justice based arguments fail on *both* sides of the animal rights debate.

...

Divine permission and nonhuman inferiority are the most generally applied techniques for forestalling sympathetic opposition to animal exploitation. Each of the major animal exploitation industries — animal farming, hunting, and vivisection — also develops its own particular protective devices. Though these devices differ in their specific content, the various industries tend to follow a common set of strategies, such as: promulgating a cover story, denying the harm done to the animals, denying the animals' subjectivity, and derogating human sympathies for animals. Each of these strategies works through one of two processes: either by blocking some part of our awareness of what is happening so that sympathetic connection with the suffering animals cannot arise, or by providing strong disincentives for acting on any sympathetic feelings we may still have. The extensive network of academics, scientists, marketing experts, and popular writers who set themselves the task of easing the public mind shows that those in the business of exploiting animals have no doubts about the human tendency to sympathize with animals.

Cover stories. Industry cover stories work to disincline us from sympathetic intervention. They all say in effect, "Well, there may be animals being harmed here, but what we're doing is so important, you better let us continue." The cover story for the animal farming industry, of course, is that they are providing food for people. Human consumption of animal flesh is portrayed as an unremarkable given, leading to a consumer "demand" for meat that simply must be met. For example: "[slaughtering] work is honest and necessary in a society which consumes beef" and "the most commonly reported justification for slaughtering . . . was that people eat meat, so that slaughtering must be done by someone." This story obscures the crucial facts that the taste for meat is culturally variable, not innate, that animal flesh is not a nutritional necessity for humans (indeed, the standard North American flesh-based diet is unhealthy), and that the animal farming industries do not passively respond to some mass insistence for meat, but rather actively construct markets for their products in order to accumulate profits.

Animal vivisectionists similarly claim to be providing for significant human needs, in this case, our health needs. This story has successfully preempted sympathetic opposition to their routine confinement, injury, and killing of animals, inasmuch as most people who have awareness or concern about animal vivisection at all tend to oppose only the most egregiously cruel and useless experiments, but support the continuation of all the medical experimentation we have been told is so "necessary." Vivisectionists respond to any challenges to animal experimentation by publicly pronouncing that we would all be dying earlier if not for their work, as in the following public service announcement made by former U.S. Surgeon General C. Everett Koop for the National Association for Biomedical Research:

> When I was born there was no vaccine for polio, no antibiotics, no way to treat diabetes or heart disease. As a result our life expectancy was just 52 years. Today, thanks to animal-based research, that figure is more than 72 years, which means that even those against animal research live to protest at least 20 years longer.

Such fear-mongering, though invaluable for maintaining funding and public support, is scientifically invalid insofar as crediting increased life expectancy to "animal-based research" ignores contributions from public health improvements and from non-vivisectionist research. Koop's analysis also completely passes over the iatrogenic effects of vivisection—the many ways people have been harmed by medicines developed through animal experimentation. We really do not know whether the animal vivisection paradigm has been more beneficial than harmful to society as a whole. Modern medicine, including animal vivisection, is a hierarchically organized male-dominated practice oriented around the control and invasive manipulation of bodies. This practice has developed at the expense of and in opposition to the previously existing woman-centered healing practices that were holistic, noninvasive, and community-based. We simply cannot say what the overall health of our society would be if the enormous resources poured into modern medicine over the last century had instead been used to support women's ways of healing.

Defenders of the hunting system have faced an even greater challenge than vivisectionists and animal farmers. How do you explain the social necessity of men killing animals for the sheer joy of it? So far, they have come up with two cover stories: hunters kill animals for meat, and we need the hunting system to control population levels. Both these stories are exact reversals of reality. In many U.S. states we are told that deer population levels are so high that we must have a hunting system. Apart from sliding over the fact that in the U.S. deer are only 2 percent of the animals killed by hunters (most of the animals killed are doves, rabbits, squirrels, quail, pheasant, and ducks, and it is never claimed that they are overpopulated), this statement disingenuously obscures that deer population levels are high *because* men like to kill bucks. Wildlife managers manipulate flora, exterminate natural predators, regulate hunting permits, and even at times breed and release deer, all in order to maintain herd sizes large enough to insure what they call a "harvestable surplus" of the animals men most like to kill.

Denying the harms.   Representatives of all the animal exploitation industries attempt to deny the harms done to animals. Toward this end there is routine and self-conscious use of euphemisms:

> A recent edition of the British *Meat Trades Journal* recommended a change in terminology designed to "conjure up an image of meat divorced from the act of slaughter." Suggestions included getting rid of the words "butcher" and "slaughterhouse" and replacing them with the American euphemisms "meat plant" and "meat factory."

Similarly, vivisectors do not kill their animal subjects, they "dispatch," "terminate," or "sacrifice" them; while hunters are only "harvesting," "bagging," or "taking" the animals they shoot to death. This manipulation of language becomes manifestly deceitful, as when a fur industry spokeswoman recently spoke of the animals trapped or anally electrocuted in order to sell their fur for profit as being *euthanized,* a word that actually means "killed painlessly to relieve suffering."

Vivisectors routinely hide their injurious work, by restricting tours of research laboratories to the holding facilities, by attempting to block media portrayals of animal vivisection and, notoriously, by the process known as *debarking*:

> Recently I visited the compound where animals are "conditioned" for the ordeal of experimentation at the University of California laboratories at La Jolla. There were well over a hundred dogs, all large: collies, German shepherds, huskies, and others. But there was not a sound from the four rows of crowded kennels: the helpless victims had their vocal chords severed, which rendered them truly voiceless.

If we cannot see them or hear them, we cannot sympathize with them, a point well appreciated by the founder of professional vivisection, Claude Bernard. He remarked that "laboratories are no less valuable to us for sheltering overly impressionable people."

Hunters often attempt to minimize the harm they inflict by suggesting that death by bullet or arrow is less traumatic than the deaths these targeted animals would otherwise experience. This ignores the fact that human hunters specifically target large, healthy animals, exactly those least likely to die from disease, starvation, or nonhuman predation. One hunter, attempting to deflect sympathetic opposition to his sport, goes so far as to call deaths from bowhunting *peaceful:*

> if a bullet or broadhead [arrow] damages a vital organ, hemorrhagic shock will send a deer to a swift, painless, and peaceful demise. If the general public was aware of this knowledge, their minds could be set at ease and a major argument against hunting would fall by the wayside.

The general public should also be aware that for every deer killed and retrieved by a bowhunter, one is hit and wounded but not retrieved.

Especially by the animal farming industry, for whom every person is a potential customer, there is an ongoing effort to deny the harms done to animals.

In recognition of the potential business loss threatened by a growing movement that explicitly advocates vegetarianism based on compassion for animals, meat industry representatives are attempting to frame animal farmers as the true animal welfarists:

> Our research shows that we can prevent long-term erosion of public support for the livestock industry. . . . We've got to do a better job of communicating with consumers, and letting them know that we, not the animals rights groups, are the animal welfare experts.

The usual argument is that farmers have a business interest in maintaining the well-being of their "stock" since sick or unhappy animals do not grow as well or cannot be sold and therefore are not as profitable. In fact, today's factory farming systems (that is, farming systems in which animals are kept confined and immobilized for long periods of time) do turn a profit from animals generally unhealthy and in pain, since economies of scale allow the absorption of the early deaths of a small but not insignificant percentage of the animals. Pharmaceuticals are used to keep animals crowded in noxious conditions growing long enough to turn a profit. Even in the most oppressive animal farming industries, such as egg laying by hens in battery cages, animal agriculturalists attempt to deny the harms to the animals: "Generally we try to provide exactly the environment which is most suitable for the bird." One farmer, who keeps calves tethered for the entirety of their brief lives (so their unexercised flesh has the distinctive veal taste of a newborn), struggles to deny the cruelty:

> Some feel that it's rather cruel to the animals to keep them tied in there, but I point out that they're in a controlled environment, they, uh, the weather is, they never get real hot, or in the winter time it's never zero weather, there's no fly problem. And as a result, really, they've got a pretty good life in there . . . although they are chained.

This description evokes the old halcyon picture of the farming family living in harmony and mutual affection with their animals. Even for traditional, less intensive animal farming, this picture erases the reality that farmers profit from the slaughter and commodification of farmed animals. The image persists, nonetheless, particularly in children's books. Animals, including farmed animals, are a favorite subject of children's books, but farmed animals are never shown being branded, castrated, debeaked, or slaughtered, they are always portrayed as protected friends.

...

Denying animal subjectivity. In the second Genesis creation story, God created the animals as helpers for the lone first man, then brought them to the man, "to see what he would call them; and whatever the man called every living creature, that was its name" (2:19). Today some people call other living creatures "livestock," "game," "pets," "laboratory animals," "meat," and so forth, and in so doing they deny the animals' own subjectivity. Projecting human uses for these animals into their definitional essences forestalls sympathy by blocking our awareness that other animals have interests of their own that are systematically overridden by the animal exploitation industries.

Those who take an active role in exploiting animals—vivisectors, hunters, farmers, purchasers of meat—are particularly likely to apply the notion that the purpose of an animal's life comes from human interests. As one animal vivisector puts it:

> I grew up in the city, but we were very close to a farm community, and my values are farm values. I grew up thinking of animals as *for* something: some were for food, others were pets . . . each type of animal had its purpose. I think of laboratory animals in the same way: they were bred for research; that's what they're for.

It can certainly smooth the exploitation process to heed the counsel of agricultural scientists: "Forget the pig is an animal. Treat him just like a machine in a factory." And "the modern [egg] layer is, after all, only a very efficient converting machine." Animals come to be seen as voids, beings whose inherently empty lives are redeemed only through the imposition of human purposes. A veterinarian giving me a tour of a vivisection facility pointed to a group of beagle puppies in a cage and said, "Beautiful, aren't they? At least this way they have a purpose." One vivisection textbook defines "experimental animal" as "part instrument, part reagent, a complicated and incidentally sentient system." The breeders who supply vivisectors further this view of animals as tools with advertisement headlines such as "Now available in standard and stripped down model" (referring to guinea pigs with and without hair), "Building a Better Beagle," and "Specific Disease Model Available."

Apparently the mere erasure of animal subjectivity is not sufficient to allow us to accept the harms done to animals—in each of the exploitation industries we see a definite construction of the animals as *willing* victims. The day after the 1990 March on Washington for the Animals, I heard a National Public Radio reporter discuss a slaughterhouse tour she had taken to see for herself whether the animal liberationist call for vegetarianism had any merit. She declared that she could see in the terrified animals' eyes that they would willingly go to slaughter if they understood the human purpose being served. This fantasy of animals longing to end up dead on our plates is promulgated through industry advertisements, such as the long-running Charlie the Tuna campaign (in which the fish repeatedly tries to get hooked), and more recently, a Domino's Pizza billboard displaying winged bison stampeding toward the viewer over the caption: "Buffalo Wings—They Come When You Call." Just for kids, the meat industry provides schools with coloring books that show steers grinning all the way to the "meat packing company."

Derogating sympathies for animals. When harms to animals are effectively concealed or animals are convincingly portrayed as tools or willing victims, our sympathies cannot become engaged. But these strategies are not always successful. When people do sympathize with exploited animals, the animal exploitation industries protect themselves by belittlement, intending that such sympathies never be taken seriously as the basis of individual action or public policy. An example of this is the characterization of antihunters as "Bambi-lovers." Many people have been emotionally affected by the movie *Bambi*, and it is true that the movie is biologically inaccurate (deer do not really speak). But the suggestion that opposition to hunting stems solely from exposure to anthropomorphic depictions of animals derides sympathies for targeted animals by implying that they are always irrationally based.

The derogation of sympathies is typically done in gender-specific ways. Women's expressions of sympathetic concern are expected and tolerated, but they are not respected; rather, they are dismissed as female hysteria. Men, on the other hand, are typically not allowed to express such feelings. For example, on one occasion at the annual live pigeon shoot in Hegins, Pennsylvania, a boy, about eight years old or so, was crying at the sight of pigeons being blown out of the air and then having their heads pulled off by "trapper boys." As this boy turned away in tears, his dad grabbed and twisted his head, forcing him to face the shooting, saying "you *will* watch."

In the vivisection industry, founded by men and still male-dominated, compassion for animals has been simultaneously feminized and derogated:

> As a young graduate student, he was running an experiment with rats. The experiment was over, and he was faced with the problem of what to do with the animals. He approached his advisor, who replied, "Sacrifice them." . . . "How?" asked my friend. . . . "Like this," replied the instructor, dashing the head of the rat on the side of the workbench, breaking its neck. . . . My friend, a kind man, was horrified and said so. The professor fixed him in a cold gaze and said, "What's the matter, Smith, are you soft? Maybe you're not cut out to be a psychologist!"

In this environment "softness" is not allowed, so men who would be scientists must establish their hard callousness, and women who would be scientists must be like the men. Susan Sperling tells of her graduate work in the early seventies under the supervision of a "great man" and "famous scientist." Her severe emotional turmoil after dissecting eight guinea pigs led her to conclude that she "would disappoint the famous man."

...

To sum up: justice-based arguments for animal liberation fail. But my own experience and the reports of others lead me to believe that direct responsiveness to need is more central to animal liberationism than concerns about consistency anyway. And contrary to the suppositions of the justice-oriented writers, the capacity to respond to animals is a deep and recurring feature of human life. That is precisely why societies that institutionalize animal exploitation must and do find ways to override and to undercut our sympathetic capacities.

The lesson I draw from this analysis is twofold, part heartening and part sobering. Heartening is the realization that the ethical basis of animal liberation is very simple and generally moving. A straightforward presentation of what the animals are like and what is done to them by hunters, vivisectors, and farmers can stir people, especially if the ideologies that block sympathy are simultaneously debunked.

But sobering is a grasp of the nature of the social forces allied against a true perception of animals, against an understanding of what is done to them, against the possibility of acting from compassion. The substantial power of institutionalized animal exploitation sustains ignorance, promotes fear, rewards cruelty, and punishes kindness. So, though the ethics of animal liberation are inherently appealing, the obstacles placed in the way of radical social change based on sympathy are daunting. This is not to say that those obstacles are insurmountable. Moving away from unsound and irrelevant justice-based arguments, taking instead a caring perspective that expects a human-animal bond, and that challenges any hindrances to this natural, normal, and healthy bond, allows us to continue moving toward a society in which animals have been liberated from human tyranny.

Discussion Questions

1. Are most people aware of how animals are treated? For example, do they know how the animals that they consume were raised, killed, and treated? What do you suppose would happen if they were to become fully aware of how animals are treated? Would they still continue to consume as much meat? Why or why not?

2. Many farmers who raise animals consider themselves to have a relationship of 'care' toward these animals, especially since animals that are well cared for are more valuable when sold. How is this 'care' like or unlike Luke's notion of 'caring for animals'? Is the perspective of farmers who care for animals, but also sell them for slaughter, compatible with the analysis offered by Luke? If so, how? If not, why not?

3. Luke rejects standard defenses of animal liberation. Suppose he is right that we have caring responses to animals. What reasons might be offered to say that these responses are irrelevant? Can the same criticisms that Luke makes of Singer and Regan be made of Luke? Why or why not? Are there convincing reasons why we should disregard our 'care' responses to animals and not care for them?

4. Is it possible to have a relationship with a nonhuman animal? If so, how is the relationship different from each perspective? Do humans have the same relationships to animals that animals have to humans? Explain your answer. Does your answer challenge Luke's theory? Why or why not?

5. Would you ever let a family member suffer in order to care for a nonhuman animal? For example, would you save the life of an animal if doing so harmed a family member? Would you ever let another human, not a family member, suffer harm in order to care for a family pet? If so, when? What does your answer say about the adequacy of Luke's theory?

For Further Reading

Luke's article is anthologized in *Beyond Animal Rights: A Feminist Caring Ethic for the Treatment of Animals,* edited by Josephine Donovan and Carol J. Adams (1996). See also their other anthology, *Animals and Women: Feminist Theoretical Explorations* (1995). Carol Adams is a major feminist advocate of animal rights; see also her *The Sexual Politics of Meat: A Feminist-Vegetarian Critical Theory* (1990) and *Neither Man nor Beast: Feminism and the Defense of Animals* (1994).

Classic philosophical treatments of animal rights include Peter Singer, *Animal Rights* (1977), and Tom Regan, *The Case for Animal Rights* (1983). Regan and Singer have also edited a book together with a number of helpful articles, *Animal Rights and Human Obligations* (1976). More current discussion of animal rights can be found in Eugene C. Hargrove, editor, *The Animal Rights, Environmental Ethics Debate* (1992).

CHAPTER 10

WHAT GIVES THE STATE
ITS AUTHORITY?

Philosophical investigations into the nature of 'justice' are as old as Plato and Aristotle. This chapter, however, focuses on updated, modern investigations into the nature of political authority: the legitimacy of the democratic state and the relationship between political liberty and equality.

Political philosophy asks some basic questions about our political institutions: What legitimizes government authority? What is a right? What does equality mean? Consider this example: What gives the government authority to punish a criminal? If we assume that some individual deserves punishment, then why should the *government* mete out the punishment? Why not a group of neighbors or the victim? Other basic and commonplace functions of the state pose equally basic problems: What gives the state the authority to tax? What is the basis for the state's ability to create laws? Why are these laws binding on citizens?

One of the most influential political theories is **political liberalism.** Political liberals are not called liberals because of their left-leaning political views, but because they take 'liberties' or rights to be the fundamental starting point of all political dialogue. Used in this sense, both the National Rifle Association and the American Civil Liberties Union are politically liberal organizations. The chief attraction of liberalism is its success in providing insightful and definitive answers to many of the basic questions posed by political philosophy.

Political liberalism begins with a description of persons as free, equal, and autonomous. These self-ruling moral agents are initially obligated to no one; they exist in a state of nature, before the creation of a government. But they soon discover that it is in their interest to cooperate with one another in order both to promote common interests, such as trade, as well as to punish criminals who violate their rights to life and property. What is essential to this theory is the fact that there is no government prior to the voluntary and free consent of individuals to create that government to rule over them. Thus the state has no authority that its citizens did not freely grant it, and whatever authority it wields, it does so only with the implicit approval of its citizens. Consider how this view of the state answers some basic philosophical questions: The state has authority to punish criminals because the criminal himself has given that authority to the state, and the state has the authority to pass laws that are binding upon citizens because they themselves have given this authority to the state. Theoretically, then, the state never restricts our liberties without our consent; if it does so, its actions are deemed inappropriate, and we have the right to take proper recourse to protect our fundamental liberties.

But liberty is only one political value; another important political value is equality. The readings in this chapter vary from one another not so much according to their views on liberty, but more because of their views on equality. For **libertarians,** such as Hospers and Locke, equal political liberties are sufficient to guarantee equality: The state has no other role in promoting or guaranteeing equality. **Socialist egalitarians,** on the other hand, while they consider equal liberties necessary for equality, do not regard them as sufficient to guarantee equality. Egalitarian political theories consider it a necessary function of the state to actively promote and secure the equality of its citizens. Is there a way to create a compromise between these two groups? In the final reading, John Rawls offers what some consider a hybrid between socialism and libertarianism. While Rawls' political theory guarantees our liberties and assigns them priority over egalitarian goals, he nonetheless argues that the state's duties to promote egalitarianism may well require a thorough revision of contemporary social institutions.

51   LETTER FROM BIRMINGHAM JAIL
Martin Luther King, Jr.

Philosophical debates over the nature of justice, equality, and liberty can be endless—but as Martin Luther King, Jr. (1929–1968), so effectively demonstrates, the demands of justice cannot wait for the end of debate. Justice delayed, King argues, is justice denied.

In April 1963 King found himself in the Birmingham, Alabama, jail as a result of organizing protests to fight racial segregation. While he was jailed, a letter from a group of Christian and Jewish clergy was published in which they argued that the protest was untimely, ill conceived, and, ultimately, indefensible. As a clergyman himself, King was particularly wounded by this criticism. Availing himself of the time he had in prison, King drafted a response, first in the margins of the newspaper, then on scraps of paper, and finally on pads of paper his lawyers were able to secure for him. The result is both a scathing critique of moderate responses to injustice and a clarion call for justice for all persons here and now.

Reading Questions

1. What are the four steps necessary for nonviolent protest? How did the protests that King organized meet these four steps?
2. Why does King believe we cannot wait for justice from the oppressor?
3. What is the difference between unjust laws and just laws?
4. How does the requirement for a parade permit become unjust?
5. Why is King disappointed with white moderates?
6. Why is King disappointed with the white church?

SOURCE: Reprinted by arrangement with The Heirs to the Estate of Martin Luther King, Jr., c/o Writers House, Inc., as agents for the proprietor. Copyright renewed 1991 by Coretta Scott King.

April 16, 1963

My Dear Fellow Clergymen:

While confined here in the Birmingham city jail, I came across your recent statement calling my present activities "unwise and untimely." Seldom do I pause to answer criticism of my work and ideas. If I sought to answer all the criticisms that cross my desk, my secretaries would have little time for anything other than such correspondence in the course of the day, and I would have no time for constructive work. But since I feel that you are men of genuine good will and that your criticisms are sincerely set forth, I want to try to answer your statement in what I hope will be patient and reasonable terms.

· · ·

You deplore the demonstrations taking place in Birmingham. But your statement, I am sorry to say, fails to express a similar concern for the conditions that brought about the demonstrations. I am sure that none of you would want to rest content with the superficial kind of social analysis that deals merely with effects and does not grapple with underlying causes. It is unfortunate that demonstrations are taking place in Birmingham, but it is even more unfortunate that the city's white power structure left the Negro community with no alternative.

In any nonviolent campaign there are four basic steps: collection of the facts to determine whether injustices exist; negotiation; self-purification; and direct action. We have gone through all these steps in Birmingham. There can be no gainsaying the fact that racial injustice engulfs this community. Birmingham is probably the most thoroughly segregated city in the United States. Its ugly record of brutality is widely known. Negroes have experienced grossly unjust treatment in the courts. There have been more unsolved bombings of Negro homes and churches in Birmingham than in any other city in the nation. These are the hard, brutal facts of the case. On the basis of these conditions, Negro leaders sought to negotiate with the city fathers. But the latter consistently refused to engage in good-faith negotiation.

Then, last September, came the opportunity to talk with leaders of Birmingham's economic community. In the course of the negotiations, certain promises were made by the merchants—for example, to remove the stores' humiliating racial signs. On the basis of these promises, the Reverend Fred Shuttlesworth

and the leaders of the Alabama Christian Movement for Human Rights agreed to a moratorium on all demonstrations. As the weeks and months went by, we realized that we were the victims of a broken promise. A few signs, briefly removed, returned; the others remained.

As in so many past experiences, our hopes had been blasted, and the shadow of deep disappointment settled upon us. We had no alternative except to prepare for direct action, whereby we would present our very bodies as a means of laying our case before the conscience of the local and national community. Mindful of the difficulties involved, we decided to undertake a process of self-purification. We began a series of workshops on nonviolence, and we repeatedly asked ourselves: "Are you able to accept blows without retaliating?" "Are you able to endure the ordeal of jail?" We decided to schedule our direct-action program for the Easter season, realizing that except for Christmas, this is the main shopping period of the year. Knowing that a strong economic-withdrawal program would be the by-product of direct action, we felt that this would be the best time to bring pressure to bear on the merchants for the needed change.

· · ·

One of the basic points in your statement is that the action that I and my associates have taken in Birmingham is untimely. Some have asked: "Why didn't you give the new city administration time to act?" The only answer that I can give to this query is that the new Birmingham administration must be prodded about as much as the outgoing one, before it will act. We are sadly mistaken if we feel that the election of Albert Boutwell as mayor will bring the millennium to Birmingham. While Mr. Boutwell is a much more gentle person than Mr. Connor, they are both segregationists, dedicated to maintenance of the status quo. I have hope that Mr. Boutwell will be reasonable enough to see the futility of massive resistance to desegregation. But he will not see this without pressure from devotees of civil rights. My friends, I must say to you that we have not made a single gain in civil rights without determined legal and nonviolent pressure. Lamentably, it is an historical fact that privileged groups seldom give up their privileges voluntarily. Individuals may see the moral light and voluntarily give up their unjust posture; but, as Reinhold Niebuhr has reminded us, groups tend to be more immoral than individuals.

We know through painful experience that freedom is never voluntarily given by the oppressor; it must be demanded by the oppressed. Frankly, I have yet to engage in a direct-action campaign that was "well timed" in the view of those who have not suffered unduly from the disease of segregation. For years now I have heard the word "Wait!" It rings in the ear of every Negro with piercing familiarity. This "Wait" has almost always meant "Never." We must come to see, with one of our distinguished jurists, that "justice too long delayed is justice denied."

We have waited for more than 340 years for our constitutional and God-given rights. The nations of Asia and Africa are moving with jetlike speed toward gaining political independence, but we still creep at horse-and-buggy pace toward gaining a cup of coffee at a lunch counter. Perhaps it is easy for those who have never felt the stinging darts of segregation to say, "Wait." But when you have seen vicious mobs lynch your mothers and fathers at will and drown your sisters and brothers at whim; when you have seen hate-filled policemen curse, kick, and even kill your black brothers and sisters; when you see the vast majority of your twenty million Negro brothers smothering in an airtight cage of poverty in the midst of an affluent society; when you suddenly find your tongue twisted and your speech stammering as you seek to explain to your six-year-old daughter why she can't go to the public amusement park that has just been advertised on television, and see tears welling up in her eyes when she is told that Funtown is closed to colored children, and see ominous clouds of inferiority beginning to form in her little mental sky, and see her beginning to distort her personality by developing an unconscious bitterness toward white people; when you have to concoct an answer for a five-year-old son who is asking: "Daddy, why do white people treat colored people so mean?"; when you take a cross-country drive and find it necessary to sleep night after night in the uncomfortable corners of your automobile because no motel will accept you; when you are humiliated day in and day out by nagging signs reading "white" and "colored"; when your first name becomes "nigger," your middle name becomes "boy" (however old you are) and your last name becomes "John," and your wife and mother are never given the respected title "Mrs."; when you are harried by day and haunted by night by the fact that you are a Negro, living constantly at tiptoe stance, never quite knowing what to expect next, and are plagued with inner fears and outer resentments; when you are forever fighting a degenerating sense of "nobodiness"—then you will understand why we find it difficult to wait. There comes a time when the cup of endurance runs over, and men are no longer willing to be plunged into the abyss of despair. I hope, sirs, you can understand our legitimate and unavoidable impatience.

You express a great deal of anxiety over our willingness to break laws. This is certainly a legitimate concern. Since we so diligently urge people to obey the Supreme Court's decision of 1954 outlawing segregation in the public schools, at first glance it may seem rather paradoxical for us consciously to break laws. One may well ask: "How can you advocate breaking some laws and obeying others?" The answer lies in the fact that there are two types of laws: just and unjust. I would be the first to advocate obeying just laws. One has not only a legal but a moral responsibility to obey just laws. Conversely, one has a moral responsibility to disobey unjust laws. I would agree with St. Augustine that "an unjust law is no law at all."

Now, what is the difference between the two? How does one determine whether a law is just or unjust? A just law is a man-made code that squares with the moral law or the law of God. An unjust law is a code that is out of harmony with the moral law. To put it in the terms of St. Thomas Aquinas: An unjust law is a human law that is not rooted in eternal law and natural law. Any law that uplifts human personality is just. Any law that degrades human personality is unjust. All segregation statutes are unjust because segregation distorts the soul and damages the personality. It gives the segregator a false sense of superiority and the segregated a false sense of inferiority. Segregation, to use the terminology of the Jewish philosopher Martin Buber, substitutes an "I-it" relationship for an "I-thou" relationship and ends up relegating persons to the status of things. Hence segregation is not only politically, economically and sociologically unsound, it is morally wrong and sinful. Paul Tillich has said that sin is separation. Is not segregation an existential expression of man's tragic separation, his awful estrangement, his terrible sinfulness? Thus it is that I can urge men to obey the 1954 decision of the Supreme Court, for it is morally right; and I can urge them to disobey segregation ordinances, for they are morally wrong.

Let us consider a more concrete example of just and unjust laws. An unjust law is a code that a numerical or power majority group compels a minority group to obey but does not make binding on itself. This is *difference* made legal. By the same token, a just law is a code that a majority compels a minority to follow and that it is willing to follow itself. This is *sameness* made legal.

Let me give another explanation. A law is unjust if it is inflicted on a minority that, as a result of being denied the right to vote, had no part in enacting or devising the law. Who can say that the legislature of Alabama which set up that state's segregation laws was democratically elected? Throughout Alabama all sorts of devious methods are used to prevent Negroes from becoming registered voters, and there are some counties in which, even though Negroes constitute a majority of the population, not a single Negro is registered. Can any law enacted under such circumstances be considered democratically structured?

Sometimes a law is just on its face and unjust in its application. For instance, I have been arrested on a charge of parading without a permit. Now, there is nothing wrong in having an ordinance which requires a permit for a parade. But such an ordinance becomes unjust when it is used to maintain segregation and to deny citizens the First-Amendment privilege of peaceful assembly and protest.

I hope you are able to see the distinction I am trying to point out. In no sense do I advocate evading or defying the law, as would the rabid segregationist. That would lead to anarchy. One who breaks an unjust law must do so openly, lovingly, and with a willingness to accept the penalty. I submit that an individual who breaks a law that conscience tells him is unjust, and who willingly accepts the penalty of imprisonment in order to arouse the conscience of the community over its injustice, is in reality expressing the highest respect for law.

Of course, there is nothing new about this kind of civil disobedience. It was evidenced sublimely in the refusal of Shadrach, Meshach and Abednego to obey the laws of Nebuchadnezzar, on the ground that a higher moral law was a stake. It was practiced superbly by the early Christians, who were willing to face hungry lions and the excruciating pain of chopping blocks rather than submit to certain unjust laws of the Roman Empire. To a degree, academic freedom is a reality today because Socrates practiced civil disobedience. In our own nation, the Boston Tea Party represented a massive act of civil disobedience.

We should never forget that everything Adolf Hitler did in Germany was "legal" and everything the Hungarian freedom fighters did in Hungary was "illegal." It was "illegal" to aid and comfort a Jew in Hitler's Germany. Even so, I am sure that, had I lived in Germany at the time, I would have aided and comforted my Jewish brothers. If today I lived in a Communist country where certain principles dear to the Christian faith are suppressed, I would openly advocate disobeying that country's antireligious laws.

I must make two honest confessions to you, my Christian and Jewish brothers. First, I must confess that over the past few years I have been gravely disappointed with the white moderate. I have almost reached the regrettable conclusion that the Negro's great stumbling block in his stride toward freedom is not the White Citizen's Counciler or the Ku Klux Klanner, but the white moderate, who is more devoted to "order" than to justice; who prefers a negative peace which is the absence of tension to a positive peace which is the presence of justice; who constantly says: "I agree with you in the goal you seek, but I cannot agree with your methods of direct action"; who paternalistically believes he can set the timetable for another man's freedom; who lives by a mythical concept of time and who constantly advises the Negro to wait for a "more convenient season."

Shallow understanding from people of good will is more frustrating than absolute misunderstanding from people of ill will. Lukewarm acceptance is much more bewildering than outright rejection.

I had hoped that the white moderate would understand that law and order exist for the purpose of establishing justice and that when they fail in this purpose they become the dangerously structured dams that block the flow of social progress. I had hoped that the white moderate would understand that the present tension in the South is a necessary phase of the transition from an obnoxious negative peace, in which the Negro passively accepted his unjust plight, to a substantive and positive peace, in which all men will respect the dignity and worth of human personality. Actually, we who engage in nonviolent direct action are not the creators of tension. We merely bring to the surface the hidden tension that is already alive. We bring it out in the open, where it can be seen and dealt with. Like a boil that can never be cured so long as it is covered up but must be opened with all its ugliness to the natural medicines of air and light, injustice must be exposed, with all the tension its exposure creates, to the light of human conscience and the air of national opinion before it can be cured.

In your statement you assert that our actions, even though peaceful, must be condemned because they precipitate violence. But is this a logical assertion? Isn't this like condemning a robbed man because his possession of money precipitated the evil act of robbery? Isn't this like condemning Socrates because his unswerving commitment to truth and his philosophical inquiries precipitated the act by the misguided populace in which they made him drink hemlock? Isn't this like condemning Jesus because his unique God-consciousness and never-ceasing devotion to God's will precipitated the evil act of crucifixion? We must come to see that, as the federal courts have consistently affirmed, it is wrong to urge an individual to cease his efforts to gain his basic constitutional rights because the quest may precipitate violence. Society must protect the robbed and punish the robber.

I had also hoped that the white moderate would reject the myth concerning time in relation to the struggle for freedom. I have just received a letter from a white brother in Texas. He writes: "All Christians know that the colored people will receive equal rights eventually, but it is possible that you are in too great a religious hurry. It has taken Christianity almost two thousand years to accomplish what it has. The teachings of Christ take time to come to earth." Such an attitude stems from a tragic misconception of time, from the strangely irrational notion that there is something in the very flow of time that will inevitably cure all ills. Actually, time itself is neutral; it can be used either destructively or constructively. More and more I feel that the people of ill will have used time much more effectively than have the people of good will. We will have to repent in this generation not merely for the hateful words and actions of the bad people but for the appalling silence of the good people. Human progress never rolls in on wheels of inevitability; it comes through the tireless efforts of men willing to be co-workers with God, and without this hard work, time itself becomes an ally of the forces of social stagnation. We must use time cre-

atively, in the knowledge that the time is always ripe to do right. Now is the time to make real the promise of democracy and transform our pending national elegy into a creative psalm of brotherhood. Now is the time to lift our national policy from the quicksand of racial injustice to the solid rock of human dignity.

You speak of our activity in Birmingham as extreme. At first I was rather disappointed that fellow clergymen would see my nonviolent efforts as those of an extremist. I began thinking about the fact that I stand in the middle of two opposing forces in the Negro community. One is a force of complacency, made up in part of Negroes who, as a result of long years of oppression, are so drained of self-respect and a sense of "somebodiness" that they have adjusted to segregation; and in part of a few middle-class Negroes who, because of a degree of academic and economic security and because in some ways they profit by segregation, have become insensitive to the problems of the masses. The other force is one of bitterness and hatred, and it comes perilously close to advocating violence. It is expressed in the various black nationalist groups that are springing up across the nation, the largest and best-known being Elijah Muhammad's Muslim movement. Nourished by the Negro's frustration over the continued existence of racial discrimination, this movement is made up of people who have lost faith in America, who have absolutely repudiated Christianity, and who have concluded that the white man is an incorrigible "devil."

I have tried to stand between these two forces, saying that we need emulate neither the "do-nothingism" of the complacent nor the hatred and despair of the black nationalist. For there is the more excellent way of love and nonviolent protest. I am grateful to God that, through the influence of the Negro church, the way of nonviolence became an integral part of our struggle.

If this philosophy had not emerged, by now many streets of the South would, I am convinced, be flowing with blood. And I am further convinced that if our white brothers dismiss as "rabble-rousers" and "outside agitators" those of us who employ nonviolent direct action, and if they refuse to support our nonviolent efforts, millions of Negroes will, out of frustration and despair, seek solace and security in black-nationalist ideologies—a development that would inevitably lead to a frightening racial nightmare.

Oppressed people cannot remain oppressed forever. The yearning for freedom eventually manifests itself, and that is what has happened to the American Negro. Something within has reminded him of his birthright of freedom, and something without has reminded him that it can be gained. Consciously or unconsciously, he has been caught up by the *Zeitgeist,* and with his black brothers of Africa and his brown and yellow brothers of Asia, South America and the Caribbean, the United States Negro is moving with a sense of great urgency toward the promised land of racial justice. If one recognizes this vital urge that has engulfed the Negro community, one should readily understand why public demonstrations are taking place. The Negro has many pent-up resentments and latent frustrations, and he must release them. So let him march; let him make prayer pilgrimages to the city hall; let him go on freedom rides—and try to understand why he must do so. If his repressed emotions are not released in nonviolent ways, they will seek expression through violence; this is not a threat but a fact of history. So I have not said to my people: "Get rid of your discontent." Rather, I have tried to say that this normal and healthy discontent can be channeled into the creative outlet of nonviolent direct action. And now this approach is being termed extremist.

But though I was initially disappointed at being categorized as an extremist, as I continued to think about the matter I gradually gained a measure of satisfaction from the label. Was not Jesus an extremist for love: "Love your enemies, bless them that curse you, do good to them that hate you, and pray for them which despitefully use you, and persecute you." Was not Amos am extremist for justice: "Let justice roll down like waters and righteousness like an ever-flowing stream." Was not Paul an extremist for the Christian gospel: "I bear in my body the marks of the Lord Jesus." Was not Martin Luther an extremist: "Here I stand; I cannot do otherwise, so help me God." And John Bunyan: "I will stay in jail to the end of my days before I make a butchery of my conscience." And Abraham Lincoln: "This nation cannot survive half slave and half free." And Thomas Jefferson: "We hold these truths to be self-evident, that all men are created equal . . . " So the question is not whether we will be extremists, but what kind of extremists we will be. Will we be extremists for hate or for love? Will we be extremists for the preservation of injustice or for the extension of justice? In that dramatic scene on Calvary's hill three men were crucified. We must never forget that all three were crucified for the same crime—the crime of extremism. Two were extremists for immorality, and thus fell below their environment. The other, Jesus Christ, was an extremist for love, truth and goodness, and thereby rose above his environment. Perhaps the South, the nation and the world are in dire need of creative extremists.

. . .

Let me take note of my other major disappointment. I have been so greatly disappointed with the white church and its leadership. Of course, there are some notable exceptions. I am not unmindful of the fact that each of you has taken some significant stands on this issue. I commend you, Reverend Stallings, for your Christian stand on this past Sunday, in welcoming Negroes to your worship service on a nonsegregated basis. I commend the Catholic leaders of this state for integrating Spring Hill College several years ago.

But despite these notable exceptions, I must honestly reiterate that I have been disappointed with the church. I do not say this as one of those negative critics who can always find something wrong with the church. I say this as a minister of the gospel, who loves the church; who was nurtured in its bosom; who has been sustained by its spiritual blessings and who will remain true to it as long as the cord of life shall lengthen.

When I was suddenly catapulted into the leadership of the bus protest in Montgomery, Alabama, a few years ago, I felt we would be supported by the white church. I felt that the white ministers, priests and rabbis of the South would be among our strongest allies. Instead, some have been outright opponents, refusing to understand the freedom movement and misrepresenting its leaders; all too many others have been more cautious than courageous and have remained silent behind the anesthetizing security of stained-glass windows.

In spite of my shattered dreams, I came to Birmingham with the hope that the white religious leadership of this community would see the justice of our cause and, with deep moral concern, would serve as the channel through which our just grievances could reach the power structure. I had hoped that each of you would understand. But again I have been disappointed.

I have heard numerous southern religious leaders admonish their worshippers to comply with a desegregation decision because it is the law, but I have longed to hear white ministers declare: "Follow this decree because integration is morally right and because the Negro is your brother." In the midst of blatant injustices inflicted upon the Negro, I have watched white churchmen stand on the sideline and mouth pious irrelevancies and sanctimonious trivialities. In the midst of a mighty struggle to rid our nation of racial and economic injustice, I have heard many ministers say: "Those are social issues, with which the gospel has no real concern." And I have watched many churches commit themselves to a completely otherworldly religion which makes a strange, un-Biblical distinction between body and soul, between the sacred and the secular.

I have traveled the length and breadth of Alabama, Mississippi and all the other southern states. On sweltering summer days and crisp autumn mornings I have looked at the South's beautiful churches with their lofty spires pointing heavenward. I have beheld the impressive outlines of her massive religious-education buildings. Over and over I have found myself asking: "What kind of people worship here? Who is their God? Where were their voices when the lips of Governor Barnett dripped with words of interposition and nullification? Where were they when Governor Wallace gave a clarion call for defiance and hatred? Where were their voices of support when bruised and weary Negro men and women decided to rise from the dark dungeons of complacency to the bright hills of creative protest?

...

Never before have I written so long a letter. I'm afraid it is much too long to take your precious time. I can assure you that it would have been much shorter if I had been writing from a comfortable desk, but what else can one do when he is alone in a narrow jail cell, other than write long letters, think long thoughts and pray long prayers?

If I have said anything in this letter that overstates the truth and indicates an unreasonable impatience, I beg you to forgive me. If I have said anything that understates the truth and indicates my having a patience that allows me to settle for anything less than brotherhood, I beg God to forgive me.

I hope this letter finds you strong in faith. I also hope that circumstances will soon make it possible for me to meet each of you, not as an integrationist or a civil-rights leader but as a fellow clergyman and a Christian brother. Let us all hope that the dark clouds of racial prejudice will soon pass away and the deep fog of misunderstanding will be lifted from our fear-drenched communities, and in some not too distant tomorrow the radiant stars of love and brotherhood will shine over our great nation with all their scintillating beauty.

Yours for the cause of Peace and Brotherhood,
Martin Luther King, Jr.

Discussion Questions

1. Does religious faith help or harm the pursuit of political justice? What does history teach us about the role of religion in promoting social justice?
2. What did King consider to be the difference between a just and an unjust law? Was King right that some laws can be unjust? If so, then how can we know that they are unjust? Should citizens regularly disobey unjust laws? Why or why not?
3. Suppose nonviolent protests had been ineffective. Would King and his followers have been justified in using violent methods? Why or why not? Why did King refuse to use violence to achieve his goals? Do you agree with his position or not?

For Further Reading

This essay was published by King in *Why We Can't Wait* (1964). For more writings by King see *A Testament of Hope: The Essential Writings of Martin Luther King, Jr.*, edited by James

Melvin Washington (1986). For a bibliography of work about King see Sherman E. Pyatt, *Martin Luther King, Jr.: An Annotated Bibliography* (1986). King's "Letter from Birmingham Jail" is the subject of two essays that explore its rhetorical force; see *Martin Luther King, Jr., and the Sermonic Power of Public Discourse*, edited by Carol Calloway-Thomas and John Louis Lucaites (1993). The civil rights movement in Birmingham itself is explored in *Birmingham, Alabama, 1956–1993: The Black Struggle for Civil Rights*, edited by David J. Garrow (1989).

King's nonviolence was strongly influenced by his reading of Mahatma Gandhi. See Gandhi's collected writings in *Satyagraha: Non-Violent Resistance* (1951). For a selection of King's views on Gandhi and nonviolence, see the Washington anthology indicated above.

52 SECOND TREATISE OF GOVERNMENT
John Locke

The English philosopher John Locke (1632–1704) wrote one of several highly influential versions of the **social contract** (Hobbes and Rousseau also wrote important early modern accounts). The social contract is a way of explaining how governments are created and what gives them legitimacy. Social contract theories were developed against the backdrop of widespread cultural acceptance of the divine right of kings to rule, and they sought to provide a new conception of the state that could be defended both rationally and morally.

Locke's account begins by imagining what human society was like before the advent of human government, the so-called state of nature. Unlike other social contract theorists, especially Hobbes, Locke's imagined state of nature was relatively peaceful, being populated by basically peace-loving members of families. But for various reasons, especially to advance commerce, people join together to form a commonwealth. This state is created by its citizens, who endow it with the authority to tax, pass laws, enforce criminal justice, and advance the good of all members of society. Locke's social contract theory, then, is able to provide a philosophical account of all the major features of political government. He explains not only when the government is legitimate but, equally important, when it is not. Locke's account of the social contract shows why the rights of persons limit the authority of the state—since these rights exist logically prior to the state—and clearly defines the purpose of the state and circumscribes its authority. Moreover Locke can explain how all citizens are equal, rooting it in the preexisting equality of all persons in the state of nature.

The following is taken from Locke's *Two Treatises of Government*, which was published anonymously in 1690. During the late 1680s, Locke had been banished to Holland after the ascendancy of James II to the throne of England. Locke returned to England in 1689, only after he became politically active behind the scenes to place William of Orange on the throne the previous year.

Reading Questions

1. Describe the state of nature. What qualities do people have in that state?
2. How does one person come to have power over another in the state of nature?
3. What is the state of war? What is the difference between the state of war and the state of nature?
4. How does Locke define freedom?
5. According to Locke, in what does property consist? How do the examples of gathering acorns or killing deer illustrate Locke's view about who properly owns a thing? How do we come to own land?
6. What puts men out of the state of nature and into the commonwealth?
7. What is the only way we can divest ourselves of our natural liberty?
8. How does Locke defend rule by a majority?
9. In what four ways are the legislative powers of the state restrained?

. . .

CHAP. II
OF THE STATE OF NATURE

4. To understand political power right, and derive it from its original, we must consider, what state all men are naturally in, and that is, a state of perfect freedom to order their actions, and dispose of their possessions and persons, as they think fit, within the bounds of the law of nature, without asking leave, or depending upon the will of any other man.

A *state* also of *equality,* wherein all the power and jurisdiction is reciprocal, no one having more than another; there being nothing more evident, than that creatures of the same species and rank, promiscuously born to all the same advantages of nature, and the use of the same faculties, should also be equal one amongst another without subordination or subjection, unless the lord and master of them all should, by any manifest declaration of his will, set one above another, and confer on him, by an evident and clear appointment, an undoubted right to dominion and sovereignty.

. . .

6. But though this be a *state of liberty,* yet *it is not a state of license:* though man in that state have an uncontrollable liberty to dispose of his person or possessions, yet he has not liberty to destroy himself, or so much as any creature in his possession, but where some nobler use than its bare preservation calls for it. The *state of nature* has a law of nature to govern it, which obliges every one: and reason, which is that law, teaches all mankind, who will but consult it, that being all *equal and independent,* no one ought to harm another in his life, health, liberty, or possessions: for men being all the workmanship of one omnipotent, and infinitely wise maker; all the servants of one sovereign master, sent into the world by his order, and about his business; they are his property, whose workmanship they are, made to last during his, not one another's pleasure: and being furnished with like faculties, sharing all in one community of nature, there cannot be supposed any such *subordination* among us, that may authorize us to destroy one another, as if we were made for one another's uses, as the inferior ranks of creatures are for ours. Every one, as he is *bound to preserve himself,* and not to quit his station willfully, so by the like reason, when his own preservation comes not in competition, ought he, as much as he can, *to preserve the rest of mankind,* and may not, unless it be to do justice on an offender, take away, or impair the life, or what tends to the preservation of the life, the liberty, health, limb, or goods of another.

7. And that all men may be restrained from invading others rights, and from doing hurt to one another, and the law of nature be observed, which willeth the peace and *preservation of all mankind,* the *execution* of the law of nature is, in that state, put into every man's hands, whereby every one has a right to punish the transgressors of that law to such a degree, as may hinder its violation: for the *law of nature* would, as all other laws that concern men in this world, be in vain, if there were no body that in the state of nature had a *power to execute* that law, and

thereby preserve the innocent and restrain offenders. And if any one in the state of nature may punish another for any evil he has done, every one may do so: for in that *state of perfect equality,* where naturally there is no superiority or jurisdiction of one over another, what any may do in prosecution of that law, every one must needs have a right to do.

8. And thus, in the state of nature, *one man comes by a power over another;* but yet no absolute or arbitrary power, to use a criminal, when he has got him in his hands, according to the passionate heats, or boundless extravagancy of his own will; but only to retribute to him, so far as calm reason and conscience dictate, what is proportionate to his transgression, which is so much as may serve for *reparation* and *restraint:* for these two are the only reasons, why one man may lawfully do harm to another, which is that we call *punishment.* In transgressing the law of nature, the offender declares himself to live by another rule than that of reason and common equity, which is that measure God has set to the actions of men, for their mutual security; and so he becomes dangerous to mankind, the tie, which is to secure them from injury and violence, being slighted and broken by him. Which being a trespass against the whole species, and the peace and safety of it, provided for by the law of nature, every man upon this score, by the right he hath to preserve mankind in general, may restrain, or where it is necessary, destroy things noxious to them, and so may bring such evil on any one, who hath transgressed that law, as may make him repent the doing of it, and thereby deter him, and by his example others, from doing the like mischief. And in the case, and upon this ground, *every man hath a right to punish the offender, and be executioner of the law of nature.*

...

CHAP. III
OF THE STATE OF WAR

16. The *state of war* is a state of *enmity* and *destruction:* and therefore declaring by word or action, not a passionate and hasty, but a sedate settled design upon another man's life, *puts him in a state of war* with him against whom he has declared such an intention, and so has exposed his life to the other's power to be taken away by him, or any one that joins with him in his defense, and espouses his quarrel; it being reasonable and just, I should have a right to destroy that which threatens me with destruction: for, *by the fundamental law of nature, man being to be preserved* as much as possible, when all cannot be preserved, the safety of the innocent is to be preferred: and one may destroy a man who makes war upon him, or has discovered an enmity to his being, for the same reason that he may kill a *wolf* or a *lion;* because such men are not under the ties of the commonlaw of reason, have no other rule, but that of force and violence, and so may be treated as beasts of prey, those dangerous and noxious creatures, that will be sure to destroy him whenever he falls into their power.

17. And hence it is, that he who attempts to get another man into his absolute power, does thereby *put himself into a state of war* with him; it being to be understood as a declaration of a design upon his life: for I have reason to conclude, that he who would get me into his power without my consent, would use me as he pleased when he had got me there, and destroy me too when he had a fancy to it; for no body can desire to *have me in his absolute power,* unless it be to compel me by force to that which is against the right of my freedom, i.e., make me a slave. To be free from such force is the only security of my preservation; and reason bids me look on him, as an enemy to my preservation, who would take away that *freedom* which is the fence to it; so that he who makes an *attempt to enslave* me, thereby puts himself into a state of war with me. He that, in the state of nature, *would take away the freedom* that belongs to any one in that state, must necessarily be supposed to have a design to take away every thing else, that *freedom* being the foundation of all the rest; as he that, in the state of society, would take away the *freedom* belonging to those of that society or common-wealth, must be supposed to design to take away from them every thing else, and so be looked on as *in a state of war.*

18. This makes it lawful for a man to *kill a thief,* who has not in the least hurt him, nor declared any design upon his life, any farther than, by the use of force, so to get him in his power, as to take away his money, or what he pleases, from him; because using force, where he has no right, to get me into his power, let his pretense be what it will, I have no reason to

suppose, that he, who would *take away my liberty*, would not, when he had me in his power, take away every thing else. And therefore it is lawful for me to treat him as one who has *put himself into a state of war* with me, i.e., kill him if I can; for to that hazard does he justly expose himself, whoever introduces a state of war, and is aggressor in it.

19. And here we have the plain *difference between the state of nature and the state of war*, which however some men have confounded, are as far distant, as a state of peace, good will, mutual assistance and preservation, and a state of enmity, malice, violence and mutual destruction, are one from another. Men living together according to reason, without a common superior on earth, with authority to judge between them, is *properly the state of nature.* But force, or a declared design of force, upon the person of another, where there is no common superior on earth to appeal to for relief, *is the state of war:* and it is the want of such an appeal gives a man the right of war even against an *aggressor,* tho' he be in society and a fellow subject. Thus a *thief,* whom I cannot harm, but by appeal to the law, for having stolen all that I am worth, I may kill, when he sets on me to rob me but of my horse or coat; because the law, which was made for my preservation, where it cannot interpose to secure my life from present force, which, if lost, is capable of no reparation, permits me my own defense, and the right of war, a liberty to kill the aggressor, because the aggressor allows not time to appeal to our common judge, nor the decision of the law, for remedy in a case where the mischief may be irreparable. Want of a common judge with authority, puts all men in a state of nature: force without right, upon a man's person, makes a state of war, both where there is, and is not, a common judge.

...

21. To avoid this *state of war* (wherein there is no appeal but to heaven, and wherein every the least difference is apt to end, where there is no authority to decide between the contenders) is one great reason of men's putting themselves into society, and quitting the state of nature: for where there is an authority, a power on earth, from which relief can be had by *appeal,* there the continuance of the *state of war* is excluded, and the controversy is decided by that power. . . .

...

CHAP. V
OF PROPERTY

...

26. God, who hath given the world to men in common, hath also given them reason to make use of it to the best advantage of life, and convenience. The earth, and all that is therein, is given to men for the support and comfort of their being. And tho' all the fruits it naturally produces, and beasts it feeds, belong to mankind in common, as they are produced by the spontaneous hand of nature; and no body has originally a private dominion, exclusive of the rest of mankind, in any of them, as they are thus in their natural state: yet being given for the use of men, there must of necessity be *a means to appropriate* them some way or other, before they can be of any use, or at all beneficial to any particular man. The fruit, or venison, which nourishes the wild *Indian,* who knows no inclosure, and is still a tenant in common, must be his, and so his, i.e., a part of him, that another can no longer have any right to it, before it can do him any good for the support of his life.

27. Though the earth, and all inferior creatures, be common to all men, yet every man has a *property* in his own *person:* this no body has any right to but himself. The *labor* of his body, and the *work* of his hands, we may say, are properly his. Whatsoever then he removes out of the state that nature hath provided, and left it in, he hath mixed his *labor* with, and joined to it something that is his own, and thereby makes it his *property.* It being by him removed from the common state nature hath placed it in, it hath by this *labor* something annexed to it, that excludes the common right of other men: for this *labor* being the unquestionable property of the laborer, no man but he can have a right to what that is once joined to, at least where there is enough, and as good, left in common for others.

28. He that is nourished by the acorns he picked up under an oak, or the apples he gathered from the trees in the wood, has certainly appropriated them to himself. No body can deny but the nourishment is his. I ask then, when did they begin to be his? when he digested? or when he eat? or when he boiled? or when he brought them home? or when he picked them up? and it is plain, if the first gathering made

them not his, nothing else could. That *labor* put a distinction between them and common: that added something to them more than nature, the common mother of all, had done; and so they became his private right. And will any one say, he had no right to those acorns or apples, he thus appropriated, because he had not the consent of all mankind to make them his? Was it a robbery thus to assume to himself what belonged to all in common? If such a consent as that was necessary, man had starved, notwithstanding the plenty God had given him. We see in *commons,* which remain so by compact, that it is the taking any part of what is common, and removing it out of the state nature leaves it in, which *begins the property:* without which the common is of no use. And the taking of this or that part, does not depend on the express consent of all the commoners. Thus the grass my horse has bit; the turfs my servant has cut; and the ore I have digged in any place, where I have a right to them in common with others, become my *property,* without the assignation or consent of any body. The *labor* that was mine, removing them out of that common state they were in, hath *fixed* my *property* in them.

...

30. Thus this Law of reason makes the Deer, that *Indian's* who hath killed it; 'tis allowed to be his goods who hath bestowed his labor upon it, though before, it was the common right of every one. And amongst those who are counted the Civilized part of Mankind, who have made and multiplied positive Laws to determine Property, this original Law of Nature for the *beginning of Property,* in what was before common, still takes place; and by virtue thereof, what Fish any one catches in the Ocean, that great and still remaining Common of Mankind; or what Ambergriese any one takes up here, is *by* the *Labor* that removes it out of that common state Nature left it in, *made* his *Property* who takes that pains about it. And even amongst us the Hare that any one is Hunting, is thought his who pursues her during the Chase. For being a Beast that is still looked upon as common, and no Man's private Possession; whoever has imploy'd so much *labor* about any of that kind, as to find and pursue her, has thereby removed her from the state of Nature, wherein she was common, and hath *begun a Property.*

31. It will perhaps be objected to this, That if gathering the Acorns, or other Fruits of the Earth, etc. makes a right to them, then any one may *ingross* as much as he will. To which I Answer, Not so. The same Law of Nature, that does by this means give us Property, does also *bound* that *Property* too. *God has given us all things richly,* 1 Tim. vi. 17. is the Voice of Reason confirmed by Inspiration. But how far has he given it us? *To enjoy.* As much as any one can make use of to any advantage of life before it spoils; so much he may by his labor fix a Property in. Whatever is beyond this, is more than his share, and belongs to others. Nothing was made by God for man to spoil or destroy. And thus, considering the plenty of natural provisions there was a long time in the world, and the few spenders; and to how small a part of that provision the industry of one man could extend itself, and ingross it to the prejudice of others; especially keeping within the *bounds,* set by reason, of what might serve for his *use;* there could be then little room for quarrels or contentions about property so established.

...

87. Man being born, as has been proved, with a title to perfect freedom, and an uncontrolled enjoyment of all the rights and privileges of the law of nature, equally with any other man, or number of men in the world, hath by nature a power, not only to preserve his property, that is, his life, liberty and estate, against the injuries and attempts of other men; but to judge of, and punish the breaches of that law in others, as he is persuaded the offense deserves, even with death itself, in crimes where the heinousness of the fact, in his opinion, requires it. But because no *political society* can be, nor subsist, without having in itself the power to preserve the property, and in order thereunto, punish the offenses of all those of that society; there, and there only is *political society,* where every one of the members hath quitted this natural power, resigned it up into the hands of the community in all cases that exclude him not from appealing for protection to the law established by it. And thus all private judgment of every particular member being excluded, the community comes to be umpire, by settled standing rules, indifferent, and the same to all parties; and by men having authority from the

community, for the execution of those rules, decides all the differences that may happen between any members of that society concerning any matter of right; and punishes those offenses which any member hath committed against the society, with such penalties as the law has established: whereby it is easy to discern, who are, and who are not, in *political society* together. Those who are united into one body, and have a common established law and judicature to appeal to, with authority to decide controversies between them, and punish offenders, are in *civil society* one with another: but those who have no such common appeal, I mean on earth, are still in the state of nature, each being, where there is no other, judge for himself, and executioner; which is, as I have before showed it, the perfect *state of nature.*

88. And thus the commonwealth comes by a power to set down what punishment shall belong to the several transgressions which they think worthy of it, committed amongst the members of that society, (which is the *power of making laws*) as well as it has the power to punish any injury done unto any of its members, by any one that is not of it, (which is the *power of war and peace;*) and all this for the preservation of the property of all the members of that society, as far as is possible. But though every man who has entered into civil society, and is become a member of any commonwealth, has thereby quitted his power to punish offenses, against the law of *nature,* in prosecution of his own private judgment, yet with the judgment of offenses, which he has given up to the legislative in all cases, where he can appeal to the magistrate, he has given a right to the commonwealth to employ his force, for the execution of the judgments of the commonwealth, whenever he shall be called to it; which indeed are his own judgments, they being made by himself, or his representative. And herein we have the original of the *legislative* and *executive power* of civil society, which is to judge by standing laws, how far offenses are to be punished, when committed within the commonwealth; and also to determine, by occasional judgments founded on the present circumstances of the fact, how far injuries from without are to be vindicated; and in both these to employ all the force of all the members, when there shall be need.

...

CHAP. VIII
OF THE BEGINNING OF POLITICAL SOCIETIES

95. Men being, as has been said, by nature, all free, equal, and independent, no one can be put out of this estate, and subjected to the political power of another, without his own consent. The only way whereby any one divests himself of his natural liberty, and puts on the *bonds of civil society,* is by agreeing with other men to join and unite into a community for their comfortable, safe, and peaceable living one amongst another, in a secure enjoyment of their properties, and a greater security against any, that are not of it. This any number of men may do, because it injures not the freedom of the rest; they are left as they were in the liberty of the state of nature. When any number of men have so *consented to make one community or government,* they are thereby presently incorporated, and make *one body politic,* wherein the *majority* have a right to act and conclude the rest.

96. For when any number of men have, by the consent of every individual, made a *community,* they have thereby made that *community* one body, with a power to act as one body, which is only by the will and determination of the *majority:* for that which acts any community, being only the consent of the individuals of it, and it being necessary to that which is one body to move one way; it is necessary the body should move that way whither the greater force carries it, which is the *consent of the majority:* or else it is impossible it should act or continue one body, *one community,* which the consent of every individual that united into it, agreed that it should; and so every one is bound by that consent to be concluded by the *majority.* And therefore we see, that in assemblies, empowered to act by positive laws, where no number is set by that positive law which empowers them, the *act of the majority* passes for the act of the whole, and of course determines as having, by the law of nature and reason, the power of the whole.

...

CHAP. XI
OF THE EXTENT OF THE LEGISLATIVE POWER

134. The great end of men's entering into society, being the enjoyment of their properties in peace and safety, and the great instrument and means of that

being the laws established in that society; the *first and fundamental positive law* of all commonwealths *is the establishing of the legislative* power; as the *first and fundamental natural law,* which is to govern even the legislative itself, *is the preservation of the society,* and (as far as will consist with the public good) of every person in it. This *legislative* is not only *the supreme power* of the commonwealth, but sacred and unalterable in the hands where the community have once placed it; nor can any edict of any body else, in what form soever conceived, or by what power soever backed, have the force and obligation of a *law,* which has not its *sanction from* that *legislative* which the public has chosen and appointed: for without this the law could not have that, which is absolutely necessary to its being a *law—the consent of the society,* over whom no body can have a power to make laws, but by their own consent, and by authority received from them; and therefore all the *obedience,* which by the most solemn ties any one can be obliged *to* pay, ultimately terminates in this *supreme power,* and is directed by those laws which it enacts: nor can any oaths to any foreign power whatsoever, or any domestic subordinate power, discharge any member of the society from his *obedience to the legislative,* acting pursuant to their trust; nor oblige him to any obedience contrary to the laws so enacted, or farther than they do allow; it being ridiculous to imagine one can be tied ultimately to *obey* any *power* in the society, which is not the *supreme.*

135. Though the *legislative,* whether placed in one or more, whether it be always in being, or only by intervals, though it be the *supreme* power in every commonwealth; yet,

First, It is *not,* nor can possibly be absolutely *arbitrary* over the lives and fortunes of the people: for it being but the joint power of every member of the society given up to that person, or assembly, which is legislator; it can be no more than those persons had in a state of nature before they entered into society, and gave up to the community: for no body can transfer to another more power than he has in himself; and no body has an absolute arbitrary power over himself, or over any other, to destroy his own life, or take away the life or property of another. A man, as has been proved, cannot subject himself to the arbitrary power of another; and having in the

state of nature no arbitrary power over the life, liberty, or possession of another, but only so much as the law of nature gave him for the preservation of himself, and the rest of mankind; this is all he doth, or can give up to the commonwealth, and by it to the *legislative power,* so that the legislative can have no more than this. Their power, in the utmost bounds of it, *is limited to the public good* of the society. It is a power, that hath no other end but preservation, and therefore can never have a right to destroy, enslave, or designedly to impoverish the subjects. The obligations of the law of nature cease not in society, but only in many cases are drawn closer, and have by human laws known penalties annexed to them, to enforce their observation. Thus the law of nature stands as an eternal rule to all men, *legislators* as well as others. The *rules* that they make for other men's actions must, as well as their own and other men's actions, be conformable to the law of nature, i.e., to the will of God, of which that is a declaration, and the *fundamental law of nature being the preservation of mankind,* no human sanction can be good, or valid against it.

136. *Secondly,* The *legislative,* or supreme authority, cannot assume to its self a power to rule by extemporary arbitrary decrees, but *is bound to dispense justice,* and decide the rights of the subject *by promulgated standing laws, and known authorized judges:* for the law of nature being unwritten, and so no where to be found but in the minds of men, they who through passion or interest shall miscite, or misapply it, cannot so easily be convinced of their mistake where there is no established judge: and so it serves not, as it ought, to determine the rights, and fence the properties of those that live under it, especially where every one is judge, interpreter, and executioner of it too, and that in his own case: and he that has right on his side, having ordinarily but his own single strength, hath not force enough to defend himself from injuries, or to punish delinquents. To avoid these inconveniences, which disorder men's properties in the state of nature, men unite into societies, that they may have the united strength of the whole society to secure and defend their properties, and may have *standing rules* to bound it, by which every one may know what is his. To this end it is that men give up all their natural power to the society which they enter into, and the community put the legislative

power into such hands as they think fit, with this trust, that they shall be governed by *declared laws,* or else their peace, quiet, and property will still be at the same uncertainty, as it was in the state of nature.

...

138. *Thirdly,* The *supreme power cannot take* from any man any part of his *property* without his own consent: for the preservation of property being the end of government, and that for which men enter into society, it necessarily supposes and requires, that the people should *have property,* without which they must be supposed to lose that, by entering into society, which was the end for which they entered into it; too gross an absurdity for any man to own. *Men therefore in society having property,* they have such a right to the goods, which by the law of the community are theirs, that no body hath a right to take their substance or any part of it from them, without their own consent: without this they have no *property* at all; for I have truly no *property* in that, which another can by right take from me, when he pleases, against my consent. Hence it is a mistake to think, that the *supreme or legislative power* of any commonwealth, can do what it will, and dispose of the estates of the subject *arbitrarily,* or take any part of them at pleasure. This is not much to be feared in governments where the *legislative* consists, wholly or in part, in assemblies which are variable, whose members, upon the dissolution of the assembly, are subjects under the common laws of their country, equally with the rest. But in governments, where the *legislative* is in one lasting assembly always in being, or in one man, as in absolute monarchies, there is danger still, that they will think themselves to have a distinct interest from the rest of the community; and so will be apt to increase their own riches and power, by taking what they think fit from the people: for a man's *property* is not at all secure, tho' there be good and equitable laws to set the bounds of it between him and his fellow subjects, if he who commands those subjects have power to take from any private man, what part he pleases of his *property,* and use and dispose of it as he thinks good.

141. *Fourthly,* The *legislative cannot transfer the power of making laws* to any other hands: for it being but a delegated power from the people, they who have it cannot pass it over to others. The people alone can appoint the form of the commonwealth, which is by constituting the legislative, and appointing in whose hands that shall be. And when the people have said, We will submit to rules, and be governed by *laws* made by such men, and in such forms, no body else can say other men shall make *laws* for them; nor can the people be bound by any *laws,* but such as are enacted by those whom they have chosen, and authorized to make *laws* for them. The power of the *legislative,* being derived from the people by a positive voluntary grant and institution, can be no other than what that positive grant conveyed, which being only to make *laws,* and not to make *legislators,* the *legislative* can have no power to transfer their authority of making laws, and place it in other hands. . . .

Discussion Questions

1. Locke apparently regarded the Indians of America as living in the state of nature. Is this consistent with Locke's theory about the state of nature? In what ways might Locke's characterization of North American Indians be problematic? Does this pose any critical problems for Locke's theory?

2. Why does Locke believe that a commonwealth must be run by majority rule? Does majority rule pose any problems for Locke? Do the four restrictions Locke places on the extent of legislative powers ensure that majority rule will not be misused? Why or why not?

3. In Locke's description of the state of nature, untilled property was readily available. This meant that any person could claim property and make a living by working the land. Obviously, such possibilities are no longer available. Does this matter to Locke's theory? Are there other 'bootstrap' economic opportunities available? Should the change in available property and economic opportunities change Locke's theory in any way? Why or why not?

4. Locke's political philosophy influenced the shaping of the U.S. Constitution. What particular features of Locke's political theory are evident in the U.S. Constitution? What features are not?

For Further Reading

For an introduction to the life and thought of Locke, see Roger S. Woolhouse, *Locke* (1983), and John W. Yolton, *Locke, An Introduction* (1985). The entry on Locke in *The Encyclopedia of Philosophy* (Macmillan, 1964) is also helpful. Roland Hall and Roger Woolhouse have compiled a bibliography of scholarly investigations of Locke; see *80 Years of Locke Scholarship* (1983).

Besides Locke's, there are many other versions of the social contract, including Kant's "The Contractual Basis for a Just Society," which can be found in *Kant's Political Writings,* edited by H. Nisbet (1970); Thomas Hobbes, *Leviathan;* and various works by Jean-Jacques Rousseau. Modern versions of the social contract include John Rawls, *A Theory of Justice* (1971); Ronald Dworkin, *Taking Rights Seriously* (1977); and David Gauthier, *Morals by Agreement* (1986).

53 ON LIBERTY
John Stuart Mill

John Stuart Mill (1806–1873) was one of the most important progressive voices in nineteenth-century England and the first prominent philosopher to advocate for equal rights for women. He combined a thorough commitment to empiricism with a basic commitment to individual liberty and freedom. This selection is from one of Mill's most famous essays, *On Liberty.* Here Mill gives his famous formulation of the **Harm Principle,** a basic principle of human government. The Harm Principle asserts that the only time it is legitimate to restrict the liberty of a citizen is to prevent that citizen from harming another or the state. While Mill regarded the Harm Principle as nothing genuinely new, it was important that the principle be publicly acknowledged and philosophically defended. Contemporary threats to liberty came not so much from tyrant kings and rulers, but from fellow citizens who used the powers of popular opinion and religion to constrain personal liberties.

One of the most appealing features of Mill's Harm Principle is its apparent simplicity: It draws a clear line between private behavior and public authority. The state's ability to interfere in personal lives is sharply circumscribed by a clear boundary—no public intervention in the life of an individual citizen is legitimate unless that person has harmed another.

The Harm Principle is often appealed to by various groups in order to bolster a claim to individual rights, but Mill himself had a sophisticated and complex notion of individual rights. He was careful not to characterize the Harm Principle in terms of what he called "Abstract Right." As an empiricist, Mill regarded natural rights as "nonsense on stilts," to use

Jeremy Bentham's phrase. How then can the Harm Principle be defended? Only by the testimony of experience: We know the Harm Principle is true because it promotes the greatest amount of happiness. If so, then the Harm Principle can be grounded in Mill's utilitarian moral theory and its appeal to the 'testimony of experience' (see Chapter 8, Reading 43).

Reading Questions

1. How was liberty originally conceived? In what two ways did it limit the powers of a ruler?
2. Does Mill believe that self-government actually existed? Do the people actually rule over themselves?
3. What is the tyranny of the majority? In what ways besides using political means does the majority tyrannize society?
4. What reasons does Mill believe most people have for their acceptance of rules and principles? Are these reasons adequate?
5. How did Mill characterize the current state of England when he wrote this essay? Is there a general principle recognizing personal liberty?
6. What are the two versions of the Harm Principle? What do they prevent society and the government from doing?
7. Does Mill believe that the general tendency of people was in accordance with the Harm Principle? Why or why not?
8. Do religious communities act in accordance with Mill's principle? Do they seek to interfere with individual liberty?

The subject of this Essay is not the so-called Liberty of the Will, so unfortunately opposed to the misnamed doctrine of Philosophical Necessity; but Civil, or Social Liberty: the nature and limits of the power which can be legitimately exercised by society over the individual. A question seldom stated, and hardly ever discussed, in general terms, but which profoundly influences the practical controversies of the age by its latent presence, and is likely soon to make itself recognized as the vital question of the future. It is so far from being new, that, in a certain sense, it has divided man-kind, almost from the remotest ages; but in the stage of progress into which the more civilized portions of the species have now entered, it presents itself under new conditions, and requires a different and more fundamental treatment.

The struggle between Liberty and Authority is the most conspicuous feature in the portions of history with which we are earliest familiar, particularly in that of Greece, Rome, and England. But in old times this contest was between subjects, or some classes of subjects, and the Government. By liberty, was meant protection against the tyranny of the political rulers.

The rulers were conceived (except in some of the popular governments of Greece) as in a necessarily antagonistic position to the people they ruled. They consisted of a governing One, or a governing tribe or caste, who derived their authority from inheritance or conquest, who, at all events, did not hold it at the pleasure of the governed, and whose supremacy men did not venture, perhaps did not desire, to contest, whatever precautions might be taken against its oppressive exercise. Their power was regarded as necessary, but also as highly dangerous; as a weapon which they would attempt to use against their subjects, no less than against external enemies. To prevent the weaker members of the community from being preyed upon by innumerable vultures, it was needful that there should be an animal of prey stronger than the rest, commissioned to keep them down. But as the king of the vultures would be no less bent upon preying on the flock than any of the minor harpies, it was indispensable to be in a perpetual attitude of defense against his beak and claws. The aim, therefore, of patriots was to set limits to the power which the ruler should be suffered to exercise over the community; and this limitation was what they meant by liberty. It was attempted in two ways. First, by obtaining a recognition of certain immunities, called political liberties or rights, which it was to be regarded as a breach of duty in the ruler to infringe, and which if he did infringe, specific resistance, or general rebellion, was held to be justifiable. A second, and generally a later expedient, was the establishment of constitutional checks, by which the consent of the community, or of a body of some sort, supposed to represent its interests, was made a necessary condition to some of the more important acts of the governing power. To the first of these modes of limitation, the ruling power, in most European countries, was compelled, more or less, to submit. It was not so with the second; and, to attain this, or when already in some degree possessed, to attain it more completely, became everywhere the principal object of the lovers of liberty. And so long as mankind were content to combat one enemy by another, and to be ruled by a master, on condition of being guaranteed more or less efficaciously against his tyranny, they did not carry their aspirations beyond this point.

A time, however, came, in the progress of human affairs, when men ceased to think it a necessity of nature that their governors should be an independent power, opposed in interest to themselves. It appeared to them much better that the various magistrates of the State should be their tenants or delegates, revocable at their pleasure. In that way alone, it seemed, could they have complete security that the powers of government would never be abused to their disadvantage. By degrees this new demand for elective and temporary rulers became the prominent object of the exertions of the popular party, wherever any such party existed; and superseded, to a considerable extent, the previous efforts to limit the power of rulers. As the struggle proceeded for making the ruling power emanate from the periodical choice of the ruled, some persons began to think that too much importance had been attached to the limitation of the power itself. *That* (it might seem) was a resource against rulers whose interests were habitually opposed to those of the people. What was now wanted was, that the rulers should be identified with the people; that their interest and will should be the interest and will of the nation. The nation did not need to be protected against its own will. There was no fear of its

tyrannizing over itself. Let the rulers be effectually responsible to it, promptly removable by it, and it could afford to trust them with power of which it could itself dictate the use to be made. Their power was but the nation's own power, concentrated, and in a form convenient for exercise. This mode of thought, or rather perhaps of feeling, was common among the last generation of European liberalism, in the Continental section of which it still apparently predominates. Those who admit any limit to what a government may do, except in the case of such governments as they think ought not to exist, stand out as brilliant exceptions among the political thinkers of the Continent. A similar tone of sentiment might by this time have been prevalent in our own country, if the circumstances which for a time encouraged it, had continued unaltered.

But, in political and philosophical theories, as well as in persons, success discloses faults and infirmities which failure might have concealed from observation. The notion, that the people have no need to limit their power over themselves, might seem axiomatic, when popular government was a thing only dreamed about, or read of as having existed at some distant period of the past. Neither was that notion necessarily disturbed by such temporary aberrations as those of the French Revolution, the worst of which were the work of a usurping few, and which, in any case, belonged, not to the permanent working of popular institutions, but to a sudden and convulsive outbreak against monarchical and aristocratic despotism. In time, however, a democratic republic came to occupy a large portion of the earth's surface, and made itself felt as one of the most powerful members of the community of nations; and elective and responsible government became subject to the observations and criticism which wait upon a great existing fact. It was now perceived that such phrases as "self-government," and "the power of the people over themselves," do not express the true state of the case. The "people" who exercise the power are not always the same people with those over whom it is exercised; and the "self-government" spoken of is not the government of each by himself, but of each by all the rest. The will of the people, moreover, practically means the will of the most numerous or the most active *part* of the people; the majority, or those who succeed in making themselves accepted as the majority; the people, consequently *may* desire to oppress a part of their number; and precautions are as much needed against this as against any other abuse of power. The limitation, therefore, of the power of government over individuals loses none of its importance when the holders of power are regularly accountable to the community, that is, to the strongest party therein. This view of things, recommending itself equally to the intelligence of thinkers and to the inclination of those important classes in European society to whose real or supposed interests democracy is adverse, has had no difficulty in establishing itself; and in political speculations "the tyranny of the majority" is now generally included among the evils against which society requires to be on its guard.

Like other tyrannies, the tyranny of the majority was at first, and is still vulgarly, held in dread, chiefly as operating through the acts of the public authorities. But reflecting persons perceived that when society is itself the tyrant—society collectively over the separate individuals who compose it—its means of tyrannizing are not restricted to the acts which it may do by the hands of its political functionaries. Society can and does execute its own mandates: and if it issues wrong mandates instead of right, or any mandates at all in things with which it ought not to meddle, it practices a social tyranny more formidable than many kinds of political oppression, since, though not usually upheld by such extreme penalties, it leaves fewer means of escape, penetrating much more deeply into the details of life, and enslaving the soul itself. Protection, therefore, against the tyranny of the magistrate is not enough: there needs protection also against the tyranny of the prevailing opinion and feeling; against the tendency of society to impose, by other means than civil penalties, its own ideas and practices as rules of conduct on those who dissent from them; to fetter the development, and, if possible, prevent the formation, of any individuality not in harmony with its ways, and compels all characters to fashion themselves upon the model of its own. There is a limit to the legitimate interference of collective opinion with individual independence: and to find that limit, and maintain it against encroachment, is as indispensable to a good condition of human affairs, as protection against political despotism.

But though this proposition is not likely to be contested in general terms, the practical question, where to place the limit—how to make the fitting adjustment between individual independence and social control—is a subject on which nearly everything remains to be done. All that makes existence valuable to any one, depends on the enforcement of restraints upon the actions of other people. Some rules of conduct, therefore, must be imposed, by law in the first place, and by opinion on many things which are not fit subjects for the operation of law. What these rules should be is the principal question in human affairs; but if we except a few of the most obvious cases, it is one of those which least progress has been made in resolving. No two ages, and scarcely any two countries, have decided it alike; and the decision of one age or country is a wonder to another. Yet the people of any given age and country no more suspect any difficulty in it, than if it were a subject on which mankind had always been agreed. The rules which obtain among themselves appear to them self-evident and self-justifying. This all but universal illusion is one of the examples of the magical influence of custom, which is not only, as the proverb says, a second nature, but is continually mistaken for the first. The effect of custom, in preventing any misgivings respecting the rules of conduct which mankind impose on one another, is all the more complete because the subject is one on which it is not generally considered necessary that reasons should be given, either by one person to others or by each to himself. People are accustomed to believe, and have been encouraged in the belief by some who aspire to the character of philosophers, that their feelings, on subjects of this nature, are better than reasons, and render reasons unnecessary. The practical principle which guides them to their opinions on the regulation of human conduct, is the feeling in each person's mind that everybody should be required to act as he, and those with whom he sympathizes, would like them to act. No one, indeed, acknowledges to himself that his standard of judgment is his own liking; but an opinion on a point of conduct, not supported by reasons, can only count as one person's preference; and if the reasons, when given, are a mere appeal to a similar preference felt by other people, it is still only many people's liking instead of one. To an ordinary man, however, his own preference, thus supported, is not only a perfectly satisfactory reason, but the only one he generally has for any of his notions of morality, taste, or propriety, which are not expressly written in his religious creed; and his chief guide in the interpretation even of that. Men's opinions, accordingly, on what is laudable or blamable, are affected by all the multifarious causes which influence their wishes in regard to the conduct of others, and which are as numerous as those which determine their wishes on any other subject.

...

In England, from the peculiar circumstances of our political history, though the yoke of opinion is perhaps heavier, that of law is lighter, than in most other countries of Europe; and there is considerable jealousy of direct interference, by the legislative or the executive power, with private conduct; not so much from any just regard for the independence of the individual, as from the still subsisting habit of looking on the government as representing an opposite interest to the public. The majority have not yet learned to feel the power of the government their power, or its opinions their opinions. When they do so, individual liberty will probably be as much exposed to invasion from the government, as it already is from public opinion. But, as yet, there is a considerable amount of feeling ready to be called forth against any attempt of the law to control individuals in things in which they have not hitherto been accustomed to be controlled by it; and this with very little discrimination as to whether the matter is, or is not, within the legitimate sphere of legal control; insomuch that the feeling, highly salutary on the whole, is perhaps quite as often misplaced as well grounded in the particular instances of its application. There is, in fact, no recognized principle by which the propriety or impropriety of government interference is customarily tested. People decide according to their personal preferences. Some, whenever they see any good to be done, or evil to be remedied, would willingly instigate the government to undertake the business; while others prefer to bear almost any amount of social evil, rather than add one to the departments of human interests amenable to governmental control. And men range themselves on one or the other side in any particular case, according to this general direction of their sentiments; or according to the degree of interest which they feel in the particular thing which it is proposed that the government should do, or according to the belief they entertain that the government would, or would not, do it in the manner they prefer; but very rarely on account of any opinion to which they consistently adhere, as to what things are fit to be done by a government. And it seems to me that in consequence of this absence of rule or principle, one side is at present as often wrong as the other; the interference of government is, with about equal frequency, improperly invoked and improperly condemned.

The object of this Essay is to assert one very simple principle, as entitled to govern absolutely the dealings of society with the individual in the way of compulsion and control, whether the means used be physical force in the form of legal penalties, or the moral coercion of public opinion. That principle is, that the sole end for which mankind are warranted, individually or collectively, in interfering with the liberty of action of any of their number, is self-protection. That the only purpose for which power can be rightfully exercised over any member of a civilized community, against his will, is to prevent harm to others. His own good, either physical or moral, is not a sufficient warrant. He cannot rightfully be compelled to do or forbear because it will be better for him to do so, because it will make him happier, because, in the opinions of others, to do so would be wise, or even right. These are good reasons for remonstrating with him, or reasoning with him, or persuading him, or entreating him, but not for compelling him, or visiting him with any evil in case he do otherwise. To justify that, the conduct from which it is desired to deter him must be calculated to produce evil to some one else. The only part of the conduct of any one, for which he is amenable to society, is that which concerns others. In the part which merely concerns himself, his independence is, of right, absolute. Over himself, over his own body and mind, the individual is sovereign.

It is, perhaps, hardly necessary to say that this doctrine is meant to apply only to human beings in the maturity of their faculties. We are not speaking of children, or of young persons below the age which the law may fix as that of manhood or womanhood. Those who are still in a state to require being taken care of by others, must be protected against their own actions as well as against external injury. For the same reason, we may leave out of consideration those backward states of society in which the race itself may be considered as in its nonage. The early difficulties in the way of spontaneous progress are so great, that there is seldom any choice of means for overcoming them; and a ruler full of the spirit of improvement is warranted in the use of any expedients that will attain an end, perhaps otherwise unattainable. Despotism is a legitimate mode of government in dealing with barbarians, provided the end be their improvement, and the means justified by actually effecting that end. Liberty, as a principle, has no application to any state of things anterior to the time when mankind have become capable of being improved by free and equal discussion. Until then, there is nothing for them but implicit obedience to an Akbar or a Charlemagne, if they are so fortunate as to find one. But as soon as mankind have attained the capacity of being guided to their own improvement by conviction or persuasion (a period long since reached in all nations with whom we need here concern ourselves), compulsion, either in the direct form or in that of pains and penalties for non-compliance, is no longer admissible as a means to their own good, and justifiable only for the security of others.

It is proper to state that I forego any advantage which could be derived to my argument from the idea of abstract right, as a thing independent of utility. I regard utility as the ultimate appeal on all ethical questions; but it must be utility in the largest sense, grounded on the permanent interests of a man as a progressive being. Those interests, I contend, authorize the subjection of individual spontaneity to external control, only in respect to those actions of each, which concern the interest of other people. If any one does an act hurtful to others, there is a *prima facie* case for punishing him, by law, or, where legal penalties are not safely applicable, by general disapprobation. There are also many positive acts for the benefit of others, which he may rightfully be compelled to perform; such as to give evidence in a court of justice; to bear his fair share in the common defense or in any other joint work necessary to the interest of the society of which he enjoys the protection; and to perform certain acts of individual beneficence, such as saving a fellow-creature's life, or interposing to protect the defenseless against ill-usage, things which whenever it is obviously a man's duty to do, he may rightfully be made responsible to society for not doing. A person may cause evil to others not only by his actions but by his inaction, and in either case he is justly accountable to them for the

injury. The latter case, it is true, requires a much more cautious exercise of compulsion than the former. To make any one answerable for doing evil to others is the rule; to make him answerable for not preventing evil is, comparatively speaking, the exception. Yet there are many cases clear enough and grave enough to justify that exception. . . .

But there is a sphere of action in which society, as distinguished from the individual, has, if any, only an indirect interest; comprehending all that portion of a person's life and conduct which affects only himself, or if it also affects others, only with their free, voluntary, and undeceived consent and participation. When I say only himself, I mean directly, and in the first instance; for whatever affects himself, may affect others through himself; and the objection which may be grounded on this contingency, will receive consideration in the sequel. This, then, is the appropriate region of human liberty. It compromises, first, the inward domain of consciousness; demanding liberty of conscience in the most comprehensive sense; liberty of thought and feeling; absolute freedom of opinion and sentiment on all subjects, practical or speculative, scientific, moral, or theological. The liberty of expressing and publishing opinions may seem to fall under a different principle, since it belongs to that part of the conduct of an individual which concerns other people; but, being almost of as much importance as the liberty of thought itself, and resting in great part on the same reasons, is practically inseparable from it. Secondly, the principle requires liberty of tastes and pursuits; of framing the plan of our life to suit our own character; of doing as we like, subject to such consequences as may follow: without impediment from our fellow-creatures, so long as what we do does not harm them, even though they should think our conduct foolish, perverse, or wrong. Thirdly, from this liberty of each individual, follows the liberty, within the same limits, of combination among individuals; freedom to unite, for any purpose not involving harm to others: the persons combining being supposed to be of full age, and not forced or deceived.

No society in which these liberties are not, on the whole, respected, is free, whatever may be its form of government; and none is completely free in which they do not exist absolute and unqualified. The only freedom which deserves the name, is that of pursuing our own good in our own way, so long as we do not attempt to deprive others of theirs, or impede their efforts to obtain it. Each is the proper guardian of his own health, whether bodily, *or* mental and spiritual. Mankind are greater gainers by suffering each other to live as seems good to themselves, than by compelling each to live as seems good to the rest.

Though this doctrine is anything but new, and, to some persons, may have the air of a truism, there is no doctrine which stands more directly opposed to the general tendency of existing opinion and practice. Society has expended fully as much effort in the attempt (according to its lights) to compel people to conform to its notions of personal as of social excellence. The ancient commonwealths thought themselves entitled to practice, and the ancient philosophers countenanced, the regulation of every part of private conduct by public authority, on the ground that the State had a deep interest in the whole bodily and mental discipline of every one of its citizens; a mode of thinking which may have been admissible in small republics surrounded by powerful enemies, in constant peril of being subverted by foreign attack or internal commotion, and to which even a short interval of relaxed energy and self-command might so easily be fatal that they could not afford to wait for the salutary permanent effects of freedom. In the modern world, the greater size of political communities, and above all, the separation between spiritual and temporal authority (which placed the direction of men's consciences in other hands than those which controlled their worldly affairs), prevented so great an interference by law in the details of private life; but the engines of moral repression have been wielded more strenuously against divergence from the reigning opinion in self-regarding, than even in social matters; religion, the most powerful of the elements which have entered into the formation of moral feeling, having almost always been governed either by the ambition of a hierarchy, seeking control over every department of human conduct, or by the spirit of Puritanism. And some of those modern reformers who have placed themselves in strongest opposition to the religions of the past, have been noway behind either churches or sects in their assertion of the right of spiritual domination: M. Comte, in particular, whose social system, as unfolded in his *Système de Politique Positive,* aims at establishing (though by moral more than by legal appliances) a despotism of society over the individual, surpassing anything contemplated in the political ideal of the most rigid disciplinarian among the ancient philosophers.

Apart from the peculiar tenets of individual thinkers, there is also in the world at large an increasing inclination to stretch unduly the powers of society over the individual, both by the force of opinion and even by that of legislation; and as the tendency of all the changes taking place in the world is to strengthen society, and diminish the power of the individual, this encroachment is not one of the evils which tend spontaneously to disappear, but, on the contrary, to grow more and more formidable. The disposition of mankind, whether as rulers or as fellow-citizens, to impose their own opinions and inclinations as a rule of conduct on others, is so energetically supported by some of the best and by some of the worst feelings incident to human nature, that it is hardly ever kept under restraint by anything but want of power; and as the power is not declining, but growing, unless a strong barrier of moral conviction can be raised against the mischief, we must expect, in the present circumstances of the world, to see it increase.

. . .

Discussion Questions

1. For Mill, the threat of tyranny came not so much from monarchs and aristocrats as from the 'majority.' In what ways can society tyrannize individual citizens? List some ways in which individuals are threatened and coerced by popular society. Do we still require protection from the tyranny of "prevailing opinion and feeling"? Why or why not?

2. To be consistent, Mill must defend the Harm Principle according to his broader philosophical commitments. This means Mill must argue that the Harm Principle can be known as true because it promotes the greatest happiness of all (see the selection from Mill in Chapter 8, Reading 43 of this book). Do you believe this is true? Does the Harm

Principle actually promote the greatest happiness of society? How exactly would 'not interfering with the liberty of action' of a person promote the general happiness?

3. Immediately after stating the Harm Principle, in the following paragraph Mill excludes certain groups from falling under this principle. What groups and individuals does he exclude? Does he have legitimate reasons for doing so? Does it matter that Mill had financial interests in the British presence in India and, for example, that he defended the East India Company before Parliament in 1857?

4. What does 'harm' mean? Does harm include loud noises from next door? Is it limited to physical injury? Is slander harm? Is unfair business competition harm? Can you give a precise definition of 'harm'? Does Mill have a clear idea of harm? Is this a problem for his theory?

5. Suppose some individual is acting in a way that harms himself or herself, but does not harm others. Is society ever justified in interfering in this person's life? Why or why not? Would any level of interference be acceptable? If so, then what? Are some people allowed, or even expected, to interfere? If so, who?

For Further Reading

There are numerous books on Mill. Suggested readings include John Skorupski, editor, *The Cambridge Companion to Mill* (1998); Wendy Donner, *The Liberal Self: John Stuart Mill's Moral and Political Philosophy* (1991); and Peter Radcliff, editor, *Limits of Liberty: Studies of Mill's* On Liberty (1966).

54   WHAT LIBERTARIANISM IS
John Hospers

John Hospers (1918–), a professor emeritus at the University of Southern California and once a libertarian candidate for president, provides a simple presentation of the core commitments of libertarianism. Libertarians, as the name suggests, hold liberties to be basic, but they have a particular notion about these rights and liberties. Liberties, for libertarians, are negative rights, that is, rights to be free from outside interference, free to be left alone. Considered this way, a right is like a bubble, or space, within which we are free to do as we like; the only restriction is the prohibition from going outside our own 'personal bubble' into the 'private bubble' of another person without that person's consent. A positive right, on the other hand, would be the right to demand something from another citizen, such as health care or welfare benefits. Libertarians reject any notion of rights as positive rights, however, since conceived as such, positive rights require us to violate the negative rights of others.

What about equality? On a libertarian conception, equality is guaranteed by equal liberties. Economic and class differences, including any difference in opportunity, are acceptable as long as all persons have the same negative liberties. No person has the right to demand of others that they act in such

SOURCE: Reprinted with permission of Nelson-Hall Publishers. From "What Libertarianism Is" by John Hospers in *The Libertarian Alternative*, edited by Tibor R. Machan, 1974.

a way as to promote equality or equal opportunity, other than that they are required not to impede others from achieving their goals.

Political theories, besides describing the relationship between liberty and equality, also generally provide some account of the optimal economic system. Here, libertarians rely heavily on the idea of contracts. Insofar as all contractual agreements are voluntarily entered into, any trading or bartering that results from these uncoerced, voluntary associations are thereby deemed legitimate and fair. In free market capitalism, transactions between buyer and seller, as well as employer and employee agreements, are all voluntary. Moreover, since the free markets reward hard work and initiative and because no liberties are infringed upon by voluntary transactions, unrestrained capitalism is the only acceptable economic system for libertarians.

Reading Questions

1. What does the example of the opera illustrate?
2. Why is the right to property so valuable according to libertarians?
3. How does the right to property sometimes limit the freedom of speech?
4. What does Hospers predict will happen if everyone shares in the ownership of property?
5. What is Hospers' definition of 'force'?
6. What is the only proper role of the government according to Hospers?
7. What does Hospers propose we do about pollution, such as air pollution?
8. What class of laws do libertarians accept? Which classes of laws do they reject?
9. What is wrong with demanding a free service?

The political philosophy that is called libertarianism (from the Latin *libertas,* liberty) is the doctrine that every person is the owner of his own life, and that no one is the owner of anyone else's life; and that consequently every human being has the right to act in accordance with his own choices, unless those actions infringe on the equal liberty of other human beings to act in accordance with *their* choices.

There are several other ways of stating the same libertarian thesis:

1. *No one is anyone else's master, and no one is anyone else's slave.* Since I am the one to decide how my life is to be conducted, just as you decide about yours, I have no right (even if I had the power) to make you my slave and be your master, nor have you the right to become the master by enslaving me. Slavery is *forced* servitude, and since no one owns the life of anyone else, no one has the right to enslave another. Political theories past and present have traditionally been concerned with who should be the master (usually the king, the dictator, or government bureaucracy) and who should be the slaves, and what the extent of the slavery should be. Libertarianism holds that no one has the right to use force to enslave the life of another, or any portion or aspect of that life.

2. *Other men's lives are not yours to dispose of.* I enjoy seeing operas; but operas are expensive to produce. Opera-lovers often say, "The state (or the city, etc.) should subsidize opera, so that we can all see it. Also it would be for people's betterment, cultural benefit, etc." But what they are advocating is nothing more or less than legalized plunder. They can't pay for the productions themselves, and yet they want to see opera, which involves a large number of people and their labor; so what they are saying in effect is, "Get the money through legalized force. Take a little bit more out of every worker's paycheck every week to pay for the operas we want to see." But I have no right to take by force from the workers' pockets to pay for what I want.

Perhaps it would be better if he *did* go to see opera—then I should try to convince him to go voluntarily. But to take the money from him forcibly, because in my opinion it would be good for *him,* is still seizure of his earnings, which is plunder.

Besides, if I have the right to force him to help pay for my pet projects, hasn't he equally the right to force me to help pay for his? Perhaps he in turn wants the government to subsidize rock-and-roll, or his new car, or a house in the country? If I have the right to milk him, why hasn't he the right to milk me? If I can be a moral cannibal, why can't he too?

We should beware of the inventors of utopias. They would remake the world according to their vision—with the lives and fruits of the labor of *other* human beings. Is it someone's utopian vision that others should build pyramids to beautify the landscape? Very well, then other men should provide the labor; and if he is in a position of political power, and he can't get men to do it voluntarily, then he must *compel* them to "cooperate"—i.e., he must enslave them.

A hundred men might gain great pleasure from beating up or killing just one insignificant human being; but other men's lives are not theirs to dispose of. "In order to achieve the worthy goals of the next five-year-plan, we must forcibly collectivize the peasants . . . "; but other men's lives are not theirs to dispose of. Do you want to occupy, rent-free, the mansion that another man has worked for twenty years to buy? But other men's lives are not yours to dispose of. Do you want operas so badly that everyone is forced to work harder to pay for their subsidization through taxes? But other men's lives are not yours to dispose of. Do you want to have free medical care at the expense of other people, whether they wish to provide it or not? But this would require them to work longer for you whether they want to or not, and other men's lives are not yours to dispose of.

3. *No human being should be a nonvoluntary mortgage on the life of another.* I cannot claim your life, your work, or the products of your effort as mine. The fruit of one man's labor should not be fair game for every freeloader who comes along and demands it as his own. The orchard that has been carefully grown, nurtured, and harvested by its owner should not be ripe for the plucking for any bypasser who has a yen for the ripe fruit. The wealth that some men have produced should not be fair game for looting by government, to be used for whatever purposes its representatives determine, no matter what their motives in so doing may be. The theft of your money by a robber is not justified by the fact that he used it to help his injured mother.

It will already be evident that libertarian doctrine is embedded in a view of the rights of man. Each human being has the right to live his life as he chooses, compatibly with the equal right of all other human beings to live their lives as they choose.

All man's rights are implicit in the above statement. Each man has the right to life: any attempt by others to take it away from him, or even to injure him, violates this right, through the use of coercion against him. Each man has the right to liberty: to conduct his life in accordance with the alternatives open to him without coercive action by others. And every man has the right to property: to work to sustain his life (and the lives of whichever others he chooses to sustain, such as his family) and to retain the fruits of his labor.

People often defend the rights of life and liberty but denigrate property rights, and yet the right to property is as basic as the other two; indeed, without property rights no other rights are possible. Depriving you of property is depriving you of the means by which you live.

I have no right to decide how *you* should spend your time or your money. I can make that decision for myself, but not for you, my neighbor. I may deplore your choice of life-style, and I may talk with you about it provided you are willing to listen to me. But I have no right to use force to change it. Nor have I the right to decide how you should spend the money you have earned. I may appeal to you to give it to the Red Cross, and you may prefer to go to prizefights. But that is your decision, and however much I may chafe about it I do not have the right to interfere forcibly with it, for example by robbing you in order to use the money in accordance with *my* choices. (If I have the right to rob you, have you also the right to rob me?)

When I claim a right, I carve out a niche, as it were, in my life, saying in effect, "This activity I must be able to perform without interference from others.

For you and everyone else, this is off limits." And so I put up a "no trespassing" sign, which marks off the area of my right. Each individual's right is his "no trespassing" sign in relation to me and others. I may not encroach upon his domain any more than he upon mine, without my consent. Every right entails a duty, true—but the duty is only that of *forbearance*—that is, of *refraining* from violating the other person's right. If you have a right to life, I have no right to take your life; if you have a right to the products of your labor (property), I have no right to take it from you without your consent. The non-violation of these rights will not guarantee you protection against natural catastrophes such as floods and earthquakes, but it will protect you against the aggressive activities *of other men*. And rights, after all, have to do with one's relations to other human beings, not with one's relations to physical nature.

Nor were these rights created by government; governments—some governments, obviously not all—*recognize* and *protect* the rights that individuals already have. Governments regularly forbid homicide and theft; and, at a more advanced stage, protect individuals against such things as libel and breach of contract.

The *right to property* is the most misunderstood and unappreciated of human rights, and it is one most constantly violated by governments. "Property" of course does not mean only real estate; it includes anything you can call your own—your clothing, your car, your jewelry, your books and papers.

The right of property is not the right to just *take* it from others, for this would interfere with *their* property rights. It is rather the right to work for it, to obtain non-coercively, the money or services which you can present in voluntary exchange.

The right to property is consistently underplayed by intellectuals today, sometimes even frowned upon, as if we should feel guilty for upholding such a right in view of all the poverty in the world. But the right to property is absolutely basic. It is your hedge against the future. It is your assurance that what you have worked to earn will still be there, and be yours, when you wish or need to use it, especially when you are too old to work any longer.

Government has always been the chief enemy of the right to property. The officials of government, wishing to increase their power, and finding an increase of wealth an effective way to bring this about, seize some or all of what a person has earned—and since government has a monopoly of physical force within the geographical area of the nation, it has the power (but not the right) to do this. When this happens, of course, every citizen of that country is insecure: he knows that no matter how hard he works the government can swoop down on him at any time and confiscate his earnings and possessions. A person sees his life savings wiped out in a moment when the tax-collectors descend to deprive him of the fruits of his work; or, an industry which has been fifty years in the making and cost millions of dollars and millions of hours of time and planning, is nationalized overnight. Or the government, via inflation, cheapens the currency, so that hard-won dollars aren't worth anything any more. The effect of such actions, of course, is that people lose hope and incentive: if no matter how hard they work the government agents can take it all away, why bother to work at all, for more than today's needs? Depriving people of property is *depriving them of the means by which they live*—the freedom of the individual citizen to do what he wishes with his own life and to plan for the future. Indeed, only if property rights are respected is there any point to planning for the future and working to achieve one's goals. *Property rights are what makes long-range planning possible*—the kind of planning which is a distinctively human endeavor, as opposed to the day-by-day activity of the lion who hunts, who depends on the supply of game tomorrow but has no real insurance against starvation in a day or a week. Without the right to property, the right to life itself amounts to little: how can you sustain your life if you cannot plan ahead? And how can you plan ahead if the fruits of your labor can at any moment be confiscated by government?

Indeed, the right to property may well be considered second only to the right to life. Even the freedom of speech is limited by considerations of property. If a person visiting in your home behaves in a way undesired by you, you have every right to evict him; he can scream or agitate elsewhere if he wishes, but not in your home without your consent. Does a person have a right to shout obscenities in a cathedral? No, for the owners of the cathedral (presumably the Church) have not allowed others on their property for that purpose; one may go there to worship or to visit, but not just for any purpose one wishes. Their property right is prior to your or my wish to scream or expectorate or write graffiti on their building. Or, to take the stock example, does a person have a right to shout "Fire!" falsely in a crowded theater? No, for the theater owner has permitted others to enter and use his property only for a specific purpose, that of seeing a film or watching a stage show. If a person heckles or otherwise disturbs other members of the audience, he can be thrown out. (In fact, he can be removed for any reason the owner chooses, provided his admission money is returned.) And if he shouts "Fire!" when there is no fire, he may be endangering other lives by causing a panic or a stampede. The right to free speech doesn't give one the right to say anything anywhere; it is circumscribed by property rights.

Again, some people seem to assume that the right to free speech (including written speech) means that they can go to a newspaper publisher and demand that he print in his newspaper some propaganda or policy statement for their political party (or other group). But of course they have no right to the use of his newspaper. Ownership of the newspaper is the product of his labor, and he has a right to put into his newspaper whatever he wants, for whatever reason. If he excludes material which many readers would like to have in, perhaps they can find it in another newspaper or persuade him to print it himself (if there are enough of them, they will usually do just that). Perhaps they can even cause his newspaper to fail. But as long as he owns it, he has the right to put in it what he wishes; what would a property right be if he could not do this? They have no right to place their material in his newspaper without his consent—not for free, nor even for a fee. Perhaps other newspapers will include it, or perhaps they can start their own newspaper (in which case they have a right to put in it what they like). If not, an option open to them would be to mimeograph and distribute some handbills.

In exactly the same way, no one has a right to "free television time" unless the owner of the television station consents to give it; it is his station, he has the property rights over it, and it is for him to decide how to dispose of his time. He may not decide wisely, but it is his right to decide as he wishes. If he makes enough unwise decisions, and courts enough unpopularity with the viewing public or the sponsors, he may have to

go out of business; but as he is free to make his own decisions, so is he free to face their consequences. (If the government owns the television station, then government officials will make the decisions, and there is no guarantee of *their* superior wisdom. The difference is that when "the government" owns the station, you are forced to help pay for its upkeep through your taxes, whether the bureaucrat in charge decides to give you television time or not.)

"But why have *individual* property rights? Why not have lands and houses owned by everybody together?" Yes, this involves no violation of individual rights, as long as everybody consents to this arrangement and no one is forced to join it. The parties to it may enjoy the communal living enough (at least for a time) to overcome certain inevitable problems: that some will work and some not, that some will achieve more in an hour than others can do in a day, and still they will all get the same income. The few who do the most will in the end consider themselves "workhorses" who do the work of two or three or twelve, while the others will be "freeloaders" on the efforts of these few. But as long as they can get out of the arrangement if they no longer like it, no violation of rights is involved. They got in voluntarily, and they can get out voluntarily; no one has used force.

"But why not say that everybody owns everything? That we *all* own everything there is?"

To some this may have a pleasant ring—but let us try to analyze what it means. If everybody owns everything, then everyone has an equal right to go everywhere, do what he pleases, take what he likes, destroy if he wishes, grow crops or burn them, trample them under, and so on. Consider what it would be like in practice. Suppose you have saved money to buy a house for yourself and your family. Now suppose that the principle, "everybody owns everything," becomes adopted. Well then, why shouldn't every itinerant hippie just come in and take over, sleeping in your beds and eating in your kitchen and not bothering to replace the food supply or clean up the mess? After all, it belongs to all of us, doesn't it? So we have just as much right to it as you, the buyer, have. What happens if we *all* want to sleep in the bedroom and there's not room for all of us? Is it the strongest who wins?

What would be the result? Since no one would be responsible for anything, the property would soon be destroyed, the food used up, the facilities nonfunctional. Beginning as a house that *one* family could use, it would end up as a house that *no one* could use. And if the principle continued to be adopted, no one would build houses any more—or anything else. What for? They would only be occupied and used by others, without remuneration.

Suppose two men are cast ashore on an island, and they agree that each will cultivate half of it. The first man is industrious and grows crops and builds a shelter, making the most of the situation with which he is confronted. The second man, perhaps thinking that the warm days will last forever, lies in the sun, picks coconuts while they last, and does a minimum of work to sustain himself. At the time of harvest, the second man has nothing to harvest, nor does he assist the first man in his labors. But later when there is a dearth of food on the island, the second man comes to the first man and demands half of the harvest as his right. But of course he has no right to the product of the first man's labors. The first man may freely choose to give part of his harvest to the second out of charity rather than see him starve; but that is just what it is—charity, not the second man's right.

How can any of man's rights be violated? Ultimately, only by the use of force. I can make suggestions to you, I can reason with you, entreat you (if you are willing to listen), but I cannot *force* you without violating your rights; only by forcing you do I cut the cord between your free decisions and your actions. Voluntary relations between individuals involve no deprivation of rights, but murder, assault, and rape do, because in doing these things I make you the unwilling victim of my actions. A man beating his wife involves no violation of rights if she *wanted* to be beaten. *Force is behavior that requires the unwilling involvement of other persons.*

Thus the use of force need not require the use of physical violence. If I trespass on your property, or dump garbage on it, I am violating your property rights, as indeed I am when I steal your watch; although this is not force in the sense of violence, it *is* a case of your being an unwilling victim of my action. Similarly, if you shout at me so that I cannot be heard when I try to speak, or blow a siren in my ear, or start a factory next door which pollutes my land, you are again violating my rights (to free speech, to property); I am, again, the unwilling victim of your ac-

tions. Similarly, if you steal a manuscript of mine and publish it as your own, you are confiscating a piece of my property and thus violating my right to keep what is the product of my labor. Of course, if I give you the manuscript with permission to sign your name to it and keep the proceeds, no violation of rights is involved—any more than if I give you permission to dump garbage in my yard.

According to libertarianism, the role of government should be limited to the retaliatory use of force against those who have initiated its use. It should not enter into any other areas, such as religion, social organization, and economics.

Government is the most dangerous institution known to man. Throughout history it has violated the rights of men more than any individual or group of individuals could do: it has killed people, enslaved them, sent them to forced labor and concentration camps, and regularly robbed and pillaged them of the fruits of their expended labor. Unlike individual criminals, government has the power to arrest and try; unlike individual criminals, it can surround and encompass a person totally, dominating every aspect of one's life, so that one has no recourse from it but to leave the country (and in totalitarian nations even that is prohibited). Government throughout history has a much sorrier record than any individual, even that of a ruthless mass murderer. The signs we see on bumper stickers are chillingly accurate: "Beware: the Government Is Armed and Dangerous."

The only proper role of government, according to libertarians, is that of protector of the citizen against aggression by other individuals. The government, of course, should never initiate aggression; its proper role is the embodiment of the *retaliatory* use of force against anyone who initiates its use.

If each individual had constantly to defend himself against possible aggressors, he would have to spend a considerable portion of his life in target practice, karate exercises, and other means of self-defenses, and even so he would probably be helpless against groups of individuals who might try to kill, maim, or rob him. He would have little time for cultivating those qualities which are essential to civilized life, nor would improvements in science, medicine, and the arts be likely to occur. The function of the government is to take this responsibility off his shoulders: the government undertakes to defend him against aggressors and to punish them if they attack him. When the government is effective in doing this, it enables the citizen to go about his business unmolested and without constant fear for his life. To do this, of course, government must have physical power—the police, to protect the citizen from aggression within its borders, and the armed forces, to protect the citizen from aggressors outside. Beyond that, the government should not intrude upon his life, either to run his business, or adjust his daily activities, or prescribe his personal moral code.

Government, then, undertakes to be the individual's protector; but historically governments have gone far beyond this function. Since they already have the physical power, they have not hesitated to use it for purposes far beyond that which was entrusted to them in the first place. Undertaking initially to protect its citizens against aggression, it has often itself become an aggressor—a far greater aggressor, indeed, than the criminals against whom it was supposed to protect its citizens. Governments have done what no private citizens can do: arrest and imprison individuals without trial and send them to slave labor camps. Government must have power in order to be effective—and yet the very means by which alone it can be effective make it vulnerable to the abuse of power, leading to managing the lives of individuals and even inflicting terror upon them.

What then should be the function of government? In a word, the *protection of human rights*.

1. *The right to life:* libertarians support all such legislation as will protect human beings against the use of force by others, for example, laws against killing, attempted killing, maiming, beating, and all kinds of physical violence.
2. *The right to liberty:* there should be no laws compromising in any way freedom of speech, of the press, and of peaceable assembly. There should be no censorship of ideas, books, films, or of anything else by the government.
3. *The right to property:* libertarians support legislation that protects the property rights of individuals against confiscation, nationalization, eminent domain, robbery, trespass, fraud and misrepresentation, patent and copyright, libel and slander.

Someone has violently assaulted you. Should he be legally liable? Of course. He has violated one of your rights. He has knowingly injured you, and since he has initiated aggression against you he should be made to expiate.

Someone has negligently left his bicycle on the sidewalk where you trip over it in the dark and injure yourself. He didn't do it intentionally; he didn't mean you any harm. Should he be legally liable? Of course; he has, however unwittingly, injured you, and since the injury is caused by him and you are the victim, he should pay.

Someone across the street is unemployed. Should you be taxed extra to pay for his expenses? Not at all. You have not injured him, you are not responsible for the fact that he is unemployed (unless you are a senator or bureaucrat who agitated for further curtailing of business, which legislation passed, with the result that your neighbor was laid off by the curtailed business). You may voluntarily wish to help him out, or better still, try to get him a job to put him back on his feet again; but since you have initiated no aggressive act against him, and neither purposely nor accidentally injured him in any way, you should not be legally penalized for the fact of his unemployment. (Actually it is just such penalties that increase unemployment.)

One man, A, works hard for years and finally earns a high salary as a professional man. A second man, B, prefers not to work at all, and to spend wastefully what money he has (through inheritance), so that after a year or two he has nothing left. At the end of this time he has a long siege of illness and lots of medical bills to pay. He demands that the bills be paid by the government—that is, by the taxpayers of the land, including Mr. A.

But of course B has no such right. He chose to lead his life in a certain way—that is his voluntary decision. One consequence of that choice is that he must depend on charity in case of later need. Mr. A chose not to live that way. (And if everyone lived like Mr. B, on whom would he depend in case of later need?) Each has a right to live in the way he pleases, but each must live with the consequences of his own decision (which, as always, falls primarily on himself). He cannot, in time of need, claim A's beneficence as his right.

If a house-guest of yours starts to carve his initials in your walls and break up your furniture, you have a right to evict him, and call the police if he makes trouble. If someone starts to destroy the machinery in a factory, the factory-owner is also entitled to evict him and call the police. In both cases, persons other than the owner are permitted on the property only under certain conditions, at the pleasure of the owner. If those conditions are violated, the owner is entitled to use force to set things straight. The case is exactly the same on a college or university campus: if a campus demonstrator starts breaking windows, occupying the president's office, and setting fire to a dean, the college authorities are certainly within their rights to evict him forcibly; one is permitted on the college grounds only under specific conditions, set by the administration: study, peaceful student activity, even political activity if those in charge choose to permit it. If they do not choose to permit peaceful political activity on campus, they may be unwise, since a campus is after all a place where all sides of every issue should get discussed, and the college that doesn't permit this may soon lose its reputation and its students. All the same, the college official who does not permit it is quite within his rights; the students do not own the campus, nor do the hired trouble-makers imported from elsewhere. In the case of a privately owned college, the owners, or whoever they have delegated to administer it, have the right to make the decisions as to who shall be permitted on the campus and under what conditions. In the case of a state university or college, the ownership problem is more complex: one could say that the "government" owns the campus or that "the people" do since they are the taxpayers who support it; but in either case, the university administration has the delegated task of keeping order, and until they are removed by the state administration or the taxpayers, it is theirs to decide who shall be permitted on campus, and what non-academic activities will be permitted to their students on the premises.

Property rights can be violated by physical trespass, of course, or by anyone entering on your property for any reason without your consent. (If you *do* consent to having your neighbor dump garbage on your yard, there is no violation of your rights.) But the physical trespass of a person is only a special case of violation of property rights. Property rights can be violated by sound-waves, in the form of a loud noise, or the sounds of your neighbor's hi-fi set while you are trying to sleep. Such violations of property rights are of course the subject of action in the courts.

But there is another violation of property rights that has not thus far been honored by the courts: this has to do with the effects of *pollution* of the atmosphere.

What about automobiles, the chief polluters of the air? One can hardly sue every automobile owner. But one can sue the manufacturers of automobiles who do not install anti-smog devices on the cars which they distribute—and later (though this is more difficult), owners of individual automobiles if they discard the equipment or do not keep it functional.

The violation of rights does not apply only to air-pollution. If someone with a factory upstream on a river pollutes the river, anyone living downstream from him, finding his water polluted, should be able to sue the owner of the factory. In this way the price of adding the anti-pollutant devices will be the owner's responsibility, and will probably be added to the cost of the products which the factory produces and thus spread around among all consumers, rather than the entire cost being borne by the users of the river in the form of polluted water, with the consequent impossibility of fishing, swimming, and so on. In each case, pollution would be stopped at the source rather than having its ill effects spread around to numerous members of the population.

What about property which you do not work to earn, but which you *inherit* from someone else? Do you have a right to that? You have no right to it until someone decides to give it to you. Consider the man who willed it to you: it was his, he had the right to use and dispose of it as *he* saw fit; and if he decided to give it to you, this is a windfall for you, but it was only the exercise of *his* right. Had the property been seized by the government at the man's death, or distributed among numerous other people designated by the government, it *would* have been a violation of his rights: for he, who worked to earn and sustain it, would not have been able to dispose of it according to his own judgment. If he doesn't have the right to determine who shall have it, who does?

· · ·

Laws may be classified into three types: (1) laws protecting individuals against themselves, such as laws against fornication and other sexual behavior, alcohol, and drugs; (2) laws protecting individuals against aggressions by other individuals, such as laws against murder, robbery, and fraud; (3) laws requiring people to help one another; for example, all laws which rob Peter to pay Paul, such as welfare.

Libertarians reject the first class of laws totally. Behavior which harms no one else is strictly the individual's own affair. Thus, there should be no laws against becoming intoxicated, since whether or not to become intoxicated is the individual's own decision; but there should be laws against driving while intoxicated, since the drunken driver is a threat to every other motorist on the highway (drunken driving falls into type 2). Similarly, there should be no laws against drugs (except the prohibition of sale of drugs to minors) as long as the taking of these drugs poses no threat to anyone else. Drug addiction is a psychological problem to which no present solution exists. Most of the social harm caused by addicts, other than to themselves, is the result of thefts which they perform in order to continue their habit—and then the *legal* crime is the theft, not the addiction. The actual cost of heroin is about ten cents a shot; if it were legalized, the enormous traffic in illegal sale and purchase of it would stop, as well as the accompanying proselytization to get new addicts (to make more money for the pusher) and the thefts performed by addicts who often require eighty dollars a day just to keep up the habit. Addiction would not stop, but the crimes would: it is estimated that 75 percent of the burglaries in New York City today are performed by addicts, and all these crimes could be wiped out at one stroke through the legalization of drugs. (Only when the taking of drugs could be shown to constitute a threat to *others*, should it be prohibited by law. It is only laws protecting people against *themselves* that libertarians oppose.)

Laws should be limited to the second class only: aggression by individuals against other individuals. These are laws whose function is to protect human beings against encroachment by others; and this, as we have seen, is (according to libertarianism) the sole function of government.

Libertarians also reject the third class of laws totally: no one should be forced by law to help others, not even to tell them the time of day if requested, and certainly not to give them a portion of one's weekly paycheck. Governments, in the guise of humanitarianism, have given to some by taking from others (charging a "handling fee" in the process, which, because of the government's waste and inefficiency,

sometimes is several hundred percent). And in so doing they have decreased incentive, violated the rights of individuals, and lowered the standard of living of almost everyone.

All such laws constitute what libertarians call *moral cannibalism*. A cannibal in the physical sense is a person who lives off the flesh of other human beings. A *moral* cannibal is one who believes he has the right to live off the "spirit" of other human beings—who believes that he has a moral claim on the productive capacity, time, and effort expended by others.

It has become fashionable to claim virtually everything that one needs or desires as one's *right*. Thus, many people claim that they have a right to a job, the right to free medical care, to free food and clothing, to a decent home, and so on. Now if one asks, apart from any specific context, whether it would be desirable if everyone had these things, one might as well say yes. But there is a gimmick attached to each of them: *At whose expense?* Jobs, medical care, education, and so on, don't grow on trees. These are goods and services *produced only by men*. Who, then, is to provide them, and under what conditions?

If you have a right to a job, who is to supply it? Must an employer supply it even if he doesn't want to hire you? What if you are unemployable or incurably lazy? (If you say "the government must supply it," does that mean that a job must be created for you which no employer needs done, and that you must be kept in it regardless of how much or little you work?) If the employer is forced to supply it at his expense even if he doesn't need you, then isn't *he* being enslaved to that extent? What ever happened to *his* right to conduct his life and his affairs in accordance with his choices?

If you have a right to free medical care, then, since medical care doesn't exist in nature as wild apples do, some people will have to supply it to you for free: that is, they will have to spend their time and money and energy taking care of you whether they want to or not. What ever happened to *their* right to conduct their lives as they see fit? Or do you have a right to violate theirs? Can there be a right to violate rights?

All those who demand this or that as a "free service" are consciously or unconsciously evading the fact that there is in reality no such thing as free services. All man-made goods and services are the result of human expenditure of time and effort. There is no such thing as "something for nothing" in this world. If you demand something free, you are demanding that other men give their time and effort to you without compensation. If they voluntarily choose to do this, there is no problem; but if you demand that they be *forced* to do it, you are interfering with their right not to do it if they so choose. "Swimming in this pool ought to be free!" says the indignant passerby. What he means is that others should build a pool, others should provide the materials, and still others should run it and keep it in functioning order, so that *he* can use it without fee. But what right has he to the expenditure of *their* time and effort? To expect something "for free" is to expect it *to be paid for by others* whether they choose to or not.

Many questions, particularly about economic matters, will be generated by the libertarian account of human rights and the role of government. Should government have no role in assisting the needy, in providing social security, in legislating minimum wages, in fixing prices and putting a ceiling on rents, in curbing monopolies, in erecting tariffs, in guaranteeing jobs, in managing the money supply? To these and all similar questions the libertarian answers with an unequivocal no.

"But then you'd let people go hungry!" comes the rejoinder. This, the libertarian insists, is precisely what would not happen; with the restrictions removed, the economy would flourish as never before. With the controls taken off business, existing enterprises would expand and new ones would spring into existence satisfying more and more consumer needs; millions more people would be gainfully employed instead of subsisting on welfare, and all kinds of research and production, released from a stranglehold of government, would proliferate, fulfilling man's needs and desires as never before. It has always been so whenever government has permitted men to be free traders on a free market. But *why* this is so, and how the free market is the best solution to all problems relating to the material aspect of man's life, is another and far longer story. . . .

Discussion Questions

1. Why are people poor according to Hospers? What do his examples, such as of the two men on an island, suggest about why Hospers believes persons are poor? Is Hospers correct about this? Why or why not?

2. Throughout the article, Hospers uses the words 'he' and 'man.' Does Hospers intend these words to be used generically and inclusively, that is, to include women? At what point in the article does Hospers mention women and family members? Is this a problem?

3. Hospers writes that it is okay to beat your wife "if she *wanted* to be beaten." In what context is this statement made? Why would, in fact, a woman want to be beaten? Under what conditions would she prefer to be physically abused? Is this a problem for Hospers' account of force and voluntary consent?

4. Is it ever legitimate for the state to fund an opera? How about recreational programs or concerts-in-the-park? If not, why not? If so, then what conditions have to be met in order for local and national governments to legitimately spend money in these ways? Do you agree with Hospers' position that it is never legitimate? How is Hospers' view different from Locke's in Reading 52 of this chapter?

For Further Reading

This essay is anthologized in *The Libertarian Alternative*, edited by Tibor R. Machan (1974). This is a useful anthology that introduces most themes in libertarian political theory. Machan also edited *The Main Debate: Communism versus Capitalism* (1987); this anthology is also helpful, but as the name implies it tends to dichotomize political theory into two incompatible, widely divergent social systems. One especially worthwhile article in that collection is Erin Mack's "In Defense of 'Unbridled' Freedom of Contract." Two other books by Machan include *Individuals and Their Rights* (1989) and *The Libertarian Reader* (1982), an anthology.

Hospers' main discussion of libertarianism and political philosophy occurs in *Libertarianism: A Political Philosophy* (1971). The most influential libertarian text, however, is Robert Nozick's *Anarchy, State, and Utopia* (1974). The distinction between negative and positive liberties is from a classic piece of political philosophy by Isaiah Berlin, "Two Concepts of Liberty," in his *Four Essays on Liberty* (1969).

55   A THEORY OF JUSTICE
John Rawls

The clash between liberty and equality is an old and troublesome problem for political philosophy. Which of these two impressive ideals should be weighted the heavier? Is it possible to combine them into a single theory— a hybrid of libertarianism and socialist egalitarianism, something like a socialist version of liberalism?

One theory has attempted to do just this—and moreover, it has been widely regarded as enormously successful. John Rawls' political liberalism, or what is sometimes called 'justice as fairness,' is the most influential political theory in the past 20 years and is largely credited with the revival of serious political philosophy. Literally hundreds of scholarly articles and papers have been written on Rawls' ideas, as well as numerous books.

Several features of Rawls' argument are significant. The first is how he combines equality and liberty. As we will see, Rawls gives priority to liberty over equality, but the egalitarian component of 'justice as fairness', is so strong that some authors have used Rawls to defend a socialist state. For this reason, Rawls' theory is sometimes referred to as a form of 'welfare liberalism', which, as the name implies, offers both guaranteed liberties and guaranteed income (or welfare, to use a term with unfortunate pejorative connotations).

Second, Rawls' theory is notable because it is **deontological.** A 'deonto-logical' theory is one that relies on principles or rules as the basis of its normative claims as opposed to determining right from wrong based on the consequences of actions. Thus while some theories justify political institutions according to whether these institutions produce good results (for example, Mill's appeal to the Harm Principle), for a deontological theory, the right thing to do is determined by following a set of rules that can be objectively defended. For Rawls, these rules are called 'principles of justice.'

But which rules? This is the third significant feature of Rawls' political theory. Far more than any other recent deontological theory, Rawls has arguably shown why two particular principles of justice are superior to all others. To argue this, Rawls describes an ideal hypothetical situation in which individuals throughout society are asked to legislate principles of justice.

SOURCE: Reprinted by permission of the publisher from *A Theory of Justice* by John Rawls, pp. 11–22, 60–63, 136–142, Cambridge, Mass.: The Belknap Press of Harvard University Press, Copyright © 1971, 1999 by The President and Fellows of Harvard College.

This hypothetical choice is made in what Rawls calls the *original position.* Imagine, he writes, that you were asked to choose the principles of justice for your society. These principles would be binding upon all citizens of that society. Which principles would you choose? You might choose principles that benefited persons like yourself. (That, of course, is precisely what socialists say libertarians have done: picked principles of justice that are self-serving.) But this would not be fair according to Rawls, so he develops what is called the *veil of ignorance:* When you enter into the original position, you go behind the veil of ignorance, behind which you 'forget' who you are in particular, including your gender, race, socioeconomic position, and so forth. You do know general facts about society, including that there are a great many diverse views about the best way to live life. You also know that persons in your society value their autonomy highly, so you won't legislate any principles that violate personal autonomy. But neither will you legislate any principles that might unjustly harm the interests of some group in society, since you yourself might be a member of that group. If you don't know your religious persuasion, for example, and did not know if you were Buddhist, Catholic, or an atheist, you would be careful to protect the interests of everyone. As a result, we can be more assured that the principles you select will be fair for everyone. Thus Rawls calls his theory 'justice as fairness'.

Reading Questions

1. When can our social situation be considered just according to Rawls?
2. Why is the principle of utility incompatible with social cooperation in a situation of equality?
3. What is the original position? How does it make vivid certain reasonable restrictions?
4. How is the equality of the parties represented in the original position?
5. What is reflective equilibrium? What role does it play in Rawls' argument?
6. How does Rawls respond to the objection that the original position is purely hypothetical?
7. What are the two principles of justice? To what features of society does each primarily apply?
8. In what order are the two principles of justice to be arranged? What does this ordering mean for conflicts between the principles?
9. What kinds of particular facts do parties situated behind the veil of ignorance not know?
10. What follows from the fact that no one knows his or her situation or natural asset? What does this mean for selecting principles or forming coalitions?

···

My aim is to present a conception of justice which generalizes and carries to a higher level of abstraction the familiar theory of the social contract as found, say, in Locke, Rousseau, and Kant. In order to do this we are not to think of the original contract as one to enter a particular society or to set up a particular form of government. Rather, the guiding idea is that the principles of justice for the basic structure of society are the object of the original agreement. They are the principles that free and rational persons concerned to further their own interests would accept in an initial position of equality as defining the fundamental terms of their association. These principles are to regulate all further agreements; they specify the kinds of social cooperation that can be entered into and the forms of government that can be established. This way of regarding the principles of justice I shall call justice as fairness.

Thus we are to imagine that those who engage in social cooperation choose together, in one joint act, the principles which are to assign basic rights and duties and to determine the division of social benefits. Men are to decide in advance how they are to regulate their claims against one another and what is to be the foundation charter of their society. Just as each person must decide by rational reflection what constitutes his good, that is, the system of ends which it is rational for him to pursue, so a group of persons must decide once and for all what is to count among them as just and unjust. The choice which rational men would make in this hypothetical situation of equal liberty, assuming for the present that this choice problem has a solution, determines the principles of justice.

In justice as fairness the original position of equality corresponds to the state of nature in the traditional theory of the social contract. This original position is not, of course, thought of as an actual historical state of affairs, much less a primitive condition of culture. It is understood as a purely hypothetical situation characterized so as to lead to a certain conception of justice. Among the essential features of this situation is that no one knows his place in society, his class position or social status, nor does anyone know his fortune in the distribution of natural assets and abilities, his intelligence, strength, and the like. I shall even assume that the parties do not know their conceptions of the good or their special psychological propensities. The principles of justice are chosen behind a veil of ignorance. This ensures that no one is advantaged or disadvantaged in the choice of principles by the outcome of natural chance or the contingency of social circumstances. Since all are similarly situated and no one is able to design principles to favor his particular condition, the principles of justice are the result of a fair agreement or bargain. For given the circumstances of the original position, the symmetry of everyone's relations to each other, this initial situation is fair between individuals as moral persons, that is, as rational beings with their own ends and capable, I shall assume, of a sense of justice. The original position is, one might say, the appropriate initial status quo, and thus the fundamental agreements reached in it are fair. This explains the propriety of the name "justice as fairness": it conveys the idea that the principles of justice

are agreed to in an initial situation that is fair. The name does not mean that the concepts of justice and fairness are the same, any more than the phrase "poetry as metaphor" means that the concepts of "poetry and metaphor" are the same.

Justice as fairness begins, as I have said, with one of the most general of all choices which persons might make together, namely, with the choice of the first principles of a conception of justice which is to regulate all subsequent criticism and reform of institutions. Then, having chosen a conception of justice, we can suppose that they are to choose a constitution and a legislature to enact laws, and so on, all in accordance with the principles of justice initially agreed upon. Our social situation is just if it is such that by this sequence of hypothetical agreements we would have contracted into the general system of rules which defines it. Moreover, assuming that the original position does determine a set of principles (that is, that a particular conception of justice would be chosen), it will then be true that whenever social institutions satisfy these principles those engaged in them can say to one another that they are cooperating on terms to which they would agree if they were free and equal persons whose relations with respect to one another were fair. They could all view their arrangements as meeting the stipulations which they would acknowledge in an initial situation that embodies widely accepted and reasonable constraints on the choice of principles. The general recognition of this fact would provide the basis for a public acceptance of the corresponding principles of justice. No society can, of course, be a scheme of cooperation which men enter voluntarily in a literal sense; each person finds himself placed at birth in some particular position in some particular society, and the nature of this position materially affects his life prospects. Yet a society satisfying the principles of justice as fairness comes as close as a society can to being a voluntary scheme, for it meets the principles which free and equal persons would assent to under circumstances that are fair. In this sense its members are autonomous and the obligations they recognize self-imposed.

One feature of justice as fairness is to think of the parties in the initial situation as rational and mutually disinterested. This does not mean that the parties are egoists, that is, individuals with only certain kinds of interests, say in wealth, prestige, and domination. But they are conceived as not taking an interest in one another's interests. They are to presume that even their spiritual aims may be opposed, in the way that the aims of those of different religions may be opposed. Moreover, the concept of rationality must be interpreted as far as possible in the narrow sense, standard in economic theory, of taking the most effective means to given ends. I shall modify this concept to some extent, as explained later, but one must try to avoid introducing into it any controversial ethical elements. The initial situation must be characterized by stipulations that are widely accepted.

In working out the conception of justice as fairness one main task clearly is to determine which principles of justice would be chosen in the original position. To do this we must describe this situation in some detail and formulate with care the problem of choice which it presents. These matters I shall take up in the immediately succeeding chapters. It may be observed, however, that once the principles of justice are thought of as arising from an original agreement in a situation of equality, it is an open question whether the principle of utility would be acknowledged. Offhand it hardly seems likely that persons who view themselves as equals, entitled to press their claims upon one another, would agree to a principle which may require lesser life prospects for some simply for the sake of a greater sum of advantages enjoyed by others. Since each desires to protect his interests, his capacity to advance his conception of the good, no one has a reason to acquiesce in an enduring loss for himself in order to bring about a greater net balance of satisfaction. In the absence of strong and lasting benevolent impulses, a rational man would not accept a basic structure merely because it maximized the algebraic sum of advantages irrespective of its permanent effects on his own basic rights and interests. Thus it seems that the principle of utility is incompatible with the conception of social cooperation among equals for mutual advantage. It appears to be inconsistent with the idea of reciprocity implicit in the notion of a well-ordered society. Or, at any rate, so I shall argue.

I shall maintain instead that the persons in the initial situation would choose two rather different principles; the first requires equality in the assignment of basic rights and duties, while the second holds that social and economic inequalities, for example inequalities of wealth and authority, are just only if they result in compensating benefits for everyone, and in particular for the least advantaged members of society. These principles rule out justifying institutions on the grounds that the hardships of some are offset by a greater good in the aggregate. It may be expedient but it is not just that some should have less in order that others may prosper. But there is no injustice in the greater benefits earned by a few provided that the situation of persons not so fortunate is thereby improved. The intuitive idea is that since everyone's well-being depends upon a scheme of cooperation without which no one could have a satisfactory life, the division of advantages should be such as to draw forth the willing cooperation of everyone taking part in it, including those less well situated. . . . The two principles mentioned seem to be a fair agreement on the basis of which those better endowed, or more fortunate in their social position, neither of which we can be said to deserve, could expect the willing cooperation of others when some workable scheme is a necessary condition of the welfare of all. Once we decide to look for a conception of justice that nullifies the accidents of natural endowment and the contingencies of social circumstance as counters in quest for political and economic advantage, we are led to these principles. They express the result of leaving aside those aspects of the social world that seem arbitrary from a moral point of view.

The problem of the choice of principles, however, is extremely difficult. I do not expect the answer I shall suggest to be convincing to everyone. It is, therefore, worth noting from the outset that justice as fairness, like other contract views, consists of two parts: (1) an interpretation of the initial situation and of the problem of choice posed there, and (2) a set of principles which, it is argued, would be agreed to. One may accept the first part of the theory (or some variant thereof), but not the other, and conversely. The concept of the initial contractual situation may seem reasonable although the particular principles proposed are rejected. . . .

Justice as fairness is an example of what I have called a contract theory. Now there may be an objection to the term "contract" and related expressions, but I think it will serve reasonably well. Many words have misleading connotations which at first are likely to confuse. The terms "utility" and "utilitarianism" are surely no exception. They too have unfortunate suggestions which hostile critics have been willing to exploit; yet they are clear enough for those prepared to study utilitarian doctrine. The same should be true of the term "contract" applied to moral theories. As I have mentioned, to understand it one has to keep in mind that it implies a certain level of abstraction. In particular, the content of the relevant agreement is not to enter a given society or to adopt a given form of government, but to accept certain moral principles. Moreover, the undertakings referred to are purely hypothetical: a contract view holds that certain principles would be accepted in a well-defined initial situation.

The merit of the contract terminology is that it conveys the idea that principles of justice may be conceived as principles that would be chosen by rational persons, and that in this way conceptions of justice may be explained and justified. The theory of justice is a part, perhaps the most significant part, of the theory of rational choice. Furthermore, principles of justice deal with conflicting claims upon the advantages won by social cooperation; they apply to the relations among several persons or groups. The word "contract" suggests this plurality as well as the condition that the appropriate division of advantages must be in accordance with principles acceptable to all parties. The condition of publicity for principles of justice is also connoted by the contract phraseology. Thus, if these principles are the outcome of an agreement, citizens have a knowledge of the principles that others follow. It is characteristic of contract theories to stress the public nature of political principles. Finally there is the long tradition of the contract doctrine. Expressing the tie with this line of thought helps to define ideas and accords with natural piety. There are then several advantages in the use of the term "contract." With due precautions taken, it should not be misleading.

...

THE ORIGINAL POSITION AND JUSTIFICATION

I have said that the original position is the appropriate initial status quo which insures that the fundamental agreements reached in it are fair. This fact yields the name "justice as fairness." It is clear, then, that I want to say that one conception of justice is more reasonable than another, or justifiable with respect to it, if rational persons in the initial situation would choose its principles over those of the other for the role of justice. Conceptions of justice are to be ranked by their acceptability to persons so circumstanced. Understood in this way the question of justification is settled by working out a problem of deliberation: we have to ascertain which principles it would be rational to adopt given the contractual situation. This connects the theory of justice with the theory of rational choice.

If this view of the problem of justification is to succeed, we must, of course, describe in some detail the nature of this choice problem. A problem of rational decision has a definite answer only if we know the beliefs and interests of the parties, their relations with respect to one another, the alternatives between which they are to choose, the procedure whereby they make up their minds, and so on. As the circumstances are presented in different ways, correspondingly different principles are accepted. The concept of the original position, as I shall refer to it, is that of the most philosophically favored interpretation of this initial choice situation for the purposes of a theory of justice.

But how are we to decide what is the most favored interpretation? I assume, for one thing, that there is a broad measure of agreement that principles of justice should be chosen under certain conditions. To justify a particular description of the initial situation one shows that it incorporates these commonly shared presumptions. One argues from widely accepted but weak premises to more specific conclusions. Each of the presumptions should by itself be natural and plausible; some of them may seem innocuous or even trivial. The aim of the contract approach is to establish that taken together they impose significant bounds on acceptable principles of justice. The ideal outcome would be that these conditions determine a unique set of principles; but I shall be satisfied if they suffice to rank the main traditional conceptions of social justice.

One should not be misled, then, by the somewhat unusual conditions which characterize the original position. The idea here is simply to make vivid to ourselves the restrictions that it seems reasonable to impose on arguments for principles of justice, and therefore on these principles themselves. Thus it seems reasonable and generally acceptable that no one should be advantaged or disadvantaged by natural fortune or social circumstances in the choice of principles. It also seems widely agreed that it should be impossible to tailor principles to the circumstances of one's own case. We should insure further that particular inclinations and aspirations, and persons' conceptions of their good do not affect the principles adopted. The aim is to rule out those principles that it would be rational to propose for acceptance, however little the chance of success, only if one knew certain things that are irrelevant from the standpoint of justice. For example, if a man knew that he was wealthy, he might find it rational to advance the principle that various taxes for welfare measures be counted unjust; if he knew that he was poor, he would most likely propose the contrary principle. To represent the desired restrictions one imagines a situation in which everyone is deprived of this sort of information. One excludes the knowledge of those contingencies which sets men at odds and allows them to be guided by their prejudices. In this manner the veil of ignorance is arrived at in a natural way. This concept should cause no difficulty if we keep in mind the constraints on arguments that it is meant to express. At any time we can enter the original position, so to speak, simply by following a certain procedure, namely, by arguing for principles of justice in accordance with these restrictions.

It seems reasonable to suppose that the parties in the original position are equal. That is, all have the same rights in the procedure for choosing principles; each can make proposals, submit reasons for their acceptance, and so on. Obviously the purpose of these conditions is to represent equality between human beings as moral persons, as creatures having a conception of their good and capable of a sense of justice. The basis of equality is taken to be similarity in these two respects. Systems of ends are not ranked in value; and each man is presumed to have the requisite ability to understand and to act upon whatever principles are adopted. Together with the veil of ignorance, these conditions define the principles of justice as those which rational persons concerned to advance their interests would consent to as equals when none are known to be advantaged or disadvantaged by social and natural contingencies.

There is, however, another side to justifying a particular description of the original position. This is to see if the principles which would be chosen match our considered convictions of justice or extend them in an acceptable way. We can note whether applying these principles would lead us to make the same judgments about the basic structure of society which we now make intuitively and in which we have the greatest confidence; or whether, in cases where our present judgments are in doubt and given with hesitation, these principles offer a resolution which we can affirm on reflection. There are questions which we feel sure must be answered in a certain way. For example, we are confident that religious intolerance and racial discrimination are unjust. We think that we have examined these things with care and have reached what we believe is an impartial judgment not likely to be distorted by an excessive attention to our own interests. These convictions are provisional fixed points which we presume any conception of justice must fit. But we have much less assurance as to what is the correct distribution of wealth and authority. Here we may be looking for a way to remove our doubts. We can check an interpretation of the initial situation, then, by the capacity of its principles to accommodate our firmest convictions and to provide guidance where guidance is needed.

In searching for the most favored description of this situation we work from both ends. We begin by describing it so that it represents generally shared and preferably weak conditions. We then see if these conditions are strong enough to yield a significant set of principles. If not, we look for further premises equally reasonable. But if so, and these principles match our considered convictions of justice, then so far well and good. But presumably there will be discrepancies. In this case we have a choice. We can either modify the account of the initial situation or we can revise our existing judgments, for even the judgments we take provisionally as fixed points are liable to revision. By going back and forth, sometimes altering the conditions of the contractual circumstances, at others withdrawing our judgments and conforming them to principle, I assume that eventually we shall find a description of the initial situation that both expresses reasonable conditions and yields principles which match our considered judgments duly pruned and adjusted. This state of affairs I refer to as reflective equilibrium. It is an equilibrium because at last our principals and judgments coincide; and it is reflective since we know to what principles our judgments conform and the premises of their derivation. At the moment everything is in order. But this equilibrium is not necessarily stable. It is liable to be upset by further examination of the conditions which should be imposed on the contractual situation and by particular cases which may lead us to revise our judgments. Yet for the time being we have done what we can to render coherent and to justify our convictions of social justice. We have reached a conception of the original position.

...

A final comment. We shall want to say that certain principles of justice are justified because they would be agreed to in an initial situation of equality. I have emphasized that this original position is purely hypothetical. It is natural to ask why, if this agreement is never actually entered into, we should take any interest in these principles, moral or otherwise. The answer is that the conditions embodied in the description of the original position are ones that we do in fact accept. Or if we do not, then perhaps we can be persuaded to do so by philosophical reflection. Each aspect of the contractual situation can be given supporting grounds. Thus what we shall do is to collect together into one conception a number of conditions on principles that we are ready upon due consideration to recognize as reasonable. These constraints express what we are prepared to regard as limits on fair terms of social cooperation. One way to look at the idea of the original position, therefore, is to see it as an expository device which sums up the meaning of these conditions and helps us to extract their consequences. On the other hand, this conception is also an intuitive notion that suggests its own elaboration, so that led on by it we are drawn to define more clearly the standpoint from which we can best interpret moral relationships. We need a conception that enables us to envision our objective from afar: the intuitive notion of the original position is to do this for us.

...

11. TWO PRINCIPLES OF JUSTICE

I shall now state in a provisional form the two principles of justice that I believe would be chosen in the original position. In this section I wish to make only the most general comments, and therefore the first formulation of these principles is tentative. As we go on I shall run through several formulations and approximate step by step the final statement to be given much later. I believe that doing this allows the exposition to proceed in a natural way.

The first statement of the two principles reads as follows.

> First: each person is to have an equal right to the most extensive scheme of equal basic liberties compatible with a similar scheme of liberties for others.
>
> Second: social and economic inequalities are to be arranged so that they are both (a) reasonably expected to be to everyone's advantage, and (b) attached to positions and offices open to all.

There are two ambiguous phrases in the second principle, namely "everyone's advantage" and "open to all." ...

These principles primarily apply, as I have said, to the basic structure of society and govern the assignment of rights and duties and regulate the distribution of social and economic advantages. Their formulation pre-supposes that, for the purposes of a theory of justice, the social structure may be viewed as having two more or less distinct parts, the first principle applying to the one, the second principle to the other. Thus we distinguish between the aspects of the social system that define and secure the equal basic liberties and the aspects that specify and establish social and economic inequalities. Now it is essential to observe that the basic liberties are given by a list of such liberties. Important among these are political liberty (the right to vote and to hold public office) and freedom of speech and assembly; liberty of conscience and freedom of thought; freedom of the person, which includes freedom from psychological oppression and physical assault and dismemberment (integrity of the person); the right to hold personal property and freedom from arbitrary arrest and seizure as defined by the concept of the rule of law. These liberties are to be equal by the first principle.

The second principle applies, in the first approximation, to the distribution of income and wealth and to the design of organizations that make use of differences in authority and responsibility. While the distribution of wealth and income need not be equal, it must be to everyone's advantage, and at the same time, positions of authority and responsibility must be accessible to all. One applies the second principle by holding positions open, and then, subject to this constraint, arranges social and economic inequalities so that everyone benefits.

These principles are to be arranged in a serial order with the first principle prior to the second. This ordering means that infringements of the basic equal liberties protected by the first principle cannot be justified, or compensated for, by greater social and economic advantages. These liberties have a central range of application within which they can be limited and compromised only when they conflict with other basic liberties. Since they may be limited when they clash with one another, none of these liberties is absolute; but however they are adjusted to form one system, this system is to be the same for all. It is difficult, and perhaps impossible, to give a complete specification of these liberties independently from the particular circumstances—social, economic, and technological—of a given society. The hypothesis is that the general form of such a list could be devised with sufficient exactness to sustain this conception of justice. Of course, liberties not on the list, for example, the right to own certain kinds of property (e.g., means of production) and freedom of contract as understood by the doctrine of laissez-faire are not basic; and so they are not protected by the priority of the first principle. Finally, in regard to the second principle, the distribution of wealth and income, and positions of authority and responsibility, are to be consistent with both the basic liberties and equality of opportunity.

The two principles are rather specific in their content, and their acceptance rests on certain assumptions that I must eventually try to explain and justify. For the present, it should be observed that these principles are a special case of a more general conception of justice that can be expressed as follows.

All social values—liberty and opportunity, income and wealth, and the social bases of self-respect—are to be distributed equally unless an unequal distribution of any, or all, of these values is to everyone's advantage.

Injustice, then, is simply inequalities that are not to the benefit of all. Of course, this conception is extremely vague and requires interpretation.

As a first step, suppose that the basic structure of society distributes certain primary goods, that is, things that every rational man is presumed to want. These goods normally have a use whatever a person's rational plan of life. For simplicity, assume that the chief primary goods at the disposition of society are rights, liberties, and opportunities, and income and wealth. (Later on in Part Three the primary good of self-respect has a central place.) These are the social primary goods. Other primary goods such as health and vigor, intelligence and imagination, are natural goods; although their possession is influenced by the basic structure, they are not so directly under its control. Imagine, then, a hypothetical initial arrangement in which all the social primary goods are equally distributed: everyone has similar rights and duties, and income and wealth are evenly shared. This state of affairs provides a benchmark for judging improvements. If certain inequalities of wealth and differences in authority would make everyone better off than in this hypothetical starting situation, then they accord with the general conception.

Now it is possible, at least theoretically, that by giving up some of their fundamental liberties men are sufficiently compensated by the resulting social and economic gains. The general conception of justice imposes no restrictions on what sort of inequalities are permissible; it only requires that everyone's position be improved. We need not suppose anything so drastic as consenting to a condition of slavery. Imagine instead that people seem willing to forego certain political rights when the economic returns are significant. It is this kind of exchange which the two principles rule out; being arranged in serial order they do not permit exchanges between basic liberties and economic and social gains except under extenuating circumstances. . . .

24. THE VEIL OF IGNORANCE

The idea of the original position is to set up a fair procedure so that any principles agreed to will be just. The aim is to use the notion of pure procedural justice as a basis of theory. Somehow we must nullify the effects of specific contingencies which put men at odds and tempt them to exploit social and natural circumstances to their own advantage. Now in order to do this I assume that the parties are situated behind a veil of ignorance. They do not know how the various alternatives will affect their own particular case and they are obliged to evaluate principles solely on the basis of general considerations.

It is assumed, then, that the parties do not know certain kinds of particular facts. First of all, no one knows his place in society, his class position or social status; nor does he know his fortune in the distribution of natural assets and abilities, his intelligence and strength, and the like. Nor, again, does anyone know his conception of the good, the particulars of his rational plan of life, or even the special features of his psychology such as his aversion to risk or liability to optimism or pessimism. More than this, I assume that the parties do not know the particular circumstances of their own society. That is, they do not know its economic or political situation, or the level of civilization and culture it has been able to achieve. The persons in the original position have no information as to which generation they belong. These broader restrictions on knowledge are appropriate in part because questions of social justice arise between generations as well as within them, for example, the question of the appropriate rate of capital saving and of the conservation of natural resources and the environment of nature. There is also, theoretically anyway, the question of a reasonable genetic policy. In these cases too, in order to carry through the idea of the original position, the parties must not know the contingencies that set them in opposition. They must choose principles the consequences of which they are prepared to live with whatever generation they turn out to belong to.

As far as possible, then, the only particular facts which the parties know is that their society is subject to the circumstances of justice and whatever this implies. It is taken for granted, however, that they know the general facts about human society. They understand political affairs and the principles of economic theory; they know the basis of social organization and the laws of human psychology. Indeed, the parties are presumed to know whatever general facts affect the choice of the principles of justice. There are no limitations on general information, that is, on general laws and theories, since conceptions of justice must be adjusted to the characteristics of the systems of social cooperation which they are to regulate, and there is no reason to rule out these facts. It is, for example, a consideration against a conception of justice that, in view of the laws of moral psychology, men would not acquire a desire to act upon it even when the institutions of their society satisfied it. For in this case there would be difficulty in securing the stability of social cooperation. An important feature of a conception of justice is that it should generate its own support. Its principles should be such that when they are embodied in the basic structure of society men tend to acquire the corresponding sense of justice and develop a desire to act in accordance with its principles. In this case a conception of justice is stable. This kind of general information is admissible in the original position. . . .

Thus there follows the very important consequence that the parties have no basis for bargaining in the usual sense. No one knows his situation in society nor his natural assets, and therefore no one is in a position to tailor principles to his advantage. We might imagine that one of the contractees threatens to hold out unless the others agree to principles favorable to him. But how does he know which principles are especially in his interests? The same holds for the formation of coalitions: if a group were to decide to band together to the disadvantage of the others, they would not know how to favor themselves in the choice of principles. Even if they could get everyone to agree to their proposal, they would have no assurance that it was to their advantage, since they cannot identify themselves either by name or description. . . .

The restrictions on particular information in the original position are, then, of fundamental importance. Without them we would not be able to work out any definite theory of justice at all. We would have to be content with a vague formula stating that justice is what would be agreed to without being able to say much, if anything, about the substance of the agreement itself. The formal constraints of the concept of right, those applying to principles directly, are not sufficient for our purpose. The veil of ignorance makes possible a unanimous choice of a particular conception of justice. Without these limitations on knowledge the bargaining problem of the original position would be hopelessly complicated. Even if theoretically a solution were to exist, we would not, at present anyway, be able to determine it. . . .

Now the reasons for the veil of ignorance go beyond mere simplicity. We want to define the original position so that we get the desired solution. If a knowledge of particulars is allowed, then the outcome is biased by arbitrary contingencies. As already observed, to each according to his threat advantage is not a principle of justice. If the original position is to yield agreements that are just, the parties must be fairly situated and treated equally as moral persons. The arbitrariness of the world must be corrected for by adjusting the circumstances of the initial contractual situation. Moreover, if in choosing principles we required unanimity even when there is full information, only a few rather obvious cases could be decided. A conception of justice based on unanimity in these circumstances would indeed be weak and trivial. But once knowledge is excluded, the requirement of unanimity is not out of place and the fact that it can be satisfied is of great importance. It enables us to say of the preferred conception of justice that it represents a genuine reconciliation of interests. . . .

Discussion Questions

1. On Rawls' theory, are the principles of justice *discovered* or *created*? Do the principles of justice exist prior to the original position or are they the outcome of the original position? Explain how Rawls would answer these questions. How does his answer protect the autonomy of citizens?

2. Consider the Difference Principle carefully. In what ways does contemporary society not meet the requirements of the Difference Principle? What changes would have to occur in order for our society to be completely just according to this principle? Can you imagine these changes? How hard would they be to institute?

3. Suppose economic wealth could be distributed in such a way that all full-time workers earned at least $40,000, but that no persons in society made more than $250,000 per year. (Imagine also that the value of money does not change in this scenario.) Would you prefer to live in this society? Would it make a difference if you didn't know who you were? Why or why not? Would it violate your rights under the Equal Liberties Principle? Could the Difference Principle require such a redistribution of wealth?

4. Vast societal redistribution of wealth would occur in a few decades if inheritance was capped, for example, at $200,000 per person over a lifetime. For the majority of people, a policy such as this would have no effect since they would never inherit that much wealth. Is such a policy possible according to Rawls' principles of justice? Is it desirable to do so according to the Difference Principle? Does it violate the Equal Liberties Principle? Why or why not?

For Further Reading

Rawls' *A Theory of Justice* is widely available and, although not completely representative of his current thought, is the first and best source for Rawls' political philosophy. His 1993 book, *Political Liberalism*, is also recommended. Some of the most important theoretical work by Rawls is also the most difficult; see "Kantian Constructivism in Moral Theory," *Journal of Philosophy* 77 (1980), 515–572. Although difficult at times, that essay rewards the careful reader with many insights into the Kantian roots of "justice as fairness."

There are many books and articles on Rawls, too many to list here. Some interesting titles include Thomas W. Pogge, *Realizing Rawls* (1989); Kenneth Baynes, *The Normative Grounds of Social Criticism: Kant, Rawls, and Habermas;* and Stephen L. Darwall, "Is There a Kantian Foundation for Rawlsian Justice?" in *John Rawls's Theory of Social Justice,* edited by H. Gene Blocker and Elizabeth H. Smith (1980). The most widely read feminist critique of Rawls can be found in Susan Moller Okin, *Justice, Gender, and the Family* (1989). Gerald Doppelt has written several socialist critiques of Rawls; see "Rawls' System of Justice: A Critique from the Left," in *Noûs* 15 (1981), 259–308.

Rawls has inspired other contractarian approaches to political philosophy and morality. See Ronald Dworkin, *Taking Rights Seriously* (1977), and David Gauthier, *Morals by Agreement* (1986).

CHAPTER 11

HOW ELSE CAN I THINK ABOUT THE STATE?

Liberal political theories, such as those of Locke, Hospers, and Rawls presented in Chapter 10, use versions of the social contract to combine certain basic notions in order to defend the liberal political state. These basic concepts include the importance of voluntary consent, the claim that obligations arise only freely, and a particular conception of the person as a separately existing individual. Many critics of liberalism claim that these basic concepts misrepresent our actual nature as persons, in part because they treat society as an idealization. Political liberalism, its critics contend, relies on abstractions that fail to address the harsh realities that systematically disadvantage many groups, especially along lines of race, class, and gender.

The first selection, Karl Marx and Friedrich Engels' rousing *Communist Manifesto,* is a powerful critique of liberal democracies as failing to create an egalitarian society. Marx's political theory treats the antagonism between social classes—the conflict between those who earn their wealth through the power of privately owned capital and those who must struggle to survive by selling their labor—as the most fundamental feature of industrial society. The class structure of society, according to Marx, not only shapes our economic fortunes but, equally as important, also determines the nature of our thought, that is, how we conceptualize the world. The second selection in this chapter picks up on this theme. Jeffrey Reiman writes about the failure of the criminal justice system to curb crime, a failure he attributes to the vested interests of a wealthy elite to shape the social perception of crime and criminals in a manner that preserves and reinforces the advantages of their social class. For both Marx and Reiman, then, our mental picture of the world is shaped by the most powerful persons in society, or, as Marx put it, "The ruling ideas of an age are the ideas of the ruling class."

The next reading addresses liberalism from the point of view of race, certainly one of the single greatest causes of political inequality over the last several centuries. Charles Mills argues that what some philosophers like Locke describe as the social contract is better described as a *Racial Contract:* a hidden contract between whites to privilege themselves by agreeing to systematically deny fair political rights to blacks, to create an unjust and exploitative economic system, and to obscure these injustices by agreeing to forget that white supremacy underlies contemporary society. Mills introduces the concept of a Racial Contract in order to illuminate not only the actual history of white supremacy but, more importantly, the way in which it is a political system.

The last two articles are feminist critiques of liberal political theory. Carole Pateman, in the first selection, questions whether social contract theorists such as Hobbes and Locke have truly incorporated voluntary consent into their theories as they claim to have done. Recall that according to the standard version of the social contract, the state is legitimate only insofar as its citizens have authorized it through voluntary consent. But Pateman regards this use of voluntary consent to be primarily an ideological smoke screen designed to promote the interests of only a few citizens. True voluntary consent, she argues, has such radical implications that social contract theorists have shied away from taking it seriously.

The last selection of this chapter attempts to apply some of the insights of recent work in moral theory by feminists to political theory. Joan Tronto investigates what would happen to our conception of the proper roles and limits of the political state if we took the idea of 'care' seriously. She derives her care ethic in part from the work of Carol Gilligan (see Chapter 9, Reading 48). Both Tronto and Gilligan can be understood as challenging typical liberal conceptions of the person. For social contract theorists, persons are conceived of as independent, self-motivating, and autonomous. What would happen, asks Tronto, if we began our political reflection from a conception of the self that matched women's self-identity? Beginning with a picture of the self that depends on women's experience means that care must now be recognized as a valid public responsibility, instead of being partitioned off into the private, domestic sphere.

56   THE COMMUNIST MANIFESTO
Karl Marx and Friedrich Engels

Libertarians are often criticized for employing a very generic and abstract view of human persons. Gone are all the distinctions between persons due to natural ability, luck, race, and gender. The difficulty of this approach is that since individuals are legally equal, in practice they cannot complain about the social inequality that arises from protected practices (that is, from the voluntary practices of free market capitalism). This simple homogeneous viewpoint, critics of libertarians contest, serves to hide differences between persons that affect the worth of their liberties: For persons who have inherited wealth, have bought a premium education, and are connected to the 'good-ole-boys network', the negative rights guaranteed by libertarianism are of tremendous value; for those who are impoverished, have received only a barely adequate education, and are outside of the informal network within which most jobs are filled and contracts negotiated—and to whom banks are unwilling to lend capital—the value of the libertarian's esteemed liberties is seriously discounted.

No one has pursued this criticism against the liberal tradition more forcefully than socialist egalitarians. Socialism, of course, owes its historic roots to the work of Karl Marx (1818–1893) and Friedrich Engels (1820–1895). The following selection is from the *Communist Manifesto*, written in 1848. In this popular and influential account of communism, Marx and

SOURCE: From "Karl Marx: The Communist Manifesto," in Frederic L. Bender (ed.), *Karl Marx: The Essential Writings* (New York: Harper & Row, 1972), pp. 254–263. Copyright © 1972 Frederich L. Bender.

Engels identify how property (or capital) perpetuates a class-structured society. One class, the **bourgeoisie,** owns investment capital (factories, stocks, real estate, banks, and so forth) and increases its wealth through the labors of others, that is, through the return on their capital investments. The other class, the **proletariat,** lacking access to investment capital, sells its labor to others. The wage-laborer proletariat works to create property, but the property they create is wrongly held by the bourgeoisie, who alienate the proletariat from the products of their labor. This is the fundamental inequity of the capitalist system, which, according to Marx and Engels, will eventually cause its own destruction at the hands of the workers of the world. Capital, the tool that makes production possible, ought to be owned by all workers. Private property, they argue, ought to be abolished—but not the property of the proletariat (which amounts to nothing anyway), just bourgeois property (which was stolen to begin with).

Reading Questions

1. How do Marx and Engels respond to the criticism that they wish to get rid of property?
2. How is labor different in a bourgeois society as opposed to an ideal communist society?
3. Why is it not a problem that individuality and freedom are going to be abolished?
4. Why do Marx and Engels wish the bourgeois family to vanish?
5. What will happen to the status of women in a communist society?
6. How do Marx and Engels respond to the criticism that communists seek to abolish countries?
7. What will happen to political power after class distinctions have disappeared?

...

The distinguishing feature of Communism is not the abolition of property generally, but the abolition of bourgeois property. But modern bourgeois private property is the final and most complete expression of the system of producing and appropriating products, that is based on class antagonisms, on the exploitation of the many by the few.

In this sense, the theory of the Communists may be summed up in the single sentence: Abolition of private property.

We Communists have been reproached with the desire of abolishing the right of personally acquiring property as the fruit of a man's own labor, which property is alleged to be the groundwork of all personal freedom, activity and independence.

Hard-won, self-acquired, self-earned property! Do you mean the property of the petty artisan and of the small peasant, a form of property that preceded the bourgeois form? There is no need to abolish that; the development of industry has to a great extent already destroyed it, and is still destroying it daily.

Or do you mean modern bourgeois private property?

But does wage labor create any property for the laborer? Not a bit. It creates capital, i.e., that kind of property which exploits wage labor, and which cannot increase except upon condition of begetting a new supply of wage labor for fresh exploitation. Property, in its present form, is based on the antagonism of capital and wage labor. Let us examine both sides of this antagonism.

To be a capitalist is to have not only a purely personal, but a social *status* in production. Capital is a collective product, and only by the united action of many members, nay, in the last resort, only by the united action of all members of society, can it be set in motion.

Capital is, therefore, not a personal, it is a social power.

When, therefore, capital is converted into common property, into the property of all members of society, personal property is not thereby transformed into social property. It is only the social character of the property that is changed. It loses its class character.

Let us now take wage labor.

The average price of wage labor is the minimum wage, i.e., that quantum of the means of subsistence, which is absolutely requisite to keep the laborer in bare existence as a laborer. What, therefore, the wage laborer appropriates by means of his labor, merely suffices to prolong and reproduce a bare existence. We by no means intend to abolish this personal appropriation of the products of labor, an appropriation that is made for the maintenance and reproduction of human life, and that leaves no surplus wherewith to command the labor of others. All that we want to do away with is the miserable character of this appropriation, under which the laborer lives merely to increase capital, and is allowed to live only insofar as the interest of the ruling class requires it.

In bourgeois society, living labor is but a means to increase accumulated labor. In Communist society, accumulated labor is but a means to widen, to enrich, to promote the existence of the laborer.

In bourgeois society, therefore, the past dominates the present; in Communist society, the present dominates the past. In bourgeois society capital is independent and has individuality, while the living person is dependent and has no individuality.

And the abolition of this state of things is called by the bourgeois, abolition of individuality and freedom! And rightly so. The abolition of bourgeois individuality, bourgeois independence, and bourgeois freedom is undoubtedly aimed at.

By freedom is meant, under the present bourgeois conditions of production, free trade, free selling and buying.

But if selling and buying disappears, free selling and buying disappears also. This talk about free selling and buying, and all the other "brave words" of our bourgeoisie about freedom in general, have a meaning, if any, only in contrast with restricted selling and buying, with the fettered traders of the Middle Ages, but have no meaning when opposed to the Communistic abolition of buying and selling, of the bourgeois conditions of production, and of the bourgeoisie itself.

You are horrified at our intending to do away with private property. But in your existing society, private property is already done away with for nine-tenths of the population; its existence for the few is solely due to its nonexistence in the hands of those nine-tenths. You reproach us, therefore, with intending to do away with a form of property, the necessary condition for whose existence is the nonexistence of any property for the immense majority of society.

In one word, you reproach us with intending to do away with your property. Precisely so; that is just what we intend.

From the moment when labor can no longer be converted into capital, money, or rent, into a social power capable of being monopolized, i.e., from the moment when individual property can no longer be transformed into bourgeois property, into capital, from that moment, you say, individuality vanishes.

You must, therefore, confess that by "individual" you mean no other person than the bourgeois, than the middle-class owner of property. This person must, indeed, be swept out of the way, and made impossible.

Communism deprives no man of the power to appropriate the products of society; all that it does is to deprive him of the power to subjugate the labor of others by means of such appropriation.

It has been objected that upon the abolition of private property all work will cease, and universal laziness will overtake us.

According to this, bourgeois society ought long ago to have gone to the dogs through sheer idleness; for those of its members who work acquire nothing, and those who acquire anything do not work. The whole of this objection is but another expression of the tautology: that there can no longer be any wage labor when there is no longer any capital.

All objections urged against the Communistic mode of producing and appropriating material products, have, in the same way, been urged against the Communistic modes of producing and appropriating intellectual products. Just as, to the bourgeois, the disappearance of class property is the disappearance of production itself, so the disappearance of class culture is to him identical with the disappearance of all culture.

That culture, the loss of which he laments, is, for the enormous majority, a mere training to act as a machine.

But don't wrangle with us so long as you apply, to our intended abolition of bourgeois property, the standard of your bourgeois notions of freedom, culture, law, etc. Your very ideas are but the outgrowth of the conditions of your bourgeois production and bourgeois property, just as your jurisprudence is but the will of your class made into a law for all, a will whose essential character and direction are determined by the economical conditions of existence of your class.

The selfish misconception that induces you to transform into eternal laws of nature and of reason, the social forms springing from your present mode of production and form of property—historical relations that rise and disappear in the progress of production—this misconception you share with every ruling class that has preceded you. What you see clearly in the case of ancient property, what you admit in the case of feudal property, you are of course forbidden to admit in the case of your own bourgeois form of property.

Abolition of the family! Even the most radical flare up at this infamous proposal of the Communists.

On what foundation is the present family, the bourgeois family, based? On capital, on private gain. In its completely developed form this family exists only among the bourgeoisie. But this state of things finds its complement in the practical absence of the family among the proletarians, and in public prostitution.

The bourgeois family will vanish as a matter of course when its complement vanishes, and both will vanish with the vanishing of capital.

Do you charge us with wanting to stop the exploitation of children by their parents? To this crime we plead guilty.

But, you will say, we destroy the most hallowed of relations, when we replace home education by social.

And your education! Is not that also social, and determined by the social conditions under which you educate, by the intervention, direct or indirect, of society, by means of schools, etc? The Communists have not invented the intervention of society in education; they do but seek to alter the character of that intervention, and to rescue education from the influence of the ruling class.

The bourgeois clap-trap about the family and education, about the hallowed co-relation of parent and child, becomes all the more disgusting, the more, by the action of Modern Industry, all family ties among the proletarians are torn asunder, and their children transformed into simple articles of commerce and instruments of labor.

But you Communists would introduce community of women, screams the whole bourgeoisie in chorus.

The bourgeois sees in his wife a mere instrument of production. He hears that the instruments of production are to be exploited in common, and, naturally, can come to no other conclusion than that the lot of being common to all will likewise fall to the women.

He has not even a suspicion that the real point aimed at is to do away with the status of women as mere instruments of production.

For the rest, nothing is more ridiculous than the virtuous indignation of our bourgeois at the community of women which, they pretend, is to be openly and officially established by the Communists. The Communists have no need to introduce community of women; it has existed almost from time immemorial.

Our bourgeois, not content with having the wives and daughters of their proletarians at their disposal, not to speak of common prostitutes, take the greatest pleasure in seducing each other's wives.

Bourgeois marriage is in reality a system of wives in common and thus, at the most, what the Communists might possibly be reproached with, is that they desire to introduce, in substitution for a hypocritically concealed, an openly legalized community of women. For the rest, it is self-evident that the abolition of the present system of production must bring with it the abolition of the community of women springing from that system, i.e., of prostitution both public and private.

The Communists are further reproached with desiring to abolish countries and nationality.

The working men have no country. We cannot take from them what they have not got. Since the proletariat must first of all acquire political supremacy, must rise to be the leading class of the nation, must constitute itself *the* nation, it is, so far, itself national, though not in the bourgeois sense of the word.

National differences and antagonisms between peoples are daily more and more vanishing, owing to the development of the bourgeoisie, to freedom of commerce, to the world market, to uniformity in the mode of production and in the conditions of life corresponding thereto.

The supremacy of the proletariat will cause them to vanish still faster. United action, of the leading civilized countries at least, is one of the first conditions for the emancipation of the proletariat.

In proportion as the exploitation of one individual by another is put an end to, the exploitation of one nation by another will also be put an end to. In proportion as the antagonism between classes within the nation vanishes, the hostility of one nation to another will come to an end.

The charges against Communism made from a religious, a philosophical, and, generally, from an ideological standpoint, are not deserving of serious examination.

Does it require deep intuition to comprehend that man's ideas, views and conceptions, in one word, man's consciousness, changes with every change in the conditions of his material existence, in his social relations and in his social life?

What else does the history of ideas prove, than that intellectual production changes its character in proportion as material production is changed? The ruling ideas of each age have ever been the ideas of its ruling class.

When people speak of ideas that revolutionize society, they do but express the fact that within the old society, the elements of a new one have been created, and that the dissolution of the old ideas keeps even pace with the dissolution of the old conditions of existence.

When the ancient world was in its last throes, the ancient religions were overcome by Christianity. When Christian ideas succumbed in the eighteenth century to rationalist ideas, feudal society fought its death battle with the then revolutionary bourgeoisie. The ideas of religious liberty and freedom of conscience merely gave expression to the sway of free competition within the domain of knowledge.

"Undoubtedly," it will be said, "religious, moral, philosophical and juridical ideas have been modified in the course of historical development. But religion, morality, philosophy, political science, and law constantly survived this change."

"There are, besides, eternal truths, such as Freedom, Justice, etc., that are common to all states of society. But Communism abolishes eternal truths, it abolishes all religion, and all morality,

instead of constituting them on a new basis; it therefore acts in contradiction to all past historical experience."

What does this accusation reduce itself to? The history of all past society has consisted in the development of class antagonisms, antagonisms that assumed different forms at different epochs.

But whatever form they may have taken, one fact is common to all past ages, viz., the exploitation of one part of society by the other. No wonder, then, that the social consciousness of past ages, despite all the multiplicity and variety it displays, moves within certain common forms, or general ideas, which cannot completely vanish except with the total disappearance of class antagonisms.

The Communist revolution is the most radical rupture with traditional property relations; no wonder that its development involves the most radical rupture with traditional ideas.

But let us have done with the bourgeois objections to Communism.

We have seen above that the first step in the revolution by the working class is to raise the proletariat to the position of ruling class, to win the battle of democracy.

The proletariat will use its political supremacy to wrest, by degrees, all capital from the bourgeoisie, to centralize all instruments of production in the hands of the State, i.e., of the proletariat organized as the ruling class; and to increase the total of productive forces as rapidly as possible.

Of course, in the beginning, this cannot be effected except by means of despotic inroads on the rights of property, and on the conditions of bourgeois production; by means of measures, therefore, which appear economically insufficient and untenable, but which, in the course of the movement, outstrip themselves, necessitate further inroads upon the old social order, and are unavoidable as a means of entirely revolutionizing the mode of production.

These measures will of course be different in different countries.

Nevertheless in the most advanced countries, the following will be pretty generally applicable.

1. Abolition of property in land and application of all rents of land to public purposes.
2. A heavy progressive or graduated income tax.

3. Abolition of all right of inheritance.
4. Confiscation of the property of all emigrants and rebels.
5. Centralization of credit in the hands of the State, by means of a national bank with State capital and an exclusive monopoly.
6. Centralization of the means of communication and transport in the hands of the State.
7. Extension of factories and instruments of production owned by the State; the bringing into cultivation of wastelands, and the improvement of the soil generally in accordance with a common plan.
8. Equal liability of all to labor. Establishment of industrial armies, especially for agriculture.
9. Combination of agriculture with manufacturing industries; gradual abolition of the distinction between town and country, by a more equable distribution of the population over the country.
10. Free education for all children in public schools. Abolition of children's factory labor in its present form. Combination of education with industrial production, etc., etc.

When, in the course of development, class distinctions have disappeared, and all production has been concentrated in the hands of a vast association of the whole nation, the public power will lose its political character. Political power, properly so called, is merely the organized power of one class for oppressing another. If the proletariat during its contest with the bourgeoisie is compelled, by the force of circumstances, to organize itself as a class, if, by means of a revolution, it makes itself the ruling class, and, as such, sweeps away by force the old conditions of production, then it will, along with these conditions, have swept away the conditions for the existence of class antagonisms and of classes generally, and will thereby have abolished its own supremacy as a class.

In place of the old bourgeois society, with its classes and class antagonisms, we shall have an association in which the free development of each is the condition for the free development of all.

Discussion Questions

1. Is it unfair that the owners of a company and factory accumulate large profits (that is, that they acquire additional capital) while their employees earn only modest incomes? Why would Marx and Engels consider this a problem? Is it actually a problem? Why or why not?
2. Is it ever acceptable to buy and sell the labor of individuals? In what ways is selling our labor to the highest bidder in an open market like sexual prostitution? In what ways is it not? Do Marx and Engels believe it is a problem to buy and sell labor? Why? Do you agree?
3. According to Marx and Engels, what is commonly referred to as 'individuality' is actually 'bourgeois individuality.' What do they mean by 'bourgeois individuality'? Why do they consider this to be a problem? Is there another sense of "individuality" that is not problematic?
4. Has the collapse of communism worldwide shown that the political philosophy of Marx and Engels is mistaken? Why or why not?

For Further Reading

You can find this selection and other important works by Marx in *Karl Marx: The Essential Writings,* edited by Frederic L. Bender (1972). An influential and recommended biography of Marx is Isaiah Berlin's *Karl Marx* (1939). For a collection of essays debating communism and capitalism see *The Main Debate,* edited by Tibor R. Machan (1987).

57   WHO IS WINNING THE LOSING WAR AGAINST CRIME?
Jeffrey Reiman

While many persons have focused on the impact Marx's political theory would have on our economic system, it also has important implications for other aspects of contemporary society. In this reading, Jeffrey Reiman (1942–), a philosopher at the American University in Washington, D.C., provides us with a practical example of how the themes first raised by Marx can be used to address significant social problems besides poverty, in this case, crime.

Reiman is concerned about the way that various ideologies prevent us from seeing the true nature of crime. What is an 'ideology'? This concept took on an increasingly important role in Western philosophy after Marx. For philosophers in this tradition, ideologies are sets of tightly related beliefs that not only are false, but are harmful because they serve the political interests of some persons and not others. Ideologies make it appear rational to organize our political life in a certain manner, which turns out to be harmful to our actual interests. For example, for Marx, a number of beliefs about freedom, personal responsibility, and the nature of human happiness comprise an ideology that supports the social foundations of capitalism, an economic system Marx regarded as harmful.

In the same way, Reiman argues that ideologies such as 'free choice' and 'human nature' deflect our attention from the complex reality of crime, much to our detriment. For example, a number of researchers approach criminal behavior by exploring the role that human nature plays in criminal activity. Reiman attempts to reframe and recast the problem. The unjust and inept criminal justice system is not, he argues, the result of a failure to recognize the contribution human nature makes to criminal behavior. The real truth, he contends, is that powerful groups in society have a vested interest in perpetuating an inept, unjust criminal justice system. This is what Reiman calls the *Pyrrhic defeat theory*, the hypothesis that the failure of the criminal justice system to actually prevent crime benefits those in positions of power. When crime control fails, powerful persons win. Or, as he puts it, "*Nothing succeeds like failure.*"

Reading Questions

1. How does the Pyrrhic defeat theory explain the failure of the criminal justice system?
2. Why does crime primarily affect the poor?
3. Why is crime so widely represented in the media and in the minds of most Americans? Why is it a natural choice to be a vehicle of class ideology?
4. What problem is there with focusing on individual criminals and individual responsibility?
5. What problem is posed by supposing that criminal law is the politically neutral minimum of a civilized society?

6. According to Reiman, what are the greatest dangers that face average citizens?
7. Why must the criminal justice system fail to reduce crime?
8. What ideological message does the criminal justice system send?

In every case the laws are made by the ruling party in its own interest; a democracy makes democratic laws, a despot autocratic ones, and so on. By making these laws they define as "just" for their subjects whatever is for their own interest, and they call anyone who breaks them a "wrongdoer" and punish him accordingly.

Thrasymachus, in Plato's *Republic*

WHY IS THE CRIMINAL JUSTICE SYSTEM FAILING?

The streams of my argument flow together at this point in a question: *Why is it happening?* I have shown how it is no accident that "the offender at the end of the road in prison is likely to be a member of the lowest social and economic groups in the country." I have shown that this is not an accurate group portrait of who threatens society—it is a picture of whom the criminal justice systems *selects* for arrest and imprisonment from among those who threaten society. It is an image distorted by the shape of the criminal justice carnival mirror. This much we have seen and now we want to know why: *Why is the criminal justice system allowed to function in a fashion that neither protects society nor achieves justice? Why is the criminal justice system failing?*

My answer to these questions will require looking at who benefits from this failure and who suffers from it. More particularly, I will argue that the rich and powerful in America, those who derive the greatest advantage from the persistence of the social and economic system as it is currently organized, reap benefits from the failure of criminal justice that has been documented in this book. . . .

. . .

To understand how the Pyrrhic defeat theory explains the current shape of our failing criminal justice policy, note that this failure is really *three* failures that work together. First, there is the failure to implement policies that stand a good chance of reducing crime and the harm it causes. Second, there is the failure to identify as crimes the harmful acts of the rich and powerful. Third, there is the failure to eliminate economic bias in the criminal justice

system, so that the poor continue to have a substantially greater chance than better-off people of being arrested, charged, convicted, and penalized for committing the acts that are treated as crimes. The effect of the first failure is that there remains a large amount of crime—even if crime rates occasionally dip as a result of factors outside the control of the criminal justice system, such as the decline in the number of 15- to 24-year-olds. The effect of the second failure is that the acts identified as crimes are predominantly done by the poor. The effect of the third failure is that the individuals who are arrested and convicted for crimes are predominantly poor people. The effect of the three failures working together is that we are largely unprotected against the harmful acts of the well off, while at the same time we are confronted on the streets and in our homes with a real and large threat of crime and in the courts and prisons with a large and visible population of poor criminals. In short, the effect of current criminal justice policy is at once to narrow the public's conception of what is dangerous to acts of the poor *and* to present a convincing embodiment of this danger.

The Pyrrhic defeat theory aims to explain the *persistence* of this failing criminal justice policy, rather than its origins. The criminal justice system we have originated as a result of complex historical factors that have to do with the development of the common law tradition in England, the particular form in which this was transplanted on American soil, and the zigzagging course of reform and reaction that has marked our history since the English colonies were transformed into an independent American nation. The study of these factors would surely require another book longer than this one—but, more important, for our purposes it would be unnecessary because it is not the origin of criminal justice policy and practices that is puzzling. The focus on one-on-one harm reflects the main ways in which people harmed each other in the days before large-scale industrialization; the refusal to implement policies that might reduce crime (such as gun control or legalization of heroin or amelioration of poverty) reflects a defensive and punitive response to crime that is natural and understandable, if not noble and far-sighted; and the existence of economic bias in the criminal justice system reflects the real economic and political inequalities that characterize the society in which that system is embedded. What is puzzling, then, is not how these policies came to be what they are but why they persist in the face of their failure to achieve either security or justice. The explanation I shall offer for this persistence I call "historical inertia."

The historical inertia explanation argues that current criminal justice policy persists because it fails in a way that does not give rise to an effective demand for change, for two reasons: First, this failing system provides benefits for those with the power to make changes, while it imposes costs on those without such power. Second, because the criminal justice system shapes the public's conception of what is dangerous, it creates the impression that the harms it is fighting are *the real* threats to society—thus, even when people see that the system is less than a roaring success, they generally do no more than demand more of the same: more police, more prisons, longer prison sentences, and so on.

Consider first the benefits that the system provides for those with wealth and power. I have argued that the triple failure of criminal justice policy diverts attention from the harmful (noncriminal) acts of the well off and confronts us in our homes and on our streets with a real substantial threat of crime and in the courts and prisons with a large and visible population of poor criminals. This in turn conveys a vivid image to the American people, namely, that *there is a real threat to our lives and limbs, and it is a threat from the poor.* This image provides benefits to the rich and powerful in America. It carries an *ideological message* that serves to protect their wealth and privilege. Crudely put, the message is this:

• The threat to "law-abiding Middle America" comes from below them on the economic ladder, not above them.
• The poor are morally defective, and thus their poverty is their own fault, not a symptom of social or economic injustice.

The effect of this message is to funnel the discontent of middle Americans into hostility toward, and fear of, the poor. It leads Americans to ignore the ways in which they are injured and robbed by the acts of the affluent and leads them to demand harsher doses of "law and order" aimed mainly at the lower classes. Most important, it nudges middle Americans toward a *conservative* defense of American society with its large disparities of wealth, power, and opportunity—and nudges them away from a progressive demand for equality and an equitable distribution of wealth and power.

On the other hand, but equally important, is that those who are mainly victimized by the "failure" to reduce crime are by and large the poor themselves. The people who are hurt the most by the failure of the criminal justice system are those with the least power to change the system. The Department of Justice's *National Criminal Victimization Survey* says of 1991, "In general, persons from households with low incomes experienced higher violent crime victimization rates than did persons from wealthier households. Persons from households with an income under $7,500 had significantly higher rates of robbery and assault than persons in most other income groups, particularly those from households earning $50,000 or more." For 1992, households with annual incomes less than $7,500 were victims of violent crimes at a rate more than double those of families earning $30,000 to $49,999, and three times those of families earning $50,000 and above (see Table 1).

The difference in the rates of property crime victimization between rich and poor understates the difference in the harms that result. The poor are far less likely than the affluent to have insurance against theft, and because they have little to start with, what they lose to theft takes a much deeper bite out of their ability to meet their basic needs. Needless to add, the various noncriminal harms documented [earlier] (occupational hazards, pollution, poverty, and so on) also fall more harshly on workers and those at the bottom of society than on those at the top.

To summarize, those who suffer most from the failure to reduce crime (and the failure to treat noncriminal harms as crimes) are not in a position to change criminal justice policy. Those who are in a position to change the policy are not seriously harmed by its failure—indeed, there are actual benefits to them from that failure. Note that I have not said that criminal justice policy is created to achieve this distribution of benefits and burdens. Instead, my claim is that the criminal justice policy that has emerged piecemeal over time and

TABLE 11-1
Criminal Victimization by Family Income, 1992 (estimated rate of personal victimization per 1,000 persons age 12 and older)

Type of Victimization	Family Income			
	Less than $7,500	$25,000 to $29,999	$30,000 to $49,000	$50,000 or More
Crimes of violence	64.4	35.6	26.6	21.2
Robbery with injury	4.2	1.2*	0.8*	0.8*
Aggravated assault	23.1	6.3	6.6	5.5
Crimes of theft	72.3	57.6	56.6	71.0

* Estimate is based on about 10 or fewer sample cases.

usually with the best of intentions happens to produce this distribution of benefits. And because criminal justice policy happens to produce this distribution, there is no inclination to change the criminal justice system among people with the power to do so. Moreover, because the criminal justice system shapes the public's conception of what is dangerous, it effectively limits its conception of how to protect itself to more of the same. Thus, though it fails, it persists.

. . .

THE POVERTY OF CRIMINALS AND THE CRIME OF POVERTY

Criminal justice is a very visible part of the American scene. As fact and fiction, countless images of crime and the struggle against it assail our senses daily, even hourly. In every newspaper, in every TV or radio newscast, there is at least one criminal justice story and often more. It is as if we live in an embattled city, besieged by the forces of crime and bravely defended by the forces of the law, and as we go about our daily tasks, we are always conscious of the war raging not very far away. Newspapers bring us daily and newscasts bring us hourly reports from the "front." Between reports, we are vividly reminded of the stakes and the desperateness of the battle by fictionalized portrayals of the struggle between the forces of the law and the breakers of the law. There is scarcely an hour on television without some dramatization of the struggle against crime. (A report to the Federal Communications Commission estimates that by the time the average American child reaches age 14, he or she has seen 13,000 human beings

killed by violence on television. Although a few of these are killed by science fiction monsters, the figure still suggests that the extent of the impact of the televised portrayal of crime and the struggle against it on the imaginations of Americans is nothing short of astounding—particularly on children: As of 1990, American children aged 2 to 5 were watching on average 27 hours of TV a week.) In the mid-1980s, it was estimated that "detective, police, and other criminal justice-related programs accounted for some eighty percent of prime-time TV viewing." If we add to this the news accounts, the panel discussions, the movies, the novels, the comic books, and the TV cartoon shows that imitate the comics, as well as the political speeches about crime, there can be no doubt that as fact or fantasy or both, criminal justice is vividly present in the imagination of most Americans.

This is no accident. Everyone can relate to criminal justice in personal and emotional terms. Everyone has some fear of crime, and as we saw [earlier], just about everyone has committed some. Everyone knows the primitive satisfaction of seeing justice done and the evildoers served up their just deserts. Furthermore, in reality or in fiction, criminal justice is naturally dramatic. It contains the acts of courage and cunning, the high risks and high stakes, and the life-and-death struggle between good and evil missing from the routine lives so many of us lead. To identify with the struggle against crime is to expand one's experience vicariously to include the danger, the suspense, the triumphs, the meaningfulness—in a word, the drama—often missing in ordinary life. How else can we explain the seemingly bottomless appetite Americans have for the endless repetition, in only slightly altered form, of the same theme: the struggle of the forces of law against the forces of crime? Criminal justice has a firm grip on the imaginations of Americans and is thus in a unique position to convey a message to Americans and to convey it with drama and with conviction.

Let us now look at this message in detail. Our task falls naturally into two parts. There is an ideological message supportive of the status quo, built into *any* criminal justice system by its very nature. Even if the criminal justice system were not failing, even if it were not biased against the poor, it would still—by its very nature—broadcast a message supportive of established institutions. This is the *implicit ideology of criminal justice*. Beyond this, there is an additional ideological message conveyed by the *failure* of the system and by its *biased* concentration on the poor. I call this the *bonus of bias*.

The Implicit Ideology of Criminal Justice

Any criminal justice system like ours conveys a subtle yet powerful message in support of established institutions. It does this for two interconnected reasons: first, because it concentrates on *individual* wrongdoers. This means that *it diverts our attention away from our institutions, away from consideration of whether our institutions themselves are wrong or unjust or indeed "criminal."*

Second, the criminal law is put forth as the *minimum neutral ground rules* for any social living. We are taught that no society can exist without rules against theft and violence, and thus the criminal law seems to be politically neutral, the minimum requirements for *any* society, the minimum obligations that any individual owes his or her fellows to make social life of any decent sort possible. Thus, it not only diverts our attention away from the possible injustice of our social institutions, but the criminal law bestows upon those institutions the mantle of its own neutrality.

Because the criminal law protects the established institutions (e.g., the prevailing economic arrangements are protected by laws against theft, and so on), attacks on those established institutions become equivalent to violations of the minimum requirements for any social life at all. In effect, the criminal law enshrines the established institutions as equivalent to the minimum requirements for *any* decent social existence—and it brands the individual who attacks those institutions as one who has declared war on *all* organized society and who must therefore be met with the weapons of war.

This is the powerful magic of criminal justice. By virtue of its focus on *individual* criminals, it diverts us from the evils of the social order. By virtue of its presumed neutrality, it transforms the established social (and economic) order from being merely *one* form of society open to critical comparison with others into the conditions of *any* social order and thus immune from criticism. Let us look more closely at this process.

What is the effect of focusing on individual guilt? Not only does this divert our attention from the possible evils in our institutions but it puts forth half the problem of justice as if it were the *whole* problem. To focus on individual guilt is to ask whether the individual citizen has fulfilled his or her obligations to his or her fellow citizens. *It is to look away from the issue of whether the fellow citizens have fulfilled their obligations to him or her.* To look only at individual responsibility is to look away from social responsibility. Writing about her stint as a "story analyst" for a prime-time TV "real crime" show based on videotapes of actual police busts, Debra Seagal describes the way focus on individual criminals deflects attention away from the social context of crime, and how television reproduces this effect in millions of homes daily:

> By the time our 9 million viewers flip on their tubes, we've reduced fifty or sixty hours of mundane and compromising video into short, action-packed segments of tantalizing, crack-filled, dope-dealing, junkie-busting cop culture. How easily we downplay the pathos of the suspect; how cleverly we breeze past the complexities that cast doubt on the very system that has produced the criminal activity in the first place.

Seagal's description illustrates as well how a television program that shows nothing but videos of actual events, that uses no reenactments whatsoever, can distort reality by selecting and recombining pieces of real events.

To look only at individual criminality is to close one's eyes to social injustice and to close one's ears to the question of whether our social institutions have exploited or violated the individual. *Justice is a two-way street—but criminal justice is a one-way street.* Individuals owe obligations to their fellow citizens because their fellow citizens owe obligations to them. Criminal justice focuses on the first and looks away from the second. *Thus, by focusing on individual responsibility for crime, the criminal justice system literally acquits the existing social order of any charge of injustice!*

...

Judges are prone to hold that an individual's responsibility for a violent crime is diminished if it was provoked by something that might lead a "reasonable man" to respond violently and that criminal responsibility is eliminated if the act was in response to conditions so intolerable that any "reasonable man" would have been likely to respond in the same way. In this vein, the law acquits those who kill or injure in self-defense and treats leniently those who commit a crime when confronted with extreme provocation. The law treats understandingly the man who kills his wife's lover and the woman who kills her brutal husband, even when neither has acted directly in self-defense. By this logic, when we hold an individual completely responsible for a crime, we are saying that the conditions in which it occurred are such that a "reasonable man" should find them tolerable. In other words, by focusing on individual responsibility for crimes, *the criminal justice system broadcasts the message that the social order itself is reasonable and not intolerably unjust.*

Thus, the criminal justice system focuses moral condemnation on individuals and deflects it away from the social order that may have either violated the individual's rights or dignity or literally pushed him or her to the brink of the crime. This not only serves to carry the message that our social institutions are not in need of fundamental questioning, but it further suggests that the justice of our institutions is obvious, not to be doubted. Indeed, because it is deviations from these institutions that are crimes, the established institutions become the implicit standard of justice from which criminal deviations are measured.

This leads to the second way in which a criminal justice system always conveys an implicit ideology. It arises from the presumption that the criminal law is nothing but the politically neutral minimum requirements of any decent social life. What is the consequence of this? As already suggested, this presumption transforms the prevailing social order into justice incarnate and all violations of the prevailing order into

injustice incarnate. This process is so obvious that it may be easily missed.

Consider, for example, the law against theft. It does seem to be one of the minimum requirements of social living. As long as there is scarcity, any society—capitalist or socialist—will need rules preventing individuals from taking what does not belong to them. The law against theft, however, is more: It is a law against stealing what individuals *presently* own. *Such a law has the effect of making present property relations a part of the criminal law.*

Because stealing is a violation of the law, this means that present property relations become the implicit standard of justice against which criminal deviations are measured. Because criminal law is thought of as the minimum requirements of any social life, this means that present property relations become the equivalent to the minimum requirements of *any* social life. The criminal who would alter the present property relations becomes nothing less than someone who is declaring war on all organized society. The question of whether this "war" is provoked by the injustice or brutality of the society is swept aside. Indeed, this suggests yet another way in which the criminal justice system conveys an ideological message in support of the established society.

The Bonus of Bias

We now consider the additional ideological bonus derived from the criminal justice system's bias against the poor. This bonus is a product of the association of crime and poverty in the popular mind. This association, the merging of the "criminal classes" and the "lower classes" into the "dangerous classes," was not invented in America. The word *villain* is derived from the Latin *villanus,* which means a farm servant. The term *villein* was used in feudal England to refer to a serf who farmed the land of a great lord and who was literally owned by that lord. In this respect, our present criminal justice system is heir to a long tradition.

The value of this association was already seen when we explored the average citizen's concept of the typical criminal and the typical crime. It is quite obvious that throughout the great mass of middle America, far more fear and hostility are directed toward the predatory acts of the poor than toward the acts of the rich. Compare the fate of politicians in recent history who call for tax reform, income redistribution, prosecution of corporate crime, and any sort of regulation of business that would make it better serve American social goals with that of politicians who erect their platform on a call for "law and order," more police, fewer limits on police power, and stiffer prison sentences for criminals—and consider this in light of what we have already seen about the real dangers posed by corporate crime and "business as usual."

It seems clear that Americans have been effectively deceived as to what are the greatest dangers to their lives, limbs, and possessions. The very persistence with which the system functions to apprehend and punish poor crooks and ignore or slap on the wrist equally or more dangerous individuals is testimony to the sticking power of this deception. That Americans continue to tolerate the comparatively gentle treatment meted out to white-collar criminals, corporate price fixers, industrial polluters, and political-influence peddlers while voting in droves to lock up more poor people faster and longer indicates the degree to which they harbor illusions as to who most threatens them. It is perhaps also part of the explanation for the continued dismal failure of class-based politics in America. American workers rarely seem able to forget their differences and unite to defend their shared interests against the rich whose wealth they produce. Ethnic divisions serve this divisive function well, but undoubtedly the vivid portrayal of the poor—and, of course, the blacks—as hovering birds of prey waiting for the opportunity to snatch away the workers' meager gains serves also to deflect opposition away from the upper classes. A politician who promises to keep working-class communities free of blacks and their prisons full of them can get their votes even if the major portion of his or her policies amount to continuation of the favored treatment of the rich at their expense. The sensationalistic use, in the 1988 presidential election, of photos of Willie Horton (a convicted black criminal who committed a brutal rape while out of prison on furlough) suggests that such tactics are still effective politics.

The most important "bonus" derived from the identification of crime and poverty is that it paints the picture that the threat to decent middle Americans comes from those below them on the economic ladder, not those above. For this to happen the system must not only identify crime and poverty, but it must also fail to reduce crime so that it remains a real

threat. By doing this, it deflects the fear and discontent of middle Americans, and their possible opposition, away from the wealthy.

There are other bonuses as well. For instance, if the criminal justice system sends out a message that bestows legitimacy on present property relations, the dramatic impact is greatly enhanced if the violator of the present arrangements is without property. In other words, the crimes of the well-to-do "redistribute" property among the haves. In that sense, they do not pose a symbolic challenge to the larger system in which some have much and many have little or nothing. If the criminal threat can be portrayed as coming from the poor, then the punishment of the poor criminal becomes a morality play in which the sanctity and legitimacy of the system in which some have plenty and others have little or nothing is dramatically affirmed. It matters little whom the poor criminals really victimize. What counts is that middle Americans come to fear that those poor criminals are out to steal what they own.

There is yet another bonus for the powerful in America, produced by the identification of crime and poverty. It might be thought that the identification of crime and poverty would produce sympathy for the criminals. My suspicion is that it produces or at least reinforces the reverse: *hostility toward the poor.*

...

My view is that, because the criminal justice system, in fact and fiction, deals with *individual legal and moral guilt,* the association of crime with poverty does not mitigate the image of individual moral responsibility for crime, the image that crime is the result of an individual's poor character. It does the reverse: It generates the association of poverty and individual moral failing and thus *the belief that poverty itself is a sign of poor or weak character.* The clearest evidence that Americans hold this belief is to be found in the fact that attempts to aid the poor are regarded as acts of charity, rather than as acts of justice. Our welfare system has all the demeaning attributes of an institution designed to give handouts to the undeserving and none of the dignity of an institution designed to make good on our responsibilities to our fellow human beings. If we acknowledged the degree to which our economic and social institutions themselves breed poverty, we would have to recognize our own responsibilities toward the poor. If we can convince ourselves that the poor are poor because of their own shortcomings, particularly moral shortcomings like incontinence and indolence, then we need acknowledge no such responsibility toward the poor. Indeed, we can go further and pat ourselves on the back for our generosity in handing out the little that we do, and, of course, we can make our recipients go through all the indignities that mark them as the undeserving objects of our benevolence. By and large, this has been the way in which Americans have dealt with their poor. It is a way that enables us to avoid asking the question of why the richest nation in the world continues to produce massive poverty. It is my view that this conception of the poor is subtly conveyed by the way our criminal justice system functions.

Obviously, no ideological message could be more supportive of the present social and economic order than this. It suggests that poverty is a sign of individual failing, not a symptom of social or economic injustice. It tells us loud and clear that massive poverty in the midst of abundance is not a sign pointing toward the need for fundamental changes in our social and economic institutions. It suggests that the poor are poor because they deserve to be poor or at least because they lack the strength of character to overcome poverty. When the poor are seen to be poor in character, then economic poverty coincides with moral poverty and the economic order coincides with the moral order. As if a divine hand guided its workings, capitalism leads to everyone getting what he or she morally deserves!

If this association takes root, then when the poor individual is found guilty of a crime, the criminal justice system acquits the society of its responsibility not only for crime *but for poverty as well.*

With this, the ideological message of criminal justice is complete. The poor rather than the rich are seen as the enemies of the majority of decent middle Americans. Our social and economic institutions are held to be responsible for neither crime nor poverty and thus are in need of no fundamental questioning or reform. The poor are poor because they are poor of character. The economic order and the moral order are one. To the extent that this message sinks in, the wealthy can rest easily—even if they can't sleep the sleep of the just.

We can understand why the criminal justice system is allowed to create the image of crime as the work of the poor and fails to reduce it so that the threat of crime remains real and credible. The result is ideological alchemy of the highest order. The poor are seen as the real threat to decent society. The ultimate sanctions of criminal justice dramatically sanctify the present social and economic order, and *the poverty of criminals makes poverty itself an individual moral crime!*

Such are the ideological fruits of a losing war against crime whose distorted image is reflected in the criminal justice carnival mirror and widely broadcast to reach the minds and imaginations of America.

Discussion Questions

1. Have you ever been a victim of a crime? How serious was that crime? Was the person who committed the crime prosecuted? Why do you believe the crime was committed; that is, what explanation would you offer? Do you think that law enforcement responded properly to this crime? Could it have been prevented? If so, how? If not, why not? Do your answers to these questions support Reiman's thesis that the failure to prevent crime is in the interest of society's elite? Explain your view.

2. Explain how Reiman's analysis illustrates the Marxist dictum that "the ruling ideas are the ideas of the ruling class." Do you agree that in the case of the criminal justice system, the ruling (normative) ideas are the concepts that serve the interests of society's elite?

3. One way advertising works in today's society is by associating socioeconomic class status with the consumption of certain products. Give some examples of advertising that works this way. Next, explain some ways in which a media outlet, such as a television network or production company, might benefit from exaggerating the threat of crime. Do advertisers have an interest in the misrepresentation of the nature of crime? Why or why not? How are advertising and economic class divisions a part of what enables the media to benefit from erroneous perceptions of crime?

For Further Reading

For a position similar to Reiman's, see Nils Christie, *Crime Control as Industry* (1993). For philosophical discussions of the justification of punishment, see *Punishment*, edited by A. John Simmons, Marshall Cohen, Joshua Cohen, and Charles R. Beitz (1995); and *Punishment and Rehabilitation*, edited by Jeffrie G. Murphy (1995).

58   THE RACIAL CONTRACT
Charles W. Mills

At the same time that social contract theory was developing among philosophers in Europe and an increasing emphasis was placed on human rights and justice, other developments contributed to some of the most virulent injustices of European and American history. Chief among these historical developments were the colonization of much of the world by European powers and, in the United States, the destruction of Native American culture and the enslavement of African peoples. The divergence between theory and reality could hardly have been more striking: even as freedom, equality, and rights were championed, European and American societies systematically enslaved, oppressed, and conquered nonwhite peoples.

In this selection by Charles Mills from his award-winning book *The Racial Contract*, Mills takes seriously not only the history of racism, but the problem of how political philosophy was related to that history. Mills proposes that we adopt what he calls the 'Racial Contract' as a superior explanation of the actual history of racism, colonialism, and slavery than its philosophical cousin, the social contract. For Mills, while the social contract is what white America and Europe professed and proclaimed, the Racial Contract is the true and actual philosophical foundation of three centuries of systematic discrimination and crimes against nonwhite persons. If so, then not only have social contract theorists and philosophers—with their *hypothetical, imaginary* thought experiment—failed to create a just world with freedom and equality for all but—because they have ignored the *actual, nonhypothetical*, and *real* contract between whites—they too share in the guilt of centuries of racial injustice.

The Racial Contract is like the social contract in many ways, but distinct in certain key areas, including the following three: First, both the racial and social contracts are contracts between persons to create a government; but while the social contract is supposedly a contract between all persons, the Racial Contract is a contract only between a subset of humans, 'whites'. As such the Racial Contract also constructs the category of 'nonwhite' and assigns to persons in that group a subordinate social standing. Second, both the racial and social contracts postulate a progression of humans from a 'state of nature' to a 'civil state'; but again, for the Racial Contract, civil society is only open to whites, while nonwhites remain in a state of nature.

As such, the Racial Contract also defines geographical space: while Europe and America are 'civilized countries' with 'civilized peoples', the rest of the world is comprised of uncivilized wildernesses and jungles populated by savages and barbarians. Third, the Racial Contract is unlike the social contract in one key way: the Racial Contract requires its signatories to forget what they have agreed to. Mills calls this 'inverted epistemology', by which he means not a method to know the truth, but the requirement that whites behave in a dysfunctional manner and live in a state of ignorance, failing to recognize the racial realities that they themselves have created.

Is Mills' claim correct? Is it true that the Racial Contract actually explains Western political history while the social contract merely obscures it? Read and evaluate this question for yourself.

(*Note:* The following article contains the use of racial terms that some consider offensive.)

Reading Questions

1. What does the Racial Contract explain that the classic social contract model also explains? What else in addition does it explain?
2. What is the difference between the consent of whites and nonwhites to the Racial Contract?
3. What 'metamorphosis' occurs to humans according to the social contract? How does that contrast with the Racial Contract?
4. How does the role of the 'state of nature' differ between the social contract and the Racial Contract? How is that related to the concept of 'savages'?
5. How are the freedom and equality of all persons in the state of nature used to guarantee rights and freedoms in contemporary society? How is this different for the Racial Contract?
6. What is 'inverted epistemology' and what does it require?
7. What evidence does Mills give that the Racial Contract has the best claim to being actual historical reality?
8. What was the *requerimiento* and how did it help to justify conquest of non-European peoples?
9. What evidence does Mills provide that the United States is a white state that used military force to establish itself by destroying the native peoples?

I will start with an overview of the Racial Contract, highlighting its differences from, as well as its similarities to, the classical and contemporary social contract. The Racial Contract is political, moral, and epistemological, the Racial Contract is real; and economically, in determining who gets what, the Racial Contract is an exploitation contract.

THE RACIAL CONTRACT IS POLITICAL, MORAL, AND EPISTEMOLOGICAL

The "social contract" is actually several contracts in one. Contemporary contractarians usually distinguish, to begin with, between the *political* contract and the *moral* contract, before going on to make (subsidiary) distinctions within both. I contend, however, that the orthodox social contract also tacitly presupposes an "epistemological" contract, and that for the Racial Contract it is crucial to make this explicit. . . .

Now the Racial Contract—and the "Racial Contract" as a theory, that is, the distanced, critical examination of the Racial Contract—follows the classical model in being both sociopolitical and moral. It explains how society was created or crucially transformed, how the individuals in that society were reconstituted, how the state was established, and how a particular moral code and a certain moral psychology were brought into existence. (As I have emphasized, the "Racial Contract" seeks to account for the way things are and how they came to be that way—the descriptive—*as well as* the way they should be—the normative—since indeed one of its complaints about white political philosophy is precisely its otherworldiness, its ignoring of basic political realities.) But the Racial Contract, as we will see, is also epistemological, prescribing norms for cognition to which its signatories must adhere. A preliminary characterization would run something like this:

The Racial Contract is that set of formal or informal agreements or meta-agreements (higher-level contracts *about* contracts, which set the limits of the contracts' validity) between the members of one subset of humans, henceforth designated by (shifting) "racial" (phenotypical/genealogical/cultural) criteria $C_1, C_2, C_3 \ldots$ as "white," and coextensive (making due allowance for gender differentiation) with the class of full persons, to categorize the remaining subset of humans as "nonwhite" and of a different and inferior moral status, subpersons, so that they have a subordinate civil standing in the white or white-ruled polities the whites either already inhabit or establish or in transactions as aliens with these polities, and the moral and juridical rules normally regulating the behavior of whites in their dealings with one another either do not apply at all in dealings with nonwhites or apply only in a qualified form (depending in part on changing historical circumstances and what particular variety of nonwhite is involved), but in any case the general purpose of the Contract is always the differential privileging of the whites as a group with respect to the nonwhites as a group, the exploitation of their bodies, land, and resources, and the denial of equal socioeconomic opportunities to them. All whites are *beneficiaries* of the Contract, though some whites are not *signatories* to it.

It will be obvious, therefore, that the Racial Contract is not a contract to which the nonwhite subset of humans can be a genuinely consenting party (though, depending again on the circumstances, it may sometimes be politic to pretend that this is the case). Rather, it is a contract between those categorized as white *over* the nonwhites, who are thus the objects rather than the subjects of the agreement.

The logic of the classic social contract, political, moral, and epistemological, then undergoes a corresponding refraction, with shifts, accordingly, in the key terms and principles.

Politically, the contract to establish society and the government, thereby transforming abstract raceless "men" from denizens of the state of nature into social creatures who are politically obligated to a neutral state, becomes the founding of a *racial polity*, whether white settler states (where preexisting populations already are or can be made sparse) or what are sometimes called "sojourner colonies," the establishment of a white presence and colonial rule over existing societies (which are somewhat more populous, or whose inhabitants are more resistant to being made sparse). In addition, the colonizing mother country is also changed by its relation to these new polities, so that its own citizens are altered.

In the social contract, the crucial human metamorphosis is from "natural" man to "civil/political" man, from the resident of the state of nature to the citizen of the created society. This change can be more or less extreme, depending on the theorist involved. For Rousseau it is a dramatic transformation, by which animallike creatures of appetite and instinct become citizens bound by justice and self-prescribed laws. For Hobbes it is a somewhat more laid-back affair by which people who look out primarily for themselves learn to constrain their self-interest for their own good. But in all cases the original "state of nature" supposedly indicates the condition of *all* men, and the social metamorphosis affects them all in the same way.

In the Racial Contract, by contrast, the crucial metamorphosis is the preliminary conceptual partitioning and corresponding transformation of human populations into "white" and "nonwhite" men. The role played by the "state of nature" then becomes radically different. In the white settler state, its role is not primarily to demarcate the (temporarily) prepolitical state of "all" men (who are really white men), but rather the permanently prepolitical state or, perhaps better, *non*political state (insofar as "pre-" suggests eventual internal movement toward) of nonwhite men. The establishment of society thus implies the denial that a society already existed; the creation of society *requires* the intervention of white men, who are thereby positioned as *already* sociopolitical beings.

White men who are (definitionally) already part of society encounter nonwhites who are not, who are "savage" residents of a state of nature characterized in terms of wilderness, jungle, wasteland. These the white men bring partially into society as subordinate citizens or exclude on reservations or deny the existence of or exterminate. In the colonial case, admittedly preexisting but (for one reason or another) deficient societies (decadent, stagnant, corrupt) are taken over and run for the "benefit" of the nonwhite natives, who are deemed childlike, incapable of self-rule and handling their own affairs, and thus appropriately wards of the state. Here the natives are usually characterized as "barbarians" rather than "savages," their state of nature being somewhat farther away (though not, of course, as remote and lost in the past—if it ever existed in the first place—as the Europeans' state of nature). But in times of crisis the conceptual distance between the two, barbarian and savage, tends to shrink or collapse, for this technical distinction within the nonwhite population is vastly less important than the *central* distinction between whites and nonwhites.

In both cases, then, though in different ways, the Racial Contract establishes a racial polity, a racial state, and a racial juridical system, where the status of whites and nonwhites is clearly demarcated, whether by law or custom. And the purpose of this state, by contrast with the neutral state of classic contractarianism, is, inter alia, specifically to maintain and reproduce this racial order, securing the privileges and advantages of the full white citizens and maintaining the subordination of nonwhites. Correspondingly, the "consent" expected of the white citizens is in part conceptualized as a consent, whether explicit or tacit, to the racial order, to white supremacy, what could be called Whiteness. To the extent that those phenotypically/genealogically/culturally categorized as white fail to live up to the civic and political responsibilities of Whiteness, they are in dereliction of their duties as citizens. From the inception, then, race is in no way an "afterthought," a "deviation" from ostensibly raceless Western ideals, but rather a central shaping constituent of those ideals.

In the social contract tradition, there are two main possible relations between the moral contract and the political contract. On the first view, the moral contract represents *preexisting* objectivist morality (theological or secular) and thus constrains the terms of the political contract. This is the view found in Locke and Kant. In other words, there is an objective moral code in the state of nature itself, even if there are no policemen and judges to enforce it. So any society, government, and legal system that are established should be based on that moral code. On the second view, the political contract *creates* morality as a conventionalist set of rules. So there is no independent objective moral criterion for judging one moral code to be superior to another or for indicting a society's established morality as unjust. On this conception, which is famously attributed to Hobbes, morality is just a set of rules for expediting the rational pursuit and coordination of our own interests without conflict with those other people who are doing the same thing.

The Racial Contract can accommodate both versions, but as it is the former version (the contract as described in Locke and Kant) rather than the latter version (the contract as described in Hobbes) which represents the mainstream of the contract tradition, I focus on that one. Here, the good polity is taken to rest on a preexisting moral foundation. Obviously, this is a far more attractive conception of a political system than Hobbes's view. The ideal of an objectively just polis to which we should aspire in our political activism goes back in the Western tradition all the way to Plato. In the medieval Christian worldview which continued to influence contractarianism well into the modern period, there is a "natural law" immanent in the structure of the universe which is supposed to direct us morally in striving for this ideal. (For the later, secular versions of contractarianism, the idea would simply be that people have rights and duties even in the state of nature because of their nature as human beings.) So it is wrong to steal, rape, kill in the state of nature even if there are no human laws written down saying it is wrong. These moral principles must constrain the human laws that are made and the civil rights that are assigned once the polity is established. In part, then, the political contract simply *codifies* a morality that already exists, writing it down and filling in the details, so we don't have to rely on a divinely implanted moral sense, or conscience, whose perceptions may on occasion be distorted by self-interest. What is right and wrong, just and unjust, in society will largely be determined by what is right and wrong, just and unjust, in the state of nature.

The character of this objective moral foundation is therefore obviously crucial. For the mainstream of the contractarian tradition, it is the *freedom and equality of all men in the state of nature*. As Locke writes in the *Second Treatise*, "To understand Political Power right, and derive it from its Original, we must consider what State all Men are naturally in, and that is, a *State of perfect Freedom* to order their Actions. . . . A *State* also *of Equality*, wherein all the Power and Jurisdiction is reciprocal, no one having more than another." For Kant, similarly, it is our equal moral personhood. Contractarianism is (supposedly) committed to moral egalitarianism, the moral equality of all men, the notion that the interests of all men matter equally and all men must have equal rights. Thus, contractarianism is also committed to a principled and foundational opposition to the traditionalist hierarchical ideology of the old feudal order, the ideology of inherent ascribed status and natural subordination. It is this language of equality which echoes in the American and French Revolutions, the Declaration of Independence, and the Declaration of the Rights of Man. And it is this moral egalitarianism that must be retained in the allocation of rights and liberties in civil society. When in a modern Western society people insist on their rights and freedoms and express their outrage at not being treated equally, it is to these classic ideas that, whether they know it or not, they are appealing.

But as we will see in greater detail later on, the color-coded morality of the Racial Contract restricts the possession of this natural freedom and equality to *white* men. By virtue of their complete nonrecognition, or at best inadequate, myopic recognition, of the duties of natural law, nonwhites are appropriately relegated to a lower rung on the moral ladder (the Great Chain of Being). They are designated as born *un*free and *un*equal. A partitioned social ontology is therefore created, a universe divided between persons and racial subpersons, *Untermenschen*, who may variously be black, red, brown, yellow—slaves, aborigines, colonial populations—but who are collectively appropriately known as "subject races." And these subpersons—niggers, injuns, chinks, wogs, greasers, blackfellows, kaffirs, coolies, abos, dinks, googoos, gooks—are biologically destined never to penetrate the normative rights ceiling established for them below white persons. Henceforth; then, whether openly admitted or not, it is taken for granted that the grand ethical theories propounded in the development of Western moral and political thought are of restricted scope, explicitly or implicitly intended by their proponents to be restricted to persons, whites. The terms of the Racial Contract set the parameters for white morality as a whole, so that competing Lockean and Kantian contractarian theories of natural rights and duties, or later anticontractarian theories such as nineteenth-century utilitarianism, are all limited by its stipulations.

Finally, the Racial Contract requires its own peculiar moral and empirical epistemology, its norms and procedures for determining what counts as moral and factual knowledge of the world. In the standard accounts of contractarianism it is not usual to speak of there being an "epistemological" contract, but there *is* an epistemology associated with contractarianism, in the form of natural law. This provides us with a moral compass, whether in the traditional version of Locke—the light of reason implanted in us by God so we can discern objective right and wrong—or in the revisionist version of Hobbes—the ability to assess the objectively optimal prudential course of a action and what it requires of us for self-interested cooperation with others. So through our natural faculties we come to know reality in both its factual and valuational aspects, the way things objectively are and what is objectively good or bad about them. I suggest we can think of this as an idealized consensus about cognitive norms and, in this respect, an agreement or "contract" of sorts. There is an understanding about what counts as a correct, objective interpretation of the world, and for agreeing to this view, one is ("contractually") granted full cognitive standing in the polity, the official epistemic community.

But for the Racial Contract things are necessarily more complicated. The requirements of "objective" cognition, factual and moral, in a racial polity are in a sense more demanding in that officially sanctioned reality is divergent from actual reality. So here, it could be said, one has an agreement to *mis*interpret the world. One has to learn to see the world wrongly, but with the assurance that this set of mistaken perceptions will be validated by white epistemic authority, whether religious or secular.

Thus in effect, on matters related to race, the Racial Contract prescribes for its signatories an inverted epistemology, an epistemology of ignorance, a particular pattern of localized and global cognitive dysfunctions (which are psychologically and socially functional), producing the ironic outcome that whites will in general be unable to understand the world they themselves have made. Part of what it means to be constructed as "white" (the metamorphosis of the sociopolitical contract), part of what it requires to achieve Whiteness, successfully to become a white person (one imagines a ceremony with certificates attending the successful rite of passage: "Congratulations, you're now an official white person!"), is a cognitive model that precludes self-transparency and genuine understanding of social realities. To a significant extent, then, white signatories will live in an invented delusional world, a racial fantasyland, a "consensual hallucination," to quote William Gibson's famous characterization of cyberspace, though this particular hallucination is located in real space. There will be white mythologies, invented Orients, invented Africas, invented Americas, with a correspondingly fabricated population, countries that never were, inhabited by people who never were—Calibans and Tontos, Man Fridays and Sambos—but who attain a virtual reality through their existence in travelers' tales, folk myth, popular and highbrow fiction, colonial reports, scholarly theory, Hollywood cinema, living in the white imagination and determinedly imposed on their alarmed real-life counterparts. One could say then, as a general rule, that *white misunderstanding, misrepresentation, evasion, and self-deception on matters related to race* are among the most pervasive mental phenomena of the past few hundred years, a cognitive and moral economy psychically required for conquest, colonization, and enslavement. And these phenomena are in no way *accidental,* but *prescribed* by the terms of the Racial Contract, which requires a certain schedule of structured blindnesses and opacities in order to establish and maintain the white polity.

THE RACIAL CONTRACT IS A HISTORICAL ACTUALITY

The social contract in its modern version has long since given up any pretensions to be able to explain the historical origins of society and the state.

Whereas the classic contractarians were engaged in a project both descriptive and prescriptive, the modern Rawls-inspired contract is purely a prescriptive thought experiment. And even Pateman's Sexual Contract, though its focus is the real rather than the ideal, is not meant as a literal account of what men in 4004 B.C. decided to do on the plains of Mesopotamia. Whatever accounts for what Frederick Engels once called "the *world historical defeat of the female sex*"—whether the development of an economic surplus, as he theorized, or the male discovery of the capacity to rape and the female disadvantage of being the childbearing half of the species, as radical feminists have argued—it is clearly lost in antiquity.

By contrast, ironically, the Racial Contract, never so far as I know explored as such, has the best claim to being an actual historical fact. Far from being lost in the mists of the ages, it is clearly historically locatable in the series of events marking the creation of the modern world by European colonialism and the voyages of "discovery" now increasingly and more appropriately called expeditions of conquest. The Columbian quincentenary a few years ago, with its accompanying debates, polemics, controversies, counterdemonstrations, and outpourings of revisionist literature, confronted many whites with the uncomfortable fact, hardly discussed in mainstream moral and political theory, that we live in a world which has been *foundationally shaped for the past five hundred years by the realities of European domination and the gradual consolidation of global white supremacy.* Thus not only is the Racial Contract "real," but—whereas the social contract is characteristically taken to be establishing the legitimacy of the nation-state, and codifying morality and law within its boundaries—the Racial Contract is *global,* involving a tectonic shift of the ethicojuridical basis of the planet as a whole, the division of the world, as Jean-Paul Sartre put it long ago, between "men" and "natives."

Europeans thereby emerge as "the lords of human kind," the "lords of all the world," with the increasing power to determine the standing of the non-Europeans who are their subjects. Although no single act literally corresponds to the drawing up and signing of a contract, there is a series of acts—papal bulls and other theological pronouncements;

European discussions about colonialism, "discovery," and international law; pacts, treaties, and legal decisions; academic and popular debates about the humanity of nonwhites; the establishment of formalized legal structures of differential treatment; and the routinization of informal illegal or quasi-legal practices effectively sanctioned by the complicity of silence and government failure to intervene and punish perpetrators—which collectively can be seen, not just metaphorically but close to literally, as its conceptual, juridical, and normative equivalent.

Anthony Pagden suggests that a division of the European empires into their main temporal periods should recognize "two distinct, but interdependent histories": the colonization of the Americas, 1492 to the 1830s, and the occupation of Asia, Africa, and the Pacific, 1730s to the period after World War II. In the first period, it was, to begin with, the nature and moral status of the Native Americans that primarily had to be determined, and then that of the imported African slaves whose labor was required to build this "New World." In the second period, culminating in formal European colonial rule over most of the world by the early twentieth century, it was the character of colonial peoples that became crucial. But in all cases "race" is the common conceptual denominator that gradually came to signify the respective global statuses of superiority and inferiority, privilege and subordination. There is an opposition of us against them with multiple overlapping dimensions: Europeans versus non-Europeans (geography), civilized versus wild/savage/barbarians (culture), Christians versus heathens (religion). But they all eventually coalesced into the *basic* opposition of white versus nonwhite.

A Lumbee Indian legal scholar, Robert Williams, has traced the evolution of the Western legal position on the rights of native peoples from its medieval antecedents to the beginnings of the modern period, showing how it is consistently based on the assumption of "the rightness and necessity of subjugating and assimilating other peoples to [the European] worldview." Initially the intellectual framework was a theological one, with normative inclusion and exclusion manifesting itself as the demarcation between Christians and heathens. The pope's powers over the *Societas Christiana*, the universal Christian commonwealth, were seen as "extending not only over all Christians within the universal commonwealth, but over unregenerated heathens and infidels as well," and this policy would subsequently underwrite not merely the Crusades against Islam but the later voyages to the Americas. Sometimes papal pronouncements did grant rights and rationality to nonbelievers. As a result of dealing with the Mongols in the thirteenth century, for example, Pope Innocent IV "conceded that infidels and heathens possessed the natural law right to elect their own secular leaders," and Pope Paul III's famous *Sublimis Deus* (1537) stated that Native Americans were rational beings, not to be treated as "dumb brutes created for our service" but "as truly men . . . capable of understanding the Catholic faith." But as Williams points out, the latter qualification was always crucial. A Eurocentrically normed conception of rationality made it coextensive with acceptance of the Christian message, so that rejection was proof of bestial irrationality.

Even more remarkably, in the case of Native Americans this acceptance was to be signaled by their agreement to the *Requerimiento*, a long statement read aloud to them in, of course, a language they did not understand, failing which assent a just war could lawfully be waged against them. One author writes:

> The *requerimiento* is the prototypical example of *text* justifying conquest. Informing the Indians that their lands were entrusted by Christ to the pope and thence to the kings of Spain, the document offers freedom from slavery for those Indians who accept Spanish rule. Even though it was entirely incomprehensible to a non-Spanish speaker, reading the document provided sufficient justification for dispossession of land and immediate enslavement of the indigenous people. [Bartolomé de] Las Casas's famous comment on the *requerimiento* was that one does not know "whether to laugh or cry at the absurdity of it." . . . While appearing to respect "rights" the *requerimiento*, in fact, takes them away.

In effect, then, the Catholic Church's declarations either formally legitimated conquest or could be easily circumvented where a weak prima facie moral barrier was erected. . . .

Indian laws, slave codes, and colonial native acts formally codified the subordinate status of nonwhites and (ostensibly) regulated their treatment, creating a juridical space for non-Europeans as a separate category of beings. So even if there was sometimes an attempt to prevent "abuses" (and these codes were honored far more often in the breach than the observance), the point is that "abuse" as a concept presupposes as a norm the *legitimacy* of the subordination. Slavery and colonialism are not conceived as wrong in their denial of autonomy to persons; what is wrong is the improper administration of these regimes.

It would be a fundamental error, then—a point to which I will return—to see racism as anomalous, a mysterious deviation from European Enlightenment humanism. Rather, it needs to be realized that, in keeping with the Roman precedent, *European humanism usually meant that only Europeans were human.* European moral and political theory, like European thought in general, developed within the framework of the Racial Contract and, as a rule, took it for granted. As Edward Said points out in *Culture and Imperialism,* we must not see culture as "antiseptically quarantined from its worldly affiliations." But this occupational blindness has in fact infected most "professional humanists" (and certainly most philosophers), so that "as a result [they are] unable to make the connection between the prolonged and sordid cruelty of practices such as slavery, colonialist and racial oppression, and imperial subjection on the one hand, and the poetry, fiction, philosophy of the society that engages in these practices on the other." By the nineteenth century, conventional white opinion casually assumed the uncontroversial validity of a hierarchy of "higher" and "lower," "master" and "subject" races, for whom, it is obvious, different rules must apply.

The modern world was thus expressly created as a *racially hierarchical* polity, globally dominated by Europeans. A 1969 *Foreign Affairs* article worth rereading today reminds us that as late as the 1940s the world "was still by and large a Western white-dominated world. The long-established patterns of white power and nonwhite non-power were still the generally accepted order of things. All the accompanying assumptions and mythologies about race and color were still mostly taken for granted. . . . [W]hite supremacy was a generally assumed and accepted state of affairs in the United States as well as in Europe's empires." But statements of such frankness are rare or nonexistent in mainstream white opinion

today, which generally seeks to rewrite the past so as to deny or minimize the obvious fact of global white domination.

Yet the United States itself, of course, is a white settler state on territory expropriated from its aboriginal inhabitants through a combination of military force, disease, and a "century of dishonor" of broken treaties. The expropriation involved literal genocide (a word now unfortunately devalued by hyperbolic overuse) of a kind that some recent revisionist historians have argued needs to be seen as comparable to the Third Reich's. Washington, Father of the Nation, was, understandably, known somewhat differently to the Senecas as "Town Destroyer." In the Declaration of Independence, Jefferson characterized Native Americans as "merciless Indian Savages," and in the Constitution, blacks, of course, appear only obliquely, through the famous "60 percent solution." Thus, as Richard Drinnon concludes: "The Framers manifestly established a government under which non-Europeans were not men created equal—in the white polity . . . they were nonpeoples." Though on a smaller scale and not always so ruthlessly (or, in the case of New Zealand, because of more successful indigenous resistance), what are standardly classified as the other white settler states—for example, Canada, Australia, New Zealand, Rhodesia, and South Africa—were all founded on similar policies: the extermination, displacement, and/or herding onto reservations of the aboriginal population. Pierre van den Berghe has coined the illuminating phrase "*Herrenvolk* democracies" to describe these polities, which captures perfectly the dichotomization of the Racial Contract. Their subsequent evolution has been somewhat different, but defenders of South Africa's system of apartheid often argued that U.S. criticism was hypocritical in light of its own history of jim crow, especially since de facto segregation remains sufficiently entrenched that even today, forty years after *Brown v. Board of Education,* two American sociologists can title their study *American Apartheid.* The racist record of preliberation Rhodesia (now Zimbabwe) and South Africa is well known; not so familiar may be the fact that the United States, Canada, and Australia all maintained "white" immigration policies until a few decades ago, and native peoples in all three countries suffer high poverty, infant mortality, and suicide rates.

Elsewhere, in Latin America, Asia, and Africa, large parts of the world were colonized, that is, formally brought under the rule of one or another of the European powers (or, later, the United States): the early Spanish and Portuguese empires in the Americas, the Philippines, and south Asia; the jealous competition from Britain, France, and Holland; the British conquest of India; the French expansion into Algeria and Indochina; the Dutch advance into Indonesia; the Opium Wars against China; the late nineteenth-century "scramble for Africa"; the U.S. war against Spain, seizure of Cuba, Puerto Rico, and the Philippines, and annexation of Hawaii. The pace of change this century has been so dramatic that it is easy to forget that less than a hundred years ago, in 1914, "Europe held a grand total of roughly 85 percent of the earth as colonies, protectorates, dependencies, dominions, and commonwealths. No other associated set of colonies in history was as large, none so totally dominated, none so unequal in power to the Western metropolis." One could say that the Racial Contract creates a transnational white polity, a virtual community of people linked by their citizenship in Europe at home and abroad (Europe proper, the colonial greater Europe, and the "fragments" of Euro–America, Euro–Australia, etc.), and constituted in opposition to their indigenous subjects. In most of Africa and Asia, where colonial rule ended only after World War II, rigid "color bars" maintained the separation between Europeans and indigenes. As European, as white, one knew oneself to be a member of the superior race, one's skin being one's passport: "Whatever a white man did must in some grotesque fashion be 'civilized.'" So though there were local variations in the Racial Contract, depending on circumstances and the particular mode of exploitation—for example, a bipolar racial system in the (Anglo) United States, as against a subtler color hierarchy in (Iberian) Latin America—it remains the case that the white tribe, as the global representative of civilization and modernity, is generally on top of the social pyramid.

We live, then, in a world built on the Racial Contract. That we do is simultaneously quite obvious if you think about it (the dates and details of colonial conquest, the constitutions of these states and their exclusionary juridical mechanisms, the histories of official racist ideologies, the battles against slavery and colonialism, the formal and informal structures of discrimination, are all within recent historical memory and, of course, massively documented in other disciplines) and nonobvious, since most whites *don't* think about it or don't think about it as the outcome of a history of political oppression but rather as just "the way things are." ("You say we're all over the world because we *conquered* the world? Why would you put it that way?") In the Treaty of Tordesillas (1494) which divided the world between Spain and Portugal, the Valladolid (Spain) Conference (1550–1551) to decide whether Native Americans were really human, the later debates over African slavery and abolitionism, the Berlin Conference (1884–1885) to partition Africa, the various inter-European pacts, treaties, and informal arrangements on policing their colonies, the post–World War I discussions in Versailles after a war to make the world safe for democracy—we see (or should see) with complete clarity a world being governed by white people. So though there is also internal conflict—disagreements, battles, even world wars—the dominant movers and shapers will be Europeans at home and abroad, with non-Europeans lining up to fight under their respective banners, and the system of white domination itself rarely being challenged. (The exception, of course, is Japan; which escaped colonization, and so for most of the twentieth century has had a shifting and ambivalent relationship with the global white polity.) The legacy of this world is, of course, still with us today, in the economic, political, and cultural domination of the planet by Europeans and their descendants. The fact that this racial structure, clearly political in character, and the struggle against it, equally so, have *not* for the most part been deemed appropriate subject matter for mainstream Anglo-American political philosophy and the fact that the very concepts hegemonic in the discipline are refractory to an understanding of these realities, reveal at best, a disturbing provincialism and an ahistoricity profoundly at odds with the radically foundational questioning on which philosophy prides itself and, at worst, a complicity with the terms of the Racial Contract itself. . . .

Discussion Questions

1. Mills argues that part of the Racial Contract was the requirement that those who bene-fited from the contract would forget through an *epistemology of ignorance* the true nature and history of racial oppression. Is it true that, as a society, we have forgotten the history of racism and colonial destruction of native peoples? Were you aware of all the evidence that Mills gave for the historical actuality of the Racial Contract? Are these parts of history taught as part of history in public education? Do your answers support Mills' claims about inverted epistemology? Why or why not?

2. Is it wrong for political philosophers to work with hypothetical and abstract concepts instead of working with historical realities? Is this true for historical figures such as Locke, Hobbes, and Kant? Should contemporary political philosophers direct their attention to hypothetical and abstract descriptions of society or should they limit their analysis to actual historical realities? Are there dangers in either or both approaches? Explain your views.

3. At the same time the Constitution of the United States, along with the Bill of Rights, was being written, slavery was becoming a more and more entrenched feature of American society. How did these two events occur simultaneously? What explanation would you give for the fact that at the same time Africans are being enslaved, basic concepts of rights and freedoms are being written into the founding documents of the United States? How could these two events occur simultaneously? What does your answer imply for contemporary society about the rights and freedoms guaranteed by the Constitution?

4. According to Mills, all whites are beneficiaries of the Racial Contract, although not all are signatories. In your view, is this a historically accurate statement? Is it still true in contemporary society? Explain your view. What does your answer imply about the collective responsibility of whites today?

For Further Reading

This selection was taken from *The Racial Contract* (1997), which was highly praised upon publication. Mills has also written *Blackness Visible: Essays on Philosophy and Race* (1998), and several articles on Marxism. A useful anthology of selections by enlightenment philosophers on the topic of race can be found in *Race and the Enlightenment: A Reader*, edited by Emmanuel Chukwudi Eze.

59   WOMEN AND CONSENT
Carole Pateman

Voluntary consent is a central and indispensable feature of social contract theories: The state legitimately exercises authority over its citizens only insofar as these citizens have authorized it to do so through voluntary consent. Social contract theorists have considered such consent to be rational (in the best interests of individuals) and thus have not worried too much about the fact that no one has actually and formally ever consented to be ruled over by the state. Because such consent is assumed to be

SOURCE: From *Political Theory*, Vol. 8, May 1980, 149–168. © 1980 Sage Publications, Inc. Reprinted by permission of the publisher.

rational, social contract theorists are satisfied to conceptualize the consent of citizens as hypothetical.

But, according to Carole Pateman (1940–), a political scientist at the University of California, Los Angeles, our conceptions of voluntariness and consent are so unclear and so distorted by the cultural history of the West, that voluntary consent serves more to bolster an ideology that promotes the interests of a few than it does to ensure that all citizens are protected from tyranny. The radical political implications of true voluntary consent remain hidden, according to Pateman, behind the facade of hypothetical consent. To defend these claims, Pateman turns to the history of women and consent. She discovers not only that women were not considered capable of consent by traditional social contract theorists such as Hobbes, Locke, and Rousseau, but that the harmful effects of the ongoing misrepresentation of women's agency still persist, as her analysis of rape law shows.

Reading Questions

1. What fundamental problems with consent does Pateman believe political consent theorists avoid?
2. How does the history of women and consent bring out suppressed problems with our understanding of consent?
3. What is Pateman's critique of Locke's notion of 'tacit consent'?
4. How does Pateman believe that Hobbes represents consent?
5. Why does Rousseau exclude women from the political order?
6. Why can a woman's consent or refusal never be taken at face value according to Rousseau?
7. How does the problem of whether or not a woman can be raped in marriage illustrate the difficulties in traditional political notions of consent?
8. What possibility for defense against a rape charge does the Morgan case provide? Why does Pateman reject the claim that rapists are not criminal or vicious, but merely stupid?
9. What wider implications does Pateman believe her analysis of rape and consent have for other institutions of liberal democratic culture?

The history of modern consent theory over the last three centuries largely consists of attempts by theorists to suppress the radical and subversive implications of their own arguments. More recently, writers on consent have been assisted in this endeavor by the contemporary consensus that women, and the relationship between the sexes, are of no special relevance to political theory. Yet an examination of the question of women and consent highlights all the problems that generations of consent theorists have tried to avoid.

Contemporary consent theory has no room for two fundamental questions: first, why consent is of central importance to liberal theory and practice; second, how far theory and practice coincide, and whether genuine consent is possible within the institutions of the liberal-democratic state. Consent is usually discussed only in a narrowly conceived political context in the course of arguments about political obligation. Most consent theorists are content to accept the verdict that

> the idea of 'consent' has survived as a constituent element of democratic ideology: as a specification of an essential characteristic of democratic regimes which distinguish them from the non-democratic.

The straightforward assertion that liberal democracies *are* based on consent avoids the 'standard embarrassment' that occurs when theorists attempt to show how and when citizens perform this act. This assertion also avoids the question of who consents, and therefore glosses over the ambiguity, inherent in consent theory from its beginnings, about which individuals or groups are capable of consenting and so count as full members of the political order. However, embarrassment is spared by reducing the concept of consent to meaninglessness. Consent as ideology cannot be distinguished from habitual acquiescence, assent, silent dissent, submission or even enforced submission. Unless refusal of consent or withdrawal of consent are real possibilities, we can no longer speak of 'consent' in any genuine sense.

The relationship of consent in everyday life to the (postulated) consent of citizens to the liberal-democratic state remains unexplored. Consent theorists fail to consider those areas of social life where consent is of practical importance to individuals, but the problems involved form part of the general difficulties and evasions of consent theory. Women are thus easily ignored, because consent in everyday life particularly concerns them. The most intimate relations of women with men are held to be governed by consent; women consent to marriage, and sexual intercourse without a woman's consent constitutes the criminal offense of rape. To begin to examine the unwritten history of women and consent brings the suppressed problems of consent theory to the surface. Women exemplify the individuals whom consent theorists have declared to be incapable of consenting. Yet, simultaneously, women have been presented as always consenting, and their explicit non-consent has been treated as irrelevant or has been reinterpreted as 'consent'.

...

From the beginning, consent theorists have attempted to avoid the revolutionary implications of voluntarism. They have adopted two main strategies to neutralize the impact of their arguments: first, they have turned to hypothetical voluntarism; second, they have excluded certain individuals and social relationships from the scope of consent. The most familiar example of hypothetical voluntarism is Locke's notorious 'tacit consent'. Not only did Locke argue from a hypothetical social contract, but his 'consent' is merely an inference from, or reinterpretation of, the existence of specific social practices and institutions. Most contemporary discussions of consent are little more than modernized versions of Locke's claim that the consent of future generations

(to the social contract made by their forefathers) can always be said to be given if individuals are going peacefully about their daily lives, even though there are 'no Expressions of it at all'. The reinterpretation of certain actions as 'consent' appears at its extreme in Hobbes's theory. His willingness to take individualism to its logical conclusion allowed him to argue that all authority relationships are based on consent, even between parent and infant. The parents' domination over a child derives not from procreation but from 'Consent, either expressed, or by other sufficient arguments declared'. For Hobbes, overwhelming power is sufficient argument, so that in the state of nature the infant's 'consent' to its mother's rule can be assumed. Hobbes's concept of 'consent' merely reinterprets the fact of power and submission; it makes no difference whether submission is voluntary or obtained through threats, even the threat of death. Because Hobbes argues that fear and liberty are compatible, 'consent' has the same meaning whether it arises from submission in fear of a conqueror's sword or in fear of exposure by a parent, or whether it is a consequence of the (hypothetical) social contract.

Hypothetical voluntarism avoids the 'standard embarrassment' of arguing from actual consent, and the embarrassment is more securely circumvented if only some of the inhabitants of the state of nature or civil society are included in the category of 'free and equal individuals'. Voluntarism presupposes that individuals are rational, that they have, or are able to develop, the moral and intellectual capacities necessary to enable free commitment to be given. 'Free and equal individuals', to use Lockean terminology, own the property in their persons and their attributes, including their capacity to give consent. The individual is the 'guardian of his own consent'. However, the latter formulation should be read literally; the consent is *his* consent. Neither the classic contract theorists nor their successors incorporated women into their arguments on the same footing as men. Contract and consent theory developed partly as an attack on patriarchal theory, but it is necessary to emphasize the limited character of the attack on patriarchal claims that political authority had a 'natural' basis in a father's procreative powers and that sons were 'naturally' in subjection to their fathers. Contract theorists did not extend their criticism to the relationship between men and women, or more specifically, husbands and wives (who are also fathers and mothers).

...

The implications of the convention that a wife must bow to the authority of and be economically dependent upon her husband, who is 'head of the household', are obscured more thoroughly in the late twentieth century than in earlier times, because it is now firmly held that marriage can properly be based only on the consent of two individuals. But this appearance of equality between two individuals cloaks the unequal status of husband and wife created through the marriage contract. In the 1980s, the authority of husbands can be explained only because the apparent 'consent' of one 'individual' is not consent at all. The contemporary significance of the contract theorists' reconciliation with patriarchalism has been hidden behind the liberal conviction that marriage is a matter of 'individual' choice.

Ironically, Rousseau, the only contract theorist who pursued the radical implications of the doctrine, is the most explicit about the reasons why women must be excluded from its scope. Rousseau accepted the patriarchal assertion that women were 'naturally' subordinate to men. He gives a full account of the contrasting 'natural' characters of the sexes, a contrast which, he argues, must be given expression in the sexual double standard. Rousseau provides a clear statement of the claim that women are incapable of consent, but, at the same time, he also denies this and reinterprets explicit non-consent as its opposite. Rousseau attacked the hypothetical voluntarism of Hobbes's and Locke's versions of the contract argument as a fraud which was tantamount to a contract of slavery, but he advocated precisely such a contract as the basis of the relationship between the sexes. In Rousseau's participatory, voluntarist political order, women must remain excluded because of their 'natural' moral characters and their deleterious influence upon the morals and civic virtue of men. In time-honored tradition, Rousseau divides women into the good and the dissolute, or whores. Women can remain good only if they stay within the shelter of domestic life. . . .

The successive transformations of human consciousness or 'nature' that Rousseau charts in the *Discourse on Inequality* and the *Social Contract* are actually transformations of male consciousness. Emile alone can be educated in the independence and judgement necessary in a citizen who gives consent and is capable of further education through political participation. Sophie's education fosters the characteristics—a concern with reputation, dependence, and deceitfulness, for example—that Rousseau condemns as 'vices' in men. She is educated to serve and obey Emile. Women, Rousseau declares, 'must be trained to bear the yoke from the first . . . and to submit themselves to the will of others', that is, the will of men. The influence of women, even good women, always corrupts men, because women are 'naturally' incapable of attaining the status of free and equal individuals, or citizens, and incapable of developing the capacities required to give consent.

Yet, at the same time, in sexual relationships, the 'consent' of women is all-important. Moreover, their consent can always be assumed to be given—even though apparently it is being refused. According to Rousseau, men are the 'natural' sexual aggressors; women are 'destined to resist'. Rousseau asks 'what would become of the human species if the order of attack and defense were changed?' Modesty and chasteness are the preeminent female virtues, but because women are also creatures of passion, they must use their natural skills of duplicity and dissemblance to maintain their modesty. In particular, *they must always say 'no' even when they desire to say 'yes'*. And here Rousseau reveals the heart of the problem of women and consent. Apparent refusal of consent can *never*, in a woman, be taken at face value:

> Why do you consult their words when it is not their mouths that speak? . . . The lips always say 'No,' and rightly so; but the tone is not always the same, and that cannot lie. . . . Must her modesty condemn her to misery? Does she not require a means of indicating her inclinations without open expression?

A man must learn to interpret a woman's 'consent' when, as in Locke's civil society, there are no obvious expressions of it at all.

...

Rousseau's view of the relationship between husbands and wives also shows that the contradiction between the appearance of consent in the marriage contract and the reality of its content goes far deeper than I indicated in my earlier remarks. . . . The consequence of entering into the marriage contract is that the subsequent 'consent' of the woman to her husband's sexual demands is legally and socially presupposed. The legal basis for the belief that the initial 'consent' of the woman in the marriage contract can never be retracted remains unexamined. This fact, together with the difficulties encountered in attempts at reforming rape law to extend its provisions to women within marriage (success to some degree has been achieved only in Sweden and South Australia and in some states of the United States) testifies to the tenacity with which popular and legal opinion clings to the conviction that rape is impossible within marriage.

…

In certain areas of the law where 'consent' is central, notably in the law concerning rape, social reluctance to recognize women as 'free and equal individuals' denies in practice what the law proclaims in principle. Rape is central to the problem of women and consent in everyday life. Rape is widespread, both in and out of marriage, but although women of all ages and classes are attacked, the majority of rapes are not reported. Here I shall concentrate on the implementation of the criminal law in the courts, because evidence is available, and because it reveals in a dramatic fashion how contradictory beliefs about women and consent are embedded in liberal-democratic social institutions.

Rape law has recently been described as a 'parody of justice'. Of the many reasons for this, the most fundamental is the manner in which the 'consent' of the victim is interpreted—or ignored. In this matter, popular opinion and the courts are Hobbesian; they identify submission, including enforced submission, with consent. Accused rapists almost invariably offer the defense that the woman actually consented, or that they believed she did (and I shall return to the question of belief in a moment). One reason why this defense is so successful, and why such a small proportion of cases of rape are ever reported, is that a woman is unlikely to convince either the public, the police or a judge and jury that she did not consent

to sexual intercourse unless she is badly physically injured or unless she can prove that she resisted. However, the criterion for resistance, too, tends to be physical injury. To prove non-consent, 'the showing of physical damage beyond the simple evidence of penetration has, almost, the status of a legal standard'.

The identification of submission with consent, unless resistance can be proved, is bound up historically with a legal distinction (that obtained before the Criminal Law Amendment Act of 1885) between acts 'against the will' of a woman, which were performed by force in the face of her resistance, and acts which were 'without her consent'. This distinction was crucial in cases where intercourse was obtained through impersonation or subterfuge. Such cases have fascinated legal writers on consent and rape, and one commentator has stated that 'since 1925 the sparse legal discussion . . . has remained focused on cases of intercourse induced by fraud'—not perpetrated by force. For example, in cases where a husband, to whom the woman would have consented, was impersonated and no force was used, it was generally held that the act was not 'against her will' and so was not rape. . . . Moreover, there is still a large area of legal uncertainty about the acts that constitute an instance of 'force' or 'threat' that separate forced 'submission' from voluntary 'consent'.

In a rape case in Britain in 1975, the judge stated of the accused: 'I have no doubt you instilled terror into this woman when you went into that room and made your intentions quite clear'—yet the accused was found not guilty of rape. Although the law holds that submission gained under threat of death or severe bodily harm is not 'consent', in practice, threats that 'instill terror', or lesser threats, may not be held by the courts to show non-consent. The Maryland Court of Appeals recently overturned a conviction for rape 'on the grounds that the victim did not have sufficient cause to think she was in danger', although she had unwillingly entered a house and was 'lightly choked'. The court held that the circumstances did not give grounds for 'reasonable fear' that harm would result if she resisted. There is also considerable legal doubt about 'consent' and threats by persons other than the rapist, or threats to persons other than the victim, for example, her children or relatives. The law provides that a contract entered into under 'threat' or 'duress' is voidable, and a person can offer as a defense to a criminal charge that an offense was committed only under threat of severe bodily harm or death. But although, historically, contracts in economic life and consent in sexual relations derive their importance from the same complex of social and theoretical developments, it is significant that legal interpretation of 'duress' in (non-criminal) contract law is much wider than the interpretation of 'threat' in rape cases. The standard of 'consent' in rape has been formulated within the same narrow boundaries as 'duress' in the performance of criminal acts.

The legal failure to distinguish between 'acts of sexual assault and consenting sexual relations among adults', or between enforced submission and consent, is grounded in a complex of beliefs about the 'natural' characters of the sexes. Eminent lawyers as well as the public are convinced that the 'naturally' sexually aggressive male must disregard a woman's refusal as merely a token gesture that hides her true desires. Rape victims are divided into 'good' and 'bad' women, and even where violence has unquestionably been used, 'consent' can be held to have been given if the victim can be said to be of 'doubtful reputation' or have 'poor' sexual morals. It is also very difficult for a woman to convince a court that she did not consent when standard works on evidence reinforce the view that women, especially 'unchaste' women, are 'naturally' deceitful and prone to make false statements, including false accusations of rape. Hale's words have been regularly cited in courtrooms for three centuries: 'rape . . . is an accusation easily to be made and hard to be proved, and harder to be defended by the party accused, tho never so innocent.' Yet a high proportion of rapes that are actually reported are rejected by the police as 'unfounded'. Even allowing for problems of evidence, it is hard to account for these practices except as a direct outcome of an extraordinary perception of women's 'natural' characters. The same perception underlies the conventional requirement that the rape victim's evidence must be corroborated; it is 'only rape complainants, along with children, accomplices and witnesses in treason trials who are [treated as] notoriously unreliable witnesses.'

Because so few cases of rape are reported, and because so many of these are rejected, the offenses that come before the courts are usually only the most vicious and brutal. It has recently been claimed that 'the facts about rape are even more elusive than most', but there is rarely much that is very elusive if a case is prosecuted—at least, not if 'consent' has any meaning. Ambiguous cases that involve complex matters of social convention and expectation do not usually reach the courts. For example, the courts are not usually judging cases where a woman unwillingly submits to a man who has taken her out for the evening, because it is 'expected' that she should 'pay' for her supper, or where she submits to an employer or foreman to retain employment. In cases where an accused comes to trial, 'consent' in any genuine sense of the concept is not usually at issue. This does *not* mean, however, that the victim's non-consent is therefore taken seriously. Instead, the beliefs of the accused about a woman's consent, even his unreasonable beliefs, are often taken to be the most relevant 'fact about rape' for the verdict of the court.

The beliefs and intentions of accused persons are a central criterion for establishing criminal responsibility. A mental or subjective element, *mens rea*, must be shown to be present for guilt to be proved. It must be shown that an accused intended to commit a criminal act; 'intention to do the act forbidden by law, or something like it, is . . . generally *necessary* for serious crime. . . .' The problem in rape cases is not this criterion as such but the manner in which it has been interpreted, in particular in the Morgan case in Britain and in the Mayberry case in the state of California. These cases created 'a totally new defense to the crime' of rape, the defense of a mistake-of-fact as to consent. It was ruled in Morgan that a man's belief in a woman's consent did not have to be a reasonable belief, and in Mayberry that a jury must specifically reject a defense of reasonable but mistaken belief in consent. The impact of this defense can be illustrated by the case referred to earlier, in which the man had 'instilled terror' into the victim. The defense was successfully presented that—although the accused had broken into the woman's flat—he genuinely believed she consented. In another case, the bizarre results of the Morgan ruling, and also the peculiar legal view of the relations between husbands and wives, were further reinforced. It is impossible for a husband to be prosecuted for the rape of his wife in Britain. However, in common law, he can be prosecuted for aiding another man to do so. In *R. v. Cogan* and *R. v. Leak* (1976), a drunken man punished his wife by forcing her to have intercourse with his drunken friend, and he was found guilty of aiding and abetting the rape of his wife—but the friend was found not guilty of rape. The defense was that the latter believed the wife to consent, even though there were no reasonable grounds for the belief and an appeal judge stated that intercourse took place 'without her consent'.

One writer on rape has argued that the legal reasoning in Morgan is 'clearly correct if the rights of the man accused of rape [are] to be maintained.' But it is far from obvious that it is 'clearly correct' (even if it is held that the belief must be 'reasonable'). In Morgan, a judge argued that if a sexual act took place because a man had falsely believed that the woman consented, then it would generally be held that, although the man might be careless, he did not commit rape. But would it so be held? And should it? Certainly, many lawyers seem to think so. The Morgan decision has been defended on the grounds that

> the opposing view was that a man could be convicted of rape . . . if he was stupid (unreasonable) in forming that belief. To convict the stupid man would be to convict him of . . . inadvertent negligence—honest conduct which may be the best this man can do but that does not come up to the standard of the so-called reasonable man . . . it would be wrong to have a law of negligent rape.

Such legal opinions imply that many, perhaps most, rapists are not criminal or vicious men, or men clearly deficient in concern for the well-being, integrity and respect of other persons, but merely stupid or careless. This ignores the empirical evidence about rape. As many as 70 per cent of rapes are planned in advance, a high proportion involve two or more men in an attack upon one woman, and there are 'documented incidences of organized rape as a social institution'.

. . .

The problem of 'objective standards' and 'reasonable mistakes' in rape highlights the extent to which 'consent' and 'non consent' have been emptied of meaning. That this fact appears unremarkable is tribute to the success of three centuries of mutual accommodation between liberalism and patriarchalism, which reinforced the contradictory perception of women and their consent and resulted in their present highly uncertain and ambiguous status as 'individuals'. Despite the apparent importance of women's consent, it is legally and socially declared irrelevant within marriage, and a woman's explicit 'no' can all too frequently be disregarded or reinterpreted as 'consent'. However, if 'no', when uttered by a woman, is to be reinterpreted as 'yes', then all the comfortable assumptions about her 'consent' are also thrown into disarray. Why should a woman's 'yes' be more privileged, be any the less open to invalidation, than her 'no'?

There can be no answer to this question until women are admitted unequivocally as 'free and equal individuals', guardians of their own consent. At present, notwithstanding their formal civic status, women are regarded as men's 'natural' subordinates, and hence as incapable of consent. In the light of the character of existing relations between the sexes, it is therefore not surprising that in matters of women's consent in our everyday lives, so wide a gulf exists between appearance and reality. Moreover, the problem extends further than our everyday lives. If the problem of women and consent is to be resolved, some radical changes are required, reaching much further than necessary reform of rape law into the heart of the theory and practice of the liberal democratic state. The consent of women, and the example of rape, is only one dimension of the problem of consent—of men and women—which itself is part of the more fundamental problem of whether the ideal of free commitment, or voluntarism, is to be taken seriously in liberal democratic theory and practice.

Consent is central to liberal democracy, because it is essential to maintain individual freedom and equality; but it is a problem for liberal democracy, because individual freedom and equality is also a precondition for the practice of consent. The identification of enforced submission with consent in rape is a stark example of the wider failure in liberal-democratic theory and practice to distinguish free commitment and agreement by equals from domination, subordination, and inequality. Writers on consent link 'consent', 'freedom' and 'equality', but the realities of power and domination in our sexual and political lives are ignored. Contemporary consent theory presents our institutions as if they were actually as consent demands, as if they were actually constituted through the free agreement of equal persons. The reduction of 'consent' to a mere 'constituent' of liberal-democratic ideology leaves consent theorists unable to ask many vital questions. This includes the question whether the character of our socio-political institutions is such that consent ought to be given to (all or some of) them, by men or women. Most liberal theorists would wish to argue that there is one relationship, at least, to which consent ought not to be given. A person ought never to consent to be a slave, because this totally negates the individual's freedom and equality and hence, in a self contradiction, denies that the individual is capable of consent. . . .

At present, consent theorists have failed to recognize even the obvious problems posed for arguments about political obligation by popular belief and the ambiguous status of women as 'individuals'. Furthermore, if the subordination of women to men is not considered, neither is the class structure of the liberal-democratic state. If consent theorists do not discuss the marriage contract, neither do they discuss the employment contract or the 'despotic organization' of capitalist production. The consent of women is treated as irrelevant, and the consent of men is assumed to be given in political and everyday life when there are 'no expressions of it at all'. . . .

Discussion Questions

1. Are our choices ever truly voluntary? What background conditions are necessary in order to have true consent? Can persons voluntarily consent, for example, when they are hungry or in danger? Can they do so when they lack important knowledge?
2. Do parents voluntarily consent to being parents? Do they consent to being the parent of *that particular child*? Do they know the true nature of parenthood before they agree to become parents? If not, does this challenge the notion that free, voluntary consent is necessary in order to become obligated? Why or why not?
3. Is a woman's 'no' still interpreted as a 'yes' in contemporary society? If not, why not? What has changed? If yes, why does this phenomenon still exist? Is it harmful? Why or why not?
4. Suppose you are an unemployed woman and the parent of two young children. Suppose a local businessman offered you a well-paying position in exchange for having sex with him twice a week. Would such an offer be coercive? Would it be wrong to make such an offer? Why or why not? Does it matter that the employer is clear about the terms of employment before you are employed?

For Further Reading

This essay can be found in Pateman's *The Disorder of Women* (1989). See also her *The Sexual Contract* (1988). Both books contain extended critiques of social contract theory. For other feminist critiques of the social contract tradition and classic political theory see Susan Moller Okin's books *Women in Western Political Thought* (1979) and *Justice, Gender, and the Family* (1989). See also Christine Di Stefano, "Masculinity as Ideology in Political Theory," in *Hypatia Reborn: Essays in Feminist Political Philosophy* (1990), edited by Azizah Y. al-Hibri and Margaret A. Simons.

For more recent feminist political theory, not necessarily critiques of the liberal tradition, see *Feminists Theorize the Political*, edited by Judith Butler and Joan W. Scott (1992), and *Feminism & Political Theory*, edited by Cass R. Sunstein (1990). For a helpful annotated bibliography on feminism and the law, including articles on rape, see *Feminist Legal Literature: A Selective Annotated Bibliography*, compiled by F. C. DeCoste, K. M. Munro, and Lillian MacPherson (1991). A classic feminist investigation of rape is Susan Brownmiller's *Against Our Will: Men, Women, and Rape* (1975).

60 CARE AND POLITICAL THEORY
Joan C. Tronto

The value and necessity of 'care' have been largely ignored by liberal political philosophy. As traditionally conceived, care was something that belonged to the private, domestic sphere and was thus not the business of the state to either provide or promote. The state was concerned only with such public values as justice. But of course, this was partly because care was conceptualized primarily as women's work, and women and their work were not properly considered part of the public sphere. Suppose, however, we began our political thought from the lives of women. Could 'care' be considered a serious political ideal? If it was, what would change?

In this selection, Joan Tronto (1952–) offers an extended definition of what constitutes care. She then argues that care ought to be taken seriously as a political value and goal. Liberal theories have ignored the ongoing activity of care, writes Tronto, making care and caregivers politically invisible. But placing care at the center of our political theorizing challenges our conception of the purpose of political institutions and has far-reaching implications. For example, Tronto argues that we ought to conceive of ourselves as interdependent, not independent as liberal theory does. Autonomy changes as well: Rather than seeing autonomy as a given, an assumed fact about citizens, once giving and receiving care is taken seriously, autonomy becomes reconceptualized as a goal. If we are autonomous, it is only through mutual cooperation, only through receiving and giving care.

Reading Questions

1. What basic change to political ideals results when a care perspective is adopted? How does this affect the view of humans as autonomous?
2. According to Tronto, how is autonomy achieved?
3. How does a care perspective change political conceptions of needs and interests?
4. How does care challenge traditional views about the separation of private and public?
5. Why does Tronto believe that care would make us better citizens?
6. What two dangers does care as a political ideal pose? How does Tronto propose to avoid these dangers?
7. What differences are there between those who take care and those who receive care? Does the marketplace provide adequate care for everyone?
8. What does a care perspective reveal about the adequacy of the current political order?
9. How does Tronto respond to the criticism that care goes against the basic American value of individualism?

Care is a central but devalued aspect of human life. To care well involves engagement in an ethical practice of complex moral judgments. Because our society does not notice the importance of care and the moral quality of its practice, we devalue the work and contributions of women and other disempowered groups who care in this society. I now arrive at my final argument: only if we understand care as a political idea will we be able to change its status and the status of those who do caring work in our culture.

This change requires a shift in our values. We are blocked from perceiving the need for this shift in values by the ways in which we currently construct our moral boundaries. To change these moral boundaries requires political action. In this chapter I outline the elements for such change.

While it is true that I am suggesting a "paradigm shift" in this book, I have deliberately used the metaphor of redrawn boundaries rather than the metaphor more usually invoked in describing paradigm change, the metaphor of revolutionary overthrow. I do not mean to destroy or undermine current moral premises, but simply to show that they are incomplete. Expanding the boundaries of moral life so that new terrain is included, of course, will change the ways that we perceive the existing landscape. But it does not require that we disavow older beliefs or ideas entirely. Indeed, I argue that care is only viable as a political ideal in the context of liberal, pluralistic, democratic institutions.

...

CARE AS A POLITICAL IDEAL

Nevertheless there is a way to incorporate care into our political vision. The practice of care that I have developed and described in the last two chapters can itself be understood not only as a moral concept, but as a political concept as well. Because the practice of care *is* also a political idea, I do not face the problem of trying to import a moral concept into a political order. Indeed, I will further suggest that the practice of care describes the qualities necessary for democratic citizens to live together well in a pluralistic society, and that only in a just, pluralistic, democratic society can care flourish.

Changing Assumptions about Humans

Perhaps the most fundamental level of change in our political ideals that results from the adoption of a care perspective is in our assumptions about human nature. From this standpoint, not only will we be able to see changes in conceptions of self, but also in relations with others.

Dependence and Autonomy The simple fact that care is a fundamental aspect of human life has profound implications. It means, in the first instance, that humans are not fully autonomous, but must always be understood in a condition of interdependence. While not all people need others' assistance at all times, it is a part of the human condition that our autonomy occurs only after a long period of dependence, and that in many regards, we remain dependent upon others throughout our lives. At the same time, we are often called upon to help others, and to care, as well. Since people are sometimes autonomous, sometimes dependent, sometimes providing care for those who are dependent, humans are best described as interdependent. Thinking of people as interdependent allows us to understand both autonomous and involved elements of human life.

That all humans need care has been a difficult fact to accept within the framework of liberal political and moral thought, because the liberal models accord only the choices of autonomy or a relationship of dependence. One of the major impetuses for liberal theory has been to avoid the kind of dependence that was described in medieval and other pre-liberal accounts of social order. Dependence, implying as it does that those who care for dependents can exercise power over them, has been anathema to liberal notions of individual autonomy. But as many feminist theorists have observed, the conception of the rational, autonomous man has been a fiction constructed to fit with liberal theories.

Nevertheless, dependence does not truly describe the condition of care. When political theorists such as Smith and Rousseau have condemned dependence, they have done so because of their peculiar views on dependency. Rather than viewing dependency as a natural part of the human experience, political theorists emphasize dependence as the character-destroying condition. For them, to be dependent is to be without autonomy. To become dependent is to learn how to act on behalf of others, not on behalf of the self. Dependent people lose the ability to make judgments for themselves, and end up at the mercy of others on whom they are dependent.

In order to make these claims, political theorists must ignore the reality that all humans are born into a condition of dependency, but manage to learn to become autonomous. Our description of care as a practice clarifies how judgment continues within the context of processes of care. Further, dependency at some moments or in some aspects of life need not lead to dependency in all parts of life. The threat of dependence has been greatly exaggerated by thinkers who have not really considered its nature. Indeed, we can probably assert that one of the goals of care is to end dependence, not to make it a permanent state.

The grave dangers of dependence can influence political life; if some become too dependent then they cannot participate as citizens. This fact, however, does not make care incompatible with democratic values; it makes democratic values all the more urgent. Only if caring takes place in the context of a democratic social order can human dependence be recognized as a necessity but also as a condition to overcome.

...

Needs and Interests   A second shift in our conceptions of human nature appears if we connect our notion of "interests" with the broader cultural concern with "needs." Too often moral and political thinkers conceive of human activity in terms that are either logically or culturally individualistic, such as "interest" or "project." In contrast, to use "needs" is necessarily intersubjective, cultural rather than individual, and almost surely disputed within the culture. For someone to say, "I have a need," is less indisputable from the care perspective and invokes a different response than the notion, "I have an interest." How one arrives at a need is a matter of social concern, how one arrives at an interest is not.

Moral Engagement   Third, from the perspective of care, individuals are presumed to be in a state of moral engagement, rather than a condition of detachment. Thus, one of the profound moral questions of contemporary moral theory, the problem of moral motivation, is less serious. If we take our activities of care

as examples of moral action, then all of us engage in moral actions much of the time. This does not mean, however, that it is simple to translate our moral perspectives from one care situation to another, or from a less narrow to a broader perspective. Further, as I suggested before, the opposite problem, how to make certain that one is sufficiently detached to recognize the moral difficulties that inhere within caring situations, is more profound. Connection presents a different set of difficulties than the problem of moral motivation; and makes the problem of moral motivation less central.

What does this transformed account of human nature mean about the way that democratic citizens live their lives? Rather than assuming the fiction that all citizens are equal, a care perspective would have us recognize the achievement of equality as a political goal. At present, we presume that people are equal though we know that they are not. If we attempted to achieve some type of equality as a political goal, it would make facts about inequality more difficult to dismiss. Questions such as: at what point do inequalities of resources prevent citizens from equal power? would become important political questions; they would not remain simply theoretical questions.

Including the Private

It is a fact of great moral significance that, in our society, some must work so that others can achieve their autonomy and independence. This fact, however, is obscured by the separation of public and private lives, and by the way care is parceled out into different parts of private life. Here, the split between public and private life refers to the ways in which some concerns are presumed to be the responsibilities of private individuals rather than of society. Many aspects of women's lives, and of caring, are obscured by this distinction. A political ideal of care would force us to reconsider this delineation of life into public and private spheres.

Consider, for example, how working parents solve the problem of day care. There is no national day care policy in the United States, except for some tax relief for middle class taxpayers who have spent money on child care. But the notion that the care of young children when their parents work is a social responsibility is an idea that has little resonance in the United States.

Caring is also displaced by other cultural ideas that accord with the separation between public and private life. As many discussions of what constitutes citizenship have shown, notions of citizenship have in the twentieth century embodied "the work ethic" as a public good. The work ethic, that one's rewards depend upon the amount of hard work that one does, starts from an assumption that people are ready and able to work, and that one meets one's needs by working. This image of what constitutes responsible human action misses entirely the care work that is necessary to keep human society functioning, except insofar as that work is also paid work. It is from the work ethic that the distinctions of public and private worth begin to emerge, that autonomy is associated with worthiness, etc. The moral boundaries that surround a world constituted by the work ethic cannot recognize the importance of care.

Members of the commonweal who work, who earn an income, are viewed as productive citizens, those who do not are viewed as lesser citizens, either because they are wards of the state or because they have no public self. It was in response to this construction that feminists at the turn of the century tried to argue that care activities should count as citizenly activities as well. But the notion that work is a (quasi-) public activity so permeates our understanding of what work is that this understanding has never proceeded very far. Furthermore, just as Weber's original Calvinists could only demonstrate that they worked religiously by acquisition, so too contemporary understandings of what constitutes valuable "work" follow the view that work which is well remunerated is more valuable. We have noticed that caring work is the least well-paid and respected work, with the exception of doctors. As long as we accept "the work ethic" as a valuable cultural norm, then those who engage in activities of care, rather than activities of production, will not be deemed especially socially valuable.

A False Dichotomy: Care and Justice

An argument that stands in the way of revaluing care is the presumed distinction between care and justice, and the assumption that if one takes care seriously then justice will be displaced. This assumption arises from the view that caring and justice arise out of two different metaethical starting points, and are thus incompatible. This argument presumes that care is particular, justice universal; that care draws out of compassion, justice out of rationality. We argued in the last chapter that this perception of the incompatibility of justice and care is inaccurate; many feminist authors have insisted that a theory of care is incomplete unless it is embedded in a theory of justice as well. Some theorists of care do seem to miss the point of a conception of justice. This misperception has led some feminist theorists of justice to dismiss or to be suspicious of notions of care.

But justice without a notion of care is incomplete. The best evidence for this argument probably derives from an argument by Susan Okin. Long skeptical of the value of a care approach, Okin nevertheless seems to argue that the kind of view of human nature inherent in the caring approach is necessary to remedy the defects of Rawls' theory of justice. Okin argues that there is no reason why Rawls' original position should assume that people are mutually disinterested rather than mutually engaged. In so arguing, Okin describes a view of human nature that is similar to the view of interdependence I have linked to care.

The separation of care and justice grows out of using the old moral boundaries as a starting point for describing moral life. But with a different sense of the relationship of how humans are interdependent, how human practices inform human rationality, and therefore how human activity can change what we accept as rational, the relationship between justice and care can be a relationship of compatibility rather than hostility.

Care Adept Practices as Democratic Training

Some writers think of care in an apolitical context by tying it to a narrow psychological concern, or argue that it is a kind of practice that is corrupted by broader social and political concerns. On the contrary, I claim that care as a practice can inform the practices of democratic citizenship. If through the practices of giving and receiving care we were to become adept at caring, I suggest that not only would we have become more caring and more moral people, but we would also have become better citizens in a democracy.

The qualities of attentiveness, of responsibility, of competence, or responsiveness, need not be restricted to the immediate objects of our care, but can also inform our practices as citizens. They direct us to a politics in which there is, at the center, a public discussion of needs, and an honest appraisal of the intersection of needs and interests. If attentiveness is presumed to be a part of public values, then the absence of attentiveness to the plight of some group in the society (or the world) becomes a public issue, worthy of public debate. We can imagine vigorous challenges to assumptions that we are not responsible for misfortunes that are distant from us. Public agencies may be held responsible for their policies or challenged for their incompetence. Most importantly, care-receivers' lives can serve as the basis for social policy concerning them. In all, a society that took caring seriously would engage in a discussion of the issues of public life from a vision not of autonomous, equal, rational actors each pursuing separate ends, but from a vision of interdependent actors, each of whom needs and provides care in a variety of ways and each of whom has other interests and pursuits that exist outside of the realm of care.

...

What this vision requires is that individuals and groups be frankly assessed in terms of the extent to which they are permitted to be care demanders and required to be care providers. Care as a political concept requires that we recognize how care—especially the question, who cares for whom?—marks relations of power in our society and marks the intersection of gender, race, and class with care-giving that we noted earlier. These facts must be judged according to what a just distribution of caring tasks and benefits might be.

Images of societies committed to care have understood care primarily in terms of superseding or supporting familial patterns of care: care has been a process of adequately raising children, of providing for the basic material needs of people. In a society where these tasks are inadequately accomplished, this vision seems remarkable and a necessary corrective to improper understandings of politics. Nevertheless, there is a danger if we think of caring as making the public realm into an enlarged family. Family is a necessarily private and parochial understanding of caring. The only way that transforming the political realm into "one big happy family" can work is to import with that notion some ideas that seem inherent in family life: hierarchy, unity, partiality, that are anathema to a liberal, democratic society. Indeed, it was to escape from a familistic understanding of politics that modern liberalism was born in the seventeenth century. But care need not be associated with family in order to become a political ideal.

My account of care's power as a political vision does not require that we ignore the fact that conflict will arise in deciding who should care for whom and how. My account does not require that we ignore inequalities of wealth and power. In all, to include the value of caring in addition to commitments to other liberal values (such as a commitment to people's rights, to due process, to obeying laws and following agreed-upon political procedures) makes citizens more thoughtful, more attentive to the needs of others, and therefore better democratic citizens.

Thus, the value of care as a basis for political practice does not derive from importing the substantive concerns of private caring into public life. As Mary Dietz observed, "All women-as-mothers can do is to chasten arrogant public power; they cannot democratize it." Yet care can contribute to the process of democratizing political life, if it is understood as a practice that makes it easier for citizens to recognize their situations vis-à-vis others.

Dangers of Care

There are two primary dangers of care as a political ideal, and they arise inherently out of the nature of care itself. These dangers are: paternalism or maternalism, and parochialism. . . .

...

The only solution that I see to these two problems is to insist that care needs to be connected to a theory of justice and to be relentlessly democratic in its disposition. It would be very easy for nondemocratic forms of care to emerge. What would make care democratic is to draw upon two elements of the theory of care that I have already mentioned: its focus on needs, and on the balance between care-givers and care-receivers.

Although all humans have different needs and thus we can say that some people are more needy than others, nonetheless the concept of needs can be useful in helping us to understand the possibilities for democracy in human society. Needs are culturally determined; if some people in society seem to have disproportionate needs, that is a matter for the individuals in the society to evaluate and perhaps to change. Further, a focus on care and on needs provides us with a better understanding of what and who democratic citizens are; needs vary not only from one person to another, they also vary over a life: all people are exceedingly needy as children and most are also quite needy as they approach death. If citizens understood that each of us ourselves have and will have varying needs over our lifetimes, then we might be in a better situation to understand how to allocate resources, and what equality and inequality might mean.

We might also want to rethink the distribution of caring tasks in society. Currently the tasks of care-giving fall disproportionately on those who have been excluded traditionally from politics. Low pay and prestige for their work makes it still more difficult for care-givers to become politically engaged. From the standpoint of a democratic assessment of needs, we should change this situation.

The promising scenario of a politics of care, then, requires that we think about care in its broadest possible public framework. It requires that care's focus on needs change the content of our public discussion so that we talk about the needs of all humans, not just those who are already sufficiently powerful to make their needs felt. It requires a re-commitment to democratic processes, for example, to listening and to including care-receivers in determining the processes of care. It requires a hard look at questions of justice, as we determine which needs to meet. And it requires, on the most profound level, that we rethink questions of autonomy and otherness, what it means to be a self-sufficient actor, and so forth.

...

CARE AND POLITICAL STRATEGY

How Care Reveals Relations of Power

Care becomes a tool for critical political analysis when we use this concept to reveal relationships of power. Care provides us with a critical standpoint from which we can view how effectively caring processes are meeting needs.

Especially in the twentieth century, questions of "care" have become "public" through government action and through the market. In the United States, these public questions of care are often treated as much as possible as if they were private questions of care. Hence, welfare, though clearly a public form of "taking care," has often followed conventional and repressive patterns of private "taking care." As many feminist critics of the welfare system have noted, the role of the male head of household who provided "care" for his family has been assumed by the state. The state came to police women's lives just as a husband would have were he present.

Similarly, insofar as non-domestic care has been rendered by the marketplace, the prevailing notion that the market is self-regulating has often informed how the market provides and distributes care. Those who can pay for more care often receive it, regardless of any assessment of need. As a result, inequalities in the distribution of care, creating a class of "care demanders," has been a result of the unequal distribution of wealth in the United States.

Finally, other facts about American society, such as the structures of inequality that make ours a race-structured and a gender-structured society, become more visible from the perspective of care. All of these forms of inequity become more visible once we begin to use the ability to command and to dispense care as a tool to recognize unequal amounts of power.

In the first place, to think of care concerns in systematic terms requires that the interconnections of different policy realms, and the consequences of capitalist development, be judged from the standpoint of the adequacy of care in society. That health care is not available for all, and that children are disproportionately represented among the poor, are evidence of profound failures of caring. To notice these failures would raise questions about our political values.

In the second place the vocabulary and description of care that I have proposed allow us to see more thoroughly the ways in which power is distributed and not distributed in our society. It allows us to recognize the powerful because they can act as care-demanders, and the weak who provide care to others, and turn to their own caring needs only after the powerful's needs have been met.

The notion of "privileged irresponsibility" takes on new meaning when we use it as a way to analyze power. Some people need not care about what is important to them. While on one level, this point seems simply an empirical assertion, notice what is hidden behind it. It means that caring needs are being met through a process that distorts reality and renders care invisible. Such an invisible process cannot be easily challenged.

Many political theorists have begun to recognize that the most profound question facing us is the question of "otherness": how to get along with others who are not like us. Yet the disdain of "others" who do caring (women, slaves, servants) has been virulent in our culture. This dismissal is inextricably bound up with an attempt to deny the importance of care. Those who are powerful are unwilling to admit their dependence upon those who care for them. To treat care as shabby and unimportant helps to maintain the positions of the powerful vis-à-vis those who do care for them. The mechanisms of this dismissal are subtle. One form of dismissal is to equate people of color and women with caring roles. Hence, all women are mothers or unnatural women, people of color are "naturally" servants. Another approach is to project that which is despised about "nature" onto others and out of the self, which makes the "other" more natural. Regardless of the mechanism, though, the result is that the others who are thus created are seen as fit only for functional roles, are seen as utterly different from the privileged selves who have dismissed them, and are not thought of as potential equals.

By analyzing care relationships in society, we are able to cast in stark relief where structures of power and privilege exist in society. Because questions of care are so concrete, an analysis of who cares for whom and for what reveals possible inequities much more clearly than do other forms of analysis.

Political Change

...

The United States is usually described as the world's oldest democracy, but it might better be described as an oligarchy, that is, the rule of the few. Leaders in the United States are disproportionately male, white, and wealthy, and disproportionately drawn from the professions. The percentage of Americans who vote is low. Most Americans have no further involvement in politics. Disproportionately, the excluded consist of people from the lower classes. While women vote in proportion to men, women are underrepresented in any other form of political participation, in large part because their private duties keep them out of public life. The formal mechanisms for increasing the participation of the disenfranchised are in place; they need only use them. But because people who are not actively involved in the political process do not generally see any advantage to becoming involved in the process, they are in fact excluded.

Can anything break this pattern? There have been times of extraordinary political involvement on the part of citizens in the United States. What theorists of social movements suggest about these times is that when there appears to be some kind of crack in the wall of solid "politics as usual," then the opportunity for a massive infusion of new people into the political process occurs. Frances Fox Piven and Richard Cloward observe,

> For a protest movement to arise out of these traumas of daily life, people have to perceive the deprivation and disorganization they experience as both wrong, and subject to redress.

Relatively disempowered individuals are often effective when they attempt to become politically involved.

The introduction of questions about the adequacy of care into the political order will reveal quickly how little the current social services agencies, corporations, and other bureaucratic organizations serve the interests of clients and of average citizens. As a result, citizens will be moved to require that, for example, care-receivers be included in the administration of social services, and other democratic reforms.

The trick, of course, is how to make politics more democratic. Once again, care may prove useful here. One of the reasons why citizens are so removed from politics is that it seems distant from them. When politics seems to touch people directly, they become much involved. Consider the difference between a vague discussion of "the economy" and the concern of unemployment. Care is a way of framing political issues that makes their impact, and concern with human lives, direct and immediate. Within the care framework, political issues can make sense and connect to each other. Under these conditions, political involvement increases dramatically.

Objections may be raised that this commitment to care seems to contradict the basic American value of individualism. While on a superficial level this argument carries some weight and is sure to serve as the basis for opposition to my position, let us examine the question more closely. The argument about individualism obviously rests upon a false notion that people are entirely "self-made." We can no longer assume that the wealthy and powerful accomplished what they have accomplished without the support and assistance of many others.

At the same time that care provides a way to collect the "powers of the weak" into a whole, care also provides a way to try to persuade those who are most powerful to surrender some of their power. Those with power rarely surrender it willingly; what I have suggested, though, is that care as a political value can help transform our public discussion in such a way that it exposes the ways in which the powerful have access to too many resources. At the same time care provides the powerful with a vision of what they stand to gain in a well-ordered and well-cared-for society.

The care ethic will have profound effects on political life. It will change our conceptions of citizens and of merit, affect forms of political education, and mobilize some excluded political groups. . . .

Discussion Questions

1. What is autonomy? Can we assume that each person is autonomous? What is required for a person to become an autonomous individual? What is required to ensure that an individual remains autonomous?
2. Is care necessary in order to thrive as a human being? Is care necessary for children to thrive? Is care necessary in order for adults to survive? If not, why not? If so, then should care become a central political value? Why or why not?
3. How do other persons care for you? Is care necessary in order for you to flourish?
4. Care has primarily been conceptualized as a private activity, something that occurs in domestic settings. Consider these questions. First, is it true that care primarily occurs in private, domestic settings? Why or why not? Second, should care become something that is publicly provided for? How would this be better? How might it be worse?

For Further Reading

This essay is from Tronto's book *Political Boundaries: A Political Argument for an Ethic of Care* (1993). Another recommended treatment of care and political theory is Nancy Hirschmann, *Rethinking Obligation: A Feminist Method for Political Theory* (1992). In that text, Hirschmann pays special attention to the psychological origins of women's moral voice, commenting extensively on Gilligan and Chodorow. Many of the essays in *Feminism & Political Theory,* edited by Cass R. Sunstein (1990), are also helpful. See also the suggested readings at the end of Reading 48 in Chapter 9.

CHAPTER 12

WHAT IS THE NATURE AND STATUS OF GOD'S EXISTENCE?

Consider this question: If God exists, what difference would it make? Would it change our moral obligations? Would our rights and obligations as citizens and our political obligations to one another be different? Would our lives have meaning that they would not have otherwise?

Conspicuously absent from the discussions in previous chapters on morality and political obligations have been authors that appeal to the will of God for direction concerning these matters. But is this not a mistake? After all, if God exists, would God not have something important to say about how we live our lives? Why, then, have the previous selections not appealed to God as the basis of their answers?

Is it legitimate to appeal to the will of God when investigating political and moral problems? It is not clear that it is. Suppose, for example, that someone argues that elective abortion is immoral because it violates the will of God. Is this argument likely to be persuasive? For those who believe in God it might be, assuming of course that they also believe that God is opposed to abortion—a view theists do not necessarily hold. But how will the argument fare when the audience consists of atheists and agnostics? The argument is likely to be unpersuasive because it assumes God's existence, precisely the assumption denied by the atheist and questioned by the agnostic. Hence, 'religious' answers to ethical and political questions are unlikely to be persuasive to an audience that includes nonbelievers. This is not to say, however, that the question of God's existence is not important—proof of God's existence would certainly make an impact on the way persons live their lives. So it makes sense to investigate whether or not God does exist before appealing to God's will for guidance.

The question "Does God exist?" poses another, equally important question: "Which God?" Indeed, in today's multicultural world, the question of God's existence is not as simple as it once was. Which God are we talking about? The God of Islam, Christianity, or Judaism? The God of Abraham or the God of New Age Mystics? The God of Thomas Jefferson or the God of John Calvin? Since Western philosophy's roots are Judeo-Christian, this chapter explores various arguments for and against the existence of the God of the Judeo-Christian tradition, as well as several new ways of conceptualizing God by beginning from a racial or gender standpoint. A particular sort of argument against belief in God, the problem of evil, is considered in Chapter 13.

How has the God of the Judeo-Christian tradition been conceived? God is supposedly perfect in every way possible. Hence, there are many attributes—or perfections—that God possesses by virtue of being perfect. For example, God is (and must be) eternal, having no beginning or end in time. God is reportedly immutable as well; this means that God's nature or essence does not change throughout time. God is also said to be omnipotent (all powerful) and omniscient (all knowing). And finally, by nature God is said to be all good, or morally perfect, an attribute called omnibenevolence.

Philosophical arguments concerning the existence of God typically fall into three categories. The first type of argument trades on the very idea or concept of God. For example, and roughly put, the **ontological argument** holds that God must exist because God—by definition—is the most perfect being and perfection entails existence. In addition to the selection from Anselm in this chapter, a version of the ontological argument also appears (in Chapter 6, Reading 28) in Descartes' *Meditations on First Philosophy*. A second type of argument claims that God is necessary to explain certain observable features about the world, for example, that motion exists or that the world seems designed for a purpose. **Cosmological** and **teleological arguments** fall into this category.

Ontological, cosmological, and teleological arguments aim to prove the existence of God, but arguments from the third category hope only to show that it is (or might be) reasonable to believe in God without proof of His existence. Two other selections from this chapter, "The Wager" by Pascal and "The Will to Believe" by William James, are examples of this type.

The final two selections of this chapter ask us to reconceptualize God in different terms. Perhaps if we imagined God differently, questions about the nature and existence of God could be more satisfactorily answered, or, at the very least, we would have a conception of God compatible with our modern conceptions of the world. For James Cone, the history of racism and racial oppression requires us to think about God as black, while Sallie McFague invites us to jettison our patriarchal language about God and replace it with metaphors that emphasize God as Mother, Lover, and Friend.

61   THE ONTOLOGICAL ARGUMENT
St. Anselm

St. Anselm (1033–1109) was a Benedictine monk who became Archbishop of Canterbury in 1093. Anselm believed in God without need of proof. However, Anselm also believed that God had given humans rational minds capable of understanding, although not completely, God and the universe that He created. In fact, Anselm believed that he could prove through reason what he already knew by faith—that God exists. The fact that Anselm dared to buttress his faith with rational argument was very risqué for the time period; religious leaders believed that philosophical investigations into religious matters would only end up confounding one's faith. Even today, theologians and philosophers still debate the proper relationship between faith and reason.

The following selection contains Anselm's most celebrated proof of God's existence—commonly referred to as the ontological argument. The ontological

SOURCE: Reprinted by permission of Open Court Publishing Company, a division of Carus Publishing Company, Peru, IL, from *Saint Anselm: Basic Writings*, translated by S. N. Deane. Copyright © 1962 by Open Court Publishing.

argument is an *a priori* argument for God's existence, which means that the argument doesn't depend on empirical data (facts gained through sensory experience). Rather, the ontological argument is similar in form to a geometric proof and attempts to deduce God's existence from the mere idea of God: By definition, God is perfect; hence, God must exist or He would be less than perfect.

Can the proof of God's existence be so simple?

Reading Questions

1. In terms of perfection, how is God conceived?
2. When a person hears of a being, and understands what he hears, where does this being exist?
3. According to Anselm, why can God not exist in the understanding alone?
4. Explain why the attribute of existence belongs to God more truly than all other beings.
5. Explain the two ways in which an object can be conceived.
6. Explain why God must be just, truthful, and blessed.

···

CHAPTER II

Truly there is a God, although the fool hath said in his heart, There is no God.

And so, Lord, do thou, who dost give understanding to faith, give me, so far as thou knowest it to be profitable, to understand that thou art as we believe; and that thou art that which we believe. And, indeed, we believe that thou art a being than which nothing greater can be conceived. Or is there no such nature, since the fool hath said in his heart, there is no God? (Psalms xiv. 1). But, at any rate, this very fool, when he hears of this being of which I speak—a being than which nothing greater can be conceived—understands what he hears, and what he understands is in his understanding; although he does not understand it to exist.

For, it is one thing for an object to be in the understanding, and another to understand that the object exists. When a painter first conceives of what he will afterwards perform, he has it in his understanding, but he does not yet understand it to be, because he has not yet performed it. But after he has made the painting, he both has it in his understanding, and he understands that it exists, because he has made it.

Hence, even the fool is convinced that something exists in the understanding, at least, than which nothing greater can be conceived. For, when

he hears of this, he understands it. And whatever is understood, exists in the understanding. And assuredly that, than which nothing greater can be conceived, cannot exist in the understanding alone. For, suppose it exists in the understanding alone: then it can be conceived to exist in reality; which is greater.

Therefore, if that, than which nothing greater can be conceived, exists in the understanding alone, the very being, than which nothing greater can be conceived, is one, than which a greater can be conceived. But obviously this is impossible. Hence, there is no doubt that there exists a being, than which nothing greater can be conceived, and it exists both in the understanding and in reality.

CHAPTER III

God cannot be conceived not to exist.—God is that, than which nothing greater can be conceived.—That which can be conceived not to exist is not God.

And it assuredly exists so truly, that it cannot be conceived not to exist. For, it is possible to conceive of a being which cannot be conceived not to exist; and this is greater than one which can be conceived not to exist. Hence, if that, than which nothing greater can be conceived, can be conceived not to exist, it is not that, than which nothing greater can be conceived. But this is an irreconcilable contradiction. There is, then, so truly a being than which nothing greater can be conceived to exist, that it cannot even be conceived not to exist; and this being thou art, O Lord, our God.

So truly, therefore, dost thou exist, O Lord, my God, that thou canst not be conceived not to exist; and rightly. For, if a mind could conceive of a being better than thee, the creature would rise above the Creator; and this is most absurd. And, indeed, whatever else there is, except thee alone, can be conceived not to exist. To thee alone, therefore, it belongs to exist more truly than all other beings, and hence in a higher degree than all others. For, whatever else exists does not exist so truly, and hence in a less degree it belongs to it to exist. Why, then, has the fool said in his heart, there is no God (Psalms xiv. 1), since it is so evident, to a rational mind, that thou dost exist in the highest degree of all? Why, except that he is dull and a fool?

CHAPTER IV

How the fool has said in his heart what cannot be conceived.—A thing may be conceived in two ways: (1) when the word signifying it is conceived; (2) when the thing itself is understood. As far as the word goes, God can be conceived not to exist; in reality he cannot.

But how has the fool said in his heart what he could not conceive; or how is it that he could not conceive what he said in his heart? since it is the same to say in the heart, and to conceive.

But, if really, nay, since really, he both conceived, because he said in his heart; and did not say in his heart, because he could not conceive; there is more than one way in which a thing is said in the heart or conceived. For, in one sense, an object is conceived, when the word signifying it is conceived; and in another, when the very entity, which the object is, is understood.

In the former sense, then, God can be conceived not to exist; but in the latter, not at all. For no one who understands what fire and water are can conceive fire to be water, in accordance with the nature of the facts themselves, although this is possible according to the words. So, then, no one who understands what God is can conceive that God does not exist; although he says these words in his heart, either without any, or with some foreign, signification. For, God is that than which a greater cannot be conceived. And

he who thoroughly understands this, assuredly understands that this being so truly exists, that not even in concept can it be non-existent. Therefore, he who understands that God so exists, cannot conceive that he does not exist.

I thank thee, gracious Lord, I thank thee; because what I formerly believed by thy bounty, I now so understand by thine illumination, that if I were unwilling to believe that thou dost exist, I should not be able not to understand this to be true.

CHAPTER V

God is whatever it is better to be than not to be; and he, as the only self-existent being, creates all things from nothing.

What art thou, then, Lord God, than whom nothing greater can be conceived? But what art thou, except that which, as the highest of all beings, alone exists through itself, and creates all other things from nothing? For, whatever is not this is less than a thing which can be conceived of. But this cannot be conceived of thee. What good, therefore, does the supreme Good lack, through which every good is? Therefore, thou art just, truthful, blessed, and whatever it is better to be than not to be. For it is better to be just than not just; better to be blessed than not blessed.

CHAPTER VI

How God is sensible (sensibilis) although he is not a body.—God is sensible, omnipotent, compassionate, passionless; for it is better to be these than not be. He who in any way knows, is not improperly said in some sort to feel.

But, although it is better for thee to be sensible, omnipotent, compassionate, passionless, than not to be these things; how art thou sensible, if thou art not a body; or omnipotent, if thou hast not all powers; or at once compassionate and passionless? For, if only corporeal things are sensible, since the senses encompass a body and are in a body, how art thou sensible, although thou art not a body, but a supreme Spirit, who is superior to body? But, if feeling is only cognition, or for the sake of cognition,—for he who feels obtains knowledge in accordance with the proper functions of his senses; as through sight, of colors; through taste, of flavors,—whatever in any way cognizes is not inappropriately said, in some sort, to feel.

Therefore, O Lord, although thou art not a body, yet thou art truly sensible in the highest degree in respect of this, that thou dost cognize all things in the highest degree; and not as an animal cognizes, through a corporeal sense.

Discussion Questions

1. Suppose that the ontological argument is sound, that is, suppose that you believe that the premises of the argument are true and that the conclusion follows from the premises. If you accepted the argument, would you then believe that God existed? If not, why not? What do you think Anselm would say?
2. In general, do you believe that arguments can establish the existence or nonexistence of God? Why? Does Anselm believe that arguments can establish God's existence all by themselves or is faith a necessary part of the equation?
3. Do members of your culture believe in God or not? If so, why? Would they accept Anselm's argument as a basis for believing in God? If they do not believe in God, what would change their minds?
4. Imagine a most perfect unicorn. Must such a unicorn exist? Is there a difference between a most perfect unicorn and a most perfect being that implies that the most perfect being necessarily exists while the most perfect unicorn does not?

For Further Reading

For a collection of Anselm's work see *St. Anselm* (1903) translated by S. N. Deane. This translation includes Anselm's ontological argument as found in his *Proslogion.* For biographical information see *Saint Anselm* (1990), by R. W. Southern.

For discussions of the ontological argument see *The Ontological Argument* (1972), by J. Barnes; *From Belief to Understanding* (1976), by R. Campbell; *God, Reason, and Theistic Proofs* (1997), by S. T. Davis; *Anselm's Discovery* (1965), by Charles Hartshorne; *The Many-Faced Argument* (1968), edited by John Hick and A. C. McGill; and *The Ontological Argument from St. Anselm to Contemporary Philosophers* (1965), by Alvin Plantinga.

62 THE FIVE WAYS
St. Thomas Aquinas

An Italian, St. Thomas Aquinas (1225–1274) was both a theologian and philosopher. His importance as a theologian cannot be overestimated. Today, Aquinas' works are required reading in most seminaries, and key elements of his writings are officially endorsed by the Roman Catholic Church.

Like Anselm before him, Aquinas believed that God's existence could be known through both faith and reason; unlike Anselm, however, Aquinas did

SOURCE: From Anton C. Pegis, *Basic Writings of St. Thomas Aquinas.* Reprinted by permission. Copyright 1945 by Random House, Inc., reprinted 1997 by Hackett Publishing Co., Inc. All rights reserved.

not believe that God's existence was 'self-evident' for humans. For Anselm, the existence of God could be demonstrated by an *a priori* argument, by merely reflecting on the concept of God—prior to the testimony of experience. For Aquinas, however, any rational proof of God's existence would have to be *a posteriori*, a proof partially dependent on sense-data. For example, in the following selection, an excerpt from his masterwork, *Summa Theologica*, the first of Aquinas' five arguments for God's existence begins with the observation that motion exists in the universe, something known from experience. But since motion could not have existed forever or come into existence all by itself, Aquinas concludes that motion must have come from an unmoved mover—namely, from God.

While all of Aquinas' arguments are based on empirical evidence, his last argument is a bit different. The first four arguments are 'cosmological arguments' and argue for the existence of God from an observable fact about the world (or **cosmos**); the final argument is called the 'teleological argument' and argues for the existence of God from the fact that the world seems to be directed toward some goal or purpose (**telos**).

Reading Questions

1. In the first argument for God's existence, what fact, evident to our senses, is in need of explanation?
2. Why can the existence of motion not be explained by an infinity of previous movers?
3. In the second argument for God's existence, Aquinas claims that there is no (actual or possible) example of what?
4. Why is it impossible for efficient causes to go on to infinity?
5. Why, if at one time nothing was in existence, would it have been impossible for anything to have begun to exist?
6. What causal role does the maximum in any genus play according to Aristotle?

...

. . . The existence of God can be proved in five ways.

The first and more manifest way is the argument from motion. It is certain, and evident to our senses, that in the world some things are in motion. Now whatever is moved is moved by another, for nothing can be moved except it is in potentiality to that towards which it is moved; whereas a thing moves inasmuch as it is in act. For motion is nothing else than the reduction of something from potentiality to actuality. But nothing can be reduced from potentiality to actuality, except by something in a state of actuality. Thus that which is actually hot, as fire, makes wood, which is potentially hot, to be actually hot, and thereby moves and changes it. Now it is not possible that the same thing should be at once in actuality and potentiality in the same respect, but only in different respects. For what is actually hot cannot simultaneously be potentially hot; but it is simultaneously potentially cold. It is therefore impossible that in the same respect and in the same way a thing should be both mover and moved, i.e., that it should move itself. Therefore, whatever is moved must be moved by another. If that by which is moved be itself moved, then this also must needs be moved by another, and that by another again. But this cannot go on to infinity, because then there would be no first mover, and, consequently, no other mover, seeing that subsequent movers move only inasmuch as they are moved by the first mover; as the staff moves only because it is moved by the hand. Therefore it is necessary to arrive at a first mover, moved by no other; and this everyone understands to be God.

The second way is from the nature of efficient cause. In the world of sensible things we find there is an order of efficient causes. There is no case known (neither is it, indeed, possible) in which a thing is found to be the efficient cause of itself; for so it would be prior to itself, which is impossible. Now in efficient causes it is not possible to go on to infinity, because in all efficient causes following in order, the first is the cause of the intermediate cause, and the intermediate is the cause of the ultimate cause, whether the intermediate cause be several, or one only. Now to take away the cause is to take away the effect. Therefore, if there be no first cause among efficient causes, there will be no ultimate, nor any intermediate, cause. But if in efficient causes it is possible to go on to infinity, there will be no first efficient cause, neither will there be an ultimate effect, nor any intermediate efficient causes; all of which is plainly false. Therefore it is necessary to admit a first efficient cause, to which everyone gives the name of God.

The third way is taken from possibility and necessity, and runs thus. We find in nature things that are possible to be and not to be, since they are found to be generated, and to be corrupted, and consequently, it is possible for them to be and not to be. But it is impossible for these always to exist, for that which can not-be at some time is not. Therefore, if everything can not-be, then at one time there was nothing in existence. Now if this were true, even now there would be nothing in existence, because that which does not exist begins to exist only through something already existing. Therefore, if at one time nothing was in existence, it would have been impossible for anything to have begun to exist; and thus even now nothing would be in existence—which is absurd. Therefore, not all beings are merely possible, but there must exist something the existence of which is necessary. But every necessary thing either has its necessity caused by another, or not. Now it is impossible to go on to infinity in necessary things which have their necessity caused by another, as has been already proved in regard to efficient causes. Therefore we cannot but admit the existence of some being having of itself its own necessity, and not receiving it from another, but rather causing in others their necessity. This all men speak of as God.

The fourth way is taken from the gradation to be found in things. Among beings there are some more and some less good, true, noble, and the like. But *more* and *less* are predicated of different things according as they resemble in their different ways something which is the maximum, as a thing is said to be hotter according as it more nearly resembles that which is hottest; so that there is something which is truest, something best, something noblest, and, consequently, something which is most being, for those things that are greatest in truth are greatest in being, as it is written in *Metaph. ii.* Now the maximum in any genus is the cause of all in that genus, as fire, which is the maximum of heat, is the cause of all hot things, as is said in the same book. Therefore there must also be something which is to all beings the cause of their being, goodness, and every other perfection; and this we call God.

The fifth way is taken from the governance of the world. We see that things which lack knowledge, such as natural bodies, act for an end, and this is evident from their acting always, or nearly always, in the same way, so as to obtain the best result. Hence it is plain that they achieve their end, not fortuitously, but designedly. Now whatever lacks knowledge cannot move towards an end, unless it be directed by some being endowed with knowledge and intelligence; as the arrow is directed by the archer. Therefore some intelligent being exists by whom all natural things are directed to their end; and this being we call God. . . .

Discussion Questions

1. In each proof, Aquinas believes that God is causally necessary to explain the existence of a fact about the world. For example, he argues that an unmoved mover must exist in order to explain the fact that motion exists in the world today. Suppose Aquinas proves the existence of an unmoved mover; has he also proved that this thing is the Judeo-Christian God? Do his arguments prove that God has other traditional attributes, such as omnibenevolence?

2. Suppose the universe could remain in motion from now until eternity. Could we also say that the universe *has been in motion since eternity?* Why or why not? Explain your answer.

3. In the fifth argument for God's existence, Aquinas claims that whatever lacks knowledge cannot move toward an end, unless directed by some being endowed with knowledge and intelligence. Give some examples of what he means. Can you come up with any counterexamples, in which things move toward an end, but without any knowledge or intelligence guiding them?

For Further Reading

For biographical information concerning Aquinas see *The Life of Saint Thomas Aquinas* (1959), by K. Foster. For an introduction to the philosophy of Aquinas see *Aquinas* (1955), by F. C. Copleston; *The Thought of Thomas Aquinas* (1992), by B. Davies; and *Aquinas* (1980), by A. Kenny.

For discussions concerning arguments for God's existence and Aquinas' arguments for God's existence see *The Five Ways: St. Thomas Aquinas' Proofs of God's Existence* (1980), by A. Kenny, and *Arguments for the Existence of God* (1971), by John Hick. For discussions of the cosmological argument see *The Cosmological Arguments* (1967), edited by D. Burrill; *The Cosmological Argument from Plato to Leibniz* (1980), by W. Craig; and *The Cosmological Argument* (1975), by W. Rowe.

63   THE BLIND WATCHMAKER
Richard Dawkins

Aquinas argued that the universe contains extremely complex creations undeniably designed for particular purposes. For example, eyes are infinitely complex and obviously designed for the purpose of seeing. Aquinas believed that the existence of objects such as eyes could be explained only by the existence of an intelligent designer, that is, God.

Modern science, however, challenges this view. In 1859, Charles Darwin published *The Origin of Species* and challenged the **creationists'** explanation of the origins of life. Darwin argued that, through the process of **natural selection,** life evolved from nonlife and that complex life evolved from simpler life forms. If true, Darwin's theory appears to challenge the theist's belief that God is necessary to explain the biological complexity of our world.

A common objection to Darwin's theory is that complex organisms, such as plants and animals, could not have come into existence by chance or by accident. Critics of **evolution** contend that, just as no one would ever expect the parts of a watch placed into a tumbler to ever produce a functioning watch, no one should expect complex life forms to arise from random events. Darwin's theory, they contend, might offer a theoretical explanation of the origins of life, but it is so highly improbable that it can be discounted altogether.

Modern evolutionary theorists have responded to this objection. Oxford zoologist Richard Dawkins (1941–) claims that this objection to evolutionary theory rests on a fundamental misunderstanding of Darwin's theory. Although chance plays a role in Darwin's explanation of life, Dawkins argues that natural selection—properly understood as "cumulative selection"—is, in fact, nonrandom. Dawkins suggests that the evolution of life and the evolution of complex forms from simpler forms via natural selection isn't improbable at all—it's inevitable. Moreover, all of this is possible without divine guidance or intervention.

Reading Questions

1. In essence, Darwinism amounts to what simple idea?
2. According to Dawkins, why did it take so long for someone to think of Darwinism?
3. Explain William Paley's version of the argument from design.
4. What does Dawkins mean by saying that the watchmaker is blind?
5. Give an example of order that has come from disorder without the help of an overseeing intelligence. What natural device allows for generation of nonrandomness?
6. Is simple sieving able to account for the massive amounts of nonrandom order that we see in living things? Explain your answer.
7. Explain the difference between single-step selection and cumulative selection.

This book is written in the conviction that our own existence once presented the greatest of all mysteries, but that it is a mystery no longer because it is solved. Darwin and Wallace solved it, though we shall continue to add footnotes to their solution for a while yet. I wrote the book because I was surprised that so many people seemed not only unaware of the elegant and beautiful solution to this deepest of problems but, incredibly, in many cases actually unaware that there was a problem in the first place!

The problem is that of complex design. The computer on which I am writing these words has an information storage capacity of about 64 kilobytes (one byte is used to hold each character of text). The computer was consciously designed and deliberately manufactured. The brain with which you are understanding my words is an array of some ten million kiloneurones. Many of these billions of nerve cells have each more than a thousand 'electric wires' connecting them to other neurones. Moreover, at the molecular genetic level, every single one of more than a trillion cells in the body contains about a thousand times as much precisely-coded digital information as my entire computer. The complexity of living organisms is matched by the elegant efficiency of their apparent design. If anyone doesn't agree that this amount of complex design cries out for an explanation, I give up. No, on second thoughts I don't give up, because one of my aims in the book is to convey something of the sheer wonder of biological complexity to those whose eyes have not been opened to it. But having built up the mystery, my other main aim is to remove it again by explaining the solution.

For reasons that are not entirely clear to me, Darwinism seems more in need of advocacy than similarly established truths in other branches of science. Many of us have no grasp of quantum theory, or Einstein's theories of special and general relativity, but this does not in itself lead us to *oppose* these theories! Darwinism, unlike 'Einsteinism', seems to be regarded as fair game for critics with any degree of ignorance. I suppose one trouble with Darwinism is that, as Jacques Monod perceptively remarked, everybody *thinks* he understands it. It is, indeed, a remarkably simple theory; childishly so, one would have thought, in comparison with almost all of physics and mathematics. In essence, it amounts simply to the idea that non-random reproduction, where there is hereditary variation, has consequences that are far-reaching if there is time for them to be cumulative.

But we have good grounds for believing that this simplicity is deceptive. Never forget that, simple as the theory may seem, nobody thought of it until Darwin and Wallace in the mid-nineteenth century, nearly 300 years after Newton's *Principia,* and more than 2,000 years after Eratosthenes measured the Earth. How could such a simple idea go so long undiscovered by thinkers of the caliber of Newton, Galileo, Descartes, Leibnitz, Hume and Aristotle? Why did it have to wait for two Victorian naturalists? What was *wrong* with philosophers and mathematicians that they overlooked it? And how can such a powerful idea go still largely unabsorbed into popular consciousness?

It is almost as if the human brain were specifically designed to misunderstand Darwinism, and to find it hard to believe. Take, for instance, the issue of 'chance', often dramatized as *blind* chance. The great majority of people that attack Darwinism leap with almost unseemly eagerness to the mistaken idea that there is nothing other than random chance in it. Since living complexity embodies the very antithesis of chance, if you think that Darwinism is tantamount to chance you'll obviously find it easy to refute Darwinism! One of my tasks will be to destroy this eagerly believed myth that Darwinism is a theory of 'chance'. Another way in which we seem predisposed to disbelieve Darwinism is that our brains are built to deal with events on radically different *timescales* from those that characterize evolutionary change. We are equipped to appreciate processes that take seconds, minutes, years or, at most, decades to complete. Darwinism is a theory of cumulative processes so slow that they take between thousands and millions of decades to complete. All our intuitive judgments of what is probable turn out to be wrong by many orders of magnitude. Our well-tuned apparatus of skepticism and subjective probability-theory misfires by huge margins, because it is tuned—ironically, by evolution itself—to work within a lifetime of a few decades. It requires effort of the imagination to escape from the prison of familiar timescale, an effort that I shall try to assist.

A third respect in which our brains seem predisposed to resist Darwinism stems from our great success as creative designers. Our world is dominated by feats of engineering and works of art. We are entirely accustomed to the idea that complex elegance is an indicator of premeditated, crafted design. This is probably the most powerful reason for the belief, held by the vast majority of people that have ever lived, in some kind of supernatural deity. It took a very large leap of the imagination for Darwin and Wallace to see that, contrary to all intuition, there is another way and, once you have understood it, a far more plausible way, for complex 'design' to arise out of primeval simplicity. A leap of the imagination so large that, to this day, many people seem still unwilling to make it. It is the main purpose of this book to help the reader to make this leap.

···

. . . [M]ost of us don't understand in detail how an airliner works. Probably its builders don't comprehend it fully either: engine specialists don't in detail understand wings, and wing specialists understand engines only vaguely. Wing specialists don't even understand wings with full mathematical precision: they can predict how a wing will behave in turbulent conditions, only by examining a model in a wind tunnel or a computer simulation—the sort of thing a biologist might do to understand an animal. But however incompletely we understand how an airliner works, we all understand by what general process it came into existence. It was designed by humans on drawing boards. Then other humans made the bits from the drawings, then lots more humans (with the aid of other machines designed by humans) screwed, riveted, welded or glued the bits together, each in its right place. The process by which an airliner came into existence is not fundamentally mysterious to us, because humans built it. The systematic putting together of parts to a purposeful design is something we know and understand, for we have experienced it at first hand, even if only with our childhood Meccano or Erector set.

What about our own bodies? Each one of us is a machine, like an airliner only much more complicated. Were we designed on a drawing board too, and were our parts assembled by a skilled engineer? The answer is no. It is a surprising answer, and we have known and understood it for only a century or so. When Charles Darwin first explained the matter, many people either wouldn't or couldn't grasp it. I myself flatly refused to believe Darwin's theory when I first heard about it as a child. Almost everybody throughout history, up to the second half of the nineteenth century, has firmly believed in the opposite—the Conscious Designer theory. Many people still do, perhaps because the true, Darwinian explanation of our own existence is still, remarkably, not a routine part of the curriculum of a general education. It is certainly very widely misunderstood.

The watchmaker of my title is borrowed from a famous treatise by the eighteenth-century theologian William Paley. His *Natural Theology—or Evidences of the Existence and Attributes of the Deity Collected from the Appearances of Nature,* published in 1802, is the best-known exposition of the 'Argument from Design', always the most influential of the arguments for the existence of a God. It is a book that I greatly admire, for in his own time its author succeeded in doing what I am struggling to do now. He had a point to make, he passionately believed in it, and he spared no effort to ram it home clearly. He had a proper reverence for the complexity of the living world, and he saw that it demands a very special kind of explanation. The only thing he got wrong—admittedly quite a big thing!—was the explanation itself. He gave the traditional religious answer to the riddle, but he articulated it more clearly and convincingly than anybody had before. The true explanation is utterly different, and it had to wait for one of the most revolutionary thinkers of all time, Charles Darwin.

Paley begins *Natural Theology* with a famous passage:

In crossing a heath, suppose I pitched my foot against a *stone,* and were asked how the stone came to be there; I might possibly answer, that, for anything I knew to the contrary, it had lain there forever: nor would it perhaps be very easy to show the absurdity of this answer. But suppose I had found a *watch* upon the ground, and it should be inquired how the watch happened to be in that place; I should hardly think of the answer which I had before given, that for anything I knew, the watch might have always been there.

Paley here appreciates the difference between natural physical objects like stones, and designed and manufactured objects like watches. He goes on to expound the precision with which the cogs and springs of a watch are fashioned, and the intricacy with which they are put together. If we found an object such as a watch upon a heath, even if we didn't know how it had come

into existence, its own precision and intricacy of design would force us to conclude

that the watch must have had a maker: that there must have existed, at some time, and at some place or other, an artificer or artificers, who formed it for the purpose which we find it actually to answer; who comprehended its construction, and designed its use.

Nobody could reasonably dissent from this conclusion, Paley insists, yet that is just what the atheist, in effect, does when he contemplates the works of nature, for:

every indication of contrivance, every manifestation of design, which existed in the watch, exists in the works of nature; with the difference, on the side of nature, of being greater or more, and that in a degree which exceeds all computation.

Paley drives his point home with beautiful and reverent descriptions of the dissected machinery of life, beginning with the human eye, a favorite example which Darwin was later to use and which will reappear throughout this book. Paley compares the eye with a designed instrument such as a telescope, and concludes that 'there is precisely the same proof that the eye was made for vision, as there is that the telescope was made for assisting it'. The eye must have had a designer, just as the telescope had.

Paley's argument is made with passionate sincerity and is informed by the best biological scholarship of his day, but it is wrong, gloriously and utterly wrong. The analogy between telescope and eye, between watch and living organism, is false. All appearances to the contrary, the only watchmaker in nature is the blind forces of physics, albeit deployed in a very special way. A true watchmaker has foresight: he designs his cogs and springs, and plans their interconnections, with a future purpose in his mind's eye. Natural selection, the blind, unconscious, automatic process which Darwin discovered, and which we now know is the explanation for the existence and apparently purposeful form of all life, has no purpose in mind. It has no mind and no mind's eye. It does not plan for the future. It has no vision, no foresight, no sight at all. If it can be said to play the role of watchmaker in nature, it is the *blind* watchmaker.

...

We have seen that living things are too improbable and too beautifully 'designed' to have come into existence by chance. How, then, did they come into existence? The answer, Darwin's answer, is by gradual, step-by-step transformations from simple beginnings, from primordial entities sufficiently simple to have come into existence by chance. Each successive change in the gradual evolutionary process was simple enough, *relative to its predecessor,* to have arisen by chance. But the whole sequence of cumulative steps constitutes anything but a chance process, when you consider the complexity of the final end-product relative to the original starting point. The cumulative process is directed by nonrandom survival. The purpose of this chapter is to demonstrate the power of this *cumulative selection* as a fundamentally nonrandom process.

If you walk up and down a pebbly beach, you will notice that the pebbles are not arranged at random. The smaller pebbles typically tend to be found in segregated zones running along the length of the beach, the larger ones in different zones or stripes. The pebbles have been sorted, arranged, selected. A tribe living near the shore might wonder at this evidence of sorting or arrangement in the world, and might develop a myth to account for it, perhaps attributing it to a Great Spirit in the sky with a tidy mind and a sense of order. We might give a superior smile at such a superstitious notion, and explain that the arranging was really done by the blind forces of physics, in this case the action of waves. The waves have no purposes and no intentions, no tidy mind, no mind at all. They just energetically throw the pebbles around, and big pebbles and small pebbles respond differently to this treatment so they end up at different levels of the beach. A small amount of order has come out of disorder, and no mind planned it.

The waves and the pebbles together constitute a simple example of a system that automatically generates non-randomness. The world is full of such systems. The simplest example I can think of is a hole. Only objects smaller than the hole can pass through it. This means that if you start with a random collection of objects above the hole, and some force shakes and jostles them about at random, after a while the objects above and below the hole will come to be nonrandomly sorted. The space below the hole will tend to contain objects smaller than the hole, and the

space above will tend to contain objects larger than the hole. Mankind has, of course, long exploited this simple principle for generating non-randomness, in the useful device known as the sieve.

The Solar System is a stable arrangement of planets, comets and debris orbiting the sun, and it is presumably one of many such orbiting systems in the universe. The nearer a satellite is to its sun, the faster it has to travel if it is to counter the sun's gravity and remain in stable orbit. For any given orbit, there is only one speed at which a satellite can travel and remain in that orbit. If it were travelling at any other velocity, it would either move out into deep space, or crash into the Sun, or move into another orbit. And if we look at the planets of our solar system, lo and behold, every single one of them is travelling at exactly the right velocity to keep it in its stable orbit around the Sun. A blessed miracle of provident design? No, just another natural 'sieve'. Obviously all the planets that we see orbiting the sun must be travelling at exactly the right speed to keep them in their orbits, or we wouldn't see them there because they wouldn't be there! But equally obviously this is not evidence for conscious design. It is just another kind of sieve.

Sieving of this order of simplicity is not, on its own, enough to account for the massive amounts of nonrandom order that we see in living things. Nowhere near enough. Remember the analogy of the combination lock. The kind of non-randomness that can be generated by simple sieving is roughly equivalent to opening a combination lock with only one dial: it is easy to open it by sheer luck. The kind of nonrandomness that we see in living systems, on the other hand, is equivalent to a gigantic combination lock with an almost uncountable number of dials. To generate a biological molecule like hemoglobin, the red pigment in blood, by simple sieving would be equivalent to taking all the amino-acid building blocks of hemoglobin, jumbling them up at random, and hoping that the hemoglobin molecule would reconstitute itself by sheer luck. The amount of luck that would be required for this feat is unthinkable, and has been used as a telling mind-boggler by Isaac Asimov and others.

A hemoglobin molecule consists of four chains of amino acids twisted together. Let us think about just one of these four chains. It consists of 146 amino acids. There are 20 different kinds of amino acids commonly found in living things. The number of possible ways of arranging 20 kinds of thing in chains 146 links long is an inconceivably large number, which Asimov calls the 'hemoglobin number'. It is easy to calculate, but impossible to visualize the answer. The first link in the 146-long chain could be any one of the 20 possible amino acids. The second link could also be any one of the 20, so the number of possible 2-link chains is 20 × 20, or 400. The number of possible 3-link chains is 20 × 20 × 20, or 8,000. The number of possible 146-link chains is 20 times itself 146 times. This is a staggeringly large number. A million is a 1 with 6 noughts after it. A billion (1,000 million) is a 1 with 9 noughts after it. The number we seek, the 'hemoglobin number', is (near enough) a 1 with 190 noughts after it! This is the chance against happening to hit upon hemoglobin by luck. And a hemoglobin molecule has only a minute fraction of the complexity of a living body. Simple sieving, on its own, is obviously nowhere near capable of generating the amount of order in a living thing. Sieving is an essential ingredient in the generation of living order, but it is very far from being the whole story. Something else is needed. To explain the point, I shall need to make a distinction between 'single-step' selection and 'cumulative' selection. The simple sieves we have been considering so far in this chapter are all examples of single-step selection. Living organization is the product of cumulative selection.

The essential difference between single-step selection and cumulative selection is this. In single-step selection the entities selected or sorted, pebbles or whatever they are, are sorted once and for all. In cumulative selection, on the other hand, they 'reproduce'; or in some other way the results of one sieving process are fed into a subsequent sieving, which is fed into . . . , and so on. The entities are subjected to selection of sorting over many 'generations' in succession. The end-product of one generation of selection is the starting point for the next generation of selection, and so on for many generations. It is natural to borrow such words as 'reproduce' and 'generation', which have associations with living things, because living things are the main examples we know of things that participate in cumulative selection. They may in practice be the only things that do. But for the moment I don't want to beg that question by saying so outright.

Sometimes clouds, through the random kneading and carving of the winds, come to look like familiar objects. There is a much published photograph, taken by the pilot of a small airplane, of what looks a bit like the face of Jesus, staring out of the sky. We have all seen clouds that reminded us of something—a sea horse, say, or a smiling face. These resemblances come about by single-step selection, that is to say by a single coincidence. They are, consequently, not very impressive. The resemblance of the signs of the zodiac to the animals after which they are named, Scorpio, Leo, and so on, is as unimpressive as the predictions of astrologers. We don't feel overwhelmed by the resemblance, as we are by biological adaptations—the products of cumulative selection. We describe as weird, uncanny or spectacular, the resemblance of, say, a leaf insect to a leaf or a praying mantis to a cluster of pink flowers. The resemblance of a cloud to a weasel is only mildly diverting, barely worth calling to the attention of our companion. Moreover, we are quite likely to change our mind about exactly what the cloud most resembles.

Hamlet: Do you see yonder cloud that's almost in shape of a camel?
Polonius: By the mass, and 'tis like a camel, indeed.
Hamlet: Methinks it is like a weasel.
Polonius: It is backed like a weasel.
Hamlet: Or like a whale?
Polonius: Very like a whale.

I don't know who it was first pointed out that, given enough time, a monkey bashing away at random on a typewriter could produce all the works of Shakespeare. The operative phrase is, of course, given enough time. Let us limit the task facing our monkey somewhat. Suppose that he has to produce, not the complete works of Shakespeare but just the short sentence 'Methinks it is like a weasel', and we shall make it relatively easy by giving him a typewriter with a restricted keyboard, one with just the 26 (capital) letters, and a space bar. How long will he take to write this one little sentence?

The sentence has 28 characters in it, so let us assume that the monkey has a series of discrete 'tries', each consisting of 28 bashes at the keyboard. If he types the phrase correctly, that is the end of the experiment. If not, we allow him another 'try' of 28 characters. I don't know any monkeys, but fortunately my 11-month old daughter is an experienced randomizing device, and she proved only too eager to step into the role of monkey typist. Here is what she typed on the computer:

UMMK JK CDZZ F ZD DSDSKSM
S SS FMCV PU I DDRGLKDXRRDO
RDTE QDWFDVIOY UDSKZWDCCVYT
H CHVY NMGNBAYTDFCCVD D
RCDFYYYRM N DFSKD LD K WDWK
JJKAUIZMZI UXDKIDISFUMDKUDXI

She has other important calls on her time, so I was obliged to program the computer to simulate a randomly typing baby or monkey:

WDLDMNLT DTJBKWIRZREQLMQCO P
Y YVMQKZPGJXWVHGLAWFVCHQYOPY
MWR SWTNUXMLCDLEUBXTQHNZVJQF
FU OVAODVYKDGXDEKYVMOGGS VT
HZQZDSFZIHIVPHZPETPWVOVPMZGF
GEWRGZRPBCTPGQMCKHFDBGW ZCCF

And so on and on. It isn't difficult to calculate how long we should reasonably expect to wait for the random computer (or baby or monkey) to type METHINKS IT IS LIKE A WEASEL. Think about the total number of *possible* phrases of the right length that the monkey or baby or random computer *could* type. It is the same kind of calculation as we did for hemoglobin, and it produces a similarly large result. There are 27 possible letters (counting 'space' as one letter) in the first position. The chance of the monkey happening to get the first letter—M—right is therefore 1 in 27. The chance of it getting the first two letters—ME—right is the chance of it getting the second letter—E—right (1 in 27) *given that* it has also got the first letter—M—right, therefore $1/27 \times 1/27$, which equals 1/729. The chance of it getting the first word—METHINKS—right is 1/27 for each of the 8 letters, therefore $(1/27) \times (1/27) \times (1/27) \times (1/27)$ . . ., etc. 8 times, or (1/27) to the power 8. The chance of it getting the entire phrase of 28 characters right is (1/27) to the power 28, i.e., (1/27) multiplied by itself 28 times. These are very small odds, about 1 in 10,000 million million million million million. To put it mildly, the phrase we seek would be a long time coming, to say nothing of the complete works of Shakespeare.

So much for single-step selection of random variation. What about cumulative selection; how much more effective should this be? Very very much more effective, perhaps more so than we at first realize, although it is almost obvious when we reflect further. We again use our computer monkey, but with a crucial difference in its program. It again begins by choosing a random sequence of 28 letters, just as before:

WDLMNLT DTJBKWIRZREZLMQCO P

It now 'breeds from' this random phrase. It duplicates it repeatedly, but with a certain chance of random error—'mutation'—in the copying. The computer examines the mutant nonsense phrases, the 'progeny' of the original phrase, and chooses the one which, *however slightly*, most resembles the target phrase, METHINKS IT IS LIKE A WEASEL. In this instance the winning phrase of the next 'generation' happened to be:

WDLTMNLT DTJBSWIRZREZLMQCO P

Not an obvious improvement! But the procedure is repeated, again mutant 'progeny' are 'bred from' the phrase, and a new 'winner' is chosen. This goes on, generation after generation. After 10 generations, the phrase chosen for 'breeding' was:

MDLDMNLS ITJISWHRZREZ MECS P

After 20 generations it was:

MELDINLS IT ISWPRKE Z WECSEL

By now, the eye of faith fancies that it can see a resemblance to the target phrase. By 30 generations there can be no doubt:

METHINGS IT ISWLIKE B WECSEL

Generation 40 takes us to within one letter of the target:

METHINKS IT IS LIKE I WEASEL

And the target was finally reached in generation 43. A second run of the computer began with the phrase:

Y YVMQKZPFJXWVHGLAWFVCHQXYOPY,

passed through (again reporting only every tenth generation):

Y YVMQKSPFTXWSHLIKEFV HQYSPY
YETHINKSPITXISHLIKEFA WQYSEY
METHINKS IT ISSLIKE A WEFSEY
METHINKS IT ISBLIKE A WEASES
METHINKS IT ISJLIKE A WEASEO
METHINKS IT IS LIKE A WEASEP

and reached the target phrase in generation 64. In a third run the computer started with:

GEWRGZRPBCTPGQMCKHFDBGW ZCCF

and reached METHINKS IT IS LIKE A WEASEL in 41 generations of selective 'breeding'.

The exact time taken by the computer to reach the target doesn't matter. If you want to know, it completed the whole exercise for me, the first time, while I was out to lunch. It took about half an hour. (Computer enthusiasts may think this unduly slow. The reason is that the program was written in BASIC, a sort of computer baby-talk. When I rewrote it in Pascal, it took 11 seconds.) Computers are a bit faster at this kind of thing than monkeys, but the difference really isn't significant. What matters is the difference between the time taken by *cumulative* selection, and the time which the same computer, working flat out at the same rate, would take to reach the target phrase if it were forced to use the other procedure of *single-step selection*: about a million million million million million years. This is more than a million million million times as long as the universe has so far existed. Actually it would be fairer just to say that, in comparison with the time it would take either a monkey or a randomly programmed computer to type our target phrase, the total age of the universe so far is a negligibly small quantity, so small as to be well within the margin of error for this sort of back-of-an-envelope calculation. Whereas the time taken for a computer working randomly but with the constraint of *cumulative selection* to perform the same task is of the same order as humans ordinarily can understand, between 11 seconds and the time it takes to have lunch.

There is a big difference, then, between cumulative selection (in which each improvement, however slight, is used as a basis for future building), and single-step selection (in which each new 'try' is a fresh one). If evolutionary progress had had to rely on single-step selection, it would never have got anywhere. If, however, there was any way in which the necessary conditions for *cumulative* selection could have been set up by the blind forces of nature, strange and wonderful might have been the consequences. As a matter of fact that is exactly what happened on this planet, and we ourselves are among the most recent, if not the strangest and most wonderful, of those consequences. . . .

Discussion Questions

1. Could single-step selection or cumulative selection be the mechanism behind the complexity and design observed in nature? Explain how it would work according to Dawkins. Do you believe this mechanism can explain how life arose? Explain your answer.
2. In your view, why do some persons not believe the theory of evolution? What sorts of reasons do they typically give? Are these good reasons? If they do not believe in evolution, would Dawkins' article convince them?
3. Granted the thesis of cumulative selection, what are the chances that simple (and complex) forms of life exist elsewhere in the universe? What do you think Dawkins believes about the possibility of intelligent extraterrestrial life? Would the presence of life on another planet count for or against the existence of God?
4. Is evolution compatible with theism? Why or why not?

For Further Reading

For Dawkins' work related to evolution see *The Blind Watchmaker* (1986), *The Selfish Gene* (1989), and *Climbing Mount Improbable* (1996). For discussions concerning evolution versus creation science (from a pro-evolution perspective) see *Abusing Science: The Case against Creationism* (1982), by P. Kitcher, and *Darwinism Defended* (1982), by M. Ruse.

64   THE WAGER
Blaise Pascal

A boy genius, Blaise Pascal (1623–1662) completed his first important
work in geometry, *Essai pour les Coniques,* at the age of 16. From there
Pascal went on to make other major contributions in the areas of
mathematics and physics. His major philosophical works were published
posthumously, however. The following selection comes from one of those
works, *Pensées,* or *Thoughts.* In it Pascal argues that we can never hope to
grasp God's nature, nor can we ever be sure that God exists. Nevertheless,
Pascal maintains that reason demands that we believe in God.

Pascal reasoned that one had to make a choice: to believe in God (and
follow His commandments) or not. By believing in God you stand to
gain eternal salvation while forfeiting very little, only the finite quantity
of pleasure that might be gained by not having to answer to God's
commandments. But by not believing in God, you risk eternal damnation
for a mere finite quantity of pleasure. What should you do? Pascal
suggests "maximizing your minimum outcome"; that is, it is rational
to avoid the worst possible outcome, in this case, eternal damnation.
Faith in God, then, is the only rational choice.

Reading Questions

1. Can one know what God is, or if He is, according to Pascal? Explain.
2. Explain why Pascal believes one must make a wager concerning God's existence.
3. What reasons are there for wagering that God exists?
4. Given the rationality of wagering on God, what should you do if you cannot bring yourself to believe in God?
5. Since one must give up sin—corrupt pleasures—as a believer, are our lives as believers
   likely to be less pleasurable than they would be if we were nonbelievers?

...

If there is a God, he is infinitely beyond our comprehension, since, having neither parts nor limits,
he bears no relation to ourselves. We are therefore
incapable of knowing either what he is, or if he is.
That being so, who will dare to undertake a resolution of this question? It cannot be us, who bear no
relationship to him.

Who will then blame the Christians for being
unable to provide a rational basis for their belief, they
who profess a religion for which they cannot provide
a rational basis? They declare that it is a folly, *stulti-
tiam* (I Cor. 1: 18) in laying it before the world: and
then you complain that they do not prove it! If they
did prove it, they would not be keeping their word.
It is by the lack of proof that they do not lack sense.
'Yes, but although that excuses those who offer their
religion as it is, and that takes away the blame from
them of producing it without a rational basis, it does
not excuse those who accept it.'

SOURCE: From *Pensées and Other Writings,* translated by Honor Levi, 1995. Used by permission of Oxford
University Press.

Let us therefore examine this point, and say: God is, or is not. But towards which side will we lean? Reason cannot decide anything. There is an infinite chaos separating us. At the far end of this infinite distance a game is being played and the coin will come down heads or tails. How will you wager? Reason cannot make you choose one way or the other, reason cannot make you defend either of the two choices.

So do not accuse those who have made a choice of being wrong, for you know nothing about it! 'No, but I will blame them not for having made this choice, but for having made any choice. For, though the one who chooses heads and the other one are equally wrong, they are both wrong. The right thing is not to wager at all.'

Yes, but you have to wager. It is not up to you, you are already committed. Which then will you choose? Let us see. Since you have to choose, let us see which interests you the least. You have two things to lose: the truth and the good, and two things to stake: your reason and will, your knowledge and beatitude; and your nature has two things to avoid: error and wretchedness. Your reason is not hurt more by choosing one rather than the other, since you do have to make the choice. That is one point disposed of. But your beatitude? Let us weigh up the gain and the loss by calling heads that God exists. Let us assess the two cases: if you win, you win everything; if you lose, you lose nothing. Wager that he exists then, without hesitating! 'This is wonderful. Yes, I must wager. But perhaps I am betting too much.' Let us see. Since there is an equal chance of gain, and loss, if you won only two lives instead of one, you could still put on a bet. But if there were three lives to win, you would have to play (since you must necessarily play), and you would be unwise, once forced to play, not to chance your life to win three in a game where there is an equal chance of losing and winning. But there is an eternity of life and happiness. And that being so, even though there were an infinite number of chances of which only one were in your favor, you would still be right to wager one in order to win two, and you would be acting wrongly, since you are obliged to play, by refusing to stake one life against three in a game where out of an infinite number of chances there is one in your favor, if there were an infinitely happy infinity

of life to be won. But here there is an infinitely happy infinity of life to be won, one chance of winning against a finite number of chances of losing, and what you are staking is finite. That removes all choice: wherever there is infinity and where there is no infinity of chances of losing against one of winning, there is no scope for wavering, you have to chance everything. And thus, as you are forced to gamble, you have to have discarded reason if you cling on to your life, rather than risk it for the infinite prize which is just as likely to happen as the loss of nothingness.

For it is no good saying that it is uncertain if you will win, that it is certain you are taking a risk, and that the infinite distance between the *certainty* of what you are risking and the *uncertainty* of whether you win makes the finite good of what you are certainly risking equal to the uncertainty of the infinite. It does not work like that. Every gambler takes a certain risk for an uncertain gain; nevertheless he certainly risks the finite uncertainty in order to win a finite gain, without sinning against reason. There is no infinite distance between this certainty of what is being risked and the uncertainty of what might be gained: that is untrue. There is, indeed, an infinite distance between the certainty of winning and the certainty of losing. But the uncertainty of winning is proportional to the certainty of the risk, according to the chances of winning or losing. And hence, if there are as many chances on one side as on the other, the odds are even, and then the certainty of what you risk is equal to the uncertainty of winning. It is very far from being infinitely distant from it. So our argument is infinitely strong, when the finite is at stake in a game where there are equal chances of winning and losing, and the infinite is to be won.

That is conclusive, and, if human beings are capable of understanding any truth at all, this is the one.

'I confess it, I admit it, but even so . . . Is there no way of seeing underneath the cards?' 'Yes, Scripture and the rest, etc.' 'Yes, but my hands are tied and I cannot speak a word. I am being forced to wager and I am not free, they will not let me go. And I am made in such a way that I cannot believe. So what do you want me to do?' 'That is true. But at least realize that your inability to believe, since reason urges you to do so and yet you cannot, arises from your passions. So concentrate not on convincing yourself by increasing the number of proofs of God but on diminishing your passions. You want to find faith and you do not know the way? You want to cure yourself of unbelief and you ask for the remedies? Learn from those who have been bound like you, and who now wager all they have. They are people who know the road you want to follow and have been cured of the affliction of which you want to be cured. Follow the way by which they began: by behaving just as if they believed, taking holy water, having masses said, etc. That will make you believe quite naturally, and according to your animal reactions.' 'But that is what I am afraid of.' 'Why? What do you have to lose? In order to show you that this is where it leads, it is because it diminishes the passions, which are your great stumbling-blocks,' etc.

'How these words carry me away, send me into raptures,' etc. If these words please you and seem worthwhile, you should know that they are spoken by a man who knelt both before and afterwards to beg this infinite and indivisible Being, to whom he submits the whole of himself, that you should also submit yourself, for your own good and for his glory, and that strength might thereby be reconciled with this lowliness.

END OF THIS DISCOURSE

But what harm will come to you from taking this course? You will be faithful, honest, humble, grateful, doing good, a sincere and true friend. It is, of course, true; you will not take part in corrupt pleasure, in glory, in the pleasures of high living. But will you not have others?

I tell you that you will win thereby in this life, and that at every step you take along this path, you will see so much certainty of winning and so negligible a risk, that you will realize in the end that you have wagered on something certain and infinite, for which you have paid nothing.

We owe a great deal to those who warn us of our faults, for they mortify us; they teach us that we have been held in contempt, but they do not prevent it from happening to us in the future, for we have many other faults to merit it. They prepare us for the exercise of correction, and the removal of a fault.

Custom is natural to us. Anyone who becomes accustomed to faith believes it, and can no longer not fear hell, and believes in nothing else. Anyone who becomes accustomed to believing that the king is to be feared, etc. Who can then doubt that our soul, being accustomed to seeing number, space, movement, believes in this and nothing else?

Do you believe that it is impossible that God should be infinite and indivisible? 'Yes.' I want to show you, then (*an image of God in his boundlessness*), an infinite and indivisible thing: it is a point moving everywhere at infinite speed.

For it is a single entity everywhere, and complete in every place.

Let this fact of nature, which previously seemed to you impossible, make you understand that there may be others which you do not yet know. Do not draw the conclusion from your apprenticeship that there is nothing left for you to learn, but that you have an infinite amount to learn.

It is not true that we are worthy of being loved by others. It is unfair that we should want to be loved. If we were born reasonable and impartial, knowing ourselves and others, we would not incline our will in that direction. However, we are born with it. We are therefore born unfair. For everything is biased towards itself: this is contrary to all order. The tendency should be towards the generality, and the leaning towards the self is the beginning of all disorder: war, public administration, the economy, the individual body.

The will is therefore depraved. If the members of the natural and civil communities tend towards the good of the body, the communities themselves should tend towards another, more general body, of which they are the members. We should therefore tend towards the general. We are born, then, unjust and depraved.

No religion apart from our own has taught that man is born sinful. No philosophical sect has said so. So none has told the truth.

No sect or religion has always existed on earth, apart from the Christian religion.

Only the Christian religion makes men together both *lovable* and *happy*. We cannot be both capable of being loved and happy in formal society.

It is the heart that feels God, not reason: that is what faith is. God felt by the heart, not by reason.

Discussion Questions

1. Pascal's wager supports belief in God—but only so long as God promises an infinite reward for obedience. But how do we know that God will reward us for believing in Him? Is it possible that God would reward disbelief? Do you think this is an important objection to Pascal's argument?
2. As part of his argument, Pascal claims that the odds of God's existence are fifty-fifty. Is this appraisal of the situation accurate? Suppose that the odds of God's existence were different (higher or lower). Would this affect the outcome of Pascal's argument?
3. Can a nonbeliever come to believe in God by acting and behaving as if God exists? Suppose you didn't believe in God, but attended worship services regularly anyway. What do you predict would happen? What does this imply about the rationality of belief in God?

For Further Reading

For the complete works of Pascal (in French) see *Oeuvres Complhtes* (1963), edited by L. Lafuma. For biographical information see *Pascal* (1981), by R. J. Nelson. For an introduction to Pascal's philosophy see *Pascal* (1980), by A. Krailsheimer, and *Discourses of the Fall* (1967), by S. E. Metzer. For studies of Pascal's wager see *Gambling on God* (1994), edited by J. Jordon, and *Pascal's Wager* (1985), by Nicholas Rescher.

65 THE WILL TO BELIEVE
William James

Anselm and Aquinas believed that reason could be used to establish the existence of God. Pascal disagreed, but he still believed that reason could be used to demonstrate that it was better to believe in God than not to believe. In the following selection, American philosopher and psychologist, William James (1842–1910), asks what one should do when faced with a question, an option, *that cannot by its nature be decided on intellectual grounds.* Should we refrain from making a judgment?

Why is James concerned about this? In part, because there are some judgments that one cannot avoid making. Additionally, suspending belief on every issue that cannot be decided on purely intellectual grounds would strip us of a major share of our beliefs. So, in practice, it is not possible to simply suspend judgment when adequate or compelling evidence is lacking.

But certainly we can say something more about when it is and is not permissible to form and hold a belief concerning an issue that cannot be decided on purely intellectual grounds. For James, it is permissible to form, hold, and act on an uncertain belief, or option, of this sort when (1) we are forced to form an opinion regarding the option, (2) the option is believed to be a real possibility, and (3) the decision holds great import.

How does this apply to belief in God? Consider whether or not God exists. Can this matter be resolved by force of rational argument alone, simply on intellectual grounds? It appears doubtful. But according to James, one is *forced* to form a belief concerning God's existence, since **agnosticism** is tantamount to **atheism** in God's eyes. So a decision must be made. Moreover, the decision to believe or not to believe in God is clearly *momentous*—it would have a great impact on our lives. Hence, if God's existence is a *live* option, and James believes it is, then it is reasonable to form a belief concerning God's existence and to act on that belief—even though, strictly speaking, God's existence remains uncertain.

Reading Questions

1. What is the difference between a live and dead hypothesis? How is the liveness of a hypothesis measured?
2. What does James mean by a "genuine option"?
3. Are most scientific hypotheses living hypotheses? Explain. Is science on any more solid ground than moral reasoning according to James?
4. Is religion a momentous option? Is it a forced option?
5. Why should we reject the agnostic rules of truth seeking?

...

I

Let us give the name of *hypothesis* to anything that may be proposed to our belief; and just as the electricians speak of live and dead wires, let us speak of any hypothesis as either *live* or *dead*. A live hypothesis is one which appeals as a real possibility to him to whom it is proposed. If I ask you to believe in the Mahdi, the notion makes no electric connection with your nature—it refuses to scintillate with any credibility at all. As an hypothesis it is completely dead. To an Arab, however (even if he be not one of the Mahdi's followers), the hypothesis is among the mind's possibilities: it is alive. This shows that deadness and liveness in an hypothesis are not intrinsic properties, but relations to the individual thinker. They are measured by his willingness to act. The maximum of liveness in an hypothesis means willingness to act irrevocably. Practically, that means belief; but there is some believing tendency wherever there is willingness to act at all.

Next, let us call the decision between two hypotheses an *option*. Options may be of several kinds. They may be—1, *living* or *dead*; 2, *forced* or *avoidable*; 3, *momentous* or *trivial*; and for our purposes we may call an option a *genuine* option when it is of the forced, living, and momentous kind.

1. A living option is one in which both hypotheses are live ones. If I say to you: "Be a theosophist or be a Mohammedan," it is probably a dead option, because for you neither hypothesis is likely to be alive. But if I say: "Be an agnostic or be a Christian," it is otherwise: trained as you are, each hypothesis makes some appeal, however small, to your belief.

2. Next, if I say to you: "Choose between going out with your umbrella or without it," I do not offer you a genuine option, for it is not forced. You can easily avoid it by not going out at all. Similarly, if I say, "Either love me or hate me," "Either call my theory true or call it false," your option is avoidable. You may remain indifferent to me, neither loving nor hating and you may decline to offer any judgment as to my theory. But if I say, "Either accept this truth or go without it," I put on you a forced option, for there is no standing place outside of the alternative. Every dilemma based on a complete logical disjunction, with no possibility of not choosing, is an option of this forced kind.

...

It will facilitate our discussion if we keep all these distinctions well in mind.

IV

. . . The thesis I defend is, briefly stated, this: *Our passional nature not only lawfully may, but must, decide an option between propositions, whenever it is a genuine option that cannot by its nature be decided on intellectual grounds; for to say, under such circumstances, "Do not decide, but leave the question open," is itself a passional decision—just like deciding yes or no—and is attended with the same risk of losing the truth.* The thesis thus abstractly expressed will, I trust, soon become quite clear. . . .

...

VIII

...

. . . Wherever the option between losing truth and gaining it is not momentus, we can throw the chance of *gaining truth* away, and at any rate save ourselves from any chance of *believing falsehood,* by not making up our minds at all till objective evidence has come. In scientific questions, this is almost always the case; and even in human affairs in general, the need of acting is seldom so urgent that a false belief to act on is better than no belief at all. Law courts, indeed, have to decide on the best evidence attainable for the moment, because a judge's duty is to make law as well as to ascertain it, and (as a learned judge once said to me) few cases are worth spending much time over: the great thing is to have them decided on *any* acceptable principle, and got out of the way. But in our dealings with objective nature we obviously are recorders, not makers, of the truth; and decisions for the mere sake of deciding promptly and getting on to the next business would be wholly out of place. Throughout the breadth of physical nature facts are what they are quite independently of us, and seldom is there any such hurry about them that the risks of being duped by believing a premature theory need be faced. The questions here are always trivial options, the hypotheses are hardly living (at any rate not living for us spectators), the choice between believing truth or falsehood is

seldom forced. The attitude of skeptical balance is therefore the absolutely wise one if we would escape mistakes. What difference indeed, does it make to most of us whether we have or have not a theory of the roentgen rays, whether we believe or not in mind stuff, or have a conviction about the causality of conscious states? It makes no difference. Such options are not forced on us. On every account it is better not to make them, but still keep weighing reasons *pro et contra* with an indifferent hand.

...

IX

...

But now, it will be said, these . . . have nothing to do with great cosmical matters, like the question of religious faith. Let us then pass on to that. Religions differ so much in their accidents that in discussing the religious question we must make it very generic and broad. What then do we now mean by the religious hypothesis? Science says things are; morality says some things are better than other things; and religion says essentially two things.

First, she says that the best things are the more eternal things, the overlapping things, the things in the universe that throw the last stone, so to speak, and say the final word. "Perfection is eternal"—this phrase of Charles Secrétan seems a good way of putting this first affirmation of religion, an affirmation which obviously cannot yet be verified scientifically at all.

The second affirmation of religion is that we are better off even now if we believe her first affirmation to be true.

Now, let us consider what the logical elements of this situation are *in case the religious hypothesis in both its branches be really true.* (Of course, we must admit that possibility at the outset. If we are to discuss the question at all, it must involve a living option. If for any of you religion be a hypothesis that cannot, by any living possibility be true, then you need go no farther. I speak to the "saving remnant" alone.) So proceeding, we see, first, that religion offers itself as a *momentous* option. We are supposed to gain even now, by our belief, and to lose by our nonbelief, a certain vital good.

Secondly, religion is a *forced* option, so far as that good goes. We cannot escape the issue by remaining skeptical and waiting for more light, because, although we do avoid error in that way *if religion be untrue*, we lose the good, *if it be true*, just as certainly as if we positively chose to disbelieve. It is as if a man should hesitate indefinitely to ask a certain woman to marry him because he was not perfectly sure that she would prove an angel after he brought her home. Would he not cut himself off from that particular angel possibility as decisively as if he went and married someone else? Skepticism, then, is not avoidance of option; it is option of a certain particular kind of risk. *Better risk loss of truth than chance of error*—that is your faith vetoer's exact position. He is actively playing his stake as much as the believer is; he is backing the field against the religious hypothesis, just as the believer is backing the religious hypothesis against the field. To preach skepticism to us as a duty until "sufficient evidence" for religion be found, is tantamount therefore to telling us, when in presence of the religious hypothesis, that to yield to our fear of its being error is wiser and better than to yield to our hope that it may be true. It is not intellect against all passions, then; it is only intellect with one passion laying down its law. And by what, forsooth, is the supreme wisdom of this passion warranted? Dupery for dupery, what proof is there that dupery through hope is so much worse than dupery through fear? I, for one, can see no proof; and I simply refuse obedience to the scientist's command to imitate his kind of option, in a case where my own stake is important enough to give the right to choose my own form of risk. If religion be true and the evidence for it be still insufficient, I do not wish, by putting your extinguisher upon my nature (which feels to me as if it had after all some business in this matter), to forfeit my sole chance in life of getting upon the winning side—that chance depending, of course, on my willingness to run the risk of acting as if my passional need of taking the world religiously might be prophetic and right.

All this is on the supposition that it really may be prophetic and right, and that, even to us who are discussing the matter, religion is a live hypothesis which may be true. Now, to most of us religion comes in a still further way that makes a veto on our active faith even more illogical. The more perfect and more eternal aspect of the universe is represented in our religions as having personal form. The universe is no longer a mere *It* to us, but a *Thou*, if we are religious; and any relation that may be possible from person to person might be possible here. For instance, although in one sense we are passive portions of the universe, in another we show a curious autonomy, as if we were small active centers on our own account. We feel, too, as if the appeal of religion to us were made to our own active good will, as if evidence might be forever withheld from us unless we met the hypothesis halfway. To take a trivial illustration: just as a man who in a company of gentlemen made no advances, asked a warrant for every concession, and believed no one's word without proof, would cut himself off by such churlishness from all social rewards that a more trusting spirit would earn—so here, one who should shut himself up in snarling logicality and try to make the gods extort his recognition willy-nilly, or not get it at all, might cut himself off forever from his only opportunity of making the gods' acquaintance. This feeling, forced on us we know not whence, that by obstinately believing that there are gods (although not to do so would be so easy both for our logic and our life) we are doing the universe the deepest service we can, seems part of the living essence of the religious hypothesis. If the hypothesis *were* true in all its parts, including this one, then pure intellectualism, with its veto on our making willing advances, would be an absurdity; and some participation of our sympathetic nature would be logically required. I, therefore, for one, cannot see my way to accepting the agnostic rules for truth seeking, or wilfully agree to keep my willing nature out of the game. I cannot do so for this plain reason, that *a rule of thinking which would absolutely prevent me from acknowledging certain kinds of truth if those kinds of truth were really there would be an irrational rule.* That for me is the long and short of the formal logic of the situation, no matter what the kinds of truth might materially be.

I confess I do not see how this logic can be escaped. But sad experience makes me fear that some of you may still shrink from radically saying with me, *in abstracto,* that we have the right to believe at our own risk any hypothesis that is live enough to tempt our will. I suspect, however, that if this is so, it is because you have got away from the abstract logical point of view altogether, and are thinking (perhaps without realizing it) of some particular religious hypothesis which for you is dead. The freedom to "believe what we will" you apply to the case of some patent superstition; and the faith you think of is the faith defined by the schoolboy when he said, "Faith is when you believe something that you know ain't true." I can only repeat that this is misapprehension. *In concreto,* the freedom to believe can only cover living options which the intellect of the individual cannot by itself resolve; and living options never seem absurdities to him who has them to consider. When I look at the religious question as it really puts itself to concrete men, and when I think of all the possibilities which both practically and theoretically it involves, then this command that we shall put a stopper on our heart, instincts, and courage, and *wait*—acting of course meanwhile more or less as if religion were *not* true—till doomsday, or till such time as our intellect and senses working together may have raked in evidence enough—this command, I say, seems to me the queerest idol ever manufactured in the philosophic cave. Were we scholastic absolutists, there might be more excuse. If we had an infallible intellect with its objective certitudes, we might feel ourselves disloyal to such a perfect organ of knowledge in not trusting to it exclusively, in not waiting for its releasing word. But if we are empiricists, if we believe that no bell in us tolls to let us know for certain when truth is in our grasp, then it seems a piece of idle fantasticality to preach so solemnly our duty of waiting for the bell. Indeed we *may* wait if we will—I hope you do not think that I am denying that—but if we do so, we do so at our peril as much as if we believed. In either case we *act,* taking our life in our hands. No one of us ought to issue vetoes to the other, nor should we bandy words of abuse. We ought, on the contrary, delicately and profoundly to respect one another's mental freedom: then only shall we bring about the intellectual republic; then only shall we have that spirit of inner tolerance without which all our outer tolerance is soulless, and which is empiricism's glory; then only shall we live and let live, in speculative as well as in practical things. . . .

Discussion Questions

1. Is belief in UFOs or extraterrestrials a momentous choice? Is it a live option? How would James respond to the criticism that his pragmatism would mean it is also acceptable to believe in leprechauns and unicorns?
2. In what ways is belief in God a momentous choice? Do you believe people's actions are affected by their belief or disbelief in God? If so, how? If not, why not?

For Further Reading

For James' collected works see *The Works of William James* (1975), edited by Burkhardt, Bowers, and Skrupselis. For biographical information see *William James: A Biography* (1967), by G. W. Allen, and *William James: His Life and Thought* (1987), by G. E. Myers. For an introduction to the philosophy of James see R. B. Perry's texts *In the Spirit of William James* (1958), and *The Thought and Character of William James* (1948).

 For information concerning pragmatism and James' philosophy of religion see *The Religious Investigations of William James* (1981), by H. S. Levinson; *Pragmatism: The Classic Writings* (1982), edited by H. S. Thayer; and *The Religious Philosophy of William James* (1981), by R. J. Vanden Burgt.

66   GOD IN BLACK THEOLOGY
James H. Cone

The most often repeated commandment in the Pentateuch (the first five books of the Hebrew Bible, traditionally said to have been authored by Moses) is the commandment that we should care for and shepherd the "widows, aliens, and orphans"; that is, we must pay special attention to those who are on the margins of society. **Liberation theology** takes this commandment seriously and aims to relieve the suffering of all persons in whatever form it is found and wherever it is discovered.

Liberation theology is a relatively recent religious movement that has had a wide impact on modern theology and philosophy of religion. Liberation theology has roots in both **Marxism** and religious faith. (The majority of liberation theologians are Christians, but not all.) In Marxism, liberation theologians discover tools for analyzing the sources of social oppression, especially instruments for exposing how social and economic institutions—including religious institutions such as churches—create oppressive social conditions. Moreover, they take from Marx not only his radical commitment to equality, but also his method of analyzing social problems from the standpoint of the **proletariat**.

Liberation theologians mix these basic Marxist ideals with religious faith, often with surprising results. God, they contend, is not omnipresent per se; rather, God is present wherever there is suffering and oppression. Nor is this God, they argue, neutral; instead God takes sides in historical struggles— *for* the poor and suffering and *against* the powerful and wealthy. This reinterpretation of God leads to an interesting new reading of the Bible as well, one in which God is shown as being present with the poor and suffering. The exodus of the Hebrew slaves from Egypt, for example, is taken to be a central event of the Hebrew Bible, an event in which God was revealed as partisan with the slaves, not with their masters. (Note that liberation theology defends violence, such as that of the exodus, as a necessary feature of political and personal liberation—a fact that continues to be true today as well.) In Jesus, liberation theologians also see a champion of the poor. Here God, they argue, present in Jesus, is thus also present with the outcasts of first-century Palestine with whom Jesus regularly associated, including lepers, prostitutes, tax collectors, the ritually unclean, and persons of suspicious racial heritage. The death and crucifixion of Jesus only continues God's identification with the suffering and oppressed.

This reconceptualization of God is advantageous in several ways. First, it responds to the criticism that religion has supported oppressive practices. Liberation theologians don't deny that religion has been a coconspirator in many great injustices, but they would regard these as aberrations of true religious faith. Second, because liberation theologians replace the abstract

SOURCE: From *A Theology of Black Liberation* by James H. Cone, pp. 55–81 (1990; 20th Anniversary Edition); used by permission of Orbis Books and James H. Cone. Copyright © 1986, 1990 James H. Cone.

God of philosophy with a concrete moral force active in history, they can argue for God's existence on different grounds. Knowledge of God, if the liberation theologian is correct, is achieved not so much through metaphysical reflection as through a proper moral perception of history. Thus if God's nature includes God's identification with the poor, then God is only known by us when we also identify with the poor and suffering. Third, liberation theology attempts to respond to the problem of evil by characterizing God both as actively present in history liberating the poor and oppressed, and as participating in our sufferings along with us.

Many liberation theologians are from Central and South America, often associated with the Catholic Church, on which they have had a wide influence. In North America, many of the most influential liberation theologians have been black theologians, including the author of the following selection, James Cone (1938–), professor of theology at Union Theological Seminary in New York City.

Reading Questions

1. Why must those who proclaim the true gospel be both 'anti-Christian' and 'unpatriotic'?
2. Why is authentic speech about God difficult?
3. Why does Cone think that black theology should not drop God-language?
4. What does Cone mean that the question is not whether people believe in God, but rather 'whose God' they believe in?
5. How has religion been related to black liberation movements according to Cone?
6. What is meant by 'God is black'?
7. How are oppression and liberation related to God's essence?
8. What must we do in order to know God?
9. How does Cone define salvation? How is it achieved?

The reality of God is presupposed in Black Theology. Black Theology is an attempt to analyze the nature of that reality, asking what we can say about the nature of God in view of his self-disclosure in biblical history and the oppressed condition of black people.

If we take the question seriously, it becomes evident that there is no simple answer to it. To speak of God and his participation in the liberation of the oppressed of the land is a risky venture in any society. But if the society is racist and also uses God-language as an instrument to further the cause of human humiliation, then the task of authentic theological speech is even more dangerous and difficult.

It is *dangerous* because the true prophet of the gospel of God must become both "anti-Christian" and "unpatriotic." It is impossible to confront a racist society, with the meaning of human existence grounded in commitment to the divine, without at the same time challenging the very existence of the national structure and all of its institutions, especially the established church. All national institutions represent the interests of the society as a whole. We live in a nation which is committed to the perpetuation of white supremacy, and it will try to exterminate all who fail to assist it in this ideal. The genocide of the American Indian is evidence of that fact. Black Theology represents that community of black people who refuse to cooperate in the exaltation of whiteness and the degradation of blackness. It proclaims the reality of the biblical God who is actively destroying everything that is against the manifestation of human dignity among black people.

Because whiteness by its very nature is against blackness, the black prophet is a prophet of national doom. He proclaims the end of the "American Way," for God has stirred the soul of the black community, and now that community will stop at nothing to claim the freedom that is 350 years overdue. The black prophet is a rebel with a cause, the cause of over twenty-five million American blacks and all oppressed men everywhere. It is God's cause because he has chosen the blacks as his own. And he has chosen them not for redemptive suffering but for freedom. Black people are not elected to be Yahweh's suffering people. Rather we are elected because we are oppressed against our will and God's, and he has decided to make our liberation his own. We are elected to be free now to do the work of him who has called us into being, namely the breaking of the chains. The black theologian must assume the dangerous responsibility of articulating the revolutionary mood of the black community. This means that his speech about God, in the authentic prophetic tradition, will always move on the brink of treason and heresy in an oppressive society.

The task of authentic theological speech is *difficult* because all religionists in the society claim to be for God and thus for man. Even the executioners are for God. They carry out punitive acts against certain segments of society because "decent" people need protection against the undesirables. That is why blacks were enslaved and Indians exterminated—in the name of God and freedom. That is why today blacks are forced into ghettos and shot down like dogs if they raise a hand in protest. When George Washington, Thomas Jefferson, Lyndon Johnson, Richard Nixon and other "great" Americans can invoke the name of God at the same time they are defining the society for white people only, then Black Theology knows that it cannot approach the God-question too casually. It must ask, "How can we speak of God without being associated with the oppressors of the land?" Whiteness is so pervasive that the oppressors can destroy the revolutionary mood among the oppressed by introducing the complacent white God into the black community, thereby reducing the spirit of freedom.

Therefore if black people want to break the chains, they must recognize the need for going all the way if liberation is to be a reality. The white God will point to a heavenly bliss as a means of directing black people away from earthly rage. Freedom comes when we realize that it is against our interests, as a self-determining black community, to point out the "good" elements in an oppressive structure. *There are no assets to slavery!* Every segment of the society participates in black oppression. To accept the white God, to see good in the evil, is to lose sight of the goal of the revolution—the destruction of everything "masterly" in the society. "All or nothing" is the only possible attitude for the black community.

MUST WE DROP GOD-LANGUAGE?

Realizing that it is very easy to be co-opted by the enemy and his God-language, it is tempting to discard all references to God and to seek to describe a way of living in the world that could not possibly be associated with "Christian" murderers. Some existentialist writers like Camus and Sartre have taken this course, and many black revolutionaries find this procedure appealing. Seeing the ungodly behavior of white churches and the timid, Uncle Tom approach of black churches, many black militants have no time for God and all that religious crap with its deadly prattle about loving your enemies and turning the other cheek. Christianity, they argue, participates in the enslavement of black Americans. Therefore an emancipation from white oppression means also liberation from the ungodly influences of the white man's religion. This approach is certainly understandable, and the merits of the argument warrant a serious investigation of this claim. As black theologians seeking to analyze the meaning of black liberation, we cannot ignore this mood. Indeed, it is quite tempting intellectually to follow the procedure. Nevertheless two observations are in order at this juncture.

(1) Black Theology affirms that there is nothing special about the English word "God" in itself. What is important is the dimension of reality to which it points. The word "God" is a symbol that opens up depths of reality in the world. If the symbol loses its power to point to the meaning of black liberation, then we must destroy it. Black Theology asks whether the symbol God has lost its liberating power. Must we conclude that as a meaningful symbol the word "God" is hopelessly dead and thus cannot be resurrected? Certainly Black Theology realizes that, when a society performs all ungodly acts against the poor in the name of God, there may come a time when the

oppressed might have to renounce all claims of "faith" in God in order to affirm authentic faith in him. Sometimes because of the very nature of oppressed-existence, the oppressed must define their being by negating everything the oppressors affirm, including belief in God. The oppressed must demonstrate that all communications are cut off. In Camus's words: "There is, in fact, nothing in common between a master and a slave; it is impossible to speak and communicate with a person who has been reduced to servitude." Therefore, the oppressed and the oppressors cannot possibly mean the same thing when they speak of God. The God of the oppressed is a God of revolution who breaks the chains of slavery. The oppressors' God is a God of slavery and must be destroyed along with the oppressors. The question then, as Black Theology sees it, is not whether black people believe in God, but whose God?

(2) In response to those inclined to drop God-language, Black Theology also believes that the destiny of black people is inseparable from the religious dimensions inherent in the black community. Theologically, one way of describing this reality is to call it general revelation. This means that all men have a sense of the presence of God, a feeling of awe, and it is precisely this experience that makes men creatures who always rebel against domestication. The black community is thus a religious community, a community that views its liberation as the work of the divine.

Here it is important to note that every significant black liberation movement has had its religious dimensions. Black liberation as a movement began with the pre-Civil War black churches who recognized that Christian freedom grounded in Jesus Christ was inseparable from civil freedom. That is why black preachers were the leaders in the struggle for abolition of slavery, and why southern slave owners refused to allow the establishment of the independent black churches in the South. It is true, however, that the post–Civil War black church lost its emphasis on civil freedom and began to identify Christianity with moral purity. But this does not mean that religion is irrelevant altogether; it only means that religion unrelated to black liberation is irrelevant. To try to separate black liberation from black religion is a mistake, because black religion is authentic only when it is

identified with the struggle for black freedom. The influences of Marcus Garvey, Elijah Muhammed, Malcolm X, and Martin Luther King, Jr., demonstrate the role of religion in the black community.

It is not the task of Black Theology to remove the influences of the divine in the black community. Its task is to interpret the forces of black liberation as divine activity. Black Theology must retain God-language despite its perils, because the black community perceives its identity in terms of divine presence. Black Theology cannot create new symbols independent of the black community and expect black people to respond. It must stay in the black community and get down to the real issue at hand ("cutting throats" to use LeRoi Jones' phrase) and not waste too much time discussing the legitimacy of religious language. The legitimacy of any language, religious or otherwise, is determined by its usability in the struggle for liberation. That the God-language of white religion has been used to create a docile spirit among black people while whites aggressively attacked them is beyond question. But that does not mean that we cannot kill the white God, so that the God of black people can make his presence known in the black-white encounter. The white God is an idol, created by the racist bastards, and we black people must perform the iconoclastic task of smashing false images.

...

GOD IS BLACK

Because black people have come to know themselves as *black,* and because that blackness is the cause of their own love of themselves and hatred of whiteness, God himself must be known only as he reveals himself in his blackness. The blackness of God, and everything implied by it in a racist society, is the heart of Black Theology's doctrine of God. There is no place in Black Theology for a colorless God in a society when people suffer precisely because of their color. The black theologian must reject any conception of God which stifles black self-determination by picturing God as a God of all peoples. Either God is identified with the oppressed to the point that their experience becomes his or he is a God of racism. Authentic identification, as Camus pointed out, is not "a question of psychological identification—a mere subterfuge by which the individual imagines that it is he himself who is being offended." It is "identification of one's destiny with that of others and a choice of sides." Because God has made the goal of black people his own goal, Black Theology believes that it is not only appropriate but necessary to begin the doctrine of God with an insistence on his blackness.

The blackness of God means that God has made the oppressed condition his own condition. This is the essence of the biblical revelation. By electing Israelite slaves as his people and by becoming the Oppressed One in Jesus Christ, God discloses to men that he is known where men experience humiliation and suffering. It is not that he feels sorry and takes pity on them (the condescending attitude of those racists who need their guilt assuaged for getting fat on the starvation of others); quite the contrary, his election of Israel and incarnation in Christ reveal that the *liberation* of the oppressed is a part of the innermost nature of God himself. This means that liberation is not an afterthought, but the essence of divine activity.

The blackness of God then means that the essence of the nature of God is to be found in the concept of liberation. Taking seriously the Trinitarian view of the Godhead, Black Theology says that as Father, God identified with oppressed Israel participating in the bringing into being of this people; as Son, he became the Oppressed One in order that all may be free from oppression; as Holy Spirit, he continues his work of liberation. The Holy Spirit is the Spirit of the Father and the Son at work in the forces of human liberation in our society today. In America, the Holy Spirit is black people making decisions about their togetherness, which means making preparation for an encounter with white people.

It is Black Theology's emphasis on the blackness of God that distinguishes it sharply from contemporary white views of God. White religionists are not capable of perceiving the blackness of God because their satanic *whiteness* is a denial of the very essence of divinity. That is why whites are finding and will continue to find the black experience a disturbing reality. White theologians would prefer to do theology without reference to color, but this only reveals how deeply racism is embedded in the thought forms of this culture. To be sure, they would *probably* concede that the concept of liberation is essential to the biblical view of God. But it is still impossible for

them to translate the biblical emphasis on liberation to the black-white struggle today. Invariably they quibble on this issue, moving from side to side, always pointing out the dangers of extremism on both sides. (In the black community, we call this shuffling.) They really cannot make a decision, because it has been made already for them. The way in which scholars would analyze God and black people was decided when black slaves were brought to this land, while churchmen sang "Jesus, Lover of My Soul." Their attitude today is no different from that of the Bishop of London who assured the slaveholders that

> Christianity, and the embracing of the Gospel, does not make the least Alteration in Civil property, or in any Duties which belong to Civil Relations; but in all these Respects, it continues Persons just in the same State as it found them. The Freedom which Christianity gives, is a Freedom from the Bondage of Sin and Satan, and from the dominion of Man's Lust and Passions and inordinate Desires; but as to their outward Condition, whatever that was before, whether bond or free, their being baptized and becoming Christians, makes no matter of change in it.

Of course white theologians today have a "better" way of putting it, but what difference does that make? It means the same thing to black people. "Sure," as the so-called radicals would say, "God is concerned about black people." And then they go on to talk about God and secularization or some other white problem unrelated to emancipation of black people. This style is a contemporary white way of saying that "Christianity . . . does not make the least alteration in civil property."

In contrast to this racist view of God, Black Theology proclaims his blackness. People who want to know who God is and what he is doing must know who black people are and what they are doing. This does not mean lending a helping hand to the poor and unfortunate blacks of the society. It does not mean joining the war on poverty! Such acts are sin offerings that represent a white way of assuring themselves that they are basically a "good" people. Knowing God means being on the side of the oppressed, becoming *one* with them and participating in the goal of liberation. *We must become black with God!*

It is to be expected that white people will have some difficulty with the idea of "becoming *black* with God." The experience is not only alien to their existence as they know it to be, it appears to be an impossibility. "How can *white* people become black?" they ask. This question always amuses me because they do not really want to lose their precious white identity, as if it is worth saving. They know, as everyone in this country knows, a black man is anyone who says he is black, despite his skin color. In the literal sense a black man is anyone who has "even one drop of black blood in his veins."

But "becoming black with God" means more than just saying "I am black," if it involves that at all. The question "How can white people become black?" is analogous to the Philippian jailer's question to Paul and Silas, "What must I do to be saved?" The implication is that if we work hard enough at it, we can reach the goal. But the misunderstanding here is the failure to see that blackness or salvation (the two are synonymous) is the work of God and not man. It is not something we accomplish; it is a gift. That is why they said, "Believe in the Lord Jesus and you will be saved." To *believe* is to receive the gift and utterly to reorient one's existence on the basis of the gift. The gift is so unlike what humans expect that when it is offered and accepted, we become completely new creatures. This is what the Wholly Otherness of God means. God comes to us in his blackness which is wholly unlike whiteness, and to receive his revelation is to become black with him by joining him in his work of liberation.

Even some black people will find this view of God hard to handle. Having been enslaved by the God of white racism so long, they will have difficulty believing that God is identified with their struggle for freedom. Becoming one of his disciples means rejecting whiteness and accepting themselves as they are in all their physical blackness. This is what the Christian view of God means for black people. . . .

Discussion Questions

1. How do you think Cone would respond to the problem of evil, that is, the objection that God's existence is incompatible with the presence of evil in the world? Why does evil occur? What is God's role in evil? Is God responsible for causing some evil? Is God responsible for preventing evil? Is Cone's reinterpretation of God as black a satisfactory response to the problem of evil? Why or why not?

2. God is traditionally defined as 'omniscient' (all knowing), 'omnipresent' (everywhere at once), 'omnipotent' (all powerful), and 'omnibenevolent' (all good). In what ways, if any, is Cone's God not like the God of traditional theism? If there are changes, do these changes strengthen or weaken Cone's account of God as black?

3. How is Cone's approach to theology and theological reasoning similar to that proposed by standpoint theorists? Review the positions of Harding (Chapter 7, Reading 38) and hooks (Chapter 7, Reading 39). What commonalities are there between Cone and standpoint theory? What differences are there? Does your comparison strengthen or weaken Cone's account of God as black? Could we use a similar method to say that God is female?

For Further Reading

This selection is from Cone's book *A Black Theology of Liberation* (1970). Other books of interest by Cone include *God of the Oppressed* (1975); *For My People: Black Theology and the Black Church* (1984); *Black Theology and Black Power* (1969); and *Martin & Malcolm & America: A Dream or a Nightmare?* (1991). Each of these books is both readable and provoking.

There are liberation theologies from many different countries and many different ethnic and cultural perspectives. One publisher that has published more liberation theology than any other is Orbis Books in Maryknoll, New York. Some recommended authors from

Orbis who represent the breadth and scope of liberation theology include Enrique Dussel, *Ethics and the Theology of Liberation* (1978); Aloysius Pieris, *An Asian Theology of Liberation* (1988); Andres G. Guerro, *A Chicano Theology* (1987); Ignatius Jesudasan, *A Gandhian Theology of Liberation* (1984); and Hyun Chung Kyung, *Struggle to Be the Sun Again: Introducing Asian Women's Theology* (1990).

67   A NEW SENSIBILITY
Sallie McFague

Sallie McFague (1933–), a professor of theology at Vanderbilt University Divinity School, advocates for radical changes in the language used to describe God. Current religious language, she argues, reflects past ways of viewing the world—ways that are seriously out of step with new, better, and more defensible conceptions of the world. According to McFague, traditional language about God is not only out of date, but also harmful. It is based on male-centered, hierarchical conceptions of reality and humanity, conceptions no longer believed to be true. She believes that an ecological, holistic model of the world is the most adequate picture of reality and our place in it. To the extent that this is true, our language for God ought to change as well. Among the possible new metaphors for God, McFague proposes Mother, Lover, and Friend.

But can past language for God simply be exchanged for new God-language whenever it has become outdated? Should we adopt new metaphors for God whenever our picture of the world changes? McFague answers a cautious 'yes'. Theological language, she argues, is necessarily metaphorical. If so, then it is no more correct (or incorrect) to say that God *is like* a Father (to use traditional Christian language) than to say that God *is like* a Mother, Lover, or Friend. But why then use one metaphor instead of another? McFague also rejects the view that just any metaphor is as good as any other. Here her defense becomes more difficult. What makes some metaphors for God better than others? How can we evaluate our choice of metaphors? Ultimately, says McFague, a metaphor for God is better when and if it reflects the particular issues and problems of our own time.

Reading Questions

1. How is our language anachronistic? Why must it be reexamined?
2. What fault does McFague find with recent attempts to make Christian theology more inclusive?
3. Why is language about 'atomistic individualism' problematic? How has it affected the Western tradition?
4. Describe the 'organic model.' How is it different from the 'mechanistic model'?

SOURCE: Reprinted from *Models of God* by Sallie McFague. Copyright © 1987 Fortress Press. Used by permission of Augsburg Fortress.

5. What language about God would be appropriate for our times, according to McFague?
6. What is wrong with past personal metaphors for God? What new personal metaphors does McFague propose?
7. What is wrong with fundamentalism, according to McFague?
8. What value does McFague believe deconstructionism has for Christian theology? What does it mean to say "our nostalgia for Presence" is "childish"?
9. What problem does McFague have with deconstructionism? What does she propose in response to this limitation?

"Sticks and stones may break my bones, but names can never hurt me." This taunt from childhood is haunting in its lying bravado. It *is* the "names" that hurt; one would prefer the sticks and stones. Names matter because what we call something, how we name it, is to a great extent what it is to us. We are the preeminent creatures of language, and though language does not exhaust human reality, it, qualifies it in profound ways. It follows, then, that naming can be hurtful, and that it can also be healing or helpful. The ways we name ourselves, one another, and the world cannot be taken for granted; we must look at them carefully to see if they heal or hurt.

How are we naming reality in the twilight years of the twentieth century? I would suggest that we live most of the time and in most ways by outmoded, anachronistic names. We are not naming ourselves, one another, and our earth in ways commensurate *with our own times* but are using names from a bygone time. However helpful and healing these names may have been once upon a time, they are hurtful now. And Christian theology that is done on the basis of anachronistic naming is also hurtful.

We live in our imaginations and our feelings in a bygone world, one under the guidance of a benevolent but absolute deity, a world that is populated by independent individuals (mainly human beings) who relate to one another and to other forms of life in hierarchical patterns. But this is not *our* world, and to continue doing theology on its assumptions is hurtful, for it undermines our ability to accept the new sensibility of our time, one that is holistic and responsible, that is inclusive of all forms of life, and that acknowledges the interdependence of all life.

A HOLISTIC VIEW OF REALITY

During the last twenty years, feminist Christian theologians have made a strong case against the androcentric, hierarchical character of the Western religious tradition. They have insisted that the humanity of women be given equal status and that the divisions that separate people—male/female, rich/poor, old/young, white/colored, straight/gay, Christian/non-Christian—be minimized in order to create an inclusive vision. As Elisabeth Schlssler Fiorenza puts it, "Not the holiness of the elect but the wholeness *of all* is the central vision of Jesus." But only in a few instances has this vision been extended to the nonhuman world. The feminist theologians, who have given attention to the nonhuman world have been, for the most part, those involved in Goddess traditions and witchcraft, for whom the body, the earth, and nature's cycles are of critical importance. Those of us within the Christian tradition have much to learn from these sources, but even these feminists have not, I believe, focused primarily on the intrinsic value of the nonhuman in a way sufficient to bring about the needed change of consciousness. Nor have other forms of liberation theology, which generally speaking are more anthropocentric than is feminist theology. All forms of liberation theology insist on the "deprivatizing" of theology, but to date this has been for the most part limited to human beings and has not included the destiny of the cosmos. The principal insight of liberation theologies—that redemption is not the rescue of certain individuals for eternal life in another world but the fulfillment of all humanity in the political and social realities of this world—must be further deprivatized to include the well-being of all life. This is the case not only because unless we adopt an ecological perspective recognizing human dependence on its environment, we may well not survive, but also, of equal theological if not pragmatic importance, because such a perspective is the dominant paradigm of our time and theology that is not done in conversation with this paradigm is not theology *for our time.*

What is at stake here is not a sentimental love of nature or a leveling of all distinctions between human beings and other forms of life but the realization, as Teilhard de Chardin, says, that his and everyone else's "poor trifling existence" is "one with the immensity of all that is and all that is still in the process of becoming." We are not separate, static, substantial individuals relating in external ways—and in ways of our choice—to other individuals, mainly human ones, and in minor ways to other forms of life. On the contrary, the evolutionary, ecological perspective insists that we are, in the most profound ways, "not our own": we belong, from the cells of our bodies to the finest creations of our minds, to the intricate, constantly changing cosmos. The ecosystem of which we are part is a whole: the rocks and waters, atmosphere and soil, plants, animals, and human beings interact in dynamic, mutually supportive ways that make all talk of atomistic individualism indefensible. Relationship and interdependence, change and transformation, not substance, changelessness, and perfection, are the categories within which a theology for our day must function.

To appreciate the extent to which we are embedded in the evolutionary ecosystem requires an act of imagination, since the Western sensibility has traditionally been nurtured by an atomistic, reductionistic perspective that separates human beings from other beings and reduces all that is not human to objects for human use. But the example of the human mind shows that human development is both culture- and nature-dependent. Infants have brains, but the human mind depends not only on other human beings in order to develop the distinctive characteristics of human existence but also on the stimuli of nature such as light, sound, smell, and heat: without the "warbling birds, blossoming cherry trees, sighing wind, and speaking humans, there would be no sources of signals—and thus no intellects." We do not ordinarily feel indebted to birds and trees for our minds, but recognizing and appreciating that debt is an aspect of the new sensibility necessary for today's theology.

...

To feel in the depths of our being that we are part and parcel of the evolutionary ecosystem of our cosmos is a prerequisite for contemporary Christian theology. It is the beginning of a turn from the anthropocentrism and individualism so deeply embedded in the Western religious tradition, which is nowhere more precisely put than in Augustine's statement in the *Confessions:* "God and the soul, nothing more, nothing at all." That tradition, with its stress on the human individual, continued in much of Protestantism, flowering in the existentialism of the twentieth century. To be sure, another more political context for theology, with deep roots in the Hebrew Scriptures and certainly also in Augustine's two cities, as well as in Calvin's insistence that God is sovereign over the secular state, emerges in our time in the liberation theologies. But what has received less attention—and that largely from the Greek cosmological rather than the Hebraic historical tradition—is the creation which also "groans" for fulfillment. Such lack of attention leads at the very least to an attitude of unconcern for the earth that is not only our home but, if we accept the evolutionary, ecological paradigm, also the giver and sustainer of our lives in basic and concrete ways. It has created a mentality of human domination and ruthlessness aptly captured in a remark by Huston Smith contrasting Western and Eastern attitudes toward nature:

> When Mount Everest was scaled the phrase commonly used in the West to describe the feat was "the conquest of Everest." An Oriental whose writings have been deeply influenced by Taoism remarked, "We would put the matter differently. We would speak of 'the befriending of Everest.'"

One is reminded of Oriental nature paintings, in which human beings are often depicted not only as diminutive in comparison with the surrounding water and trees but also in a pose of mutual deference with a mountain—each bent, as it were, toward the other.

...

It is obvious how this [new] perspective breaks through the old dualisms generated by the mechanical model—spirit/flesh, human/nonhuman, objective/subjective, reason/passion, supernatural/natural—for in the organic model hard lines cannot be drawn between matter and energy, the organic and the inorganic, the mind and the body, human beings and other forms of life. In addition, the organic or evolutionary, ecological model is one that unites entities in a way basically different from the mechanistic model: instead of bringing entities together by means of common laws that govern all, creating a pattern of external relations, it unites by symbiotic, mutual interdependencies, creating a pattern of internal relations. In the organic model, one does not "enter into relations" with others but finds oneself in such relationships as the most basic given of existence. What separates entities differs as well: whereas in the mechanistic model entities are separated dualistically and hierarchically, in the organic model (or "mutualistic" model—a term that avoids the suggestion of reducing life to bodies which is implied in "organic") all entities are considered to be subjects as well as objects, to have intrinsic value as well as instrumental worth. "The ecological model is a model of living things which are acted upon and which respond by acting in their turn. They are patients and agents. In short they are subjects." To take this perspective does not mean granting consciousness to amoebas, let alone to rocks, but it is to relativize the differences that have in the past been viewed as absolutes. It is to adopt the view toward the world so well captured in Martin Buber's famous distinction between I-Thou and I-It. It is the difference between an aesthetic and a utilitarian perspective, between one that appreciates the other (*all* others) and one that merely uses the other. An aesthetic sensibility toward the cosmos is one that values what is unselfishly, with a sense of delight in others for their own sakes. Such appreciation and delight are a necessary step in turning from an anthropocentric to an ecological sensibility. Thus, in the evolutionary, mutualistic model, all entities are united symbiotically and internally in levels of interdependence but are also separated as centers of action and response, each valuable in its own "beingness," however minimal or momentary that may appear to us. The symbol of the mountain and the human being bent toward each other, if allowing more agency and response to the mountain than can be empirically defended, does express an attitude of respect for otherness rare in the traditional Western sensibility.

Moreover, such an attitude is a basic ingredient in the development of the kind of global consciousness and conscience in relation to human solidarity and solidarity with other levels of life which is the required sensibility for the twenty-first century. Although it is manifestly utopian to imagine that the appreciation of otherness, whether human or nonhuman, will revolutionize our national and international behavior, it is surely folly to continue to encourage in ourselves and those whom we influence individualistic, hierarchical, dualistic, and utilitarian ways of thinking that are outmoded and have proved to be destructive of life at all levels.

...

If one were to do Christian theology from the holistic perspective, it is evident that some significant changes from traditional models and concepts would be necessary for expressing the relationships between God and the world and between ourselves and the world. Language that supports hierarchical, dualistic, external, unchanging, atomistic, anthropocentric, and deterministic ways of understanding these relationships is not appropriate *for our time,* whatever its appropriateness might have been for other times. It would appear that the appropriate language for our time, in the sense of being true to the paradigm of reality in which we actually live, would support ways of understanding the God-world and human-world relationships as open, caring, inclusive, interdependent, changing, mutual, and creative.

Needless to say, I am not proposing that the only criterion for theology is its fit with the reigning understanding of reality. But for theology to do *less* than fit our present understanding—for it to accept basic assumptions about reality from a very different time—seems blatantly wrongheaded. Nor am I suggesting that the holistic perspective and the guidelines it suggests for interpreting the relationships between God and the world and between ourselves and the world will necessarily be more permanent than earlier paradigms and guidelines. The evolutionary, ecological model insists above all else that the only permanence is change and hence that a theology appropriate to the holistic model will, at the very least, have to overcome what Rosemary Radford Ruether calls the "tyranny of the absolutizing imagination," which supposes that revolutions, theological or any other kind, are for all time. What is needed is attention to the needs of one's own time. It is my contention that a theology that does not work within the context of the holistic view of reality cannot address the needs of our time.

...

The question, then, is this: In what metaphors and models should we conceive of God as Thou who is related to the world in a unified and interdependent way? To understand God as Thou, it seems to me, is basic for our relating to all reality in the mode of mutuality, respect, care, and responsibility. The qualities of personal relationship are needed in our time not only in the God-world relation but in the human-world relation as well. The problem, I believe, is not that personal metaphors and concepts have been used for God; it is not the personal aspect that has brought about the asymmetrical dualism. The problem lies, rather, in the particular metaphors and concepts chosen. The primary metaphors in the tradition are hierarchical, imperialistic, and dualistic, stressing the distance between God and the world and the total reliance of the world on God. Thus, the metaphors of God as king, ruler, lord, master, and governor, and the concepts that accompany them of God as absolute, complete, transcendent, and omnipotent permit no sense of mutuality, shared responsibility, reciprocity, and love (except in the sense of gratitude). Even the one primary metaphor for God that would allow for a more unified, interdependent view, that of father, has been so qualified by being associated with the metaphors of king and lord (as, for instance, in the phrase, "almighty Father") that its potential as an expression of a unified, interdependent view of God and the world is undercut.

It has become increasingly and painfully evident to many Westerners, both those within the Judeo-Christian tradition and those outside who nonetheless are influenced by its imagery, values, and concepts, that the language used to express the relationship between God and the world needs revision. It is my contention that this revision must begin at the level of the imagination, in a "thought experiment" with metaphors and their accompanying concepts that, unlike the principal ones in the tradition, express a unified, interdependent framework for understanding God-world and human-world relations. I see this experiment in part as a response to Kaufman's call to students of religion to combat the

ways the traditional imagery for God supports either militarism or escapism in this nuclear age, by entering "into the most radical kind of deconstruction and reconstruction of the traditions they have inherited, including especially the most central and precious symbols of these traditions, *God* and *Jesus Christ* and *Torah*." There are, undoubtedly, many ways to respond to this call, but *one* critical aspect of the deconstruction and reconstruction of religious symbols involves both a critique of the triumphalist, imperialistic, patriarchal model and a "thought experiment" with some alternative models that are, I believe, commensurate with the evolutionary, ecological sensibility and with the Christian faith. No one, of course, can create images of God; religious symbols are born and die in a culture for complex reasons. At most, one can try to attend carefully to the images in the culture and church which appear to be emerging and to experiment imaginatively with them, reflecting on their implications for life with God and with others.

The models of God as mother, lover, and friend offer possibilities for envisioning power in unified, interdependent ways quite different from the view of power as either domination or benevolence. I believe these models are uniquely suited for theology in a nuclear age and could serve as well to recontextualize the present dominant metaphor of father in a parental rather than patriarchal direction. We asked earlier about power that is not domination or benevolence and suggested that we hold in abeyance a consideration of the "power of love." The kind of power associated with the models of mother (and father), lover, and friend is indeed love, and love that is unified and interdependent. That is, if one reflects on the characteristics of the love shown by parents, lovers, and friends, the words that come to mind include "fidelity," "nurture," "attraction," "self-sacrifice," "passion," "responsibility," "care," "affection," "respect," and "mutuality." In fact, all the qualities of love so neatly demarcated in the ancient divisions of agape, eros, and philia come into play. These words suggest power but a very different kind of power from that associated with the models of lord, king, and patriarch.

If theologians and students of religion are to be part of the solution to the problem posed by the unprecedented nuclear knowledge that human beings now possess, they must, I believe, answer the call to deconstruct and reconstruct the traditional symbols of Christian faith. This task suggests that Christian theology, in our time at least, cannot be merely or mainly hermeneutics, that is, interpretation of the tradition, a translation of ancient creeds and concepts to make them relevant for contemporary culture. Rather, theology must be self-consciously constructive, willing to think differently than in the past. If one reflects on the contrasts between the theologies of Paul, Augustine, Luther, Schleiermacher, and Barth (just to take a sampling of the tradition) as to their basic images, root metaphors, concepts, and assumptions about reality, one has to acknowledge an enormous variety, all of it, however, capable of being accommodated within the Christian paradigm. Theology in our day needs to be self-consciously constructive in order to free itself from traditional notions of divine sovereignty sufficiently to be able to experiment with other and more appropriate metaphors and models that may help us cope with the "question now before the human species . . . whether life or death will prevail on earth."

THEOLOGICAL CONSTRUCTION

In addition to the holistic vision and acceptance of responsibility for nuclear knowledge, a third aspect of the new sensibility for doing theology in our time is consciousness of the constructive character of all human activities, especially of those within which we live and therefore of which we are least aware: our world views, including our religions. One of the distinctive features of the twentieth century, evident in all fields including science, is increasing awareness of the creative, interpretive character of human existence. But it is important that our interpretive creations not be reified or petrified. Paul de Man, the deconstructionist literary critic, makes the point vividly with his comment that the story of language is "like the plot of a Gothic novel in which someone compulsively manufactures a monster" on which one "then becomes totally dependent" and which one "does not have the power to kill." We are reminded of Nietzsche's description of truth as worn-out metaphors that have become "fixed, canonic and binding" so that we forget that they are "illusions." The double-edged allegation of Nietzsche concerning

the constructive as well as the illusory character of human language—in our case the language of theology—must be squarely faced. I do not believe that recognition of, even celebration of, the constructive character of theology necessarily involves the admission that all construction is merely play and that hence one construction is no better than another. At this point, the absolutism of fundamentalism and the absolutism of deconstruction are similar: the first insists that only one construction (which is not admitted to be a construction) is true, right, and good, and the second insists that all constructions (which are solely the products of aesthetic playfulness) are equally illusory, with none more true, more right, or better than any of the others. What links these positions, in my view, is related to metaphor: fundamentalism fails to appreciate that the language of theology is metaphorical, and deconstruction refuses to acknowledge that there is anything but metaphor.

It is evident that fundamentalism does not accept the metaphorical character of religious and theological language, for its basic tenet is the identification of the Word of God with human words, notably those human words in the canonical Scriptures of the church. The essence of metaphorical theology, however, is precisely the refusal to identify human constructions with divine reality. Since a metaphor is a word or phrase appropriate to one context but used in another, no metaphorical construction can be univocally applied, that is, applied in the form of identity. To say that "God is mother" is not to identify God with mother, but to understand God in light of some of the characteristics associated with mothering. It is, then, also to say, "God is not mother," or, to combine the positive and negative aspects of metaphorical assertion, "God is/is not mother," or yet again, "God *as* mother" (which underscores the comparative nature of metaphor: God viewed in the capacity, character, or role of mother). In other words, the constructive character of metaphor is self-evident, since the appropriate, literal, or conventional context for applying the title of mother is obviously not the divine. Yet much if not all religious language and a great deal of theological language is of this type; that is, language that is literally appropriate to personal, social, or political human relationships or to the natural world is applied metaphorically to God. Thus, the fundamentalist's assertion of univocity between human language about God and God or "God's Word" fails to appreciate the most basic characteristic of religious and theological language: its iconoclastic character, what the tradition calls the *via negativa*. All language about God is human construction and as such perforce "misses the mark."

On the other hand, deconstruction, in many ways a highly perceptive critique of Western metaphysics, focuses on metaphor, for one way of describing deconstruction is as an insistence that there is nothing but metaphor. As the latest stage of a journey beginning with Nietzsche—who saw how language deceives us into believing it is fixed and definite, referring to something outside ourselves, when in fact it is nothing but the play of metaphors—deconstruction concludes that the root metaphor of human existence is writing and interprets writing literally as metaphoricity itself. The increasing realization of the power of language as the most distinctive attribute of human existence, and the realization of the ways in which we construct the worlds we inhabit through it, have during this century come to the point of claiming with the French deconstructionist Jacques Derrida that "there is nothing outside the text"—and this statement includes author and referent. If there is only text, or writing, this means there is only the play of words, interpretation upon interpretation, referring to nothing but other words, an endless spiral with no beginning or end. This is language as "metaphoricity itself." There is nothing but metaphor; metaphor is the ultimate metaphor, for all words miss the mark, are inappropriate, and out of context, because there is no mark, there is no way to judge appropriateness, there is no conventional or literal context for a word or phrase.

I disagree with this understanding of metaphor, but before going into that, I would first underscore the value of deconstruction's critique of Western metaphysics for the new sensibility needed to do Christian theology in our time. Its extreme position gives it a base for launching a full-scale attack on what it calls the "metaphysics of presence" in Western thought. This metaphysics takes many forms, but in essence it is an attempt to cover up the absence, emptiness, and uncertainty we sense (and fear) may be at the heart of things. What metaphor

does, say the deconstructionists, is to insist on absence, for if metaphor is a word or sign standing for another word or sign in endless repetition with no reference outside itself, then there is no possibility of words conveying "presence": not our presence to one another, or the world's presence to us, or God's to us. The metaphysics of presence is most evident in the desire for completeness and totality, full presence, in the Judeo-Christian tradition, and especially in the orthodox christological assertion that God is present, fully and completely, in one human being. Jesus Christ, fully God and fully man, is the ultimate assurance that the universe is not blank emptiness: on the contrary, full and unmediated presence, not just of other selves or the reality of the world but of Presence itself is ours in the Christ, and through him we are assured of the return of what we have lost, the garden of Eden, as well as of even greater fulfillment in the paradise to come. And, says deconstruction, Western theology claims also to have assurance of this Presence in the Book, the Text of texts, in which human words truly refer to the Word itself. Hence, in our language about this Presence we need not take *aporia*, absence, seriously into account nor acknowledge the uncertainty, incompleteness, or relativity of our interpretations so long as we stay close to the Book. But, deconstruction continues, the history of Western metaphysics is one of massive forgetfulness, forgetfulness that metaphor lies at the base of all our constructions, including that most sacred Text: it too is but the play of words, interpretation upon interpretation, creating a shimmering surface that has no author and no referent.

...

Deconstruction criticizes as childish our nostalgia for Presence. It calls Christian theology (and all other constructions or world views) to adulthood. In this it makes a major contribution to adjusting the sensibility of our time. The desire for full presence, whether in the form of nostalgia for the garden of Eden, or the quest for the historical Jesus, or the myth of God incarnate, is a denial of what we know as adults to be the case in human existence: such innocence, certainty, and absoluteness are not possible. What deconstruction, with its denial of all presence, brings out powerfully even for nondeconstructionists is that absence is at least more prevalent than presence: the world in which we live is one in which we create structures to protect us against the chaos, absence, death, oppression, and exclusion that surround us—a negativity symbolized by the ultimate absence, a nuclear holocaust. . . .

What deconstruction does not do, however, is offer any assistance on the question of *which* constructions are better than others. It deals eloquently with the "is not" of metaphor, but it refuses to deal with the "is." I agree with the deconstructionists that all constructions are metaphorical and hence miss the mark; I nevertheless disagree with them when they say that language (writing) is about only itself and that no construction is any better than any other. To claim that all constructions are metaphorical is to insist that one never experiences reality "raw"; it does not follow from this, however, that there is nothing outside language. All that follows is that our access to reality is in every case mediated and hence partial and relative. Nor is the admission of the metaphoricity of our constructions a denial that interpretations can genuinely conflict. In fact, the opposite is the case, for the presence of many constructions, many metaphors, assumes conflict and the need for criteria.

There is indeed no way behind our constructions to test them for their correspondence with the reality they presume to represent, but the constructions do, I believe, have a twofold relationship with reality which deconstruction ignores. First, they are productive of reality; that is, our metaphorical constructions are redescriptions or new readings of what lies outside them, in place of old or conventional descriptions or readings. All renderings of reality are metaphorical (that is, none is literal), but in our novel constructions we offer new possibilities in place of others. In this sense we create the reality in which we live; we do not copy it, or to put it more

pointedly, there are no copies, only creations. The assumption here, however, is that there is a reality to which our constructions refer, even though the only way we have of reaching it is by creating versions of it. This is altogether different from the deconstructionist's position that there is nothing to which the text refers.

Second, our constructions are intended to be better than the ones they refute or replace. This is of course a very difficult issue, because if one admits that all are readings, with the new replacing the old, on what basis can some be better than others? They certainly cannot claim to be better absolutely, or from all perspectives, or for all time. At the most, they might be better relatively (to other constructions) from a particular perspective, and for a particular time. And this is the claim I would make: that a construction of the Christian faith in the context of a holistic vision and the nuclear threat is from our particular perspective and for our particular time relatively better than constructions that ignore these issues. It is relatively better in part because of what Christian faith at base is about. The claim is that to understand the Christian faith in terms of the holistic vision and in response to the nuclear threat is in continuity with the basic Christian paradigm as well as being an appropriate construction of that faith for our time. I will attempt to make that case, but it cannot be proved. As with any construction, the most one can do is to "live within" it, testing it for its disclosive power, its ability to address and cope with the most pressing issues of one's day, its comprehensiveness and coherence, its potential for dealing with anomalies, and so forth. Theological constructions are "houses" to live in for a while, with windows partly open and doors ajar; they become prisons when they no longer allow us to come and go, to add a room or take one away—or if necessary, to move out and build a new house. . . .

Discussion Questions

1. How does McFague defend her new metaphors as better than past metaphors? Are there standards that determine the suitability of a particular metaphor? What reasons might there be to reject a particular metaphor as inappropriate according to McFague? Review her reasons carefully. Do you believe she has an adequate method to evaluate metaphors? Why or why not?

2. Is all traditional language about God metaphorical? For example, if God is described as 'omnipotent' and 'omniscient,' is this language metaphorical? Why or why not? Does your answer strengthen McFague's account or not?

3. Could all world religions be using different metaphorical language for the same transcendent reality behind these conflicting metaphors? Why or why not? Does your answer support McFague's position? Do you think McFague would consider this as a possibility? Why or why not?

4. Are there other metaphors that we ought to use for God? If so, what other metaphors would you propose for speaking about God? Why would you propose them? If not, why not? Are there compelling reasons to use additional new metaphors for God? Why or why not?

For Further Reading

This selection is from McFague's book *Models of God: Theology for an Ecological, Nuclear Age* (1987). Many of the themes in this selection are expanded or developed in her other books, including *The Body of God: An Ecological Theology* (1993), and *Super, Natural Christians: How We Should Love Nature* (1997). For other perspectives on feminism, religion, and ecology, see Carol J. Adams, editor, *Ecofeminism and the Sacred* (1993).

　　There are a number of other important authors who propose feminist-based approaches to religion and theism. One of the most important is Rosemary Ruether; see her *Sexism and God-Talk: Toward a Feminist Theology* (1983), and *New Woman, New Earth: Sexist Ideologies and Human Liberation* (1975). Another influential author is Mary Daly; see her *Beyond God the Father: Toward a Philosophy of Women's Liberation* (1973). For other perspectives, see Carol P. Christ and Judith Plaskow, editors, *Womanspirit Rising: A Feminist Reader in Religion* (1979); Elizabeth A. Johnson, *She Who Is: The Mystery of God in Feminist Theological Discourse* (1992); and Ann Loades, *Feminist Theology: A Reader* (1990).

CHAPTER 13

IS EVIL COMPATIBLE WITH THE EXISTENCE OF GOD?

The God of the Judeo-Christian tradition is typically defined as perfect in every possible way. Hence, there are many attributes—or perfections—that God possesses in virtue of being perfect, including omniscience (being all knowing) and omnipotence (being all powerful). Among other things, one of God's perfections involves the attribute of complete goodness, what is called omnibenevolence (being all good). But if God is all good, the existence of evil, or at least the existence of certain evils, demands explanation. Why does a wholly good God allow (or propagate, as the case may be) evils such as disease, drought, famine, and pestilence? Couldn't God prevent these evils? And why does a wholly good God allow humans to slaughter one another in war? Why do innocent and helpless children suffer? Isn't God powerful enough to prevent these sorts of evil? These questions comprise what is known as the **problem of evil.**

An attempt to explain or reconcile God's goodness with the existence of evil is called a **theodicy.** Theodicies normally make a distinction between two sorts of evils, natural evil and moral evil, and attempt to explain how the existence of both sorts of evil are compatible with God's existence. Moral evils include those evils which are a direct result of human volition, including murder, rape, and torture. Natural evils, on the other hand, are evils that occur because of natural processes such as disease and drought, flood and famine, earthquakes, tornadoes, and typhoons, to mention but a few.

Of course, no matter how good God might be, the problem of evil does not arise if God is powerless to prevent evil from occurring: We cannot demand an explanation for the existence of evil from a God who cannot prevent it. Hence, the problem of evil requires more than God being wholly good; one must also assume that God *possesses the power* to do something about evil before one can reasonably ask God why He allows evil. On top of this, God must also *know how* to use His power against evil before the problem of evil is truly upon us, since God might wish to eradicate evil and be powerful enough to do so but not know how.

These additional assumptions, however, that God is powerful enough to do something about evil and that God is smart enough to know how to use His power against evil, are not hard to come by. The Judeo-Christian tradition claims that God is not just all good but all powerful (omnipotent) and all knowing (omniscient) as well. Hence, the problem of evil presents itself as a real problem for the Judeo-Christian tradition. Is there a workable theodicy that can rectify this problem?

In this chapter, J. L. Mackie argues that no such theodicy is possible. Mackie considers several proposed solutions to the problem of evil, arguing that each defense is inadequate. According to Mackie, believers in God invariably, although implicitly, deny one of God's essential attributes when they propose a theodicy, usually God's omnipotence or omnibenevolence. For example, consider the following explanation for the existence of evil: "Good cannot exist without evil." Mackie begins by asking why good cannot exist without evil. After all, if God is all powerful, then God could have created good without evil. If the believer responds by claiming that God cannot make good without evil, then Mackie responds by claiming that God is not omnipotent. If, on the other hand, the believer claims that God could have made good without evil but chose not to, Mackie stands ready to assert that God must not be all good, since an omnibenevolent God capable of creating good without evil would have done so. Either way, Mackie believes that the believer is forced to give up one of his essential beliefs about the nature of God. That is, the believer is forced to admit that God does not exist as he conceives Him.

On the other hand, Richard Swinburne believes that arguments like Mackie's against the possibility of a theodicy rest on bogus moral principles. Once these faulty principles are identified and dismissed, Swinburne believes that an adequate theodicy is possible. For example, some arguments might assume that a good God would never create creatures capable of harming each other, but according to Swinburne, this assumption cannot be defended. Therefore, all arguments against God based on this premise fail.

A question still remains, however: Why does evil exist in a world governed by an omnibenevolent God? To this Swinburne responds with the free-will defense: God gave humans free will and evil exists in the world as a result of humans abusing their free will, that is, because they have chosen evil over good.

The final two selections of this chapter offer two very different responses to the problem of evil—responses that are not so much philosophical as practical. Both articles are rooted in particular, historical evils of great magnitude: the holocaust and slavery. Emil Fackenheim, in the fourth selection, believes that some evils defy explanation. As a Jew and survivor of the Nazi Holocaust, Fackenheim can fathom no explanation for the horrors of concentration camps such as Auschwitz. Nonetheless, he refuses to abandon his religious faith; rather, according to Fackenheim, the attempt to annihilate Jews and Judaism is all the more reason to proclaim his faith and his Jewishness. Refusing to grant Hitler a posthumous victory, Fackenheim aims to ensure that the Jewish race shall never perish.

The final selection, by M. Shawn Copeland, considers responses by slaves to the evils of slavery. Copeland belongs to a relatively recent theological movement called liberation theology. While traditional Christian theology is *otherworldly* in the sense that its ultimate concern is for whether one shall receive salvation in the afterlife, liberation theology, in contrast, is characterized by a concern for liberation (that is, salvation) first and foremost *in this life*. Liberation theology can be characterized as a theology of action: The duty of religious communities is to relieve the suffering of the oppressed and the impoverished here and now. Thus liberation theology responds to the problem of evil by claiming that God in fact is present with the poor and suffering, acting in history to liberate them.

First, however, in a selection from his novel *The Brothers Karamazov*, Fyodor Dostoevsky invites us to reflect soberly on the horrors of evil in this world and ask ourselves whether anything could possibly justify the kinds of evils humans inflict upon one another.

68 "REBELLION" FROM *THE BROTHERS KARAMAZOV*
Fyodor Dostoevsky

One of the difficulties in discussing the problem of evil is to hold a clear picture in our mind of the depth and kind of evil that is the most serious challenge to theistic belief. It is perhaps easy enough to talk about evil in the abstract, but difficult to feel and fully comprehend the atrocities that mark human history. Too often, those who defend theistic beliefs do so by inadvertently denying that anything bad actually does happen, typically by arguing that what evil does occur is outweighed by a higher good to be achieved (whether in this life or the next). But this way of arguing has the unfortunate effect of denying the full force of human suffering by explaining away too quickly tremendous evils of an incomprehensible magnitude.

Literature is one way of counteracting this tendency because literature can help us to emotionally respond to and cognitively imagine experiences we ourselves have not known. The following selection is from *The Brothers Karamazov*, written in 1879 by one of the greatest Russian novelists of the nineteenth century, Fyodor Dostoevsky (1821–1881). Listen in on the conversation between the brothers as Ivan attempts to demonstrate to Alyosha that if he himself would not consent to create a world like ours, how could a supposedly more loving and caring God create such a miserable place.

Reading Questions

1. What does Alyosha observe about Christ-like love and humankind? How does Ivan respond?
2. What does Ivan propose is the relationship between the devil and humanity? How does Alyosha turn his words against him?
3. According to Ivan, why is Richard beheaded? How does he respond?
4. What does Ivan say that he has been told about why God does not protect innocent young children?
5. According to Ivan, what is the relationship of the absurd to this world? What does Ivan claim to know and understand about this?
6. What challenge does Ivan issue Alyosha after Alyosha has charged him with rebellion? How does Alyosha reply?

CHAPTER 4. REBELLION

"I must make you one confession," Ivan began. "I could never understand how one can love one's neighbours. It's just one's neighbours, to my mind, that one can't love, though one might love those at a distance. I once read somewhere of John the Merciful, a saint, that when a hungry, frozen beggar came to him, he took him into his bed, held him in his arms, and began breathing into his mouth, which was putrid and loathsome from some awful disease. I am convinced that he did that from 'self-laceration,' from the self-laceration of falsity, for the sake of the charity imposed by duty, as a penance laid on him. For anyone to love a man, he must be hidden, for as soon as he shows his face, love is gone."

"Father Zossima has talked of that more than once," observed Alyosha; "he, too, said that the face of a man often hinders many people not practised in love, from loving him. But yet there's a great deal of love in mankind, and almost Christ-like love. I know that myself, Ivan."

"Well, I know nothing of it so far, and can't understand it, and the innumerable mass of mankind are with me there. The question is, whether that's due to men's bad qualities or whether it's inherent in their nature. To my thinking, Christ-like love for men is a miracle impossible on earth. He was God. But we are not gods. Suppose I, for instance, suffer intensely. Another can never know how much I suffer, because he is another and not I. And what's more, a man is rarely ready to admit another's suffering (as though it were a distinction). Why won't he admit it, do you think? Because I smell unpleasant, because I have a stupid face, because I once trod on his foot. Besides, there is suffering and suffering; degrading, humiliating suffering such as humbles me—hunger, for instance—my benefactor will perhaps allow me; but when you come to higher suffering—for an idea, for instance—he will very rarely admit that, perhaps because my face strikes him as not at all what he fancies a man should have who suffers for an idea. And so he deprives me instantly of his favour, and not at all from badness of heart. Beggars, especially genteel beggars, ought never to show themselves, but to ask for charity through the newspapers. One can love one's neighbours in the abstract, or even at a distance, but at close quarters it's almost impossible. If it were as on the stage, in the ballet, where if beggars come in, they wear silken rags and tattered lace and beg for alms dancing gracefully, then one might like looking at them. But even then we should not love them. But enough of that. I simply wanted to show you my point of view. I meant to speak of the suffering of mankind generally, but we had better confine ourselves to the sufferings of the children. That reduces the scope of my argument to a tenth of what it would be. Still we'd better keep to the children, though it does weaken my case. But, in the first place, children can be loved even at close quarters, even when they are dirty, even when they are ugly (I fancy, though, children never are ugly). The second reason why I won't speak of grown-up people is that, besides being disgusting and unworthy of love, they have a compensation—they've eaten the apple and know good and evil, and they have become 'like gods.' They go on eating it still. But the children haven't eaten anything, and are so far innocent. Are you fond of children, Alyosha? I know you are, and you will understand why I prefer to speak of them. If they, too, suffer horribly on earth, they must suffer for their fathers' sins, they must be punished for their fathers, who have eaten the apple; but that reasoning is of the other world and is incomprehensible for the heart of man here on earth. The innocent must not suffer for another's sins, and especially such innocents! You may be surprised at me, Alyosha, but I am awfully fond of children, too. And observe, cruel people, the violent, the rapacious, the Karamazovs are sometimes very fond of children. Children while they are quite little—up to seven, for instance—are so remote from grown-up people; they are different creatures, as it were, of a different species. I knew a criminal in prison who had, in the course of his career as a burglar, murdered whole families, including several children. But when he was in prison, he had a strange affection for them. He spent all his time at his window, watching the children playing in the prison yard. He trained one little boy to come up to his window and made great friends with him. . . . You don't know why I am telling you all this, Alyosha? My head aches and I am sad."

"You speak with a strange air," observed Alyosha uneasily, "as though you were not quite yourself."

"By the way, a Bulgarian I met lately in Moscow," Ivan went on, seeming not to hear his brother's words, "told me about the crimes committed by Turks and Circassians in all parts of Bulgaria through fear of a general rising of the Slavs. They burn villages, murder, outrage women and children, they nail their prisoners by the ears to the fences, leave them so till morning, and in the morning they hang them—all sorts of things you can't imagine. People talk sometimes of bestial cruelty, but that's a great injustice and insult to the beasts; a beast can never be so cruel as a man, so artistically cruel. The tiger only tears and gnaws, that's all he can do. He would never think of nailing people by the ears, even if he were able to do it. These Turks took a pleasure in torturing children, too; cutting the unborn child from the mother's womb, and tossing babies up in the air and catching them on the points of their bayonets before their mothers' eyes. Doing it before the mothers' eyes was what gave zest to the amusement. Here is another scene that I thought very interesting. Imagine a trembling mother with her baby in her arms, a circle of invading Turks around her. They've planned a diversion: they pet the baby, laugh to make it laugh. They succeed, the baby laughs. At that moment a Turk points a pistol four inches from the baby's face. The baby laughs with glee, holds out its little hands to the pistol, and he pulls the trigger in the baby's face and blows out its brains. Artistic, wasn't it? By the way, Turks are particularly fond of sweet things, they say."

"Brother, what are you driving at?" asked Alyosha.

"I think if the devil doesn't exist, but man has created him, he has created him in his own image and likeness."

"Just as he did God, then?" observed Alyosha.

"'It's wonderful how you can turn words,' as Polonius says in *Hamlet*," laughed Ivan. "You turn my words against me. Well, I am glad. Yours must be a fine God, if man created Him in his image and likeness. You asked just now what I was driving at. You see, I am fond of collecting certain facts, and, would you believe, I even copy anecdotes of a certain sort from newspapers and books, and I've already got a fine collection. The Turks, of course, have gone into it, but they are foreigners. I have specimens from home that are even better than the Turks. You know we prefer beating—rods and scourges—that's our national institution. Nailing ears is unthinkable for us, for we are, after all, Europeans. But the rod and the scourge we have always with us and they cannot be taken from us. Abroad now they scarcely do any beating. Manners are more humane, or laws have been passed, so that they don't dare to flog men now. But they make up for it in another way just as national as ours. And so national that it would be practically impossible among us, though I believe we are being inoculated with it, since the religious movement began in our aristocracy. I have a charming pamphlet, translated from the French, describing how, quite recently, five years ago, a murderer, Richard, was executed—a young man, I believe, of three and twenty, who repented and was converted to the Christian faith at the very scaffold. This Richard was an illegitimate child who was given as a child of six by his parents to some shepherds on the Swiss moun-

tains. They brought him up to work for them. He grew up like a little wild beast among them. The shepherds taught him nothing, and scarcely fed or clothed him, but sent him out at seven to herd the flock in cold and wet, and no one hesitated or scrupled to treat him so. Quite the contrary, they thought they had every right, for Richard had been given to them as a chattel, and they did not even see the necessity of feeding him. Richard himself describes how in those years, like the Prodigal Son in the Gospel, he longed to eat of the mash given to the pigs, which were fattened for sale. But they wouldn't even give him that, and beat him when he stole from the pigs. And that was how he spent all his childhood and his youth, till he grew up and was strong enough to go away and be a thief. The savage began to earn his living as a day labourer in Geneva. He drank what he earned, he lived like a brute, and finished by killing and robbing an old man. He was caught, tried, and condemned to death. They are not sentimentalists there. And in prison he was immediately surrounded by pastors, members of Christian brotherhoods, philanthropic ladies, and the like. They taught him to read and write in prison, and expounded the Gospel to him. They exhorted him, worked upon him, drummed at him incessantly, till at last he solemnly confessed his crime. He was converted. He wrote to the court himself that he was a monster, but that in the end God had vouchsafed him light and shown grace. All Geneva was in excitement about him—all philanthropic and religious Geneva. All the aristocratic and well-bred society of the town rushed to the prison, kissed Richard and embraced him; 'You are our brother, you have found grace.' And Richard does nothing but weep with emotion, 'Yes, I've found grace! All my youth and childhood I was glad of pigs' food, but now even I have found grace. I am dying in the Lord.' 'Yes, Richard, die in the Lord; you have shed blood and must die. Though it's not your fault that you knew not the Lord, when you coveted the pigs' food and were beaten for stealing it (which was very wrong of you, for stealing is forbidden); but you've shed blood and you must die.' And on the last day, Richard, perfectly limp, did nothing but cry and repeat every minute: 'This is my happiest day. I am going to the Lord.' 'Yes,' cry the pastors and the judges and philanthropic ladies. 'This is the happiest day of your life, for you are going to the Lord!' They all walk or drive to the scaffold in procession behind the prison van. At the scaffold they call to Richard: 'Die, brother, die in the Lord, for even thou hast found grace!' And so, covered with his brothers' kisses, Richard is dragged on to the scaffold, and led to the guillotine. And they chopped off his head in brotherly fashion, because he had found grace. Yes, that's characteristic. That pamphlet is translated into Russian by some Russian philanthropists of aristocratic rank and evangelical aspirations, and has been distributed gratis for the enlightenment of the people. The case of Richard is interesting because it's national. Though to us it's absurd to cut off a man's head, because he has become our brother and has found grace, yet we have our own speciality, which is all but worse. Our historical pastime is the direct satisfaction of inflicting pain. There are lines in Nekrassov describing how a peasant lashes a horse on the eyes, 'on its meek eyes,' everyone must have seen it. It's peculiarly Russian. He describes how a feeble little nag has foundered under too heavy a load and cannot move. The peasant beats it, beats it savagely, beats it at last not knowing what he is doing in the intoxication of cruelty, thrashes it mercilessly over and over again. 'However weak you are, you must pull, if you die for it.' The nag strains, and then he begins lashing the poor defenceless creature on its weeping, on its 'meek eyes.' The frantic beast tugs and draws the load, trembling all over, gasping for breath, moving sideways, with a sort of unnatural spasmodication— it's awful in Nekrassov. But that's only a horse, and God has given horses to be beaten. So the Tatars have taught us, and they left us the knout as a remembrance of it. But men, too, can be beaten. A well-educated, cultured gentleman and his wife beat their own child with a birch-rod, a girl of seven. I have an exact account of it. The papa was glad that the birch was covered with twigs. 'It stings more,' said he, and so he began stinging his daughter. I know for a fact there are people who at every blow are worked up to sensuality, to literal sensuality, which increases progressively at every blow they inflict. They beat for a minute, for five minutes, for ten minutes, more often and more savagely. The child screams. At last the child cannot scream, it gasps, 'Daddy! daddy!' By some diabolical unseemly chance the case was brought into court. A counsel is engaged. The Russian people have long called a barrister 'a conscience for hire.' The counsel protests in his client's defence. 'It's such a simple thing,' he says, 'an everyday domestic event. A father corrects his child. To our shame be it said, it is brought into court.' The jury, convinced by him, give a favourable verdict. The public roars with delight that the torturer is acquitted. Ah, pity I wasn't there! I would have proposed to raise a subscription in his honour! Charming pictures.

"But I've still better things about children. I've collected a great, great deal about Russian children, Alyosha. There was a little girl of five who was hated by her father and mother, 'most worthy and respectable people, of good education and breeding.' You see, I must repeat again, it is a peculiar characteristic of many people, this love of torturing children, and children only. To all other types of humanity these torturers behave mildly and benevolently, like cultivated and humane Europeans; but they are very fond of tormenting children, even fond of children themselves in that sense. It's just their defencelessness that tempts the tormentor, just the angelic confidence of the child who has no refuge and no appeal, that sets his vile blood on fire. In every man, of course, a demon lies hidden—the demon of rage, the demon of lustful heat at the screams of the tortured victim, the demon of lawlessness let off the chain, the demon of diseases that follow on vice, gout, kidney disease, and so on."

"This poor child of five was subjected to every possible torture by those cultivated parents. They beat her, thrashed her, kicked her for no reason till her body was one bruise. Then, they went to greater refinements of cruelty—shut her up all night in the cold and frost in a privy, and because she didn't ask to be taken up at night (as though a child of five sleeping its angelic, sound sleep could be trained to wake and ask), they smeared her face and filled her mouth with excrement, and it was her mother, her mother did this. And that mother could sleep, hearing the poor child's groans! Can you understand why a little creature, who can't even understand what's done to her, should beat her little aching heart with her tiny fist in the dark and the cold, and weep her meek unresentful tears to dear, kind God to protect her? Do you understand that, friend and brother, you pious and humble novice? Do you understand why this infamy must be and is permitted? Without it, I am told, man could not have existed on earth, for he could not have known good and evil. Why should he know that diabolical good and evil when it costs so much? Why, the whole world of knowledge is not worth that child's prayer to 'dear, kind God'! I say nothing of the sufferings of grown-up people, they have eaten the apple, damn them, and the devil take them all! But these little ones! I am making you suffer, Alyosha, you are not yourself. I'll leave off if you like."

"Never mind. I want to suffer too," muttered Alyosha.

"One picture, only one more, because it's so curious, so characteristic, and I have only just read it in some collection of Russian antiquities. I've forgotten the name. I must look it up. It was in the darkest days of serfdom at the beginning of the century, and long live the Liberator of the People! There was in those days a general of aristocratic connections, the owner of great estates, one of those men—somewhat exceptional, I believe, even then—who, retiring from the service into a life of leisure, are convinced that they've earned absolute power over the lives of their subjects. There were such men then. So our general, settled on his property of two thousand souls, lives in pomp, and domineers over his poor neighbours as though they were dependents and buffoons. He has kennels of hundreds of hounds and nearly a hundred dog-boys—all mounted, and in uniform. One day a serf-boy, a little child of eight, threw a stone in play and hurt the paw of the general's favourite hound. 'Why is my favourite dog lame?' He is told that the boy threw a stone that hurt the dog's paw. 'So you did it.' The general looked the child up and down. 'Take him.' He was taken—taken from his mother and kept shut up all night. Early that morning the general comes out on horseback, with the hounds, his dependents, dog-boys, and huntsmen, all mounted around him in full hunting parade. The servants are summoned for their edification, and in front of them all stands the mother of the child. The child is brought from the lock-up. It's a gloomy, cold, foggy autumn day, a capital day for hunting. The general orders the child to be undressed; the child is stripped naked. He shivers, numb with terror, not daring to cry. . . . 'Make him run.' commands the general. 'Run! run!' shout the dog-boys. The boy runs. . . .'At him!'

yells the general, and he sets the whole pack of hounds on the child. The hounds catch him, and tear him to pieces before his mother's eyes! . . . I believe the general was afterwards declared incapable of administering his estates. Well—what did he deserve? To be shot? To be shot for the satisfaction of our moral feelings? Speak, Alyosha!"

"To be shot," murmured Alyosha, lifting his eyes to Ivan with a pale, twisted smile.

"Bravo!" cried Ivan delighted. "If even you say so . . . You're a pretty monk! So there is a little devil sitting in your heart, Alyosha Karamazov!"

"What I said was absurd, but———"

"That's just the point, that 'but'!" cried Ivan. "Let me tell you, novice, that the absurd is only too necessary on earth. The world stands on absurdities, and perhaps nothing would have come to pass in it without them. We know what we know!"

"What do you know?"

"I understand nothing," Ivan went on, as though in delirium. "I don't want to understand anything now. I want to stick to the fact. I made up my mind long ago not to understand. If I try to understand anything, I shall be false to the fact, and I have determined to stick to the fact."

"Why are you trying me?" Alyosha cried, with sudden distress. "Will you say what you mean at last?"

"Of course, I will; that's what I've been leading up to. You are dear to me, I don't want to let you go, and I won't give you up to your Zossima."

Ivan for a minute was silent, his face became all at once very sad.

"Listen! I took the case of children only to make my case clearer. Of the other tears of humanity with which the earth is soaked from its crust to its centre, I will say nothing. I have narrowed my subject on purpose. I am a bug, and I recognise in all humility that I cannot understand why the world is arranged as it is. Men are themselves to blame, I suppose; they were given paradise, they wanted freedom, and stole fire from heaven, though they knew they would become unhappy, so there is no need to pity them. With my pitiful, earthly, Euclidian understanding, all I know is that there is suffering and that there are none guilty; that cause follows effect, simply and directly; that everything flows and finds its level— but that's only Euclidian nonsense, I know that, and I can't consent to live by it! What comfort is it to me that there are none guilty and that cause follows effect simply and directly, and that I know it?—I must have justice, or I will destroy myself. And not justice in some remote infinite time and space, but here on earth, and that I could see myself. I have believed in it. I want to see it, and if I am dead by then, let me rise again, for if it all happens without me, it will be too unfair. Surely I haven't suffered simply that I, my crimes and my sufferings, may manure the soil of the future harmony for somebody else. I want to see with my own eyes the hind lie down with the lion and the victim rise up and embrace his murderer. I want to be there when everyone suddenly understands what it has all been for. All the religions of the world are built on this longing, and I am a believer. But then there are the children, and what am I to do about them? That's a question I can't answer. For the hundredth time I repeat, there are numbers of questions, but I've only taken the children, because in their case what I mean is so unanswerably clear. Listen! If all must suffer to pay for the eternal harmony, what have children to do with it, tell me, please? It's beyond all comprehension why they should suffer, and why they should pay for the harmony. Why should they, too, furnish material to enrich the soil for the harmony of the future? I understand solidarity in sin among men. I understand solidarity in retribution, too; but there can be no such solidarity with children. And if it is really true that they must share responsibility for all their fathers' crimes, such a truth is not of this world and is beyond my comprehension. Some jester will say, perhaps, that the child would have grown up and have sinned, but you see he didn't grow up, he was torn to pieces by the dogs, at eight years old. Oh, Alyosha, I am not blaspheming! I understand, of course, what an upheaval of the universe it will be when everything in heaven and earth blends in one hymn of praise and everything that lives and has lived cries aloud: 'Thou art just, O Lord, for Thy ways are revealed.' When the mother embraces the fiend who threw her child to the dogs, and all three cry aloud with tears, 'Thou art just, O Lord!' then, of course, the crown of knowledge will be reached and all will be made clear. But what pulls me up here is that I can't accept that harmony. And while I am on earth, I make haste to take my own measures. You see, Alyosha, perhaps it really may happen that if

I live to that moment, or rise again to see it, I, too, perhaps, may cry aloud with the rest, looking at the mother embracing the child's torturer, 'Thou art just, O Lord!' but I don't want to cry aloud then. While there is still time, I hasten to protect myself, and so I renounce the higher harmony altogether. It's not worth the tears of that one tortured child who beat itself on the breast with its little fist and prayed in its stinking outhouse, with its unexpiated tears to 'dear, kind God'! It's not worth it, because those tears are unatoned for. They must be atoned for, or there can be no harmony. But how? How are you going to atone for them? Is it possible? By their being avenged? But what do I care for avenging them? What do I care for a hell for oppressors? What good can hell do, since those children have already been tortured? And what becomes of harmony, if there is hell? I want to forgive. I want to embrace. I don't want more suffering. And if the sufferings of children go to swell the sum of sufferings which was necessary to pay for truth, then I protest that the truth is not worth such a price. I don't want the mother to embrace the oppressor who threw her son to the dogs! She dare not forgive him! Let her forgive him for herself, if she will, let her forgive the torturer for the immeasurable suffering of her mother's heart. But the sufferings of her tortured child she has no right to forgive; she dare not forgive the torturer, even if the child were to forgive him! And if that is so, if they dare not forgive, what becomes of harmony? Is there in the whole world a being who would have the right to forgive and could forgive? I don't want harmony. From love for humanity I don't want it. I would rather be left with the unavenged suffering. I would rather remain with my unavenged suffering and unsatisfied indignation, *even if I were wrong*. Besides, too high a price is asked for harmony; it's beyond our means to pay so much to enter on it. And so I hasten to give back my entrance ticket, and if I am an honest man I am bound to give it back as soon as possible. And that I am doing. It's not God that I don't accept, Alyosha, only I most respectfully return Him the ticket."

"That's rebellion," murmured Alyosha, looking down.

"Rebellion? I am sorry you call it that," said Ivan earnestly. "One can hardly live in rebellion, and I want to live. Tell me yourself, I challenge you—

answer. Imagine that you are creating a fabric of human destiny with the object of making men happy in the end, giving them peace and rest at last, but that it was essential and inevitable to torture to death only one tiny creature—that baby beating its breast with its fist, for instance—and to found that edifice on its unavenged tears, would you consent to be the architect on those conditions? Tell me, and tell the truth."

"No, I wouldn't consent," said Alyosha softly . . . .

Discussion Questions

1. What makes something evil? What is it about an experience or an event that makes that thing itself evil? Could it be pain and suffering? What difference does it matter that not all pain and suffering is bad? Is anything besides pain and suffering necessary to make something evil?
2. Suppose the children that are made to suffer in Dostoevsky's story are rewarded with riches and pleasures after they die. Would this make their suffering acceptable? Is it possible to compensate them for their pain? Could anything justify these experiences? If so, do they then stop becoming evil experiences?
3. Dostoevsky suggests through Ivan that we've created the devil in our own image. What did he mean? What would this imply about the source of evil in the world? Why do people believe in the devil to begin with? Is there any justification for believing in the devil or in demons besides appeal to religious authority? Does your answer support Ivan's view that the devil is merely a projection of our own capacity for evil? Why or why not?

For Further Reading

There is a vast literature on Dostoevsky, whose works have been the object of scholarly study and speculation for generations. Reference works on Dostoevsky include *The Cambridge Companion to Dostoevskii*, edited by W. J. Leatherbarrow (2002), *A Dostoevsky Dictionary*, by Richard Chapple (1983), and *Critical Essays on Dostoevsky*, edited by Robin Miller (1986). Other worthwhile titles include *The Brothers Karamazov and The Poetics of Memory*, by Diane Thompson (1991), *Dialogues with Dostoevsky*, by Robert Jackson (1993), and *Fyodor Dostoyevsky: The Brothers Karamazov*, by W. J. Leatherbarrow (1992).

69   EVIL AND OMNIPOTENCE
J. L. Mackie

A British citizen, J. L. Mackie (1917–1981) spent the first part of his academic career teaching philosophy in Australia before taking a position at the University of York (1963), followed ultimately by a post at University College, Oxford (1967). Influenced by the philosophy of David Hume, Mackie applied his empiricist perspective to the nature of causation, ethics, and God's existence. His more important publications on these themes include *The Cement of the Universe: A Study of Causation* (1974), *Ethics: Inventing Right and Wrong* (1977), *Hume's Moral Theory* (1980), and *The Miracle of Theism*, published posthumously (1982).

Source: "Evil and Omnipotence" by J. L. Mackie, from *Mind,* Vol. LXIV, no. 254. Oxford University Press, 1955. Reprinted with the permission of Oxford University Press.

In the following essay Mackie attempts to critique various theodicies. His strategy is to show that the proponent of the theodicy always backs down on one of his or her claims concerning God's nature—either the claim that God is omnipotent or the claim that God is omnibenevolent. If Mackie is correct, then the theist can only solve the problem of evil by modifying the nature of the Judeo-Christian God.

It should be noted, however, that much of the force of Mackie's criticism depends on how the concept of omnipotence is construed. If God's omnipotence is defined in such a way that God can do *absolutely anything*—including the logically impossible, making $2 + 2 = 5$ for example—then it is more difficult to respond to Mackie's criticism than if God can do only that which is logically possible. For example, Mackie might claim that a good God should have done such-and-such, and since God has failed to do so, either God does not exist or God is not all good. If the theist can successfully argue that such-and-such is *logically impossible* and that God's powers are limited to performing the logically possible, then the fact that God did not do such-and-such is not an argument against God's goodness or existence. The philosophical question becomes, then, a debate about the nature of omnipotence or, perhaps, a debate about what is logically possible.

Reading Questions

1. According to Mackie, the problem of evil shows much more than the fact that religious belief is without foundation. What does it show?
2. Explain the problem of evil. What auxiliary premises are needed to make the problem viable?
3. Are there any adequate solutions to the problem of evil? What does Mackie mean by half-hearted solutions to the problem of evil?
4. Why does Mackie believe that "good cannot exist without evil" is not an adequate solution to the problem of evil?
5. Are there any limits to God's omnipotence?
6. Why does Mackie believe that "evil is a necessary means to good" is not an adequate solution to the problem of evil?
7. What are the different ways in which the phrase "the universe is better with some evil in it than it could be if there were no evil" can be interpreted?
8. Why does Mackie believe that "the universe is better with some evil in it than it could be if there were no evil" is not an adequate solution to the problem of evil?
9. Explain the difference between "first order evil," "first order good," "second order good," and "second order evil."
10. Why does Mackie believe that "evil is due to human free will" is not an adequate solution to the problem of evil? What sort of being does Mackie believe that God should have made?
11. Explain the paradox of omnipotence.

The traditional arguments for the existence of God have been fairly thoroughly criticized by philosophers. But the theologian can, if he wishes, accept this criticism. He can admit that no rational proof of God's existence is possible. And he can still retain all that is essential to his position, by holding that God's existence is known in some other, non-rational way. I think, however, that a more telling criticism can be made by way of the traditional problem of evil. Here it can be shown, not that religious beliefs lack rational support, but that they are positively irrational, that the several parts of the essential theological doctrine are inconsistent with one another, so that the theologian can maintain his position as a whole only by a much more extreme rejection of reason than in the former case. He must now be prepared to believe, not merely what cannot be proved, but what can be *disproved* from other beliefs that he also holds.

The problem of evil, in the sense in which I shall be using the phrase, is a problem only for someone who believes that there is a God who is both omnipotent and wholly good. And it is a logical problem, the problem of clarifying and reconciling a number of beliefs: it is not a scientific problem that might be solved by further observations, or a practical problem that might be solved by a decision or an action. These points are obvious; I mention them only because they are sometimes ignored by theologians, who sometimes parry a statement of the problem with such remarks as "Well, can you solve the problem yourself?" or "This is a mystery which may be revealed to us later" or "Evil is something to be faced and overcome, not merely discussed."

In its simplest form the problem is this: God is omnipotent; God is wholly good; and yet evil exists. There seems to be some contradiction between these three propositions, so that if any two of them were true the third would be false. But at the same time all three are essential parts of most theological positions: the theologian, it seems, at once *must* adhere and *cannot consistently* adhere to all three. (The problem does not arise only for theists, but I shall discuss it in the form in which it presents itself for ordinary theism.)

However, the contradiction does not arise immediately; to show it we need some additional premises, or perhaps some quasi-logical rules connecting the terms 'good', 'evil', and 'omnipotent'. These additional principles are that good is opposed to evil, in such a way that a good thing always eliminates evil as far as it can, and that there are no limits to what an omnipotent thing can do. From these it follows that a good omnipotent thing eliminates evil completely, and then the propositions that a good omnipotent thing exists, and that evil exists, are incompatible.

A. ADEQUATE SOLUTIONS

Now once the problem is fully stated it is clear that it can be solved, in the sense that the problem will not arise if one gives up at least one of the propositions that constitute it. If you are prepared to say that God is not wholly good, or not quite omnipotent, or that evil does not exist, or that good is not opposed to the kind of evil that exists, or there are limits to what an omnipotent thing can do, then the problem of evil will not arise for you.

There are, then, quite a number of adequate solutions of the problem of evil, and some of these have been adopted, or almost adopted, by various thinkers. For example, a few have been prepared to deny God's omnipotence, and rather more have been prepared to keep the term 'omnipotence' but severely to restrict its meaning, recording quite a number of things that an omnipotent being cannot do. Some have said that evil is an illusion, perhaps because they held that the whole world of temporal, changing things is an illusion, and that what we call evil belongs only to this world, or perhaps because they held that although temporal things *are* much as we see them, those that we call evil are not really evil. Some have said that what we call evil is merely the privation of good, that evil in a positive sense, evil that would really be opposed to good, does not exist. Many have agreed with Pope that disorder is harmony not understood, and that partial evil is universal good. Whether any of these views is *true* is, of course, another question. But each of them gives an adequate solution of the problem of evil in the sense that if you accept it this problem does not arise for you, though you may, of course, have *other* problems to face.

But often enough these adequate solutions are only *almost* adopted. The thinkers who restrict God's power, but keep the term 'omnipotence', may reasonably be suspected of thinking in other contexts, that his power is really unlimited. Those who say that evil is an illusion may also be thinking, inconsistently, that this illusion is itself an evil. Those who say that "evil" is merely privation of good may also be thinking, inconsistently, that the privation of good is an evil. (The fallacy here is akin to some forms of the "naturalistic fallacy" in ethics, where some think, for example, that "good" is just what contributes to evolutionary progress, and that evolutionary progress is itself good.) If Pope meant what he said in the first line of his couplet, that "disorder" is only harmony not understood, the "partial evil" of the second line must, for consistency, mean "that which, taken in isolation, falsely appears to be evil," but it would more naturally mean "that which, in isolation, really is evil." The second line, in fact, hesitates between two views, that "partial evil" isn't really evil, since only the universal quality is real, and that "partial evil" is really an evil, but only a little one.

In addition, therefore, to adequate solutions, we must recognize unsatisfactory inconsistent solutions, in which there is only half-hearted or temporary rejection of one of the propositions which together constitute the problem. In these, one of the constituent propositions is explicitly rejected, but it is covertly re-asserted or assumed elsewhere in the system.

B. FALLACIOUS SOLUTIONS

Besides these half-hearted solutions, which explicitly reject but implicitly assert one of the constituent propositions, there are definitely fallacious solutions which explicitly maintain all the constituent propositions, but implicitly reject at least one of them in the course of the argument that explains away the problem of evil.

There are, in fact, many so-called solutions which purport to remove the contradiction without abandoning any of its constituent propositions. These must be fallacious, as we can see from the very statement of the problem, but it is not so easy to see in each case precisely where the fallacy lies. I suggest that in all cases the fallacy has the general form suggested above: in order to solve the problem one (or perhaps more) of its constituent propositions is given up, but in such a way that it appears to have been retained, and can therefore be asserted without qualification in other contexts. Sometimes there is a further complication: the supposed solution moves to and fro between, say, two of the constituent propositions, at one point asserting the first of these but covertly abandoning the second, at another point asserting the second but covertly abandoning the first. These fallacious solutions often turn upon some equivocation with the words 'good' and 'evil', or upon some vagueness about the way in which good and evil are opposed to one another, or about how much is meant by 'omnipotence'.

I propose to examine some of these so-called solutions, and to exhibit their fallacies in detail. Incidentally, I shall also be considering whether an adequate solution could be reached by a minor modification of one or more of the constituent propositions, which would, however, still satisfy all the essential requirements of ordinary theism.

1. "Good cannot exist without evil" or "Evil is necessary as a counterpart to good"

It is sometimes suggested that evil is necessary as a counterpart to good, that if there were no evil there could be no good either, and that this solves the problem of evil. It is true that it points to an answer to the question "Why should there be evil?" But it does so only by qualifying some of the propositions that constitute the problem.

First, it sets a limit to what God can do, saying that God *cannot* create good without simultaneously creating evil, and this means either that God is not omnipotent or that there are *some* limits to what an omnipotent thing can do. It may be replied that these limits were always presupposed, that omnipotence has never meant the power to do what is logically impossible, and on the present view the existence of good without evil would be a logical impossibility. This interpretation of omnipotence may, indeed, be accepted as a modification of our original account which does not reject anything that is essential to theism, and I shall in general assume it in the subsequent discussion. It is, perhaps, the most common theistic view, but I think that some theists at least have maintained that God can do what is logically impossible. Many theists, at any rate, have held that logic itself is created or laid down by God, that logic is the way in which God arbitrarily chooses to think. (This is, of course, parallel to the ethical view that morally right actions are those which God arbitrarily chooses to command, and the two views encounter similar difficulties.) And *this* account of logic is clearly inconsistent with the view that God is bound by logical necessities—unless it is possible for an omnipotent being to bind himself, an issue we shall consider later, when we come to the Paradox of Omnipotence. The solution of the problem of evil cannot, therefore, be consistently adopted along with the view that logic is itself created by God.

But, secondly, this solution denies that evil is opposed to good in our original sense. If good and evil are counterparts, a good thing will not "eliminate evil as far as it can." Indeed, this view suggests that good and evil are not strictly qualities of things at all. Perhaps the suggestion is that good and evil are related in much the same way as great and small. Certainly, when the term 'great' is used relatively as a condensation of 'greater than so-and-so', and 'small' is used correspondingly, greatness and smallness are counterparts and cannot exist without each other. But in this sense greatness is not a quality, not an intrinsic feature of anything; and it would be absurd to think of a movement in favor of greatness and against smallness in this sense. Such a movement would be self-defeating, since relative greatness can be promoted only by a simultaneous promotion of relative smallness. I feel sure that no theists would be content to regard God's goodness as analogous to this—as if what he supports were not the *good* but the *better,* and as if he had the paradoxical aim that all things should be better than other things.

This point is obscured by the fact that 'great' and 'small' seem to have an absolute as well as a relative sense. I cannot discuss here whether there is an absolute magnitude or not, but if there is, there could be an absolute sense for 'great', it could mean of at least a certain size, and it would make sense to speak of all things getting bigger, of a universe that was expanding all over, and therefore it would make sense to speak of promoting greatness. But in *this* sense great and small are not logically necessary counterparts: either quality could exist without the other. There would be no logical impossibility in everything's being small or in everything's being great.

Neither in the absolute nor in the relative sense, then, of 'great' and 'small' do these terms provide an analogy of the sort that would be needed to support this solution of the problem of evil. In neither case are greatness and smallness *both* necessary counterparts *and* mutually opposed forces or possible objects for support and attack.

It may be replied that good and evil are necessary counterparts in the same way as any quality and its logical opposite: redness can occur, it is suggested, only if non-redness also occurs. But unless evil is merely the privation of good, they are not logical opposites, and some further argument would be needed

to show that they are counterparts in the same way as genuine logical opposites. Let us assume that this could be given. There is still doubt of the correctness of the metaphysical principle that a quality must have a real opposite: I suggest that it is not really impossible that everything should be, say, red, that the truth is merely that if everything were red we should not notice redness, and so we should have no word 'red'; we observe and give names to qualities only if they have real opposites. If so, the principle that a term must have an opposite would only belong to our language or to our thought, and would not be an ontological principle, and, correspondingly, the rule that good cannot exist without evil would not state a logical necessity of a sort that God would just have to put up with. God might have made everything good, though *we* should not have noticed it if he had.

But, finally, even if we concede that this *is* an ontological principle, it will provide a solution for the problem of evil only if one is prepared to say, "Evil exists, but only just enough evil to serve as the counterpart of good." I doubt whether any theist will accept this. After all, the *ontological* requirement that non-redness should occur would be satisfied even if all the universe, except for a minute speck, were red, and, if there were a corresponding requirement for evil as a counterpart to good, a minute dose of evil would presumably do. But theists are not usually willing to say, in all contexts, that all the evil that occurs is a minute and necessary dose.

2. "Evil is necessary as a means to good"

It is sometimes suggested that evil is necessary for good not as a counterpart but as a means. In its simple form this has little plausibility as a solution of the problem of evil, since it obviously implies a severe restriction of God's power. It would be a *causal* law that you cannot have a certain end without a certain means, so that if God has to introduce evil as a means to good, he must be subject to at least some causal laws. This certainly conflicts with what a theist normally means by omnipotence. This view of God as limited by causal laws also conflicts with the view that causal laws are themselves made by God, which is more widely held than the corresponding view about the laws of logic. This conflict would, indeed, be resolved if it were possible for an omnipotent being to bind himself, and this possibility has still to be considered. Unless a favorable answer can be given to this question, the suggestion that evil is necessary as a means to good solves the problem of evil only by denying one of its constituent propositions, either that God is omnipotent or that 'omnipotent' means what it says.

3. "The universe is better with some evil in it than it could be if there were no evil"

Much more important is a solution which at first seems to be a mere variant of the previous one, that evil may contribute to the goodness of a whole in which it is found, so the universe as a whole is better as it is, with some evil in it, that it would be if there were no evil. This solution may be developed in either of two ways. It may be supported by an aesthetic analogy, by the fact that contrasts heighten beauty, that in a musical work, for example, there may occur discords which somehow add to the beauty of the work as a whole. Alternatively, it may be worked out in connection with the notion of progress, that the best possible organization of the universe will not be static, but progressive, that the gradual overcoming of evil by good is really a finer thing than would be the eternal unchallenged supremacy of good.

In either case, this solution usually starts from the assumption that the evil whose existence gives rise to the problem of evil is primarily what is called physical evil, that is to say, pain. In Hume's rather half-hearted presentation of the problem of evil, the evils that he stresses are pain and disease, and those who reply to him argue that the existence of pain and disease makes possible the existence of sympathy, benevolence, heroism, and the gradually successful struggle of doctors and reformers to overcome these evils. In fact, theists often seize the opportunity to accuse those who stress the problem of evil of taking a low, materialistic view of good and evil, equating these with pleasure and pain, and of ignoring the more spiritual goods which can arise in the struggle against evils.

But let us see exactly what is being done here. Let us call pain and misery 'first order evil' or 'evil (1)'. What contrasts with this, namely, pleasure and happiness, will be called 'first order good' or 'good (1)'. Distinct from this is 'second order good' or 'good

(2)' which somehow emerges in a complex situation in which evil (1) is a necessary component—logically, not merely causally, necessary. (Exactly *how* it emerges does not matter: in the crudest version of this solution good (2) is simply the heightening of happiness by the contrast with misery, in other versions it includes sympathy with suffering, heroism in facing danger, and the gradual decrease of first order evil and increase in first order good.) It is also being assumed that second order good is more important than first order good or evil, in particular that it more than outweighs the first order evil it involves.

Now this is a particularly subtle attempt to solve the problem of evil. It defends God's goodness and omnipotence on the ground that (on a sufficiently long view) this is the best of all logically possible worlds, because it includes the important second order goods, and yet it admits that real evils, namely first order evils, exist. But does it still hold that good and evil are opposed? Not, clearly, in the sense that we set out originally: good does not tend to eliminate evil in general. Instead, we have a modified, a more complex pattern. First order good (e.g., happiness) *contrasts with* first order evil (e.g., misery): these two are opposed in a fairly mechanical way; some second order goods (e.g., benevolence) try to maximize first order good and minimize first order evil; but God's goodness is not this, it is rather the will to maximize *second* order good. We might, therefore, call God's goodness an example of a third order goodness, or good (3). While this account is different from our original one, it might well be held to be an improvement on it, to give a more accurate description of the way in which good is opposed to evil, and to be consistent with the essential theist position.

There might, however, be several objections to this solution.

First, some might argue that such qualities as benevolence—and *a fortiori* the third order goodness which promotes benevolence—have a merely derivative value, that they are not higher sorts of good, but merely means to good (1), that is, to happiness, so that it would be absurd for God to keep misery in existence in order to make possible the virtues of benevolence, heroism, etc. The theist who adopts the present solution must, of course, deny this, but he can do so with some plausibility, so I should not press this objection.

Secondly, it follows from this solution that God is not in our sense benevolent or sympathetic: he is not concerned to minimize evil (1), but only to promote good (2); and this might be a disturbing conclusion for some theists.

But, thirdly, the fatal objection is this. Our analysis shows clearly the possibility of the existence of a *second* order evil, an evil (2) contrasting with good (2) as evil (1) contrasts with good (1). This would include malevolence, cruelty, callousness, cowardice, and states in which good (1) is decreasing and evil (1) increasing. And just as good (2) is held to be the important kind of good, the kind that God is concerned to promote, so evil (2) will, by analogy, be the important kind of evil, the kind which God, if he were wholly good and omnipotent, would eliminate. And yet evil (2) plainly exists, and indeed most theists (in other contexts) stress its existence more than that of evil (1). We should, therefore, state the problem of evil in terms of second order evil, and against this form of the problem the present solution is useless.

An attempt might be made to use this solution again, at a higher level, to explain the occurrence of evil (2): indeed the next main solution that we shall examine does just this, with the help of some new notions. Without any fresh notions, such a solution would have little plausibility: for example, we could hardly say that the really important good was a good (3), such as the increase of benevolence in proportion to cruelty, which logically required for its occurrence the occurrence of some second order evil. But even if evil (2) could be explained in this way, it is fairly clear that there would be third order evils contrasting with this third order good: and we should be well on the way to an infinite regress, where the solution of a problem of evil, stated in terms of evil (n), indicated the existence of an evil ($n + 1$), and a further problem to be solved.

4. "Evil is due to human freewill"

Perhaps the most important proposed solution of the problem of evil is that evil is not to be ascribed to God at all, but to the independent actions of human beings, supposed to have been endowed by God with freedom of the will. This solution may be combined with the preceding one: first order evil (e.g., pain) may be justified as a logically necessary component in the second order good (e.g., sympathy) while second order evil (e.g., cruelty) is not *justified*, but is so ascribed to human beings that God cannot be held responsible for it. This combination evades my third criticism of the preceding solution.

The freewill solution also involves the preceding solution at a higher level. To explain why a wholly good God gave men freewill although it would lead to some important evils, it must be argued that it is better on the whole that men should act freely, and sometimes err, than that they should be innocent automata, acting rightly in a wholly determined way. Freedom, that is to say, is now treated as a third order good, and as being more valuable than second order goods (such as sympathy and heroism) would be if they were deterministically produced, and it is being assumed that second order evils, such as cruelty, are logically necessary accompaniments of freedom, just as pain is a logically necessary precondition of sympathy.

I think that this solution is unsatisfactory primarily because of the incoherence of the notion of freedom of the will: but I cannot discuss this topic adequately here, although some of my criticisms will touch upon it.

First I should query the assumption that second order evils are logically necessary accompaniments of freedom. I should ask this: if God has made men such that in their free choices they sometimes prefer what is good and sometimes what is evil, why could he not have made men such that they always freely choose the good? If there is no logical impossibility in a man's freely choosing the good on one, or on several, occasions, there cannot be a logical impossibility in choosing the good on every occasion. God was not, then, faced with a choice between making innocent automata and making beings who, in acting freely, would sometimes go wrong: there was open to him the obviously better possibility of making beings who would act freely but always go right. Clearly, his failure to avail himself of this possibility is inconsistent with his being both omnipotent and wholly good.

If it is replied that this objection is absurd, that the making of some wrong choices is logically necessary for freedom, it would seem that 'freedom' must here mean complete randomness or indeterminacy, including randomness with regard to the alternatives good and evil, in other words that men's choices and consequent actions can be "free" only if they are not determined by their characters. Only on this assumption can God escape the responsibility for men's actions; for if he made them as they are, but did not determine their wrong choices, this can only be because the wrong choices are not determined by men as they are. But then if freedom is randomness, how can it be a characteristic of *will?* And, still more, how can it be the most important good? What value or merit would there be in free choices if these were random actions which were not determined by the nature of the agent?

I conclude that to make this solution plausible two different senses of 'freedom' must be confused, one sense which will justify the view that freedom is a third order good, more valuable than other goods would be without it, and another sense, sheer randomness, to prevent us from ascribing to God a decision to make men such that they sometimes go wrong when he might have made them such that they would always freely go right.

This criticism is sufficient to dispose of this solution. But besides this there is a fundamental difficulty in the notion of an omnipotent God creating men with freewill, for if men's wills are really free this must mean that even God cannot control them, that is, that God is no longer omnipotent. It may be objected that God's gift of freedom to men does not mean that he *cannot* control their wills, but that he always *refrains* from controlling their wills. But why, we may ask, should God refrain from controlling evil wills? Why should he not leave men free to will rightly, but intervene when he sees them beginning to will wrongly? If God could do this, but does not, and if he is wholly good, the only explanation could be that even a wrong free act of will is not really evil, that its freedom is a value that outweighs its wrongness, so that there would be a loss of value if God took away the wrongness and the freedom together. But this is utterly opposed to what theists say about sin in other contexts. The present solution of the problem of evil, then, can be maintained only in the form that God has made men so free that he *cannot* control their wills.

This leads us to what I call the Paradox of Omnipotence: can an omnipotent being make things which he cannot subsequently control? Or, what is practically equivalent to this, can an omnipotent being make rules which then bind himself? (These

are practically equivalent because any such rules could be regarded as setting certain things beyond his control, and *vice versa*.) The second of these formulations is relevant to the suggestions that we have already met, that an omnipotent God creates the rules of logic or causal laws, and is then bound by them.

It is clear that this is a paradox: the questions cannot be answered satisfactorily either in the affirmative or in the negative. If we answer "Yes," it follows that if God actually makes things which he cannot control, or makes rules which bind himself, he is not omnipotent once he has made them: there are *then* things which he cannot do. But if we answer "No," we are immediately asserting that there are things which he cannot do, that is to say that he is already not omnipotent.

It cannot be replied that the question which sets this paradox is not a proper question. It would make perfectly good sense to say that a human mechanic has made a machine which he cannot control: if there is any difficulty about the question it lies in the notion of omnipotence itself.

This, incidentally, shows that although we have approached this paradox from the free will theory, it is equally a problem for a theological determinist. No one thinks that machines have free will, yet they may well be beyond the control of their makers. The determinist might reply that anyone who makes anything determines its ways of acting, and so determines its subsequent behavior: even the human mechanic does this by his *choice* of materials and structure for his machine, though he does not know all about either of these: the mechanic thus determines, though he may not foresee, his machine's actions. And since God is omniscient, and since his creation of things is total, he both determines and foresees the ways in which the creatures will act. We may grant this, but it is beside the point. The question is not whether God *originally* determined the future actions of his creatures, but whether he can *subsequently* control their actions, or whether he was able in his original creation to put things beyond his subsequent control. Even on determinist principles the answers "Yes" and "No" are equally irreconcilable with God's omnipotence.

Before suggesting a solution of this paradox, I would point out that there is a parallel Paradox of Sovereignty. Can a legal sovereign make a law restricting its own future legislative power? For example, could the British parliament make a law forbidding any future parliament to socialize banking, and also forbidding the future repeal of this law itself? Or could the British parliament, which was legally sovereign in Australia in, say, 1899, pass a valid law, or series of laws, which made it no longer sovereign in 1933? Again, neither the affirmative nor the negative answer is really satisfactory. If we were to answer "Yes," we should be admitting the validity of a law which, if it were actually made, would mean that parliament was no longer sovereign. If we were to answer "No," we should be admitting that there is a law, not logically absurd, which parliament cannot validly make, that is, that parliament is not now a legal sovereign. This paradox can be solved in the following way. We should distinguish between first order laws, that is laws governing the actions of individuals and bodies other than the legislature, and second order laws, that is laws about laws, laws governing the actions of the legislature itself. Correspondingly, we should distinguish two orders of sovereignty, first order sovereignty (sovereignty (1)) which is unlimited authority to make first order laws, and second order sovereignty (sovereignty (2)) which is unlimited authority to make second order laws. If we say that parliament is sovereign we might mean that any parliament at any time has sovereignty (1), or we might mean that parliament has both sovereignty (1) and sovereignty (2) at present, but we cannot without contradiction mean both that the present parliament has sovereignty (2) and that every parliament at every time has sovereignty (1), for if the present parliament has sovereignty (2) it may use it to take away sovereignty (1) of later parliaments. What the paradox shows is that we cannot ascribe to any continuing institution legal sovereignty in an inclusive sense.

The analogy between omnipotence and sovereignty shows that the paradox of omnipotence can be solved in a similar way. We must distinguish between first order omnipotence (omnipotence (1)), that is

unlimited power to act, and second order omnipotence (omnipotence (2)), that is unlimited power to determine what powers to act things shall have. Then we could consistently say that God all the time has omnipotence (1), but if so no beings at any time have powers to act independently of God. Or we could say that God at one time had omnipotence (2), and used it to assign independent powers to act to certain things, so that God thereafter did not have omnipotence (1). But what the paradox shows is that we cannot consistently ascribe to any continuing being omnipotence in an inclusive sense.

An alternative solution of this paradox would be simply to deny that God is a continuing being, that any times can be assigned to his actions at all. But on this assumption (which also has difficulties of its own) no meaning can be given to the assertion that God made men with wills so free that he could not control them. The paradox of omnipotence can be avoided by putting God outside time, but the freewill solution of the problem of evil cannot be saved in this way, and equally it remains impossible to hold that an omnipotent God *binds himself* by causal or logical laws.

CONCLUSION

Of the proposed solutions of the problem of evil which we have examined, none has stood up to criticism. There may be other solutions which require examination, but this study strongly suggests that there is no valid solution of the problem which does not modify at least one of the constituent propositions in a way which would seriously affect the essential core of the theistic position.

Quite apart from the problem of evil, the paradox of omnipotence has shown that God's omnipotence must in any case be restricted in one way or another, that unqualified omnipotence cannot be ascribed to any being that continues through time. And if God and his actions are not in time, can omnipotence, or power of any sort, be meaningfully ascribed to him?

Discussion Questions

1. What is the scope of God's omnipotence? Can God do that which is logically impossible, or are God's powers limited to doing only that which is logically possible? Could God make a 'round square', for example? Why or why not?

2. Can God be considered good if He or She fails to prevent persons from harming each other? Could a person be considered good if he or she fails to prevent persons from harming each other? What do your answers imply about the problem of evil and God's existence?

3. Suppose that much of the evil in the world is a result of human free will and therefore God is not responsible for it since humans freely cause it. Is God nonetheless responsible for the evil that results from earthquakes and other natural disasters? Why or why not? Could it be impossible to create a world without natural evil in it?

4. Some persons claim that God allows evil to happen but for reasons that are too mysterious for humans to understand. What are the advantages and disadvantages of such a response? Is it a reasonable response to the problem of evil to argue that God is good in some way beyond human understanding?

For Further Reading

For Mackie's major work concerning issues in the philosophy of religion see *The Miracle of Theism* (1982). For a collection of Mackie's work see the two-volume set *Selected Papers* (1985), edited by J. Mackie and P. Mackie. For a commentary on the work of Mackie see *Morality and Objectivity* (1985), edited by T. Honderich.

For a collection of essays concerning the problem of evil see *God and Evil* (1964), edited by N. Pike; *The Problem of Evil* (1991), edited by Marilyn Adams and Robert Adams; and *The Problem of Evil: Selected Readings* (1992), edited by M. Peterson. Also see *Evil and the God of Love* (1966), by John Hick, and *The Nature of Necessity* (1974), by Alvin Plantinga. For a defense of atheism see *Atheism: A Philosophical Analysis* (1990), by M. Martin. For an excellent collection of essays concerning various issues within the philosophy of religion see *Philosophical Perspectives, 5: Philosophy of Religion* (1991), edited by J. Tomberlin.

70 THE PROBLEM OF EVIL
Richard Swinburne

In the following selection, Richard Swinburne (1934–), one of the most important contemporary defenders of theism, constructs a theodicy. Roughly, Swinburne blames the existence of evil on the misuse of human free will: God is not responsible for the existence of evil; humans are. This is what is called 'the free will defense.' But surely God could have foreseen the havoc that humans would wreak on one another when they were created. Why, then, did God give humans free will in the first place? Why did God not make people who were wholly good, even if that meant taking away their free will? Or why did God simply not create people at all, given that they create such misery? Swinburne's response is that for all of the evil in this world, a world in which men and women must struggle—and sometimes fail—to choose good over evil, a world in which evil is eventually overcome by good is a far better place than no world at all, far better than a world in which men and women never have to overcome temptation and evil. This is exactly why, says Swinburne, God created this world.

SOURCE: Reprinted from Richard Swinburne, "The Problem of Evil" in *Reason and Religion*, ed. Stuart Brown, pp. 81–102. Copyright © 1977 The Royal Institute of Philosophy. Used by permission of the publisher, Cornell University Press.

Reading Questions

1. What characteristics does Swinburne attribute to God?
2. According to Swinburne, the mere existence of evil is no real threat to theism. What, then, is the real threat to theism?
3. Explain the difference between a theodicist and an antitheodicist.
4. Explain the difference between physical, mental, state, and moral evil. What are passive evils?
5. What is the antitheodicist's moral principle *P1*? How does Swinburne respond to *P1*? Why is it a good thing that there exist free agents even if they sometimes do evil?
6. What is the antitheodicist's moral principle *P2*? How does Swinburne respond to *P2*? Why is it a good thing that there exist free agents even if they sometimes create passive evils for other creatures?
7. What is the antitheodicist's moral principle *P3*? How does Swinburne respond to *P3*?
8. It is generally supposed to be a duty of persons to stop other persons from hurting each other. So why is it not God's duty to stop persons from hurting each other? Why might God's moral responsibilities be different from our moral responsibilities?
9. How does Swinburne account for the pain caused to men, women, and children by disease or earthquake or cyclone?
10. What is the antitheodicist's moral principle *P4*? How does Swinburne respond to *P4*?
11. Which is better, a finished universe in which nothing needs improving or a basically good but half-finished universe? Why?
12. How does Swinburne respond to the claim that there is just too much evil in the world?

God is, by definition, omniscient, omnipotent, and perfectly good. By "omniscient" I understand "one who knows all true propositions." By "omnipotent" I understand "able to do anything logically possible." By "perfectly good" I understand "one who does no morally bad action," and I include among actions omissions to perform some action. The problem of evil is then often stated as the problem whether the existence of God is compatible with the existence of evil. Against the suggestion of compatibility, an atheist often suggests that the existence of evil entails the nonexistence of God. For, he argues, if God exists, then being omniscient, he knows under what circumstances evil will occur, if he does not act; and being omnipotent, he is able to prevent its occurrence. Hence, being perfectly good, he will prevent its occurrence and so evil will not exist. Hence the existence of God entails the nonexistence of evil. Theists have usually attacked this argument by denying the claim that necessarily a perfectly good being, foreseeing the occurrence of evil and able to prevent it, will prevent it. And indeed, if evil is understood in the very wide way in which it normally is understood in this context, to include physical pain of however slight a degree, the cited claim is somewhat implausible. For it implies that if through my neglecting frequent warnings to go to the dentist, I find myself one morning with a slight toothache, then necessarily, there does not exist a perfectly good being who foresaw the evil and was able to have prevented it. Yet it seems fairly obvious that such a being might well choose to allow me to suffer some mild consequences of my folly—as a lesson for the future which would do me no real harm.

The threat to theism seems to come, not from the existence of evil as such, but rather from the existence of evil of certain kinds and degrees—severe undeserved physical pain or mental anguish, for example. I shall therefore list briefly the kinds of evil which are evident in our world, and ask whether their existence in the degrees in which we find them is compatible with the existence of God. I shall call the man who argues for compatibility the theodicist, and his opponent the antitheodicist. The theodicist will claim that it is not morally wrong for God to create or permit the various evils, normally on the grounds that doing so is providing the logically necessary conditions of greater goods. The antitheodicist denies these claims by putting forward moral principles which have as consequences that a good God would not under any circumstances create or permit the evils in question. I shall argue that these moral principles are not, when carefully examined, at all obvious, and indeed that there is a lot to be said for their negations. Hence I shall conclude that it is plausible to suppose that the existence of these evils is compatible with the existence of God.

Since I am discussing only the compatibility of various evils with the existence of God, I am perfectly entitled to make occasionally some (non-self-contradictory) assumption, and argue that if it was true, the compatibility would hold. For if p is compatible with q, given r (where r is not self-contradictory), then p is compatible with q simpliciter. It is irrelevant to the issue of compatibility whether these assumptions are true. If, however, the assumptions which I make are clearly false, and if also it looks as if the existence of God is compatible with the existence of evil *only* given those assumptions, the formal proof of compatibility will lose much of interest. To avoid this danger, I shall make only such assumptions as are not clearly false—and also in fact the ones which I shall make will be ones to which many theists are already committed for entirely different reasons.

What then is wrong with the world? First, there are painful sensations, felt both by men, and, to a lesser extent, by animals. Second, there are painful emotions, which do not involve pain in the literal sense of this word—for example, feelings of loss and failure and frustration. Such suffering exists mainly among men, but also, I suppose, to some small extent among animals too. Third, there are evil and undesirable states of affairs, mainly states of men's minds, which do not involve suffering. For example, there are the states of mind of hatred and envy; and such states of the world as rubbish tipped over a beauty spot. And fourth, there are the evil actions of men, mainly actions having as foreseeable consequences evils of the first three types, but perhaps other actions as well—such as lying and promise breaking with no such foreseeable consequences. As before, I include among actions, omissions to perform some actions. If there are rational agents other than men and God

(if he exists), such as angels or devils or strange beings on distant planets, who suffer and perform evil actions, then their evil feelings, states, and actions must be added to the list of evils.

I propose to call evil of the first type physical evil, evil of the second type mental evil, evil of the third type state evil, and evil of the fourth type moral evil. Since there is a clear contrast between evils of the first three types, which are evils that happen to men or animals or the world, and evils of the fourth type, which are evils that men do, there is an advantage in having one name for evils of any of the first three types—I shall call these passive evils. I distinguish evil from mere absence of good. Pain is not simply the absence of pleasure. A headache is a pain, whereas not having the sensation of drinking whiskey is, for many people, mere absence of pleasure. Likewise, the feeling of loss in bereavement is an evil involving suffering, to be contrasted with the mere absence of the pleasure of companionship. Some thinkers have, of course, claimed that a good God would create a "best of all (logically) possible worlds" (i.e., a world than which no better is logically possible), and for them the mere absence of good creates a problem since it looks as if a world would be a better world if it had that good. For most of us, however, the mere absence of good seems less of a threat to theism than the presence of evil, partly because it is not clear whether any sense can be given to the concept of a best of all possible worlds (and if it cannot then of logical necessity there will be a better world than any creatable world) and partly because even if sense can be given to this concept it is not at all obvious that God has an obligation to create such a world—to whom would he be doing an injustice if he did not? My concern is with the threat to theism posed by the existence of evil.

Now much of the evil in the world consists of the evil actions of men and the passive evils brought about by those actions. (These include the evils brought about intentionally by men, and also the evils which result from long years of slackness by many generations of men. Many of the evils of 1975 are in the latter category, and among them many state evils. The hatred and jealousy which many men and groups feel today result from an upbringing consequent on generations of neglected opportunities for reconciliations.) The antitheodicist suggests as a moral principle (*P1*) that a creator able to do so ought to create only creatures such that necessarily they do not do evil actions. From this it follows that God would not have made men who do evil actions. Against this suggestion the theodicist naturally deploys the free-will defense, elegantly expounded in recent years by Alvin Plantinga. This runs roughly as follows: it is not logically possible for an agent to make another agent such that necessarily he freely does only good actions. Hence if a being G creates a free agent, he gives to the agent power of choice between alternative actions, and how he will exercise that power is something which G cannot control while the agent remains free. It is a good thing that there exist free agents, but a logically necessary consequence of their existence is that their power to choose to do evil actions may sometimes be realized. The price is worth paying, however, for the existence of agents performing free actions remains a good thing even if they sometimes do evil. Hence it is not logically possible that a creator create free creatures "such that necessarily they do not do evil actions." But it is not a morally bad thing that he create free creatures, even with the possibility of their doing evil. Hence the cited moral principle is implausible.

The free-will defense as stated needs a little filling out. For surely there could be free agents who did not have the power of moral choice, agents whose only opportunities for choice were between morally indifferent alternatives—between jam and marmalade for breakfast, between watching the news on BBC 1 or the news on ITV. They might lack this power either because they lacked the power of making moral judgments (i.e., lacked moral discrimination); or because all their actions which were morally assessable were caused by factors outside their control; or because they saw with complete clarity what was right and wrong and had no temptation to do anything except the right. The free-will defense must claim, however, that it is a good thing that there exist free agents with the power and opportunity of choosing between morally good and morally evil actions, agents with sufficient moral discrimination to have some idea of the difference and some (though not overwhelming) temptation to do other than the morally good. Let us call such agents humanly free agents. The defense must then go on to claim that it is not logically possible to create humanly free agents such that necessarily they do not do morally evil actions.

Unfortunately, this latter claim is highly debatable, and I have no space to debate it. I propose therefore to circumvent this issue as follows. I shall add to the definition of humanly free agents, that they are agents whose choices do not have fully deterministic precedent causes. Clearly then it will not be logically possible to create humanly free agents whose choices go one way rather than another, and so not logically possible to create humanly free agents such that necessarily they do not do evil actions. Then the free-will defense claims that (P1) is not universally true; it is not morally wrong to create humanly free agents—despite the real possibility that they will do evil. Like many others who have discussed this issue, I find this a highly plausible suggestion. Surely as parents we regard it as a good thing that our children have power to do free actions of moral significance—even if the consequence is that they sometimes do evil actions. This conviction is likely to be stronger, not weaker, if we hold that the free actions with which we are concerned are ones which do not have fully deterministic precedent causes. In this way we show the existence of God to be compatible with the existence of moral evil—but only subject to a very big assumption—that men are humanly free agents. If they are not, the compatibility shown by the free-will defense is of little interest. For the agreed exception to (P1) would not then justify a creator making men who did evil actions; we should need a different exception to avoid incompatibility. The assumption seems to me not clearly false, and is also one which most theists affirm for quite other reasons. Needless to say, there is no space to discuss the assumption here.

All that the free-will defense has shown so far, however (and all that Plantinga seems to show), is grounds for supposing that the existence of moral evil is compatible with the existence of God. It has not given grounds for supposing that the existence of evil consequences of moral evils is compatible with the existence of God. In an attempt to show an incompatibility, the antitheodicist may suggest instead of (P1), (P2)—that a creator able to do so ought always to ensure that any creature whom he creates does not cause passive evils, or at any rate passive evils which hurt creatures other than himself. For could not God have made a world where there are humanly free creatures, men with the power to do evil actions, but where those actions do not have evil consequences, or at any rate evil consequences which affect others—e.g., a world where men cannot cause pain and distress to other men? Men might well do actions which are evil either because they were actions which they believed would have evil consequences or because they were evil for some other reason (e.g., actions which involved promise breaking) without them in fact having any passive evils as consequences. Agents in such a world would be like men in a simulator training to be pilots. They can make mistakes, but no one suffers through those mistakes. Or men might do evil actions which did have the evil consequences which were foreseen but which damaged only themselves. Some philosophers might hold that an action would not be evil if its foreseen consequences were ones damaging only to the agent, since, they might hold, no one has any duties to himself. For those who do not hold this position, however, there are some plausible candidates for actions evil solely because of their foreseeable consequences for the agent—e.g., men brooding on their misfortunes in such a way as foreseeably to become suicidal or misanthropic.

I do not find (P2) a very plausible moral principle. A world in which no one except the agent was affected by his evil actions might be a world in which men had freedom but it would not be a world in which men had responsibility. The theodicist claims that it would not be wrong for God to create interdependent humanly free agents, a society of such agents responsible for each other's well being, able to make or mar each other.

Fair enough, the antitheodicist may again say. It is not wrong to create a world where creatures have responsibilities for each other. But might not those responsibilities simply be that creatures had the opportunity to benefit or to withhold benefit from each other, not a world in which they had also the opportunity to cause each other pain? One answer to this is that if creatures have only the power to benefit and not the power to hurt each other, they obviously lack any very strong responsibility for each other. To bring out the point by a caricature—a world in which I could choose whether or not to give you sweets, but not whether or not to break your leg or make you unpopular, is not a world in which I have a very strong influence on your destiny, and so not a world in which I have a very full responsibility for you.

Further, however, there is a point which will depend on an argument which I will give further on. In the actual world very often a man's withholding benefits from another is correlated with the latter's suffering some passive evil, either physical or mental. Thus if I withhold from you certain vitamins, you will suffer disease. Or if I deprive you of your wife by persuading her to live with me instead, you will suffer grief at the loss. Now it seems to me that a world in which such correlations did not hold would not necessarily be a better world than the world in which they do. The appropriateness of pain to bodily disease or deprivation, and of mental evils to various losses or lacks of a more spiritual kind, is something for which I shall argue in detail a little later.

So then the theodicist objects to (P2) on the grounds that the price of possible passive evils for other creatures is a price worth paying for agents to have great responsibilities for each other. It is a price which (logically) must be paid if they are to have those responsibilities. Here again a reasonable antitheodicist may see the point. In bringing up our own children, in order to give them responsibility, we try not to interfere too quickly in their quarrels—even at the price, sometimes, of younger children getting hurt physically. We try not to interfere, first, in order to train our children for responsibility in later life and second because responsibility here and now is a good thing in itself. True, with respect to the first reason, whatever the effects on character produced by training, God would produce without training. But if he did so by imposing a full character on a humanly free creature, this would be giving him a character which he had not in any way chosen or adopted for himself. Yet it would seem a good thing that a creator should allow humanly free creatures to influence by their own choices the sort of creatures they are to be, the kind of character they are to have. That means that the creator must create them immature, and allow them gradually to make decisions which affect the sort of beings they will be. And one of the greatest privileges which a creator can give to a creature is to allow him to help in the process of education, in putting alternatives before his fellows.

Yet though the antitheodicist may see the point, in theory, he may well react to it rather like this. "Certainly some independence is a good thing. But surely a father ought to interfere if his younger son is really getting badly hurt. The ideal of making men free and responsible is a good one, but there are limits to the amount of responsibility which it is good that men should have, and in our world men have too much responsibility. A good God would certainly have intervened long ago to stop some of the things which happen in our world." Here, I believe, lies the crux—it is simply a matter of quantity. The theodicist says that a good God could allow men to do to each other the hurt they do, in order to allow them to be free and responsible. But against him the antitheodicist puts forward as a moral principle (*P3*) that a creator able to do so ought to ensure that any creature whom he creates does not cause passive evils as many and as evil as those in our world. He says that in our world freedom and responsibility have gone too far—produced too much physical and mental hurt. God might well tolerate a boy hitting his younger brothers, but not Belsen.

The theodicist is in no way committed to saying that a good God will not stop things getting too bad. Indeed, if God made our world, he has clearly done so. There are limits to the amount and degree of evil which are possible in our world. Thus there are limits to the amount of pain which a person can suffer—persons live in our world only so many years and the amount which they can suffer at any given time (if mental goings-on are in any way correlated with bodily ones) is limited by their physiology. Further, theists often claim that from time to time God intervenes in the natural order which he has made to prevent evil which would otherwise occur. So the theodicist can certainly claim that a good God stops too much sufferings—it is just that he and his opponent draw the line in different places. The issue as regards the passive evils caused by men turns ultimately to the quantity of evil. To this crucial matter I shall return toward the end of the paper.

We shall have to turn next to the issue of passive evils not apparently caused by men. But, first, I must consider a further argument by the theodicist in support of the free-will defense and also an argument of the antitheodicist against it. The first is the argument that various evils are logically necessary conditions for the occurrence of actions of certain especially good kinds. Thus for a man to bear his suffering cheerfully there has to be suffering for him to bear. There have to be acts which irritate for another to

show tolerance of them. Likewise, it is often said, acts of forgiveness, courage, self-sacrifice, compassion, overcoming temptation, etc., can be performed only if there are evils of various kinds. Here, however, we must be careful. One might reasonably claim that all that is necessary for some of these good acts (or acts as good as these) to be performed is belief in the existence of certain evils, not their actual existence. You can show compassion toward someone who appears to be suffering, but is not really; you can forgive someone who only appeared to insult you, but did not really. But if the world is to be populated with imaginary evils of the kind needed to enable creatures to perform acts of the above specially good kinds, it would have to be a world in which creatures are generally and systematically deceived about the feelings of their fellows—in which the behavior of creatures generally and unavoidably belies their feelings and intentions. I suggest, in the tradition of Descartes (*Meditations* 4, 5 and 6), that it would be a morally wrong act of a creator to create such a deceptive world. In that case, given a creator, then, without an immoral act on his part, for acts of courage, compassion, etc., to be acts open to men to perform, there have to be various evils. Evils give men the opportunity to perform those acts which show men at their best. A world without evils would be a world in which men could show no forgiveness, no compassion, no self-sacrifice. And men without that opportunity are deprived of the opportunity to show themselves at their noblest. For this reason God might well allow some of his creatures to perform evil acts with passive evils as consequences, since these provide the opportunity for especially noble acts.

Against the suggestion of the developed free-will defense that it would be justifiable for God to permit a creature to hurt another for the good of his or the other's soul, there is one natural objection which will surely be made. This is that it is generally supposed to be the duty of men to stop other men hurting each other badly. So why is it not God's duty to stop men hurting each other badly? Now the theodicist does not have to maintain that it is never God's duty to stop men hurting each other but he does have to maintain that it is not God's duty in circumstances where it clearly is our duty to stop such hurt if we can—e.g., when men are torturing each other in mind or body in some of the ways in which they do this in our world and when, if God exists, he does not step in.

Now different views might be taken about the extent of our duty to interfere in the quarrels of others. But the most which could reasonably be claimed is surely this—that we have a duty to interfere in three kinds of circumstances—(1) if an oppressed person asks us to interfere and it is probable that he will suffer considerably if we do not, (2) if the participants are children or not of sane mind and it is probable that one or other will suffer considerably if we do not interfere, or (3) if it is probable that considerable harm will be done to others if we do not interfere. It is not very plausible to suppose that we have any duty to interfere in the quarrels of grown sane men who do not wish us to do so, unless it is probable that the harm will spread. Now note that in the characterization of each of the circumstances in which we would have a duty to interfere there occurs the word "probable," and it is being used in the "epistemic" sense—as "made probable by the total available evidence." But then the "probability" of an occurrence varies crucially with which community or individual is assessing it, and the amount of evidence which they have at the time in question. What is probable relative to your knowledge at t_1 may not be at all probable relative to my knowledge at t_2. Hence a person's duty to interfere in quarrels will depend on their probable consequences relative to that person's knowledge. Hence it follows that one who knows much more about the probable consequences of a quarrel may have no duty to interfere where another with less knowledge does have such a duty—and conversely. Hence a God who sees far more clearly than we do the consequences of quarrels may have duties very different from ours with respect to particular such quarrels. He may know that the suffering that A will cause B is not nearly as great as B's screams might suggest to us and will provide (unknown to us) an opportunity to C to help B recover and will thus give C a deep responsibility which he would not otherwise have. God may very well have reason for allowing particular evils which it is our bounden duty to attempt to stop at all costs simply because he knows so much more about them than we do. And this is no ad hoc hypothesis—it follows directly

from the characterization of the kind of circumstances in which persons have a duty to interfere in quarrels.

We may have a duty to interfere in quarrels when God does not for a very different kind of reason. God, being our creator, the source of our beginning and continuation of existence, has rights over us which we do not have over our fellow-men. To allow a man to suffer for the good of his or someone else's soul one has to stand in some kind of parental relationship toward him. I don't have the right to let some stranger Joe Bloggs suffer for the good of his soul or of the soul of Bill Snoggs, but I do have *some* right of this kind in respect of my own children. I may let the younger son suffer *somewhat* for the good of his and his brother's soul. I have this right because in small part I am responsible for his existence, its beginning and continuance. If this is correct, then *a fortiori*, God who is, *ex hypothesi*, so much more the author of our being than are our parents, has so many more rights in this respect. God has rights to allow others to suffer, while I do not have those rights and hence have a duty to interfere instead. In these two ways the theodicist can rebut the objection that if we have a duty to stop certain particular evils which men do to others, God must have this duty too.

In the free-will defense, as elaborated above, the theist seems to me to have an adequate answer to the suggestion that necessarily a good God would prevent the occurrence of the evil which men cause—if we ignore the question of the quantity of evil, to which I will return at the end of my paper. But what of the passive evil apparently not due to human action? What of the pain caused to men by disease or earthquake or cyclone, and what too of animal pain which existed before there were men? There are two additional assumptions, each of which has been put forward to allow the free-will defense to show the compatibility of the existence of God and the existence of such evil. The first is that, despite appearances, men are ultimately responsible for disease, earthquake, cyclone, and much animal pain. There seem to be traces of this view in Genesis 3:16-20. One might claim that God ties the goodness of man to the well-being of the world and that a failure of one leads to a failure of the other. Lack of prayer, concern, and simple goodness lead to the evils in nature. This assumption, though it may do some service for the free-will defense, would seem unable to account for the animal pain which existed before there were men. The other assumption is that there exist humanly free creatures other than men, which we may call fallen angels, who have chosen to do evil, and have brought about the passive evils not brought about by men. These were given the care of much of the material world and have abused that care. For reasons already given, however, it is not God's moral duty to interfere to prevent the passive evils caused by such creatures. This defense has recently been used by, among others, Plantinga. This assumption, it seems to me, will do the job, and is not *clearly* false. It is also an assumption which was part of the Christian tradition long before the free-will defense was put forward in any logically rigorous form. I believe that this assumption may indeed be indispensable if the theist is to reconcile with the existence of God the existence of passive evils of certain kinds, e.g., certain animal pain. But I do not think that the theodicist need deploy it to deal with the central cases of passive evils not caused by men—mental evils and the human pain that is a sign of bodily malfunctioning. Note, however, that if he does not attribute such passive evils to the free choice of some other agent, the theodicist must attribute them to the direct action of God himself, or rather, what he must say is that God created a universe in which passive evils must necessarily occur in certain circumstances, the occurrence of which is necessary or at any rate not within the power of a humanly free agent to prevent. The antitheodicist then naturally claims, that although a creator might be justified in allowing free creatures to produce various evils, nevertheless (P4) a creator is never justified in creating a world in which evil results except by the action of a humanly free agent. Against this the theodicist tries to sketch reasons which a good creator might have for creating a world in which there is evil not brought about by humanly free agents. One reason which he produces is one which we have already considered earlier in the development of the free-will defense. This is the reason that various evils are logically necessary conditions for the occurrence of actions of certain especially noble kinds. This was adduced earlier as a reason why a creator might allow creatures to perform evil acts with passive evils as consequences. It can also be adduced as a reason why he might

himself bring about passive evils—to give further opportunities for courage, patience, and tolerance. I shall consider here one further reason that, the theodicist may suggest, a good creator might have for creating a world in which various passive evils were implanted, which is another reason for rejecting (P4). It is, I think, a reason which is closely connected with some of the other reasons which we have been considering why a good creator might permit the existence of evil.

A creator who is going to create humanly free agents and place them in a universe has a choice of the kind of universe to create. First, he can create a finished universe in which nothing needs improving. Humanly free agents know what is right, and pursue it; and they achieve their purposes without hindrance. Second, he can create a basically evil universe, in which everything needs improving, and nothing can be improved. Or, third, he can create a basically good but half-finished universe—one in which many things need improving, humanly free agents do not altogether know what is right, and their purposes are often frustrated; but one in which agents can come to know what is right and can overcome the obstacles to the achievement of their purposes. In such a universe the bodies of creatures may work imperfectly and last only a short time; and creatures may be morally ill-educated, and set their affections on things and persons which are taken from them. The universe might be such that it requires long generations of cooperative effort between creatures to make perfect. While not wishing to deny the goodness of a universe of the first kind, I suggest that to create a universe of the third kind would be no bad thing, for it gives to creatures the privilege of making their own universe. Genesis 1 in telling of a God who tells men to "subdue" the earth pictures the creator as creating a universe of this third kind; and fairly evidently—given that men are humanly free agents—our universe is of this kind.

Now a creator who creates a half-finished universe of this third kind has a further choice as to how he molds the humanly free agents which it contains. Clearly he will have to give them a nature of some kind, that is, certain narrow purposes which they have a natural inclination to pursue until they choose or are forced to pursue others—e.g., the immediate attainment of food, sleep, and sex. There could hardly be humanly free agents without some such initial purposes. But what is he to do about their knowledge of their duty to improve the world—e.g., to repair their bodies when they go wrong, so that they can realize long-term purposes, to help others who cannot get food to do so, etc.? He could just give them a formal hazy knowledge that they had such reasons for action without giving them any strong inclination to pursue them. Such a policy might well seem an excessively laissez-faire one. We tend to think that parents who give their children no help toward taking the right path are less than perfect parents. So a good creator might well help agents toward taking steps to improve the universe. We shall see that he can do this in one of two ways.

An action is something done for a reason. A good creator, we supposed, will give to agents some reasons for doing right actions—e.g., that they are right, that they will improve the universe. These reasons are ones of which men can be aware and then either act on or not act on. The creator could help agents toward doing right actions by making these reasons more effective causally; that is, he could make agents so that by nature they were inclined (though not perhaps compelled) to pursue what is good. But this would be to impose a moral character on agents, to give them wide general purposes which they naturally pursue, to make them naturally altruistic, tenacious of purpose, or strong-willed. But to impose a character on creatures might well seem to take away from creatures the privilege of developing their own characters and those of their fellows. We tend to think that parents who try too forcibly to impose a character, however good a character, on their children, are less than perfect parents.

The alternative way in which a creator could help creatures to perform right actions is by sometimes providing additional reasons for creatures to do what is right, reasons which by their very nature have a strong causal influence. Reasons such as improving the universe or doing one's duty do not necessarily have a strong causal influence, for as we have seen creatures may be little influenced by them. Giving a creature reasons which by their nature were strongly causally influential on a particular occasion on any creature whatever his character, would not impose a particular character on a creature. It would, however, incline him to do what is right on that occasion and

maybe subsequently too. Now if a reason is by its nature to be strongly causally influential it must be something of which the agent is aware which causally inclines him (whatever his character) to perform some action, to bring about some kind of change. What kind of reason could this be except the existence of an unpleasant feeling, either a sensation such as a pain or an emotion such as a feeling of loss or deprivation? Such feelings are things of which agents are conscious, which cause them to do whatever action will get rid of those feelings, and which provide reason for performing such action. An itch causally inclines a man to do whatever will cause the itch to cease, e.g., scratch, and provides a reason for doing that action. Its causal influence is quite independent of the agent—saint or sinner, strong-willed or weak-willed, will all be strongly inclined to get rid of their pains (though some may learn to resist the inclination). Hence a creator who wished to give agents some inclination to improve the world without giving them a character, a wide set of general purposes which they naturally pursue, would tie some of the imperfections of the world to physical or mental evils.

To tie desirable states of affairs to pleasant feelings would not have the same effect. Only an existing feeling can be causally efficacious. An agent could be moved to action by a pleasant feeling only when he had it, and the only action to which he could be moved would be to keep the world as it is, not to improve it. For men to have reasons which move men of any character to actions of perfecting the world, a creator needs to tie its imperfections to unpleasant feelings, that is, physical and mental evils.

There is to some considerable extent such tie-up in our universe. Pain normally occurs when something goes wrong with the working of our body which is going to lead to further limitations on the purposes which we can achieve; and the pain ends when the body is repaired. The existence of the pain spurs the sufferer, and others through the sympathetic suffering which arises when they learn of the sufferer's pain, to do something about the bodily malfunctioning. Yet giving men such feelings which they are inclined to end involves the imposition of no character. A man who is inclined to end his toothache by a visit to the dentist may be saint or sinner, strong-willed or weak-willed, rational or irrational. Any other way of which I can conceive of giving men an inclination to correct what goes wrong, and generally to improve the universe, would seem to involve imposing a character. A creator could, for example, have operated exclusively by threats and promises, whispering in men's ears, "unless you go to the dentist, you are going to suffer terribly," or "if you go to the dentist, you are going to feel wonderful." And if the order of nature is God's creation, he does indeed often provide us with such threats and promises—not by whispering in our ears but by providing inductive evidence. There is plenty of inductive evidence that unattended cuts and sores will lead to pain; that eating and drinking will lead to pleasure. Still, men do not always respond to threats and promises or take the trouble to notice inductive evidence (e.g., statistics showing the correlation between smoking and cancer). A creator could have made men so that they naturally took more account of inductive evidence. But to do so would be to impose character. It would be to make men, apart from any choice of theirs, rational and strong-willed.

Many mental evils too are caused by things going wrong in a man's life or in the life of his fellows and often serve as a spur to a man to put things right, either to put right the cause of the particular mental evil or to put similar things right. A man's feeling of frustration at the failure of his plans spurs him either to fulfill those plans despite their initial failure or to curtail his ambitions. A man's sadness at the failure of the plans of his child will incline him to help the child more in the future. A man's grief at the absence of a loved one inclines him to do whatever will get the loved one back. As with physical pain, the spur inclines a man to do what is right but does so without imposing a character—without say, making a man responsive to duty, or strong-willed.

Physical and mental evils may serve as spurs to long-term cooperative research leading to improvement of the universe. A feeling of sympathy for the actual and prospective suffering of many from tuberculosis or cancer leads to acquisition of knowledge and provision of cure for future sufferers. Cooperative and long-term research and cure is a very good thing, the kind of thing toward which men need a spur. A man's suffering is never in vain if it leads through sympathy to the work of others which eventually provides a long-term cure. True, there could be

sympathy without a sufferer for whom the sympathy is felt. Yet in a world made by a creator, there cannot be sympathy on the large scale without a sufferer, for whom the sympathy is felt, unless the creator planned for creatures generally to be deceived about the feelings of their fellows; and that, we have claimed, would be morally wrong.

So generally many evils have a biological and psychological utility in producing spurs to right action without imposition of character, a goal which it is hard to conceive of being realized in any other way. This point provides a reason for the rejection of (P4). There are other kinds of reason which have been adduced reasons for rejecting (P4)—e.g., that a creator could be justified in bringing about evil as a punishment—but I have no space to discuss these now. I will, however, in passing, mention briefly one reason why a creator might make a world in which certain mental evils were tied to things going wrong. Mental suffering and anguish are a man's proper tribute to losses and failures, and a world in which men were immunized from such reactions to things going wrong would be a worse world than ours. By showing proper feelings a man shows his respect for himself and others. Thus a man who feels no grief at the death of his child or the seduction of his wife is rightly branded by us as insensitive, for he has failed to pay the proper tribute of feeling to others, to show in his feeling how much he values them and thereby failed to value them properly—for valuing them properly involves having proper reactions of feeling to their loss. Again, only a world in which men feel sympathy for losses experienced by their friends, is a world in which love has full meaning.

So, I have argued, there seem to be kinds of justification for the evils which exist in the world, available to the theodicist. Although a good creator might have very different kinds of justification for producing, or allowing others to produce, various different evils, there is a central thread running through the kind of theodicy which I have made my theodicist put forward. This is that it is a good thing that a creator should make a half-finished universe and create immature creatures, who are humanly free agents, to inhabit it; and that he should allow them to exercise some choice over what kind of creatures they are to become and what sort of universe is to be (while at the same time giving them a slight push in the direction of doing what is right); and that the creatures should have power to affect not only the development of the inanimate universe but the well-being and moral character of their fellows, and that there should be opportunities for creatures to develop noble characters and do especially noble actions. My theodicist has argued that if a creator is to make a universe of this kind, then evils of various kinds may inevitably—at any rate temporarily—belong to such a universe; and that it is not a morally bad thing to create such a universe despite the evils.

Now a morally sensitive antitheodicist might well in principle accept some of the above arguments. He may agree that in principle it is not wrong to create humanly free agents, despite the possible evils which might result, or to create pains as biological warnings. But where the crunch comes, it seems to me, is in the amount of evil which exists in our world. The antitheodicist says, all right, it would not be wrong to create men able to harm each other, but it would be wrong to create men able to put each other in Belsen. It would not be wrong to create backaches and headaches, even severe ones, as biological warnings, but not the long severe incurable pain of some diseases. In reply the theodicist must argue that a creator who allowed men to do little evil would be a creator who gave them little responsibility; and a creator who gave them only coughs and colds, and not cancer and cholera would be a creator who treated men as children instead of giving them real encouragement to subdue the world. The argument must go on with regard to particular cases. The antitheodicist must sketch in detail and show his adversary the horrors of particular wars and diseases. The theodicist in reply must sketch in detail and show his adversary the good which such disasters make possible. He must show to his opponent men working together for good, men helping each other to overcome disease and famine; the heroism of men who choose the good in spite of temptation, who help others not merely by giving them food but who teach them right and wrong, give them something to live for and something to die for. A world in which this is possible can only be a world in which there is much evil as well as great good. Interfere to stop the evil and you cut off the good.

Like all moral arguments this one can be settled only by each party pointing to the consequences of his opponent's moral position and trying to show that his opponent is committed to implausible consequences. They must try, too, to show that each other's moral principles do or do not fit well with other moral principles which each accepts. The exhibition of consequences is a long process, and it takes time to convince an opponent even if he is prepared to be rational, more time than is available in this paper. All that I claim to have *shown* here is that there is no *easy proof* of incompatibility between the existence of evils of the kinds we find around us and the existence of God. Yet my sympathies for the outcome of any more detailed argument are probably apparent, and indeed I may have said enough to convince some readers as to what that outcome would be.

My sympathies lie, of course, with the theodicist. The theodicist's God is a god who thinks the higher goods so worthwhile that he is prepared to ask a lot of man in the way of enduring evil. Creatures determining in cooperation their own character and future, and that of the universe in which they live, coming in the process to show charity, forgiveness, faith, and self-sacrifice is such a worthwhile thing that a creator would not be unjustified in making or permitting a certain amount of evil in order that they should be realized. No doubt a good creator would put a limit on the amount of evil in the world and perhaps an end to the struggle with it after a number of years. But if he allowed creatures to struggle with evil, he would allow them a real struggle with a real enemy, not a parlor game. The antitheodicist's mistake lies in extrapolating too quickly from *our* duties when faced with evil to the duties of a creator, while ignoring the enormous differences in the circumstances of each. Each of us at one time can make the existing universe better or worse only in a few particulars. A creator can choose the kind of universe and the kind of creatures there are to be. It seldom becomes us in our ignorance and weakness to do anything more than remove the evident evils—war, disease, and famine. We seldom have the power or the knowledge or the right to use such evils to forward deeper and longer-term goods. To make an analogy, the duty of the weak and ignorant is to eliminate cowpox and not to spread it, while the doctor has a duty to spread it (under carefully controlled conditions). But a creator who made or permitted his creatures to suffer much evil and asked them to suffer more is a very demanding creator, one with high ideals who expects a lot. For myself I can say that I would not be too happy to worship a creator who expected too little of his creatures. Nevertheless such a God does ask a lot of creatures. A theodicist is in a better position to defend a theodicy such as I have outlined if he is prepared also to make the further additional claim—that God knowing the worthwhileness of the conquest of evil and the perfecting of the universe by men, shared with them this task by subjecting himself as man to the evil in the world. A creator is more justified in creating or permitting evils to be overcome by his creatures if he is prepared to share with them the burden of the suffering and effort.

Discussion Questions

1. Swinburne assumes that God's powers are limited to doing what is logically possible. Is this assumption necessary for Swinburne's theodicy to succeed? Is it a defensible assumption?
2. Suppose that a small child is kidnaped, tortured, and then killed. How would Swinburne's theodicy handle a case like this? In what ways do you think his response is inadequate? In what ways is it adequate? Explain your answer.
3. Certain natural evils appear as if they could be easily prevented. For example, many cancers are the result of genetic defects. Could God have prevented these cancers by preventing these genes from arising or by not creating them? Why or why not?

For Further Reading

Swinburne's main publications in the philosophy of religion are *The Concept of Miracle* (1970), *The Coherence of Theism* (1977), *The Existence of God* (1979), *Faith and Reason* (1983), *The Evolution of the Soul* (1986), *Responsibility and Atonement* (1989), *Revelation* (1991), and *Is There a God?* (1996). For a collection of essays concerning the problem of evil see *God and Evil* (1964), edited by Nelson Pike; *The Problem of Evil* (1991), edited by Marilyn Adams and Robert Adams; and *The Problem of Evil: Selected Readings* (1992), edited by M. Peterson. See also *Evil and the God of Love* (1966), by John Hick, and *The Nature of Necessity* (1974), by Alvin Plantinga. For a defense of atheism see *Atheism: A Philosophical Analysis* (1990), by M. Martin. For an excellent collection of essays concerning various issues within the philosophy of religion see *Philosophical Perspectives, 5: Philosophy of Religion* (1991), edited by J. Tomberlin.

71 THE JEWISH RETURN TO HISTORY
Emil Ludwig Fackenheim

A German Jew and rabbi, Emil Fackenheim (1916–) fled Nazi Germany for safe haven in Canada. There he earned his Ph.D. in 1945 from the University of Toronto, where he has taught philosophy ever since. Fackenheim is best known for his studies of Judaism and his thoughts concerning the Holocaust and its meaning for Jews.

The following selection comes from Fackenheim's *The Jewish Return to History* (1978). In it, Fackenheim considers the question of Auschwitz: Why was there ever such a thing as Auschwitz? How could God have permitted it? Is it because God found the Jews to be sinners deserving of punishment?

Was it to serve as a reminder of Christ's sacrifice? Or was it justified on the grounds that it paved the way for the Jewish state of Israel? According to Fackenheim, all of these explanations fail to explain the magnitude of evil in the Holocaust. Moreover, he finds the very search for such a justification or purpose morally offensive: There can be no humanly comprehensible justification or purpose for the particular horrors of Auschwitz. This does not mean, however, that there is no proper response to the horrors of Auschwitz. The proper response, according to Fackenheim, is to be ever mindful of the horrors of Auschwitz and ever vigilant against future holocausts.

Reading Questions

1. What is the difference between the evil of Auschwitz and Dresden?
2. Should the memory of Auschwitz be pushed from our minds?
3. Does Fackenheim believe that there is a rational, religious explanation for the horrors of Auschwitz?
4. What does Fackenheim make of "for our sins we are punished" as an explanation for Auschwitz?
5. What discovery did Fackenheim make in response to Auschwitz? What is the commandment of Auschwitz?

I

Within the past two centuries, three events have shaken and are still shaking Jewish religious existence—the Emancipation and its aftereffects, the Nazi Holocaust, and the rise of the first Jewish state in two thousand years—and of these, two have occurred in our own generation. From the point of view of Jewish religious existence, as from so many other points of view, the Holocaust is the most shattering. Doubtless the Emancipation and all its works have posed and continue to pose powerful challenges, with which Jewish thought has been wrestling all along— scientific agnosticism, secularism, assimilation, and the like. The Emancipation presents, however, a challenge *ab extra*, from without, and for all its well-demonstrated power to weaken and undermine Jewish religious existence, I have long been convinced that the challenge can be met, religiously and intellectually. The state of Israel, by contrast, is a challenge *ab intra*, from within—at least to much that Jewish existence has been throughout two millennia. But this challenge is positive—the fact that in one sense (if not in many others) a long exile has ended. That it represents a positive challenge was revealed during and immediately after the Six Day War, when biblical (i.e., pre-exilic) language suddenly came to life.

The Holocaust, too, challenges Jewish faith from within, but the negativity of its challenge is total, without light or relief. After the events associated with the name of Auschwitz, everything is shaken, nothing is safe.

To avoid Auschwitz, or to act as though it had never occurred, would be blasphemous. Yet how face it and be faithful to its victims? No precedent exists either within Jewish history or outside it. Even when a Jewish religious thinker barely begins to face Auschwitz, he perceives the possibility of a desperate choice between the faith of a millennial Jewish past, which has so far persisted through every trial, and faithfulness to the victims of the present. But at the edge of this abyss there must be a great pause, a lengthy silence, and an endurance.

II

Men shun the scandal of the particularity of Auschwitz. Germans link it with Dresden; American liberals, with Hiroshima. Christians deplore anti-semitism-in-general, while Communists erect monuments to victims-of-Fascism-in-general, depriving the dead of Auschwitz of their Jewish identity even in death. Rather than face Auschwitz, men everywhere seek refuge in generalities, comfortable precisely because they are generalities. And such is the extent to which reality is shunned that no cries of protest are heard even when in the world community's own forum obscene comparisons are made between Israeli soldiers and Nazi murderers.

The Gentile world shuns Auschwitz because of the terror of Auschwitz—and because of real or imagined implication in the guilt for Auschwitz. But Jews shun Auschwitz as well. Only after many years did significant Jewish responses begin to appear. Little of real significance is being or can be said even now. Perhaps there should still be silence. It is certain, however, that the voices, now beginning to be heard, will grow ever louder and more numerous. For Jews now know that they must ever after remember Auschwitz, and be its witnesses to the world. Not to be a witness would be a betrayal. In the murder camps the victims often rebelled with no other hope than that one of them might escape to tell the tale. For Jews now to refrain from telling the tale would be unthinkable. Jewish faith still recalls the Exodus, Sinai, the two destructions of the Temple. A Judaism that survived at the price of ignoring Auschwitz would not deserve to survive.

It is because the world shrinks so fully from the truth that once a Jew begins to speak at all he must say the most obvious. Must he say that the death of a Jewish child at Auschwitz is no more lamentable than the death of a German child at Dresden? He must say it. And in saying it, he must also refuse to dissolve Auschwitz into suffering-in-general, even though he is almost sure to be considered a Jewish particularist who cares about Jews but not about mankind. Must he distinguish between the mass-killing at Hiroshima and that at Auschwitz? At the risk of being thought a sacrilegious quibbler, he must, with endless patience, forever repeat that Eichmann was moved by no such "rational" objective as victory when he diverted trains needed for military purposes in order to dispatch Jews to their death. He must add that there was no "irrational" objective either. Torquemada burned bodies in order to save souls. Eichmann sought to destroy both bodies and souls. Where else and at what other time have executioners ever separated those to be murdered now from those to be murdered later to the strain of Viennese waltzes? Where else has human skin ever been made into lamp

shades, and human body-fat into soap—not by isolated perverts but under the direction of ordinary bureaucrats? Auschwitz is a unique descent into hell. It is an unprecedented celebration of evil. It is evil for evil's sake.

A Jew must bear witness to this truth. Nor may he conceal the fact that Jews in their particularity were the singled-out victims. Of course, they were by no means the sole victims. And a Jew would infinitely prefer to think that to the Nazis, Jews were merely a species of the genus "inferior race." This indeed was the theme of Allied wartime propaganda, and it is still perpetuated by liberals, Communists, and guilt-ridden Christian theologians. Indeed, "liberal"-minded Jews themselves perpetuate it. The superficial reason is that this view of Auschwitz unites victims of all races and creeds: it is "brotherly" propaganda. Under the surface, however, there broods at least in Jewish if not in some Gentile minds an idea horrible beyond all description. Would even Nazis have singled out Jews for such a terrible fate unless Jews had done *something* to bring it upon themselves? Most of the blame attaches to the murderers: must not at least some measure of blame attach to the victims as well? Such are the wounds that Nazism has inflicted on some Jewish minds. And such is the extent to which Nazism has defiled the world that, while it should have destroyed every vestige of antisemitism in every Gentile mind on earth, Auschwitz has, in some Gentile minds, actually increased it.

These wounds and this defilement can be confronted only with the truth. And the ineluctable truth is that Jews at Auschwitz were not a species of the genus "inferior race," but rather the prototype by which "inferior race" was defined. Not until the Nazi revolution had become an anti-Jewish revolution did it begin to succeed as a movement; and when all its other works came crashing down only one of its goals remained: the murder of Jews. This is the scandal that requires, of Germans, a ruthless examination of their whole history; of Christians, a pitiless reckoning with the history of Christian anti-Semitism; of the whole world, an inquiry into the grounds of its indifference for twelve long years. Resort to theories of suffering-in-general or persecution-in-general permits such investigations to be evaded.

Yet even where the quest for explanations is genuine there is not, and never will be, an adequate explanation. Auschwitz is the scandal of evil for evil's sake, an eruption of demonism without analogy; and the singling-out of Jews, ultimately, is an unparalleled expression of what the rabbis call groundless hate. This is the rock on which throughout eternity all rational explanations will crash and break apart.

How can a Jew respond to thus having been singled out, and to being singled out even now whenever he tries to bear witness? Resisting rational explanations, Auschwitz will forever resist religious explanations as well. Attempts to find rational causes succeed, at least up to a point, and the search for the religious, ideological, social, and economic factors leading to Auschwitz must be relentlessly pressed. In contrast, the search for a purpose in Auschwitz is foredoomed to total failure. Not that good men in their despair have not made the attempt. Good Orthodox Jews have resorted to the ancient "for our sins we are punished," but this recourse, unacceptable already to Job, is in this case all the more impossible. A good Christian theologian sees the purpose of Auschwitz as a divine reminder of the sufferings of Christ, but this testifies to a moving sense of desperation—and to an incredible lapse of theological judgment. A good Jewish secularist will connect the Holocaust with the rise of the state of Israel, but while to see a causal connection here is possible and necessary, to see a purpose is intolerable. A total and uncompromising sweep must be made of these and other explanations, all designed to give purpose to Auschwitz. No purpose, religious or non-religious, will ever be found in Auschwitz. The very attempt to find one is blasphemous.

Yet it is of the utmost importance to recognize that seeking a purpose is one thing, but seeking a response quite another. The first is wholly out of the question. The second is inescapable. Even after two decades any sort of adequate response may as yet transcend the power of any Jew. But his faith, his destiny, his very survival will depend on whether, in the end, he will be able to respond.

How can a Jew begin to seek a response? Looking for precedents, he finds none either in Jewish or in non-Jewish history. Jewish (like Christian) martyrs have died for their faith, certain that God needs martyrs. Job suffered despite his faith, able to protest within the sphere of faith. Black Christians have died for their race, unshaken in a faith which was not at issue. The one million Jewish children murdered in the Nazi Holocaust died neither because of their faith, nor in spite of their faith, nor for reasons unrelated to faith. They were murdered because of the faith of their great-grandparents. Had these great-grandparents abandoned their Jewish faith, and failed to bring up Jewish children, then their fourth-generation descendants might have been among the Nazi executioners, but not among their Jewish victims. Like Abraham of old, European Jews some time in the mid-nineteenth century offered a human sacrifice, by the mere minimal commitment to the Jewish faith of bringing up Jewish children. But unlike Abraham they did not know what they were doing, and there was no reprieve. This is the brute fact which makes all comparisons odious or irrelevant. This is what makes Jewish religious existence today unique, without support from analogies anywhere in the past. This is the scandal of the particularity of Auschwitz which, once confronted by Jewish faith, threatens total despair.

I confess that it took me twenty years until I was able to look at this scandal, but when at length I did, I made what to me was, and still is, a momentous discovery: that while religious thinkers were vainly struggling for a response to Auschwitz, Jews throughout the world—rich and poor, learned and ignorant, religious and nonreligious—had to some degree been responding all along. For twelve long years Jews had been exposed to a murderous hate which was as groundless as it was implacable. For twelve long years the world had been lukewarm or indifferent, unconcerned over the prospect of a world without Jews. For twelve long years the whole world had conspired to make Jews wish to cease to be Jews wherever, whenever, and in whatever way they could. Yet to this unprecedented invitation to group suicide, Jews responded with an expected will to live—with, under the circumstances, an incredible commitment to Jewish group survival.

In ordinary times, a commitment of this kind may be a mere mixture of nostalgia and vague loyalties not far removed from tribalism; and, unable to face Auschwitz, I had myself long viewed it as such, placing little value on a Jewish survival which was, or seemed to be, only survival for survival's sake. I was wrong, and even the shallowest Jewish survivalist philosophy of the postwar period was right by comparison. For in the age of Auschwitz a Jewish commitment to Jewish survival is in itself a monumental, albeit as yet fragmentary, act of faith. Even to do no more than remain a Jew after Auschwitz is to confront the demons of Auschwitz in all their guises, and to bear witness against them. It is to believe that these demons cannot, will not, and must not prevail, and to stake on that belief one's own life and the lives of one's children, and of one's children's children. To be a Jew after Auschwitz is to have wrested hope—for the Jew and for the world—from the abyss of total despair. In the words of a speaker at a recent gathering of Bergen-Belsen survivors, the Jew after Auschwitz has a second *Shema Yisrael:* no second Auschwitz, no second Bergen-Belsen, no second Buchenwald—anywhere in the world, for anyone in the world!

What accounts for this commitment to Jewish existence when there might have been, and by every rule of human logic should have been, a terrified and demoralized flight from Jewish existence? Why, since Auschwitz, have all previous distinctions among Jews—between religious and secularist, Orthodox and liberal—diminished in importance, to be replaced by a new major distinction between Jews committed to Jewish survival, willing to be singled out and counted, and Jews in flight, who rationalize this flight as a rise to humanity-in-general? In my view nothing less will do than to say that a commanding Voice speaks from Auschwitz, and that there are Jews who hear it and Jews who stop their ears.

The ultimate question is: where was God at Auschwitz? For years I sought refuge in Buber's image of an eclipse of God. This image, still meaningful in other respects, no longer seems to me applicable to Auschwitz. Most assuredly no *redeeming* Voice is heard from Auschwitz, or ever will be heard. However, a *commanding* Voice is being heard, and has, however faintly, been heard from the start. Religious Jews hear it, and they identify its source. Secularist Jews also hear it, even though perforce they leave it unidentified. At Auschwitz, Jews came face to face with absolute evil. They were and still are singled out by it, but in the midst of it they hear an absolute commandment: *Jews are forbidden to grant posthumous victories to Hitler.* They are commanded to survive as Jews, lest the Jewish people perish. They are commanded to remember the victims of Auschwitz, lest their memory perish. They are forbidden to despair of man and his world, and to escape into either cynicism or otherworldliness, lest they cooperate in delivering the world over to the forces of Auschwitz. Finally, they are forbidden to despair of the God of Israel, lest Judaism perish. A secularist Jew cannot make himself believe by a mere act of will, nor can he be commanded to do so; yet he can perform the commandment of Auschwitz. And a religious Jew who has stayed with his God may be forced into new, possibly revolutionary, relationships with him. One possibility, however, is wholly unthinkable. A Jew may not respond to Hitler's attempt to destroy Judaism by himself cooperating in its destruction. In ancient times, the unthinkable Jewish sin was idolatry. Today, it is to respond to Hitler by doing his work. . . .

Discussion Questions

1. Fackenheim rejects constructing a theodicy for the horrors of Auschwitz. Why does he think this is not a legitimate philosophical project? Do you agree? Why or why not? Is this a sign of a strong faith or a weak faith?

2. Was Auschwitz an anomaly? Have there been or are there other evils on the same order of magnitude as the Holocaust? If so, what are they? Is the United States, for example, guilty of atrocities comparable to Auschwitz?

3. How would Swinburne's theodicy handle Auschwitz? Compare Swinburne's response to the response of Fackenheim. What are the strengths and weaknesses of each? Which author do you believe is making the better response? Why?

For Further Reading

Fackenheim's major publications concerning Judaism and the meaning of the Holocaust include *Paths to Jewish Belief* (1960); *Quest for Past and Future: Essays in Jewish Theology* (1968); *God's Presence in History: Jewish Affirmations and Philosophical Reflections* (1970); *Encounters between Judaism and Modern Philosophy* (1973); *The Jewish Return into History* (1978); *To Mend the World: Foundations of Future Jewish Thought* (1982); *What Is Judaism: An Interpretation for the Present Ages* (1988); and *Jewish Philosophers and Jewish Philosophy* (1996), edited by E. Fackenheim and M. Morgan. For commentaries on the work of Fackenheim see *Fackenheim* (1992), edited by L. Greenspan and G. Nicholson; *Post-Holocaust Dialogues* (1983), by S. Katz; and *The Jewish Thought of Emil Fackenheim* (1987), edited by M. Morgan and E. Fackenheim.

72   "WADING THROUGH MANY SORROWS": TOWARD A THEOLOGY OF SUFFERING IN A WOMANIST PERSPECTIVE
M. Shawn Copeland

M. Shawn Copeland (1947–) teaches in the department of theology at Marquette University and is the author of several articles in the area of liberation theology and theological anthropology. The following selection touches on both areas. Copeland begins by establishing the (historical) need for a liberation theology for women—at least for female African American slaves of the Southern plantations. The evidence offered is overwhelming and consists of gut-wrenching testimonials from female slaves, often mere teenagers, of unspeakable abuse—emotional, spiritual, physical, and sexual—at the hands of their owners. While these testimonials are tragic, they are at the same time inspirational; Copeland highlights the resourceful resistance of slaves such as Louisa Picquet, Mary Prince, and Harriet Jacobs. Finally, Copeland closes by outlining a liberation theology for women or "a Theology of Suffering in Womanist Perspective."

Sadly, the truth is often brutal and upsetting; the following selection contains language and descriptions of events that may be upsetting or offensive to some readers.

Reading Questions

1. To what extent did a slave owner have dominion over his (female) slaves? Was it complete or partial?
2. Slave Louisa Picquet is forced to have sex with her owner, Mr. Williams. How does this make Louisa feel? Does she feel as if *she* has done something wrong?
3. What motivation does slave Harriet Jacobs have for narrating her story?
4. What were the circumstances of the death of slave Hetty?

SOURCE: "Wading through Many Sorrows" by M. Shawn Copeland, from *A Troubling in My Soul*, edited by Emilie M. Townes. Used by permission of Orbis Books.

5. What assumptions are black women's narratives intended to counter?
6. What did Christian biblical revelation offer slaves?
7. Characterize a theology of suffering in womanist perspective.

. . .

As a working definition, I understand suffering as the disturbance of our inner tranquillity caused by physical, mental, emotional, and spiritual forces that we grasp as jeopardizing our lives, our very existence. Evil is the negation and deprivation of good; suffering, while never identical with evil, is inseparable from it. Thus, and quite paradoxically, the suffering caused by evil can result in interior development and perfection as well as in social and cultural good. African Americans have encountered monstrous evil in chattel slavery and its legacy of virulent institutionalized racism and have been subjected to unspeakable physical, psychological, social, moral, and religious affliction and suffering. Yet, from the anguish of our people rose distinctive religious expression, exquisite music and song, powerful rhetoric and literature, practical invention and creative art. If slavery was the greatest evil, freedom was the greatest good and women and men struggled, suffered, sacrificed, and endured much to attain it.

. . .

The focus of this three-part essay is not the formal, self-conscious and bold contemporary articulation of womanist theology for an authentic new world order, but rather its roots in the rich historic soil of Black women's experiences of suffering and affliction during the centuries of chattel slavery. In the first section of the essay, enslaved or fugitive Black women speak for themselves . . . .

. . .

. . . Drawing from these narratives, the second section discusses those resources that support Black women's resistance to evil and the third section sketches the basic elements of a theology of suffering from womanist perspective.

BLACK WOMEN'S EXPERIENCES OF SUFFERING

Composite narratives and interviews with emancipated men and women, as well as their children and grandchildren, have given us a picture of daily planta-

tion life. These include chronicles of the horrors and anguish they endured under chattel slavery: the auction block with its rupture of familial bonds, the brutalization of human feeling, savage beatings and mutilation, petty cruelty, and chronic deprivation of human physical and psychological needs. But accounts of the rape and sexual abuse of enslaved Black women are told reluctantly, if at all. James Curry, after his escape, recounting some of the "extreme cruel[ties] practiced upon [some] plantations" around Person County, North Carolina, asserted "that there is no sin which man [sic] can commit, that those slaveholders are not guilty of." And Curry lamented, "It is not proper to be written; but the treatment of females in slavery is dreadful." Still, some men and women dared to write and speak about that dreadful treatment—the coarse and vulgar seduction, rape, abuse, and concubinage of Black women under chattel slavery.

Lizzie Williams, who had been held on a plantation near Selma, Alabama, relayed the fear and resignation that overtook so many Black women. "Many de poor nigger women have chillen for de massa, dat is if de massa mean man. Dey just tell de niggers what to do and dey know better dan to fuss." The following reports are bitter reinforcements:

One former slave repeated this story:

> Ma mama said that a nigger 'oman couldn't help herself, fo' she had to do what de marster say. Ef he come to de field whar de women workin' and tell gal to come on, she had to go. He would take one down in de woods an' use her all de time he wanted to, den send her on back to work.

And another former slave told this plaintive account:

> My sister was given away when she was a girl. She told me and ma that they'd make her go out and lay on a table and two or three white men would have sex with her before they'd let her up. She was just a small girl. She died when she was still in her young days, still a girl.

Fourteen-year-old Louisa Picquet escaped from the sexual advances of one slave owner, only to be sold to another with similar intentions. Years later in an interview, the emancipated Picquet recalled:

> Mr. Williams told me what he bought me for, soon as we started for New Orleans. He said he was getting old, and when he saw me he thought he'd buy me and end his days with me. He said if I behave myself he'd treat me well: but, if not, he'd whip me almost to death.

Compelled to serve as Williams' housekeeper, caretaker for his sons from a former marriage, and his mistress, Picquet also bears four children by Williams. When the interviewer questions her about her life with Williams, Picquet reveals her innermost anguish: "I thought, now I shall be committin' adultery, and there's no chance for me, and I'll have to die and be lost. Then I had this trouble with him and my soul the whole time." Picquet tells her interviewer that she had broached these concerns with Williams often. But his response, she says, was to curse and to argue that her life with him was not an impediment to her religious conversion. Picquet continues:

> But I knew better than that. I thought it was of no use to be prayin', and livin' in sin . . . . I begin then to pray that he might die, so that I might get religion; and then I promise the Lord one night, faithful, in prayer, if he would just take him out of the way, I'd get religion and be true to Him as long as I lived.

Sometime later, Williams became ill and died.

In what is most likely the first female slave narrative from the Americas, Mary Prince describes her anger at a slaveholder's lewd intentions and her own efforts at personal modesty:

> [Mr. D—] had an ugly fashion of stripping himself quite naked, and ordering me then to wash him in the tub of water. This was worse to me than all the [beatings]. Sometimes when he called me to wash him I would not come, my eyes were so full of shame. He would then come to beat me. One time I had plates and knives in my hand, and I dropped both plates and knives, and some of the plates broke.

Mr. D—struck her and Mary Prince declares, "at last I defended myself, for I thought it was high time to do so. I then told him I would not live longer with him, for he was a very indecent man—very spiteful, and too indecent; with no shame for his servants, no shame for his own flesh." With that, she walked out and went to a neighboring house. And although

Mary Prince is compelled to return the next morning, the slaveholder hires her out to work. Her daring gains her some small measure of relief.

Under the pseudonym Linda Brent, Harriet Jacobs gives us a detailed presentation of the psychological and sexual torment to which she was subjected. Like other fugitive female narrators, Jacobs writes her story neither "to attract attention" to herself, nor "to excite sympathy for [her] own sufferings." Rather, she seeks "to arouse the women of the North to a realizing sense of the condition of millions of women in the South, still in bondage, suffering what I suffered, and most of them far worse."

Born in 1818 to an enslaved mulatto couple, Jacobs describes a childhood in which she and her brother were "fondly shielded" from the harsh reality of their condition. Neither dreamt that they were like "merchandise, [only] trusted to [their parents] for safe keeping, and liable to be demanded of them at any moment." Jacobs' father's reputation and skill as a carpenter earned him unusual privileges and a substantial income, a portion of which he paid annually to the woman who owned him. Allowed to manage his own affairs, her father provided a relatively comfortable home and living for his wife and two children. "His strongest wish," Brent writes, "was to purchase his children; but, though he several times offered his hard earnings for that purpose, he never succeeded." The little girl's happiness is marred irrevocably by the death, first of her mother, then, that of the female slaveholder, who was also her mother's foster sister. Family and friends had expected the woman to emancipate the children; after all, their mother and grandmother had been trusted family servants and she had promised Jacobs' dying mother that "her children should never suffer for any thing." Yet, the slaveholder's will bequeathed Linda to a five-year-old niece. Looking back more than thirty years, Jacobs wrote mournfully and sagely that "the memory of a faithful slave does not avail much to save her children from the auction block." It is this broken promise that consigns twelve-year-old Linda and her ten-year-old brother William to the household of Dr. and Mrs. Flint.

At fifteen with the onset of her puberty, like Louisa Picquet and Mary Prince, Harriet Jacobs' Linda Brent is confronted by the persistent, unwelcome lewd advances by the male head of the household.

I now entered my fifteenth year—a sad epoch in the life of a slave girl. [Dr. Flint] began to whisper foul words in my ear. Young as I was, I could not remain ignorant of their import. I tried to treat them with indifference or contempt. . . . He tried his utmost to corrupt the pure principles my grandmother had instilled. He peopled my young mind with unclean images, such as only a vile monster could think of. I turned from him with disgust and hatred. But he was my master. I was compelled to live under the same roof with him—where I saw a man forty years my senior daily violating the most sacred commandments of nature. He told me I was his property; that I must be subject to his will in all things. My soul revolted against the mean tyranny. But where could I turn for protection? No matter whether the slave girl be as black as ebony or as fair as her mistress. In either case, there is no shadow of law to protect her from insult, from violence, or even from death; all these are inflicted by fiends who bear the shape of men. The mistress, who ought to protect the helpless victim, has no other feelings toward her but those of jealousy and rage.

Flint sought not only to satiate his lust, but to wreak his twisted will-to-power, to conquer Linda Brent's body and defile her spirit.

My master met me at every turn, reminding me that I belonged to him, and swearing by heaven and earth that he would compel me to submit to him. If I went out for a breath of fresh air, after a day of unwearied toil, his footsteps dogged me. If I knelt by my mother's grave, his dark shadow fell on me even there.

When I succeeded in avoiding opportunities for him to talk to me at home, I was ordered to come to his office, to do some errand. When there, I was obliged to stand and listen to such language as he saw fit to address to me.

Brent's revulsion and repulsion are unshakable, even as the physician is consumed by a life of revenge. Flint refuses to sell Brent to the freeborn colored man who wishes to marry her. Flint's insults, taunting, and physical abuse force Brent to break off her engagement.

[The doctor] had an iron will and was determined to keep me, and to conquer me. My lover was an intelligent and religious man. Even if he could have obtained permission to marry me while I was a slave, the marriage would give him no power to protect me from my master. It would have made him miserable to witness the insults I should have been subjected to. And then, if we had children, I knew they must "follow the condition of the mother." What a terrible blight that would be on the heart of a free, intelligent father! For his sake, I felt that I ought not to link his fate with my own unhappy destiny.

Flint has a small house built in a secluded place, a few miles outside of town—away from his wife and home. He intends to keep Brent as his mistress; but she vows "never [to] enter it." Brent writes, "I had rather toil on the plantation from dawn till dark; I had rather live and die in jail, than drag on, from day to day, through such a living death." Emotionally distraught, feeling "forsaken by God and man [sic]," Brent acquiesces emotionally and sexually to the sympathy, romantic overtures, and eloquence of the white unmarried gentleman, Mr. Sands.

So much attention from a superior person was, of course, flattering; for human nature is the same in all. . . . It seemed to me a great thing to have such a friend. By degrees, a more tender feeling crept into my heart. . . . Of course, I saw whither all this was tending. I knew the impassable gulf between us; but to be an object of interest to a man who is not married, and who is not her master, is agreeable to the pride and feelings of a slave, if her miserable situation has left her any pride or sentiment. It seems less degrading to give one's self, than to submit to compulsion.

Brent describes her decision as "a headlong plunge into the abyss," and admits a mixture of motives: "Revenge and calculations of interest were added to flattered vanity and sincere gratitude for kindness. . . . [A]nd it was something to triumph over my tyrant even in that small way." Jacobs' Brent is convinced that the physician will be so outraged at her sexual and emotional choice of Sands that he will sell her. She is just as convinced that Sands will buy her and that she easily can obtain her freedom from him. When Flint orders Brent to move into the completed cottage, she adamantly and triumphantly refuses.

I told him I would never enter it. He said, "I have heard enough of such talk as that. You shall go, if you are carried by force; and you shall remain there."

I replied, "I will never go there. In a few months I shall be a mother."

He stood and looked at me in dumb amazement, and left the house without a word. I thought I should be happy in my triumph over him. But now that the truth was out, and my relatives would hear of it, I felt wretched. Humble as were their circumstances, they had pride in my good character. Now, how could I look them in the face? My self-respect was gone! I had resolved that I would be virtuous, though I was a slave. I have said, "Let the storm beat! I will brave it till I die." And now how humiliated I felt.

Brent used her body, her sex, to gain some measure of psychological freedom from Flint. Although she wounds her grandmother in this process, she is never completely alienated from this good woman, even when she bears her second child by Sands. When Brent hears that her newborn is a girl, she is pained. "Slavery is terrible for men; but it is far more terrible for women. Superadded to the burden common to all, *they* have wrongs, and sufferings, and mortifications peculiarly their own."

Flint is relentless; Brent takes the only and hazardous course open to her. She runs away, resolving "that come what would, there should be no turning back," staking her future on liberty or death. Concealed, first by a friend, then by the wife of a prominent slaveholder, Brent eludes meticulous search for some weeks. Then, following a carefully devised plan involving Brent disguising herself as a sailor, hiding for a few days in a swamp, and darkening her face with charcoal, friends and relatives hide Brent beneath the sloping crawl space of her grandmother's house. For nearly seven years, Linda Bent lived undetected in this garret—nine feet long, seven feet wide, three feet high, accessible only through a carefully constructed and hidden trapdoor that led to a storeroom. Deprived of light and air, with no space to stand or move about, Brent is assailed by insects and heat in the summer and frostbite in winter. But she insists, she was not without comfort: brief conversations with her relatives, the discovery of a small gimlet that she uses to bore three small holes to increase light and air, and the voices—and most importantly the purchased freedom—of her son and daughter. Only her grandmother, aunt, uncle, brother, and a trusted friend knew her whereabouts. During those nearly seven years, Flint threatened and harassed her family and traveled three times to New York to search for Linda Brent who was "practically in his own back yard."

...

Mary Prince remembers the brutal death of Hetty, an enslaved woman who was especially kind to her in her youth. She and the other slaves of this plantation believe that Hetty's premature death was caused by a beating she received during her pregnancy.

> One of the cows had dragged the rope away from the stake to which Hetty had fastened it, and got loose. My master flew into a terrible passion, and ordered the poor creature to be stripped quite naked, notwithstanding her pregnancy, and to be tied up to a tree in the yard. He then flogged her as hard as he could lick, both with the whip and the cow-skin, till she was all over streaming with blood. He rested, and then beat her again and again. Her shrieks were terrible. Poor Hetty was brought to bed before her time, and was delivered after severe labor of a dead child. She appeared to recover after her confinement, so far that she was repeatedly flogged by both master and mistress afterward; but her former strength never returned to her. Ere long her body and limbs swelled to a great size; and she lay on a mat in the kitchen, till the water burst out of her body and she died. All the slaves said that death was a good thing for poor Hetty; but I cried very much for her death. The manner of it filled me with horror. I could not bear to think about it; yet it was always present to my mind for many a day.

Prince is forced to take over many of Hetty's duties, including the care of the cows. Once again, a cow slips its tether. The cow wanders into a garden, and eats some sweet-potato slips; Prince is blamed. Capt. I—, the slave master, finds Prince milking a cow. He takes off his boot and strikes her with it in the small of the back. The frightened cow kicks over the pan, spilling the milk. The accident is the slaveholder's fault, but it fuels his rage at Prince and he beats her. "I cannot remember how many licks he gave me then, but he beat me until I was unable to stand, and till he himself was weary." Prince runs away to her mother who is held on a nearby farm. Her mother, Prince tells us, "was both grieved and glad" to see her: "grieved because [Prince] had been so ill used, and glad because she had not seen [her daughter] for a long, long, while." Prince's mother hid her in a hole in nearby rocks and brought her food late each evening. But her father takes her back to the slaveholder. Not surprisingly, Prince is fearful of return. When they arrive, her father entreats Capt. I—"to be a kind master" to his daughter in the future. But Prince speaks up boldly:

> I then took courage and said that I could stand the floggings no longer; that I was weary of my life, and therefore I had run away to my mother; but mothers could only weep and mourn over their children, they could not save them from cruel masters—from whip, the rope, and the cow-skin. [Capt. I—] told me to hold my tongue and go about my work, or he would find a way to settle me. He did not, however, flog me that day.

For five years Prince remained a slave in this household, flogged and mistreated almost daily, until she was sold and shipped away from her parents and siblings.

Harriet Jacobs, Mary Prince, Louisa Picquet, Mattie Jackson and all the many thousand women gone were caught in the vicious nexus spawned in chattel slavery—full and arrogant self-assertion of white male power and privilege, white female ambivalence and hatred, the subjugation of Black women and men. These and so many other women were caught, but not trapped. To be sure, these are narratives of staggering affliction—human lives are seized, uprooted, and attacked directly and indirectly, in psychological, cultural, social, physical dimensions. Clearly these narratives expose maldistributed suffering, for Black women endured torments precisely because they were Black women and all Black women—enslaved or free—were potential victims. Neither is the suffering disclosed here pedagogically motivated, nor is it some form of spiritually beneficial asceticism. And since such suffering was meant to break, not temper, the spirit, it is of negative quality. Not infrequently, the beatings and abuse these women withstood ended in death. And, finally, their suffering extended for more than three hundred years, striking mother, daughter, granddaughter, great-granddaughter, great-great-granddaughter. Again: These are narratives of affliction, but not narratives of despair; the women may be caught, but they are not trapped. These Black women wade through their sorrows, managing their suffering, rather than being managed by it. In the next section, we turn to look at their resistance, a characteristic feature of their suffering and struggle and potent element in a theology of suffering in womanist perspective.

RESOURCES OF WOMANIST RESISTANCE

Almost from its emergence, Christianity has been described as the religion of slaves. Space does not allow me to elaborate here the nature and character of the psychic moments, spiritual experiences, preaching and teaching, rituals of passage and praise, spirituals and shouts and dance, visions and vocations that signify the distinctive Afric appropriation, if not reception, of biblical revelation by the enslaved Africans in the Americas. From their aural appropriation of the Bible and critical reflection on their own condition, these men and women shaped and "fitted" Christian practices, rituals, and values to their own particular experiences, religio-cultural expectations, and personal needs. The slave community formed a distinctive image of itself and fashioned "an inner world, a scale of values and fixed points of vantage from which to judge the world around them and themselves."

Christian religion was a fundamental resource for womanist resistance. Many women drank from its well, yet selectively so. Harriet Jacobs was critical of religious hypocrisy speaking of the "great difference between Christianity and the religion of the south." Slaveholders who beat, tortured, and sexually harassed slaves prided themselves on church membership. The planter class held one set of morals for white women, another for white men, and assumed that enslaved women and men had little, if any, capacity for real moral experience, moral agency, and moral virtue. All too often, Christian preaching, teaching, and practice complied. Black women's narratives counter these assumptions and stereotypes as well as discern and embrace a religious standard that exposes the moral hypocrisy of the planter class. Moreover, these women are living witnesses to the power of divine grace, not merely to sustain men and women through such evil, but to enable them to turn victimization into Christian triumph. Jacobs records the lines of this old slave hymn that sings the distinction between a pure or true Christianity and that poisoned by slavery: "Ole Satan's church is here below/ Up to God's free church I hope to go."

The attitude of the master class toward worship by slaves was not uniform. On some plantations slaves held independent, and sometimes, unsupervised services of worship; on other plantations, they attended white churches, sitting or standing in designated areas; on still others, they were forbidden to worship at all and they were punished if found praying and singing. Yet the people persisted. Christian biblical revelation held out formidable power. It offered the slaves the "dangerous" message of freedom, for indeed, Jesus did come to bring "freedom for the captive and release for those held in economic, social, and political bondage." It offered them the great and parallel event of Exodus, for indeed, it was for a people's freedom that the Lord God chose, called, and sent Moses. Christian biblical revelation provided the slaves with material for the singular mediation of their pain. The spirituals, "forged of sorrow in the heat of religious fervor," were an important resource of resistance. In and through these moaned or sung utterances, one woman's, one man's suffering or shout of jubilation became that of a people. The spirituals reshaped and conflated the characters and stories, parables and periscopes, events and miracles of the Hebrew and Christian scriptures. These songs told the mercy of God anew and testified to the ways in which the enslaved people met God at the whipping post, on the auction block, in the hush arbor, in the midnight flight to freedom. The maker of the spiritual sang: "God dat lived in Moses' time/Is jus' de same today." The spirituals served as coded messages, signaling the arrival of Moses in the person of Harriet Tubman or other ex-slaves who went back into Egypt to "tell ole Pharaoh, Let My People Go." "Steal away," sang the maker of the spiritual, "the chariot is comin'." And, if the makers of the spirituals gloried in singing of the cross of Jesus, it was not because they were masochistic and enjoyed suffering. Rather, the enslaved Africans sang because they saw on the rugged wooden planks One who had endured what was their daily portion. The cross was treasured because it enthroned the One who went all the way with them and for them. The enslaved Africans sang because they saw the result of the cross—triumph over the principalities and powers of death, triumph over evil in this world.

...

AN OUTLINE FOR A THEOLOGY OF SUFFERING IN WOMANIST PERSPECTIVE

It is ironic, perhaps, that a theology of suffering is formed from resources of resistance. It is not womanist perspective that makes it so, but the Christianity of the plantation. In its teaching, theologizing, preaching, and practice, this Christianity sought to bind the slaves to their condition by inculcating caricatures of the cardinal virtues of patience, long-suffering, forbearance, love, faith, and hope. Thus, to distance itself from any form of masochism, even Christian masochism, a theology of suffering in womanist perspective must reevaluate those virtues in light of Black women's experiences. Such reevaluation engages a hermeneutic of suspicion and a hermeneutic of resistance; but that reevaluation and reinterpretation must be rooted in a critical realism that rejects both naive realism and idealism as adequate foundations for a theology of suffering.

Chattel slavery disclosed the impoverished idealism that vitiated the Gospels, left Christianity a mere shell of principles and ideals, and obviated the moral and ethical implications of slavery—for master and slave alike. Likewise, a naive biblicism is impossible: "the Bible has been the most consistent and effective book that those in power have used to restrict and censure the behavior of African American women." Womanist Christian realism eschews naive biblicism, dogmatic moralism, and idealism distantiated from critical knowledge of experience, of human reality—of Black women's reality. Thus, a theology of suffering in womanist perspective begins with the acknowledgement of Black women's critical cognitive practice and develops through their distinctive Christian response to suffering.

Recalling her father's stories of slavery, Ruth Shays reflected: "The mind of the man and the mind of the woman is the same. But this business of living makes women use their minds in ways that men don' even have to think about. . . . it is life that makes all these differences, not nature." As a mode of critical consciousness and emancipatory struggle, Black women's critical cognitive practice is glimpsed in the earliest actuated meanings of resistance by captured and enslaved African women in North America. This practice emerged even more radically in the patterned operations of seeing, hearing, touching, smelling, tasting, inquiring, imagining, understanding, conceiving, formulating, reflecting, marshaling and weighing the evidence, judging, deliberating, evaluating, and deciding, speaking, writing. As a mode of critical self-consciousness, Black women's cognitive practice emphasizes the dialectic between oppression, conscious reflection on the experience of that oppression, and activism to resist and change it. The matrix of domination is responsive to human agency: the struggle of Black women suggests that there is choice and power to act—and to do so mindfully, artfully.

A theology of suffering in womanist perspective grows in the dark soil of the African-American religious tradition and is intimate with the root paradigms of African-American culture, in general, and African-American women's culture, in particular. Such a theology of suffering attends critically and carefully to the differentiated range of Black women's experiences. It holds itself accountable to Black women's self-understandings, self-judgment, and self-evaluation.

A theology of suffering in womanist perspective repels every tendency toward any *ersatz* spiritualization of evil and suffering, of pain and oppression. Such a theology of suffering seeks, on behalf of the African-American community whose lives and struggles it honors and serves, to understand and to clarify the meaning of the liberating Word and deed of God in Jesus of Nazareth for all women and men who strive against the principalities and structures, the powers and forces of evil. A theology of suffering in womanist perspective is characterized by remembering and retelling, by resisting, by redeeming.

- A theology of suffering in womanist perspective remembers and retells the lives and sufferings of those who "came through" and those who have "gone on to glory land." This remembering honors the sufferings of the ancestors, known and unknown, victims of chattel slavery and its living legacy. As Karen Holloway indicates, this "telling . . . is testimony that recenters the spirits of women, mythic and ancestral, into places where their passionate articulation assures them that

neither geography nor history can separate them from the integrity of the essential Word." And that "recentering" revives the living as well. Black women remember and draw strength in their own anguish from hearing and imitating the strategies adopted by their mothers, grandmothers, great-grandmothers, great-great-grandmothers to handle their suffering. These stories evoke growth and change, proper outrage and dissatisfaction, and enlarge Black women's moral horizon and choices.

- A theology of suffering in womanist perspective is *redemptive*. In their narratives, Black women invite God to partner them in the redemption of Black people. They make meaning of their suffering. Over and over again, Black women under chattel slavery endured pain, privation, and injury; risked their very lives, for the sake of the lives and freedom of their children. Praying in her garret, Linda Brent offers her suffering as part of the price of the emancipation of her children. Mattie Jackson recounts that during their escape, her mother fasted for two days, saving what food she had been able to carry away for Mattie and her sister. And, by their very suffering and privation, Black women under chattel slavery freed the cross of Christ. Their steadfast commitment honored that cross and the One who died for all and redeemed it from Christianity's vulgar misuse.

- A theology of suffering in womanist perspective is *resistant*. With motherwit, courage, sometimes their fists, and most often sass, Black women resisted the degradation of chattel slavery. Sass gave Black women a weapon of self-defense. With sass, Black women defined themselves and dismantled the images that had been used to control and demean them. With sass, Black women turned back the shame that others tried to put on them. With sass, Black women survived, even triumphed over emotional and psychic assault.

Moreover, in their resistance, Black women's suffering redefined caricatured Christian virtues. Because of the lives and suffering of Black women held in chattel slavery—the meanings of forbearance, long-suffering, patience, love, hope, and faith can never again be ideologized. Because of the rape, seduction, and concubinage of Black women under chattel slavery, chastity or virginity begs new meaning.

Harriet Jacobs' sexual liaison with Mr. Sands causes her great remorse and she experiences a loss of self-esteem. Indeed, for Jacobs, this spiritual and existential agony shadows the remainder of her life. A theology of suffering in womanist perspective ought to offer her comfort: Does not the sacrifice of her virgin body shield and preserve the virginity of her spirit and her heart? And, of what importance is a virgin body if the spirit and heart are violated, raped, crushed? And can we not hope that in the life of death, Harriet Jacobs has found "god in [her]self and loves her/loves her fiercely?"

Discussion Questions

1. Do all oppressed groups need a liberation theology? For example, do women and homosexuals require a liberation theology? What about members of ethnic minorities and racially oppressed groups? Why or why not?
2. In what ways is religion changed when suffering is placed in the center of its mission and theology? Do you think religion in America today would change if it took full account of the suffering of persons? Why or why not?
3. What does it mean to say that Christianity is a "religion of slaves"? In what ways is it beneficial for it to be considered a religion of slaves? In what ways is it detrimental? Explain your answer.

For Further Reading

For an entire series of texts concerning the liberation struggles of blacks in the United States see the Bishop Henry McNeal Turner Studies in North American Black Religion: *For My People* (1984), edited by James H. Cone; *Black and African Theologies* (1986), edited by J. U. Young; *Troubling Biblical Waters* (1989), edited by C. H. Felder; *Black Theology in the USA and South Africa* (1989), edited by D. N. Hopkins; *Empower the People* (1981), edited by Theodore Walker, Jr.; *A Common Journey* (1993), edited by G. C. L. Cummings; and *Dark Symbols, Obscure Signs* (1993), edited by R. R. Earl, Jr. Also see *Black Theology and Black Power* (1969), by James H. Cone. For a collection of essays by Martin Luther King, Jr., see *A Testament of Hope* (1986), edited by J. M. Washington. For an introduction to feminist theology see *The Church and the Second Sex* (1968) and *Beyond God the Father* (1973), by Mary Daly. See also the work of Rosemary Ruether: *Liberation Theology* (1973); *New Women, New Earth* (1975); *Sexism and God Talk* (1983); *Women-Church* (1985); and *Gaia and God* (1992).

CHAPTER 14

HOW SHOULD I LIVE MY LIFE?

$\mathbf{M}$any of the previous chapters have focused on specific problems, such as what is freedom, in what does personal identity consist, and how might my identity be shaped. Although these problems are important, philosophy, as 'the-love-of-wisdom,' aims at something more than solving these isolated, particular problems. Philosophers are also concerned with larger problems—problems as large as life itself—in particular, with the practical question, How should I live my life?

In this section, four philosophers with very different personal histories and intellectual journeys give divergent answers to the practical question "what should I do now?" In the first selection, Aristotle offers a traditional answer to this question. His commitments to reason, science, and philosophy match his vision of the ideal life: the life of study. Aristotle argues, somewhat suspiciously perhaps, that the life devoted to reflection and study—that is, the life of the philosopher—is the best. While his argument has often been criticized, the life of study remains an attractive ideal to many practitioners of philosophy. And although it is not easily done, many persons continue to give up lucrative careers in other fields in order to pursue a less financially rewarding and more difficult life of study.

Jean-Paul Sartre, in the second selection, offers a very different view of how we should live our lives, a view that emerged only after millennia of philosophical investigations by numerous philosophers before him. Sartre considers philosophy to have established one central truth: that *the world is only what we make it.* Therefore, we are faced with the inescapable responsibility of defining ourselves and the world we inhabit. Unfortunately, most persons refuse to accept this responsibility and instead fall into the roles defined by others for them.

Whereas Sartre and Aristotle stand at opposite ends of the long tradition of **Western philosophy,** the last two authors represent younger, more recent philosophical voices. For Cornel West, the problems facing black America are very different from those that motivate Sartre's **existentialism.** West seeks to identify the destructive forces that are ravaging the hearts of communities and lives of individuals; one destructive force is 'nihilism.' According to West, the source of nihilism is the colonial occupation of our culture by corporate market institutions. These corporate market institutions pander hedonistic visions of life that undercut nonmarket values such as love and deferred gratification, and in turn, the loss of nonmarket values encourages the growth and expansion of nihilism.

In the final article, feminist philosopher Sandra Lee Bartky considers a different type of colonialization: the colonial occupation of the imagination by the eroticization of domination, that is, by the desire for sadomasochistic forms of sexuality. Bartky's analysis suggests limits to the value of philosophical reflection. While philosophy may enlighten us intellectually, mere knowledge is not enough to liberate humanity from the shackles of oppression and injustice.

73 EUDAIMONIA
Aristotle

The Greek word **eudaimonia** plays a special role in the ethics of Aristotle (384–322 B.C.E.). Translated into English as 'happiness', *eudaimonia* has a fuller and richer meaning. Certainly *eudaimonia* is not exhausted by the concept of pleasure, although, of course a 'happy' life will be one with pleasure in it. Aristotle's idea of *eudaimonia* is closer to the idea of 'living well' or 'flourishing'.

In what does *eudaimonia* consist? What is 'happiness' for humans? To answer this, Aristotle looks at what he calls the 'proper function' of human beings. The **function** of a thing is the unique purpose of that thing—the unique 'work' that it does. For example, the function of a can opener is to open cans. The function of a knife is to cut. Once the function of a thing is known, then that thing can be assessed as being either good or bad. Thus, to continue the examples, if the function of a can opener is to open cans, a *good* can opener is one that opens cans *well*. If the function of a knife is to cut, a *good* knife is one that cuts *well*. So what is the unique function of a human? Aristotle says that the unique function of humanity is to reason: Humans are by definition 'rational animals.' If that is our unique function, then a good human will be one that functions well, that is, one that reasons well. What does this have to do with *eudaimonia?* Persons are 'happy' insofar as they fulfill their function, that is, if they live well or flourish as a human. To live well and to flourish means, given the definition of the human function, to reason well.

Persons have *eudaimonia* then insofar as they reason well, that is, insofar as they exhibit rationality throughout their life. But in this passage, Aristotle extends his argument in a new direction. The best life is not just a life in which reason and rationality are exhibited throughout; rather, the best life is the life devoted to reason exclusively, that is, the life of study—the life of the philosopher.

Reading Questions

1. Why is happiness not to be found in amusement?
2. Why is complete happiness to be found in the activity of study? What reasons does Aristotle give for its superiority?
3. What is the relationship between happiness and leisure?
4. How is the life of study related to the divine element in humans?
5. Does the life of study require external goods?
6. How does Aristotle conclude that the superior activity of the Gods is the activity of study?
7. Does a person require prosperity to be happy?

HAPPINESS IS GOOD ACTIVITY, NOT AMUSEMENT

Now that we have spoken of the virtues, the forms of friendship, and the varieties of pleasure, what remains is to discuss in outline the nature of happiness, since this is what we state the end of human nature to be. Our discussion will be the more concise if we first sum up what we have said already.

We said, then, that it is not a disposition; for if it were it might belong to someone who was asleep throughout his life, living the life of a plant, or, again, to someone who was suffering the greatest misfortunes. If these implications are unacceptable, and we must rather class happiness as an activity, as we have said before, and if some activities are necessary, and desirable for the sake of something else, while others are so in themselves, evidently happiness must be placed among those desirable in themselves, not among those desirable for the sake of something else; for happiness does not lack anything, but is self-sufficient. Now those activities are desirable in themselves from which nothing is sought beyond the activity. And of this nature virtuous actions are thought to be; for to do noble and good deeds is a thing desirable for its own sake.

Pleasant amusements also are thought to be of this nature: we choose them not for the sake of other things; for we are injured rather than benefited by them, since we are led to neglect our bodies and our property. But most of the people who are deemed happy take refuge in such pastimes, which is the reason why those who are ready-witted at them are highly esteemed at the courts of tyrants; they make themselves pleasant companions in the tyrants' favourite pursuits, and that is the sort of man they want. Now these things are thought to be of the nature of happiness because people in despotic positions spend their leisure in them, but perhaps such people prove nothing; for virtue and reason, from which good activities flow, do not depend on despotic position; nor, if these people, who have never tasted pure and generous pleasure, take refuge in the bodily pleasures, should these for that reason be thought more desirable; for boys, too, think the things that are valued among themselves are the best. It is to be expected, then, that, as different things

seem valuable to boys and to men, so they should to bad men and to good.

Now, as we have often maintained, those things are both valuable and pleasant which are such to the good man; and to each man the activity in accordance with his own disposition is most desirable, and therefore to the good man that which is in accordance with virtue. Happiness, therefore, does not lie in amusement; it would, indeed, be strange if the end were amusement, and one were to take trouble and suffer hardship all one's life in order to amuse oneself. For, in a word, everything that we choose we choose for the sake of something else—except happiness, which is an end. Now to exert oneself and work for the sake of amusement seems silly and utterly childish. But to amuse oneself in order that one may exert oneself, as Anacharsis puts it, seems right; for amusement is a sort of relaxation, and we need relaxation because we cannot work continuously. Relaxation, then, is not an end; for it is taken for the sake of activity.

The happy life is thought to be virtuous; now a virtuous life requires exertion, and does not consist in amusement. And we say that serious things are better than laughable things and those connected with amusement, and that the activity of the better of any two things—whether it be two elements of our being or two men—is the more serious; but the activity of the better is *ipso facto* superior and more of the nature of happiness. And any chance person—even a slave—can enjoy the bodily pleasures no less than the best man; but no one assigns to a slave a share in happiness—unless he assigns to him also a share in human life. For happiness does not lie in such occupations, but, as we have said before, in virtuous activities.

HAPPINESS IN THE HIGHEST SENSE IS THE CONTEMPLATIVE LIFE

If happiness is activity in accordance with virtue, it is reasonable that it should be in accordance with the highest virtue; and this will be that of the best thing in us. Whether it be reason or something else that is this element which is thought to be our natural ruler and guide and to take thought of things noble and divine, whether it be itself also divine or only the most divine element in us, the activity of this in accordance with its proper virtue will be perfect happiness. That this activity is contemplative we have already said.

Now this would seem to be in agreement both with what we said before and with the truth. For, firstly, this activity is the best (since not only is reason the best thing in us, but the objects of reason are the best of knowable objects); and, secondly, it is the most continuous, since we can contemplate truth more continuously than we can *do* anything.

And we think happiness ought to have pleasure mingled with it, but the activity of philosophic wisdom is admittedly the pleasantest of virtuous activities; at all events the pursuit of it is thought to offer pleasures marvellous for their purity and their enduringness, and it is to be expected that those who know will pass their time more pleasantly than those who inquire.

And the self-sufficiency that is spoken of must belong most to the contemplative activity. For while a philosopher, as well as a just man or one possessing any other virtue, needs the necessaries of life, when they are sufficiently equipped with things of that sort the just man needs people towards whom and with whom he shall act justly, and the temperate man, the brave man, and each of the others is in the same case, but the philosopher, even when by himself, can contemplate truth, and the better the wiser he is; he can perhaps do so better if he has fellow workers, but still he is the most self-sufficient.

And this activity alone would seem to be loved for its own sake; for nothing arises from it apart from the contemplating, while from practical activities we gain more or less apart from the action. And happiness is thought to depend on leisure; for we are busy that we may have leisure, and make war that we may live in peace.

Now the activity of the practical virtues is exhibited in political or military affairs, but the actions concerned with these seem to be unleisurely. Warlike actions are completely so (for no one chooses to be at war, or provokes war, for the sake of being at war; anyone would seem absolutely murderous if he were to make enemies of his friends in order to bring about battle and slaughter); but the action of the statesman also is unleisurely, and aims—beyond the political action itself—at despotic power and honours, or at all events happiness, for him and his fellow citizens—a happiness different from

political action, and evidently sought as being different. So if among virtuous actions political and military actions are distinguished by nobility and greatness, and these are unleisurely and aim at an end and are not desirable for their own sake, but the activity of reason, which is contemplative, seems both to be superior in serious worth and to aim at no end beyond itself, and to have its pleasure proper to itself (and this augments the activity), and the self-sufficiency, leisureliness, unweariedness (so far as this is possible for man), and all the other attributes ascribed to the supremely happy man are evidently those connected with this activity, it follows that this will be the complete happiness of man, if it be allowed a complete term of life (for none of the attributes of happiness is *in*complete).

But such a life would be too high for man; for it is not in so far as he is man that he will live so, but in so far as something divine is present in him; and by so much as this is superior to our composite nature is its activity superior to that which is the exercise of the other kind of virtue. If reason is divine, then, in comparison with man, the life according to it is divine in comparison with human life. But we must not follow those who advise us, being men, to think of human things, and, being mortal, of mortal things, but must, so far as we can, make ourselves immortal, and strain every nerve to live in accordance with the best thing in us; for even if it be small in bulk, much more does it in power and worth surpass everything. This would seem, too, to be each man himself, since it is the authoritative and better part of him. It would be strange, then, if he were to choose not the life of his self but that of something else. And what we said before will apply now: that which is proper to each thing is by nature best and most pleasant for each thing; for man, therefore, the life according to reason is best and pleasantest, since reason more than anything else *is* man. This life therefore is also the happiest.

SUPERIORITY OF THE CONTEMPLATIVE LIFE FURTHER CONSIDERED

...

The excellence of the reason is a thing apart: we must be content to say this much about it, for to describe it precisely is a task greater than our purpose requires. It would seem, however, also to need external equipment but little, or less than moral virtue does. Grant that both need the necessaries, and do so equally, even if the statesman's work is the more concerned with the body and things of that sort; for there will be little difference there; but in what they need for the exercise of their activities there will be much difference. The liberal man will need money for the doing of his liberal deeds, and the just man too will need it for the returning of services (for wishes are hard to discern, and even people who are not just pretend to wish to act justly); and the brave man will need power if he is to accomplish any of the acts that correspond to his virtue, and the temperate man will need opportunity; for how else is either he or any of the others to be recognized?

It is debated, too, whether the will or the deed is more essential to virtue, which is assumed to involve both; it is surely clear that its perfection involves both; but for deeds many things are needed, and more, the greater and nobler the deeds are. But the man who is contemplating the truth needs no such thing, at least with a view to the exercise of his activity; indeed they are, one may say, even hindrances, at all events to his contemplation; but in so far as he is a man and lives with a number of people, he chooses to do virtuous acts; he will therefore need such aids to living a human life.

But that perfect happiness is a contemplative activity will appear from the following consideration as well. We assume the gods to be above all other beings blessed and happy; but what sort of actions must we assign to them? Acts of justice? Will not the gods seem absurd if they make contracts and return deposits, and so on? Acts of a brave man, then, confronting dangers and running risks because it is noble to do so? Or liberal acts? To whom will they give? It will be strange if they are really to have money or anything of the kind. And what would their temperate acts be? Is not such praise tasteless, since they have no bad appetites? If we were to run through them all, the circumstances of action would be found trivial and unworthy of gods. Still, everyone supposes that they *live* and therefore that they are active; we cannot suppose them to sleep like Endymion. Now if you take away from a living being

action, and still more production, what is left but contemplation? Therefore the activity of God, which surpasses all others in blessedness, must be contemplative; and of human activities, therefore, that which is most akin to this must be most of the nature of happiness.

This is indicated, too, by the fact that the other animals have no share in happiness, being completely deprived of such activity. For while the whole life of the gods is blessed, and that of men too in so far as some likeness of such activity belongs to them, none of the other animals is happy, since they in no way share in contemplation. Happiness extends, then, just so far as contemplation does, and those to whom contemplation more fully belongs are more truly happy, not as a mere concomitant but in virtue of the contemplation; for this is in itself precious. Happiness, therefore, must be some form of contemplation.

But, being a man, one will also need external prosperity; for our nature is not self-sufficient for the purpose of contemplation, but our body also must be healthy and must have food and other attention. Still, we must not think that the man who is to be happy will need many things or great things, merely because he cannot be supremely happy without external goods; for self-sufficiency and action do not involve excess, and we can do noble acts without ruling earth and sea; for even with moderate advantages one can act virtuously (this is manifest enough; for private persons are thought to do worthy acts no less than despots—indeed even more); and it is enough that we should have so much as that; for the life of the man who is active in accordance with virtue will be happy. . . . Now he who exercises his reason and cultivates it seems to be both in the best state of mind and most dear to the gods. For if the gods have any care for human affairs, as they are thought to have, it would be reasonable both that they should delight in that which was best and most akin to them (i.e., reason) and that they should reward those who love and honour this most, as caring for the things that are dear to them and acting both rightly and nobly. And that all these attributes belong most of all to the philosopher is manifest. He, therefore, is the dearest to the gods. And he who is that will presumably be also the happiest; so that in this way too the philosopher will more than any other be happy.

Discussion Questions

1. Are there important ways of human flourishing beyond the life of study? Do you agree with Aristotle that the best life is the life of study? Why or why not? Are there some ways in which a life of study might be incomplete? Are there some ways in which a life of study might be dangerous or distorted? Explain your answer.
2. Can a person truly flourish if reason and rationality play little or no part in his or her life? Is rationality a necessary condition for *eudaimonia*? Why or why not?
3. Could everyone pursue a 'life of study'? Could everyone be a philosopher even if they are not employed as a professional philosopher? For example, could all the various ways in which humans work and play be the objects of philosophical reflection? Would this be a worthwhile ideal? Why or why not?
4. Are intellectuals (that is, persons who have devoted themselves to a life of study) valued in every culture? Is a life of study valued in your culture? Are individuals who devote themselves to a life of study, philosophical reflection, and intellectual pursuits valued in your culture? Why or why not? Compare your culture to another cultural group. What differences are there? Which way of valuing intellectual pursuits do you believe is most valuable?
5. Are external goods necessary in order to flourish as a human being? Why or why not? If so, should all persons be guaranteed access to these external goods? Why or why not?

For Further Reading

For additional readings on Aristotle's ethics, see the suggested readings after Reading 45 in Chapter 8. For a specific discussion on *eudaimonia* see Richard Kraut, *Aristotle on the Human Good* (1989); Don Asselin, *Human Nature and Eudaimonia in Aristotle* (1989); J. M. Cooper, *Reason and Human Good in Aristotle* (1975); and J. L. Ackrill, "Aristotle on Eudaimonia" in Amélie Rorty, editor, *Essays on Aristotle's Ethics* (1980).

74 EXISTENTIALISM IS A HUMANISM
Jean-Paul Sartre

In place of a definition of existentialism, Walter Kaufmann in his 1956 essay "Existentialism from Dostoevsky to Sartre" offered this description of existentialism:

> The refusal to belong to any school of thought, the repudiation of the adequacy of any body of beliefs whatsoever, and especially of systems, and a marked dissatisfaction with traditional philosophy as superficial, academic, and remote from life—this is the heart of existentialism.[1]

Although existentialism is dependent on the historical philosophy that precedes it, existentialism is nonetheless predicated on the failure of grand philosophical programs. Epistemology, ethics, aesthetics, metaphysics, philosophy of religion—all lead to one unavoidable, sobering result for the existentialist: that humanity is absolutely free and cannot escape from the awesome responsibility of creating meaning for itself.

SOURCE: From *Being and Nothingness* (1956), by Jean-Paul Sartre. Reprinted with permission of Philosophical Library, Inc., New York.

[1] Walter Kaufmann, from *Existentialism from Dostoevsky to Sartre* (1956), p. 12

In this essay, Jean-Paul Sartre (1905–1980), perhaps the leading exponent of existentialism, defines many of the key terms used by existentialists, including the meaning of 'existence precedes essence', 'abandonment,' 'the absence of God', and 'despair.' Having witnessed firsthand two world wars that ravaged Europe, Sartre's portrait of humanity is stern and austere. Existentialism, Sartre writes, places the entire responsibility for human reality firmly upon the shoulders of humanity. We are nothing other than what we make ourselves. Furthermore, it is not merely that each person is responsible for him or herself; rather, each person is responsible for all.

Reading Questions

1. What does the example of the paper-knife illustrate? How is this like God creating man?
2. What does 'existence precedes essence' mean?
3. How does existentialism respond to the fact that God does not exist? How is this different from other responses?
4. Summarize Sartre's example of the young man who must choose between joining the resistance or staying with his mother. How does this illustrate the concept of 'abandonment'?
5. What problems does Sartre have with materialist explanations of humanity?
6. How is art like morality?
7. How does Sartre respond to the criticism that existentialists are unable to judge others?
8. What meaning of 'humanism' does Sartre accept? Which does he reject?

...

... What, then, is this that we call existentialism?

Most of those who are making use of this word would be highly confused if required to explain its meaning. For since it has become fashionable, people cheerfully declare that this musician or that painter is "existentialist." A columnist in *Clartés* signs himself "The Existentialist," and, indeed, the word is now so loosely applied to so many things that it no longer means anything at all. It would appear that, for the lack of any novel doctrine such as that of surrealism, all those who are eager to join in the latest scandal or movement now seize upon this philosophy in which, however, they can find nothing to their purpose. For in truth this is of all teachings the least scandalous and the most austere: it is intended strictly for technicians and philosophers. All the same, it can easily be defined.

The question is only complicated because there are two kinds of existentialists. There are, on the one hand, the Christians, amongst whom I shall name Jaspers and Gabriel Marcel, both professed Catholics; and on the other the existential atheists, amongst whom we must place Heidegger as well as the French existentialists and myself. What they have in common is simply the fact that they believe that *existence* comes before *essence*—or, if you will, that we must begin from the subjective. What exactly do we mean by that?

If one considers an article of manufacture—as, for example, a book or a paper-knife—one sees that it has been made by an artisan who had a conception of it; and he has paid attention, equally, to the conception of a paper-knife and to the pre-existent technique of production which is a part of that conception and is, at bottom, a formula. Thus the paper-knife is at the same time an article producible in a certain manner and one which, on the other hand, serves a definite purpose, for one cannot suppose that a man would produce a paper-knife without knowing what it was for. Let us say, then, of the paper-knife that its essence—that is to say the sum of the formulae and the qualities which made its production and its definition possible—precedes its existence. The presence of such-and-such a paper-knife or book is thus determined before my eyes. Here, then, we are viewing the world from a technical standpoint, and we can say that production precedes existence.

When we think of God as the creator, we are thinking of him, most of the time, as a supernal artisan. Whatever doctrine we may be considering, whether it be a doctrine like that of Descartes, or of Leibnitz himself, we always imply that the will follows, more or less, from the understanding or at least accompanies it, so that when God creates he knows precisely what he is creating. Thus, the conception of man in the mind of God is comparable to that of the paper-knife in the mind of the artisan: God makes man according to a procedure and a conception, exactly as the artisan manufactures a paper-knife, following a definition and a formula. Thus each individual man is the realization of a certain conception which dwells in the divine understanding. In the philosophic atheism of the eighteenth century, the notion of God is suppressed, but not, for all that, the idea that essence is prior to existence; something of that idea we still find everywhere, in Diderot, in Voltaire and even in Kant. Man possesses a human nature; that "human nature," which is the conception of human being, is found in every man; which means that each man is a particular example of a universal conception, the conception of Man. In Kant, this universality goes so far that the wild man of the woods, man in the state of nature and the bourgeois are all contained in the same definition and have the same fundamental qualities. Here again, the essence of man precedes that historic existence which we confront in experience.

Atheistic existentialism, of which I am a representative, declares with greater consistency that if God does not exist there is at least one being whose existence comes before its essence, a being which exists before it can be defined by any conception of it. That being is man or, as Heidegger has it, the human reality. What do we mean by saying that existence precedes essence? We mean that man first of all exists, encounters himself, surges up in the world—and defines himself afterwards. If man as the existentialist sees him is not definable, it is because to begin with he is nothing. He will not be anything until later, and then he will be what he makes of himself. Thus, there is no human nature, because there is no God to have a conception of it. Man simply is. Not that he is sim-

ply what he conceives himself to be, but he is what he wills, and as he conceives himself after already existing—as he wills to be after that leap towards existence. Man is nothing else but that which he makes of himself. That is the first principle of existentialism. And this is what people call its "subjectivity," using the word as a reproach against us. But what do we mean to say by this, but that man is of a greater dignity than a stone or a table? For we mean to say that man primarily exists—that man is, before all else, something which propels itself towards a future and is aware that it is doing so. Man is, indeed, a project which possesses a subjective life, instead of being a kind of moss, or a fungus or a cauliflower. Before that projection of the self nothing exists; not even in the heaven of intelligence: man will only attain existence when he is what he purposes to be. Not, however, what he may wish to be. For what we usually understand by wishing or willing is a conscious decision taken—much more often than not—after we have made ourselves what we are. I may wish to join a party, to write a book or to marry—but in such a case what is usually called my will is probably a manifestation of a prior and more spontaneous decision. If, however, it is true that existence is prior to essence, man is responsible for what he is. Thus, the first effect of existentialism is that it puts every man in possession of himself as he is, and places the entire responsibility for his existence squarely upon his own shoulders. And, when we say that man is responsible for himself, we do not mean that he is responsible only for his own individuality, but that he is responsible for all men. The word "subjectivism" is to be understood in two senses, and our adversaries play upon only one of them. Subjectivism means, on the one hand, the freedom of the individual subject and, on the other, that man cannot pass beyond human subjectivity. It is the latter which is the deeper meaning of existentialism. When we say that man chooses himself, we do mean that every one of us must choose himself; but by that we also mean that in choosing for himself he chooses for all men. For in effect, of all the actions a man may take in order to create himself as he wills to be, there is not one which is not creative, at the same time, of an image of man such as he believes he ought to be. To choose between this or that is at the same time to affirm the value of that which is chosen; for we are unable ever to choose the worse. What we choose is always the better; and nothing can be better for us unless it is better for all. If, moreover, existence precedes essence and we will to exist at the same time as we fashion our image, that image is valid for all and for the entire epoch in which we find ourselves. Our responsibility is thus much greater than we had supposed, for it concerns mankind as a whole. If I am a worker, for instance, I may choose to join a Christian rather than a Communist trade union. And if, by that membership, I choose to signify that resignation is, after all, the attitude that best becomes a man, that man's kingdom is not upon this earth, I do not commit myself alone to that view. Resignation is my will for everyone, and my action is, in consequence, a commitment on behalf of all mankind. Or if, to take a more personal case, I decide to marry and to have children, even though this decision proceeds simply from my situation, from my passion or my desire, I am thereby committing not only myself, but humanity as a whole, to the practice of monogamy. I am thus responsible for myself and for all men, and I am creating a certain image of man as I would have him to be. In fashioning myself I fashion man.

This may enable us to understand what is meant by such terms—perhaps a little grandiloquent—as anguish, abandonment and despair. As you will soon see, it is very simple. First, what do we mean by anguish? The existentialist frankly states that man is in anguish. His meaning is as follows—When a man commits himself to anything, fully realizing that he is not only choosing what he will be, but is thereby at the same time a legislator deciding for the whole of mankind—in such a moment a man cannot escape from the sense of complete and profound responsibility. There are many, indeed, who show no such anxiety. But we affirm that they are merely disguising their anguish or are in flight from it. Certainly, many people think that in what they are doing they commit no one but themselves to anything: and if you ask them, "What would happen if everyone did so?" they shrug their shoulders and reply, "Everyone does not do so." But in truth, one ought always to ask oneself what would happen if everyone did as one is doing; nor can one escape from that disturbing thought except by a kind of self-deception. The man who lies in self-excuse, by saying "Everyone will not do it"

must be ill at ease in his conscience, for the act of lying implies the universal value which it denies. By its very disguise his anguish reveals itself. This is the anguish that Kierkegaard called "the anguish of Abraham." You know the story: An angel commanded Abraham to sacrifice his son: and obedience was obligatory, if it really was an angel who had appeared and said, "Thou, Abraham, shalt sacrifice thy son." But anyone in such a case would wonder, first, whether it was indeed an angel and secondly, whether I am really Abraham. Where are the proofs? A certain mad woman who suffered from hallucinations said that people were telephoning to her, and giving her orders. The doctor asked, "But who is it that speaks to you?" She replied: "He says it is God." And what, indeed, could prove to her that it was God? If an angel appears to me, what is the proof that it is an angel; or, if I hear voices, who can prove that they proceed from heaven and not from hell, or from my own subconsciousness or some pathological condition? Who can prove that they are really addressed to me?

Who, then, can prove that I am the proper person to impose, by my own choice, my conception of man upon mankind? I shall never find any proof whatever; there will be no sign to convince me of it. If a voice speaks to me, it is still I myself who must decide whether the voice is or is not that of an angel. If I regard a certain course of action as good, it is only I who choose to say that it is good and not bad. There is nothing to show that I am Abraham: nevertheless I also am obliged at every instant to perform actions which are examples. Everything happens to every man as though the whole human race had its eyes fixed upon what he is doing and regulated its conduct accordingly. So every man ought to say, "Am I really a man who has the right to act in such a manner that humanity regulates itself by what I do." If a man does not say that, he is dissembling his anguish. Clearly, the anguish with which we are concerned here is not one that could lead to quietism or inaction. It is anguish pure and simple, of the kind well known to all those who have borne responsibilities. When, for instance, a military leader takes upon himself the responsibility for an attack and sends a number of men to their death, he chooses to do it and at bottom he alone chooses. No doubt he acts under a higher command, but its orders, which are more general, require interpretation by him and upon that interpretation depends the life of ten, fourteen or twenty men. In making the decision, he cannot but feel a certain anguish. All leaders know that anguish. It does not prevent their acting, on the contrary it is the very condition of their action, for the action presupposes that there is a plurality of possibilities, and in choosing one of these, they realize that it has value only because it is chosen. Now it is anguish of that kind which existentialism describes, and moreover, as we shall see, makes explicit through direct responsibility towards other men who are concerned. Far from being a screen which could separate us from action, it is a condition of action itself.

And when we speak of "abandonment"—a favorite word of Heidegger—we only mean to say that God does not exist, and that it is necessary to draw the consequences of his absence right to the end. The existentialist is strongly opposed to a certain type of secular moralism which seeks to suppress God at the least possible expense. Towards 1880, when the French professors endeavored to formulate a secular morality, they said something like this:— God is a useless and costly hypothesis, so we will do without it. However, if we are to have morality, a society and a law-abiding world, it is essential that certain values should be taken seriously; they must have an *a priori* existence ascribed to them. It must be considered obligatory *a priori* to be honest, not to lie, not to beat one's wife, to bring up children and so forth; so we are going to do a little work on this subject, which will enable us to show that these values exist all the same, inscribed in an intelligible heaven although, of course, there is no God. In other words—and this is, I believe, the purport of all that we in France call radicalism—nothing will be changed if God does not exist; we shall rediscover the same norms of honesty, progress and humanity, and we shall have disposed of God as an out-of-date hypothesis which will die away quietly of itself. The existentialist, on the contrary, finds it extremely embarrassing that God does not exist, for there disappears with Him all possibility of finding values in an intelligible heaven. There can no longer be any good *a priori,* since there is no infinite and perfect consciousness to think it. It is nowhere written that "the good" exists, that one must be honest or must not lie, since we are now upon the plane where there are only men. Dostoevsky once wrote "If God did not exist, everything would be

permitted"; and that, for existentialism, is the starting point. Everything is indeed permitted if God does not exist, and man is in consequence forlorn, for he cannot find anything to depend upon either within or outside himself. He discovers forthwith, that he is without excuse. For if indeed existence precedes essence, one will never be able to explain one's action by reference to a given and specific human nature; in other words, there is no determinism— man is free, man *is* freedom. Nor, on the other hand, if God does not exist, are we provided with any values or commands that could legitimize our behavior. Thus we have neither behind us, nor before us in a luminous realm of values, any means of justification or excuse. We are left alone, without excuse. That is what I mean when I say that man is condemned to be free. Condemned, because he did not create himself, yet is nevertheless at liberty, and from the moment that he is thrown into this world he is responsible for everything he does. The existentialist does not believe in the power of passion. He will never regard a grand passion as a destructive torrent upon which a man is swept into certain actions as by fate, and which, therefore, is an excuse for them. He thinks that man is responsible for his passion. Neither will an existentialist think that a man can find help through some sign being vouchsafed upon earth for his orientation: for he thinks that the man himself interprets the sign as he chooses. He thinks that every man, without any support or help whatever, is condemned at every instant to invent man. As Ponge has written in a very fine article, "Man is the future of man." That is exactly true. Only, if one took this to mean that the future is laid up in Heaven, that God knows what it is, it would be false, for then it would no longer even be a future. If, however, it means that, whatever man may now appear to be, there is a future to be fashioned, a virgin future that awaits him—then it is a true saying. But in the present one is forsaken.

As an example by which you may the better understand this state of abandonment, I will refer to the case of a pupil of mine, who sought me out in the following circumstances. His father was quarreling with his mother and was also inclined to be a "collaborator"; his elder brother had been killed in the German offensive of 1940 and this young man, with a sentiment somewhat primitive but generous, burned to avenge him. His mother was living alone with him, deeply afflicted by the semi-treason of his father and by the death of her eldest son, and her one consolation was in this young man. But he, at this moment, had the choice between going to England to join the Free French Forces or of staying near his mother and helping her to live. He fully realized that this woman lived only for him and that his disappearance—or perhaps his death—would plunge her into despair. He also realized that, concretely and in fact, every action he performed on his mother's behalf would be sure of effect in the sense of aiding her to live, whereas anything he did in order to go and fight would be an ambiguous action which might vanish like water into sand and serve no purpose. For instance, to set out for England he would have to wait indefinitely in a Spanish camp on the way through Spain; or, on arriving in England or in Algiers he might be put into an office to fill up forms. Consequently, he found himself confronted by two very different modes of action; the one concrete, immediate, but directed towards only one individual; and the other an action addressed to an end infinitely greater, a national collectivity, but for that very reason ambiguous—and it might be frustrated on the way. At the same time, he was hesitating between two kinds of morality; on the one side the morality of sympathy, of personal devotion and, on the other side, a morality of wider scope but of more debatable validity. He had to choose between those two. What could help him to choose? Could the Christian doctrine? No. Christian doctrine says: Act with charity, love your neighbor, deny yourself for others, choose the way which is hardest, and so forth. But which is the harder road? To whom does one owe the more brotherly love, the patriot or the mother? Which is the more useful aim, the general one of fighting in and for the whole community, or the precise aim of helping one particular person to live? Who can give an answer to that *a priori*? No one. Nor is it given in any ethical scripture. The Kantian ethic says, Never regard another as a means, but always as an end. Very well; if I remain with my mother, I shall be regarding her as the end and not as a means: but by the same token I am in danger of treating as means those who are fighting on my behalf; and the converse is also true, that if I go to the aid of the combatants I shall be treating them as the end at the risk of treating my mother as a means.

If values are uncertain, if they are still too abstract to determine the particular, concrete case under consideration, nothing remains but to trust in our instincts. That is what this young man tried to do; and when I saw him he said, "In the end, it is feeling that counts; the direction in which it is really pushing me is the one I ought to choose. If I feel that I love my mother enough to sacrifice everything else for her—my will to be avenged, all my longings for action and adventure—then I stay with her. If, on the contrary, I feel that my love for her is not enough, I go." But how does one estimate the strength of a feeling? The value of his feeling for his mother was determined precisely by the fact that he was standing by her. I may say that I love a certain friend enough to sacrifice such or such a sum of money for him, but I cannot prove that unless I have done it. I may say, "I love my mother enough to remain with her," if actually I have remained with her. I can only estimate the strength of this affection if I have performed an action by which it is defined and ratified. But if I then appeal to this affection to justify my action, I find myself drawn into a vicious circle.

...

As for "despair," the meaning of this expression is extremely simple. It merely means that we limit ourselves to a reliance upon that which is within our wills, or within the sum of the probabilities which render our action feasible. Whenever one wills anything, there are always these elements of probability. If I am counting upon a visit from a friend, who may be coming by train or by tram, I presuppose that the train will arrive at the appointed time, or that the tram will not be derailed. I remain in the realm of possibilities; but one does not rely upon any possibilities beyond those that are strictly concerned in one's action. Beyond the point at which the possibilities under consideration cease to affect my action, I ought to disinterest myself. For there is no God and no prevenient design, which can adapt the world and all its possibilities to my will. When Descartes said, "Conquer yourself rather than the world," what he meant was, at bottom, the same—that we should act without hope.

...

What is at the very heart and center of existentialism, is the absolute character of the free commitment, by which every man realizes himself in realizing a type of humanity—a commitment always understandable, to no matter whom in no matter what epoch—and its bearing upon the relativity of the cultural pattern which may result from such absolute commitment. One must observe equally the relativity of Cartesianism and the absolute character of the Cartesian commitment. In this sense you may say, if you like, that every one of us makes the absolute by breathing, by eating, by sleeping or by behaving in any fashion whatsoever. There is no difference between free being—being as self-committal, as existence choosing its essence—and absolute being. And there is no difference whatever between being as an absolute, temporarily localized—that is, localized in history—and universally intelligible being.

This does not completely refute the charge of subjectivism. Indeed that objection appears in several other forms, of which the first is as follows. People say to us, "Then it does not matter what you do," and they say this in various ways. First they tax us with anarchy; then they say, "You cannot judge others, for there is no reason for preferring one purpose to another"; finally, they may say, "Everything being merely voluntary in this choice of yours, you give away with one hand what you pretend to gain with the other." These three are not very serious objections. As to the first, to say that it does not matter what you choose is not correct. In one sense choice is possible, but what is not possible is not to choose. I can always choose, but I must know that if I do not choose, that is still a choice. This, although it may appear merely formal, is of great importance as a limit to fantasy and caprice. For, when I confront a real situation—for example, that I am a sexual being, able to have relations with a being of the other sex and able to have children—I am obliged to choose my attitude to it, and in every respect I bear the responsibility of the choice which, in committing myself, also commits the whole of humanity. Even if my choice is determined by no *a priori* value whatever, it can have nothing to do with caprice: and if anyone thinks that this is only Gide's theory of the *acte gratuit* over again, he has failed to see the enormous difference between this theory and that of Gide. Gide does not know what a situation is, his "act" is one of pure caprice. In our view, on the contrary, man finds himself in an organized situation in which he is himself involved: his choice involves mankind in its entirety, and he cannot avoid choosing.

Either he must remain single, or he must marry without having children, or he must marry and have children. In any case, and whichever he may choose, it is impossible for him, in respect of this situation, not to take complete responsibility. Doubtless he chooses without reference to any pre-established values, but it is unjust to tax him with caprice. Rather let us say that the moral choice is comparable to the construction of a work of art.

But here I must at once digress to make it quite clear that we are not propounding an aesthetic morality, for our adversaries are disingenuous enough to reproach us even with that. I mention the work of art only by way of comparison. That being understood, does anyone reproach an artist, when he paints a picture, for not following rules established *a priori*? Does one ever ask what is the picture that he ought to paint? As everyone knows, there is no pre-defined picture for him to make; the artist applies himself to the composition of a picture, and the picture that ought to be made is precisely that which he will have made. As everyone knows, there are no aesthetic values *a priori*, but there are values which will appear in due course in the coherence of the picture, in the relation between the will to create and the finished work. No one can tell what the painting of tomorrow will be like; one cannot judge a painting until it is done. What has that to do with morality? We are in the same creative situation. We never speak of a work of art as irresponsible; when we are discussing a canvas by Picasso, we understand very well that the composition became what it is at the time when he was painting it, and that his works are part and parcel of his entire life.

It is the same upon the plane of morality. There is this in common between art and morality, that in both we have to do with creation and invention. We cannot decide *a priori* what it is that should be done. I think it was made sufficiently clear to you in the case of that student who came to see me, that to whatever ethical system he might appeal, the Kantian or any other, he could find no sort of guidance whatever; he was obliged to invent the law for himself. Certainly we cannot say that this man, in choosing to remain with his mother—that is, in taking sentiment, personal devotion and concrete charity as his moral foundations—would be making an irresponsible choice, nor could we do so if he preferred the sacrifice of going away to England. Man makes himself; he is not found ready-made; he makes himself by the choice of his morality, and he cannot but choose a morality, such is the pressure of circumstances upon him. We define man only in relation to his commitments; it is therefore absurd to reproach us for irresponsibility in our choice.

In the second place, people say to us, "You are unable to judge others." This is true in one sense and false in another. It is true in this sense, that whenever a man chooses his purpose and his commitment in all clearness and in all sincerity, whatever that purpose may be, it is impossible for him to prefer another. It is true in the sense that we do not believe in progress. Progress implies amelioration; but man is always the same, facing a situation which is always changing, and choice remains always a choice in the situation. The moral problem has not changed since the time when it was a choice between slavery and anti-slavery—from the time of the war of Secession, for example, until the present moment when one chooses between the M.R.P. [*Mouvement Rèpublicain Populaire*] and the Communists.

We can judge, nevertheless, for, as I have said, one chooses in view of others, and in view of others one chooses himself. One can judge, first—and perhaps this is not a judgment of value, but it is a logical judgment—that in certain cases choice is founded upon an error, and in others upon the truth. One can judge a man by saying that he deceives himself. Since we have defined the situation of man as one of free choice, without excuse and without help, any man who takes refuge behind the excuse of his passions, or by inventing some deterministic doctrine, is a self-deceiver. One may object: "But why should he not choose to deceive himself?" I reply that it is not for me to judge him morally, but I define his self-deception as an error. Here one cannot avoid pronouncing a judgment of truth. The self-deception is evidently a falsehood, because it is a dissimulation of man's complete liberty of commitment. Upon this same level, I say that it is also a self-deception if I choose to declare that certain values are incumbent upon me; I am in contradiction with myself if I will these values and at the same time say that they impose themselves upon me. If anyone says to me, "And what if I wish to deceive myself?" I answer, "There is no reason why you should not, but I declare that you are doing so, and

that the attitude of strict consistency alone is that of good faith." Furthermore, I can pronounce a moral judgment. For I declare that freedom, in respect of concrete circumstances, can have no other end and aim but itself; and when once a man has seen that values depend upon himself, in that state of forsakenness he can will only one thing, and that is freedom as the foundation of all values. That does not mean that he wills it in the abstract: it simply means that the actions of men of good faith have, as their ultimate significance, the quest of freedom itself as such. A man who belongs to some communist or revolutionary society wills certain concrete ends, which imply the will to freedom but that freedom is willed in community. We will freedom for freedom's sake, in and through particular circumstances. And in thus willing freedom, we discover that it depends entirely upon the freedom of others and that the freedom of others depends upon our own. Obviously, freedom as the definition of a man does not depend upon others, but as soon as there is a commitment, I am obliged to will the liberty of others at the same time as my own. I cannot make liberty my aim unless I make that of others equally my aim. Consequently, when I recognize, as entirely authentic, that man is a being whose existence precedes his essence, and that he is a free being who cannot, in any circumstances, but will his freedom, at the same time I realize that I cannot not will the freedom of others. Thus, in the name of that will to freedom which is implied in freedom itself, I can form judgments upon those who seek to hide from themselves the wholly voluntary nature of their existence and its complete freedom. Those who hide from this total freedom, in a guise of solemnity or with deterministic excuses, I shall call cowards. Others, who try to show that their existence is necessary, when it is merely an accident of the appearance of the human race on earth—I shall call scum. But neither cowards nor scum can be identified except upon the plane of strict authenticity. Thus, although the content of morality is variable, a certain form of this morality is universal. Kant declared that freedom is a will both to itself and to the freedom of others. Agreed: but he thinks that the formal and the universal suffice for the constitution of a morality. We think, on the contrary, that principles that are too abstract break down when we come to defining action. To take once again the case of that student; by what authority, in the name of what golden rule of morality, do you think he could have decided, in perfect peace of mind, either to abandon his mother or to remain with her? There are no means of judging. The content is always concrete, and therefore unpredictable; it has always to be invented. The one thing that counts, is to know whether the invention is made in the name of freedom.

...

The third objection, stated by saying, "You take with one hand what you give with the other," means, at bottom, "your values are not serious, since you choose them yourselves." To that I can only say that I am very sorry that it should be so; but if I have excluded God the Father, there must be somebody to invent values. We have to take things as they are. And moreover, to say that we invent values means neither more nor less than this; that there is no sense in life *a priori*. Life is nothing until it is lived; but it is yours to make sense of, and the value of it is nothing else but the sense that you choose. Therefore, you can see that there is a possibility of creating a human community. I have been reproached for suggesting that existentialism is a form of humanism: people have said to me, "But you have written in your *Nausée* that the humanists are wrong, you have even ridiculed a certain type of humanism, why do you now go back upon that?" In reality, the word humanism has two very different meanings. One may understand by humanism a theory which upholds man as the end-in-itself and as the supreme value. Humanism in this sense appears, for instance, in Cocteau's story *Round the World in 80 Hours,* in which one of the characters declares, because he is flying over mountains in an airplane, "Man is magnificent!" This signifies that although I, personally, have not built airplanes I have the benefit of those particular inventions and that I personally, being a man, can consider myself responsible for, and honored by, achievements that are peculiar to some men. It is to assume that we can ascribe value to man according to the most distinguished deeds of certain men. That kind of humanism is absurd, for only the dog or the horse would be in a position to pronounce a general judgment upon man and declare that he is magnificent, which they have never been such fools as to do—at least, not as far as I know. But neither is it admissible that a man should pronounce judgment upon Man. Existentialism dispenses with any judgment of this sort: an existentialist will never take man as the end, since man is still to be determined. And we have no right to believe that humanity is something to which we could set up a cult, after the manner of Auguste Comte. The cult of humanity ends in Comtian humanism, shut-in upon itself, and—this must be said—in Fascism. We do not want a humanism like that.

But there is another sense of the word, of which the fundamental meaning is this: Man is all the time outside of himself: it is in projecting and losing himself beyond himself that he makes man to exist; and, on the other hand, it is by pursuing transcendent aims that he himself is able to exist. Since man is thus self-surpassing, and can grasp objects only in relation to his self-surpassing, he is himself the heart and center of his transcendence. There is no other universe except the human universe, the universe of human subjectivity. This relation of transcendence as constitutive of man (not in the sense that God is transcendent, but in the sense of self-surpassing) with subjectivity (in such a sense that man is not shut up in himself but forever present in a human universe)—it is this that we call existential humanism. This is humanism, because we remind man that there is no legislator but himself; that he himself, thus abandoned, must decide for himself; also because we show that it is not by turning back upon himself, but always by seeking, beyond himself, an aim which is one of liberation or of some particular realization, that man can realize himself as truly human. . . .

Discussion Questions

1. Define what Sartre means by 'existence precedes essence'. Do you agree that this is true for humans? What reasons are there to accept or reject this central component of existentialism? Do such sciences as psychology and sociology provide reasons to reject Sartre's view? Why or why not?

2. Is Sartre's existentialism compatible with theism? Why or why not? Do you think it would be possible to be an existentialist and also to be religious? Why or why not?

3. According to Sartre, what is wrong with materialist explanations of humanity? How would a materialist respond to Sartre? Do you agree that existentialism and materialist explanations are incompatible with each other? Why or why not? If so, which view do you consider stronger, if either? If not, how would you propose to combine these two views?

4. Toward the end of his life, Sartre defended a form of socialism/Marxism. Is this consistent with the views he defends in this essay? Why or why not?

For Further Reading

This selection can be found in *Existentialism from Dostoevsky to Sartre* (1956), edited by Walter Kaufmann. For additional suggested readings on existentialism and Sartre, see Chapter 1, Reading 7.

75 NIHILISM IN BLACK AMERICA
Cornel West

In this selection, Cornel West (1953–), a professor at Harvard University, addresses the crises of hope and meaning that threaten black Americans. This interesting and provoking article works on many levels at once. West's analysis is simultaneously political, moral, economic, philosophical, and religious. He addresses issues that are both deeply personal and political, while arguing for solutions that are at once radical and conservative. It is not surprising, then, that West begins by discarding the division between liberal and conservative perspectives that characterizes most investigations into the problems facing black America. These tiresome categories, states West, only exacerbate the problem and further paralyze responsive actions. Sometimes, he suggests, these dated analyses inadvertently contribute to making the problem worse.

What exactly is this problem that faces black America? West identifies it as 'nihilism'. Nihilism literally means the doctrine that nothing matters and that nothing has meaning or value; the word 'nihilism' shares similar Latin roots with other English words such as 'annihilate', 'nil', and 'null'. West, however, uses nihilism in another sense: Nihilism is a pervasive sense of hopelessness and despair that characterizes many parts of contemporary black American life. Notice the rich multiple dimensions of 'nihilism' as West uses it. It is at once a function of both communities and individuals, something that is both economic and spiritual. For West, the problem of what gives life meaning is not a simple issue, easily reducible to single categories or polarized agendas. It requires a subtle eye and a careful hand to uncover.

SOURCE: From *Race Matters* by Cornel West. © 1993 by Cornel West. Reprinted by permission of Beacon Press, Boston.

Reading Questions

1. What are the two sides in the debate over the plight of African Americans? What does each side consider central in their analysis?
2. In what three ways does West believe we must go beyond the current shape of the debate?
3. Why have liberal structuralists failed?
4. Why have conservative behaviorists failed to address the central issues?
5. Define nihilism. Describe its effects.
6. How did past black American society ward off the threat of nihilism?
7. How have corporate market institutions contributed to the collapse of black civil society? How is pleasure related to this collapse?
8. What is the politics of conversion? How is a love ethic related to it?

We black folk, our history and our present being, are a mirror of all the manifold experiences of America. What we want, what we represent, what we endure is what America is. If we black folk perish, America will perish. If America has forgotten her past, then let her look into the mirror of our consciousness and she will see the living past living in the present, for our memories go back, through our black folk of today, through the recollections of our black parents, and through the tales of slavery told by our black grandparents, to the time when none of us, black or white, lived in this fertile land. The differences between black folk and white folk are not blood or color, and the ties that bind us are deeper than those that separate us. The common road of hope which we all traveled has brought us into a stronger kinship than any words, laws, or legal claims.

—**Richard Wright**, *12 Million Black Voices* (1941)

Recent discussions about the plight of African Americans—especially those at the bottom of the social ladder—tend to divide into two camps. On the one hand, there are those who highlight the *structural* constraints on the life chances of black people. Their viewpoint involves a subtle historical and sociological analysis of slavery, Jim Crowism, job and residential discrimination, skewed unemployment rates, inadequate health care, and poor education. On the other hand, there are those who stress the *behavioral* impediments on black upward mobility. They focus on the waning of the Protestant ethic—hard work, deferred gratification, frugality, and responsibility—in much of black America.

Those in the first camp—the liberal structuralists—call for full employment, health, education, and child-care programs, and broad affirmative action

practices. In short, a new, more sober version of the best of the New Deal and the Great Society: more government money, better bureaucrats, and an active citizenry. Those in the second camp—the conservative behaviorists—promote self-help programs, black business expansion, and non-preferential job practices. They support vigorous "free market" strategies that depend on fundamental changes in how black people act and live. To put it bluntly, their projects rest largely upon a cultural revival of the Protestant ethic in black America.

Unfortunately, these two camps have nearly suffocated the crucial debate that should be taking place about the prospects for black America. This debate must go far beyond the liberal and conservative positions in three fundamental ways. First, we must acknowledge that structures and behavior are inseparable, that institutions and values go hand in hand. How people act and live are shaped—though in no way dictated or determined—by the larger circumstances in which they find themselves. These circumstances can be changed, their limits attenuated, by positive actions to elevate living conditions.

Second, we should reject the idea that structures are primarily economic and political creatures—an idea that sees culture as an ephemeral set of behavioral attitudes and values. Culture is as much a structure as the economy or politics; it is rooted in institutions such as families, schools, churches, synagogues, mosques, and communication industries (television, radio, video, music). Similarly, the economy and politics are not only influenced by values but also promote particular cultural ideals of the good life and good society.

Third, and most important, we must delve into the depths where neither liberals nor conservatives dare to tread, namely, into the murky waters of despair and dread that now flood the streets of black America. To talk about the depressing statistics of unemployment, infant mortality, incarceration, teenage pregnancy, and violent crime is one thing. But to face up to the monumental eclipse of hope, the unprecedented collapse of meaning, the incredible disregard for human (especially black) life and property in much of black America is something else.

The liberal/conservative discussion conceals the most basic issue now facing black America: *the nihilistic threat to its very existence.* This threat is not simply a matter of relative economic deprivation and political powerlessness—though economic well-being and political clout are requisites for meaningful black progress. It is primarily a question of speaking to the profound sense of psychological depression, personal worthlessness, and social despair so widespread in black America.

The liberal structuralists fail to grapple with this threat for two reasons. First, their focus on structural constraints relates almost exclusively to the economy and politics. They show no understanding of the structural character of culture. Why? Because they tend to view people in egoistic and rationalist terms according to which they are motivated primarily by self-interest and self-preservation. Needless to say, this is partly true about most of us. Yet, people, especially degraded and oppressed people, are also hungry for identity, meaning, and self-worth.

The second reason liberal structuralists overlook the nihilistic threat is a sheer failure of nerve. They hesitate to talk honestly about culture, the realm of meanings and values, because doing so seems to lend itself too readily to conservative conclusions in the narrow way Americans discuss race. If there is a hidden taboo among liberals, it is to resist talking *too much* about values because such discussions remove the focus from structures and especially because they obscure the positive role of government. But this failure by liberals leaves the existential and psychological realities of black people in the lurch. In this way, liberal structuralists neglect the battered identities rampant in black America.

As for the conservative behaviorists, they not only misconstrue the nihilistic threat but inadvertently contribute to it. This is a serious charge, and it rests upon several claims. Conservative behaviorists talk about values and attitudes as if political and economic structures hardly exist. They rarely, if ever, examine the innumerable cases in which black people do act on the Protestant ethic and still remain at the bottom of the social ladder. Instead, they highlight the few instances in which blacks ascend to the top, as if such success is available to all blacks, regardless of circumstances. Such a vulgar rendition of Horatio Alger in blackface may serve as a source of inspiration to some—a kind of model for those already on the right track. But it cannot serve as a substitute for serious historical and social analysis of the predicaments of and prospects for all black people, especially the grossly disadvantaged ones.

Conservative behaviorists also discuss black culture as if acknowledging one's obvious victimization by white supremacist practices (compounded by sexism and class condition) is taboo. They tell black people to see themselves as agents, not victims. And on the surface, this is comforting advice, a nice cliché for downtrodden people. But inspirational slogans cannot substitute for substantive historical and social analysis. While black people have never been simply victims, wallowing in self-pity and begging for white giveaways, they have been—and are—*victimized.* Therefore, to call on black people to be agents makes sense only if we also examine the dynamics of this victimization against which their agency will, in part, be exercised. What is particularly naive and peculiarly vicious about the conservative behavioral outlook is that it tends to deny the lingering effect of black history—a history inseparable from though not reducible to victimization. In this way, crucial and indispensable themes of self-help and personal responsibility are wrenched out of historical context and contemporary circumstances—as if it is all a matter of personal will.

This ahistorical perspective contributes to the nihilistic threat within black America in that it can be used to justify right-wing cutbacks for poor people struggling for decent housing, child care, health care, and education. As I pointed out above, the liberal perspective is deficient in important ways, but even so liberals are right on target in their critique of conservative government cutbacks for services to the poor. These ghastly cutbacks are one cause of the nihilist threat to black America.

The proper starting point for the crucial debate about the prospects for black America is an examination of the nihilism that increasingly pervades black communities. *Nihilism is to be understood here not as a philosophic doctrine that there are no rational grounds for legitimate standards or authority; it is, far more, the lived experience of coping with a life of horrifying meaninglessness, hopelessness, and (most important) lovelessness.* The frightening result is a numbing detachment from others and a self-destructive disposition toward the world. Life without meaning, hope, and love breeds a coldhearted, mean-spirited outlook that destroys both the individual and others.

Nihilism is not new in black America. The first African encounter with the New World was an encounter with a distinctive form of the Absurd. The initial black struggle against degradation and devaluation in the enslaved circumstances of the New World was, in part, a struggle against nihilism. In fact, the major enemy of black survival in America has been and is neither oppression nor exploitation but rather the nihilistic threat—that is, loss of hope and absence of meaning. For as long as hope remains and meaning is preserved, the possibility of overcoming oppression stays alive. The self-fulfilling prophecy of the nihilistic threat is that without hope there can be no future, that without meaning there can be no struggle.

The genius of our black foremothers and forefathers was to create powerful buffers to ward off the nihilistic threat, to equip black folk with cultural armor to beat back the demons of hopelessness, meaninglessness, and lovelessness. These buffers consisted of cultural structures of meaning and feeling that created and sustained communities; this armor constituted ways of life and struggle that embodied values of service and sacrifice, love and care, discipline and excellence. In other words, traditions for black surviving and thriving under usually adverse New World conditions were major barriers against the nihilistic threat. These traditions consist primarily of black religious and civic institutions that sustained familial and communal networks of support. If cultures are, in part, what human beings create (out of antecedent fragments of other cultures) in order to convince themselves not to commit suicide, then black foremothers and forefathers are to be applauded. In fact, until the early seventies black Americans had the lowest suicide rate in the United States.

But now young black people lead the nation in suicides.

What has changed? What went wrong? The bitter irony of integration? The cumulative effects of a genocidal conspiracy? The virtual collapse of rising expectations after the optimistic sixties? None of us fully understands why the cultural structures that once sustained black life in America are no longer able to fend off the nihilistic threat. I believe that two significant reasons why the threat is more powerful now than ever before are the saturation of market forces and market moralities in black life and the present crisis in black leadership. The recent market-driven shattering of black civil society—black families, neighborhoods, schools, churches, mosques—leaves more and more black people vulnerable to daily lives endured with little sense of self and fragile existential moorings.

Black people have always been in America's wilderness in search of a promised land. Yet many black folk now reside in a jungle ruled by a cutthroat market morality devoid of any faith in deliverance or hope for freedom. Contrary to the superficial claims of conservative behaviorists, these jungles are not primarily the result of pathological behavior. Rather, this behavior is the tragic response of a people bereft of resources in confronting the workings of U.S. capitalist society. Saying this is not the same as asserting that individual black people are not responsible for their actions—black murderers and rapists should go to jail. But it must be recognized that the nihilistic threat contributes to criminal behavior. It is a threat that feeds on poverty and shattered cultural institutions and grows more powerful as the armors to ward against it are weakened.

But why is this shattering of black civil society occurring? What has led to the weakening of black cultural institutions in asphalt jungles? Corporate market institutions have contributed greatly to their collapse. By corporate market institutions I mean that complex set of interlocking enterprises that have a disproportionate amount of capital, power, and exercise a disproportionate influence on how our society is run and how our culture is shaped. Needless to say, the primary motivation of these institutions is to make profits, and their basic strategy is to convince the public to consume. These institutions have helped create a seductive way of life, a culture of consumption that capitalizes on every opportunity to make money. Market calculations and cost-benefit analyses hold sway in almost every sphere of U.S. society.

The common denominator of these calculations and analyses is usually the provision, expansion, and intensification of *pleasure*. Pleasure is a multivalent term; it means different things to many people. In the American way of life pleasure involves comfort, convenience, and sexual stimulation. Pleasure, so defined, has little to do with the past and views the future as no more than a repetition of a hedonistically driven present. This market morality stigmatizes others as objects for personal pleasure or bodily stimulation. Conservative behaviorists have alleged that traditional morality has been undermined by radical feminists and the cultural radicals of the sixties. But it is clear that corporate market institutions have greatly contributed to undermining traditional morality in order to stay in business and make a profit. The reduction of individuals to objects of pleasure is especially evident in the culture industries—television, radio, video, music—in which gestures of sexual foreplay and orgiastic pleasure flood the marketplace.

Like all Americans, African Americans are influenced greatly by the images of comfort, convenience, machismo, femininity, violence, and sexual stimulation that bombard consumers. These seductive images contribute to the predominance of the market-inspired way of life over all others and thereby edge out nonmarket values—love, care, service to others—handed down by preceding generations. The predominance of this way of life among those living in poverty-ridden conditions, with a limited capacity to ward off self-contempt and self-hatred, results in the possible triumph of the nihilistic threat in black America.

A major contemporary strategy for holding the nihilistic threat at bay is a direct attack on the sense of worthlessness and self-loathing in black America. This *angst* resembles a kind of collective clinical depression in significant pockets of black America. The eclipse of hope and collapse of meaning in much of black America is linked to the structural dynamics of corporate market institutions that affect all Americans. Under these circumstances black existential *angst* derives from the lived experience of ontological

wounds and emotional scars inflicted by white supremacist beliefs and images permeating U.S. society and culture. These beliefs and images attack black intelligence, black ability, black beauty, and black character daily in subtle and not-so- subtle ways. Toni Morrison's novel *The Bluest Eye*, for example, reveals the devastating effect of pervasive European ideals of beauty on the self-image of young black women. Morrison's exposure of the harmful extent to which these white ideals affect the black self-image is a first step toward rejecting these ideals and overcoming the nihilistic self-loathing they engender in blacks.

The accumulated effect of the black wounds and scars suffered in a white-dominated society is a deep-seated anger, a boiling sense of rage, and a passionate pessimism regarding America's will to justice. Under conditions of slavery and Jim Crow segregation, this anger, rage, and pessimism remained relatively muted because of a well-justified fear of brutal white retaliation. The major breakthroughs of the sixties—more psychically than politically—swept this fear away. Sadly, the combination of the market way of life, poverty-ridden conditions, black existential *angst,* and the lessening of fear of white authorities has directed most of the anger, rage, and despair toward fellow black citizens, especially toward black women who are the most vulnerable in our society and in black communities. Only recently has this nihilistic threat—and its ugly inhumane outlook and actions—surfaced in the larger American society. And its appearance surely reveals one of the many instances of cultural decay in a declining empire.

What is to be done about this nihilistic threat? Is there really any hope, given our shattered civil society, market-driven corporate enterprises, and white supremacism? If one begins with the threat of concrete nihilism, then one must talk about some kind of *politics of conversion.* New models of collective black leadership must promote a version of this politics. Like alcoholism and drug addiction, nihilism is a disease of the soul. It can never be completely cured, and there is always the possibility of relapse. But there is always a chance for conversion—a chance for people to believe that there is hope for the future and a meaning to struggle. This chance rests neither on an agreement about what justice consists of nor on an analysis of how racism, sexism, or class subordination operate. Such arguments and analyses are indispensable. But a politics of conversion requires more. Nihilism is not overcome by arguments or analyses; it is tamed by love and care. Any disease of the soul must be conquered by a turning of one's soul. This turning is done through one's own affirmation of one's worth—an affirmation fueled by the concern of others. A love ethic must be at the center of a politics of conversion.

A love ethic has nothing to do with sentimental feelings or tribal connections. Rather it is a last attempt at generating a sense of agency among a downtrodden people. The best exemplar of this love ethic is depicted on a number of levels in Toni Morrison's great novel *Beloved*. Self-love and love of others are both modes toward increasing self-valuation and encouraging political resistance in one's community. These modes of valuation and resistance are rooted in a subversive memory—the best of one's past without romantic nostalgia—and guided by a universal love ethic. For my purposes here, *Beloved* can be construed as bringing together the loving yet critical affirmation of black humanity found in the best of black nationalist movements, the perennial hope against hope for trans-racial coalition in progressive movements, and the painful struggle for self-affirming sanity in a history in which the nihilistic threat *seems* insurmountable.

The politics of conversion proceeds principally on the local level—in those institutions in civil society still vital enough to promote self-worth and self-affirmation. It surfaces on the state and national levels only when grassroots democratic organizations put forward a collective leadership that has earned the love and respect of and, most important, has proved itself *accountable* to these organizations. This collective leadership must exemplify moral integrity, character, and democratic statesmanship within itself and within its organizations.

Like liberal structuralists, the advocates of a politics of conversion never lose sight of the structural conditions that shape the sufferings and lives of people. Yet, unlike liberal structuralism, the politics of conversion meets the nihilistic threat head-on. Like conservative behaviorism, the politics of conversion openly confronts the self-destructive and inhumane actions of black people. Unlike conservative behaviorists, the politics of conversion situates these actions within inhumane circumstances (but does not thereby exonerate them). The politics of conversion shuns the limelight—a limelight that solicits status seekers and ingratiates egomaniacs. Instead, it stays on the ground among the toiling everyday people, ushering forth humble freedom fighters—both followers and leaders—who have the audacity to take the nihilistic threat by the neck and turn back its deadly assaults.

Discussion Questions

1. What are corporate-market institutions? How do corporate-market institutions affect the lives of individuals in our society? Identify some ways in which these institutions influence the lives of individuals in contemporary society. Do you agree with West that they operate by expanding hedonism? Do you agree that corporate-market institutions ultimately generate nihilism?

2. How do different cultures ensure that life and meaning have purpose? What is the meaning and purpose of life in your ethnic, cultural, or religious group? How is it achieved?

3. What are nonmarket values? Are these values threatened by the way corporate-market institutions dominate contemporary culture? Should we work to preserve nonmarket values? If so, how?

4. What is the "politics of conversion"? How is it different than other responses to nihilism? How is it related to hope and love? What practical ways can you think of to implement a politics of conversion? What concrete steps can be taken to achieve its goals? What institutions would be most likely to implement a politics of conversion: individuals, families, civic organizations, religious organizations, schools, the government? Why?

For Further Reading

This article was originally published in the magazine *Dissent*. It is most widely available as Chapter 1 of West's best-selling book, *Race Matters* (1993). It is also anthologized in *Legacy of Dissent: 40 Years of Writing from Dissent Magazine,* edited by Nicolaus Mills (1994), which contains a number of other interesting essays.

Other books by Cornel West include *Keeping Faith: Philosophy and Race in America* (1994), *Prophetic Fragments* (1988), and *Restoring Hope: Conversations on the Future of Black America* (1997). West has coauthored with Henry Louis Gates, Jr., *The Future of the Race* (1996). For some of West's philosophical influences, see his *The American Evasion of Philosophy: A Genealogy of Pragmatism* (1989) and *Post-Analytic Philosophy,* edited by John Rajchman and Cornel West (1985).

76 FEMININE MASOCHISM AND THE POLITICS OF PERSONAL TRANSFORMATION
Sandra Lee Bartky

Can knowledge transform the deepest parts of the self? Can philosophical reflection transform behavior? Can it remove the shackles created by false, distorting traditional beliefs? Can our socially constructed conceptions of ourselves and the world we inhabit be voluntarily exchanged for a new enlightened model?

In this article, Sandra Lee Bartky (1935–), a professor at the University of Illinois at Chicago, investigates these problems as she struggles with the difficulty of aligning one's life, self, and desires with what one is intellectually committed to. Many persons, Bartky considers, have internalized conceptions of sexuality that eroticize domination. She considers this eroticization of dominance to be *prima facie* wrong and harmful, not only in its extreme sadomasochistic forms, but also in its more common, popular forms (such as that found in romance novels and women's magazines).

Suppose an individual, Bartky names her "P.", comes to discover that her sexuality falls far short of her intellectual, philosophical, and political commitments to gender equality. Suppose, that is, that P. discovers that her own sexual fantasies are a reflection of our culture's eroticization of male sexual dominance. As a result, she might come to regard her own sexuality as something humiliating and shameful. Would this be a mistake? Should P. embrace her own sexuality as good, despite her contradictory intellectual commitments? Can P. change her sexual desires? If she could, should she? Will she discover a path that unites the deepest parts of her psyche with her best political reflection? Can she, as Bartky puts it, "decolonize the imagination"?

These questions raise more important questions about the limits of philosophical reflection. Bartky's account suggests that philosophical reflection is valuable and important, but not, in the end, sufficient to transform the personal and the political.

Reading Questions

1. What does "the personal is political" mean? What implications does it have for a feminist conception of sexuality?
2. What is sadomasochism? How is it represented in popular women's media?
3. What does it mean that male dominance is eroticized?
4. On what three grounds is sadomasochism defended?
5. Does Bartky believe that women should have the right to engage in any sexual activity? Does she believe they should exercise that right? Why?
6. How might a person experience his or her sexuality as arbitrary and alien?
7. According to Bartky, why might therapy not be a good option for P.?
8. What is 'sexual voluntarism'? Why does Bartky believe it is mistaken?
9. What advice does Bartky have for women who find themselves in P.'s position?

To be at once a sexual being and a moral agent can be troublesome indeed: no wonder philosophers have wished that we could be rid of sexuality altogether. What to do, for example, when the structure of desire is at war with one's principles? This is a difficult question for any person of conscience, but it has a particular poignancy for feminists. A prime theoretical contribution of the contemporary feminist analysis of women's oppression can be captured in the slogan "the personal is political." What this means is that the subordination of women by men is pervasive, that it orders the relationship of the sexes in every area of life, that a sexual politics of domination is as much in evidence in the private spheres of the family, ordinary social life, and sexuality as in the traditionally public spheres of government and the economy. The belief that the things we do in the bosom of the family or in bed are either "natural" or else a function of the personal idiosyncrasies of private individuals is held to be an "ideological curtain that conceals the reality of women's systematic oppression." For the feminist, two things follow upon the discovery that sexuality too belongs to the sphere of the political. The first is that whatever pertains to sexuality—not only actual sexual behavior, but sexual desire and sexual fantasy as well—will have to be understood in relation to a larger system of subordination; the second, that the deformed sexuality of patriarchical culture must be moved from the hidden domain of "private life" into an arena for struggle, where a "politically correct" sexuality of mutual respect will contend with an "incorrect" sexuality of domination and submission.

A number of questions present themselves at once. What is a politically correct sexuality, anyhow? What forms would the struggle for such a sexuality assume? Is it possible for individuals to prefigure more liberated forms of sexuality in their own lives now, in a society still marked by the subordination of women in every domain? Finally, the question with which we began, the moral worry about what to do when conscience and sexual desire come into conflict, will look like this when seen through the lens of feminism: What to do when one's own sexuality is "politically incorrect," when desire is wildly at variance with feminist principles? I turn to this question first.

THE STORY OF P.

If any form of sexuality has a *prima facie* claim to be regarded as politically incorrect, it would surely be sadomasochism. I define sadomasochism as any sexual practice that involves the eroticization of relations of domination and submission. Consider the case of P., a feminist, who has masochistic fantasies. If P. were prepared to share her secret life with us, this is what she might say:

> For as long as I can remember (from around age six . . .), my sexual fantasies have involved painful exposure, embarrassment, humiliation, mutilation, domination by Gestapo-like characters.

P. regarded her fantasies as unnatural and perverse until she discovered that of all women who have sexual fantasies, 25 percent have fantasies of rape.

Indeed, much material which is often arousing to women, material not normally regarded as perverse, is thematically similar to P.'s fantasies. Many women of her mother's generation were thrilled when the masterful Rhett Butler overpowered the struggling Scarlett O'Hara and swept her triumphantly upstairs in an act of marital rape: "treating 'em rough" has enhanced the sex appeal of many a male film star ever since. The feminine taste for fantasies of victimization is assumed on virtually every page of the large pulp literature produced specifically for women. Confession magazines, Harlequin romances, and that genre of historical romance known in the publishing trade as the "bodice-ripper" have sales now numbering in the billions, and they can be bought in most drugstores and supermarkets across the land. The heroes of these tales turn out to be nice guys in the end, but only in the end; before that they dominate and humiliate the heroines in small "Gestapo-like" ways. In the Harlequin romance *Moth to the Flame* (she the moth, he the flame), the hero, Santino, "whose mouth, despite its sensual curve looked as if it had never uttered the word 'compromise' in its life," insults the heroine, Juliet, mocks her, kidnaps her, steals her clothes, imprisons her in his seaside mansion in Sicily, and threatens repeatedly to rape her. Ginny, the heroine of *Sweet Savage Love,* is "almost raped, then almost seduced, then deflowered — half by rape and half by seduction, then alternately raped and seduced" — all this by Steve, who is by turns her assailant and lover. The purity and constancy of women like Juliet and Ginny finally restrain the brutality of their lovers and all ends happily in marriage, but one cannot escape the suspicion that the ruthlessness of these men constitutes a good part of their sex appeal. When at last brutality recedes and the couple is reconciled, the fantasy ends: *the story is over.*

It might be ventured that standard heterosexual desire in women has often a masochistic dimension, though such desire would fall out far lower on a continuum of masochistic desire than P.'s fantasies or the average Harlequin romance. Essential to masochism is the eroticization of domination. Now women are regularly attracted by power, its possession and exercise. Male power manifests itself variously as physical prowess, muscular strength, intellectual brilliance, worldly position, or the kind of money that buys respect. One or another of these kinds of power may become erotically charged for a woman depending on her values, her history, or her personal idiosyncracies. In a sexually inegalitarian society, these manifestations of male power are precisely the instruments by which men are able to accomplish the subordination of women. Hence, insofar as male power is eroticized, male dominance itself becomes erotically charged.

...

P. is deeply ashamed of her fantasies. Shame, according to John Deigh, is typically expressed in acts of concealment; it is a reaction to the threat of demeaning treatment one would invite in appearing to be a person of lesser worth. P. would be mortified if her fantasies were somehow to be made public. But she suffers a continuing loss of esteem in her own eyes as well. While one of Schlafly's lieutenants might be embarrassed by such fantasies, too, P.'s psychic distress is palpable, for she feels obliged to play out in the theater of her mind acts of brutality which are not only abhorrent to her but which, as a political activist, she is absolutely committed to eradicating. She experiences her own sexuality as doubly humiliating; not only does the content of her fantasies concern humiliation but the very having of such fantasies, given her politics, is humiliating as well. Two courses of action seem open to someone in P.'s predicament; she can either get rid of her shame and keep her desire, or else get rid of her desire. I shall discuss each of these alternatives in turn.

SADOMASOCHISM AND SEXUAL FREEDOM

Sadomasochism has been roundly denounced in feminist writing, in particular the sadism increasingly evident in much male-oriented pornography. Feminists have argued that sadomasochism is one inevitable expression of a women-hating culture. It powerfully reinforces male dominance and female subordination because, by linking these phenomena to our deepest sexual desires — desires defined by an ideologically tainted psychology as instinctual — it makes them appear natural. To participate willingly in this mode of sexuality is thus to collude in women's subordination. No wonder, then, that the emergence of Samois has shocked and offended many in the feminist community. Samois is an organization of and for sadomasochistic women which describes itself both as "lesbian" and "feminist."

In several recent publications, members of Samois have tried to justify their sexual tastes against the standard feminist condemnation. Women like P. are urged to set aside shame, to accept their fantasies fully, to welcome the sexual satisfaction such fantasies provide and even, in controlled situations, to act them out. Most manifestations of sexuality are warped anyhow, they argue, so why the particular scorn heaped upon sadomasochism? Why are the acts of sadomasochistic women—"negotiated mutual pleasure"—in which no one is really hurt worse than, e.g., conventional heterosexuality where the structure of desire in effect ties a woman erotically to her oppressor? The critics of sadomasochism conflate fantasy and reality: Representations of violent acts should not be regarded with the same loathing as the acts themselves. Sadomasochism is ritual or theater in which the goings-on are entirely under the control of the actors; the participants are no more likely to want to engage in real acts of domination or submission than are the less sexually adventurous. Further, sadomasochism is liberatory, say its defenders, in that it challenges the sexual norms of the bourgeois family, norms still rooted to a degree in an older, more repressive sexual ethic that saw sexual acts as legitimate only if they were performed in the service of reproduction. Sadomasochism is the "quintessence of nonreproductive sex": its devotees have a "passion for making use of the entire body, every nerve fiber and every wayward thought." Some members of Samois claim that there are moral values inherent in the sadomasochistic encounter itself, for example in the heightened trust the submissive member of a pair practicing bondage must have in the dominant member. An unusual attentiveness and sensitivity to the partner are required of one who has permission to inflict pain ("Good tops are the most compassionate and sensitive beings on earth"), while overt physical aggression "can function to keep a relationship clean," i.e., free of festering guilt and psychological manipulation.

Finally, sadomasochism is defended on general grounds of sexual freedom. Here, three arguments are brought forward. First, since sex is a basic human need and the right to seek sexual satisfaction is a basic human right, it follows that sexual freedom, in and of itself, is an intrinsic good, provided of course that the sexual activity in question is consensual. Second, the feminist condemnation of sadomasochism is said to be sexually repressive, perpetuating shame and secrecy in sexual matters and discouraging sexual experimentation and the exploration of unfamiliar terrain. Third, anything less than a total commitment to sexual freedom is said to endanger the future of the women's movement by giving ground to the newly militant Right. . . .

How convincing is Samois's defense of sadomasochism? There is, first of all, some question whether the arguments they adduce are mutually consistent. It seems odd to insist that sadomasochistic practices are isolated and compartmentalized rituals which do not resonate with the rest of one's life activity and at the same time to claim that they can enhance the quality of ongoing real relationships, e.g., in the development of trust or the "clean" acting out of aggression. The claim that sadomasochism creates unique opportunities for the building of trust, while true in some sense, strikes me as peculiar. If someone—the "bottom"—allows herself to be tied helplessly to the bedpost, she must of course trust the one doing the tying up—the "top"—not to ignore whatever limits have been agreed upon in advance. If the bottom already knows her top and has reason to believe in her trustworthiness, how can this trust have come about except in the ordinary ways in which we all develop trust in intimate relationships? But if top and bottom are not well acquainted and the activity in question caps a chance meeting in a bar, the awarding of trust in such circumstances is an act of utter foolhardiness. Further, there is little consolation in the observation that sadomasochistic sexuality is no worse than the usual forms of sexuality under patriarchy. If true, this claim does not establish the allowability of sadomasochism at all but only highlights once more the thoroughgoing corruption of much of what we do and the urgent need for a radical revision of erotic life. Nor can sadomasochistic sexuality be justified solely on the grounds that it is frequently non-procreative or that it violates the norms of the bourgeois family, for there are morally reprehensible practices, e.g., necrophilia, which shock respectable people too and are non-procreative in the bargain.

I agree entirely with Gayle Rubin's demand that feminists defend sexual freedom, most tested in the case of sexual minorities, against a newly militant Right. But a political movement may defend some type of erotic activity against prudery or political conservatism without implying in any way that the activity in question is mandated by or even consistent with its own principles. Prostitution is a case in point. There are reasons, in my view, why feminists ought to support the decriminalization of prostitution. If prostitution were legalized, prostitutes would no longer be subject to police or Mafia shakedowns or to the harassment of fines and imprisonment, nor would they need the protection of pimps who often brutalize them. However, none of this implies approval of prostitution as an institution or an abandonment of the feminist vision of a society without prostitutes.

The most convincing defense of sadomasochism, no doubt, is the claim that since sexual satisfaction is an intrinsic good, we are free to engage in any sexual activities whatsoever, provided of course that these activities involve neither force nor fraud. But this is essentially a *liberal* response to a *radical* critique of sexuality and, as such, it fails entirely to engage this critique. As noted earlier, one of the major achievements of contemporary feminist theory is the recognition that male supremacy is perpetuated not only openly, through male domination of the major societal institutions, but more covertly, through the manipulation of desire. Moreover, desires may be produced and managed in ways which involve neither force nor fraud nor the violation of anyone's legal rights. . . .

···

The right, staunchly defended by liberals, to desire what and whom we please and, under certain circumstances, to act on our desire, is not an issue here; the point is that women would be better off if we learned when to refrain from the exercise of this right. A thorough overhaul of desire is clearly on the feminist agenda: the fantasy that we are overwhelmed by Rhett Butler should be traded in for one in which we seize state power and reeducate him. P. has no choice, then, except to reject the counsel of Samois that, unashamed, she make space in her psyche for the free and full enjoyment of every desire. Samois in effect advises P. to ignore in her own life a general principle to which, as a feminist, she is committed and which she is therefore bound to represent to all other women: the principle that we struggle to decolonize our sexuality by removing from our minds the internalized forms of oppression that make us easier to control.

In their enthusiasm for sexual variation, liberals ignore the extent to which a person may experience her own sexuality as arbitrary, hateful, and alien to the rest of her personality. Each of us is in pursuit of an inner integration and unity, a sense that the various aspects of the self form a harmonious whole. But when the parts of the self are at war with one another, a person may be said to suffer from self-estrangement. That part of P. which is compelled to produce sexually charged scenarios of humiliation is radically at odds with the P. who devotes much of her life to the struggle against oppression. Now perfect consistency is demanded of no one, and our little inconsistencies may even lend us charm. But it is no small thing when the form of desire is disavowed by the personality as a whole. The liberal is right to defend the value of sexual satisfaction, but the struggle to achieve an integrated personality has value too and the liberal position does not speak to those situations in which the price of sexual satisfaction is the perpetuation of self-estrangement.

···

It is often the case that the less unwanted desires are acknowledged as belonging to the self and the more they are isolated and compartmentalized, the more psychic distress is minimized. The more extreme the self-estrangement, in other words, the less intense the psychic discomfort. P.'s shame and distress may well be a sign that she is *not* reconciled to her lack of inner harmony and integration and that she clings to the hope that the warring factions within her personality will still somehow be reconciled.

···

Let us suppose that P., determined to bring her desires into line with her ideology, embarks upon a course of traditional psychotherapy, and let us further suppose that her psychotherapy is unsuccessful. As part of her political education, P. is now exposed to a radical critique of psychotherapy: Psychotherapy is sexist; it is authoritarian and hierarchical; it is mired in the values of bourgeois society. P. now resolves to consult a "politically correct" therapist, indeed, a feminist therapist. In order to bring our discussion forward, let us suppose that this second attempt is unsuccessful too, for in spite of its popularity there is evidence that therapy fails as often as it succeeds, whatever the theoretical orientation of the therapist. P. is finding it no simple thing to change her desires. Ought she to try again? In a society with little cohesiveness and less confidence in its own survival, an obsessional preoccupation with self has come to replace more social needs and interests. For many people, there is no higher obligation than to the self—to get it "centered," to realize its "potentialities," to clear out its "hangups"—and little to life apart from a self-absorbed trek through the fads, cults, and therapies of our time. But how compatible is such a surrender to the "new narcissism" (the old "bourgeois individualism") with a serious commitment to radical reform? Few but the relatively privileged can afford psychotherapy anyhow, and the search for what may well be an unrealizable ideal of mental health can absorb much of a person's time, energy, and money. It is not at all clear that the politically correct course of action for P. is to continue in this way whatever the cost; perhaps she is better advised to direct her resources back toward the women's movement. She is, after all, not psychologically disabled; within the oppressive realities of the contemporary world, her life is richer and more effective than the lives of many other people, and she is reconciled to her life—in every respect but one.

PARADISE LOST AND NOT REGAINED: THE FAILURE OF A POLITICS OF PERSONAL TRANSFORMATION

The view is widespread among radical feminists, especially among certain lesbian separatists, that female sexuality is malleable and diffuse and that a woman can, if she chooses, alter the structure of her desire. Here then is a new source of moral instruction for P., a source at the opposite pole from Samois. Without the help of any paid professional—for no such help is really needed—P. is now to pull herself up by her own psychological bootstraps.

The idea that we can alter our entire range of sexual feelings I shall call "sexual voluntarism." Sexual voluntarism has two sources: first, the fact that for many women, thoroughgoing and unforeseen personal changes, including the rejection of heterosexuality for lesbian sexuality, have often accompanied the development of a feminist politics; second, a theory of sexuality that relies heavily on Skinnerian-style behaviorism. While it is a fact that many women (and even some men) have been able to effect profound personal transformations under the influence of feminist ideas, a theory of sexuality I believe to be both false and politically divisive has taken this fact as evidence for the practicability of a willed transformation of self.

For the sexual voluntarist, individuals are thought to be blank tablets on which the culture inscribes certain patterns of behavior. Sexual norms are embedded in a variety of cultural forms, among them "common sense," religion, the family, books, magazines, television, films, and popular music. Individuals are "positively reinforced," i.e., rewarded, when they model their behavior on images and activities held out to them as normal and desirable, "negatively reinforced," i.e., punished, when their modeling behavior is done incorrectly or not done at all.

. . .

"Any woman can"—such is the motto of voluntarism. Armed with an adequate feminist critique of sexuality and sufficient will power, any woman should be able to alter the pattern of her desires. While the feminist theory needed for this venture is known to be the product of collective effort, and while groups of women—even, in the case of lesbian separatism, organized communities of women—may be waiting to welcome the reformed pervert, the process of transformation is seen, nonetheless, as something a woman must accomplish alone. How can it be otherwise, given the fact that no tendency within the contemporary women's liberation movement has developed a genuinely collective *praxis* which would make it possible for women like P. to bring their desires into line with their principles? (I shall return to this point later.) A pervasive and characteristic feature of bourgeois ideology has here been introduced into feminist theory, namely, the idea that the victims, the colonized, are responsible for their own colonization and that they can change the circumstances of their lives by altering their consciousness. Of course, no larger social transformation can occur unless individuals change as well, but the tendency I am criticizing places the burden for effecting change squarely upon the individual, an idea quite at variance with radical feminist thinking generally.

One final point, before I turn to another mode of theorizing about sexuality—one not as subject to moralism and divisiveness. Those who claim that any woman can reprogram her consciousness if only she is sufficiently determined hold a shallow view of the nature of patriarchal oppression. Anything done can be undone, it is implied; nothing has been permanently damaged, nothing irretrievably lost. But this is tragically false. One of the evils of a system of oppression is that it may damage people in ways that cannot always be undone. Patriarchy invades the intimate recesses of personality where it may maim and cripple the spirit forever. No political movement, even a movement with a highly developed analysis of sexual oppression, can promise an end to sexual alienation or a cure for sexual dysfunction. Many human beings, P. among them, may have to live with a degree of psychic damage that can never be fully healed.

...

INSTEAD OF A CONCLUSION

P. will search the foregoing discussion in vain for practical moral advice. The way out of her predicament seemed to be the abandonment either of her shame or of her desire. But I have suggested that there is a sense in which she is "entitled" to her shame, insofar as shame is a wholly understandable response to behavior which is seriously at variance with principles. In addition, I have argued that not every kind of sexual behavior, even behavior that involves consenting adults or is played out in the private theater of the imagination, is compatible with feminist principles, a feminist analysis of sexuality, or a feminist vision of social transformation. To this extent, I declare the incompatibility of a classical liberal position on sexual freedom with my own understanding of feminism.

P.'s other alternative, getting rid of her desire, is a good and sensible project if she can manage it, but it turns out to be so difficult in the doing that to preach to her a feminist code of sexual correctness in the confident anticipation that she will succeed would be a futility—and a cruelty. Since many women (perhaps even most women) are in P.'s shoes, such a code would divide women within the movement and alienate those outside of it. "Twix't the conception and creation,"

writes the poet, "falls the shadow." Between the conception of a sexuality in harmony with feminism and the creation of a feminist standard of political correctness in sexual matters, fall not one but two shadows: first, the lack of an adequate theory of sexuality; the second the lack of an effective political practice around issues of personal transformation. The second shadow need not wait upon the emergence of the first, for to take seriously the principle of the inseparability of theory and practice is to see that a better theoretical understanding of the nature of sexual desire might well begin to emerge in the course of a serious and sustained attempt to alter it.

I am not suggesting that human sexuality is entirely enigmatic. Quite the contrary. There have been revolutionary advances in our knowledge of human sexual psychology over the last ninety years, and the work of feminist theorists such as Nancy Chodorow, Esther Person, and Dorothy Dinnerstein promises to extend our understanding still further. Nor do I want to substitute a sexual determinism for sexual voluntarism. Some people try to reorganize their erotic lives and they succeed. Others, caught up in the excitement of a movement that calls for the radical transformation of every human institution, find that they have changed without even trying. But more often than not, sexuality is mysterious and opaque, seemingly unalterable because its meaning is impenetrable. The significance of a particular form of desire as well as its persistence may lie in a developmental history only half-remembered or even repressed altogether. However embarrassing from a feminist perspective, a tabooed desire may well play a crucial and necessary role in a person's psychic economy.

The order of the psyche, here and now, in a world of pain and oppression, is not identical to the ideal order of a feminist political vision. We can teach a woman how to plan a demonstration, how to set up a phone bank, or how to lobby. We can share what we have learned about starting up a women's studies program or a battered women's shelter. But we cannot teach P. or the women of Samois or even ourselves how to decolonize the imagination: This is what I meant earlier by the claim that the women's movement has an insufficiently developed practice around issues of sexuality. The difficulties which stand in the way of the emergence of such a practice are legion; another paper would be required to identify them and also to examine the circumstances in which many women and some men have been able to effect dramatic changes in their lives. But in my view, the prevalence in some feminist circles of the kind of thinking I call "sexual voluntarism," with its simplistic formulas, moralism, intolerance, and refusal to acknowledge the obsessional dimension of sexual desire, is itself an obstacle to the emergence of an adequate practice. . . .

Discussion Questions

1. Bartky is not the first to note that there are contradictory desires at war within us and that knowledge does not necessarily result in corresponding action. What other resources are there for individuals who are faced with such struggles? How would members of your own cultural, religious, or ethnic group counsel individuals who struggle with similar difficulties? What would they consider the value of therapy, prayer, meditation, confrontation, self-acceptance, and so forth?
2. What does Bartky mean by 'colonized imagination'? What is this? How does it happen? Is this an explanation for why people eroticize domination? Do you think this is a good explanation? What other explanations are there? Which explanation do you consider the best? Why?
3. What advice would you offer P.?

For Further Reading

This article can be found in Bartky's book *Femininity and Domination: Studies in the Phenomenology of Oppression* (1990), which contains a number of other interesting articles. For a variety of different perspectives on feminism and sadomasochistic sexual practices see Lorena Leigh Saxe, "Sadomasochism and Exclusion," in *Hypatia* 7 (1994), 64–77; Pat Califia, "A Personal View of the History of the Lesbian S/M Community and Movement in San Francisco," in *Coming to Power,* edited by Samois (1981); Lynda Hart, *Between the Body and the Flesh: Performing Sadomasochism* (1998); Carol Queen, *Real Live Nude Girl: Chronicles of a Sex Positive Culture* (1994); and Alison M. Jaggar, editor, *Living with Contradictions: Controversies in Feminist Social Ethics* (1994).

GLOSSARY

ad hoc Latin phrase meaning "for this (specific purpose)"; an *ad hoc* assumption is an unsupported claim (or "made up" reason) added to an argument or philosophical position merely to prevent it from being defeated by a specific objection.

ad hominem Latin phrase meaning "to the person"; an *ad hominem* argument is fallacious because it attacks the person who is making the argument, rather than the argument itself.

ad infinitum Latin phrase meaning "to infinity" or "endlessly"; in common usage it means "and so on without end."

aesthetics A branch of philosophy concerned with the nature of beauty and art.

a fortiori Latin phrase meaning "for a still stronger reason" or "all the more"; for example, if sexual harassment is immoral, then *a fortiori* rape is immoral.

agnostic A person who neither affirms nor denies God's existence.

alienation Used by Marxists to indicate the indifference or aversion laborers have toward the products they labor to produce; industrial workers in a capitalist system are said to be alienated or estranged from the products of their labor, from the processes of production, and from other coproducers.

analytic statement A statement that is true by virtue of the meaning of its words; for example, "all bachelors are unmarried men" can be known to be true simply by analyzing the concept of "bachelor."

antecedent The thing that precedes; in a conditional statement of the form "If X, then Y," the antecedent is "X." See also *conditional statement.*

antecedent conditions The circumstances or events that precede another event; the free will/determinism debate is over whether or not the antecedent conditions determine a person's actions.

a posteriori Latin phrase meaning "from what is behind or after"; *a posteriori* knowledge is knowledge that can be gained only through or *after* experience or observation.

a priori Latin phrase meaning "from what is prior or before"; *a priori* knowledge is knowledge that can be known independent of experience or prior to experience.

Arabic philosophy See *Islamic philosophy.*

argument from design An argument for the existence of God, also called *the teleological argument;* it asserts that God's existence is required to explain some feature about the world, such as its complexity.

artificial intelligence The attempt to create computers that mimic human reasoning processes, perhaps including consciousness.

atheism The belief that there is no God.

automaton A person or thing that appears to act purposely but actually acts without thought, such as a robot.

autonomy Literally, "self-rule": the ability or right to govern one's own actions.

begging the question A fallacious argument in which the conclusion is (implicitly) assumed within its premises; an argument begs the question if it assumes what it sets out to prove.

behaviorism School of psychology founded by J. B. Watson and B. F. Skinner; behaviorists reject appeal to mental events as an explanation for human behavior, relying instead solely upon observable behavior as the basis of the science of human psychology.

bourgeoisie In Marxism, the class of persons who own capital or the means of producing wealth; the bourgeoisie are contrasted with the wage-earning *proletariat* class.

brute fact Used by David Hume to signify a fact that has no explanation.

capitalism An economic system in which the means of production—that is, factories, land, and investment capital—are owned and controlled by private individuals.

Cartesianism Philosophical beliefs that rely on the philosophy or philosophical methods of René Descartes.

Cartesian dualism The doctrine that there are two substances, immaterial mind and corporeal body, that are capable of interacting with one another; a form of dualism defended by René Descartes.

categorical imperative An unconditional command, of the form "Do such-and-such"; according to Kant, the categorical imperative, the supreme principle of moral duty, commands us to act always according to a law or principle we could will to be universal without exception.

category-mistake A term coined by Gilbert Ryle; a conceptual confusion caused by mistakenly applying descriptive terms proper for one particular category of thing to an item belonging to another category for which these terms are inappropriate.

ceteris paribus Latin phrase meaning "other things being equal" or "excluding unusual circumstances."

circular reasoning An argument in which the conclusion is considered evidence for a premise, which in turn is evidence for the conclusion. See also *begging the question.*

cogito ergo sum Latin phrase meaning "I think, therefore I am (or exist)"; used by Descartes as a foundational truth that can be known even when all other beliefs are doubted.

cognitivist A person who believes that something can be known; in contrast, a skeptic believes that little or nothing can be known.

communism A social, political, and economic system in which industry and its profits are owned and controlled by the public; the communal owning of capital.

compatibilism The philosophy that persons can be both morally free and determined; soft-determinists are considered compatibilists because they maintain that moral freedom is compatible with determinism.

computational theory of mind A theory that maintains that mental processes are computational processes; cognitive scientists who believe the computational theory of mind believe that mental processes can be modeled on computer or machine algorithms.

conceptual truth A statement that is true by virtue of the meaning of its words alone; for example, it is a conceptual truth that "bachelors are unmarried men" or that "it is raining or it is not raining." See also *analytic statement.*

conditional statement A statement with the form "if . . ., then . . ."; the if-clause is known as the antecedent, and the then-clause is called the consequent.

Confucian A doctrine or philosophy associated with the thought of Confucius; Confucius (551–479 B.C.E.) was one of the most important Chinese philosophers, devoting himself to the study of the excellent person of virtue and his leadership role in society.

connectionism An approach to designing cognitive systems that mimic human thought processes by "networking" processors together in a manner similar to the way that neurons are connected in the human brain; also called the "neural network" or the "parallel-distributed processing" method.

consequentialism An ethical theory in which the correct action to perform is the one that produces the best results (or consequences); utilitarianism is a form of consequentialism that holds that the best consequences are determined by measuring the amount of happiness or pleasure produced.

contingent Something that is possible but not necessary; a contingent being is a being whose existence is not necessary, a being that may not have existed.

contractarianism Moral and political theories that hold that moral and political obligations are justified by appeal to (actual or hypothetical) agreements or contracts between persons.

corporeal Having the quality of being bodily or physical; a corporeal body is a physical or material body.

cosmological argument An argument for the existence of God that depends on the idea that the cosmos must have had a first cause; proponents argue that because causal series cannot extend back forever, there must have been a first cause, which they identify as God.

cosmology The study of the nature of the universe.

cosmos Greek word meaning "world" or "universe."

counterfactual A conditional statement (an "if . . . then . . ." statement) in which the antecedent (the if-clause) is false; for example, the statement "if it were not raining, then we could play golf" is a counterfactual when, in fact, it is raining.

creationism The belief that God created the universe and all its contents; a belief that denies evolutionary theory.

cultural relativism The view that standards of morality are specific to the culture in which they originate; cultural relativists hold that it is improper to make moral judgments about other cultures.

Darwinism The theory that new species arise from other species as the result of the combined effects of genetic mutation and natural selection.

deductive argument An argument in which the conclusion is supposedly true in light of its premises; deductive arguments are contrasted with inductive arguments, in which the conclusion is likely to be true.

deontological theory A moral theory that is principle- or rule-based; deontological theories assert that the right action is the action that conforms to the proper rule; from the Greek root *deon*, meaning "duty."

dependent being A being that owes its existence to another being; humans are considered dependent (or contingent) beings.

determinism The view that every event, including all human thought and activity, is the necessary result of antecedent conditions.

divine command theory The view that moral duties acquire their obligatory nature because they are commanded by God.

dualism The belief that humans are composed of two substances, the immaterial mind and a corporeal body.

dualistic interactionism A form of dualism that holds that mental events can causally affect the body and vice versa. See also *Cartesian dualism*.

Eastern philosophy Philosophical systems that trace their roots to the religious and cultural traditions of Asia, including India, China, and Japan.

efficient cause That which creates, constructs, or causes a thing to come into being; for example, the efficient cause of a pot is the potter.

egoism, ethical The claim that it is morally proper to always and only act in one's own self-interest.

egoism, psychological The view that all human activity is unavoidably self-interested.

eliminative materialism The view that mental phenomena do not exist and that what is called "mind" can be described in purely material terms.

emotivism The view that moral claims or judgments are nothing more than expressions of positive or negative emotional responses; emotivists reject the claim that the terms "good" and "bad" describe objective qualities of acts, events, or persons, and instead hold that they describe merely subjective responses that possess no interpersonal validity.

empiricism The view that all meaningful knowledge is dependent on sense experience; empiricists also deny the existence of innate ideas. Compare *rationalism*.

Epicureanism A philosophical system that holds that pleasure is the highest good; its name derives from the ancient Greek philosopher Epicurus.

epiphenomenalism A form of dualism that maintains that mental events are caused by physical events in the body, but that mental events have no causal effect on the body.

epistemology The branch of philosophy that studies the nature and limits of knowledge.

equivocation Using a word, for example, in an argument, in two different senses; the fallacy of equivocation occurs when the conclusion of the argument is reached by shifting the meaning of a word.

eros Sensual or erotic love; for the followers of Plato, the type of love one has for eternal truths (the Forms).

ethical relativism The view that there are no objective moral claims that are interpersonally true.

ethical skepticism The view that ethical truths, even if they exist, cannot be known.

ethics The branch of philosophy that studies the nature of morality.

eudaimonia Greek word, translated as "happiness"; as used by Aristotle, *eudaimonia* means "human flourishing" or "the good life of an excellent human."

evolution The theory that new species arise from other species as a result of the combined effects of genetic mutation and natural selection.

ex hypothesis Latin phrase meaning "by hypothesis"; used to refer back to a premise assumed at the beginning of an argument.

existentialism A school of thought that holds that humans are utterly free and must decide for themselves what meaning their lives are to have.

ex nihilo Latin phrase meaning "from nothing."

fallacy An illegitimate argument.

falsifiable A statement that can be tested, that is, a statement for which we can conceive of circumstances under which it would be false; a falsifiable statement is not a *false* statement, but one that can be tested and therefore verified as either true or false.

fatalism The view that no matter what we do, our future or destiny is beyond our control; a fatalist believes that one's future is inevitable no matter what choice or course of action one undertakes.

final cause The end or purpose for which a thing was created; for example, the final cause of a jug may be to hold water.

free will The ability to act and make choices independent of the influence of antecedent conditions; a person is free if he or she could have done otherwise in the same circumstances.

function The characteristic product or achievement of a thing; the work that a thing uniquely does; in Aristotle's ethics, the unique function of a human being is the unique characteristic activity of humans, their use of reason.

functionalism The view that mental states can be understood in terms of cause-and-effect relationships or behavior; for example, "being in pain" can be understood as reacting to certain sorts of stimuli (injury, for example) in specific ways (groaning, for example).

hard determinism See *determinism*.

Harm Principle A principle of human government that states that the only time it is legitimate to restrict the liberty of a citizen is to prevent that citizen from harming another or the state.

hedonism The view that pleasure is the ultimate good; utilitarianism is a hedonic form of consequentialism.

historical materialism The theory that all social thought and philosophy is the result of material or economic forces, which in turn result from necessary (historical) processes and which follow necessary processes of change and development; used commonly as a synonym for Marxism and communism.

humanism The view that humans and their interests are of primary importance; generally contrasted with religious views holding that God and the relationship of humans to God is of primary importance.

idealism The view that only minds and their contents exist; idealism denies the existence of material entities.

ideology A system of thought or doctrine; often used to indicate a hidden and therefore harmful system of thought that distorts social reality; examples of ideologies include humanism, theism, communism, and capitalism.

immaterialism The view that noncorporeal (nonphysical) entities, such as souls and minds, exist; dualism and idealism are forms of immaterialism.

immutable Unchanging and unchangeable; traditional forms of theism regard God as immutable.

imperfect duty According to Kant, a duty that is not owed to any particular person; charity, for example, is an imperfect duty because we have an obligation to be charitable, but no particular person can claim that they are entitled to our charitable contributions.

incompatibilism The theory that moral freedom is not compatible with determinism; hard determinists and libertarians are incompatibilists.

indeterminism The view that some events are not determined or caused; indeterminists hold that at least some human activity is not determined.

indubitable Beyond rational doubt.

inductive argument An argument in which the premises provide evidentiary weight or support for the conclusion; when the conclusion is made *likely* or *probable* by the evidence, that argument is inductive.

innate idea An idea or truth that humans possess at birth; empiricists deny the existence of innate ideas.

interactionism The view that (immaterial) mind and (corporeal) body causally interact with one another. See also *Cartesian dualism.*

intersubjective world A reality that various humans share and that lies behind their individual experiences, as opposed to an *intra*-subjective world, which is a reality that only a single person participates in; a shared, intersubjective world may or may not exist independently of humans and human society.

Islamic philosophy A philosophical movement that flourished primarily from the eighth century to the twelfth century within the Islamic religious community; Aristotle's philosophy was an important influence on Islamic philosophy, which created an extensive technical vocabulary in Arabic.

liberation theology A form of theism in which God is primarily interested in liberating persons from suffering.

libertarianism, metaphysical The belief in the existence of free will.

libertarianism, political The view that the rights of the individual are paramount; libertarians hold that the government should be minimal and that a free market form of capitalism is the only justified economic system.

logical impossibility Something that logically could not exist or be true because it is self-contradictory; for example, a "round triangle" is a logical impossibility.

logical positivism The philosophical school that holds that a sentence must be scientifically verifiable in order to be meaningful; logical positivists therefore assert that most metaphysical statements are meaningless.

logical possibility Something that could have been different or could occur; a statement or state of affairs that is not self-contradictory.

logical truth A sentence that is true by virtue of its *logical* structure alone; for example, "pigs can fly or pigs cannot fly" is a logical truth; logical truths are different from analytic or conceptual truths, which are true by virtue of the meaning of their words.

Marxism The political and economic theory of Karl Marx; Marxism holds that ideas and concepts are the result of historical forces, which in turn are best understood as primarily the result of economic institutions and processes; Marxists advocate for communism.

material cause The material cause of a thing is that from which the thing is constructed; for example, the material cause of a pot is clay.

materialism The metaphysical view that everything that exists is material.

matters of fact According to Hume, facts that can be discovered only through sensory experience; for example, "the car is green" is known only after perceiving the car's color.

maxim A rule or principle of conduct.

metaphysics The branch of philosophy devoted to the study of the ultimate nature of reality and existence.

modus operandi Latin phrase meaning "mode of operation"; the unique style or method in which a person or thing operates.

monism The belief that there is only one sort of substance in the universe; for example, materialists are monists, as are idealists.

monotheism The belief that there is only one God; polytheists, on the other hand, believe in multiple Gods,

whereas pantheists believe that everything exists as part of God.

moral freedom The sort of freedom for which one is held morally responsible or accountable.

mutatis mutandis Latin phrase meaning "the necessary changes having been made."

natural selection The process through which evolution is thought to occur; life forms with genes that favor survival are more likely to pass these genes on to their offspring.

nature/nurture debate The controversy over whether human behavior is shaped by genetic factors (nature) or by upbringing and environment (nurture).

necessary being A being that exists necessarily, by virtue of its very nature; God is thought to be a necessary being.

necessary condition X is a necessary condition for Y if X is required for Y, but X by itself does not guarantee Y; for example, a battery is a necessary condition for starting a car but is not enough to guarantee that the car will start (gasoline, for example, is also required). See also *sufficient condition.*

necessary truth A statement that is necessarily true; either a conceptual or logical truth.

neural network See *connectionism.*

normative moral theory An ethical theory that identifies what people ought to do, or what obligations they have; deontological ethics and consequentialism are normative moral theories; *descriptive* moral theories, by contrast, describe the values and norms of a culture or person.

objective Refers to a judgment (or claim) the truth of which does not depend on the person (or subject) making the judgment or claim; sometimes taken to refer to a judgment or claim not influenced by personal opinion or feelings.

occasionalism A form of dualism in which the mind and body are separate and do not directly interact; God is considered the link between the body and the mind.

omnibenevolence The state of being all good, all loving, or morally perfect; according to many forms of theism, God is considered to be omnibenevolent.

omnipotence The state of being all powerful, capable of doing anything logically possible; a traditional attribute of God.

omniscience The state of being all knowing; God is omniscient in traditional theism.

ontological argument An argument for the existence of God that depends on the concept of God; God is held to be perfect, and therefore must exist, since failure to exist would mean that God is less than perfect.

ontology The study of the existence and nature of "being."

paradigm A way of seeing things, a world view, or model of how things operate. See also *ideology.*

parallelism A form of dualism in which the mind and body are separate and do not interact; God sets the mind and body in motion in a predetermined "parallel" but separate fashion.

parallel-processing A problem-solving strategy in computer science in which larger problems are divided into smaller problems and worked on simultaneously by multiple processors.

patriarchy Literally "rule by fathers"; used in feminist philosophy to indicate an interlocking system of beliefs and institutions, largely hidden, that favor male supremacy to the detriment of women (in particular, but not exclusively).

perfect duty According to Kant, a moral duty that admits of no exceptions; for example, according to Kant we have a perfect duty to tell the truth no matter the circumstances. See also *imperfect duty.*

peripatetic From the Greek, meaning someone who walks about; refers to followers of Aristotle, who was said to deliver his lectures as he walked about.

phenomenology The branch of philosophy concerned with the study of the subjective nature of existence which stresses the careful description of phenomena as subjectively experienced.

philosophy of language The branch of philosophy concerned with the *philosophical* nature of language, such as how words refer to entities and come to have meaning.

philosophy of religion The branch of philosophy concerned with questions about religion, especially the existence and nature of God and the ability to know religious truth.

philosophy of science A branch of philosophy concerned with the nature of science, including the nature of explanation, prediction, and methods of discovery and confirmation.

physicalism See *materialism.*

Platonist A school of thought that derives from Plato and holds that what is ultimately real are nonphysical ideas or truths (the Forms).

pluralism The coexistence of multiple and diverse belief systems in a single culture, usually referring to religious and moral beliefs; liberal political theories attempt to accommodate pluralism.

political liberalism A political theory or system in which rights or liberties are taken as basic and in which governmental authority is legitimized through an ideal social contract.

polytheism The belief that many gods exist.

postmodernism The critique of philosophical appeals to the efficacy of reason and rationality to create a unified system of thought and truth (that is, the Enlightenment and Modernism), which postmodernists believe must be defeated and unmasked as tyrannizing.

pragmatism A school of thought that holds (roughly) that the truth of a belief is a function of its pragmatic, practical usefulness or value; derives from the philosophy of C. S. Peirce and William James.

predicate The part of a sentence that describes the subject of a sentence.

prima facie Latin phrase for "at first appearance" or "at first glance"; a *prima facie* judgment or belief is one that can be justifiably held until further reflection shows that it is true or false.

primary qualities According to Locke, the qualities of an object that cannot be separated from that object and that produce sensations in us; the primary qualities of a material object include solidity and extension. See also *secondary qualities.*

principle of sufficient reason The principle that states that every thing and every fact must have an explanation, thus denying the existence of brute facts.

problem of evil The seeming inconsistency that an all-knowing, all-powerful, morally perfect God exists and so does natural and moral evil; an argument against the existence of God from the fact that innocent persons suffer great evils.

proletariat The class of persons that meet their basic needs by selling their wage labor; according to Marx and Engels, in a capitalist society, the proletariat is alienated from the products of its labor by the ruling, capital-owning class. See also *bourgeoisie.*

qua Latin word meaning "as" or "in the character or capacity of."

qualia The qualitative characteristics of sense experience, such as the feeling of pain.

ratiocination Logical or scientific reasoning.

rationalism The view that knowledge is discoverable by using reason independent of sense experience; rationalism is contrasted with *empiricism*, which holds that all knowledge comes from or is dependent on experience.

reductio ad absurdum Literally, "reduce to an absurdity"; an argument in which an absurd or false conclusion is derived from an initial claim hypothetically taken as true, thus showing that the initial claim is false.

Sapir-Whorf hypothesis The claim that the grammatical structure of language determines and shapes our experience of the world; according to the Sapir-Whorf hypothesis, users of grammatically distinct languages

share fundamentally different worlds; also called the "language relativity principle."

secondary qualities According to Locke, the qualities of a thing that produce sensations in us, but that are not essential parts of that object; qualities that can be separated from an object; for example, color and temperature are secondary qualities of an object.

skepticism The belief that humans are capable of little or no certain knowledge about the world.

social contract A method of defending political authority by appealing to a hypothetical agreement (contract) between persons, from which all legitimate political authority derives.

socialist egalitarianism A political philosophy that advocates for an economic system in which capital is socially owned and for the active role of the state in promoting equality. Compare *communism, historical materialism,* and *Marxism.*

soft determinism The view that human freedom is compatible with determinism.

sophism A school of ancient Greek philosophers who taught for a fee; sophists are usually characterized as persons who offer arguments that are convincing on the surface, but ultimately false and misleading.

sound argument A deductive argument in which the premises are true and the conclusion necessarily follows from the premises.

substance The basic stuff out of which things are composed; materialism and idealism are theories about the basic substance of the universe.

substratum Substance or that which lies beyond appearance.

sufficient condition X is a sufficient condition for Y if X guarantees Y; for example, a car starting is a sufficient condition for knowing that the car has gasoline. See also *necessary condition.*

supererogation A praiseworthy act that is not morally obligatory; an act one is not required to do, but is praised for performing.

synthetic judgment According to Kant, a statement in which the predicate is not contained in the subject; a judgment that requires joining or combining (synthesizing) judgments; for example, "Frank is a bachelor" is synthetic because the idea of being a bachelor is not contained in the subject, Frank.

tabula rasa Latin phrase meaning "blank slate"; empiricists hold that because humans lack innate knowledge, they are a *tabula rasa* at birth.

tautology A sentence that is always true by virtue of its logical structure; sometimes used to indicate an empty truth.

teleological argument An argument for God's existence that depends on the fact that the universe appears to have been designed for some purpose and therefore must have been created by a designer, that is, by God.

teleology The study of the end, function, or purpose of a thing.

telos Greek word translated as "end," but also meaning "purpose" or "goal"; the *telos* of an action is the goal or purpose that the act aims to achieve; the *telos* of a human is the goal or purpose of human existence. See also *function.*

theism The belief in God or gods.

theodicy The defense of God's existence against the objection of the problem of evil. See also *problem of evil.*

Turing Test A test devised by A. M. Turing to determine whether a machine is intelligent.

universals Abstract entities such as love, honor, and justice, or the idea of a ship or triangle, that Platonists believe exist; true knowledge for Platonists is knowledge of universals, as opposed to physical things.

utilitarianism A type of consequentialist theory according to which an action is good insofar as it produces happiness (that is, pleasure and the absence of pain); many utilitarians, such as John Stuart Mill, are hedonists and consider pleasure to be the primary good.

valid Describes an argument in which the conclusion follows with logical necessity from the premises.

verifiability criterion A standard of meaning according to which all sentences (except conceptual truths and logical truths) must be scientifically testable in order to be meaningful; logical positivists advocated for the verifiability criterion. See also *falsifiable.*

virtue A morally excellent quality of an individual's character; virtue ethicists hold that actions are good insofar as they flow from the character of a virtuous person; primarily associated with Aristotle's ethics; the opposite of a virtue is a "vice."

virtue epistemology A theory in epistemology that holds that in order to assess if a belief is justified, philosophical analysis should focus on the mental qualities (virtues) of persons who are good or excellent at acquiring correct belief, rather than abstract analyses of the concept of knowledge; accordingly, a belief is justified just in cases where it is the belief that a virtuous knower (with adequate time and information) believes.

virtue theory A moral theory that holds that good or proper actions flow from the character (the virtue) of a person.

Western philosophy A philosophical tradition rooted primarily in ancient Greek philosophy, now the dominant philosophical system in Europe and the Americas.

Notes

Notes

Notes

Notes

Notes

Notes

Notes

Notes

The Canon and Its Critics

. . . offers readers a flexible format in which a central philosophical topic is explored in each of the 14 chapters. *The Canon and Its Critics* introduces central figures important to liberal arts education, such as Plato, Descartes, Locke, Hume, Kant, Mill, and Nietzsche. Todd Furman and Mitchell Avila have included a wide array of authors—for example, Cornel West, Alison Jaggar, Carol Gilligan, bell hooks, and Paul Feyerabend—who challenge the canon but in so doing are in dialogue with it.

The Canon and Its Critics contains 15 articles by woman authors and 7 articles by African American authors—more than any other introductory anthology. This new edition includes 10 new readings by Blatchford, Sartre, de Beauvoir, J. J. C. Smart, Greco, Nietzsche, Yeager, Singer, Charles Mills, and Dostoyevsky.

Visit us on the Web at www.mhhe.com/philosophy

The McGraw·Hill Companies

McGraw Hill

Higher Education

ISBN 0-07-283237-1

9 780072 832372

90000

www.mhhe.com

W9-AVG-647